Foundations of
Behavioral Research

FOUNDATIONS OF BEHAVIORAL RESEARCH

THIRD EDITION

Fred N. Kerlinger

UNIVERSITY OF OREGON

Harcourt Brace College Publishers
Fort Worth   Philadelphia   San Diego
New York   Orlando   Austin   San Antonio
Toronto   Montreal   London   Sydney   Tokyo

Library of Congress Cataloging-in-Publication Data

Kerlinger, Fred N. (Fred Nichols), 1910 –
    Foundations of behavioral research.
    Bibliography: p.
    Includes index.
    1. Psychology – Research – Statistical methods.
2. Sociology – Research – Statistical methods.
I. Title.
BF76.5.K4   1986   150′.72   85-8693
ISBN   0-03-041761-9

Printed in the United States of America.
15 14 13 12 11 10

To BETTY, PAUL, and STEPHEN

Preface

SOME ACTIVITIES command more interest, devotion, and enthusiasm than do others. So it seems to be with science and with art. Why this is so is an interesting and significant psychological question to which there is no unequivocal answer. All that seems to be clear is that once we become immersed in scientific research or artistic expression we devote most of our thoughts, energies, and emotions to these activities. It seems a far cry from science to art. But in one respect at least they are similar: we make passionate commitments to them.[1]

This is a book on scientific behavioral research. Above everything else, it aims to convey the exciting quality of research in general, and in the behavioral sciences and education in particular. A large portion of the book is focused on abstract conceptual and technical matters, but behind the discussion is the conviction that research is a deeply absorbing and vitally interesting business.

It may seem strange in a book on research that I talk about interest, enthusiasm, and passionate commitment. Shouldn't we be objective? Shouldn't we develop a hardheaded attitude toward psychological, sociological, and educational phenomena? Yes, of course. But more important is somehow to catch the essential quality of the excitement of discovery that comes from research well done. Then the difficulties and frustrations of the research enterprise, while they never vanish, are much less significant. What I am trying to say is that strong subjective involvement is a powerful motivator for acquiring an objective approach to the study of phenomena. It is doubtful that any significant work is ever done without great personal involvement. It is doubtful that students can learn much

---

[1] The term "passionate commitment" is Polanyi's. M. Polanyi, *Personal Knowledge*. Chicago: University of Chicago Press, 1958.

about science, research design, and research methods without considerable personal involvement. Thus I would encourage students to discuss, argue, debate, and even fight about research. Take a stand. Be opinionated. Later try to soften the opinionation into intelligent conviction and controlled emotional commitment.

The writing of this book has been strongly influenced by the book's major purpose: to help students understand the fundamental nature of the scientific approach to problem solution. Technical and methodological problems have been considered at length. One cannot understand any complex human activity, especially scientific research activity, without some technical and methodological competence. But technical competence is empty without an understanding of the basic intent and nature of scientific research: the controlled and objective study of the relations among phenomena. All else is subordinate to this. Thus the book, as its name indicates, strongly emphasizes the *fundamentals* or *foundations* of behavioral research.

To accomplish the major purpose indicated above, the book has four distinctive general features. First, it is a treatise on scientific research; it is limited to what is generally accepted as the scientific approach. It does not discuss historical research, legal research, library research, philosophical inquiry, and so on.[2] It emphasizes, in short, understanding scientific research problem solution.

Second, the student is led to grasp the intimate and often difficult relations between a research problem and the design and methodology of its solution. While methodological problems are treated at length, the book is not a "methods" book. Stress is always on the research problem, the design of research, and the relation between the two. The student is encouraged to think relationally and structurally.

Third, the content of much of the book is tied together with the notions of set, relation, and variance. These ideas, together with those of probability theory, statistics, and measurement, are used to integrate the diverse content of research activity into a unified and coherent whole.

Fourth, a good bit of the book's discussion is slanted toward psychological, sociological, and educational research problems. It seemed to me that a foundational research book was needed in education. But there is little scientific research in education that is uniquely educational; for the most part it is behavioral research, research basically psychological and sociological in nature. In sum, while this is a book on the intellectual and technical foundations of scientific behavioral research in general, it emphasizes psychological, sociological, and educational problems and examples, while not ignoring other behavioral disciplines.

The book's content is organized into ten parts. In Part 1, the language and approach of science are studied. Its three chapters discuss the nature of science, scientific problems and hypotheses, and the notions of variables, constructs, and definitions. Part 2 presents the conceptual and mathematical foundations. Much of the presentation of conceptual and technical matters, as indicated above, is based on the ideas of set, relation, and variance. These terms are defined using modern mathematical theory. Fortunately the theory is simple, though the reader may feel a bit strange at first. After becoming accustomed to the language and thinking, however, he will find that he possesses powerful instruments for understanding later subjects.

It is impossible to do competent research or to read and understand research reports without understanding the probabilistic and statistical thinking of scientists. Parts 3, 4, and 5 are thus devoted mainly to probabilistic thinking, sampling, randomness, and the nature and purpose of statistics and statistical inference, including a generous exposure to that great invention, analysis of variance. The first chapter of this part, however, discus-

---

[2]Historical inquiry and methodological research are briefly discussed in Appendix A.

ses the highly important subject of the principles of analysis and interpretation. This chapter and the following chapter on the analysis of frequencies were inserted at this point to make clear the purpose of quantitative analysis and statistics. Indeed, this is what Parts 3, 4, and 5 are about: drawing inferences from data with quantitative methods. Interpretation is in essence drawing inferences, and the ultimate purpose of quantitative analysis and statistics is interpretation.

Parts 1 through 5, then, provide an important part of the conceptual and mathematical foundations of behavioral research. The remainder of the book uses these foundations to attack problems of design, measurement, and observation and data collection.

Part Six, ''Designs of Research,'' is the structural heart of the book. Here the major designs of experimental and nonexperimental research are outlined and explained. Part Seven, on types of research, follows naturally from Part Six: nonexperimental research and the distinctions among laboratory experiments, field experiments, field studies, and survey research are explored.

Part Eight addresses itself mainly to theoretical measurement problems, while Part Nine addresses itself to practical and technical problems of gathering the data necessary for scientific problem solution. Standard methods of observation and data collection— interviews, objective tests and scales, direct observation of behavior, projective methods, content analysis, the use and analysis of available materials, and sociometry—are extensively discussed and illustrated. Q methodology has been given a separate chapter because of its importance and research potential, its distinctive nature, and evident lack of understanding of its characteristics by behavioral researchers.[3]

The book ends with fairly extended but elementary discussions of multiple regression, multivariate analysis, factor analysis, and analysis of covariance structures. The very nature of behavioral research is multivariable: many variables act in complex ways to influence other variables. While some of the complexity can be handled with analysis of variance, it is only with multivariate methods that the complexity of many psychological, sociological, and educational problems can be adequately attacked. We are in the midst of a revolution in research thinking and practice. Behavioral research has been changing from a predominantly univariate emphasis to a multivariate emphasis. The change is extensive and profound. Even the nature of theory and problems is changing. Before finishing the book, I hope the reader will become convinced of the necessity of considering at some length such relatively difficult subjects as multiple regression and factor analysis.

We need to explain further why Part Ten on multivariate analysis, and especially Chapter 36 on analysis of covariance structures, seemed necessary. Some experts may say that the chapter does not belong in an elementary text. Of course some will say this about the whole of Part Ten on multivariate approaches. I readily grant that many students may profit little from Chapters 33 through 36, especially if their instruction lacks enthusiasm for multivariate analysis. There can be little doubt, however, of the great importance and widespread and profitable use of the powerful and fundamental approaches of multiple regression and factor analysis in psychology, sociology, and education. One cannot conceive of modern behavioral research without also recognizing the necessity for students of research to study these admittedly difficult yet indispensable approaches to research problems.

Even the relatively advanced student may have trouble with the mathematics and the scientific reasoning of analysis of covariance structures, not only because of the intrinsic difficulty of the mathematics (yet it isn't all that difficult), but also because of the ab-

---

[3]This lack of understanding has again been demonstrated recently when researchers have used Q sorts as though they were normative measures and neglected the original thinking and work of Q's originator, William Stephenson (see Chapter 32).

stractness and generality of the system. I recall vividly my own perplexity when a Dutch colleague got me started. The so-called structural equation mystified me and I asked my colleague, ''What does it mean?'' His reply stuck with me: ''Anything you want it to mean.'' I didn't really know what he meant at the time, and I certainly didn't understand the structural equation of the LISREL system. Only faith in my colleague kept me going—fortunately.

His answer was profound. It meant that the LISREL system was abstract and general and could be applied to many different problems in the behavioral disciplines. And its abstractness and generality made it flexible in the sense that, with ingenuity, persistence, and patience, it can be differently structured for different problems. Most important, however, analysis of covariance structures and LISREL restructure our thinking and conceptualization of research problems. They force us to study and grasp the very core of what we are doing when we study and test theories, hypotheses, and models. That the system is hard to learn and to use can of course be used as an argument against it—and against including it in this book. Its great importance, however, does not permit its omission.[4]

Some word on the book's level and audience is in order. The book is a behavioral science text intended for graduate students who have elementary backgrounds in psychology, statistics, and measurement. While many terms and ideas used in educational and psychological problems are defined, some familiarity with terms like intelligence, aptitude, socioeconomic status, authoritarianism, and the like is assumed. All technical terms are defined, though many students will probably need instructor help with some of them.

As usual, statistical terms and ideas may hinder the student's progress. While it is possible to study the book and master its contents without statistical background, the student who has had an elementary statistics course will probably find the going easier. Suggestions are given in Part Four to help the student conquer certain statistical difficulties.

Foundations of Behavioral Research can be used in courses of either one or two semesters. When used in one-semester courses, it should be selectively studied. Although individual instructors will of course make their own selection decisions, the following parts and chapters are suggested for a single-semester course: Parts 1 and 2 and Chapters 8–12, 17, 19, 23, and 25–29. (Chapters 25, 26, and 27 can also be omitted.) For a two-semester course, all or most of the chapters may well be studied. Whatever selection is made, it should be borne in mind that later discussions often presuppose understanding of earlier discussions.

To aid student study and understanding, and to help surmount some of the inherent difficulties of the subject, several devices have been used. One, many topics have been discussed at length. If a choice had to be made between repetition and possible lack of student understanding, material was repeated, though in different words with different examples. Two, many examples from actual research as well as many hypothetical examples have been used. The student who reads the book through will have been exposed to a large number and a wide variety of problems, hypotheses, designs, and data and to many actual research studies in the social sciences and education.

Three, an important feature of the book is the frequent use of simple numerical examples in which the numbers are only those between 0 and 9. The fundamental ideas of statistics, measurement, and design can be conveyed as well with small numbers as with large numbers, without the additional burden of tedious arithmetic computations. It is suggested that the reader work through each example at least once. Intelligent handling of data is indispensable to understanding research design and methodology.

---

[4] If readers experience undue difficulty with the chapter, I suggest omitting it from formal study.

Four, most chapters have study suggestions that include readings as well as problems designed to help integrate and consolidate the material presented in the chapters. Many of them arose from practical use with graduate students. Answers to most of the computational problems have been given immediately after the problems. An answer, if checked against a supplied answer and found to be correct, reassures students about computational details. They should not have to waste time wondering about right answers. Understanding the procedures is what is important and not the calculations as such.

How does this edition of *Foundations* differ from the first and second editions? One, many of the errors and gaucheries in the earlier editions have been detected and corrected. Two, most of the research examples have been replaced with more recent and, in many cases, more interesting studies. Moreover, a greater effort has been made to include more studies from psychology, sociology, and other behavioral disciplines rather than such a heavy concentration of educational studies. Three, the examples used have in most cases been taken from multivariate studies and research problems. Four, the attitude toward computers and computer use remains highly favorable, but this enthusiasm has been tempered by skepticism and doubt of the wisdom of unsupervised and uncontrolled use of computer package programs by graduate students and faculty. These doubts have been expressed mainly in Appendix B, but they have also influenced the presentation in other parts of the book.

Although much of the text and some of the organization of the book have been changed, its basic approach and purpose remain the same: understanding of principles of research through relatively lengthy explanation and many examples. No one can be completely satisfied with the organization and content of a book. One of the goals of all three editions has been to supply enough materials for instructors and students of diverse background and taste to select what they need. Even so, the content of the book is still highly selective when one considers the great diversity and depth of modern behavioral research and methods. I hope my selection will serve the teaching and learning needs of most instructors and students.

All books are cooperative enterprises. Though one person may undertake the actual writing, he is dependent on many others for ideas, criticism, and support. Among the many persons who contributed to this book, I am most indebted to those mentioned below. I here express my sincere thanks to them.

Three individuals read the entire original manuscript of the first edition and made many valuable and constructive suggestions for improvement: Professors T. Newcomb, D. Harris, and J. Nunnally. Professor Newcomb also furnished the early prodding and encouragement needed to get the book going. Professor Harris contributed from his wide research experience insights whose worth cannot be weighed. The late Professor Nunnally's trenchant and penetrating analysis was invaluable, especially with a number of difficult technical matters.

I am grateful to the many teachers and students who have corresponded with me about aspects of the book (especially the errors). All suggested corrections and changes have been given careful consideration. I owe a large debt in the writing of both revisions to my colleague and friend, Professor E. Pedhazur, and to Professor E. Page. They have ferreted out weaknesses and made many suggestions for improvement. I also want to express my gratitude to my former colleagues of the Psychology Laboratory, University of Amsterdam, who pointed out errors and ambiguities in the text, some of which I have been able to correct.

The editors of Holt, Rinehart and Winston who were responsible for the first two editions of the book and a substantial part of this edition, Richard Owen and David Boynton, both contributed greatly to the content and style of the book itself with perspicacious insights and suggestions and with steady and unfailing psychological support. I am very grateful to them for their work with me and for being conscientious, scrupulous, and creative editors.

Authors rarely recognize and acknowledge the work and contributions of project editors. Project editors—I prefer to say ''super editors''—are those individuals who solve the many technical communication problems encountered in preparing book manuscripts for publication. I would like to mention the extraordinary competence, insight, and aesthetic and technical creativity of the individual who has prepared this book for the printer: Jeanette Ninas Johnson. I am very grateful and here acknowledge her valuable contribution.

It is doubtful that this book could have been written without the sabbatical leaves given me in 1961–1962 and 1970–1971 by New York University. I am grateful to the University for its generous sabbatical policy.

The price a family pays for an author's book is high. Its members put up with his obsession and his unpredictable writing ups and downs. I express my gratitude and indebtedness to my wife and sons by dedicating the book to them. I must say more than this, however. My wife has had to cope with two overseas moves and one transcontinental move, two retirements, and innumerable logistical and temperamental problems. To express thanks and gratitude in the face of this extraordinary example of coping seems pale and inadequate. Nevertheless, I here express both.

FRED N. KERLINGER

Eugene, Oregon
June 1985

Contents

PART FIVE
Analysis of Variance

PART SIX
Designs of Research

PART SEVEN
Types of Research

PART EIGHT
Measurement

reliability coefficient. The standard error of the mean and the standard error of measurement. The improvement of reliability. The value of reliability.

significance. Interpretation of multiple regression statistics. Other analytic and interpretative problems. Research examples. Multiple regression analysis and scientific research.

One-way analysis of variance and multiple regression analysis. Coding and data analysis. Factorial analysis of variance, analysis of covariance, and related analyses. Discriminant analysis, canonical correlation, multivariate analysis of variance, and path analysis. Multivariate analysis and behavioral research. Study suggestions.

Foundations. Extraction and rotation of factors, factor scores, and second-order factor analysis. Research examples. Factor analysis and scientific research. Addendum. Study suggestions.

Testing alternative factor hypotheses: Duality versus bipolarity of social attitudes. Latent variable influences: The full LISREL system. Research studies. Conclusions—And reservations. Study suggestions.

Appendixes

Foundations of
Behavioral Research

PART ONE

THE LANGUAGE AND APPROACH OF SCIENCE

Chapter 1

Science and the Scientific Approach

To UNDERSTAND any complex human activity we must grasp the language and approach of the individuals who pursue it. So it is with understanding science and scientific research. One must know and understand, at least in part, scientific language and the scientific approach to problem-solving.

One of the most confusing things to the student of science is the special way scientists use ordinary words. To make matters worse, they invent new words. There are good reasons for this specialized use of language; they will become evident later. For now, suffice it to say that we must understand and learn the language of social scientists. When investigators tell us about their independent and dependent variables, we must know what they mean. When they tell us that they have randomized their experimental procedures, we must not only know what they mean—we must understand why they do as they do.

Similarly, the scientist's approach to problems must be clearly understood. It is not so much that this approach is different from the layman's. It *is* different, of course, but it is not strange and esoteric. Quite the contrary. When understood, it will seem natural and almost inevitable that the scientist does what he does. Indeed, we will probably wonder why much more human thinking and problem-solving are not consciously structured along such lines.

The purpose of Part One of this book is to help the student learn and understand the language and approach of science and research. In the chapters of this part many of the basic constructs of the social and educational scientist will be studied. In some cases it will not be possible to give complete and satisfactory definitions because of lack of background at this early point in our development. In such cases we shall attempt to formulate and use reasonably accurate first approximations to later, more satisfactory definitions. Let us begin our study by considering how the scientist approaches problems and how this approach differs from what might be called a commonsense approach.

SCIENCE AND COMMON SENSE

Whitehead has pointed out that in creative thought common sense is a bad master. "Its sole criterion for judgment is that the new ideas shall look like the old ones."[1] This is well said. Common sense may often be a bad master for the evaluation of knowledge. But how are science and common sense alike and how are they different? From one viewpoint, science and common sense are alike. This view would say that science is a systematic and controlled extension of common sense, since common sense, as Conant points out, is a series of concepts and conceptual schemes satisfactory for the practical uses of mankind.[2] But these concepts and conceptual schemes may be seriously misleading in modern science—and particularly in psychology and education. It was self-evident to many educators of the last century—it was only common sense—to use punishment as a basic tool of pedagogy. Now we have evidence that this older commonsense view of motivation may be quite erroneous. Reward seems more effective than punishment in aiding learning.

Science and common sense differ sharply in five ways. These disagreements revolve around the words "systematic" and "controlled." First, the uses of conceptual schemes and theoretical structures are strikingly different. While the man in the street uses "theories" and concepts, he ordinarily does so in a loose fashion. He often blandly accepts fanciful explanations of natural and human phenomena. An illness, for instance, may be thought to be a punishment for sinfulness. An economic depression may be attributed to Jews. Scientists, on the other hand, systematically build theoretical structures, test them for internal consistency, and subject aspects of them to empirical test. Furthermore, they realize that the concepts they use are man-made terms that may or may not exhibit a close relation to reality.

Second, scientists systematically and empirically test their theories and hypotheses. Nonscientists test "hypotheses," too, but they test them in what may be called a selective fashion. They often "select" evidence simply because it is consistent with the hypotheses. Take the stereotype: Blacks are musical. If people believe this, they can easily "verify" the belief by noting that many blacks are musicians. Exceptions to the stereotype, the unmusical or tone-deaf black, for example, are not perceived. Sophisticated social scientists, knowing this "selection tendency" to be a common psychological phenomenon, carefully guard their research against their own preconceptions and predilections and against selective support of hypotheses. For one thing, they are not content with armchair exploration of relations; they must test the relations in the laboratory or in the

---

[1] A. Whitehead, *An Introduction to Mathematics*. New York: Holt, Rinehart and Winston, 1911, p. 157.

[2] J. Conant, *Science and Common Sense*. New Haven: Yale University Press, 1951, pp. 32–33. A *concept* is a word that expresses an abstraction formed by generalization from particulars. "Aggression" is a concept, an abstraction that expresses a number of particular actions having the similar characteristic of hurting people or objects. A *conceptual scheme* is a set of concepts interrelated by hypothetical and theoretical propositions. (See *ibid.*, pp. 25, 47–48.) A *construct* is a concept with the additional meaning of having been created or appropriated for special scientific purposes. "Mass," "energy," "hostility," "introversion," and "achievement" are constructs. They might more accurately be called "constructed types" or "constructed classes," classes or sets of objects or events bound together by the possession of common characteristics defined by the scientist. The term "variable" will be defined in a later chapter. For now let it mean a symbol or name of a characteristic that takes on different numerical values.

field. They are not content, for example, with the presumed relations between methods of teaching and achievement, between intelligence and creativity, between values and administrative decisions. They insist upon systematic, controlled, and empirical testing of these relations.

A third difference lies in the notion of control. In scientific research, control means several things. For the present, let it mean that the scientist tries systematically to rule out variables that are possible "causes" of the effects under study other than the variables hypothesized to be the "causes." Laymen seldom bother to control systematically their explanations of observed phenomena. They ordinarily make little effort to control extraneous sources of influence. They tend to accept those explanations that are in accord with their preconceptions and biases. If they believe that slum conditions produce delinquency, they tend to disregard delinquency in nonslum neighborhoods. The scientist, on the other hand, seeks out and "controls" delinquency incidence in different kinds of neighborhoods. The difference, of course, is profound.

Another difference between science and common sense is perhaps not so sharp. It was said earlier that the scientist is constantly preoccupied with relations among phenomena. So is the layman who invokes common sense for his explanations of phenomena. But the scientist consciously and systematically pursues relations. The layman's preoccupation with relations is loose, unsystematic, uncontrolled. He often seizes, for example, on the fortuitous occurrence of two phenomena and immediately links them indissolubly as cause and effect.

Take the relation tested in a study done many years ago by Hurlock.[3] In more recent terminology, this relation may be expressed: Positive reinforcement (reward) produces greater increments of learning than does punishment. The relation is between reinforcement (or reward and punishment) and learning. Educators and parents of the nineteenth century often assumed that punishment was the more effective agent in learning. Educators and parents of the present often assume that positive reinforcement (reward) is more effective. Both may say that their viewpoints are "only common sense." It is obvious, they may say, that if you reward (or punish) a child, he or she will learn better. The scientist, on the other hand, while personally espousing one or the other or neither of these viewpoints, would probably insist on systematic and controlled testing of both (and other) relations, as Hurlock did.

A final difference between common sense and science lies in different explanations of observed phenomena. The scientist, when attempting to explain the relations among observed phenomena, carefully rules out what have been called "metaphysical explanations." A metaphysical explanation is simply a proposition that cannot be tested. To say, for example, that people are poor and starving because God wills it, or that it is wrong to be authoritarian, is to talk metaphysically.

None of these propositions can be tested; thus they are metaphysical. As such, science is not concerned with them. This does not mean that scientists would necessarily spurn such statements, say they are not true, or claim they are meaningless. It simply means that *as scientists* they are not concerned with them. In short, science is concerned with things that can be publicly observed and tested. If propositions or questions do not contain implications for such public observation and testing, they are not scientific propositions or questions.

[3] E. Hurlock, "An Evaluation of Certain Incentives Used in Schoolwork," *Journal of Educational Psychology,* 16 (1925), 145–159.

FOUR METHODS OF KNOWING

Charles Peirce said that there are four general ways of knowing or, as he put it, fixing belief.[4] The first is the *method of tenacity*. Here men hold firmly to the truth, the truth that they know to be true because they hold firmly to it, because they have always known it to be true. Frequent repetition of such "truths" seems to enhance their validity. People often cling to their beliefs in the face of clearly conflicting facts. And they will also infer "new" knowledge from propositions that may be false.

A second method of knowing or fixing belief is the *method of authority*. This is the method of established belief. If the Bible says it, it is so. If a noted physicist says there is a God, it is so. If an idea has the weight of tradition and public sanction behind it, it is so. As Peirce points out, this method is superior to the method of tenacity, because human progress, although slow, can be achieved using the method. Actually, life could not go on without the method of authority. We must take a large body of facts and information on the basis of authority. Thus, it should not be concluded that the method of authority is unsound; it is unsound only under certain circumstances.

The *a priori method* is the third way of knowing or fixing belief. (Cohen and Nagel call it the *method of intuition*.) It rests its case for superiority on the assumption that the propositions accepted by the "a priorist" are self-evident. Note that a priori propositions "agree with reason" and not necessarily with experience. The idea seems to be that people, through free communication and intercourse, can reach the truth because their natural inclinations tend toward truth. The difficulty with this position lies in the expression "agree with reason." Whose reason? Suppose two honest and well-meaning individuals, using rational processes, reach different conclusions, as they often do. Which one is right? Is it a matter of taste, as Peirce puts it? If something is self-evident to many people—for instance, that learning hard subjects trains the mind and builds moral character, that American education is inferior to Russian and European education—does this mean it is so? According to the a priori method, it does—it just "stands to reason."

The fourth method is the *method of science*. Peirce says:

> To satisfy our doubts, . . . therefore, it is necessary that a method should be found by which our beliefs may be determined by nothing human, but by some external permanency—by something upon which our thinking has no effect. . . . The method must be such that the ultimate conclusion of every man shall be the same. Such is the method of science. Its fundamental hypothesis . . . is this: There are real things, whose characters are entirely independent of our opinions about them. . . .[5]

The scientific approach[6] has a characteristic that no other method of attaining knowledge has: self-correction. There are built-in checks all along the way to scientific knowledge. These checks are so conceived and used that they control and verify scientific activities and conclusions to the end of attaining dependable knowledge. Even if a hypothesis seems to be supported in an experiment, the scientist will test alternative plausible hypotheses that, if also supported, may cast doubt on the first hypothesis. Scientists do not accept statements as true, even though the evidence at first looks promising. They insist upon testing them. They also insist that any testing procedure be open to public inspection.

---

[4]J. Buchler, ed., *Philosophical Writings of Peirce*. New York: Dover, 1955, chap. 2. In the ensuing discussion, I am taking some liberties with Peirce's original formulation in an attempt to clarify the ideas and to make them more germane to the present work. For a good discussion of the four methods, see M. Cohen and E. Nagel, *An Introduction to Logic and Scientific Method*. New York: Harcourt, 1934, pp. 193–196.

[5]Buchler, *op. cit.*, p. 18.

[6]This book's position is that there is no one scientific method as such. Rather, there are a number of methods that scientists can and do use, but it can probably be said that there is one scientific approach.

As Peirce says, the checks used in scientific research are anchored as much as possible in reality lying outside the scientist's personal beliefs, perceptions, biases, values, attitudes, and emotions. Perhaps the best single word to express this is "objectivity." *Objectivity* is agreement among "expert" judges on what is observed or what is to be done or has been done in research.[7] But, as we shall see later, the scientific approach involves more than this. The point is that more dependable knowledge is attained because science ultimately appeals to evidence: propositions are subjected to empirical test. An objection may be raised: Theory, which scientists use and exalt, comes from people, the scientists themselves. But, as Polanyi points out, "A theory is something other than myself";[8] thus a theory helps the scientist to attain greater objectivity. In short, scientists systematically and consciously use the self-corrective aspect of the scientific approach.

SCIENCE AND ITS FUNCTIONS

What is science? The question is not easy to answer. Indeed, no definition of science will be directly attempted. We shall, instead, talk about notions and views of science and then try to explain the functions of science.

Science is a badly misunderstood word. There seem to be three popular stereotypes that impede understanding of scientific activity. One is the white coat-stethoscope-laboratory stereotype. Scientists are perceived as individuals who work with facts in laboratories. They use complicated equipment, do innumerable experiments, and pile up facts for the ultimate purpose of improving the lot of mankind. Thus, while somewhat unimaginative grubbers after facts, they are redeemed by noble motives. You can believe them when, for example, they tell you that such-and-such toothpaste is good for you or that you should not smoke cigarettes.

The second stereotype of scientists is that they are brilliant individuals who think, spin complex theories, and spend their time in ivory towers aloof from the world and its problems. They are impractical theorists, even though their thinking and theory occasionally lead to results of practical significance like atomic bombs.

The third stereotype equates science with engineering and technology. The building of bridges, the improvement of automobiles and missiles, the automation of industry, the invention of teaching machines, and the like are thought to be science. The scientist's job, in this conception, is to work at the improvement of inventions and artifacts. The scientist is conceived to be a sort of highly skilled engineer working to make life smooth and efficient.

These notions impede student understanding of science, the activities and thinking of the scientist, and scientific research in general. In short, they make the student's task harder than it would otherwise be. Thus they should be cleared away to make room for more adequate notions.

There are two broad views of science: the static and the dynamic.[9] The *static view,* the view that seems to influence most laymen and students, is that science is an activity that contributes systematized information to the world. The scientist's job is to discover new facts and to add them to the already existing body of information. Science is even conceived to be a body of facts. In this view, science is also a way of explaining observed phenomena. The emphasis, then, is on the *present state of knowledge and adding to it* and on the present set of laws, theories, hypotheses, and principles.

---

[7]For discussions of objectivity, its meaning, and its controversial character, see F. Kerlinger, *Behavioral Research: A Conceptual Approach*. New York: Holt, Rinehart and Winston, 1979, pp. 8–13; 262–264.

[8]M. Polanyi, *Personal Knowledge*. Chicago: University of Chicago Press, 1958, p. 4.

[9]Conant, *op. cit.,* pp. 23–27.

The *dynamic view,* on the other hand, regards science more as an *activity,* what scientists *do.* The present state of knowledge is important, of course. But it is important mainly because it is a base for further scientific theory and research. This has been called a *heuristic view.* The word "heuristic," meaning serving to discover or reveal, now has the notion of self-discovery connected with it. A heuristic method of teaching, for instance, emphasizes students' discovering things for themselves. The heuristic view in science emphasizes theory and interconnected conceptual schemata that are fruitful for further research. A heuristic emphasis is a discovery emphasis.

It is the heuristic aspect of science that distinguishes it in good part from engineering and technology. On the basis of a heuristic hunch, the scientist takes a risky leap. As Polanyi says, "It is the plunge by which we gain a foothold at another shore of reality. On such plunges the scientist has to stake bit by bit his entire professional life."[10] Heuristic may also be called problem-solving, but the emphasis is on imaginative and not routine problem-solving. The heuristic view in science stresses problem-solving rather than facts and bodies of information. Alleged established facts and bodies of information are important to the heuristic scientist because they help lead to further theory, further discovery, and further investigation.

Still avoiding a direct definition of science—but certainly implying one—we now look at the function of science. Here we find two distinct views. The practical man, the nonscientist generally, thinks of science as a discipline or activity aimed at improving things, at making progress. Some scientists, too, take this position. The function of science, in this view, is to make discoveries, to learn facts, to advance knowledge in order to improve things. Branches of science that are clearly of this character receive wide and strong support. Witness the continuing generous support of medical and military research. The criteria of practicality and "payoff" are preeminent in this view, especially in educational research.[11]

A very different view of the function of science is well expressed by Braithwaite: "The function of science . . . is to establish general laws covering the behaviors of the empirical events or objects with which the science in question is concerned, and thereby to enable us to connect together our knowledge of the separately known events, and to make reliable predictions of events as yet unknown."[12] The connection between this view of the function of science and the dynamic-heuristic view discussed earlier is obvious, except that an important element is added: the establishment of general laws—or theory, if you will. If we are to understand modern behavioral research and its strengths and weaknesses, we must explore the elements of Braithwaite's statement. We do so by considering the aims of science, scientific explanation, and the role and importance of theory.

THE AIMS OF SCIENCE, SCIENTIFIC EXPLANATION, AND THEORY

The basic aim of science is theory. Perhaps less cryptically, the basic aim of science is to explain natural phenomena. Such explanations are called theories. Instead of trying to explain each and every separate behavior of children, the scientific psychologist seeks general explanations that encompass and link together many different behaviors. Rather

[10] Polanyi, *op. cit.,* p. 123.
[11] See F. Kerlinger, "Research in Education," in R. Ebel, V. Noll, and R. Bauer, eds., *Encyclopedia of Educational Research,* 4th ed. New York: Macmillan, 1969, pp. 1127–1144; "The Influence of Research on Educational Practice," *Educational Researcher,* 16 (1977), 5–12.
[12] R. Braithwaite, *Scientific Explanation.* Cambridge: Cambridge University Press, 1955, p. 1.

than try to explain children's methods of solving arithmetic problems, for example, he seeks general explanations of all kinds of problem-solving. He might call such a general explanation a theory of problem-solving.

This discussion of the basic aim of science as theory may seem strange to the student, who has probably been inculcated with the notion that human activities have to pay off in practical ways. If we said that the aim of science is the betterment of mankind, most readers would quickly read the words and accept them. But the *basic* aim of science is not the betterment of mankind. It is theory. Unfortunately, this sweeping and really complex statement is not easy to understand. Still, we must try because it is important.[13]

Other aims of science that have been stated are: explanation, understanding, prediction, and control. If we accept theory as the ultimate aim of science, however, explanation and understanding become subaims of the ultimate aim. This is because of the definition and nature of theory:

> A theory is a set of interrelated constructs (concepts), definitions, and propositions that present a systematic view of phenomena by specifying relations among variables, with the purpose of explaining and predicting the phenomena.

This definition says three things. One, a theory is a set of propositions consisting of defined and interrelated constructs. Two, a theory sets out the interrelations among a set of variables (constructs), and in so doing, presents a systematic view of the phenomena described by the variables. Finally, a theory explains phenomena. It does so by specifying what variables are related to what variables and how they are related, thus enabling the researcher to predict from certain variables to certain other variables.

One might, for example, have a theory of school failure. One's variables might be intelligence, verbal and numerical aptitudes, anxiety, social class membership, and achievement motivation. The phenomenon to be explained, of course, is school failure— or, perhaps more accurately, school achievement. School failure is explained by specified relations between each of the six variables and school failure, or by combinations of the six variables and school failure. The scientist, successfully using this set of constructs, then "understands" school failure. He is able to "explain" and, to some extent at least, "predict" it.

It is obvious that explanation and prediction can be subsumed under theory. The very nature of a theory lies in its explanation of observed phenomena. Take reinforcement theory. A simple proposition flowing from this theory is: If a response is rewarded (reinforced) when it occurs, it will tend to be repeated. The psychological scientist who first formulated some such proposition did so as an explanation of the observed repetitious occurrences of responses. *Why* did they occur and reoccur with dependable regularity? Because they were rewarded. This is an explanation, although it may not be a satisfactory explanation to many people. Someone else may ask *why* reward increases the likelihood of a response's occurrence. A full-blown theory would have the explanation. Today, however, there is no really satisfactory answer. All we can say is that, with a high degree of probability, the reinforcement of a response makes the response occur and reoccur.[14] In other words, the propositions of a theory, the statements of relations, constitute the explanation, as far as that theory is concerned, of observed natural phenomena.

Now, about prediction and control. It can be said that scientists do not really have to be concerned with explanation and understanding. Only prediction and control are necessary. Proponents of this point of view may say that the adequacy of a theory is its

---

[13] See Kerlinger, *Behavioral Research: A Conceptual Approach, op. cit.*, pp. 15–18, chap. 16.

[14] Even this statement must be qualified. See R. Nisbett and L. Ross, *Human Inference: Strategies and Shortcomings of Social Judgment*. Englewood Cliffs, N.J.: Prentice-Hall, 1980, pp. 101ff.

predictive power. If by using the theory we are able to predict successfully, then the theory is confirmed and this is enough. We need not necessarily look for further underlying explanations. Since we can predict reliably, we can control because control is deducible from prediction.

The prediction view of science has validity. But as far as this book is concerned, prediction is considered to be an aspect of theory. By its very nature, a theory predicts. That is, when from the primitive propositions of a theory we deduce more complex ones, we are in essence "predicting." When we explain observed phenomena, we are always stating a relation between, say, the class A and the class B. Scientific explanation inheres in specifying the relations between one class of empirical events and another, under certain conditions. We say: If A, then B, A and B referring to classes of objects or events.[15] But this *is* prediction, prediction from A to B. Thus a theoretical explanation implies prediction. And we come back to the idea that theory is the ultimate aim of science. All else flows from theory.

There is no intention here to discredit or denigrate research that is not specifically and consciously theory-oriented. Much valuable social scientific and educational research is preoccupied with the shorter-range goal of finding specific relations; that is, merely to discover a relation is part of science. The ultimately most usable and satisfying relations, however, are those that are the most generalized, those that are tied to other relations in a theory.

The notion of generality is important. Theories, because they are general, apply to many phenomena and to many people in many places. A specific relation, of course, is less widely applicable. If, for example, one finds that test anxiety is related to test performance, this finding, though interesting and important, is less widely applicable and less understood than if one first found the relation in a network of interrelated variables that are parts of a theory. Modest, limited, and specific research aims, then, are good. Theoretical research aims are better because, among other reasons, they are more general and more widely applicable.

SCIENTIFIC RESEARCH—A DEFINITION

It is easier to define scientific research than it is to define science. It would not be easy, however, to get scientists and researchers to agree on such a definition. Even so, we attempt one here:

> Scientific research is systematic, controlled, empirical, and critical investigation of natural phenomena guided by theory and hypotheses about the presumed relations among such phenomena.

This definition requires little explanation since it is mostly a condensed and formalized statement of much that was said earlier or that will be said soon. Two points need emphasis, however. First, when we say that scientific research is systematic and controlled, we mean, in effect, that scientific investigation is so ordered that investigators can have critical confidence in research outcomes. As we shall see later, scientific research observations are tightly disciplined. Moreover, among the many alternative explanations of a phenomenon, all but one are systematically ruled out. One can thus have greater confi-

---

[15] Statements of the form "If p, then q," called conditional statements in logic, are the core of scientific inquiry. They and the concepts or variables that go into them are the central ingredient of theories. The logical foundation of scientific inquiry that underlies much of the reasoning in this book has been outlined in Kerlinger, "Research in Education," *op. cit.*, 1132–1134.

dence that a tested relation is as it is than if one had not controlled the observations and ruled out alternative possibilities.

Second, scientific investigation is empirical. If the scientist believes something is so, he must somehow or other put his belief to a test outside himself. Subjective belief, in other words, must be checked against objective reality. The scientist must always subject his notions to the court of empirical inquiry and test. He is hypercritical of the results of his own and others' research. Every scientist writing a research report has other scientists reading what he writes while he writes it. Though it is easy to err, to exaggerate, to overgeneralize when writing up one's own work, it is not easy to escape the feeling of scientific eyes constantly peering over one's shoulder.

THE SCIENTIFIC APPROACH

The scientific approach is a special systematized form of all reflective thinking and inquiry. Dewey, in his influential *How We Think,* outlined a general paradigm of inquiry.[16] The present discussion of the scientific approach is based largely on Dewey's analysis.

Problem-Obstacle-Idea

The scientist will usually experience an obstacle to understanding, a vague unrest about observed and unobserved phenomena, a curiosity as to why something is as it is. His first and most important step is to get the idea out in the open, to express the problem in some reasonably manageable form. Rarely or never will the problem spring full-blown at this stage. He must struggle with it, try it out, live with it. Dewey says, "There is a troubled, perplexed, trying situation, where the difficulty is, as it were, spread throughout the entire situation, infecting it as a whole."[17] Sooner or later, explicitly or implicitly, he states the problem, even if his expression of it is inchoate and tentative. Here he intellectualizes, as Dewey puts it, "what at first is merely an *emotional* quality of the whole situation."[18] In some respects, this is the most difficult and most important part of the whole process. Without some sort of statement of the problem, the scientist can rarely go further and expect his work to be fruitful.

Hypothesis

After intellectualizing the problem, after turning back on experience for possible solutions, after observing relevant phenomena, the scientist may formulate a hypothesis. A hypothesis is a conjectural statement, a tentative proposition about the relation between two or more phenomena or variables. Our scientist will say, "If such-and-such occurs, then so-and-so results."

Reasoning-Deduction

This step or activity is frequently overlooked or underemphasized. It is perhaps the most important part of Dewey's analysis of reflective thinking. The scientist deduces the conse-

[16] J. Dewey, *How We Think*. Boston: Heath, 1933, pp. 106–118.
[17] *Ibid.,* p. 108.
[18] *Ibid.* p. 109.

quences of the hypothesis he has formulated. Conant, in talking about the rise of modern science, said that the new element added in the seventeenth century was the use of deductive reasoning.[19] Here is where experience, knowledge, and perspicacity are important.

Often the scientist, when deducing the consequences of a hypothesis he has formulated, will arrive at a problem quite different from the one he started with. On the other hand, he may find that his deductions lead him to believe that the problem cannot be solved with present technical tools. For example, before modern statistics was developed, certain behavioral research problems were insoluble. It was difficult, if not impossible, to test two or three interdependent hypotheses at one time. It was next to impossible to test the interactive effect of variables. And we now have reason to believe that certain problems are insoluble unless they are tackled in a multivariate manner. An example of this is teaching methods and their relation to achievement and other variables. It is likely that teaching methods, *per se,* do not differ much if we study only their simple effects. Teaching methods probably work differently under different conditions, with different teachers, and with different pupils. It is said that the methods ''interact'' with the conditions and with the characteristics of teachers and of pupils.

An example may help us understand this reasoning-deduction step. Suppose an investigator becomes intrigued with aggressive behavior. He wonders why people are often aggressive in situations where aggressiveness may not be appropriate. He has noted that aggressive behavior seems to occur when people have experienced difficulties of one kind or another. (Note the vagueness of the problem here.) After thinking for some time, reading the literature for clues, and making further observations, he formulates a hypothesis: Frustration leads to aggression. He defines ''frustration'' as prevention from reaching a goal and ''aggression'' as behavior characterized by physical or verbal attack on other persons or objects.

He may now reason somewhat as follows. If frustration leads to aggression, then we should find a great deal of aggression among children who are in schools that are restrictive, schools that do not permit children much freedom and self-expression. Similarly, in difficult social situations, assuming such situations are frustrating, we should expect more aggression than is ''usual.'' Reasoning further, if we give experimental subjects interesting problems to solve and then prevent them from solving them, we can predict some kind of aggressive behavior.

Reasoning may, as indicated above, change the problem. We may realize that the initial problem was only a special case of a broader, more fundamental and important problem. We may, for example, start with a narrower hypothesis: Restrictive school situations lead to negativism in children. Then we can generalize the problem to the form: Frustration leads to aggression. While this is a different form of thinking from that discussed earlier, it is important because of what can almost be called its heuristic quality. Reasoning can help lead to wider, more basic, and thus more significant problems, as well as provide operational (testable) implications of the original hypothesis.

Observation-Test-Experiment

It should be clear by now that the observation-test-experiment phase is only part of the scientific enterprise. If the problem has been well stated, the hypothesis or hypotheses adequately formulated, and the implications of the hypotheses carefully deduced, this step is almost automatic—assuming that the investigator is technically competent.

---

[19] Conant, *op. cit.,* p. 46.

The essence of testing a hypothesis is to test the *relation* expressed by the hypothesis. We do not test variables, as such; we test the relation between the variables. Observation, testing, and experimentation are for one large purpose: putting the problem relation to empirical test. To test without knowing at least fairly well what and why one is testing is to blunder. Simply to state a vague problem, like How does Open Education affect learning? and then to test pupils in schools presumed to differ in "openness," or to ask What are the effects of cognitive dissonance? and then, after experimental manipulations to create dissonance, to search for presumed effects can lead only to questionable information. Similarly, to say one is going to study attribution processes without really knowing why one is doing it or without stating relations between variables is research nonsense.

Another point about testing hypotheses is that we usually do not test hypotheses directly. As indicated in the previous step on reasoning, we test deduced implications of hypotheses. Our test hypothesis may be: "Subjects induced to lie will comply more with later requests than will subjects not induced to lie," which was deduced from a broader and more general hypothesis: "Increased guilt leads to increased compliance." We do not test "inducement to lie" nor "comply with requests." We test the relation between them, in this case the relation between lying (deduced guilt) and compliance with later requests.[20]

Dewey emphasized that the temporal sequence of reflective thinking or inquiry is not fixed. We can repeat and reemphasize what he says in our own framework. The steps of the scientific approach are not neatly fixed. The first step is not neatly completed before the second step begins. Further, we may test before adequately deducing the implications of the hypothesis. The hypothesis itself may seem to need elaboration or refinement as a result of deducing implications from it.[21]

Feedback to the problem, the hypotheses, and, finally, the theory of the results of research is highly important. Learning theorists and researchers, for example, have frequently altered their theories and research as a result of experimental findings.[22] Theorists and researchers have been studying the effects of early environment and training on later development. Their research has yielded varied evidence converging on this extremely important theoretical and practical problem.[23] Part of the essential core of scientific research is the constant effort to replicate and check findings, to correct theory on the basis of empirical evidence, and to find better explanations of natural phenomena. One can even go so far as to say that science has a cyclic aspect. A researcher finds, say, that *A* is related to *B* in such-and-such a way. He then does more research to determine under what other conditions *A* is similarly related to *B*. Other researchers challenge his theory and his research, offering explanations and evidence of their own. The original researcher, it is hoped, alters his work in the light of his own and others' evidence. The process never ends.

Let us summarize the so-called scientific approach to inquiry. First there is doubt, a barrier, an indeterminate situation crying out to be made determinate. The scientist experiences vague doubts, emotional disturbance, inchoate ideas. He struggles to formulate the problem, even if inadequately. He studies the literature, scans his own experience and

---

[20] This hypothesis was taken from an ingenious and interesting study: J. Freedman, S. Wallington, and E. Bless, "Compliance Without Pressure: The Effect of Guilt," *Journal of Personality and Social Psychology,* 7 (1967), 117–124.

[21] Hypotheses and their expression will often be found inadequate when implications are deduced from them. A frequent difficulty occurs when a hypothesis is so vague that one deduction is as good as another—that is, the hypothesis may not yield to precise test.

[22] E. Hilgard and G. Bower, *Theories of Learning,* 4th ed. Englewood Cliffs, N. J.: Prentice-Hall, 1975.

[23] For example, E. Bennett et al., "Chemical and Anatomical Plasticity of Brain," *Science,* 146 (1964), 610–619; J. Hunt, *Intelligence and Experience.* New York: Ronald, 1961.

the experience of others. Often he simply has to wait for an inventive leap of the mind. Maybe it will occur; maybe not. With the problem formulated, with the basic question or questions properly asked, the rest is much easier. Then the hypothesis is constructed, after which its empirical implications are deduced. In this process the original problem, and of course the original hypothesis, may be changed. It may be broadened or narrowed. It may even be abandoned. Last, but not finally, the relation expressed by the hypothesis is tested by observation and experimentation. On the basis of the research evidence, the hypothesis is accepted or rejected. This information is then fed back to the original problem, and the problem is kept or altered as dictated by the evidence. Dewey pointed out that one phase of the process may be expanded and be of great importance, another may be skimped, and there may be fewer or more steps involved. Research is rarely an orderly business anyway. Indeed, it is much more disorderly than the above discussion may imply. Order and disorder, however, are not of primary importance. What is much more important is the controlled rationality of scientific research as a process of reflective inquiry, the interdependent nature of the parts of the process, and the paramount importance of the problem and its statement.

Study Suggestion

Some of the content of this chapter is highly controversial. The views expressed are accepted by some thinkers and rejected by others. Readers can enhance understanding of science and its purpose, the relation between science and technology, and basic and applied research by selective reading of the literature. Such reading can be the basis for class discussions.

Extended treatment of the controversial aspects of science, especially behavioral science, is given in my book, *Behavioral Research: A Conceptual Approach*. New York: Holt, Rinehart and Winston, 1973, chaps. 1, 15, and 16.

Many fine articles on science and research have been published in the journal *Science*. Here are seven of them. All are pertinent to this chapter's substance.

BRAIN, W. R. "Science and Antiscience," 148 (1965), 192–198. On misunderstanding of science. Especially pertinent for psychologists.

BROOKS, H. "Can Science Survive in the Modern Age?" 174 (1971), 21–30. Penetrating analysis.

DUBOS, R. "Scientist and Public," 133 (1961), 1207–1211. Stresses danger of utilitarian view of science.

DuBRIDGE, L. A. "Science Serves Society," 164 (1969), 1137–1140. Emphasizes moral aspects of science, and says that it "has been the most brilliantly successful enterprise in human history."

Panel on Basic Research and Graduate Education of the President's Science Advisory Committee. "Scientific Progress and the Federal Government," 132 (1960), 1802–1815. Long, important, and excellent report.

SIMPSON, G. G. "Biology and the Nature of Science," 139 (1963), 81–88. Outstanding article on the nature of science. Strongly recommended.

THOMSON, G. "The Two Aspects of Science," 132 (1960), 996–1000. Stresses the importance—and fascination—of understanding as the aim of science.

Chapter 2

Problems and Hypotheses

MANY PEOPLE think that science is basically a fact-gathering activity. It is not. As Cohen says:

> There is . . . no genuine progress in scientific insight through the Baconian method of accumulating empirical facts without hypotheses or anticipation of nature. Without some guiding idea we do not know what facts to gather . . . we cannot determine what is relevant and what is irrelevant.[1]

The scientifically uninformed person often has the idea that the scientist is a highly objective individual who gathers data without preconceived ideas. Poincaré long ago pointed out how wrong this idea is. He said:

> It is often said that experiments should be made without preconceived ideas. That is impossible. Not only would it make every experiment fruitless, but even if we wished to do so, it could not be done.[2]

PROBLEMS

It is not always possible for a researcher to formulate his problem simply, clearly, and completely. He may often have only a rather general, diffuse, even confused notion of the problem. This is in the nature of the complexity of scientific research. It may even take an investigator years of exploration, thought, and research before he can clearly say what questions he has been seeking answers to. Nevertheless, adequate statement of the research problem is one of the most important parts of research. That it may be difficult or

---

[1] M. Cohen, *A Preface to Logic*. New York: Meridian, 1956, p. 148.
[2] H. Poincaré, *Science and Hypothesis*. New York: Dover, 1952, p. 143.

impossible to state a research problem satisfactorily at a given time should not allow us to lose sight of the ultimate desirability and necessity of doing so.

Bearing this difficulty in mind, a fundamental principle can be stated: If one wants to solve a problem, one must generally know what the problem is. It can be said that a large part of the solution lies in knowing what it is one is trying to do. Another part lies in knowing what a problem is and especially what a scientific problem is.

What is a good problem statement? Although research problems differ greatly and there is no one "right" way to state a problem, certain characteristics of problems and problem statements can be learned and used to good advantage. To start, let us take two or three examples of published research problems and study their characteristics. First, take the problem of the study by Hurlock mentioned in Chapter 1: What are the effects on pupil performance of different types of incentives?[3] Note that the problem is stated in question form. The simplest way is here the best way. Also note that the problem states a relation between variables, in this case between the variables incentives and pupil performance (achievement). ("Variable" will be formally defined in Chapter 3. For now, a variable is the name of a phenomenon, or a construct, that takes a set of different numerical values.)

A *problem,* then, is an interrogative sentence or statement that asks: What relation exists between two or more variables? The answer is what is being sought in the research. A problem in most cases will have two or more variables. In the Hurlock example, the problem statement relates incentive to pupil performance. Another problem, studied in an ingenious experiment by Glucksberg and King, is associated with an adage: We remember what we want to remember, and with Freud's concept of repression: Are memory items associated with unpleasant events more readily forgotten than neutral items?[4] One variable is items associated with unpleasantness, and the other variable is remembering (or forgetting). Still another problem, by Jones and Cook, is quite different: Do attitudes toward blacks influence judgments of the effectiveness of alternative racial social policies?[5] One variable is attitudes toward blacks and the other is judgments of the effectiveness of social policies.[6]

Criteria of Problems and Problem Statements

There are three criteria of good problems and problem statements. One, the problem should express a relation between two or more variables. It asks, in effect, questions like: Is *A* related to *B*? How are *A* and *B* related to *C*? How is *A* related to *B* under conditions *C* and *D*? The exceptions to this dictum occur mostly in taxonomic or methodological research. (See Appendix A and footnote 6.)

[3] E. Hurlock, "An Evaluation of Certain Incentives Used in Schoolwork," *Journal of Educational Psychology,* 16 (1925), 145–149. When citing problems and hypotheses from the literature, I have not always used the words of the authors. In fact, the statements of many of the problems are mine and not those of the cited authors. Some authors use only problem statements; some use only hypotheses; others use both.

[4] S. Glucksberg and L. King, "Motivated Forgetting Mediated by Implicit Verbal Chaining: A Laboratory Analog of Repression," *Science,* 158 (1967), 517–519.

[5] S. Jones and S. Cook, "The Influence of Attitude on Judgments of the Effectiveness of Alternative Social Policies," *Journal of Personality and Social Psychology,* 32 (1975), 767–773.

[6] Not all research problems clearly have two or more variables. For example, in experimental psychology, the research focus is often on psychological processes like memory and categorization. In her justifiably well-known and influential study of perceptual categories, Rosch in effect asked the question: Are there nonarbitrary ("natural") categories of color and form? (E. Rosch, "Natural Categories," *Cognitive Psychology,* 4 [1973], 328–350.) Although the relation between two or more variables is not apparent in this problem statement, in the actual research the categories were related to learning. Toward the end of this book we will see that factor analytic research problems also lack the relation form discussed above. In most behavioral research problems, however, the relations among two or more variables are studied, and we will therefore emphasize such relation statements.

Two, the problem should be stated clearly and unambiguously in question form. Instead of saying, for instance, "The problem is . . . ," or "The purpose of this study is . . . ," ask a question. Questions have the virtue of posing problems directly. The purpose of a study is not necessarily the same as the problem of a study. The purpose of the Hurlock study, for instance, was to throw light on the use of incentives in school situations. The problem was the question about the relation between incentives and performance. Again, the simplest way is the best way: ask a question.

The third criterion is often difficult to satisfy. It demands that the problem and the problem statement should be such as to *imply* possibilities of empirical testing. A problem that does not contain implications for testing its stated relation or relations is not a scientific problem. This means not only that an actual relation is stated, but also that the variables of the relation can somehow be measured. Many interesting and important questions are not scientific questions simply because they are not amenable to testing. Certain philosophic and theological questions, while perhaps important to the individuals who consider them, cannot be tested empirically and are thus of no interest to the scientist as a scientist. The epistemological question, "How do we know?," is such a question. Education has many interesting but nonscientific questions, such as, "Does democratic education improve the learning of youngsters?" "Are group processes good for children?" These questions can be called metaphysical in the sense that they are, at least as stated, beyond empirical testing possibilities. The key difficulties are that some of them are not relations, and most of their constructs are very difficult or impossible to so define that they can be measured.[7]

HYPOTHESES

A *hypothesis* is a conjectural statement of the relation between two or more variables. Hypotheses are always in declarative sentence form, and they relate, either generally or specifically, variables to variables. There are two criteria for "good" hypotheses and hypothesis statements. They are the same as two of those for problems and problem statements. One, hypotheses are statements about the relations between variables. Two, hypotheses carry clear implications for testing the stated relations. These criteria mean, then, that hypothesis statements contain two or more variables that are measurable or potentially measurable and that they specify how the variables are related.

Let us take three hypotheses from the literature and apply the criteria to them. The first hypothesis seems to defy common sense: Overlearning leads to performance decrement (or, as the authors say: Practice makes imperfect!).[8] Here a relation is stated between one variable, overlearning, and another variable, performance decrement. Since the two variables are readily defined and measured, implications for testing the hypothesis, too, are readily conceived. The criteria are satisfied. A second hypothesis is related to the first (though formulated many years earlier). It is also unusual because it states a relation in the so-called null form: Practice in a mental function has no effect on the future learning of that function.[9] The relation is stated clearly: one variable, practice in a mental function

---

[7] Webb, working from a different point of view, has proposed the following criteria of research problems: knowledge (of the researcher); dissatisfaction (skepticism, going against the tide, etc.); generality (wideness of applicability). Webb's article is doubly valuable because he effectively disposes of irrelevant criteria, such as conformability, cupidity ("payola"), conformity ("Everybody's doing it"). W. Webb, "The Choice of Problem," *American Psychologist*, 16 (1961), 223–227.

[8] E. Langer and L. Imber, "When Practice Makes Imperfect: Debilitating Effects of Overlearning," *Journal of Personality and Social Psychology*, 37 (1980), 2014–2024.

[9] A. Gates and G. Taylor, "An Experimental Study of the Nature of Improvement Resulting from Practice in a Mental Function," *Journal of Educational Psychology*, 16 (1925), 583–592.

(like memory), is related to another variable by the words "has no effect on." On the criterion of potential testability, however, we meet with difficulty. We are faced with the problem of so defining "mental function" and "future learning" that they are measurable. If we can solve this problem satisfactorily, then we definitely have a hypothesis. Indeed, we have a famous one—but one that has usually not been stated as a hypothesis but as a fact by many educators of the past and present.

The third hypothesis represents a numerous and important class. Here the relation is indirect, concealed, as it were. It customarily comes in the form of a statement that Groups *A* and *B* will differ on some characteristic. For example: Middle-class children more often than lower-class children will avoid finger-painting tasks.[10] Note that this statement is one step removed from the actual hypothesis, which may be stated: Finger-painting behavior is in part a function of social class. If the latter statement were the hypothesis stated, then the first might be called a subhypothesis, or a specific prediction based on the original hypothesis.

Let us consider another hypothesis of this type but removed one step further: Individuals having the same or similar occupational role will hold similar attitudes toward cognitive objects significantly related to the occupational role.[11] ("Cognitive objects" are any concrete or abstract things perceived and "known" by individuals. People, groups, the government, and education are examples.) The relation in this case, of course, is between occupational role and attitudes (toward a cognitive object related to the role, for example, role of educator and attitudes toward education). In order to test this hypothesis, it would be necessary to have at least two groups, each representing a different occupational role, and then to compare the attitudes of the groups. For instance, we might take a group of teachers and compare their attitudes toward education to those of, say, a group of businessmen. In any case, the criteria are satisfied.

THE IMPORTANCE OF PROBLEMS AND HYPOTHESES

There is little doubt that hypotheses are important and indispensable tools of scientific research. There are three main reasons for this belief. One, they are, so to speak, the working instruments of theory. Hypotheses can be deduced from theory and from other hypotheses. If, for instance, we are working on a theory of aggression, we are presumably looking for causes and effects of aggressive behavior. We might have observed cases of aggressive behavior occurring after frustrating circumstances. The theory, then, might include the proposition: Frustration produces aggression.[12] From this broad hypothesis we may deduce more specific hypotheses, such as: To prevent children from reaching desired goals (frustration) will result in their fighting each other (aggression); if children are deprived of parental love (frustration), they will react in part with aggressive behavior.

The second reason is that hypotheses can be tested and shown to be probably true or probably false. Isolated facts are not tested, as we said before; only relations are tested. Since hypotheses are relational propositions, this is probably the main reason they are used in scientific inquiry. They are, in essence, predictions of the form, "If *A*, then *B*,"

---

[10]T. Alper, H. Blane, and B. Adams, "Reactions of Middle and Lower Class Children to Finger Paints as a Function of Class Differences in Child-Training Practices," *Journal of Abnormal and Social Psychology*, 51 (1955), 439–448.

[11]F. Kerlinger, "The Attitude Structure of the Individual: A *Q*-Study of the Educational Attitudes of Professors and Laymen," *Genetic Psychology Monographs*, 53 (1956), 283–329.

[12]J. Dollard, L. Doob, N. Miller, O. Mowrer, and R. Sears, *Frustration and Aggression*. New Haven: Yale University Press, 1939.

which we set up to test the relation between *A* and *B*. We let the facts have a chance to establish the probable truth or falsity of the hypothesis.

Three, hypotheses are powerful tools for the advancement of knowledge because they enable scientists to get outside themselves. Though constructed by man, hypotheses exist, can be tested, and can be shown to be probably correct or incorrect apart from man's values and opinions. This is so important that we venture to say that there would be no science in any complete sense without hypotheses.

Just as important as hypotheses are the problems behind the hypotheses. As Dewey has well pointed out, research usually starts with a problem. He says that there is first an indeterminate situation in which ideas are vague, doubts are raised, and the thinker is perplexed.[13] He further points out that the problem is not enunciated, indeed cannot be enunciated, until one has experienced such an indeterminate situation.

The indeterminacy, however, must ultimately be removed. Though it is true, as stated earlier, that a researcher may often have only a general and diffuse notion of his problem, sooner or later he has to have a fairly clear idea of what the problem is. Though this statement seems self-evident, one of the most difficult things to do is to state one's research problem clearly and completely. In other words, you must know what you are trying to find out. When you finally do know, the problem is a long way toward solution.

VIRTUES OF PROBLEMS AND HYPOTHESES

Problems and hypotheses, then, have important virtues. One, they direct investigation. The relations expressed in the hypotheses tell the investigator, in effect, what to do. Two, problems and hypotheses, because they are ordinarily generalized relational statements, enable the researcher to deduce specific empirical manifestations implied by the problems and hypotheses. We may say, following Allport and Ross: If it is indeed true that people of extrinsic religious orientation (they *use* religion) are prejudiced, whereas people of intrinsic religious orientation (they *live* religion) are not, then it follows that churchgoers should be more prejudiced than nonchurchgoers. They should perhaps also have a "jungle" philosophy: general suspicion and distrust of the world.[14]

There are important differences between problems and hypotheses. Hypotheses, if properly stated, can be tested. While a given hypothesis may be too broad to be tested directly, if it is a "good" hypothesis, then other testable hypotheses can be deduced from it. Facts or variables are not tested as such. The relations stated by the hypotheses are tested. And a problem cannot be scientifically solved unless it is reduced to hypothesis form, because a problem is a question, usually of a broad nature, and is not directly testable. One does not test the questions: Does efficiency enhance organizational effectiveness and profitability?[15] Does differential experience modify the brain?[16] One tests one or more hypotheses implied by these questions. For example, to study the latter problem, one may hypothesize that animals with different levels of experience will have different thicknesses of the brain cortex.

[13] J. Dewey, *Logic: The Theory of Inquiry*. New York: Holt, Rinehart and Winston, 1938, pp. 105–107.

[14] G. Allport and J. Ross, "Personal Religious Orientation and Prejudice," *Journal of Personality and Social Psychology*, 5 (1967), 432–443.

[15] D. Katz and R. Kahn, *The Social Psychology of Organizations*, 2nd ed. New York: Wiley, 1978, pp. 237ff.

[16] M. Rosenzweig, "Environmental Complexity, Cerebral Change, and Behavior," *American Psychologist*, 21 (1966), 321–332.

Problems and hypotheses advance scientific knowledge by helping the investigator confirm or disconfirm theory. Suppose a psychological investigator gives a number of subjects three or four tests, among which is a test of anxiety and an arithmetic test. Routinely computing the intercorrelations between the three or four tests, he finds that the correlation between anxiety and arithmetic is negative. He concludes, therefore that the greater the anxiety the lower the arithmetic score. But it is quite conceivable that the relation is fortuitous or even spurious. If, however, he had hypothesized the relation on the basis of theory, the investigator could have greater confidence in the results. Investigators who do not hypothesize relations in advance, in short, do not give give the facts a chance to prove or disprove anything.[17]

This use of the hypothesis is similar to playing a game of chance. The rules of the game are set up in advance, and bets are made in advance. One cannot change the rules after an outcome, nor can one change one's bets after making them. That would not be "fair." One cannot throw the dice first and then bet. Similarly, if one gathers data first and then selects a datum and comes to a conclusion on the basis of the datum, one has violated the rules of the scientific game. The game is not "fair" because the investigator can easily capitalize on, say, two significant relations out of five tested. What happens to the other three? They are usually forgotten. But in a fair game every throw of the dice is counted, in the sense that one either wins or does not win on the basis of the outcome of each throw.

Hypotheses direct inquiry. As Darwin pointed out long ago, observations have to be for or against some view if they are to be of any use. Hypotheses incorporate aspects of the theory under test in testable or near-testable form. Earlier, an example of reinforcement theory was given in which testable hypotheses were deduced from the general problem. The importance of recognizing this function of hypotheses may be shown by going through the back door and using a theory that is very difficult, or perhaps impossible, to test. Freud's theory of anxiety includes the construct of repression. Now, by repression Freud meant the forcing of unacceptable ideas deep into the unconscious. In order to test the Freudian theory of anxiety it is necessary to deduce relations suggested by the theory. These deductions will, of course, have to include the repression notion, which includes the construct of the unconscious. Hypotheses can be formulated using these constructs; in order to test the theory, they have to be so formulated. But testing them is another, more difficult matter because of the extreme difficulty of so defining terms such as "repression" and "unconscious" that they can be measured. To the present, no one has succeeded in defining these two constructs without seriously departing from the original Freudian meaning and usage. Hypotheses, then, are important bridges between theory and empirical inquiry.

PROBLEMS, VALUES, AND DEFINITIONS

To clarify further the nature of problems and hypotheses, two or three common errors will now be discussed. First, scientific problems are not moral and ethical questions. Are

[17] The words "prove" and "disprove" are not to be taken here in their usual literal sense. It should be remembered that a hypothesis is never really proved or disproved. To be more accurate we should probably say something like: The weight of evidence is on the side of the hypothesis, or the weight of the evidence casts doubt on the hypothesis. Braithwaite says: "Thus the empirical evidence of its instance never proves the hypothesis: in suitable cases we may say that it *establishes* the hypothesis, meaning by this that the evidence makes it reasonable to accept the hypothesis; but it never *proves* the hypothesis in the sense that the hypothesis is a logical consequence of the evidence." (R. Braithwaite, *Scientific Explanation*. Cambridge: Cambridge University Press, 1955, p. 14.)

punitive disciplinary measures bad for children? Should an organization's leadership be democratic? What is the best way to teach college students? To ask these questions is to ask value and judgmental questions that science cannot answer. Many so-called hypotheses are not hypotheses at all. For instance: The small-group method of teaching is better than the lecture method. This is a value statement; it is an article of faith and not a hypothesis. If it were possible to state a relation between the variables, and if it were possible to define the variables so as to permit testing the relation, then we might have a hypothesis. But there is no way to test value questions scientifically.

A quick and relatively easy way to detect value questions and statements is to look for words such as "should," "ought," "better than" (instead of "greater than"), and similar words that indicate cultural or personal judgments or preferences. Value statements, however, are tricky. While a "should" statement is obviously a value statement, certain other kinds of statements are not so obvious. Take the statement: Authoritarian methods of teaching lead to poor learning. Here there is a relation. But the statement fails as a scientific hypothesis because it uses two value expressions or words, "authoritarian methods of teaching" and "poor learning," neither of which can be defined for measurement purposes without deleting the words "authoritarian" and "poor."[18]

Other kinds of statements that are not hypotheses or are poor ones are frequently formulated, especially in education. Consider, for instance: The core curriculum is an enriching experience. Another type, too frequent, is the vague generalization: Reading skills can be identified in the second grade; the goal of the unique individual is self-realization; Prejudice is related to certain personality traits.

Another common defect of problem statements often occurs in doctoral theses: the listing of methodological points or "problems" as subproblems. These methodological points have two characteristics that make them easy to detect: (1) they are not substantive problems that spring from the basic problem; and (2) they relate to techniques or methods of sampling, measuring, or analyzing. They are usually not in question form, but rather contain the words "test," "determine," "measure," and the like. "To determine the reliability of the instruments used in this research," "To test the significance of the differences between the means," and "To assign pupils at random to the experimental groups" are examples of this mistaken notion of problems and subproblems.

GENERALITY AND SPECIFICITY OF PROBLEMS AND HYPOTHESES

One difficulty that the research worker usually encounters and that almost all students working on a thesis find bothersome is the generality and specificity of problems and hypotheses. If the problem is too general, it is usually to vague to be tested. Thus, it is scientifically useless, though it may be interesting to read. Problems and hypotheses that are too general or too vague are common. For example: Creativity is a function of the self-actualization of the individual; Democratic education enhances social learning and citizenship; Authoritarianism in the college classroom inhibits the creative imagination of students. These are interesting problems. But, in their present form, they are worse than useless scientifically, because they cannot be tested and because they give one the spurious assurance that they are hypotheses that can "some day" be tested.

Terms such as "creativity," "self-actualization," "democracy," "authoritarian-

---

[18] An almost classic case of the use of the word "authoritarian" is the statement sometimes heard among educators: The lecture method is authoritarian. This seems to mean that the speaker does not like the lecture method and he is telling us that it is bad. Similarly, one of the most effective ways to criticize a teacher is to say that he is authoritarian.

ism,'' and the like have, at the present time at least, no adequate empirical referents.[19] Now, it is quite true that we can define ''creativity,'' say, in a limited way by specifying one or two creativity tests. This may be a legitimate procedure. Still, in so doing, we run the risk of getting far away from the original term and its meaning. This is particularly true when we speak of artistic creativity. We are often willing to accept the risk in order to be able to investigate important problems, of course. Yet terms like ''democracy'' are almost hopeless to define. Even when we do define it, we often find we have destroyed the original meaning of the term.[20]

The other extreme is too great specificity. Every student has heard that it is necessary to narrow problems down to workable size. This is true. But, unfortunately, we can also narrow the problem out of existence. In general, the more specific the problem or hypothesis the clearer are its testing implications. But triviality may be the price we pay. While researchers cannot handle problems that are too broad because they tend to be too vague for adequate research operations, in their zeal to cut the problems down to workable size or to find a workable problem, they may cut the life out of it. They may make it trivial or inconsequential. A thesis, for instance, on the simple relation between the speed of reading and size of type, while important and maybe even interesting, is too thin for doctoral study. Too great specificity is perhaps a worse danger than too great generality. At any rate, some kind of compromise must be made between generality and specificity. The ability effectively to make such compromises is a function partly of experience and partly of critical study of research problems.

THE MULTIVARIATE NATURE OF BEHAVIORAL RESEARCH AND PROBLEMS

Until now the discussion of problems and hypotheses has been pretty much limited to two variables, x and y. We must hasten to correct any impression that such problems and hypotheses are the norm in behavioral research. Researchers in psychology, sociology, education, and other behavioral sciences have become keenly aware of the multivariate nature of behavioral research. Instead of saying: If p, then q, it is often more appropriate to say: If $p_1, p_2, \ldots, p_k$, then q; or: If p_1, then q, under conditions r, s, and t.

An example may clarify the point. Instead of simply stating the hypothesis: If frustration, then aggression, it is more realistic to recognize the multivariate nature of the determinants and influences of aggression by saying, for example: If high intelligence, middle class, male, and frustrated, then aggression. Or: If frustration, then aggression, under the conditions of high intelligence, middle class, and male. Instead of one x, we now have four x's. Although one phenomenon may be the most important in determining or influencing another phenomenon, it is unlikely that most of the phenomena of interest to behavioral scientists are determined simply. It is much more likely that they are determined multiply. It is much more likely that aggression is the result of several influences working in complex ways. Moreover, aggression itself has multiple aspects. After all, there are different kinds of aggression.

Problems and hypotheses thus have to reflect the multivariate complexity of psycho-

---

[19] Although many studies of authoritarianism have been done with considerable success, it is doubtful that we know what authoritarianism in the classroom means. For instance, an action of a teacher that is authoritarian in one classroom may not be authoritarian in another classroom. The alleged democratic behavior exhibited by one teacher may even be called authoritarian if exhibited by another teacher. Such elasticity is not the stuff of science.

[20] An outstanding exception to this statement is Bollen's definition and measurement of ''democracy.'' We will examine both in subsequent chapters. K. Bollen, ''Issues in the Comparative Measurement of Political Democracy,'' *American Sociological Review,* 45 (1980), 370–390.

logical, sociological, and educational reality. Although we will talk of one x and one y, especially in the early part of the book, it *must* be understood that contemporary behavioral research, which used to be almost exclusively univariate in its approach, is rapidly becoming multivariate. (For now, "univariate" means one x and one y. "Univariate," strictly speaking, applies to y. If there is more than one x or more than one y, the word "multivariate" is used, at least in this book.) We will soon encounter multivariate conceptions and problems. And later parts of the book will be especially concerned with a multivariate approach and emphasis.

CONCLUDING REMARKS—THE SPECIAL POWER OF HYPOTHESES

One will sometimes hear that hypotheses are unnecessary in research, that they unnecessarily restrict the investigative imagination, that the job of science and scientific investigation is to find out things and not to belabor the obvious, that hypotheses are obsolete, and the like. Such statements are quite misleading. They misconstrue the purpose of hypotheses.

It can almost be said that the hypothesis is one of the most powerful tools yet invented to achieve dependable knowledge. We observe a phenomenon. We speculate on possible causes. Naturally, our culture has answers to account for most phenomena, many correct, many incorrect, many a mixture of fact and superstition, many pure superstition. It is the business of scientists to doubt most explanations of phenomena. Such doubts are systematic. Scientists insist upon subjecting explanations of phenomena to controlled empirical test. In order to do this, they formulate the explanations in the form of theories and hypotheses. In fact, the explanations *are* hypotheses. Scientists simply discipline the business by writing systematic and testable hypotheses. If an explanation cannot be formulated in the form of a testable hypothesis, then it can be considered to be a metaphysical explanation and thus not amenable to scientific investigation. As such, it is dismissed by scientists as being of no interest.

The power of hypotheses goes further than this, however. A hypothesis is a prediction. It says that if x occurs, y will also occur. That is, y is predicted from x. If, then, x is made to occur (vary), and it is observed that y also occurs (varies concomitantly), then the hypothesis is confirmed. This is more powerful evidence than simply observing, without prediction, the covarying of x and y. It is more powerful in the betting-game sense discussed earlier. The scientist makes a bet that x leads to y. If, in an experiment, x does lead to y, then he has won the bet. He cannot just enter the game at any point and pick a perhaps fortuitous common occurrence of x and y. Games are not played this way (at least in our culture). He must play according to the rules, and the rules in science are made to minimize error and fallibility. Hypotheses are part of the rules of the game.

Even when hypotheses are not confirmed, they have power. Even when y does not covary with x, knowledge is advanced. Negative findings are sometimes as important as positive ones, since they cut down the total universe of ignorance and sometimes point up fruitful further hypotheses and lines of investigation. *But the scientist cannot tell positive from negative evidence unless he uses hypotheses*. It is possible to conduct research without hypotheses, of course, particularly in exploratory investigations. But it is hard to conceive modern science in all its rigorous and disciplined fertility without the guiding power of hypotheses.

Study Suggestions

1. Use the following variable names to write research problems and hypotheses: frustration, academic achievement, intelligence, verbal ability, race, social class (socioeconomic status), sex, reinforcement, teaching methods, occupational choice, conservatism, education, income, authority, need for achievement, group cohesiveness, obedience, social prestige, permissiveness.

2. Eight problems from the research literature are given below. Study them carefully, choose two or three, and construct hypotheses based on them.

(a) If people are given more time than necessary to do a task, will they continue to take more time than necessary on subsequent similar tasks?[21]

(b) How does organizational climate affect administrative performance?[22]

(c) Is comprehension of text facilitated by constructing meaningful elaborations of the text?[23]

(d) Do colleges discriminate against women applicants?[24]

(e) How does equalization of extrinsic environmental factors and conditions affect the mental performance of school children?[25]

(f) Are "natural" categories of color and form developed around basic prototypes (basic colors, basic forms) more readily learned than less prototypical categories?[26]

(g) What is the influence of massive rewards on the reading achievement of potential school dropouts?[27]

(h) Does extrinsic reward undermine intrinsic motivation?[28]

3. Eight hypotheses are given below. Discuss possibilities of testing them. Then read two or three of the studies to see how the authors tested them.

(a) The greater the cohesiveness of a group, the greater its influence on its members.[29]

(b) The greater the state's control of the economic system, the lower the level of democracy of the political system.[30]

(c) Revolutionary leaders who were successful before and after the success of the revolutionary movement exhibit a low level of conceptual complexity before the revolution and a high level of complexity after its success.[31]

(d) Role conflict is a function of incompatible expectations placed on or held by the individual.[32]

(e) Prejudiced (anti-Semitic) subjects, when frustrated, will displace aggression on to individuals not necessarily related to the source of the frustration.[33]

---

[21] E. Aronson and E. Gerard, "Beyond Parkinson's Law: The Effect of Excess Time on Subsequent Performance," *Journal of Personality and Social Psychology,* 3 (1966), 336–339.

[22] N. Frederiksen, O. Jensen, and A. Beaton, *Organizational Climates and Administrative Performance.* Princeton, N. J.: Educational Testing Service, 1968.

[23] M. Doctorow, M. Wittrock, and C. Marks, "Generative Processes in Reading Comprehension," *Journal of Educational Psychology,* 70 (1978), 109–118.

[24] E. Walster, T. Cleary, and M. Clifford, "The Effect of Race and Sex on College Admissions," *Journal of Educational Sociology,* 44 (1970), 237–244.

[25] A. Firkowska, A. Ostrowska, M. Sokolowska, Z. Stein, M. Susser, and I. Wald, "Cognitive Development and Social Policy," *Science,* 200 (1978), 1357–1362.

[26] E. Rosch, "Natural Categories," *Cognitive Psychology,* 4 (1973), 328–350.

[27] C. Clark and H. Walberg, "The Influence of Massive Rewards on Reading Achievement in Potential School Dropouts," *American Educational Research Journal,* 5 (1968), 305–310.

[28] E. Deci, "Effects of Externally Mediated Rewards on Intrinsic Motivation," *Journal of Personality and Social Psychology,* 18 (1971), 105–115; M. Lepper, D. Greene, and R. Nisbett, "Undermining Children's Intrinsic Interest with Extrinsic Reward: A Test of the 'Overjustification' Hypothesis," *Journal of Personality and Social Psychology,* 28 (1973), 129–137.

[29] S. Schachter, N. Ellertson, D. McBride, and D. Gregory, "An Experimental Study of Cohesiveness and Productivity," *Human Relations,* 4 (1951), 229–238.

[30] K. Bollen, "Political Democracy and the Timing of Development," *American Sociological Review,* 44 (1979), 572–587.

[31] P. Suedfeld and A. Rank, "Revolutionary Leaders: Long-Term Success as a Function of Changes in Conceptual Complexity," *Journal of Personality and Social Psychology,* 34 (1976), 169–178.

[32] J. Getzels and E. Guba, "Role, Role Conflict, and Effectiveness: An Empirical Study," *American Sociological Review,* 19 (1954), 164–175.

[33] L Berkowitz, "Anti-Semitism and the Displacement of Aggression," *Journal of Abnormal and Social Psychology,* 59 (1959), 182–187.

(f) Teachers who are perceived by students as dissimilar (to the students) in traits relevant to teaching are more attractive to students than teachers perceived as similar.[34]

(g) The more continuous and unlagging the provisions of lessons, the greater the task involvement of pupils.[35]

(h) Vivid information is better remembered than pallid information and is more likely to influence subsequent inference.[36]

4. Multivariate (for now, more than two variables) problems and hypotheses have become common in behavioral research. To give the student a preliminary feeling for such problems, we here append several of them. Try to imagine how you would do research to study them.

(a) What are the relative contributions to the verbal achievement of white and black elementary school pupils of home background, school facilities, and pupil attitudes?[37]

(b) How do self-esteem, educational attainment, and family background influence occupational attainment?[38]

(c) How do communication, urbanization, education, and agriculture influence the political development of nations?[39]

(d) How are ethnic group membership and home learning environment related to mental ability?[40]

(e) How do air pollution and socioeconomic status effect pulmonary mortality?[41]

(f) Do primary candidates' campaign expenditures, regional exposure, and past performance influence voting outcomes in primary elections?[42]

(g) How do sex-role stereotyping, sexual conservatism, adversial sexual beliefs, and acceptance of interpersonal violence affect attitudes toward rape and sexual violence?[43]

(h) How is rank in the U.S. Civil Service related to social class, race, and sex?[44]

(i) How do home conditions, classroom processes, and peer group environment influence science and mathematics achievement and attitudes?[45]

(j) Does stimulus exposure have two effects, one cognitive and one affective, which in turn affect liking, familiarity, and recognition confidence and accuracy?[46]

[34] J. Grush, G. Clore, and F. Costin, "Dissimilarity and Attraction: When Difference Makes a Difference," *Journal of Personality and Social Psychology,* 32 (1975), 783–789.

[35] J. Kounin and P. Doyle, "Degree of Continuity of a Lesson's Signal System and the Task Involvement of Children," *Journal of Educational Psychology,* 67 (1975), 159–164.

[36] R. Nisbett and L. Ross, *Human Inference: Strategies and Shortcomings of Social Judgment.* Englewood, Cliffs N. J.: Prentice-Hall, 1980, chap. 3.

[37] J. Coleman, E. Campbell, C. Hobson, J. Partland, A. Mood, F. Weinfeld, and R. York, *Equality of Educational Opportunity.* Washington, D.C.: U. S. Office of Education, 1966.

[38] J. Bachman and P. O'Malley, "Self-Esteem in Young Men: A Longitudinal Analysis of the Impact of Educational and Occupational Attainment," *Journal of Personality and Social Psychology,* 35 (1977), 365–380.

[39] P. Cutright, "National Political Development: Measurement and Analysis," *American Sociological Review,* 27 (1963), 229–245.

[40] K. Marjoribanks, "Ethnic and Environmental Influences on Mental Abilities," *American Journal of Sociology,* 78 (1972), 323–337.

[41] L. Lave and E. Seskin, "Air Pollution and Human Health," *Science,* 169 (1970), 723–733.

[42] J. Grush, "Impact of Candidate Expenditures, Regionality, and Prior Outcomes on the 1976 Democratic Presidential Primaries," *Journal of Personality and Social Psychology,* 38 (1980), 337–347.

[43] M. Burt, "Cultural Myths and Supports for Rape," *Journal of Personality and Social Psychology,* 38 (1980), 217–230.

[44] K. Meier, "Representative Bureaucracy: An Empirical Analysis," *American Political Science Review,* 69 (1975), 526–542.

[45] J. Keeves, *Educational Environment and Student Achievement.* Melbourne: Australian Council for Educational Research, 1972.

[46] R. Zajonc, "Feeling and Thinking: Preferences Need No Inferences," *American Psychologist,* 35 (1980), 151–175. The last two problems and studies are quite complex because the relations stated are complex. The other problems and studies, though also complex, have only one phenomenon presumably affected by other phenomena, whereas the last two problems have several phenomena influencing two or more other phenomena. Readers should not be discouraged if they find these problems a bit difficult. By the end of the book they should appear interesting and natural.

Chapter 3

Constructs, Variables, and Definitions

SCIENTISTS operate on two levels: theory-hypothesis-construct and observation. More accurately, they shuttle back and forth between these levels. A psychological scientist may say, "Early deprivation produces learning deficiency." This statement is a hypothesis consisting of two concepts, "early deprivation" and "learning deficiency," joined by a relation word, "produces." It is on the theory-hypothesis-construct level. Whenever scientists utter relational statements and whenever they use concepts, or constructs as we shall call them, they are operating at this level.

Scientists must also operate at the level of observation. They must gather data to test hypotheses. To do this, they must somehow get from the construct level to the observation level. They cannot simply make observations of "early deprivation" and "learning deficiency." They must so define these constructs that observations are possible. The problem of this chapter is to examine and clarify the nature of scientific concepts or constructs and the way in which behavioral scientists get from the construct level to the observation level, how they shuttle from one to the other.

CONCEPTS AND CONSTRUCTS

The terms "concept" and "construct" have similar meanings. Yet there is an important distinction. A *concept* expresses an abstraction formed by generalization from particulars. "Weight" is a concept: it expresses numerous observations of things that are more or less "heavy" or "light." "Mass," "energy," and "force" are concepts used by physical scientists. They are, of course, much more abstract than concepts such as "weight," "height," and "length."

A concept of more interest to readers of this book is "achievement." It is an abstraction formed from the observation of certain behaviors of children. These behaviors are associated with the mastery or "learning" of school tasks—reading words, doing arithmetic problems, drawing pictures, and so on. The various observed behaviors are put together and expressed in a word—"achievement." "Intelligence," "aggressiveness," "conformity," and "honesty" are all concepts used to express varieties of human behavior.

A *construct* is a concept. It has the added meaning, however, of having been deliberately and consciously invented or adopted for a special scientific purpose. "Intelligence" is a concept, an abstraction from the observation of presumably intelligent and nonintelligent behaviors. But as a scientific construct, "intelligence" means both more and less than it may mean as a concept. It means that scientists consciously and systematically use it in two ways. One, it enters into theoretical schemes and is related in various ways to other constructs. We may say, for example, that school achievement is in part a function of intelligence and motivation. Two, "intelligence" is so defined and specified that it can be observed and measured. We can make observations of the intelligence of children by administering X intelligence test to them, or we can ask teachers to tell us the relative degrees of intelligence of their pupils.

VARIABLES

Scientists somewhat loosely call the constructs or properties they study "variables." Examples of important variables in sociology, psychology, and education are: sex, income, education, social class, organizational productivity, occupational mobility, level of aspiration, verbal aptitude, anxiety, religious affiliation, political preference, political development (of nations), task orientation, anti-Semitism, conformity, recall memory, recognition memory, achievement. It can be said that a variable is a property that takes on different values. Putting it redundantly, a variable is something that varies. While this way of speaking gives us an intuitive notion of what variables are, we need a more general and yet more precise definition.

A *variable* is a symbol to which numerals or values are assigned. For instance, x is a variable: it is a *symbol* to which we assign numerical values. The variable x may take on any justifiable set of values—for example, scores on an intelligence test or an attitude scale. In the case of intelligence we assign to x a set of numerical values yielded by the procedure designated in a specified test of intelligence. This set of values ranges from low to high, from, say, 50 to 150.

A variable, x, however, may have only two values. If sex is the construct under study, then x can be assigned 1 and 0, 1 standing for one of the sexes and 0 standing for the other. It is still a variable. Other examples of two-valued variables are: alive-dead, citizen-noncitizen, middle class-working class, teacher-nonteacher, Republican-Democrat, and so on. Such variables are called dichotomies or dichotomous variables.

Some of the variables used in behavioral research are true dichotomies—that is, they are characterized by the presence or absence of a property: male-female, alive-dead, employed-unemployed. Some variables are polytomies. A good example is religious preference: Protestant, Catholic, Jew, Other.[1] Most variables, however, are theoretically capable of taking on continuous values. It has been common practice in behavioral research to convert continuous variables to dichotomies or polytomies. For example, intelli-

---

[1] Such dichotomies and polytomies have been called "qualitative variables." The questionable nature of this designation will be discussed later.

gence, a continuous variable, has been broken down into high and low intelligence, or into high, medium, and low intelligence. Variables such as anxiety, introversion, and authoritarianism have been treated similarly. While it is not possible to convert a truly dichotomous variable such as sex to a continuous variable, it is always possible to convert a continuous variable to a dichotomy or a polytomy. As we will see later, such conversion can serve a useful conceptual purpose, but is poor practice in the analysis of data because it throws information away.

CONSTITUTIVE AND OPERATIONAL DEFINITIONS OF CONSTRUCTS AND VARIABLES

The distinction made earlier between "concept" and "construct" leads naturally to another important distinction: that between kinds of definitions of constructs and variables. Words or constructs can be defined in two general ways. First, we can define a word by using other words, which is what a dictionary usually does. We can define "intelligence" by saying it is "operating intellect," "mental acuity," or "the ability to think abstractly." Such definitions use other concepts or conceptual expressions in lieu of the expression being defined.

Second, we can define a word by telling what actions or behaviors it expresses or implies. Defining "intelligence" this way requires that we specify what behaviors of children are "intelligent" and what behaviors are "not intelligent." We may say that a child of seven who successfully reads a story we give him to read is "intelligent." If the child cannot read the story, we may say he is "not intelligent." In other words, this kind of definition can be called a behavioral or observational definition. Both "other word" and "observational" definitions are used constantly in everyday living.

There is a disturbing looseness about this discussion. Although scientists use the types of definition just described, they do so in a more precise manner. We express this usage by defining and explaining Margenau's distinction between constitutive and operational definitions.[2] A *constitutive definition* defines a construct with other constructs. For instance, we can define "weight" by saying that it is the "heaviness" of objects. Or we can define "anxiety" as "subjectified fear." In both cases we have substituted one concept for another. Some of the constructs of a scientific theory may be defined constitutively. Torgerson, borrowing from Margenau, says that all constructs, in order to be scientifically useful, must possess constitutive meaning.[3] This means that they must be capable of being used in theories.

An *operational definition* assigns meaning to a construct or a variable by specifying the activities or "operations" necessary to measure it. Alternatively, an operational definition is a specification of the activities of the researcher in measuring a variable or in manipulating it. An operational definition is a sort of manual of instructions to the investigator. It says, in effect, "Do such-and-such in so-and-so a manner." In short, it defines or gives meaning to a variable by spelling out what the investigator must do to measure it.

A well-known, if extreme, example of an operational definition is: Intelligence (anxiety, achievement, and so forth) is scores on X intelligence test, or intelligence is what X intelligence test measures. This definition tells us what to do to measure intelligence. It says nothing about how well intelligence is measured by the specified instrument. (Pre-

---

[2] H. Margenau, *The Nature of Physical Reality*. New York: McGraw-Hill, 1950, chaps. 4, 5, and 12. The present discussion leans heavily on Margenau and on Torgerson's excellent presentation of the same distinction: W. Torgerson, *Theory and Methods of Scaling*. New York: Wiley, 1958, pp. 2–5.

[3] *Ibid.*, p. 5.

sumably the adequacy of the test was ascertained prior to the investigator's use of it.) In this usage, an operational definition is an equation where we say, "Let intelligence equal the scores on X test of intelligence." We also seem to be saying, "The meaning of intelligence (in this research) is expressed by the scores on X intelligence test."

There are, in general, two kinds of operational definitions: (1) *measured* and (2) *experimental*. The definition given above is more closely tied to measured than to experimental definitions. A *measured* operational definition describes how a variable will be measured. For example, achievement may be defined by a standardized achievement test, by a teacher-made achievement test, or by grades. Hiller, Fisher, and Kaess, studying effective classroom lecturing, defined vagueness of lecturing by specifying words and phrases that make lectures vague, for example, "a couple," "a few," "sometimes," "all of this," "and things," "not very," "pretty much." Videotapes of actual lectures were analyzed using this "definition" of vagueness and other operationally defined verbal variables, like interest, information, and verbal fluency.[4] A study may include the variable *consideration*. It can be defined operationally by listing behaviors of children that are presumably considerate behaviors and then requiring teachers to rate the children on a five-point scale. Such behaviors might be when the children say to each other, "I'm sorry," or "Excuse me," when one child yields a toy to another on request (but not on threat of aggression), or when one child helps another with a school task.

An *experimental* operational definition spells out the details (operations) of the investigator's manipulation of a variable. Reinforcement can be operationally defined by giving the details of how subjects are to be reinforced (rewarded) and not reinforced (not rewarded) for specified behaviors. In the Hurlock study discussed earlier, for example, some children were praised, some blamed, and some ignored. Dollard et al. define frustration as prevention from reaching a goal, or ". . . interference with the occurrence of an instigated goal response at its proper time in the behavior sequence. . . ."[5] This definition contains clear implications for experimental manipulation. Freedman, Wallington, and Bless operationally defined "guilt" by inducing their subjects to lie. Telling lies was presumed to engender guilt. (Apparently it did.)[6] Other examples of both kinds of operational definitions will be given later.

Scientific investigators must sooner or later face the necessity of measuring the variables of the relations they are studying. Sometimes measurement is easy, sometimes difficult. To measure sex or social class is easy; to measure creativity, conservatism, or organizational effectiveness is difficult. The importance of operational definitions cannot be overemphasized. They are indispensable ingredients of scientific research because they enable researchers to measure variables and because they are bridges between the theory-hypothesis-construct level and the level of observation. There can be no scientific research without observations, and observations are impossible without clear and specific instructions on what and how to observe. Operational definitions are such instructions.

Though indispensable, operational definitions yield only limited meanings of constructs. No operational definition can ever express all of a variable. No operational definition can ever express the rich and diverse aspects of human prejudice, for example. This means that the variables measured by scientists are always limited and specific in meaning. The "creativity" studied by psychologists is not the "creativity" referred to by artists, though there will of course be common elements.

[4] J. Hiller, G. Fisher, and W. Kaess, "A Computer Investigation of Verbal Characteristics of Effective Classroom Lecturing," *American Educational Research Journal,* 6 (1969), 661–675.

[5] J. Dollard et al., *Frustration and Aggression.* New Haven: Yale University Press, 1939, p. 7.

[6] J. Freedman, S. Wallington, and E. Bless, "Compliance Without Pressure: The Effect of Guilt," *Journal of Personality and Social Psychology,* 7 (1967), 117–124.

Some scientists say that such limited operational meanings are the only meanings that "mean" anything, that all other definitions are metaphysical nonsense. They say that discussions of anxiety are metaphysical nonsense, unless adequate operational definitions of anxiety are available and are used. This view is extreme, though it has healthy aspects. To insist that every term we use in scientific discourse be operationally defined would be too narrowing, too restrictive, and, as we shall see, scientifically unsound.[7]

Despite the dangers of extreme operationism, it can be safely said that operationism has been and still is a healthy influence because, as Skinner puts it, "The operational attitude, in spite of its shortcomings, is a good thing in any science but especially in psychology because of the presence there of a vast vocabulary of ancient and nonscientific origin."[8] When the terms used in education are considered, it is clear that education, too, has a vast vocabulary of ancient and nonscientific terms. Consider these: the whole child, horizontal and vertical enrichment, meeting the needs of the learner, core curriculum, emotional adjustment, and curricular enrichment.

To clarify constitutive and operational definitions—and theory, too—look at Figure 3.1, which has been adapted after Margenau and Torgerson. The diagram is supposed to illustrate a well-developed theory. The single lines represent theoretical connections or relations between constructs. These constructs, labeled with lower-case letters, are defined constitutively; that is, c_4 is defined somehow by c_3, or vice versa. The double lines represent operational definitions. The C constructs are directly linked to observable data; they are indispensable links to empirical reality. But it is important to note that not all constructs in a scientific theory are defined operationally. Indeed, it is a rather thin theory that has all its constructs so defined.

Let us build a "small theory" of underachievement to illustrate these notions. Suppose an investigator believes that underachievement is, in part, a function of pupils'

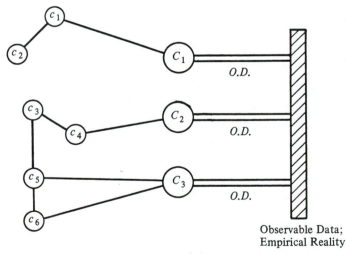

Figure 3.1

[7] For a good discussion of this point, see F. Northrop, *The Logic of the Sciences and the Humanities*. New York: Macmillan, 1947, chaps. VI and VII. Northrop says, for example, "The importance of operational definitions is that they make verification possible and enrich meaning. They do not, however, exhaust scientific meaning" (p. 130). Margenau makes the same point in his extended discussion of scientific constructs. (See Margenau, *op. cit.*, pp. 232ff.)

[8] B. Skinner, "The Operational Analysis of Psychological Terms." In H. Feigl and M. Brodbeck, eds., *Readings in the Philosophy of Science*. New York: Appleton, 1953, p. 586.

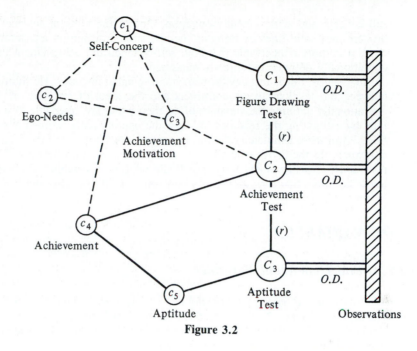

Figure 3.2

self-concepts. He believes that pupils who perceive themselves "inadequately," who have negative self-percepts, also tend to achieve less than their potential capacity and aptitude indicate they should achieve. He further believes that ego-needs (which we will not define here) and motivation for achievement (call this *n*-ach, or need for achievement) are tied to underachievement. Naturally, he is also aware of the relation between aptitude and intelligence and achievement in general. A diagram to illustrate this "theory" might look like Figure 3.2.

The investigator has no *direct* measure of self-concept, but he assumes that he can draw inferences about an individual's self-concept from a figure-drawing test. He operationally defines self-concept, then, as certain responses to the figure-drawing test. This is probably the most common method of measuring psychological (and educational) constructs. The heavy single line between c_1 and C_1 indicates the relatively direct nature of the presumed relation between self-concept and the test. (The double line between C_1 and the level of observation indicates an operational definition, as it did in Figure 3.1.) Similarly, the construct achievement (c_4) is operationally defined as the discrepancy between measured achievement (C_2) and measured aptitude (c_5). In this model the investigator has no direct measure of achievement motivation, no operational definition of it. In another study, naturally, he may specifically hypothesize a relation between achievement and achievement motivation, in which case he will try to define achievement motivation operationally.

A single solid line between concepts—for example, the one between the construct achievement (c_4) and achievement test (C_2)—indicates a relatively well-established relation between postulated achievement and what standard achievement tests measure. The single solid lines between C_1 and C_2 and between C_2 and C_3 indicate obtained relations between the test scores of these measures. (The lines between C_1 and C_2 and between C_2 and C_3 are labeled *r* for "relation," or "coefficient of correlation.")

The broken single lines indicate postulated relations between constructs that are not relatively well established. A good example of this is the postulated relation between self-concept and achievement motivation. One of the aims of science is to make these broken lines solid lines by bridging the operational definition-measurement gap. In this case, it is quite conceivable that both self-concept and achievement motivation can be operationally defined and directly measured.

In essence, this is the way the behavioral scientist operates. He shuttles back and forth between the level of theory-constructs and the level of observation. He does this by operationally defining the variables of his theory that are amenable to such definition and then by estimating the relations between the operationally defined and measured variables. From these estimated relations he makes inferences as to the relations between the constructs. In the above example, he calculates the relation between C_1 (figure-drawing test) and C_2 (achievement test) and, if the relation is established on this observational level, he infers that a relation exists between c_1 (self-concept) and c_4 (achievement).

TYPES OF VARIABLES

Independent and Dependent Variables

With definitional background behind us, we return to variables. Variables can be classified in several ways. In this book three kinds of variables are very important and will be emphasized: (1) independent and dependent variables, (2) active and attribute variables, and (3) continuous and categorical variables.

The most useful way to categorize variables is as independent and dependent. This categorization is highly useful because of its general applicability, simplicity, and special importance in conceptualizing and designing research and in communicating the results of research. An *independent variable* is the *presumed* cause of the *dependent variable*, the *presumed* effect. The independent variable is the antecedent; the dependent is the consequent. When we say: If A, then B, we have the conditional conjunction of an independent variable (A) and a dependent variable (B).

The terms "independent variable" and "dependent variable" come from mathematics, where X is the independent and Y the dependent variable. This is probably the best way to think of independent and dependent variables, because there is no need to use the touchy word "cause" and related words, and because such use of symbols applies to most research situations. There is no theoretical restriction on numbers of X's and Y's. When, later, we consider multivariate thinking and analysis, we will deal with several independent and several dependent variables.

In experiments the independent variable is the variable manipulated by the experimenter. When, for example, educational investigators study the effects of different teaching methods, they may manipulate method, the independent variable, by using different methods. In nonexperimental research, where there is no possibility of experimental manipulation, the independent variable is the variable that "logically" has some effect on a dependent variable. For example, in the research on cigarette-smoking and lung cancer, cigarette-smoking, which has already been done by many subjects, is the independent variable.

The dependent variable, of course, is the variable predicted *to,* whereas the independent variable is predicted *from*. The dependent variable, Y, is the presumed effect, which varies concomitantly with changes or variation in the independent variable, X. It is the variable that is not manipulated. Rather, it is observed for variation as a presumed result of variation in the independent variable. In predicting from X to Y, we can take any value of X we wish, whereas the value of Y we predict to is "dependent on" the value of X we have selected. The dependent variable is ordinarily the condition we are trying to explain. The most common dependent variable in education, for instance, is achievement or "learning." We want to account for or explain achievement. In doing so we have a large number of possible X's or independent variables to choose from.

When the relation between intelligence and school achievement is studied, intelligence is the independent and achievement the dependent variable. (Is it conceivable that it might be the other way around?) Other independent variables that can be studied in relation to the dependent variable, achievement, are social class, methods of teaching, personality types, types of motivation (reward and punishment), attitudes toward school, class atmosphere, and so on. When the presumed determinants of delinquency are studied, such determinants as slum conditions, broken homes, lack of parental love, and the like, are independent variables and, naturally, delinquency (more accurately, delinquent behavior) is the dependent variable. In the frustration-aggression hypothesis mentioned earlier, frustration is the independent variable and aggression the dependent variable. Sometimes a phenomenon is studied by itself, and either an independent or a dependent variable is implied. This is the case when teacher behaviors and characteristics are studied. The usual implied dependent variable is achievement or child behavior in general. Teacher behavior can of course be a dependent variable.

The relation between an independent variable and a dependent variable can perhaps be more clearly understood if we lay out two axes at right angles to each other, one axis representing the independent variable and the other axis the dependent variable. (When two axes are at right angles to each other, they are called *orthogonal* axes.) Following mathematical custom, X, the independent variable, is the horizontal axis and Y, the dependent variable, the vertical axis. (X is called the *abscissa* and Y the *ordinate*.) X values are laid out on the X axis and Y values on the Y axis. A very common and useful way to "see" and interpret a relation is to plot the pairs of XY values, using the X and Y axes as a frame of reference. Let us suppose, in a study of child development, that we have two sets of measures: the X measures chronological age, the Y measures reading age:[9]

$X:$ Chronological Age (in Months)	$Y:$ Reading Age (in Months)
72	48
84	62
96	69
108	71
120	100
132	112

These measures are plotted in Figure 3.3.

The relation between chronological age (*CA*) and reading age (*RA*) can now be "seen" and roughly approximated. Note that there is a pronounced tendency, as might be expected, for more advanced *CA* to be associated with higher *RA*, medium *CA* with medium *RA*, and less advanced *CA* with lower *RA*. In other words, the relation between the independent and dependent variables, in this case between *CA* and *RA*, can be seen from a graph such as this. A straight line has been drawn in to "show" the relation. It is a rough average of all the points of the plot. Note that if one has knowledge of independent variable measures and a relation such as that shown in Figure 3.3, one can predict with considerable accuracy the dependent variable measures. Plots like this can of course be used with any independent and dependent variable measures.

---

[9]*Reading age* is a so-called growth age. Seriatim measurements of individuals' growths—in height, weight, intelligence, and so forth—are expressed as the average chronological age at which they appear in the standard population.

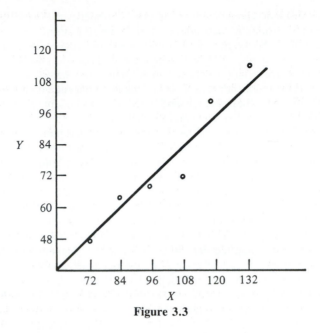

Figure 3.3

The student should be alert to the possibility of a variable being an independent variable in one study and a dependent variable in another, or even both in the same study. An example is economic development. McClelland, for instance, used it as a dependent variable in studying the relation between Protestantism and economic development.[10] Cutright, on the other hand, used it as an independent variable predicting to political development as a dependent variable.[11] Anxiety has been studied as an independent variable affecting the dependent variable achievement.[12] But it can readily be conceived and used as a dependent variable—for example, if we wished to study the effectiveness of types of teaching or types of teacher supportive behavior, or types of tests, in reducing anxiety.[13] In other words, the independent and dependent variable classification is really a classification of *uses* of variables rather than a distinction between different *kinds* of variables.

Active and Attribute Variables

A classification that will be useful in our later study of research design is based on the distinction between experimental and measured variables. It is important when planning and executing research to distinguish between these two types of variables. Manipulated variables will be called *active* variables; measured variables will be called *attribute* variables.

Any variable that is manipulated, then, is an active variable. "Manipulation" means, essentially, doing different things to different groups of subjects, as we will see clearly in a later chapter where we discuss in depth the differences between experimental and nonexperimental research. When a researcher does one thing to one group—for example,

[10] D. McClelland, *The Achieving Society*. Princeton, N.J.: Van Nostrand, 1961, pp. 50ff.
[11] P. Cutright, "National Political Development," *American Sociological Review*, 28 (1963), 229–245.
[12] E.g., F. Dowaliby and H. Schumer, "Teacher-Centered Versus Student-Centered Mode of College Classroom Instruction as Related to Manifest Anxiety," *Journal of Educational Psychology*, 64 (1978), 125–132.
[13] See S. Tobias, "Anxiety Research in Educational Psychology," *Journal of Educational Psychology*, 71 (1979), 573–582.

positively reinforces a certain kind of behavior—and does something different to another group, or has the two groups follow different instructions, this is manipulation. When one uses different methods of teaching, or rewards the subjects of one group and punishes those of another, or creates anxiety through worrisome instructions, one is *actively* manipulating the variables methods, reinforcement, and anxiety.

Variables that cannot be manipulated are attribute variables. It is impossible, or at least difficult, to manipulate many variables. All variables that are human characteristics—intelligence, aptitude, sex, socioeconomic status, conservatism, field dependence, need for achievement, and attitudes, for example—are attribute variables. Subjects come to our studies with these variables (attributes) ready-made. Early environment, heredity, and other circumstances have made individuals what they are.[14] The word "attribute," moreover, is accurate enough when used with inanimate objects or referents. Organizations, institutions, groups, populations, homes, and geographical areas have attributes. Organizations are variably productive; institutions become outmoded; groups differ in cohesiveness; geographical areas vary widely in resources.

This active-attribute distinction is general, flexible, and useful. We will see that some variables are by their very nature always attributes, but other variables that are attributes can also be active. This latter characteristic makes it possible to investigate the "same" relations in different ways. A good example, again, is the variable anxiety. We can measure the anxiety of subjects. Anxiety is in this case obviously an attribute variable. But we can manipulate anxiety, too. We can induce different degrees of anxiety, for example, by telling the subjects of one experimental group that the task they are about to do is difficult, that their intelligence is being measured, and that their futures depend on the scores they get. The subjects of another experimental group are told to do their best but to relax, the outcome is not too important and will have no influence on their futures. Actually, we cannot assume that the measured (attribute) and the manipulated (active) "anxieties" are the same. We may assume that both are "anxiety" in a broad sense, but they are certainly not the same.

CONTINUOUS AND CATEGORICAL VARIABLES

A distinction especially useful in the planning of research and the analysis of data—that between continuous and categorical variables—has already been introduced. Its later importance, however, justifies more extended consideration.

A *continuous* variable is capable of taking on an ordered set of values within a certain range. This definition means, first, that the values of a continuous variable reflect at least a rank order, a larger value of the variable meaning more of the property in question than a smaller value. The values yielded by a scale to measure dependency, for instance, express differing amounts of dependency from high through medium to low. Second, continuous measures in actual use are contained in a range, and each individual obtains a "score" within the range. A scale to measure dependency may have the range 1 through 7. Most

[14] Such variables are also called *organismic* variables. Any property of an individual, any characteristic or attribute, is an organismic variable. It is part of the organism, so to speak. In other words, organismic variables are those characteristics that individuals have in varying degrees when they come to the research situation. The term individual differences implies organismic variables.

Another related classification, used mainly by psychologists, is *stimulus* and *response* variables. A *stimulus variable* is any condition or manipulation by the experimenter of the environment that evokes a response in an organism. A *response variable* is any kind of behavior of the organism. The assumption is made that for any kind of behavior there is always a stimulus. Thus the organism's behavior is a response. This classification is reflected in the well-known equation: $R = f(O,S)$, which is read: "Responses are a function of the organism and stimuli," or "Response variables are a function of organismic variables and stimulus variables."

scales in use in the behavioral sciences also have a third characteristic: there is a theoretically infinite set of values within the range. (Rank-order scales are somewhat different; they will be discussed later in the book.) That is, a particular individual's score may be 4.72 rather than simply 4 or 5.

Categorical variables, as I will call them, belong to a kind of measurement called nominal. (It will be explained in Chapter 25.) In nominal measurement, there are two or more subsets of the set of objects being measured. Individuals are categorized by their possession of the characteristic that defines any subset. "To categorize" means to assign an object to a subclass or subset of a class or set on the basis of the object's having or not having the characteristic that defines the subset. The individual being categorized either has the defining property or does not have it; it is an all-or-none kind of thing. The simplest examples are dichotomous categorical variables: sex, Republican-Democrat, white-black. Polytomies, variables with more than two subsets or partitions, are fairly common, especially in sociology and economics: religious preference, education (usually), nationality, occupational choice, and so on.

Categorical variables—and nominal measurement—have simple requirements: all the members of a subset are considered the same and all are assigned the same name (nominal) and the same numeral. If the variable is religious preference, for instance, all Protestants are the same, all Catholics are the same, and all "others" are the same. If an individual is a Catholic—operationally defined in a suitable way—he is assigned to the category "Catholic" and also assigned a "1" in that category. In brief, he is counted as a "Catholic." Categorical variables are "democratic": there is no rank order or greater-than and less-than among the categories, and all members of a category have the same value: 1.

The expression "qualitative variables" has sometimes been applied to categorical variables, especially to dichotomies, probably in contrast to "quantitative variables" (our continuous variables). Such usage reflects a somewhat distorted notion of what variables are. They are always quantifiable, or they are not variables. If x has only two subsets and can take on only two values, 1 and 0, these are still values, and the variable varies. If x is a polytomy, like religious preference, we quantify again by assigning 1's and 0's to individuals. If an individual, say, is a Catholic, then put him in the Catholic subset and assign him a 1. It is extremely important to understand this because, for one thing, it is the basis of quantifying many variables—even experimental treatments—for complex analysis. In multiple regression analysis, as we will see later in the book, all variables, continuous and categorical, are entered as variables into the analysis. Earlier, the example of sex was given, 1 being assigned to one sex and 0 to the other. We can set up a column of 1's and 0's just as we would set up a column of dependency scores. The column of 1's and 0's is the quantification of the variable sex. There is no mystery here. The method is easily extended to polytomies.[15]

CONSTRUCTS, OBSERVABLES, AND LATENT VARIABLES

In much of the previous discussion of this chapter it has been implied, though not explicitly stated, that there is a sharp difference between constructs and observed variables. In fact, we can say that constructs are nonobservables, and variables, when operationally

[15] Such variables have been called "dummy variables." Since they are highly useful and powerful, even indispensable, in modern research data analysis, they should be clearly understood. See F. Kerlinger and E. Pedhazur, *Multiple Regression Analysis in Behavioral Research*. New York: Holt, Rinehart and Winston, 1973, chaps. 6 and 7, and Chapter 34 of this volume. A *polytomy* is a division of the members of a group into three or more subdivisions.

defined, are observables. The distinction is important, because if we are not always keenly aware of the level of discourse we are on when talking about variables, we can hardly be clear about what we are doing.

An important and fruitful expression, which we will encounter and use a good deal later in the book, is "latent variable." A latent variable is an unobserved "entity" presumed to underlie observed variables. The best-known example of an important latent variable is "intelligence." We note, say, that three ability tests, verbal, numerical, and spatial, are positively and substantially related. This means, in general, that persons high on one tend to be high on the others; similarly, persons low on one tend to be low on the others. We believe that something is common to the three tests or observed variables and name this something "intelligence." It is a latent variable.

We have encountered many examples of latent variables in previous pages: achievement, creativity, social class, anti-Semitism, conformity, and so on. Indeed, whenever we utter the names of phenomena on which people or objects vary, we are talking about latent variables. In science our real interest is more in the relations among latent variables than it is in the relations among observed variables because we seek to explain phenomena and their relations. When we enunciate a theory, we enunciate in part systematic relations among latent variables. We are not too interested in the relation between observed frustrated behaviors and observed aggressive behaviors, for example, though we must of course work with them at the empirical level. We are really interested in the relation between the latent variable frustration and the latent variable aggression.

We must be cautious, however, when dealing with nonobservables. Scientists, using such terms as "hostility," "anxiety," and "learning," are aware that they are talking about invented constructs the "reality" of which has been inferred from behavior. If they want to study the effects of different kinds of motivation, they must know that "motivation" is a latent variable, a construct invented to account for presumably "motivated" behavior. They must know that its "reality" is only a postulated reality. They can only judge that youngsters are motivated or not motivated by observing their behavior. Still, in order to study motivation, they must measure it or manipulate it. But they cannot measure it directly because it is an "in-the-head" variable, an unobservable entity, a latent variable, in short. The construct was invented for "something" *presumed to be* inside individuals, "something" prompting them to behave in such-and-such manners. This means that researchers must always measure presumed indicants of motivation and not motivation itself. They must, in other words, always measure some kind of behavior, be it marks on paper, spoken words, or meaningful gestures, and then make inferences about presumed characteristics—or latent variables.

Other terms have been used to express more or less the same ideas. For example, constructs have been called intervening variables.[16] *Intervening variable* is a term invented to account for internal, unobservable psychological processes that in turn account for behavior. An intervening variable is an "in-the-head" variable. It cannot be seen, heard, or felt. It is inferred from behavior. "Hostility" is inferred from presumably hostile or aggressive acts. "Anxiety" is inferred from test scores, skin responses, heart beat, and certain experimental manipulations. Another term is "hypothetical construct." Since this expression means much the same as latent variable with somewhat less generality, we need not pause over it. We should mention, however, that "latent variable" appears to be a more general and applicable expression than "intervening variable" and "hypothetical construct" because, as we will later see, it can be used for virtually any phenomena that presumably influence or are influenced by other phenomena. In other

---

[16]E. Tolman, *Behavior and Psychological Man*. Berkeley, Calif.: University of California Press, 1958, pp. 115–129.

words, "latent variable" can be used with psychological, sociological, and other phenomena. "Latent variable" seems to me to be the preferable term because of its generality and because it is now possible in the analysis of covariance structures approach to assess the effects of latent variables on each other and on so-called manifest or observed variables. This rather abstract discussion will later be made more concrete and, it is hoped, meaningful. We will then see that the idea of latent variables and the relations between them is an extremely important, fruitful, and useful one that is helping to change fundamental approaches to research problems.

EXAMPLES OF VARIABLES AND OPERATIONAL DEFINITIONS

A number of constructs and operational definitions have already been given. To illustrate and clarify the preceding discussion, especially that in which the distinction was made between experimental and measured variables and between constructs and operationally defined variables, several examples of constructs or variables and operational definitions are given below. If a definition is experimental, it is labeled (E); if it is measured, it is labeled (M).

Operational definitions differ in degree of specificity. Some are quite closely tied to observations. "Test" definitions, like "Intelligence is defined as a score on X intelligence test," are very specific. A definition like "Frustration is prevention from reaching a goal" is more general and requires further specification to be measurable.

Social Class ". . . two or more orders of people who are believed to be, and are accordingly ranked by the members of a community, in socially superior and inferior positions."[17] (M) To be operational, this definition has to be specified by questions aimed at people's beliefs about other people's positions. This is a subjective definition of social class. Social class, or social status, is also defined more objectively by using such indices as occupation, income, and education, or by combinations of such indices. For example, ". . . primary emphasis has been placed on the educational attainment and occupational status of the head of the family in which an individual is reared."[18] (M)

Achievement (School, Arithmetic, Spelling) Achievement is customarily defined operationally by citing a standardized test of achievement (for example, Iowa Tests of Basic Skills, Elementary), by grade-point averages, or by teacher judgments.

> The criterion of school achievement, grade-point average . . . was generally obtained by assigning weights of 4, 3, 2, 1, and 0 to grades of A, B, C, D, and F, respectively. Only courses in the so-called "solids," that is, mathematics, science, social studies, foreign language, and English, were used in computing grade-point averages.[19] (M)

Popularity Popularity is often defined operationally by the number of sociometric choices an individual receives from other individuals (in his class, play group, and so on). Individuals are asked: "With whom would you like to work?," "With whom would you like to play?," and the like. Each individual is required to choose one, two, or more individuals from his group on the basis of such criterion questions. (M)

Visceral Response (Intestinal Contractions) "We decided on intestinal contractions, and recorded them in the curarized rat with a little balloon filled with water thrust approxi-

---

[17] W. Warner and P. Lunt, *The Social Life of a Modern Community*. New Haven: Yale University Press, 1941, p. 82.

[18] O. Duncan, D. Featherman, and B. Duncan, *Socioeconomic Background and Achievement*. New York: Seminar Press, 1972, p. 6.

[19] W. Holtzman and W. Brown, "Evaluating the Study Habits and Attitudes of High School Students," *Journal of Educational Psychology,* 59 (1968), 404–409.

mately 4 centimeters beyond the anal sphincter. Changes in pressure in the balloon were transduced into electric voltages which produced a record on a polygraph.''[20] (M)

Task Involvement ''. . . each child's behavior during a lesson was coded every 6 sec as being appropriately involved, or deviant. The task involvement scores for a lesson was the percentage of 6-sec units in which the children were coded as 'appropriately involved.' ''[21] (M)

Reinforcement Reinforcement definitions come in a number of forms. Most of them involve, in one way or another, the principle of reward. But both positive and negative reinforcement may be used.

''. . . statements of *agreement* or *paraphrase*.''[22] (E) Then the author gives specific experimental definitions of ''reinforcement.'' For example,

> In the second 10 minutes, every opinion statement S made was recorded by E and reinforced. For two groups, E agreed with every opinion statement by saying: ''Yes, you're right,'' ''That's so,'' or the like, or by nodding and smiling affirmation if he could not interrupt. (E)
>
> . . . the model and the child were administered alternately 12 different sets of story items. . . . To each of the 12 items, the model consistently expressed judgmental responses in opposition to the child's moral orientation . . . and the experimenter reinforced the model's behavior with verbal approval responses such as ''Very good,'' ''That's fine,'' and ''That's good.'' The child was similarly reinforced whenever he adopted the model's class of moral judgments in response to his own set of items.[23] (E) [This is called ''social reinforcement.'']

Attitudes Toward Blacks ''Racial attitudes were determined . . . by the use of the Multifactor Racial Attitude Inventory (Woodmansee & Cook, 1967).''[24] (M) This is a common form of operational definition: specification of the instrument used to measure a variable or variables. It is good practice to refer to original sources, as was done here.

Self-Esteem ''. . . is measured by a 10-item index. . . .''[25] (M) The authors then describe the sources of the items, the kind of scale, and the scoring.

Achievement (Academic Performance) ''Academic performance . . . is operationalized as the respondents' report in 1966 of their overall grades for the previous year (which was the ninth grade, 1965–1966).''[26] (M) Note that this is a self-report measure, which may be subject to considerable error.

Race ''All students . . . were administered the TAQ (an anxiety scale) by either a white or a Negro experimenter.''[27] (E) It was noted that the assignment of subjects was done at random. This operational definition is unusual. Race is usually a measured variable.

Memory: Recall and Recognition ''. . . two basic methods. One, *recall,* is to ask the subject to recite what he remembers of the items shown him, giving him a point for each item that matches one on the stimulus list. The other testing procedure, *recognition,* is to

[20] N. Miller, ''Learning of Visceral and Glandular Responses,'' *Science,* 163 (1969), 434–445 (438).

[21] J. Kounin and P. Doyle, ''Degree of Continuity of a Lesson's Signal System and the Task Involvement of Children,'' *Journal of Educational Psychology,* 67 (1975), 159–164.

[22] W. Verplanck, ''The Control of the Content of Conversation: Reinforcement of Statements of Opinion,'' *Journal of Abnormal and Social Psychology,* 51 (1955), 668–676.

[23] A. Bandura and F. McDonald, ''Influence of Social Reinforcement and the Behavior of Models in Shaping Children's Moral Judgments,'' *Journal of Abnormal and Social Psychology,* 67 (1963), 274–281.

[24] S. Jones and S. Cook, ''The Influence of Attitude on Judgments of the Effectiveness of Alternative Social Policies,'' *Journal of Personality and Social Psychology,* 32 (1975), 767–773.

[25] J. Bachman and P. O'Malley, ''Self-Esteem in Young Men: A Longitudinal Analysis of the Impact of Educational and Occupational Attainment,'' *Journal of Personality and Social Psychology,* 35 (1977), 365–380 (368).

[26] *Ibid.,* p. 369.

[27] S. Baratz, ''Effect of Race of Experimenter, Instructions, and Comparison Population Upon Level of Reported Anxiety in Negro Subjects,'' *Journal of Personality and Social Psychology,* 7 (1967), 194–196.

show the subject test items and ask him to decide whether or not they were part of the stimulus list.''[28] (M)

Ingratiation "Half of the subject groups were given the following instructions which were designed to create an *accuracy set*." (Then instructions to give accurate answers in an interview were given.) "Subjects in the remaining groups were given instructions to create an *ingratiation set*."[29] (Appropriate instructions followed.) (E)

Discrimination Against Jews "This tendency was assessed through the extent of the manager's agreement with four . . . questionnaire items."[30] (The items then followed. One of them was: "Anyone who employs many people should be careful not to hire a large percentage of Jews." Subjects expressed agreement and disagreement on a six-point scale.) (M)

Values " 'Rank the ten goals in the order of *their importance to you*.' (1) financial success; (2) being liked; (3) success in family life; (4) being intellectually capable; (5) living by religious principles; (6) helping others; (7) being normal, well-adjusted; (8) cooperating with others; (9) doing a thorough job; (10) occupational success."[31] (M)

Democracy (Political Democracy) "The index [of political democracy] consists of three indicators of popular sovereignty and three of political liberties. The three measures of popular sovereignty are: (1) fairness of elections, (2) effective executive selection, and (3) legislative selection. The indicators of political liberties are: (4) freedom of the press, (5) freedom of group opposition, and (6) government sanctions."[32] (M) The author gives operational details of the six indicators in an appendix (pp. 585–586). Note that he used the term "indicators." Indicators—usually called social indicators—are variables that measure (indicate) the main features of a society: traffic safety, mental disease, wealth (and its distribution), access to education, crime, home ownership, teachers' salaries, investments, and so on.[33]

The benefits of operational thinking have been great. Indeed, operationism has been and is one of the most significant and important movements of our times. Extreme operationism, of course, can be dangerous because it clouds recognition of the importance of constructs and constitutive definitions in behavioral science, and because it can also restrict research to trivial problems. There can be little doubt, however, that it is a healthy influence. It is the indispensable key to achieving objectivity—without which there is no science—because its demand that observations must be public and replicable helps to put research activities outside of and apart from researchers and their predilections. And, as Underwood has said:

> . . . I would say that operational thinking makes better scientists. The operationist is forced to remove the fuzz from his empirical concepts. . . .
>
> . . . operationism facilitates communication among scientists because the meaning of concepts so defined is not easily subject to misinterpretation.[34]

[28] D. Norman, *Memory and Attention: An Introduction to Human Information Processing,* 2nd ed. New York: Wiley, 1976, p. 97.

[29] E. Jones, *Ingratiation: A Social Psychological Analysis*. New York: Appleton-Century-Crofts, 1964, p. 53.

[30] R. Quinn, R. Kahn, J. Tabor, and L. Gordon, *The Chosen Few: A Study of Discrimination in Executive Selection*. Ann Arbor: Institute for Social Research, Survey Research Center, University of Michigan, 1968, pp. 7–8.

[31] T. Newcomb, *The Acquaintance Process*. New York: Holt, Rinehart and Winston, 1961, pp. 40 and 83.

[32] K. Bollen, "Political Democracy and the Timing of Development," *American Sociological Review,* 44 (1979), 572–587 (580). This is a particularly good example of the operational definition of a complex concept. Moreover, it is an excellent description of the ingredients of democracy.

[33] See R. Bauer, ed., *Social Indicators*. Cambridge, Mass.: MIT Press, 1966; E. Sheldon and R. Parke, "Social Indicators," *Science,* 188 (1975), 693–699.

[34] B. Underwood, *Psychological Research*. New York: Appleton, 1957, p. 53.

Study Suggestions

1. Write operational definitions for five or six of the following constructs. When possible, write two such definitions: an experimental one and a measured one.

reinforcement	punitiveness
achievement	reading ability
underachievement	needs
leadership	interests
transfer of training	delinquency
level of aspiration	need for affiliation
organizational conflict	conformity
political preference	marital satisfaction

Some of these concepts or variables—for example, needs and transfer of training—may be difficult to define operationally. Why?

2. Can any of the variables in 1, above, be both independent and dependent variables? Which ones?

3. It is instructive and broadening for specialists to read outside their fields. This is particularly true for students of behavioral research. It is suggested that the student of a particular field read two or three research studies in one of the best journals of another field. If you are in psychology, read a sociology journal, say the *American Sociological Review*. If you are in education or sociology, read a psychology journal, say the *Journal of Personality and Social Psychology* or the *Journal of Experimental Psychology*. Students not in education can sample the *Journal of Educational Psychology* or the *American Educational Research Journal*. When you read, jot down the names of the variables and compare them to the variables in your own field. Are they primarily active or attribute variables? Note, for instance, that psychology's variables are more "active" than sociology's. What implications do the variables of a field have for its research?

PART TWO

SETS, RELATIONS, AND VARIANCE

Chapter 4

Sets

THE CONCEPT of ''set'' is one of the most powerful and useful of mathematical ideas in understanding methodological aspects of research. Sets and their elements are the primitive materials with which mathematics works. Even if we are unaware of it, sets and set theory are foundations of our descriptive, logical, and analytic thinking and operating. They are the basis of virtually all else in this book. They are the foundations upon which we erect the complexities of numerical, categorical, and statistical analysis, even though we do not always make the set basis of our thinking and work explicit. For example, set theory provides us with an unambiguous definition of relations. It helps us approach and understand probability and sampling. It is first cousin to logic. And it helps us to understand the highly important subject of categories and categorizing the objects of the world. Moreover, set thinking can even help us to understand that difficult problem of human communication: confusion caused by mixing levels of discourse.

Science works basically with group, class, or set concepts. When scientists discuss individual events or objects, they do so by considering such objects as members of sets of objects. But this is true of human discourse in general. We say ''goose,'' but the word ''goose'' is meaningless without the concept of a goose-like group called ''geese.'' When we talk about a child and his problems, we inevitably must talk of the groups, classes, or sets of objects to which he belongs: A seven-year old (first set), second-grade (second set), bright (third set), and healthy (fourth set), boy (fifth set).

A *set* is a well-defined collection of objects or elements.[1] A set is well defined when it

[1]J. Kemeny, J.Snell, and G. Thompson, *Introduction to Finite Mathematics*, 2d ed. Englewood Cliffs, N.J.: Prentice-Hall, 1966, p. 58.

is possible to tell whether a given object does or does not belong to the set. Terms like class, school, family, flock, and group indicate sets. There are two ways to define a set: (1) by listing all the members of the set, and (2) by giving a rule for determining whether objects do or do not belong to the set. Call (1) a "list" definition and (2) a "rule" definition. In research the rule definition is usually used, although there are cases where all members of a set are actually or imaginatively listed. For example, suppose we study the relation between voting behavior and political preference. Political preference can be defined as being a registered Republican or Democrat. We then have a large set of all people with political preferences with two smaller *subsets:* the subset of Republicans and the subset of Democrats. This is a rule definition of sets. Of course, we might list all registered Democrats and all registered Republicans to define our two subsets, but this is often difficult if not impossible. Besides, it is unnecessary; the rule is usually sufficient. Such a rule might be: A Republican is any person who is registered in the Republican party. Another such rule might be: A Republican is any person who says he is a Republican.

SUBSETS

A *subset* of a set is a set that results from selecting sets from an original set. Each subset of a set is part of the original set. More succinctly and accurately, "A set B is a subset of a set A whenever all the elements of B are elements of A."[2] We designate sets by capital letters: $A, B, K, L, X, Y,$ and so forth. If B is a subset of A, we write $B \subset A$, which means "B is a subset of A," "B is contained in A," or "All members of B are also members of A."

Whenever a population is sampled, the samples are subsets of the population. Suppose an investigator samples four eleventh-grade classes out of all the eleventh-grade classes in a large high school. The four classes form a subset of the population of all the eleventh-grade classes. Each of the four classes of the the sample, too, can be considered a subset of the four classes—and also of the total population of classes. All the children of the four classes can be broken down into two subsets of boys and girls. Whenever a researcher breaks down or partitions a population or a sample into two or more groups he is "creating" subsets using a "rule" or criterion to do so. Examples are numerous: religious preferences into Protestant, Catholic, Jew; intelligence into high and low; and so on. Even experimental conditions can be so viewed. The classic experimental-control group idea is a set-subset idea. Individuals are put into the experimental group; this is a subset of the whole sample. All other individuals used in the experiment (the control-group individuals) form a subset, too.

SET OPERATIONS

There are two basic set operations: *intersection* and *union*. An operation is simply "a doing-something to." In arithmetic we add, subtract, multiply, and divide. We "intersect" and "union" sets. We also "negate" them.

Intersection is the overlapping of two or more sets; it is the elements shared in common by the two or more sets. The symbol for intersection is ∩ (read "intersection" or "cap"). The intersection of the sets A and B is written $A \cap B$, and $A \cap B$ is itself a set.

[2]R. Kershner and L. Wilcox, *The Anatomy of Mathematics.* New York: Ronald, 1950, p. 35.

More precisely, it is the set that contains those elements of *A* and *B* that belong to *both A and B*. Intersection is also written $A \cdot B$, or simply *AB*.

Let $A = \{0, 1, 2, 3\}$; let $B = \{2, 3, 4, 5\}$. (Note that we use braces, "{ }," to symbolize sets.) Then $A \cap B = \{2, 3\}$. This is shown in Figure 4.1. $A \cap B$, or $\{2, 3\}$, is a new set composed of the members *common* to both sets. Note that $A \cap B$ also indicates the *relation* between the sets, the elements shared in common by *A* and *B*.

The *union* of two sets is written $A \cup B$. $A \cup B$ is a set that contains all the members of *A* and all the members of *B*. Mathematicians define $A \cup B$ as a set that contains those elements that belong either to *A* or to *B* or to both. In other words, we "add" the elements of *A* to those of *B* to form a new set $A \cup B$. Take the example of Figure 4.1. *A* included 0, 1, 2, and 3; *B* included 2, 3, 4, and 5. $A \cup B = \{0, 1, 2, 3, 4, 5\}$. The union of *A* and *B* in Figure 4.1 is indicated by the whole area of the two circles. Note that we do not count the members of $A \cap B$, $\{2, 3\}$, twice.

Examples of union in research would be putting males and females together, $M \cup F$, or Republican and Democrats together, $R \cup D$. Let *A* be all the children of the elementary schools and *B* all the children of the secondary schools of X school district. Then $A \cup B$ is the set of all the school children in the district

THE UNIVERSAL AND EMPTY SETS; SET NEGATION

The *universal set,* labeled *U,* is the set of all elements under discussion. It can be called the *universe of discourse* or *level of discourse*. (It is much like the terms *population* and *universe* in sampling theory.) This means that we limit our discussion to the fixed set of elements—all of them—from this fixed class, *U.* If we were to study determinants of achievement in the elementary school, for example, we might define *U* as all pupils in grades one through six. We can define *U,* alternatively, as the scores on an achievement test of these same pupils. Subsets of *U,* perhaps to be studied separately, might be the scores of Grade 1 pupils, the scores of Grade 2 pupils, and so on.

U can be large or small. Returning to the example of Figure 4.1, $A = \{0, 1, 2, 3\}$ and $B = \{2, 3, 4, 5\}$. If $A \cup B = U$, then $U = \{0, 1, 2, 3, 4, 5\}$. Here *U* is quite small. Let $A = \{$Jane, Mary, Phyllis, Betty$\}$, and $B = \{$Tom, John, Paul$\}$. If these individuals are all we are talking about, then $U = \{$Jane, Mary, Phyllis, Betty, Tom, John, Paul$\}$. And, of course, $U = A \cup B$. This is another example of a small *U*. In research *U*'s are more often large. If we sample the schools of a large county, then *U* is all the schools in the county, a rather large *U*. *U* might also be all the children or all the teachers in these schools, still larger *U*'s.

In research it is important to know the *U* one is studying. Ambiguity in the definition of *U* can lead to erroneous conclusions. It is known, for example, that social classes differ

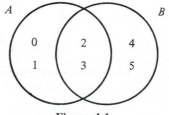

Figure 4.1

in incidences of neurosis and psychosis.[3] If we were studying presumed determinants of mental illness and used only middle-class people as subjects, our conclusions would of course be limited to the middle class. But it is easy to generalize to all people, and such generalization can be grossly in error. In such a case we have generalized to all people, U, when in fact we have studied our relations only in U_1, middle class. It is quite possible, perhaps even likely, that the relations are different in U_2, working class.

The *empty set* is the set with no members in it. We label it E. It can also be called the *null set*. Though it may seem peculiar to the student that we bother with sets with no members, the notion is quite useful, even indispensable. With it we can convey certain ideas economically and unambiguously. To indicate that there is no relation between two sets of data for example, we can write the set equation $A \cap B = E$, which simply says that the intersection of the sets A and B is empty, meaning that no member of A is a member of B, and vice versa.

Let $A = \{1, 2, 3\}$; Let $B = \{4, 5, 6\}$. Then $A \cap B = E$. Clearly there are no members common to A and B. The set of possibilities of the Democratic and Republican presidential candidates both winning the national election is empty. The set of occurrences of rain without clouds is empty. The empty set, then, is another way of expressing the falsity of propositions. In this case we can say that the statement ''Rain without clouds'' is false. In set language this can be expressed $P \cap {\sim}Q = E$, where $P =$ the set of all occurrences of rain, $Q =$ the set of all occurrences of clouds, and ${\sim}Q =$ the set of all occurrences of no clouds.

The *negation* or *complement* of the set A is written ${\sim}A$. It means all members of U not in A. If we let $A =$ all men, when $U =$ all human beings, then ${\sim}A =$ all women (not-men). Simple dichotomization seems to be a fundamental basis of human thinking. In order to think, categorization is necessary: one must, at the most elementary level, separate objects into those belonging to a certain set and those not belonging to the set. We must distinguish men and not-men, me and not-me, early and not-early, good and not-good.

If $U = \{0, 1, 2, 3, 4\}$, and $A = \{0, 1\}$, then ${\sim}A = \{2, 3, 4\}$. A and ${\sim}A$ are of course subsets of U. An important property of sets and their negation is expressed in the set equation: $A \cup {\sim}A = U$. Note, too, that $A \cap {\sim}A = E$.

SET DIAGRAMS

We now pull together and illustrate the basic set ideas already presented by diagramming them. Sets can be depicted with various kinds of figures, but rectangles and circles are

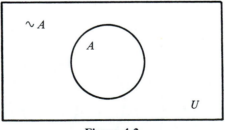

Figure 4.2

[3] E. Hilgard, R. C. Atkinson, and R. L. Atkinson, *Introduction to Psychology*, 6th ed. New York: Harcourt Brace Jovanovich, 1975, p. 490.

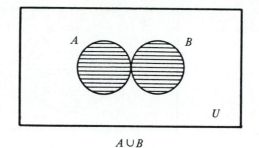

$A \cup B$

Figure 4.3

ordinarily used. They have been adapted from a system invented by John Venn. In this book rectangles, circles, and ovals will be used. Look at Figure 4.2. U is represented by the rectangle. All members of the universe under discussion are in U. All members of U not in A form another subset of U: $\sim A$. Note, again, that $A \cup \sim A = U$. Note, too, that $A \cap \sim A = E$, that is, there are no members common to both A and $\sim A$.

Next, we depict, in Figure 4.3, two sets, A and B, both subsets of U. From the diagram it can be seen that $A \cap B = E$. We adopt a convention: when we wish to indicate a set or a subset, we shade it either horizontally, vertically, or diagonally. The set $A \cup B$ has been shaded in Figure 4.3.

Intersection, probably the most important set notion from the point of view of this book, is indicated by the shaded portion of Figure 4.4. The situation can be expressed by the equation $A \cap B \neq E$; the intersection of the sets A and B is *not* empty.

When two sets, A and B, are equal, they have the same set elements or members. The Venn diagram would show two congruent circles in U. In effect, only one circle would show. When $A = B$, then $A \cap B = A \cup B = A = B$.

We diagram $A \subset B$; A is a subset of B, in Figure 4.5. B has been shaded horizontally, A vertically. Note that $A \cup B = B$ (whole shaded area) and $A \cap B = A$ (area shaded both horizontally and vertically). All members of A are also in B, or all a's are also b's, if we let $a = $ any member of A and $b = $ any member of B.

SET OPERATIONS WITH MORE THAN TWO SETS

Set operations are not limited to two subsets of U. Let A, B, and C be three subsets of U. Suppose the intersection of these three subsets of U is not empty, as shown in Figure 4.6.

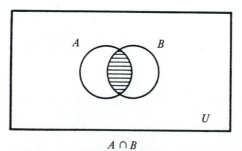

$A \cap B$

Figure 4.4

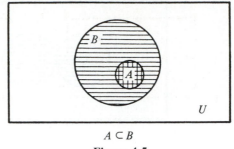

$A \subset B$

Figure 4.5

The triply hatched area shows $A \cap B \cap C$. There are four intersections, each hatched differently: $A \cap B$, $A \cap C$, $B \cap C$, and $A \cap B \cap C$.

Although four or more sets can be diagrammed, such diagrams become cumbersome and not easy to draw and inspect. There is no reason, however, why the intersection and union operations cannot be applied symbolically to four or more sets.

PARTITIONS AND CROSS PARTITIONS

Our discussion of sets has been abstract and perhaps a bit dull. We leaven the discussion by examining an aspect of set theory of great importance in clarifying principles of categorization, analysis, and research design: partitioning. U can be broken down (partitioned) into subsets that do not intersect and that exhaust all of U. When this is done the process is called partitioning. Formally stated, *partitioning* breaks a universal set down into subsets that are *disjoint* and *exhaustive* of the universal set.

Let U be a universe, and let A and B be subsets of U that are partitions. We label subsets of A: $A_1, A_2, \ldots, A_k$ and of B: $B_1, B_2, \ldots, B_m$. Now, $[A_1 A_2]$ and $[B_1 B_2]$,[4] for example, are partitions if:

$$A_1 \cup A_2 = U \quad \text{and} \quad A_1 \cap A_2 = E$$
$$B_1 \cup B_2 = U \quad \text{and} \quad B_1 \cap B_2 = E$$

Diagrams make this clearer. The partitioning of U, represented by a rectangle, separately into the subsets A_1 and A_2 and into B_1 and B_2, is shown in Figure 4.7. Both

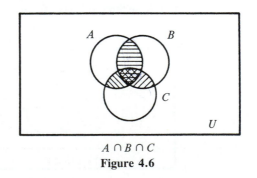

$A \cap B \cap C$

Figure 4.6

[4]Partitions are usually set off by square brackets, [ ], while sets and subsets are set off by curled brackets or braces, { }.

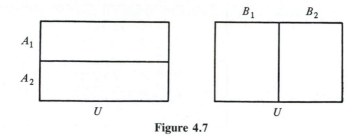

Figure 4.7

partitionings have been performed on the same U. We have met examples of such partitions: male-female, middle class-working class, high income-low income, Democrat-Republican, pass-fail, approve-disapprove, and so on. Some of these are true dichotomies; some are not.

It is possible to put the two partitions together into a *cross partition*. A *cross partition* is a new partitioning that arises from successively partitioning the same set U by forming all subsets of the form $A \cap B$. In other words, perform the A partitioning, then the B partitioning on the same U, or the same square. This is shown in Figure 4.8. Each cell of the partitioning is an intersection of the subsets of A and B. We shall find in a later chapter that such cross-partitioning is very important in research design and in the analysis of data.

Anticipating later developments, we give a research example of a cross partition. Such examples are called *crossbreaks*. Crossbreaks provide the most elementary way to show a relation between two variables. The example is from Miller and Swanson's study of child-rearing practices. One of the tables they report is a crossbreak in which the variables are social class (middle class and working class) and weaning (early and late). The data, converted to percentages by the writer, are given in Table 4.1.[5] The frequencies reported by Miller and Swanson are given in the lower right corner of each cell. Evidently there is a relation between social class and weaning. Middle-class mothers show a tendency to wean their children earlier than lower-class mothers do. The two conditions of disjointness and exhaustiveness are satisfied. The intersection of any two cells is empty, for example, $(A_1 \cap B_1) \cap (A_2 \cap B_2) = E$. And the cells exhaust all the cases: $(A_1 \cap B_1) \cup \cdots \cup (A_2 \cap B_2) = U$.

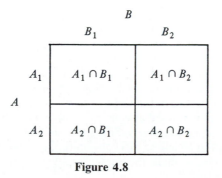

Figure 4.8

[5]D. Miller and G. Swanson, *Inner Conflict and Defense*. New York: Holt, Rinehart and Winston, 1960, p. 426.

Table 4.1   Crossbreak Table: Relation Between Social Class and Weaning, Miller and Swanson Study

		Weaning			
		Early (B_1)		Late (B_2)	
	Middle Class (A_1)	60%	(33)	40%	(22)
Social Class	Working Class (A_2)	35%	(17)	65%	(31)

Partitioning extends beyond two partitions, of course. Instead of dichotomies, we can have polytomies; instead of success-failure, for instance, we can have success-partial success-failure. A variable can theoretically be partitioned into any number of subsets, though there are usually practical limitations. There is no theoretical limitation, either, on the number of variables in a cross partition, but practical considerations usually limit the number to three or four. In a later chapter we will extend partitioning to three variables.

LEVELS OF DISCOURSE

When we talk about anything we talk about it in a context or frame of reference. The expressions context and frame of reference are closely related to U, the universe of discourse. The universe of discourse must be able to include any objects we talk about. If we go to another U, another level of discourse, the new level will not include all the objects. Indeed, it may not include any of the objects. If we are talking about people, for instance, we do not—or perhaps I should say "should not"—start talking about birds and their habits unless we somehow relate birds and their habits to people and make it clear that this is what we are doing. There are two levels of discourse or universes (U's) of discourse here: people and birds. When discussing the democratic implications of segregation, we should not abruptly shift to religious problems—unless, of course, we somehow relate the latter to the former. Otherwise we lose our original universe of discourse, or we cannot assign the objects of the level, religion, perhaps, to the old level, the education of black children.

To color the picture differently, let's change our level of discourse to music and judging and understanding different kinds of music. One of the great difficulties in listening to modern music is that the classical system of rules our ears have learned is not suited to the music of composers like Bartók, Schoenberg, and Ives. One has less difficulty with Bartók and much more difficulty with Schoenberg and Ives because Bartók maintains more of the classical basis than do Schoenberg and Ives. Take Ives' Concord Sonata, a truly great work. At first hearing one is bewildered by the seeming cacophony and lack of structure. After a number of hearings, however, one begins to suspend classical judgmental frames of reference and to hear the beauty, meaning, and structure of the work. Ives' universe of musical discourse is simply quite different from the classical universe of discourse, and it is extremely difficult for us to shift from the classical U to Ives' U. Many people are even unable to make the shift: they find Ives' music strange, even repugnant. They are unable to shake the classical aesthetic and judgmental level of discourse enough to make the shift.[6]

[6]I do not want to imply that it is necessarily desirable to make the shift, nor do I want to imply that all modern music, even all of Ives' music, is great or good music. I am simply trying to illustrate the generality and applicability of the ideas of sets and levels of discourse.

In research, we must be very careful not to mix or shift our levels of discourse, or to do so only knowingly and consciously. Set-thinking helps us avoid such mixing and shifting. As an extreme example, suppose an investigator decided to study the toilet training, authoritarianism, musical aptitude, creativity, intelligence, reading achievement, and general scholastic achievement of ninth-grade youngsters. While it is conceivable that some sort of relations can be teased out of this array of variables, it is more conceivable that it is an intellectual mess. At any rate, remember sets. Ask yourself: "Do the objects I am discussing or am about to discuss belong to the set or sets of my present discussion?" If so, then you are on one level of discourse. If not, then another level of discourse, another set, or set of sets, is entering the discussion. If this happens without your knowing it, the result is confusion. In short, ask: "What are U and the subsets of U?"

Research requires precise definitions of universal sets. "Precise" means: give a clear rule that tells you when an object is or is not a member of U. Similarly, define subsets of U and the subsets of the subsets of U. If the objects of U are people, then you cannot have a subset with objects that are not people. (Though you might have a set A of people and the set $\sim A$ of "not-people," this logically amounts to U being people. "Not-people" is in this case a subset of "people," by definition or convention.)

The set idea is fundamental in human thinking. This is because all or most thinking probably depends on putting things into categories and labeling the categories, as indicated earlier.[7] What we do is to group together classes of objects—things, people, events, phenomena in general—and name these classes. Such names are then concepts, labels that we no longer need to learn anew and that we can use for efficient thinking.

Set theory is also a general and widely applicable tool of conceptual and analytic thinking. Its most important applications pertinent to research methodology are probably to the study of relations, logic, sampling, probability, measurement, and data analysis, as indicated earlier. But sets can be applied to other areas and problems that are not considered technical in the sense, say, that probability and measurement are. Piaget, for example, has used set algebra to help explain the thinking of children.[8] Hunt has applied sets to his study of concept learning.[9] Coombs presented his important theory of data largely in set terms.[10] Warr and Smith, with remarkable ingenuity and insight, used set theory to test different models of inference about personal traits—with rather surprising results.[11] Later in this book, measurement will be defined using a single set-theoretic equation. In addition, basic principles of sampling, analysis, and of research design will be clarified with sets and set theory. Unfortunately, most social scientists and educators are still not aware of the generality, power, and flexibility of set thinking. It can be safely predicted, however, that researchers in the social sciences and education will find set thinking and theory increasingly useful in the conceptualization of theoretical and research problems.

Study Suggestions

1. Draw two overlapping circles, enclosed in a rectangle. Label the following parts: the universal set U, the subsets A and B, the intersection of A and B, and the union of A and B.

---

[7] J. Bruner, J. Goodnow, and G. Austin, *A Study of Thinking*. New York: Wiley, 1956, chap. 1; E. Rosch, "Principles of Categorization." In E. Rosch and B. Lloyd, eds., *Cognition and Categorization*. Hillsdale, N. J.: Erlbaum Associates, 1978, chap. 2.

[8] J. Piaget, *Logic and Psychology*. New York: Basic Books, 1957. Also, B. Inhelder and J. Piaget, *The Growth of Logical Thinking from Childhood to Adolescence*. New York: Basic Books, 1958.

[9] E. Hunt, *Concept Learning*. New York: Wiley, 1962.

[10] C. Coombs, "A Theory of Data," *Psychological Review*, 67 (1960), 143–159.

[11] P. Warr and J. Smith, "Combining Information about People: Comparisons Between Six Models," *Journal of Personality and Social Psychology*, 16 (1970), 55–65.

(a) If you were working on a research problem involving fifth-grade children, what part of the diagram would indicate the children from which you might draw samples?

(b) What might the sets A and B represent?

(c) What meaning might the intersection of A and B have?

(d) How would you have to change the diagram to represent the empty set? Under what conditions would such a diagram have research meaning?

2. Consider the following cross partition:

$$\text{Republican } (B_1) \quad \text{Democrat } (B_2)$$

$$\text{Male } (A_1)$$
$$\text{Female } (A_2)$$

What is the meaning of the following sets—that is, what would we call any object in the sets?

(a) $(A_1 \cap B_1)$; $(A_2 \cap B_2)$

(b) A_1; B_1

(c) $(A_1 \cap B_1) \cup (A_1 \cap B_2) \cup (A_2 \cap B_1) \cup (A_2 \cap B_2)$

(d) $(A_1 \cap B_1) \cup (A_2 \cap B_1)$

3. Make a cross partition using the variables socioeconomic status and voting preference (Democrat and Republican). Can a sample of American individuals be unambiguously assigned to the cells of the cross partition? Are the cells exhaustive? Are they disjoint? Why are these two conditions necessary?

4. Under what conditions will the following set equation be true?

$$n(A \cup B) = n(A) + n(B)$$

[*Note:* $n(A)$ means the number of objects in the set A.]

5. Suppose a researcher in sociology wants to do a study of the influence of race on occupational status. How can he conceptualize the problem in set terms?

6. How are sets related to variables? Can we talk about the partitioning of variables? Is it meaningful to talk about subsets and variables? Explain.

7. Let $A = \{\text{Opus 101, Opus 106, Opus 109, Opus 110, Opus 111}\}$, which is the set of Beethoven's last five piano sonatas. This is a list definition. Here is a rule definition:

$$A = \{a \mid a \text{ is one of the last five Beethoven sonatas}\}$$

(The sign "$\mid$" is read "given.")

Under what conditions are rule definitions better than list definitions?

Chapter 5

Relations

RELATIONS are the essence of knowledge. What is important in science is not knowledge of particulars but knowledge of the relations among phenomena. We know that large things are large only by comparing them to smaller things. We thus establish the relations "greater than" and "less than." Educational scientists can "know" about achievement only as they study achievement in relation to nonachievement and in relation to other variables. When they learn that children of higher intelligence generally do well in school and that children of lower intelligence often do less well, they "know" an important facet of achievement. When they also learn that middle-class children tend to do better in school than working-class children, they are beginning to understand "achievement." They are learning about the relations that give meaning to the concept of achievement. The relations between intelligence and achievement, between social class and achievement, and, indeed, between any variables are the basic "stuff" of science.

The relational nature of human knowledge is clearly seen even when seemingly obvious "facts" are analyzed. Is a stone hard? To say whether this statement is true or false we must examine sets and subsets of different kinds of stones. Then, after operationally defining "hard," we compare the "hardness" of stones to other "hardnesses." The "simplest" facts turn out, on analysis, to be not so simple. Northrop, discussing concepts and facts, says, "The only way to get pure facts, independent of all concepts and theory, is merely to look at them and forthwith to remain perpetually dumb. . . . "[1]

The dictionary tells us that a relation is a bond, a connection, a kinship. For most people this definition is good enough. But what do "bond," "connection," and "kin-

[1]F. Northrop, *The Logic of the Sciences and the Humanities*. New York: Macmillan, 1947, p. 317. See also, M. Cohen and E. Nagel, *An Introduction to Logic and Scientific Method*. New York: Harcourt, 1934, pp. 217–219.

ship'' mean? Again, the dictionary says that a bond is a tie, a binding force, and that a connection is, among other things, a union, a relationship, an alliance. But a union, a tie, between what? And what do ''union,'' ''tie,'' and ''binding force'' mean? Such definitions, while intuitively helpful, are too ambiguous for scientific use.

RELATIONS AS SETS OF ORDERED PAIRS

Relations in science are always between classes or sets of objects. One cannot ''know'' the relation between social class and school achievement by studying one child. ''Knowing'' the relation is achieved only by abstracting the relation from sets of children, or more accurately, from sets of characteristics of children. Let us take examples of relations and intuitively develop a notion of what a relation is.

Let A be the set of all fathers and B the set of all sons. If we pair each father with his son (or sons), we have the relation ''father-son.'' We might also call this relation ''fatherhood,'' even though daughters have not been considered. Similarly we might pair parents (elements of A, each pair of parents being considered as an element) with their children. This would be the relation of ''parenthood,'' or maybe ''family.'' Let A be the set of all husbands and B the set of all wives. The set of pairs then defines the relation ''marriage.'' In other words, a new set is formed, a set of pairs with husbands always listed first and wives second and each husband paired only with his own wife.

Suppose the set A consists of the scores of a specified group of children on an intelligence test and the set B scores on an achievement test. If we pair each child's IQ with his achievement score, we define a relation between intelligence and achievement. Notice that we cannot so easily assign a name like ''parenthood'' or ''marriage'' to this relation. Suppose the sets of scores are as follows:

Intelligence	Achievement
136	55
125	57
118	42
110	48
100	42
97	35
90	32

Consider the two sets as one set of pairs. Then this set is a relation.

If we graph the two sets of scores on X and Y axes, as we did in Chapter 3 (Figure 3.3), the relation becomes easier to ''see.'' This has been done in Figure 5.1. Each point is defined by two scores. For example, the point farthest to the right is defined by (136, 55), and the point farthest to the left is (90, 32). Graphs like Figure 5.1 are highly useful and succinct ways to express relations. One sees at a glance, for instance, that higher values of X are accompanied by higher values of Y, and lower values of X by lower values of Y. As we will see in a later chapter, it is also possible to draw a line through the plotted points of Figure 5.1, from lower left to upper right. (The reader should try this.) This line, called a regression line, also expresses the relation between X and Y, between intelligence and achievement, but it also succinctly gives us considerably more information about the relation: namely its direction and magnitude.

We are now ready to define ''relation'' formally: *A relation is a set of ordered pairs.* Any relation *is* a set, a certain kind of set: a set of ordered pairs. An *ordered pair* is two objects, or a set of two elements, in which there is a fixed order for the objects to appear. Actually, we speak of ordered pairs which means, as indicated earlier, that the members

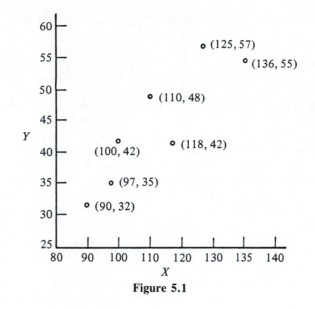

Figure 5.1

of each pair always appear in a certain order. If the members of the sets *A* and *B* are paired, then we must specify whether the members of *A* or the members of *B* come first in each pair. If we define the relation of marriage, for example, we specify the set of ordered pairs with, say, husbands always placed first in each pair. In other words, the pair (*a,b*) is not the same as the pair (*b,a*). (Ordered pairs are enclosed thus: ( ).) A set of ordered pairs is indicated in this manner: {(*a,k*), (*b,l*), (*c,m*)}.

We have fortunately left the previous ambiguity of the dictionary definition behind. The definition of relations as sets of ordered pairs, though it may seem a bit strange and even curious to the reader, is unambiguous and general. Moreover, the scientist, like the mathematician, can work with it.

DETERMINING RELATIONS IN RESEARCH

Although we have avoided ambiguity with our definition of relations, we have not cleared up the definitional and especially the practical problem of "determining" relations. There is another way to define a relation that may help us. Let *A* and *B* be sets. If we pair each individual member of *A* with every member of *B*, we obtain *all the possible pairs* between the two sets. This is called the *Cartesian product* of the two sets and is labeled *A* × *B*. A relation is then defined as a subset of *A* × *B*, that is, *any* subset of ordered pairs drawn from *A* × *B* is a relation.[2]

To illustrate this idea very simply, let the set *A* = {a_1, a_2, a_3} and the set *B* = {b_1, b_2, b_3}.[3] Then the Cartesian product, *A* × *B*, can be diagrammed as in Figure 5.2. That is, we generate nine ordered pairs: (*a₁,b₁*), (*a₁,b₂*), . . . , (*a₃,b₃*). With large sets, of course, there would be many pairs, in fact *mn* pairs, where *m* and *n* are the numbers of elements in *A* and *B*, respectively.

[2] See R. Kershner and L. Wilcox, *The Anatomy of Mathematics*. New York: Ronald, 1950, chap. 5, for an excellent discussion of relations.

[3] The subscript integers merely label and distinguish individual members of sets. They do not imply order. Note, too, that there do not have to be equal numbers of members in the two sets.

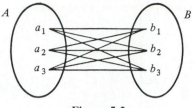

Figure 5.2

This is not very interesting—at least in the present context. What do we do to determine or "discover" a relation? We determine empirically which elements of A "go with" which elements of B according to some criterion. Obviously there are many subsets of pairs of $A \times B$, most of which do not "make sense" or which do not interest us. Kershner and Wilcox say that a relation is "a method for distinguishing some ordered pairs from others; it is a scheme for singling out certain pairs from all of them."[4] According to this way of viewing relations, the relation of "marriage" is a method or procedure for distinguishing married couples from all possible pairings of men and women. In this way we can even think of religion as a relation. Let $A = \{a_1, a_2, \ldots, a_n\}$ be the set of all people in the United States, and let $B = \{$Catholic, Protestant, Jew, and so forth$\}$ be the set of religions. If we order pairs, in this case each person with his religion, then we have the "relation" of religion, or perhaps more accurately, "religious affiliation."

Lest the student be too disturbed by the perhaps jarring sensation of defining a relation as a subset of $A \times B$, we may hastily add, again, that many of the possible subsets of ordered pairs of $A \times B$, naturally, will make no sense. Perhaps the main point to be made is that our definition of relation is unambiguous and completely general. No matter what sets of ordered pairs we pick, it *is* a relation. It is up to *us* to decide whether or not the sets we pick make scientific sense according to the dictates of the problems to which we are seeking answers.

The reader may wonder why so much trouble has been taken to define relations. The basic answer is simple: Almost all science pursues and studies relations. There is literally no empirical way to "know" anything except through its relations to other things, as indicated earlier. If, like Suedfeld and Rank, we are interested in the success of revolutionary leaders (for example, Jefferson, Mao Tse-tung, and Castro), we have to relate that success or lack of success to other variables.[5] To explain a phenomenon like revolutionary success, we must "discover" its determinants, the relations it has with other pertinent variables. Suedfeld and Rank "explained" revolutionary success by relating such success to the conceptual complexity of revolutionary leaders. For revolutionary success *before* a revolution, conceptual simplicity is needed, but *after* a revolution conceptual complexity is necessary. Obviously, if relations are fundamental in science, then we must know clearly what they are, as well as how to study them.[6]

Rules of Correspondence and Mapping

Any objects—people, numbers, gambling outcomes, points in space, symbols, and so on and on—can be members of sets and can be related in the ordered-pair sense. It is said

---

[4] Kershner and Wilcox, *op. cit.,* p. 46.

[5] P. Suedfeld and A. Rank, "Revolutionary Leaders: Long-Term Success as a Function of Changes in Conceptual Complexity," *Journal of Personality and Social Psychology,* 34 (1976), 169–178.

[6] The definition of "relation" has been neglected in behavioral research. It seems to be a concept whose meaning is assumed to be known by everyone. It is also confused with "relationship," which is a connection of some kind between people, or between people and groups, like a mother-child relationship. It is not the same as a relation.

that the members of one set are *mapped* on to the members of another set by means of a rule of correspondence. A *rule of correspondence* is a prescription or a formula that tells us how to map the objects of one set on to the objects of another set. It tells us, in brief, how the correspondence between set members is achieved. Study Figure 5.3, which shows the relation between the names of five individuals and the symbols 1 and 0, which stand for male (1) and female (0). We have here a mapping of sex (1 and 0) on to the names. This is of course a relation, each name having either 1 or 0, male or female, assigned to it.

In a relation the two sets whose "objects" are being related are called the *domain* and the *range*, or *D* and *R*. *D* is the set of first elements, and *R* the set of second elements. In Figure 5.3, we assigned 1 to male and 0 to female. To each member of the domain the appropriate member of the range is assigned. *D* = {Jane, Arthur, Michael, Alberta, Ruth}, and *R* = {0, 1}. The rule of correspondence says: If the object of *D* is female assign a 0, if male assign a 1.

In other words, objects, especially numbers, are assigned to other objects—persons, places, numbers, and so on—according to rules. The process is highly varied in its applications but simple in its conception. Instead of thinking of all the different ways of expressing relations separately, we realize that they are all sets of ordered pairs and that the objects of one set are simply mapped on to the objects of another set. All the varied ways of expressing relations—as mappings, correspondences, equations, sets of points, tables, or statistical indices—can be reduced to sets of ordered pairs.

SOME WAYS TO STUDY RELATIONS

Relations can be and are expressed in various ways. In the previous discussion, some of these were illustrated. One way is simply to list and pair the members of sets, as in Figures 5.2 and 5.3. Actually, this method is not often used in the research literature. We now examine more useful ways.

Graphs

A *graph* is a drawing in which the two members of each ordered pair of a relation are plotted on two axes, *X* and *Y* (or any appropriate designation). Figure 5.1 is a graph of the ordered pairs of the fictitious intelligence and achievement scores given earlier. We can see from that graph that the ordered pairs tend to "go together": high values of *Y* go with high values of *X*, and low values of *Y* go with low values of *X*.

A more interesting set of ordered pairs is graphed in Figure 5.4. The numbers used to make the graph are from a fascinating study by Miller and DiCara, in which seven rats

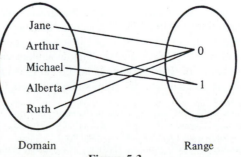

Domain   Range

Figure 5.3

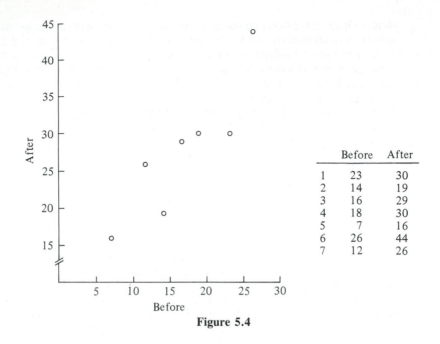

Figure 5.4

were "trained" to secrete urine.[7] (Since urine secretion is an autonomic function, it is normally beyond control and thus training and learning.) The "Before" or X axis of the graph indicates values of urine secretion before the training; the "After" or Y axis indicates values after the training. Since we will use these same data in another context later in the book—at which time the study will be described in more detail—no further details are given here. The relation between the two sets of urine secretion values is pronounced. Again, high values before training are accompanied by high values after training, and similarly with low values. The graph and the relation it expresses reflect individual differences in urine secretion. The full meaning of this statement will be made clear when we later describe the statistical analysis of these data.

Tables

Perhaps the most common way to present data to show relations is in tables. The variables of the relations presented are usually given at the top and the sides of the table and the data in the table itself. The statistical data are most often means, frequencies, and percentages. Consider Table 5.1, which is a summary presentation of the frequency data presented by Freedman, Wallington, and Bless, who tested the notion that compliance is related to guilt: the greater the feeling of guilt, the greater the compliance with demands.[8] The experimenters induced half their subjects to lie; they assumed that lying would engender guilt (apparently it did). The Guilt or Lie variable is labeled at the top of the table. This is the independent variable, of course. The dependent variable was compliance to demands made of all subjects. This variable is labeled at the side of the table. The data in the cells of the table are frequencies, the numbers of subjects who fell into the subsets or subcate-

[7] N. Miller and L. DiCara, "Instrumental Learning of Urine Formation by Rats: Changes in Renal Blood Flow," *American Journal of Physiology,* 215 (1968), 677–683. (The numbers used and given in Figure 5.4 have been multiplied by 1000 to facilitate graphing.)

[8] J. Freedman, S. Wallington, and E. Bless, "Compliance Without Pressure: The Effect of Guilt," *Journal of Personality and Social Psychology,* 7 (1967), 117–124.

gories. Of the 31 subjects induced to lie, 20 complied with the demands of the experimenter; 11 did not comply with the demands. Of the 31 subjects who were not induced to lie, 11 complied and 20 did not comply. The data are consistent with the hypothesis. In a later chapter we will study in detail how to analyze and interpret frequency data and tables of this kind.

Table 5.1 Frequency Results of Experiment to Study Relation Between Guilt and Compliance, Freedman et al. Study

	Lie (Guilt)	Not Lie (No Guilt)
Comply	20	11
Not-Comply	11	20
	—	—
	31	31

The point of Table 5.1 is that a relation and the evidence on the nature of the relation are expressed in the table. In this case the tabled data are in frequency form. (A frequency is the number of members of sets and subsets.) The table itself is a cross partition, often called a crossbreak, in which one variable of the relation is set up against another variable of the relation. The two variable labels appear on the top and side of the table, as indicated earlier. The direction and magnitude of the relation itself is expressed by the relative sizes of the frequencies in the cells of the table. In Table 5.1 many more of the subjects induced to lie (20 of 31) complied than did the subjects not induced to lie (11 of 31).

A different kind of table presents means, arithmetic averages, in the body of the table. The means express the dependent variable. If there is only one independent variable, its categories are labeled at the top of the table. If there are two or more independent variables, their categories can be presented in various ways at the top and sides of tables, as we will see in later chapters. An example is given in Table 5.2, which is the simplest form such a table can take. In this study by Clark and Walberg, the effect of massive reinforcement on the reading achievement of underachieving black children was studied.[9] It was expected that the reinforcement given to the experimental group children would increase their reading scores compared to those of a similar group of children who were not reinforced ("Control" in the table). As can be seen, the experimental group mean is larger than the control group mean. Is the difference between the means "large" or "small"? We will later learn how to assess the size and meaning of such differences. Here we are interested only in why the table expresses a relation.

Table 5.2 Means of Experimental and Control Groups, Clark and Walberg Study

Experimental	Control
31.62[a]	26.86

[a] The means were calculated from a reading test.

In tables of this kind a relation is always expressed or implied.[10] In the present case there are two variables being related: reinforcement and reading achievement. The rubric

[9] C. Clark and H. Walberg, "The Influence of Massive Rewards on Reading Achievement in Potential Urban School Dropouts," *American Educational Research Journal,* 5 (1968), 305–310.

[10] Tables as simple as this one are rarely given in the literature. It saves space merely to mention the two means in the text of a report. Moreover, there can be more than two means compared. The principle is the same, however: the means "express" the dependent variable, and the differences among them the presumed effect of the independent variable.

"Experimental-Control" expresses the reinforcement that the experimental group received and the control group did not receive. This is the independent variable. The two means in the table express the reading achievement of the two groups of children, the dependent variable. If the means differ sufficiently, then it can be assumed that reinforcement had an effect on reading achievement.

Tables of means are extremely important in behavioral research, especially in experimental research. There can be two, three, or more independent variables, and they can express the separate and combined effects of these variables on a dependent variable, or even on two or more dependent variables. The central point is that relations are always studied, even though it is not always easy to conceptualize and to state the relations.

Graphs and Correlation

Although we briefly examined relations and graphs earlier, it will be profitable to pursue this important topic further. Suppose we have two sets of scores of the same individuals on two tests, X and Y:

X	Y
1	1
2	1
2	2
3	3

The two sets form a set of ordered pairs. This set is of course a relation. It can also be written, letting R stand for relation, $R = \{(1,1), (2,1), (2,2), (3,3)\}$. It is plotted in the graph of Figure 5.5.

We can often get a rough idea of the direction and degree of a relation by inspection of lists of ordered pairs, but such a method is imprecise. Graphs, such as those of Figures 5.1 and 5.5, tell us more. It can more easily be "seen" that Y values "go along" with X values: higher values of Y accompany higher values of X, and lower values of Y accompany lower values of X. In this case the relation, or correlation, as it is also called, is positive. (If we had the equation, $R = \{(1,3), (2,1), (2,2), (3,1)\}$, the relation would be negative. The student should plot these values and note their direction and meaning.) If the equation were $R = \{(1,2), (2,1), (2,2), (3,2)\}$, the relation would be null or zero. This is plotted in Figure 5.6. It can be seen that Y values do not "go along" with X values in any systematic way. This does not mean that there is "no" relation. There is always a relation—by definition—since there is a set of ordered pairs. It is commonly said, however, that there is "no" relation. It is more accurate to say that the relation is null or zero.

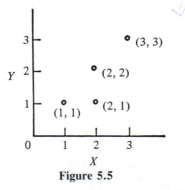

Figure 5.5

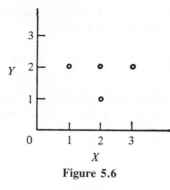

Figure 5.6

Social scientists commonly calculate indices of relation, usually called coefficients of correlation, between sets of ordered pairs in order to obtain more precise estimates of the direction and degree of relations. If one such index, the product-moment coefficient of correlation, or r, is calculated for the ordered pairs of Figure 5.5, $r = .85$ is obtained. For the pairs of $R = \{(1,3), (2,1), (2,2), (3,1)\}$, the relation we said was negative, $r = -.85$. For the pairs of Figure 5.6, the set of pairs that showed a null or zero relation, $r = 0$.[11]

Product-moment and related coefficients of correlation, then, are based on the concomitant variation of the members of sets of ordered pairs. If they *covary,* vary together—high values with high values, medium values with medium values, and low values with low values, or high values with low values, and so on—it is said that there is a positive or negative relation as the case may be. If they do not covary, it is said there is ''no'' relation. The most useful such indices range from $+1.00$ through 0 to -1.00, $+1.00$ indicating a perfect positive relation, -1.00 a perfect negative relation, and 0 no discernible relation, or zero relation. Some indices range only from 0 to $+1.00$. Other indices may take on other values.

Most coefficients of relation tell us how similar the rank orders of two sets of measures are. Table 5.3 presents three examples to illustrate this going together of rank orders. The coefficients of correlation are given with each of the sets of ordered pairs. I is obvious: the rank orders of the X and Y scores of I go together perfectly. So do the X and Y scores of II, but in the opposite direction. In III, no relation between the rank orders can be discerned. In I and II, one can predict perfectly from X to Y, but in III one cannot predict

Table 5.3   Three Sets of Ordered Pairs Showing Different Directions and Degrees of Correlation

(I) $r = 1.00$		(II) $r = -1.00$		(III) $r = 0$	
X	Y	X	Y	X	Y
1	1	1	5	1	2
2	2	2	4	2	5
3	3	3	3	3	3
4	4	4	2	4	1
5	5	5	1	5	4

[11] Methods of calculating these r's and other coefficients of correlation are discussed in statistics texts. These texts also discuss at greater length than is possible in this book the interpretation of correlation coefficients.

values of Y from knowledge of X. Coefficients of correlation are rarely 1.00 or 0. They ordinarily take on intermediate values.

Two Research Examples

To put some flesh on the rather abstract bones of our discussion of relations, let's look at two interesting examples of relations and correlation. In studying emotional aspects of prejudice, Cooper calculated two sets of ranks. He had his subjects respond to nine national and ethnic groups by choosing from each of all the possible pairs of such groups— for example, from Swedes-Austrians, Jews-Japanese, English-Poles, and so on—those groups they preferred.[12] The numbers of choices the groups received were then assigned ranks from 1 through 9, 1 indicating the most preferred and 9 the least preferred. Cooper also measured the subjects' psychogalvanic skin response to each of the groups. This response indicates emotional change by measuring skin resistance. These measures were also ranked, 1 indicating the least response and 9 the most response. The results are given in Table 5.4. The hypothesis tested was: Strongly prejudiced (negative) attitudes are supported by high levels of emotion. Examination of the two sets of rank orders—the set of ordered pairs—shows that they tend to covary, thus supporting the hypothesis. The actual coefficient of correlation—called a rank-order coefficient of correlation—was .82, a high value. Evidently different groups evoke different emotional responses, and groups perceived negatively evoke the stronger responses, as Cooper predicted.

Table 5.4 Rank Orders of Physiological and Paired-Comparison Responses to National and Ethnic Groups, Cooper Study[a]

Group	Physiological	Paired-Comparison
Swedes	1	2
Canadians	2	1
Austrians	3	5
English	4	4
Poles	5	7
Germans	6	3
Japanese	7	6
Jews	8	9
Mexicans	9	8

[a]Physiological: 1 = least response; 9 = greatest response; Paired-Comparison: 1 = most preferred; 9 = least preferred.

Our second example is not quantitative, though quantity is implied and it would not be difficult to quantify the variables. Hardy studied, among other things, the relation between religious affiliation and doctoral productivity.[13] Which religious groups produce the most scholarly doctorates and which the least? (Hardy was really studying values and their influence on scholarship.) The results are given in Table 5.5. They need little comment. It is apparent that the relation is strong: the more liberal a religious group the higher the production of doctoral degrees. The ordered pairs of religious groups and their productivity ratings are easily seen.

[12]J. Cooper, "Emotion in Prejudice," *Science*, 130 (1959), 314–318.
[13]K. Hardy, "Social Origins of American Scientists and Scholars," *Science*, 185 (1974), 497–506.

Table 5.5 The Relation Between Religious Affiliation and Output of Scholarly Doctorates in the United States, Hardy Study

Religious Group	Religious Type	Productivity Rating
Unitarian Quaker (Friends) Secularized Jewish	Liberal, secularized Protestants and Jews	Highly productive
Church of the Brethren Evangelical E. U. Brethren Mormon Reformed Christian Reformed Congregational	Moderately liberal, dissident, antitraditional Protestants	Productive
Presbyterian Methodist Baptist	Traditional Protestants	Fair productivity
Southern Protestant Disciples of Christ Lutheran	Fundamentalist, conservative Protestants	Low productivity
Roman Catholic	Catholic	Very low productivity

MULTIVARIATE RELATIONS AND REGRESSION

In our discussion of relations we may have given the impression that scientists and researchers are always preoccupied with the relations between two variables. When, for instance, we talked about the relations between intelligence and achievement, guilt and compliance, religious values and production of doctorates, we perhaps erroneously conveyed the idea that scientists are preoccupied with studying only two-variable relations. Not so. Indeed, much research has been two-variable research, but in the behavioral sciences this has changed dramatically. The preoccupation of behavioral researchers is today more likely to be with multiple relations. While modern researchers know that the relation between intelligence and achievement is substantial and positive, they also know that there are many determinants of both achievement and intelligence. They know, for instance, that social class has a substantial influence on both variables. They also believe, though the evidence is conflicting, that self-esteem affects both intelligence and achievement. Moreover, methodologists have developed powerful analytic approaches and methods to handle what we will call multivariate problems. Let us look briefly at the logic and substance of such problems.

Some Logic of Multivariate Inquiry

The hidden structure of our argument to now is epitomized by the expression "If p, then q": "If intelligence, then achievement," "If guilt, then compliance," "If conceptual complexity, then revolutionary success." These are implied relations, of course. But they go further: they also imply direction—from independent variables to dependent variables. They can all be conceptualized as If p, then q statements. In logic, If p, then q is called a conditional statement, and it is possible to conceptualize most research problems and study the structure of scientific arguments using conditional and related statements.[14] But the relations of behavioral research are more complex than simple If p, then q statements. Contemporary researchers are more likely to say: If p, then q, under conditions r and t. This conditional statement can be written: $p \to q|r$, t, which is read as in the preceding sentence ("|" means "under conditions," or "given"). Or, somewhat simpler, we can write: $(p_1, p_2, p_3) \to q$, which means: If p_1 and p_2 and p_3, then q. More concretely, this means that the variables p_1, p_2, and p_3 influence the variable q in certain ways. We might say, for instance, that intelligence, social class, and self-esteem affect school achievement in such-and-such ways.

The simplest way to show the relations graphically is with so-called "path diagrams." A path diagram for the above statement is given in Figure 5.7. In this diagram—in which we use x_1, x_2, and x_3 for the independent variables and y for the dependent variable—specifies, in effect, that the three independent variables all directly affect the dependent variable. This is what is called a straightforward multiple regression problem (see below), in which k (=3) independent variables mutually influence a dependent variable. This approach, too, has changed dramatically in the past decade. Researchers are now likely to talk about and test both direct and indirect influences. An alternative model and path analytic diagram is given in Figure 5.8. Here Intelligence and Self-Esteem influence School Achievement directly, but Social Class does not. Instead, it influences School Achievement indirectly *through* Intelligence and Self-Esteem, quite a different conception.

Multiple Relations and Regression

The research situation depicted in Figure 5.7 is a multiple regression problem: k (=3) independent variables mutually and simultaneously influence a dependent variable. Later in the book we will show how such a problem is solved. (The method is technically complex but conceptually simple, and it will give us little trouble.) For now, the problem is one of first finding the relation between the three independent variables, taken simultaneously, and the dependent variable, and second, of determining how much each independent variable, x_1, x_2, and x_3, influences the dependent variable, y. Though now much more complex, the problem is still a relation, a set of ordered pairs.

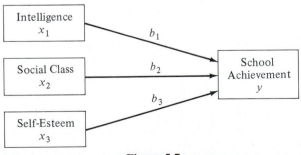

Figure 5.7

---

[14] F. Kerlinger, "Research in Education." In R. Ebel, V. Noll, and R. Bauer, eds., *Encyclopedia of Educational Research*, 4th ed. New York: Macmillan, 1969, pp. 1127–1144 (pp. 1133–1134). We will examine this logic further when we later discuss experimental and nonexperimental research.

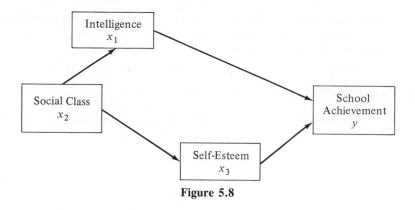

Figure 5.8

What the method does essentially—and beautifully—is to find the best possible combination of x_1, x_2, and x_3, given y and the relations among the four variables, so that the correlation between the three-variable combination and y is a maximum. In the problem of Figure 5.7, multiple regression finds those values of b_1, b_2, and b_3 (see the figure) that will make the correlation between x_1, x_2, and x_3, taken together, and y as high as possible. (The student of mathematics will recognize this as a calculus problem.) The b weights, called regression weights or coefficients, are then used with the three variables in predicting the dependent variable, y. The method in effect creates a new variable which is a combination of x_1, x_2, and x_3. Call this variable y'. Then the multiple correlation is between y, the observed dependent variable, and y', the dependent variable predicted from knowledge of x_1, x_2, and x_3.

The alert reader will have seen that relations and correlations are symmetric: it often doesn't matter much which variable is independent and which dependent. In regression analysis, however, it does make a difference; regression is asymmetric. We say, If x, then y, or: If x_1, x_2, x_3, then y. Many writers talk about ''causal analysis,'' especially when talking about problems such as those given in Figure 5.7 and 5.8. I prefer to avoid the words ''cause'' and ''causal'' because they are exceedingly sticky ideas—What is a cause? for instance—and because their use is not necessary. We can adequately operate with conditional statements, though not always easily.[15]

Regression, in other words, deals with relations, but the traffic is mostly one-way: from independent to dependent variables. To further anticipate a later discussion, let's look at a regression equation:

$$Y = a + b_1 X_1 + b_2 X_2$$

If we ignore the a—it is not important for the argument—we see that Y is the sum of X_1 and X_2, each weighted by its b. When we solve the equation for the b's (and the a, of course) we use them to produce a score Y' for each person in the sample. Y and Y'—keep in mind that Y and Y' stand for values for each person in the sample—are then a set of ordered pairs and thus a relation. The correlation between them is merely an ordinary correlation coefficient, r. But it is labeled R and is called the multiple coefficient of correlation, or the coefficient of multiple correlation. We will later examine the use and interpretation of multiple regression, the coefficient of multiple correlation, and regression weights in greater detail and with actual research examples. At that time, the stu-

---

[15] I must admit that the language is saturated with words that imply cause, for example, ''influence'' and ''depend upon.'' Yet we will avoid causal expressions as much as possible, if for no other reason than that it is never possible to say unambiguously that one thing causes another. More pragmatically, we don't need the word or concept of ''cause''; conditional statements of the if p, then q kind are sufficient for scientific purposes.

dent's natural bewilderment with the presumed mysteries of multivariate thinking should be dissipated and replaced by admiration and perhaps a bit of awe and excitement at these engaging and very powerful ideas and methods.

Study Suggestions

1. Discussions of relations appear to be confined to mathematics texts. The best discussion I have found, albeit abstract and somewhat difficult, is:

KERSHNER R., and WILCOX, L. *The Anatomy of Mathematics.* New York: Ronald, 1950, pp. 41–60.

2. Six examples of relations are given below. Assume that the first-named set is the domain and the second the range. Why are all of these relations?

(a) Book pages and page numbers
(b) Chapter numbers and pages of a book
(c) Population table headings or categories and population figures in a census report
(d) A class of third-grade children and their scores on a standardized achievement test
(e) $y = 2x$
(f) $Y = a + b_1X_1 + b_2X_2$

3. An educational investigator has studied the relation between anxiety and school achievement. Express the relation in set language.

4. Suppose that you wish to study the relations among the following variables: intelligence, socioeconomic status, need for achievement, and school achievement. Set up two alternative models that "explain" school achievement. Draw path diagrams of the two models.

Chapter 6

Variance and Covariance

To STUDY scientific problems and to answer scientific questions, we must study differences among phenomena. In Chapter 5, we examined relations among variables; in a sense, we were studying similarities. Now we concentrate on differences because without differences, without variation, there is no technical way to determine the relations among variables. If we want to study the relation between race and achievement, for instance, we are helpless if we have only achievement measures of white children. We must have achievement measures of children of more than one race. In short, race must vary; it must have variance. It is necessary to explore the variance notion analytically and in some depth. To do so adequately, it is also necessary to skim some of the cream off the milk of statistics.

Studying sets of numbers as they are is unwieldy. It is usually necessary to reduce the sets in two ways: by calculating averages or measures of central tendency, and by calculating measures of variability. The measure of central tendency used in this book is the *mean*. The measure of variability most used is the *variance*. Both kinds of measures epitomize sets of scores, but in different ways. They are both ''summaries'' of whole sets of scores, ''summaries'' that express two important facets of the sets of scores: their central or average tendency and their variability. Solving research problems without these measures is next to impossible. We start our study of variance, then, with some simple computations.

CALCULATION OF MEANS AND VARIANCES

Take the set of numbers $X = \{1, 2, 3, 4, 5\}$. The mean is defined:

$$M = \frac{\Sigma X}{n} \tag{6.1}$$

n = the number of cases in the set of scores; Σ means "the sum of" or "add them up." X stands for any one of the scores, that is, each score is an X. The formula, then, says, "Add the scores and divide by the number of cases in the set." Thus:

$$M = \frac{1 + 2 + 3 + 4 + 5}{5} = \frac{15}{5} = 3$$

The mean of the set X is 3.

Calculating the variance, while not as simple as calculating the mean, is still simple. The formula is:[1]

$$V = \frac{\Sigma x^2}{n} \tag{6.2}$$

V means variance; n and Σ are the same as in Equation 6.1. Σx^2 is called the *sum of squares;* it needs some explanation. The scores are listed in a column:

X	x	x^2
1	-2	4
2	-1	1
3	0	0
4	1	1
5	2	4

ΣX:	15	
M:	3	
Σx^2		10

In this calculation x is a deviation from the mean. It is defined:

$$x = X - M \tag{6.3}$$

Thus, to obtain x, simply subtract from X the mean of all the scores. For example, when $X = 1$, $x = 1 - 3 = -2$; when $X = 4$, $x = 4 - 3 = 1$; and so on. This has been done above. Equation 6.2, however, says to square each x. This has also been done above. (Remember, that the square of a negative number is always positive.) In other words, Σx^2 tells us to subtract the mean from each score to get x, square each x to get x^2, and then add up the x^2's. Finally, the average of the x^2's is taken by dividing Σx^2 by n, the number of cases. Σx^2, the *sum of squares,* is a very important statistic which we will use often.

The variance, in the present case, is

$$V = \frac{(-2)^2 + (-1)^2 + (0)^2 + (1)^2 + (2)^2}{5} = \frac{4 + 1 + 0 + 1 + 4}{5} = \frac{10}{5} = 2$$

The variance is also called the *mean square* (when calculated in a slightly different way).

---

[1] "V" will be used for variance in this book. Other symbols commonly used are σ^2 and s^2. The former is a so-called population value; the latter is a sample value. N is used for the total number of cases in a total sample or in a population. ("Sample" and "population" will be defined in a later chapter.) n is used for a subsample or subset of U of a total sample. Appropriate subscripts will be added and explained as necessary. For example, if we wish to indicate the number of elements in a set A, a subset of U, we can write n_A or n_a. Similarly we attach subscripts to x, V, and so on. When double subscripts are used, such as r_{xy}, the meaning will usually be obvious.

It is called this because, obviously, it is the mean of the x^2's. Clearly it is not difficult to calculate the mean and the variance.[2]

The question is: Why calculate the mean and the variance? The rationale for calculating the mean is easily disposed of. The mean expresses the general level, the center of gravity, of a set of measures. It is, in general, a good representative of the level of a group's characteristics or performance. It also has certain desirable statistical properties, and is the most ubiquitous statistic of the behavioral sciences. In much behavioral research, for example, means of different experimental groups are compared to study relations, as pointed out in Chapter 5. We may be testing the relation between organizational climates and productivity, for instance. We may have used three kinds of climates and may be interested in the question of which climate has the greatest effect on productivity. In such cases means are customarily compared. For instance, of three groups, each operating under one of three climates, A_1, A_2, and A_3, which has the greatest mean on, say, a measure of productivity?

The rationale for computing and using the variance in research is more difficult to explain. In the usual case of ordinary scores the variance is a measure of the dispersion of the set of scores. It tells us how much the scores are spread out. If a group of pupils is very heterogeneous in reading achievement, then the variance of their reading scores will be large compared to the variance of a group that is homogeneous in reading achievement. The variance, then, is a measure of the spread of the scores; it describes the extent to which the scores differ from each other.[3] The remainder of this chapter and later parts of the book will explore other aspects of the use of the variance statistic.

KINDS OF VARIANCE

Variances come in a number of forms. When you read the research and technical literature, you will frequently come across the term, sometimes with a qualifying adjective, sometimes not. To understand the literature, it is necessary to have a good idea of the characteristics and purposes of these different variances. And to design and do research, one must have a rather thorough understanding of the variance concept as well as considerable mastery of statistical variance notions and manipulations.

Population and Sample Variances

The *population variance* is the variance of U, a universe or population of measures. If all the measures of a defined universal set, U, are known, then the variance is known. More likely, however, all the measures of U are not available. In such cases the variance is estimated by calculating the variance of one or more samples of U. A good deal of statistical energy goes into this important activity. A question may arise: How variable is the intelligence of the citizens of the United States? This is a U or population question. If there were a complete list of all the millions of people in the United States—and there

---

[2] The method of calculating the variance used in this chapter differs from the methods ordinarily used. In fact, the method given above is impracticable in most situations. Our purpose is not to learn statistics, as such. Rather, we are pursuing basic ideas. Methods of computation, examples, and demonstrations have been constructed to aid this pursuit of basic ideas. The student should therefore *not* learn the computational methods of this chapter.

[3] For descriptive purposes, the square root of the variance is ordinarily used. It is called the *standard deviation*. Because of certain mathematical properties, however, the variance is more useful in research. It is suggested that the student supplement his study with study of appropriate sections of an elementary statistics text, since it will not be possible in this book to discuss all the facets of meaning and interpretation of means, variances, and standard deviations.

were also a complete list of intelligence test scores of these people—the variance could be simply if wearily computed. No such list exists. So samples—representative samples—of Americans are tested and means and variances computed. The samples are used to estimate the mean and variance of the whole population.

Sampling variance is the variance of statistics computed from samples. The means of four random samples drawn from a population will differ. If the sampling is random and the samples are large enough, the means should not vary too much. That is, the *variance of the means* should be relatively small.[4]

Systematic Variance

Perhaps the most general way to classify variances is as *systematic variance* and *error variance*. *Systematic variance* is the variation in measures due to some known or unknown influences that "cause" the scores to lean in one direction more than another. Any natural or man-made influences that cause events to happen in a certain predictable way are systematic influences. The achievement test scores of the children in a wealthy suburban school will tend to be *systematically* higher than the scores of the children in a city slum area school. Expert teaching may systematically influence the achievement of children—as compared to the achievement of children taught inexpertly.

There are many, many causes of systematic variance. Scientists seek to separate those in which they are interested from those in which they are not interested. They also try to separate from systematic variance variance that is random. Indeed, research may narrowly and technically be defined as the controlled study of variances.

Between-Groups (Experimental) Variance

One important type of systematic variance in research is between-groups or experimental variance. *Between-groups* or *experimental variance*, as the name indicates, is the variance that reflects systematic differences between *groups* of measures. The variance discussed previously as score variance reflects the differences between individuals in a group. We can say, for instance, that, on the basis of present evidence and current tests, the variance in intelligence of a random sample of eleven-year-old children is about 225 points.[5] This figure is a statistic that tells us how much the individuals differ from each other. Between-groups variance, on the other hand, is the variance due to the differences between *groups* of individuals. If the achievement of northern and southern children in comparable schools is measured, there would be differences between the northern and southern groups. Groups as well as individuals differ or vary, and it is possible and appropriate to calculate the variance between these groups.

---

[4]Unfortunately, in much actual research only one sample is usually available—and this one sample is frequently small. We can, however, estimate the sampling variance of the means by using what is called the *standard variance of the mean(s)*. (The term "standard error of the mean" is usually used. The standard error of the mean is the square root of the standard variance of the mean.) The formula is

$$V_M = \frac{V_s}{n_s}$$

where V_M is the standard variance of the mean, V_s the variance of the sample, and n_s, the size of the sample.

Notice an important conclusion that can be reached from this equation. If the size of the sample is increased, V_m is decreased. In other words, to be more confident that the sample is close to the population mean, make n large. Conversely, the smaller the sample, the riskier the estimate. (See Study Suggestions 5 and 6 at the end of the chapter.)

[5]This is obtained by squaring the standard deviation reported in a test manual. The standard deviation of the California Test of Mental Maturity for 11-year-old children, for instance, is about 15, and $15^2 = 225$.

Between-groups variance and experimental variance are fundamentally the same. Both arise from differences between groups. Between-groups variance is a term that covers all cases of systematic differences between groups, experimental and nonexperimental. Experimental variance is usually associated with the variance engendered by active manipulation of independent variables by experimenters.

Here is an example of between-groups variance—in this case experimental variance. Suppose an investigator tests the relative efficacies of three different kinds of reinforcement on learning. After differentially reinforcing the three groups of subjects, the experimenter calculates the means of the groups. Suppose that they are 30, 23, and 19. The mean of the three means is 24, and we calculate the variance *between the means* or *between the groups:*

	x	x^2
30	6	36
23	−1	1
19	−5	25

$\Sigma X:$	72	
$M:$	24	
$\Sigma x^2:$		62

$$V_b = \frac{62}{3} = 20.67$$

In the experiment just described, presumably the different methods of reinforcement tend to "bias" the scores one way or another. This is, of course, the experimenter's purpose: he wants Method A, say, to increase all the learning scores of an experimental group. He may believe that Method B will have no effect on learning, and that Method C will have a depressing effect. If he is correct, the scores under Method A should all tend to go up, whereas under Method C they should all tend to go down. Thus the scores of the groups, as wholes—and, of course, their means—differ systematically. Reinforcement is an *active* variable, a variable deliberately manipulated by the experimenter with the conscious intent to "bias" the scores differentially. Thus any experimenter-manipulated variables are intimately associated with systematic variance. When Bennett et al. gave their experimental groups of rats different degrees of early experience—environmental complexity and training (enriched experiences), control condition (the usual rat colony condition), and reduced experience (isolation)—they were deliberately attempting the build systematic variance into their outcome measures (weight, thickness, and chemical activity of the brain).[6]

The basic idea behind the famous "classical design" of scientific research, in which experimental and control groups are used, is that, through careful control and manipulation, the experimental group's outcome measures (also called "criterion measures") are made to vary systematically, to all go up or down together, while the control group's measures are ordinarily held at the same level. The variance, of course, is between the two groups, that is, the two groups are made to differ. For example, Braud and Braud manipulated experimental groups in a most unusual way. They trained the rats of an experimental group to choose the larger of two circles in a choice task; the control group rats received no training.[7] Extracts from the brains of the animals of both groups were injected into the brains of two new groups of rats. Statistically speaking, they were trying to increase the

[6] E. Bennett, M. Diamond, D. Krech, and M. Rosenzweig, "Chemical and Anatomical Plasticity of Brain," *Science,* 146 (1964), 610–619.

[7] L. Braud and W. Braud, "Biochemical Transfer of Relational Responding," *Science,* 176 (1972), 942–944.

between-groups variance. They succeeded: the new "experimental group" animals exceeded the new "control group" animals in choosing the larger circle in the same choice task!

This is clear and easy to see in experiments. In research that is not experimental, in research where already existing differences between groups are studied, it is not always so clear and easy to see that one is studying between-groups variance. But the idea is the same. The principle may be stated in a somewhat different way: The greater the differences between groups, the more an independent variable or variables can be presumed to have operated. If there is little difference between groups, on the other hand, then the presumption must be that an independent variable or variables have not operated, that their effects are too weak to be noticed, or that different influences have canceled each other out. We judge the effects of independent variables that have been manipulated or that have worked in the past, then, by between-groups variance. Whether the independent variables have or have not been manipulated, the principle is the same.

To illustrate the principle, we use the well-studied problem of the effect of anxiety on school achievement. It is possible to manipulate anxiety by having two experimental groups and inducing anxiety in one and not in the other. This can be done by giving each group the same test with different instructions. We tell the members of one group that their grades depend wholly on the test. We tell the members of the other group that the test does not matter particularly, that its outcome will not affect grades. On the other hand, the relation between anxiety and achievement may also be studied by comparing groups of individuals on whom it can be assumed that different environmental and psychological circumstances have acted to produce anxiety. (Of course, the experimentally induced anxiety and the already existing anxiety—the stimulus variable and the organismic variable—are not assumed to be the same.) A study to test the hypothesis that different environmental and psychological circumstances act to produce different levels of anxiety was done by Sarnoff et al.[8] The investigators predicted that, as a result of the English 11-plus examinations, English school children would exhibit greater test anxiety than would American school children. In the language of this chapter, the investigators hypothesized a between-groups variance larger than could be expected by chance because of the differences between English and American environmental, educational, and psychological conditions. (The hypothesis was supported.)

Error Variance

It is probably safe to say that the most ubiquitous kind of variance in research is error variance. *Error variance* is the fluctuation or varying of measures due to chance. Error variance is random variance. It is the variation in measures due to the usually small and self-compensating fluctuations of measures—now here, now there; now up, now down. The sampling variance discussed earlier in the chapter, for example, is random or error variance.[9]

It can be said that error variance is the variance in measures due to ignorance. Imagine a great dictionary in which everything in the world—every occurrence, every event,

[8] I. Sarnoff, F. Lighthall, R. Waite, K. Davidson, and S. Sarason, "A Cross-Cultural Study of Anxiety among American and English School Children," *Journal of Educational Psychology,* 49 (1958), 129–136.

[9] It will be necessary in this chapter and the next to use the notion of "random" or "randomness." Ideas of randomness and randomization will be discussed in considerable detail in Chapter 8. For the present, however, *randomness* means that there is no known way that can be expressed in language of correctly describing or explaining events and their outcomes. Random events cannot be predicted, in other words. A *random sample* is a subset of a universe, its members so drawn that each member of the universe has an equal chance of being selected. This is another way of saying that, if members are randomly selected, there is no way to predict which member will be selected on any one selection—other things equal.

every little thing, every great thing—is given in complete detail. To understand any event that has occurred, that is now occurring, or that will occur, all one needs to do is look it up in the dictionary. With this dictionary there are obviously no random or chance occurrences. Everything is accounted for. In brief, there is no error variance; all is systematic variance. Unfortunately—or more likely, fortunately—we do not have such a dictionary. Many, many events and occurrences cannot be explained. Much variance eludes identification and control. This is error variance—at least as long as identification and control elude us.

While seemingly strange and even a bit bizarre, this mode of reasoning is useful, provided we remember that some of the error variance of today may not be the error variance of tomorrow. Suppose that we do an experiment on teaching problem-solving in which we assign pupils to three groups at random. After we finish the experiment, we study the differences between the three groups to see if the teaching has had an effect. We know that the scores and the means of the groups will always show minor fluctuations, now plus a point or two or three, now minus a point or two or three, which we can probably never control. Something or other makes the scores and the means fluctuate in this fashion. According to the view under discussion, they do not just fluctuate for no reason; there is probably no "absolute randomness." Assuming determinism, there must be some cause or causes for the fluctuations. True, we can learn some of them and possibly control them. When we do this, however, we have systematic variance.

We find out, for instance, that sex "causes" the scores to fluctuate, since boys and girls are mixed in the experimental groups. (We are, of course, talking figuratively here. Obviously sex does not make scores fluctuate.) So we do the experiment and control sex by using, say, only boys. The scores still fluctuate, though to a somewhat lesser extent. We remove another presumed cause of the perturbations: intelligence. The scores still fluctuate, though to a still lesser extent. We go on removing such sources of variance. We are controlling systematic variance. We are also gradually identifying and controlling more and more unknown variance.

Now note that before we controlled or removed these systematic variances, before we "knew" about them, we would have to label all such variance error variance—partly through ignorance, partly through inability to do anything about such variance. We could go on and on doing this and there will still be variance left over. Finally we give in; we "know" no more; we have done all we can. There will still be variance. A practical definition of error variance, then, would be: *Error variance* is the variance left over in a set of measures after all known sources of systematic variance have been removed from the measures. This is so important it deserves a numerical example.

An Example of Systematic and Error Variance

Suppose I am interested in knowing whether vagueness in lecturing lowers the effectiveness of university professors. Call "vague" and "not vague" the variable A, partitioned into A_1 and A_2.[10] I assign 10 students at random to two groups and assign treatments A_1 and A_2 at random to the two groups. I do an experiment in which, say, the students of A_1 listen to a lecture with many vague expressions in it—like "a few," "in fact," "kind of," "something." The students of A_2, on the other hand, hear virtually the same lecture but with no vague expressions in it. The students are subsequently tested for knowledge of the lecture content. The scores are as follows:

---

[10] The idea for this variable was gotten from: J. Hiller, G. Fisher, and W. Kaess, "A Computer Investigation of Verbal Characteristics of Effective Classroom Lecturing," *American Educational Research Journal*, 6 (1969), 661–675. These authors, however, *measured* vagueness; in the above example, vagueness is an experimental or manipulated variable.

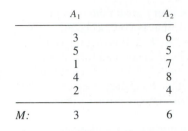

	A_1	A_2
	3	6
	5	5
	1	7
	4	8
	2	4
M:	3	6

The means are different; they vary. There is between-groups variance. Taking the difference between the means at face value—later we will be more precise—we may conclude that vagueness in lecturing had an effect. Calculating the between-groups variance just as we did earlier, we get:

		x	x^2
	3	−1.5	2.25
	6	1.5	2.25
M:	4.5		
x^2:			4.50

$$V_b = \frac{4.50}{2} = 2.25$$

In other words, we calculate the between-groups variance just as we earlier calculated the variance of the five scores 1, 2, 3, 4, and 5. We simply treat the two means as though they were individual scores, and go ahead with an ordinary variance calculation. The between-groups variance, V_b, is, then, 2.25. An appropriate statistical test would show that the difference between the means of the two groups is what is called a "statistically significant" difference. (The meaning of this will be taken up in another chapter.)[11] Evidently, the vagueness of the lecture helped to depress the scores of the students of A_1.

If we put the 10 scores in a column and calculate the variance we get:

	X	x	x^2
	3	−1.5	2.25
	5	.5	.25
	1	−3.5	12.25
	4	− .5	.25
	2	−2.5	6.25
	6	1.5	2.25
	5	.5	.25
	7	2.5	6.25
	8	3.5	12.25
	4	− .5	.25
M:	4.5		
x^2:			42.50

[11] The method of computation used here is *not* what would be used to test statistical significance. It is used here purely as a pedagogical device. Note, too, that the small numbers of cases in the examples given and the small size of the numbers are used only for simplicity of demonstration. Actual research data, of course, are usually more complex, and many more cases are needed. In actual analysis of variance the correct expression for the between sum of squares is: $ss_b = n\Sigma x_b^2$. For pedagogical simplicity, however, we retain Σx_b^2, later replacing it with ss_b.

$$V_t = \frac{42.50}{10} = 4.25$$

This is the total variance, V_t. $V_t = 4.25$ contains all sources of variation in the scores. We already know that one of these is the between-groups variance, $V_b = 2.25$. Let us calculate still another variance. We do this by calculating the variance of A_1 alone and the variance of A_2 alone and then averaging the two:

A_1	x	x^2	A_2	x	x^2
3	0	0	6	0	0
5	2	4	5	−1	1
1	−2	4	7	1	1
4	1	1	8	2	4
2	−1	1	4	−2	4
$X:$ 15			30		
$M:$ 3			6		
$x^2:$		10			10

$$V_{A_1} = \frac{10}{5} = 2 \qquad V_{A_2} = \frac{10}{5} = 2$$

The variance of A_1 is 2, and the variance of A_2 is 2. The average is 2. Since each of these variances was calculated *separately* and then *averaged,* we call the average variance calculated from them the "within-groups variance." We label this variance V_w, meaning within variance, or within-groups variance. Thus $V_w = 2$. *This variance is unaffected by the difference between the two means.*[12]

Now write an equation: $V_t = V_b + V_w$. This equation says that the total variance is made up of the variance between the groups and the variance within the groups. Is it? Substitute the numerical values: $4.25 = 2.25 + 2.00$. Our method works—it shows us, too, that these variances are additive (as calculated).

The variance ideas under discussion can perhaps be clarified with a diagram. In Figure 6.1, a circle broken up into two parts has been drawn. Let the area of the total circle represent the total variance of the 10 scores, or V_t. The larger shaded portion represents the between-groups variance, or V_b. The smaller unshaded portion represents the error variance, or V_w or V_e. From the diagram one can see that $V_t = V_b + V_e$. (Note the similarity to set thinking and the operation of union.)

A measure of all sources of variance is represented by V_t and a measure of the between-groups variance (or a measure of the effect of the experimental treatment) by V_b. But what is V_w, the within-groups variance? Since, of the total variance, we have accounted for a known source of variance, via the between-groups variance, we assume that the variance remaining is due to chance or random factors. We call it error variance. But, you may say, surely there must be other sources of variance? How about individual differences in intelligence, sex, and so on? Since I assigned the students to the experimental groups at random, assume that these sources of variance are equally, or approximately equally, distributed between A_1 and A_2. And because of the random assignment we cannot isolate and identify any other sources of variance. So we call the variance remaining error variance, knowing full well that there are probably other sources of variance but assum-

---

[12] This is easily shown by subtracting a constant of 3 from the scores of A_2. This makes the mean of A_2 equal to 3. Then, if the variance of A_2 is calculated, it will be the same as before: 2. Obviously the within-groups variance will be the same: 2.

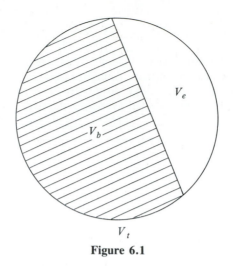

Figure 6.1

ing, and hoping our assumption is correct, that they have been equally distributed between the two groups.

A Subtractive Demonstration: Removing Between-Groups Variance from Total Variance

Let us demonstrate all this another way by removing from the original set of scores the between-groups variance, using a simple subtractive procedure. First, we let each of the means of A_1 and A_2 be equal to the total mean; we remove the between-groups variance. The total mean is 4.5. (See above where the mean of all 10 scores was calculated.) Second, we adjust each individual score of A_1 and A_2 by subtracting or adding, as the case may be, an appropriate constant. Since the mean of A_1 is 3, we add $4.5 - 3 = 1.5$ to each of the A_1 scores. The mean of A_2 is 6, and $6 - 4.5 = 1.5$ is the constant to be *subtracted* from each of the A_2 scores.

Study the "corrected" scores. Compare them with the original scores. Note that they vary less than they did before. Naturally. We removed the between-groups variance, a sizable portion of the total variance. The variance that remains is that portion of the total variance due, presumably, to chance. We calculate the variance of the "corrected" scores of A_1, A_2, and the total, and note these surprising results:

Correction:	+1.5	−1.5
	A_1	A_2
	$3 + 1.5 = 4.5$	$6 - 1.5 = 4.5$
	$5 + 1.5 = 6.5$	$5 - 1.5 = 3.5$
	$1 + 1.5 = 2.5$	$7 - 1.5 = 5.5$
	$4 + 1.5 = 5.5$	$8 - 1.5 = 6.5$
	$2 + 1.5 = 3.5$	$4 - 1.5 = 2.5$
X:	22.5	22.5
M:	4.5	4.5

A_1	x	x^2	A_2	x	x^2
4.5	0	0	4.5	0	0
6.5	2	4	3.5	−1	1
2.5	−2	4	5.5	1	1
5.5	1	1	6.5	2	4
3.5	−1	1	2.5	−2	4

X:	22.5		22.5		
M:	4.5		4.5		
x^2:		10			10

$$V_{A_1} = \frac{10}{5} = 2 \qquad V_{A_2} = \frac{10}{5} = 2$$

The within-groups variance is the same as before. It is unaffected by the correction operation. Obviously the between-groups variance is now zero. What about the total variance, V_t? Calculating it, we obtain $\Sigma x_t^2 = 20$, and $V_t = 20/10 = 2$. Thus the within-groups variance is now equal to the total variance. The reader should study this example carefully until he has firmly grasped what has happened and *why*.

Although the previous example is perhaps sufficient to make the essential points, it may solidify the student's understanding of these basic variance ideas if we extend the example by putting in and pulling out another source of variance. The reader may recall that we knew that the within-groups variance contained variation due to individual differences. Now assume that, instead of randomly assigning the students to the two groups, I had matched them on intelligence—and intelligence is related to the dependent variable. That is, I put pair members with approximately equal intelligence test scores into the two groups. The outcome of the experiment might be:

	A_1	A_2
	3	6
	1	5
	4	7
	2	4
	5	8
M:	3	6

Note carefully that the *only* difference between this setup and the previous one is that the matching has caused the scores to covary: the A_1 and A_2 measures now have nearly the same rank order. In fact, the coefficient of correlation between the two sets of scores is 0.90. We have here another source of variance: that due to individual differences in intelligence which is reflected in the rank order of the pairs of criterion measures. (The precise relation between the rank order and matching ideas and their effects on variance will be taken up in another chapter. The student should take it on faith for the present that matching produces systematic variance.)

This variance can be calculated and extracted as before, except that there is an additional operation. First equalize the A_1 and A_2 means and "correct" the scores as before. This yields:

Correction:	+1.5	−1.5
	4.5	4.5
	2.5	3.5
	5.5	5.5
	3.5	2.5
	6.5	6.5
M:	4.5	4.5

Second, by equalizing the rows (making each *row* mean equal to 4.5 and "correcting" the row scores accordingly) we find the following data:

Correction:	A_1	A_2	Original Means	Corrected Means
0	4.5 + 0 = 4.5	4.5 + 0 = 4.5	4.5	4.5
+1.5	2.5 + 1.5 = 4.0	3.5 + 1.5 = 5.0	3.0	4.5
−1.0	5.5 − 1.0 = 4.5	5.5 − 1.0 = 4.5	5.5	4.5
+1.5	3.5 + 1.5 = 5.0	2.5 + 1.5 = 4.0	3.0	4.5
−2.0	6.5 − 2.0 = 4.5	6.5 − 2.0 = 4.5	6.5	4.5
M:	4.5	4.5	$M_t = 4.5$	

The doubly corrected measures now show very little variance. The variance of the 10 doubly corrected scores is 0.10, very small indeed. There is no between-groups (columns) or between-individuals (rows) variance left in the measures, of course. After double correction, all of the total variance is error variance. (As we will see later, when the variances of both columns and rows are extracted like this—although with a quicker and more efficient method—there is no within-groups variance.)

This has been a long operation. A brief recapitulation of the main points may be useful. Any set of measures has a total variance. If the measures from which this variance is calculated have been derived from the responses of human beings, then there will always be at least two sources of variance. One will be due to systematic sources of variation like individual differences of the subjects whose characteristics or accomplishments have been measured and differences between the groups or subgroups involved in research. The other will be due to chance or random error, fluctuations of measures that cannot be accounted for. Sources of systematic variance tend to make scores lean in one direction or another. This is reflected in differences in means, of course. If sex is a systematic source of variance in a study of school achievement, for instance, then the sex variable will tend to act in such a manner that the achievement scores of girls will tend to be higher than those of boys. Sources of random error, on the other hand, tend to make measures fluctuate now this way now that way. Random errors, in other words, are self-compensating; they tend to balance each other out.

In any experiment or study, the independent variable (or variables) is a source of systematic variance—at least it should be. The researcher "wants" the experimental groups to differ systematically. He usually seeks to maximize such variance while controlling or minimizing other sources of variance, both systematic and error. The experimental example given above illustrates the additional idea that these variances are additive, and that because of this additive property, it is possible to analyze a set of scores into systematic and error variances.

COMPONENTS OF VARIANCE

The discussion so far may have convinced the student that any total variance has what will be called "components of variance." The case just considered, however, included one experimental component due to the difference between A_1 and A_2, one component due to individual differences, and a third component due to random error. We now study the case of two components of systematic experimental variance. To do this, we synthesize the experimental measures, creating them from *known* variance components. We go backwards, in other words. Because we start from "known" sources of variance, from "known" scores, there will be no error in the synthesized scores.

We have a variable X which has three values. Let $X = \{0, 1, 2\}$. We also have another variable Y, which has three values. Let $Y = \{0, 2, 4\}$. X and Y, then, are *known* sources of variance. We assume an ideal experimental situation where there are two independent variables acting *in concert* to produce effects on a dependent variable, Z. That is, each score of X operates with each score of Y to produce a dependent variable score Z. For example, the X score, 0, has no influence. The X score, 1, operates with Y as follows: $\{(1 + 0), (1 + 2), (1 + 4)\}$. Similarly, the X score, 2, operates with Y: $\{(2 + 0), (2 + 2), (2 + 4)\}$. All this is easier to see if we generate Z in clear view:

		Y						Z		
		0	2	4			0	2	4
	0	0 + 0	0 + 2	0 + 4		0	0	2	4
X	1	1 + 0	1 + 2	1 + 4	=	1	1	3	5
	2	2 + 0	2 + 2	2 + 4		2	2	4	6

The set of scores in the 3×3 matrix (a matrix is any rectangular set of numbers) is the set of Z scores. The purpose of this example will be lost unless the reader remembers that in practice we do *not* know the X and Y scores; we only know the Z scores. In actual experimental situations we manipulate or set up X and Y. But we only hope they are effective. They may not be. In other words, the sets $X = \{0, 1, 2\}$ and $Y = \{0, 2, 4\}$ can never be known like this. The best we can do is to estimate their influence by estimating the amount of variance in Z due to X and to Y.

The sets X and Y have the following variances:

X	x	x^2		Y	y	y^2
0	−1	1		0	−2	4
1	0	0		2	0	0
2	1	1		4	2	4

ΣX: 3 ΣY: 6

M: 1 M: 2

Σx^2: 2 Σy^2: 8

$$V_x = \frac{2}{3} = .67 \qquad V_y = \frac{8}{3} = 2.67$$

The set Z has variance as follows:

Z	z	z^2
0	-3	9
2	-1	1
4	1	1
1	-2	4
3	0	0
5	2	4
2	-1	1
4	1	1
6	3	9

ΣX:	27	
M:	3	
Σx^2:		30

$$V_x = \frac{30}{9} = 3.33$$

Now $.67 + 2.67 = 3.34$, or $V_z = V_x + V_y$, within errors of rounding.

This example illustrates that, under certain conditions, variances operate additively to produce the experimental measures we analyze. While the example is "pure" and therefore unrealistic, it is not unreasonable. It is possible to think of X and Y as independent variables. They might be level of aspiration and pupil attitudes. And Z might be verbal achievement, a dependent variable. That real scores do not behave exactly this way does not alter the idea. They behave approximately this way. We plan research to make this principle as true as possible, and we analyze data as though it were true. And it works!

COVARIANCE

Covariance is really nothing new. Recall, in an earlier discussion of sets and correlation, that we talked about the relation between two or more variables being analogous to the intersection of sets. Let X be $\{0, 1, 2, 3\}$, a set of attitude measures for four children. Let Y be $\{1, 2, 3, 4\}$, a set of achievement measures of the same children, but not in the same order. Let R be a set of ordered pairs of the elements of X and Y, the rule of pairing being: each individual's attitude and achievement measures are paired, with the attitude measure placed first. Assume that this yields $R = \{(0, 2), (1, 1), (2, 3), (3, 4)\}$. By our previous definition of relation, this set of ordered pairs is a relation, in this case the relation between X and Y. The results of the calculations of the variance of X and the variance of Y are:

X	x	x^2		Y	y	y^2
0	-1.5	2.25		2	$-.5$	.25
1	$-.5$	.25		1	-1.5	2.25
2	$.5$	.25		3	$.5$	.25
3	1.5	2.25		4	1.5	2.25

ΣX:	6			10		
M:	1.5			2.5		
Σx^2:		5.00				5.00

$$V_x = \frac{5}{4} = 1.25 \qquad V_y = \frac{5}{4} = 1.25$$

We now set ourselves a problem. (Note carefully in what follows that we are going to work with deviations from the mean, x's and y's, and not with the original raw scores.) We have calculated the variances of X and Y above by using the x's and y's, that is, the deviations from the respective means of X and Y. If we can calculate the variance of any set of scores, is it not possible to calculate the relation *between* any two sets of scores in a similar way? Is it conceivable that we can calculate the variance of the two sets simultaneously? And if we do so, will this be a measure of the variance of the two sets together? Will this variance also be a measure of the relation between the two sets?

What we want to do is to use some statistical operation analogous to the set operation of intersection, $X \cap Y$. To calculate the variance of X or of Y, we squared the deviations from the mean, the x's or the y's, and then added and averaged them. A natural answer to our problem is to perform an analogous operation on the x's and y's *together*. To calculate the variance of X, we did this first: $(x_1 \cdot x_1), \ldots, (x_4 \cdot x_4) = x_1^2, \ldots, x_4^2$. Why, then, not follow this through with *both* x's and y's, multiplying the ordered pairs like this: $(x_1 \cdot y_1), \ldots, (x_4 \cdot y_4)$? Then, instead of writing Σx^2 or Σy^2, we write Σxy, as follows:

x	·	y	=	xy
-1.5	·	$-.5$	=	.75
$-.5$	·	-1.5	=	.75
.5	·	.5	=	.25
1.5	·	1.5	=	2.25

$$\Sigma xy = 4.00$$

$$V_{xy} = CoV_{xy} = \frac{4}{4} = 1.00$$

If we calculate the variance of these products—symbolized as V_{xy} or CoV_{xy}—we obtain 1.00, as indicated above. This 1.00, then, can be taken as an index of the relation between two sets. But it is an unsatisfactory index because its size fluctuates with the ranges and scales of different X's and Y's. That is, it might be 1.00 in this case and 8.75 in another case, making comparisons from case to case difficult and unwieldy.

Before going further, let use give names to Σxy and V_{xy}. Σxy is called the *cross product*, or the sum of the cross products. V_{xy} is called the *covariance*. We will write it CoV with suitable subscripts. Returning to the problem, we need a measure that is comparable from problem to problem. Such a measure—an excellent one, too—is obtained simply by writing a fraction or ratio: the covariance, CoV_{xy}, divided by an average of the variances of X and Y. The average usually taken is the square root of the product of V_x and V_y. The whole formula for our index of relation, then, is

$$R = \frac{CoV_{xy}}{\sqrt{V_x \cdot V_y}}$$

This is one form of the well-known product-moment coefficient of correlation. Using it with our little problem, we obtain:

$$R = \frac{1.00}{\sqrt{(1.25)(1.25)}} = \frac{1.00}{1.25} = .80$$

This index, usually written r, can range from $+1.00$ through 0 to -1.00, as we learned in Chapter 5.

So we have another important source of variation in sets of scores, provided the set elements, the X's and Y's, have been ordered into pairs after conversion into deviation scores. The variation is aptly called *covariance* and is a measure of the relation between the sets of scores.

It can be seen that the definition of relation as a set of ordered pairs leads to several ways to define the relation of the above example:

$$R = \{(x, y); x \text{ and } y \text{ are numbers, } x \text{ always coming first}\}$$

$$xRy = \text{the same as above or ``} x \text{ is related to } y\text{''}$$

$$R = \{(0, 2), (1, 1), (2, 3), (3, 4)\}$$

$$R = \{(-1.5, -5), (-.5, -1.5), (.5, .5), (1.5, 1.5)\}$$

$$R_{xy} = \frac{CoV_{xy}}{\sqrt{V_x \cdot V_y}} = \frac{1.00}{1.25} = .80$$

Variance and covariance are concepts of the highest importance in research and in the analysis of research data. There are two main reasons. One, they summarize, so to speak, the variability of variables and the relations among variables. This is most easily seen when we realize that correlations are covariances. But the term also means the covarying of variables in general. In much or most of our research we literally pursue and study covariation of phenomena. Two, variance and covariance form the statistical backbone of multivariate analysis, as we will see toward the end of the book. Most discussions of the analysis of data are based on variances and covariances. Analysis of variance, for example, studies different sources of variance of observations, mostly in experiments, as indicated earlier. Factor analysis is in effect the study of covariances, one of whose major purposes is to isolate and identify common sources of variation. The contemporary ultimate in analysis, the most powerful and advanced multivariate approach yet devised, is called analysis of covariance structures because the system studies complex sets of relation by analyzing the covariances among variables. Variances and covariances will obviously be the core of much of our discussion and preoccupation from this point on.

Study Suggestions

1. A social psychologist has done an experiment in which one group, A_1, was given a task to do in the presence of an audience, and another group, A_2, was given the same task to do without an audience. The scores of the two groups on the task, a measure of digital skill, were:

A_1	A_2
5	3
5	4
9	7
8	4
3	2

(a) Calculate the means and variances of A_1 and A_2, using the method described in the text.
(b) Calculate the between-groups variance, V_b, and the within-groups variance, V_w.
(c) Arrange all ten scores in a column, and calculate the total variance, V_t.
(d) Substitute the calculated values obtained in (b) and (c), above, in the equation: $V_t = V_b + V_w$. Interpret the results.
[*Answers:* (a) $V_{a1} = 4.8$; $V_{a2} = 2.8$; (b) $V_b = 1.0$; $V_w = 3.8$; (c) $V_t = 4.8$.]

2. Add 2 to each of the scores of A_1 in 1, above, and calculate V_t, V_b, and V_w. Which of these variances changed? Which stayed the same? Why?
[*Answers:* $V_t = 7.8$; $V_b = 4.0$; $V_w = 3.8$.]

3. Equalize the means of A_1 and A_2, in 1, above, by adding a constant of 2 to each of the scores of A_2. Calculate V_t, V_b, and V_w. What is the main difference between these results and those of 1, above? Why?

4. Suppose a sociological researcher obtained measures of conservatism (A), attitude toward religion (B), and anti-Semitism (C) from 100 individuals. The correlations between the variables were: $r_{ab} = .70$; $r_{ac} = .40$; $r_{bc} = .30$. What do these correlations mean? [*Hint:* Square the r's before trying to interpret the relations. Also, think of ordered pairs.]

5. The purpose of this study suggestion and Study Suggestion 6 is to give the student an intuitive feeling for the variability of sample statistics, the relation between population and sample variances, and between-groups and error variances. Appendix C contains 40 sets of 100 random numbers 0 through 100, with calculated means, variances, and standard deviations. Draw 10 sets of 10 numbers each from 10 different places in the table.

    a.   Calculate the mean, variance, and standard deviation of each of the 10 sets. Find the highest and lowest means and the highest and lowest variances. Do they differ much from each other? What value "should" the means be? (50) While doing this, save the 10 totals and calculate the mean of all 100 numbers. Do the 10 means differ much from the total mean? Do they differ much from the means reported in the table of means, variances, and standard deviations given after the random numbers?

    b.   Count the odd and even numbers in each of the 10 sets. Are they what they "should be"? Count the odd and even numbers of the 100 numbers. Is the result "better" than the results of the 10 counts? Why should it be?

    c.   Calculate the variance of the 10 means. This is, of course, the between-groups variance, V_b. Calculate the error variance, using the formula: $V_e = V_t - V_b$.

    d.   Discuss the meaning of your results after reviewing the discussion in the text.

6. As early as possible in their study, students of research should start to understand and use the computer. Study Suggestion 5 can be better and less laboriously accomplished with the computer. It would be better, for example, to draw 20 samples of 100 numbers each. Why? In any case, students should learn how to do simple statistical operations using existing computer facilities and programs at their institutions. All institutions have programs for calculating means and standard deviations (variances can be obtained by squaring the standard deviations[13]) and for generating random numbers. If you can use your institution's facilities, use them for Study Suggestion 5, but increase the number of samples and their n's. You can have much more fun by writing your own program to calculate simple statistics. For guidance—and even programs—see Lohnes and Cooley's very useful elementary statistics book.[14]

---

[13] There may be small discrepancies between your hand-calculated standard deviations and variances and those of the computer because existing programs and built-in routines of hand-held calculators usually use a formula with $N - 1$ rather than N in the denominator of the formula. The discrepancies will be small, however, especially if N is large. (The reason for the different formulas will be explained later when we take up sampling and other matters.)

[14] P. Lohnes and W. Cooley, *Introduction to Statistical Procedures: With Computer Exercises*. New York: Wiley, 1968.

PART THREE

PROBABILITY, RANDOMNESS, AND SAMPLING

Chapter 7

Probability

PROBABILITY is an obvious and simple subject. It is a baffling and complex subject. It is a subject we know a great deal about, and a subject we know nothing about. Kindergartners can study probability, and philosophers do. It is dull; it is interesting. Such contradictions are the stuff of probability.

Take the expression "laws of chance." The expression itself is contradictory. Chance or randomness, by definition, is the absence of law. If events can be explained lawfully, they are not random. Then why say "laws of chance"? The answer, too, is contradictory—seemingly. It is possible to gain knowledge from ignorance if we view randomness as ignorance. This is because random events, *in the aggregate,* occur in lawful ways with monotonous regularity. From the disorder of randomness the scientist welds the order of scientific prediction and control.

It is not easy to explain these disconcerting statements. Indeed, philosophers disagree on the answers. Fortunately there is no disagreement on the empirical probabilistic events—or at least very little. Almost all scientists and philosophers will agree that if two dice are thrown a number of times, there will probably be more sevens than twos or twelves. They will also agree that certain events like finding a hundred-dollar bill or winning a sweepstakes are extremely unlikely.

DEFINITION OF PROBABILITY

What is probability? We ask this question and immediately strike a perplexing problem. Philosophers cannot seem to agree on the answer.[1] This seems to be because there are two broad definitions, among others, which seem irreconcilable: the a priori and the a posteriori. The *a priori definition* we owe to a controversial, interesting, and very human genius, Simon Laplace.[2] The probability of an event is the number of favorable cases divided by the total number of (equally possible) cases, or $p = f/(f + u)$, where p is probability, f the number of favorable cases, and u the number of unfavorable cases. The method of calculating probability implied by the definition is a priori in the sense that probability is given, that we can determine the probabilities of events before empirical investigation. This definition is the basis of theoretical mathematical probability.

The *a posteriori,* or *frequency, definition* is empirical in nature. It says that, in an actual series of tests, probability is the ratio of the number of times an event occurs to the total number of trials. With this definition, one approaches probability empirically by performing a series of tests, counting the number of times a certain kind of event happens, and then calculating the ratio. The result of the calculation is the probability of the certain kind of event. Frequency definitions have to be used when theoretical enumeration over classes of events is not possible. For example, to calculate longevity and horse race probabilities one has to use actuarial tables and calculate probabilities from past counts and calculations.[3]

Practically speaking and for our purposes, the distinction between the a priori and a posteriori definition is not too vital. Following Margenau (p. 264), we put the two together by saying that the a priori approach supplies a constitutive definition of probability, whereas the a posteriori approach supplies an operational definition of probability. We need to use both approaches; we need to supplement one with the other.

SAMPLE SPACE, SAMPLE POINTS, AND EVENTS

To calculate the probability of any outcome, first determine the total number of possible outcomes. With a die the outcomes are 1, 2, 3, 4, 5, 6. Call this set U. U is the *sample space,* or universe of possible outcomes. The sample space includes all possible outcomes of an "experiment" that are of interest to the experimenter. The primary elements of U are called *elements* or *sample points.* Then let us write $U = \{1, 2, 3, 4, 5, 6\}$, and bring this chapter in line with the set reasoning and method of Part Two. Letting x_i = any sample point or element in U, we write $U = \{x_1, x_2, \ldots, x_n\}$. Examples of different U's are: all possible outcomes of tossing two dice (see below); all kindergarten children in such-and-such a school system; all eligible voters in X County.

Sometimes the determination of the sample space is easy; sometimes it is difficult. The problem is analogous to the definition of sets of Chapter 4: sets can be defined by

---

[1] For discussions of the disagreement, see J. Kemeny, *A Philosopher Looks at Science.* New York: Van Nostrand Reinhold, 1959, chaps. 4, 11. H. Margenau, *The Nature of Physical Reality.* New York: McGraw-Hill, 1950, chap. 13. W. Salmon, *The Foundations of Scientific Inference.* Pittsburgh: University of Pittsburgh Press, 1966, chap. V. (Salmon presents five interpretations of probability!)

[2] For a good brief discussion of Laplace and his work, see J. Newman, *The World of Mathematics,* vol. 2. New York: Simon and Schuster, 1956, pp. 1316–1324. For Laplace's own definition of probability, see *ibid.,* pp. 1325–1333. Discussions of the two kinds of definitions are given by Margenau, *op. cit.,* chap. 13. (Laplace was famous for using that exasperating expression of mathematicians and statisticians, "It is easy to see that . . . ."

[3] M. Turner, *Philosophy and the Science of Behavior.* New York: Appleton-Century-Crofts, 1967, p. 384.

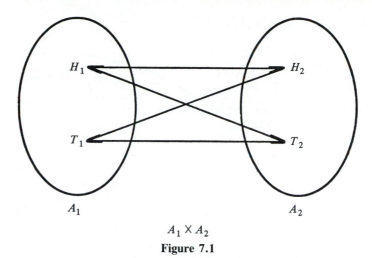

$$A_1 \times A_2$$

Figure 7.1

listing all the members of the set, and by giving a rule for the inclusion of elements in a set. In probability theory, both kinds of definition are used. What is U in tossing two coins? We list all the possibilities: $U = \{(H, H), (H, T), (T, H), (T, T)\}$. This is a list definition of U. A rule definition—although we would not use it—might be: $U = \{x; x$ is all combinations of H and $T\}$. In this case U is the Cartesian product. Let $A_1 = \{H_1, T_1\}$, the first coin; let $A_2 = \{H_2, T_2\}$, the second coin. Recalling that a Cartesian product of two sets is the set of *all* ordered pairs whose first entry is an element of one set and whose second entry is an element of another set, we can diagram the generation of the Cartesian product of this case, $A_1 \times A_2$, as in Figure 7.1. Notice that there are four lines connecting A_1 and A_2. Thus there are four possibilities: $\{(H_1, H_2), (H_1, T_2), (T_1, H_2), (T_1, T_2)\}$. This thinking and procedure can be used in defining many sample spaces of U's, although the actual procedure can be tedious.

With two dice, what is U? Think of the Cartesian product of two sets and you will probably have little trouble. Let A_1 be the outcomes or points of the first die: $\{1, 2, 3, 4, 5, 6\}$. Let A_2 be the outcomes or points of the second die. Then $U = A_1 \times A_2 = \{(1, 1), (1, 2), \ldots, (6, 5), (6, 6)\}$. We can diagram this as we diagrammed the coin example, but counting the lines is more difficult; there are too many of them. We can know the number of possible outcomes simply by $6 \times 6 = 36$, or in a formula: *mn*, where m is the number of possible outcomes of the first set, and n is the number of possible outcomes of the second set.

It is often possible to solve difficult probability problems by using trees. Trees define sample spaces, logical possibilities, with clarity and precision. A *tree* is a diagram that gives all possible alternatives or outcomes for combinations of sets by providing paths and set points. This definition is a bit unwieldy. Illustration is better. Take the coin example (we turn the tree on its side). Its tree is shown in Figure 7.2.

To determine the number of possible alternatives, just count the number of alternatives or points at the "top" of the tree. In this case, there are four alternatives. To name the alternatives, read off, for each end point, the points that led to it. For example, the first alternative is (H_1, H_2). Obviously, three, four, or more coins can be used. The only trouble is that the procedure is tedious because of the large number of alternatives. The tree for three coins is illustrated in Figure 7.3. There are eight possible alternatives, outcomes, or sample points: $U = \{(H_1, H_2, H_3), (H_1, H_2, T_3), \ldots, (T_1, T_2, T_3)\}$. (The elements of this set are called ordered triples.)

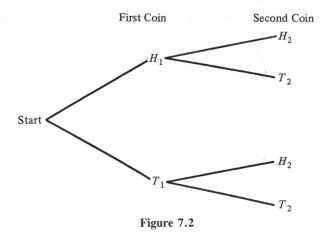

Figure 7.2

Sample points of a sample space may seem a bit confusing to the reader, because two kinds of points have been discussed without differentiation. Another term and its use may help clear up this possible confusion. An *event* is a subset of U. Any element of a set is also a subset of the set. Recall that with set $A = \{a_1, a_2\}$, for example, both $\{a_1\}$ and $\{a_2\}$ are subsets of A, as well as $\{a_1, a_2\}$, and $\{\ \}$, the empty set. Identically, all the outcomes of Figures 7.2 and 7.3, for example, (H_1, T_2), (T_1, H_2), and $(T_1, H_2 T_3)$, are subsets of their respective U's. Therefore they are events, too—by definition. But in the usual usage, events are more encompassing than points. All points are events (subsets), but not all events are points. Or, a point or outcome is a special kind of event, the simplest kind. Any time we state a proposition, we describe an event. We ask, for instance, "If two coins are thrown, what is the probability of getting two heads?" The "two heads" is an event. It

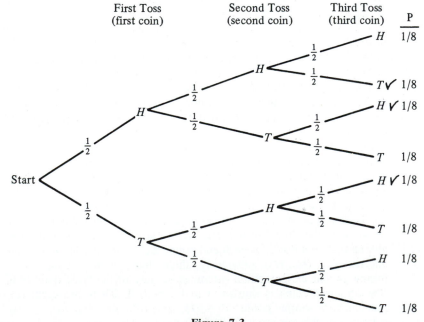

Figure 7.3

so happens, in this case, that it is also a sample point. But suppose we asked, ''What is the probability of getting at least one head?'' ''At least one head'' is an event, but not a sample point, because it includes, in this case, three sample points: (H_1, H_2), (H_1, T_2), and (T_1, H_2). (See Figure 7.2.)

DETERMINING PROBABILITIES WITH COINS

Suppose we toss a new coin three times. We write $p(H) = 1/2$ and $p(T) = 1/2$, meaning the probability of heads is 1/2, and similarly for tails. We assume, then, equiprobability. The sample space for three tosses of a coin (or one toss of three coins) is: $U = \{(H, H, H), (H, H, T), (H, T, H), (H, T, T), (T, H, H), (T, H, T), (T, T, H), (T, T, T)\}$. Note that if we pay no attention to the order of heads and tails, we obtain one case of 3 heads, one case of 3 tails, three cases of 2 heads and 1 tail, and three cases of 2 tails and 1 head. The probability of each of the eight outcomes is obviously 1/8. Thus the probability of 3 heads is 1/8, and the probability of 3 tails is 1/8. The probability of 2 heads and 1 tail, on the other hand, is 3/8, and similarly for the probability of 2 tails and 1 head.

The probabilities of all the points in the sample space must add up to 1.00. It also follows that *probabilities are always positive.* If we write a probability tree for the three-toss experiment, it looks like Figure 7.3. Each complete path of the tree (from the start to the third toss) is a sample point. All the paths comprise the sample space. The single path sections are labeled with the probabilities, in this case all of them are labeled with ''1/8.'' This leads naturally to the statement of a basic principle: If the outcomes at the different points in the tree, that is, at the first, second, and third tosses, are independent of each other (that is, if one outcome does not influence another in any way), then the probability of any sample point (*HHH* perhaps) is the product of the probabilities of the separate outcomes. For example, the probability of 3 heads is $1/2 \times 1/2 \times 1/2 = 1/8$.

Another principle is: *To obtain the probability of any event, add the probabilities of the sample points that comprise that event.* For example, what is the probability of tossing 2 heads and 1 tail? We look at the paths in the tree that have 2 heads and 1 tail. There are 3 of them. (They are checked in Figure 7.3.) Thus, $1/8 + 1/8 + 1/8 = 3/8$. In set language, we find the subsets (events) of U and note their probabilities. The subset of U of the type ''2 heads and 1 tail'' are, from the tree or the previous definition of U, $\{(H, H, T), (H, T, H), (T, H, H)\}$. Call this the set A_1. Then $p(A_1) = 3/8$.

This procedure can be followed with an experiment of 100 tosses, but it is much too laborious. Instead, to get the theoretical expectations, we merely multiply the number of tosses by the probability of any one of them, $100 \times 1/2 = 50$, to get the *expected* number of heads (or tails). This can be done because all the probabilities are the same. A big and important question is: In actual experiments in which we throw 100 coins, will we get *exactly* 50 heads? No, not often: about 8 times in 100 such experiments. This can be written: $p = 8/100$ or .08. (Probabilities can be written in fractional or decimal forms, more usually in decimal form.)

AN EXPERIMENT WITH DICE

I threw two new dice 72 times under carefully controlled conditions. If I add the number of spots on the two dice on all 72 throws, I will obtain a set of sums from 2 to 12. Some of these outcomes (sums) will turn up more frequently than others simply because there are more ways for them to do so. For example, there is only one way for 2 or for 12 to turn up:

1 + 1 and 6 + 6, but there are three ways for a 4 to turn up: 1 + 3, 3 + 1, and 2 + 2. If this is so, then the probabilities for getting different sums must be different. The game of craps is based on these differences in frequency expectations.

To solve the a priori probability problem, we must first define the sample space: $U = \{(1, 1), (1, 2), (1, 3), \ldots ,(6, 4), (6, 5), (6, 6)\}$. That is, we pair each number of the first die with each number of the second die in turn (the Cartesian product again). This can easily be seen if we set up this procedure in a matrix (see Table 7.1). Suppose we want to know the probability of the event—a very important event, too— "a 7 turns up." Simply count the number of 7's in the table. There are six of them nicely arrayed along the center diagonal. There are 36 sample points in U, obtained by some method of enumerating them, as above, or by using the formula mn, which says: Multiply the number of possibilities of the first thing by the number of possibilities of the second thing. This method can be defined: When there are m ways of doing something, A, and n ways of doing something else, B, then, if the n ways of doing B are independent of the m ways of doing A, there are $m \cdot n$ ways of doing both A and B.[4]

Table 7.1 Matrix of Possible Outcomes With Two Dice

		Second Die					
		1	2	3	4	5	6
	1	2	3	4	5	6	7
	2	3	4	5	6	7	8
First	3	4	5	6	7	8	9
Die	4	5	6	7	8	9	10
	5	6	7	8	9	10	11
	6	7	8	9	10	11	12

Applied to the dice problem, $mn = 6 \times 6 = 36$. Assuming equipossibility again, the probability of any *single* outcome is 1/36. The probability of a 12, for instance, is 1/36. The probability of a 4, however, is different. Since 4 occurs three times in the table above, we must add the probabilities for each of these elements of the sample space: 1/36 + 1/36 + 1/36 = 3/36. Thus $p(4) = 3/36 = 1/12$. As we have seen, the probability of a 7 is $p(7) = 6/36 = 1/6$. The probability of an 8 is $p(8) = 5/36$. Note, too, that we can calculate the probabilities of combinations of events. Gamblers often bet on such combinations. For example, what is the probability of a 4 *or* a 10? In set language, this is a *union* question: $p(4 \cup 10)$. Count the number of 4's and 10's in the table. There are three 4's and three 10's. Thus $p(4 \cup 10) = 6/36$.

Counting, in Table 7.1, the probabilities of each kind of outcome, we lay out a table of expected frequencies (f_e) for 36 throws. Then double these frequencies to get the expected (a priori) frequencies for 72 throws. We juxtapose against these expected frequencies the frequencies obtained when two dice were actually thrown 72 times. The absolute differences between expected and obtained frequencies are then apparent. The results are laid out in Table 7.2. The discrepancies are not great. In fact, by actual statistical test, they do not differ significantly from chance expectation. The a priori method seems to have virtue.

[4]This principle can be extended to more than two things. If, for example, there are three things, A, B, and C, then the formula is mnr.

Table 7.2 Expected and Obtained Frequencies of Sums of Two Dice Thrown 72 Times

Sum of Dice	2	3	4	5	6	7	8	9	10	11	12
$f_e(36)$	1	2	3	4	5	6	5	4	3	2	1
$f_e(72)$	2	4	6	8	10	12	10	8	6	4	2
$f_o(72)$	4	2	6	6	10	15	7	11	6	4	1
Difference	2	2	0	2	0	3	3	3	0	0	1

SOME FORMAL THEORY

We have the *sample space* U, with subsets A, B, ... The elements of U—and of A, B, . . . —are $a_i, b_i, \ldots$, that is, $a_1, a_2, \ldots, a_n$ and $b_1, b_2, \ldots, b_n$, and so forth. A, B, and so forth, are *events*. Actually, although we have often talked about the probability of a single occurrence, we really mean the probability of a type of occurrence. When we talk about the probability of any single event of U, for instance, we can only do so because any particular member of U is conceived as representative of all of U. And similarly for the probabilities of subsets A, B, . . . , K of U. The probability of U is 1; the probability of E, the empty set, is 0. Or $p(U) = 1.00$; $p(E) = 0$. To determine the probability of any subset of U, a *measure* of the set must be assigned. In order to assign such a measure, we must assign a *weight* to each element of U and thus to each element of the subsets of U. A weight is defined.[5]

A *weight* is a positive number assigned to each element, x, in U, and written $w(x)$, such that the sum of all these weights, $\Sigma w(x)$, is equal to 1.

This is a function notion; w is called a *weight function*. It is a rule that assigns weights to elements of a set, U, in such a way that the sum of the weights is equal to 1, that is, $w_1 + w_2 + w_3 + \cdots + w_n = 1.00$, and $w_i = 1/n$. The weights are equal, assuming equiprobability; each weight is a fraction with 1 in the numerator and the number of cases, n, in the denominator. In the previous experiment of the tosses of a coin (Figure 7.3), the weights assigned to each element of U, U being all the outcomes, are all 1/8. The sum of all the weight functions, $w(x)$, is $1/8 + 1/8 + \cdots + 1/8 = 1$. In probability theory, the sum of the elements of the sample space must always equal 1.

To get from weights to the measure of a set is easy: The *measure* of a set is the sum of the weights of the elements of the set.[6]

$$\sum_{x \text{ in } U} w(x) \quad or \quad \sum_{x \text{ in } A} w(x)$$

We write $m(A)$, meaning "The measure of the set A." This simply means the sum of the weights of the elements in the set A.

Suppose we randomly sample children from the 400 children of the fourth grade of a school system. Then U is all 400 children. Each child is a sample point of U. Each child is an x in U. The probability of selecting any one child at random is 1/400. Let A = the boys in U, and B = the girls in U. There are 100 boys and 300 girls. Each boy is assigned the

---

[5] The approach used here follows to some extent that found in J. Kemeny, J. Snell, and G. Thompson, *Introduction to Finite Mathematics*, 2d ed. Englewood Cliffs, N.J.: Prentice-Hall, 1966, chap. IV.

[6] Note that the sum of the weights in a subset A of U does not have to equal 1. In fact, it is usually less than 1.

weight 1/400, and each girl is assigned the weight 1/400. Suppose we wish to sample, all together, 100 children. Our expectation is, then, 25 boys and 75 girls in the sample. The measure of the set A, $m(A)$, is the sum of the weights of all the elements in A. Since there are 100 boys in U, we sum the 100 weights: $1/400 + 1/400 + \cdots + 1/400 = 100/400 = 1/4$, or

$$m(A) = \sum_{x \; in \; A} w(x) = \frac{1}{4}$$

Similarly,

$$m(B) = \sum_{x \; in \; B} w(x) = \frac{3}{4}$$

For the set B, the girls, we sum 300 weights, each of them being 1/400. In short, the sums of the weights are the probabilities. That is, the measure of a set is the probability of a member of the set being chosen. Thus we can say that the probability that a member of the sample of 400 children will be a boy is 1/4, and the probability that the selected member will be a girl is 3/4. To determine the expected frequencies, multiply the sample size by these probabilities: $1/4 \times 100 = 25$ and $3/4 \times 100 = 75$.

Probability has three fundamental properties:

1. The measure of any set, as defined above, is greater than or equal to 0 and less than or equal to 1. In brief, probabilities (measures of sets) are either 0, 1, or in between.
2. The measure of a set, $m(A)$, equals 0 if and only if there are no members in A, that is, A is empty.
3. Let A and B be sets. If A and B are disjoint, that is, $A \cap B = E$, then:

$$m(A \cup B) = m(A) + m(B)$$

This equation says that when no members of A and B are shared in common, then the probability of either A or B or both is equal to the combined probabilities of A and B.

There is no need to give an example to illustrate (1). We have had several earlier. To illustrate (2), assume, in the boys-girls example, that we asked the probability of drawing a teacher in the sample. But U did not include teachers. Let C be the set of fourth-grade teachers. In this case, the set C is empty, and $m(C) = 0$. Use the same boys-girls example to illustrate (3). Let A be the set of boys, B the set of girls. Then $m(A \cup B) = m(A) + m(B)$. But $m(A \cup B) = 1.00$, because they were the only subsets of U. And we learned that $m(A) = 1/4$ and $m(B) = 3/4$. The equation holds.

COMPOUND EVENTS AND THEIR PROBABILITIES

We said earlier that an *event* is a subset of U, but we need to elaborate this a bit. An event is a set of possibilities; it is a possible set of events; it is an outcome of a probability "experiment." A *compound event* is the co-occurrence of two or more single (or compound) events. The two set operations of intersection and union—the operations of most interest to us—imply compound events. If we toss a coin and roll a die, the outcome is a compound event, and we can calculate the probability of such an event. More interesting, we might ask how race, sex, and status are related. One way to do this is to seek answers to such questions as: What is the probability of a female white Anglo-Saxon Protestant being listed in *Who's Who in America*?[7] or What is the probability of a black male holding a high rank in the Civil Service?[8]

Compound events are more interesting than single events—and more useful in research. Relations can be studied with them. To understand this, we first define and illustrate compound events and then examine certain counting problems and the ways in which counting is related to set theory and probability theory. It will be found that if the basic theory is understood, the application of probability theory to research problems is considerably facilitated. In addition, the interpretation of data becomes less subject to error.

Assume that a group of sixth-grade children has been studied, that there are 100 children altogether in the group, 60 boys and 40 girls. A useful function is the *numerical function,* which assigns to any set the number of members in the set. The number of members in A is $n(A)$. In this case $n(U) = 100$, $n(A) = 60$, and $n(B) = 40$, where A is the set of boys and B the set of girls, both subsets of U, the 100 sixth-grade children. If there is no overlap between two sets, $A \cap B = E$, then the following equation holds:

$$n(A \cup B) = n(A) + n(B) \tag{7.1}$$

Recall that earlier the frequency definition of probability was given as:

$$p = \frac{f}{f + u} \tag{7.2}$$

where f is the number of favorable cases, and u the number of unfavorable cases. The numerator is $n(F)$ and the denominator $n(U)$, the total number of possible cases. Similarly, we can divide through the terms of Equation 7.1 by $n(U)$:

$$\frac{n(A \cup B)}{n(U)} = \frac{n(A)}{n(U)} + \frac{n(B)}{n(U)} \tag{7.3}$$

This reduces to probabilities, analogously to Equation 7.2:

$$p(A \cup B) = p(A) + p(B) \tag{7.4}$$

Using the example of the 100 children, and substituting values in Equation 7.3, we get

$$\frac{100}{100} = \frac{60}{100} + \frac{40}{100}$$

which yields for Equation 7.4:

$$1.00 = .60 + .40$$

In many cases, two (or more) sets in which we are interested are not disjoint. Rather, they overlap. When this is so, then $A \cap B \neq E$, and it is not true that $n(A \cup B) = n(A) + n(B)$. Look at Figure 7.4.

Here A and B are subsets of U; sample points are indicated by dots. The number of sample points in A is 8; the number in B is 6. There are two sample points in $A \cap B$. Thus the equation above does not hold. If we calculate all the points in $A \cup B$ with Equation

[7] S. Lieberson and D. Carter, "Making It in America: Differences between Eminent Black and White Ethnic Groups," *American Sociological Review,* 44 (1979), 347–366.

[8] K. Meier, "Representative Bureaucracy: An Empirical Analysis," *American Political Science Review,* 69 (1975), 526–542.

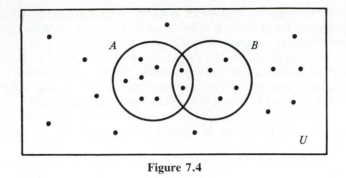

Figure 7.4

7.1, we get $8 + 6 = 14$ points. But there are only 12 points. The equation has to be altered to a more general equation that fits all cases:

$$n(A \cup B) = n(A) + n(B) - n(A \cap B) \qquad (7.5)$$

It should be clear that the error when Equation 7.1 is used results from counting the two points of $A \cap B$ twice. Therefore we subtract $n(A \cap B)$ once, which corrects the equation. It now fits any possibility. If, for example, $n(A \cap B) = E$, the empty set, Equation 7.5 reduces to (7.1). Equation 7.1 is a special case of (7.5). Calculating the number of sample points in $A \cup B$ of Figure 7.4, then, we get: $n(A \cup B) = 8 + 6 - 2 = 12$. If we divide Equation 7.5 through by $n(U)$, as in (7.3):

$$p(A \cup B) = p(A) + p(B) - p(A \cap B) \qquad (7.6)$$

Substituting our number of dots or sample points, we find that

$$\frac{12}{24} = \frac{8}{24} + \frac{6}{24} - \frac{2}{24}$$

$$.50 = .33 + .25 - .08$$

In a random sample of U, then, the probabilities of an element being a member of A, B, $A \cap B$, and $A \cup B$, respectively, are .33, .25, .08, and .50.

INDEPENDENCE, MUTUAL EXCLUSIVENESS, AND EXHAUSTIVENESS

Consider the following questions, variants of which must be asked by researchers. Does the occurrence of this event, A, preclude the possibility of the occurrence of this other event, B? Does the occurrence of event A have an influence on the occurrence of event B? Are the events A, B, and C related? When A has occurred, does this influence the outcomes of B—and, perhaps, C? Do the events A, B, C, and D exhaust the possibilities? Or are there, perhaps, other possibilities E, F, and so on? Suppose, for instance, that a researcher is studying board of education decisions and their relation to political preference, religious preference, education, and other variables. In order to relate these variables to board decisions, he has to have some method of classifying the decisions. One of the first questions he must ask is, "Have I exhausted all possibilities in my classification system?" He should also ask, "If a board makes one kind of decision, does this preclude the possibility of making another kind of decision?" Perhaps the most important question the researcher can ask is, "If a board makes a particular decision, does this decision influence its action on any other decision?"

We have been talking about exhaustiveness, mutual exclusiveness, and independence. We now define these ideas in a more detailed manner and use them in probability examples. Their general applicability and importance will also become apparent in Part Four when we take up analysis of data.

Let A and B be subsets of U. We ask the questions: Are there any other subsets of U (other than the empty set)? Do A and B exhaust the sample space? Are all the sample points of the sample space U included in A or in B? A simple example is: Let $A = \{H, T\}$; let $B = \{1, 2, 3, 4, 5, 6\}$. If we toss a coin and throw a die together, what are the possibilities? Unless *all* the possibilities are exhausted, we cannot solve the probability problem. There are 12 possibilities (2×6). The sets A and B exhaust the sample space. (This is of course obvious, since A and B generated the sample space.) Now take a more realistic example. Suppose a researcher is studying religious preferences. He sets up the following system to categorize individuals: {Protestants, Catholics, Jews}. What he has done, implicitly, is to set up U = all people (with or without religious preferences) and subsets of U, A = Protestants, B = Catholics, C = Jews. The set question is: Does $A \cup B \cup C = U$? Has he exhausted all religious preferences? How about Buddhists? How about atheists? And so on.

Exhaustiveness, then, means that the subsets of U use up all the sample space, or $A \cup B \cup \cdots \cup K = U$, where $A, B, \ldots, K$ are subsets of U, the sample space. In probability language, this means: $p(A \cup B \cup \cdots \cup K) = 1.00$. Unless the sample space, U, is used up, so to speak, probabilities cannot be adequately calculated. For example, in the religious-preference example, suppose we thought that $A \cup B \cup C = U$, but in fact there were a large number of individuals with no particular religious preference. So, really, $A \cup B \cup C \cup D = U$, where D is the subset of individuals with no religious preference. The probabilities calculated on the assumption of this equation would be quite different than those based on the assumption of the earlier equation.

Two events, A and B, are *mutually exclusive* when they are disjoint, or when $A \cap B = E$. That is, when the intersection of two (or more) sets is the empty set—or when two sets have no elements in common—the sets are said to be mutually exclusive. This is the same as saying, again in probability language, $p(A \cap B) = 0$. It is more convenient for researchers when events are mutually exclusive, because they can then add the probabilities of events. We state a principle in set and probability terms: If the events (sets) A, B, and C are *mutually exclusive,* then $p(A \cup B \cup C) = p(A) + p(B) + p(C)$. This is the special case of the more general principle we discussed in the previous sections. (See Equations 7.1, 7.4, 7.5, and 7.6 and the accompanying discussion, above.)

One of the chief purposes of research design is to set up conditions of independence of events so that conditions of dependence of events can be adequately studied. Two events, A and B, are *statistically independent* if the following equation holds:

$$p(A \cap B) = p(A) \cdot p(B) \qquad (7.7)$$

which says that the probability of A and B *both* occurring is equal to the probability of A times the probability of B. Easy and clear examples of independent events are dice throws and coin tosses. If A is the event of a die throw and B is the event of a coin toss, and $p(A) = 1/6$ and $p(B) = 1/2$, then, if $p(A) \cdot p(B) = 1/6 \cdot 1/2 = 1/12$, A and B are independent. If we toss a coin 10 times, one toss has no influence on any other toss. The tosses are independent. So are the throws of dice. Similarly, when we simultaneously throw a die and toss a coin, the events of throwing a die, A, and tossing a coin, B, are independent. The outcome of a die throw has no influence on the toss of a coin—and vice versa. Unfortunately, this neat model does not always apply in research situations.

The commonsense notion of the so-called law of averages is utterly erroneous, but it nicely illustrates lack of understanding of independence. It says that if there is a large number of occurrences of an event, then the chance of that event occuring on the next trial is smaller. Suppose a coin is being tossed. Heads has come up five times in a row. The commonsense notion of the "law of averages" would lead one to believe that there is a greater chance of getting tails on the next toss. Not so. The probability is still 1/2. Each toss is an independent event.

Suppose students in a college class are taking an examination. They are working under the usual conditions of no communication, no looking at each other's papers, and so forth. The responses of any student can be considered independent of the responses of any other student. Can the responses to the items within the test be considered independent? Suppose that the answer to one item later in the test is embedded in an item earlier in the test. The probability of getting the later item correct by chance, say, is 1/4. But the fact that the answer was given earlier can change this probability. With some students it might even become 1.00. What is important for the researcher to know is that independence is often difficult to achieve and that lack of independence when research operations assume independence can seriously affect the interpretation of data.

Suppose we rank order examination papers and then assign grades on the basis of the ranks. This is a perfectly legitimate and useful procedure. But it must be realized that the grades given by the rank-order method are not independent (if they ever could be). Take five such papers. After reading them one is ranked as the first (the best), the second next, and so on through the five papers. We assign the number "1" to the first, "2" to the second, "3" to the third, "4" to the fourth, and "5" to the fifth. After using up 1, we have only 2, 3, 4, and 5 left. After using up 2, only 3, 4, and 5 remain. When we assign 4, obviously we must assign 5 to the remaining examination. In short, the assignment of 5 was influenced by the assignment of 4—and also 1, 2, and 3. The assignment events are not independent. One may ask, "Does this matter?" Suppose we take the ranks, treat them as scores, and make inferences about mean differences between groups, say between two classes. The statistical test used to do this is probably based on the coin-dice paradigm with its pristine independence. But we have not followed this model—one of its most important assumptions, independence, has been ignored.

When research events lack independence, statistical tests lack a certain validity. A χ^2 test, for example, assumes that the events—responses of individuals to an interview question, say—recorded in the cells of a crossbreak table, are independent of each other. If the recorded events are not independent of each other, then the basis of the statistical test and the inferences drawn from it are corrupted.

In a fascinating account of research on the aggressive behavior of apes, Hebb and Thompson present the data of Table 7.3.[9] The problem was the relation between sex and aggression. Samples of the behavior of 30 adult chimpanzees were taken in an effort to study individual differences in ape temperament. Without going into details, it can be said that one analysis of the observations showed that males and females displayed friendly behavior about equally often, but that males were more aggressive. Hebb and Thompson's data on this observation seem to say: "Watch out for males!" But, the authors point out, this is quite out of line with the experience of the apes' caretakers. Nineteen out of 20 cuts and scratches were inflicted by females! Then Hebb and Thompson pursued the interesting, if disconcerting, idea of tabulating incidence of aggressive acts in two ways: when such were preceded by quasi-aggression, that is, by warning of attack, and when aggressive acts were preceded by friendly behavior. The resulting incidences of behavior are given in Table 7.3. The table seems to indicate: "Watch out for female apes when they are friendly!"

[9]D. Hebb and W. Thompson, "The Social Significance of Animal Studies." In G. Lindzey and E. Aronson, eds., *The Handbook of Social Psychology,* 2d ed., vol. 2. New York: Random House, Inc., 1968, pp. 729–774. The table is on p. 751.

Table 7.3 Example Exhibiting Possible Lack of
Independence, Hebb and Thompson
Data[a]

	Males (n = 8)	Females (n = 22)
Quasi-Aggression, then Aggression	37	0
Friendly Behavior, then Aggression	0	15

[a]Table entries are numbers of acts of male and female chimpanzees of the kinds indicated by the margin labels on the left.

The data in the table cannot be validly analyzed statistically, since the numbers indicate the frequency of kinds of acts. But all 37 acts by males may have been committed by only one or two of them. If one ape had committed all 37 acts, then it should be clear that the acts were not independent of each other. The ape might have had a bad temper. And bad tempers notoriously create lack of independence in animal and human acts.

The second example is hypothetical. Suppose a researcher decides to sample 100 board of education decisions. He has a variety of ways to do this. He can sample many decisions from a few boards, or he can sample many decisions from many boards. Or he may do both. If he wants to be assured of the independence of the decisions, then he should sample many decisions from many boards of education. Theoretically, he should take only one decision from each board. Then he is assured of independence—at least as much as such assurance is possible. As soon as he takes more than one decision from the same board, however, he must entertain the notion that decisions of the kind A may influence decisions of the kind B. Decision A may influence decision B, for example, because the board members may wish to appear consistent. Both decisions may involve expenditures for instructional equipment, and since the board adopted a liberal policy on A it must adopt a liberal policy on B.

Suppose an investigator calculated the probability that an obtained result—for example, the difference between two means—was due to chance. This probability was 5/100, or .05. This means that there were approximately five chances in 100 that his result was due to chance. That is, if he repeated the experimental conditions 100 times *without* the experimental manipulation, approximately five of those times he could obtain a mean difference as large as the one he obtained *with* the experimental manipulation. Feeling shaky about the result—after all, there *are* five chances in 100 that the result could have been due to chance—he carefully repeated the whole experiment. He obtained substantially the same result (luck!). Having controlled everything carefully to be sure the two experiments were independent, he calculated the probability that the two results were due to chance. This probability was approximately .02. Thus we see both one of the values of independence in experimentation and the importance of replication of results.[10]

Note, finally, that the formula for independence works two ways. One, it tells us, if events are independent and we know the probabilities of the separate events, the probabil-

[10]The method of calculating these combined probabilities was proposed by Fisher and is described in F. Mosteller and R. Bush, ''Selected Quantitative Techniques.'' In G. Lindzey, ed., *Handbook of Social Psychology*, vol. I. Reading, Mass.: Addison-Wesley, 1954, pp. 328–331. The astute student may wonder why the set principle applied to probability, $P(A \cap B) = p(A) \cdot p(B)$, is not applicable. That is, why not calculate .05 × .05 = .0025? Mosteller and Bush explain this point. Since it is a rather difficult and moot point, we do not consider it in this book. All the reader need do is to remember that the probability of getting, say, a substantial difference between means in the same direction on repeated experiments is considerably smaller than getting such a difference once. Thus one can be more sure of one's data and conclusions, other things equal.

ity of both events occurring *by chance*. If it is found that dice repeatedly show 12's, say, then there is probably something wrong with the dice. If a gambler notes that another gambler seems always to win, he will of course get suspicious. The chances of continually winning a fair game are small. It can happen, of course, but it is unlikely to happen. In research, it is unlikely that one would get two or three significant results by chance. *Something* beyond chance is probably operating—the independent variable, we hope.

Two, the formula can be turned around, so to speak. It can tell the researchers what he must do to allow himself the advantage of the multiplicative probabilities. He must, if it is at all possible, plan his research so that events are independent. That this is easier said than done will become quite evident before this book is finished.

CONDITIONAL PROBABILITY

In all research and perhaps especially in social scientific and educational research, events are often not independent. Look at independence in another way. When two variables are related they are not independent. Our previous discussion of sets makes it clear; if $A \cap B = E$, then there is no relation (more accurately, a zero relation), or A and B are independent; if $A \cap B \neq E$, then there is a relation, or A and B are not independent. When events are not independent, scientists can sharpen their probabilistic inferences. The meaning of this statement can be explicated to some extent by studying conditional probability.

When events are not independent, the probability approach must be altered. Here is a simple example. What is the probability that, of any married couple picked at random, both mates are Republicans? First, assuming equiprobability and that everything else is equal, the sample space U (all the possibilities) is $\{RR, RD, DR, DD\}$, where the husband comes first in each possibility or sample point. Thus the probability that both husband and wife are Republicans is $p(RR) = 1/4$. But suppose we know that one of them is a Republican. What is the probability of both being Republicans now? U is reduced to $\{RR, RD, DR\}$. The knowledge that one is a Republican deletes the possibility DD, thus reducing the sample space. Therefore, $p(RR) = 1/3$. Suppose we have the further information that the wife is a Republican. Now, what is the probability that both mates are Republicans? Now $U = \{RR, DR\}$. Thus $p(RR) = 1/2$. The new probabilities are, in this case, "conditional" on prior knowledge or facts.

Definition of Conditional Probability

Let A and B be events in the sample space, U, as usual. The conditional probability is denoted: $P(A \mid B)$, which is read, "The probability of A, given B." For example, we might say, "The probability that a husband and wife are both Republicans, given that the husband is a Republican," or, much more difficult to answer, though more interesting, "The probability of high effectiveness in college teaching, given the Ph.D. degree." Of course, we can write $p(B \mid A)$, too. The formula for the conditional probability involving two events is:[11]

$$p(A \mid B) = \frac{p(A \cap B)}{p(B)} \tag{7.8}$$

The formula takes an earlier notion of probability and alters it for the conditional probability situations. Remember that in probability problems the denominator has to be the sample space. The formula above changes the denominator of the ratio and thus *changes*

[11] The theory extends to more than two events, but will not be discussed in this book.

the sample space. The sample space has, through knowledge, been cut down from U to B. To demonstrate this point take two examples, one of independence or simple probability and one of dependence or conditional probability.

Toss a coin twice. The events are independent. What is the probability of getting heads on the second toss if heads appeared on the first toss? We already know: 1/2. Let us calculate the probability using Equation 7.8. First we write a probability matrix (see Table 7.4). For the probabilities of heads (*H*) and tails (*T*) on the first toss, read the marginal entries on the right side of the matrix. Similarly for the probabilities of the second toss: they are on the bottom of the matrix. Thus $p(H_1) = 1/2$, $p(H_2) = 1/2$, and $p(H_2 \cap H_1) = 1/4$. Therefore,

$$p(H_2 \mid H_1) = \frac{p(H_2 \cap H_1)}{p(H_1)} = \frac{1/4}{1/2} = \frac{1}{2}$$

Table 7.4 Probability Matrix Showing Joint Probabilities of Two Independent Events

		Second Toss		
		H_2	T_2	
	H_1	¼	¼	½
First Toss				
	T_1	¼	¼	½
		½	½	

The result agrees with our previous simpler reasoning. If we make the problem a bit more complex, however, maybe the formula will be more useful. Suppose, somehow, that the probability of getting heads on the second toss were .60 instead of .50, and the events are still independent. Does this change the situation? The new situation is set up in Table 7.5. (The .30 in the cell $H_1 \cap H_2$ is calculated with the probabilities on the margins: $.50 \times .60 = .30$. This is permissible since we know that the events are independent. If they are not independent, conditional probability problems cannot be solved without knowledge of at least one of the values.) The formula gives us:

$$p(H_2 \mid H_1) = \frac{p(H_2 \cap H_1)}{p(H_1)} = \frac{.30}{.50} = .60$$

Table 7.5 Matrix of Joint Probabilities of Events

		Second Toss		
		H_2	T_2	
	H_1	.30	.20	.50
First Toss				
	T_1	.30	.20	.50
		.60	.40	1.00

But this .60 is the same as the simple probability of H_2. When events are independent, we get the same results. That is, in this case:

$$p(H_2 \mid H_1) = p(H_2)$$

and in the general case:

$$p(A \mid B) = p(A) \tag{7.9}$$

We have another definition or condition of independence. If Equation 7.9 holds, the events are independent.

An Academic Example

There are more interesting examples of conditional probability than coins and other such chance devices. Take the baffling and frustrating problem of predicting the success of doctoral students in graduate school. Can the coin-dice models be used in such a complex situation? Yes—under certain conditions. Unfortunately, these conditions are difficult to arrange. There is some limited success, however. Provided that we have certain empirical information, the model can be quite useful. Assume that the administrators of a graduate school are interested in predicting the success of their doctoral students. They are distressed by the poor performance of many of their graduates and want to set up a selection system. The school continues to admit all doctoral applicants as in the past, but for three years all incoming students take the Miller Analogies Test (MAT), a test that has been found to be fairly successful in predicting doctoral success. An arbitrary cutoff point of a raw score of 65 is selected.

The school administration finds that 30 percent of all the candidates of the three-year period score 65 or above. Each is categorized as a success (s) or failure (f). The criterion is simple: Does he or she get the degree? If so, this is defined as success. It is found that 40 percent of the total number succeed. To determine the relation between MAT score and success or failure, the administration, again using a cutoff point of 65, determines the proportions shown in Table 7.6.

Table 7.6 Joint Probabilities, Graduate-School Problem

	Success (s)	Failure (f)	
≥ 65	.20	.10	.30
< 65	.20	.50	.70
	.40	.60	1.00

The MAT divides the successful group in half (.20 and .20), but sharply differentiates in the failure group (.10 and .50). Now, the questions are asked: What is the probability of getting the doctor's degree if a candidate gets an MAT score of 65 or higher? What is the probability of a candidate's getting the degree if the MAT score is lower than 65? The computations are:

$$p(S \mid \geq 65) = \frac{p(S \cap \geq 65)}{p(\geq 65)} = \frac{.20}{.30} = .67$$

$$p(S \mid < 65) = \frac{p(S \cap < 65)}{p(< 65)} = \frac{.20}{.70} = .29$$

Clearly, it would seem that the MAT is a good predictor of success in the program.

Note carefully what happens in all these cases. When we write $p(A \mid B)$ instead of simply $p(A)$, in effect we cut down the sample space from U to B. Take the example just given. The probability of success without any other knowledge is a probability problem on the whole sample space U. This probability is .40. But given knowledge of MAT score, the sample space is cut down from U to a subset of U, ≥ 65. The actual number of occurrences of the success event, of course, does not change; the same number of persons succeed. But the probability fraction gets a new denominator. Put differently, the probability estimate is refined by knowledge of "pertinent" subsets of U. In this case, ≥ 65 and <65 are "pertinent" subsets of U. By "pertinent" subsets we mean that the variable implied is related to the criterion variable, success and failure.

Maybe the following mode of looking at the problem will help. An area interpretation of the graduate-student problem is diagrammed in Figure 7.5. The idea of a *measure of a set* is used here. Recall that a measure of a set or subset is the sum of the weights of the set or subset. The weights are assigned to the elements of the set or subset. Figure 7.5 is a square with ten equal parts on each side. Each part is equal to 1/10 or .10. The area of the whole square is the sample space U, and the measure of U, $m(U)$, equals 1.00. This means that all the weights assigned to all the elements of the square add up to 1.00. The measures of the subsets have been inserted: $m(F) = .60$, $m(<65) = .70$, $m(S \cap \geq 65) = .20$. The measures of these subsets can be calculated by multiplying the lengths of their sides. For example, the area of the upper left (doubly hatched) box is $.5 \times .4 = .20$. Recall that the probability of any set (or subset) is the measure of the set (or subset). So the probability of any of the boxes in Figure 7.5 is as indicated. We can find the probability of any two boxes by adding the measures of sets; for example, the probability of success is $.20 + .20 = .40$.

These measures (or probabilities) are defined on the whole area, or $U = 1.00$. The probability of success is equal to $.40/1.00$. We have knowledge of the students' performances on the MAT. The areas indicating the probabilities associated with ≥ 65 and <65 are marked off by horizontal dashed lines. The simple probability of ≥ 65 is equal to $.20 + .10 = .30$, or $.30/1.00$. The whole shaded area on the top indicates this probability. The areas of the "success" and "failure" measures are indicated by the heavy lines separating them on the square.

Our conditional probability problem is: What is the probability of success, given knowledge of MAT scores, or given ≥ 65 (it could also be <65, of course)? We have a new small sample space, indicated by the whole shaded area at the top of the square. In effect U has been cut down to this smaller space because we know the "truth" of the smaller space. Instead of letting this smaller space be equal to .30, we now let it be equal to 1.00. (You might say it becomes a new U.) Consequently the measures of the boxes that constitute the new sample space must be recalculated. For instance, instead of calculating the probability of $p(\geq 65 \cap S) = .20$ because it is 2/10 of the area of the whole

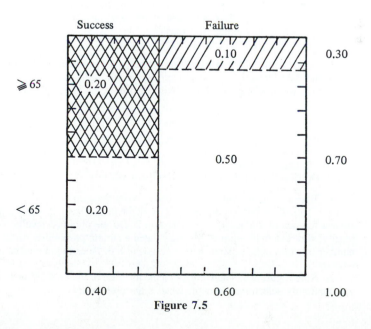

Figure 7.5

square, we must calculate, since we now know that the elements in the set ≥ 65 do have MAT scores greater than or equal to 65, the probability on the basis of the area of ≥ 65 (the whole shaded area at the top of the square). Having done this, we get $.20/.30 = .67$, which is exactly what we got when we used Equation 7.8.

What happens is that additional knowledge makes U no longer relevant as the sample space. *All probability statements are relative to sample spaces*. The basic question, then, is that of adequately defining sample spaces. In the earlier problem of husbands and wives, we asked the question: What is the probability of both mates being Republican? The sample space was $U = \{RR, RD, DR, DD\}$. But when we add the knowledge that one of them is certainly a Republican and ask the same question, in effect we make the original U irrelevant to the problem. A new sample space, call it U', is required. Consequently the probability that both are Republicans is different when we have more knowledge.

We can calculate other probabilities similarly. Suppose we wanted to know the probability of failure, given an MAT score less than 65. Look at Figure 7.5. The probability we want is the box on the lower right, labeled .50. Since we know that the score is <65, we use this knowledge to set up a new sample space. The two lower boxes whose area equals $.20 + .50 = .70$ represent this sample space. Thus we calculate the new probability: $.50/.70 = .71$. The probability of failure to get the degree if one has an MAT score less than 65 is .71.

Study Suggestions

1. Suppose that you are sampling ninth-grade youngsters for research purposes. There are 250 ninth graders in the school system, 130 boys and 120 girls.

(a) What is the probability of selecting any youngster?
(b) What is the probability of selecting a girl? A boy?
(c) What is the probability of selecting either a boy or a girl? How would you write this problem in set symbols? [*Hint:* Is it equivalent to set intersection or union?]
(d) Suppose you drew a sample of 100 boys and girls. You got 90 boys and 10 girls. What conclusions might you reach?
[*Answers:* (a) 1/250; (b) 120/250, 130/250; (c) 1.]

2. Toss a coin and throw a die once. What is the probability of getting heads on the coin *and* a six on the die? Draw a tree to show all the possibilities. Label the branches of the tree with the appropriate weights or probabilities. Now answer some questions. What is the probability of getting:

(a) tails and either a 1, a 3, or a 6?
(b) heads and either a 2 or a 4?
(c) heads or tails and a 5?
(d) heads or tails and a 5 or a 6?
[*Answers:* (a) 1/4; (b) 1/6; (c) 1/6; (d) 1/3.]

3. Toss a coin and roll a die 72 times. Write the results side-by-side on a ruled sheet as they occur. Check the obtained frequencies against the theoretical expected frequencies. Now check your answer to each of the questions in question 2. Do the obtained results come close to the expected results? (For example, suppose you calculated a certain probability for 2(a), above. Now count the number of times tails is paired with a 1, a 3, or a 6. Does the obtained fraction equal the expected fraction?)

4. Note Figure 7.6. There are 20 elements in U, of which 4 are in A, 6 in B, and 2 in $A \cap B$. If you randomly select one element, what is the probability

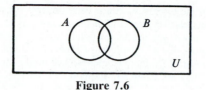

Figure 7.6

(a) that it will be in A?
(b) that it will be in B?
(c) that it will be in $A \cap B$?
(d) that it will be either in A or B? [*Hint:* Remember the equation: $p(A \cup B) = p(A) + p(B) - p(A \cap B)$.]
(e) that it will be neither in A nor in B?
(f) that it will be in B but not in A?

5. Consider Figure 7.7. There are 20 elements in U, 4 in B, and 8 in A. If an element of U is selected at random, what are the probabilities that the element will be in

(a) A?   (d) $A \cup B$?
(b) B?   (e) U?
(c) $A \cap B$?

[*Answers:* (a) 2/5; (b) 1/5; (c) 1/5; (d) 2/5; (e)1.]

6. Using Figure 7.7, answer the following questions:

(a) Given A (knowing that a sampled element came from A), what is the probability of B?
(b) Given B, what is the probability of A?
[*Answers:* (a) 1/2; (b) 1.]

7. Using Figure 7.6, answer the following questions:

(a) Given B, what is the probability of A?
(b) Given A, what is the probability of B?
[*Answers:* (a) 1/3; (b) 1/2.]

8. Suppose one had a two-item four-choice multiple-choice test, with the four choices of each item labeled a, b, c, and d. The correct answers to the two items are c and a.

(a) Write out the sample space. (Draw a tree; see Figure 7.3.)
(b) What is the probability of any testee getting both items correct by guessing?
(c) What is the probability of getting at least one of the items correct by guessing? (*Hint:* This may be a bit troublesome. Draw the tree and think of the possibilities. Count them.)
(d) What is the probability of getting both items wrong by guessing?
(e) Given that a testee gets the first item correct, what is the probability of him getting the second item correct by guessing?
[*Answers:* (b) 1/16; (c) 7/16; (d) 9/16; (e) 1/4.]

9. Most of the discussion in the text has been based on the assumption of equiprobability. This assumption is often not justified, however. What is wrong with the following argument, for instance? The probability of one's dying tomorrow is one-half. Why? Because one will either die

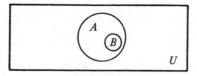

Figure 7.7

tomorrow or not die tomorrow. Since there are two possibilities, they each have a probability of occurrence of one-half. How would insurance companies fare with this reasoning? Suppose, now, that a political scientist studied the relation between religious and political preferences, and assumed that the probabilities that a Catholic was Democrat or Republican were equal. What would you think of his research results? Do these examples have implications for researchers knowing something of the phenomena they are studying? Explain.

Chapter 8

Sampling and Randomness

IMAGINE the many situations in which we want to know something about people, about events, about things. To learn something about people, for instance, we take some few people whom we know—or do not know—and study them. After our "study," we come to certain conclusions, often about people in general. Some such method is behind much folk wisdom. Commonsensical observations about people, their motives, and their behaviors derive, for the most part, from observations and experiences with relatively few people. We make such statements as: "People nowadays have no sense of moral values"; "Politicians are corrupt"; and "Public school pupils are not learning the three R's."

The basis for making such statements is simple. People, mostly through their limited experiences, come to certain conclusions about other people and about their environment. In order to come to such conclusions, they must *sample* their "experiences" of other people. Actually, they take relatively small samples of all possible experiences. The term "experiences" here has to be taken in a broad sense. It can mean direct experience with other people—for example, first-hand interaction with, say, Germans or Jews. Or it can mean indirect experience: hearing about Germans or Jews from friends, acquaintances, parents, and others. Whether experience is direct or indirect, however, does not concern us too much at this point. Let us assume that all such experience is direct. An individual believes he "knows" something about Jews and says he "knows" they are clannish, because he has had direct experience with a number of Jews. He may even say, "Some of my best friends are Jews, and I know that . . . " The point is that his conclusions are based on a sample of Jews, or a sample of the behaviors of Jews, or both. He can never "know" all Jews; he must depend, in the last analysis, on samples. Indeed, most of the world's knowledge is based on samples, most often on inadequate samples.

SAMPLING, RANDOM SAMPLING, AND REPRESENTATIVENESS

Sampling is taking any portion of a population or universe as representative of that population or universe. This definition does not say that the sample taken—or drawn, as researchers say—*is* representative. It says, rather, taking a portion of the population and *considering* it to be representative. When a school administrator visits certain classrooms in his system "to get the feel of the system," he is sampling classes from all the classes in the system. He is probably assuming that if he visits, say, eight to ten classes out of forty "at random," as he may say, he will get a fair notion of the quality of teaching going on in the system. Or he may visit one teacher's class two or three times to sample her teaching. He is now sampling behaviors, in this case teaching behaviors, from the universe of all possible behaviors of the teacher. Such sampling is necessary and legitimate.

Random sampling is that method of drawing a portion (or sample) of a population or universe so that each member of the population or universe has an equal chance of being selected. This definition has the virtue of being easily understood. Unfortunately, it is not entirely satisfactory because it is limited. A better definition is: *Random sampling* is that method of drawing a portion (sample) of a population or universe so that all possible samples of fixed size n have the same probability of being selected.[1] This definition is general and thus more satisfactory than the earlier definition.

Define a universe to be studied as all fourth-grade children in X school system. Suppose there are 200 such children. They comprise the population (or universe). We select one child at random from the population. His (or her) chance of being selected is 1/200, if the sampling procedure is random. Likewise, a number of other children are similarly selected. Let us assume that after selecting a child we return him (or the symbol assigned to him) to the population. Then the chance of selecting any second child is also 1/200. (If we do not return him to the population, then the chance each of the remaining children has, of course, is 1/199. This is called *sampling without replacement*. When the sample elements are returned to the population after being drawn, the procedure is called *sampling with replacement*.)

Suppose from the population of the 200 fourth-grade children in X school system we decide to draw a random sample of 50 children. This means, if the sample is random, that all possible samples of 50 have the same probability of being selected—a very large number of possible samples. To make the ideas involved comprehensible, suppose a population consists of four children, *a, b, c,* and *d,* and we draw a random sample of two children. Then the list of all the possibilities, or the *sample space,* is: (a,b), (a,c), (a,d), (b,c), (b,d), (c,d). There are six possibilities. If the sample of two is drawn at random, then its probability is 1/6. Each of the pairs has the same probability of being drawn. This sort of reasoning is needed to solve many research problems, but we will usually confine ourselves to the simpler idea of sampling connected with the first definition. The first definition, then, is a special case of the second general definition—the special case in which $n = 1$.

Unfortunately, we can never be sure that a random sample is representative of the population from which it is drawn. Remember that any particular sample of size n has the same probability of being selected as any other sample of the same size. Thus, a particular sample may not be representative at all. We should know what "representative" means. Ordinarily, "representative" means to be typical of a population, that is, to exemplify the

---

[1] W. Feller, *An Introduction to Probability Theory and Its Applications,* 2nd ed. New York: Wiley, 1957, p. 29.

characteristics of the population. From a research point of view, "representative" must be more precisely defined, though it is often difficult to be precise. We must ask: What characteristics are we talking about? So, in research, a "representative sample" means that the sample has approximately the characteristics of the population relevant to the research in question. If sex and socioeconomic class are variables (characteristics) relevant to the research, a representative sample will have approximately the same proportions of men and women and middle-class and working-class individuals as the population. When we draw a random sample, we *hope* that it will be representative, that the relevant characteristics of the population will be present in the sample in approximately the same way they are present in the population. But we can never be sure; there is no guarantee.

What we rely on is the fact, as Stilson points out, that the characteristics typical ("characteristic") of a population are those that are the most frequent and therefore most likely to be present in any particular random sample.[2] When sampling is random, the sampling variability is predictable. We learned in Chapter 7, for example, that if we throw two dice a number of times, the probability of a 7 turning up is greater than that of a 12 turning up. (See Table 7.1.)

A sample drawn at random is unbiased in the sense that no member of the population has any more chance of being selected than any other member. We have here a democracy in which all members are equal before the bar of selection. Rather than using coins or dice, let's use a research example. Suppose we have a population of 100 children. The children differ in intelligence, a variable relevant to our research. We want to know the mean intelligence score of the population, but for some reason we can only sample 30 of the 100 children. If we sample randomly, there are a large number of possible samples of 30 each. The samples have equal probabilities of being selected. The means of most of the samples will be relatively close to the mean of the population. A few will not be close. The probability of selecting a sample with a mean close to the population mean, then, is greater than the probability of selecting a sample with a mean not close to the population mean—if the sampling has been random.

If we do not draw our sample at random, however, some factor or factors unknown to us may predispose us to select a biased sample, in this case perhaps one of the samples with a mean not close to the population mean. The mean intelligence of this sample will then be a biased estimate of the population mean. If the 100 children were known to us, we might unconsciously tend to select the more intelligent children. It is not so much that we *would* do so; it is that our method *allows* us to do so. Random methods of selection do not allow our own biases or any other systematic selection factors to operate. The procedure is objective, divorced from our own predilections and biases.

The reader may be experiencing a vague and disquieting sense of uneasiness. If we can't be sure that random samples are representative, how can we have confidence in our research results and their applicability to the populations from which we draw our samples? Why not select samples systematically so that they *are* representative? The answer is complex. First—and again—we cannot ever be sure. Second, random samples are more likely to include the characteristics typical of the population if the characteristics are frequent in the population. In actual research, we draw random samples whenever we can and hope and assume that the samples are representative. We learn to live with uncertainty, but try to cut it down whenever we can—just as we do in ordinary day-to-day

---

[2] D. Stilson, *Probability and Statistics in Psychological Research and Theory*. San Francisco: Holden-Day, 1966, p. 35.

living, but more systematically and with considerable knowledge of and experience with random sampling and random outcomes. Fortunately, our lack of certainty does not impair our research functioning.

RANDOMNESS

The notion of randomness is at the core of modern probabilistic methods in the natural and behavioral sciences. But it is difficult to define "random." The dictionary notion of haphazard, accidental, without aim or direction, does not help us much. In fact, scientists are quite systematic about randomness; they carefully select random samples and plan random procedures.

The position can be taken that nothing happens at random, that for any event there is a cause. The only reason, this position might say, that one uses the word random is that human beings do not know enough. To omniscience nothing is random. Suppose an omniscient being has an omniscient newspaper. It is a gigantic newspaper in which every event down to the last detail—for tomorrow, the next day, and the next day, and on and on into indefinite time—is carefully inscribed.[3] There is nothing unknown. And, of course, there is no randomness. Randomness is, as it were, ignorance, in this view.

Taking a cue from this argument, we define randomness in a backhand way. We say events are random if we cannot predict their outcomes. For instance, there is no known way to win a penny-tossing game. Whenever there is no system for playing a game that ensures our winning (or losing), then the event-outcomes of the game are random. More formally put, *randomness* means that there is no known law, capable of being expressed in language, that correctly describes or explains events and their outcomes.[4] In a word, when events are random we cannot predict them individually. Strange to say, however, we can predict them quite successfully in the aggregate. That is, we can predict the outcomes of large numbers of events. We cannot predict whether a coin tossed will be heads or tails. But, if we toss the coin 1000 times, we can predict, with considerable accuracy, the total numbers of heads and tails.

An Example of Random Sampling

To give the reader a feeling for randomness and random samples, we now do a demonstration using a table of random numbers. A table of random numbers contains numbers generated mechanically so that there is no discernible order or system in them. It was said above that if events are random they cannot be predicted. But now we are going to predict the *general nature* of the outcomes of our experiment. We select, from a table of random digits, 10 samples of 10 digits each. Since the numbers are random, each sample "should" be representative of the universe of digits. The universe can be variously defined. We simply define it as the complete set of digits in the Rand Corporation table of random digits.[5] We now draw samples from the table. The means of the 10 samples will, of course, be different, but they should fluctuate within a relatively narrow range, with most of them fairly close to the mean of all 100 numbers and to the theoretical mean of

[3] See J. Kemeny, *A Philosopher Looks at Science*. New York: Van Nostrand Reinhold, 1959, p. 39.
[4] *Ibid.*, pp. 68–75.
[5] The source of random numbers used was: Rand Corporation, *A Million Random Digits with 100,000 Normal Deviates*. New York: Free Press, 1955. This is a large and carefully constructed table of random numbers. There are many other such tables, however, that are good enough for most practical purposes. Modern statistics texts have such tables. Appendix C at the end of this book contains 4,000 computer-generated random numbers.

the whole population of random numbers. And the number of even numbers in each sample of 10 should be approximately equal to the number of odd numbers—though, again, there will be fluctuations, some of them perhaps extreme but most of them comparatively modest. The samples are given in Table 8.1.

TABLE 8.1   Ten Samples of Random Numbers

	1	2	3	4	5	6	7	8	9	10
	9	0	8	0	4	6	0	7	7	8
	7	2	7	4	9	4	7	8	7	7
	6	2	8	1	9	3	6	0	3	9
	7	9	9	1	6	4	9	4	7	7
	3	3	1	1	4	1	0	3	9	4
	8	9	2	1	3	9	6	7	7	3
	4	8	3	0	9	2	7	2	3	2
	1	4	3	0	0	2	6	9	7	5
	3	1	8	8	4	5	2	1	0	3
	2	1	4	8	9	2	9	3	0	1

Mean: 5.0   3.9   5.3   2.4   5.7   3.8   5.2   4.4   5.0   4.9   Total mean = 4.56

The means of the samples are given below each sample. The mean of U, the theoretical mean of the whole population of Rand random numbers, {0, 1, 2, 3, 4, 5, 6, 7, 8, 9}, is 4.5. The mean of all 100 numbers, which can be considered a sample of U, is 4.56. This is, of course, very close to the mean of U. It can be seen that the means of the 10 samples vary around 4.5, the lowest being 2.4 and the highest 5.7. Only two of these means differ from 4.5 by more than 1. A statistical test—later we will learn the rationale of such tests—shows that the 10 means do not differ from each other significantly. (The expression "do not differ from each other significantly" means that the differences are not greater than the differences that would occur by chance.) And by another statistical test nine of them are "good" estimates of the population mean of 4.5 and one (2.4) is not.

Changing the sampling problem, we can define the universe to consist of odd and even numbers. Let's assume that in the entire universe there is an equal number of both. In our sample of 100 numbers there should be approximately 50 odd and 50 even numbers. There are actually 54 odd and 46 even numbers. A statistical test shows that the deviation of 4 for odd and 4 for even does not depart significantly from chance expectation.[6]

Similarly, if we sample human beings, then the numbers of men and women in the samples should be approximately in proportion to the numbers of men and women in the population—if the sampling is random and the samples are large enough. If we measure the intelligence of a sample, and the mean intelligence score of the population is 100, then the mean of the sample should be close to 100. Of course, we must always bear in mind the possibility of selection of the deviant sample, the sample with a mean, say, of 80 or less or 120 or more. Deviant samples *do* occur, but they are less likely to occur. The reasoning is similar to that for coin-tossing demonstrations. If we toss a coin three times, it is less likely that 3 heads or 3 tails will turn up than it is that 2 heads and 1 tail or 2 tails and 1 head will turn up, because $U = \{HHH, HHT, HTH, HTT, THH, THT, TTH, TTT\}$. There is only one *HHH* point and one *TTT* point, while there are three points with two *H*'s and three with two *T*'s.

---

[6] The nature of such statistical tests, as well as the reasoning behind them, will be explained in detail in Part Four. The student should not be too concerned if he does not completely grasp the statistical ideas expressed here. Indeed, one of the purposes of this chapter is to introduce some of the basic elements of such ideas.

RANDOMIZATION

Suppose an investigator wishes to test the hypothesis that counseling helps underachievers. He wants to set up two groups of underachievers, one to be counseled, one not to be counseled. Naturally, he also wishes to have the two groups equal in other independent variables that may have a possible effect on achievement. One way he can do this is to assign the children to both groups at random by, say, tossing a coin for each child in turn and assigning the child to one group if the toss is heads and to the other group if the toss is tails. (Note that if he had three experimental groups he would probably not use coin-tossing. He might use a die.) Or he can use a table of random numbers and assign the children as follows: if an odd number turns up, assign a child to one group, and if an even number turns up, assign the child to the other group. He can now assume that the groups are approximately equal in all possible independent variables. The larger the groups, the safer the assumption. Just as there is no guarantee, however, of not drawing a deviant sample, as discussed earlier, there is no guarantee that the groups *are* equal or even approximately equal in all possible independent variables. Nevertheless, it can be said that the investigator has used randomization to equalize his groups, or, as it is said, to control influences on the dependent variable other than that of the manipulated independent variable.

An "ideal" experiment is one in which *all* the factors or variables likely to affect the experimental outcome are controlled. If we *knew* all these factors, in the first place, and *could* control them, in the second place, then we might have an ideal experiment. But the sad case is that we can never know all the pertinent variables nor could we control them even if we did know them. Randomization, however, comes to our aid.

Randomization is the assignment to experimental treatments of members of a universe in such a way that, for any given assignment to a treatment, every member of the universe has an equal probability of being chosen for that assignment. The basic purpose of random *assignment*, as indicated earlier, is to apportion subjects (objects, groups) to treatments so that individuals with varying characteristics are spread approximately equally among the treatments so that variables that might affect the dependent variable other than the experimental variables have "equal" effects in the different treatments.[7] There is no guarantee that this desirable state of affairs will be attained, but it is more likely to be attained with randomization than otherwise. The idea of randomization seems to have been discovered or invented by Sir Ronald Fisher, who virtually revolutionized statistical and experimental design thinking and methods using random notions as part of his leverage.[8] In any case, randomization and what can be called the principle of randomization is one of the great intellectual achievements of our time. It is not possible to overrate the importance of both the idea and the practical measures that come from it to improve experimentation and inference.

[7] Randomization also has a statistical rationale and purpose. If random assignment has been used, then it is possible to distinguish between systematic or experimental variance and error variance. Biasing variables—Hays calls them "nuisance" variables—are distributed to experimental groups according to chance. As Wendel, in a letter to *Science* (1978, 199, p. 368), says "the biasing errors become random errors." Wendel also says that the "equalization" function is secondary to the statistical function. Strictly speaking, the tests of statistical significance that we will discuss later logically depend on random assignment. Without it the significance tests lack logical foundation. (See following footnote.)

[8] See R. A. Fisher, *The Design of Experiments*. New York: Hafner, 1951, Chap. II. This chapter begins with Fisher's famous lady who said that by tasting a cup of tea she could tell whether the milk or the tea was first added to the cup. He uses the example to illustrate the necessity and importance of randomization. The chapter is a fine statement of the physical and statistical conditions of experiments.

Randomization can perhaps be clarified in two or three ways: by stating the principle of randomization, by describing how one uses it in practice, and by demonstrating how it works with objects and numbers. The importance of the idea deserves all three.

The *principle of randomization* may be stated thus: Since, in random procedures, every member of a population has an equal chance of being selected, members with certain distinguishing characteristics—male or female, high or low intelligence, conservative or liberal, and so on and on—will, if selected, probably be offset in the long run by the selection of other members of the population with counterbalancing quantities or qualities of the characteristics. We can say that this is a practical principle of what usually happens; we cannot say that it is a law of nature. It is simply a statement of what most often happens when random procedures are used.

We say that subjects are assigned at random to experimental groups, and that experimental treatments are assigned at random to groups. For instance, in the example cited above of an experiment to test the effectiveness of counseling on achievement, subjects can be assigned to two groups at random by using random numbers or by tossing a coin. When the subjects have been so assigned, the groups can be randomly designated as experimental and control groups using a similar procedure. We will encounter a number of examples of randomization as we go along.

A Senatorial Randomization Demonstration

To show how, if not why, the principle of randomization works, we now set up a sampling and design experiment. We have a population of 100 members of the United States Senate from which we can sample. In this population (in 1981), there are 53 Republicans and 47 Democrats. I have selected two important votes, one (Issue 162) on aid programs for welfare children and the other (Issue 121) on proposed reductions in Social Security benefits.[9] While these votes were important since each of them reflected presidential proposals, a Nay vote on 162 and a Yea vote on 121 indicating support of the President, we here ignore their substance and treat the actual votes, or rather, the senators who cast the votes, as populations from which we sample.

We pretend we are going to do an experiment using three groups of senators, with 20 in each group. The nature of the experiment is not too relevant here, but let us say that we want to test the efficacy of a film depicting the horrors of nuclear warfare in changing the attitudes of the senators toward nuclear test bans. We want the three groups of senators to be approximately equal in all possible characteristics. Using a programmable calculator-computer I generated random numbers between 1 and 100.[10] The first 60 numbers drawn, with no repeated numbers (sampling without replacement), were recorded in groups of 20 each. Political party affiliation, 1 = Republican, 0 = Democrat, and the senators' votes on the two issues, 1 = Yea and 0 = Nay, were also recorded.

How "equal" are the groups? In the total population of 100 senators, 53 are Republicans and 47 Democrats, or 53 percent and 47 percent. In the total sample of 60 there are 30 Republicans and 30 Democrats, or 50 percent each, a difference of 3 percent from the expectation of 53 percent and 47 percent. The obtained and expected frequencies of Republicans in the three groups and the total sample are given in Table 8.2. The devia-

---

[9]*Congressional Quarterly,* 1981 (39), pp. 920 (No. 121) and 1156 (No. 162).

[10]Hewlett-Packard HP-67. *Hewlett-Packard HP-67/HP-97: Stat Pac I,* pp. 04-01–04-05. This program is based on a method described in: D. E. Knuth, *The Art of Computer Programming,* vol. 2. Reading, Mass.: Addison-Wesley, 1971. In this chapter we have used three different methods of generating pseudo-random numbers (as they are more properly called): drawing them from a random numbers table, generating them with a programmable hand-held calculator, and generating them on a large computer.

tions from expectation are obviously small. The three groups are ''equal'' in the sense that they have equal numbers of Republican senators—and, of course, Democrats.[11]

TABLE 8.2 Obtained and Expected Frequencies of Political Party (Republican) in Random Samples of 20 U.S. Senators[a]

	Groups			Total
	I	II	III	
Obtained	10	10	10	30
Expected[b]	10.60	10.60	10.60	31.80
Deviation	.60	.60	.60	1.80

[a]Only the larger of the two expectations of the Republican-Democrat split, the Republican (.53), is reported.
[b]The expected frequencies were calculated as follows: $20 \times .53 = 10.60$. Similarly, the total is calculated: $60 \times .53 = 31.80$.

Remember that we are demonstrating both random sampling and randomization, but especially randomization. We therefore ask whether the random assignment of senators to the three groups has resulted in ''equalizing'' the groups in all characteristics. We can never test all characteristics, of course; we can only test those available. In the present case we have only political party affiliation, which we tested above, and the votes on the two issues: aid programs for welfare children (Issue 162) and proposed reductions in Social Security benefits (Issue 121). How did the random assignment work with the two issues? The results are presented in Table 8.3. The original vote on Issue 162 of the 98 senators who voted were 46 Yeas and 52 Nays. These total votes yield expected Yea frequencies in the total group of 46/98 = .47, or 47 percent. We therefore expect $20 \times .47 = 9.40$, or 9 rounded, in each experimental group. The original vote of the 97 senators who voted on Issue 121 was 49 Yeas, or 51 percent (49/97 = .51). The expected group Yea frequencies, then, are: $20 \times .51 = 10.20$, or rounded, 10. The obtained and expected frequencies and the deviations from expectation for the three groups of 20 senators and for the total sample of 60 on Issue 121 are also given in Table 8.3.

TABLE 8.3 Obtained and Expected Frequencies on Yea Votes on Issues 162 and 121 in Random Groups of Senators

	Groups						Total	
	I		II		III			
	162	121	162	121	162	121	162	121
Obtained	8	11	10	10	11	9	29	30
Expected[a]	9	10	9	10	9	10	28	31
Deviation	1	1	1	0	2	1	1	1

[a]The expected frequencies were calculated for Group I, Issue 162, as follows: there were 46 Yeas of a total of 98 votes, or 46/98 = .47; $20 \times .47 = 9.40$, or rounded, 9. For the total group, the calculation is: $60 \times .47 = 28.20$, or rounded, 28.

It is obvious that the deviations from chance expectation are all small. Evidently the three groups are approximately ''equal'' in the sense that the incidence of the votes on the

[11]Obtaining 10 Republicans—and, of course, 10 Democrats—in each experimental group is unusual. But this is the sort of ''unusual'' outcome that occasionally happens with random sampling.

two issues is approximately the same in each of the groups. The deviations from chance expectation of the Yea votes (and, of course, the Nay votes) are small. So far as we can see, then, the randomization has been "successful."[12] We can now do our experiment believing that the three groups are "equal." They may not be, of course, but the probabilities are in our favor. And as we have seen, the procedure usually works well.[13] Our checking of the characteristics of the senators in the three groups showed that the groups were fairly "equal" in political preference and Yea (and Nay) votes on the two issues. Thus we can have greater confidence that if the groups become unequal in attitudes toward a nuclear test ban, the differences are probably due to our experimental manipulation and not to differences between the groups before we started.

SAMPLE SIZE

A rough-and-ready rule taught to beginning students of research is: Use as large samples as possible. Whenever a mean, a percentage, or other statistic is calculated from a sample, a population value is being estimated. A question that must be asked is: How much error is likely to be in statistics calculated from samples of different sizes? The curve of Figure 8.1 roughly expresses the relations between sample size and error, error meaning deviation from population values. The curve says that the smaller the sample the larger the error, and the larger the sample the smaller the error.

Consider the following rather extreme example. Total reading and total mathematics scores of 327 Eugene, Oregon, sixth-grade children on the Metropolitan Achievement

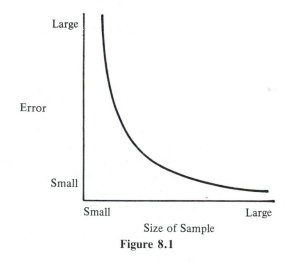

Figure 8.1

---

[12] This demonstration can also be interpreted as a random sampling problem. We may ask, for example, whether the three samples of 20 each and the total sample of 60 are representative. Do they accurately reflect the characteristics of the population of 100 senators? For instance, do the samples reflect the proportions of Republicans and Democrats in the Senate? The proportions in the samples were all .50 and .50. The actual proportions are .53 and .47. Although there are 3 percent deviations in the samples, the deviations are within chance expectation. We can say, therefore, that the samples are representative insofar as political party membership is concerned. Similar reasoning applies to the samples and the votes on the two issues.

[13] No less an expert than Feller, however, writes: "In sampling human populations the statistician encounters considerable and often unpredictable difficulties, and bitter experience has shown that it is difficult to obtain even a crude image of randomness." Feller, *op. cit.*, p. 29.

Tests (administered in 1978), together with the sex of the pupils, were made available to me.[14] From this "population," 10 samples of two pupils each were randomly selected.[15] These sample scores and the sample means are given in Table 8.4. The deviations of the means from the means of the population are also given in the table.

TABLE 8.4 Samples ($n = 2$) of Reading and Mathematics Scores of 327 Sixth-Grade Children, Means of the Samples, and Deviations of the Sample Means from the Population Mean[a]

					Reading					
	83	88	88	61	83	82	62	37	74	66
	80	60	83	86	67	83	67	84	74	73
Mean	81.5	74.0	85.5	73.5	75.0	82.5	64.5	60.5	74.0	69.5
Dev.	12.33	4.83	16.33	4.33	5.83	13.33	−4.67	−8.67	4.83	.33

Total Mean (20) = 74.05
Population Mean (327) = 69.17

					Mathematics					
	110	91	102	69	91	108	56	36	71	50
	100	63	95	108	57	88	93	79	62	87
Mean	105.0	77.0	98.5	88.5	74.0	98.0	59.5	57.5	66.5	68.5
Dev.	27.85	−.15	21.35	11.35	−3.15	20.85	−17.65	−19.65	−10.65	−8.65

Total Mean (20) = 80.80
Population Mean (327) = 77.15

[a]These data and the data of Table 8.5 are reproduced with the permission of Dr. Larry Barber, Director of Research, School District 4-J, Eugene, Oregon.

The reading means range from 60.5 to 85.5, and the mathematics means from 57.5 to 105.0. The two total means (calculated from the 20 reading and the 20 mathematics scores) are 74.05 and 80.80. These small sample means vary considerably. The reading and arithmetic means of the population ($N = 327$) were 69.17 and 77.15. The deviations of the reading means range a good deal: from −8.67 to 16.33. The mathematics deviations range from −19.65 to 27.85. With very small samples like these we cannot depend on any one mean as an estimate of the population value, but we can depend more on the means calculated from all 20 scores, although both have an upward bias.

Four more random samples of 20 reading and 20 mathematics scores were drawn from the population. The four reading and the four mathematics means are given in Table 8.5. The deviations (Dev.) of each of the means of the samples of 20 from the population means are also given in the table, as well as the means of the sample of 80 and of the total population. The reading deviations range from −2.02 to 4.88, and the mathematics deviations from −2.00 to 1.55. The mean of the 80 reading scores is 69.91, and the mean of all 327 reading scores is 69.17. The comparable mathematics means are 76.95 ($n = 80$) and 77.15 ($N = 327$). These means are quite clearly much better estimates of the population means.

[14]These data were generously made available by Dr. Larry Barber and Dr. Charles Stephens, research directors of the 4-J School District, Eugene, Oregon. I express my thanks and appreciation to Dr. Barber and Dr. Stephens and to the Eugene 4-J School District.

[15]The random selection of these samples and of others soon to be described was done on a large computer using a program to generate random numbers between 1 and 327.

TABLE 8.5 Means and Deviations from Population Means of Four Reading and Four Mathematics Samples, $n = 20$, Total Sample, $n = 80$, and Population, $N = 327$, Eugene Data[a]

Reading	Samples ($n = 20$)				Total ($n = 80$)	Population ($N = 327$)
Reading	70.65	74.05	67.80	67.15	69.91	69.17
Dev.	1.48	4.88	−1.37	−2.02	.74	
Mathematics	75.15	78.35	78.70	75.60	76.95	77.15
Dev.	−2.00	1.20	1.55	−1.55	−.20	

[a] See footnote a, Table 8.4.

We can now draw conclusions. First, statistics calculated from large samples are more accurate, other things equal, than those calculated from small samples. A glance at the deviations of Tables 8.4 and 8.5 will show that the means of the samples of 20 deviated much less from the population mean than did the means of the samples of 2. Moreover, the means of the samples of 80 deviated little from the population means (.74 and −.20).

It should now be fairly clear why the research and sampling principle is: Use large samples.[16] Large samples are not advocated because large numbers are good in and of themselves. They are advocated in order to give the principle of randomization, or simply randomness, a chance to "work," to speak somewhat anthropomorphically. With small samples, the probability of selecting deviant samples is a greater than with large samples. For example, in one random sample of 20 senators drawn some years ago, the first 10 senators (of 20) drawn were all Democrats! Such a run of 10 Democrats is most unusual. *But it can and does happen.* If we had chosen to do an experiment with only two groups of 10 each and one of the groups was the one with the 10 Democrats and the other had both Democrats and Republicans, the results could have been seriously biased, especially if the experiment had anything to do with political preference or social attitudes. With large groups, say 30 or more, there is less danger.

KINDS OF SAMPLES

The discussion of sampling has until now been confined to simple random sampling. The purpose is to help the student understand fundamental principles; thus the idea of simple random sampling, which is behind much of the thinking and procedures of modern research, is emphasized. The student should realize, however, that simple random sampling is not the only kind of sampling used in behavioral research. Indeed, it is relatively uncommon, at least for describing characteristics of populations and the relations between such characteristics. It is, nevertheless, the model on which all scientific sampling is based.

Other kinds of samples can be broadly classified into probability and nonprobability samples (and certain mixed forms). *Probability samples* use some form of random sampling in one or more of their stages. *Nonprobability samples* do not use random sampling; they thus lack the virtues being discussed. Still, they are often necessary and unavoidable. Their weakness can to some extent be mitigated by using knowledge, expertise, and care in selecting samples and by replicating studies with different samples.

One form of nonprobability sampling is *quota sampling,* in which knowledge of strata of the population—sex, race, region, and so on—is used to select sample members that

[16] The situation is more complex than this simple statement indicates. Samples that are too large can be dangerous; the reasons will be explained in a later chapter.

are representative, "typical," and suitable for certain research purposes. Quota sampling derives its name from the practice of assigning quotas, or proportions of kinds of people, to interviewers. Such sampling has been used a good deal in public opinion polls. Another form of nonprobability sampling is *purposive sampling*, which is characterized by the use of judgment and a deliberate effort to obtain representative samples by including presumably typical areas or groups in the sample. So-called *"accidental" sampling*, the weakest form of sampling, is probably also the most frequent. In effect, one takes available samples at hand; classes of seniors in high school, sophomores in college, a convenient PTA, and the like. This practice is hard to defend. Yet, used with reasonable knowledge and care, it is probably not as bad as it has been said to be. The most sensible advice seems to be: Avoid accidental samples unless you can get no others (random samples are usually expensive and, in general, hard to come by) and, if you do use them, use extreme circumspection in analysis and interpretation of data.

Probability sampling includes a variety of forms. The most general of these are stratified sampling and cluster sampling. In *stratified sampling*, the population is divided into strata, such as men and women, black and white, and the like, from which random samples are drawn. *Cluster sampling*, the most used method in surveys, is the successive random sampling of units, or sets and subsets. In educational research, for example, school districts of a state or county can be randomly sampled, then schools, then classes, and finally pupils. Another kind of probability sampling—if, indeed, it can be called probability sampling—is *systematic sampling*. Here the first sample element is randomly chosen from numbers 1 through k and subsequent elements are chosen at every kth interval. For example, if the element randomly selected from the elements 1 through 10 is 6, then the subsequent elements are 16, 26, 36, and so on. The student who will pursue research further should, of course, know much more about these methods and should consult one or more of the excellent references on the subject.[17]

Randomness, randomization, and random sampling are among the great ideas of science, as indicated earlier. While research can, of course, be done without using ideas of randomness, it is difficult to conceive how it can have viability and validity, at least in most aspects of behavioral scientific research. Modern notions of research design, sampling, and inference, for example, are literally inconceivable without the idea of randomness. One of the most remarkable of paradoxes is that through randomness, or "disorder," we are able to achieve control over the often obstreperous complexities of psychological, sociological, and educational phenomena. We impose order, in short, by exploiting the known behavior of sets of random events. One is perpetually awed by what can be called the structural beauty of probability, sampling, and design theory and by its great usefulness in solving difficult problems of research design and planning and the analysis and interpretation of data.

Before leaving the subject, let's return to a view of randomness mentioned earlier. To an omniscient being, there is no randomness. By definition such a being would "know" the occurrence of any event with complete certainty.[18] As Poincaré points out, to gamble with such a being would be a losing venture. Indeed, it would not *be* gambling. When a

[17] A clear exposition of different kinds of sampling can be found in: F. Stephan and P. McCarthy, *Sampling Opinions*. New York: Wiley, 1963 (1958), chap. 3. An excellent account of general principles of sampling, together with examples and formulas for estimates, is: G. Snedecor and W. Cochran, *Statistical Methods*, 5th ed. Ames, Iowa: Iowa State University Press, 1967, chap. 17. Although oriented toward biology and agriculture, the principles and methods of this authoritative book are easily applied to behavioral disciplines. Another authoritative reference is: L. Kish, "Selection of the Sample." In L. Festinger and D. Katz, eds., *Research Methods in the Behavioral Sciences*. New York: Holt, Rinehart and Winston, 1953, pp. 175–239. On sampling and estimation, see D. Warwick and C. Lininger, *The Sample Survey: Theory and Practice*. New York: McGraw-Hill, 1975, chap. 4.

[18] For an eloquent discussion of this point, see Poincaré's essay on chance: H. Poincaré, *Science and Method*. New York: Dover, 1952, pp. 64–90.

coin was tossed ten times, he (or she) would predict heads and tails with complete certainty and accuracy. When dice were thrown, he would know infallibly what the outcomes will be. He would even be able to predict every number in a table of random numbers! And certainly he would have no need for research and science. What I seem to be saying is that randomness is a term for ignorance. If we, like the omniscient being, knew all the contributing causes of events, then there would be no randomness. The beauty of it, as indicated above, is that we use this "ignorance" and turn it to knowledge. How we do this should become more and more apparent as we go on with our study.

Study Suggestions

A variety of experiments with chance phenomena is recommended: games using coins, dice, cards, roulette wheels, and tables of random numbers. Such games, properly approached, can help one learn a great deal about fundamental notions of modern scientific research, statistics, probability, and, of course, randomness. Try the problems given in the suggestions below. Do not become discouraged by the seeming laboriousness of such exercises here and later on in the book. It is evidently necessary and, indeed, helpful occasionally to go through the routine involved in certain problems. After working the problems given, devise some of your own. If you can devise intelligent problems, you are probably well on your way to understanding.

1. From a table of random numbers draw 50 numbers, 0 through 9. (Use the random numbers of Appendix C, if you wish.) List them in columns of 10 each.

(a) Count the total number of odd numbers; count the total number of even numbers. What would you expect to get by chance? Compare the obtained totals with the expected totals.

(b) Count the total number of numbers 0, 1, 2, 3, 4. Similarly count 5, 6, 7, 8, 9. How many of the first group should you get? The second group? Compare what you do get with these chance expectations. Are you far off?

(c) Count the odd and even numbers in each group of 10. Count the two groups of numbers 0, 1, 2, 3, 4 and 5, 6, 7, 8, 9 in each group of 10. Do the totals differ greatly from chance expectations?

(d) Add the columns of the five groups of 10 numbers each. Divide each sum by 10. (Simply move the decimal point one place to the left.) What would you expect to get as the mean of each group if only chance were "operating"? What did you get? Add the five sums and divide by 50. Is this mean close to the chance expectation? [*Hint:* To obtain the chance expectation, remember the population limits.]

2. This is a class exercise and demonstration. Assign numbers arbitrarily to all the members of the class from 1 through N, N being the total number of members of the class. Take a table of random numbers and start with any page. Have a student wave a pencil in the air and blindly stab at the page of the table. Starting with the number the pencil indicates, choose n two-digit numbers between 1 and N (ignoring numbers greater than N and repeated numbers) by, say, going down columns (or any other specified way). n is the numerator of the fraction n/N, which is decided by the size of the class. If $N = 30$, for instance, let $n = 10$. Repeat the process twice on different pages of the random numbers table. You now have three equal groups (if N is not divisible by 3, drop one or two persons at random). Write the random numbers on the blackboard in the three groups. Have each class member call out his height in inches. Write these values on the blackboard separate from the numbers, but in the same three groups. Add the three sets of numbers in each of the sets on the blackboard, the random numbers and the heights. Calculate the means of the six sets of numbers. Also calculate the means of the total sets.

(a) How close are the means in each of the sets of numbers? How close are the means of the groups to the mean of the total group?

(b) Count the number of men and women in each of the groups. Are the sexes spread fairly evenly among the three groups?

(c) Discuss this demonstration. What do you think is its meaning for research?

3. In Chapter 6, it was suggested that the student generate 20 sets of 100 random numbers between 0 and 100 and calculate means and variances. If you did this, use the numbers and statistics in this exercise. If you did not, use the numbers and statistics of Appendix C at the end of the book.

(a) How close to the population mean are the means of the 20 samples? Are any of the means "deviant"? (You might judge this by calculating the standard deviation of the means and adding and subtracting two standard deviations to the total mean.)

(b) On the basis of (a), above, and your judgment, are the samples "representative"? What does "representative" mean?

(c) Pick out the third, fifth, and ninth group means. Suppose that 300 subjects had been assigned at random to the three groups and that these were scores on some measure of importance to a study you wanted to do. What can you conclude from the three means, do you think?

4. Most published studies in the behavioral sciences and education have not used random samples, especially random samples of large populations. Occasionally, however, studies based on random samples are done. One such study is:

J. BACHMAN and P. O'MALLEY, "Self-Esteem in Young Men: A Longitudinal Analysis of the Impact of Educational and Occupational Attainment," *Journal of Personality and Social Psychology,* 35 (1977), 365–380.

This study is worth careful reading, even though its level of methodological sophistication puts a number of its details beyond our present grasp. Try not to be discouraged by this sophistication. Get what you can out of it, especially its sampling of a large population of young men. Later in the book we will return to the interesting problem pursued. At that time, perhaps the methodology will no longer appear so formidable. (In studying research, it is sometimes helpful to read beyond our present capacity—provided we don't do too much of it!)

5. Random assignment of subjects to experimental groups is much more common than random sampling of subjects. A particularly good, even excellent, example of research in which subjects were assigned at random to two experimental groups, is:

S. THOMPSON, "Do Individualized Mastery and Traditional Instructional Systems Yield Different Course Effects in College Calculus?" *American Educational Research Journal,* 17 (1980), 361–375.

Again, don't be daunted by the methodological details of this study. Get what you can out of it. Note at this time how the subjects were classified into aptitude groups and then assigned at random to experimental treatments. We will also return to this study later. At that time, we should be able to understand its purpose and design and be intrigued by its carefully controlled experimental pursuit of a difficult substantive educational problem: the comparative merits of so-called individualized mastery instruction and conventional lecture-discussion-recitation instruction.

Special Note. In some of the above study suggestions and in those of Chapter 6, instructions were given to draw numbers from tables of random numbers or to generate sets of random numbers using a computer. If you have a microcomputer or have access to one, you may well prefer to generate the random numbers using the built-in random number generator (function) of the microcomputer. Study the computer manual to find out how to produce such numbers. It should be simple. On the widely available TRS-80, Apple, and IBM machines, for example, random numbers can be produced quite easily with a few instructions in BASIC, the language common to most microcomputers. How "good" are the random numbers generated? ("How good?" means "How random?") Since they are produced in line with the best contemporary theory and practice, they should be satisfactory, although they might not meet the exacting requirements of some experts. In my experience, they are quite satisfactory, and I recommend their use to teachers and students. (See, also, footnotes 10 and 15.)

PART FOUR

ANALYSIS, INTERPRETATION, STATISTICS, AND INFERENCE

Chapter 9

Principles of Analysis and Interpretation

THE RESEARCH analyst breaks down data into constituent parts to obtain answers to research questions and to test research hypotheses. The analysis of research data, however, does not in and of itself provide the answers to research questions. Interpretation of the data is necessary. To interpret is to explain, to find meaning. It is difficult or impossible to explain raw data; one must first analyze the data and then interpret the results of the analysis.[1]

Analysis means the categorizing, ordering, manipulating, and summarizing of data to obtain answers to research questions. The purpose of analysis is to reduce data to intelligible and interpretable form so that the relations of research problems can be studied and tested. A primary purpose of statistics, for example, is to manipulate and summarize numerical data and to compare the obtained results with chance expectations. A researcher hypothesizes that styles of leadership affect group-member participation in certain ways. He plans an experiment, executes the plan, and gathers data from his subjects. Then he must so order, break down, and manipulate the data that he can answer the question: How do styles of leadership affect group-member participation? It should be apparent that this view of analysis means that the categorizing, ordering, and summarizing of data should be

---

[1] "Data," as used in behavioral research, means research results from which inferences are drawn: usually numerical results, like scores of tests and statistics such as means, percentages, and correlation coefficients. The word is also used to stand for the results of mathematical and statistical analysis; we will soon study such analysis and its results. "Data" can be more, however: newspaper and magazine articles, biographical materials, diaries, and so on—indeed, verbal materials in general. In other words, "data" is a general term with several meanings. Think of research data, too, as the results of systematic observation and analysis used to make inferences and arrive at conclusions. Scientists make observations, assign symbols and numbers to the observations, manipulate the symbols and numbers to put them into interpretable form, and then, from these "data," make inferences about the relations among the variables of research problems. ("Data" is usually a plural noun, and we will so use it in this book. The singular is the seldom-used "datum.")

planned early in the research. The researcher should lay out analysis paradigms or models even when working on the problem and hypotheses. Only in this way can he see, even if only dimly, whether his data and its analysis can and will answer the research questions.

Interpretation takes the results of analysis, makes inferences pertinent to the research relations studied, and draws conclusions about these relations. The researcher who interprets research results searches them for their meaning and implications. This is done in two ways. One, the relations *within* the research study and its data are interpreted. This is the narrower and more frequent use of the term interpretation. Here interpretation and analysis are closely intertwined. One almost automatically interprets as one analyzes. That is, when one calculates, say, a coefficient of correlation, one almost immediately infers the existence of a relation.

Two, the broader meaning of research data is sought. One compares the results and the inferences drawn from the data to theory and to other research results. One seeks the meaning and implications of research results within the study results, and their congruence or lack of congruence with the results of other researchers. More important, one compares results with the demands and expectations of theory.

An example that may illustrate these ideas is research on perception of teacher characteristics.[2] On the basis of so-called directive-state and social perception theory,[3] it was predicted that perceptions or judgments of desirable characteristics of effective teachers will in part be determined by the attitudes toward education of the individuals making the judgments. Suppose, now, that we have measures of attitudes toward education and measures of the perceptions or judgments of the characteristics of effective teachers. We correlate the two sets of measures: the correlation is substantial. This is the analysis. The data have been broken down into the two sets of measure, which are then compared by means of a statistical procedure.

The result of the analysis, a correlation coefficient, now has to be interpreted. What is its meaning? Specifically, what is its meaning within the study? What is its broader meaning in the light of previous related research findings and interpretations? And what is its meaning as confirmation or lack of confirmation of theoretical prediction? If the ''internal'' prediction holds up, one then relates the finding to other research findings which may or may not be consistent with the present finding.

The correlation was substantial. Within the study, then, the correlation datum is consistent with theoretical expectation. Directive-state theory says that central states influence perceptions. Attitude is a central state; it should therefore influence perception. The specific inference is that attitudes toward education influence perceptions of the effective teacher. We measure both variables and correlate the measures. From the correlation coefficient we make an inferential leap to the hypothesis: since it is substantial, as predicted, the hypothesis is supported. We then attempt to relate the finding to other research and other theory.

FREQUENCIES AND CONTINUOUS MEASURES

Quantitative data come in two general forms: frequencies and continuous measures. Obviously, continuous measures are associated with continuous variables. (See discussion of

[2] F. Kerlinger and E. Pedhazur, ''Educational Attitudes and Perceptions of Desirable Traits of Teachers,'' *American Educational Research Journal*, 5 (1968), 543–560.

[3] *Directive-state theory* is a broad theory of perception that says in effect that our perceptions of cognitive objects are colored by our emotions, needs, wants, motives, attitudes, and values. These latter are, so to speak, directive states within the individual influencing his perceptions and judgments. F. Allport, *Theories of Perception and the Concept of Structure*. New York: Wiley, 1955, chaps. 13, 14, and 15.

continuous and categorical variables in Chapter 3.) Although both kinds of variables and measures can be subsumed under the same measurement frame of reference, in practice it is necessary to distinguish them.

Frequencies are the numbers of objects in sets and subsets. Let U be the universal set with N objects. Then N is the *number* of objects in U. Let U be partitioned into $A_1, A_2, \ldots, A_k$. Let $n_1, n_2, \ldots, n_k$ be the numbers of objects in $A_1, A_2, \ldots, A_k$. Then $n_1, n_2, \ldots, n_k$ are called frequencies.

It is helpful to look at this as a function. Let X be any set of objects with members $\{x_1, x_2, \ldots, x_n\}$. We wish to measure an attribute of the members of the set; call it M. Let $Y = \{0,1\}$. Let the measurement be described as a function:

$$f = \{(x,y); \ x \text{ is a member of the set } X, \text{ and } y \text{ is either}$$
$$1 \text{ or } 0 \text{ depending on } x\text{'s possessing or not possessing } M\}$$

This is read: f, a function, or rule of correspondence, equals the set of ordered pairs (x,y) such that x is a member of X, y is 1 or 0, and so on. If x possesses M (determined in some empirical fashion), then assign a 1. If x does not possess M, assign a 0. To find the frequency of objects with characteristic M, count the number of objects that have been assigned 1.

With continuous measures, the basic idea is the same. Only the rule of correspondence, f, and the numerals assigned to objects change. The rule of correspondence is more elaborate and the numerals are generally 0, 1, 2, . . . and fractions of these numerals. In other words, we write a measurement equation:

$$f = \{(x,y); \ x \text{ is an object, and } y = \text{any numeral}\}$$

which is the generalized form of the function.[4] This digression is important, because it helps us to see the basic similarity of frequency analysis and continuous measure analysis.

RULES OF CATEGORIZATION

The first step in any analysis is categorization. It was said earlier (Chapter 4) that partitioning is the foundation of analysis. We will now see why. Categorization is merely another word for partitioning—that is, a *category* is a partition or a subpartition. If a set of objects is categorized in some way, it is partitioned according to some rule. The rule tells us, in effect, how to assign set objects to partitions and subpartitions. If this is so, then the rules of partitioning we studied earlier apply to problems of categorization. We need only explain the rules, relate them to the basic purposes of analysis, and put them to work in practical analytic situations.

Five rules of categorization are given below. Two of them, (2) and (3), are the exhaustiveness and disjointness rules discussed in Chapter 4. Two others, (4) and (5), can actually be deduced from the fundamental rules, (2) and (3). Nevertheless, we list them as separate rules for practical reasons.

1. Categories are set up according to the research problem and purpose.
2. The categories are exhaustive.
3. The categories are mutually exclusive and independent.
4. Each category (variable) is derived from one classification principle.
5. Any categorization scheme must be on one level of discourse.

Rule 1 is the most important. If categorizations are not set up according to the de-

---

[4]This equation and the ideas behind it will be explained in detail in Chapter 25.

mands of the research problem, then there can be no adequate answers to the research questions. We constantly ask: Does my analysis paradigm conform to the research problem? Suppose the research question asked was: What is the influence of race on the self-esteem of children? It has been said that conditions of life for black Americans are such as to produce low self-esteem in black children. Is this so? Whatever data are gathered and analyses done must bear on the research problem, which in this case is the relation between race and self-esteem.

The simplest kind of analysis is frequency analysis. Rosenberg and Simmons, in their study of race and self-esteem,[5] randomly sampled a large number of white and black children, and, among other things, measured their self-esteem. On the basis of these measures, they divided their sample into the categories low, medium, and high self-esteem. The paradigm for the frequency analysis looked like this:

Self-Esteem	Black	White
Low Medium High	Frequencies	

Since Rosenberg and Simmons had continuous measures of self-esteem, they might have used this paradigm:

Black	White
Self-Esteem Measures	

It is obvious that both paradigms bear directly on the problem: it is possible in both to test the relation between race and self-esteem, albeit in different ways. The authors chose the first method—and found, contrary to common expectation, that black children's self-esteem was higher, not lower, than that of white children. The second paradigm would undoubtedly have led to the same conclusion. The point is that an analytical paradigm is, in effect, another way to state a problem, a hypothesis, a relation. That one paradigm uses frequencies while the other uses continuous measures in no way alters the relation tested. In other words, both modes of analysis are logically similar: they both test the same proposition. They differ in the data they use, in statistical tests, and in sensitivity and power.

There are several things a researcher might do that would be irrelevant to the problem. If he included one, two, or three variables in the study with no theoretical or practical reason for doing so, then the analytic paradigm would be at least partly irrelevant to the problem. Suppose a researcher, in a study of the hypothesis that religious education enhances the moral character of children, collected achievement test data from public and parochial school children. This would probably have no bearing on the problem, since the researcher is interested in the moral differences and not the achievement differences between the two types of schools and, of course, between religious instruction and no religious instruction. He might bring other variables into the picture that have little or no bearing on the problem, for example, differences in teacher experience and training or teacher-pupil ratios. If, on the other hand, he thought that certain variables, like sex, family religious background, and perhaps personality variables, might interact with reli-

[5]M. Rosenberg and R. Simmons, *Black and White Self-Esteem: The Urban Child*. Washington, D.C.: American Sociological Association, 1971.

gious instruction to produce differences, then he might be justified in building such variables into the research problem and consequently into the analytic paradigm.[6]

Rule 2, on exhaustiveness, means that all subjects, all objects of U, must be used up. All individuals in the universe must be capable of being assigned to the cells of the analytic paradigm. With the example just considered, each child either goes to parochial school or to public school. If, somehow, the sampling had included children who attend private schools, then the rule would be violated because there would be a number of children who could not be fitted into the implied paradigm of the problem. (What would a frequency analysis paradigm look like? Conceive the dependent variable as honesty.) If, however, the research problem called for private school pupils, then the paradigm would have to be changed by adding the rubric Private to the rubrics Parochial and Public.

The exhaustiveness criterion is not always easy to satisfy. With some categorical variables, there is no problem. If sex is one of the variables, any individual has to be male or female. Suppose, however, that a variable under study were religious preference and we set up, in a paradigm, Protestant-Catholic-Jew. Now suppose some subjects were atheists or Buddhists. Clearly the categorization scheme violates the exhaustiveness rule: some subjects would have no cells to which to be assigned. Depending on numbers of cases and the research problem, we might add another rubric, Others, to which we assign subjects who are not Protestants, Catholics, or Jews. Another solution, especially when the number of Others is small, is to drop these subjects from the study. Still another solution is to put these other subjects, if it is possible to do so, under an already existing rubric. Other variables where this problem is encountered are political preference, social class, types of education, and so on.

Rule 3 is one that often causes research workers concern. To demand that the categories be mutually exclusive means, as we learned earlier, that each object of U, each research subject (actually the measure assigned to each subject), must be assigned to one cell and one cell only of an analytic paradigm. This is a function of operational definition. Definitions of variables must be clear and unambiguous so that it is unlikely that any subject can be assigned to more than one cell. If religious preference is the variable being defined, then the definition of membership in the subsets Protestant, Catholic, and Jew must be clear and unambiguous. It may be "registered membership in a church." It may be "born in the church." It may simply be the subject's identification of himself as a Protestant, a Catholic, or a Jew. Whatever the definition, it must enable the investigator to assign any subject to one and only one of the three cells.

The independence part of Rule 3 is often difficult to satisfy, especially with continuous measures—and sometimes with frequencies. *Independence* means that the assignment of one object to a cell in no way affects the assignment of any other object to that cell or to any other cell. Random assignment from an infinite or very large universe, of course, satisfies the rule. Without random assignment, however, we run into problems. When assigning objects to cells on the basis of the object's possession of certain characteristics, the assignment of an object now may affect the assignment of another object later.

Rule 4, that each category (variable) be derived from one classificatory principle, is sometimes violated by the neophyte. If one has a firm grasp of partitioning, this error is easily avoided. The rule means that, in setting up an analytic design, each variable has to be treated separately, because each variable is a separate dimension. One does not put two

---

[6]In the next chapter, elementary consideration will be given to frequency analysis with more than one independent variable. In later chapters there will be much more detailed consideration of both frequency and continuous measure analysis with several independent variables. The reader should not now be concerned with complete understanding of examples like those given above. They will be clarified later.

or more variables in one category or one dimension. If one were studying, for instance, the relations between social class, sex, and drug addiction, one would not put social class and sex on one dimension.

If one were studying the relations among race, sex, and college admissions, as Walster, Cleary, and Clifford did,[7] one would not include race and sex on one dimension. Such an error might look like this:

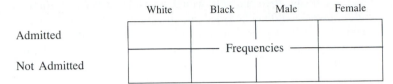

It is clear that this paradigm violates the rule: it has one category derived from two variables. Each variable must have its own category. A correct paradigm might look like this:

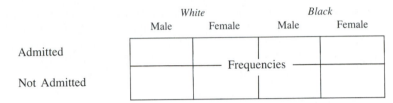

Rule 5 is the hardest to explain because the term "level of discourse" is hard to define. It was defined in an earlier chapter as a set that contains all the objects that enter into a discussion. If we use the expression "universe of discourse," we tie the idea to set ideas. When talking about U_1, do not bring in U_2 without good reason and without making it clear that you are doing so.[8]

In research analysis, it is usually the measures of the dependent variable that are analyzed. Take the problem of the relations among race, sex, and college admission. Race and sex are the independent variables; college admission is the dependent variable. The objects of analysis are the college admission measures. The independent variables and their categories are actually used to structure the dependent variable analysis. The universe of discourse, U, is the set of dependent variable measures. The independent variables can be conceived as the partitioning principles that are used to break down or partition the dependent variable measures. If, suddenly, we switch to another kind of dependent variable measure, then we may have switched levels or universes of discourse.

KINDS OF STATISTICAL ANALYSIS

There are many kinds of statistical analysis and presentation that cannot be discussed in detail in this book. Later discussions of certain more advanced forms of statistical analysis

[7] E. Walster, T. Cleary, and M. Clifford, "The Effect of Race and Sex on College Admission," *Journal of Educational Sociology,* 44 (1971), 237–244. The above examples were only suggested by this report. The actual research, which we will examine later, was both more ingenious and more complex. Another independent variable, ability (of student applicants) was included, all three independent variables were experimental or manipulated variables, and the dependent variable, admission, was a continuous variable.

[8] For a discussion of levels of discourse and relevance, see F. Kerlinger, "Research in Education." In R. Ebel, V. Noll, and R. Bauer, eds., *Encyclopedia of Educational Research,* 4th ed. New York: Macmillan, 1969, pp. 1127–1144, especially p. 1131.

have as their purpose basic understanding of statistics and statistical inference and the relation of statistics and statistical inference to research. In this section, the major forms of statistical analysis are discussed briefly to give the reader an overview of the subject; they are discussed, however, only in relation to research. It is assumed that the reader has already studied the simpler descriptive statistics. Those who have not can find good discussions in elementary textbooks.[9]

Frequency Distributions

Although frequency distributions are used primarily for descriptive purposes, they can be used for other research purposes. For example, one can test whether two or more distributions are sufficiently similar to warrant merging them. Suppose one were studying the verbal learning of boys and girls in the sixth grade. After obtaining large numbers of verbal learning scores, one can compare and test the differences between the boy and girl distributions.[10] If the test shows the distributions to be the same—and other criteria are satisfied—they can perhaps be combined for other analysis.

Observed distributions can also be compared to theoretical distributions. The best-known such comparison is with the so-called normal distribution. It may be important to know that obtained distributions are normal in form, or, if not normal, depart from normality in certain specifiable ways. Such analysis can be useful in other theoretical and applied work and research. In theoretical study of abilities it is important to know whether such abilities are in fact distributed normally. Since a number of human characteristics have been found to be normally distributed,[11] researchers can ask significant questions about "new" characteristics being investigated.

Applied educational research can profit from careful study of distributions of intelligence, aptitude, and achievement scores. Is it conceivable that an innovative learning program can change the distributions of the achievement scores, say, of third and fourth graders? Can it be that massive early education programs can change the shape of distributions, as well as the general levels of scores?

Allport's study of social conformity many years ago showed that even a complex behavioral phenomenon like conformity can be profitably studied using distribution analysis.[12] Allport was able to show that a number of social behaviors—stopping for red lights, parking violations, religious observances, and so on—were distributed in the form of a J curve, with most people conforming, but with predictable smaller numbers not conforming in different degrees.

Distributions have probably been too little used in the behavioral sciences and education. The study of relations and the testing of hypotheses are almost automatically associated with correlations and comparisons of averages. The use of distributions is considered less often. Some research problems, however, can be solved better by using distribution analysis. Studies of pathology and other unusual conditions are perhaps best approached through a combination of distribution analysis and probabilistic notions.

[9] For example, A. Edwards, *Statistical Analysis,* 3d ed. New York: Holt, Rinehart and Winston, 1969; D. Freedman, R. Pisani, and R. Purves, *Statistics.* New York: Norton, 1978.

[10] See W. Hays, *Statistics,* 3d ed. New York: Holt, Rinehart and Winston, 1981, pp. 576ff.

[11] A. Anastasi, *Individual Differences,* 3d ed. New York: Macmillan, 1958, pp. 26ff. The student of research in education, psychology, and sociology should study Anastasi's outstanding contribution to our understanding of individual differences. Her book also contains many examples of distributions of empirical data.

[12] F. Allport, "The J-Curve Hypothesis of Conforming Behavior." In T. Newcomb and E. Hartley, eds., *Readings in Social Psychology.* New York: Holt, Rinehart and Winston, 1947, pp. 55–67.

Graphs and Graphing

One of the most powerful tools of analysis is the graph. A *graph* is a two-dimensional representation of a relation or relations. It exhibits pictorially sets of ordered pairs in a way no other method can. If a relation exists in a set of data, a graph will not only clearly show it; it will show its nature: positive, negative, linear, quadratic, and so on. While graphs have been used a good deal in the behavioral sciences, they, like distributions, probably have not been used enough. To be sure, there are objective ways of epitomizing and testing relations, such as correlation coefficients, comparison of means, and other statistical methods, but none of these so vividly and uniquely describes a relation as a graph.[13]

Look back at the graphs in Chapter 5 (Figures 5.1, 5.4, 5.5, and 5.6). Note how they convey the nature of the relations. Later we will use graphs in a more interesting way to show the nature of rather complex relations among variables. To give the student just a taste of the richness and interest of such analysis, we anticipate later discussion; in fact, we will try to teach a complex idea through graphs.

The three graphs of Figure 9.1 show three hypothetical relations between age, as an independent variable, and verbal achievement (VA), as dependent variable, of middle-class children (A), and working-class children (B). One can call these growth graphs. The horizontal axis is the abscissa; it is used to indicate the independent variable, or X. The vertical axis is the ordinate; it is used to indicate the dependent variable, or Y. Graph (a) shows the same positive relation between age and VA with both A and B samples. It also shows that the A children exceed the B children. Graph (b), however, shows that both relations are positive, but that as time goes on the A children's achievement increases more than the B children's achievement. This seems to be the sort of phenomenon that Coleman et al. found when comparing the verbal achievement of majority- and minority-group children in grades 3, 6, 9, and 12.[14] Graph (c) is more complex. It shows that the A children were superior to the B children at an early age and remained the same to a later

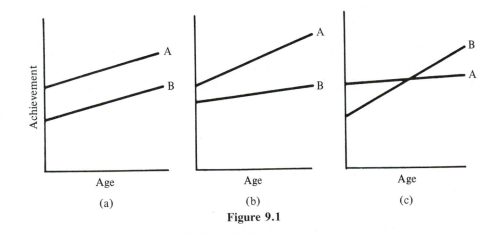

Figure 9.1

[13] Drawing graphs is today greatly expedited by the availability of computers and computer programs with graphic capabilities. For instance, some computer programs routinely incorporate the possibility of printing so-called scatter plots of data. The labor of drawing graphs—except in special circumstances—has virtually been eliminated. Interpretation, of course, remains a problem.

[14] J. Coleman et al., *Equality of Educational Opportunity*. Washington, D.C.: U.S. Government Printing Office, 1966. See, especially, pp. 20ff. and 220ff.

age, but the B children, who started lower, advanced and continued to advance over time until they exceeded the A children. This sort of relation is unlikely with verbal achievement, but it can occur with other variables.

The phenomenon shown in graphs (b) and (c) is known as *interaction*. Briefly, it means that two (or more) variables interact in their "effect" on a dependent variable. In this case, age and group status interact in their relation to verbal achievement. Expressed differently, interaction means that the relation of an independent variable to a dependent variable is different in different groups, as in this case, or at different levels of another independent variable. It will be explained in detail and more accurately when we study analysis of variance and multiple regression analysis.

While means are one of the best ways to report complex data, complete reliance on them can be unfortunate. Most cases of significant mean differences between groups are also accompanied by considerable overlap of the distributions. Clear examples are given by Anastasi, who points out the necessity of paying attention to overlapping and gives examples and graphs of sex distribution differences, among others.[15] In short, students of research are advised to get into the habit, from the beginning of their study, of paying attention to and understanding distributions of variables and to graphing relations of variables.

Measures of Central Tendency and Variability

There is little doubt that measures of central tendency and variability are the most important tools of behavioral data analysis. Since much of this book will be preoccupied with such measures—indeed, a whole section is called "The Analysis of Variance"—we need only characterize averages and variances. The three main averages, or measures of central tendency, used in research, the mean, median, and mode, are epitomes of the sets of measures from which they are calculated. Sets of measures are too many and too complex to grasp and understand readily. They are "represented" or epitomized by measures of central tendency. They tell what sets of measures "are like" on the average. But they are also compared to test relations. Moreover, individual scores can be usefully compared to them to assess the status of the individual. We say, for instance, that individual A's score is such-and-such a distance above the mean.

While the mean is the most used average in research, and while it has desirable properties that justify its preeminent position, the median, the midmost measure of a set of measures, and the mode, the most frequent measure, can sometimes be useful in research. For instance, the median, in addition to being an important descriptive measure, can be used in tests of statistical significance where the mean is inappropriate.[16] The mode is used mostly for descriptive purposes, but it can be useful in research for studying characteristics of populations and relations. Suppose that a mathematical aptitude test was given to all incoming freshmen in a college that has just initiated open admissions, and that the distribution of scores was bimodal. Suppose, further, that only a mean was calculated, compared to means of previous years, and found to be considerably lower. The simple conclusion that the average mathematical aptitude of incoming freshmen was considerably lower than in previous years conceals the fact that because of the open admissions policy many freshmen were admitted who had deficient backgrounds in mathematics. While this

---

[15] Anastasi, *op. cit.*, pp. 453ff.

[16] Consult: J. Bradley, *Distribution-Free Statistical Tests*. Englewood Cliffs, N.J.: Prentice-Hall, 1968, pp. 103–105; 170–174; 203–209; 237–239. Types of means and other measures of central tendency are exceptionally well discussed in: M. Tate, *Statistics in Education*. New York: Macmillan, 1955, chap. II. Tate also gives a number of good examples of distributions and graphs of various kinds. Though old, this is a valuable book.

is an obvious example, deliberately chosen because it *is* obvious, it should be noted that obscuring important sources of differences can be more subtle. It often pays off in research, in other words, to calculate medians and modes as well as means.[17]

The principal measures of variability are the variance and the standard deviation. They have already been discussed and will be discussed further in later chapters. We therefore forego discussion of them here, except to say that research reports should always include variability measures. Means should almost never be reported without standard deviations (and N's, the sizes of samples), because adequate interpretation of research by readers is virtually impossible without variability indices. Another measure of variability that has in recent years become more important is the *range,* the difference between the highest and lowest measures of a set of measures. It has become possible, especially with small samples (with N about 20 or 15 or less), to use the range in tests of statistical significance.

Measures of Relations

There are many useful measures of relations: the product-moment coefficient of correlation (r), the rank-order coefficient of correlation (*rho*), the distance measure (D), the coefficient of contingency (C), the coefficient of multiple correlation (R), and so on. Almost all coefficients of relation, no matter how different in derivation, appearance, calculation, and use, do essentially the same thing: express the extent to which the pairs of sets of ordered pairs vary concomitantly. In effect, they tell the researcher the magnitude and (usually) the direction of the relation. Some of them vary in value from -1.00 through 0 to $+1.00$, -1.00 and 1.00 indicating perfect negative and positive association, respectively, and 0 indicating no discernible relation.

Measures of relations are comparatively direct indices of relations in the sense that from them one has some direct idea of the degree of the covarying of the variables. The square of the product-moment coefficient of correlation, for example, is a direct estimate of the amount of the variance shared by the variables. One can say, at least roughly, how high or low the relation is. This is in contrast to measures of statistical significance which say, in effect, that a relation is or is not "significant" at some specified level of significance. Ideally, any analysis of research data should include both kinds of indices, measures of the significance of a relation and measures of the magnitude of the relation.

Measures of relations, but especially product-moment coefficients of correlation, are unusual in that they themselves are subject to extensive and elaborate forms of analysis, mainly multiple regression analysis and factor analysis (see below). They are thus extremely useful and powerful tools of the researcher.

Analysis of Differences

The analysis of differences, particularly the analysis of differences between means, occupies a rather large part of statistical analysis and inference. It is important to note two things about differences analysis. One, it is by no means confined to the differences between measures of central tendency. Almost any kind of difference—between frequencies, proportions, percentages, ranges, correlations, and variances—can be so analyzed. Take variances. Suppose an educational psychologist wants to know if a certain form of instruction has the effect of making pupils more heterogeneous in concept learning. The difference between the variances of groups taught by different methods can be easily

---

[17] See *ibid.*, pp. 79ff.

tested. Or one might want to know whether groups set up to be homogeneous are homogeneous on variables other than those used to form the groups.[18]

The second point is more important. All analysis of differences is really for the purpose of studying relations. Suppose one believes that changing art preferences toward greater complexity will transfer to music preferences and sets up three experimental groups, one of which is given the greater complexity manipulation.[19] One finds the predicted differences between the means of the three groups on music preferences, with the one given the complexity manipulation the highest. It is not really these differences that interest us, however. It is the relation of the study; that between the complexity modification on art preference and the modification toward greater music complexity preference. Differences between means, then, really reflect the relation between the independent variable and the dependent variable. If there are no significant differences among means, the correlation between independent variable and dependent variable is zero. And, conversely, the greater the differences the higher the correlation, other things equal.

Suppose an experiment to study the effect of random reinforcement of opinion utterance on rate of opinion utterance has been done and the experimental group, which received random reinforcement, had a mean of 6 utterances in a specified period of time, and the control group, which received a regular rate of reinforcement, had a mean of 4 utterances.[20] The difference is statistically significant, and we conclude from the significant difference that there is a relation between reinforcement and opinion utterance rate. In earlier chapters, relations between measured variables were plotted to show the nature of the relations. It is possible, too, to graph the present relation between the experimental (manipulated) independent variable and the measured dependent variable. This has been done in Figure 9.2, where the means have been plotted as indicated. While the plotting is more or less arbitrary—for instance, there are no real baseline units for the independent variable—the similarity to the earlier graphs is apparent and the basic idea of a relation is clear.

If the reader will always keep in mind that relations are sets of ordered pairs, the conceptual similarity of Figure 9.2 to earlier graphs will be evident. In the earlier graphs, each member of each pair was a score. In Figure 9.2, an ordered pair consists of an experimental treatment and a score. If we assign 1 to the experimental group and 0 to the control group, two ordered pairs might be: (1, 6), (0, 4).

Analysis of Variance and Related Methods

A sizable part of this book will be devoted to analysis of variance and related methods. So there is little need to say much here. The reader need only put this important method of analysis in perspective. Analysis of variance is what its name implies—and more: a method of identifying, breaking down, and testing for statistical significance variances that come from different sources of variation. That is, a dependent variable has a total amount of variance, some of which is due to the experimental treatment, some to error,

---

[18] A quick, easy, and effective test of variances is given in E. Pearson and H. Hartley, eds., *Biometrika Tables for Statisticians,* vol. I. Cambridge: University of Cambridge Press, 1954, pp. 60–61 and 179. This well-known volume of statistical tables and its examples and explanations are most useful to researchers. Another useful and well-known volume of statistical tables is: R. Fisher and F. Yates, eds., *Statistical Tables for Biological, Agricultural and Medical Research.* New York: Hafner, 1963.

[19] V. Renner, "Effects of Modification of Cognitive Style on Creative Behavior," *Journal of Personality and Social Psychology,* 14 (1970), 257–262.

[20] The idea for this problem comes from: W. Verplanck, "The Control of the Content of Conversation: Reinforcement of Statements of Opinion." *Journal of Abnormal and Social Psychology,* 51 (1955), 668–676.

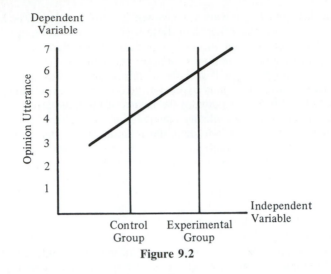

Figure 9.2

and some to other causes. Analysis of variance's job is to work with these different variances and sources of variance. Strictly speaking, analysis of variance is more appropriate for experimental than for nonexperimental data, even though its inventor, Fisher, used it with both kinds.[21] We will consider it, then, a method for the analysis of data yielded by experiments in which randomization and manipulation of at least one independent variable have been used.

There is probably no better way to study research design than through an analysis of variance approach. Those proficient with the approach almost automatically think of alternative analysis of variance models when confronted with new research problems. Suppose an experienced social psychological investigator is asked to assess the differential effects of three kinds of group cohesiveness on learning. He will immediately think of a simple one-way analysis of variance, which will look like the paradigm on the left [marked (a)] of Figure 9.3. If he also thinks that cohesiveness may affect children of higher intelligence differently than children of lower intelligence, then the paradigm will look like that on the right (b).[22] Clearly, analysis of variance is an important method of studying differences.

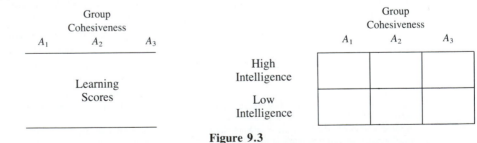

Figure 9.3

[21] R. Fisher, *Statistical Methods for Research Workers*, 11th ed. New York: Hafner, 1950, pp. 227ff.

[22] The idea for this problem came from: A. Lott and B. Lott, "Group Cohesiveness and Individual Learning," *Journal of Educational Psychology*, 57 (1966), 61–73.

Profile Analysis

Profile analysis is basically the assessment of the similarities of the profiles of individuals or groups. A *profile* is a set of different measures of an individual or group, each of which is expressed in the same unit of measure. An individual's scores on a set of different tests constitute a profile, if all scores have been converted to a common measure system, like percentiles, ranks, and standard scores. Profiles have been used mostly for diagnostic purposes—for instance, the profiles of scores from test batteries are used to assess and advise high school pupils. But profile analysis is becoming increasingly important in psychological and sociological research, as we will see later when we study, among other things, *Q* methodology.

Profile analysis has special problems that require researchers' careful consideration. Similarity, for example, is not a general characteristic of persons; it is similarity only of specified characteristics or complexes of characteristics.[23] Another difficulty lies in what information one is willing to sacrifice in calculating indices of profile similarity. When one uses the product-moment coefficient of correlation—which is a profile measure—one loses level; that is, differences between means are sacrificed. This is loss of *elevation*. Product-moment *r*'s take only *shape* into account. Further, *scatter*—differences in variability of profiles—is lost in the calculation of certain other kinds of profile measures. In short, information can be and is lost. The student will find excellent help and guidance with profile analysis in Nunnally's book on psychometrics, though the treatment is not elementary.[24]

Multivariate Analysis

Perhaps the most important forms of statistical analysis, especially at the present stage of development of the behavioral sciences, are multivariate analysis and factor analysis. *Multivariate analysis* is a general term used to categorize a family of analytic methods whose chief characteristic is the simultaneous analysis of *k* independent variables and *m* dependent variables.[25] If an analysis includes, for instance, four independent variables and two dependent variables, handled simultaneously, it is a multivariate analysis.

It can be argued that, of all methods of analysis, multivariate methods are the most powerful and appropriate for scientific behavioral research. The argument to support this statement is long and involved and would sidetrack us from our subject. Basically, it rests on the idea that behavioral problems are almost all multivariate in nature and cannot be solved with a bivariate (two-variable) approach—that is, an approach that considers only one independent and one dependent variable at a time. This has become strikingly clear in much educational research where, for instance, the determinants of learning and achievement are complex: intelligence, motivation, social class, instruction, school and class atmosphere and organization, and so on. Evidently variables like these work with each other, sometimes against each other, mostly in unknown ways, to affect learning and

---

[23] L. Cronbach and G. Gleser, "Assessing Similarity Between Profiles," *Psychological Bulletin,* 50 (1953), 456–473 (p. 457).

[24] J. Nunnally, *Psychometric Theory,* 2d ed. New York: McGraw-Hill, 1978, chap. 12.

[25] In this book we will not be excessively concerned about the terminology used with multivariate analysis. To some, multivariate analysis includes factor analysis and other forms of analysis, like multiple regression analysis. "Multivariate" to these individuals means more than one independent variable *or* more than one dependent variable, *or* both. Others in the field use "multivariate analysis" only for the case of *both* multiple independent and multiple dependent variables.

achievement. In other words, to account for the complex psychological and sociological phenomena of education requires design and analytic tools that are capable of handling the complexity, which manifests itself above all in multiplicity of independent and dependent variables. A similar argument can be given for psychological and sociological research.

This argument and the reality behind it impose a heavy burden on those individuals teaching and learning research approaches and methods. It is unrealistic, even wrong, to study and learn only an approach that is basically bivariate in conception. Multivariate methods, however, are like the behavioral reality they try to reflect: complex and difficult to understand. The pedagogical necessity, as far as this book is concerned, is to try to convey the fundamentals of research thinking, design, methods, and analysis mainly through a modified bivariate approach, to extend this approach as much as possible to multivariate conceptions and methods, and to hope that the student will pursue matters further after having gotten an adequate foundation.

Multiple regression, probably the single most useful form of multivariate methods, analyzes the common and separate influences of two or more independent variables on a dependent variable.[26] We gave an educational example above. The method is used similarly in other kinds of behavioral research. Cutright, as we saw in an earlier chapter, used multiple regression to study the effects of communication, urbanization, education, and agriculture on political development.[27] Lave and Seskin used it to study the influences of air pollution and social class on human mortality.[28] The method has been used in hundreds of studies probably because of its flexibility, power, and general applicability to many different kinds of research problems. (It also has limitations!) We can hardly ignore it, then, in this book. Fortunately, it is not too difficult to understand and to learn to use—given sufficient desire to do so.

Canonical correlation is a logical extension of multiple regression. Indeed, it *is* a multiple regression method. It adds more than one dependent variable to the multiple regression model. In other words, it handles the relations between sets of independent variables and sets of dependent variables. As such, it is a theoretically powerful method of analysis. It has limitations, however, that can restrict its usefulness: in the interpretation of the results it yields and in its limited ability to test theoretical models.

Discriminant analysis is also closely related to multiple regression. Its name indicates its purpose: to discriminate groups from one another on the basis of sets of measures. It is also useful in assigning individuals to groups on the basis of their scores on tests. While this explanation is not adequate, it is sufficient for now.

It is difficult at this stage to characterize, even at a superficial level, the technique known as multivariate analysis of variance, because we have not yet studied analysis of variance. We therefore postpone its discussion.

Factor analysis is essentially different in kind and purpose from the other multivariate methods. Its fundamental purpose is to help the researcher discover and identify the unities or dimensions, called *factors,* behind many measures. We now know, for example, that behind many measures of ability and intelligence lie fewer general dimensions or factors. Verbal aptitude and mathematical aptitude are two of the best known such factors. In measuring social attitudes, religious, economic, and educational factors have been found.

[26] This statement has limitations, especially about the separate contributions of independent variables, that will be discussed in Chapter 33.

[27] P. Cutright, "National Political Development: Measurement and Analysis," *American Sociological Review,* 27 (1963), 229–245.

[28] L. Lave and E. Seskin, "Air Pollution and Human Health," *Science,* 169 (1970), 723–733.

The above-mentioned multivariate methods are ''standard'' in the sense that they are usually what is meant by ''multivariate methods.'' There are, however, other multivariate methods of equal, even greater, importance. As I said in the Preface, it is not possible in a book of this kind to give adequate and correct technical explanations of all multivariate methods. While enormously important, for example, analysis of covariance structures and log-linear models analysis are far too complex and difficult to describe and explain adequately. Similarly, multidimensional scaling and path analysis cannot be adequately presented. What to do, then? Some of these approaches and procedures are so powerful and important—indeed, they are revolutionizing behavioral research—that a book that ignores them will be sadly deficient. The solution of the problem was also outlined in the Preface. It is worth repeating. The most common and accessible approaches—analysis of variance, multiple regression, and factor analysis—will be presented in sufficient technical detail that a motivated and diligent student can at least use them and interpret their results, with the aid, of course, of desk calculators or computers (especially programmable calculators and microcomputers). Certain other highly complex methods like analysis of covariance structures and log-linear models will be described and explained ''conceptually.'' That is, their purpose and rationale will be explained, with generous citation and description of fictitious and actual research use. Such an approach will be used in later chapters with the following three methodologies.

Path analysis is a graphic method of studying the presumed direct and indirect influences of independent variables on each other and on dependent variables. It is a method, in other words, of portraying and testing ''theories.''[29] Perhaps its main virtue is that it requires researchers to make explicit the theoretical framework of research problems. To accomplish its goals, path analysis uses so-called causal or path diagrams and regression analysis. Readers can assuage a little of their curiosity by turning to Chapter 34 and examining one or two of the path analytic examples given there. It is highly likely that path analysis will in the future be used more as an adjunct method to other more general methods rather than as a self-contained and complete analytic method. For instance, path analysis can be and should be used as an integral part of analysis of covariance structures, as we will see in a later chapter.

Analysis of covariance structures—or causal modeling, or structural equation models—is the ultimate approach to the analysis of complex data structures. It means, essentially, the analysis of the varying together of variables that are in a structure dictated by theory. For example, we can test the adequacy of theories of intelligence mentioned in earlier chapters by fitting the theories into the analysis of covariance structure framework and then testing how well they account for actual intelligence test data. The method—or rather, methodology—is an ingenious mathematical and statistical synthesis of factor analysis, multiple regression, path analysis, and psychological measurement into a single comprehensive system that can express and test complex theoretical formulations of research problems.

Log-linear models is the ultimate multivariate method—or again, methodology—of analyzing frequency data. The above-mentioned multivariate methods are for the most part geared to analyzing data obtained from continuous measures: test scores, attitude and personality scale measures, measures of ecological variables, and the like. As we will see in the next chapter, however, behavioral research data are often in the form of frequen-

---

[29] F. Kerlinger and E. Pedhazur, *Multiple Regression in Behavioral Research*. New York: Holt, Rinehart and Winston, 1973, pp. 305ff.; E. Pedhazur, *Multiple Regression in Behavioral Research: Explanation and Prediction,* 2d ed. New York: Holt, Rinehart and Winston, 1982, chap 15.

cies, mostly counts of individuals, for example, numbers of males and females, blacks and whites, teachers and non-teachers, middle- and working-class individuals, Catholics, Protestants, and Jews. Log-linear analysis makes it possible to study complex combinations of such nominal variables and, like analysis of covariance structures, to test theories of the relations and influences of such variables on each other. We will briefly characterize the methodology in the next chapter, though space limitations and technical difficulties will force us to limit the discussion to the basic ideas involved. We will at least see, however, that, like analysis of covariance structures, it is one of the most powerful and important methodological breakthroughs of the century.

INDICES

Index can be defined in two related ways. One, an index is an observable phenomenon that is substituted for a less observable phenomenon. A thermometer, for example, gives readings of numbers that stand for degrees of temperature. The numerals on a speedometer dial indicate the speed of a vehicle. Test scores indicate achievement levels, verbal aptitudes, degrees of anxiety, and so on.

A definition perhaps more useful to the researcher is: An index is a number that is a composite of two or more numbers. An investigator makes a series of observations, for example, and derives some single number from the measures of the observations to summarize the observations, to express them succinctly. By this definition, all sums and averages are indices: they include in a single measure more than one measure. But the definition also includes the idea of indices as composites of different measures. Coefficients of correlation are such indices. They combine different measures in a single measure or index.

There are indices of social-class status. For example, one can combine income, occupation, and place of residence to obtain a rather good index of social class. An index of cohesiveness can be obtained by asking members of a group whether they would like to stay in the group. Their responses can be combined in a single number.

Indices are most important in research. They simplify comparisons. Indeed, they enable research workers to make comparisons that otherwise cannot be made or that can be made only with considerable difficulty. Raw data are usually much too complex to be grasped and used in mathematical and statistical manipulations. They must be reduced to manageable form. The percentage is a good example. Percentages transform raw numbers into comparable form.

Indices generally take the form of quotients: one number is divided by another number. The most useful such indices range between 0 and 1.00 or between -1.00 through 0 to $+1.00$. This makes them independent of numbers of cases and aids comparison from sample to sample and study to study. (They are generally expressed in decimal form.) There are two forms of quotients: ratios and proportions. A third form, the percentage, is a variation of the proportion.

A *ratio* is a composite of two numbers that relates one number to the other in fractional or decimal form. Any fraction, any quotient, is a ratio. Either or both the numerator and denominator of a ratio can themselves be ratios. The chief purpose and utility of a ratio is relational: it permits the comparison of numbers. In order to do this, it is perhaps best to put the larger of the two numbers of the quotient in the denominator. This of course satisfies the condition mentioned above of having the ratio values range between 0 and 1.00, or between -1.00 through 0 to $+1.00$. This is not absolutely necessary, however.

If, for example, we wished to compare the ratio of male to female high school graduates to the ratio of male and female graduates of junior high school over several years, the ratio will sometimes be less than 1.00 and sometimes greater than 1.00, since it is possible that the preponderance of one sex over the other in one year may change in another year.

Sometimes ratios give more accurate information (in a sense) than the parts of which they are composed. If one were studying the relation between educational variables and tax rate, for instance, and if one were to use actual tax rates, an erroneous notion of the relation may be obtained. This is because tax rates on property are often misleading. Some communities with high *rates* actually have relatively low levels of taxation. The assessed valuation of property may be low. To avoid the discrepancies between one community and another, one can calculate, for each community, the ratio of assessed valuation to true valuation. Then an adjusted tax rate, a "true" tax rate, can be calculated by multiplying the tax rate in use by this fraction. This will yield a more accurate figure to use in calculations of relations between the tax rate and other variables.

A *proportion* is a fraction with the numerator one of two or more observed frequencies and the denominator the sum of the observed frequencies. The probability definition given earlier, $p = s/(s + f)$, where s = number of successes and f = number of failures, is a proportion. Take any two numbers, say 20 and 60. The ratio of the two numbers is $20/60 = .33$. (It could also be $60/20 = 3$.) If these two numbers were the observed frequencies of the presence and lack of presence of an attribute in a total sample, where $N = 60 + 20 = 80$, then a proportion would be: $20/(60 + 20) = .25$. Another proportion, of course, is $60/80 = .75$.

A *percentage* is simply a proportion multiplied by 100. With the above example, $20/80 \times 100 = 25$ percent. The main purpose of proportions and percentages is to reduce different sets of numbers to comparable sets of numbers with a common base. Any set of frequencies can be transformed to proportions or percentages in order to facilitate statistical manipulation and interpretation.[30]

A word of caution is in order. Because they are often a mixture of two fallible measures, indices can be dangerous. The old method of computing IQ is a good example. The numerator of the fraction is itself an index since MA, mental age, is a composite of a number of measures. A better example is the so-called Achievement Quotient: AQ = $100 \times$ EA/MA, where EA = Educational Age, and MA = Mental Age. Here, both the numerator and the denominator of the fraction are complex indices. Both are mixtures of measures of varying reliability. What is the meaning of the resulting index? How can we interpret it sensibly? It is hard to say. In short, while indices are indispensable aids to scientific analysis, they must be used with circumspection and care.

SOCIAL INDICATORS

Indicators, although closely related to indices—indeed, they are frequently indices as defined above—form a special class of variables. Variables like income, life expectancy, fertility, quality of life, educational level (of people), and environment can be called social indicators. It is evident that these are variables. Since statistics on them are usually

---

[30] Percentages should not be used with small numbers, though proportions may always be used. The reason for the percentage computation restriction is that the relatively larger percentages give a sense of accuracy not really present in the data. For example, suppose 6 and 4 are two observed frequencies. To transform these frequencies to 60 percent and 40 percent is a bit absurd.

calculated, social indicators are both variables and statistics. Unfortunately, it is difficult to define "social indicators,"[31] and no formal attempt will be made here to do so. Readers should know, however, that the idea of social indicators is important and is likely to become increasingly important in the future. Their use is expanding into all fields and eventually they will be systematically studied from a scientific viewpoint, as well as from a "public" and social viewpoint.

In this book we are interested in social indicators as a class of sociological and psychological variables that in the future may be useful in developing and testing scientific theories of the relations among social and psychological phenomena. Certain social indicators, for example, are now used in so-called causal modeling studies of educational and occupational achievement—social class, parents' occupation, and earnings, for example.[32] Psychological indicators, such as perceived quality of life, or "happiness," have also been used.[33] In general, however, there seems to have been little systematic methodological work done to categorize and study social indicators, their relations to each other, and their relations to other variables. Most of the work can be called demographic and narrowly pragmatic—in essence, descriptive. Nevertheless, the field, after problems of reliability and validity are addressed and perhaps solved,[34] is richly promising and should, within a decade, offer behavioral scientists more than such statistics as 51.2 percent of the population was female in 1976, or 54 percent of the population over 18 had nine to twelve years of education. Instead, we can expect factor analytic studies of indicators, analysis of covariance studies in which indicators are variables of the analyzed structures, and an increasing general use of the idea of indicators in social and psychological research. One can easily see this in educational research where the achievement of children appears to be affected in complex ways by different kinds of variables, some of them of the social indicator kind.[35] One of the virtues of the social indicator movement is that these influences on achievement will be more consciously and systematically used in studying and testing theories of achievement.[36]

THE INTERPRETATION OF RESEARCH DATA

Scientists, in evaluating research, can disagree on two broad fronts: data and the interpretation of data. Disagreements on data focus on such problems as the validity and reliability of measurement instruments, and the adequacy and inadequacy of research design, methods of observation, and analysis. Assuming competence, however, major disagreements ordinarily focus upon the interpretation of data. Most psychologists, for example, will

[31] R. Jaeger, "About Educational Indicators: Statistics on the Conditions and Trends in Education." In L. Shulman, ed., *Review of Reseach in Education,* vol. 6. Itasca, Ill.: Peacock Publishers, 1978, chap. 7. (The title is misleading. This review is mostly about *social* indicators.)

[32] O. Duncan, D. Featherman, and B. Duncan, *Socioeconomic Background and Achievement.* New York: Seminar Press, 1972.

[33] A. Campbell, P. Converse, and W. Rodgers, *The Quality of American Life: Perceptions, Evaluations, Satisfactions.* New York: Russell Sage Foundation, 1976.

[34] C. Turner and E. Krauss, "Fallible Indicators of the Subjective State of the Nation," *American Psychologist,* 35 (1978), 456–470.

[35] Pedhazur, *op. cit.*

[36] The pioneering book on social indicators is: R. Bauer, ed., *Social Indicators.* Cambridge, Mass.: MIT Press, 1966. The Jaeger article, cited earlier, is a good introduction. For sources, see: O. Duncan, *Toward Social Reporting: Next Steps.* New York: Russell Sage Foundation, 1969. The following article outlines the development of this new field: E. Sheldon and R. Parke, "Social Indicators," *Science,* 188 (1975), 693–699. An important discussion of social indicators is: A. Campbell, "Subjective Measures of Well-Being," *American Psychologist,* 31 (1976), 117–124. The field is disappointing in one sense, however, because the emphasis has been almost wholly on the use of indicators in descriptive research and not in scientific-explanatory research.

agree on the data of reinforcement experiments. Yet they disagree vigorously on the interpretation of the data of the experiments. Such disagreements are in part a function of theory. In a book like this we cannot labor interpretation from theoretical standpoints. We must be content with a more limited objective: the clarification of some common precepts of the interpretation of data *within* a particular research study or series of studies.

Adequacy of Research Design, Methodology, Measurement, and Analysis

One of the major themes of this book is the appropriateness of methodology to the problem under investigation. The researcher usually has a choice of research designs, methods of observation, methods of measurement, and types of analysis. All of these must be congruent; they must fit together. One does not use, for example, an analysis appropriate to frequencies with, say, the continuous measures yielded by an attitude scale. Most important, the design, methods of observation, measurement, and statistical analysis must all be appropriate to the research problem.

Investigators must carefully scrutinize the technical adequacy of methods, measurements, and statistics. The adequacy of data interpretation depends on such scrutiny. A frequent source of interpretative weakness, for example, is neglect of measurement problems. It is urgently necessary to pay particular attention to the reliability and validity of the measures of variables, as we will see in later chapters. Even the best research organizations and individuals sometimes falter. For many years, for example, the measurement in sociology and psychology of the social attitudes commonly called liberalism and conservatism has been questionable. For one thing, it has been assumed—even in the face of contrary evidence—that liberalism and conservatism form a single continuum. For another, social attitudes have been measured with far too few items. Even the highly respected and competent Survey Research Center of the University of Michigan has erred in both respects.[37] It is not a grievous sin so to err; the real sin is in drawing sweeping conclusions as to the attitudes of the people of the United States on the basis of measurement of questionable reliability and validity.[38]

Simply to accept without question the reliability and validity of the measures of variables, then, is a gross error. Researchers must be especially careful to question the validity of their measures, since the whole interpretative framework can collapse on this one point alone. If a psychologist's problem includes the variable anxiety, for instance, and the statistical analysis shows a positive relation between anxiety and, say, achievement, the investigator must ask himself and the data whether the anxiety measured (or manipulated) is the type of anxiety germane to the problem. He may, for example, have measured test anxiety when the problem variable is really general anxiety. Similarly, he must ask himself whether his measure of achievement is valid for the research purpose. If the research problem demands application of principles but the measure of achievement is a standardized test that emphasizes factual knowledge, the interpretation of the data can be erroneous.

[37] See J. Robinson, J. Rusk, and K. Head, *Measures of Political Attitudes*. Ann Arbor, Michigan: Institute for Social Research, University of Michigan, 1968, chap. 13. Survey Research Center national survey data have been used by others. Thus, if the measurement is inadequate, the inadequacy spreads. See, for example: N. Nie, J. Verba, and J. Petrocik, *The Changing American Voter*. Cambridge, Mass.: Harvard University Press, 1976.

[38] One of the most influential of such sweeping conclusions is contained in: P. Converse, "The Nature of Belief Systems in Mass Publics." In D. Apter, ed., *Ideology and Discontent*. New York: Free Press, 1964, pp. 206–261. Converse says, in effect, that the American mass public has no systematic attitude structure. He also says that the liberal-conservative continuum [*sic*] is a higher-order abstraction that the man-in-the-street knows little about. Ignoring the empirical validity of either claim, note that both conclusions were based on the analysis of relatively few attitude items with a restricted range of content.

In other words, we face here the obvious, but too easily overlooked, fact that adequacy of interpretation is dependent on each link in the methodological chain, as well as on the appropriateness of each link to the research problem and the congruence of the links to each other. This is clearly seen when we are faced with negative or inconclusive results.

Negative and Inconclusive Results

Negative or inconclusive results are much harder to interpret than positive results. When results are positive, when the data support the hypotheses, one interprets the data along the lines of the theory and the reasoning behind the hypotheses. Although one carefully asks critical questions, upheld predictions are evidence for the validity of the reasoning behind the problem statement.

This is one of the great virtues of scientific prediction. When we predict something and plan and execute a scheme for testing the prediction, and things turn out as we say they will, then the adequacy of our reasoning and our execution seems supported. We are never sure, of course. The outcome, though predicted, may be as it is for reasons quite other than those we fondly espouse. Still, that the whole complex chain of theory, deduction from theory, design, methodology, measurement, and analysis has led to a predicted outcome is cogent evidence for the adequacy of the whole structure. We make a complex bet with the odds against us, so to speak. We then throw the research dice or spin the research wheel. If our predicted number comes up, the reasoning and the execution leading to the successful prediction would seem to be adequate. If we can repeat the feat, then the evidence of adequacy is even more convincing.

But now take the negative case. Why were the results negative? Why did the results not come out as predicted? Note that any weak link in the research chain can cause negative results. They can be due to any one, or several, or all of the following: incorrect theory and hypotheses, inappropriate or incorrect methodology, inadequate or poor measurement, and faulty analysis. All these must be carefully examined. All must be scrutinized and the negative results laid at the door of one, several, or all of them. If we can be fairly sure that the methodology, the measurement, and the analysis are adequate, then negative results can be definite contributions to scientific advance, since only then can we have some confidence that our hypotheses are not correct.

Unhypothesized Relations and Unanticipated Findings

The testing of hypothesized relations is strongly emphasized in this book. This does not mean, however, that other relations in the data are not sought and tested. Quite the contrary. Practicing researchers are always keen to seek out and study relations in their data. The unpredicted relation may be an important key to deeper understanding of theory. It may throw light on aspects of the problem not anticipated when the problem was formulated. Therefore researchers, while emphasizing hypothesized relations, should always be alert to unanticipated relations in their data.

Suppose we have hypothesized that the homogeneous grouping of pupils will be beneficial to bright pupils but not beneficial to pupils of lesser ability. The hypothesis is upheld, say. But we notice an apparent difference between suburban and rural areas: the relation seems stronger in the suburban areas; it is reversed in some rural areas! We analyze the data using the suburban-rural variable. We find that homogeneous grouping seems to have a marked influence on bright children in the suburbs, but that it has little or no influence in rural areas. This would be an important finding indeed.

One of the strongest and best-supported of findings in modern psychology has been that positive reinforcement strengthens response tendencies.[39] For example, it has been believed that to enhance the learning of children their correct responses to problems should be positively reinforced. Unexpectedly, however, it has also been found that external motivation sometimes has deleterious effects. Lepper, Greene, and Nisbett, for instance, found that extrinsic positive reinforcement undermined children's intrinsic interest in a drawing activity, a result certainly not predictable from reinforcement theory.[40]

Unpredicted and unexpected findings must be treated with more suspicion than predicted and expected findings. Before being accepted, they should be substantiated in independent research in which they are specifically predicted and tested. Only when a relation is deliberately and systematically tested with the necessary controls built into the design can we have much faith in it. The unanticipated finding may be fortuitous or spurious.

Proof, Probability, and Interpretation

The interpretation of research data culminates in conditional probabilistic statements of the "If p, then q" kind. We enrich such statements by qualifying them in some such way as: If p, then q, under conditions r, s, and t. Ordinarily we eschew causal statements, because we are aware that they cannot be made without grave risk of error.

Perhaps of greater practical importance to the researcher interpreting data is the problem of proof. Let us flatly assert that nothing can be "proved" scientifically. All one can do is to bring evidence to bear that such-and-such a proposition is true. Proof is a deductive matter, and experimental methods of inquiry are not methods of proof. They are controlled methods of bringing evidence to bear on the probable truth or falsity of relational propositions. In short, no scientific investigation ever proves anything. Thus the interpretation of the analysis of research data can never use the term proof.

Fortunately, for practical research purposes it is not necessary to worry excessively about causality and proof. Evidence at satisfactory levels of probability is sufficient for scientific progress. Causality and proof were discussed in this chapter to sensitize the reader to the danger of loose usage of the terms. The understanding of scientific reasoning, and practice and reasonable care in the interpretation of research data, while no guarantees of the validity of one's interpretations, are helpful guards against inadequate inference from data to conclusions.

Study Suggestions

1. Suppose you wish to study the relation between social class and test anxiety. What are the two main possibilities for analyzing the data (omitting the possibility of calculating a coefficient of correlation)? Set up two analytic structures.

2. Assume that you want to add sex as a variable to the problem above. Set up the two kinds of analytic paradigms.

3. Suppose an investigator has tested the effects of three methods of teaching reading on

[39] G. Bower and E. Hilgard, *Theories of Learning,* 5th ed. New York: Appleton-Century-Crofts, 1981, chap. 15.

[40] M. Lepper, D. Greene, and R. Nisbett, "Undermining Children's Intrinsic Interest with Extrinsic Reward: A Test of the Overjustification Hypothesis," *Journal of Personality and Social Psychology,* 28 (1973), 129–137. Condry has competently reviewed research on extrinsic and intrinsic motivation: J. Condry, "Enemies of Exploration: Self-Initiated versus Other-Initiated Learning," *Journal of Personality and Social Psychology,* 35 (1977), 459–477.

reading achievement. He had 30 subjects in each group and a reading achievement score for each subject. He also included sex as an independent variable: half the subjects were male and half female. What does his analytic paradigm look like? What goes into the cells?

4. Study Figure 9.3. Do these analysis of variance designs or paradigms represent partitioning of variables? Why? Why is partitioning important in setting up research designs and in analyzing data? Do the rules of categorization (and partitioning) have any effect on the interpretation of data? If so, what effects might they have? (Consider the effects of violations of the two basic partitioning rules.)

Chapter 10

The Analysis of Frequencies

So FAR, we have talked mostly *about* analysis. Now we learn how to do analysis. The simplest way to analyze data to study relations is by cross-partitioning frequencies. A cross partition, as we learned in Chapter 4, is a new partitioning of the set U by forming all subsets of the form $A \cap B$. That is, we form subsets of the form $A \cap B$ from the known subsets A and B of U. Examples were given in Chapter 4; more will be given shortly. The expression "cross partition" refers to an abstract process of set theory. Now, however, when the cross partition idea is applied to the analysis of frequencies to study relations between variables, we call the cross partitions *crossbreaks*. The kind of analysis to be shown is also called *contingency analysis,* or contingency table analysis.

We can no longer get along without statistics. So we introduce a form of statistical analysis commonly associated with frequencies, the χ^2 (chi square) test, and the idea of statistical "significance." This study of crossbreaks and χ^2 should help ease us into statistics.

The political struggle between Republicans and Democrats is often dramatically shown by votes in the Congress. One of these important recent votes in the U. S. Senate was taken on a proposed amendment by Senator Moynihan (Democrat). The Republican-Democrat struggle during the spring of 1981 centered on proposals of President Reagan, the Republicans being generally for the Reagan proposals and the Democrats against. One of these proposals was to cut certain welfare services. Moynihan's amendment was to preserve parts of existing law for aid to the states for maintenance of welfare children and child welfare services to prevent breakup of low-income families. The amendment was defeated, 52 to 46, thus supporting Reagan. More interesting to us is how the Republican-Democrat vote turned out. This is given in Table 10.1[1]

[1] The data are from *Congressional Quarterly,* 39 (1981), 1156.

Table 10.1 Relation Between Political Party Affiliation and Welfare Vote (Moynihan Amendment), U. S. Senate, 1981

	Yea		Nay		
Republican	5	9%	48	91%	53
Democrat	41	91%	4	9%	45
	46		52		98

It is clear from the frequencies (in this case) that there is a strong relation between political party membership and vote on the Moynihan amendment: Republicans voted Nay and Democrats Yea. Not all frequency crossbreaks are this clear. It is common practice, therefore, to calculate percentages. If we do so in a way to be described later, the percentages are those given in the lower right of each cell. We see the strength of the relation between political party membership and vote: 91 percent of the Republicans voted Nay, and 91 percent of the Democrats voted Yea. (The same percentage, 91, is unusual and accidental.)

Study of similar votes at about the same time show the same general relation. For instance, the vote to lower the capital gains tax from 28 percent to 15 percent is given in Table 10.2.[2] The relation is again strong, though not as strong as in the Moynihan amendment vote (note the Democrat percentages).

Table 10.2 Vote of the U. S. Senate to Lower the Capital Gains Tax, 1981

	Yea		Nay		
Republican	51	98%	1	2%	52
Democrat	11	24%	35	76%	46
	62		36		98

DATA AND VARIABLE TERMINOLOGY

In Chapter 3 a distinction was made between active and attribute variables, the former meaning an experimental or manipulated variable and the latter a measured variable. The term "attribute" was used because it is general and can cover the properties of any objects, animate or inanimate. Unfortunately, however, "attribute" has sometimes been used to mean what have been called categorical variables in this book. In this usage, for example, sex, race, religion, and similar categorical variables have been called attributes. They have also been called "qualitative variables." Both usages seem ill-advised. An attribute is any property of any object, whether the object is measured in an all-or-none way or with a set of continuous measures. We so use it in this book not to upset any conventional usage, if that were possible, but rather to clarify the distinction between experimental and measured variables.

[2]*Congressional Quarterly,* 39 (1981), 1313.

What we have called categorical variables are also called, perhaps more accurately, "nominal variables." This is because they belong to what we will later learn is the level of measurement called "nominal." Since in this and later chapters we have to be quite clear about the difference between continuous and categorical variables, let us briefly anticipate a later discussion and define measurement. When the numbers or symbols assigned to objects have no number meaning beyond presence or absence of the property or attribute being measured, the measurement is called "nominal." A variable that is nominal is, of course, what we have been calling "categorical." To name something ("nominal") is to put it into a category ("categorical").

All this is perhaps clarified by the following set equation, which is a general definition of measurement:[3]

$$f = \{(x, y): x = \text{any object, and } y = \text{any numeral}\}$$

which is read: f is a rule of correspondence that is defined as a set of ordered pairs, (x, y), such that x is some object and y is some numeral assigned to x. This is a general definition that covers all cases of measurement. Obviously, y can be a set of continuous measures or simply the set $\{0, 1\}$. Categorical or nominal variables are those variables where $y = \{0, 1\}$, 0 and 1 being assigned on the basis of the object x either possessing or not possessing some defined property or attribute. Continuous variables are those variables where $y = \{0, 1, 2, \ldots, k\}$, or some numerical system where the numbers mean more or less of the attribute in question. (It is mathematically difficult to define "continuous measures," and the definition just given is not satisfactory. Nevertheless, the reader will know what is meant.)

The level of measurement of this chapter is mostly nominal. Even when continuous variables are used, they are converted to nominal variables. In general, this should not be done, because it throws information (variance) away. Nevertheless, there are times when, in the judgment of the researcher, it is necessary or desirable to treat a continuous variable as a nominal variable. For example, it may be possible to measure a potentially continuous variable only in a crude way by, say, having an observer judge whether or not objects possess or do not possess an attribute. While there are degrees of aggressive behavior, it may only be possible to say that an individual did or did not exhibit aggressive behavior.

CROSSBREAKS: DEFINITIONS AND PURPOSE

A *crossbreak* is a numerical tabular presentation of data, usually in frequency or percentage form, in which variables are cross-partitioned in order to study the relations between them.[4] It is a common form of analysis that can be used with almost any kind of data. Its principal use, however, is with categorical or nominal data. Apart from its actual research use, the crossbreak is a valuable pedagogical device. Its clarity and simplicity make it an effective tool for learning how to structure research problems and how to analyze data. Crossbreaks are cross partitions, as indicated earlier. Therefore the partitioning rules and the set notions already learned can be easily applied to their analysis.

Crossbreaks enable the researcher to determine the nature of the relations between

---

[3]F. Kerlinger, "Research in Education." In R. Ebel, V. Noll, and R. Bauer, eds., *Encyclopedia of Educational Research,* 4th ed. New York: Macmillan, 1969, pp. 1127–1114 (1137).

[4]Crossbreaks are also used in descriptive ways. The investigator may not be interested in relations, as such: he may want only to describe a situation that exists. For instance, take the case where a table breaks social-class membership against possession of TV sets, refrigerators, and so on. This is a descriptive comparison rather than a variable crossbreak, even though we might conceivably call possession of a TV set, for instance, by some variable name. Our concern is exclusively with the analysis of data gathered to test or explore relations.

variables. But they have other side purposes. They can be used to organize data in convenient form for statistical analysis. A statistical test is then applied to the data. Indices of association, too, are readily calculated.

Another purpose of crossbreaks is to control variables. As we will see later, crossbreaks enable us to study and test a relation between two variables while controlling a third variable. In this way "spurious" relations can be unmasked and the relations between variables can be "specified"—that is, differences in degree of relation at different levels of a control variable can be determined.

Still another purpose of crossbreaks was alluded to above: their study and use sensitize the student and practicing researcher to the design and structure of research problems. There is something salutary about reducing a research problem to a crossbreak. In fact, if you cannot write a diagrammatic paradigm of your research problem in either analysis of variance or crossbreak form, then the problem is not clear in your mind, or you do not really have a research problem.

SIMPLE CROSSBREAKS AND RULES FOR CROSSBREAK CONSTRUCTION

The simplest form a crossbreak can take is a 2-by-2, or 2×2, table. Two examples were given above. A third example is given in Table 10.3. The data are from a study of what the authors call the New Left, or New Liberals, and the Silent Minority.[5] The two rubrics amount to "liberal" and "conservative." Call this variable ideology. The tabled data are the numbers of respondents who felt that the responsibility for the condition of the poor was either the poor themselves or the society. Appropriate percentages (proportions) have been calculated and entered in the cells. It is clear that there is a strong relation between ideology and attribution of responsibility: The New Liberals assign responsibility more to

Table 10.3 Attribution of Responsibility for Poverty of Liberals and Silent Minority, Miller-Levitin Study[a]

Ideology	Responsibility Attribution		
	Poor	Society	
New Liberals	46 .32	97 .68	143
Silent Minority	29 .83	6 .17	35
	75	103	178

[a]The figures in the center of each cell are frequencies. The figures in the lower right of each cell are percentages, calculated *from* Ideology *to* Responsibility, e.g., $46/143 = .32$, and $6/35 = .17$. The latter are written as proportions: multiply by 100 and the proportions become percentages. We follow the convention henceforth of writing proportions.

[5] W. Miller and T. Levitin, *Leadership and Change: The New Politics and the American Electorate.* Cambridge, Mass.: Winthrop Publishers, 1976. The frequencies in the table were reconstructed from the percentages and *N*'s in the authors' Table 6-6. The middle categories of their 3×3 table were omitted for pedagogical reasons.

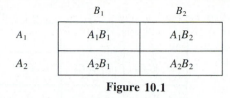

Figure 10.1

society than to the poor (.32 and .68), whereas the Silent Minority attributes responsibility to the poor and not to society (.83 and .17). Right now, however, we are more interested in how the table was set up.

There seem to be no generally accepted rules on the setup of crossbreaks. We know, however, that they are cross partitions and thus must follow the rules of partitioning or categorization discussed earlier: the categories are set up according to the research hypotheses; they are independent and mutually exclusive; they are exhaustive; each category is derived from one and only one classification principle; all categories are on one level of discourse.

A 2×2 crossbreak, in variable symbols, is given in Figure 10.1. A_1 and A_2 are the partitions of the variable A; B_1 and B_2 are the partitions of the variable B. The cells A_1B_1, . . . , A_2B_2 are simply the intersections of the subsets of A and B: $A_1 \cap B_1$, . . . , $A_2 \cap B_2$. Any object in U, the universe of objects, can be categorized as A_1B_1, A_1B_2, A_2B_1, or A_2B_2. If U is a sample of children, and A is sex and B is delinquency, then an A_1B_1 member is a delinquent boy, whereas an A_2B_2 child is a nondelinquent girl. In Table 10.3, A = Ideology; B = Attribution of Responsibility; A_1 = New Liberal; A_2 = Silent Minority; B_1 = Attribution of Responsibility to Poor; B_2 = Attribution of Responsibility to Society. Then A_1B_1 is New Liberals who attribute responsibility to the poor, and A_2B_2 is members of the Silent Minority who attribute responsibility to society. Larger tables— 2×3, 2×4, 3×2, and so on—are merely extensions of the idea.

In the three-variable case, strictly speaking, a cube is necessary. Let there be three variables A, B, C, each dichotomized (for simplicity). The actual situation would look like Figure 10.2. Each cell is a cube with a triple label. All visible cubes have been properly labeled. If the variables A, B, and C were sex, social class, and delinquency, then, for example, an $A_2B_2C_1$ cell member would be a working-class girl who is delinquent. Since handling cubes is cumbersome, we use a simpler system. The three-variable crossbreak table can look like that of Figure 10.3. We return to three-variable crossbreaks later.

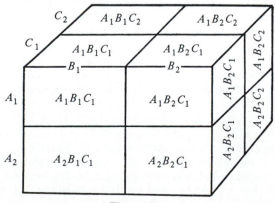

Figure 10.2

	B_1		B_2	
	C_1	C_2	C_1	C_2
A_1	$A_1B_1C_1$	$A_1B_1C_2$	$A_1B_2C_1$	$A_1B_2C_2$
A_2	$A_2B_1C_1$	$A_2B_1C_2$	$A_2B_2C_1$	$A_2B_2C_2$

Figure 10.3

CALCULATION OF PERCENTAGES

Calculate percentages from the independent variable to the dependent variable. In studies where it is not possible to label the variables as independent and dependent, the rule, of course, does not apply. But in most cases it does apply. In Tables 10.1 and 10.2, the percentages were calculated *from* Republican and Democrat *to* Yea and Nay, e.g., 5/53 = .09 and 48/53 = .91 in Table 10.1, and 11/46 = .24 and 35/46 = .76 in Table 10.2. In the three tables above, the convention was followed of putting the independent variable on the side of the table and the dependent variable at the top. It could just as well have been the other way around, however. Indeed, when there is more than one independent variable, published contingency tables are frequently printed from the top down. In Figure 10.3, for example, *B* and *C* would be the independent variables and *A* the dependent variable.

Return to Table 10.3, the data from the Miller-Levitin study. Does the table indicate a relation greater than chance expectation between ideology and attribution of responsibility for poverty? Do the proportions in the four cells of the table depart significantly from the proportions to be expected by chance? If they do, we say that there is a relation between the variables. Suppose a statistical test has been done and its result indicates greater than chance departure of the proportions. (We will see how to do such a test shortly.) We say, then, that there is a statistically significant relation between ideology and responsibility attribution.

But what is the nature of the relation? This is determined by study of the table, especially the percentages (proportions). The weightiest part of the relation seems to be the Silent Minority line: 83 percent of the responses attribute responsibility for poverty to the poor themselves and only 17 percent to society. Among the New Liberals, on the other hand, the difference in attribution, while substantial, is not as sharp: 68 percent versus 32 percent.

Crossbreaks with frequencies can sometimes be interpreted the way they are, but it is usually better to convert the frequencies to percentages following the rule given above: calculate from the independent variable to the dependent variable one row (or column) at a time. To do this, first add the frequencies in the rows and in the columns and enter these sums at the bottom and side of the table. In Table 10.3, these sums have been entered. They are called "marginal frequencies," or "marginals." (Actually, to calculate the percentages, only the row sums of Table 10.3 need be calculated. Both row and column sums will be needed later.) In the relations of Tables 10.1 and 10.2, the independent variable is clearly political party affiliation and the dependent variable is vote on the issue. In Table 10.3, the independent variable is ideology and the dependent variable responsibility attribution. Sometimes, however, determining which variable is which is not so simple. At any rate, in all three tables we calculate the percentages across the rows, or from the independent variable (rows) to the dependent variable (columns).

To be sure we know what we are doing, let's calculate the percentages of Table 10.3. Take the rows separately: the New Liberal row: 46/143 = .32, and 97/143 = .68. These are the proportions. Multiplying by 100—which amounts to moving the decimal point two places to the right—yields, of course, 32 percent and 68 percent. Now the Silent Minority row: 29/35 = .83, and 6/35 = .17, or 83 percent and 17 percent. (Notice that each row must total 1.00, or 100 percent.) The relation is now clear: the Silent Minority attributes responsibility for poverty to the poor, whereas the New Liberals tend to attribute responsibility to society. Notice how the percentage crossbreak highlights the relation, which is not clear in the frequencies because of unequal numbers of New Liberals (143) and Silent Minority (35). In other words, the percentage calculation transforms both rows to a common base and enhances the comparison—and the relation.

The reader may wonder about two things: Why not calculate the percentages the other way: from the dependent variable to the independent variable? Why not calculate the percentages over the whole table? There is nothing inherently wrong with either of these calculations. In the first case, however, we would be asking the data a different question. In the second case, we merely transform the frequency data to percentage or proportion data without changing the pattern of the frequencies.

The Miller-Levitin problem is pointed toward accounting for attribution of responsibility for poverty—to the poor or to society. An hypothesis implied by the problem is: Conservatives attribute responsibility for poverty to the poor. This is a statement of the if p, then q kind: If conservative, then attribution of responsibility to the poor. There can be no doubt of the independent and dependent variables. Therefore the calculation of the percentages is determined, since we must ask: Given conservatism, what proportion of responses is attribution of responsibility to the poor? The question is answered in the second row of Table 10.3: .83, or 83 percent. (The first row is of course also important in the overall relation.) If the percentages are calculated down the columns, this is tantamount to the hypothesis: If attribution of responsibility for poverty is to the poor, then conservative ideology. But we are not trying to account for ideology; ideology is not the dependent variable. Naturally, if we go ahead anyway and calculate percentages, they will be misleading. (See Study Suggestion 3.)[6]

STATISTICAL SIGNIFICANCE AND THE χ^2 TEST

We must now interrupt our study of crossbreaks to learn a little statistics and thus anticipate the work and study of the next chapter. While it is possible to talk about crossbreaks and how they are constructed without statistics, it is not really possible to go into the analysis and interpretation of frequency data without at least some statistics. So we examine one of the simplest and yet most useful of statistical tests, the χ^2 (chi square) test.

[6] The theoretical rationale for the percentage calculation from the independent variable to the dependent variable is based on the consideration that percentages calculated in this way are conditional probabilities (see Chapter 7), whose correct statements are derived from the research problem. For example, for Table 10.1 we can say: If Republican, then vote Nay, a conditional statement. In set and probability theory language, this is: the probability of B_2, a Nay vote, given A_1, Republican, or:

$$p(B_2|A_1) = \frac{p(A_1 \cap B_2)}{p(A_1)} = \frac{48/98}{53/98} = .91,$$

and this is the conditional probability: the probability of B_2, given A_1. It is also the percentage in the A_1B_2 cell of Table 10.1. For a more complete discussion, see F. Kerlinger, *Foundations of Behavioral Research*, 2d ed. New York: Holt, Rinehart and Winston, 1973, pp. 164–166.

Look at the frequencies of Table 10.3. Do they really express a relation between ideology and attribution of responsibility for poverty? Or could they have happened by chance? Are they one pattern among many patterns of frequencies that one would get picking numbers from a table of random numbers, such selection being limited only by the given marginal frequencies? Such questions have to be asked of every set of frequency results obtained from samples. Until they *are* answered, there is little or no point in going further with data interpretation. If our results could have happened by chance, of what use is our effort to interpret them?

What does it mean to say that an obtained result is "statistically significant"—that it departs "significantly" from chance expectation? Suppose that we were to do an actual experiment 100 times just as we toss a coin 100 times. Each experiment is like a coin toss or a throw of the dice. The outcome of each experiment can be considered a sample point. The sample space, properly conceived, is an infinite number of such experiments or sample points. For convenience, we conceive of the 100 replications of the experiment as the sample space U. This is nothing new. It is what we did with the coins and the dice.

Take a simple example. A university administration is considering the wisdom of changing the marking system, but it wants to know faculty attitudes toward the proposed change, since it has found from experience that if most of the faculty does not approve a change the new system can run into serious trouble. By means of a suitable procedure 100 faculty members, selected at random, are asked their attitudes toward the proposed change. Sixty faculty members approve the change, and 40 disapprove. The administration now has to ask: Is this a "significant" majority? The administration reasons this way. If the faculty members were completely indifferent, their responses would be like chance: now this way, now that way. The expected frequency on an indifference hypothesis would of course be 50/50, the result to be expected by chance.

To answer the question whether 60/40 differs significantly from indifference or chance a statistical test known as χ^2 is performed. A table (Table 10.4) is set up to obtain the necessary terms for the calculation of χ^2. The term f_o means "frequency obtained" and f_e means "frequency expected." The function of statistical tests is to compare obtained results with those to be expected on the basis of chance. Here, then, we compare f_o with f_e. On the indifference or chance assumption, we write 50 and 50. But 60 and 40 were obtained. The difference is 10. Could a difference as large as 10 have happened by chance? Another way to put the question is: If we performed the same experiment 100 times and only chance were operating—that is, the faculty members answered the questions indifferently or, in effect, randomly—how many times in the 100 could we expect to get a deviation as large as 60/40? If we tossed a coin 100 times, we know that sometimes we would get 60 heads and 40 tails and 40 heads and 60 tails. How many times would

Table 10.4   Calculation of χ^2: Faculty Approval and Disapproval of Proposed Change in Marking System

	Approve	Disapprove
f_o	60	40
f_e	50	50
$f_o - f_e$	10	-10
$(f_o - f_e)^2$	100	100
$\dfrac{(f_o - f_e)^2}{f_e}$	$\dfrac{100}{50} = 2$	$\dfrac{100}{50} = 2$

such a large discrepancy, if it *is* a large discrepancy, happen by chance? The χ^2 test is a convenient way to get an answer.

We now write a χ^2 formula:

$$\chi^2 = \sum \left[\frac{(f_o - f_e)^2}{f_e} \right]$$

which simply says: "Subtract each expected frequency, f_e, from the comparable obtained frequency, f_o, square this difference, divide the difference squared by the expected frequency, f_e, and then add up these quotients." This was done in Table 10.4. To make sure the reader knows what is happening, we write it out:

$$\chi^2 = \frac{(60 - 50)^2}{50} + \frac{(40 - 50)^2}{50} = \frac{100}{50} + \frac{100}{50} = 4$$

But what does $\chi^2 = 4$ mean? χ^2 is a measure of the departure of obtained frequencies from the frequencies expected by chance. Provided we have some way of knowing what the chance expectations are, and provided the observations are independent, we can always calculate χ^2. The larger χ^2 is the greater the obtained frequencies deviate from the expected chance frequencies. The value of χ^2 ranges from 0, which indicates no departure of obtained from expected frequencies, through a large number of increasing values.

In addition to the formula above, it is necessary to know the so-called *degrees of freedom* of the problem and to have a χ^2 table. Chi square tables are found in almost any statistics book, together with instructions on how to use them. So are explanations of degrees of freedom. We may say here that "degrees of freedom" means the latitude of variation a statistical problem has. In the problem above, there is one degree of freedom because the total number of cases is fixed, 100, and as soon as one of the frequencies is given the other is immediately determined. That is, there are no degrees of freedom when two numbers must sum to 100 and one of them, say 40, is given. Once 40, or 45, or any other number is given, there are no more places to go. The remaining number has no freedom to vary.[7]

To understand more about what is going on here, suppose we calculate all the χ^2's for all possibilities: 40/60, 41/59, 42/58, . . . , 50/50, . . . , 60/40. Doing so, we get the set of values given in Table 10.5. (In reading the table, it is helpful to conceive of the first frequency of each pair as "Heads," or "Agrees with," or "Male," or any other variable.) Only two of these χ^2's, the values of 4.00 associated with 40/60 and 60/40, are statistically significant. They are statistically significant because by checking the χ^2 table for one degree of freedom we find an entry of 3.841 at what is called the .05 level of significance. All the other χ^2's in Table 10.5 are less than 3.841. Take the χ^2 for 42/58, which is 2.56. If we consult the table, 2.56 falls between the values of χ^2 with probabilities of .10 and .25, or 2.706 and 1.323, respectively. This is actually a probability of about .14. In most cases, we do not need to bother finding out where it falls. All we need to do is to note that it does not make the .05 grade of 3.841. If it does not, we say that it is not statistically significant—*at the .05 level.* The reader may now ask: "What is the .05

[7] Similarly, if one calculates a mean of 100 scores, one uses up one degree of freedom, by imposing one restriction on the data. Probably the best explanation of degrees of freedom is Walker's. See H. Walker, "Degrees of Freedom," *Journal of Educational Psychology,* 31 (1940), 253–269, and H. Walker, *Mathematics Essential for Elementary Statistics,* rev. ed. New York: Holt, Rinehart and Winston, 1951, chap. 22.

Table 10.5 Frequencies and Corresponding χ^2's [a]

Frequencies	χ^2
40/60	4.00
41/59	3.24
42/58	2.56
43/57	1.96
44/56	1.44
45/55	1.00
46/54	.64
47/53	.36
48/52	.16
49/51	.04
50/50	0

[a] The values of χ^2 for 51/49. . . . , 60/40 are, of course, the same as those in the table but in reverse order.

level?'' and ''Why the .05 level?'' ''Why not .10 or even .15?'' To answer these questions, we must digress a little.

LEVELS OF STATISTICAL SIGNIFICANCE

The .05 level means that an obtained result that is significant at the .05 level could occur *by chance* only 5 times in 100 trials. With our responses to the administration's question of 60 Agrees and 40 Disagrees, we can say that a discrepancy as large as this *will happen by chance* only about 5 times in 100 trials. It *can* happen more often or less often, but it probably will happen about 5 times in 100.

A level of statistical significance is to some extent chosen arbitrarily.[8] But it is certainly not completely arbitrary. Another level of significance frequently used is the .01 level. The .05 and .01 levels correspond fairly well to two and three standard deviations from the mean of a normal probability distribution. (A normal probability distribution is the symmetric bell-shaped curve which the student has probably often seen. We take it up later.)

Think back to the coin-tossing experiment, when a penny was tossed 100 times. Heads turned up 52 times and tails 48 times. Consult Table 10.5. $\chi^2 = .16$, a result clearly not significant. But suppose the coin had been tossed not one set of 100 tosses but 100 sets of 100 tosses, which would be tantamount to 100 experiments. From these 100 experiments we would get a variety of results: 58/42, 46/54, 51/49, and so on. About 95 or 96 of these experiments would yield heads within the bounds of 40 and 60. That is, only 4 or 5 of the experiments would yield less than 40 or greater than 60 heads. Similarly, if we perform an experiment and find a difference between two means which, after an appropriate statistical test, is at the .05 level of significance, then we have reason to believe that the obtained mean difference is not merely a chance difference. It *could* be a chance difference, however. If the experiment were done 100 times and there really were no

[8] The .05 level was apparently first chosen by Fisher. See R. Fisher, *Statistical Methods for Research Workers,* 11th ed. New York: Hafner, 1950, pp. 80ff.

difference between the means, 5 of these 100 replications might show differences as large as the actual obtained differences.

While this discussion may help to clarify the meaning of statistical significance, it does not yet answer all the questions asked before. The .05 level was originally chosen—and has persisted with researchers—because it is considered a reasonably good gamble. It is neither too high nor too low for most social scientific research. Many researchers prefer the .01 level of significance. This is quite a high level of certainty. Indeed, it is "practical certainty." Some researchers say that the .10 level may sometimes be used. Others say that 10 chances in 100 are too many, so that they are not willing to risk a decision with such odds. Others say that the .01 level, or 1 chance in 100, is too stringent, that "really" significant results may be discarded in this manner.

Should a certain level of significance be chosen and adhered to? This is a difficult question. The .05 and .01 levels have been widely advocated. There is a newer trend of thinking that advocates reporting the significance levels of all results. That is, if a result is significant at the .12 level, say, it should be reported accordingly. Some practitioners object to this practice. They say that one should make a bet and stick to it. Another school of thought advocates working with what are called "confidence intervals."[9] In this book, the statistical "levels" approach will be used because it is simpler. For the student who does not plan to do any research, the matter is not serious. But it is emphasized that those who will engage in research should study other procedures, such as statistical estimation methods, confidence intervals, and exact probability methods.

To illustrate the calculation and use of the χ^2 test with crossbreaks, we now apply it to the frequency data of Table 10.3. The formula given above is used, but with crossbreak tables its application is more complicated than its use in Table 10.4. The main difference is the calculation of the expected frequencies. The necessary calculations are given in Table 10.6. The expected frequencies, f_e, are in the upper left corner of each cell; they are calculated as shown in footnote a of the table. The obtained frequencies, f_o, are given in the right center of each cell. The $f_o - f_e$ terms, required by the formula, are given in the lower left corner of the cells. They are the same in all cells, except for sign. This will be true in 2 × 2 tables. The χ^2 formula simply requires squaring these differences, dividing the squares by the expected frequencies, and summing the results. These calculations are indicated below. $\chi^2 = 65.1863$, at one degree of freedom. (Why one degree of freedom?) Looking up the tabled χ^2 value, one degree of freedom at the .01 level, we read 6.635. Since our value exceeds this substantially, it can be said that χ^2 is statistically significant, the obtained results are probably not chance results, and the relation expressed in the table is a "real" one in the sense that it is probably not due to chance.[10]

[9] Most investigators say that the results are not significant if they do not make the .05 or .01 grade. For a penetrating discussion of this obviously difficult issue, which cannot be adequately discussed here, see W. Rozeboom, "The Fallacy of the Null-Hypothesis Significance Test," *Psychological Bulletin,* 57 (1960), 416–428. Rozeboom advocates the use of confidence intervals and the reporting of precise probability values of experimental outcomes. See also J. Nunnally, "The Place of Statistics in Psychology," *Educational and Psychological Measurement,* 20 (1960), 641–650. The basic idea is that, instead of categorically rejecting hypotheses if the .05 grade is not made, we say the probability is .95 that the unknown value falls between .30 and .50. Now, if the obtained empirical proportion is, say, .60, then this is evidence for the correctness of the investigator's substantive hypothesis, or in null hypothesis language, the null hypothesis is rejected. A convenient and excellent source of these and similar problems is: R. Kirk, ed., *Statistical Issues: A Reader for the Behavioral Sciences.* Monterey, Calif.: Brooks/Cole, 1972, chap 4. See, especially, essays by Chandler, by Edwards, and by Lykken.

[10] Note that χ^2 needs a correction if N is small. The approximate rule is that the so-called correction for continuity is used—it consists merely of subtracting .5 from the absolute difference between f_0 and f_e in the χ^2 formula *before squaring*—when *expected* frequencies are less than 5 in 2 × 2 tables.

Table 10.6 Calculation of χ^2, Data of Table 10.3

24.8776[a] −19.8776[b]	5	28.1224 19.8776	48	53
21.1224 −19.8776	41	23.8776 19.8776	4	45
	46		52	98

[a]$f_e = (53 \times 46)/98 = 24.8776$; $(53 \times 52)/98 = 28.1224$; etc.
[b]$f_o - f_e = 5 - 24.8776 = -19.8776$; etc.

$$\chi^2 = \sum \left[\frac{(f_o - f_e)^2}{f_e} \right]$$

$$= \frac{(5. - 24.8776)^2}{24.8776} + \frac{(48. - 28.1224)^2}{28.1224} + \frac{(41. - 21.1224)^2}{21.1224}$$

$$+ \frac{(4. - 23.8776)^2}{23.8776} = 15.8825 + 14.0500 + 18.7062$$

$$+ 16.5477 = 65.1864$$

χ^2, like other statistics that indicate statistical significance, tells us nothing about the magnitude of the relation. It is a test of the independence of the variables in the sense of independence discussed in Chapter 9. It is not, strictly speaking, a measure of association. One of the oldest problems of statistics is indexing the strength or magnitude of association or relation between categorical variables. Its complexity forbids discussion here. But we give one statistic, even though it is not the best one, because it is easily applicable and can be used with any size contingency or crossbreak table. It is C, the *coefficient of contingency:*

$$C = \sqrt{\frac{\chi^2}{\chi^2 + N}}$$

If we substitute the value of χ^2 calculated above and insert it and N in the equation, we obtain:

$$C = \sqrt{\frac{65.1864}{65.1864 + 98}} = \sqrt{.3995} = .63$$

which is a rough and conservative index of the strength of the relation.

C is inadequate partly because it cannot reach 1.00, has no sign, and is not readily interpretable in various terms, as is r, for instance. Nevertheless, it yields a measure of association that is useful if used with circumspection.[11] Generally speaking, the best advice for handling categorical data is to calculate χ^2 to determine statistical significance,

---

[11] The reader is urged to study the subject further. See Hays, *op. cit.*, pp. 289ff. Hays has for many years advocated using measures of the strength of association as well as significance tests. This advice is strongly supported in this book. For good discussions of indices of association or correlation, see H. Reynolds, *The Analysis of Cross-Classifications*. New York: Free Press, 1977, chap. 2; H. Reynolds, *Analysis of Nominal Data*. Beverly Hills, Calif.: Sage Publications, 1977, chap. 2.

calculate C (or other measures: see footnote 11), calculate the percentages as outlined earlier, and then interpret the data using all the information.

TYPES OF CROSSBREAKS AND TABLES

In general there are three types of tables: one-dimensional, two-dimensional, and k-dimensional. The number of dimensions of a table is determined by the number of variables: a one-dimensional table has one variable, a two-dimensional table has two variables, and so on. It makes no difference how many categories any single variable has; the dimensions of a table are always fixed by the number of variables. We have already considered the two-dimensional table where two variables, one independent and one dependent, are set against each other. It is often fruitful and necessary to consider more than two variables simultaneously. Theoretically, there is no limit to the number of variables that can be considered at one time. The only limitations are practical ones: insufficient sample size and difficulty of comprehension of the relations contained in a multidimensional table.

One-Dimensional Tables

There are two kinds of one-dimensional table. One is a "true" one-dimensional table; it is of little interest to us since it does not express a relation. Such tables occur commonly in newspapers, government publications, magazines, and so forth. In reporting the number or proportion of males and females in San Francisco, the number of cars of different makes produced in 1982, the number of children in each of the grades of X school system, we have "true" one-dimensional tables. One variable only is used in the table.

Social scientists sometimes choose to report their data in tables that look one-dimensional but are really two-dimensional. Consider a table reported by Child, Potter, and Levine.[12] In this study the values expressed in third-grade children's textbooks were content-analyzed. Table 10.7 shows the percentages of instances in which rewards were given for various modes of acquisition. (In the original table, only the column of percentages on the left was given.) The table looks one-dimensional, but it really expresses a relation between two variables, mode of acquisition and reward.

The key point is that tables of this kind are not really one-dimensional. In Table 10.7, one of the variables, reward, is incompletely expressed. To make this clear, simply add another column of percentages beside those in the original table. (This has been done in the table.) This column can be labeled "Not Rewarded." Now we have a complete two-dimensional table, and the relation becomes obvious. (Sometimes this cannot be done because data for "completing" the table are lacking.)

Table 10.7 Child, Potter, and Levine Data

Mode of Acquisition	% in which rewarded	(% in which not rewarded)
Effort	93	(7)
Buying, Selling, Trading	80	(20)
Asking, Wishing, Taking What Is Offered	68	(32)
Dominance, Aggression, Stealing, Trickery	41	(59)

[12] I. Child, E. Potter, and E. Levine, "Children's Textbooks and Personality Development: An Exploration in the Social Psychology of Education," *Psychological Monographs*, 60 (1946), No. 3.

Two-Dimensional Tables

Two-dimensional tables or crossbreaks have two variables, each with two or more sub-classes. The simplest form of a two-dimensional table, as we have seen, is called two-by-two, or simply 2 × 2. Two-dimensional tables are by no means limited to the 2 × 2 form. In fact, there is no logical limitation on the number of subclasses that each variable can have. Let us look at a few examples of $m \times n$ tables.

Baum and Greenberg studied the effects of anticipated crowding on seating behavior.[13] They reported the 2 × 3 crossbreak of Table 10.8. The results support their hypothesis, which was: Persons who anticipate crowding will sit in corners of rooms, as contrasted to persons who do not anticipate crowding. $\chi^2 = 39.42$, which is highly significant. $C = .58$, a substantial relation. (The authors did not calculate a measure of association.) We see here a simple but effective method of testing the hypothesis and analyzing the data. Under the anticipation of crowding, the subjects sat in corners, as contrasted to subjects who did not anticipate crowding.

Table 10.8 Seat Positions Taken by Subjects Who Anticipated Crowding (10 Persons) and No Crowding (4 Persons), Baum and Greenberg Study[a]

	Seat Position		
Expectation	Corner	Wall	Middle
4 Persons	5	11	23
10 Persons	31	8	1

[a]$\chi^2 = 39.42$ ($p < .001$); $C = .58$.

Another example of a two-dimensional table that can help us make two or three important points, as well as give us interesting data to study, is from Stouffer's conformity-tolerance study.[14] Stouffer studied the relation between tolerance, on the one hand, and several other sociological variables, on the other hand. One of the latter was education. Stouffer sought an answer to the question: What is the relation between the amount of education and degree of tolerance? The crossbreak given in Table 10.9 is instructive because: it is a 5 × 3 type and thus more complex than previous types; it juxtaposes an ordinal variable, education, against a classification of a presumably continuous variable, tolerance; and it illustrates a point that seems to confuse students, namely that the m and n numbers of an $m \times n$ crossbreak tell the number of subclasses or subcategories, and not the number of variables. Study of the tables shows that a relation between the two variables exists: evidently the more education the more tolerance.

[13] A. Baum and C. Greenberg, "Waiting for a Crowd: The Behavioral and Perceptual Effects of Anticipated Crowding," *Journal of Personality and Social Psychology,* 32 (1975), 671–679.

[14] S. Stouffer, *Communism, Conformity, and Civil Liberties.* New York: Doubleday, 1955. Copyright © 1955 by Samuel A. Stouffer. Reprinted by Permission of Doubleday & Company, Inc. This book contains exhaustive crossbreak analyses. It can almost be considered a text and model of how to analyze relations via crossbreaks. Stouffer's untiring specifications of his data are especially valuable. For example, see chap. 4 where he juxtaposes age, education, tolerance, and other variables.

Table 10.9   Relation Between Education and Tolerance, Stouffer Study

| | *Percentage of Distribution of Scores on Scale of Tolerance* | | | |
Education	Less Tolerant	In-Between	More Tolerant	N
College Graduates	5	29	66	308
Some College	9	38	53	319
High School Graduates	12	46	42	768
Some High School	17	54	29	576
Grade School	22	62	16	792

Let's look briefly at a similar analysis of a different kind of research problem. Meier studied the relations between rank in the U.S. Civil Service and social class, sex, and race.[15] Table 10.10 presents his findings on social class. The main numbers in the cells are frequencies; I calculated them from Meier's percentages and N's. Percentages (proportions) are given in the lower right corners of the cells. It is evident from the percentages that social class and Civil Service rank are related. $\chi^2 = 63.27$, highly significant, and $C = .28$, a moderate relation. Although relatively few individuals hold high rank, those who do tend to be middle class. The lower ranks are disproportionately filled with working-class individuals.

Table 10.10   Relation Between Social Class and Rank in the U.S. Civil Service, Meier Study[a]

| Social Class | Civil Service Rank | | | | |
	GS 1-4	GS 5-10	GS 11-13	GS 14 +	
Middle Class	118 .28	159 .38	122 .29	20 .05	419
Working Class	150 .47	135 .43	30 .09	2 .01	317
	268	294	152	22	736

[a]Frequencies were calculated using Meier's percentages and N's.

Two-Dimensional Tables, "True" Dichotomies, and Continuous Measures

Many two-dimensional tables report "true" nominal data, data of variables that are truly dichotomous: sex, alive-dead, and the like. Yet many such tables have one or both variables presumably continuous and artificially dichotomized or trichotomized. In their study of the self-esteem of black children in the Baltimore public schools, Rosenberg and Simmons showed that black self-esteem was not, as thought, lower than white self-esteem.[16] One of their tables, in percentages, is given in Table 10.11. Note that the table

[15] K. Meier, "Representative Bureaucracy: An Empirical Analysis," *American Political Science Review,* 69 (1975), 526–542.

[16] M. Rosenberg and R. Simmons, *Black and White Self-Esteem: The Urban Child.* Washington, D.C.: American Sociological Association, 1971.

Table 10.11 Relation of Self-Esteem and Race, Baltimore School Children, Rosenberg and Simmons Study

Self-Esteem	Race	
	Black	White
Low	19%	37%
Medium	35	30
High	46	33
	100%	100%
N:	1213	682

has been set up differently than previous tables: the independent variable, race, is at the top and the dependent variable, self-esteem, at the side. (Thus, the percentages are calculated down the columns.) Note, too, that a continuous variable, self-esteem, has been converted to a nominal variable.

Three- and k-Dimensional Tables

It is theoretically possible to crossbreak any number of variables, but in practice the limit is three or four, more often three. The reasons for such limitation are obvious: very large N's are required and, more important, the interpretation of data becomes considerably more difficult. Another point to bear in mind is: Never use a complex analysis when a simpler one will accomplish the analytic job. Still, three- and four-dimensional tables can be useful and can supply indispensable information.

The analysis of three or more variables simultaneously has two main purposes. One is to study the relations among three or more variables. Take a three-dimensional example, and call the variables A, B, and C. We can study the following relations: between A and B, between A and C, between B and C, and between A, B, and C. The second purpose is to control one variable while studying the relation between the other two variables. For instance, we can study the relation between B and C while controlling A. An important use of this notion is to help detect spurious relations. Another use is to "specify" a relation, to tell us when or under what conditions a relation is more or less pronounced.

SPECIFICATION

Specification is a process of describing the conditions under which a relation exists or does not exist, or exists to a greater or a lesser extent. An example will help to clarify what is meant. We also take this opportunity to introduce k-dimensional contingency tables and multivariate analysis of frequency data.

Suppose an investigator was interested in the hypothesis that level of aspiration is positively related to success in college: the higher the level of aspiration, the greater the probability of graduating. Suppose further that he had a relatively crude dichotomous measure of level of aspiration. He also had, of course, a measure of success in college: Did a student graduate, or didn't he? The variables and categories, then, are Hi *LA* (high level of aspiration), Lo *LA*, *SC* (success in college), and *NSC* (not successful in college). He drew a random sample of 400 sophomores from a college and obtained level of aspiration measures from them. He divided the 400 students into halves on the basis of the

Table 10.12 Relation Between Level of Aspiration and School Achievement, Hypothetical Data

	SC	NSC	
Hi *LA*	140	60	200
Lo *LA*	60	140	200
	200	200	(400)

level-of-aspiration measures. At the end of three years he further categorized the students on the basis of having graduated or not. Suppose the results were those shown in Table 10.12.[17] There is evidently a relation between the variables: $\chi^2 = 64$, significant at the .001 level, and $C = .37$.

The investigator shows the results to a colleague, a rather sour individual, who says they are questionable, that if social class were brought into the picture the relation might be quite different. He reasons that social class and level of aspiration are strongly related, and that the original relation might hold for middle-class students but not for working-class students. Disconcerted, the investigator goes back to his data, and, since he luckily has indices of social class for all the subjects, he finds, when he works out the three-variable crossbreak, the results shown in Table 10.13. Inspection of the data shows that the investigator's colleague was right: the relation between level of aspiration and success in college is considerably more pronounced with middle-class students than with working-class students.

The investigator can study the relations in more depth by calculating percentages separately for the middle-class and working-class sides of Table 10.13. In this case, since the frequencies in each row of the halves of the table total to 100, the frequencies are, in effect, percentages. It can be seen that the relation between level of aspiration and college success is stronger with middle-class students than it is with working-class students.

In the above analysis, the data were specified: it was shown, by introducing the social-class variable, that the relation between level of aspiration and success in college was stronger in one group (middle class) than in another group (working class). This is

Table 10.13 Relations Among Level of Aspiration, Social Class, and School Achievement, Hypothetical Data

	MC		WC		
	Hi *LA*	Lo *LA*	Hi *LA*	Lo *LA*	
SC	80	20	60	40	200
NSC	20	80	40	60	200
	100	100	100	100	(400)
	(200)		(200)		

[17] The marginal totals of Table 10.12 (and those of Table 10.13, below) have been made equal to simplify the discussion and to highlight certain points to be made here and later. This is of course unrealistic: frequency tables are rarely this obliging.

similar to the phenomenon of interaction discussed in Chapter 9. We said, then, that interaction means that an independent variable affects a dependent variable differently at different levels or facets of another independent variable. Strictly speaking, ''interaction'' is a term used in experimental research and analysis of variance, as we will see in subsequent chapters. There is some question, therefore, whether the term can be applied in nonexperimental research and in the kind of analysis we are now examining. The position taken in this book is that interaction is a general phenomenon of great importance and that it occurs in both experimental and nonexperimental research. The ''validity'' of interaction in nonexperimental research, however, is much harder to establish than in experimental research. Indeed, this is true of the ''validity'' of all relations in nonexperimental research, as we will see clearly and in detail in Chapter 22. In sum, the specified relations of Table 10.13 can be viewed as interaction or simply as specification of relations. The main thing, of course, is that we understand what is going on: Relations are stronger, weaker, or even zero at different levels of other independent variables. In the above example, the relation between level of aspiration and college success is different in the two social classes. With such multivariate statements, we are getting closer to the heart and spirit of scientific investigation, analysis, and interpretation.

CROSSBREAKS, RELATIONS, AND ORDERED PAIRS

A relation is a set of ordered pairs. Two of the ways in which we can express a set of ordered pairs are by listing the pairs and by graphing them. A coefficient of correlation is an index that expresses the magnitude of a relation. A crossbreak expresses the ordered pairs in a table of frequencies.

To show how these ideas are related, take the fictitious data of Table 10.14. The relation studied is between state control of the economic system and political democracy. In a study of political democracy in modern nations, Bollen hypothesized that the greater the control of the economic system of a country, the lower its level of political democracy.[18] Suppose that of a sample of 23 countries, we count 12 countries with low economic control (Low EC) and 11 countries with high economic control (High EC). We also count 13 countries with high political development (High PD) and 10 countries with low political development (Low PD). This gives us the marginal totals of a 2×2 crossbreak. It does not tell us how many countries are in each of the cells, however.

We now count the number of Low EC countries that have High PD and the number of

Table 10.14 Relation Between State Control of Economic System and Political Development, Fictitious Data

		B_1 High PD		B_2 Low PD		
A_1	Low EC	(1,1)	10	(1,0)	2	12
A_2	High EC	(0,1)	3	(0,0)	8	11
		13		10		

[18] K. Bollen, ''Political Democracy and the Timing of Development,'' *American Sociological Review,* 44 (1979), 572–587. This was one of several hypotheses on political democracy. We use this hypothesis only as suggestive. The data of Table 10.14 are entirely fictitious.

High EC countries that have Low PD. These counts are entered in the appropriate cells of the 2 × 2 crossbreak of Table 10.14. We find that the cell frequencies depart significantly from chance expectation.[19] There is thus a significant relation between state economic control and political development.

So that we can see the ordered pairs clearly, let's change the variable notation. Let A_1 = Low EC, A_2 = High EC, B_1 = High PD, and B_2 = Low PD. The A and B labels have been appropriately inserted in Table 10.14. Now, how do we set up the ordered pairs of the crossbreak? We do so by assigning each of the 23 countries one of the following subset combinations: (1,1), (0,1), (1,0), (0,0). (See the designations in Table 10.14.) In other words, A_1 and B_1 are assigned 1's, and A_2 and B_2 are assigned 0's. If a country has Low EC *and* High PD, then it is A_1B_1; consequently the ordered pair assigned to it is (1,1). The first 10 countries of Table 10.15 belong to the A_1B_1 category and are thus assigned (1,1). Similarly, the remaining countries are assigned ordered pairs of numbers according to their subset membership. The full list of 23 ordered pairs is given in Table 10.15. The categories or crossbreak (set) intersections have been indicated.

Table 10.15 Ordered-pair Arrangement of the Data of Table 10.14

Countries	A	B	
1	1	1	
2	1	1	
3	1	1	
4	1	1	
5	1	1	
6	1	1	A_1B_1
7	1	1	
8	1	1	
9	1	1	
10	1	1	
11	0	1	
12	0	1	A_2B_1
13	0	1	
14	1	0	
15	1	0	A_1B_2
16	0	0	
17	0	0	
18	0	0	
19	0	0	
20	0	0	A_2B_2
21	0	0	
22	0	0	
23	0	0	

The relation is the set of ordered pairs of 1's and 0's. Table 10.15 is simply a different way of expressing the same relation shown in Table 10.14. We can calculate a coefficient of correlation for both tables. If, for example, we calculate a coefficient of correlation, a

[19] As determined by Finney's tables: E. Pearson and H. Hartley, eds., *Biometrika Tables for Statisticians,* Vol. I. Cambridge: Cambridge University Press, 1954, pp. 188ff. When the frequencies of a 2 × 2 contingency table are relatively small, the Finney tables give a more accurate test of significance than χ^2 does.

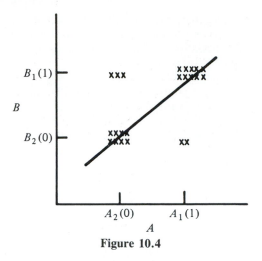

Figure 10.4

product-moment r, of the Table 10.15 data, we obtain .56. (The product-moment r calculated with 1's and 0's is called a *phi* (ϕ) coefficient.[20])

Graph the relation. Let there be two axes, A and B, at right angles to each other, and let A and B represent the two variables of Tables 10.14 and 10.15. We are interested in studying the relation between A and B. Figure 10.4 shows the graphed ordered pairs. It also shows a "relation" line run through the larger clusters of pairs. Where is the relation? We ask: Is there a set of ordered pairs that defines a significant relation between A and B? We have *paired* each individual's score on A with his "score" on B and plotted the pairs on the A and B axes. Going back to the substance of the relation, we pair each individual country's "score" on economic control with its "score" on political development. In this manner we obtain a set of ordered pairs and this set *is* a relation. Our real question, however, is not: Is there a relation between A and B? but rather: What is the nature of the relation between A and B?

We can see from Figure 10.4 that the relation between A and B is fairly strong. This is determined by the ordered pairs: the pairs are mostly (a_1b_1) and (a_2b_2). There are comparatively few (a_1b_2) and (a_2b_1) pairs. In words, low economic control scores pair with high political development scores (1,1), and high economic control scores pair with political development scores (0,0), with comparatively few exceptions (5 cases out of 23). We cannot name this relation succinctly, as we can such relations as "marriage," "brotherhood," and the like. We might, however, call it "state economic control–political development," meaning that there is a relation of these variables in the ordered-pair sense.

ADDENDUM

Multivariate Analysis of Frequency Data: Log-Linear Models

Most of the above discussion was limited to two variables, an independent variable and a dependent variable. Many frequency data analyses, however, are of three and more variables. A fictitious example with three variables was given earlier in Table 10.13. While most three-variable cases can be analyzed and interpreted using percentages, study data

---

[20]This is not a recommended procedure. It is used here to help clarify analytic procedures and not to illustrate how ϕ is calculated.

with four or more variables are not so amenable to analysis and interpretation. Another approach is needed. Even with three variables another approach is often needed because the data are too complex and subtle for simple interpretation. With a two-variable cross-break there is only one relation: between A and B. With three variables, however, there are four relations of possible interest: AB, AC, BC, and ABC. The three two-variable crossbreaks are the kind we have been studying. The one three-variable crossbreak, ABC, is like that shown in Table 10.13, and in this case can be viewed most fruitfully as follows: study of the relation between level of aspiration and success in college in two samples: middle class and working class. That is, we study whether the relation between level of aspiration and college success is the same in the middle class as it is in the working class. If it is the same we have "established" an invariance. If it is different, however, we have an interaction: the relation is such-and-such in the middle class, but it is so-and-so in the working class.

In the last decade or so, remarkable changes in conceptualization of research problems and in data analysis have taken place. Before the development of multivariate analysis of both continuous measures and frequencies, analysis—and the conceptualization of analysis—was mostly bivariate. Investigators studied the relations between pairs of variables, as we have pretty much done in Chapter 10. While the idea of studying the operation of several variables simultaneously was well-known, the practical means of doing so had to wait for both the computer and a different way of thinking. Later in this book we will examine the nature of the computer and its important role in research. We want now to explore, but briefly and only in an introductory way, part of the newer kind of thinking in behavioral research in relation to frequency analysis.

Doing research is in effect setting up models of what "reality" is supposed to be and then testing the models against empirical data. The trouble is that the world is which influences and variables operate is almost always complex, and scientists are always limited to aspects of this complexity. The whole "reality" of anything is forever beyond reach. Perhaps we can only rarely say that A is related to B in all times and all circumstances. Indeed, the variables A and B are themselves complex. We have already seen this. Intelligence, achievement, level of aspiration, social class, and political development, for example, are all complex ideas that reflect the natural complexity of the behavioral world. Now add to this individual variable complexity the additional complexity of the relations among the variables and one wonders how it is possible to study the complexity and actually advance knowledge. Indeed, in the face of these difficulties it is remarkable that science has been as successful as it has been.

In the contemporary approach to multivariate data, we test data to determine what model fits the data. A *model* is an abstract outline specifying hypothesized relations in a set of data.[21] Let's use the data and the paradigm of Table 10.13 again. Let S = success (in college); L = level of aspiration; C = social class, the three variables of the table. If I believe that the relation between level of aspiration and success in college is the same in the middle class and in the working class, then I am hypothesizing a certain complex outcome; I am specifying a model. For example, if I believe that level of aspiration (L) "determines" or "influences" success in college (S), without regard to social class (C), I can simply write:

LS

This means that L and S are related, and that they have the same relation in both social

---

[21] This definition is hardly satisfactory. Indeed, it is extremely difficult if not impossible to define "model" satisfactorily. Yet we have to have something to go on and the above definition should work. See M. Brodbeck, "Models, Meaning, and Theories." In M. Brodbeck, ed., *Readings in the Philosophy of the Social Sciences.* New York: Macmillan, 1968, pp. 579–600. Brodbeck virtually demolishes the use of "models" in the social sciences and shows how difficult and complex the idea is.

classes. It also means that social class and success in college are not related and that social class and level of aspiration are not related.

Suppose, however, that level of aspiration and success in college are related, but that they are related differently in the middle class and working class, as indicated by the data of Table 10.13. Then the model is quite different:[22]

SLC

This means that success in college (*S*) and the level of aspiration (*L*) are related, but that they are somehow related differently in the two social classes (*C*). The difference may take one of several forms. One, the relation (*SL*) may exist in both social classes, but it may be stronger in one social class than in the other, as in Table 10.13. Two, the relation may exist in one social class but not in the other. And three, the relation may take a certain form (positive, for example) in one social class but a different form (negative, for example) in the other social class. The *SLC* means that all three variables have to be taken into account in order for the model to be satisfactory (fit the data).

This should be sufficient discussion for a preliminary conceptual idea of an elementary multivariate approach to frequency data. A crucial idea in contemporary methodological approaches to frequency data analysis is that of "fit." One proposes a model that springs from a theory, or that somehow seems reasonable. One sets up the model and, through appropriate analysis, one generates data consistent with the model. Then one compares the generated data to the actual data. If they are alike, then the model fits. If they are different, then the model does not fit. It so happens that the only model that fits the data of Table 10.13 is that just given: *SLC*. And study of the table (and appropriate computer output) shows that the first possibility outlined in the preceding paragraph seems "correct": the relation between level of aspiration and success in college "exists" in both the middle class and the working class, and it is stronger in the middle class than it is in the working class.

When crossbreak data tables have more than three variables they become difficult to analyze because of the many possible relations. With two variables, there is only the relation *AB* to examine, as was pointed out earlier. With three variables, the possible relations are: *AB, AC, BC, ABC*. There are three first-order relations and one second-order relation. With four variables, there are many more: 11 in all. *AB, AC, AD, BC, CD* are the first-order possibilities; *ABC, ABD, ACD, BCD* are the second-order possible relations; *ABCD* is the third-order possibility. (Each of these would have a table like Table 10.13— or larger.) Obviously frequency data studies with four variables can be very complex. With five or more variables, the numbers of relations become so high as to be virtually unmanageable. Fortunately, problems in the published literature rarely have more than four variables. This is in sharp contrast to studies with continuous measures and continuous measure analysis where five and more variables are common.

As said earlier, another approach and another mode of analysis are needed. There are several such approaches and modes of analysis, but the most useful and most-used is called log-linear analysis. Without more background it is not possible to describe and explain this approach adequately. We can try, however, to take the mystery out of the name and to characterize the approach. Recall that to calculate χ^2 it was necessary to calculate expected frequencies. Take an easy example from a Senate vote on the budget reported in the *New York Times*.[23] This vote is given in Table 10.16, together with calculations of expected frequencies. The frequency of the first cell to be expected on the

---

[22] In doing an actual analysis, this model is not stated correctly in the sense that it does not follow conventional log-linear rules. It is, however, good enough for our pedagogical purpose.

[23] *New York Times*, May 13, 1981. The title of the article was: "Compliant but Reluctant Democrats."

basis of chance is 46/98ths of 78, or $(46)(78)/98 = 36.612$. The expected frequencies for the other three cells are calculated similarly (see footnote a of Table 10.16). It is possible to do an analysis based on such multiplicative calculations.[24]

Table 10.16   Senate Vote on the Budget, May 12, 1981

	For		Against		
Democrat	36.612[a]	28	9.388	18	46
Republican	41.388	50	10.612	2	52
		78		20	98

[a]Calculation of expected frequencies: $(46)(78)/98 = 36.612$; $(46)(20)/98 = 9.388$; etc. Logarithmic calculations: $l(46) + l(78) - l(98) = 3.829 + 4.357 - 4.585 = 3.600$. Antilog $(3.600) = 36.612$.

Log-linear models are virtually the same as multiplicative models except that they are expressed in natural logarithms.[25] Various models can be specified to "fit" any set of crossbreak frequency data. If one were to say that there is no relation between political party membership and vote on the budget in Table 10.16, then the following model can be written for the first cell of the table:

$$E_{11} = u + u_A + u_B \tag{10.1}$$

where E_{11} = expectation for cell 11; u is a grand mean, u_A is a row effect, or the difference between 46 and 52, and u_B is the column effect, or the difference between 78 and 20. This model really states that there is no relation between A and B, that the only effects evident in the table are due to the sum of the grand mean (a constant), the difference between the rows and the difference between the columns. Such a model is unlikely to fit many data tables and certainly not that of Table 10.16. It is more likely that there is some relation between A and B in the table. If so, the model would be:

$$E_{11} = u + u_A + u_B + u_{AB} \tag{10.2}$$

where u_{AB} in effect expresses the relation between A and B. (Remember: the u's, the effects, will be in logarithmic form.)

How these terms are calculated is of no concern to us. We want only to focus on possible models and to get an intuitive idea of log-linear analysis. The empirically valid model of Table 10.13, the model that fits the data, is written:

$$E_{11} = u + u_A + u_B + u_C + u_{AB} + u_{AC} + u_{BC} + u_{ABC} \tag{10.3}$$

[24] D. Knoke and P. Burke, *Log-Linear Models*. Beverly Hills, Calif.: Sage Publications, 1980. The first part of this brochure describes and illustrates multiplicative models.

[25] Readers are more likely to be familiar with logarithms to the base 10. For example, the number 100 expressed in a logarithm to the base 10 is 2.00, or $10^2 = 100$. That is, 2 is the logarithm. The number 43 is expressed $10^{1.6335}$. The value 1.6335 is the logarithm, or the power of 10 required to produce 43. Natural logarithms, which are used in log-linear models analysis, have certain properties that make them desirable. They are logarithms to the base $e = 2.71828$. The number 43 is then expressed: $l_e(43) = 3.7612$, or $43 = 2.71828^{3.7612}$. The number 3.7612 is the natural logarithm of 43. Using logarithms, it is possible to change multiplicative to additive operations. The expected frequency, in logarithms, for the first cell of Table 10.16 has been calculated in footnote a of the table. (It used to be cumbersome to work with logarithms: one had to look them up in tables, write them down, and then calculate with them. Today, however, computer functions make logarithms readily accessible and easy to use. Even many hand-held calculators have both kinds of logarithms as functions.)

This states that, to account for the data, all possible relations of A, B, and C must be taken into account.[26] Strictly speaking, this is not literally true because some of the terms equalled zero. For instance, the relation between social class and college success, and the differences between the marginal frequencies were all zero. So, a more accurate way to write the model would be:

$$E_{11} = u + u_{BC} + u_{ABC} \tag{10.4}$$

which means, in effect, that level of aspiration and college success are related, and that they are differently related in the middle class and the working class (see Table 10.13). The rules of log-linear analysis, however, require the specification of *all* the terms that "precede" the highest order term, u_{ABC}.

In log-linear analysis, the u's of whatever model is specified (hypothesized) are calculated and called "effects." If they are significantly different from zero, they indicate relations (except u_A, u_B, and u_C, which only express the differences in marginal frequencies). The point is that log-linear analysis shows where relations "exist" and gives estimates of their magnitude and their statistical significance. Perhaps more important, log-linear analysis provides a method for telling which model (or models) among the many possible in complex frequency tables fits the empirical data. For the data of Table 10.13, for example, the only model that fits the data is expressed in Equation 10.3 (or 10.4), which means essentially what we expressed earlier in words: there is a second-order interaction in the data, or level of aspiration is related to college success more strongly in the middle class than in the working class.

The reader should not feel chagrined if he has had trouble following the above discussion. Log-linear analysis, while powerful and highly useful, is a complex method that requires careful and deep study. The discussion of some of its characteristics was attempted here to introduce the highly important ideas of model and testing for fit, to apprise the reader of log-linear analysis, one of the most important contemporary methodological developments, and to widen our knowledge of multivariate analysis and multivariate research problems.

Study Suggestions

1. In an experimental study of the hypothesis that guilt leads to compliance, Freedman, Wallington, and Bliss induced guilt in their experimental subjects by having them lie about a test they were to take.[27] Control subjects were not made to lie. The subjects were then asked whether they would be willing the participate in an unrelated study (dependent variable: compliance). The authors report the following frequency table:

	Experimental (Lie)	Control (Not Lie)
Comply	20	11
Not Comply	11	20

Calculate χ^2, C, and percentages. Interpret the results. Is the hypothesis supported? Is the relation

[26] Users of log-linear analysis, however, would usually only write the model as *ABC*. The other terms are implied. Or it could be written:

A, B, C, AB, AC, BC, ABC.

[27] J. Freedman, S. Wallington, and E. Bless, "Compliance Without Pressure: The Effect of Guilt," *Journal of Personality and Social Psychology*, 7 (1967), 117–124.

weak, moderate, strong? (*Answers:* $\chi^2 = 5.23$ ($p < .05$); $C = .28$. Yes, the hypothesis is supported. The relation is weak to moderate.)

2. On June 10, 1981, the U.S. Senate voted on requiring households to pay in part for food stamps. The vote was:[28]

	For	Against
Republican	26	27
Democrat	7	39

Calculate χ^2, C, and percentages. Interpret the results. (*Answers:* $\chi^2 = 12.69$; $C = .34$.)

3. In the important Kerner Commission Report on civil disorders (riots) in the United States, a large number of relations are presented in table form. Here is one of the tables, from a Newark survey, which gives the percentages of responses to the question, "Sometimes I hate white people," given by rioters (R) and people not involved (NI).[29]

	R ($N = 105$)	NI ($N = 126$)
Agree	72.4%	50.0%
Disagree	27.6	50.0

(a) Interpret the table. Examine the data carefully before interpreting.
(b) Calculate the frequencies (e.g., $.724 \times 105 = 76$). Are the percentages calculated the "right" way? Calculate them across the rows, e.g., $76/139 = .55$. Does the interpretation change? How?
(c) If you think the percentages are calculated incorrectly in the data above, why are they incorrect?

4. The analysis of crossbreaks and contingency tables is a large and deep subject. We have only examined elementary principles and methods in this chapter. The student who is going to do research and the practicing professional should go deeper. The following references are a good beginning. They are oriented to behavioral science data and are highly recommended.

Everitt, B. *The Analysis of Contingency Tables*. New York: Wiley (Halsted Press) and London: Chapman and Hall, 1977. A fine book.

Gilbert, F. *Modelling Society: An Introduction to Loglinear Analysis for Social Researchers*. London: George Allen & Unwin, 1981. Valuable book. Has perhaps the clearest explanation of how to conceptualize and calculate expected frequencies for different models.

Kennedy, J. *Analyzing Qualitative Data: Introductory Log-Linear Analysis for Behavioral Research*. New York: Praeger, 1983. Thorough and fine treatment. Puts strong emphasis on the structural and mathematical similarity of analysis of variance and log-linear models analysis.

Reynolds, H. *Analysis of Nominal Data*. Beverly Hills and London: Sage Publications, 1977. A very good, clear, and useful brief introduction.

Reynolds, H. *The Analysis of Cross-Classifications*. New York: Free Press; London: Collier Macmillan, 1977. Reynolds's extended treatment. Excellent.

All five references discuss log-linear models.

5. It is both possible and desirable to calculate coefficients of association for frequency data. C, the coefficient of contingency, was described in this chapter. Many such coefficients are possible, especially for 2×2 tables. (The discussions of Everitt, chaps. 2 and 3, and Reynolds, chap. 2, are very good.) For example, the product-moment coefficient of correlation is possible: $r = \sqrt{\chi^2/N}$. It is also called ϕ (phi) for nominal data. For the data of Table 10.2, a strong relation, $\chi^2 = 57.77$,

---

[28] *Congressional Quarterly*, 39 (1981).
[29] *Report of the National Advisory Commission on Civil Disorders*. New York: Bantam, 1968, p. 176.

$C = .61$, and $r = .77$. It is suggested that readers study Everitt's or Reynolds' extended treatment and then calculate χ^2, C, and r for the 2×2 tables of this chapter. For the tables with more than two classifications, calculate χ^2 and C. The advanced student should study newer approaches and measures, like Goodman and Kruskal's lambda, the odds ratio, and the log odds ration.

6. Except for large tables, the calculation of χ^2, C, and other coefficients of association is not difficult and can be done with good small calculators. For those students who have programmable calculators or microcomputers, it is fairly easy to write programs that will calculate χ^2, C, and other indices. Some machines (e.g., Hewlett-Packard HP-67 and HP-41CV) have accompanying software (programs) that do the calculations. Virtually any computer installation will have programs for contingency table analysis. One of the easiest to use is the widely available Minitab set of programs, which has a program, Tables, that calculates χ^2 for various tables. Unfortunately, Minitab calculates no indices of association. (Note, however, that if you have χ^2 you can easily calculate C and r with a hand calculator.) Log-linear models can be calculated "by hand," but such calculations are often difficult and risky. The Goodman computer program ECTA is not hard to use and is efficient. The BMDP computer programs, BMDP3F (1977 and 1979 manuals) and BMDP4F (1981 manual)[30] are highly sophisticated programs that are harder to use than ECTA but that yield more analytic results.

7. Have occupations of women changed under the impact of the women's liberation movement? Here are interesting data from a U.S. Census Report (in thousands):[31]

	1970		1977	
	Male	Female	Male	Female
Professional, Managerial, Administrative	12,005	5,637	15,261	7,943
Clerical, Sales Service	10,413	16,489	11,213	21,471

(*Note:* The above figures were obtained by adding the categories Professional + Managerial + Administrative; Clerical + Sales + Service.)

(a) Calculate percentages. (Be careful: calculate from the independent variables to the dependent variable, as usual.)

(b) Calculate χ^2 and C for 1970 and 1977 separately. (Use the above figures, i.e., neglect the fact that the figures indicate thousands. This affects χ^2 but not C.)

(c) Interpret the results of your calculations. (Be circumspect. The method of adding the category numbers may have been biased or even incorrect.)

(d) In b, above, you calculated χ^2 and C using the tabled frequencies as they are. Now do the same calculations using the numbers in the thousands, i.e., instead of 12,005, for instance, use 12,005,000. Note the enormous increase in χ^2 but C is the same. Here is a generalization: With very large numbers virtually everything is statistically significant. This is one reason for measures of association that are unaffected by the magnitude of the numbers.

[30] W. Dixon and M. Brown, eds., *BMDP-77: Biomedical Computer Programs, P-Series*. Berkeley: University of California Press, 1977, pp. 297–332; W. Dixon, ed., *BMDP Statistical Software*. Berkeley: University of California Press, 1981, pp. 143–206. The 1977 program is excellent and, with application and study, readily used. The 1981 4F program is an extensive revision of the earlier program and, while also excellent, is harder to use because so many possibilities and options have been incorporated into one program. Although praised by some, the trend toward highly complex programs that do "everything" is perhaps unfortunate because it puts programs beyond the understanding of many users and makes their intelligent and discerning use more difficult. (*Advice:* Don't try to use log-linear analysis and programs without deep and long study. *This is a powerful methodology; it is also highly complex and difficult.*)

[31] U.S. Dept. of Commerce, Bureau of the Census, *Social and Economic Characteristics of the Metropolitan and Nonmetropolitan Population: 1977 and 1970*. Washington, D.C.: U.S. Government Printing Office, 1978, pp. 74–79. (Current Population Reports, Special Studies P-23, No. 75.) (The efficient citation of government publications is an arcane art. For some reason such publications have long and complex sources and names.)

8. Here are some interesting frequency data obtained in a now well-known study by the Survey Research Center, University of Michigan, on the determinants of feelings of political efficacy. The 1,223 subjects of the crossbreak were a random sample of the people of the United States. In this case the relation was between education and feelings of political efficacy among men and women.[32]

Sex	Education	*Political Efficacy* Hi PE	Med PE	Lo PE
Men	Grade School	48	46	56
	High School	126	77	64
	College	96	14	6
Women	Grade School	26	39	133
	High School	153	130	99
	College	75	27	8

(a) Calculate percentages and interpret.

(b) Does education seem to influence sense of political efficacy? Strongly? Moderately? Is the relation the same with women as it is with men?

COMPUTATIONAL ADDENDUM

The results you obtain from your calculations may not agree exactly with those of the text. This is often because of so-called errors of rounding. In calculations with fractional numbers—for instance, 1234.567, 482.791, and the like—it is often necessary to round off results to, say, two decimal places. Multiply 1234.567 by 482.791; the result is 596,037.8365. Round this product to two decimal places: 596,037.84. Now imagine hundreds of such multiplications, and you will realize that obtained products will not be completely accurate because small errors cumulate. Large computers with large memories and processors that work with very large numbers give the most accurate results. Results obtained with microcomputers and handheld calculators, on the other hand, are much less accurate. For example, the χ^2 calculated with the data of Table 10.6 was reported as 65.1864. This was calculated with a handheld calculator (but a highly accurate one). The χ^2 obtained with a microcomputer of greater capacity and accuracy, however, was 65.1860.

[32] A. Campbell, P. Converse, W. Miller, and P. Stokes, *The American Voter*. New York: Wiley, 1960. The above tabled frequencies were calculated from the authors' Table 17-9, p. 491, in which percentages were reported. (This table included another variable: South. The above data were from the non-South.)

Chapter 11

Statistics: Purpose, Approach, Method

THE BASIC APPROACH

THE BASIC principle behind the use of statistical tests of significance can be summed up in one sentence: *Compare obtained results to chance expectation*. When a research study is done and statistical results obtained, they are checked against the results expected by chance. In Chapter 7 we met examples of checking empirical results of coin-tossing and dice-throwing against theoretical expectations. For example, if a die is thrown a large number of times, the expected proportion of occurrences of a 4, say, is one-sixth of the total number of throws. In Chapter 10 we learned that the rationale of the χ^2 test was the comparison of numbers of observed frequencies of events to the numbers of frequencies expected by chance. Indeed, the statistical ideas of Chapter 10 were presented before those of this chapter in part to give the student preliminary experience with obtained and expected results.

Two dice were thrown 72 times in a demonstration described in Chapter 7. Theoretically, 7 should turn up $1/6 \times 72 = 12$. But Table 7.2 showed that 7 turned up 15 times in 72 throws rather than 12 times. We ask an important question: Does this obtained result differ significantly from the theoretically expected result? Or: Does this obtained result differ from chance expectation enough to warrant a belief that something other than chance is at work?

Such questions are the essence of the statistical approach. Statisticians are skeptics. They do not believe in the "reality" of empirical results until they have applied statistical tests to them. They assume that results are chance results until shown to be otherwise. They are inveterate probabilists. The core of their approach to empirical data is to set up chance expectation as their hypothesis and to try to fit empirical data to the chance model. If the empirical data "fit" the chance model, then it is said that they are "not significant." If they do not fit the chance model, if they depart "sufficiently" from the chance model, it is said that they are "significant."

This and several succeeding chapters are devoted to the statistical approach to research problems. In this chapter we extend the discussion of Chapter 7 on probability to basic conceptions of the mean, variance, and standard deviation. The so-called law of large numbers and the normal probability curve are also explained and interpreted, and some idea is given of their potent use in statistics. In the next chapter we tackle the idea of statistical testing itself. These two chapters are the foundation.

DEFINITION AND PURPOSE OF STATISTICS

Statistics is the theory and method of analyzing quantitative data obtained from samples of observations in order to study and compare sources of variance of phenomena, to help make decisions to accept or reject hypothesized relations between the phenomena, and to aid in making reliable inferences from empirical observations.

Four purposes of statistics are suggested in this definition. The first is the commonest and most traditional: to reduce large quantities of data to manageable and understandable form. It is impossible to digest 100 scores, for instance, but if a mean and a standard deviation are calculated, the scores can be readily interpreted by a trained person. The definition of "statistic" stems from this traditional usage and purpose of statistics. A *statistic* is a measure calculated from a sample. A statistic contrasts with a *parameter*, which is a population value. If, in U, a population or universe, we calculate the mean, this is a parameter. Now take a subset (sample) A of U. The mean of A is a statistic. For our purpose, parameters are of theoretical interest only. They are not usually known. They are *estimated* with statistics. Thus we deal mostly with sample or subset statistics. These samples are usually conceived to be representative of U. Statistics, then, are epitomes or summaries of the samples—and often, presumably, of the populations—from which they are calculated. Means, medians, variances, standard deviations, percentiles, percentages, and so on, calculated from samples, are statistics.

A second purpose of statistics is to aid in the study of populations and samples. This use of statistics is so well known that it will not be discussed. Besides, we studied something of populations and samples in earlier chapters.

A third purpose of statistics is to aid in decision making. If an educational psychologist needs to know which of three methods of instruction promotes the most learning with the least cost, he can use statistics to help him gain this knowledge. This use of statistics is comparatively recent.

Although most decision situations are more complex, we use an example that is quite familiar by now. A decision-maker dice gambler would first lay out the outcomes for dice throws. These are, of course, 2 through 12. He notes the differing frequencies of the numbers. For example, 2 and 12 will probably occur much less often than 7 or 6. He calculates the probabilities for the various outcomes. Finally, on the basis of how much money he can expect to make, he devises a betting system. He decides, for instance, that, since 7 has a probability of 1/6, he will require that his opponent give him, say, odds of 5 to 1 instead of even money on the first throw. (We here take liberties with craps.) To make this whole thing a bit more dramatic, suppose that two players operate with different decision-makers.[1] One player, A, proposes the following game: A will win if 2, 3, or 4

[1] This example was suggested by I. Bross, *Design for Decision*. New York: Macmillan, 1953, p. 28.

turns up; his opponent, *B*, will win if 5, 6, or 7 turns up (outcomes 8 through 12 are to be disregarded). It is obvious that *A*'s decision-maker is faulty. It is based on the assumption that 2, 3, 4, 5, 6, and 7 are equiprobable. *B* should have a good time with this game.

The fourth and last purpose of statistics, to aid in making reliable inferences from observational data, is closely allied to, indeed, is part of, the purpose of helping to make decisions among hypotheses. An *inference* is a proposition or generalization derived by reasoning from other propositions, or from evidence. Generally speaking, an inference is a conclusion arrived at through reasoning. In statistics, a number of inferences may be drawn from tests of statistical hypotheses. We "conclude" that methods A and B really differ. We conclude from evidence, say $r = .67$, that two variables are really related.

Statistical inferences have two characteristics. One, the inferences are usually made *from samples to populations*. When we say that the variables *A* and *B* are related because the statistical evidence is $r = .67$, we are inferring that because $r = .67$ in *this* sample it is $r = .67$, or near .67, in the population from which the sample was drawn. The second kind of inference is used when investigators are not interested in the populations, or only interested secondarily in them. An educational investigator is studying the presumed effect of the relationships between board of education members and chief educational administrators, on the one hand, and teacher morale, on the other hand. His hypothesis is that, when relationships between boards and chief administrators are strained, teacher morale is lower than otherwise. He is interested only in testing this hypothesis in Y County. He makes the study and obtains statistical results that support the hypothesis, for example, morale is lower in system A than in systems B and C. He *infers*, from the statistical evidence of a difference between system A, on the one hand, and systems B and C, on the other hand, that his hypothetical proposition is correct—in Y County. And it is possible for his interest to be limited strictly to Y County.

To summarize much of the above discussion, the purposes of statistics can be reduced to one major purpose: *to aid in inference-making*. This is one of the basic purposes of research design, methodology, and statistics. Scientists want to draw inferences from data. Statistics, through its power to reduce data to manageable forms (statistics) and its power to study and analyze variances, enables scientists to attach probability estimates to the inferences they draw from data. Statistics says, in effect, "The inference you have drawn is correct at such-and-such a level of significance. You may act as though your hypothesis were true, remembering that there is such-and-such a probability that it is untrue." It should be reasonably clear why some contemporary statisticians call statistics the discipline of decision making under uncertainty. It should also be reasonably clear that, whether you know it or not, you are always making inferences, attaching probabilities to various outcomes or hypotheses, and making decisions on the basis of statistical reasoning. Statistics, using probability theory and mathematics, makes the process more systematic and objective.

BINOMIAL STATISTICS

When things are counted, the number system used is simple and useful. Whenever objects are counted, they are counted on the basis of some criterion, some variable or attribute, in research language. Many examples have already been given: heads, tails, numbers on dice, sex, aggressive acts, political preference, and so on. If a person or a thing possesses the attribute, the person or thing is "counted in," we say. When something is "counted in" because it possesses the attribute in question, it is assigned a 1. If it does not possess the attribute, it is assigned a 0. This is a binomial system.

Earlier, the mean was defined as $M = \Sigma X/n$. The variance is $V = \Sigma x^2/n$, where $x =$

$X - M$ (each x is a deviation from the mean). The standard deviation is $SD = \sqrt{V}$. Of course, these formulas work with any scores. Here we use them only with 1's and 0's. And it is useful to alter the formula for the mean. The formula $\Sigma X/n$ is not general enough. It assumes that all scores are equiprobable. A more general formula, which can be used when equiprobability is not assumed, is

$$M = \Sigma[X \cdot w(X)] \qquad (11.1)$$

where $w(X)$ is the weight assigned to an X. $w(X)$ simply means the probability each X has of occurring. The formula says: Multiply each X, each score, by its weight (probability), and then add them all up. Notice that if all X's are equally probable, this formula is the same as $\Sigma X/n$.

The mean of the set $\{1, 2, 3, 4, 5,\}$ is

$$M = \frac{1 + 2 + 3 + 4 + 5}{5} = \frac{15}{5} = 3$$

By Formula 11.1 it is, of course, the same, but its computation looks different:

$$M = 1 \cdot 1/5 + 2 \cdot 1/5 + 3 \cdot 1/5 + 4 \cdot 1/5 + 5 \cdot 1/5 = 3$$

Why the hair-splitting? Let a coin be tossed. $U = \{H, T\}$. The *mean number of heads* is, by Equation 11.1,

$$M = 1 \cdot 1/2 + 0 \cdot 1/2 = 1/2$$

Let two coins be tossed. $U = \{HH, HT, TH, TT\}$. The mean number of heads, or the *expectation* of heads, is

$$M = 2 \cdot 1/4 + 1 \cdot 1/4 + 1 \cdot 1/4 + 0 \cdot 1/4 = 4/4 = 1$$

This means that if two coins are tossed many times, the average number of heads per toss is 1. If we sample one person from 30 men and 70 women, the mean of men is: $M = 3/10 \cdot 1 + 7/10 \cdot 0 = .3$. The mean for women is: $M = 3/10 \cdot 0 + 7/10 \cdot 1 = .7$. These are the means for one outcome. (This is a little like saying "an average of 2.5 children per family.")

What has been said in these examples is that the mean of any single experiment (a single coin toss, a sample of one person) is the probability of the occurrence of one of two possible outcomes (heads, a man) which, if the outcome occurs, is assigned a 1 and, if it does not occur, is assigned a 0. This is tantamount to saying: $p(1) = p$ and $p(0) = 1 - p$. In the one-toss experiment, let 1 be assigned if heads turns up and 0 if tails turns up. Then $p(1) = 1/2$ and $p(0) = 1 - 1/2 = 1/2$. In tossing a coin twice, let 1 be assigned to each head that occurs and 0 to each tail. We are interested in the outcome "heads." $U = \{HH, HT, TH, TT\}$. The mean is

$$M = 1/4 \cdot 2 + 1/4 \cdot 1 + 1/4 \cdot 1 + 1/4 \cdot 0 = 1$$

Can we arrive at the same result in an easier manner? Yes. Just add the means for each outcome. The mean of the outcome of one coin toss is 1/2. For two coin tosses it is $1/2 + 1/2 = 1$. To assign probabilities with one coin toss, we weight 1 (heads) with its probability and 0 (tails) with its probability. This gives $M = p \cdot 1 + (1 - p) \cdot 0 = p$. Take the men-women sampling problem. Let $p =$ the probability of a man's being sampled on a single outcome and $1 - p = q =$ the probability of a woman's being sampled on a single outcome. Then $p = 3/10$ and $q = 7/10$. We are interested in the mean of a man being sampled. Since $M = p \cdot 1 + q \cdot 0 = p$, $M = 3/10 \cdot 1 + 7/10 \cdot 0 = 3/10 = p$. The mean is 3/10 and the probability is 3/10. Evidently $M = p$, or the mean is equal to the probability.

How about a series of outcomes? We write S_n for the sum of n outcomes. One example, the tossing of two coins, was given above. Let us take the men-women sampling problem. The mean of a man's occurring is 3/10 and of a woman's occurring 7/10. We sample 10 persons. What is the mean number of men? Put differently, what is the *expectation* of men? If we sum the 10 means of the individual outcomes, we get the answer:

$$M(S_{10}) = M_1 + M_2 + \cdots + M_{10} \tag{11.2}$$
$$= 3/10 + 3/10 + \cdots + 3/10 = 30/10 = 3$$

In a sample of 10, we expect to get the answer: 3 men. The same result could have been obtained by $3/10 \cdot 10 = 3$. But $3/10 \cdot 10$ is pn, or

$$M(S_n) = pn \tag{11.3}$$

In n trials the mean number of occurrences of the outcome associated with p is pn.

THE VARIANCE

Recall that in Chapter 6 the variance was defined as $V = \Sigma x^2/n$. Of course, it will be the same in this chapter, with a change in symbols (for the same reason given with the formula for the mean):

$$V = \Sigma[w(X)(X - M)^2] \tag{11.4}$$

To make clear what a variance—and a standard deviation—is in probability theory, we work two examples. Recall that, binomially, only two outcomes are possible: 1 and 0. Therefore X is equal to 1 or 0. We set up a table to help us calculate the variance of the heads outcome of a coin throw:

Outcome	X	w(X) = p	(X − M)²
H	1	1/2	$(1 - 1/2)^2 = 1/4$
T	0	1/2	$(0 - 1/2)^2 = 1/4$

The variance is, then,

$$V = 1/2(1 - 1/2)^2 + 1/2(0 - 1/2)^2 = 1/2 \cdot 1/4 + 1/2 \cdot 1/4 = 1/4$$

The mean is 1/2 and the variance is 1/4. The standard deviation is the square root of the variance, or $\sqrt{1/4} = 1/2$.

The variance of an individual outcome, however, does not have much meaning. We really want the variance of the sum of a number of outcomes. If the outcomes are independent, the variance of the sum of the outcomes is the sum of the variances of the outcomes:

$$V(S_n) = V_1 + V_2 + \cdots + V_n \tag{11.5}$$

For 10 coin tosses, the variance of heads is $V(H_{10}) = 10 \cdot 1/4 = 10/4 = 2.5$.

Earlier we showed that $M(S_n) = np$. We now want a formula for the variance. That is, instead of Equation 11.5 we want a direct, simple formula. With a little algebraic manipulation we can arrive at such a formula:

$$V = p(1 - p) = pq \tag{11.6}$$

This is the variance of one outcome. The variance of the number of times that an outcome occurs is, analogously to Equations 11.2, 11.3, and 11.5, the sum of the individual outcome variances, or

$$V(S_n) = npq \qquad (11.7)$$

The standard deviation is

$$SD(S_n) = \sqrt{npq} \qquad (11.8)$$

Equations 11.3, 11.7, and 11.8 are important and useful. They can be applied in many statistical situations. Take two or three applications of the formula: first, the Agree-Disagree problem of the last chapter. Since a sample of 100 was taken, $n = 100$. On the assumption of equiprobability, $p = 1/2$ and $q = 1/2$. Therefore, $M(S_{100}) = np = 100 \cdot 1/2 = 50$, $V(S_{100}) = npq = 100 \cdot 1/2 \cdot 1/2 = 25$, and $SD(S_{100}) = \sqrt{25} = 5$. It was found that there were 60 Agrees. So, this is a deviation of two standard deviations from the mean of 50, $60 - 50 = 10$, and $10/5 = 2$. Second, take the coin-tossing experiment of the chapter on probability. In one experiment, 52 heads turned up in 100 tosses. The calculations are the same as those just given. Since there were 52 heads, the deviation from the mean, or expected frequency, is $52 - 50 = 2$. In standard deviation terms or units, this is $2/5 = .4$ standard deviation units from the mean. We now get back to one of the original questions we asked: Are these differences "statistically significant"? We found, via χ^2, that the result of 60 Agrees was statistically significant and that the result of 52 heads was not statistically significant. Can we do the same thing with the present formula? Yes, we can. Further, the beauty of the present method is that it is applicable to all kinds of numbers, not just to binomial numbers. Before demonstrating this, however, we must study, if only briefly, the so-called law of large numbers and the properties of the standard deviation and the normal probability curve.

THE LAW OF LARGE NUMBERS

The law of large numbers took Jacob Bernoulli twenty years to work out. In essence it is so simple that one wonders why he took so long to develop it.[2] Roughly, the law says that as you increase the size of samples, you also decrease the probability that the observed value of an event, *A*, will deviate from the "true" value of *A* by no more than a fixed amount, *k*. Provided the members of the samples are drawn independently, the larger the sample the closer the "true" value of the population is approached. The law is also a gateway to the testing of statistical hypotheses, as we shall see.

Toss a coin 1, 10, 50, 100, 400, and 1000 times. Let heads be the outcome in which we are interested. We calculate means, variances, standard deviations, and two new measures. The first of these new measures is the proportion of favorable outcomes, heads in this case, in the total sample. We call this measure H_n and define it as $H_n = S_n/n$. (Recall that S_n is the total number of times the favorable outcome occurs in n trials.) Then, the fraction of the time that the favorable outcome occurs is H_n. The mean of H_n is p, or $M(H_n) = p$. [This follows from Equation 11.3, where $M(S_n) = pn$, and since $H_n = S_n/n$, $M(H_n) = M(S_n)/n = np/n = p$.] In short, $M(H_n)$ equals the expected probability. The second measure is the variance of H_n. It is defined: $V(H_n) = pq/n$. The variance, $V(H_n)$, is a

---

[2] A brief statement of the law by Bernoulli himself can be found in: J. Newman, *The World of Mathematics*, vol. 3. New York: Simon and Schuster, 1956, pp. 1452–1455. For more exact statements than are possible in this text, see *ibid.*, pp. 1448–1449.

measure of the variability of the mean, $M(H_n)$. Later more will be said about the square root of $V(H_n)$, called the *standard error of the mean*. The results of the calculation are given in Table 11.1

TABLE 11.1   Means, Variances, Standard Deviations, and Expected Probabilities of the Outcome Heads with Different Size Samples[a]

n	$M(S_n) = np$	$V(S_n) = npq$	$SD(S_n)$	$M(H_n) = p$	$V(H_n) = pq/n$
1	½	.25	.50	½	¼
10	5	2.50	1.58	½	$\frac{1}{40}$
50	25	12.50	3.54	½	$\frac{1}{200}$
100	50	25.00	5.00	½	$\frac{1}{400}$
400	200	100.00	10.00	½	$\frac{1}{1600}$
1000	500	250.00	15.81	½	$\frac{1}{4000}$

[a] See text for explanation of symbols in this table.

Notice that, although the means, variances, and standard deviations of the sums increase with the sizes of the samples, the $M(H_n)$'s or p's remain the same. That is, the average number of heads, or $M(H_n)$, is always 1/2. But the variance of the average number of heads, $V(H_n)$, gets smaller and smaller as the sizes of the samples increase. Again, $V(H_n)$ is a measure of the *variability of the averages*. As Table 11.1 clearly indicates, the average number of outcomes should come closer and closer to the "true" value, in this case 1/2. (The student should ponder this example carefully before going further.)

THE NORMAL PROBABILITY CURVE AND THE STANDARD DEVIATION

The normal probability curve is the lovely bell-shaped curve encountered so often in statistics and psychology textbooks. Its importance stems from the fact that chance events in large numbers tend to distribute themselves in the form of the curve. The so-called theory of errors uses the curve. Many natural phenomena, physical and psychological, distribute themselves in approximately normal form. Height, intelligence, and achievement are three familiar examples. The means of samples distribute themselves normally.[3] It is hard to conceive of modern statistics without this curve. Every statistics text has a table called the "table of the normal deviate," or "table of the normal curve."

The most important statistical reason for using the normal curve is to be able easily to interpret the probabilities of the statistics one calculates. If the data are, as is said, "normal" or approximately normal, one has a clear interpretation for what one does.

There are two types of graphs ordinarily used in behavioral research. In one of these, as we have seen, the values of a dependent variable are plotted against the values of an

[3] The reader should avoid the untested belief that all or even most phenomena are normally distributed. Whenever possible, data should be checked by appropriate methods, especially by plotting or graphing. Data are often subtle. Take height, for example. In the whole population, height is probably normally distributed. But suppose we are studying men of high talent. Is height normally distributed? (Some people may think short people are more talented; others that tall people are more talented.) Havelock Ellis, in his study of British genius, lists 270 men of high talent according to their heights: 103 tall, 57 medium, and 100 short. Although we can well question the sampling and the source data, the example is instructive. (See H. Ellis, *A Study of British Genius*. Boston: Houghton Mifflin, 1926, pp. 278–281.) Margenau gives a powerful *rational* argument for normality: H. Margenau, *The Nature of Physical Reality*. New York: McGraw-Hill, 1950, pp. 114–115.

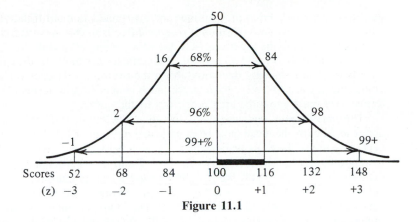

Figure 11.1

independent variable. The second major type of graph has a different purpose: to show the distribution of a single variable. On the horizontal axis, values are laid out similarly to the first type of graph. But, on the vertical axis, *frequencies* or frequency intervals or probabilities are laid out.

We draw a normal curve and lay out two sets of values on the horizontal axis. In one set of values, we use intelligence test scores with a mean of 100 and a standard deviation of 16. Say we have a sample of 400 and the data (the scores) are in approximately normal form. (It is said that the data are "normally distributed.") The curve looks like that of Figure 11.1. Imagine a Y (vertical) axis with frequencies (or proportions) marked off on the axis. The major characteristics of normal curves are unimodality (one curve), symmetry (one side the same as the other), and certain mathematical properties. It is the mathematical properties that interest us, because they allow us to make statistical inferences of considerable power.

A standard deviation can be conceived as a length along the base line of the curve from the mean or middle of the base line out to the right or left to the point where the curve inflects. It can also be visualized as a point on the base line a certain distance from the mean. One standard deviation from the mean of this particular distribution is $100 + 16 = 116$. The distance from 100 to 116 has been indicated by a heavy line in Figure 11.1. Similarly, one standard deviation below the mean is $100 - 16 = 84$. Two standard deviations are represented by $100 + (2)(16) = 132$ and $100 - (2)(16) = 68$. If one can be reasonably confident that one's data are normally distributed, then one can draw a curve like the one above, mark the mean, and lay out the standard deviations. This has also been done in Figure 11.1. The base line has also been labeled in *standard deviation units* (labeled z in the figure). That is, instead of scores of 100, 116, and 68, for instance, standard deviation scores can be used. They are $0, + 1, - 2$, and so on; points between these marked points can be indicated. For example, one half of a standard deviation above the mean, in raw scores, is $100 + (1/2)(16) = 108$. In standard deviation scores, it is $0 + .5 = .5$. These standard deviation scores are called *standard scores* or z scores. z scores range, in practical usage, from about -3 through 0 to about $+3$.[4]

If z scores are used, and the total area under the curve is set equal to 1.00, the curve is said to be in *standard form*. This immediately suggests probability. Portions of the area of

[4]To transform any raw score to a z score, use the formula $z = x/s$, where $x = X - M$ and s is the sample standard deviation. The x's are called deviation scores. Now we can divide the standard deviation into any x to convert the X (raw score) to a z score. As an example, take $X = 120$. Then $z = (120 - 100)/16 = 20/16 = 1.25$. That is, a raw score of 120 is equivalent to a z score of 1.25. Or, it is one and a quarter standard deviations above the mean.

the curve are conceived as probabilities and interpreted as such. If the total area under the whole curve is equal to 1.00, then if a vertical line is drawn upward from the base line at the mean ($z = 0$) to the top of the bell, the areas to the left and to the right of the vertical line are each equal to 1/2 or 50 percent. But vertical lines might be drawn elsewhere on the base line, at one standard deviation above the mean ($z = 1$) or two standard deviations below the mean ($z = -2$). To interpret such points in area terms—and in probability terms—we must know the area properties of the curve.

The *approximate* percentages of the areas one, two, and three standard deviations above and below the mean have been indicated in Figure 11.1. For our purposes, it is not necessary to use the exact percentages. The area between $z = -1$ and $z = +1$ is approximately 68 percent. The area between $z = -2$ and $z = +2$ is approximately 96 percent. (The exact figure is .9544. We use .96 because it makes interpretation easier.) The area between $z = -3$ and $z = +3$ is 99+ percent. Similarly all other possible baseline distances and their associated areas can be translated into percentages of the whole curve. An important point to remember is that, since the area of the whole curve is equal to 1.00, or 100 percent, and thus is equivalent to U in probability theory, the percentages of area can be interpreted as probabilities. In fact, the normal probability table entries are given in percentages of areas corresponding to z scores.

INTERPRETATION OF DATA USING THE NORMAL PROBABILITY CURVE—FREQUENCY DATA

We now inquire about the probabilities of events. To do this, we first go back to tossing coins. Strictly speaking, the frequencies of heads and tails are discontinuous events, whereas the normal probability curve is continuous. But this need not worry us, since the approximations are close. It is possible to specify with great accuracy and considerable ease the probabilities that chance events will occur. Instead of calculating exact probabilities, as we did before, we can estimate probabilities from knowledge of the properties of the normal curve.

Suppose we again, somewhat wearily perhaps, toss 100 coins. We found that the mean number of times heads will probably turn up is $M(S_{100}) = np = 100 \cdot 1/2 = 50$, and the standard deviation was $SD(S_{100}) = \sqrt{V(S_{100})} = \sqrt{npq} = \sqrt{100 \cdot 1/2 \cdot 1/2} = \sqrt{25} = 5$. Using the percentages of the curve (probabilities), we can make probability statements. We can say, for example, that in 100 tosses the probability that heads will turn up between one standard deviation below the mean ($z = -1$) and one standard deviation above the mean ($z = +1$) is approximately .68. Roughly, then, there are two out of three chances that the number of heads will be between 45 and 55 (50 ± 5). There *is* one chance in three, approximately, that the number of heads will be less than 45 or greater than 55. That is, $q = 1 - p = 1 - .68 = .32$, approximately.

Take two standard deviations above and below the mean. These points would be $50 - (2)(5) = 40$ and $50 + (2)(5) = 60$. Since we know that about 95 or 96 percent of the cases will probably fall into this band, that is, between $z = -2$ and $z = +2$, or between 40 and 60, we can say that the probability that the number of heads will not be less than 40 nor greater than 60 is about .95 or .96. That is, there are only about 4 or 5 chances in 100 that less than 40, or more than 60, heads will occur. It can happen. But it is unlikely to happen.

If we want or need to be practically certain (as in certain kinds of medical or engineering research), then we can go out to three standard deviations, $z = -3$ and $z = +3$, or perhaps somewhat less than three standard deviations. (The .01 level is about two and a half standard deviations.) Three standard deviations means the numbers of heads between 35 and 65. Since three standard deviations above and below the mean in Figure 11.1 take up more than 99 percent of the area of the curve, we can say that we are practically certain that the number of heads in 100 tosses of a fair coin will not be less than 35 nor more than 65. The probability is greater than .99. If you tossed a coin 100 times and got, say, 68 heads, you might conclude that there was probably something wrong with the coin. Of course, 68 heads can occur, but it is very, very unlikely that they will.

The earlier Agree-Disagree problem is treated exactly the same as the coin problem above. The result of 60 Agrees and 40 disagrees is unlikely to happen. There are only about 4 chances in 100 that 60 Agrees and 40 Disagrees will happen by chance. We knew this before from the χ^2 test and from the exact probability test. Now we have a third way that is generally applicable to all kinds of data—provided the data are distributed normally or approximately so.

INTERPRETATION OF DATA USING THE NORMAL PROBABILITY CURVE—CONTINUOUS DATA

Suppose we have the mathematics test scores of a sample of 100 fifth-grade children. The mean of the scores is 70; the standard deviation is 10. From previous knowledge we know that the distribution of test scores on this test is approximately normal. Obviously we can interpret the data using the normal curve. Our interest is in the reliability of the mean. How much can we depend on this mean? With future samples of similar fifth-grade children, will we get the same mean? If the mean is undependable, that is, if it fluctuates widely from sample to sample, obviously any interpretation of the test scores of individual children is in jeopardy. A score of 75 might be average this time, but if the mean is unreliable this 75 might be, on a future testing, a superior score. In other words, we must have a dependable or reliable mean.

Imagine giving this same test to the same group of children again and again and again. Go further. Imagine giving the test under exactly the same conditions 100,000 times. Assume that all other things are equal: the children learn nothing new in all these repetitions; they do not get fatigued; environmental conditions remain the same; and so on.

If we calculate a mean and a standard deviation for each of the many times, we obtain a gigantic distribution of means (and standard deviations). What will this distribution be like? First, it will form a beautiful bell-shaped normal curve. Means do. They have the property of falling nicely into the normal distribution, even when the original distributions from which they are calculated are not normal. This is because we assumed "other things equal" and thus have no source of mean fluctuations other than chance. The means will fluctuate, but the fluctuations will all be chance fluctuations. Most of these fluctuations will cluster around what we will call the "true" mean, the "true" value of the gigantic population of means. A few will be extreme values. If we repeated the 100 coin-tosses experiment many many times, we would find that heads would cluster around what we know is the "true" value: 50. Some would be a little higher, some a little lower, a few considerably higher, a few considerably lower. In brief, the heads and the means will obey the same "law." Since we assumed that nothing else is operating, we must come to the conclusion that these fluctuations are due to chance. And chance errors, given enough of them, distribute themselves into a normal distribution. This is the theory. It is called the *theory of errors.*

Continuing our story of the mean, if we had the data from the very many administrations of the mathematics test to the same group, we could calculate a mean and a standard deviation. The mean so calculated would be close to the "true" mean. If we had an infinite number of means from an infinite number of test administrations and calculated the mean of the means, we would then obtain the "true" mean. Similarly for the standard deviation of the means. Naturally, we cannot do this, for we do not have an infinite or even a very large number of test administrations. There is fortunately a simple way to solve the problem. It consists in accepting the mean calculated from the sample as the "true" mean and then estimating how accurate this acceptance (or assumption) is. To do this, a statistic known as the *standard error of the mean* is calculated. It is defined:

$$SE_M = \frac{\sigma_{\text{pop}}}{\sqrt{n}} \qquad (11.9)$$

where the standard error of the mean is SE_M; the standard deviation of the population (σ is read "sigma"), σ_{pop}; and the number of cases in the sample, n.

There is a little snag here. We do not know, nor can we know, the standard deviation of the population. Recall that we also did not know the mean of the population, but that we estimated it with the mean of the sample. Similarly, we estimate the standard deviation of the population with the standard deviation of the sample. Thus the formula to use is

$$SE_M = \frac{SD}{\sqrt{n}} \qquad (11.10)$$

The mathematics test mean can now be studied for its reliability. We calculate:

$$SE_M = \frac{10}{\sqrt{100}} = \frac{10}{10} = 1$$

Again imagine a large population of means of this test. If they are put into a distribution and the curve of the distribution plotted, the curve would look something like the curve of Figure 11.2. Keep firmly in mind: this is an imaginary distribution of means of samples. It is *not* a distribution of scores. It is easy to see that the means of this distribution are not very variable. If we double the standard error of the mean we get 2. Subtract and add this to the mean of 70: 68 to 72. The probability is approximately .95 that the population ("true") mean lies within the interval 68 to 72, that is, approximately 5 percent of the time the means of random samples of this size will lie outside this interval.

If we do the same calculation for the intelligence test data of Figure 11.1, we obtain

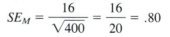

$$SE_M = \frac{16}{\sqrt{400}} = \frac{16}{20} = .80$$

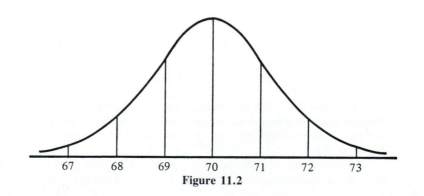

Figure 11.2

Three standard errors above and below the mean of 100 give the range 97.60 to 102.40, or we can say that the "true" mean very probably (less than 1 percent chance of being wrong) lies within the interval 98 to 102. Means *are* reliable—with fair-size samples.[5]

The standard error of the mean, then, is a standard deviation. It is a standard deviation of an infinite number of means. Only chance error makes the means fluctuate. Thus the standard error of the mean—or the standard deviation of the means, if you like—is a measure of chance or error in its effect on one measure of central tendency.

A caution is in order. All of the theory discussed is based on the assumptions of random sampling and independence of observations. If these assumptions are violated, the reasoning, while not entirely invalidated, practically speaking, is open to question. Estimates of error may be biased to a greater or lesser extent. The trouble is we cannot tell how much a standard error is biased. Years ago Guilford gave interesting examples of the biases encountered when the assumptions are violated.[6] With large numbers of Air Force pilots, he found that estimates of standard errors were sometimes considerably off. No one can give hard-and-fast rules. The best maxim probably is: Use random sampling and keep observations independent, if at all possible.

If random sampling cannot be used, and if there is doubt about the independence of observations, calculate the statistics and interpret them. But be circumspect about interpretations and conclusions; they may be in error. Because of such possibilities of error, it has been said that statistics are misleading, and even useless. Like any other method—consulting authority, using intuition, and the like—statistics *can* be misleading. But even when statistical measures are biased, they are usually less biased than authoritative and intuitive judgements. It is not that numbers lie. The numbers do not know what they are doing. It is that the human beings using the numbers may be informed or misinformed, biased or unbiased, knowledgeable or ignorant, intelligent or stupid. Treat numbers and statistics neither with too great respect nor too great contempt. Calculate statistics and act as though they were "true," but always maintain a certain reserve toward them, a willingness to disbelieve them if the evidence indicates such disbelief.[7]

[5] Even with relatively small samples, the mean is quite stable. (See the intelligence test data in Chapter 8.) Five samples of 20 intelligence scores each were drawn from a population of such scores with a mean of 95. The means of the five samples were calculated. Standard errors of the mean were calculated for the first two samples, and interpretations were made. Then comparisons were made to the "true" value of 95. The mean of the first sample was 93.55 with a standard deviation of 12.22. $SE_M = 2.73$. The .05 level range of means was: 88.09 to 99.01. Obviously 95 falls within this range. The mean of the second sample was more deviant: 90.20. The standard deviation was 9.44. $SE_M = 2.11$. The .05 level range was 85.98 to 94.42. Our 95 does not fall in this range. The .01 level range is: 83.87 to 96.53. Now 95 is encompassed. This is not bad at all for samples of only 20. For samples of 50 or 100 it would be even better. The mean of the five means was 93.31; the standard deviation of these means was 2.73. Compare this to the standard errors calculated from the two samples: 2.73 and 2.11. In the next chapter a more convincing demonstration of the stability of means will be given.

[6] J. Guilford, *Fundamental Statistics in Psychology and Education,* 3d ed. New York: McGraw-Hill, 1956, pp. 169–173.

[7] Study suggestions for this chapter are given at the end of the next chapter.

Chapter 12

Testing Hypotheses and the Standard Error

THE STANDARD error, as an estimate of chance fluctuation, is the measure against which the outcomes of experiments are checked. Is there a difference between the means of two experimental groups? If so, is the difference a "real" difference or merely a consequence of the many relatively small differences that could have arisen by chance? To answer this question, the standard error of the differences between means is calculated and the obtained difference is compared to this standard error. If it is sufficiently greater than the standard error, it is said to be a "significant" difference. Similar reasoning can be applied to any statistic. Thus, there are many standard errors: of correlation coefficients, of differences between means, of means, of medians, of proportions, and so on. The purpose of this chapter is to examine the general notion of the standard error and to see how hypotheses are tested using the standard error.

EXAMPLES: DIFFERENCES BETWEEN MEANS

A particularly difficult problem in contemporary psychology centers around the question whether behavior is controlled more by situational or environmental factors, or by dispositions of individuals. McGee and Snyder, using a presumed difference between those individuals who salt their food before they taste it and those who taste their food before they salt it, hypothesized that those individuals who construe their behavior dispositionally salt their food before tasting it, whereas those individuals who construe their behavior situationally taste their food before salting it.[1] They further reasoned that the former individuals would ascribe more traits to themselves than the latter individuals. They found that the former group, the "salters," ascribed a mean of 14.87 traits to themselves, whereas the latter group, the "tasters," ascribed a mean of 6.90 traits to themselves. The direction of the difference was as the authors predicted. Is the size of the difference between the means, 7.97, sufficient to warrant the authors' claim that their hypothesis was supported? A test of the statistical significance of this difference showed that it was highly significant.

The point of this example in the present context is that the difference between means was tested for statistical significance with a standard error. The standard error in this case was the standard error of the difference between two means. The difference was found to be significant. This means that those individuals who perceive behavior as influenced by individual traits tend to salt their food before tasting it, whereas those individuals whose perception is more environmentally oriented taste their food before salting it. (This statement is a generalization of the original.) Now let us look at an example in which the difference between means was not significant.

Gates and Taylor, in a well-known early study of transfer of training, set up two matched groups of 16 pupils each.[2] The experimental group was given practice in digit memory; the control was not. The mean gain of the experimental group right after the practice period was 2.00; the mean gain of the control group was .67, a mean difference of 1.33. Four to five months later, the children of both groups were tested again. The mean score of the experimental group was 4.71; the mean score of the control group was surprising: 4.77. The mean gains over the initial tests were .35 and .36. Statistical tests are hardly necessary with data like these.

ABSOLUTE AND RELATIVE DIFFERENCES

Since differences between statistics, especially between means, are tested and reported a great deal in the literature, we must try to get some perspective on the absolute and relative sizes of such statistics. Although the discussion uses differences between means as examples, the same points apply to differences between proportions, correlation coefficients, and so on. In a study by Goldberg, Gottesdiner, and Abramson, women perceived as supporting the women's liberation movement were rated less attractive than women perceived as not supporting the movement.[3] The latter mean was 2.86 and the former 2.75, a difference of .11, which was statistically significant. Is such a small difference meaningful? Contrast this small difference to one of the mean differences between experimental and control groups obtained by Mann and Janis in their study of the long-term effects of role playing on smoking: 13.50 and 5.20.[4] (These are mean decreases in number of cigarettes smoked each day; the difference is statistically significant.)

The problem here is actually two problems: one of absolute and relative size of differ-

[1]M. McGee and M. Snyder, "Attribution and Behavior: Two Field Studies," *Journal of Personality and Social Psychology,* 32 (1975), 185–190.

[2]A. Gates and G. Taylor, "An Experimental Study of the Nature of Improvement Resulting from Practice in a Mental Function," *Journal of Educational Psychology,* 16 (1925), 583–592.

[3]P. Goldberg, M. Gottesdiener, and P. Abramson, "Another Put-Down of Women?: Perceived Attractiveness as a Function of Support for the Feminist Movement," *Journal of Personality and Social Psychology,* 32 (1975), 113–115.

[4]L. Mann and I. Janis, "A Follow-Up on the Long-Term Effects of Emotional Role Playing," *Journal of Personality and Social Psychology,* 8 (1968), 339–342.

ences and one of practical or "real" significance versus statistical significance. What appears to be a very small difference may, upon close examination, not be so small. In the Goldberg et al. study, to be sure, the difference of .11 is probably trivial even though statistically significant. The .11 was derived from a five-point scale of attractiveness, and is thus really small. Now take an entirely different sort of example from an important study by Miller and DiCara on the instrumental conditioning of urine secretion.[5] The means of a group of rats before and after training to secrete urine were .017 and .028, and the difference was highly statistically significant. But the difference was only .011. Is this not much too small to warrant serious consideration? But now the nature of the measures has to be considered. The small means of .017 and .028 were obtained from measures of urine secretion of rats. When one considers the size of rats' bladders and that the mean difference of .011 was produced by instrumental conditioning (reward for secreting urine), the meaning of the difference is dramatic: it is even quite large! (We will analyze the data in a later chapter and perhaps see this more clearly.)

One should ordinarily not be enthusiastic about mean differences like .20, .15, .08, and so on, but one has to be intelligent about it. Suppose that a very small difference is reported as statistically significant, and you think this ridiculous. But also suppose that it was the mean difference between the cerebral cortex weights of groups of rats under enriched and deprived experiences in the early days of their lives.[6] To obtain *any* difference in brain weight due to experience is an outstanding achievement and, of course, an important scientific discovery.

CORRELATION COEFFICIENTS

Correlation coefficients are reported in large quantities in research journals. Questions as to the significance of the coefficients—and the "reality" of the relations they express— must be asked. For example, to be statistically significant a coefficient of correlation calculated between 30 pairs of measures has to be approximately .31 at the .05 level and .42 at the .01 level. With 100 pairs of measures the problem is less acute (the law of large numbers again). To carry the .05 day, an r of .16 is sufficient; to carry the .01 day, an r of about .23 does it. If r's are less than these values, they are considered to be not significant.

If one draws, say, 30 pairs of numbers from a table of random numbers and correlates them, theoretically the r should be near zero. Clearly, there should be near-zero relations between sets of random numbers, but occasionally sets of pairs can yield statistically significant and reasonably high r's *by chance*. At any rate, coefficients of correlation, as well as means and differences, have to be weighed in the balance for statistical significance by stacking them up against their standard errors. Fortunately, this is easy to do, since r's for different levels of significance and for different sizes of samples are given in tables in most statistics texts. Thus, with r's it is not necessary to calculate and use the standard error of an r. The reasoning behind the tables has to be understood, however.[7]

[5] N. Miller and L. DiCara, "Instrumental Learning of Urine Formation by Rats: Changes in Renal Flow," *American Journal of Physiology*, 215 (1968), 677–683.

[6] E. Bennett et al., "Chemical and Anatomical Plasticity of Brain," *Science*, 146 (1964), 610–619. (See, especially, remarks on p. 618.)

[7] There has been a good deal of misunderstanding about the assumptions that have to be satisfied to calculate coefficients of correlation. No assumptions have to be satisfied simply to calculate r's. The assumptions come in only when we wish to infer from the sample to the population. See W. Hays, *Statistics*, 3d ed. New York: Holt, Rinehart and Winston, 1981, pp. 459–461.

Of the thousands of correlation coefficients reported in the research literature, many are of low magnitude. How low is low? At what point is a correlation coefficient too low to warrant treating it seriously? Usually, r's less than .10 cannot be taken too seriously: an r of .10 means that only one percent ($.10^2$) of the variance of y is shared with x! If an r of .30, on the other hand, is statistically significant, it may be important because it may point to an important relation. r's between .20 and .30 make the problem more difficult. (And remember that with large N's, r's between .20 and .30 are statistically significant.) To be sure, an r, say, of .20 means that the two variables share only four percent of their variance. But an r of .26—seven percent of the variance shared—or even one of .20 may be important because it may provide a valuable lead for theory and subsequent research. The problem *is* complex. In basic research, low correlations—of course, they should be statistically significant—may enrich theory and research. It is in applied research, where prediction is important, that value judgments about low correlations and the trivial amounts of variance shared have grown. In basic research, however, the picture is more complicated. One conclusion is fairly sure: correlation coefficients, like other statistics, must be tested for statistical significance.

HYPOTHESIS TESTING: SUBSTANTIVE AND NULL HYPOTHESES

The main research purpose of inferential statistics is to test research hypotheses by testing statistical hypotheses. Broadly speaking, the scientist uses two types of hypothesis, substantive and statistical. A *substantive hypothesis* is the usual type of hypothesis discussed in Chapter 2 in which a conjectural statement of the relation between two or more variables is expressed, for example, "The greater the cohesiveness of a group the greater its influence on its members"[8] is a substantive hypothesis. An investigator's theory dictates that this variable is related to that variable. The statement of the relation is a substantive hypothesis.

A substantive hypothesis itself, strictly speaking, is not testable. It has first to be translated into operational terms. One very useful way to test substantive hypotheses is through statistical hypotheses. A *statistical hypothesis* is a conjectural statement, in statistical terms, of statistical relations deduced from the relations of the substantive hypothesis. This rather clumsy statement needs translation. A statistical hypothesis expresses an aspect of the original substantive hypothesis in quantitative and statistical terms. $M_A > M_B$, Mean A is greater than Mean B; $r > +.20$, the coefficient of correlation is greater than $+.20$; $M_A > M_B > M_C$, at the .01 level; χ^2 is significant at the .05 level; and so on. A statistical hypothesis is a prediction of how the statistics used in analyzing the quantitative data of a research problem will turn out.

Statistical hypotheses must be tested against something, however. It is not possible simply to test a statistical hypothesis as it stands. That is, we do not directly test the statistical proposition $M_A > M_B$ in and of itself. We test it against an alternative proposition. Naturally, there can be several alternatives to $M_A > M_B$. The alternative usually selected is the null hypothesis, which was invented by Sir Ronald Fisher. The *null hypothesis* is a statistical proposition which states, essentially, that there is no relation between the variables (of the problem). The null hypothesis says, "You're wrong, there is no

---

[8]S. Schachter el al., "An Experimental Study of Cohesiveness and Productivity," *Human Relations*, 4 (1951), 229–238.

relation; disprove me if you can.'' It says this in statistical terms such as $M_A = M_B$, or $M_A - M_B = 0$; $r_{xy} = 0$; χ^2 is not significant; t is not significant; and so on.[9]

Fisher says, ''Every experiment may be said to exist only in order to give the facts a chance of disproving the null hypothesis.''[10] Aptly said. What does it mean? Suppose you entertain a hypothesis to the effect that method A is superior to method B. If you satisfactorily solve the problems of defining what you mean by ''superior,'' of setting up an experiment, and the like, you now must specify a statistical hypothesis. In this case, you might say $M_A > M_B$ (the mean of method A is, or will be greater than the mean of method B on such-and-such a criterion measure). Assume that after the experiment the two means are 68 and 61, respectively. It would seem that your substantive hypothesis is upheld since $68 > 61$, or M_A is greater than M_B. As we have already learned, however, this is not enough since this difference may be one of the many possible similar differences due to chance.

In effect, we set up what can be called the chance hypothesis: $M_A = M_B$, or $M_A - M_B = 0$. These are null hypotheses. What we do, then, is write hypotheses. First we write the statistical hypothesis that reflects the operational-experimental meaning of the substantive hypothesis. Then we write the null hypothesis against which we test the first type of hypothesis. Here are the two kinds of hypothesis suitably labeled:

$$H_1: M_A > M_B$$
$$H_0: M_A = M_B$$

H_1 means ''Hypothesis 1.'' There is often more than one such hypothesis. They are labeled H_1, H_2, H_3, and so on. H_0 means ''null hypothesis.'' Note that the null hypothesis could in this case have been written:

$$H_0: M_A - M_B = 0$$

This form shows where the null hypothesis got its name: the difference between M_A and M_B is zero. But it is a little unwieldy in this form, especially when there are three or more means or other statistics being tested. $M_A = M_B$ is general, and of course means the same as $M_A - M_B = 0$ and $M_B - M_A = 0$. Notice that we can write quite easily $M_A = M_B = M_C = \cdots = M_N$.

---

[9] Researchers sometimes unwittingly use null hypotheses as substantive hypotheses. Instead of saying that one method of presenting textual materials has a greater effect on recall memory than another method, for instance, they may say that there is no difference between the two methods. This is poor practice because it in effect uses the statistical null hypothesis as a substantive hypothesis and thus confuses the two kinds of hypotheses. Strictly speaking, any significant result, positive or negative, then, supports the hypothesis. But this is certainly not the intention. The intention is to bring statistical evidence to bear on the substantive hypothesis, for example, on $M_A > M_B$. If the result is statistically significant—that is, that $M_A \neq M_B$, or the null hypothesis is rejected—and $M_A > M_B$, then the substantive hypothesis is supported. Using the null hypothesis substantively loses the power of the substantive hypothesis, which amounts to the investigator making a specific nonchance prediction.

There is of course always the rather rare possibility that a null hypothesis is the substantive hypothesis. If, for example, an investigator seeks to show that two methods of teaching make no difference in achievement, then the null hypothesis is presumably appropriate. The trouble now is that the investigator is in a difficult logical position because it is extremely difficult, perhaps impossible, to demonstrate the empirical ''validity'' of a null hypothesis. After all, if the hypothesis $M_A = M_B$ is supported, it could well be one of the many chance results that are possible rather than a meaningful nondifference! Good discussions of hypothesis testing are given in: R. Giere, *Understanding Scientific Reasoning*. New York: Holt, Rinehart and Winston, 1979, chaps. 6, 8, 11, and 12, especially chap. 11.

[10] R. Fisher, *The Design of Experiments*, 6th ed. New York: Hafner, 1951, p. 16.

THE GENERAL NATURE OF A STANDARD ERROR

If this were the best of all possible research worlds, there would be no random error. And if there were no random error, there would be no need for statistical tests of significance. The word "significance" would be meaningless, in fact. Any difference at all would be a "real" difference. But such is never the case, alas. There are *always* chance errors (and biased errors, too), and in behavioral research they often contribute substantially to the total variance. Standard errors are measures of this error, and are used, as has repeatedly been said, as a sort of yardstick against which experimental or "variable" variance is checked.

The *standard error* is the standard deviation of the sampling distribution of any given measure—the mean or the correlation coefficient, for instance. In most cases, population or universe values (parameters) cannot be known; they must be estimated from sample measures, usually from single samples.

Suppose we draw a random sample of 100 children from eighth-grade classes in such-and-such a school system. It is difficult or impossible, say, to measure the whole universe of eighth-grade children. We calculate the mean and the standard deviation from a test we give the children and find these statistics to be $M = 110$; $SD = 10$. An important question we must ask ourselves is "How accurate is this mean?" Or, if we were to draw a large number of random samples of 100 eighth-grade pupils from this same population, will the means of these samples be 110 or near 110? And, if they are near 110, how near? What we do, in effect, is to set up a *hypothetical distribution of sample means,* all calculated from samples of 100 pupils each drawn from the parent population of eighth-grade pupils. If we could calculate the mean of this population *of means,* or if we knew what it was, everything would be simple. But we do not know this value, and we are not able to know it since the possibilities of drawing different samples are so numerous. The best we can do is to *estimate it with our sample value, or sample mean.* We simply say, in this case, let the sample mean equal the mean of the population mean—and hope we are right. Then we must test our equation. This we do with the standard error.

A similar argument applies to the standard deviation of the whole population (of the original scores). We do not know and probably can never know it. But we can estimate it with the standard deviation calculated from our sample. Again, we say, in effect, let the standard deviation of the sample equal the standard deviation of the population. We know they are probably not the same value, but we also know, if the sampling has been random, that they are probably close.

In Chapter 11 the sample standard deviation was used as a substitute for the standard deviation of the population in the formula for the *standard error of the mean:*

$$SE_M = \frac{SD}{\sqrt{n}} \qquad (12.1)$$

This is also called the *sampling error.* Just as the standard deviation is a measure of the dispersion of the original scores, the standard error of the mean is a measure of the dispersion of the distribution of sample means. It is *not* the standard deviation of the population of individual scores if, for example, we could test every member of the population and calculate the mean and standard deviation of this population.

A MONTE CARLO DEMONSTRATION

To give us material to work with, we now resort to the computer and what are called Monte Carlo methods. Monte Carlo methods are computer-assisted simulation methods designed to obtain solutions to mathematical, statistical, numerical, and even verbal problems by using random procedures and samples of random numbers. Usually associated with mathematical problems whose solutions are intractable, Monte Carlo methods have been extended to "testing" the statistical characteristics of samples of large populations. For example, the consequences of violating the assumptions behind statistical tests of significance can be effectively studied by simulating statistical distributions with random numbers and introducing violations of assumptions into the procedure to study the consequences. In the behavioral sciences, Monte Carlo procedures are usually empirical studies of statistical and other models using the computer-generated random numbers to help simulate the random processes needed to study the models. In any case, we now use an elementary form of Monte Carlo to test a most important theorem of statistics and to explore the variability of means and the use of the standard error of the mean. We also want to lay a foundation for understanding the computer in studying random processes.

The Procedure

A computer program was written to generate 4000 random numbers evenly distributed between 0 and 100 (so that each number has an equal chance of being "drawn") in 40 sets of 100 numbers each, and to calculate various statistics with the numbers. Consider this set of 4000 numbers a population, or U. The mean of U is 50.33 (by actual computer calculation) and the standard deviation 29.17. We wish to estimate this mean from samples that we draw randomly from U. Of course, in a real situation we would usually not know the mean of the population. One of the virtues of Monte Carlo procedures is that we can know what we ordinarily do not know.

Five of the 40 sets of 100 numbers were drawn at random. (The sets drawn were 5, 7, 8, 16, and 36. See Appendix C.) The means and standard deviations of the five sets were calculated. So were the five standard errors of the mean. These statistics are reported in Table 12.1. We want to give an intuitive notion of what the standard error of the mean is and then we want to show how it is used.

Table 12.1   Means, Standard Deviations, and Standard Errors of the Mean, Five Samples of 100 Random Numbers (0 through 100)[a]

			Samples		
	1	2	3	4	5
M:	53.21	49.64	51.37	49.02	55.51
SD:	29.62	27.91	29.83	26.72	29.23
SE_M:	2.96	2.79	2.98	2.67	2.92

[a] Population statistics: $M = 50.33$; $SD = 29.17$; $N = 4000$.

First, calculate the *standard deviation of this sample of means*. If we simply treat the five means as ordinary scores and calculate the mean and standard deviation, we obtain: $M_1 = 51.75$; $SD = 2.38$. The mean of all 4000 scores is 50.33. Each of the five means is a sample estimate of this population mean. Notice that three of them, 49.64, 51.37, and

49.02, are rather close to the population mean, and two of them, 53.21 and 55.51, are farther away from it. So it seems that three of the samples provide good estimates of the population mean and two do not—or do they?

The standard deviation of 2.38 is *akin to* the standard error of the mean. (It is, of course, not the standard error of the mean, because it has been calculated from only five means.) Suppose only one sample, the first with $M = 53.21$ and $SD = 29.62$, had been drawn—and this is the usual situation in research—and the standard error of the mean calculated:

$$SE_M = \frac{SD}{\sqrt{N}} = \frac{29.62}{\sqrt{100}} = 2.96$$

This value is an estimate of the standard deviation of the population *means* of many, many samples of 100 cases, each randomly drawn from the population. Our population has 40 groups and thus 40 means. (Of course, this is not many, many means.) The standard deviation of these means is actually 3.10. The SE_M calculated with the first sample, then, is close to this population value: 2.96 as an estimate of 3.10.

The five standard errors of the mean are given in the third data line of Table 12.1. They fluctuate very little—from 2.67 to 2.98—even though the means of the sets of 100 scores vary considerably. The standard deviation of 2.38 calculated from the five means is only a fair estimate of the standard deviation of the population of means. Yet it *is* an estimate. The interesting and important point is that the standard error of the mean, which is a "theoretical" estimate, calculated from the data of any one of the five groups, is an accurate estimate of the variability of the means of samples of the population.

To reinforce these ideas, let's now look at another Monte Carlo demonstration of much greater magnitude. The computer program used to produce the 4000 random numbers for example discussed above was used to produce 15 more sets of 4000 random numbers each, evenly distributed between 0 and 100. That is, a total of 80,000 random numbers, in 20 sets of 4000 each, were generated. The theoretical mean, again, of numbers between 0 and 100 is 50. Consider each of the 20 sets as a sample of 4000 numbers. The means of the 20 sets are given in Table 12.2.

Table 12.2 Means from 20 Sets of 4000 Computer-generated Random Numbers (0 through 100)[a]

50.3322	49.9447	50.1615	50.0995
50.1170	49.5960	51.0585	51.1450
49.8200	49.3175	49.5822	50.6440
49.8227	49.9022	49.7505	49.8437
49.5875	50.6180	50.0990	49.3605

[a]Mean of means = 50.0401; standard deviation of the means = .4956; standard error of the mean, first sample = .4611.

The 20 means cluster closely around 50: the lowest is 49.3175, the highest is 51.1450, and most of them are near 50. The mean of the 20 means is 50.0401, very close indeed to the theoretical expectation of 50. The standard deviation of the 20 means is .4956. The standard deviation of the first sample of 4000 cases (see footnote a, Table 12.1) is 29.1653. If we use this standard deviation to calculate the standard error of the mean, we obtain: $SE_M = 29.1653\sqrt{4000} = .4611$. Note that this estimate of the standard error of the mean is close to the calculated standard deviation of the 20 means. We would not go wrong using it to assess the variability of the means of samples of 4000 random numbers. Clearly, means of large samples are highly stable statistics, and standard errors are good estimates of their variability.

Generalizations

Three or four generalizations of great usefulness in research can now be made. One, means of samples are stable in the sense that they are much less variable than the measures from which they are calculated. This is, of course, true by definition. Variances, standard deviations, and standard errors of the mean are even more stable; they fluctuate within relatively narrow ranges. Even when the sample means of our example varied by as much as four or five points, the standard errors fluctuated by no more than a point and a half. This means that we can have considerable faith that estimates of sample means will be rather close to the mean of a population of such means. And the law of large numbers tells us that the larger the sample size, the closer to the population values the statistics will probably be.

A difficult question for researchers is: Do these generalizations always hold, especially with nonrandom samples? The validity of the generalizations depends on random sampling. If the sampling is not random, we cannot really know whether the generalizations hold. Nevertheless, we often have to act as though they do hold, even with nonrandom samples. Fortunately, if we are careful about studying our data to detect substantial sample idiosyncrasy, we can use the theory profitably. For example, samples can be checked for easily verified expectations. If one expects about equal numbers of males and females in a sample, or known proportions of young and old or Republican and Democrat, it is simple to count these numbers. There are experts who insist on random sampling as a condition of the validity of the theory—and they are correct. But if the theory is forbidden to us with nonrandom samples, much use of statistics and the inferences that accompany statistics would have to be abandoned. The reality is that the statistics seem to work very well even with nonrandom samples—provided the researcher knows the limitations of such samples, is even more careful than he would be with random samples, and replicates his studies.

The Central Limit Theorem

Before studying the actual use of the standard error of the mean, we should look, if briefly, at an extremely important generalization about means: *If samples are drawn from a population at random, the means of the samples will tend to be normally distributed.* The larger the *n*'s, the more this is so. And the shape and kind of distribution of the original population makes no difference. That is, the population distribution does not have to be normally distributed.[11]

For example, the distribution of the 4000 random numbers in Appendix C is rectangular, since the numbers are evenly distributed. If the central limit theorem is empirically valid, then the means of the 40 sets of 100 scores each should be approximately normally distributed. If so, this is a remarkable thing. And it is so, though one sample of 40 means is hardly sufficient to show the trend too well. Therefore, three more populations of 4000 different evenly distributed random numbers, partitioned into 40 subsets of 100 numbers

---

[11] See Hays, *op. cit.*, pp. 215–220. Hays gives a neat example to show how the theorem works (pp. 219–220). Another good discussion with examples is given by G. Snedecor and W. Cochran, *Statistical Methods,* 6th ed. Ames, Iowa: Iowa State University Press, 1967, pp. 51–56.

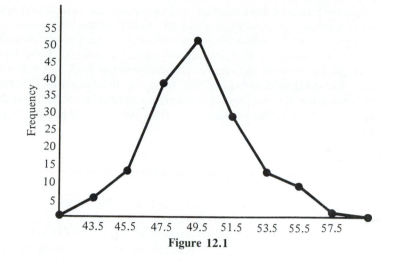

Figure 12.1

each, were generated on the computer. The means calculated for the $4 \times 40 = 160$ subsets of 100 numbers each were calculated and put into one distribution. A frequency polygon of the means is given in Figure 12.1. It can be seen that the 160 means look almost like the bell-shaped normal curve. Apparently the central limit theorem "works." And bear in mind that this distribution of means was obtained from rectangular distributions of numbers.

Why go to all this bother? Why is it important to show that distributions of means approximate normality? We work with means a great deal in data analysis, and if they are normally distributed then one can use the known properties of the normal curve to interpret obtained research data. Knowing that approximately 96 percent of the means will lie between two standard deviations (standard errors) above and below the mean is valuable information, because an obtained result can be assessed against the known properties of the normal curve. In the last chapter we saw the use of the normal curve in interpreting means. We now turn to what is perhaps a more interesting use of the curve in assessing the differences between means.

The Standard Error of the Differences Between Means

One of the most frequent and useful strategies in research is to compare means of samples. From differences in means we infer effects of independent variables. Any linear combination of means is also governed by the central limit theorem. That is, differences in means will be normally distributed, given large enough samples. (A linear combination is any equation of the first degree, e.g., $Y = M_1 - M_2$. $Y = M_1^2 - M_1$ is not linear.) Therefore we can use the same theory with differences between means that we use with means.

Suppose we have randomly assigned 200 subjects to two groups, 100 to each group. We show a movie on intergroup relations to one group, for example, and none to the other group. Next, we give both groups an attitude measure. The mean score of Group A (saw the movie) is 110 and the mean score of Group B (did not see the movie) is 100. Our problem is: Is the difference of 10 units a "real" difference, a statistically significant difference? Or is it a difference that could have arisen by chance—more than 5 times in 100, say, or some other amount—when no difference actually exists?

If we similarly create double samples of 100 each and calculate the differences between the means of these samples, and go through the same experimental procedure, will we consistently get this difference of 10? Again, we use the standard error to evaluate our differences, but this time we have a *sampling distribution of differences between means*. It is as if we took each $M_i - M_j$ and considered it as an X. Then the several differences between the means of the samples are considered as the X's of a new distribution. At any rate, the standard deviation of this sampling distribution of differences is *akin* to the standard error. But this procedure is only for illustration; actually we do not do this. Here, again, we estimate the standard error from our first two groups, A and B, by using the formula:

$$SE_{M_A - M_B} = \sqrt{SE_{M_A}{}^2 + SE_{M_B}{}^2} \tag{12.2}$$

where $SE_{M_A}{}^2$ *and* $SE_{M_B}{}^2$ are the standard errors squared, respectively, of Groups A and B, as previously stated.[12]

Suppose we did the experiment with five double groups, that is, ten groups, two at a time. The five differences between the means were 10, 11, 12, 8, 9. The mean of these differences is 10; the standard deviation is 1.414. This 1.414 is again *akin to* the standard error of the sampling distribution of the differences between the means, in the same sense as the standard error of the mean in the earlier discussion. Now, if we calculate the standard error of the mean for each group (by making up standard deviations for the two groups, $SD_A = 8$ and $SD_B = 9$), we obtain:

$$SE_{M_A} = \frac{SD_A}{\sqrt{n_A}} = \frac{8}{\sqrt{100}} = .8, \qquad SE_{M_B} = \frac{SD_B}{\sqrt{n_B}} = \frac{9}{\sqrt{100}} = .9$$

By Equation 12.2 we calculate the standard error of the differences between the means:

$$SE_{M_A - M_B} = \sqrt{SE_{M_A}{}^2 + SE_{M_B}{}^2} = \sqrt{(.8)^2 + (.9)^2} = \sqrt{.64 + .81}$$

$$= \sqrt{1.45} = 1.20$$

What do we do with the 1.20 now that we have it? If the scores of the two groups had been chosen from a table of random numbers and there were no experimental conditions, we would expect no difference between the means. But we have learned that there are always relatively small differences due to chance factors. These differences are random. *The standard error of the differences between the means is an estimate of the dispersion of these differences*. But it is a measure of these differences that is an estimate for the whole population of such differences. For instance, the standard error of the differences between the means is 1.20. This means that, by chance alone, around the difference of 10 between M_A and M_B there will be random fluctuations—now 10, now 10.2, now 9.8, and so on. Only rarely will the differences exceed, say, 13 or 7 (about three times the SE). Another way of putting it is to say that the standard error of 1.20 indicates the limits (if we multiply the 1.20 by the appropriate factor) beyond which sample differences between the means probably will not go.

What has all this to do with our experiment? It is precisely here that we evaluate the experimental results. The standard error of 1.20 estimates random fluctuations. Now, $M_A - M_B = 10$. Could this have arisen by chance, as a result of random fluctuations as just described? It should by now be halfway clear that this cannot be, except under very unusual circumstances. We evaluate this difference of 10 by comparing it to our estimate

---

[12] Other formulas are applicable under other circumstances, for example, if we start off with matched pairs of subjects.

of random or chance fluctuations. *Is it one of them?* We make the comparison by means of the *t* ratio, or *t* test:

$$t = \frac{M_A - M_B}{SE_{M_A - M_B}} = \frac{110 - 100}{1.20} = \frac{10}{1.20} = 8.33$$

This means that our measured difference between M_A and M_B would be 8.33 standard deviations away from a hypothesized mean of zero (zero difference, no difference between the two means).

We would not have any difference, theoretically, if our subjects were well randomized and there had been no experimental manipulation. We would have, in effect, two distributions of random numbers from which we could expect only chance fluctuations. But here we have, comparatively, a huge difference of 10, compared to an insignificant 1.20 (our estimate of random deviations). Decidedly, something is happening here besides chance. And this something is just what we are looking for. It is, presumably, the effect of the movie, or the effect of the experimental condition, other conditions having been sufficiently controlled, of course.

Look at Figure 12.2. It represents *a population of differences between means* with a mean of zero and a standard deviation of 1.20. (The mean is set at zero, because we assume that the mean of all the mean differences is zero.) Where would the difference of 10 be placed on the base line of the diagram? In order to answer this question, the 10 must first be converted into standard deviation (or standard error) units. (Recall standard scores from the last chapter.) This is done by dividing by the standard deviation (standard error), which is 1.20: 10/1.2 = 8.33. But this is what we got when we calculated the *t* ratio. It is, then, simply the difference between M_A and M_B, 10, expressed in standard deviation (standard error) units. Now we can put it on the base line of the diagram. Look far to the right for the dot. Clearly the difference of 10 is a deviate. It is so far out, in fact, that it probably does not belong to the population in question. In short, the difference between M_A and M_B is statistically significant, so significant that it amounts to what Bernoulli called "moral certainty." Such a large difference, or deviation from chance expectation,

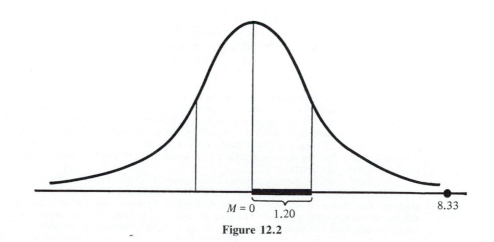

$M = 0$ 1.20 8.33

Figure 12.2

can hardly be attributed to chance. The odds are actually greater than a billion to one. It *can* happen. But it is hardly likely to happen.[13]

Such is the standard error and its use. The standard errors of other statistics are used in the same way. A very important and useful tool. It is a basic instrument in contemporary research. Indeed, it would be hard to imagine modern research methodology, and impossible to imagine modern statistics, without the standard error. As a key to statistical inference its importance cannot be overestimated. Much of statistical inference boils down to a family of fractions epitomized by the fraction:

$$\frac{\text{Statistic}}{\text{Standard error of the statistic}}$$

STATISTICAL INFERENCE

To *infer* is to derive a conclusion from premises or from evidence. To *infer statistically* is to derive probabilistic conclusions from probabilistic premises. We conclude probabilistically, that is, at a specified level of significance. We infer, probabilistically, if an experimental result deviates from chance expectation, if the null hypothesis is not "true," that a "real" influence is at work. If, in the methods experiment, $M_A > M_B$ and $M_A \neq M_B$, or H_1 is "true" and H_0 is not "true," we infer that method A is "superior" to method B, "superior" being accepted in the sense defined in the experiment.

Another form of inference, discussed at length in the chapter on sampling, is that from a sample to a population. Since, for instance, 55 percent of a random sample of 2000 people in the United States say they will vote for a certain presidential candidate, it is inferred that the whole population of the United States, if asked, will respond similarly. This is a rather big inference. One of the gravest dangers of research—or perhaps I should say, of any human reasoning—is the inferential leap from sample data to population fact. Inferential leaps of no mean size are constantly made—in politics, economics, education, and other areas of large concern. If the government cuts spending, inflation will decrease, for example. If we use teaching machines, children will learn more. But scientists, too, make inferential leaps, often very large ones—with one important difference. The scientist is (or should be) aware that he is making such leaps and that they are always risky.

It can be said, in sum, that statistics enables scientists to test substantive hypotheses indirectly by enabling them to test statistical hypotheses directly (if it is at all possible to test anything directly). In this process, they use null hypotheses, hypotheses written by chance. They test the "truth" of substantive hypotheses by subjecting null hypotheses to statistical tests on the bases of probabilistic reasoning. They then make appropriate inferences. Indeed, the objective of all statistical tests is to test the justifiability of inferences.[14]

[13] An important question is: How large a difference, or in the language of statistics, how far away from the hypothetical mean of zero must a deviation be to be significant? This question cannot be answered definitively in this book. The .05 level is 1.96 standard deviations from the mean, and the .01 level is 2.58 standard deviations from the mean. But there are complications, especially with small samples. The student must, as usual, study a good statistics text. A simple rule is: 2 standard deviations (*SE*'s) are significant (about the .05 level); 2.5 standard deviations are very significant (about the .01 level); and 3 standard deviations are highly significant (a little less than the .001 level).

[14] A reviewer of this chapter has questioned the message the chapter implies, namely that all statistical tests of hypotheses involve standard errors. This implication would be unfortunate. Indeed, as we will see in later chapters, other means of assessing statistical significance are often used. For example, the nonparametric analysis of variance tests presented in Chapter 16 depend on ranking, and the complex tests of analysis of covariance structures of Chapter 36 depend on comparisons of covariances (correlations).

Study Suggestions

1. Good references on statistics, fortunately, are plentiful. Ask your instructor for recommendations. The books mentioned below may be helpful. Choose one or two books to supplement your study. In reading a statistics book, do not be discouraged if you do not completely understand everything you read. Indeed, sometimes you may be completely bewildered. As you acquire understanding of the language and methods of the statistician, most of the difficulties will disappear.

EDWARDS, A. *Statistical Analysis,* 3d ed. New York: Holt, Rinehart and Winston, 1969. A good book for the beginning student: clear and readable. See, especially, chaps. 3, 4, 10, and 11.

FREEDMAN, A., PISANI, R., and PURVES, R. *Statistics.* New York: Norton, 1978. Accessible to the beginning student. Good discussions of interesting studies and problems. Applications oriented.

HAYS, W. *Statistics,* 3d ed. New York: Holt, Rinehart and Winston, 1981. Superb: thorough, authoritative, research-oriented—but not elementary. Its careful study should be a goal of serious students and researchers.

McNEMAR, Q. *Psychological Statistics,* 4th ed. New York: Wiley, 1969. Excellent book: clear, comprehensive, helpful.

SNEDECOR, G., and COCHRAN, W. *Statistical Methods,* 6th ed. Ames, Iowa: Iowa State University Press, 1967. Solid, authoritative, helpful, but not elementary. Excellent reference book.

2. The proportions of men and women voters in a certain county are .70 and .30, respectively. In one election district of 400 people, there are 300 men and 100 women. Can it be said that the district's proportions of men and women voters differ significantly from those of the county?
    [*Answer:* Yes. $\chi^2 = 4.76$. χ^2 table entry, .05 level, for df = 1: 3.84.]

3. An investigator in the field of prejudice experimented with various methods of answering the prejudiced person's remarks about minority group members. He randomly assigned 32 subjects to two groups, 16 in each group. With the first group he used method A; with the second group he used method B. The means of the two groups on an attitude test, administered after the methods were used, were A: 27; B: 25. Each group had a standard deviation of 4. Do the two group means differ significantly?
    [*Answer:* No. $(27 - 25)/1.414 = 1.414$.]

4. The evenly distributed 4000 random numbers discussed in the text and the statistics calculated from the random numbers are given in Appendix C at the end of the book. Use a table of random numbers—the 4000 random numbers will do—and wave a pencil in the air with eyes closed and let it come to rest at any point in the table. Going down the columns from the place the table was entered, copy out 10 numbers in the range from 1 through 40. Let these be the numbers of ten of the 40 groups. The means, variances, and standard deviations are given right after the table of 4000 random numbers. Copy out the means of the groups randomly selected. Round the means; i.e., 54.33 becomes 54, 47.87 becomes 48, and so on.

(a) Calculate the mean of the means, and compare it to the population mean of 50 (really 50.33). Did you come close?
(b) Calculate the standard deviation of the 10 means.
(c) Take the first group selected and calculate the standard error of the mean, using $N = 100$ and the reported standard deviation. Do the same for the fourth and ninth groups. Are the SE_M's alike? Interpret the first SE_M. Compare the results of (b) and (c).
(d) Calculate the differences between the first and sixth means and the fourth and tenth means. Test the two differences for statistical significance. Should they be statistically significant? Give the reason for your answer. Make up an experimental situation and imagine that the fourth and tenth means are your results. Interpret.
(e) Discuss the central limit theorem in relation to (d), above.

5. To now, the variance and the standard deviation have been calculated with N in the denominator. In statistics books, the student will encounter the variance formula as: $V = \Sigma\ x^2/N$, or $V = \Sigma\ x^2/(N-1)$. The first formula is used when only describing a sample or population. The second is used when estimating the variance of a population with the sample variance (or standard deviation). With N large, there is little practical difference. In Part Five, we will see that the denominators of variance estimates always have $N-1$, $k-1$, and so on. These are really degrees of freedom. Most computer programs use $N-1$ to calculate standard deviations. Perhaps the best advice is to use $N-1$ always. Even when it is not appropriate, it will not make that much difference.

6. Statistics is not always viewed favorably. Marxists, for example, are not too sympathetic. (Why, do you suppose?) Here is an interesting study in education in which a design with a control group was used, but no statistical tests of significance or measures of the magnitude of relations were used!: E. DeCorte and L. Verschaffel, "Children's Solution Processes in Elementary Arithmetic Problems: Analysis and Improvement," *Journal of Educational Psychology*, 73 (1981), 765–779. The student may find it interesting to read this study.

7. There has been much discussion in education about the presumed virtues of the "open" educational environment. In a study by Wright of the difference between "open" and "traditional" school environments, a number of interesting mean differences were reported.[15] Among these mean differences, those in word-meaning knowledge and verbal creativity (p. 453) were:

	Word Meaning		Verbal Creativity	
	Traditional	Open	Traditional	Open
N:	50	50	50	50
M:	4.84	4.35	135.38	129.60
s:	1.19	.78	23.5	19.2

Calculate the two t ratios and interpret the results. (Use formula 12.1 and substitute in formula 12.2.)

[*Answers:* Word Meaning: $t = 2.43$ ($p < .05$); Verbal Creativity: $t = 1.35$ (n.s.).]

8. Review the brief summary of the McGee and Snyder study at the beginning of the chapter. Note that the authors did a t test of the dispositional means. These means, however, reflect the independent variable. Analysis of data with t tests and similar statistics is usually done on dependent variable measures. Were the authors wrong? If so, why? Could a t test of the dependent variable, or "salting," measures conceivably have been not significant? If so, what happens to the authors' hypothesis? (We ignore here other possible kinds of analysis.)

[*Hint:* What is predicted in problems of this kind? Think of hypotheses as If p, then q statements.]

---

[15] R. Wright, "The Affective and Cognitive Consequences of an Open Education Elementary School," *American Educational Research Journal*, 12 (1975), 449–465.

PART FIVE

ANALYSIS
OF VARIANCE

Chapter 13

Analysis of Variance: Foundations

THE ANALYSIS of variance is not just a statistical method. It is an approach and a way of thinking. It is also one of the many expressions of what is known as the general linear model. The linear model is actually a linear equation—"linear" means that no terms of the equation have powers greater than 1—that expresses the sources of variance of a set of measures. In a form suitable for analysis of variance, it can be written:

$$y_i = b_0 x_0 + b_1 x_{i1} + b_2 x_{i2} + \ldots + b_k x_{ik} + e_i$$

(Notice that none of the x's has a power greater than 1, that is, there are no x^2's or x^3's.) If we conceive a score of one individual, y, as having one or more sources of variance, x_1, x_2, . . . , then we can roughly grasp the idea of the model.[1] The b's are weights that express the relative degrees of influence of the x's in accounting for y. e is error; it expresses the unknown factors that influence y plus, of course, ubiquitous random error. The equation is general: it fits most analytic situations in which we wish to explain the variation of a set of measures of a dependent variable, y. For analysis of variance models, the equation simplifies to one of several specific forms, which we need not now examine. The point is that dependent variable measures are conceived as having two or more components, and the task of analysis of variance is to determine the relative contributions of these components to the dependent variable variation. As we will see toward the end of the book, this is one of the goals of multiple regression, as well as of other analytic methods. We must try to make these abstractions concrete and understandable, however. For now, just bear this in mind: the total dependent variable variance of any statistical situation is broken down into component sources of variance.

[1] For a lucid, brief explanation of the general linear model and analysis of variance models, see W. Hays, *Statistics*, 3d ed. New York: Holt, Rinehart and Winston, 1981, pp. 327ff.

In this chapter and in Chapters 14 and 15 we explore the analysis of variance. The emphasis will be on the few fundamental and general notions that underlie the method. The chapters are not meant merely to teach analysis of variance and related methods as statistics. Their intent is to convey the basic ideas of the methods in relation to research and research problems. To accomplish the pedagogical purpose, simple examples will be used. It makes little difference whether 5 scores or 500 scores are used, or if 2 or 20 variables are used. The fundamental ideas, the theoretical conceptions, are the same. In this chapter, *simple one-way analysis of variance* is discussed. The next two chapters consider so-called factorial analysis of variance and the analysis of variance of correlated groups or subjects. By then the student should have a good basis for the study of research design.[2]

VARIANCE BREAKDOWN: A SIMPLE EXAMPLE

In Chapter 6, two sets of scores were analyzed in a variance fashion. The *total variance* of all the scores was broken down into a *between-groups variance* and a *within-groups variance*. We now pick up the theme of Chapter 6 by using, in altered form, the two-group example given there, and by correcting the method of calculation. Then we extend analysis of variance ideas considerably.

Suppose an investigator is interested in the relative efficacies of two methods, A_1 and A_2.[3] Selecting ten students as a sample, he divides them into two groups at random and assigns the experimental treatments to the two groups at random. After a suitable length of time, he measures, let's say, the learning of the students of both groups on a measure of achievement. The results, together with certain computations, are given in Table 13.1.

Our job is to locate and calculate the different variances that make up the total variance. The total variance and the other variances are calculated as before, with an important difference. Instead of using N or n in the denominator of variance fractions, we use so-called degrees of freedom. Degrees of freedom are ordinarily defined as one case less than N or n, that is, $N - 1$ and $n - 1$. In the case of groups, instead of k (the number of groups), we use $k - 1$. While this method has a great advantage from a statistical point of

Table 13.1   Two Sets of Hypothetical Experimental Data with Sums, Means, and Sums of Squares

	A_1	x	x^2	A_2	x	x^2	
	4	0	0	3	0	0	
	5	1	1	1	−2	4	
	3	−1	1	5	2	4	
	2	−2	4	2	−1	1	
	6	2	4	4	1	1	
ΣX:	20			15			$\Sigma X_t = 35$
M:	4			3			$M_t = 3.5$
Σx^2:			10			10	

---

[2] At this point the student should review Chapter 6. The basic ideas presented in that chapter will be applied in this one.

[3] We use "methods" here and elsewhere because the term is general and easily grasped. The student can supply the substance of different methods of his own field. In education, for example, it might be methods of teaching, in psychology methods of reinforcement or attention arousal, in political science methods of participation in political processes.

Table 13.2   Calculation of V_t of Data of Table 13.1

X	x	x^2
4	.5	.25
5	1.5	2.25
3	− .5	.25
2	−1.5	2.25
6	2.5	6.25
3	− .5	.25
1	−2.5	6.25
5	1.5	2.25
2	−1.5	2.25
4	.5	.25

ΣX:	35	
M:	3.5	
Σx^2:		22.50

view, from a mathematical-conceptual point of view it makes our job a bit more difficult. First, we do the computations, and then return to the difficulty.

To calculate the total variance, we use the formula:

$$V_t = \frac{\Sigma x^2}{N - 1} \qquad (13.1)$$

where Σx^2 = the sum of squares, as before, $x = X - M$, or deviation from the mean of any score, and N = number of cases in the total sample. To calculate V_t, simply take all the scores, regardless of their grouping, and calculate the necessary terms of Equation 13.1, as in Table 13.2. Since $N - 1 = 10 - 1 = 9$, $V_t = 22.50/9 = 2.5$. Thus, if we arrange the data of Table 13.1 without regard to the two groups, $V_t = 2.5$.

There is variance between the groups and this variance is due, presumably, to the experimental manipulation. That is, the experimenter did something to one group and something different to the other group. These different treatments should make the groups and their means different. They will have *between-groups variance*. Take the two means, treat them like any other scores (X's), and calculate their variance (see Table 13.3).

There is a remaining source of variance left over: the ubiquitous random error. We saw in Chapter 6 that this could be obtained by calculating the variance *within* each group

Table 13.3   Calculation of V_b of Data of Table 13.1

X	x	x^2
4	.5	.25
3	.5	.25

ΣX:	7	
M:	3.5	
Σx^2:		.50

$$V_b = \frac{\Sigma x_b^2}{k - 1} = \frac{.50}{2 - 1} = .50$$

separately and then averaging these separate variances. We do this using the figures given in Table 13.1. Each group has $\Sigma x^2 = 10$. Dividing each of these sums of squares by its degrees of freedom, we get:

$$\frac{\Sigma x_{A_1}^2}{n_{A_1} - 1} = \frac{10}{4} = 2.5$$

and

$$\frac{\Sigma x_{A_2}^2}{n_{A_2} - 1} = \frac{10}{4} = 2.5$$

The averaging yields, of course, 2.5. Therefore the *within-groups variance*, V_w, is 2.5.

Three variances have been calculated: $V_t = 2.5$, $V_b = .50$, $V_w = 2.5$. The theoretical equation given in Chapter 6 says that the total variance is made up of separate sources of variance: the between-groups and the within-groups variances. Logically, they should add up to the total variance. The theoretical equation is

$$V_t = V_b + V_w \qquad (13.2)$$

Since 2.5 is not equal to .50 and 2.5, something must be wrong. The trouble is that degrees of freedom were used in the denominators of the variance formula instead of N, n, and k. Had N, n, and k been used, the relation of Equation 13.2 would have held (see Chapter 6).

The student may ask: Why not follow the N, n, and k procedure? And if you cannot follow it, why bother with all this? The answer is that the calculation of the variances with N, n, and k is mathematically correct but statistically "unsatisfactory." Another important aspect of the analysis of variance is the estimation of population values. It can be shown that using degrees of freedom in the denominators of the variance formula yields unbiased estimates of the population values, a matter of great statistical concern. The reason we bother going through the present procedure is to show the reader clearly the mathematical basis of the reasoning. One should remember, though, that variances, as used in the analysis of variance, are not necessarily additive.

Sums of squares, on the other hand, are always additive. (They are calculated from the scores and not divided by anything.) And sums of squares, of course, are also measures of variability. Except at the final stage of analysis of variance, sums of squares are calculated, studied, and analyzed. To convince ourselves of the additive property of sums of squares, note that the between-groups and the within-groups sums of squares add to the total sum of squares. If we multiply the between-groups sum of squares by n, the number of cases in each group:

$$\Sigma x_t^2 = n\Sigma x_b^2 + \Sigma x_w^2$$

or numerically, $22.50 = (5)(.50) + 20$.[4]

THE *t*-RATIO APPROACH

Using the data of Table 13.1, we calculate several statistics for the A_1 and A_2 data separately: the variances, standard deviations, standard errors of the means, and standard

[4] The reasoning behind the expression $n\Sigma x_b^2$ in this equation is as follows. The definition of an unbiased estimate of the variance of the population of means is $V_M = \Sigma x^2/(n - 1)$. But from our reasoning on the standard error and the standard variance, we know that $V_M = SV_M = V/n$. Substituting in the first equation, we get $V/n = \Sigma x^2/(k - 1)$, and thus $V = n\Sigma x^2/(k - 1)$. It should be noted here that the expression, $n\Sigma x_b^2$, indicated in footnote 11, Chapter 6, is really the *between sum of squares*—and not Σx_b^2, as indicated in Chapter 6 and subsequent chapters. That is, instead of writing Σx_b^2, statisticians write ss_b, which is really $n\Sigma x_b^2$.

Table 13.4   Various Statistics Calculated from Table 13.1 Data

	A_1	A_2
V:	$\dfrac{\Sigma x^2}{n-1} = \dfrac{10}{4} = 2.5$	$\dfrac{10}{4} = 2.5$
SD:	$\sqrt{2.5} = 1.58$	$\sqrt{2.5} = 1.58$
SE_M:	$\dfrac{SD}{\sqrt{n}} = \dfrac{1.58}{\sqrt{5}} = .705$	$\dfrac{1.58}{\sqrt{5}} = .705$
SV_M:	$\dfrac{V}{n} = \dfrac{2.5}{5} = .50$	$\dfrac{2.5}{5} = .50$

variances of the means.[5] These calculations are shown in Table 13.4. (Note that V is now calculated with $n - 1$ instead of n.)

Now we consider the central statistical idea behind the analysis of variance. The question the investigator has to ask himself is: Do the means differ significantly? It is obvious that 4 does not equal 3, but the question has to be asked statistically. We know that if sets of random numbers are drawn, the means of the sets will not be equal. They should, however, not be too different, that is, they should differ only within the bounds of chance fluctuations. Thus the question becomes: Does 4 differ from 3 *significantly?* Again the null hypothesis is set up: $H_o: M_{A_1} - M_{A_2} = 0$, or $M_{A_1} = M_{A_2}$. The substantive hypothesis was: $H_1: M_{A_1} > M_{A_2}$. Which hypothesis does the evidence support? In other words, it is not simply a question of 4 being absolutely greater than 3. It is, rather, a question of whether 4 differs from 3 beyond the differences to be expected by chance.

This question can be quickly answered using the method of the last chapter. First, calculate the standard error of the differences between the means:

$$SE_{M_{A1}-M_{A2}} = \sqrt{SE_{M_{A1}}{}^2 + SE_{M_{A2}}{}^2} = \sqrt{(.705)^2 + (.705)^2}$$
$$= \sqrt{.994} = .997 = 1.00 \text{ (rounded)}$$

Now, the t ratio:

$$t = \frac{M_{A1} - M_{A2}}{SE_{M_{A1}-M_{A2}}} = \frac{4-3}{1.00} = \frac{1}{1} = 1$$

Since the difference being evaluated is no greater than the measure of error, it is obvious that it is not significant. The numerator and the denominator of the t ratio are equal. The difference, $4 - 3 = 1$, is clearly one of the differences that could have occurred with random numbers. Remember that a ''real'' difference would be reflected in the t ratio by a considerably larger numerator than denominator.

THE ANALYSIS OF VARIANCE APPROACH

In the analysis of variance, the approach is conceptually similar, although the method differs. The method is general: differences of more than two groups can be tested for

---

[5]The methods of analysis used in the first part of this chapter are not used in actual calculation. They are too cumbersome. They are used here for pedagogical reasons. Unfortunately, the usual method of calculation tends to obscure the important relations and operations underlying the analysis of variance.

statistical significance, whereas the *t* test applies only to two groups. (With two groups, as we shall see shortly, the results of the two methods are really identical.) The method of analysis of variance uses variances entirely, instead of using actual differences and standard errors, even though the actual difference-standard error reasoning is behind the method. Two variances are always pitted against each other. One variance, that presumably due to the experimental (independent) variable or variables, is pitted against another variance, that presumably due to error or randomness. This is a case, again, of information versus error, as Diamond put it,[6] or, as information theorists say, information versus noise. To get a grip on this idea, go back to the problem.

We found that the between-groups variance was .50. Now we must find a variance that is a reflection of error. This is the within-groups variance. After all, since we calculate the within-groups variance, essentially, by calculating the variance of each group separately and then averaging the two (or more) variances, this estimate of error is unaffected by the differences between the means. Thus, *if nothing else is causing the scores to vary*, it is reasonable to consider the within-groups variance a measure of chance fluctuation. If this is so, then we can *stack up the variance due to the experimental effect, the between-groups variance, against this measure of chance error, the within-groups variance.* The only question is: How is the within-groups variance calculated?

Remember that the variance of a population of means can be estimated with the standard variance of the mean (the standard error squared). One way to obtain the within-groups variance is to calculate the standard variance of each of the groups and then average them for all of the groups. This should yield an estimate of error that can be used to evaluate the variance of the means of the groups. The reasoning here is basic. To evaluate the differences between the means, it is necessary to refer to a theoretical population of means that would be gotten from the random sampling of groups of scores like the groups of scores we have. In the present case, we have two means from samples with five scores in each group. (It is well to remember that we might have three, four, or more means from three, four, or more groups. The reasoning is the same.) If subjects were assigned to the groups at random, and nothing has operated—that is, there have been no experimental manipulations and no other systematic influences at work—then it is possible to estimate the variance of the means of the population of means with the standard variance of the means (SE_M^2, or SV_M). Each group provides such an estimate. These estimates will vary to some extent among themselves. We can pool them by averaging to form an overall estimate of the variance of the population means.

Recall that the standard error of the mean formula was: $SE_M = SD/\sqrt{n}$. Simply square this expression to get the standard variance of the mean: $SE_M^2 = (SD)^2/n = SV_M = V/n$. The variances of each of the groups was 2.5. Calculating the standard variances, we obtain for each group: $SV_M = V/n = 2.50/5 = .50$. Averaging them obviously yields .50. Note carefully that each standard variance was calculated from each group *separately and then averaged*. Therefore this average standard variance is uninfluenced by differences between the means, as noted earlier. The average standard variance, then, is a *within-groups variance*. It is an estimate of random errors.

But if random numbers had been used, the same reasoning applies to the between-groups variance, the variance calculated from the actual means. We calculated a variance from the means of 4 and 3: it was .50. If the numbers were random, estimating the variance of the population of means should be possible by calculating the variance of the obtained means.

Note carefully, however, that if any extraneous influence has been at work, if any-

[6]S. Diamond, *Information and Error*. New York: Basic Books, 1959.

thing like experimental effects have operated, then no longer will the variance calculated from the obtained means be a good estimate of the population variance of means. If an experimental influence—or some influence other than chance—has operated, the effect may be to increase the variance of the obtained means. In a sense, this is the purpose of experimental manipulation: to increase the variance between means, to make the means different from each other. This is the crux of the analysis of variance matter. *If an experimental manipulation has been influential, then it should show up in differences between means above and beyond the differences that arise by chance alone.* And the between-groups variance should show the influence by becoming greater than expected by chance. Clearly we can use V_b, then, as a measure of experimental influence. Equally clearly, as we showed above, we can use V_w as a measure of chance variation. Therefore, we have almost reached the end of a rather long but profitable journey: we can evaluate the between-groups variance, V_b, with the within-groups variance, V_w. Or information, experimental information, can be weighed against error or chance.

It might be possible to evaluate V_b by subtracting V_w from it. In the analysis of variance, however, V_b is divided by V_w. The ratio so formed is called the F ratio. (The F ratio was named by Snedecor in honor of Ronald Fisher, the inventor of the analysis of variance. It was Snedecor who worked out the F tables used to evaluate F ratios.) One calculates the F ratio from observed data and checks the result against an F table. (The F table with direction for its use can be found in any statistics text.) If the obtained F ratio is as great or greater than the appropriate tabled entry, the differences that V_b reflects are statistically significant. In such a case the null hypothesis of no differences between the means is rejected at the chosen level of significance. In the present case:

$$F = \frac{V_b}{V_w} = \frac{.50}{.50} = 1$$

One obviously does not need the F table to see that the F ratio is not significant. Evidently the two means of 4 and 3 do not differ from each other significantly. In other words, of the many possible random samples of pairs of groups of five cases each, this particular case could easily be one of them. Had the difference been considerably greater, great enough to tip the F-ratio balance scale, then the conclusion would have been quite different, as we shall see.[7]

AN EXAMPLE OF A STATISTICALLY SIGNIFICANT DIFFERENCE

Suppose that the investigator had obtained quite different results. Say the means had been 6 and 3, rather than 4 and 3. We now take the above example and *add a constant of 2 to each A_1 score.* This operation of course merely restores the scores used in Chapter 6. It was said earlier that adding a constant to a set of scores (or subtracting a constant) changes the mean by the constant *but has no effect whatever on the variance.* The figures are given in Table 13.5.

---

[7] Note that the t test and analysis of variance yielded the same result. With only two groups, or one degree of freedom $(k - 1)$, $F = t^2$, or $t = \sqrt{F}$. This equality shows that it does not matter, in the case of two groups, whether t or F is calculated. (But the analysis of variance is a bit easier to calculate than t, in most cases.) With three or more groups, however, the equality breaks down; F must always be calculated. Thus F is the general test of which t is a special case.

Table 13.5 Hypothetical Experimental Data for Two Groups: Table 13.1 Data Altered

	A_1	x	x^2	A_2	x	x^2
	$4 + 2 = 6$	0	0	3	0	0
	$5 + 2 = 7$	1	1	1	-2	4
	$3 + 2 = 5$	-1	1	5	2	4
	$2 + 2 = 4$	-2	4	2	-1	1
	$6 + 2 = 8$	2	4	4	1	1
ΣX:	30			15		
M:	6			3		
Σx^2:			10			10
V:	$\dfrac{10}{4} = 2.5$			$\dfrac{10}{4} = 2.5$		
SV:	$\dfrac{V}{n} = \dfrac{2.5}{5} = .50$			$\dfrac{2.5}{5} = .50$		

It is important to note carefully that the Σx^2 values are the same as they were before, 10. Note, too, that the variances, V, are the same, 2.5. So are the standard variances, each being .50. As far as these statistics are concerned, then, there is no difference between this example and the previous example. But now we calculate the between-groups variance (Table 13.6). V_b is nine times greater than it was before: 4.50 versus .50. But V_w *is exactly the same as it was before.* This is an important point. To repeat: adding a constant to one set of scores—which is tantamount to an experimental manipulation, since one of the purposes of an experiment of this kind is to augment or diminish one set of measures (the experimental group measures) while the other set does not change (the control group measures)—has no effect on the within-groups variance while the between-groups variance changes drastically. Note that *the estimates of V_b and V_w are independent of each other.* (If they are not, by the way, the F test is vitiated.)

The F ratio is $F = V_b/V_w = 4.50/.50 = 9$. Evidently information is much greater than error. Does this mean that the difference $6 - 3 = 3$ is a statistically significant difference? If we check an F table, we find that, in this case, an F ratio of 5.32 or greater is significant at the .05 level. (The details of how to read an F table are omitted here. They are not essential to the argument.) To be significant at the .01 level, the F ratio in this case would have to be 11.26 or greater. Our F ratio is 9. It is greater than 5.32 but less than 11.26. It

Table 13.6 Calculation of Between-groups Variance of Table 13.5 Data

	X	x	x^2
	6	1.5	2.25
	3	-1.5	2.25
ΣX:	9		
M:	4.5		
Σx^2:			4.50

$$V_b = \frac{\Sigma x_b^2}{k - 1} = \frac{4.50}{2 - 1}$$

$$= 4.50$$

seems that the difference of 3 is statistically significant difference at the .05 level. Therefore, $6 \neq 3$, and the null hypothesis is rejected.

CALCULATION OF ONE-WAY ANALYSIS OF VARIANCE

Simple one-way analysis of variance is easier to do than the above procedure and discussion have indicated. To show the method, the example just considered will be used. By now the reader should be able to follow the procedure without difficulty. Note that deviation scores (x's) are not used at all. One can calculate entirely with raw scores. There will be certain differences in the variances. In the preceding examples, standard variances were used in order to show the underlying rationale of the analysis of variance. In the following method, however, although the same method is used, certain steps are omitted because it is possible to do the calculation in a much easier way.

The calculations of Table 13.7 can easily be followed. First, in the body of the table, note that the raw scores, the X's, are each squared.[8] Then they are added to yield the ΣX^2's at the bottom of the table (190 and 55). The purpose of doing this is to obtain $\Sigma X_t^2 = 245$ (190 + 55), at the right and bottom. Read ΣX_t^2. "The total sum of all the squared X's." The ΣX's and M's are calculated as usual (even though we do not really need the M's, except for later interpretation). Next, each group sum is squared and written $(\Sigma X)^2$. They are $(30)^2 = 900$ and $(15)^2 = 225$. (Be careful here. A frequent mistake is to confuse ΣX^2 and $(\Sigma X)^2$.) At the bottom right of the table proper, ΣX_t, $(\Sigma X_t)^2$, M_t, and ΣX_t^2 are entered. They are statistics of all the scores and are calculated in the same way as the individual group statistics.

Next, the calculations of the sums of squares (hereafter, ss). In the analysis of variance, mostly sums of squares are calculated and used. The variances or mean squares are reserved for the final analysis of variance table (at the bottom of Table 13.7). What we are after in this procedure are the total, the between and the within *sums of squares,* or ss_t, ss_b, and ss_w. First, the calculation of C, the correction term. Since we are using raw scores, and since we are aiming at sums of squares, which are the *sums of the deviations* squared, we must reduce the raw scores to deviation scores. To accomplish this, we subtract C from every calculation. This accomplishes the reduction: it changes, in effect, X's to x's. The actual calculation of C is obvious. Here it is 202.50.

The total sum of squares, ss_t, is now calculated: 42.50. The between, or between-groups, or between-means, sum of squares is not as obvious. The sum of each group's scores is squared and then divided by the number of scores in the group. These averages are then added. From this sum C is subtracted. The result is the between-groups sum of squares, or ss_b. And this is all there is to the simple one-way analysis of variance. The within sum of squares, ss_w is calculated by subtraction. The following equation is important and should be remembered:

$$ss_t = ss_b + ss_w \tag{13.3}$$

---

[8] To do the calculations in this book, students are urged to use only desk or hand-held calculators that can cumulate sums and sums of squares. Occasionally access to a microcomputer or larger computer will be helpful, even necessary. In general, however, one should get the feel of analysis of variance (and other methods) "through the hands." Students are strongly advised against using package programs (SPSS, BMDP, SAS, and the like) to do the exercises, except when explicitly advised to do so. Some calculations, of course, cannot be done "by hand," or are extremely difficult to do. The principle is (or should be): Understand what you're doing all along the way. To relieve the monotony of repetitive calculations of sums and sums of squares, it is highly useful if one has a programmable calculator or a microcomputer and an easily used program to calculate sums and sums of squares.

Table 13.7 Calculation of Analysis of Variance: Fictitious Data

X_{A_1}	$X_{A_1}^2$	X_{A_2}	$X_{A_2}^2$	
6	36	3	9	$N = 10$
7	49	1	1	$n = 5$
5	25	5	25	$k = 2$
4	16	2	4	
8	64	4	16	

ΣX:	30	15		$\Sigma X_t = 45$
$(\Sigma X)^2$:	900	225		$(\Sigma X_t)^2 = 2025$
M:	6	3		$M_t = 4.5$
ΣX^2:		190	55	$\Sigma X_t^2 = 245$

$$C = \frac{(\Sigma X_t)^2}{N} = \frac{(45)^2}{10} = \frac{2025}{10} = 202.50$$

$$\text{Total} = \Sigma X_t^2 - C = 245 - 202.50 = 42.50$$

$$\text{Between} = \left[\frac{(\Sigma X_{A_1})^2}{n_{A_1}} + \frac{(\Sigma X_{A_2})^2}{n_{A_2}} \right] - C$$

$$= \left[\frac{(30)^2}{5} + \frac{(15)^2}{5} \right] - 202.50 = (180 + 45) - 202.50 = 22.50$$

Source	df	ss	ms	F
Between Groups	$k - 1 = 1$	22.50	22.50	9. (.05)
Within Groups	$N - k = 8$	20.00	2.50	
Total	$N - 1 = 9$	42.50		

Recall Equation 13.2: $V_t = V_b + V_w$. Equation 13.3 is the same equation in the sums of squares form. Equation 13.2 cannot be used since, as was pointed out earlier, it is a theoretical formulation that only works exactly under the conditions specified. Equation 13.3 always works; that is, sums of squares in the analysis of variance are always additive. So, with a little algebraic manipulation we see that $ss_w = ss_t - ss_b$. To obtain the within sum of squares, in other words, simply subtract the between from the total sum of squares. In the table, $42.50 - 22.50 = 20$. (It is, of course, possible to calculate the within sum of squares directly.)

After completing the above calculation, we enter the degrees of freedom (df) in the final table. Although formulas have been entered, they are not necessary to the operation. For the total degrees of freedom, simply take one less than the total number of subjects used. If, for example, there were three experimental groups with 30 S's in each group, the total degrees of freedom are $N - 1 = 90 - 1 = 89$. The between-groups degrees of freedom are one less than the number of experimental groups. With three experimental groups, $k - 1 = 3 - 1 = 2$. With the example of Table 13.7, $k - 1 = 2 - 1 = 1$. The within-groups degrees of freedom, like the within-groups sum of squares, are obtained by subtraction. In this case, $9 - 1 = 8$. Next, divide the degrees of freedom into the sums of squares (ss/df) to obtain the between and within mean squares, labeled "ms" in the table. In the analysis of variance, the variances are called "mean squares." Finally, obtain the F ratio by dividing the within or error variance or mean square into the between variance or mean square: $F = ms_b/ms_w = 22.50/2.50 = 9$. This final F ratio, also called the variance ratio, is checked against appropriate entries in an F table to determine its significance, as discussed previously.

A RESEARCH EXAMPLE

To illustrate the research use of one-way analysis of variance, data from an early experimental study by Hurlock, described earlier in this book, are given in Table 13.8.[9] The data were not analyzed in this manner by Hurlock, the analysis of variance not being available at the time of the study. Hurlock divided 106 fourth- and sixth-grade pupils into four groups, E_1, E_2, E_3, and C. Five forms of an addition test, A, B, C, D, and E, were used. Form A was administered to all the S's on the first day. For the next four days the experimental groups, E_1, E_2, and E_3, were given a different form of the test. The control group, C, was separated from the other groups and given different forms of the test on four separate days. The S's of Group C were told to work as usual. But each day before the tests were given, the E_1 group was brought to the front of the room and *praised* for its good work. Then the E_2 group was brought forward and *reproved* for its poor work. The members of the E_3 group were *ignored*. On the fifth day of the experiment, Form E was administered to all groups. Scores were the number of correct answers on this form of the test. Summary data are given in Table 13.8, together with the table of the final analysis of variance.

Since $F = 10.08$, which is significant at the .001 level, the null hypothesis of no differences between the means has to be rejected. Evidently the experimental manipulations were effective. There is not much difference between the Ignored and Control groups, an interesting finding. The Praised group has the largest mean, with the Reproved group mean in between the Praised group and the other two groups. The student can complete the interpretation of the data.[10]

Table 13.8 Summary Data and Analysis of Variance of Data from Hurlock Study

	E_1 Praised	E_2 Reproved	E_3 Ignored	C Control
n:	27	27	26	26
M:	20.22	14.19	12.38	11.35
SD:	7.68	6.78	6.06	4.21

Source	df	ss	ms	F
Between Groups	3	1260.06	420.02	10.08 (.001)
Within Groups	102	4249.29	41.66	
Total	105	5509.35		

[9] E. Hurlock, "An Evaluation of Certain Incentives in Schoolwork," *Journal of Education Psychology,* 16 (1925), 145–159. The first three lines in Table 13.8 were reported by Hurlock. All the other figures were calculated by the author from these figures (see Addendum to chapter).

[10] After an analysis of variance of this kind, some investigators test pairs of means with *t* tests. Unless specific differences between means, or groups of means, have been predicted, this procedure is questionable. We take up this problem later in the chapter. (See Study Suggestion 6.)

STRENGTH OF RELATIONS: CORRELATION AND THE ANALYSIS OF VARIANCE

Tests of statistical significance like t and F unfortunately do not indicate the magnitude or strength of relations. A t test of the difference between two means, if significant, simply tells the investigator that there *is* a relation. An F test, similarly, if significant, simply says that a relation exists. The relation is inferred from the significant differences between two, three, or more means. A statistical test like F says in an indirect way that there is or is not a relation between the independent variable (or variables) and the dependent variable.

In contrast to tests of statistical significance like t and F, coefficients of correlation are relatively direct measures of relations. They have an easily "seen" and direct intuitive message since the joining of two sets of scores more obviously seems like a relation; it follows our earlier definition of a relation as a set of ordered pairs. If, for example, $r = .90$, it is easy to see that the rank orders of the measures of two variables are very similar. But t and F ratios are one or two steps removed from the actual relation. An important research technical question, then, is how t and F, on the one hand, and measures like r, on the other hand, are related.

In an analysis of variance, the variable on the margins of the data table—methods of incentive in the Hurlock example—is the independent variable. The measures in the body of the table reflect the dependent variable: arithmetic achievement in the Hurlock example. The analysis of variance works with the relation between these two kinds of variables. if the independent variable has had an effect on the dependent variable, then the "equality" of the means of the experimental groups that would be expected if the numbers being analyzed were random numbers is upset. The effect of a really influential independent variable is to make means unequal. We can say, then, that any relation that exists between the independent and dependent variables is reflected in the inequality of the means. The more unequal the means, the wider apart they are, the higher the relation, other things equal.

If no relation exists between the independent variable and the dependent variable, then it is as though we had sets of random numbers, and consequently, random means. The differences between the means would only be chance fluctuations. An F test would show them not to be significantly different. If a relation does exist, if there is a tie or bond

Table 13.9 Strong Relation Between Methods of Instruction and Achievement

Independent Variable (Methods of Instruction)	Dependent Variable (Achievement)	Means
Method A_1	10 9 9 8	9
Method A_2	7 7 7 7	7
Method A_3	5 4 4 3	4

Table 13.10   Zero Relation Between Methods of Instruction and Achievement

Independent Variable (Methods of Instruction)	Dependent Variable (Achievement)	Means
Method A_1	4 8 10 7	7.25
Method A_2	3 5 4 9	5.25
Method A_3	7 7 7 9	7.50

between the independent and dependent variables, the imposition of *different* aspects of the independent variable, like different methods of instruction, should make the measures of the dependent variable vary accordingly. Method A_1 might make achievement scores go up, whereas method A_2 might make them go down or stay about the same. Note that we have the same phenomenon of concomitant variation that we did with the correlation coefficient. Take two extreme cases: a strong relation and a zero relation. We lay out a hypothetically strong relation between methods and achievement in Table 13.9. Note that the dependent variable scores vary directly with the independent variable methods: Method A_1 has high scores, method A_2 medium scores, and method A_3 low scores. The relation is also shown by comparing methods and the means of the dependent variable.

Compare the example of Table 13.9 with chance expectation. If there were no relation between methods and achievement, then the achievement means would not covary with methods. That is, the means would be nearly equal. In order to show this, I wrote the 12 achievement scores of Table 13.9 on separate slips of paper, mixed them up thoroughly in a hat, threw them all on the floor, and picked them up 4 at a time, assigning the first four to A_1, the second four to A_2, and the third four to A_3. The results are shown in Table 13.10.

Now it is difficult, or impossible, to ''see'' a relation. The means differ, but not much. Certainly the relation between methods and achievement scores (and means) is not nearly as clear as it was before. Still, we have to be sure. Analyses of variance of both sets of data were performed. The F ratio of the data of Table 13.9 (strong relation) was 57.59, highly significant, whereas the F ratio of the data of Table 13.10 (low or zero relation) was 1.29, not significant. The statistical tests confirm our visual impressions. We now know that there is a relation between methods and achievement in Table 13.9 but not in Table 13.10.

The problem, however, is to show the relation between significance tests like the F test and the correlation method. This can be done in several ways. We illustrate with two such ways, one graphical and one statistical. In Figure 13.1 the data of Tables 13.9 and 13.10 have been plotted much as continuous X and Y measures in the usual correlation problem are plotted, with the independent variable—Methods—on the horizontal axis, and the dependent variable—Achievement—on the vertical axis, as usual. To indicate the

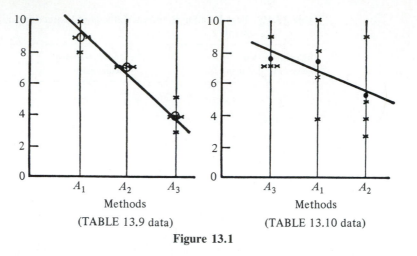

Methods
(TABLE 13.9 data)

Methods
(TABLE 13.10 data)

Figure 13.1

relation, lines have been drawn as near to the means as possible. A diagonal line making a 45-degree angle with the horizontal axis would indicate a strong relation. A horizontal line across the graph would indicate a zero relation. Note that the plotted scores of the data of Table 13.9 clearly indicate a strong relation: the height of the plotted scores (crosses) and the means (circles) varies with the method. The plot of the data of Table 13.10, even with a rearrangement of the methods for purposes of comparison, shows a weak relation or no relation.

Let us now look at the problem statistically. It is possible to calculate correlation coefficients with data of this kind. If one has done an analysis of variance, a simple (but not entirely satisfactory) coefficient is yielded by the following formula:

$$\eta = \sqrt{\frac{ss_b}{ss_t}} \tag{13.4}$$

Of course, ss_b and ss_t are the between-groups sum of squares and the total sum of squares, respectively. One simply takes these sums of squares from the analysis-of-variance table to calculate the coefficient. η, usually called the *correlation ratio,* is a general coefficient or index of relation often used with data that are not linear. (*Linear,* roughly speaking, means that, if two variables are plotted one against another, the plot tends to follow a straight line. This is another way of saying what was said in Chapter 12 about linear combinations.) Its values vary from 0 to 1.00. We are interested here only in its use with analysis of variance and in its power to tell us the magnitude of the relation between independent and dependent variables.

Recall that the means of the data of Table 13.1 were 3 and 4. They were not significantly different. Therefore there is no relation between the independent variable (methods) and the dependent variable (achievement). If an analysis of variance of the data of Table 13.1 is done, using the method outlined in Table 13.7, $ss_b = 2.50$ and $ss_t = 22.50$. $\eta = \sqrt{2.50/22.50} = \sqrt{.111} = .33$ yields the correlation between methods and achievement. Since we know that the data are not significant ($F = 1$), η is not significant. In other words, $\eta = .33$ is here tantamount to a zero relation. Had there been no difference at all between the means, then, of course, $\eta = 0$. If $ss_b = ss_t$, then $\eta = 1.00$. This can happen only if all the scores of one group are the same, and all the scores of the other group are the same as, and yet different from, those of the first group, which is highly unlikely. For example, if the A_1 scores were 4, 4, 4, 4, 4, and the A_2 scores were 3, 3, 3, 3, 3, then $ss_b = ss_t = 2.5$, and $\eta = \sqrt{2.5/2.5} = 1$. It is obvious that there is no within-groups variance—again, extremely unlikely.

Take the data of Table 13.7. The means are 6 and 3. They are significantly different, since $F = 9$. Calculate η:

$$\eta = \sqrt{\frac{ss_b}{ss_t}} = \sqrt{\frac{22.50}{42.50}} = \sqrt{.529} = .73$$

Note the substantial increase in η. And since F is significant, $\eta = .73$ is significant. There is a substantial relation between methods and achievement.

The Hurlock study is more interesting: $\eta = \sqrt{1260.06/5509.35} = \sqrt{.229} = .48$, which is of course significant. Other things equal, incentive is substantially related to arithmetic achievement, as defined.

By now the student has sufficient background to interpret η in variance terms. In Chapter 6, this was done for r, where it was explained that r^2 indicated the variance shared by two variables. η can be given a similar interpretation. If η is squared, η^2 indicates, in essence, the variance shared by the independent and dependent variables. Perhaps more to the point, η^2 indicates the proportion of the variance of the dependent variable, say achievement, determined by the variance of the independent variable, methods, or incentives. For example, in the Hurlock example, $\eta^2 = (.48)^2 = .23$, which indicates that 23 percent of the variance of the arithmetic addition scores is accounted for by the different modes of incentives used by Hurlock.

η^2 is an index of the proportion of variance accounted for in this sample. Another index, Hays' ω^2 (omega-squared) is an estimate of the strength of association between the independent variable and the population dependent variable. We recommend its use:[11]

$$\omega^2 = \frac{ss_b - (k - 1)ms_w}{ss_t + ms_w} \tag{13.5}$$

where k = number of groups in the analysis of variance and the other terms are the sums of squares and mean squares defined earlier. ω^2 is a conservative estimate of the strength of association or relation between the independent variable X and the dependent variable Y, or between the variable reflected by the experimental treatment and the dependent variable measure. Calculating ω^2 for the Hurlock example,

$$\omega^2 = \frac{1260.06 - (4 - 1)(41.66)}{5509.35 + 41.66} = .205$$

This is rather close to the value of η^2, .23. ω^2 is comparable to η^2 rather than to η. Both indices indicate the proportion of variance in a dependent variable due to the presumed influence of an independent variable.[12]

[11] Hays, *op. cit.*, p. 349.

[12] Different indices, the relations between them, and their relative merits are not easy problems. See G. Vaughan and M. Corballis, "Beyond Tests of Significance: Estimating Strength of Effects in Selected ANOVA Designs," *Psychological Bulletin*, 72 (1969), 204–213. In the previous editions of this book, the intraclass correlation coefficient, *RI*, was recommended. But this coefficient is appropriate for so-called Model II or random effects analysis of variance designs and not for so-called Model I or fixed-effects designs, which are the designs discussed in this text and which are common in the behavioral sciences. No great harm is done, however, if it is used. Actually, the three coefficients, η^2, *RI*, and ω^2, estimate the same thing: the proportion of variance of the dependent variable accounted for by the independent variable. Here is the formula for *RI*, the intraclass coefficient:

$$RI = \frac{ms_b - ms_w}{ms_b + (n_j - 1)ms_w}$$

For the Hurlock data, $RI = .26$, somewhat larger than ω^2 and η^2. To be analogous to product-moment correlation coefficients, strictly speaking, one calculates η and the square roots of *RI* and ω^2. This is not usually done, however.

The point of the above discussion has been to bring out the similarity of conception of these and other indices of association or correlation and, more important, the similarity of the principle and structure of analysis of variance and correlation methods. From a practical and applied standpoint, it should be emphasized that η^2, ω^2, or other measures of association should always be calculated and reported. It is not enough to report F ratios and whether they are statistically significant. We must know how strong relations are. After all, with large enough N's, F and t ratios can almost always be statistically significant. While often sobering in their effect, especially when they are low, coefficients of association of independent and dependent variables are indispensable parts of research results.

BROADENING THE STRUCTURE: PLANNED COMPARISONS AND POST HOC TESTS

The approach used in this chapter and the next two chapters, while pedagogically useful, is too rigid. That is, the emphasis is on neat paradigms that have as their culmination the F test and some measure of relation. Actual research, however, frequently does not fit into such nice shapes and thinking. Nevertheless, the basic analysis of variance notions can be used in a broader and freer way, with an expansion of the design and statistical possibilities. We examine such possibilities within the general framework of this chapter.

Post Hoc Tests

Suppose an experiment like Hurlock's has been done and the experimenter has the data of Table 13.8. He knows that the overall differences among the means are statistically significant. But he does not know which differences contribute to the significance. Can he simply test the differences between all pairs of means to tell which are significant? Yes and No, but generally No. Such tests are not independent and, with sufficient numbers of tests, one of them can be significant by chance. In short, such a "shotgun" procedure capitalizes on chance. Moreover, they are blind and what has been called "no-headed."

There are several ways to do post hoc tests, but we mention only one of them briefly.[13] The Scheffé test, if used with discretion, is a general method that can be applied to all comparisons of means after an analysis of variance.[14] If and only if the F test is significant, one can test all the differences between means; one can test the combined mean of two or more groups against the mean of one other group; or one can select any combination of means against any other combination. Such a test with the ability to do so much is very useful. But we pay for the generality and usefulness: the test is quite conservative. To attain significance, differences have to be rather substantial. The main point is that post hoc comparisons and tests of means can be done, mainly for exploratory and interpretative purposes. One examines one's data in detail; one rummages for insights and clues.

Since it would take us too far afield, the mechanics of the Scheffé test are not given

---

[13] For an excellent description of such tests, see T. Ryan, "Multiple Comparisons in Psychological Research," *Psychological Bulletin*, 56 (1959), 26–47. See, also, T. Ryan, "Significance Tests for Multiple Comparisons of Proportions, Variances, and Other Statistics," *Psychological Bulletin*, 57 (1960), 318–328. Perhaps the best reference is R. Kirk, *Experimental Design: Procedures for the Behavioral Sciences*. Belmont, Calif.: Brooks/Cole, 1968, chap. 3.

[14] H. Scheffé, "A Method for Judging All Contrasts in the Analysis of Variance," *Biometrika*, (1953), 87–104. See, also, Hays, *op, cit.*, p. 433ff. Hays' discussion of the problems of this section is particularly good.

here. (But see Study Suggestion 6 at the end of the chapter.) Suffice it to say that, when applied to the Hurlock data of Table 13.8, it shows that the Praised mean is significantly greater than the other three means and that none of the other differences is significant. This is important information, because it points directly to the main source of the significance of the overall F ratio: praise versus reproof, ignoring, and control. (However, the difference between an average of means 1 and 2 versus an average of means 3 and 4 is also statistically significant.) Although one can see this from the relative sizes of the means, the Scheffé test makes things precise—in a conservative way.

Planned Comparisons

While post hoc tests are important in actual research, especially for exploring one's data and for getting leads for future research, the method of planned comparisons is perhaps more important scientifically. Whenever hypotheses are formulated and systematically tested and empirical results support them, this is much more powerful evidence on the empirical validity of the hypotheses than when "interesting" (sometimes translate: "support my predilections") results are found *after* the data are obtained. This point was made in Chapter 2 where the power of hypotheses was explained.

In the analysis of variance, an overall F test, if significant, simply indicates that there are significant differences somewhere in the data. Inspection of the means can tell one, though imprecisely, which differences are important. To test hypotheses, however, more or less controlled and precise statistical tests are needed. There is a large variety of possible comparisons in any set of data that one can test. But which ones? As usual, the research problem and the theory behind the problem should dictate the statistical tests. One designs research in part to test substantive hypotheses.

Suppose the reinforcement theory behind the Hurlock study said, in effect, that any kind of attention, positive or negative, will improve performance, and that positive reinforcement will improve it more than punishment. This would mean that E_1 and E_2 of Table 13.8, taken together or separately, will be significantly greater than E_3 and C taken together or separately. That is, both Praised (positive reinforcement) and Reproved (punishment) will be significantly greater than Ignored (no reinforcement) and Control (no reinforcement). In addition, the theory says that the effect of positive reinforcement is greater than the effect of punishment. Thus Praised will be significantly greater than Reproved. These implied tests can be written symbolically:

$$H_1: C_1 = \frac{M_1 + M_2}{2} > \frac{M_3 + M_4}{2}$$

$$H_2: C_2 = M_1 > M_2$$

where C_1 indicates the first comparison and C_2 the second. We have here the ingredients of one-way analysis of variance, but the simple overall test and its democracy of means have been radically changed. That is, the plan and design of the research have changed under the impact of the theory and the research problem.

When the Scheffé test is used, the overall F ratio must be significant because none of the Scheffé tests can be significant if the overall F is not significant. When planned comparisons are used, however, no overall F test need be made. The focus is on the planned comparisons and the hypotheses. The number of comparisons and tests made are limited by the degrees of freedom. In the Hurlock example, there are three degrees of freedom $(k - 1)$; therefore, three tests can be made. These tests have to be *orthogonal* to each other—that is, they must be independent. We keep the comparisons orthogonal by using what are called *orthogonal coefficients,* which are weights to be attached to the means in the comparisons. The coefficients, in other words, specify the comparisons. The coefficients or weights for H_1 and H_2, above, are:

$$H_1: \quad 1/2 \quad\quad 1/2 \quad -1/2 \quad -1/2$$
$$H_2: \quad 1 \quad\quad -1 \quad\quad 0 \quad\quad 0$$

For comparisons to be orthogonal, two conditions must be met: the sum of each set of weights must equal 0, and the sum of the products of any two sets of weights must also be zero. It is obvious that both of the above sets sum to zero. Test the sum of the products: $(1/2)(1) + (1/2)(-1) + (-1/2)(0) + (-1/2)(0) = 0$. Thus the two sets of weights are orthogonal.

It is important to understand orthogonal weights, as well as the two conditions just given. The first set of weights simply stands for: $(M_1 + M_2)/2 - (M_3 + M_4)/2$. The second set stands for: $M_1 - M_2$. Now, suppose we also wanted to test the notion that the Ignored mean is greater than the Control mean. This is tested by: $M_3 - M_4$, and is coded: $H_3: 0\ 0\ 1\ -1$. Henceforth, we will call these *weight vectors.* The values of the vector sum to zero. What about its sum of products with the other two vectors?

$$H_1 \times H_3: \quad (1/2)(0) + (1/2)(0) + (-1/2)(1) + (-1/2)(-1) = 0$$
$$H_2 \times H_3: \quad (1)(0) + (-1)(0) + (0)(1) + (0)(-1) = 0$$

The third vector is orthogonal to, or independent of, the other two vectors. The third comparison can be made. If these three comparisons are made, no other is possible because the available $k - 1 = 4 - 1 = 3$ degrees of freedom are used up.

Suppose, now, that instead of the H_3 above, we wanted to test the difference between the average of the first three means against the fourth mean. The coding is: $1/3\ 1/3\ 1/3 - 1$. This is tantamount to: $(M_1 + M_2 + M_3)/3 - M_4$. Is the vector orthogonal to the first two? Calculate:

$$(1/2)(1/3) + (1/2)(1/3) + (-1/2)(1/3) + (-1/2)(-1) = 1/6 + 1/6 - 1/6 + 1/2 = 4/6$$
$$= 2/3$$

Since the sum of the products does not equal zero, it is not orthogonal to the first vector, and the comparison should not be made. The comparison implied by the vector would yield redundant information. In this case, the comparison using the third vector supplies information already given in part by the first vector.

The method of calculating the significance of the differences of planned comparisons need not be detailed. Besides, at this point we do not need the actual calculations. Our purpose, we hope, is a larger one: to show the flexibility and power of analysis of variance when properly conceived and understood. F tests (or t tests) are used with each comparison, or, in this case, with each degree of freedom. The details of calculations can be found in Hays' and other texts.[15] The basic idea of planned comparisons is quite general, and we use it again when we study research design.

We have come a long, perhaps hard, way on the analysis of variance road. One may wonder why so much space has been devoted to the subject. There are several reasons. One, the analysis of variance has wide practical applicability. It takes many forms that are applicable in psychology, sociology, economics, political science, agriculture, biology, education, and other fields. It frees us from working with only one independent variable at

---

[15] Hays, *op. cit.,* chap. 12. In the Hurlock example, H_1 and H_2, above, were both statistically significant at the .01 level, but H_3 was not significant.

a time and gives us a powerful lever for solving measurement problems. It increases the possibilities of making experiments exact and precise. It also permits us to test several hypotheses at one time, as well as to test hypotheses that cannot be tested in any other way, at least with precision. Thus its generality of application is great.

More germane to the purposes of this book, the analysis of variance gives us insight into modern research approaches and methods. It does this by focusing sharply and constantly on variance thinking, by making clear the close relation between research problems and statistical methods and inference, and by clarifying the structure, the architecture, of research design. It is also an important step in understanding contemporary multivariate conceptions of research because it is an expression of the general linear model.

The model of this chapter is simple and can be written:

$$y = a_o + A + e$$

where y is the dependent variable score of an individual, a_o is a term common to all individuals, for example, the general mean of y. A is the effect of the independent variable treatment, and e is error. The model of the next chapter will be a little more complex, and, before the book is finished, models will become much more complex. As we will see, the general linear model is flexible and generally applicable to many research problems and situations. Perhaps of more immediate weight to us, it can help us better understand the common threads and themes of different multivariate approaches and methods.

Study Suggestions

1. There are many good references on analysis of variance, varying in difficulty and clarity of explanation. Hays' discussion (*op. cit.*, pp. 325–348), which includes the general linear model, is as usual excellent, but not easy. It is highly recommended for careful study. The following two books are very good indeed. Both are staples of statistical diet.

> EDWARDS, A. *Experimental Design in Psychological Research*, 4th ed. New York: Holt, Rinehart and Winston, 1972.
> KIRK, R. *Experimental Designs: Procedures for the Behavioral Sciences*. Belmont, Calif.: Brooks/Cole, 1968.

Some students may like to read an interesting history of analysis of variance, especially in psychology, followed by a history of the .05 level of statistical significance.

> RUCCI, A., and TWENEY, R. "Analysis of Variance and the 'Second Discipline' of Scientific Psychology: A Historical Account." *Psychological Bulletin*, 87 (1980), 166–184.
> COWLES, M., and DAVIS, C. "On the Origins of the .05 Level of Statistical Significance." *Psychological Bulletin*, 89 (1982), 553–558.

2. A university professor has conducted an experiment to test the relative efficacies of three methods of instruction: A_1, Lecture; A_2, Large-Group Discussion; and A_3, Small-Group Discussion. From a universe of sophomores, 30 were selected at random and randomly assigned to three groups. The three methods were randomly assigned to the three groups. The students were tested for their achievement at the end of four months of the experiment. The scores for the three groups are given below.

Test the null hypothesis, using one-way analysis of variance and the .01 level of significance. Calculate η^2 and ω^2. Interpret the results. Draw a graph of the data similar to those in the text.

A_1 (Lecture)	Methods A_2 (Large-Group Discussion)	A_3 (Small-Group Discussion)
4	5	3
7	6	5
9	3	1
6	8	4
9	3	4
6	2	5
5	5	7
7	6	3
7	7	5
10	5	3

[*Answers:* $F = 7.16$ (.01); $\eta^2 = .35$; $\omega^2 = .29$][16]

3. From a table of random numbers—you can use those in Appendix C—draw three samples of 10 each of numbers 0 through 9.

(a) Make up a research study, with problem and hypotheses, and imagine that the three sets of numbers are your results.

(b) Do an analysis of variance of the three sets of numbers. Calculate η, η^2, and ω^2. Draw a graph of the results like those of Figure 13.1. Interpret the results both statistically and substantively.

(c) Add a constant of 2 to each of the scores of the group with the highest mean. Do the calculations and graph of (b), above, again. Interpret. What changes take place in the statistics? [Examine the sums of squares especially, taking careful note of the within-groups variances (mean squares) of both examples.].

4. Take the scores of the highest and lowest groups in Study Suggestion 2, above (Groups A_1 and A_3).

(a) Do an analysis of variance, and calculate the square root of F, $\sqrt{F}$. Now do a t test as described in Chapter 12. Compare the t obtained with $\sqrt{F}$.

(b) Is it legitimate, after doing the analysis of variance of the three groups, to calculate the t ratio as instructed and then to draw conclusions about the difference between the two methods? (Consult your instructor, if necessary. This point is difficult.)

[*Answers:* (a) $F = 14.46$; $\sqrt{F} = 3.80$, $t = 3.80$; (c) $\eta^2 = .45$; $\omega^2 = .40$.

5. Aronson and Mills tested the interesting and perhaps humanly perverse hypothesis that individuals who undergo an unpleasant initiation to become members of a group have more liking for the group than do members who do not undergo such an initiation.[17] Three groups of 21 young women each were subjected to three experimental conditions: (1) *severe condition,* in which the S's were asked to read obscene words and vivid descriptions of sexual activity in order to become members of a group; (2) *mild condition,* in which S's read words related to sex but not obscene; and (3) *control condition,* in which S's were not required to do anything to become members of the group. After a rather elaborate procedure, the S's were asked to rate the discussion and the members

---

[16] From now on, errors of rounding will occur. The student should carry one or two more decimal places than needed. If the answers obtained do not agree exactly with those given—say a discrepancy between the second decimal places, e.g., $F = 7.16$ and 7.12, or 7.21—do not be concerned. As calculations become more complex, errors of rounding play a more and more important part. For a discussion of rounding, see P. Dwyer, *Linear Computations*. New York: Wiley, 1951, pp. 13–14.

[17] E. Aronson and J. Mills, "The Effect of Severity of Initiation on Liking for a Group," *Journal of Abnormal and Social Psychology,* 59 (1959), 177–181.

of the group to which they then ostensibly belonged. The means and standard deviations of the total ratings are *severe: M* = 195.3, *SD* = 31.9; *mild: M* = 171.1, *SD* = 34.0; *control: M* = 166.7, *SD* = 21.6. Each *n* was 21.

(a) Do an analysis of variance of these data. Use the method outlined in the addendum to this chapter. Interpret the data. Is the hypothesis supported?
(b) Calculate ω^2. Is the relation strong? Would you expect the relation to be strong in an experiment of this kind?

[*Answers:* (a) F = 5.39 (.01); (b) ω^2 = .12.]

6. Use the Scheffé test to calculate the significance of all the differences between the three means of Study Suggestion 2, above. Here is one way to do the Scheffé test. Calculate the standard error of the differences between two means with the following formula:

$$SE_{M_i - M_j} = \sqrt{ms_w \left(\frac{1}{n_i} + \frac{1}{n_j} \right)} \tag{13.6}$$

where ms_w = within-groups mean square, and n_i and n_j are the numbers of cases in groups i and j. For the example, this is:

$$SE_{M_{A1} - M_{A2}} = \sqrt{(3.26) \left(\frac{1}{10} + \frac{1}{10} \right)} = .81$$

Then calculate the statistic S (for Scheffé):

$$S = \sqrt{(k - 1) \, F_{.05(k-1,m)}} \tag{13.7}$$

where k = number of groups in the analysis of variance, and the F term is the .05 level F ratio obtained from an F table at $k - 1$ $(3 - 1 = 2)$ and $m = N - k = 30 - 3 = 27$ degrees of freedom. This is 3.35. Thus,

$$S = \sqrt{(3 - 1)(3.35)} = \sqrt{6.70} = 2.59$$

The final step is to multiply the results of Formulas 13.6 and 13.7:

$$S \times SE_{M_i - M_j} = (2.59)(.81) = 2.10$$

Any difference, to be statistically significant at the .05 level, must be as large or larger than 2.10. Now use the statistic in the example.

7. Studies that have used one-way analysis of variance are relatively infrequent. Here are five of them. Select two for study. Pay particular attention to post hoc tests of the significance of the differences between means.

ALLEN, D. "Some Effects of Advance Organizers and Level of Questions on the Learning and Retention of Written Social Studies Materials." *Journal of Educational Psychology,* 56 (1970), 333–339.

GOLIGHTLY, C., and BYRNE, D. "Attitude Statements as Positive and Negative Reinforcements." *Science,* 146 (1964), 798–799.

JONES, S., and COOK, S. "The Influence of Attitude on Judgments of the Effectiveness of Alternative Social Policies." *Journal of Personality and Social Psychology,* 32 (1975), 767–773.

SILVERSTEIN, B. "Cigarette Smoking, Nicotine Addiction, and Relaxation." *Journal of Personality and Social Psychology,* 42 (1982), 946–950.

WITTROCK, M. "Replacement and Nonreplacement Strategies in Children's Problem Solving." *Journal of Educational Psychology,* 58 (1967), 69–74.

ADDENDUM

Analysis of Variance Calculations with Means, Standard Deviations, and n's

It is sometimes useful to be able to do analysis of variance from means, standard deviations, and n's of groups rather than from raw scores. One method of doing so is as follows. The data of Table 13.7 are used to illustrate the method:

(1) From the n's and M's calculate the sums of the groups, ΣX_j. Add these to obtain ΣX_t. Calculate total N from the n's of the groups.

$$\Sigma X_t = \Sigma[\overline{X}_j n_j] = (5)(6.) + (5)(3.) = 45.; N = 5 + 5 = 10.$$

(2) Correction term: $(\Sigma X_t)^2/N = 45^2/10 = 202.50.$ (C)

(3) Calculate the within-groups sum of squares: the average of the sums of squares within the groups:

$$(1.5811^2)(4) + (1.5811^2)(4) = 19.9990 = 20. = ss_w.$$

(4) Calculate between sums of squares:

$$ss_b = \Sigma[n_j \overline{X}^2_j] - C$$
$$ss_b = [(6^2)(5) + (3^2)(5)] - C = 225.00 - 202.50 = 22.50.$$

(5) Set up analysis of variance table (as in Table 13.7), and calculate mean squares and F ratio.

Special Note: The method assumes that the original standard deviations were calculated with $n - 1$. If they were calculated with n, alter step 3, above: $(1.4142^2)(5) + (1.4142^2)(5) = 20.$ I.e., change 4 to 5, or $n - 1$ to n.

Chapter 14

Factorial Analysis of Variance

WE NOW study the statistical and design approach that epitomizes the true beginning of the modern behavioral science research outlook. The idea of factorial design and factorial analysis of variance is one of the creative research ideas of the last fifty or more years. And its influence on contemporary behavioral research, especially in psychology and education, has been great. It is no exaggeration to say that factorial designs are the most used of all experimental designs and that factorial analysis of variance is used more in experimental psychological research than any other form of analysis. These are strong statements and require explanation. We devote this chapter to such explanation, together with description and explanation of the mechanics of factorial analysis of variance. Because of its importance and complexity, it will be necessary to labor aspects of the subject more than usual. This chapter, in other words, will be heavier than most. Readers should thus have patience, persistence, and forbearance. Believe that it is in a good cause. We begin with two instructive research examples.

TWO RESEARCH EXAMPLES

Prejudice is a deep and subtle phenomenon. Once born it penetrates large parts of our thinking. It is an obvious truism that negative prejudice against minorities is a widespread and potent phenomenon. Is prejudice so pervasive and subtle that it can work "the other way"? Do people who believe themselves free of prejudice discriminate positively toward minorities? Is there such a thing, in other words, as "inverse prejudice"? Is some of the hiring of blacks and women by business firms and universities prompted by inverse prejudice—or is it simply good business? Such questions can of course be easily asked. They are not so easily answered—at least scientifically.

In an insightful and somewhat upsetting study, Dutton and Lake hypothesized that if people are threatened by the thought that they themselves might be prejudiced, they would act in a reverse discriminatory manner toward minority group members.[1] They would discriminate, but favorably, in other words.

From a pool of 500 college students, 40 male and 40 female students, who had evaluated themselves as relatively unprejudiced in questionnaires administered before the experiment, were assigned to two experimental conditions, *threat* and *race*, partitioned into high threat and low threat and black panhandler and white panhandler. The design, then, was the simplest factorial design possible: a so-called two-by-two, or 2 × 2. It is given in Table 14.1, together with the means of the dependent variable, which was money (cents) given to a panhandler. Notice that this 2 × 2 table looks like the 2 × 2 crossbreaks discussed in Chapter 10. It is essentially different, however, and the student should clearly learn the difference: Crossbreaks have frequencies or percentages in the table cells, whereas factorial designs have measures of the dependent variable in the cells, usually means. The dependent variable is always one of the variables on the margins *of the crossbreak;* in factorial designs, the dependent variable is always the measure in the cells.

Dutton and Lake reasoned that reverse discrimination was likely to occur if subjects who saw themselves as unprejudiced were led to suspect that they might actually be prejudiced. This suspicion would be a threat to self, and a subject experiencing this threat would, under appropriate conditions, act in a reverse discriminatory manner. The high threat subjects were told that they had shown high emotional arousal—as presumably measured by galvanic skin response and pulse rate—to slides depicting interracial scenes. The low threat subjects were given no such feedback to the slides. This experimental condition is given at the top of the design in Table 14.1.

The second experimental variable, *race,* was manipulated as follows. After the completion of the threat variable manipulation, the subjects were paid in quarters and then dismissed. On their way out of the laboratory, however, they were asked by a confederate, who was black for half the subjects and white for the other half: "Can you spare some change for some food?" This second experimental variable, *race,* is given on the side margin of Table 14.1, black panhandler and white panhandler. It was predicted that the high threat subjects would give more money to the black panhandler than to the white

Table 14.1 Factorial Design, 2 × 2, of Dutton and Lake Reverse Discrimination Experiment[a]

Race	Threat		
	High Threat	Low Threat	
Black Panhandler	47.25	16.75	32.00
White Panhandler	28.25	27.75	28.00
	37.75	22.25	

[a]Numbers in the cells are means, in cents, given to panhandlers. The original design included sex, but we omit this variable here.

[1]D. Dutton and R. Lake, "Threat of Own Prejudice and Reverse Discrimination," *Journal of Personality and Social Psychology,* 28 (1973), 94–100.

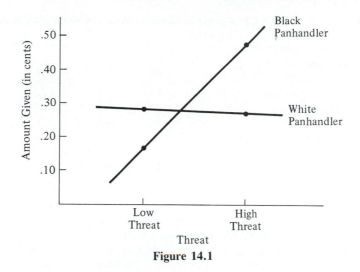

Figure 14.1

panhandler, since it was assumed that the high threat subjects would react against the idea that they were prejudiced, as suggested by the polygraph of the experimental condition, by giving more money to the black panhandler. Low threat subjects, since they had not been made to doubt their lack of prejudice, would not give money to the same extent. In other words, there would be a between-threat difference of money given to the black panhandler but no between-threat difference of money given to the white panhandler. The predicted outcome is known as an *interaction,* a term we will explain later at considerable length.

The data of Table 14.1, taken from the more extensive data reported by Dutton and Lake, seem to support the hypothesis. The means of high threat versus low threat under the black panhandler condition were 47.25 and 16.75 (cents), whereas the threat means under the white panhandler condition were 28.25 and 27.75. Statistical analysis indicated that the hypothesized outcomes were indeed as the authors indicated they would be. We try to bring out and emphasize the nature of the obtained data by the plot of the means given in Figure 14.1. The plotted points—indicated by the small circles—are the means of Table 14.1. The horizontal axis is *threat*. Since there are only two "values," their placement on the line is almost arbitrary. The vertical axis is for the amounts of money given the panhandler.

The relation is apparent: the black panhandler is given more money under the high-threat condition than under the low-threat condition, whereas there is virtually no difference in the two threat conditions with the white panhandler. Evidently the "interaction" hypothesis is supported. Reverse discrimination was practiced, and we can perhaps say that inverse prejudice "exists."

In a provocative experimental study of the effects of two important teaching variables, vagueness and discontinuity, Smith and Cotten found that both impeded mathematics achievement.[2] They assigned 100 seventh-grade mathematics students to four groups at random. The variables associated with the groups were defined by the presence and absence of vagueness and discontinuity. This is more readily understood by considering Table 14.2. One variable is *vagueness,* which is partitioned into *absent* and *present*. The other variable, on the side of the design, was *discontinuity,* partitioned similarly into

[2]L. Smith and M. Cotten, "Effect of Lesson Vagueness and Discontinuity on Student Achievement and Attitudes," *Journal of Educational Psychology,* 72 (1980), 670–675.

Table 14.2 Design and Results (Means) of Smith and Cotten Study: 2 × 2 Factorial[a]

Discontinuity	Vagueness		
	Absent	Present	
Absent	8.68	3.32	6.00
Present	4.36	2.80	3.58
	6.52	3.06	

[a]Marginal means were added to the table: they were calculated from the cell means.

absent and *present*. These were experimental conditions. Each group listened to an audiotaped geometry lesson. The lessons were characterized by whether or not they were vague, discontinuous, both, or neither. Vagueness was defined by the presence of expressions like "somehow," "I'm sorry," "actually," "and so forth," "in fact," and "a few." Discontinuity was defined by the injection of irrelevant material or by relevant material introduced at inappropriate times. The dependent variable, *mathematics achievement,* was defined by a 20-item test.

The means of the four experimental groups on the mathematics test are those of Table 14.2. In the table, for instance, 8.68 was the mean score of those students whose lesson had neither vagueness nor discontinuity, while 2.80 was the mean score of those students whose lesson had both vagueness and discontinuity. We will discuss the interpretation of these data later.

THE NATURE OF FACTORIAL ANALYSIS OF VARIANCE

In factorial analysis of variance two or more independent variables vary independently or interact with each other to produce variation in a dependent variable. *Factorial analysis of variance is the statistical method that analyzes the independent and interactive effects of two or more independent variables on a dependent variable.*

If there are two independent variables, as in the examples just discussed, the linear model is an extension of the linear model of the last chapter:

$$y = a_o + A + B + AB + e \tag{14.1}$$

where *y,* as usual, is a score of an individual on the dependent variable, a_o is the term common to all individuals, the general mean, *A* is the effect of one independent variable, *B* the effect of another independent variable, *AB* is the effect of both variables working together, or interacting, and *e* is error. In addition to the one effect, *A,* and error, *e,* in one-way analysis of variance, we now have a second effect, *B,* and a third "effect," the joint working or influence on *y* of *A* and *B,* or *AB.* There is no theoretical limit to the number of independent variables in factorial designs. Here is the model for three independent variables:

$$y = a_o + A + B + C + AB + AC + BC + ABC + e \tag{14.2}$$

Here there are three independent variables, *A, B,* and *C,* and the interactions between them, *AB, AC,* and *BC,* and the simultaneous interaction of all three, *ABC.* As complex as this model seems, there are many uses of it in the literature. We will give one or two examples later. And we can add more independent variables. The only limitations are practical ones: how to handle so many variables at one time and how to interpret interactions, especially triple and quadruple ones. What we are after, however, are the basic ideas behind factorial designs and models.

One of the most significant and revolutionary developments in modern research design and statistics is the planning and analysis of the simultaneous operation and interaction of two or more variables. Scientists have long known that variables do not act independently. Rather, they often act in concert. The virtue of one method of teaching contrasted with another method of teaching depends on the teachers using the methods. The educational effect of a certain kind of teacher depends, to a large extent, on the kind of pupil being taught. An anxious teacher may be quite effective with anxious pupils but less effective with nonanxious pupils. Different methods of teaching in colleges and universities may depend on the intelligence and personality of both professors and students. In the Dutton and Lake study, the effect of threat depended on the race of the panhandler (see Table 14.1 and Figure 14.1). In the Smith and Cotten study, the interaction was different. The joint effect of the independent variables, vagueness and discontinuity, was cumulative: when both were present, the effect was strongest (see Table 14.2).

Before the invention of analysis of variance and the designs suggested by the method, the traditional conduct of experimental research was to study the effect of one independent variable on one dependent variable. I am not implying, by the way, that this approach is wrong. It is simply limited. Nevertheless, many research questions can be adequately answered using this "one-to-one" approach. Many other research questions can be adequately answered only by considering multiple and interacting influences. Educational scientists knew that the study of the effects of different pedagogical methods and techniques on educational outcomes was in part a function of other variables, such as the intelligence of the students, the personality of the teachers, the social background of both the teacher and the students, and the general atmosphere of the class and the school. But many researchers believed that the most effective research method was to vary one independent variable while controlling, as best one could, other independent variables that might contribute to the variance of the dependent variable.

In the studies summarized above, the conclusions go beyond the simple differences between effects or groups. It was possible to qualify the conclusions in important ways because the authors studied the simultaneous working of the two independent variables. They were consequently able to talk about the *differential effect* of their variables. They could say, for example, that treatment A_1 is effective when coupled with level B_1, but not effective when alone or when coupled with level B_2, and that, perhaps, A_2 is effective only when coupled with B_1.

The implied logic behind this sort of research thinking can be understood better by returning to the conditional statements and thinking of an earlier chapter. Recall that a conditional statement takes the form If p, then q, or If p, then q, under conditions r and s. In logical notation: $p \rightarrow q$ and $p \rightarrow q | r,s$. Schematically, the conditional statement behind the one-way analysis of variable problems of Chapter 13 is the simple statement If p, then q. In the Hurlock study, if certain incentives, then certain achievement. In the Aronson and Mills study (see Study Suggestion 5, Chapter 13), if severity of initiation, then liking for the group.

The conditional statements associated with the research problems of this chapter, however, are more complex and subtle: If p, then q, under conditions r and s, or $p \rightarrow q | r,s$, where "|" means "under condition(s)." In the Dutton and Lake study, this would be $p \rightarrow q | r$, or If threat, then reverse discrimination, under the condition that the target (the panhandler) is black. While structurally similar, the "cumulative" logic of Smith and Cotten is different: If p and r, then q, or If vagueness *and* discontinuity, then lower achievement, or in logical symbols: $(p \cap r) \rightarrow q$ (read: If p *and* r, then q). Here we cannot say "under the condition" because p and q, vagueness and discontinuity, are equal partners and combine to affect achievement.

THE MEANING OF INTERACTION

Interaction is the working together of two or more independent variables in their influence on a dependent variable. More precisely, interaction means that the operation or influence of one independent variable on a dependent variable depends on the level of another independent variable. This is a rather clumsy way of saying what we said earlier in talking about conditional statements, for example, If p, then q, under condition r.[3] In other words, interaction occurs when an independent variable has different effects on a dependent variable at different levels of another independent variable.

The above definition of interaction encompasses two independent variables. This is called a first-order interaction. It is possible for three independent variables to interact in their influence on a dependent variable. This is a second-order interaction. Still higher order interactions are theoretically possible but unlikely and difficult to interpret. We therefore drop them from consideration and turn to calculation matters. Before doing so, however, the reader should be aware that interaction can occur in the absence of any separate effects of the independent variables. (Interaction can also be absent when one or more independent variables have significant separate effects.) Separate independent variable effects are called *main effects*. We will now show this possibility with a fictitious example and then later with an example from published research.

A SIMPLE FICTITIOUS EXAMPLE

As usual we take a simple, if unrealistic, example that highlights the basic problems and characteristics of factorial analysis of variance. Assume that an educational investigator is interested in the relative efficacy of two methods of teaching, A_1 and A_2. Call this variable methods. He believes that methods of teaching, in and of themselves, do not differ very much. They differ only when used with certain kinds of students, by certain kinds of teachers, in certain kinds of educational situations, and with certain kinds of motives. Studying all of these variables at one time is too large an order for him, though not necessarily impossible. So he decides to study methods and motivations, which gives him two independent variables and one dependent variable. Call the dependent variable achievement. (Some type of achievement measure will be used, perhaps scores on a standardized test.)

The investigator conducts an experiment with eight sixth-grade children. (Obviously in a real experiment he would work with many more than eight children.) He randomly assigns the eight children to four groups, two per group. He also randomly assigns methods A_1 and A_2 and motivations B_1 and B_2 to the four groups. Refer back to the earlier discussion on partitions of sets. Recall that we can partition and cross-partition sets of objects. The objects can be assigned to a partition or subpartition on the basis of the possession of certain characteristics. But they can also be assigned at random—and then

---

[3] Note that conditional statements are used a great deal in so-called Bayesian thinking and statistics, in which prior knowledge plays an important part in the analytic drama. Bayesians talk a great deal of "givens." For example, "The probability of C given A and B." This is much like an interaction statement. See the section, "Conditional Probability," in Chapter 7, *supra*.

$$\begin{array}{ccc}
 & \text{Methods} & \\
 & A_1 & A_2 \\
B_1 & A_1B_1 & A_2B_1 \\
B_2 & A_1B_2 & A_2B_2
\end{array}$$

Motivations

Figure 14.2

presumably be "given" certain characteristics by the experimenter. In either case the partitioning logic is the same. The experimenter will end up with four subpartitions: A_1B_1, A_1B_2, A_2B_1, and A_2B_2. The experimental paradigm is shown in Figure 14.2.

Each cell in the design is the intersection of two subsets. For instance, method A_1 combined with motivation B_2 is conceptually $A_1 \cap B_2$. Method A_2 combined with motivation B_2 is the intersection $A_2 \cap B_2$. In this design, we write only A_1B_2 and A_2B_2 for simplicity. Now two children have been assigned at random to each of the four cells. This means that each child will get a combination of two experimental manipulations, and each pair of children will get a different combination.

Call A_1 "recitation," and A_2 "no recitation." Call B_1 "praise," and B_2 "blame." The children in cell A_1B_1, then, will be taught with recitation and will be praised for their work. The children in cell A_1B_2 will be taught with recitation but will be "blamed" for their work. And similarly for the other two cells. If the experimental procedures have been adequately handled, it is possible to conceive of the variables as being independent, that is, two separate experiments are actually being run with the same subjects. One experiment manipulates methods; the other, types of motivations. The design of the experiment, in other words, makes it possible for the investigator to test *independently* the effects on a dependent variable, in this case, achievement, of (1) methods and (2) types of motivation. To show this and other important facets of factorial designs, let us jump to the fictitious data of the experiment. These "data" are reported in Table 14.3, together with the necessary computations for a factorial analysis of variance.

Table 14.3 Data of Hypothetical Factorial Experiment with Analysis of Variance Calculations

Types of Motivation	Methods		
	A_1	A_2	
B_1	8	4	
	6	2	
ΣX	14	6	$\Sigma X_{B_1} = 20$
$(\Sigma X)^2$	196	36	$(\Sigma X_{B_1})^2 = 400$
M	⑦	③	$M_{B_1} = $ ⑤
B_2	8	4	
	6	2	
ΣX	14	6	$\Sigma X_{B_2} = 20$
$(\Sigma X)^2$	196	36	$(\Sigma X_{B_2})^2 = 400$
M	⑦	③	$M_{B_2} = $ ⑤
ΣX_A	28	12	$\Sigma X_t = 40$
$(\Sigma X_A)^2$	784	144	$(\Sigma X_t)^2 = 1600$
M_A	⑦	③	$M_t = $ ⑤
			$\Sigma X_t^2 = 240$

First, we calculate the sums of squares that we would for a simple one-way analysis of variance. There is of course a *total sum of squares,* calculated from all the scores, using C, the correction term:

$$C = \frac{(40)^2}{8} = \frac{1600}{8} = 200$$

$$\text{Total} = 240 - 200 = 40$$

Since there are four groups, there is a sum of squares associated with the means of the four groups. Simply conceive of the four groups placed side by side as in one-way analysis of variance, and calculate the sum of squares as in the last chapter. Now, however, we call this the *"between all groups"* sum of squares to distinguish it from sums of squares to be calculated later.

$$\text{Between all groups} = \left(\frac{196}{2} + \frac{36}{2} + \frac{196}{2} + \frac{36}{2} \right) - 200 = 32$$

This sum of squares is a measure of the variability of all four group means. Therefore, if we subtract this quantity from the total sum of squares, we should obtain the sum of squares due to error, the random fluctuations of the scores within the cells (groups). This is familiar: it is the *within-groups sum of squares:*

$$\text{Within groups} = 40 - 32 = 8$$

To calculate the *sum of squares for methods,* proceed exactly as with one-way analysis of variance: treat the scores (X's) and sums of scores (ΣX's) of the columns (methods) as though there were no B_1 and B_2:

	A_1	A_2
	8	4
	6	2
	8	4
	6	2
ΣX:	28	12

The calculation is:

$$\text{Between methods} \atop (A_1, A_2) = \left(\frac{(28)^2}{4} + \frac{(12)^2}{4} \right) - 200 = \left(\frac{784}{4} + \frac{144}{4} \right) - 200 = 32$$

Similarly, treat types of motivation (B_1 and B_2) as though there were no methods:

	B_1	B_2
	8	8
	6	6
	4	4
	2	2
ΣX:	20	20

The calculation of the between-types sum of squares is really not necessary. Since the sums (and the means) are the same, the between-types sum of squares is zero:

$$\text{Between types} \atop (B_1, B_2) = \left(\frac{(20)^2}{4} + \frac{(20)^2}{4} \right) - 200 = 0$$

There is another possible source of variance, the variance due to the *interaction* of the two independent variables. The between-all-groups sum of squares comprises the variability due to the means of the four groups: 7, 3, 7, 3. This sum of squares was 32. If this were not a contrived example, part of this sum of squares would be due to methods, part to types of motivation, and a remaining part left over, *which is due to the joint action, or interaction,* of methods and types. In many cases it would be relatively small, no greater than chance expectation. In other cases, it would be large enough to be statistically significant; it would exceed chance expectation. In the present problem it is clearly zero since the between-methods sum of squares was 32, and this is equal to the between-all-groups sum of squares. To complete the computational cycle we calculate:[4]

$$\text{Interaction: methods} \times \text{types} = \text{between all groups} - (\text{between} \\ \text{methods} + \text{between types}) = 32 - (32 + 0) = 0$$

We are now in a position to set up the final analysis of variance table. We postpone this, however, until we perform a minor operation on these scores.

We use exactly the same scores, but rearrange them slightly: we reverse the scores A_1B_2 and A_2B_2. Since all the individual scores (X's) are exactly the same, the total sum of squares must also be exactly the same. Further, the sums and sums of squares of B_1 and B_2 (types) must also be exactly the same. Table 14.4 shows just what was done and its effect on the means of the four groups.

Study the numbers of Tables 14.3 and 14.4 and note the differences. To emphasize the differences, the means have been circled in both tables. To make the differences still clearer, the means of both tables have been laid out in Table 14.5. The little table on the left shows two variabilities: between all four means and between A_1 and A_2 means. In the little table on the right, there is only one variability, that between the four means. In both tables, the variability of the four means is the same since they both have the same four means: 7, 3, 7, 3. Obviously, there is no variability of the B means in both tables. There

Table 14.4 Data of Hypothetical Factorial Experiment of Table 14.3 with B_2 Figures Rearranged

Types of Motivation	Methods		
	A_1	A_2	
B_1	8	4	
	6	2	
ΣX	14	6	$\Sigma X_{B_1} = 20$
M	⑦	③	$M_{B_1} = ⑤$
B_2	4	8	
	2	6	
ΣX	6	14	$\Sigma X_{B_2} = 20$
M	③	⑦	$M_{B_2} = ⑤$
ΣX	20	20	$\Sigma X_t = 40$
M	⑤	⑤	$M_t = ⑤$
			$\Sigma X_t^2 = 240$

[4] In a more complex factorial analysis of variance it is not possible to calculate the interactions so easily. Since the purpose of these chapters is not basically computational, we do not take up the calculation of more complex forms of analysis of variance. See A. Edwards, *Experimental Design in Psychological Research,* 4th ed. New York: Holt, Rinehart and Winston, 1972, chaps. 9 and 10.

Table 14.5 Means of the Data of Tables 14.3 and 14.4

	Table 14.3 Means					Table 14.4 Means		
	A_1	A_2				A_1	A_2	
B_1	7	3	5		B_1	7	3	5
B_2	7	3	5		B_2	3	7	5
	7	3				5	5	

are two differences between the tables, then: the A means and the arrangement of the four means inside the squares. If we analyze the sum of squares of the four means, the between-all-groups sums of squares, we find that B_1 and B_2 contribute nothing to it in both tables, since there is no variability with 5, 5, the means of B_1 and B_2. In the table on the right, the A_1 and A_2 means of 5 and 5 contribute no variability. In the table on the left, however, the A_1-A_2 means differ considerably, 7 and 3, and thus they contribute variance.

Assuming for the moment that the means of 7 and 3 differ significantly, we can say that methods of the data of Table 14.3 had an effect irrespective of types of motivation. That is, $M_{A_1} \neq M_{A_2}$, or $M_{A_1} > M_{A_2}$. As far as this experiment is concerned, methods differ significantly *no matter what the type of motivation*. And, obviously, types of motivation had no effect, since $M_{B_1} = M_{B_2}$. In Table 14.4, on the other hand, the situation is quite different. Neither methods nor types of motivation had an effect *by themselves*. Yet there *is* variance. The problem is: What is the source of the variance? It is in the *interaction of the two variables*, the interaction of methods and types of motivation.

If we had performed an experiment and obtained data like those of Table 14.4, then we could come to the likely conclusion that there was an interaction between the two variables in their effect on the dependent variable. In this case, we would interpret the results as follows. Methods A_1 and A_2, operating in and of themselves, do not differ in their effect. Types of motivation B_1 and B_2, in and of themselves, do not differ in their effect. When methods and types of motivation are allowed to "work together," when they are permitted to interact, they are significantly effective. Specifically, method A_1 is superior to method A_2 when combined with type of motivation B_1. When combined with type of motivation B_2, it is inferior to A_2. This interaction effect is indicated on the right-hand side of Table 14.5 by the crisscrossed arrows. Qualitatively interpreting the original methods, we find that "recitation" seems to be superior to "no recitation" under the condition of "praise," but that it is inferior to "no recitation" under the condition of "blame" (reproof).

It is instructive to note, before going further, that interaction can be studied and calculated by a subtractive procedure. In a 2×2 design, this procedure is simple. Subtract one mean from another in each row, and then calculate the variance of these differences. Take the fictitious means of Table 14.5. If we subtract the Table 14.3 means, we get $7 - 3 = 4$; $7 - 3 = 4$. Clearly the mean square is zero. Thus, the interaction is zero. Follow the same procedure for the Table 14.4 means (right-hand side of the table): $7 - 3 = 4$; $3 - 7 = -4$. If we now treat these two differences as we did means in the last chapter and calculate the sum of squares and the mean square, we will arrive at the interaction sum of squares and the mean square, 32 in each case. The reasoning behind this procedure is simple. If there were no interaction, we would expect the differences between row means to be approximately equal to each other and to the difference between the means at the bottom of the table, the methods means, in this case. Note that this is so for the Table 14.3 means: the bottom-row difference is 4, and so are the differences of each of the rows. The row differences of Table 14.4, however, deviate from the difference

Table 14.6   Final Analysis of Variance Tables: Data of Tables 14.3 and 14.4

Source	df	\[Data of Table 14.3\] ss	ms	F	\[Data of Table 14.4\] ss	ms	F
Between Methods							
(A_1, A_2)	1	32	32	16(.05)	0	0	. . . .
Between Types							
(B_1, B_2)	1	0	0	. . . .	0	0	. . . .
Interaction:							
$A \times B$	1	0	0	. . . .	32	32	16(.05)
Within Groups	4	8	2		8	2	
Total	7	40			40		

between the bottom-row (methods) means. They are 4 and -4, whereas the bottom-row difference is $5 - 5 = 0$.

From this discussion and a little reflection, it can be seen that a significant interaction can be caused by one deviant row. For example, the means of the above example might be:

$$
\begin{array}{ccc}
7 & 3 & 5 \\
5 & 5 & 5 \\
\hline
6 & 4 &
\end{array}
$$

Subtract the rows. $7 - 3 = 4$; $5 - 5 = 0$; and $6 - 4 = 2$. There is obviously some variance in these remainders.

It will be profitable to write the final analysis of variance tables in which the different variances and F ratios are calculated. Table 14.6 gives the final analysis of variance tables for both examples.[5] The sum of squares and mean square and the resulting F ratio of 16 on the left-hand side of the table indicate what we already know from the preceding discussion: Methods are significantly different (at the .05 level), and types of motivation and interaction are not significant. The parallel figures of the right-hand side of the table indicate that only the interaction is significant.

INTERACTION: AN EXAMPLE

In the last chapter, it was said that if sampling was random the means of the k groups would be approximately equal. If, for example, there were four groups and the general mean, M_t, was 4.5, then it would be expected that each of the means would be approximately 4.5. Similarly, in factorial analysis of variance, if random samples of numbers are drawn for each of the cells, then the means of the cells should be approximately equal. If the general mean, M_t, were 10, then the best expectation for any cell means in the factorial design would be 10. These means, of course, would very rarely be exactly 10. Indeed,

---

[5] The between-all-groups sums of squares have not been included in the table. They are only useful for calculating the within-groups sums of squares. The degrees of freedom for the main effects (methods and types) and for between all groups and within groups are calculated in the same way as in one-way analysis of variance. This should become apparent upon studying the table. The interaction degrees of freedom is the product of the degrees of freedom of the main effects, that is, $1 \times 1 = 1$. If methods had had four groups and types three groups, the interaction degrees of freedom would have been $3 \times 2 = 6$.

some of them might be considerably far from 10. The fundamental statistical question is: Do they differ significantly from 10? The means of combinations of means, too, should hover around 10. For example, in a design like that of the previous example the A_1 and A_2 means should be approximately 10, and the B_1 and B_2 means should be approximately 10. In addition, the means of each of the cells, A_1B_1, A_1B_2, A_2B_1, and A_2B_2, should hover around 10.

Using a table of random numbers, I drew 60 digits, 0 through 9, to fill the six cells of a factorial design. The resulting design has two levels or independent variables, A and B. A is subdivided into A_1, A_2, and A_3, B into B_1 and B_2. This is called a 3×2 factorial design. (The examples of Tables 14.3 and 14.4 are 2×2 designs.)

Conceive of A as types of appeal. In a social psychological experiment designed to test hypotheses of the best ways to appeal to prejudiced people to change their attitudes, the question is asked: What kinds of appeal work best to change prejudiced attitudes?[6] Assume that three types of appeal, "Religious," "Fair-Play," "Democratic," have been tried with unclear results. The investigator suspects that the situation is more complex, that types of appeal interact with the manner in which appeals are made. So she sets up a 3×2 factorial design, in which the second variable, B, is divided into B_1 and B_2, impassioned and calm manner of appeal. That is, the religious appeal is given in an impassioned manner to some subjects and in a calm manner to others, and similarly for the other two types of appeal. We will not explore this research problem further, but simply use it to color the abstract and perhaps skeleton quality of our discussion. Imagine the experiment to have been done with the results given in Table 14.7, which gives the design paradigm and the means of each cell, as well as the means of the two variables, A and B, and the general mean, M_t. These means were calculated from the 60 random numbers drawn in lots of 10 each and inserted in the cells.

We hardly need a test of statistical significance to know that these means do not differ significantly. Their total range is 3.9 to 5.6. The mean expectation, of course, is the mean of the numbers 0 through 9, 4.5. The closeness of the means to $M_t = 4.45$ or to 4.5 is remarkable, even for random sampling. At any rate, if these were the results of an actual experiment, the experimenter would probably be most chagrined. Types of appeal, manner of appeal, and the interaction between them are all not significant.

Notice how many different outcome possibilities other than chance there would be if one or both variables had been effective. The three means of types of appeal, M_{A_1}, M_{A_2}, and M_{A_3}, might have been significantly different, with the means of manner, M_{B_1} and M_{B_2},

Table 14.7 Two-way Factorial Design: Means of Groups of Random Numbers 0 through 9

Manner of Appeal	A_1 Religious	A_2 Fair-Play	A_3 Democratic	Manner Means
	Type of Appeal			
B_1 Impassioned	4.1	5.0	3.9	4.33
B_2 Calm	5.6	3.9	4.2	4.57
Type means	4.85	4.45	4.05	$M_t = 4.45$

[6]The idea for this fictitious experiment was taken from an actual experiment: A. Citron, I. Chein, and J. Harding, "Anti-Minority Remarks: A Problem for Action Research," *Journal of Abnormal and Social Psychology,* 45 (1950), 99–126.

Table 14.8 Means of Table 14.7 Altered Systematically by Adding and Subtracting Constants

Manner of Appeal	Type of Appeal			Manner Means
	A_1	A_2	A_3	
B_1	(4.1 + 2) 6.1	5.0	(3.9 − 1) 2.9	4.67
B_2	(5.6 − 2) 3.6	3.9	(4.2 + 1) 5.2	4.23
Type Means	4.85	4.45	4.05	4.45

not significantly different. Or the manner means might be significantly different, with the types means not significantly different; or both sets of means could be different; or both could turn out not to be different, with their interaction significant. The possibilities of *kinds* of differences and interactions are considerable, too, although it would take too many words and numbers to illustrate even a small number of them. If the student will juggle the numbers a bit, he can get considerable insight into both statistics and design possibilities. Since our present preoccupation is with interaction, let us alter the means to create a significant interaction. We increase the A_1B_1 mean by 2, decrease the A_1B_2 mean by 2, increase the A_3B_2 mean by 1, and decrease the A_3B_1 mean by 1. We let the A_2 means stand as they are, and alter the main effect means accordingly. The changes are shown in Table 14.8.

The table should be studied carefully. Compare it to Table 14.7. Interaction has been produced by the arbitrary alterations. The cell means have been unbalanced, so to speak, while the marginal means (A_1, A_2, A_3, B_1, B_2) are almost undisturbed. The total mean remains unchanged at 4.45. The three A means are the same. (Why?) The two B means are changed very little. A factorial analysis of variance of the appropriately altered random numbers—which, of course, are no longer random—yields the final analysis of variance table given in Table 14.9.

Neither of the main effects (appeal and manner) is significant. That is, the means of A_1, A_2, and A_3 do not differ significantly from chance. Neither do the means of B_1 and B_2. The only significant F ratio is that of interaction, which is significant at the .05 level.[7]

Table 14.9 Final Analysis of Variance Table of Altered Random-Number Data

Source	df	ss	ms	F
Between All Groups	5	70.15		
Within Groups	54	476.70	8.83	
Between Appeals (A_1, A_2, A_3)	2	6.40	3.20	< 1.0 (n.s.)
Between Manners (B_1, B_2)	1	2.82	2.82	< 1.0 (n.s.)
Interaction: $A \times B$	2	60.93	30.47	3.45 (.05)
Total	59	546.85		

[7] The random numbers that generated Table 14.7 were also subjected to an analysis of variance. The F ratios were not significant.

Evidently the alteration of the scores has had an effect. If we were interpreting the results, as given in Tables 14.8 and 14.9, we would say that, in and of themselves, neither type of appeal to the bigot nor the manner of appeal differs. But a religious appeal delivered in an impassioned manner and a democratic appeal in a calm manner seem to be most effective. Perhaps a bit more clearly, the democratic appeal in an impassioned manner is relatively ineffectual, as is the religious appeal in a calm manner. (It is not possible to say much about the fair-play appeal.)

KINDS OF INTERACTION

To now, we have said nothing about kinds of interaction of independent variables in their joint influence on a dependent variable. To leap to the core of the matter of interactions, let us lay out several sets of means to show the main possibilities. There are, of course, many possibilities, especially when one includes higher-order interactions. The six examples in Table 14.10 indicate the main possibilities with two independent variables. The first three setups show the three possibilities of significant main effects. They are so obvious that they need not be discussed. (There is, naturally, another possibility: neither A nor B is significant.)

When there is a significant interaction, on the other hand, the situation is not so obvious. The setups (d), (e), and (f) show three common possibilities. In (d), the means crisscross, as indicated by the arrows in the table. It can be said that A is effective in one direction at B_1, but is effective in the other direction at B_2. Or, $A_1 > A_2$ at B_1, but $A_1 < A_2$ at B_2. This sort of interaction with this crisscross pattern is called disordinal interaction (see below). In this chapter, the fictitious example of Table 14.4 was a disordinal interaction. (See also Table 14.5.) The fictitious example of Table 14.8, where interaction was deliberately induced by adding and subtracting constants, is another disordinal interaction.

The setups in (e) and (f), however, are different. Here one independent variable is effective at one level only of the other independent variable. In (e), $A_1 > A_2$ at B_1, but $A_1 = A_2$ at B_2. In (f), $A_1 = A_2$ at B_1, but $A_1 > A_2$ at B_2. The interpretation changes accordingly. In the case of (e), we would say that A is effective at B_1 level, but makes no difference at B_2 level. The case of (f) would take a similar interpretation. Such interactions are called *ordinal* interactions.

Table 14.10 Various Sets of Means Showing Different Kinds of Main Effects and Interaction

	A_1	A_2			A_1	A_2			A_1	A_2	
B_1	30	20	25		30	30	30		30	20	25
B_2	30	20	25		20	20	20		40	30	35
	30	20			25	25			35	25	

(a) A significant; B not significant; Interaction not significant

(b) A not significant; B significant; Interaction not significant

(c) A significant; B significant; Interaction not significant

	A_1	A_2			A_1	A_2			A_1	A_2	
B_1	30	20	25		30	20	25		20	20	20
B_2	20	30	25		20	20	20		30	20	25
	25	25			25	20			25	20	

(d) Interaction significant (disordinal)

(e) Interaction significant (ordinal)

(f) Interaction significant (ordinal)

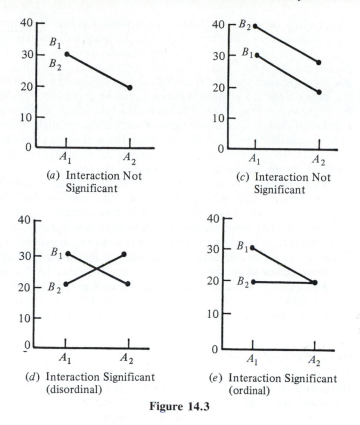

Figure 14.3

A simple way to study the interaction with a 2×2 setup (it is more complex with more complex models) is to subtract one entry from another in each row, as we did earlier. If this be done for (a), we get, for rows B_1 and B_2, 10 and 10. For (b), we get 0 and 0, and for (c), 10 and 10 again. When these two differences are equal, as in these cases, there is no interaction. But now try it with (d), (e), and (f). We get 10 and −10 for (d), 10 and 0 for (e), and 0 and 10 for (f). When these differences are significantly unequal, interaction is present. The student can interpret these differences as an exercise.

It is also possible—and often very profitable—to graph interactions, as we did in Figure 14.1. Set up one independent variable by placing the experimental groups (A_1, A_2, and so on) at equal intervals on the horizontal axis and appropriate values of the dependent variable on the vertical axis. Then plot, against the horizontal axis group positions (A_1, A_2, and so on), the mean values in the table at the levels of the other independent variable (B_1, B_2, and so on). This method can quite easily be used with 2×3, 3×3, and other such designs. The plots of (a), (c), (d), and (e) are given in Figure 14.3.

We can discuss these graphs briefly since both graphs and graphing relations have been discussed before.[8] In effect, we ask first if there is a relation between the main effects (independent variables) and the measures of the dependent variables. Each of these relations is plotted as in the preceding chapter, except that the relation between one independent variable and the dependent variable is plotted at both levels of the other

[8]Extended discussions of interactions can be found in: Edwards, *op. cit.*, chaps. 9–10. A valuable and clear discussion of ordinal and disordinal interactions and the virtue of graphing significant interactions is given in: A. Lubin, "The Interpretation of Significant Interaction," *Educational and Psychological Measurement,* 21 (1961), 807–817.

independent variables; for instance, A is plotted against the dependent variable (vertical axis) at B_1 and B_2. The slope of the lines roughly indicates the extent of the relation. In each case, we have chosen to plot the relations using A_1 and A_2 on the horizontal axis. If the plotted line is horizontal, obviously there is no relation. There is no relation between A and the dependent variable at level B_2 in (e) of Figure 14.3, but there is a relation at level B_1. In (a), there is a relation between A and the dependent variable at both levels, B_1 and B_2. The same is true of (c). The nearer the line comes to being diagonal, the higher the relation. If the two lines make approximately the same angle in the same direction (that is, they are parallel), as in (a) and (c), the relation is approximately the same magnitude at each level. To the extent that the lines make different angles with horizontal axis (are not parallel), to this extent there is interaction present.

If the graphs of Figure 14.3 were plotted from actual research data, we could interpret them as follows. Call the measures of the dependent variable (on the vertical axis) Y. In (a), A is related to Y *regardless of B*. It makes no difference what B is; A_1 and A_2 differ significantly. The interpretation of (c) is similar: A is related to Y at both levels of B. There is no interaction in either (a) or (c). In (d) and (e), however, the case is different. The graph of (d) shows interaction. A is related to Y, but the kind of relation depends on B. Under the B_1 condition, A_1 is greater than A_2. But under the B_2 condition A_2 is greater than A_1. The graph of (e) says that A is related to Y at level B_1 but not at level B_2, or A_1 is greater than A_2 at B_1 but at B_2 they are equal. (Note that it is possible to plot B on the horizontal axis. The interpretations would differ accordingly.)

NOTES OF CAUTION

Interaction is not always a result of the "true" interaction of experimental treatments. There are, rather, three possible causes of a significant interaction. One is "true" interaction, the variance contributed by the interaction that "really" exists between two variables in their mutual effect on a third variable. Another is error. A significant interaction *can* happen by chance, just as the means of experimental groups can differ significantly by chance. A third possible cause of interaction is some extraneous, unwanted, uncontrolled effect operating at one level of an experiment but not at another. Such a cause of interaction is particularly to be watched for in nonexperimental uses of the analysis of variance, that is, in the analysis of variance of data gathered after independent variables have already operated. Suppose, for example, that the levels in an experiment on methods was schools. Extraneous factors in such a case can cause a significant interaction. Assume that the principal of one school, although he had consented to having the experiment run in his school, was negative in his attitude toward the research. This attitude could easily be conveyed to teachers and pupils, thus contaminating the experimental treatment, methods. In short, significant interactions must be handled with the same care as any other research results. They are interesting, even dramatic, as we have seen. Thus they can perhaps cause us momentarily to lose our customary caution.[9]

[9] A precept that researchers should take seriously is: Whenever possible, *replicate research studies*. Replication should be routinely planned. It is especially necessary when complex relations are found. If an interaction is found in an original study and in a replication, it is probably not due to chance, though it could still be due to other causes. The term "replication" is used rather than "repetition" because in a replication, although the original relation is studied again, it might be studied with different kinds of subjects, under somewhat different conditions, and even with fewer, more, or even different variables. The trend in the psychological research literature, happily, is to do two or more related studies on the same basic problem. This trend is closely related to testing alternative hypotheses, whose virtue and necessity were discussed in an earlier chapter. For an excellent example of replication and multiple studies on the same general problem, see the Jones et al. example cited in Study Suggestion 1, below.

Table 14.11   Example of Disproportion and Unequal Cell n's Arising from Nonexperimental Variables[a]

	Republican	Democrat	
Male	30	20	50
Female	20	30	50
	50	50	

[a]The cell entries are frequencies.

Two related difficulties of factorial analysis are unequal n's in the cells of a design and the experimental and nonexperimental use of the method. If the n's in the cells of a factorial design are not equal (and are disproportionate, i.e., not in proportion from row to row or column to column), the orthogonality or independence of the independent variables is impaired. While adjustments can be made, they are a bit awkward and not too satisfactory. When doing experiments, the problem is not severe because subjects can be assigned to the cells at random—except, of course, for attribute variables—and the n's kept equal or nearly equal. But in the nonexperimental use of factorial analysis, the n's in the cells get pretty much beyond the control of the researcher. Indeed, even in experiments, when more than one categorical variable is included (like race and sex), n's almost necessarily become unequal.

To understand this, take a simple example. Suppose we split a group in two by sex and have, say, 50 males and 50 females. A second variable is political preferences and we want to come up with two equal groups of Republicans and Democrats. But suppose that sex is correlated with political preference. Then there may be, for example, more males who are Republican compared to females who are Republican, creating a disproportion. This is shown in Table 14.11. Now add another independent variable and the difficulties increase greatly.

What can we do, then, in nonexperimental research? Can't we use factorial analysis of variance? The answer is complex and is evidently not clearly understood. Factorial analysis of variance paradigms can and should be used because they guide and clarify research. There are devices for surmounting the unequal n difficulty. One can make adjustments of the data, or one can equalize the groups by elimination of subjects at random. These are unwieldy devices, however. The best analytic solution seems to be to use multiple regression analysis. While the problems do not all disappear, many of them cease to be problems in the multiple regression framework. In general, factorial analysis of variance is best suited to experimental research in which the subjects can be randomly assigned to cells, the n's thus kept equal and the assumptions behind the method more or less satisfied. Nonexperimental research or experimental research that uses a number of nonexperimental (attribute) variables is better served with multiple regression analysis. With equal n's and experimental variables, multiple regression analysis *yields exactly the same sums of squares, mean squares, and F ratios, including interaction F ratios as the standard factorial analysis*. Nonexperimental variables, which are a grave problem for factorial analysis, are routine in multiple regression analysis. We return to all this in a later chapter.

INTERACTION AND INTERPRETATION

We end this section on interaction with a complex and difficult problem: the interpretation of factorial analysis of variance results when interactions are significant. Suppose we have two variables, A and B. Both F ratios are statistically significant and the interaction F ratio is not significant. This is straightforward: there is no problem of interpretation. If, on the other hand, A, or B, or both are significant *and* the interaction of A and B is also significant, there *is* a problem. Some writers say that the interpretation of significant main effects in the presence of interaction is not possible and, if done, can lead to incorrect conclusions.[10] The reason is that when one says that a main effect is significant, one may imply that it is significant under all conditions, that M_{A_1} is greater than M_{A_2} with all kinds of individuals and in all kinds of places, for instance. If the interaction between A and B, however, is significant, the conclusion is empirically not valid. One has at least to qualify it: there is at least one condition, namely B, that has to be taken into account. One must say, instead of the simple If p, then q statement, If p, then q, under condition r, or, for example, M_{A_1} is greater than M_{A_2} under condition B_1 but not under condition B_2. A method of reinforcement, say praise, is effective with middle-class children but not with working-class children.

A general rule is that when an interaction is significant, it may not be appropriate to try to interpret main effects because the main effects are not constant but vary according to the variables that interact with them. This is especially so if the interaction is disordinal [see Figure 14.3 (d)], or if the main effect under study is weak. If a main effect is strong—the differences between means are large—and interaction is ordinal [see Figure 14.3 (e)], then one can perhaps interpret a main effect. Obviously the interpretation of research data when more than one independent variable is studied is often complex and difficult. This is no reason to be discouraged, however. Such complexity only reflects the multivariate and complex nature of psychological, sociological, and educational reality. The task of science is to understand this complexity. Such understanding can never be complete, of course, but substantial progress can be made with the help of modern methods of design and analysis. Factorial designs and analysis of variance are large achievements that substantially enhance our ability to understand complex psychological, sociological, and educational reality.

FACTORIAL ANALYSIS OF VARIANCE WITH THREE OR MORE VARIABLES

Factorial analysis of variance works with more than two independent variables. Three, four, and more variables are possible and do appear in the literature. Designs with more than four variables, however, are uncommon and perhaps not too fruitful. It is not so much because the statistics become complex and unwieldy. Rather, it is a matter of practicality. It is very difficult just to get enough subjects to fill the cells of complex designs. And it is even more difficult to manipulate four, five, or six independent variables at one time. For instance, take an experiment with four independent variables. The smallest arrangement possible is $2 \times 2 \times 2 \times 2$, which yields 16 cells into each of which some minimum number of subjects must be put. If 10 S's are placed in each cell, it will be necessary to handle the total of 160 S's in four different ways. Yet one should not be dogmatic about the number of variables. Perhaps in the next ten years factorial designs with more than four variables will become common. Indeed, when we later study multiple regression analysis we will find that factorial analysis of variance can be done with multiple regression analysis and that four and five factors are easily accommodated *ana-*

[10] For discussions of interpretation when interactions are significant, see: E. Pedhazur, *Multiple Regression in Behavioral Research*, 2d ed. New York: Holt, Rinehart and Winston, 1982, chap. 10. Pedhazur's discussion is particularly cogent when he attacks the difficulty of interpreting interactions in nonexperimental research.

Appeals

		A_1 (Religious)		A_2 (Democratic)	
Mode		C_1 Personalized	C_2 Objectified	C_1 Personalized	C_2 Objectified
Manner	B_1 (Impassioned)	$A_1B_1C_1$	$A_1B_1C_2$	$A_2B_1C_1$	$A_2B_1C_2$
	B_2 (Calm)	$A_1B_2C_1$	$A_1B_2C_2$	$A_2B_2C_1$	$A_2B_2C_2$

Figure 14.4

lytically. That is, the complexities of analysis of variance calculations with four or five independent variables are considerably simplified. Such analytic facilitation of calculations, however, in no way changes the *experimental* difficulties of managing several manipulated independent variables.

The simplest form of a three-variable factorial analysis of variance is a $2 \times 2 \times 2$ design. Consider the example of Table 14.7. Suppose the investigator decided to use, in a new experiment, a third independent variable. She drops the fair-play appeal and keeps the religious and democratic appeals. She has noticed that there seems to be a greater effect on the prejudiced person if she personalizes the appeal. So she adds another variable, C, which she calls personalization. This variable she defines as the degree of appeal to the person as an individual rather than as a member of any group. In the design this variable has two *modes* which she calls "personalized" and "objectified," C_1 and C_2. The design now looks like that in Fig. 14.4.

The researcher can now test seven hypotheses: the differences between A_1 and A_2 (appeal), between B_1 and B_2 (manner), and between C_1 and C_2 (mode). These are the *main effects.* Four interactions can also be tested: $A \times B$, $A \times C$, $B \times C$, and $A \times B \times C$. A final analysis of variance table would look like Table 14.12. It is evident that a great deal of information can be obtained from this one experiment. Contrast it with the one variable experiment in which only *one* hypothesis can be tested. The difference is not only great—it indicates a fundamentally different way of conceptualizing research problems.

Table 14.12 Final Analysis of Variance Table for the $2 \times 2 \times 2$ Design of Fig. 14.4

Source	*df*	*ss*	*ms*	*F*
Between Appeals				
(A_1, A_2)	1			
Between Manners				
(B_1, B_2)	1			
Between Modes				
(C_1, C_2)	1			
Interaction: $A \times B$	1			
Interaction: $A \times C$	1			
Interaction: $B \times C$	1			
Interaction: $A \times B \times C$	1			
Within Groups	$N - 7$			
Total	$N - 1$			

Significant first-order interactions are reported more and more in published research studies. Some years ago they were considered to be rare phenomena. This is quite evidently not so.[11] Indeed, it is now apparent that interactions of variables are hypothesized on the basis of theory.[12] Part of the essence of scientific theory, of course, is specifying the conditions under which a phenomenon can and will occur. For example, years ago Berkowitz was interested in the phenomenon of displacement of aggression.[13] When one is frustrated, one may have an aggressive reaction, says frustration-aggression theory. But it is dangerous or forbidden to express aggression directly against the sources of frustration. So aggressive urges may be displaced. In Berkowitz's study, it was displaced against Jews: he found a most interesting interaction between hostility arousal and anti-Semitism. Anti-Semitic subjects were more likely to respond to frustration with displaced aggression than less prejudiced subjects. Significant higher-order interactions, while not common, *do* occur. The trouble is: They are often hard to interpret. First- and second-order interactions can be handled, but third- and higher-order interactions make research life uncomfortable because one is at a loss as to what they mean.[14]

By now the reader no doubt realizes that in principle the breakdowns of the independent variables are not restricted to just two or three subpartitions. It is quite possible to have 2×4, 2×5, 4×6, $2 \times 3 \times 3$, $2 \times 5 \times 4$, $4 \times 4 \times 3 \times 5$, ... Laughlin et al., in their study of concept attainment, used a $2 \times 2 \times 2 \times 8 \times 3$ design.[15] As always, the problem under investigation and the judgment of the researcher are the criteria that determine what a design and its concomitant analysis shall be.

ADVANTAGES AND VIRTUES OF FACTORIAL DESIGN AND ANALYSIS OF VARIANCE

Factorial analysis of variance, as we have seen, accomplishes several things, all of which are important advantages of the approach and method. One, it enables the researcher to manipulate and control two or more variables simultaneously. In educational research, not only is it possible to study the effects of teaching methods on achievement; we can also

[11] See D. Berliner and L. Cahen, "Trait-Treatment Interaction and Learning," in F. Kerlinger, ed., *Review of Research in Education,* Vol. 1. Itasca, Ill.: Peacock, 1973, chap. 3; G. Bracht, "Experimental Factors Related to Aptitude-Treatment Interactions," *Review of Educational Research,* 40 (1970), 627–645; L. Cronbach and R. Snow, *Aptitudes and Instructional Methods: A Handbook for Research on Interaction.* New York: Irvington, 1977. Most of the methodological and substantive preoccupation with interaction in the literature is in education. It even has a name: ATI (Aptitude-Treatment Interaction) research. Evidently it has flourished because much or most educational research is preoccupied with improving instruction, and interactions of pupils' aptitudes and instructional methods are believed to be an important key to doing so.

[12] For example, F. Bishop, "The Anal Character: A Rebel in the Dissonance Family," *Journal of Personality and Social Psychology,* 6 (1967), 23–36; E. Jones, "Conformity as a Tactic of Ingratiation," *Science,* 149 (1965), 144–150; C. Ames, R. Ames, and D. Felder, "Effects of Competitive Reward Structure and Valence of Outcome on Children's Achievement Attributions," *Journal of Educational Psychology,* 69 (1977), 1–8; J. Cooper and C. Scalise, "Dissonance Produced by Deviations from Life Styles: The Interaction of Jungian Typology and Conformity," *Journal of Personality and Social Psychology,* 29 (1974), 566–571.

[13] L. Berkowitz, "Anti-Semitism and the Displacement of Aggression," *Journal of Abnormal and Social Psychology,* 59 (1959), 182–187.

[14] Here are two interesting cases of reported triple interactions: I. Katz, T. Henchy, and H. Allen, "Effects of Race of Tester, Approval-Disapproval, and Need on Negro Children's Learning," *Journal of Personality and Social Psychology,* 8 (1968), 38–42 (black boys performed better on a verbal learning task when examiners were black and when given approval); J. Rapier, "Learning Abilities of Normal and Retarded Children as a Function of Social Class," *Journal of Educational Psychology,* 59 (1968), 102–110 (the experimental treatments worked differently with subjects of higher and lower socioeconomic status and higher and lower intelligence).

[15] P. Laughlin et al., "Concept Attainment by Individuals versus Cooperative Pairs as a Function of Memory, Sex, and Concept Rule," *Journal of Personality and Social Psychology,* 8 (1968), 410–417.

study the effects of both methods *and,* say, kinds of reinforcement. In psychological research, we can study the separate and combined effects of many kinds of independent variables, such as anxiety, guilt, reinforcement, prototypes, types of persuasion, race, and group atmosphere, on many kinds of dependent variables, such as compliance, conformity, learning, transfer, discrimination, perception, and attitude change. In addition, we can control variables such as sex, social class, and home environment.

A second advantage is that factorial analysis is more precise than one-way analysis. Here we see one of the virtues of combining research design and statistical considerations. It can be said that, other things equal, factorial designs are "better" than one-way designs. This value judgment has been implicit in most of the preceding discussion. The precision argument adds weight to it and will be elaborated shortly.

A third advantage—and, from a large scientific viewpoint, perhaps the most important one—is the study of the interactive effects of independent variables on dependent variables. This has been discussed. But a highly important point must be added. Factorial analysis enables the research *to hypothesize interactions* because the interactive effects can be directly tested. If we go back to conditional statements and their qualification, we see the core of the importance of this statement. In a one-way analysis, we simply say: If p, then q; If such-and-such methods, then so-and-so outcomes. In factorial analysis, however, we utter richer conditional statements. We can say: If p, then q *and* If r, then q, which is tantamount to talking about the main effects in a factorial analysis. In the problem of Table 14.4, for instance, p is methods (A) and r is types of motivation (B). We can also say, however: If p *and* r, then q, which is equivalent to the interaction of methods and types of motivation. Interaction can also be expressed by: If p, then q, under condition r.

On the basis of theory, previous research, or hunch, researchers can hypothesize interactions. One hypothesizes that an independent variable will have a certain effect only in the presence of another independent variable. Berkowitz, in the study of anti-Semitism and displaced aggression cited earlier, asked whether prejudiced persons were more likely to respond to frustration with displaced aggression than less prejudiced persons. As we saw, this is an interaction hypothesis. Part of his results are given in Table 14.13. The means in the table reflect liking for the partner, which Berkowitz thought would be affected by the hostility arousal and anti-Semitism. Neither main effect, hostility nor anti-Semitism, was statistically significant, but the interaction between them *was* significant. When hostility is aroused, evidently, high anti-Semitic subjects responded with more displaced aggression than low anti-Semitic subjects. The interaction hypothesis was supported—a finding of both theoretical and practical significance.[16]

FACTORIAL ANALYSIS OF VARIANCE: CONTROL

In a one-way analysis of variance, there are two *identifiable* sources of variance: that presumed to be due to the experimental effects and that presumably due to error or chance

---

[16] It has become common practice to partition a continuous variable into dichotomies or other polytomies. In the Berkowitz study, for instance, a continuous measure, anti-Semitism, was dichotomized. It was pointed out earlier that creating a categorical variable out of a continuous variable throws variance away and thus should be avoided. We will learn in a later chapter that factorial analysis of variance can be done with multiple regression analysis and that, with such analysis, it is not necessary to sacrifice any variance by conversion of variables. Nevertheless, there are countervailing arguments. One, if a difference is statistically significant and the relation is substantial, the variable conversion does not matter. The danger is in concealing a relation that in fact exists. Two, there are times when conversion of a variable may be wise—for example, for exploration of a new field or problem and when measurement of a variable is at best rough and crude. In other words, while the rule is a good one, it is best not to be inflexible about it. Much good, even excellent, research has been done with continuous variables that have been partitioned for one reason or another.

Table 14.13 Mean Liking-for-Partner Scores as Related to Hostility and Anti-Semitism, Berkowitz Study[a]

	Hostility Arousal	No Hostility Arousal
High Anti-Semitism	18.4	14.2
Low Anti-Semitism	12.2	16.3

[a]The higher the score the less the liking for partner.

variation. We now look at the latter more closely. When subjects have been assigned to the experimental groups at random, the only possible estimate of chance variation is the within-groups variance. But—and this is important—it is clear that the within-groups variance contains not only variance due to error; it also contains variance due to individual differences among the subjects. Two simple examples are intelligence and sex. There are, of course, many others. If both girls and boys are used in an experiment, randomization can be used in order to balance the individual differences that are concomitant to sex. Then the number of girls and boys in each experimental group will be approximately equal. We can also arbitrarily assign girls and boys in equal numbers to the groups. This method, however, does not accomplish the overall purpose of randomization, which is to equalize the groups on *all* possible variables. It *does* equalize the groups as far as the sex variable is concerned, but we can have no assurance that other variables are equally distributed among the groups. Similarly for intelligence. Randomization, if successful, will equalize the groups such that the intelligence test means and standard deviations of the groups will be approximately equal. Here, again, it is possible arbitrarily to assign youngsters to the groups in a way to make the groups approximately equal, but then there is no assurance that other possible variables are similarly controlled, since randomization has been interfered with.

Now, let us assume that randomization has been "successful." Then theoretically there will be no differences between the groups in intelligence and all other variables. *But there will still be individual differences in intelligence—and other variables—within each group.* With two groups, for instance, Group 1 might have intelligence scores ranging from, say, 88 to 145, and Group 2 might have intelligence scores ranging from 90 to 142. This range of scores, in and of itself, shows, just as the presence of boys and girls within the groups shows, that there are individual differences in intelligence *within* the groups. If this be so, then how can we say that the within-groups variance can be an estimate of error, of chance variation?

The answer is that it is the best we can do under the design circumstances. If the design is of the simple one-way kind, there is no other measure of error obtainable. So we calculate the within-groups variance and treat it as though it were a "true" measure of error variance. It should be clear that the within-groups variance will be larger than the "true" error variance, since it contains variance due to individual differences as well as error variance. Therefore, an *F* ratio may not be significant when in fact there is "really" a difference between the groups. Obviously if the *F* ratio is significant, there is not so much to worry about, since the between-groups variance is sufficiently large to overcome the too high estimate of error variance.

To summarize what has been said, let us rewrite an earlier theoretical equation. The earlier equation was

$$V_t = V_b + V_w \qquad (14.3)$$

Since the within-groups variance contains more variance than error variance, the variance due to individual differences, in fact, we can write

$$V_w = V_i + V_e \qquad (14.4)$$

where V_i = variance due to individual differences and V_e = "true" error variance. If this be so, than we can substitute the right-hand side of Equation 14.4 for the V_w in Equation 14.3:

$$V_t = V_b + V_i + V_e \qquad (14.5)$$

In other words, Equation 14.5 is a shorthand way to say what we have been saying above.

The practical research significance of Equation 14.5 is considerable. If we can find a way to control or measure V_i, to separate it from V_w, then it follows that a more accurate measure of the "true" error variance is possible. Put differently, our ignorance of the variable situation is decreased because we identify and isolate more systematic variance. A portion of the variance that was attributed to error is identified. Consequently the within-groups variance is reduced.

Many of the principles and much of the practice of research design is occupied with this problem, which is essentially a problem of control—the control of variance. When it was said earlier that factorial analysis of variance was more precise than simple one-way analysis of variance, we meant that, by setting up levels of an independent variable, say sex or social class, we decrease the estimate of error, the within-groups variance, and thus get closer to the "true" error variance. Instead of writing Equation 14.5, let us now write a more specific equation, substituting for V_i, the variance of individual differences, V_{sc}, the variance for social class—and reintroducing V_w:

$$V_t = V_b + V_{sc} + V_w \qquad (14.6)$$

Compare this equation to Equation 14.3. More of the total variance, other than the between-groups variance, has been identified and labeled. This variance, V_{sc}, has in effect been taken out of the V_w of Equation 14.3.

RESEARCH EXAMPLES

A large number of interesting uses of factorial analysis of variance have been reported in recent years in the behavioral research literature. Indeed, one is confronted with an embarrassment of riches. A number of examples of different kinds have been selected to illustrate further the usefulness and strength of the method. We include more examples than usual because of the complexity of factorial analysis, its frequency of use, and its manifest importance.

Race, Sex, and College Admissions[17]

In an ingenious and elegantly conceived study, Walster, Cleary, and Clifford asked whether colleges in the United States discriminate against women and black applicants. They used a $2 \times 2 \times 3$ factorial design in which race (white, black), sex (male, female), and ability (high, medium, low) were the independent variables and admission (scored on a five-point scale, with 1 = rejection through 5 = acceptance with encouragement) was the dependent variable. They randomly selected 240 colleges from a standard guide and

[17] E. Walster, T. Cleary, and M. Clifford, "The Effect of Race and Sex on College Admissions," *Journal of Educational Sociology*, 44 (1970), 237–244.

Table 14.14 Results of Walster, Cleary, and Clifford Study for Sex, Ability, and Admission (Means)[a]

Sex	Ability			
	High	Medium	Low	
Male	3.75	3.48	3.00	3.41
Female	4.05	3.48	1.93	3.15
	3.90	3.48	2.47	

[a] Marginal means were calculated from cell means. The higher the mean the greater the acceptance.

sent specially prepared letters of application to the colleges from fictitious individuals who possessed, among other things, the race, sex, and ability levels mentioned above. For instance, a candidate might be black, male, with a medium level of ability. Note the clever manipulation of variables not usually amenable to experimental manipulation. Also note that the unit of analysis was institutions.

Factorial analysis of variance showed that none of the three main effects was statistically significant. If this were all the information the researchers had, they could have concluded that there was no discrimination practiced. But one of the interactions, sex by ability, was statistically significant. The means for sex and ability are given in Table 14.14. (The variable ''race'' is omitted because the race main effect and the interactions of race with the other variables were not significant.) An intriguing finding! It seems that women are discriminated against at the lower level of ability but not at the high and medium levels.

Learning During Sleep[18]

A problem that has intrigued psychologists and educators is: Can we learn while sleeping? Beh and Barratt have shown that it is evidently possible. In one of their experiments, they divided their subjects ($N = 20$) equally into experimental and control groups. They used two tones of 500 cy/sec (cycles per second) and 300 cy/sec as experimental tone stimuli. After habituating the subjects to the two tones and testing whether they could be conditioned to the 500 cy/sec tone while awake, they conducted one of their sleep experiments. In this experiment they presented both tones repeatedly to the subjects *while they were asleep*. The 300 cy/sec tone, however, was accompanied on 15 of the presentations by a shock to the right forefinger; the 500 cy/sec tone was sounded without shock. The control group subjects ''heard'' both tones without shock. After the conditioning trials, the subjects received random presentations of both tones until there was no response to either tone.

Part of the data of the experiment is given in Table 14.15. The figures in the table are means of percentages of response to the two tones as recorded by electroencephalogram records. They are average responses to the two tones of the experimental and control group subjects. $F = 68.4$, highly significant, for the interaction of stimuli and type of subject, experimental or control. This F ratio was due mostly to the Experimental–300 cy/sec cell of 48.5, thus indicating that learning of the conditioned response took place during sleep. Moreover, the conditioned stimulus evoked the electroencephalogramic

---

[18] H. Beh and P. Barratt, ''Discrimination and Conditioning During Sleep as Indicated by the Electroencephalogram,'' *Science, 147* (1965), 1470–1471. The summary of this research is highly simplified. All details, however, are not necessary to make the essential points. Recall that in classical conditioning a neutral stimulus takes on the power to evoke a response by being repeatedly paired with a stimulus capable of evoking the response.

Table 14.15 Mean Percentages of Responses to Tone Stimuli During Sleep, Beh and Barratt Study[a]

Tone	Group Experimental	Control
500 cy/sec	14.7	20.6
300 cy/sec	48.5	14.8

[a]The conditioned stimulus was the 300 cy/sec tone. Interaction $F = 68.4$, highly significant.

response during sleep. These rather remarkable results do not mean, of course, that complex verbal learning can take place during sleep. But evidently learning of at least a rudimentary kind can. (Note the nice suitability of factorial analysis of variance for the analytic problem and the applicability of the idea of interaction in this situation.)

Student Essays and Teacher Evaluation[19]

The above examples were limited to two independent variables. We now look briefly at a more complex example with more than two independent variables. The subject of the research has always been of great interest to educators: reading, scoring, and evaluating student essays. In what is probably an important study of the problem, Freedman manipulated the content, organization, mechanics, and sentence structure of essays. She rewrote eight student essays "of moderate quality" to be either stronger or weaker in the four characteristics just mentioned. (This was a difficult task, which Freedman did admirably.) The essays to be judged included both the original essays and the rewritten essays. The essays were then evaluated by twelve readers (another variable in the design). The dependent variable was quality, rated on a four-point scale. We have, then, a $2 \times 2 \times 2 \times 2 \times 12$ design (the 12 was the 12 judges). The factorial analysis of variance is summarized in Table 14.16.

These results are interesting and potentially important. First, the readers (R) did not differ, which is as it should be. Second, content and organization were both highly significant. (The author talks about "the largest main effect," which could have been

Table 14.16 Factorial Analysis of Variance Results of Rewriting Effects, Freedman Study of Evaluation of Essays

Source	df	ms	F[a]
Reader (R)	11	.448	
Content (C)	1	9.860	37.78**
Organization (O)	1	5.195	29.69**
Sentence Structure (SS)	1	1.500	2.54
Mechanics (M)	1	5.042	9.77**
C × SS	1	1.960	6.30
C × M	1	.990	3.18
O × SS	1	3.767	12.11*
O × M	1	6.155	19.79**
SS × M	1	.001	

[a]*: significant at .01 level; **: significant at .001 level.

[19]S. Freedman, "How Characteristics of Student Essays Influence Teachers' Evaluations," *Journal of Educational Psychology,* 71 (1979), 328–338.

better judged by, say ω^2.) Mechanics (M) was also significant; Sentence Structure (SS) was not. But the $0 \times$ SS and the $0 \times$ M significant interactions showed that the strength or weakness of mechanics and sentence structure mattered when essays had strong organization. This study and its essay assessment are certainly on another level of discourse from the more or less intuitive and loose methods that most of us use in judging student writing!

Study Suggestions

1. Here are some varied and interesting psychological or educational studies that have used factorial analysis of variance in one way or another. Read and study two of them and ask yourself: Was factorial analysis the appropriate analysis? That is, might the researchers have used, say, a simpler form of analysis?

> ANDERSON, R., REYNOLDS, R., SCHALLERT, D., and GOETZ, E. "Frameworks for Comprehending Discourse." *American Educational Research Journal,* 14 (1977), 367–381. 2 × 2; based on cognitive psychological theory.
>
> JONES, E., ROCK, L., SHAVER, K., GOETHALS, G., and WARD, L. "Pattern of Performance and Ability Attribution: An Unexpected Primacy Effect." *Journal of Personality and Social Psychology,* 10 (1968), 317–340. Set of excellent studies on an important psychological phenomenon. See, especially, Experiment V.
>
> LANGER, E., and IMBER, L. "When Practice Makes Imperfect: Debilitating Effects of Overlearning." *Journal of Personality and Social Psychology,* 37 (1980), 2014–2024. 3 × 3 and 3 × 2; unusual findings.
>
> SIGALL, H., and LANDY, D. "Radiating Beauty: Effects of Having a Physically Attractive Partner on Person Perception." *Journal of Personality and Social Psychology,* 28 (1973), 218–224. 3 × 2; interesting significant interaction.

2. We are interested in testing the relative efficacies of different methods of teaching foreign languages (or any other subject). We believe that foreign language aptitude is possibly an influential variable. How might an experiment be set up to test the efficacies of the methods? Now add a third variable, sex, and lay out the paradigms of both researches. Discuss the logic of each design from the point of view of statistics. What statistical tests of significance would you use? What part do they play in interpreting the results?

3. Write two problems and the hypotheses to go with them, using any three (or four) variables you wish. Scan the problems and hypotheses in Study Suggestions 2 and 3, Chapter 2, and the variables given in Chapter 3. Or use any of the variables of this chapter. Write at least one hypothesis that is an interaction hypothesis.

4. From the random numbers of Appendix C draw 40 numbers, 0 through 9, in groups of 10. Consider the four groups as A_1B_1, A_2B_1, A_1B_2, A_2B_2.

> (a) Do a factorial analysis of variance as outlined in the chapter. What should the A, B and $A \times B$ (interaction) F ratios be like?
>
> (b) Add 3 to each of the scores in the group with the highest mean. Which F ratio or ratios should be affected? Why? Do the factorial analysis of variance. Are your expectations fulfilled?

5. Some students may wish to expand their reading and study of research design and factorial analysis of variance. Much has been written, and it is hard to recommend books and articles. There are two books, however, that have rich resources and interesting chapters on design itself, statistical problems, assumptions and their testing, and the history of analysis of variance and related methods.

> COLLIER, R., and HUMMEL, T., eds. *Experimental Design and Interpretation.* Berkeley, Calif.: McCutchan, 1977. This book was sponsored by the American Educational Research Association.
>
> KIRK, R., ed. *Statistical Issues: A Reader for the Behavioral Sciences.* Monterey, Calif.: Brooks/Cole, 1972.

Chapter 15

Analysis of Variance: Correlated Groups[1]

SUPPOSE a team of researchers wants to test the effects of marijuana and alcohol on driving.[2] It can, of course, set up a one-way design or a factorial design. Instead, the investigators decide to use subjects as their own controls. That is, each subject is to undergo three experimental treatments or conditions: marijuana (A_1), alcohol (A_2), and control (A_3). After each of these treatments, the subjects will operate a driving simulator. The dependent variable measure is the number of driving errors. A paradigm of the design of the experiment, with a few fictitious scores, is given in Table 15.1. Note that the sums of both columns *and* rows are given in the table. Note, too, that the design looks like that of one-way analysis of variance, with one exception: the sums of the rows, which are the sums of each subject's scores across the three treatments, are included.

This is quite a different situation from the earlier models in which subjects were assigned at random to experimental groups. Here all subjects undergo all treatments. Therefore, each subject is his own control, so to speak. More generally, instead of independence we now have dependence or correlation between groups. What does correlation between groups mean? It is not easy to answer this question with a simple statement.

[1] The term "correlated groups" is used because it seems to express the basic and distinctive nature of the kind of analysis of variance discussed in this chapter. Other terms more commonly used are "randomized blocks" and "repeated measures." Neither of these is completely general, however. See A. Edwards, *Experimental Design in Psychological Research,* 4th ed. New York: Holt, Rinehart and Winston, 1972, chap. 14.

[2] The idea for this example came from an actual research study: A. Crancer et al., "Comparison of the Effects of Marijuana and Alcohol on Simulated Driving Performance," *Science,* 164 (1969), 851–854.

Table 15.1 Design of Marijuana, Alcohol, and Simulator Driving Experiment: Repeated Measures (Fictitious Scores)

Subjects	Marijuana (A_1)	Alcohol (A_2)	Control (A_3)	Sums, Rows
1	18	27	16	61
2	24	29	21	74
.	.	.	.	.
.	.	.	.	.
.	.	.	.	.
36	21	25	20	66
Sums	710	820	680	$\Sigma X_t = 2210$

DEFINITION OF THE PROBLEM

In one-way and factorial analysis of variance, the independence of groups, subjects, and observations is a sine qua non of the designs. In both approaches subjects are assigned to experimental groups at random. There is no question of correlation between groups—by definition. Except for variables specifically put into the design—like adding sex to treatments—variance due to individual differences is randomly distributed among the experimental groups, and the groups are thus "equalized." Variance due to individual differences is known to be substantial. If it can be isolated and extracted from the total variance, then there should be a substantial increase in precision, because this source of variation in the scores can be subtracted from the total variance. Thus a smaller error variance to use to evaluate the effects of the treatments is created.

In one of the examples of factorial analysis of variance of the last chapter, we identified and subtracted variance due to social class from the total variance (see Equations 14.3-14.6 and accompanying discussion), thus reducing the within-groups variance, the error term. The reasoning in this chapter is similar: isolate and extract variance in the dependent variable due to individual differences. To make this abstract discussion concrete, we use an easy example in which the idea of matching is introduced. Using the same subjects in the different experimental groups and matching subjects on one, two, or more variables involves the same basic idea of correlation between groups.[3]

A Fictitious Example

A principal of a school and the members of his staff decided to introduce a program of education in intergroup relations as an addition to the school's curriculum. One of the problems that arose was in the use of motion pictures. Films were shown in the initial phases of the program, but the results were not too encouraging. The staff hypothesized that the failure of the films to have impact might have resulted from their not making any particular effort to bring out the possible applications of the film to intergroup relations. They decided to test the hypothesis that seeing the films and then discussing them would improve the viewers' attitudes toward minority group members more than would just seeing the films.

For a preliminary study the staff randomly selected a group of students from the total

[3] In the example that follows, matching is used to show the applicability of correlated-groups analysis to a common research situation, because certain points about correlation and its effect can be conveniently made. Matching as a research device, however, is *not* in general advocated for reasons that will be discussed in a later chapter.

Table 15.2 Attitude Scores and Calculations for Analysis of Variance—Fictitious Example

Pairs	*Groups* A_1 (Experimental)	A_2 (Control)	Σ
1	8	6	14
2	9	8	17
3	5	3	8
4	4	2	6
5	2	1	3
6	10	7	17
7	3	1	4
8	12	7	19
9	6	6	12
10	11	9	20
ΣX:	70	50	$\Sigma X_t = 120$
M:	7	5	$\Sigma X_t^2 = 930$

student body and paired the students on intelligence until ten pairs were obtained, each pair being approximately equal in intelligence. The reasoning behind the experiment was that intelligence is related to attitudes toward minority groups and needs to be controlled. Each member of each pair was randomly assigned to either an experimental or a control group, and then both groups were shown a film on intergroup relations. The A_1 (experimental) group had a discussion session after the picture was shown; the A_2 (control) group had no such discussion after the film. Both groups were tested with a scale designed to measure attitudes toward minority groups. The attitude scores and the calculations for an analysis of variance procedure to be described are given in Table 15.2.

First we do a one-way analysis of variance as though the investigators had not matched the subjects. We disregard the matching procedure and analyze the scores as though all the subjects had been randomly assigned to the two groups without regard to intelligence. The calculations are:

$$C = \frac{14{,}400}{20} = 720$$

$$\text{Total} = 930 - 720 = \mathit{210}$$

$$\text{Between columns } (A_1, A_2) = \left(\frac{70^2}{10} + \frac{50^2}{10}\right) - 720 = \mathit{20}$$

The final analysis of variance table of this analysis is given in Table 15.3. Since the F ratio of 1.89 is not significant, the two group means of 7 and 5 do not differ significantly. The interpretation of these data would lead the experimenters to believe that the film plus discussion had no effect. This conclusion would be wrong. The difference in this case is

Table 15.3 Final Analysis of Variance Table, One-way Analysis of Fictitious Data of Table 15.2

Source	*df*	*ss*	*ms*	*F*
Between Groups (A_1, A_2)	1	20.00	20.0	1.89 (n.s.)
Within Groups	18	190.00	10.56	
Total	19	210.00		

really significant as the .01 level. Let us assume that this statement is true; if it *is* true, then there must be something wrong with the analysis.

An Explanatory Digression

When subjects are matched on variables *significantly related to the dependent variable,* correlation is introduced into the statistical picture. In Chapter 14 we saw that it was often possible to identify and control more of the total variance of an experimental situation by setting up levels of one or more variables presumably related to the dependent variable. The setting up of two or three levels of social class, for example, makes it possible to identify the variance in the dependent-variable scores due to social class. Now, simply shift gears a bit. The matching of the present experiment has actually set up ten levels, one for each pair. The members of the first pair had intelligence scores of 130 and 132, say, the members of the second pair 124 and 125, and so on to the tenth pair, the members of which had scores of 89 and 92. Each pair (level) has a different mean. Now, if intelligence is substantially and positively correlated with the dependent variable, then the dependent variable pairs of scores should reflect the matching on intelligence. That is, the dependent variable pairs of scores should also be more like each other than they are like other dependent-variable scores. So the matching on intelligence has "introduced" variance between pairs on the dependent variable, or *between-rows variance.*

Consider another hypothetical example to illustrate what happens when there is correlation between sets of scores. Suppose that an investigator has matched three groups of subjects on intelligence, and that intelligence was perfectly correlated with the dependent variable, achievement of some kind. This is highly unlikely, but let's go along with it to get the idea. The first trio of subjects had intelligence scores of 141, 142, and 140; the second trio 130, 126, and 128; and so on through the fifth trio of 82, 85, and 82. If we check the rank orders in columns of the three sets of scores, they are exactly the same: 141, 130, . . . , 82; 142, 126, . . . , 85; 140, 128, . . . , 82. Since we assume that $r = 1.00$ between intelligence and achievement, then the rank orders of the achievement scores must be the same in the three groups. The assumed achievement test scores are given on the left-hand side of Table 15.4. The rank orders of these fictitious scores, from high to low, are given in parentheses beside each achievement score. Note that the rank orders are the same in the three groups.

Now suppose that the correlation between intelligence and achievement was approximately zero. In such a case, no prediction could be made of the rank orders of the achievement scores, or, to put it another way, the achievement scores would not be matched. To simulate such a condition of zero correlation, I broke up the rank orders of

Table 15.4 Correlated and Uncorrelated Scores, Fictitious Example

I. Correlated Groups					II. Uncorrelated Groups				
A_1		A_2	A_3	M	A_1		A_2	A_3	M
73	(1)	74 (1)	72 (1)	73	63	(2)	74 (1)	46 (5)	61.00
63	(2)	65 (2)	61 (2)	63	45	(5)	55 (3)	61 (2)	53.67
57	(3)	55 (3)	59 (3)	57	50	(4)	50 (4)	59 (3)	53.00
50	(4)	50 (4)	53 (4)	51	57	(3)	65 (2)	53 (4)	58.33
45	(5)	44 (5)	46 (5)	45	73	(1)	44 (5)	72 (1)	63.00

$M_t = 57.80$ $M_t = 57.80$

the scores on the left-hand side of Table 15.4 with the help of a table of random numbers. After drawing three sets of numbers 1 through 5, I rearranged the scores in columns according to the random numbers. (Before doing this, all the column rank orders were 1, 2, 3, 4, 5.) The first set of random numbers was 2, 5, 4, 3, 1. The second number of column A_1 was put first. I next took the fifth number of A_1 and put it second. This process was continued until the former first number became the fifth number. The same procedure was used with the other two groups of numbers, with, of course, different sets of random numbers. The final results are given on the right-hand side of Table 15.4. The means of the rows are also given, as are the ranks of the column scores (in parentheses).

First, study the ranks of the two sets of scores. In the left-hand portion of the table, labeled I, are the correlated scores. Since the ranks are the same in each column, the average correlation between columns is 1.00. The numbers of the set labeled II, which are essentially random, present quite a different picture. The 15 numbers of both sets are exactly the same. So are the numbers in each column (and their means). Only the row numbers—and, of course, the row means—are different. Look at the rank orders of II. No systematic relations can be found between them. The average correlation should be approximately zero, since the numbers were randomly shuffled. Actually it is .11.

Now study the variability of the row means. Note that the variability of the means of I is considerably greater than that of II. If the numbers are random, the expectation for the mean of any row is the general mean. The means of the rows of II hover rather closely around the general mean of 57.80. The range is $63 - 53 = 10$. But the means of the rows of I do not hover closely around 57.80; their variability is much greater, as indicated by a range of $73 - 45 = 28$. Calculating the variances of these two sets of means (called *between-rows variance*), we obtain 351.60 for I and 58.27 for II. The variance of I is six times greater than the variance of II. This large difference is a direct effect of the correlation that is present in the scores of I but not in II. It may be said that the between-rows variance is a direct index of individual differences. The reader should pause here and go over this example, especially the examples of Table 15.4, until the effect of correlation on variance is clear.

What is the effect of the estimate of the error variance of correlated scores? Clearly the variance due to the correlation is *systematic* variance, which must be removed from the total variance if a more accurate estimate of error variance is desired. Otherwise the error variance estimate will include the variance due to individual differences and the result will thus be too large. In the example of Table 15.4, we know that the shuffling procedure has concealed the systematic variance due to the correlation. By rearranging the scores the possibility of identifying this variance is removed. The variance is still in the scores of II, but it cannot be extracted. To show this, we calculate the variances of the error terms of I and II; that of I is 3.10, that of II, 149.77. By removing from the total variance the variance due to the correlation, it is possible to reduce the error term greatly, with the result that the error variance of I is 48 times smaller than the error variance of II. If there is substantial systematic variance in the sets of measures, then, and it is possible to isolate and identify this variance, it is clearly worthwhile to do so.

Actual research data will not be as dramatic as the above example. Correlations are almost never 1. But they are often greater than .50 or .60. *The higher the correlation, the larger the systematic variance that can be extracted from the total variance and the more the error term can be reduced*. This principle becomes very important not only in designing research, but also in measurement theory and practice. Sometimes it is possible to build correlation into the scores and then extract the variance due to the resulting correlated scores. For example, we can obtain a ''pure'' measure of individual differences by using the same subjects on different trials. Obviously a subject's own scores will be more alike than they will be like the scores of others.

Re-examination of Table 15.2 Data

We return to the fictitious research data of Table 15.2 on the effects of films on attitudes toward minority groups. Earlier we calculated a between-columns sum of squares and variance exactly as in one-way analysis of variance. We found that the difference between the means was not significant when this method was used. From the above discussion, we can surmise that if there is correlation between the two sets of scores, then the variance due to the correlation should be removed from the total variance and, of course, from the estimate of the error variance. If the correlation is substantial, this procedure should make quite a difference: the error term should get considerably smaller. The correlation between the sets of scores of A_1 and A_2 of Table 15.2 is .93. Since this is a high degree of correlation, the error term when properly calculated should be much lower than it was before.

The additional operation required is simple. Just add the scores in each row of Table 15.2 and calculate the *between-rows* sum of squares and the variance. Square the sum of each row and divide the result by the number of scores in the row; for example, in the first row: $8 + 6 = 14$; $(14)^2/2 = 196/2 = 98$. Repeat this procedure for each row, add the quotients, and then subtract the correction term C. This yields the *between-rows* sum of squares. (Since the number of scores in each row is always 2, it is easier, especially with a desk calculator, to add all the squared sums and then divide by 2.)

$$\begin{matrix} \text{Between rows} \\ (1, 2, \ldots, 10) \end{matrix} = \left[\frac{(14)^2 + (17)^2 + \cdots + (20)^2}{2} \right] - 720 = 902 - 720 = 182$$

This between-rows sum of squares is a measure of the variability due to individual differences, as indicated earlier.

We have extracted from the total sum of squares the between-columns and the between-rows sums of squares. Now, set up a familiar equation:

$$ss_t = ss_b + ss_w \tag{15.1}$$

This is the equation used in one-way analysis of variance. The analysis of Table 15.3 is an example. We must alter this equation to suit the present circumstances. The former between-groups sum of squares, ss_b, is relabeled ss_c, which means the sum of squares of the columns. The sum of squares of the rows, ss_r, is added, and ss_w must be relabeled since we now no longer have a within-groups variance. (Why?) We label it ss_{res}, meaning the sum of squares of the *residuals*. As the name indicates, the *residual* sum of squares means the sum of squares left over after the sums of squares of columns and rows have been extracted from the total sum of squares. The equation then becomes

$$ss_t = ss_c + ss_r + ss_{res} \tag{15.2}$$

Briefly, the total variance has been broken down into two identifiable or systematic variances and one error variance. And this error variance is a more accurate estimate of error or chance variation of the scores than that of Table 15.3.

Rather than substitute in the equation, we set up the final analysis of variance table (Table 15.5). The F ratio of the columns is now $20.00/.89 = 22.47$, which is significant at the .001 level. In Table 15.3 the F ratio was not significant.

This is quite a difference. Since the between-columns variance is the same, the difference is due to the greatly decreased error term, now .89 when it was 10.56 before. By calculating the rows sum of squares and the variance, it has been possible to reduce the error term to about 1/12 of its former magnitude. In this situation, obviously, the former error variance of 10.56 was greatly over-inflated. Returning to the original problem, it is

Table 15.5 Final Complete Analysis of Variance Table: Data of Table 15.2

Source	df	ss	ms	F
Between Columns (A_1, A_2)	1	20.	20.00	22.47 (.001)
Between Rows (1, 2, . . . , 10)	9	182.	20.22	22.72 (.001)
Residual	9	8.	.89	
Total	19	210.		

now possible to say that adding discussion after the motion picture seems to have had a significant effect on attitudes toward minority groups.

Further Considerations

Before we leave this example, three or four additional points need to be made. The first involves the error term and the within-groups and residual variances. When the variances of the columns and the rows are calculated, it is not possible to calculate a within-groups variance, since there is in effect only one score per cell. Also bear in mind that both error variances, as calculated, *are only estimates of the error variance*. In the one-way situation the only estimate possible is the within-groups variance. In the present situation a better estimate is possible, "better" in the sense that it contains less systematic variance. When it is possible to extract systematic variance we do so. It was possible to do so with the data of Table 15.2.

A second point is: Why not use the t test? The answer is simple: Do so if you wish. If there is only one degree of freedom, that is, two groups, then $t = \sqrt{F}$, or $F = t^2$. The t ratio of the data of Table 15.5 is simply: $\sqrt{22.47}=4.74$. But if there is more than one degree of freedom, the t test must give way to the F test. Moreover, the analysis of variance yields more information. The analysis of Table 15.5 tells us that the difference between the mean attitude scores of the experimental and control groups is significantly different. The t test would have yielded the same information. But Table 15.5 also tells us, simply and clearly, that the matching was effective, or that the correlation between the dependent variable scores of the two groups is significant. Had the between-rows F ratio not been significant, we would know that the matching had not been successful—important information indeed. Finally, the calculations of the analysis of variance, once understood, are easily remembered, whereas the equations used for estimating the standard error of the differences between the means seem to confuse the beginning student. (The simple formula given earlier has to be altered because of the correlation.)

Three, post hoc tests of the significance of the differences between individual means can be made—of course with more than two groups. The Scheffé and other tests are applicable.[4]

Finally, and most important, the principles discussed above are applicable to a variety of research situations. Their application to matching is perhaps the least important, though maybe the easiest to understand. Whenever the same subjects and repeated measures are used, the principles apply. When different classes or different schools are used in educational research, the principles apply: variance due to class and school differences can be extracted from the data. Indeed, the principles can be invoked for any research in which

[4]Edwards, *op. cit.*, chap. 8; R. Kirk, *Experimental Design: Procedures for the Behavioral Sciences.* Belmont, Calif.: Brooks/Cole, 1968, chap. 3.

different experimental treatments are used in different units of a larger organization, institution, or even geographical area—provided these units differ in variables of significance to the research.

To see what is meant, imagine that the rows of the left side of Table 15.4 are different schools or classes in a school system, that the schools or classes differ significantly in achievement, as indicated by the row means, and that A_1, A_2, and A_3 are experimental treatments of an experiment done in each of the schools or classes. (See Study Suggestion 2.)

Two-way analysis of variance is useful in the solution of certain measurement problems, particularly in psychology and education, as we will see later in Part Eight. Individual differences are a constant source of variance that needs to be identified and analyzed. A good example is its use in the study of raters and ratings. One can separate the variance of raters from the variance of the objects being rated. The reliability of measuring instruments can be studied because the variance of the items can be separated from the variance of the persons responding to the items. We return again and again to these important points and the principles behind them.

EXTRACTING VARIANCES BY SUBTRACTION

To make sure that the reader understands the points being made, previous examples are repeated here. In Table 15.6, two sets of numbers, labeled I and II, are given. The numbers in these sets are exactly the same; only their arrangements differ. In I, there is

Table 15.6 Analyses of Variance of Randomized and Correlated Fictitious Data

| | I $r = .00$ | | | | II $r = .90$ | | |
	A_1	A_2	Σ		A_1	A_2	Σ
	1	5	6		1	2	3
	2	2	4		2	4	6
	3	4	7		3	3	6
	4	6	10		4	5	9
	5	3	8		5	6	11
ΣX:	15	20	$\Sigma X_t = 35$		15	20	$\Sigma X_t = 35$
M:	3	4	$\Sigma X_t^2 = 145$		3	4	$\Sigma X_t^2 = 145$
			$M_t = 3.5$				$M_t = 3.5$

$$C = \frac{35^2}{10} = 122.50 \qquad\qquad C = \frac{35^2}{10} = 122.50$$

$$\text{Total} = 145 - 122.50 = 22.50 \qquad\qquad \text{Total} = 145 - 122.50 = 22.50$$

$$\text{Between } C = \frac{15^2 + 20^2}{5} - 122.50 \qquad\qquad \text{Between } C = \frac{15^2 + 20^2}{5} - 122.50$$

$$= 2.50 \qquad\qquad\qquad = 2.50$$

$$\text{Between } R = \frac{6^2 + 4^2 + \cdots + 8^2}{2} \qquad\qquad \text{Between } R = \frac{3^2 + 6^2 + \cdots + 9^2}{2}$$

$$-122.50 = 132.50 - 122.50 = 10 \qquad\qquad -122.50 = 141.50 - 122.50 = 19$$

Table 15.7 Final Analysis of Variance Tables

Source	df	ss	ms	F	ss	ms	F
		I ($r = .00$)			II ($r = .90$)		
Between C	1	2.5	2.5	1. (n.s.)	2.5	2.50	10. (.05)
Between R	4	10.0	2.5		19.0	4.75	
Residual $C \times R$	4	10.0	2.5		1.0	.25	
Total	9	22.5			22.5		

no correlation between the two columns of numbers; the coefficient of correlation is exactly zero. This is analogous to the assignment of subjects to the two groups at random. One-way analysis of variance is applicable. In II, on the other hand, the A_2 numbers have been rearranged so that there is correlation between the A_1 and A_2 numbers. (Check the rank orders.) In fact, $r = .90$. One-way analysis of variance is not applicable here. If it is used with the numbers of II, the result would be exactly the same as it would be with the numbers of I, but then we would be disregarding the variance due to the correlation.

The calculations in Table 15.6 yield all the sums of squares except the residual sums of squares, which are obtained by subtraction. Since the calculations are so straightforward, we proceed directly to the final analysis of variance tables which are given in Table 15.7. The sums of squares for totals, columns, and rows are entered as indicated, with the appropriate degrees of freedom. The between-rows degrees of freedom are the number of rows minus one ($5 - 1 = 4$). The residual degrees of freedom, like the interaction degrees of freedom in factorial analysis of variance, are obtained by multiplying the between-columns and between-rows degrees of freedom: $1 \times 4 = 4$. Or simply subtract the between-columns and between-rows degrees of freedom from the total degrees of freedom: $9 - 1 - 4 = 4$. The residual sums of squares, similarly, are obtained by subtracting the between-columns and between-rows sums of squares from the total sums of squares. For I, $22.5 - 2.5 - 10.0 = 10$; for II, $22.5 - 2.5 - 19.0 = 1$.

These analyses need little elaboration. Note particularly that where there is correlation, the between-columns F ratio is significant, but where the correlation is zero it is not significant. Note, too, the error terms. For I ($r = .00$), it is 2.5. For II ($r = .90$), it is .25, which is *ten* times smaller.

Removal of Systematic Sources of Variance

We now use the subtractive procedure of Chapter 6 to remove the two systematic sources of variance in the two sets of scores. First, remove the between-columns variance by correcting each mean so that it equals the general mean of 3.5. Then correct each score in each column similarly (as done for I and II in Table 15.8).

If we now calculate the total sums of squares of I and II, in both cases we obtain 20. Compare this result to the former figure of 22.5. The correction procedure has reduced the total sums of squares by 2.5. These are of course the sums of squares between columns. Note, again, that the correction procedure has had no effect whatever on the variance within each of the four groups of scores. Nor has it had any effect on the means of the rows.

Now remove the rows variance by letting each row mean equal 3.5, the general mean, and by correcting the row scores accordingly. This has been done in Table 15.9, which should be carefully studied. Note that the variability of both sets of scores has been reduced, but that the variability of the correlated set (II) has been sharply reduced. In fact,

Table 15.8 Removal of Between-columns Variance by Equalizing Column Means and Scores

| Correction | I (r = .00) | | | | II (r = .90) | | |
| | .5 | −.5 | | | .5 | −.5 | |
	A_1	A_2	M		A_1	A_2	M
	1.5	4.5	3.0		1.5	1.5	1.5
	2.5	1.5	2.0		2.5	3.5	3.0
	3.5	3.5	3.5		3.5	2.5	3.0
	4.5	5.5	5.0		4.5	4.5	4.5
	5.5	2.5	4.0		5.5	5.5	5.5
M:	3.5	3.5	$M_t = 3.5$		3.5	3.5	$M_t = 3.5$

the scores of II have a range of only $4 - 3 = 1$, whereas the range of the I scores is $5 - 2 = 3$. The matching of the scores in II and its concomitant correlation enables us, via the corrective procedure, to reduce the error term sharply by "correcting out" the variance due to the correlation. The only variance now in the twice-corrected scores is the residual variance. "Residual variance" is an apt term. It is the variance left over after the two systematic variances have been removed. If we calculate the *total* sums of squares of I and II, we find them to be 10 and 1, respectively. If we calculate the sums of squares *within* the groups as with one-way analysis of variance, we find them also to be 10 and 1. Evidently there is no more systematic variance left in the scores—only error variance remains. The most important point to note is that the residual sum of squares of the uncorrelated scores is ten times greater than the residual sum of squares of the correlated scores. Exactly the same operation was performed on both sets of scores. With the uncorrelated scores, however, it is not possible to extract as much variance as with the correlated scores.

Table 15.9 Removal of Between-rows Variance by Equalizing Row Means and Scores

| | I (r = .00) | | | | II (r = .90) | | |
Correction	A_1	A_2	M	Correction	A_1	A_2	M
+ .5	2.0	5.0	3.5	+2.0	3.5	3.5	3.5
+1.5	4.0	3.0	3.5	+ .5	3.0	4.0	3.5
0	3.5	3.5	3.5	+ .5	4.0	3.0	3.5
−1.5	3.0	4.0	3.5	−1.0	3.5	3.5	3.5
− .5	5.0	2.0	3.5	−2.0	3.5	3.5	3.5
M:	3.5	3.5	(3.5)		3.5	3.5	(3.5)

RESEARCH EXAMPLES

Presidential Rhetoric and Conceptual Complexity

Some research circumstances and situations lead naturally to repeated measures on the same subjects or groups. Such was the case in a study of revolutionary leaders cited in an

Table 15.10 Conceptual Complexity Measures of Ten U. S. Presidents Before and After Election, Tetlock Study

President	Preelection	1st Month	2d Year	3d Year
McKinley	2.1	3.1	3.1	3.2
Taft	2.4	3.5	3.5	4.1
Wilson	3.2	3.9	3.6	3.8
Harding	2.2	2.5	2.0	2.1
Hoover	3.8	2.8	2.7	3.0
F. D. Roosevelt	2.2	3.5	3.8	3.5
Eisenhower	1.9	3.4	3.4	3.8
Kennedy	2.1	3.6	3.5	4.0
Nixon	2.5	2.9	3.1	2.9
Carter	2.7	3.1	3.1	3.4
Means	2.51	3.23	3.18	3.38

earlier chapter, in which conceptual complexity was the dependent variable.[5] This important variable was also used in a recent study of American presidential rhetoric before and after election, again a "natural" repeated measures situation.[6] Tetlock tested alternative explanations or hypotheses, one of which suggested that U. S. presidents used conceptually simple utterances before election because they were manipulating voter impressions to get elected. The second more charitable explanation, the cognitive adjustment hypothesis, suggests that presidents gradually become more complex in their thinking as they become increasingly familiar with larger policy issues. Tetlock gives conceptual complexity measures of ten recent presidents before election, one month after election, the second year after election, and the third year after election. These measures were derived through content analysis, a method we examine in a later chapter, from public spoken and written statements. His data are given in Table 15.10.

Repeated measures, or two-way, analysis of variance showed that the four means differed significantly from each other ($F = 7.81$, $df = 3,27$; $p < .01$), and that, among other things, the conceptual complexity mean one month after election was significantly greater than the preelection mean ($F = 9.12$, $df = 1,9$; $p < .05$).[7] There was no trend for the means to increase while the presidents were in office, however. Therefore, the impression-management hypothesis was supported.

Learning Sets of Isopods

In an interesting and effective demonstration of the use of subjects as their own controls, in which two-way analysis of variance and the testing of learning theory with lower organisms were used, Morrow and Smithson showed that isopods (small crustaceans) can learn to learn.[8] Many students, humanists, sociologists, educators, and even psycholo-

[5] P. Suedfeld and A. Rank, "Revolutionary Leaders: Long-Term Success as a Function of Changes in Conceptual Complexity," *Journal of Personality and Social Psychology,* 34 (1976), 169–178.

[6] P. Tetlock, "Pre- to Postelection Shifts in Presidential Rhetoric: Impression Management or Cognitive Adjustment?" *Journal of Personality and Social Psychology,* 41 (1981), 207–212. Copyright © 1981 by the American Psychological Association. Reprinted by permission of the author.

[7] I calculated the *F* ratios reported above from Tetlock's Table 1 (p. 210). Tetlock's reported *F* ratios were somewhat larger. Since the ratios were significant by either calculation, the conclusions hold. (See Study Suggestion 5.)

[8] J. Morrow and B. Smithson, "Learning Sets in an Invertebrate," *Science,* 164 (1969), 850–851.

Table 15.11 Analysis of Variance of Morrow and Smithson Data

Source	df	ss	ms	F
Between Columns	9	3095.95	343.994	4.78 (.01)
Between Rows	7	1587.40	226.771	3.15 (.01)
Residual	63	4532.85	71.950	
Total	79	9216.20		

gists have criticized learning theorists and other psychological investigators for using animals in their research. While there can be legitimate criticism of psychological and other behavioral research, criticizing it because animals are used is part of the frustrating but apparently unavoidable irrationality that plagues all human effort. Yet, it does have a certain charm and can itself be the object of scientific investigation.[9] In any case, one of the reasons for testing similar hypotheses with different species is the same reason we replicate research in different parts of the United States and in other countries: generality. How much more powerful a theory is if it holds up with southerners, northerners, easterners, and westerners, with Germans, Japanese, Israelis, and Americans—and with rats, pigeons, horses, and dogs. Morrow and Smithson's study attempted to extend learning theory to little creatures whose learning one might think to be governed by different laws than the learning of men and rats. They succeeded—to some extent at least.

They trained eight isopods, through water deprivation and subsequent reinforcement for successful performance (wet blotting paper), to make reversals of their "preferences" for one or the other arm of a T maze. When the S's had reached a specified criterion of correct turns in the maze, the training was reversed—that is, turning in the direction of the other arm of the T maze was reinforced until the criterion was reached. This was done with each isopod for nine reversals. The question is: Did the animals learn to make the reversals sooner as the trials progressed? Such learning should be exhibited by fewer and fewer errors.

Morrow and Smithson analyzed the data with two-way analysis of variance. The mean number of errors of the initial trial and the nine reversal trials consistently got smaller: 27.5, 23.6, 18.6, 14.3, 16.8, 13.9, 11.1, 8.5, 8.6, 8.6. The two-way analysis of variance table is given in Table 15.11.[10] The ten means differ significantly, since the F ratio for columns (reversal trials), 4.78, is significant at the .01 level. That there is correlation between the columns, and thus individual differences among the isopods, is shown by the F ratio for rows, 3.15, also significant at the .01 level. It is a piquant note that even little crustaceans are individuals!

Study Suggestions

1. Do two-way analysis of variance of the two sets of fictitious data of Table 15.6. Use the text as an aid. Interpret the results. Now do two-way analysis of variance of the two sets of Table 15.8; do the same for Table 15.9. Lay out the final analysis of variance tables and compare. Think through carefully how the adjustive corrections have affected the original data.

2. Three sociologists were asked to judge the general effectiveness of the administrative offices

[9] Bugelski has written an excellent defense of the use of rats in learning research that students of behavioral research should read: B. Bugelski, *The Psychology of Learning*. New York: Holt, Rinehart and Winston, 1956, pp. 33–44. Another excellent essay on a somewhat broader base is: D. Hebb and W. Thompson, "The Social Significance of Animal Studies." In G. Lindzey and E. Abelson, eds., *The Handbook of Social Psychology*, 2d ed. Reading, Mass.: Addison-Wesley, 1968, vol. II, pp. 729–774.

[10] I did the analysis of variance from the original data given by Morrow and Smithson in their Table 1.

of ten elementary schools in a school district. One of their measures was administrative flexibility. (The higher the score the greater the flexibility.) The ten ratings on this measure of the three sociologists are given below:

	S_1	S_2	S_3
1	9	7	5
2	9	9	6
3	7	5	4
4	6	5	3
5	3	4	2
6	5	6	4
7	5	3	1
8	4	2	1
9	5	4	4
10	7	5	5

(a) Do a two-way analysis of variance as described in the chapter.
(b) Do the three sociologists agree in their mean ratings? Does one of the sociologists appear to be severe in his ratings?
(c) Are there substantial differences among the schools? Which school appears to have the greatest administrative flexibility? Which school has the least flexibility?

[*Answers:* (a) F (columns) = 24.44 (.001); F (rows) = 14.89 (.001); (b) no; yes; (c) yes: no. 2; no. 8.]

3. Draw 30 digits, 0 through 9, from a table of random numbers (use Appendix C, if you wish), or generate the numbers on a computer, microcomputer, or programmable calculator. Divide them arbitrarily into three groups of 10 digits each.

(a) Do a two-way analysis of variance. Assume that the numbers in each row are data from one individual.
(b) Now add constants to the three numbers of each row as follows: 20 to the first two rows, 15 to the second two rows, 10 to the third two rows, 5 to the fourth two rows, and 0 to the last two rows. Do a two-way analysis of variance of these "data."
(c) In effect, what have you done by "biasing" the row numbers in this fashion?
(d) Compare the sum of squares and the mean squares of (a) and (b). Why are the *total* sums of squares and mean squares different? Why are the *between-columns* and the *residual* sums of squares and mean squares the same? Why are the *between-rows* sums of squares and mean squares different?
(e) Create a research problem out of all this and interpret the "results." Is the example realistic?

4. In an extraordinary series of studies, Miller and his colleagues have shown that, contrary to traditional belief, it is possible to learn to control autonomic responses like heart beat, urine secretion, and intestinal contractions.[11] In one of these studies, Miller and DiCara published all their data on the secretion of urine.[12] Parts of the data are reproduced in Table 15.12. The data of II on the right are the increases in urine secretion of seven randomly selected rats (of 14) before and after "training." The training was instrumental conditioning: whenever a rat secreted urine it was rewarded. These data, then, are repeated measures. If the conditioning "worked," the means should be significantly different. The data of I, on the left, are the *before* measures of two randomly assigned groups (for another experimental purpose). Since they are urine secretion measures *before* the experimental manipulation, the means should *not* be significantly different.

---

[11] N. Miller, "Learning of Visceral and Glandular Responses," *Science,* 163 (1969), 434–445; N. Miller, *Neal Miller: Selected Papers.* Chicago: Aldine-Atherton, 1971, Part XI.
[12] N. Miller and L. DiCara, "Instrumental Learning of Urine Formation by Rats: Changes in Renal Blood Flow," *American Journal of Physiology,* 215 (1968), 677–683. Also in the Miller volume cited in footnote 11, pp. 796–810. The data are in their Table 1. The analyses suggested above were not the analyses that Miller and DiCara did.

Table 15.12 Conditioning of Urine Secretion Data; Miller and DiCara Study[a]

(I) Two Samples Before Conditioning			(II) Sample Rewarded for Urine Increase	
Sample 1	Sample 2		Before	After
.023	.018	1	.023	.030
.014	.015	2	.014	.019
.016	.012	3	.016	.029
.018	.015	4	.018	.030
.007	.030	5	.007	.016
.026	.027	6	.026	.044
.012	.020	7	.012	.026

[a] The measures are ml/min/per 100 grams of body weight. The data of I are those of two samples of rats randomly assigned to the two groups. The data of II are the before and after reward measures of Sample 1 of I. The data of I were analyzed with one-way analysis of variance, while those of II were analyzed with two-way, or repeated measures, analysis of variance.

(a) Do a one-way analysis of variance of the measures of I (use six decimal places).

(b) Do a two-way, or repeated measures, analysis of variance of the measures of II (use six decimal places).

(*Note:* It might be easier to multiply each of the scores by 1000 before doing the analyses, i.e., move the decimal point three places to the right. Does this affect the F ratios? If you do this, three decimal places are sufficient.)

(c) Interpret the results.

[*Answers:* (a) $F = .73$ (n.s.); (b) $F = 43.88$ ($p < .01$).]

5. (a) Do a repeated measures analysis of variance of the complexity measures of the last three data sets of Table 15.10: 1st Month, 2d Year, 3d Year.

(b) What does the F ratio mean?

[*Answers:* (a) $F_C = 2.97$ (n.s.); (b) Evidently the conceptual complexity of the ten presidents did not change while they were in office.]

Chapter 16

Nonparametric Analysis of Variance and Related Statistics

IT IS, of course, possible to analyze data and to draw inferences about relations among variables without statistics. Sometimes, for example, data are so obvious that a statistical test is not really necessary. If all the scores of an experimental group are greater than (or less than) those of a control group, then a statistical test is superfluous. It is also possible to have statistics of a quite different nature than those we have been studying, statistics that use properties of the data other than the strictly quantitative. We can infer an effect of X on Y if the scores of an experimental group are mostly of one kind, say high or low, as contrasted to the scores of a control group. This is because, on the basis of randomization and chance, we expect about the same numbers of different kinds of scores in both experimental and control groups. Similarly, if we arrange all the scores of experimental and control groups in rank order, from high to low, say, then on the basis of chance alone we expect the sum or average of the ranks in each group to be about the same. If they are not, if the higher or the lower ranks tend to be clustered in one of the groups, then we infer that ''something'' other than chance has operated.

Indeed, there are many ways to approach and analyze data other than comparing means and variances. But the basic principle is always the same if we continue to work in a probabilistic world: compare obtained results to chance or theoretical expectations. If, for example, we administer four treatments to subjects and expect that one of the four will excel the others, we can compare the mean of the favored group with the average of the other three groups in an analysis of variance and planned comparisons manner. But suppose our data are highly irregular in one or more ways and we fear for the validity of the usual tests of significance. What can we do? We can rank order all the observations, for one thing. If none of the four treatments has any more influence than any other, we expect the ranks to disperse themselves among the four groups more or less evenly. If treatment A_2, however, has a preponderance of high (or low) ranks, than we conclude that the usual expectation is upset. Such reasoning is a good part of the basis of so-called nonparametric and distribution-free statistics.[1]

In this chapter we examine certain interesting forms of nonparametric analysis of variance. Other forms of nonparametric statistics will be briefly mentioned. The chapter has two main purposes: to introduce the reader to the ideas behind nonparametric statistics, but especially nonparametric analysis of variance, and to bring out the essential similarity of most inference-aiding methods.

The student should be aware that careful study of nonparametric statistics gives depth of insight into statistics and statistical inference. The insight gained is probably due to the considerable loosening of thinking that seems to occur when working tangential to the usual statistical structure. One sees, so to speak, a broader perspective; one can even invent statistical tests, once the basic ideas are well understood. In short, statistical and inferential ideas are generalized on the basis of relatively simple fundamental ideas.

PARAMETRIC AND NONPARAMETRIC STATISTICS

A parametric statistical test, the kind of test we have studied to now, depends on a number of assumptions about the population from which the samples used in the test are drawn. The best-known such assumption is that the population scores are normally distributed. A nonparametric or distribution-free statistical test depends on no assumptions as to the form of the sample population or the values of the population parameters. For example, nonparametric tests do not depend on the assumption of normality of the population scores. The problem of assumptions is difficult, thorny, and controversial. Some statisticians and researchers consider the violation of assumptions a serious matter that leads to invalidity of parametric statistical tests. Others believe that, in general, violation of the assumptions is not so serious because tests like the F and t tests are robust, which means, roughly, that they operate well even under assumption violations, provided violations are not gross and multiple.[2] Nevertheless, let's examine three important assumptions and the evidence for believing parametric methods to be robust. We also discuss a fourth assumption, independence of observations, because of its generality—it applies no matter what kind of statistical test is used—and, more important, because its violation invalidates the results of most statistical tests of significance.

---

[1] There is no single name for the statistics we are discussing. The two most appropriate names are "nonparametric statistics" and "distribution-free statistics." The latter, for instance, means that the statistical tests of significance make no assumptions about the precise form of the sampled population. See J. Bradley, *Distribution-Free Statistical Tests.* Englewood Cliffs, N. J.: Prentice-Hall, 1968, chap. 2. In this book we will use "nonparametric statistics" to mean those statistical tests of significance not based on so-called classical statistical theory, which is based largely on the properties of means and variances and the nature of distributions.

[2] For an excellent general treatment of the problems and an encouraging review of the robustness issue, see P. Gardner, "Scales and Statistics," *Review of Educational Research,* 45 (1975), 43–57. For quite a different and discouraging view, see Bradley, *op. cit.* chap. 2, or J. Bradley, "Nonparametric Statistics," in R. Kirk, ed., *Statistical Issues: A Reader for the Behavioral Sciences.* Monterey, Calif.: Brooks/Cole, 1972, Sel. 9.1. Glass and colleagues, in another treatise on the subject, also take a dim view of assumption violations: G. Glass, P. Peckham, and J. Sanders, "Consequences of Failure to Meet Assumptions Underlying the Fixed Effects Analysis of Variance and Covariance," *Review of Educational Research,* 42 (1972), 237–288. In sum, Gardner says to go ahead and use parametric statistics, whereas Bradley advocates nonparametric methods. The difficulty is that both arguments are compelling and valid! I lean toward Gardner's position. If one uses reasonable care in sampling and analysis and circumspection in interpretation of statistical results, parametric methods are useful, valuable, and irreplaceable. Nonparametric methods are useful adjuncts in the statistical armamentarium of the researcher, but they can by no means replace parametric methods.

Assumption of Normality

The best-known assumption behind the use of many parametric statistics is the *assumption of normality*. It is assumed in using the *t* and *F* tests (and thus the analysis of variance), for example, that the samples with which we work have been drawn from populations that are normally distributed. It is said that, if the populations from which samples are drawn are not normal, then statistical tests that depend on the normality assumption are vitiated. As a result, the conclusions drawn from sampled observations and their statistics will be in question. When in doubt about the normality of a population, or when one knows that the population is not normal, one should use a nonparametric test that does not make the normality assumption, it is said. Some teachers urge students of education and psychology to use *only* nonparametric tests on the questionable ground that most educational and psychological populations are not normal. The issue is not this simple.

Homogeneity of Variance

The next most important assumption is that of *homogeneity of variance*. It is assumed, in analysis of variance, that the variances within the groups are statistically the same. That is, variances are assumed to be homogeneous from group to group, within the bounds of random variation. If this is not true, the *F* test is vitiated. There is good reason for this statement. We saw earlier that the within-groups variance was an average of the variances within the two, three, or more groups of measures. If the variances differ widely, then such averaging is questionable. The effect of widely differing variances is to inflate the within-groups variance. Consequently an *F* test may be not significant when in reality there are significant differences between the means.

These two assumptions have both been examined rather thoroughly by empirical methods. Artificial populations have been set up, samples drawn from them, and *t* and *F* tests performed. The evidence to date is that the importance of normality and homogeneity is overrated, a view that is shared by the author.[3] Unless there is good evidence to believe that populations are rather seriously nonnormal and that variances are heterogeneous, it is usually unwise to use a nonparametric statistical test in place of a parametric one. The reason for this is that parametric tests are almost always more powerful than nonparametric tests. (The power of a statistical test is the probability that the null hypothesis will be rejected when it is actually false.) There is one situation, or rather, combination of situations, that may be dangerous. Boneau found that when there was heterogeneity of variance *and* differences in the sample sizes of experimental groups, significance tests were adversely affected.

[3] Two important studies were done by Norton and by Boneau. Lindquist gives an admirable summary of the Norton study: E. Lindquist, *Design and Analysis of Experiments*. Boston: Houghton Mifflin, 1953, pp. 78–86. Boneau discusses the whole problem of assumptions and reports his own definitive study in a brilliant article: C. Boneau, "The Effects of Violations of Assumptions Underlying the *t* Test," *Psychological Bulletin*, 57 (1960), 49–64. Another useful article by Boneau is C. Boneau, "A Note on Measurement Scales and Statistical Tests," *American Psychologist*, 16 (1961), 260–261. An excellent but more general article is N. Anderson, "Scales and Statistics: Parametric and Nonparametric," *Psychological Bulletin*, 58 (1961), 305–316. Additional empirical demonstrations of the robustness of analysis of variance and the *t* test are: P. Games and P. Lucas, "Power of the Analysis of Variance of Independent Groups on Non-Normal and Normally Transformed Data," *Educational and Psychological Measurement*, 26 (1966), 311–327; B. Baker, C. Hardyck, and I. Petronovich, "Weak Measurements vs. Strong Statistics: An Empirical Critique of S. S. Stevens' Proscriptions on Statistics," *Educational and Psychological Measurement*, 26 (1966), 291–309. It has also been found that tests of the significance of coefficients of correlation are insensitive to extreme violations of the assumptions of normality and measurement scale: L. Havlicek and N. Peterson, "Effect of the Violation of Assumptions Upon Significance Levels of the Pearson *r*," *Psychological Bulletin*, 84 (1977), 373–377.

Continuity and Equal Intervals of Measures

A third assumption is that the measures to be analyzed are continuous measures with equal intervals. As we shall see in a later chapter, this assumption is behind the arithmetic operations of adding, subtracting, multiplying, and dividing. Parametric tests like the *F* and *t* tests of course depend on this assumption, but many nonparametric tests do not. This assumption's importance has also been overrated. Anderson has effectively disposed of it,[4] and Lord has lampooned it in a well-known article on football numbers.[5]

Despite the conclusions of Lindquist, Boneau, Anderson, and others, it is well to bear these assumptions in mind. It is not wise to use statistical procedures—or, for that matter, any kind of research procedures—without due respect for the assumptions behind the procedures. If they are too seriously violated, the conclusions drawn from research data may be in error. To the reader who has been alarmed by some statistics books the best advice probably is: Use parametric statistics, as well as the analysis of variance, routinely, but keep a sharp eye on data for gross departures from normality, homogeneity of variance, and equality of intervals. Be aware of measurement problems and their relation to statistical tests, and be familiar with the basic nonparametric statistics so that they can be used when necessary. Also bear in mind that nonparametric tests are often quick and easy to use and are excellent for preliminary, if not always definitive, tests.

Independence of Observations

Another assumption that is important in both measurement and statistics is that of independence of observations—also called statistical independence. We have already studied statistical independence in Chapter 7, where we examined independence, mutual exclusiveness, and exhaustiveness of events and their probabilities. (The reader is urged to review that section of Chapter 7.) We reexamine independence here, however, in the context of statistics because of the special importance of the principle involved. The independence assumption applies on both parametric and nonparametric statistics. That is, one cannot escape its implications by using a different statistical approach that does not involve the assumption.

The formal definition of statistical independence is: If two events, A_1 and A_2, are statistically independent, the probability of their intersection is: $p(A_1 \cap A_2) = p(A_1) \cdot p(A_2)$.[6] If, for example, a student takes a test of ten items, the probability of getting any item correct by chance (guessing) is $\frac{1}{2}$. If the items and the responses to them are independent, then the probability of getting, say, items two, three, and seven correct by chance is: $\frac{1}{2} \times \frac{1}{2} \times \frac{1}{2} = .125$. And similarly for all ten items: .001.

It is assumed in research that observations are independent, that making one observation does not influence the making of another observation. If I am observing the cooperative behavior of children, and I note that Anna seems to very cooperative, then I am likely to violate the independence assumption because I will *expect* her future behavior to be cooperative. If, indeed, the expectation operates, then my observations are not independent.

Statistical tests assume independence of the observations that yield the numbers that

[4] Anderson, *op. cit.*

[5] F. Lord, "On the Statistical Treatment of Football Numbers," *American Psychologist,* 8 (1953), 750–751. Both the Lord and the Anderson articles are in Kirk, *op. cit.*, selections 2.3 and 2.4.

[6] W. Feller, *An Introduction to Probability Theory and Its Applications*, vol. I. New York: Wiley, 1950, p. 115.

go into the statistical calculations. If the observations are not independent, arithmetic operations and statistical tests are vitiated. For example, if item 3 in the ten-item test really contained the correct answer to item 9, then the responses to the two items will not be independent. The probability of getting all ten items right by chance is altered. Instead of .001, the probability is some larger figure. The calculation of means and other statistics will be contaminated. Violation of this assumption seems to be fairly common probably because it is easy to do.

In Chapter 7 we encountered an interesting and subtle example of violation of the assumption when we reproduced a table (Table 7.3) whose entries were aggressive *acts* rather than the numbers of animals who acted aggressively. If we have a crossbreak tabulation of frequencies and calculate χ^2 to determine whether the cell entries depart significantly from chance expectation, the total N must be the total number of units in the sample, whether the units are individuals or some sort of aggregate (like groups), the units having been independently observed. The N's of statistical formulas assume that sample sizes are the numbers of units of the calculation, each unit being independently observed.

If, for example, one has a sample of 16 subjects, then $N = 16$. Suppose one had observed varying acts of some of the subjects and entered the frequencies of occurrence of these acts. Suppose, further, that a total of 54 such acts was observed and 54 was used as N. This would be a gross violation of the independence of observations assumption. In short, the entries in frequency tables must be the numbers of independent observations. One cannot count several occurrences of a kind of event from one person. If N is the number of persons, then it cannot become the number of occurrences of events of the persons. This is a subtle and dangerous point. The statistical analyses of a number of published studies suffer from violation of the principle. I have even seen a factorial analysis of variance table in which the tabled entries were numbers of occurrences of certain events and *not* the true units of analysis, the individuals of the sample. The difficulty is not so much that violation of independence is immoral. It is a research delinquency because it can lead to quite erroneous conclusions about the relations among variables.

NONPARAMETRIC ANALYSIS OF VARIANCE

The nonparametric analysis of variance methods studied here, like so many other nonparametric methods, depend on ranking. We study basic forms: one-way analysis and two-way, or repeated measures, analysis.

One-Way Analysis of Variance: The Kruskal-Wallis Test

An investigator interested in the differences in conservatism of three boards of education is unable to administer a measure of conservatism to the board members. He therefore has an expert judge rank order all the members of the three boards on the basis of private discussions with them. The three boards have six, six, and five members, respectively. The ranks of all the board members are given in Table 16.1.

If there were no differences in conservatism between the three boards, then the ranks should be randomly distributed in the three columns. If so, then the sums of the ranks (or their means) in the three columns should be approximately equal.[7] On the other hand, if

[7] Kendall has ingeniously shown how it is appropriate to add ranks: M. Kendall, *Rank Correlation Methods*. London: Griffin, 1948, p. 1.

Table 16.1 Ranks of 17 Members of Three Boards of Education on Judged Conservatism

	Boards		
	I	II	III
	12	11	4
	14	16	3
	10	5	8
	17	7	1
	15	6	9
	13	2	
Σ Ranks:	81	47	25
M:	13.50	7.83	5.00

there are differences in conservatism between the three groups, then the ranks in one column should be higher than the ranks in another column—with a consequent higher sum or mean of ranks.

Kruskal and Wallis give formula for assessing the significance of these differences:[8]

$$H = \frac{12}{N(N + 1)} \Sigma \frac{R_j^2}{n_j} - 3(N + 1) \tag{16.1}$$

where N = total number of ranks; n_j = number of ranks in group j; and R_j = sum of the ranks in group j. Applying Equation 16.1 to the ranks of Table 16.1, we first calculate $\Sigma(R_j^2/n_j)$:

$$\Sigma \frac{R_j^2}{n_j} = \frac{(81)^2}{6} + \frac{(47)^2}{6} + \frac{(25)^2}{5} = 1093.50 + 368.17 + 125.0 = 1586.67$$

Substituting in Equation 16.1, we find:

$$H = \frac{12}{17(17 + 1)} \cdot 1586.67 - 54 = 62.22 - 54 = 8.22$$

H is approximately distributed as χ^2. The degrees of freedom are $k - 1$, where k is the number of columns or groups, or $3 - 1 = 2$. Checking the χ^2 table, we find this to be significant at the .02 level. Thus the ranks are not random.

The Kruskal and Wallis method is analogous to one-way analysis of variance. It is simple and effective. Measurement is sometimes such that it is doubtful whether parametric analysis is legitimate. Of course, doubtful measures can also be transformed.[9] But in many cases it is easily possible to rank order the scores and do the analysis on the ranks. There are also research situations in which the only form of measurement possible is rank

[8]W. Kruskal and W. Wallis, "Use of Ranks in One-Criterion Variance Analysis," *Journal of the American Statistical Association*, 47 (1952), 583–621. The test is also described in statistics texts, for example: W. Hays, *Statistics*, 3d ed. New York: Holt, Rinehart and Winston, 1981, pp. 591–594; Bradley, *op, cit.*, pp. 129–134. Note that the test can be extended to the factorial case: see *ibid.*, pp. 138–141.

[9]The problem of transformation of scores exceeds the bounds of this book. An enlightened discussion for behavioral science students is: F. Mosteller and R. Bush, "Selected Quantitative Techniques." In G. Lindzey, ed., *Handbook of Social Psychology*. Reading, Mass.: Addison-Wesley, 1954, vol. I, pp. 324–328. The essence of the idea of transformations is that measures that are not respectable, owing to lack of normality and other reasons, are transformed to respectability via a linear function of the sort $y = f(x)$, where y is a transformed score, x the original score, and f is some operation ("the square root of") on x.

order, or ordinal measurement. The Kruskal and Wallis test is most useful in such situations. But it is also useful when data are irregular but amenable to ranking.

Two-Way Analysis of Variance: The Friedman Test

In situations in which subjects are matched or the same subjects are observed more than once, a form of rank-order analysis of variance, first devised by Friedman, can be used.[10] An ordinary two-way analysis of variance of the ranks can also be used.

An educational researcher, concerned with the relation between role and perception of teaching competence, asked groups of professors to rate each other on an instructor evaluation rating instrument. He also asked administrators and students to rate the same professors. Since the numbers of professors ("peers"), administrators, and students differed, he averaged the ratings of the members of each rating group. In effect the hypothesis stated that the three groups of raters would differ significantly in their ratings. The researcher also wanted to know whether there were significant differences among the professors. The data of one part of the study are given in Table 16.2.

There are a number of ways these data can be analyzed. First, of course, ordinary two-way analysis of variance can be used. If the numbers being analyzed seem to conform reasonably well to the assumptions discussed earlier, this would be the best analysis. In the analysis of variance, the F ratio for columns (between raters) is 4.70, significant at the .05 level, and the F ratio for rows is 12.72, significant at the .01 level. The hypothesis of the investigator is supported. This is indicated by the significant differences between the means of the three groups. The professors, too, differ significantly.

Now assume that the investigator is disturbed by the type of data he has and decides to use nonparametric analysis of variance. Clearly he should not use the Kruskal-Wallis method; he decides to use the Friedman method, rank ordering the data *by rows*. In so doing he tests the differences between the columns. Obviously if two or more raters are given the same ranking system, say 1, 2, 3, 4, 5, it is apparent that the sums and means of the ranks of the different raters will always be the same. In this analysis, then, he concentrates on the differences between the raters and ignores the differences between the professors (as rated). In what follows, then, we focus on the ranks in the parentheses to the right

Table 16.2 Hypothetical Means of Ratings of Professors by Peers, Administrators, and Students, with Ranks of the Three Groups of Raters of the Mean Ratings[a]

Professors	Peers		Administrators		Students	
A	28	(3)	19	(1)	22	(2)
B	22	(1)	23	(2)	36	(3)
C	26	(2)	24	(1)	29	(3)
D	44	(2)	34	(1)	48	(3)
E	35	(1)	39	(2)	40	(3)
F	40	(2)	38	(1)	45	(3)
ΣR:		11		8		17

[a]The numbers in the table are composite ratings. The numbers in parentheses are ranks: the higher the number (or rank), the greater the perceived competence. *Note:* The ratings of each *row* are ranked, reflecting the differences among the three groups of each professor.

[10] M. Friedman, "The Use of Ranks to Avoid the Assumption of Normality Implicit in the Analysis of Variance," *Journal of the American Statistical Association,* (1937), 675–701. The Friedman test is also described in the references mentioned earlier.

of each composite rating. We also focus on the sums of the ranks at the bottom of the table.

The formula given by Friedman is:

$$\chi_r^2 = \frac{12}{kn(n+1)} \Sigma R_j^2 - 3k(n+1) \qquad (16.2)$$

where $\chi_r^2 = \chi^2$, ranks; $k =$ number of rankings; $n =$ number of objects being ranked; $\Sigma R_j =$ sum of the ranks in column (group) j; and $\Sigma R_j^2 =$ sum of the squared sums. First calculate ΣR_j^2:

$$\Sigma R_j^2 = 11^2 + 8^2 + 17^2 = 474$$

Now determine k and n. The number of rankings is k, or the number of times that the rank-order system, whatever it is, is used. Here $k = 6$. The number of objects being ranked, n, or the number of ranks, is 3. (Actually, the raters are not being ranked: 3 is the number of ranks in the rank-order system being used.) Now calculate χ_r^2.

$$\chi_r^2 = \frac{12}{(6)(3)(4)} \cdot 474 - (3)(6)(4) = 79 - 72 = 7$$

This value is checked against a χ^2 table, at $df = n - 1 = 3 - 1 = 2$. The value is significant at the .05 level.[11]

The investigator was also interested in the significance of the differences among the professors as rated. He assigns ranks to the rating composites in *columns* (in parentheses in Table 16.3). These are the ranks that the rater groups assigned to the six professors. Professors who are rated high should get the higher ranks, which can be determined by adding their ranks across the rows. (See ΣR column on the right-hand side of the table.) This time $k = 3$ and $n = 6$. We calculate χ_r^2 using Equation 16.2 again:

$$\chi_r^2 = \frac{12}{(3)(6)(7)} \cdot 787 - (3)(3)(7) = 11.95$$

Table 16.3 Hypothetical Means of Ratings of Professors by Peers, Administrators, and Students, with Ranks[a]

Professors	Peers		Administrators		Students		ΣR
A	28	(3)	19	(1)	22	(1)	5
B	22	(1)	23	(2)	36	(3)	6
C	26	(2)	24	(3)	29	(2)	7
D	44	(6)	34	(4)	48	(6)	16
E	35	(4)	39	(6)	40	(4)	14
F	40	(5)	38	(5)	45	(5)	15

[a]The numbers in the table are composite ratings. The numbers in parentheses are ranks: the higher the number, the greater the perceived competence. *Note:* The ratings of each *column* are ranked, reflecting the differences among the six professors, as rated by each group.

Checking this value in a χ^2 table, at $df = n - 1 = 6 - 1 = 5$, we find it to be significant at the .05 level. The instructors, as rated, seem to be different.

Compare these results to the ordinary analysis of variance results. In the latter, the

---

[11] With n and k relatively small, the significance level is in doubt. For details, see Bradley, *op. cit.*, pp. 125ff.

three groups were found to be significantly different at the .05 level. In the case of the significance of the differences between the professors, the analysis also showed significance. In general, the methods should agree fairly well.[12]

The Coefficient of Concordance, W

Perhaps a more direct test of the investigator's hypothesis is provided by using a measure of the association of the ranks. Such a measure, called the *coefficient of concordance, W,* has been worked out by Kendall.[13] We are now interested in the degree of agreement or association in the ranks of the columns of Table 16.2. Each rater group has virtually assigned a rank to each professor. If there were no association whatever between two of the rater groups, and a rank-order coefficient of correlation were computed between the ranks, it should be near zero. On the other hand, if there is agreement, the coefficient should be significantly different from zero.

The coefficient of concordance, W, expresses the average agreement, on a scale from .00 to 1.00, among the ranks. There are two ways to define W. The Kendall method will be presented first. According to this method W can be expressed as the ratio between the *between-groups* (or ranks) sum of squares and the *total* sum of squares of a complete analysis of variance of the ranks. This ratio, then, is the correlation ratio squared, η^2, of ranked data.

Where there are k rankings of n individual objects, Kendall's coefficient of concordance is defined by

$$W = \frac{12S}{k^2(n^3 - n)} \tag{16.3}$$

S is the sum of the deviations squared of the totals of the n ranks from their mean. S is a between-groups sum of squares for ranks. It is like ss_b. (In fact, if we divide S by k, S/k, we obtain the between sum of squares we would obtain in a complete analysis of variance of the ranks.)

$$S = (5^2 + 6^2 + \cdots + 15^2) - (63)^2/6 = 787 - 661.5 = 125.5$$

Since $k = 3$ and $n = 6$,

$$W = \frac{12 \times 125.50}{3^2(6^3 - 6)} = \frac{1506}{9(216 - 6)} = \frac{1506}{1890} = .797 = .80$$

The relation between the three sets of ranks is substantial.

To assess the significance of W, the following formula can be used, provided that $k \geq 8$ and $n \geq 7$ (degrees of freedom are $n - 1$):

$$\chi^2 = k(n - 1)W \tag{16.4}$$

---

[12] Using another method of analysis of variance based on ranges rather than variances, the results of the Friedman test are confirmed. This method, called the *studentized range test,* is useful. For details, see E. Pearson and H. Hartley, eds., *Biometrika Tables for Statisticians.* Cambridge: Cambridge University Press, 1954, vol. I, pp. 51–54 and 176–179. Ranges are good measures of variation for small samples but not for large samples. The principle of the studentized range test is similar to that of the F test in that a ''within-groups range'' is used to evaluate the range of the means of the groups. Another useful method, that of Link and Wallace, is described in detail in Mosteller and Bush, *op. cit.,* pp. 304–307. Both methods have the advantage that they can be used with one-way and two-way analyses. Still another method, which has the unique virtue of testing an *ordered* hypothesis of the ranks, is the L test: E. Page, ''Ordered Hypotheses for Multiple Treatments: A Significance Test for Linear Ranks,'' *Journal of the American Statistical Association,* 58 (1963), 216–230.

[13] Kendall, *op. cit.,* chap. 6.

If k and n are small, appropriate tables of S can be used.[14] $W = .80$ is statistically significant at the .01 level. The relation is high: evidently there is high agreement of the three groups in their rankings of the professors.

PROPERTIES OF NONPARAMETRIC METHODS[15]

A large number of good nonparametric methods are readily available, many or most of them in Bradley's book. They are usually based on some property of data that can be tested against chance expectation. For example, the odds and evens of coin-tossing are a dichotomous property that is conveniently tested with binomial statistics (see Chapter 7, above). Another data property is range. With small samples, the range is a good index of variability. A quick method of estimating the standard error of the mean (MB, pp. 323–324), for instance is:

$$SE_{M(e)} = \frac{\text{Largest observation} - \text{Smallest observation}}{N}$$

A t test of the difference between two means can be made with the following formula:

$$t_e = \frac{\bar{X}_1 - \bar{X}_2}{\frac{1}{2}(R_1 + R_2)}$$

where t_e = estimated t; R_1 = range of group 1, and R_2 = range of group 2 (see MB, p. 324).

Another property of data is what can be called periodicity. If there are different kinds of events (heads and tails, male and female, religious preference, etc.), and numerical data from different groups are combined and ranked, then by chance there should not be long runs of any particular event, like a long run of females in one experimental group. The runs test is based on this idea.

Still another property of data was discussed in Chapter 11: distribution. The distributions of different samples can be compared with each other or with a "criterion" group (like the normal distribution) for deviations. The Kolmogorov-Smirnov test (S, pp. 47–52, 127–136) tests goodness of fit of the distributions. It is a useful test, especially for small samples.

The most ubiquitous property of data, perhaps, is rank order. Whenever data can be ranked, they can be tested against chance expectation. Many, perhaps most, nonparametric tests are rank-order tests. The Kruskal-Wallace and the Friedman tests are, of course, both based on rank order. Rank-order coefficients of correlation are extremely useful. W is one of these. So are the Spearman rank-order coefficient of correlation (S, pp. 202–213) and Kendall's *tau* (S, pp. 213–223).

Nonparametric methods are virtually inexhaustible. There seems to be no end to what can be done, given the relatively simple principles involved and the various properties of data that can be exploited: range, periodicity, distribution, and rank order. While means and variances have desirable statistical properties and advantages, we are in no way restricted to them. Medians and ranges, for example, are often appropriate ingredients of statistical tests. Much of the point of this chapter has been a covert repetition of the

---

[14] Bradley, *op. cit.*, pp. 323–325. F ratios are also possible. One way is to do a two-way analysis of variance using the ranks as scores. Then $\eta^2 = W$, and the F ratio tests both the statistical significance of η^2 and of W.

[15] To expedite referencing, the following abbreviations will be used: MB: Mosteller and Bush, *op. cit.*; S: S. Siegel, *Nonparametric Statistics for the Behavioral Sciences*. New York: McGraw-Hill, 1956.

principle emphasized again and again—perhaps a bit tediously: Assess obtained results against chance expectation. There is no magic to nonparametric methods. No divine benison has been put on them. The same probabilistic principles apply.

Another point made earlier needs repetition and emphasis: Most analytic problems of behavioral research can be adequately handled with parametric methods. The F test, t test, and other parametric approaches are robust in the sense that they perform well even when the assumptions behind them are violated—unless, of course, the violations are gross or multiple. Nonparametric methods, then, are highly useful secondary or complementary techniques that can often be valuable in behavioral research. Perhaps most important, they again show the power, flexibility, and wide applicability of the basic precepts of probability and the phenomenon of randomness enunciated in earlier chapters.

Study Suggestions

1. A teacher interested in studying the effect of workbooks decides to conduct a small experiment with her class. She randomly divides the class into 3 groups of 7 pupils each, calling these groups, A_1, A_2, and A_3. A_1 was taught without any workbooks, A_2 was taught with the occasional use of workbooks at the teacher's direction, and A_3 was taught with heavy dependence on workbooks. At the end of four months, the teacher tested the children in the subject matter. The scores she obtained were in percentage form, and she thought that it might be questionable to use parametric analysis of variance.[16] So she used the Kruskal-Wallis method. The data are as follows:

A_1	A_2	A_3
.55	.82	.09
.32	.24	.35
.74	.91	.25
.09	.36	.36
.48	.86	.20
.61	.80	.07
.12	.65	.36

Convert the percentages into ranks (from 1 through 21) and calculate H. Interpret. (To be significant, H must be 5.99 or greater for the .05 level, and 9.21 for the .01 level. This is at $k - 1 = 2$ degrees of freedom, the χ^2 table.)

(*Note:* Two cases of tied percentages and consequently tied ranks occur in these data. When ties occur, simply take the median (or mean) of the ties. For example, there are three .36's in the above table. The median (or mean) of the tenth, eleventh, and twelfth ranks, is 11. All three .36's, then, will be assigned the rank of 11. The next higher rank must then be 13, since 10, 11, and 12 have been "used up." Similarly there are two .09's, which occur at the second and third ranks. The median of 2 and 3 is 2.5. Both .09's are assigned 2.5 and the next higher rank, of course, is 4.) [*Answer H* = 7.86 (.05).]

2. The relation between the discussion behavior of members of boards of education and their decisions was studied by a social psychological researcher. In this research, a particularly complex facet of discussion behavior, say antagonistic behavior, was to be measured. She wondered if this behavior could be reliably measured. She trained three observers and had them rank order the antagonistic behavior of the members of one board of education during a two-hour session. The ranks of the three observers are given below (high ranks show high antagonism):

---

[16] When scores are in percentage form, they can easily be transformed to scores amenable to parametric analysis. The appropriate transformation is called the *arc-sine transformation*, a table for which can be found in R. Fisher and F. Yates, *Statistical Tables for Biological, Agricultural, and Medical Research*, 5th ed. New York: Hafner, 1957, Table X, p. 70.

Board Members	Observers		
	O_1	O_2	O_3
1	3	2	2
2	2	4	1
3	6	6	7
4	1	1	3
5	7	7	6
6	4	3	5
7	5	5	4

(a) What is the degree of agreement or concordance among the three observers? (Use W.)

(b) Is W statistically significant? (Calculate χ^2 using Equation 16.4. If $\chi^2 \geq 12.59$, $df = 6$, it is significant at .05.)

(c) Can the social psychologist say that she is reliably measuring "antagonism" or "antagonistic behavior"?

[*Answers:* (a) $W = .86$; $\chi^2 = 15.43$ ($p < .05$); (b) Yes.]

3. Using the "data" of Study Suggestion 2, above, do a one-way analysis of variance of the board members' antagonism scores.

(a) What is the F ratio? Is it statistically significant?

(b) Calculate η^2. (Recall that $\eta^2 = ss_b/ss_t$.) Compare to W calculated in Study Suggestion 2, above.

(c) Do the board of education members differ in antagonistic behavior?

[*Answers:* (a) $F = 14.00$ ($p < .01$); (b) $\eta^2 = W = .86$; (c) Yes.]

4. Suppose you obtained the following scores on a complexity measure: 27, 21, 14, 12, 6. Do a rough and quick estimate of the standard error of the mean (see text).

[*Answer:* (27-6)/5 = 4.20.]

5. Imagine that you are an analytic specialist and that you have been asked to invent and produce a method for assessing the statistical significance of runs. A *run* is a group of values or identifications connected with one population or sample. Suppose that we have a sample of men and women and we are measuring some attribute but we have no interest in sex as a variable. We rank order the sample according to the sizes of the attribute scores. If sex has no relation to the attribute, then when we rank order the cases the men and women should be mixed as though we had placed them throughout the sample at random. In this case there would be many runs, for example, *MM F M FFF M F MM FF M F,* and thus little or no relation between sex and the attribute. (Remember: the cases were ranked by the attribute.) There are 10 runs; they are italicized. This is relatively many in a sample of 15 cases. If, on the other hand, there were relatively few runs, for example: *MMMM F MM F M FFFFFF,* or six runs, there could well be a relation between the attribute and sex.

(a) How would you go about creating a test to assess the statistical significance of numbers of runs in a sample of n cases? (*Hint:* Think of using a random number generator on a computer or a table of random numbers. Don't try to find a formula. Just use brute force!)

(b) Make up two cases of samples of 20 each containing different numbers of runs and use your test to assess the significance of numbers of runs.

(c) Outline the basic principles of what you have done so that someone who does not know or understand statistics will understand you. Is your test a nonparametric test?

[*Special note:* This is probably a difficult exercise, but one well worth working at and discussing with others, especially in class.]

PART SIX

DESIGNS OF RESEARCH

Chapter 17

Research Design: Purpose and Principles

RESEARCH DESIGN is the plan and structure of investigation so conceived as to obtain answers to research questions. The *plan* is the overall scheme or program of the research. It includes an outline of what the investigator will do from writing the hypotheses and their operational implications to the final analysis of data. The structure of research is harder to explain because "structure" is difficult to define clearly and unambiguously. Since it is a concept that becomes increasingly important as we continue our study, we here break off and attempt a definition and a brief explanation. The discourse will necessarily be somewhat abstract at this point. Later examples, however, will be more concrete. More important, we will find the concept powerful, useful, even indispensable, especially in our later study of multivariate analysis where "structure" is a key concept whose understanding is essential to understanding much contemporary research methodology.

A *structure* is the framework, organization, or configuration of elements of the structure related in specified ways. The best way to specify a structure is to write a mathematical equation that relates the parts of the structure to each other. Such a mathematical equation, since its terms are defined and specifically related by the equation (or set of equations), is unambiguous. In short, a structure is a paradigm or model of the relations among the variables of a study.[1] A research design expresses both the structure of the research problem and the plan of investigation used to obtain empirical evidence on the relations of the problem. We will soon encounter examples of both design and structure that will perhaps enliven this abstract discussion.

---

[1] The words "structure," "model," and "paradigm" are troublesome because they are hard to define clearly and unambiguously. A "paradigm" is a model, an example. Diagrams, graphs, and verbal outlines are paradigms. We use "paradigm" here rather than "model" because "model" has another important meaning in science, a meaning we return to in Chapter 36 when we discuss the testing of theory using multivariate procedure and "models" of aspects of theories.

PURPOSES OF RESEARCH DESIGN

Research design has two basic purposes: (1) *to provide answers to research questions* and (2) *to control variance*. Design helps investigators obtain answers to the questions of research and also helps them to control the experimental, extraneous, and error variances of the particular research problem under study. Since all research activity can be said to have the purpose of providing answers to research questions, it is possible to omit this purpose from the discussion and to say that research design has one grand purpose: to control variance. Such a delimitation of the purpose of design, however, is dangerous. Without strong stress on the research questions and on the use of design to help provide answers to these questions, the study of design can degenerate into an interesting, but sterile, technical exercise.

Research designs are invented to enable researchers to answer research questions as validly, objectively, accurately, and economically as possible. Research plans are deliberately and specifically conceived and executed to bring empirical evidence to bear on the research problem. Research problems can be and are stated in the form of hypotheses. At some point in the research they are stated so that they can be empirically tested. Designs are carefully worked out to yield dependable and valid answers to the research questions epitomized by the hypotheses. We can make one observation and infer that the hypothesized relation exists on the basis of this one observation, but it is obvious that we cannot accept the inference so made. On the other hand, it is also possible to make hundreds of observations and to infer that the hypothesized relation exists on the basis of these many observations. In this case we may or may not accept the inference as valid. The result depends on how the observations and the inference were made. Adequately planned and executed design helps greatly in permitting us to rely on both our observations and our inferences.

How does design accomplish this? Research design sets up the framework for study of the relations among variables. Design tells us, in a sense, what observations to make, how to make them, and how to analyze the quantitative representations of the observations. Strictly speaking, design does not "tell" us precisely what to do, but rather "suggests" the directions of observation-making and analysis. An adequate design "suggests," for example, how many observations should be made, and which variables are active and which are attribute. We can then act to manipulate the active variables and to categorize and measure the attribute variables. A design tells us what type of statistical analysis to use. Finally, an adequate design outlines possible conclusions to be drawn from the statistical analysis.

An Example

It has been said that colleges and universities discriminate against women in hiring and in admissions.[2] Suppose we wish to test discrimination in admissions. We set up an experiment as follows. To a random sample of 200 colleges we send applications for admission basing the applications on several model cases selected over a range of tested ability with all details the same except for sex. Half the applications will be those of men and half women. Other things equal, we expect approximately equal numbers of acceptances and

---

[2]The idea for the example to be used came from the unusual and ingenious experiment cited earlier: E. Walster, T. Cleary, and M. Clifford, "The Effect of Race and Sex on College Admission," *Sociology of Education*, 44 (1971), 237–244.

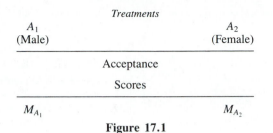

Figure 17.1

rejections. Acceptance, then, is the dependent variable. It is measured on a three-point scale: full acceptance, qualified acceptance, rejection. Call male A_1 and female A_2. The paradigm of the design is given in Figure 17.1.

The design is the simplest possible, given minimum requirements of control. The two treatments will be assigned to the colleges at random. Each college, then, will receive one application, which will be either male or female. The difference between the means, M_{A_1} and M_{A_2}, will be tested for statistical significance with a t or F test. The substantive hypothesis is: $M_{A_1} > M_{A_2}$, or more males than females will be accepted for admission. If there is no discrimination in admissions, then $M_{A_1} = M_{A_2}$, statistically. Suppose that an F test indicates that the means are not significantly different. Can we then be sure that there is no discrimination practiced (on the average)? While the design of Figure 17.1 is satisfactory as far as it goes, perhaps it does not go far enough.

A Stronger Design

Walster and her colleagues used two other independent variables, race and ability, in a factorial design. We drop race—it was not statistically significant, nor did it interact significantly with the other variables—and concentrate on sex and ability. If a college bases its selection of incoming students strictly on ability, there is no discrimination (unless, of course, ability selection is called discrimination). Add ability to the design of Figure 17.1; use three levels. That is, in addition to the applications being designated male and female, they are also designated as high, medium, and low ability. For example, three of the applications may be: male, medium ability; female, high ability; female, low ability. Now, if there is no significant difference between sexes *and* the interaction between sex and ability is not significant, this would be considerably stronger evidence for no discrimination than that yielded by the design and statistical test of Figure 17.1. We now use the expanded design to explain this statement and to discuss a number of points about research design. The expanded design is given in Figure 17.2.

The design is a 2×3 factorial. One independent variable, A, is sex, the same as in Figure 17.1. The second independent variable, B, is ability, which is manipulated by indicating in several ways what the ability levels of the students are.[3] Let's assume that we believe discrimination against women takes a more subtle form than simply across-the-board exclusion: that it is the women of lower ability who are discriminated against (compared to men). This is an interaction hypothesis. At any rate, we use this problem and the paradigm of Figure 17.2 as a basis for discussing some elements of research design.

---

[3] It is important not to be confused by the names of the variables. Sex and ability are ordinarily attribute variables and thus nonexperimental. In this case, however, they are manipulated. The student records sent to the colleges were systematically adjusted to fit the six cells of Figure 17.2. A case in the A_1B_2 cell, for instance, would be the record of a male of medium ability. It is this record that the college judges for admission.

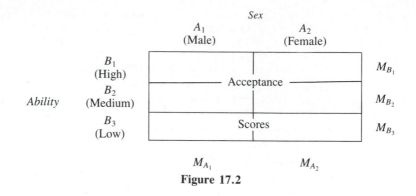

Figure 17.2

Research problems suggest research designs. Since the hypothesis just discussed is one of interaction, a factorial design is evidently appropriate. *A* is *sex; B* is *ability*. *A* is partitioned into A_1 and A_2, and *B* into B_1, B_2, and B_3.

The paradigm of Figure 17.2 suggests a number of things. First and most obvious, a fairly large number of subjects is needed. Specifically, $6n$ subjects are necessary (n = number of S's in each cell). If we decide that n should be 20, then we must have 120 S's for the experiment. Note the "wisdom" of the design here. If we were only testing the treatments and ignoring ability, only $2n$ S's would be needed.[4]

Second, the design indicates that the "subjects" (colleges, in this case) can be randomly assigned to both *A* and *B* because both are experimental variables. If ability were a nonexperimental attribute variable, however, then the subjects could be randomly assigned to A_1 and A_2, but not to B_1, B_2, and B_3. Third, according to the design the observations made on the "subjects" must be made independently. The score of one college must not affect the score of another college. Reducing a design to an outline like that of Figure 17.2 in effect prescribes the operations necessary for obtaining the measures that are appropriate for the statistical analysis. An *F* test depends on the assumption of the independence of the measures of the dependent variable. If ability here is an attribute variable and individuals are measured for intelligence, say, then the independence requirement is in greater jeopardy because of the possibility of one subject seeing another subject's paper, because teachers may unknowingly (or knowingly) "help" children with answers, and for other reasons. Researchers try to prevent such things—not on moral grounds but to satisfy the requirements of sound design and sound statistics.

A fourth point is quite obvious to us by now: Figure 17.2 suggests factorial analysis of variance, *F* tests, measures of association, and, perhaps, post hoc tests. If the research is well designed before the data are gathered—as it certainly was by Walster et al.—most statistical problems can be solved. In addition, certain troublesome problems can be avoided before they arise or can even be prevented from arising at all. With an inadequate design, however, problems of appropriate statistical tests may be very troublesome. One reason for the strong emphasis in this book on treating design and statistical problems

[4]There are ways to determine how many subjects are needed in a study. Such determination is part of the subject of "power," which refers to the ability of a test of statistical significance to detect differences in means (or other statistics) when such differences indeed exist. While important, we forego consideration of power and related ideas. See W. Hays, *Statistics,* 3d ed. New York: Holt, Rinehart and Winston, 1981, pp. 247ff. A method for determining appropriate sample sizes is given in: A. Edwards, *Experimental Design in Psychological Research,* 4th ed. New York: Holt, Rinehart and Winston, 1972, pp. 89–92; R. Krejcie and D. Morgan, "Determining Sample Size for Research Activities," *Educational and Psychological Measurement,* 30 (1970), 607–610. Both references give tables that can be helpful in determining sample sizes.

concomitantly is to point out ways to avoid these problems. If design and statistical analysis are planned simultaneously, the analytical work is usually straightforward and uncluttered.

A highly useful dividend of design is this: A clear design, like that in Figure 17.2, suggests the statistical tests that can be made. A simple one-variable randomized design with two partitions, for example, two treatments, A_1 and A_2, permits only a statistical test of the difference between the two statistics yielded by the data. These statistics might be two means, two medians, two ranges, two variances, two percentages, and so forth. Only one statistical test is ordinarily possible. With the design of Figure 17.2, however, three statistical tests are possible: (1) between A_1 and A_2; (2) among B_1, B_2, and B_3; and (3) the interaction of A and B. In most investigations, all the statistical tests are not of equal importance. The important ones, naturally, are those directly related to the research problems and hypotheses.

In the present case the interaction hypothesis [or (3), above] is the important one, since the discrimination is supposed to depend on ability level. Colleges may practice discrimination at different levels of ability. As suggested above, females (A_2) may be accepted more than males (A_1) at the higher ability level (B_1), whereas they may be accepted less at the lower ability level (B_3).

It should be evident that research design is not static. A knowledge of design can help us to plan and do better research and can also suggest the testing of hypotheses. Probably more important, we may be led to realize that the design of a study is not in itself adequate to the demands we are making of it. What is meant by this somewhat peculiar statement?

Assume that we formulate the interaction hypothesis as outlined above without knowing anything about factorial design. We set up a design consisting, actually, of two experiments. In one of these experiments we test A_1 against A_2 under condition B_1. In the second experiment we test A_1 against A_2 under condition B_2. The paradigm would look like that of Figure 17.3. (To make matters simpler, we are only using two levels of B, B_1 and B_3, but changing B_3 to B_2. The design is thus reduced to 2 × 2.)

The important point to note is that no *adequate* test of the hypothesis is possible with this design. A_1 can be tested against A_2 under both B_1 and B_2 conditions, to be sure. But it is not possible to know, clearly and unambiguously, whether there is a significant interaction between A and B. Even if $M_{A_1} > M_{A_2}|B_2$ (M_{A_1} is greater than M_{A_2}, under condition B_2), as hypothesized, the design cannot provide a clear possibility of confirming the hypothesized interaction since we cannot obtain information about the differences between A_1 and A_2 at the two levels of B, B_1 and B_2. Remember that an interaction hypothesis implies, in this case, that the difference between A_1 and A_2 is different at B_1 from what it is at B_2. In other words, information of both A and B *together in one experiment* is needed to test an interaction hypothesis. If the statistical results of separate experiments showed a significant difference between A_1 and A_2 in one experiment under the B_1 condition, and no significant difference in another experiment under the B_2 condition, then there is good *presumptive* evidence that the interaction hypothesis is correct. But pre-

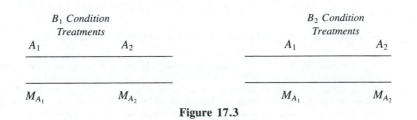

Figure 17.3

	A_1	A_2	
B_1	30	30	30
B_2	40	30	35
	35	30	

Figure 17.4

sumptive evidence is not good enough, especially when we know that it is possible to obtain better evidence.

In Figure 17.3, suppose the means of the cells were, from left to right: 30, 30; 40, 30. This result would seem to support the interaction hypothesis, since there is a significant difference between A_1 and A_2 at level B_2, but not at level B_1. But we could not know this to be certainly so, even though the difference between A_1 and A_2 is statistically significant. Figure 17.4 shows how this would look if a factorial design had been used.

(The figures in the cells and on the margins are means.) Assuming that the main effects, A_1 and A_2; B_1 and B_2, were significant, it is still possible that the interaction is not significant. Unless the interaction hypothesis is specifically tested, the evidence for interaction is merely presumptive, because the planned statistical interaction test that a factorial design provides is lacking. It should be clear that a knowledge of design could have improved this experiment.

RESEARCH DESIGN AS VARIANCE CONTROL

The main technical function of research design is *to control variance*. A research design is, in a manner of speaking, a set of instructions to the investigator to gather and analyze data in certain ways. It is therefore a control mechanism. The statistical principle behind this mechanism, as stated earlier, is: *Maximize systematic variance, control extraneous systematic variance, and minimize error variance*. In other words, we must *control variance*.

According to this principle, by constructing an efficient research design the investigator attempts (1) to maximize the variance of the variable or variables of his substantive research hypothesis, (2) to control the variance of extraneous or "unwanted" variables that may have an effect on his experimental outcomes, and (3) to minimize the error or random variance, including so-called errors of measurement. Let us look at an example.

A Controversial Example

Controversy is rich in all science. It seems to be especially rich and varied in behavioral science. Two such controversies have arisen from different theories of human behavior and learning. Reinforcement theorists have amply demonstrated that positive reinforcement can enhance learning. As usual, however, things are not so simple. The presumed beneficial effect of external rewards has been questioned; research has shown that extrinsic reward can have a deleterious influence on children's motivation, intrinsic interest, and learning.[5] Amabile has shown that external evaluation has a deleterious effect on

---

[5] For example, E. Deci, "Effects of Externally Mediated Rewards on Intrinsic Motivation," *Journal of Personality and Social Psychology*, 18 (1971), 105–115, and M. Lepper, D. Greene, and R. Nisbett, "Undermining Children's Intrinsic Interest with Extrinsic Reward: A Test of the 'Overjustification' Hypothesis," *Journal of Personality and Social Psychology*, 28 (1973), 129–137. For a review of the research, see M. Lepper and D. Greene, eds., *The Hidden Costs of Reward*. Hillsdale, N.J.: Erlbaum, 1978.

artistic creativity.[6] So even the seemingly straightforward principle of reinforcement is not so straightforward.

There is a substantial body of belief and research that indicates that college students learn well under a regime of what has been called mastery learning. Very briefly ''mastery learning'' means a system of pedagogy based on personalized instruction and requiring students to learn curriculum units to a mastery criterion.[7] If there is substantial research supporting the efficacy of mastery learning, there is at least one study—and a fine study it is—whose results indicate that students taught with the approach do no better than students taught with a conventional approach of lecture, discussion, and recitation.[8] Controversy enters the picture because mastery learning adherents seem so strongly convinced of its virtues, while its doubters are almost equally skeptical. Will research decide the matter? Hardly. But let's see how one might approach a relatively modest study capable of yielding at least a partial *empirical* answer.

An educational investigator decides to test the hypothesis that achievement in science is enhanced more by a mastery learning method (ML) than by a traditional method (T). We ignore the details of the methods and concentrate on the design of the research. Call the mastery learning method A_1 and the traditional method A_2. The investigator knows that other possible independent variables influence achievement: intelligence, sex, social class background, previous experience with science, motivation, and so on. He has reason to believe that the two methods work differently with different kinds of students. They may work differently, for example, with students of different scholastic aptitudes. The traditional approach is effective, perhaps, with students of high aptitude, whereas mastery learning is more effective with students of low aptitude. Call aptitude B: high aptitude is B_1 and low aptitude B_2.[9]

What kind of design should be set up? To answer this question it is important to label the variables and to know clearly what questions are being asked. The variables are:

Independent Variables		Dependent Variable
Methods	Aptitude	Science Achievement
Mastery Learning, A_1	High Aptitude, B_1	Test scores,
Traditional, A_2	Low Aptitude, B_2	Science

The investigator may also have included other variables in the design, especially variables potentially influential on achievement: general intelligence, social class, sex, high school average, for example. He decides, however, that random assignment will take care of intelligence and other possible influential independent variables. His dependent variable measure is provided by a standardized science knowledge test.

The problem seems to call for a factorial design. There are two reasons for this choice.

[6]T. Amabile, ''Effects of External Evaluation on Artistic Creativity,'' *Journal of Personality and Social Psychology,* 37 (1979), 221–233.

[7]For a review, see J. Block and R. Burns, ''Mastery Learning.'' In L. Shulman, ed., *Review of Research in Education,* vol. 4. Itasca, Ill.: Peacock, 1976. The mastery learning approach is more complex than the above brief characterization indicates.

[8]S. Thompson, ''Do Individualized Mastery and Traditional Instruction Systems Yield Different Course Effects in College Calculus?'' *American Educational Research Journal,* 17 (1980), 361–375. This is an exemplary study, done with careful controls over an extended time period. The example elaborated below was inspired by the Thompson study. Its design and controls, however, are much simpler than Thompson's. Note, too, that Thompson had an enormous advantage: He did his experiment in a military establishment. This means, of course, that many control problems, usually recalcitrant in educational research, are easily solved. Why?

[9]As we will see when we study multiple regression, this is not the best way to handle the aptitude variable. When a continuous measure is dichotomized or trichotomized, variance is lost. We return to this point in later discussions.

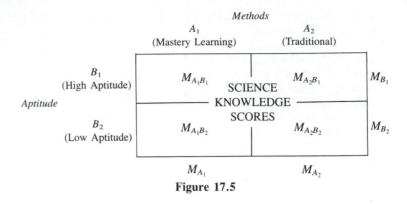

Figure 17.5

One, there are two independent variables. Two, the investigator has quite clearly an interaction hypothesis in mind, though he may not have stated it in so many words, since he has the belief that the methods will work differently with different kinds of students. We set up the design structure in Figure 17.5.

Note that all the marginal and cell means have been appropriately labeled. Note, too, that there is one *active variable,* methods, and one *attribute variable,* aptitude.[10] All he can do is to categorize his subjects as high aptitude and low aptitude and assign them accordingly to B_1 and B_2. He can, however, and *does* randomly assign the students to A_1 and A_2, the methods groups. This he does in two stages: (1) he randomly assigns the B_1 (high aptitude) students to A_1 and A_2 and (2) he assigns the B_2 (low aptitude) students to A_1 and A_2. By so randomizing the subjects the investigator can assume that before the experiment begins, the students in A_1 are approximately equal to the students in A_2 in all possible characteristics.

Our present concern is with the different roles of variance in research design and the variance principle. Before going further, we name the variance principle for easy reference—the "maxmincon" principle. The origin of this name is obvious: *max*imize the systematic variance under study; *con*trol extraneous systematic variance; and *min*imize error variance—with two of the syllables reversed for euphony.

Before tackling the application of the maxmincon principle in the present example, an important point should be discussed. Whenever we talk about variance, we must be sure to know *what* variance we are talking about. We speak of the variance of the methods, of intelligence, of sex, of type of home, and so on. This sounds as though we were talking about the independent variable variance. This is true and not true. We always mean *the variance of the dependent variable, the variance of the dependent variable measures,* after the experiment has been done.[11] Our way of saying "independent variable variance" stems from the fact that, by manipulation and control of independent variables, we *influence,* presumably, the variance of the dependent variable. Somewhat inaccurately put, we "make" the measures of the dependent variable behave or vary as a presumed result of our manipulation and control of the independent variables. In an experiment, it is the dependent variable measures that are analyzed. Then, from the analysis we *infer* that the

[10] It will be remembered from Chapter 3 that an *active variable* is an experimental or manipulated variable, and an *attribute variable* is a measured variable, or a variable that is a characteristic of people or groups, e.g., intelligence, social class, and occupation (people), and cohesiveness, productivity, and restrictive-permissive atmosphere (organizations, groups, and the like).

[11] This is not true in so-called correlational studies where, when we say "the variance of the independent variable," we mean just that. When correlating two variables, we study the variances of the independent and dependent variables "directly."

variances present in the total variance of the dependent variable measures are due to the manipulation and control of the independent variables and to error. Now, back to our principle.

MAXIMIZATION OF EXPERIMENTAL VARIANCE

The experimenter's most obvious, but not necessarily most important, concern is to maximize what we will call the *experimental variance*. This term is introduced to facilitate subsequent discussions and, in general, simply refers to the variance of the dependent variable influenced by the independent variable or variables of the substantive hypothesis. In this particular case, the experimental variance is the variance in the dependent variable presumably due to methods, A_1 and A_2, and aptitude, B_1 and B_2. Although experimental variance can be taken to mean only the variance due to a manipulated or *active* variable, like methods, we shall also consider *attribute* variables, like intelligence, sex, and, in this case, aptitude, experimental variables. One of the main tasks of an experimenter is to maximize this variance. He must "pull" the methods apart as much as possible to make A_1 and A_2 (and A_3, A_4, and so on, if they are in the design) as unlike as possible.

If the independent variable does not vary substantially, there is little chance of separating its effect from the total variance of the dependent variable. It is necessary to give the variance of a relation a chance to show itself, to separate itself, so to speak, from the total variance, which is a composite of variances due to numerous sources and chance. Remembering this subprinciple of the maxmincon principle, we can write a research precept: *Design, plan, and conduct research so that the experimental conditions are as different as possible.*[12]

In the present research example, this subprinciple means that the investigator must take pains to make A_1 and A_2, the mastery learning and traditional methods, as different as possible. Next, he must so categorize B_1 and B_2 that they are different on the aptitude dimension. This latter problem is essentially one of measurement, as we will see in a later chapter. In an experiment, the investigator is like a puppeteer making the independent variable puppets do what he wants. He holds the strings of the A_1 and A_2 puppets in his right hand and the strings of the B_1 and B_2 puppets in his left hand. (We assume there is no influence of one hand on the other, that is, the hands must be independent.) He makes the A_1 and A_2 puppets dance apart, and he makes the B_1 and B_2 puppets dance apart. He then watches his audience (the dependent variable) to see and measure the effect of his manipulations. If he is successful in making A_1 and A_2 dance apart, and if there is a relation between A and the dependent variable, the audience reaction—if separating A_1 and A_2 is funny, for instance—should be laughter. He may even observe that he only gets laughter when A_1 and A_2 dance apart and, at the same time, B_1 or B_2 dance apart (interaction again).

CONTROL OF EXTRANEOUS VARIABLES

The control of extraneous variables means that the influences of independent variables extraneous to the purposes of the study are minimized, nullified, or isolated. There are three ways to control extraneous variables. The first is the easiest, if it is possible: to

---

[12] There are, of course, exceptions to this subprinciple, but they are probably rare. An investigator might want to study the effects of small gradations of, say, motivational incentives on the learning of some subject matter. Here he would not make his experimental conditions as different as possible. Still, he would have to make them vary somewhat or there would be no discernible resulting variance in the dependent variable.

eliminate the variable as a variable. If we are worried about intelligence as a possible contributing factor in studies of achievement, its effect on the dependent variable can be virtually eliminated by using subjects of only one intelligence level, say intelligence scores within the range of 90 to 110. If we are studying achievement, and racial membership is a possible contributing factor to the variance of achievement, it can be eliminated by using only members of one race. The principle is: *To eliminate the effect of a possible influential independent variable on a dependent variable, choose subjects so that they are as homogeneous as possible on that independent variable.*

This method of controlling unwanted or extraneous variance is very effective. If we select only one sex for an experiment, then we can be sure that sex cannot be a contributing independent variable. But then we lose generalization power; for instance we can say nothing about the relation under study with girls if we use only boys in the experiment. If the range of intelligence is restricted, then we can discuss only this restricted range. Is it possible that the relation, if discovered, is nonexistent or quite different with children of high intelligence or children of low intelligence? We simply do not know; we can only surmise or guess.

The second way to control extraneous variance is through randomization. This is the best way, in the sense that you can have your cake and eat some of it, too. Theoretically, randomization is the only method of controlling *all* possible extraneous variables. Another way to phrase it is: if randomization has been accomplished, then the experimental groups can be considered statistically equal in all possible ways. This does not mean, of course, that the groups *are* equal in all the possible variables. We already know that by chance the groups can be unequal, but the probability of their being equal is greater, with proper randomization, than the probability of their not being equal. For this reason control of the extraneous variance by randomization is a powerful method of control. All other methods leave many possibilities of inequality. If we match for intelligence, we may successfully achieve statistical equality in intelligence (at least in those aspects of intelligence measured), but we may suffer from inequality in other significantly influential independent variables like aptitude, motivation, and social class. A precept that springs from this equalizing power of randomization, then, is: *Whenever it is possible to do so, randomly assign subjects to experimental groups and conditions, and randomly assign conditions and other factors to experimental groups.*

The third means of controlling an extraneous variable is to build it right into the design as an independent variable. For example, assume that sex was to be controlled in the experiment discussed earlier and it was considered inexpedient or unwise to eliminate it. One could add a third independent variable, sex, to the design. Unless one were interested in the actual difference between the sexes on the dependent variable or wanted to study the interaction between one or two of the other variables and sex, however, it is unlikely that this form of control would be used. One might want information of the kind just mentioned and also want to control sex, too. In such a case, adding it to the design as a variable might be desirable. The point is that building a variable into an experimental design "controls" the variable, since it then becomes possible to extract from the total variance of the dependent variable the variance due to the variable. (In the above case, this would be the "between-sexes" variance.)

These considerations lead to another principle: *An extraneous variable can be controlled by building it into the research design as an attribute variable, thus achieving control and yielding additional research information about the effect of the variable on the dependent variable and about its possible interaction with other independent variables.*

The fourth way to control extraneous variance is to match subjects. The control principle behind matching is the same as that for any other kind of control, the control of variance. Matching is similar—in fact, it might be called a corollary—to the principle of controlling the variance of an extraneous variable by building it into the design. The basic principle is to split a variable into two or more parts, say into high and low intelligence in a factorial design, and then randomize within each level as described above. Matching is a special case of this principle. Instead of splitting the subjects into two, three, or four parts, however, they are split into $N/2$ parts, N being the number of subjects used; thus the control of variance is built into the design.

In using the matching method several problems may be encountered. To begin with, the variable on which the subjects are matched must be substantially related to the dependent variable or the matching is a waste of time. Even worse, it can be misleading. In addition, matching has severe limitations. If we try to match, say, on more than two variables, or even more than one, we lose subjects. It is difficult to find matched subjects on more than two variables. For instance, if one decides to match intelligence, sex, and social class, one may be fairly successful in matching the first two variables but not in finding pairs that are fairly equal on all three variables. Add a fourth variable and the problem becomes difficult, often impossible to solve.

Let us not throw the baby out with the bath, however. When there is a substantial correlation between the matching variable or variables and the dependent variable ($>.50$ or .60), then matching reduces the error term and thus increases the precision of an experiment, a desirable outcome. If the same subjects are used with different experimental treatments—called repeated measures or randomized blocks design—we have powerful control of variance. How match better on all possible variables than by matching a subject with himself? Unfortunately, other negative considerations usually rule out this possibility. It should be forcefully emphasized that matching of any kind is no substitute for randomization. If subjects are matched, *they should then be assigned to experimental groups at random*. Through a random procedure, like tossing a coin or using odd and even random numbers, the members of the matched pairs are assigned to experimental and control groups. If the same subjects undergo all treatments, then the order of the treatments should be assigned randomly. This adds randomization control to the matching, or repeated measures, control.

A principle suggested by this discussion is: *When a matching variable is substantially correlated with the dependent variable, matching as a form of variance control can be profitable and desirable. Before using matching, however, carefully weigh its advantages and disadvantages in the particular research situation. Complete randomization or the analysis of covariance may be better methods of variance control.*

Still another form of control, statistical control, was discussed at length in Part Five, but one or two further remarks are in order here. Statistical methods are, so to speak, forms of control in the sense that they isolate and quantify variances. But statistical control is inseparable from other forms of design control. If matching is used, for example, an appropriate statistical test must be used, or the matching effect, and thus the control, will be lost.

MINIMIZATION OF ERROR VARIANCE

Error variance is the variability of measures due to random fluctuations whose basic characteristic is that they are self-compensating, varying now this way, now that way, now positive, now negative, now up, now down. Random errors tend to balance each other so that their mean is zero.

There are a number of determinants of error variance, for instance, factors associated with individual differences among subjects. Ordinarily we call this variance due to individual differences "systematic variance." But when such variance cannot be, or is not identified and controlled, we have to lump it with the error variance. Because many determinants interact and tend to cancel each other out (or at least we assume that they do), the error variance has this random characteristic.

Another source of error variance is that associated with what are called errors of measurement: variation of responses from trial to trial, guessing, momentary inattention, slight temporary fatigue and lapses of memory, transient emotional states of subjects, and so on.

Minimizing error variance has two principal aspects: (1) the reduction of errors of measurement through controlled conditions, and (2) an increase in the reliability of measures. The more uncontrolled the conditions of an experiment, the more the many determinants of error variance can operate. This is one of the reasons for carefully setting up controlled experimental conditions. In studies under field conditions, of course, such control is difficult; still, constant efforts must be made to lessen the effects of the many determinants of error variance. This can be done, in part, by specific and clear instructions to subjects and by excluding from the experimental situation factors that are extraneous to the research purpose.

To increase the reliability of measures is to reduce the error variance. Pending fuller discussion later in the book, reliability can be taken to be the *accuracy* of a set of scores. To the extent that scores do not fluctuate randomly, to this extent they are reliable. Imagine a completely unreliable measurement instrument, one that does not allow us to predict the future performance of individuals at all, one that gives one rank ordering of a sample of subjects at one time and a completely different rank ordering at another time. With such an instrument, it would not be possible to identify and extract systematic variances, since the scores yielded by the instrument would be like the numbers in a table of random numbers. This is the extreme case. Now imagine differing amounts of reliability and unreliability in the measures of the dependent variable. The more reliable the measures, the better we can identify and extract systematic variances and the smaller the error variance in relation to the total variance.

Another reason for reducing error variance as much as possible is to give systematic variance a chance to show itself. We cannot do this if the error variance, and thus the error term, is too large. If a relation exists, we seek to discover it. One way to discover the relation is to find significant differences between means. But if the error variance is relatively large due to uncontrolled errors of measurement, the systematic variance—earlier called "between" variance—will not have a chance to appear. Thus the relation, although it exists, will probably not be detected.

The problem of error variance can be put into a neat mathematical nutshell. Remember the equation:

$$V_t = V_b + V_e$$

where V_t is the total variance in a set of measures; V_b is the between-groups variance, the variance presumably due to the influence of the experimental variables; and V_e is the error variance (in analysis of variance, the within-groups variance and the residual variance). Obviously, the larger V_e is, the smaller V_b must be, with a given amount of V_t.

Consider the following equation: $F = V_b/V_e$. For the numerator of the fraction on the right to be accurately evaluated for significant departure from chance expectation, the denominator should be an accurate measure of random error.

A familiar example may make this clear. Recall that in the discussions of factorial analysis of variance and the analysis of variance of correlated groups we talked about variance due to individual differences being present in experimental measures. We said that, while adequate randomization can effectively equalize experimental groups, there will be variance in the scores due to individual differences, for instance, differences due to intelligence, aptitude, and so on. Now, in some situations, these individual differences can be quite large. If they are, then the error variance and, consequently, the denominator of the F equation, above, will be "too large" relative to the numerator; that is, the individual differences will have been randomly scattered among, say, two, three, or four experimental groups. Still they are sources of variance and, as such, will inflate the within-groups or residual variance, the denominator of the above equation.

Study Suggestions

1. We have noted that research design has the purposes of obtaining answers to research questions and controlling variance. Explain in detail what this statement means. How does a research design control variance? Why should a factorial design control more variance than a one-way design? How does a design that uses matched subjects or repeated measures of the same subjects control variance? What is the relation between the research questions and hypotheses and a research design? In answering these questions, make up a research problem to illustrate what you mean (or use an example from the text).

2. Sir Ronald Fisher, the inventor of analysis of variance, said, in one of his books,

it should be noted that the null hypothesis is never proved or established, but is possibly disproved, in the course of experimentation. Every experiment may be said to exist only in order to give the facts a chance of disproving the null hypothesis.[13]

Whether you agree or disagree with Fisher's statement, what do you think he meant by it? In framing your answer, think of the maxmincon principle and F tests and t tests.

[13]R. Fisher, *The Design of Experiments*, 4th ed. New York: Hafner, 1951, p. 16.

Chapter 18

Inadequate Designs and Design Criteria

ALL MAN'S disciplined creations have form. Architecture, poetry, music, painting, mathematics, scientific research—all have form. Man puts great stress on the content of his creations, often not realizing that without strong structure, no matter how rich and how significant the content, the creations may be weak and sterile.

So it is with scientific research. The scientist needs viable and plastic form with which to express scientific aims. Without content—without good theory, good hypotheses, good problems—the design of research is empty. But without form, without structure adequately conceived and created for the research purpose, little of value can be accomplished. Indeed, it is no exaggeration to say that many of the failures of behavioral research have been failures of disciplined and imaginative form.

The principal focus of this chapter is on inadequate research designs. Such designs have been so common that they must be discussed. More important, the student should be able to recognize them and understand *why* they are inadequate. This negative approach has a virtue: the study of deficiencies forces one to ask why something is deficient, which in turn centers attention on the criteria used to judge both adequacies and inadequacies. So the study of inadequate designs leads us to the study of the criteria of research design. We take the opportunity, too, to describe the symbolic system to be used and to identify an important distinction between experimental and nonexperimental research.

EXPERIMENTAL AND NONEXPERIMENTAL APPROACHES

Discussion of design must be prefaced by an important distinction: that between experimental and nonexperimental approaches to research. Indeed, this distinction is so important that a separate chapter will be devoted to it later. An *experiment* is a scientific investigation in which an investigator manipulates and controls one or more independent variables and observes the dependent variable or variables for variation concomitant to the manipulation of the independent variables. An *experimental design,* then, is one in which the investigator *manipulates* at least one independent variable. Hurlock manipulated incentives to produce different amounts of retention. Walster, Cleary, and Clifford manipulated sex, race, and ability levels to study their effects on college acceptance: the application forms submitted to colleges differed in descriptions of applicants as male-female, white-black, and high, medium, or low ability levels.

In nonexperimental research one cannot manipulate variables or assign subjects or treatments at random because the nature of the variables is such as to preclude manipulation. Subjects come to us with their differing characteristics intact, so to speak. They come to us with their sex, intelligence, occupational status, creativity, or aptitude ''already there.'' In many areas of research, likewise, random assignment is unfortunately not possible, as we will see later. Although experimental and nonexperimental research differ in these crucial respects, they share structural and design features that will be pointed out in this and subsequent chapters. In addition, their basic purpose is the same: to study relations among phenomena. Their scientific logic is also the same: to bring empirical evidence to bear on conditional statements of the form If $p,$ then $q.$

The ideal of science is the controlled experiment. Except, perhaps, in taxonomic research—research with the purpose of discovering, classifying, and measuring natural phenomena and the factors behind such phenomena—the controlled experiment is the desired model of science. It may be difficult for many students to accept this rather categorical statement since its logic is not readily apparent. Earlier it was said that the main goal of science was to discover relations among phenomena. Why, then, assign a priority to the controlled experiment? Do not other methods of discovering relations exist? Yes, of course they do. The main reason for the preeminence of the controlled experiment, however, is that researchers can have more confidence that the relations they study *are* the relations they think they are. The reason is not hard to see: they study the relations under the most carefully controlled conditions of inquiry known. The unique and overwhelmingly important virtue of experimental inquiry, then, is control. In short, a perfectly conducted experimental study is more trustworthy than a perfectly conducted nonexperimental study. Why this is so should become more and more apparent as we advance in our study of research design.

SYMBOLISM AND DEFINITIONS

Before discussing inadequate designs, explanation of the symbolism to be used in these chapters is necessary. X means an *experimentally manipulated* independent variable (or variables). $X_1, X_2, X_3,$ etc. mean independent variables 1, 2, 3, and so on, though we usually use X alone, even when it can mean more than one independent variable. (We also use $X_1, X_2,$ etc. to mean partitions of an independent variable, but the difference will always be clear.) The symbol $\widehat{X}$ indicates that the independent variable is *not manipulated*—is not under the direct control of the investigator, but is *measured* or *imagined.* The dependent variable is Y: Y_b is the dependent variable *before* the manipulation of $X,$ and Y_a the dependent variable *after* the manipulation of $X.$ With $\sim X,$ we borrow the negation sign of set theory; $\sim X$ ("not-X") means that the experimental variable, the independent variable X, *is not* manipulated. (Note: $\textcircled{X}$ is a nonmanipulable variable and $\sim X$ is a manipulable variable that is *not* manipulated.) The symbol $\boxed{R}$ will be used for the random assignment of subjects to experimental groups and the random assignment of experimental treatments to experimental groups.

The explanation of $\sim X$, just given, is not quite accurate, because in some cases $\sim X$ can mean a different aspect of the treatment X rather than merely the absence of X. In an older language, *the* experimental group was the group that was given the so-called experimental treatment, X, while the control group did not receive it, $\sim X$. For our purposes, however, $\sim X$ will do well enough, especially if we understand the generalized meaning of "control" discussed below. An *experimental group*, then, is a group of subjects receiving some aspect or treatment of X. In testing the frustration-aggression hypothesis, the experimental group is the group whose subjects are systematically frustrated. In contrast, the control group is one that is given "no" treatment.

In modern multivariate research, it is necessary to expand these notions. They are not changed basically; they are only expanded. It is quite possible to have more than one experimental group, as we have seen. Different degrees of manipulation of the independent variable are not only possible; they are often also desirable or even imperative. Furthermore, it is possible to have more than one control group, a statement that at first seems like nonsense. How can one have different degrees of "no" experimental treatment?—because the notion of *control* is generalized. When there are more than two groups, and when any two of them are treated differently, one or more groups serve as "controls" on the others. Recall that control is always control of variance. With two or more groups treated differently, variance is engendered by the experimental manipulation. So the traditional notion of X and $\sim X$, treatment and no treatment, is generalized to $X_1, X_2, \ldots, X_k$, different forms or degrees of treatment.

If X is circled, $\textcircled{X}$, this means that the investigator "imagines" the manipulation of X, or he assumes that X occurred and that it is *the* X of his hypothesis. It may also mean that X is measured and not manipulated. Actually, we are saying the same thing here in different ways. The context of the discussion should make the distinction clear. Suppose a sociologist is studying delinquency and the frustration-aggression hypothesis. He observes delinquency, Y, and imagines that his delinquent subjects were frustrated in their earlier years, or $\textcircled{X}$. All nonexperimental designs will have $\textcircled{X}$. Generally, then, $\textcircled{X}$ means an independent variable not under the experimental control of the investigator.

One more point—each design in this chapter will ordinarily have an *a* and a *b* form. The *a* form will be the experimental form, or that in which X is manipulated. The *b* form will be the nonexperimental form, that in which X is not under the control of the investigator, or $\textcircled{X}$. Obviously, $\textcircled{\sim X}$ is also possible.

FAULTY DESIGNS

There are four (or more) inadequate designs of research that have often been used—and are occasionally still used—in behavioral research. The inadequacies of the designs lead to poor control of independent variables. We number each such design, give it a name, sketch its structure, and then discuss it.

Design 18.1: One-Group

(a) X	Y	(Experimental)
(b) $\textcircled{X}$	Y	(Nonexperimental)

Design 18.1 (a) has been called the "One-Shot Case Study," an apropos name.[1] The (a) form is experimental, the (b) form nonexperimental. An example of the (a) form: a school faculty institutes a new curriculum and wishes to evaluate its effects. After one year, Y, student achievement, is measured. It is concluded, say, that achievement has improved under the new program. With such a design the conclusion is weak. Design 18.1 (b) is the nonexperimental form of the one-group design. Y, the outcome, is studied, and X is assumed or imagined. An example would be to study delinquency by searching the past of a group of juvenile delinquents for factors that may have led to antisocial behavior.

Scientifically, Design 18.1 is worthless. There is virtually no control of other possible influences on outcome. As Campbell long ago pointed out, the minimum of useful scientific information requires at least one formal comparison.[2] The curriculum example requires, *at the least*, comparison of the group that experienced the new curriculum with a group that did not experience it. The presumed effect of the new curriculum, say such-and-such achievement, might well have been about the same under any kind of curriculum. The point is not that the new curriculum did or did not have an effect, but that, in the absence of any formal, controlled comparison of the performance of the members of the "experimental" group with the performance of the members of some other group not experiencing the new curriculum, little can be said about its effect.

An important distinction should be made. It is not that the method is entirely worthless, but that it is *scientifically* worthless. In everyday life, of course, we depend on such scientifically questionable evidence; we have to. We act, we say, on the basis of our experience. We hope that we use our experience rationally. The everyday-thinking paradigm implied by Design 18.1 is not being criticized. Only when such a paradigm is used and said or believed to be scientific do difficulties arise. Even in high intellectual pursuits, the thinking implied by this design is used. Freud's careful observations and brilliant and creative analysis of neurotic behavior seem to fall into this category. The quarrel is not with Freud, then, but rather with assertions that his conclusions are "scientifically established."

Design 18.2: One-Group, before-after (Pretest-Posttest)

    (a) Y_b X Y_a (Experimental)

    (b) Y_b Ⓧ Y_a (Nonexperimental)

Design 18.2 is only a small improvement on Design 18.1. The essential characteristic of this mode of research is that a group is compared with itself. Theoretically, there is no better choice since all possible independent variables associated with the subjects' characteristics are controlled. The procedure dictated by such a design is as follows. A group is measured on the dependent variable, Y, before experimental manipulation. This is usually called a *pretest*. Assume that the attitudes toward women of a group of subjects are measured. An experimental manipulation designed to change these attitudes is used. An experimenter might expose the group to expert opinion on women's rights, for example. After the interposition of this X, the attitudes of the subjects are again measured. The difference scores, or $Y_a - Y_b$, are examined for change in attitudes.

At face value, this would seem a good way to accomplish the experimental purpose. After all, if the difference scores are statistically significant, does this not indicate a change in attitudes? The situation is not so simple, however—there are a number of other

[1]D. Campbell and J. Stanley, *Experimental and Quasi-Experimental Designs for Research*. Chicago: Rand McNally, 1963, p. 6.

[2]D. Campbell, "Factors Relevant to the Validity of Experiments in Social Settings," *Psychological Bulletin*, 54 (1957), 297–312.

factors that may have contributed to the change in scores. Campbell gives an excellent detailed discussion of these factors,[3] only a brief outline of which can be given here.

Measurement, History, Maturation

First is the possible effect of the measurement procedure: measuring subjects changes them. Can it be that the post-X measures were influenced not by the manipulation of X but by increased sensitization due to the pretest? Campbell calls such measures *reactive measures*, because they themselves cause the subject to react. Controversial attitudes, for example, seem to be especially susceptible to such sensitization. Achievement measures, though probably less reactive, are still affected. Measures involving memory are susceptible. If you take a test now, you are more likely to remember later things that were included in the test. In short, observed changes may be due to reactive effects.

Two other important sources of extraneous variance are *history* and *maturation*. Between the Y_b and Y_a testings, many things can occur other than X. The longer the period of time, the greater the chance of extraneous variables affecting the subjects and thus the Y_a measures. This is what Campbell calls *history*. These variables or events are *specific* to the particular experimental situation. *Maturation*, on the other hand, covers events that are *general*, not specific to any particular situation. They reflect change or growth in the organism studied. Mental age increases with time, an increase that can easily affect achievement, memory, and attitudes. People learn in any given time interval and the learning may affect dependent variable measures. This is one of the exasperating difficulties of research that extends over considerable time periods. The longer the time interval, the greater the possibility that extraneous, unwanted sources of systematic variance will influence dependent variable measures.

The Regression Effect

A statistical phenomenon that has misled researchers is the so-called *regression effect*. Test scores change as a statistical fact of life: on retest, on the average, they *regress* toward the mean. The regression effect operates because of the imperfect correlation between the pretest and posttest scores. If $r_{ab} = 1.00$, then there is no regression effect; if $r_{ab} = .00$, the effect is at a maximum in the sense that the best prediction of any posttest score from pretest score is the mean. With the correlations found in practice, the net effect is that lower scores on the pretest tend to be higher, and higher scores lower on the posttest—when, in fact, no real change has taken place in the dependent variable. Thus, if low-scoring subjects are used in a study, their scores on the posttest will probably be higher than on the pretest due to the regression effect. This can deceive the researcher into believing that the experimental intervention has been effective when it really has not. Similarly, one may erroneously conclude that an experimental variable has had a depressing effect on high pretest scorers. Not necessarily so. The higher and lower scores of the two groups may be due to the regression effect.

How does this work? There are many chance factors at work in any set of scores.[4] On

---

[3] *Ibid.*, pp. 298–300. The first point discussed, the possible interaction effect of the pretest, seems first to have been pointed out by Solomon in an excellent article: R. Solomon, "An Extension of Control Group Design," *Psychological Bulletin*, 46 (1949), 137–150. Also see S. Stouffer, "Some Observations on Study Design," *American Journal of Sociology*, 55 (1950), 355–361.

[4] Much of this explanation is due to Anastasi's clear discussion of the regression effect: A. Anastasi, *Differential Psychology*, 3d ed. New York: Macmillan, 1958, pp. 203–205. For an equally excellent and more complete discussion, see R. Thorndike, *Concepts of Over- and Underachievement*. New York: Teachers College Press, 1963, pp. 11–15. The statistically sophisticated student should consult J. Nesselroade, S. Stigler, and P. Baltes, "Regression Toward the Mean and the Study of Change," *Psychological Bulletin*, 88 (1980), 622–637.

the pretest some high scores are higher than "they should be" due to chance, and similarly with some low scores. On the posttest it is unlikely that the high scores will be maintained, because the factors that made them high were chance factors—which are uncorrelated on the pretest and posttest. Thus the high scorer will tend to drop on the posttest. A similar argument applies to the low scorer—but in reverse.

Research designs have to be constructed with the regression effect in mind. There is no way in Design 18.2 to control it. If there were a control group, then one could "control" the regression effect, since both experimental and control groups have pretest and posttest. If the experimental manipulation has had a "real" effect, then it should be apparent over and above the regression effect. That is, the scores of both groups, other things equal, are affected the same by regression and other influences. So if the groups differ in the posttest, it should be due to the experimental manipulation.

Design 18.2 is inadequate not so much because extraneous variables and the regression effect can operate (the extraneous variables operate whenever there is a time interval between pretest and posttest), but *because we do not know whether they have operated, whether they have affected the dependent-variable measures.* The design affords no opportunity to control or to test such possible influences.

Design 18.3:   Simulated before-after

$$X \qquad\qquad Y_a$$

Y_b

The peculiar title of this design stems in part from its very nature. Like Design 18.2 it is a before-after design. Instead of using the before and after (or pretest-posttest) measures of one group, we use as pretest measures the measures of another group, which are chosen to be as similar as possible to the experimental group and thus a control group of a sort. (The line between the two levels, above, indicates separate groups.) This design satisfies the condition of having a control group and is thus a gesture toward the comparison that is necessary to scientific investigation. Unfortunately, the controls are weak, a result of our inability to know that the two groups were equivalent before X, the experimental manipulation.

Design 18.4:   Two Groups, No Control

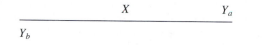

(a) $\dfrac{X \qquad Y}{\sim X \qquad Y}$ (Experimental)

(b) $\dfrac{\textcircled{X} \qquad Y}{\widetilde{\sim X} \qquad \sim Y}$ (Nonexperimental)

Design 18.4 is common. In (a) the experimental group is administered treatment X; the "control" group, taken to be, or assumed to be, similar to the experimental group, is not given X. The Y measures are compared to ascertain the effect of X. Groups or subjects are taken "as they are," or they may be matched. The nonexperimental version of the same design is labeled (b). An effect, Y, is observed to occur in one group (top line) but not in another group, or to occur in the other group to a lesser extent (indicated by the $\sim Y$ in the bottom line). The first group is found to have experienced X, the second group not to have experienced X.

This design has a basic weakness. The two groups are *assumed* to be equal in independent variables other than X. It is sometimes possible to check the equality of the groups roughly by comparing them on different pertinent variables, for example, age, sex, income, intelligence, ability, and so on. This should be done if it is at all possible, but, as

Stouffer says, "there is all too often a wide-open gate through which other uncontrolled variables can march."[5] Because randomization is not used—that is, the subjects are not assigned to the groups at random—it is not possible to assume that the groups are equal. Both versions of the design suffer seriously from lack of control of independent variables due to lack of randomization.

CRITERIA OF RESEARCH DESIGN

After examining some of the main weaknesses of inadequate research designs, we are in a good position to discuss what can be called criteria of research design. Along with the criteria, we will enunciate certain principles that should guide researchers. Finally, the criteria and principles will be related to Campbell's notions of internal and external validity, which, in a sense, express the criteria another way.

Answer Research Questions?

The main criterion or desideratum of a research design can be expressed in a question: *Does the design answer the research questions?* or *Does the design adequately test the hypotheses?* Perhaps the most serious weakness of designs often proposed by the neophyte is that they are not capable of adequately answering the research questions. A common example of this lack of congruence between the research questions and hypothesis, on the one hand, and the research design, on the other, is matching subjects for reasons irrelevant to the research and then using an experimental group-control group type of design. Students often assume, because they match pupils on intelligence and sex, for instance, that their experimental groups are equal. They have heard that one should match subjects for "control" and that one should have an experimental group and a control group. Frequently, however, the matching variables may be irrelevant to the research purposes. That is, if there is no relation between, say, sex and the dependent variable, then matching on sex is irrelevant.

Another example of this weakness is the case where three or four experimental groups are needed—for example, three experimental groups and one control group, or four groups with different amounts or aspects of X, the experimental treatment—and the investigator uses only two because he has heard that an experimental group and a control group are necessary and desirable.

The example discussed in Chapter 17 of testing an interaction hypothesis by performing, in effect, two separate experiments is another example. The hypothesis to be tested was that discrimination in college admissions is a function of both sex and ability level, that it is women of low ability who are excluded (in contrast to men of low ability). This is an interaction hypothesis and probably calls for a factorial-type design. To set up two experiments, one for college applicants of high ability and another for applicants of low ability, is poor practice because such a design, as shown earlier, cannot decisively test the stated hypothesis. Similarly, to match subjects on ability and then set up a two-group design would miss the research question entirely. These considerations lead to a general and seemingly obvious precept:

Design research to answer research questions.

[5] Stouffer, *op. cit.*, p. 522.

Control of Extraneous Independent Variables

The second criterion is *control,* which means control of independent variables: the independent variables of the research study and extraneous independent variables. Extraneous independent variables, of course, are variables that may influence the dependent variable but that are not part of the study. In the admissions study of Chapter 17, for example, geographical location (of the colleges) may be a potentially influential extraneous variable that can cloud the results of the study. If colleges in the east, for example, exclude more women than colleges in the west, then geographical location is an extraneous source of variance in the admissions measures—which should somehow be controlled. The criterion also refers to control of the variables of the study. Since this problem has already been discussed and will continue to be discussed, no more need be said here. But the question must be asked; *Does this design adequately control independent variables?*

The best single way to answer this question satisfactorily is expressed in the following principle:

> *Randomize whenever possible: select subjects at random; assign subjects to groups at random; assign experimental treatments to groups at random.*

While it may not be possible to *select* subjects at random, it may be possible to *assign* them to groups at random, thus "equalizing" the groups in the statistical sense discussed in Parts Four and Five. If such random assignment of subjects to groups is not possible, then every effort should be made to assign experimental treatments to experimental groups at random. And, if experimental treatments are administered at different times with different experimenters, times and experimenters should be assigned at random.

The principle that makes randomization pertinent is complex and difficult to implement:

> *Control the independent variables so that extraneous and unwanted sources of systematic variance have minimal opportunity to operate.*

As we have seen earlier, randomization theoretically satisfies this principle (see Chapter 8). When we test the empirical validity of an If *p,* then *q* proposition, we manipulate *p* and observe that *q* covaries with the manipulation of *p.* But how confident can we be that our If *p,* then *q* statement is really "true"? Our confidence is directly related to the completeness and adequacy of the controls. If we use a design similar to Designs 18.1 through 18.4, we cannot have too much confidence in the empirical validity of the If *p,* then *q* statement, since our control of extraneous independent variables is weak or nonexistent. Because such control is not always possible in much psychological, sociological, and educational research, should we then give up research entirely? By no means. Nevertheless, we must be aware of the weaknesses of intrinsically poor design.

Generalizability

The third criterion, *generalizability,* is independent of other criteria because it is different in kind. This is an important point that will shortly become clear. It means simply: *Can we generalize the results of a study to other subjects, other groups, and other conditions?* Perhaps the question is better put: *How much* can we generalize the results of the study? This is probably the most complex and difficult question that can be asked of research data because it touches not only on technical matters like sampling and research design, but also on larger problems of basic and applied research. In basic research, for example, generalizability is not the first consideration, because the central interest is the relations among variables and *why* the variables are related as they are.[6] This emphasizes the internal rather than the external aspects of the study. In applied research, on the other hand, the central interest forces more concern for generalizability because one certainly wishes to apply the results to the other persons and to other situations. If the reader will ponder the following two examples of basic and applied research, he can get closer to this distinction.

In Chapter 14 we examined a study by Berkowitz on hostility arousal, anti-Semitism, and displaced aggression. This is clearly basic research: the central interest was in the relations among hostility, anti-Semitism, and displaced aggression. While no one would be foolish enough to say that Berkowitz was not concerned with hostility, anti-Semitism, and displaced aggression in general, the emphasis was on the relations among the variables *of the study*. Contrast this study with the effort of Walster et al. to determine whether colleges discriminate against women. Naturally, Walster and her colleagues were particular about the internal aspects of their study. But they perforce had to have another interest: Is discrimination practiced among colleges in general? Their study is clearly applied research, though one cannot say that basic research interest was absent. The considerations of the next section may help to clarify generalizability.

Internal and External Validity

Two general criteria of research design have been discussed at length by Campbell and by Campbell and Stanley.[7] These notions constitute one of the most significant, important, and enlightening contributions to research methodology in the last two or three decades.

Internal validity asks the question: Did *X*, the experimental manipulation, really make a significant difference? The three criteria of the last chapter are actually aspects of internal validity. Indeed, anything affecting the *controls* of a design becomes a problem of internal validity. If a design is such that one can have little or no confidence in the relations, as shown by significant differences between experimental groups, say, this is a problem of internal validity.

A difficult criterion to satisfy, *external validity* means *representativeness* or *generalizability*. When an experiment has been completed and a relation found, to what populations can it be generalized? Can we say that *A* is related to *B* for *all* school children? All eighth-grade children? All eighth-grade children in this school system or the eighth-grade children of this school only? Or must the findings be limited to the eighth-grade children with whom we worked? This is a very important scientific question that should always be asked—*and answered*.

Not only must sample generalizability be questioned. It is necessary to ask questions about the ecological and variable representativeness of studies. If the social setting in which the experiment was conducted is changed, will the relation of *A* and *B* still hold? Will *A* be related to *B* if the study is replicated in a lower-class school? In a western school? In a southern school? These are questions of *ecological representativeness*.

Variable representativeness is more subtle. A question not often asked, but that should be asked, is: Are the variables of this research representative? When an investigator works with psychological and sociological variables, he assumes that his variables are "constant." If he finds a difference in achievement between boys and girls, he assumes that sex as a variable is "constant."

---

[6] For a brief discussion of basic and applied research, see F. Kerlinger, "Research in Education." In R. Ebel, V. Noll, and R. Bauer, eds., *Encyclopedia of Educational Research*, 4th ed. New York: Macmillan, 1969, pp. 1127–1143, esp. p. 1128. This article also cites a number of references on basic and applied research.

[7] Campbell, *op, cit.*; Campbell and Stanley, *op. cit.* Readers are urged to study these sources, since the above discussion can only define and highlight internal and external validity.

In the case of variables like achievement, aggression, aptitude, and anxiety, can the investigator assume that the "aggression" of his suburban subjects is the same "aggression" to be found in city slums? Is the variable the same in a European suburb? The representativeness of "anxiety" is more difficult to ascertain. When we talk of "anxiety," what kind of anxiety do we mean? Are all kinds of anxiety the same? If anxiety is manipulated in one situation by verbal instructions and in another situation by electric shock, are the two induced anxieties the same? If anxiety is manipulated by, say, experimental instruction, is this the same anxiety as that measured by an anxiety scale? Variable representativeness, then, is another aspect of the larger problem of external validity, and thus of generalizability.

Unless special precautions are taken and special efforts made, the results of research are frequently not representative, and hence not generalizable. Campbell and Stanley say that internal validity is the sine qua non of research design, but that the ideal design should be strong in both internal validity and external validity, even though they are frequently contradictory. This point is well taken. In these chapters, the main emphasis will be on internal validity, with a vigilant eye on external validity.

The negative approach of this chapter was taken in the belief that an exposure to poor but commonly used and *accepted* procedures, together with a discussion of their major weaknesses, would provide a good starting point for the study of research design. Other inadequate designs are possible, but all such designs are inadequate on design-structural principles alone. This point should be emphasized because in the next chapter we will find that a perfectly good design structure can be poorly used. Thus it is necessary to learn and understand the two sources of research weakness: intrinsically poor designs and intrinsically good designs poorly used.

Study Suggestions

1. The faculty of a liberal arts college has decided to begin a new curriculum for all undergraduates. It asks a faculty research group to study the program's effectiveness for two years. The research group, wanting to have a group with which to compare the new curriculum group, requests that the present program be continued for two years and that students be allowed to volunteer for the present or the new program. The research group believes that it will then have an experimental group and a control group.

Discuss the research group's proposal critically. How much faith would you have in the findings at the end of two years? Give reasons for positive or negative reactions to the proposal.

2. Imagine that you are a graduate school professor and have been asked to judge the worth of a proposed doctoral thesis. The doctoral student is a school superintendent who is instituting a new type of administration into his school system. He plans to study the effects of the new administration for a three-year period and then write his thesis. He will not study any other school situation during the period so as not to bias the results, he says.

Discuss the proposal. When doing so, ask yourself: Is the proposal suitable for doctoral work?

3. In your opinion, should all research be held rather strictly to the criterion of generalizability? If so, why? If not, why not? Which field is likely to have more basic research: psychology or education? Why? What implications does your conclusion have for generalizability?

4. What does replication of research have to do with generalizability? Explain. If it were possible, should all research be replicated? If so, why? What does replication have to do with external and internal validity?

Chapter 19

General Designs of Research

DESIGN IS data discipline. The implicit purpose of all research design is to impose controlled restrictions on observations of natural phenomena. The research design tells the investigator, in effect: Do this and this; don't do that or that; be careful with this; ignore that; and so on. It is the blueprint of the research architect and engineer. If the design is poorly conceived structurally, the final product will be faulty. If it is at least well conceived structurally, the final product has a greater chance of being worthy of serious scientific attention. In this chapter, our main preoccupation is seven or eight "good" basic designs of research. In addition, however, we take up certain conceptual foundations of research and two or three problems related to design—for instance, the rationale of control groups and the pros and cons of matching.

CONCEPTUAL FOUNDATIONS OF RESEARCH DESIGN

The conceptual foundation for understanding research design was laid in Chapters 4 and 5, where sets and relations were defined and discussed. Recall that a *relation* is a set of ordered pairs. Recall, too, that a *Cartesian product* is all the possible ordered pairs of two sets. A *partition* breaks down a universal set U into subsets that are *disjoint* and *exhaustive*. A *cross partition* is a new partitioning that arises from successively partitioning U by forming all subsets of the form $A \cap B$. These definitions were elaborated in Chapters 5 and 6. We now apply them to design and analysis ideas.

Take two sets, A and B, partitioned into A_1 and A_2, B_1 and B_2. The Cartesian product of the two sets is:

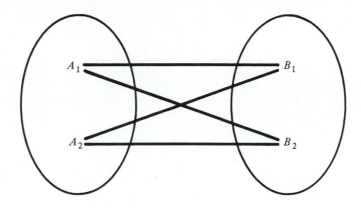

The ordered pairs, then, are: A_1B_1, A_1B_2, A_2B_1, A_2B_2. Since we have a set of ordered pairs, this is a relation. It is also a cross partition. The reader should look back at Figures 4.7 and 4.8 of Chapter 4 to help clarify these ideas, and to see the application of the Cartesian product and relation ideas to research design. For instance, A_1 and A_2 can be two aspects of any independent variable: experimental-control, two methods, male and female, and so on.

A *design* is some subset of the Cartesian product of the independent variables and the dependent variable. It is possible to pair each dependent variable measure, which we call Y in this discussion, with some aspect or partition of an independent variable. The simplest possible cases occur with one independent variable and one dependent variable. In Chapter 10, an independent variable, A, and a dependent variable, B, were partitioned into $[A_1, A_2]$ and $[B_1, B_2]$ and then cross-partitioned to form the by-now familiar 2 × 2 crossbreak, with frequencies or percentages in the cells. We concentrate, however, on similar cross partitions of A and B, but with continuous measures in the cells.

Take A alone, using a one-way analysis of variance design. Suppose we have three experimental treatments, A_1, A_2, and A_3, and, for simplicity, two Y scores in each cell. This is shown on the left of Figure 19.1, labeled (a). Say that six subjects have been assigned at random to the three treatments, and that the scores of the six individuals after the experimental treatments are those given in the figure.

The right side of Figure 19.1, labeled (b), shows the same idea in ordered-pair or relation form. The ordered pairs are A_1Y_1, A_1Y_2, A_2Y_3, . . . , A_3Y_6. This is, of course, not a Cartesian product, which would pair A_1 with all the Y's, A_2 with all the Y's, and A_3 with all the Y's, a total of 3 × 6 = 18 pairs. Rather, Figure 19.1(b) is a subset of the Cartesian product, $A \times B$. Research designs are subsets of $A \times B$, and the design and the research problem define or specify how the subsets are set up. The subsets of the design of Figure 19.1 are presumably dictated by the research problem.

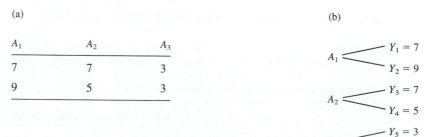

(a)

A_1	A_2	A_3
7	7	3
9	5	3

(b)

A_1 $Y_1 = 7$, $Y_2 = 9$
A_2 $Y_3 = 7$, $Y_4 = 5$
A_3 $Y_5 = 3$, $Y_6 = 3$

Figure 19.1

(a)   (b)

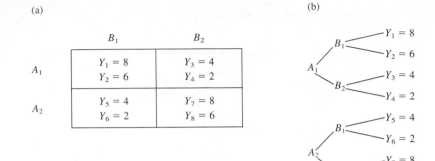

Figure 19.2

When there is more than one independent variable, the situation is more complex. Take two independent variables, A and B, partitioned into $[A_1, A_2]$ and $[B_1, B_2]$.[1] We must now have ordered triples (or two sets of ordered pairs): ABY. Study Figure 19.2. On the left side of the figure, labeled (a), the 2×2 factorial analysis of variance design and example used in Chapter 14 (see Figure 14.2 and Tables 14.3 and 14.4) is given, with the measures of the dependent variable, Y, inserted in the cells. That is, eight subjects were assigned at random to the four cells. Their scores, after the experiment, are $Y_1, Y_2, \ldots, Y_8$. The right side of the figure, labeled (b), shows the ordered triples, ABY, as a tree. Obviously these are subsets of $A \times B \times Y$ and are relations. The same reasoning can be extended to larger and more complex designs, like a $2 \times 2 \times 3$ factorial ($ABCY$) or a $4 \times 3 \times 2 \times 2$ ($ABCDY$). (In these designations, Y is usually omitted because it is implied.) Other kinds of designs can be similarly conceptualized, though their depiction in trees can be laborious.

In sum, a research design is some subset of the Cartesian product of the independent and the dependent variables. With only one independent variable, the single variable is partitioned; with more than one independent variable, the independent variables are cross-partitioned. With three or more independent variables, the conceptualization is the same; only the dimensions differ, for example, $A \times B \times C$ and $A \times B \times C \times D$ and the cross partitions thereof. Whenever possible, it is desirable to have "complete" designs—a complete design is a cross partition of the independent variables[2]—and to observe the two basic conditions of disjointness and exhaustiveness. That is, the design must not have a case (a subject's score) in more than one cell of a partition or cross partition, and all the cases must be used up. Moreover, the basic minimum of any design is at least a partition of the independent variable into two subsets, for example, A into A_1 and A_2.

The term "general designs" means that the designs given in the chapter are symbolized or expressed in their most general and abstract form. Where a simple X, meaning independent variable, is given, it must be taken to mean more than one X—that is, X is partitioned into two or more experimental groups. For instance, Design 19.1, to be studied shortly, has X and $\sim X$, meaning experimental and control groups, and thus is a

---

[1] The reader should not confuse this with the earlier AB frequency paradigm, in which A was the independent variable and B the dependent variable.

[2] There are also "incomplete" designs, but "complete" designs are emphasized more in this book. See R. Kirk, *Experimental Design: Procedures for the Behavioral Sciences.* Belmont, Calif.: Brooks/Cole, 1968, especially Table 1.4-1, p.12.

partition of X. But X can be partitioned into a number of X's, perhaps changing the design from a simple one-variable design to, say, a factorial design. The basic symbolism associated with Design 19.1, however, remains the same. These complexities will, we hope, be clarified in this and succeeding chapters.

A PRELIMINARY NOTE: EXPERIMENTAL DESIGNS AND ANALYSIS OF VARIANCE

Before taking up the designs of this chapter, we need to clarify one or two confusing and potentially controversial points not usually considered in the literature. Most of the designs we consider are experimental. As usually conceived, the rationale of research design is based on experimental ideas and conditions. They are also intimately linked to analysis of variance paradigms. This is of course no accident. Modern conceptions of design, especially factorial designs, were born when analysis of variance was invented. Although there is no hard law that says that analysis of variance is applicable only in experimental situations—indeed, it has been used many times in nonexperimental research—it is in general true that it is most appropriate for the data of experiments.[3] This is especially so for factorial designs where there are equal numbers of cases in the design paradigm cells, and where the subjects are assigned to the experimental conditions (or cells) at random.

When it is not possible to assign subjects at random, and when, for one reason or another, there are unequal numbers of cases in the cells of a factorial design, the use of analysis of variance is questionable, even inappropriate. It can also be clumsy and inelegant. This is because the use of analysis of variance assumes that the correlations between or among the independent variables of a factorial design are zero. Random assignment makes this assumption tenable since such assignment presumably apportions sources of variance equally among the cells. But random assignment can only be accomplished in experiments. In nonexperimental research, the independent variables are more or less fixed characteristics of the subjects, e.g., intelligence, sex, social class, and the like. They are usually systematically correlated. Take two independent manipulated variables, say reinforcement and anxiety. Because subjects with varying amounts of characteristics correlated with these variables are randomly distributed in the cells, the correlations between aspects of reinforcement and anxiety are assumed to be zero. If, on the other hand, the two independent variables are intelligence and social class, both ordinarily nonmanipulable and correlated, the assumption of zero correlation between them necessary for analysis of variance cannot be made. Some method of analysis that takes account of the correlation between them should be used. We will see later in the book that such a method is readily available: multiple regression.

We have not yet reached a state of research maturity to appreciate the profound difference between the two situations. For now, however, let us accept the difference and the statement that analysis of variance is basically an experimental conception and form of analysis. Strictly speaking, if our independent variables are nonexperimental, then analysis of variance is not the appropriate mode of analysis.[4] Similarly, if for some reason the

---

[3] See W. Hays, *Statistics,* 3d ed. New York: Holt Rinehart and Winston, 1981. Hays virtually equates experimental design models and analysis of variance models (pp. 328–329).

[4] There are exceptions to this statement. For instance, if one independent variable is experimental and one nonexperimental, analysis of variance is appropriate. In one-way analysis of variance, moreover, since there is only one independent variable, analysis of variance can be used with a nonexperimental independent variable, though regression analysis would probably be more appropriate. In Study Suggestion 5 at the end of the chapter, an interesting use of analysis of variance with nonexperimental data is cited.

numbers of cases in the cells are unequal (and disproportionate), then there will be correlation between the independent variables, and the assumption of zero correlation is not tenable. This rather abstract and abstruse digression from our main design theme may seem a bit confusing at this stage of our study. The problems involved should become clear after we have studied experimental and nonexperimental research and, later in the book, that fascinating and powerful approach known as multiple regression.

THE DESIGNS

In the remainder of this chapter we discuss four or five basic designs of research. Remember that a design is a plan, an outline for conceptualizing the structure of the relations among the variables of a research study. A design not only lays out the relations of the study; it also implies how the research situation is controlled and how the data are to be analyzed. A design, in the sense of this chapter, is the skeleton on which we put the variable-and-relation flesh of our research. The sketches given in Designs 19.1 through 19.8, following, *are* designs, the bare and abstract structure of the research. Sometimes analytic tables, such as Figure 19.2 (on the left) and the figures of Chapter 17 (e.g., Figures 17.2, 17.3, and 17.5) and elsewhere are called designs. While no great harm is done by calling them designs, they are, strictly speaking, analytic paradigms. We will not be fussy, however. We will call both kinds of representations "designs."

Design 19.1: Experimental Group-Control Group: Randomized Subjects

$$\boxed{R} \quad \frac{X \qquad Y}{\sim X \qquad Y} \quad \begin{array}{l} \text{(Experimental)} \\ \text{(Control)} \end{array}$$

Design 19.1, with two groups as above, and its variants with more than two groups, are probably the "best" designs for many experimental purposes in behavioral research. The $\boxed{R}$ before the paradigm indicates that subjects are *randomly assigned* to the experimental group (top line) and the control group (bottom line). This randomization removes the objections to Design 18.4 mentioned in Chapter 18. Theoretically, *all* possible independent variables are controlled. Practically, of course, this may not be so. If enough subjects are included in the experiment to give the randomization a chance to "operate," then we have strong control, and the claims of internal validity are rather well satisfied.

If extended to more than two groups and if it is capable of answering the research questions asked, Design 19.1 has the following advantages: (1) it has the best built-in theoretical control system of any design, with one or two possible exceptions in special cases; (2) it is flexible, being theoretically capable of extension to any number of groups with any number of variables; (3) if extended to more than one variable, it can test several hypotheses at one time; and (4) it is statistically and structurally elegant.

Before taking up other designs, we need to examine the notion of the control group, one of the creative inventions of the last hundred years, and certain extensions of Design 19.1. The two topics go nicely together.

The Notion of the Control Group and Extensions of Design 19.1

Evidently the word "control" and the expression "control group" did not appear in the scientific literature before the late nineteenth century.[5] The notion of controlled experi-

---

[5] E. Boring, "The Nature and History of Experimental Control," *American Journal of Psychology,* 67 (1954), 573–589.

mentation, however, is much older: Boring says that Pascal used it as early as 1648. Solomon searched the psychological literature and could not find a single case of the use of a control group before 1901.[6] He says that control-group design apparently had to await statistical developments and the development of statistical sophistication among psychologists.

Perhaps the first use of control groups in psychology and education occurred in 1901.[7] One of the two men who did this research, E. L. Thorndike, extended the basic and revolutionary ideas of this first research series to education.[8] Thorndike's controls, in this gigantic study of 8564 pupils in many schools in a number of cities, were independent educational groups. Among other comparisons, he contrasted the gains in intelligence test scores presumably engendered by the study of English, history, geometry, and *Latin* with the gains presumably engendered by the study of English, history, geometry, and *shop-work*. He tried, in effect, to compare the influence of Latin and shopwork. He also made other comparisons of a similar nature. Despite the weaknesses of design and control, Thorndike's experiments and those he stimulated others to perform were remarkable for their insight. Thorndike even berated colleges for not admitting students of stenography and typing who had not studied Latin, because he claimed to have shown that the influence of various subjects on intelligence was similar. It is interesting that he thought huge numbers of subjects were necessary—he called for 18,000 more cases. He was also quite aware, in 1924, of the need for random samples.[9]

The notion of the control group needs generalization. Assume that in an educational experiment we have four experimental groups as follows. A_1 is reinforcement of every response, A_2 reinforcement at regular time intervals, A_3 reinforcement at random intervals, and A_4 no reinforcement. Technically, there are three experimental groups and one control group, in the traditional sense of the control group. However, A_4 might be another "experimental treatment"; it might be some kind of minimal reinforcement. Then, in the traditional sense, there would be *no* control group. The traditional sense of the term "control group" lacks generality. If the notion of control is generalized, the difficulty disappears. Whenever there is more than one experimental group and any two groups are given different treatments, control is present in the sense of comparison previously mentioned. As long as there is an attempt to make two groups systematically different on a dependent variable, a comparison is possible. Thus the traditional notion that an experimental group should receive the treatment not given to a control group is a special case of the more general rule that comparison groups are necessary for the internal validity of scientific research.

If this reasoning is correct, we can set up designs such as the following:

$$\boxed{R} \quad \begin{array}{cc} X_1 & Y \\ \hline X_2 & Y \\ \hline X_3 & Y \end{array}$$

---

[6] R. Solomon, "An Extension of Control Group Design," *Psychological Bulletin*, 46 (1949), 137–150. Perhaps the notion of the control group was used in other fields, though it is doubtful that the idea was well developed. Solomon (p.175) also says that the Peterson and Thurstone study of attitudes in 1933 was the first serious attempt to use control groups in the evaluation of the effects of educational procedures. One cannot find the expression "control group" in the famous eleventh edition (1911) of the *Encyclopaedia Britannica*, even though experimental method is discussed.

[7] E. Thorndike and R. Woodworth, "The Influence of Improvement in One Mental Function upon the Efficiency of Other Functions," *Psychological Review*, 8 (1901), 247–261, 384–395, 553–564.

[8] E. Thorndike, "Mental Discipline in High School Subjects," *Journal of Educational Psychology*, 15 (1924), 1–22, 83–98.

[9] See *ibid.*, pp. 93, 97, and 85 for the three points mentioned.

or

$$\boxed{R} \quad \begin{array}{c|c} X_{1a} & Y \\ \hline X_{1b} & Y \\ \hline X_{2a} & Y \\ \hline X_{2b} & Y \end{array}$$

These designs will be more easily recognizable if they are set up in the manner of Part Five, as in Figure 19.3. The design on the left is a simple one-way analysis of variance design and the one on the right a 2×2 factorial design. In the right-hand design, X_{1a} might be experimental and X_{1b} control, with X_{2a} and X_{2b} either a manipulated variable or a dichotomous attribute variable. It is, of course, the same design as that shown in Figure 19.2(a).

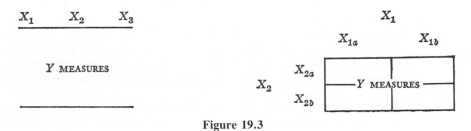

Figure 19.3

The structure of Design 19.2 is the same as that of Design 19.1. The only difference is that subjects are matched on one or more attributes. For the design to take its place as an "adequate" design, however, randomization must enter the picture, as noted by the small r attached to the M (for "matched"). It is not enough that matched subjects are used; the members of each pair must be assigned to the two groups at random. Ideally, too, whether a group is to be an experimental or a control group is also decided at random. In either case, each decision can be made by flipping a coin or by using a table of random numbers, letting odd numbers mean one group and even numbers the other group. If there are more than two groups, naturally, a random number system must be used.

Design 19.2: Experimental Group-Control Group: Matched Subjects

$$\boxed{M_r} \quad \begin{array}{c|c} X & Y \quad \text{(Experimental)} \\ \hline \sim X & Y \quad \text{(Control)} \end{array}$$

As in Design 19.1, it is possible, though often not easy, to use more than two groups. (The difficulty of matching more than two groups was discussed earlier.) There are times, however, when a matching design is an inherent element of the research situation. When the same subjects are used for two or more experimental treatments, or when subjects are given more than one trial, matching is inherent in the situation. In educational research, when schools or classes are in effect variables—when, say, two or more schools or classes are used and the experimental treatments are administered in each school or class—then Design 19.2 is the basis of the design logic. Study the paradigm of a schools design in Figure 19.4. It is seen that variance due to the differences between schools, and such variance can be substantial, can be readily estimated.

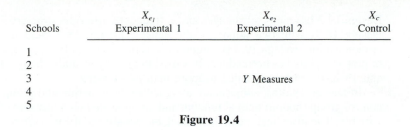

	X_{e_1}	X_{e_2}	X_c
Schools	Experimental 1	Experimental 2	Control
1			
2			
3		Y Measures	
4			
5			

Figure 19.4

MATCHING—PRO AND CON

Matching is not limited to matching subjects. If we think of the effect of matching on variance, we can understand why. When the members of certain subsets are more alike in a variable related to the dependent variable than they are to the members of other subsets, *between* subsets variance is present. If the members of one subgroup of a sample tend to have higher verbal ability, for example, than the members of other subgroups, and intelligence is substantially related to the dependent variable, then we have between subgroup variance (in the dependent variable). The extreme case is when the same subjects are used on more than one trial, because a subject is naturally more like himself than he is like other persons. The three experimental groups of Figure 19.4 can be the same subjects on different trials, which introduces systematic variance, individual differences variance. When pretests and posttests are used, matching is of course present, too. Schools are known to differ in important characteristics: classes differ, school districts differ, neighborhoods differ, teachers differ. These differences can be used in the study and the variances arising form their use can be isolated by building their sources into the design. In fact, failure to build such variables into designs can lead to the confounding of the experimental variables.[10] And to have correlation between groups, due to matching or repeated measures of individuals or units like classes and schools, and not to take advantage of the correlation is a statistical and design blunder.[11]

Design 19.3: Before and after Control Group (Pretest-Posttest)

(a)	R	Y_b	X	Y_a	(Experimental)
		Y_b	$\sim X$	Y_a	(Control)
(b)	M_r	Y_b	X	Y_a	(Experimental)
		Y_b	$\sim X$	Y_a	(Control)

[10] The terms "confounding" means the "mixing" of the variance of one or more independent variables, usually extraneous to the research purpose, with the independent variable or variables of the research problem. As a result it cannot be clearly said that the relation found is between the independent variables and the dependent variable of the research. Underwood points out that there is only one basic principle of research design: "design the experiment so that the effects of the independent variables can be evaluated unambiguously." (B. Underwood, *Psychological Research*. New York: Appleton, 1957, p. 86.) When this cannot be done—it is a difficult procedure—more likely than not the independent variables have been confounded. The term evidently came from statistics, where "confounding" is sometimes deliberately practiced.

[11] It must be emphasized that matching is in general not a desirable procedure. *And matching is never a substitute for randomization.* Remember, too, that the correlation between the matching variable or variables and the dependent variable must be substantial (greater than .50, say) to be productive, and that only the variable or variables matched on—and, perhaps, variables substantially correlated with these variables—are controlled. A better procedure, in general, is analysis of covariance or other regression procedure, a subject we will examine in later chapters.

Design 19.3 has many advantages and is frequently used. Its structure is similar to that of Design 18.2, with two important differences: Design 18.2 lacks a control group and randomization. Design 19.3 is similar to Designs 19.1 and 19.2, except that the "before" or pretest feature has been added. It is used frequently to study change. Like Designs 19.1 and 19.2, it can be expanded to more than two groups.

In Design 19.3(a), subjects are assigned to the experimental group (top line) and the control group (bottom line) at random and are pretested on a measure of Y, the dependent variable. The investigator can then check the equality of the two groups on Y. The experimental manipulation X is performed, after which the groups are again measured on Y. The difference between the two groups is tested statistically. An interesting and difficult characteristic of this design is the nature of the scores usually analyzed: difference, or change, scores, $Y_a - Y_b = D$. Unless the effect of the experimental manipulation is strong, the analysis of difference scores is not advisable. Difference scores are considerably less reliable than the scores from which they are calculated.[12] There are other problems. We discuss only the main strengths and weaknesses.[13] At the end of the discussion the analytic difficulties of difference or change scores will be taken up.

Probably most important, Design 19.3 overcomes the great weakness of Design 18.2, because it supplies a comparison control group against which the difference, $Y_a - Y_b$, can be checked. With only one group, we can never know whether history, maturation (or both), or the experimental manipulation X produced the change in Y. When a control group is added, the situation is radically altered. After all, if the groups are equated (through randomization), the effects of history and maturation, if present, should be present in both groups. If the mental ages of the children of the experimental group increase, so should the mental ages of the children of the control group. Then, if there is still a difference between the Y measures of the two groups, it should not be due to history or maturation. That is, if something happens to affect the experimental subjects between the pretest and the posttest, this something should also affect the subjects of the control group. Similarly, the effect of testing—Campbell's *reactive* measures—should be controlled. For if the testing affects the members of the experimental group it should similarly affect the members of the control group. (There is, however, a concealed weakness here, which will be discussed later.) This is the main strength of the well-planned and well-executed before-after, experimental-control group design.

On the other hand, before-after designs have a troublesome aspect, which decreases the external validity of the experiment, although the internal validity is not affected. This source of difficulty is the pretest. A pretest can have a *sensitizing effect* on subjects. For example, the subjects may possibly be alerted to certain events in their environment that they might not ordinarily notice. If the pretest is an attitude scale, it can sensitize subjects to the issues or problems mentioned in the scale. Then, when the X treatment is administered to the experimental group, the subjects of this group may be responding not so much to the attempted influence, the communication, or whatever method is used to change attitudes, as to a combination of their increased sensitivity to the issues *and* the experimental manipulation.

---

[12] For a clear explanation of why this is so, see R. Thorndike and E. Hagen, *Measurement and Evaluation in Psychology and Education*, 4th ed. New York: Wiley, 1977, pp. 98–101. See, also, R. Thorndike, *The Concepts of Over- and Underachievement*. New York: Bureau of Publications, Teachers College, Columbia University, 1963, pp. 39ff.; R. Thorndike, "Intellectual Status and Intellectual Growth," *Journal of Educational Psychology*, 57 (1966), 121–127; and E. O'Connor, "Extending Classical Theory to the Measurement of Change," *Review of Educational Research*, 42 (1972), 73–97. O'Connor recommends a better statistical procedure for handling change. We will outline the appropriate procedure later in the book in the context of multiple regression.

[13] For a more complete discussion, see D. Campbell and J. Stanley, *Experimental Designs and Quasi-Experimental Designs for Research*. Chicago, Ill.: Rand McNally, 1963, pp. 13ff.

Since such interaction effects are not immediately obvious, and since they contain a threat to the external validity of experiments, it is worthwhile to consider them a bit further. One would think that, since both the experimental and the control groups are pretested, the effect of pretesting, if any, would ensure the validity of the experiment. Let us assume that no pretesting was done, that is, that Design 19.2 was used. Other things equal, a difference between the experimental and the control groups after experimental manipulation of X can be assumed to be due to X. There is no reason to suppose that one group is more sensitive or more alert than the other, since they both face the testing situation *after X*. But when a pretest is used, the situation changes. While the pretest sensitizes both groups, it can make the experimental subjects respond to X, wholly or partially, *because of the sensitivity*. What we have, then, is a lack of generalizability: it may be possible to generalize to pretested groups but not to unpretested ones. Clearly such a situation is disturbing to the researcher, since who wants to generalize to pretested groups?

If this weakness is important, why is this a good design? While the possible interaction effect described above may be serious in some research, it is doubtful that it strongly affects much behavioral research, provided researchers are aware of its potential and take adequate precautions. Testing is an accepted and normal part of many situations, especially in education. It is doubtful, therefore, that research subjects will be unduly sensitized in such situations. Still, there may be times when they can be affected. The rule Campbell and Stanley give is a good one: When unusual testing procedures are to be used, use designs with no pretests.

Difference Scores

Look at Design 19.3 again, particularly at changes between Y_b and Y_a. One of the most difficult problems that has plagued—and intrigued—researchers, measurement specialists, and statisticians is how to study and analyze such difference, or change, scores. In a book of the scope of this one, it is impossible to go into the problems in detail. General precepts and cautions, however, can be outlined. One would think that the application of analysis of variance to difference scores yielded by Design 19.3 and similar designs would be effective. Such analysis *can* be done if the experimental effects are substantial. But difference scores, as mentioned earlier, are usually less reliable then the scores form which they are calculated. Real differences between experimental and control groups may be undetectable simply because of the unreliability of the difference scores. To detect differences between experimental and control groups, the scores analyzed must be reliable enough to reflect the differences and thus to be detectable by statistical tests. Because of this difficulty experts even say that difference or change scores should not be used.[14] So what can be done?

The generally recommended procedure is to use so-called residualized or regressed gain scores, which are scores calculated by predicting the posttest scores from the pretest scores on the basis of the correlation between pretest and posttest, and then subtracting these predicted scores from the posttest scores to obtain the residual gain scores. (The reader should not be concerned if this procedure is not too clear at this stage. Later, after we study regression and analysis of covariance, it should become clearer.) The effect of the pretest scores is removed from the posttest scores; that is, the residual scores are posttest scores purged of the pretest influence. Then the significance of the difference

---

[14] See footnotes 12 and 13 and L. Cronbach and L. Furby, "How Should We Measure 'Change'—or Should We?" *Psychological Bulletin,* 74 (1970), 68–80.

between the means of these scores is tested. All this can be accomplished by using either the procedure just described and a regression equation or by analysis of covariance.

Even the use of residual gain scores and analysis of covariance is not perfect, however. If subjects have not been assigned at random to the experimental and control groups, the procedure will not save the situation. When groups differ systematically before experimental treatment in other characteristics pertinent to the dependent variable, statistical manipulation does not correct such differences.[15] If, however, a pretest is used, use random assignment and analysis of covariance, remembering that the results must always be treated with special care. Finally, multiple regression analysis may provide the best solution of the problem, as we will see later.[16]

Design 19.4:   Simulated before-after, Randomized

The value of this design is doubtful, even though it is included among the adequate designs. The scientific demand for a comparison is satisfied: there is a comparison group (lower line). A major weakness of Design 18.3 (a pallid version of Design 19.4) is remedied by the randomization. Recall that with Design 18.3 we were unable to assume beforehand that the experimental and control groups were equivalent. Design 19.4 calls for subjects to be assigned to the two groups at random. Thus, it can be assumed that they are statistically equal. Such a design might be used when one is worried about the reactive effect of pretesting, or when, due to the exigencies of practical situations, one has no other choice. Such a situation occurs when one has the opportunity to try a method or some innovation only once. To test the method's efficacy, one provides a base line for judging the effect of X on Y by pretesting a group similar to the experimental group. Then Y_a is tested against Y_b.

This design's validity breaks down if the two groups are not both randomly selected from the same population or if the subjects are not assigned to the two groups at random. Even then, it has the weaknesses mentioned in connection with other similar designs, namely, other possible variables may be influential in the interval between Y_b and Y_a. In other words, Design 19.4 is superior to Design 18.3, but it should not be used if a better design is available.

Design 19.5:   Three-Group, before-after

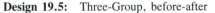

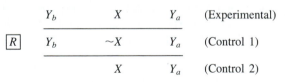

[15] *Ibid.*, p. 78.

[16] It is unfortunate that the complexities of design and statistical analysis may discourage the student, sometimes even to the point of feeling hopeless. But that is the nature of behavioral research: it merely reflects the exceedingly complex character of psychological, sociological, and educational reality. This is at one and the same time frustrating and exciting. Like marriage, behavioral research is difficult and often unsuccessful—but not impossible. Moreover, it is the only way to acquire reliable understanding of our behavioral world. The point of view of this book is that we should learn and understand as much as we can about what we are doing, use reasonable care with design and analysis, and then *do* the research without fussing too much about analytic matters. The main thing is always the research problem and our interest in it. This does not mean a cavalier disregard of analysis. It simply means reasonable understanding and care and healthy measures of both optimism and skepticism.

This design is better. In addition to the assets of Design 19.3 it provides a way to avoid possible interactive effects due to the pretest. This is achieved by the second control group (third line). (It seems a bit strange to have a control group with an X, but the group of the third line is really a control group.) With the Y_a measures of this group available, it is possible to check the interaction effect. Suppose the mean of the experimental group is significantly greater than the mean of the first control group (second line). We may doubt whether this difference was really due to X. It might have been produced by increased sensitization of the subjects after the pretest and the interaction of their sensitization and X. We now look at the mean of Y_a of the second control group (third line). It, too, should be significantly greater than the mean of the first control group. If it is, we can assume that the pretest has not unduly sensitized the subjects, or that X is sufficiently strong to over-ride a sensitization-X interaction effect.

Design 19.6: Four-Group, before-after (Solomon)

	Y_b	X	Y_a	(Experimental)
	Y_b	$\sim X$	Y_a	(Control 1)
$\boxed{R}$		X	Y_a	(Control 2)
		$\sim X$	Y_a	(Control 3)

This design, proposed by Solomon,[17] is strong and aesthetically satisfying. It has potent controls. Actually, if we change the designation of Control 2 to Experimental 2, we have a combination of Designs 19.3 and 19.1, our two best designs, where the former design forms the first two lines and the latter the second two lines. The virtues of both are combined in one design. Campbell says that this design has become the new ideal for social scientists.[18] While this is a strong statement, probably a bit too strong, it indicates the high esteem in which the design is held.

Among the reasons why it is a strong design is that the demand for comparison is well satisfied with the first two lines *and* the second two lines, the randomization enhances the probability of statistical equivalence of the groups, and history and maturation are controlled with the first two lines of the design. The interaction effect due to possible pretest subject sensitization is controlled by the first three lines. By adding the fourth line, temporary contemporaneous effects that may have occurred between Y_b and Y_a can be controlled. Because Design 19.1 and 19.3 are combined, we have the power of each test separately and the power of replication because, in effect, there are two experiments. If Y_a of Experimental is significantly greater than Control 1, and Control 2 is significantly greater than Control 3, together with a consistency of results between the two experiments, this is strong evidence, indeed, of the validity of our research hypothesis.

What is wrong with this paragon of designs? It certainly looks fine on paper. There seem to be only two sources of weakness. One is practicability—it is harder to run two simultaneous experiments than one and the researcher encounters the difficulty of locating more subjects of the same kind.

The other difficulty is statistical. Note that there is a lack of balance of groups. There are four actual groups, but not four complete sets of measures. Using the first two lines,

[17] Solomon, *op. cit.*, pp. 137–150. Although this design can have a matching form, it is not discussed here nor is it recommended. The symbolism used above is not Solomon's.

[18] D. Campbell, "Factors Relevant to the Validity of Experiments in Social Settings," *Psychological Bulletin*, 54 (1957), 297–312. See, also, D. Campbell and J. Stanley, *Experimental Designs and Quasi-Experimental Designs for Research*. Chicago: Rand McNally, 1963.

that is, with Design 19.3, one can subtract Y_b from Y_a or do an analysis of covariance. With the two lines, one can test the Y_a's against each other with a t test or F test, but the problem is how to obtain one overall statistical approach. One solution is to test the Y_a's of Controls 2 and 3 against the average of the two Y_b's (the first two lines), as well as to test the significance of the difference of the Y_a's of the first two lines. In addition, Solomon originally suggested a 2×2 factorial analysis of variance, using the four Y_a sets of measures.[19] Solomon's suggestion is outlined in Figure 19.5. A careful study will reveal that this is a fine example of research thinking, a nice blending of design and analysis. With this analysis we can study the main effects, X and $\sim X$, and Pretested and Not Pretested. What is more interesting, we can test the interaction of pretesting and X and get a clear answer to the previous problem.

	X	$\sim X$
Pretested	Y_a, Experimental	Y_a, Control 1
Not Pretested	Y_a, Control 2	Y_a, Control 3

Figure 19.5

While this and other complex designs have decided strengths, it is doubtful that they can be used routinely. In fact, they should probably be saved for very important experiments in which, perhaps, hypotheses already tested with simpler designs are again tested with greater rigor and control. Indeed, it is recommended that designs like 19.5 and 19.6 and certain variants of Designs 19.6, to be discussed later, be reserved for definitive tests of research hypotheses after a certain amount of preliminary experimentation has been done.

VARIANTS OF BASIC DESIGNS

Designs 19.1 through 19.6 are the *basic* experimental designs. Some variants of these designs have already been indicated. Additional experimental and control groups can be added as needed, but the core ideas remain the same. It is always wise to consider the possibility of adding experimental and control groups. Within reason, the addition of such groups provides more evidence of the validity of the study hypotheses as we saw clearly with Design 19.6. We saw that this design was a combination of two other basic designs, combining the strengths of both and adding replication power, as well as further controls. Such advantages lead to the principle that, whenever we consider a research design, we should consider the possibility of adding experimental groups as *replications* or *variants* of experimental and control groups.

Important variants of the basic design are *time designs*. The form of Design 19.6 can be altered to include a span of time:

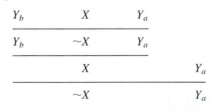

The Y_a's of the third and fourth lines are observations of the dependent variable at any specified later date. Such an alteration, of course, changes the purpose of the design and

[19] Solomon, *op. cit.*, p. 146; Campbell, *op. cit.*, p. 303.

may cause some of the virtues of Design 19.6 to be lost. We might, if we had the time, the patience, and the resources, retain all the former benefits and still extend in time by adding two more groups to Design 19.6 itself.

Compromise Designs

It is possible, indeed necessary, to use designs that are compromises with true experimentation. Recall that true experimentation requires at least two groups, one receiving an experimental treatment and one not receiving the treatment or receiving it in different form. The true experiment requires the manipulation of at least one independent variable, the random assignment of subjects to groups, and the random assignment of treatments to groups. When one or more of these prerequisites is missing for one reason or another, we have a *compromise design*. Although there are many possibilities, only one will be discussed at length below.

Compromise Experimental Group-Control Group Design

Perhaps the most commonly used design is the experimental group-control pattern in which one has no clear assurance that the experimental and control groups are equivalent. The structure of this design has already been considered in Design 19.3. The compromise form is as follows:

Design 19.7: Compromise Experimental Group-Control Group

$$
\begin{array}{cccl}
Y_b & X & Y_a & \text{(Experimental)} \\
\hline
Y_b & {\sim}X & Y_a & \text{(Control)}
\end{array}
$$

The difference between Designs 19.3 and 19.7 is sharp. In Design 19.7, there is no randomized assignment of subjects to groups, as in 19.3(a), nor is there matching of subjects and then random assignment, as in 19.3(b). Design 19.7, therefore, is subject to the weaknesses due to the possible lack of equivalence between the groups in variables other than X. Researchers commonly take pains to establish equivalence by other means, and to the extent they are successful in doing so, to this extent the design is valid. This is done in ways discussed below.

It is often difficult or impossible to equate groups by random selection or random assignment, or by matching. Should one then give up doing the research? By no means. Every effort should be made, first, to select and to assign at random. If both of these are not possible, perhaps matching and random assignment can be accomplished. If they are not, an effort should be made at least to use samples from the same population or to use samples as alike as possible. The experimental treatments should be assigned at random. Then the similarity of the groups should be checked using any information available— sex, age, social class, and so on. The equivalence of the groups should be checked using the means and standard deviations of the pretests: t tests and F tests will do. The distributions should also be checked. Although one cannot have the assurance that randomization gives, if these items all check one can go ahead with the study knowing at least that there is no evidence against the equivalence assumption.

These precautions increase the possibilities of attaining internal validity. There are still difficulties, all of which are subordinate to one main difficulty, called *selection*. (These other difficulties will not be discussed here. For detailed discussion, see the Campbell and Stanley chapter previously cited.)

Selection is one of the difficult and troublesome problems of behavioral research.

Since its aspects will be discussed in detail in Chapter 22 on nonexperimental research, only a brief description will be given here. One of the important reasons for the emphasis on random selection and assignment is to avoid the difficulties of selection. When subjects are selected into groups on bases extraneous to the research purposes, we call this "selection," or alternatively, "self-selection." Take a common example: let us assume that volunteers are used in the experimental group and other subjects are used as controls. If the volunteers differ in a characteristic related to Y, the dependent variable, the ultimate difference between the experimental and control groups may be due to this characteristic rather than to X. Volunteers, for instance, may be more intelligent (or less intelligent) than nonvolunteers. If we were doing an experiment with some kind of learning as the dependent variable, obviously the volunteers might perform better on Y because of superior intelligence, despite the initial likeness of the two groups on the pretest. (Note that, if we had used only volunteers and had assigned them to experimental and control groups at random, the selection difficulty disappears. External validity or representativeness, however, is decreased.)

Another more frequent example in educational research is to take some school classes for the experimental group and others for the control group. If a fairly large number of classes are selected and assigned at random to experimental and control groups, there is no great problem. But if they are not assigned at random, certain ones may select themselves into the experimental groups, and these classes may have characteristics that predispose them to have higher mean Y scores than the other classes. For example, their teachers may be more alert, more intelligent, more aggressive. These characteristics interact with the selection to produce, irrespective of X, higher experimental group than control group Y scores. In other words, something that influences the selection process, as do the volunteer subjects, also influences the dependent variable measures. This happens even though the pretest may show the groups to be the same on the dependent variable. The X manipulation is "effective," but it is not effective in and of itself. It is effective because of selection, or *self-selection*.

Time Designs

A common research problem, especially in studies of the development and growth of children, involves the study of individuals and groups using time as a variable. Such studies are longitudinal studies of subjects, often children, at different points in time. One such design among many might be:

Design 19.8:   A Longitudinal Time Design

$$Y_1 \quad Y_2 \quad X \quad Y_3 \quad Y_4$$

Note the similarity to Design 18.2, where a group is compared to itself. The use of Design 19.8 allows us to avoid one of the difficulties of Design 18.2. Its use makes it possible to separate reactive measurement effects from the effect of X. It also enables us to see, if the measurements have a reactive effect, whether X has an effect over and above that effect. The reactive effect should show itself at Y_2; this can be contrasted with Y_3. If there is an increase at Y_3 over and above the increase at Y_2, it can be attributed to X. A similar argument applies for maturation and history.

One difficulty with longitudinal or time studies, especially with children, is the growth or learning that occurs over time. Children do not stop growing and learning for research convenience. The longer the time period, the greater the problem. In other words, time itself is a variable in a sense. With a design like Design 18.2, $Y_b X Y_a$, the time variable can confound X, the experimental independent variable. If there is a significant difference between Y_a and Y_b, one cannot tell whether X or a time "variable" caused the change. But with Design 19.8, one has other measures of Y and thus a base line against which to compare the change in Y presumably due to X.

The statistical analysis of time measures is a special and troublesome problem: the usual tests of significance applied to time measures can yield spurious results. One reason is that such data tend to be highly variable, and it is easy to interpret changes not due to X as due to X. That is, in time data, individual and mean scores tend to move around a good bit. It is easy to fall into the trap of seeing one of these shifts as "significant," especially if it accords with our hypothesis. If we can legitimately assume that influences other than X, both random and systematic, are uniform over the whole series of Y's, the statistical problem can be solved. But such an assumption may be, and probably often is, unwarranted.

The researcher who does time studies should make a special study of the statistical problems and should consult a statistician. For the practitioner, this statistical complexity is unfortunate in that it may discourage needed practical studies. Since longitudinal single-group designs are particularly well-suited to individual class research, it is recommended that in longitudinal studies of methods or studies of children in educational situations analysis be confined to drawing graphs of results and interpreting them qualitatively. Crucial tests, especially those for published studies, however, must be buttressed with statistical tests.

Naturally, there are possible variations of Design 19.8. One important variation is to add one or more control groups; another is to add more time observations. Still another is to add more X's, more experimental interventions.[20]

Concluding Remarks

The designs of this chapter are general: they are stripped down to bare essentials to show underlying structure. Having the underlying structures well in mind—cognitive psychologists say that such structures are important in remembering and thinking—the student is in a position to use the more specific designs of analysis of variance and related paradigms. Knowing and understanding the general designs may enhance mental flexibility and the ability to cope conceptually and practically with research problems and the design means of solving the problems.

Study Suggestions

1. The first sentence of this chapter is "Design is data discipline." What does this sentence mean? Justify it.

2. Suppose you are an educational psychologist and plan to test the hypothesis that feeding back psychological information to teachers effectively enhances the children's learning by increasing the teachers' understanding of the children. Outline an *ideal* research design to test this hypothesis, assuming that you have complete command of the situation and plenty of money and help. (*These are important conditions,* which are included to free the reader from the practical limitations that so often compromise good research designs.) Set up two designs, each with complete randomization, both following the paradigm of Design 19.1. In one of these use only one independent

[20] See J. Gottman, R. McFall, and J. Barnett, "Design and Analysis of Research Using Time Series," *Psychological Bulletin*, 72 (1969), 299–306; Campbell and Stanley, *op. cit.,* pp. 37–46.

variable and one-way analysis of variance. In the second, use two independent variables and a simple factorial design.

How do these two designs compare in their control powers and in the information they yield? Which one tests the hypothesis better? Why?

3. Design research to test the hypothesis of Study Suggestion 2, above, but this time compromise the design by not having randomization. Compare the relative efficacies of the two approaches. In which of them would you put greater faith? Why? Explain in detail.

4. Suppose that a team of sociologists, psychologists, and educators believed that competent and insightful counseling can change the predominantly negative attitudes of juvenile offenders for the better. They took 30 juvenile offenders—found to be so by the courts—who had been referred for counseling in the previous year and matched each of them to another nonoffender youngster on sex and intelligence. They compared the attitudes of the two groups at the beginning and the end of the year (the duration of the counseling), and found a significant difference at the beginning of the year but no significant difference at the end. They concluded that counseling had a salutary effect on the juvenile offenders' attitudes.

Criticize the research. Bring out its strengths and weaknesses. Keep the following in mind: sampling, randomization, group comparability, matching, and control. Is the conclusion of the researchers empirically valid, do you think? If not, outline a study that will yield valid conclusions.

5. The advice in the text not to use analysis of variance in nonexperimental research does not apply so much to one-way analysis of variance as it does to factorial analysis. Nor does the problem of equal numbers of cases in the cells apply (within reason). In a number of nonexperimental studies, in fact, one-way analysis of variance has been profitably used. One such study is: S. Jones and S. Cook, ''The Influence of Attitude on Judgments of the Effectiveness of Alternative Social Policies,'' *Journal of Personality and Social Psychology,* 32 (1975), 767–773. The independent variable was attitude toward blacks, obviously not manipulated. The dependent variable was preference for social policy affecting blacks: remedial action involving social change or action involving self-improvement of blacks. One-way analysis of variance was used with social policy preference scores of four groups differing in attitudes toward blacks. (Attitudes toward blacks were also measured with an attitude scale.)

It is suggested that students read and digest this excellent and provocative study. It will be time and effort well-spent. You may also want to do an analysis of variance of the data of the authors' Table 1, using the method outlined earlier of analysis of variance using n's, means, and standard deviations (see Addendum, Chapter 13).

Chapter 20

Research Design Applications: Randomized Groups

It is difficult to tell anyone how to do research. Perhaps the best thing to do is to make sure that the beginner has a grasp of principles and possibilities. In addition, approaches and tactics can be suggested. In tackling a research problem, the investigator should let his mind roam, speculate about possibilities, even guess the pattern of results. Once the possibilities are known, intuitions can be followed and explored. Intuition and imagination, however, are not much help if we know little or nothing of technical resources. On the other hand, good research is not just methodology and technique. Intuitive thinking is essential because it helps researchers arrive at solutions that are not merely conventional and routine. It should never be forgotten, however, that analytic thinking *and* creative intuitive thinking both depend on knowledge, understanding, and experience.

The main purposes of this chapter and the next are to enrich and illustrate our design and statistical discussion with actual research examples and to suggest basic possibilities for designing research so that the student can ultimately solve research problems. Our summary purpose, then, is to supplement and enrich earlier, more abstract design and statistical discussions.

SIMPLE RANDOMIZED SUBJECTS DESIGN

In Chapters 13 and 14 the statistics of simple one-way and factorial analysis of variance were discussed and illustrated. The design behind the earlier discussions is here called *randomized subjects design*. The general design paradigm is Design 19.1:

$$\boxed{R} \quad \frac{X \qquad Y}{\sim X \qquad Y}$$

Research Examples

The simplest form of Design 19.1 is a one-way analysis of variance paradigm in which *k* groups are given *k* experimental treatments and the *k* means are compared with analysis of variance or separate tests of significance. A glance at Figure 19.3, left side, shows this simple form of 19.1 with *k* = 3. Strange to say, it is not used too often, researchers more often preferring the factorial form of Design 19.1. Two one-way examples are given below. One used random assignment; one probably did not. Unfortunately, some researchers do not report *how* subjects were assigned to groups or treatments. The need to report on method of subject selection and assignment to experimental groups should by now be obvious.

Peeck: Prior Knowledge and Memory

There has been much theorizing and research on memory, its "structure," and *how* people remember what they have learned. In one such study, Peeck tested the idea that learning is assisted if learners have and use meaningful contexts that integrate the material to be learned. This means that if learners are somehow given relevant background or context for a learning task *before* learning, they will learn (remember) more than if they are not given such a relevant background. Peeck assigned 78 students at random to three experimental conditions, which were aspects of task mobilization: Presidents, States, Control.[1] In the first, subjects were asked to write down as many presidents of the United States as they could in five minutes. (The subjects were Dutch.) The subjects of the second group were asked to write the names of as many states of the United States as they could in five minutes. The subjects of the third group, the control group, were asked to write the names of birds and other animals. All subjects were then shown, on slides, the names of 16 presidents and 16 states in random order. They were instructed to write as many of the names as they could remember.

If mobilization was effective, the subjects of the presidents-mobilization group should recall more presidents, and the subjects of the states-mobilization group should remember more states. There should be no effect, of course, on the control group members. The mean numbers of recalled presidents and recalled states in the three mobilization conditions are given in Table 20.1. One-way analyses of variance of each of the sets of three means yielded significant *F* ratios, and the patterns of the means were as predicted: the presidents-mobilized group had the highest mean (7.77) in recall of presidents, and the states-mobilized group had the highest mean (8.50) in recall of states. Post hoc tests indicated that presidents-mobilized subjects recalled significantly more presidents than the

Table 20.1 Mean Correct Recalls of Presidents and States by Mobilization Conditions, Peeck Experiment

| | Mobilization Treatment | | | |
Recall of	Presidents	States	Control	F
Presidents	7.77[a]	6.42	5.69	8.44 (.05)
States	6.23	8.50	6.35	10.58 (.05)

[a]The italicized means show the crucial predictions: If presidents mobilized, then better recall of presidents, and if states mobilized, then better recall of states.

[1] J. Peeck, "Effects of Mobilization of Prior Knowledge on Free Recall," *Journal of Experimental Psychology: Learning, Memory, and Cognition*, 8 (1982), 608–612.

other two groups, and states-mobilized subjects recalled more states than the other two groups. Peeck also did a second experiment in which the recall test was delayed 24 hours. The results were similar. Mobilization seems to be an effective means of enhancing recall. Students should especially note the use of the same design (19.1) and analyses of variance with two different categories of recall. One is considerably more convinced by such varied replication than one would be if only one recall task had been used.

Wickens: Stimulus and Response Generalization Study

This ingenious and important study of stimulus and response generalization (roughly, spread of effectiveness of stimuli to elicit the same or similar responses to other related stimuli) deserves careful study not only because of a creative use of conditioning and a clever use of analysis of variance, but also for its implications for teaching.[2] The study is also noteworthy because randomization was evidently not used. It was probably deemed unnecessary. Why? With any type of human response, especially physiological response, that is universal to *homo sapiens* and that *does not exhibit a wide range of individual differences,* it is sometimes fairly safe not to randomize. If all people are pretty much alike in a characteristic under study, it obviously makes no difference whether randomization is used. In this respect, any single individual is representative of the whole human race. The possession of blood, a heart beat, and lungs are examples. Of course, the type of blood and the rate of the heart beat and lung action, when used as variables, radically change the picture. At any rate, in Wickens' study, it was probably assumed that all subjects are conditionable. Still, it would have been better to assign subjects to groups at random, because we know that there are individual differences in conditioning or conditionability. It is conceivable that such differences might affect the experimental outcomes.

Returning to Wickens' experiment, the responses of subjects to shock were conditioned to a tone. After being conditioned, the subjects' hands were turned over and their conditioned responses to the first tone and to other tones were tested. Three experimental groups and one control group were used. Groups I, II, and III, the experimental groups, were conditioned and then tested differently. Although the details do not concern us, in general the *S*'s were conditioned to one tone and either tested with that tone or with tones one or two octaves above or below the original conditioned tone. The results, in mean number of responses (flexion in a new hand position), indicated that stimulus generalization and response generalization had occurred. The means for the four groups were: I, 5.87; II, 3.69; III, 4.19; and control, .16.

Wickens did a one-way analysis of variance of the data of Groups, I, II, and III to show that they did not differ in mean response. The *F* ratio was not significant. This demonstrated stimulus generalization (since the *S*'s responded similarly to the original tone *and* to the tones one and two octaves away from the original tone). He then tested each of the experimental groups against the control group. Each comparison was significant, which demonstrated response generalization (because the control group was shocked but not conditioned, and the responses were given with the hand turned over).

FACTORIAL DESIGNS

The basic general design is still Design 19.1, though the variation of the basic experimental group-control pattern is drastically altered by the addition of other experimental factors

[2] D. Wickens, "Studies of Response Generalization in Conditioning. I. Stimulus Generalization during Response Generalization," *Journal of Experimental Psychology,* 33 (1943), 221–227.

or independent variables. Following an earlier definition of factorial analysis of variance, *factorial design is the structure of research in which two or more independent variables are juxtaposed in order to study their independent and interactive effects on a dependent variable.*

The reader may at first find it a bit difficult to fit the factorial framework into the general experimental group-control group paradigm of Design 19.1. The discussion of the generalization of the control-group idea in Chapter 19, however, should have clarified the relations between Design 19.1 and factorial designs. The discussion is now continued. We have the independent variables A and B and the dependent variable Y. The simplest factorial design, the 2×2, has three possibilities: both A and B active; A active, B attribute (or vice versa); and both A and B attribute. (The last possibility, both independent variables attributes, is the nonexperimental case. As indicated earlier, however, it is probably not appropriate to use analysis of variance with nonexperimental independent variables.) Returning to the experimental group-control notion, A can be divided into A_1 and A_2, experimental and control, as usual, with the additional independent variable B partitioned into B_1 and B_2. Since this structure is familiar to us by now, we need only discuss one or two procedural details.

The ideal subject assignment procedure is to assign subjects to the four cells at random. If both A and B are active variables, this is possible and easy. Simply give the subjects numbers arbitrarily from 1 through N, N being the total number of subjects. Then, using a table of random numbers, write down numbers 1 through N as they turn up in the table. Place the numbers into four groups as they turn up and then assign the four groups of subjects to the four cells. To be safe, assign the groups of subjects to the experimental treatments (the four cells) at random, too. Label the groups 1, 2, 3, and 4. Then draw these numbers from a table of random numbers. Assume that the table yielded the numbers in this order: 3, 4, 1, 2. Assign Group 3 subjects to the upper left cell, Group 4 subjects to the upper right cell, and so on.

Often B will be an attribute variable, like sex, intelligence, achievement, anxiety, self-perception, race, and so on. The subject assignment must be altered. First, since B is an attribute variable, there is no possibility of assigning subjects to B_1 and B_2 at random. If B were the variable sex, the best we can do is to assign males first at random to the cells A_1B_1 and A_2B_1, and then females to the cells A_1B_2 and A_2B_2.

Factorial Designs with More than Two Variables

We can often improve the design and increase the information obtained from a study by adding groups. Instead of A_1 and A_2, and B_1 and B_2, an experiment may profit from A_1, A_2, A_3, and A_4, and B_1, B_2, and B_3. Practical and statistical problems increase and sometimes become quite difficult as variables are added. Suppose we have a $3 \times 2 \times 2$ design that has $3 \times 2 \times 2 = 12$ cells, each of which has to have at least two subjects, and preferably many more. (It is possible, but not very sensible, to have only one subject per cell if one can have more than one. There are, of course, designs that have only one subject per cell.) If we decide that 10 subjects per cell are necessary, $12 \times 10 = 120$ subjects will have to be obtained and assigned at random. The problem is more acute with one more variable and the practical manipulation of the research situation is also more difficult. But the successful handling of such an experiment allows us to test a number of hypotheses and yields a great deal of information. The combinations of three-, four-, and five-variable designs give a wide variety of possible designs: $2 \times 5 \times 3$, $4 \times 4 \times 2$, $3 \times 2 \times 4 \times 2$, $4 \times 3 \times 2 \times 2$, and so on.

Research Examples of Factorial Designs

Examples of two- and three-dimensional factorial designs were described in Chapter 14. (The restudy of these examples is recommended, because the reasoning behind the essential design can now be more easily grasped.) Since a number of examples of factorial designs were given in Chapter 14, we confine the examples given here to three studies with unusual features.

Flowers: Groupthink

In a highly provocative article, "Groupthink," Janis discussed the possible deleterious consequences of the drive for concurrence (often called consensus) in cohesive groups.[3] He said that consensus-seeking becomes so dominant in cohesive ingroups that it overrides realistic appraisal of alternative courses of action. In support of his thesis, Janis cited the Bay of Pigs, the Vietnam war, and other "fiascos." The article and its arguments are impressive. Will it hold up under experimental testing? Flowers tested Janis' basic hypothesis in the laboratory.[4] Flowers' hypothesis was that cohesiveness and leadership style in groups interact to produce groupthink. That is, in high cohesive groups with closed leadership groupthink, as measured by number of problem solutions proposed and the use of information outside the groups, will develop. Cohesiveness was operationalized as follows: groups of acquaintances = high cohesive; groups of strangers = low cohesive. Style of leadership was open—leader encouraged divergent opinions and emphasized wise decisions—or closed—leader encouraged unanimity at all costs and focused on the preferred solution of the leader. The dependent variables were: number of suggested solutions to problems and the use of information outside the group. (There were, of course, many more details in operationalizing these variables.)

Part of the results obtained are given in Table 20.2. These data were obtained from 40 *groups*, with 10 groups in each cell. The unit of analysis was the group, therefore, an unusual feature of this research. The only effect that was significant was open and closed leadership, as shown by the means of (a), 6.45 and 5.15 and (b), 16.35 and 11.75. The predicted interaction between leadership style and cohesiveness did not emerge in either set of data. Evidently style of leadership is the crucial variable. Part of Janis' thesis was supported.

Table 20.2 Mean Numbers of Solutions Proposed, (a), and Emergent Facts, (b), Flowers Study[a]

(a)

	Open	Closed	
High Coh.	6.70	4.94	5.82
Low Coh.	6.20	5.35	5.78
	6.45	5.15	

(b)

	Open	Closed	
High Coh.	16.8	11.8	14.3
Low Coh.	15.9	11.70	13.8
	16.35	11.75	

[a]$N = 40$ groups, 4 in each group. The layout of the data is mine, as are the calculations of the marginal means. F_a (open-closed) = 6.44 ($p < .05$); F_b (open-closed) = 16.76 ($p < .01$).

[3]I. Janis, "Groupthink," *Psychology Today*, Nov. 1971, 43–46, 74–86.
[4]M. Flowers, "A Laboratory Test of Some Implications of Janis' Groupthink Hypothesis," *Journal of Personality and Social Psychology*, 35 (1977), 888–896.

The student should particularly note that group measures were analyzed. Also note the use of two dependent variables and two analyses of variance. That the main effect of open and closed leadership was significant with number of proposed solutions *and* with facts used is much more convincing than if only one of these had been used. An interesting and potentially important experiment! Indeed, Flowers' operationalization of Janis' ideas of groupthink and its consequences is a good example of experimental testing of complex social ideas. It is also a good example of replication and of Design 19.1 in its simplest factorial form.

Sigall and Ostrove: Attractiveness and Crime

It has often been said that attractive women are reacted to and treated differently than men and less attractive women. In most cases, perhaps, the reactions are "favorable": attractive women are perhaps more likely than less attractive women to receive the attention and favors of the world. Is it possible, however, that their attractiveness may in some situations be disadvantageous? Sigall and Ostrove asked the question: How is physical attractiveness of a criminal defendant related to juridic sentences, and does the nature of the crime interact with attractiveness?[5] They had their subjects assign sentences, in years, to swindle and burglary offenses of attractive, unattractive, and control defendants. The factorial paradigm of the experiment, together with the results, is given in Table 20.3. (We forego describing many of the experimental details; they were well handled.)

In the burglary case, the defendant stole $2,200 in a high-rise building. In the swindle case, the defendant ingratiated herself with and swindled a middle-aged bachelor of $2,200. Note that the Unattractive and Control conditions did not differ much from each other. Both Attractive-Swindle (5.45) and Attractive-Burglary (2.80) differed from the other two conditions—but in opposite directions! Attractive-Swindle received the heaviest mean sentence: 5.45 years, whereas Attractive-Burglary received the lowest mean sentence: 2.80 years. The statistics support the preceding verbal summary: the interaction was statistically significant: The Attractiveness-Offense F, at 2 and 106 degrees of freedom, was 4.55, $p < .025$. In words, attractive defendants have an advantage over unattractive defendants, except when their crimes are attractiveness-related (swindle).

Hoyt: Teacher Knowledge and Pupil Achievement

We now outline an educational study done many years ago because it was planned to answer an important theoretical and practical question and because it clearly illustrates a

Table 20.3 Mean Sentences in Years of Attractive, Unattractive, and Control Defendants for Swindle and Burglary, Sigall and Ostrove Study

	Defendant Condition[a]		
	Attractive	Unattractive	Control
Swindle	5.45	4.35	4.35
Burglary	2.80	5.20	5.10

[a]$N = 120$, 20 per cell. F (interaction) = 4.55 ($p < .025$).

[5]H. Sigall and N. Ostrove, "Beautiful but Dangerous: Effects of Offender Attractiveness and Nature of the Crime on Juridic Judgment," *Journal of Personality and Social Psychology*, 31 (1975), 410–414. Copyright © 1975 by the American Psychological Association. Reprinted by permission of the author.

complex factorial design.[6] The research question was: What are the effects on the achievement and attitudes of pupils if teachers are given knowledge of the characteristics of their pupils? Hoyt's study explored several aspects of the basic question and used factorial design to enhance the internal and external validity of the investigation. The first design was used three times for each of three school subjects, and the second and third were used twice, once in each of two school systems.

The paradigm for the first design is shown in Figure 20.1. The independent variables were treatments, ability, sex, and schools. The three treatments were no information (N), test scores (T), and test scores plus other information (TO). These are self-explanatory. Ability levels were high, medium, and low IQ. The variables sex and schools are obvious. Eighth-grade students were assigned at random within sex and ability levels. It will help us understand the design if we examine what a final analysis of variance table of the design looks like. Before doing so, however, it should be noted that the achievement results were mostly indeterminate (or negative). The F ratios, with one exception, were not significant. Pupils' attitudes toward teachers, on the other hand, seemed to improve with increased teacher knowledge of pupils, an interesting and potentially important finding. The analysis of variance table is given in Table 20.4. One experiment yields 14 tests! Naturally, a number of these tests are not important and can be ignored. The tests of greatest importance (marked with asterisks in the table) are those involving the treatment variable. The most important test is between treatments, the first of the main effects. Perhaps equally important are the interactions involving treatments. Take the interaction treatments × sex. If this were significant, it would mean that the amount of information a teacher possesses about students has an influence on student achievement, but boys are influenced differently than girls. Boys with teachers who possess information about their pupils may do better than boys whose teachers do not have such information, whereas it may be the opposite with girls, or it may make no difference one way or the other.[7]

Second-order or triple interactions are harder to interpret. They seem to be rarely significant. If they *are* significant, however, they require special study. Crossbreak tables

		Treatments					
		N		*T*		*TO*	
	Sex	M	F	M	F	M	F
School A	High IQ						
	Medium IQ						
	Low IQ			Dependent			
School B	High IQ			Variable			
	Medium IQ			Measures			
	Low IQ						

Figure 20.1

[6] K. Hoyt, "A Study of the Effects of Teacher Knowledge of Pupil Characteristics on Pupil Achievement and Attitudes towards Classwork," *Journal of Educational Psychology*, 46 (1955), 302–310.

[7] The student will find it helpful to lay out and study the tables for these interactions. For example, the one under discussion would be:

	N	*T*	*TO*
Female			
Male			

Table 20.4 Sources of Variance and Degrees of Freedom for a $3 \times 3 \times 2 \times 2$ Factorial Design with Variables Treatments, Ability, Sex, and School (Total and Within Degrees of Freedom are Omitted)

Source	df
Main Effects:	
*Between Treatments	2
Between Ability Levels	2
Between Sexes	1
Between Schools	1
First-Order Interactions:	
*Interaction: Treatments × Ability	4
*Interaction: Treatments × Sex	2
*Interaction: Treatments × School	2
Interaction: Ability × Sex	2
Interaction: Ability × School	2
Interaction: Sex × School	1
Second-Order Interactions:	
*Interaction: Treatments × Ability × Sex	4
*Interaction: Treatment × Ability × School	4
Interaction: Ability × Sex × School	2
Third-Order Interaction:	
Interaction: Treatment × Ability × Sex × School	4
Within	
Total	

of the means are perhaps the best way, but graphic methods, as discussed earlier, are often enlightening. The student will find guidance in Edwards' book.[8]

EVALUATION OF RANDOMIZED SUBJECTS DESIGNS

Randomized subjects designs are all variants or extensions of Design 19.1, the basic experimental group-control group design in which subjects are assigned to the experimental and control groups at random. As such they have the strengths of the basic design, the most important of which is the randomization feature and the consequent ability to assume the preexperimental approximate equality of the experimental groups in all possible independent variables. History and maturation are controlled because very little time elapses between the manipulation of X and the observation and measurement of Y. There is no possible contamination due to pretesting.

Two other strengths of these designs, springing from the many variations possible, are flexibility and applicability. They can be used to help solve many behavioral research problems, since they seem to be peculiarly well-suited to the types of design problems that arise from social scientific and educational problems and hypotheses. The one-way designs, for example, can incorporate any number of methods, and the testing of methods is a major educational need. The variables that constantly need control in behavioral research—sex, intelligence, aptitude, social class, schools, and many others—can be in-

[8] A. Edwards, *Experimental Design in Psychological Research*, 4th ed. New York: Holt, Rinehart and Winston, 1972, chaps. 9, 10.

corporated into factorial designs and thus controlled. With factorial designs, too, it is possible to have mixtures of active and attribute variables, another important need.

There are also weaknesses. One criticism has been that randomized subjects designs do not permit tests of the equality of groups as do before-after designs. Actually, this is not a valid criticism for two reasons: with enough subjects and randomization, it can be assumed that the groups are equal, as we have seen; and it *is* possible to check the groups for equality on variables other than Y, the dependent variable. For educational research, data on intelligence, aptitude, and achievement, for example, are available in school records. Pertinent data for sociology and political science studies can often be found in county and election district records.

Another difficulty is statistical. One should have equal numbers of cases in the cells of factorial designs. (It is possible to work with unequal n's, but it is both clumsy and a threat to interpretation. Small discrepancies can be cured by dropping out cases at random.) This imposes a limitation on the use of such designs, because it is often not possible to have equal numbers in each cell. One-way randomized designs are not so delicate: unequal numbers are not a difficult problem.[9]

Compared to matched groups designs, randomized subjects designs are usually less precise, that is, the error term is ordinarily larger, other things equal. It is doubtful, however, whether this is cause for concern. In some cases it certainly is—for example, where a very sensitive test of a hypothesis is needed. In much behavioral research, though, it is probably desirable to consider as nonsignificant any effect that is insufficiently powerful to make itself felt over and above the random noise of a randomized subjects design.

All in all, then, these are powerful, flexible, useful, and widely applicable designs. In the opinion of the writer, they are the best all-round designs, perhaps the first to be considered when planning the design of a research study.

Study Suggestions

1. In studying research design, it is useful to do analyses of variance—as many as possible: simple one-way analyses and two-variable factorial analyses. Try even a three-variable analysis. By means of this statistical work you can get a better understanding of the designs. You may well attach variable names to your "data," rather than work with numbers alone. Some useful suggestions for projects with random numbers follow.

- (a) Draw three groups of random numbers, 0 through 9. Name the independent and dependent variables. Express a hypothesis and translate it into design-statistical language. Do a one-way analysis of variance. Interpret.
- (b) Repeat 1(a) with five groups of numbers.
- (c) Now increase the numbers of one of your groups by 2, and decrease those of another group by 2. Repeat the statistical analysis.
- (d) Draw four groups of random numbers, 10 in each group. Set them up, at random, in a 2×2 factorial design. Do a factorial analysis of variance.

[9] How to adjust and analyze data for unequal n's is a complex, thorny, and much-argued problem. For a discussion in the context mostly of analysis of variance, see G. Snedecor and W. Cochran, *Statistical Methods,* 6th ed. Ames, Iowa: Iowa State University Press, 1967, chap. 16. Discussion in the context of multiple regression, which is actually a better solution of the problem, can be found in: F. Kerlinger and E. Pedhazur, *Multiple Regression in Behavioral Research.* New York: Holt, Rinehart and Winston, 1973, pp. 140–151, 187–197; and E. Pedhazur, *Multiple Regression in Behavioral Research: Explanation and Prediction,* 2d ed. New York: Holt, Rinehart and Winston, 1982, pp. 316–323, 371–373. Pedhazur's discussions are detailed and authoritative. He reviews the issues and suggests solutions.

(e) Bias the numbers of the two right-hand cells by adding 3 to each number. Repeat the analysis. Compare with the results of 1(d).

(f) Bias the numbers of the data of 1(d), as follows: add 2 to each of the numbers in the upper left and lower right cells. Repeat the analysis. Interpret.

2. Look up Study Suggestion 2 and 3, Chapter 14. Work through both examples again. (Are they easier for you now?)

3. Suppose that you are the principal of an elementary school. Some of the fourth- and fifth-grade teachers want to dispense with workbooks. The superintendent does not like the idea, but he is willing for you to test the notion that workbooks do not make much difference. (One of the teachers even suggests that workbooks may have bad effects on both teachers and pupils.) Set up two research plans and designs to test the efficacy of the workbooks: a one-way design and a factorial design. Consider the variables achievement, intelligence, and sex. You might also consider the possibility of teacher attitude toward workbooks as an independent variable.

4. Study Table 20.1, the data of the Peeck study. Peeck used one-way analyses of variance, one analysis for the recall measures of Presidents, the other for the recall measures of States. He was of course testing the significance of the mean recall differences among the mobilization conditions. Could he have used a 3×2 factorial design? If so, what would the advantages be, if any? In Table 20.1, why were the two means italicized?

5. Suppose an investigation using methods and sex as the independent variables and achievement as the dependent variable has been done with the results shown in Table 20.5. The numbers in the cells are fictitious means. The F ratios of methods and sex are not significant. The interaction F ratio is significant at the .01 level. Interpret these results statistically and substantively. To do the latter, name the three methods.

Table 20.5 Hypothetical Data (Means) of a Fictitious Factorial Experiment

Sex	Methods			
	A_1	A_2	A_3	
Male	45	45	36	42
Female	35	39	40	38
	40	42	38	

6. Although difficult and sometimes frustrating, there is no substitute for reading and studying original research studies. A number of studies using factorial design and analysis of variance have been cited and summarized in this chapter and in earlier chapters. Select and read two of these studies. Try summarizing one of them. Criticize both studies for adequacy of design and execution of the research (to the best of your present knowledge and ability). Focus particularly on the adequacy of the design to answer the research question or questions.

Chapter 21

Research Design Applications: Correlated Groups

A BASIC principle is behind all correlated-groups[1] designs: there is systematic variance in the dependent variable measures due to the correlation between the groups *in some variable related to the dependent variable*. This correlation and its concomitant variance can be introduced into the measures—and the design—in three ways: (1) use the same units, for example, subjects, in each of the experimental groups, (2) match units on one or more independent variables that are related to the dependent variable, and (3) use more than one group of units, like classes or schools, in the design. Despite the seeming differences among these three ways of introducing correlation into the dependent variable measures, they are basically the same. We now examine the design implications of this basic principle and discuss ways of implementing the principle.

THE GENERAL PARADIGM

With the exception of correlated factorial designs and so-called nested designs, all analysis of variance paradigms of correlated-groups designs can be easily outlined. The general paradigm is given in Figure 21.1. To emphasize the sources of variance, means of columns and rows have been indicated. The individual dependent variable measures (Y's)

---

[1] The word "group" should be taken to mean set of scores. Then there is no confusion when a repeated trials experiment is classified as a multigroup design.

Units	X_1	X_2	X_3	.	.	.	X_k	
				Treatments				
1	Y_{11}	Y_{12}	Y_{13}	.	.	.	Y_{1k}	M_1
2	Y_{21}	Y_{22}	Y_{23}	.	.	.	Y_{2k}	M_2
3	Y_{31}	Y_{32}	Y_{33}	.	.	.	Y_{3k}	M_3
.	.	.	.	.	.	.	.	.
.	.	.	.	.	.	.	.	.
.	.	.	.	.	.	.	.	.
n	Y_{n1}	Y_{n2}	Y_{n3}				Y_{nk}	M_n
	M_{x_1}	M_{x_2}	M_{x_3}	.	.	.	M_{x_k}	(M_t)

Figure 21.1

have also been inserted.[2] It can be seen that there are two sources of systematic variance: that due to columns, or treatments, and that due to rows—individual or unit differences. Analysis of variance must be the two-way variety.

The student who has studied the correlation-variance argument of Chapter 15, where the statistics and some of the problems of correlated-groups designs were presented, will have no difficulty with the variance reasoning of Figure 21.1. The intent of the design is to maximize the between-treatments variance, identify the between-units variance, and minimize the error (residual) variance. The *maxmincon* principle applies here as elsewhere. The only difference, really, between designs of correlated groups and randomized subjects is the rows or units variance.

Units

The units used do not alter the variance principle. The word "unit" is deliberately used to emphasize that units can be persons or subjects, classes, schools, districts, cities, even nations. In other words, "unit" is a generalized rubric that can stand for many kinds of entities. The important consideration is whether the units, whatever they are, differ from each other. If they do, *variance between units* is introduced. In this sense, talking about correlated groups or subjects is the same as talking about variance between groups or subjects. The notion of individual differences is extended to *unit differences*.

The real value of correlated-groups designs would seem to be that not only do they enable the investigator to isolate and estimate the variance due to correlation; they also guide him to design research to capitalize on the differences that frequently exist between units. If a research study involves different classes in the same school, these classes are a possible source of variance. Thus it may be wise to use "classes" as units in the design. The well-known differences between schools are very important sources of variance in behavioral research. They may be handled factorially, or they may be handled in the manner of the designs in this chapter. Indeed, if one looks carefully at a factorial design

[2]It is useful to know the system of subscripts to symbols used in mathematics and statistics. A rectangular table of numbers is called a *matrix*. The entries of a matrix are letters and/or numbers. When letters are used, it is common to identify any particular matrix entry with two (sometimes more) subscripts. The first of these indicates the number of the *row*, the second the number of the *column*. Y_{32}, for instance, indicates the Y measure in the third row and the second column. Y_{57} indicates the Y measure of the fifth row and the seventh column. It is also customary to generalize this system by adding the letter subscripts. In this book, i symbolizes *any row number* and j *any column number*. Any number of the matrix is represented by Y_{ij}, *any* number of the third row, Y_{3j}, and *any* number of the second column, Y_{i2}.

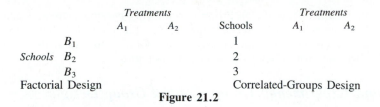

Figure 21.2

with two independent variables, one of them *schools,* and at a correlated-groups design with units *schools,* one finds, in essence, the same design. Study Figure 21.2. On the left is a factorial design and on the right a correlated-groups design. But they look the same! They are the same, in variance principle. (The only differences might be numbers of scores in the cells and statistical treatment.)

One-group Repeated Trials Design

In the one-group repeated trials design, as the name indicates, one group is given different treatments at different times. In a learning experiment, the same group of subjects may be given several tasks of different complexity, or the experimental manipulation may be to present learning principles in different orders, say from simple to complex, from complex to simple, from whole to part, from part to whole.

It was said earlier that the best possible matching of subjects is to match a subject with himself, so to speak. The difficulties in using this solution of the control problem have also been mentioned. One of these difficulties resembles pretest sensitization, which may produce an interaction between the pretest and the experimentally manipulated variable. Another is that subjects mature and learn over time. A subject who has experienced one or two trials of an experimental manipulation and is facing a third trial is a different person from the one who faced trial one. Experimental situations differ a great deal, of course. In some situations, repeated trials may not unduly affect the performances of subjects on later trials; in other situations, they may. The problem of how individuals learn or become unduly sensitized during an experiment is a difficult one to solve. In short, *history, maturation,* and *sensitization* are possible weaknesses of repeated trials. The regression effect can also be a weakness because, as we saw in an earlier chapter, low scorers tend to get higher scores and high scorers lower scores on retesting simply due to the imperfect correlation between the groups. A control group is, of course, needed.

Despite the basic time difficulties, there may be occasions when a one-group repeated trials design is useful. Certainly in analyses of "time" data this is the implicit design. If we have a series of growth measurements of children, for instance, the different times at which the measurements were made correspond to treatments. The paradigm of the design is the same as that of Figure 21.1. Simply substitute "subjects" for "units" and label X_1, X_2, . . . "trials."

From this general paradigm special cases can be derived. The simplest case is the one-group, before-after design, Design 18.2 (a), where one group of subjects was given an experimental treatment preceded by a pretest and followed by a posttest. Since the weaknesses of this design have already been mentioned, further discussion is not necessary. It should be noted, though, that this design, especially in its nonexperimental form, closely approximates much commonsense observation and thinking. A person may observe educational practices today and decide that they are not good. In order to make this judgment, he implicitly or explicitly compares today's educational practices with educational practices of the past. From a number of possible causes, depending on his particular bias, he will select one or more reasons for what he believes to be the sorry state of educational affairs: "progressive education," "educationists," "moral degeneration," "lack of firm religious principles," and so on.

Two-group, Experimental Group–Control Group Designs

This design has two forms, the better of which (repeated here) was described in Chapter 19 as Design 19.2:

$$\boxed{M_r} \quad \frac{X \qquad\qquad Y}{\sim\!X \qquad\qquad Y} \qquad \begin{array}{l}\text{(Experimental)}\\[1ex] \text{(Control)}\end{array}$$

In this design, subjects are first matched and then assigned to experimental and control groups at random. In the other form, subjects are matched but not assigned to experimental and control groups at random. The latter design can be indicated by simply dropping the subscript r from $\boxed{M_r}$ (described in Chapter 18 as Design 18.4, one of the inadequate designs).

The design-statistical paradigm of this warhorse of designs is shown in Figure 21.3. The insertion of the symbols for the means shows the two sources of systematic variance: *treatments* and *pairs, columns* and *rows*. This is in clear contrast to the randomized designs of Chapter 20, where the only systematic variance was *treatments* or *columns*.

The most common variant of the two-group, experimental group-control group design is the before-after, two-group design. [See Design 19.3 (b).] The design-statistical paradigm and its rationale are discussed later.

RESEARCH EXAMPLES OF CORRELATED-GROUPS DESIGNS

Hundreds of studies of the correlated-groups kind have been published. The most frequent designs have used matched subjects or the same subjects with pre- and posttests. Correlated-groups designs, however, are not limited to two groups; the same subjects, for example, can be given more than two experimental treatments. The studies described below have been chosen not only because they illustrate correlated-groups design, matching, and control problems, but also because they are historically, psychologically, or educationally important.

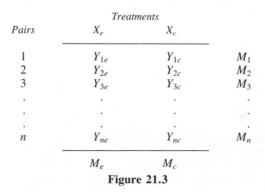

Figure 21.3

Thorndike's Transfer of Training Study

In 1924, E. L. Thorndike published a remarkable study of the presumed effect on intelligence of certain school subjects.[3] Students were matched according to scores on Form A of the measure of the dependent variable, intelligence. This test also served as a pretest. The independent variable was One Year's Study of Subjects, such as history, mathematics, and Latin. A posttest, Form B of the intelligence test, was given at the end of the year. Thorndike used an ingenious device to separate the differential effect of each school subject by matching on Form A of the intelligence test those pupils who studied, for instance, English, history, geometry, and *Latin* with those pupils who studied English, history, geometry, and *shopwork*. Thus, for these two groups, he was comparing the differential effects of *Latin* and *shopwork*. Gains in final intelligence scores were considered a joint effect of growth plus the academic subjects studied.

Despite its weaknesses, this was a colossal study. Thorndike was aware of the lack of adequate controls, as revealed in the following passage on the effects of selection:

> The chief reason why good thinkers seem superficially to have been made such by having taken certain school studies, is that good thinkers have taken such studies. . . . When the good thinkers studied Greek and Latin, these studies seemed to make good thinkers. Now that the good thinkers study Physics and Trigonometry, these seem to make good thinkers. If the abler pupils should all study Physical Education and Dramatic Art, these subjects would seem to make good thinkers.[4]

Thorndike pointed the way to controlled educational research, which has led to the decrease of metaphysical and dogmatic explanations in education. His work struck a blow against the razor-strop theory of mental training, the theory that likened the mind to a razor that could be sharpened by stropping it on "hard" subjects.

It is not easy to evaluate a study such as this, the scope and ingenuity of which is impressive. One wonders, however, about the adequacy of the dependent variable, "intelligence" or "intellectual ability." Can school subjects studied for one year have much effect on intelligence? Moreover, the study was not experimental. Thorndike measured the intelligence of students and let the independent variables, school subjects, operate. No randomization, of course, was possible. As mentioned above, he was aware of this control weakness in his study, which is still a classic that deserves respect and careful study despite its weaknesses in history and selection (maturation was controlled).

Miller and DiCara: Learning of Autonomic Functions

In Study Suggestion 4, Chapter 15, we presented data from one of the set of remarkable studies of the learning of autonomic functioning done by Miller and his colleagues.[5] It has been believed by experts and laymen that it is not possible to learn and control responses of the autonomic nervous system. That is, glandular and visceral responses—heart beat, urine secretion, and blood pressure, for example—were supposed to be beyond the "control" of the individual. Miller believed otherwise. He demonstrated experimentally that

[3] E. Thorndike, "Mental Discipline in High School Studies," *Journal of Educational Psychology*, 15 (1924), 1–22, 83–98.

[4] *Ibid.*, p. 98.

[5] N. Miller, "Learning of Visceral and Glandular Responses," *Science*, 163 (1969), 434–445. Miller reports a number of these studies in: N. Miller, *Selected Papers*. New York: Aldine, 1971, Part XI. The study now to be reported is: N. Miller and L. DiCara, "Instrumental Learning of Urine Formation by Rats: Changes in Renal Blood Flow," *American Journal of Physiology*, 215 (1968), 677–683.

such responses are subject to instrumental learning. The crucial part of his method consisted of rewarding visceral responses when they occurred. In the study whose data were cited in Chapter 15, for example, rats were rewarded when they increased or decreased the secretion of urine. Fourteen rats were assigned at random to two groups called "Increase Rats" and "Decrease Rats." The rats of the former group were rewarded with brain stimulation (which was shown to be effective for *increases* in urine secretion), while the rats of the latter group were rewarded for *decreases* in urine secretion during a "training" period of 220 trials in approximately three hours.

To show part of the experimental and analytic paradigms of this experiment, the data before and after the training periods for the Increase Rats and the Decrease Rats are given in Table 21.1 (taken from the authors' Table 1). The measures in the table are the milliliters of urine secretion per minute per 100 grams of body weight. Note that they are very small quantities. The research design is a variant of Design 19.3 (a):

$$\boxed{R} \quad \begin{array}{ccc} Y_b & X & Y_a \quad \text{(E)} \\ \hline Y_b & \sim X & Y_a \quad \text{(C)} \end{array}$$

The difference is that $\sim X$, which in the design means absence of experimental treatment for the control group, now means reward for decrease of urine secretion. The usual analysis of the after-training measures of the two groups is therefore altered.

We can better understand the analysis if we analyze the data of Table 21.1 somewhat differently than Miller and DiCara did. (They used t tests.) I did a two-way (repeated measures) analysis of variance of the Increase Rats data, Before and After, and the Decrease Rats data, Before and After. The Increase Before and After means were .017 and .028, and the Decrease means were .020 and .006. The Increase F ratio was 43.875 ($df = 1,6$); the Decrease F was 46.624. Both were highly significant. The two Before means of .017 and .020 were not significantly different, however, In this case, comparison of the means of the two After groups, the usual comparison with this design, is probably not appropriate because one was for increase and the other for decrease in urine secretion.

This whole study, with its highly controlled experimental manipulations and its "control" analyses, is a lovely example of imaginative conceptualization and disciplined com-

Table 21.1 Secretion of Urine Data, Miller and DiCara Study: Increase Rats and Decrease Rats, Before and After Training

	Increase Rats[a]				Decrease Rats[b]		
Rats	Before	After	Σ	Rats	Before	After	Σ
1	.023	.030	.053	1	.018	.007	.025
2	.014	.019	.033	2	.015	.003	.018
3	.016	.029	.045	3	.012	.005	.017
4	.018	.030	.048	4	.015	.006	.021
5	.007	.016	.023	5	.030	.009	.039
6	.026	.044	.070	6	.027	.008	.035
7	.012	.026	.038	7	.020	.003	.023
Means	.017	.028			.020	.006	

[a] Increase, Before-After: $F = 43.875$ ($p < .001$); $\omega^2 = .357$. The measures in the table are milliliters per minute per 100 grams of weight.
[b] Decrease, Before-After: $F = 46.624$ ($p < .001$); $\omega^2 = .663$.

petent analysis. The above analysis is one example. But the authors did much more. For example, to be more sure that the reinforcement affected only urine secretion, they compared the Before and After heart rates (beats per minute) of both the Increase and the Decrease rats. The means were 367 and 412 for Increase rats, and 373 and 390 for the Decrease rats. Neither difference was statistically significant. Similar comparisons of blood pressure and other bodily functions were not significant.

Students will do well to study this fine example of laboratory research until they clearly understand what was done and why. It will help students learn more about controlled experiments, research design, and statistical analysis than most textbook exercises. It is a splendid achievement!

Bandura and Menlove: Modeling and Extinction Study

Psychological researchers, perhaps because of the nature of many psychological problems that involve change, are increasingly using relatively complex designs with pre- and postmeasures and tests. We choose one such study not only for pretests and posttests but also because it is one of a fine series of researches along similar theoretical and practical lines on the problems of social learning and modeling.[6] The design is again a variant of Design 19.3 (a), even though it uses three and four groups.

The researchers first measured the animal-avoidance behavior of 48 nursery school children (the pretest). They then randomly assigned the children to three experimental groups: *single-model, multiple-model,* and *control*. *S*'s in the single-model condition observed a movie in which a five-year-old progressively approached a cocker spaniel. *S*'s in the multiple-model condition observed boys and girls interacting positively with different dogs. Children in the control condition were shown other unrelated movies. The avoidance behavior was tested after the treatment (posttest), and again in a later follow-up.

Analyses used in the study were unusual: because of nonnormality of the score distributions, nonparametric tests were used. First, to test the *trend* effect—that is, the differences among the scores of the pretest, posttest, and follow-up—a Friedman nonparametric analysis was used. χ_r^2 was 15.79, significant at the .001 level. Recall that the Friedman test takes account of the correlation. Here, the differences among the experimental treatments of the same children were tested. Thus, there was significant change. Other tests showed that the two modeling conditions changed, but the control condition did not change. The significance of the differences among the three experimental treatments was tested using the Kruskal-Wallis one-way nonparametric analysis of variance. Change or difference scores obtained between pretest and follow-up were analyzed. *H* was 5.01, significant at the .05 level. Other analyses showed that the modeling treatments were effective.

The authors then added an ingenious twist to the study: they used the multiple-modeling procedure with the control group *S*'s at the end of the experiment proper. These *S*'s already had three approach scores: pretest, posttest, follow-up. Call the new fourth set of scores posttherapy. The significance of the differences among the four sets of scores— note carefully that each *S* had four scores and thus we have correlated groups—was tested with the Friedman test. χ_r^2 was 13.42, significant at the .01 level. Thus the modeling procedure was also effective with the controls.

To be quite clear on what was done, the three principal analyses used by Bandura and Menlove are summarized in Table 21.2, using the symbolism already familiar to us or self-evident. Recall that the Kruskal-Wallis test is a one-way analysis and uses ranks of *all*

[6] A. Bandura and F. Menlove, ''Factors Determining Vicarious Extinction of Avoidance Behavior through Symbolic Modeling,'' *Journal of Personality and Social Psychology*, 8 (1968), 99–108.

Table 21.2 Paradigmatic Outline of Analyses of Bandura and Menlove Modeling Study

I.					*II.*		
		Trends				*Experimental Conditions*[a]	
S's	Pretest	Posttest	Follow-up		SM	MM	C
1	Y_{1pr}	Y_{1po}	Y_{1fu}				
2	Y_{2pr}	Y_{2po}	Y_{2fu}			Change Scores	
.	.	.	.			(Follow-up—Pretest)	
.	.	.	.				
N	Y_{Npr}	Y_{Npo}	Y_{Nfu}				
		Friedman Test				Kruskal-Wallis Test	

III.				
		Control Trends		
S's	Pretest	Posttest	Follow-up	Posttherapy
1	Y_{1pr}	Y_{1po}	Y_{1fu}	Y_{1pt}
2	Y_{2pr}	Y_{2po}	Y_{2fu}	Y_{2pt}
.	.	.	.	.
12	Y_{12pr}	Y_{12po}	Y_{12fu}	Y_{12pt}
		Friedman Test		

[a]SM = single-modeling; MM = multiple-modeling; C = control.

the scores, while the Friedman test is a two-way analysis and uses ranks of each row separately. Bandura and Menlove, then, used Designs 19.1 and 19.3, and they chose statistical tests to match the demands of their designs. The reader is urged to read the original study for its theoretical and technical sophistication and its considerable practical psychological and educational interest and significance. When reading it, keep Table 21.2 before you. (The original report is neither easy nor complete.)

MULTIGROUP CORRELATED-GROUPS DESIGNS

Units Variance

While it is difficult to match three and four sets of subjects, and while it is ordinarily not feasible or desirable in behavioral research to use the same subjects in each of the groups, there are natural situations in which correlated groups exist. These situations are particularly important in educational research. Until recently, the variances due to differences between classes, schools, school systems, and other "natural" units have not been well controlled or often used in the analysis of data. Perhaps the first indication of the importance of this kind of variance was given in Lindquist's fine book on statistical analysis in educational research.[7] In this book, Lindquist placed considerable emphasis on *schools variance*. Schools, classes, and other educational units tend to differ significantly in achievement, intelligence, aptitudes, and other variables. The educational investigator has to be alert to these *unit differences,* as well as to individual differences.

Consider an obvious example. Suppose an investigator chooses a sample of five schools for their variety and heterogeneity. He is of course seeking external validity: representativeness. He conducts an investigation using pupils from all five schools and combines the measures from the five schools to test the mean differences in some dependent variable. In so doing, he is ignoring the variance due to the differences among schools. It is understandable that the means do not differ significantly; the schools variance is mixed in with the error variance.

Gross errors can arise from ignoring the variance of units such as schools and classes. One such error is to select a number of schools and to designate certain schools as experimental schools and others as control schools. Here the between-schools variance gets entangled with the variance of the experimental variable. Similarly, classes, school districts, and other educational units differ and thus engender variance. The variances must be identified and controlled, whether it be by experimental or statistical control, or both.

FACTORIAL CORRELATED GROUPS

Factorial models can be combined with the units notion to yield a valuable design: *factorial correlated-groups design*. Such a design is appropriate when units are a natural part of a research situation. For instance, the research may require the comparison of a variable before and after an experimental intervention, or before and after an important event. Obviously there will be correlation between the before and after dependent variable measures. Another useful example is shown in Figure 21.4. This is a 3×2 factorial design with five units (classes, school, and so forth) in each level, B_1 and B_2.

The strengths and weaknesses of the factorial correlated-groups design are similar to those of the more complex factorial designs. The main strengths are the ability to isolate

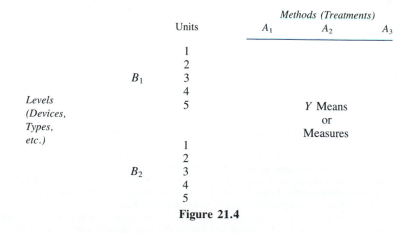

Figure 21.4

[7]E. Lindquist, *Statistical Analysis in Educational Research*. Boston: Houghton Mifflin, 1940.

and measure variances and to test interactions. Note that the two main sources of variance, *treatments (A)* and *levels (B)*, and the *units* variance can be evaluated; that is, the differences between the *A, B,* and *units* means can be tested for significance. In addition, three interactions can be tested: *treatments* by *levels, treatments* by *units,* and *levels* by *units.* If individual scores are used in the cells instead of means, the triple interaction, too, can be tested. Note how important such interaction can be, both theoretically and practically. For example, questions like the following can be answered: Do treatments work differently in different units? Do certain methods work differently at different intelligence levels or with different sexes or with children of different socioeconomic levels?[8]

Suedfeld and Rank: Revolutionary Leaders and Conceptual Complexity

Suedfeld and Rank, in a study mentioned earlier in another context, tested the intriguing notion that successful revolutionary leaders—Lenin, Cromwell, Jefferson, for example— are conceptually simple in their public communications *before* revolution and conceptually complex *after* revolution.[9] Unsuccessful revolutionary leaders, on the other hand, do not differ in conceptual complexity before and after revolution. The problem lends itself to a factorial design and to repeated measures analysis. The design and the data on conceptual complexity are shown in Table 21.3. It can be seen that the successful leaders became conceptually more complex—from 1.67 to 3.65—but unsuccessful leaders did not change—2.37 and 2.22. The interaction F ratio was 12.37, significant at the .005 level. The hypothesis was supported.

A few points should be picked up. One, note the effective combining of factorial design and repeated measures. When appropriate, as in this case, the combination is highly useful mainly because it sets aside, so to speak, the variance in the dependent variable measures due to individual (or group or block) differences. The error term is thus smaller and better able to assess the statistical significance of mean differences. Two, this

Table 21.3 Factorial Design with Repeated Measures: Suedfeld and Rank Study of Revolutionary Leaders[a]

	Pretakeover	Posttakeover	
Success	1.67	3.65	2.66
Failure	2.37	2.22	2.30
	1.96	3.05	

[a]Tabled measures are means of conceptual complexity measures. Interaction $F = 12.37$ ($p < .005$).

[8]The advanced student will want to know how to handle units (schools, classes, etc.) and units variance in factorial designs. Detailed guidance is given in A. Edwards, *Experimental Design in Psychological Research,* 4th ed. New York: Holt, Rinehart and Winston, 1972, chap. 14, and in R. Kirk, *Experimental Design: Procedures for the Behavioral Sciences.* Belmont, Calif.: Brooks/Cole, 1968, pp. 229–244 and chap. 8. The subject is difficult. Even the names of the designs become complex: randomized blocks, nested treatments, split-plot designs. Such designs are powerful, however: they combine virtues of factorial designs *and* of correlated groups designs. When needed, Edwards and Kirk are good guides. It is suggested, in addition, that help be solicited from someone who understands both statistics *and* behavioral research. It is unwise to use computer programs because their names seem appropriate. It is also unwise to seek analytic help from computer personnel. One cannot expect such people to know and understand, say, factorial analysis of variance. That is *not* their job. More will be said about computer analysis in later chapters.

[9]P. Suedfeld and A. Rank, "Revolutionary Leaders: Long-Term Success as a Function of Changes in Conceptual Complexity," *Journal of Personality and Social Psychology,* 34 (1976), 169–178.

study was nonexperimental: no experimental variable was manipulated. Three and most important, the intrinsic interest and significance of the research problem and its theory and the ingenuity of measuring and using conceptual complexity as a variable to "explain" the success of revolutionary leaders overshadow possible questionable methodological points.[10]

ANALYSIS OF COVARIANCE

The invention of the analysis of covariance by Ronald Fisher was an important event in behavioral research methodology. Here is a creative use of the variance principles common to experimental design and to correlation and regression theory—which we study later in the book—to help solve a long-standing control problem.

Analysis of covariance is a form of analysis of variance that tests the significance of the differences among means of experimental groups after taking into account initial differences among the groups *and* the correlation of the initial measures and the dependent variable measures. That is, analysis of covariance analyzes the differences between experimental groups on Y, the dependent variable, after taking into account either initial differences between the groups on Y (pretest), or differences between the groups in some pertinent independent variable or variables, X, substantially correlated with Y, the dependent variable. The measure used as a control variable—the pretest or pertinent variable—is called a *covariate*.

Clark and Walberg: Massive Reinforcement and Reading Achievement

There is little point to describing the statistical procedures and calculations of analysis of covariance. First, in their conventional form, they are complex and hard to follow. Second, we wish here only to convey the meaning and purpose of the approach. Third and most important, there is a much easier way to do what analysis of covariance does. Later in the book we will see that analysis of covariance is a special case of multiple regression and is much easier to do with multiple regression. To give the reader a feeling for what analysis of covariance accomplishes, let us look at an effective use of the procedure in an educational study.[11]

Clark and Walberg thought that their subjects, potential school dropouts doing poorly in school, needed far more reinforcement (encouragement, reward, etc.) than subjects doing well in school. So they used massive reinforcement with their experimental group subjects and moderate reinforcement with their control group subjects. Since their dependent variable, reading achievement, is substantially correlated with intelligence, they also needed to control intelligence. A one-way analysis of variance of the reading achievement means of the experimental and control groups yielded an F of 9.52, significant at the .01 level, supporting their belief. It is conceivable, however, that the difference between the experimental and control groups was due to intelligence rather than to rein-

---

[10]The above sentence, for instance, may be incongruent with the use of variables in this study. Suedfeld and Rank analyzed measures of the independent variable, conceptual complexity. But the hypothesis under study was actually: If conceptual complexity (after revolution), then successful leadership. But with a research problem of such compelling interest and a variable of such importance (conceptual complexity) imaginatively and competently measured, who wants to quibble? (The logical difficulty is similar to that of the salt-tasting study of McGee and Snyder cited in Chapter 12 in which salting food was the dependent variable, but the researchers analyzed measures of the independent variable, attribution of dispositional and environmental factors.)

[11]C. Clark and H. Walberg, "The Influence of Massive Rewards on Reading Achievement in Potential School Dropouts," *American Educational Research Journal*, 5 (1968), 305–310.

Table 21.4 Analysis of Covariance Paradigm, Clark and Walberg Study

	Experimental (Massive Reinforcement)		*Control* (Moderate Reinforcement)	
	X (Intelligence)	Y (Reading)	X (Intelligence)	Y (Reading)
Means:	92.05	31.62	90.73	26.86

forcement. That is, even though the S's were assigned at random to the experimental groups, an initial difference in intelligence in favor of the experimental group may have been enough to make the experimental group reading mean significantly greater than the control group reading mean, since intelligence is substantially correlated with reading. With random assignment, it is unlikely to happen, but it *can* happen. To control this possibility, Clark and Walberg used analysis of covariance.

Study Table 21.4, which shows in outline the design and analysis. The means of the X and Y scores, as reported by Clark and Walberg, are given at the bottom of the table. The Y means are the main concern. They were significantly different. Although it is doubtful that the analysis of covariance will change this result, it is possible that the difference between the X means, 92.05 and 90.73, may have tipped the statistical scales, in the test of the difference between the Y means, in favor of the experimental group. The analysis of covariance F test, which uses Y sums of squares and mean squares purged of the influence of X, was significant at the .01 level: $F = 7.90$. Thus the mean reading scores of the experimental and control groups differed significantly, after being adjusted or controlled for intelligence.

RESEARCH DESIGN AND ANALYSIS: CONCLUDING REMARKS

Four major objectives have dominated the organization and preparation of Part Six. The first was to acquaint the student with the principal designs of research. By so doing, it was hoped that narrowly circumscribed notions of doing research with, say, only one experimental group and one control group, or with matched subjects, or with one group, before and after, may be widened. The second objective was to convey a sense of the balanced structure of good research designs, to develop sensitive feeling for the architecture of design. Design must be formally as well as functionally fitted to the research problems we seek to solve. The third objective was to help the reader understand the logic of experimental inquiry and the logic of the various designs. Research designs are alternative routes to the same destination: reliable and valid statements of the relations among variables. Some designs, if feasible, yield stronger relational statements then other designs.

In a certain sense, the fourth objective of Part Six has been the most difficult to achieve: to help the student understand the relation between the research design and statistics. Statistics is, in one sense, the technical discipline of handling variance. And, as we have seen, one of the basic purposes of design is to provide control of systematic and error variances. This is the reason for treating statistics in such detail in Parts Four and

Five before considering design in Part Six. Fisher expresses this idea succinctly when he says, "Statistical procedure and experimental design are only two different aspects of the same whole, and that whole comprises all the logical requirements of the complete process of adding to natural knowledge by experimentation."[12]

A well-conceived design is no guarantee of the validity of research findings. Elegant designs nicely tailored to research problems can still result in wrong or distorted conclusions. Nevertheless, the chances of arriving at accurate and valid conclusions are better with sound designs than with unsound ones. This is relatively sure: if design is faulty, one can come to no clear conclusions. If, for instance, one uses a two-group, matched-subjects design when the research problem logically demands a factorial design, or if one uses a factorial design when the nature of the research situation calls for a correlated-groups design, no amount of interpretative or statistical manipulation can increase confidence in the conclusions of such research.

It is fitting that Fisher should have the last word on this subject. In the first chapter of his book, *The Design of Experiments,* he said:

> If the design of an experiment is faulty, any method of interpretation which makes it out to be decisive must be faulty too. It is true that there are a great many experimental procedures which are well designed in that they *may* lead to decisive conclusions, but on other occasions may fail to do so; in such cases, if decisive conclusions are in fact drawn when they are unjustified, we may say that the fault is wholly in the interpretation, not in the design. But the fault of interpretation . . . lies in overlooking the characteristic features of the design which lead to the result being sometimes inconclusive, or conclusive on some questions but not on all. To understand correctly the one aspect of the problem is to understand the other.[13]

Study Suggestions

1. Can memory be improved by training? William James, the great American psychologist and philosopher, did a memory experiment on himself.[14] He first learned 158 lines of a Victor Hugo poem, which took him $131\frac{5}{8}$ minutes. This was his baseline. Then he worked for 20-odd minutes daily, for 38 days, learning the entire first book of *Paradise Lost.* (Book I is 22 tightly printed pages of rather difficult verse!) This was training of his memory. He returned to the Hugo poem and learned 158 additional lines in $151\frac{1}{2}$ minutes. Thus he took longer after the training than before. Not satisfied, he had others do similar tasks—with similar results.

On the basis of this work, what conclusions could James come to? Comment on his research design. What design among those in this book does his design approximate?

2. In the Miller and DiCara study outlined in this chapter, the authors did parallel analyses. In addition to their analyses of urine secretion, for example, they analyzed heart beat rate and blood pressure. Why did they do this?

In her classic study of "natural categories," Rosch replicated the original study of colors with forms (square, circle, etc.).[15] What advantage is there in such replication?

3. I did a two-way (repeated measures) analysis of variance of the Miller and DiCara Increase Rats data of Table 21.1, with some of the results reported in the table. ω^2 (Hays omega-squared) was .357. ω^2 for the Decrease Rats data was .663. What do these coefficients mean? Why calculate them?

4. Kolb, basing his work on the outstanding work of McClelland on achievement motivation, did a fascinating experiment with underachieving high school boys of high intelligence.[16] Of 57

---

[12]R. Fisher, *The Design of Experiments,* 6th ed. New York: Hafner, 1951, p. 3.

[13]*Ibid.,* pp. 2–3.

[14]W. James, *The Principles of Psychology.* New York: Holt, 1890, pp. 666–667.

[15]E. Rosch, "Natural Categories," *Cognitive Psychology,* 4 (1973), 328–350.

[16]D. Kolb, "Achievement Motivation Training for Underachieving High-School Boys," *Journal of Personality and Social Psychology,* 2 (1965), 783–792.

boys, he assigned 20 at random to a training program in which, through various means, the boys were "taught" achievement motivation (an attempt to build a need to achieve into the boys). The boys were given a pretest of achievement motivation in the summer, and given the test again six months later. The mean *change scores* were, for experimental and control groups, respectively, 6.72 and −.34, significant at the .005 level.

    (a) Comment on the use of change scores. Does their use lessen our faith in the statistical significance of the results?

    (b) Might factors other than the experimental training have induced the change?

    5. Lest the student believe that only continuous measures are analyzed and that analysis of variance alone is used in psychological and educational experiments, read the study by Freedman et al. on guilt and compliance.[17] There was an experimental group (*S*'s induced to lie) and a control group, and the dependent variable was measured by whether a *S* did or did not comply with a request for help. The results were reported in crossbreak frequency tables.

Read the study, and, after studying the authors' design and results, design one of the three experiments another way. Bring in another independent variable, for instance. Suppose that it was known that there were wide individual differences in compliance. How can this be controlled? Name and describe two kinds of design to do it.

    6. One useful means of control by matching is to use pairs of identical twins. Why is this method a useful means of control? If you were setting up an experiment to test the effect of environment on measured intelligence and you had 20 pairs of identical twins and complete experimental freedom, how would you set up the experiment?

    7. In a study in which training on the complexities of art stimuli affected attitude toward music, among other things, Renner used analysis of covariance, with the covariate being measures from a scale to measure attitude toward music.[18] This was a pretest. There were three experimental groups. Sketch the design from this brief description. Why did Renner use the music attitude scale as a pretest? Why did she use analysis of covariance? (*Note:* The original report is well worth reading. The study, in part a study of creativity, is itself creative.)

    8. In a significant study of the effect of liberal arts education on complex concept formation, Winter and McClelland found the difference between senior and freshmen of a liberal arts college on a measure of complex concept formation to be statistically significant ($M_s = 2.00$, $M_f = 1.22$; $t = 3.76$ ($p < .001$)).[19] Realizing that a comparison was needed, they also tested similar mean differences in a teachers college and in a community college. Neither of these differences was statistically significant.

Why did Winter and McClelland test the relation in the teachers college and in the community college?

It is suggested that students look up the original report—it is well worth study—and do analysis of variance from the reported *n*'s, means, and standard deviations, using the method outlined in Chapter 13 (Addendum).

    9. One virtue of analysis of covariance seldom mentioned in texts is that three estimates of the correlation between *X* and *Y* can be calculated: the total *r* over all the scores, the between-groups *r*, which is the *r* between the *X* and *Y* means, and the within-groups *r*, the *r* calculated from an average of the *r*'s between *X* and *Y* within the *k* groups. The within-groups *r* is the "best" estimate of the "true" *r* between *X* and *Y*. Why is this so?

[*Hint:* Can a total *r*, the one usually calculated in practice, be inflated or deflated by between-groups variance?]

    10. The $2 \times 2 \times 2$ factorial design is used a good deal by social psychologists. Here are three unusual, excellent, even creative studies in which it was used:

[17] J. Freedman, S. Wallington, and E. Bless, "Compliance Without Pressure: The Effect of Guilt," *Journal of Personality and Social Psychology,* 7 (1967), 117–124.

[18] V. Renner, "Effects of Modification of Cognitive Style on Creative Behavior," *Journal of Personality and Social Psychology,* 14 (1970), 257–262.

[19] D. Winter and D. McClelland, "Thematic Analysis: An Empirically Derived Measure of the Effects of Liberal Arts Education," *Journal of Educational Psychology,* 70 (1978), 8–16.

ARONSON, E., and GERARD, E. "Beyond Parkinson's Law: The Effect of Excess Time on Subsequent Performance," *Journal of Personality and Social Psychology,* 3 (1966), 336–339.

CARLSMITH, J., and GROSS, A. "Some Effects of Guilt on Compliance," *Journal of Personality and Social Psychology,* 11 (1969), 232–239.

JONES, E., et al. "Pattern of Performance and Ability Attribution: An Unexpected Primacy Effect," *Journal of Personality and Social Psychology,* 10 (1968), 317–340.

Read one of these studies. (The Jones study is long, involved, and difficult, but well worth the effort. It has replication and systematic exploration of alternative hypotheses, as well as high theoretical and technical competence.)

PART SEVEN

TYPES OF RESEARCH

Chapter 22

Nonexperimental Research

AMONG prevalent fallacies, one of the most dangerous to science is that known as *post hoc, ergo propter hoc:* after this, therefore caused by this. We may joke, with a tinge of seriousness, "If I take an umbrella, it won't rain." We may even seriously say that delinquents are delinquent because of a lack of discipline in the schools or that religious education makes children more virtuous. It is easy to assume that one thing causes another simply because it occurs before the other, and because one has such a wide choice of possible "causes." Then, too, many explanations often seem plausible. It is easy to believe, for instance, that the learning of children improves because we institute a new educational practice or teach in a certain way. We assume that the improvement in their learning was due to the new spelling method, to the institution of group processes into the classroom situation, to stern discipline and more homework (or little discipline and less homework). We rarely realize that children will usually learn something if they are given the opportunity to learn.

The social scientist and the educational scientist constantly face the problem of the post hoc fallacy. The sociologist who seeks the causes of delinquency knows that extreme care must be used in studying the problem. Slum conditions, broken homes, lack of love—each or all of these conditions are possible causes of delinquency. The psychologist seeking the roots of adult personality faces an even subtler problem: hereditary traits, child-rearing practices, educational influences, parental personality, and environmental circumstances are all plausible explanations. The educational scientist, with the goal of understanding the basis of successful school achievement, also faces a large number of reasonable possibilities: intelligence, aptitude, motivation, home environment, teacher personality, pupil personality, and teaching methods.

The danger of the post hoc assumption is that it can, and often does, lead to erroneous and misleading interpretations of research data, the effect being particularly serious when scientists have little or no control over time and independent variables. When they seek to explain a phenomenon that has already occurred, they are confronted with the unpleasant fact that they do not have real control of the possible causes. Hence they must pursue a course of research action different in execution and interpretation from that of scientists who experiment.

Definition

Nonexperimental research is systematic empirical inquiry in which the scientist does not have direct control of independent variables because their manifestations have already occurred or because they are inherently not manipulable. Inferences about relations among variables are made, without direct intervention, from concomitant variation of independent and dependent variables.

Assume that an investigator is interested in the relation between sex and creativity in children. He measures the creativity of a sample of boys and girls and tests the significance of the difference between the means of the two sexes. The mean of boys is significantly higher than the mean of girls. He concludes that boys are more creative than girls. This may or may not be a valid conclusion. The relation exists, true. With only this evidence, however, the conclusion is doubtful. The question is: Is the demonstrated relation really between sex and creativity? Since other variables are correlated with sex, it might have been one or more of these variables that produced the difference between the creativity scores of the two sexes.

BASIC DIFFERENCE BETWEEN EXPERIMENTAL AND NONEXPERIMENTAL RESEARCH

The basis of the structure in which experimental science operates is simple. One hypothesizes: If x, then y; if frustration, then aggression. Depending on circumstances and personal predilection in research design, one uses some method to manipulate or measure x. One then observes y to see if concomitant variation, the variation expected or predicted from the variation in x, occurs. If it does, this is evidence for the validity of the proposition, $x \rightarrow y$, "If x then y." Note that we here predict from a controlled x to y. To help us achieve control, we can use the principle of randomization and active manipulation of x and can assume, other things equal, that y is varying as a result of the manipulation of x.

In nonexperimental research, on the other hand, y is observed, and an x, or several x's, are also observed, either before, after, or concomitant to the observation of y. There is no difference in the basic logic: it can be shown that the argument structure and its *logical* validity are the same in experimental and nonexperimental research.[1] And the basic purpose of both is also the same: to establish the *empirical* validity of so-called conditional statements of the form If p, then q. The essential difference is direct control of p, the independent variable. In experimental research, p can be manipulated, which is rather direct "control." When Clark and Walberg had teachers give one group of subjects massive reinforcement and other teachers give another group moderate reinforcement,

---

[1] The basic logic is set forth in: F. Kerlinger, "Research in Education." In R. Ebel, V. Noll, and R. Bauer, eds., *Encyclopedia of Educational Research*, 4th ed. New York: Macmillan, 1969, pp. 1127–1144 (pp. 1133–1134).

they were directly manipulating or controlling the variable reinforcement. Similarly, when Bandura and Menlove showed one group a movie with a single model, another group a movie with multiple models, and a third group a "neutral" movie, they were directly manipulating the variable modeling. In addition, subjects can be assigned at random to the experimental groups.

In nonexperimental research, *direct* control is not possible: neither experimental manipulation nor random assignment can be used. These are two essential differences between experimental and nonexperimental approaches. Owing to lack of relative control of x and other possible x's, the "truth" of the hypothesized relation between x and y cannot be asserted with the confidence of the experimental situation. Basically, nonexperimental research has, so to speak, an inherent weakness: lack of control of independent variables.

The most important difference between experimental research and nonexperimental research, then, is *control*. In experiments, investigators at least have manipulative control: they have at least one active variable. If an experiment is a "true" experiment, they can also exercise control by randomization. They can assign subjects to groups at random, or can assign treatments to groups at random. In the nonexperimental research situation, this kind of control of the independent variables is not possible. Investigators must take things as they are and try to disentangle them.

Take a well-known case. When we paint the skins of rats with carcinogenic substances (x), adequately control other variables, and the rats ultimately develop carcinoma (y), the argument is compelling because x (and other possible x's, theoretically) is controlled and y is predicted. But when we find cases of lung cancer (y) and then go back among the possible multiplicity of causes ($x_1, x_2, \ldots, x_n$) and pick cigarette-smoking (say x_3) as the culprit, we are in a more difficult and ambiguous situation. Neither situation is sure, of course; both are probabilistic. But in the experimental case we can be *more* sure—considerably more sure if we have adequately made "other things equal"—that the statement If x, then y is empirically valid. In the nonexperimental case, however, we are always on shakier ground because we cannot say, with nearly as much assurance, "other things equal." We cannot control the independent variables by manipulation or by randomization. In short, the probability that x is "really" related to y is greater in the experimental situation than it is in the nonexperimental situation, because the control of x is greater.

SELF-SELECTION AND NONEXPERIMENTAL RESEARCH

In an ideal behavioral research world, the drawing of random samples of subjects, and the random assignment of subjects to groups and treatments to groups, would always be possible. In the real world, however, one, two, or even all three of these possibilities do not exist. It is possible to draw subjects at random in both experimental and nonexperimental research. But it is not possible, in nonexperimental research, to assign subjects to groups at random or to assign treatments to groups at random. Thus subjects can "assign themselves" to groups, can "select themselves" into the groups on the basis of characteristics other than those in which the investigator may be interested. The subjects and the treatments come, as it were, already assigned to the groups.

Self-selection occurs when the members of the groups being studied are in the groups, in part, because they differentially possess traits or characteristics extraneous to the research problem, characteristics that possibly influence or are otherwise related to the variables of the research problem. Examples of self-selection may aid understanding.

In the well-known research on cigarette-smoking and cancer, the smoking habits of a large number of people were studied. This large group was divided into those who had lung cancer—or who had died of it—and those who did not have it. The dependent variable was thus the presence or absence of cancer. Investigators probed the subjects' backgrounds to determine whether they smoked cigarettes, and if so, how many. Cigarette-smoking was the independent variable. The investigators found that the incidence of lung cancer rose with the number of cigarettes smoked daily. They also found that the incidence was lower in the cases of light smokers and nonsmokers. They came to the conclusion that cigarette-smoking causes lung cancer.[2] This conclusion may or may not be true. But the investigators cannot come to this conclusion, although they *can* say that there is a statistically significant relation between the variables.

The reason they cannot state a causal connection is that there are a number of other variables, any one of which, or any combination of which, may have caused lung cancer. And they have not controlled other possible independent variables. They *cannot* control them, except by testing alternative hypotheses, a procedure to be explained later. Even when they also study "control groups" of people who have no cancer, self-selection may be operating. Maybe tense, anxious men are doomed to have lung cancer if they marry tall women, for instance. It may just happen that this type of man also smokes cigarettes heavily. The cigarette-smoking is not what kills him—he kills himself by being born tense and anxious—and possibly by marrying a tall woman. Such men are selected into the sample by investigators only because they smoke cigarettes. But such men select themselves into the sample because they commonly possess a temperament that happens to have cigarette-smoking as a concomitant.

Self-selection can be a subtle business. There are two kinds: self-selection into *samples* and into *comparison groups*. The latter occurs when subjects are selected because they are in one group or another: cancer and no cancer, college and no college, underachievement and no underachievement. That is, they are selected *because* they possess the dependent variable in greater or lesser degree. Self-selection into samples occurs when subjects are selected in a nonrandom fashion into a sample.

The crux of the matter is that when *assignment* is not random, there is always a loophole for other variables to crawl through. When we put subjects into groups, in the above case and in similar cases, or they "put themselves" into groups, on the basis of one variable, it is possible that another variable (or variables) correlated with this variable is the "real" basis of the relation. The usual nonexperimental study uses groups that exhibit differences in the dependent variable. In some longitudinal-type studies the groups are differentiated first on the basis of the independent variable. But the two cases are basically the same, since group membership *on the basis of a variable* always brings selection into the picture.

For example, we may select college freshmen at random and then follow them to determine the relation between intelligence and success in college. The students selected themselves into college, so to speak. One or more of the characteristics they bring with them to college, other than intelligence—socioeconomic level, motivation, family background—may be the principal determinants of college success. That we start with the independent variable, in this case intelligence, does not change the self-selective nature of the research situation. In the sampling sense, the students selected themselves into college, which would be an important factor if we were studying college students and noncollege students. But if we are interested only in the success and nonsuccess *of college*

---

[2]Careful scientific investigators will usually not say "cause." The word "cause" is used here to make the point more emphatic and because authoritative sources so use it: see *The New York Times,* Dec. 6, 1959, p. E-11, where the Surgeon General of the United States Public Health Service was directly quoted as saying: "the weight of evidence at present implicates smoking as the principal etiological [causative] factor in the increased incidence of lung cancer."

students, self-selection into college is irrelevant, whereas self-selection into success and nonsuccess groups is crucial. That we measure the intelligence of the students when they enter college and follow them through to success and nonsuccess does not change either the selection problem or the nonexperimental character of the research. In sum, the students selected themselves into college and selected themselves to succeed or not to succeed in college.

LARGE-SCALE NONEXPERIMENTAL RESEARCH

Research examples will, as usual, help us to understand the nature of nonexperimental research. Instead of summarizing only individual studies, as we have to now, we describe both individual studies and sets of studies centered around some phenomenon or variable of interest. Nonexperimental behavioral research often focuses on large problems of social and human importance: social class, political processes, segregation and desegregation, public attitudes, school achievement, for example. The importance—"relevance" is the fashionable word—of the subject of these studies should not obscure our understanding of their nonexperimental character. Because nonexperimental research has inherent weaknesses, however, does *not* mean that experimental research is more important. As said earlier, the experiment is one of the great inventions of all time, an ideal of control toward which we aspire. This does not mean that experiments are necessarily "better" than nonexperimental studies. On the other hand, nonexperimental research is not necessarily "better" than experimental research because its content and variables seem to be socially important. This would be like saying that psychological research is "better" than sociological research because psychologists more often use an experimental approach and sociologists a nonexperimental approach!

Authoritarianism and Ethnocentrism

One of the most important and influential studies of the century was the set of investigations into ethnocentrism and authoritarianism reported in the book *The Authoritarian Personality*.[3] The general hypothesis of the study was that political, economic, and social beliefs are related to deep-seated personality characteristics. Another hypothesis was that adult personality is derived from early childhood experiences. In short, attitudes and beliefs were related to underlying personality trends. The investigators, among other things, studied anti-Semitism as part of a general characteristic called *ethnocentrism.* Later, the investigators extended their thought and work to a still larger construct, *authoritarianism,* which they conceived to be a broad personality syndrome that determines in part ethnocentrism, social attitudes, and certain other behaviors. The authoritarian personality was conceived to be conventional, cynical, destructive, aggressive, power-centered, and ethnocentric.[4]

While this is an inadequate summary of the basic problems of a complex study, it is sufficient for the present purpose. The study had to be nonexperimental because authoritarianism and ethnocentrism, as defined, are nonmanipulable variables, as are most of the variables related to authoritarianism. One of the major results of the study, for instance,

[3] T. Adorno, E. Frenkel-Brunswik, D. Levinson, and R. Sanford, *The Authoritarian Personality.* New York: Harper & Row, 1950.

[4] For evidence that the authors' theory about the characteristics of the authoritarian personality and its measurement was in general well-conceived, see F. Kerlinger and M. Rokeach, "The Factorial Nature of the F and D Scales," *Journal of Personality and Social Psychology,* 4 (1966), 391–399.

was information on the relation between authoritarianism and prejudice. It is obvious that when one studies such variables one is studying already existing sets of personality characteristics and attitudes. The subjects are ready-made authoritarians or nonauthoritarians (with gradations between) and come to the research with already well-formulated attitudes. One can conceive, somehow, of manipulating such variables, but the manipulation, as indicated previously, changes their nature. Whenever one studies the relations between variables that "already exist" in the individuals studied, or whenever one studies the determinants of such variables, one is deeply embedded in nonexperimental research and its problems.

Determinants of School Achievement

A large preoccupation of educational researchers has been a search for the determinants of school achievement.[5] What are the factors that lead to successful achievement in school—and unsuccessful achievement? Intelligence is an important factor, of course. While measured intelligence, especially verbal ability, accounts for a large proportion of the variance of achievement, there are many other variables, psychological and sociological: sex, race, social class, aptitude, environmental characteristics, school and teacher characteristics, family background, teaching methods. The study of achievement is characterized by both experimental and nonexperimental approaches. We are here concerned only with the latter since it clearly illustrates problems of nonexperimental research.

In 1966 the now famous Coleman report was published.[6] As its title indicates, it was a large-scale attempt to answer the question: Do American schools offer equal educational opportunity to all children? Equally important, however, was the question of the relation between student achievement and the kinds of schools students attend. This study was a massive and admirable effort to answer these questions (and others). Its most famous and controversial finding was that the differences among schools account for only a small fraction of the differences in school achievement. Most achievement variance was accounted for by what the children bring with them to school. There was much to question about the study's methodology and conclusions.[7] Indeed, its reverberations are still with us. The principal dependent variable was verbal achievement. There were, however, more than 100 independent variables. The authors used relatively sophisticated multivariate procedures to analyze the data. Much of the core of the analytic problems, the interpretations of the findings, and the subsequent critiques inhere in the nonexperimental nature of the research.

The controversial conclusion mentioned above of the relative importance of home background variables and school variables depends on a completely reliable and valid method for assessing relative impacts of different variables. In experimental research, one is safer drawing comparative conclusions because the independent variables are not corre-

[5]The literature is large. A good guide to some of the work is: B. Bloom, *Stability and Change in Human Characteristics*. New York: Wiley, 1964, especially chap. 4. Another valuable book is: H. Hyman, C. Wright, and J. Reed, *The Enduring Effects of Education*. Chicago: University of Chicago Press, 1975. An impressive work that focuses mainly on teaching and the observation of teaching is: M. Dunkin and B. Biddle, *The Study of Teaching*. New York: Holt, Rinehart and Winston, 1974.

[6]J. Coleman, E. Campbell, C. Hobson, J. McPartland, A. Mood, F. Weinfeld, and R. York, *Equality of Educational Opportunity*. Washington, D.C.: U. S. Govt. Printing Office, 1966.

[7]An important evaluation of *Equality* is: F. Mosteller and D. Moynihan, eds., *On Equality of Educational Opportunity*. New York: Vintage Books, 1972. Another important critique and analysis is: C. Jencks and others, *Inequality: A Reassessment of the Effect of Family and Schooling in America*. New York: Basic Books, 1972 (paperback: Harper Colophon Books, 1973).

lated. In the real educational world, however, the variables are correlated, making their unique contributions to achievement hard to determine. While there are statistical methods to handle such problems, no methods can tell us unambiguously that X_1 influences Y to this or that extent because the real influence may be X_2, which influences both X_1 and Y. The ''correct'' interpretation of the findings of *Equality* and studies like it is always unattainable. While there are powerful analytic methods to use with nonexperimental data, unequivocal answers to questions of the determinants of achievement are forever beyond reach.

Participation in Political Processes

How does the participation of citizens in a democracy influence governmental processes? This difficult question was fundamental to Verba and Nie's large, complex, and sophisticated study of political participation in American democracy.[8] A representative sample of over 2,500 residents of the United States was asked questions about political participation, information on political and local leaders, opinions on political efficacy of citizens, and many others. The researchers found that participation does indeed make a difference. Political leaders are more responsive to citizens who participate more. But participants were not a representative group: the participant population tends to be the more affluent and better educated people in higher status occupations. Verba and Nie found, then, that a socioeconomic model of participation and the influence of participation on government was appropriate.

This fine study's findings are probably correct, but the ever-present possibility in all research and especially in nonexperimental research is that independent variables other than those included in the research are the ''real'' source of the variance of the dependent variable. I deliberately selected what I thought was a major study with excellent methodology to underline the difficulties of nonexperimental research. For the obtained important relation found between citizen participation and political leader responsiveness, for example, might the substantial relation be due not to citizen participation and social status but, say, to the (presumed) fact that citizens who participate more are also upper social status people and so are the political leaders? That is, the leaders are responsive not so much because citizens participate at a high level but because higher social status citizens participate more than lower status citizens, and leaders respond to the social status—and its accompanying education, influence, and attitudes—rather than the participation as such. The participation, in other words, is a variable that ''helps'' make social status visible to leaders.[9] Another reservation, as the authors themselves bring out, is that the concurrence of leaders and citizens was not measured in urban cores. Is it possible that in such cores the relation is negligible?

SMALLER SCALE NONEXPERIMENTAL RESEARCH

To illustrate nonexperimental behavioral research studies or series of studies is not easy: there are many, many of them, but few of them satisfy my criteria of methodological soundness and substantive interest. I have chosen the following three studies for three

[8] S. Verba and N. Nie, *Participation in America: Political Democracy and Social Equality*. New York: Harper & Row, 1972.
[9] See *ibid.*, pp. 336–337, especially Table 20-1, where the above argument actually turns out to be in part correct.

reasons. One, they each represent a unique, original, and interesting approach to an important sociological, psychological, or educational problem. Two, each contributes significantly to scientific knowledge. And three, each is nonexperimental.

Kounin: The Management of Classrooms

Again, this example is really a set of researches all directed to the same general question, which can be loosely expressed: What effects do teachers' classroom management procedures have on children in classrooms?[10] The research of Kounin and his colleagues has been characterized by original and significant variables, both independent and dependent, by systems of extensive observations of the behavior in classrooms of teachers and pupils specifically aimed at measuring the variables, and by careful operationalizations of the variables. In one such study, for example, Kounin and Doyle analyzed videotapes of 596 formal lessons taught by 36 teachers in a preschool aimed at measuring the variables lesson continuity and task involvement. The hypothesis tested was simple: The more continuous and unlagging a lesson, the greater the task involvement of children.

During lessons, observers coded children's behavior for appropriate involvement every six seconds. Percentages of involvement scores were calculated. Continuity of lessons was measured by noting and timing child recitations, which were thought to be more discontinuous than the "official" teacher reading and demonstrating. In other words, if a lesson had a high proportion of child recitations, it was considered discontinuous. High task-involvement and low task-involvement reading lessons, as categorized by observers, were compared using the percentages of child-recitation times. The mean percentages of child recitation for high task-involvement lessons was 8.40; the mean for low task-involvement lessons was 20.20. The difference was statistically significant. A similar analysis of demonstration lessons yielded similar results. The authors concluded: "measured degrees of continuity *within* lesson types distinguished between those lessons that had high task involvement when manned by the same occupants" (p. 163).

This is interesting and potentially important research—and all the Kounin studies are characterized by an imaginative yet objective approach to teacher and pupil observation. Unfortunately, none of the studies is experimental. How much more convincing the relation between lesson continuity and task involvement, for example, if lesson continuity had been experimentally manipulated and task involvement had been substantially affected thereby! Questions can and should also be raised about the selection of lessons for analysis and about the analysis of the data. (It seems, again, that independent variable measures were analyzed rather than, as one would normally expect, measures of the dependent variable.[11] This possible error, incidentally, could probably not have happened if the research had been experimental since there would have been k experimental groups in which different amounts of continuity [or discontinuity] had been engendered and the analysis perforce of the task-involvement scores and means of these groups.) Despite

[10] J. Kounin, *Discipline and Group Management in Classrooms*. New York: Holt, Rinehart and Winston, 1970. Other interesting studies have been published since this book's appearance. The one chosen to be summarized is: J. Kounin and P. Doyle, "Degree of Continuity of a Lesson's Signal System and the Task Involvement of Children," *Journal of Educational Psychology,* 67 (1975), 159–164.

[11] The authors report in their Table 4, for instance, means of 18.8 for the high task-involvement group and 15.1 for the low task-involvement group, not significantly different. But these are means of child recitation scores and *not* task-involvement scores. I did what amounts to an analysis of group membership scores, membership in the high and low task-involvement groups, predicting such membership from the child-recitation scores. I did similar analyses for the data of their four tables. In all cases, the conclusions were the same as theirs. It is possible, however, that they might not have been the same. (Later I will show how such analyses are done.)

these methodological caveats—which are troublesome because they becloud the substantive issues—the Kounin et al. studies, although not experimental *even when they could be,* are creative empirical approaches to long-standing teaching problems and methods of classroom discipline and management and the controlled observation of teaching variables in the classroom. Moreover, a theory of classroom management seems possible to develop on the basis of the empirical work.

McClelland: Protestantism, Capitalism, and Achievement

There has been much thought and speculation on the relations among capitalism, Protestantism, and achievement. Max Weber, for example, wrote an important book on capitalism and Protestantism.[12] His basic hypothesis was that Protestantism led to the spirit of capitalism because the Protestant ethic—self-reliance, deferment of enjoyment, asceticism, emphasis on achievement, and so on—produced individuals with the qualities necessary to capitalistic enterprise and development. McClelland, in a remarkable book, has described his many studies on the relation between Protestantism and capitalism.[13] Actually, McClelland's main interest has been on motivation and its measurement, and his research can safely be called one of the successes of psychology. The variable of his principal interest and work has been *achievement motivation,* commonly called *n* Achievement, or *n* Ach, which he has measured by asking individuals to write brief stories suggested by pictures shown them for a few seconds, the pictures representing situations related to work. The stories were then content-analyzed using a complex coding system to obtain scores of *n* Achievement for each individual. In the present study *n* Achievement was an independent variable among several independent variables used to predict the economic growth of nations.

McClelland's hypothesis was that countries whose population is predominantly Protestant will emphasize achievement. Protestant countries should thus show greater capitalistic enterprise than Catholic countries, other things equal. "Capitalistic enterprise" is reflected in economic advance, growth, or development. "Other things equal" means controlling such things as natural resources. Some countries, for example, may be economically more advanced simply because they have greater natural resources. The measure of economic growth, the dependent variable, was electricity production. McClellands's analysis is too complex to explain here. Suffice it to say that he found that Protestant countries were economically more advanced than Catholic countries, as reflected in electricity production, thus supporting the hypothesis. He also found that *n* Achievement was significantly correlated with deviations from expected growth. (The correlation was .43: *ibid.,* p. 100, Table 3.6. See pp. 88–89 for the reason he used deviation scores, or measures of over- and underachievement, rather than the electricity production scores themselves.)

The research reported in *The Achieving Society* is an excellent example of sophisticated approaches to theoretical and empirical problems of large consequence. The difficulties of collecting, analyzing, and interpreting nonexperimental empirical data are well illustrated in this remarkable book. One emerges from its study convinced of the validity of McClelland's theoretical explanations and the soundness of his analyses and interpretations of the findings. I know of no more ambitious and competent studies of complex phenomena and the testing of plausible alternative hypotheses. Yet we must constantly bear in mind the nonexperimental nature of the research and the enormous difficulty of

[12] M. Weber, *The Protestant Ethic and the Spirit of Capitalism* (transl., T. Parsons). New York: Scribner, 1930 (1904).

[13] D. McClelland, *The Achieving Society.* Princeton: Van Nostrand, 1961.

drawing valid conclusions from the evidence presented. On the other hand, McClelland's work greatly advanced scientific understanding of the presumed determinants of capitalistic enterprise and growth *and* of achievement motivation, even though one wishes for more controlled experimentation to provide a firmer foundation for understanding these important psychological, sociological, and economic phenomena.[14]

Bollen: Political Democracy and Level and Timing of Development

What are the conditions and determinants of political democracy? Sociologists and political scientists, long interested in this and related questions and perhaps stimulated by advances in analytic approaches, have recently directed empirical inquiries to the problem of political democracy. We now examine a good example of such research again to illustrate nonexperimental inquiry and the testing of alternative hypotheses.[15] The study has considerable intrinsic interest. We can also help to build our sensitivity to and knowledge of multivariate approaches to complex problems. Other points of interests are the unit of analysis used, *countries*, and the skillful measurement of complex concepts but particularly political democracy. Bollen directed his study mainly to the question of which is the more important factor in the development of political democracy: timing of development or level of development. That is, are late-developing countries less likely than early-developing countries to have attained political democracy? Plausible arguments have been advanced to answer the question. Bollen sought an empirical answer. In addition, he studied the ideas that Protestantism leads to higher political development, a nice link to McClelland's research, and that the greater a country's control of the economic system, the lower the level of democracy.

Using a sample of 99 countries with widely different levels of development, Bollen assessed the effects of time and levels of development on political democracy. To do this, he used multiple regression analysis, which has been mentioned before and will be discussed in detail later in the book. The results of the analysis supported the hypotheses, with one or two exceptions. The most important variable affecting political democracy was level of development and not timing of development: the greater the development of a country, as measured by its energy consumption, the greater its political democracy. That is, *how much* development was far more important than *when* the development took place. The proportion of the population that was Protestant and the state's control of the economy were also significant influences, the former positive and the latter negative.

With these nonexperimental studies behind us, we can discuss and evaluate nonexperimental research in general. We precede evaluative discussion, however, with a more systematic inquiry into the testing of alternative hypotheses, one of the highly important features of scientific research.

TESTING ALTERNATIVE HYPOTHESES

Most investigations begin with hypotheses; the empirical implications of these hypotheses are then tested. Although we "confirm" hypotheses in the manner described in earlier

---

[14] My appraisal of McClelland's thinking and work is perhaps too restrained. Like most good scientists, McClelland's mind has roamed over a wide assortment of human activities, and attempted to explain them with the Protestant ethic and *n* Achievement. He even speculates about preferences for colors and for travel—and then tests the speculations, or cites the work of others in testing them! (See, e.g., *ibid.*, pp. 309ff.) I should have said that the book is an imaginative classic!

[15] K. Bollen, "Political Democracy and the Timing of Development," *American Sociological Review,* 44 (1979), 572–587.

chapters, we can also "confirm" and "disconfirm" hypotheses under study by trying to show that alternative plausible hypotheses are or are not supported. First consider alternative independent variables as antecedents of a dependent variable. The reasoning is the same. If we say "alternative independent variables," for example, we are in effect stating alternative hypotheses or explanations of a dependent variable.

In nonexperimental studies, although one cannot have the confidence in the "truth" of an "If x, then y" statement that one can have in experiments, it *is* possible to set up and test alternative or "control" hypotheses. (Of course, alternative hypotheses can be and are tested in experimental studies, too.) This procedure has been formalized and explained by Platt who, influenced by Chamberlin, called it "strong inference."[16] Chamberlin aptly called the procedure the "method of working multiple hypotheses," and he outlined how the investigator's own "intellectual affections" can be guarded against. He said: "The effort is to bring up into view every rational explanation of new phenomena, and to develop every tenable hypothesis respecting their cause and history. The investigator thus becomes the parent of a family of hypotheses; and, by his parental relation to all, he is forbidden to fasten his affections unduly upon any one."[17]

Let x_1, x_2, and x_3 be three alternative independent variables, and let y be the dependent variable, the phenomenon to be "explained" with a statement of the form: If x, then y. Assume that x_1, x_2, and x_3 exhaust the possibilities. This assumption cannot actually be made—in scientific research it is practically impossible to exhaust all the possibilities. Still, it is assumed for pedagogical reasons.

An investigator has evidence that x_1 and y are substantially related. Having reason to believe that x_1 is the determinative factor, he holds x_2 and x_3 constant. He is assuming that one of the three factors is *the* factor, that either x_1 or x_2 or x_3 is *the* "true" independent variable. (Again, note the assumption. It may be none of them or some combination of all three.) Suppose that the investigator succeeds in eliminating x_2, that is, he shows that x_2 is not related to y. If he also succeeds in eliminating x_3, he can then conclude that x_1 is the influential independent variable. Since the alternative or "control" hypotheses have not been substantiated, the original hypothesis is strengthened.

Similarly, we can test alternative *dependent* variables, which also imply alternative hypotheses. We shift the alternatives to the dependent variable. This is illustrated in a study by Alper, Blane, and Abrams of the different reactions of middle- and lower-class children to finger paints as a consequence of different child-rearing practices.[18] The general question asked was: Do social-class differences in child-training practices result in class differences in personality? The theory invoked required that there be differences in reactions to finger paints. The authors reasoned that middle-class children would react differently from lower-class children to 16 different variables *when finger paints were used:* acceptance of task, washing, and so on. The reactions were significantly different on most of the variables. In a "control experiment," the same procedure was followed *using crayons instead of finger paints*. The two groups did not differ significantly on any of the 11 variables measured, in surprising contrast to the finger paint results. The study was nonexperimental because it was not possible to manipulate the independent variable and because the children came to the study with their reactions ready-made, as it were.

---

[16] J. Platt, "Strong Inference," *Science,* 146 (1964), 347–353; T. Chamberlin, "The Method of Multiple Working Hypotheses," *Science,* 147 (1965), 754–759. The Chamberlin article was originally published in *Science* in 1890 (vol. 15). A clear explanation of the logic behind testing alternative hypotheses is given in: M. Cohen and E. Nagel, *An Introduction to Logic and Scientific Method.* New York: Harcourt Brace Jovanovich, 1934, pp. 265–267.

[17] Chamberlin, *op. cit.,* p. 756.

[18] T. Alper, H. Blane, and B. Abrams, "Reactions of Middle and Lower Class Children to Finger Paints as a Function of Class Differences in Child-Training Practices," *Journal of Abnormal and Social Psychology,* 51 (1955), 439–448.

This use of a control study was ingenious and crucial. Imagine the researchers' consternation if the differences between the two groups on the crayon task had been significant!

Now consider a study by Sarnoff et al. in which it was predicted that English and American children would differ significantly in test anxiety but not in general anxiety.[19] The hypothesis was carefully delineated: If eleven-plus examinations are taken, then test anxiety results. (The eleven-plus examinations are given to English school children at eleven years of age to help determine their educational futures.) Since it was possible that there might be other independent variables causing the difference between the English and American children on test anxiety, the investigators evidently wished to rule out at least some of the major contenders. This they accomplished by carefully matching the samples: they probably reasoned that the difference in test anxiety might be due to a difference in general anxiety, since the measure of test anxiety obviously must reflect some general anxiety. If this were found to be so, the major hypothesis would not be supported. Therefore Sarnoff and his colleagues, in addition to testing the relation between examination and test anxiety, also tested the relation between examination and general anxiety.

The method of testing alternative hypotheses, though important in all research, is particularly important in nonexperimental studies, because it is one of the only ways to "control" the independent variables of such research. Lacking the possibility of randomization and manipulation, nonexperimental researchers, perhaps more so than experimentalists, must be very sensitive to alternative hypothesis-testing possibilities.

EVALUATION OF NONEXPERIMENTAL RESEARCH

The reader may have concluded from the preceding discussion that nonexperimental research is inferior to experimental research, but this conclusion would be unwarranted. It is easy to *say* that experimental research is "better" than nonexperimental research, or that experimental research tends to be "trivial," or that nonexperimental research is "merely correlational." Such statements, in and of themselves, are oversimplifications. What the student of research needs is a balanced understanding of the strengths and weaknesses of both kinds of research. To be committed unequivocally to experimentation or to nonexperimental research may be shortsighted.

The Limitations of Nonexperimental Interpretation

Nonexperimental research has three major weaknesses, two of which have already been discussed in detail: (1) the inability to manipulate independent variables, (2) the lack of power to randomize, and (3) the risk of improper interpretation. In other words, compared to experimental research, other things equal, nonexperimental research lacks control; this lack is the basis of the third weakness: the risk of improper interpretation.

The danger of improper and erroneous interpretations in nonexperimental research stems in part from the plausibility of many explanations of complex events. It is easy to accept the first and most obvious interpretation of an established relation, especially if one works without hypotheses to guide investigation. Research unguided by hypotheses, research "to find out things," is most often nonexperimental. Experimental research is more likely to be based on carefully stated hypotheses.

Hypotheses are if-then predictions. In a research experiment the prediction is from a well-controlled *x* to a *y*. If the prediction holds true, we are relatively safe in stating the

---

[19]I. Sarnoff, F. Lighthall, R. Waite, K. Davidson, and S. Sarason, "A Cross-Cultural Study of Anxiety Among American and English School Children," *Journal of Educational Psychology,* 49 (1958), 129–136.

conditional, If *x*, then *y*. In a nonexperimental study under the same conditions, however, we are considerably less safe in stating the conditional, for reasons discussed earlier. Careful safeguards are more essential in the latter case, especially in the selection and testing of alternative hypotheses, such as the predicted lack of relation between the eleven-plus examination and general anxiety in the Sarnoff study. A predicted (or unpredicted) relation in nonexperimental research may be quite spurious, but its plausibility and conformity to preconception may make it easy to accept. This is a danger in experimental research, but it is *less* of a danger than it is in nonexperimental research because an experimental situation is so much easier to control.

Nonexperimental research that is conducted without hypotheses, without predictions, research in which data are just collected and then interpreted, is even more dangerous in its power to mislead. Significant differences or correlations are located if possible and then interpreted. Assume that an educator decides to study the factors leading to underachievement. He selects a group of underachievers and a group of normal achievers and administers a battery of tests to both groups. He then calculates the means of the two groups on the tests and analyzes the differences with *t* tests. Among, say, twelve such differences, three are significant. The investigator concludes, then, that underachievers and normal achievers differ on the variables measured by these three tests. Upon analysis of the three tests, he thinks he understands what characterizes underachievers. Since all three of the tests seem to measure insecurity, the cause of underachievement is therefore insecurity.

When guided by hypotheses the credibility of the results of studies like the one just cited may be enhanced, but the results are still weak because they capitalize on chance: by chance alone one or two results of many statistical tests may be significant. Above all, plausibility can be misleading. A plausible explanation often seems compelling—even though quite wrong! It seems so obvious, for example, that conservatism and liberalism are opposites. The research evidence, however, seems to indicate that they are not opposites.[20] Another difficulty is that plausible explanations, once found and believed, are often hard to test. According to Merton, *post factum* explanations do not lend themselves to nullifiability because they are so flexible. Whatever the observations, he says, new interpretations can be found to "fit the facts."[21]

The Value of Nonexperimental Research

Despite its weaknesses, much nonexperimental research must be done in psychology, sociology, and education simply because many research problems do not lend themselves to experimental inquiry. A little reflection on some of the important variables in behavioral research—intelligence, aptitude, home background, achievement, social class, rigidity, ethnocentrism—will show that they are not manipulable. Controlled inquiry is possible, of course, but true experimentation is not.

It can even be said that nonexperimental research is more important than experimental research. This is, of course, not a methodological observation. It means, rather, that most social scientific and educational research problems do not lend themselves to experimentation, although many of them do lend themselves to controlled inquiry of the nonexperimental kind. Consider Piaget's studies of children's thinking, the authoritarianism studies

[20] See F. Kerlinger, "Social Attitudes and Their Criterial Referents: A Structural Theory," *Psychological Review,* 74 (1967), 110–122; "Analysis of Covariance Structure Tests of a Criterial Referents Theory of Attitudes," *Multivariate Behavioral Research,* 15 (1980), 403–422; *Liberalism and Conservatism: The Nature and Structure of Social Attitudes*. Hillsdale, N.J.: Erlbaum, 1984.

[21] R. Merton, *Social Theory and Social Structure*. New York: Free Press, 1949, pp. 90–91.

of Adorno et al., the highly important study *Equality of Educational Opportunity*, and McClelland's studies of need for achievement. If a tally of sound and important studies in the behavioral sciences and education were made, it is possible that nonexperimental studies would outnumber and outrank experimental studies.

CONCLUSIONS

Students of research differ widely in their views of the relative values of experimental and nonexperimental research. There are those who exalt experimental research and decry nonexperimental research. There are those who criticize the alleged narrowness and lack of "reality" of experiments, especially laboratory experiments. These critics, especially in education, emphasize the value and relevance of nonexperimental research in "real-life," "natural" situations. A rational position seems obvious. If it is possible, use experimentation because, *other things equal,* one can interpret the results of most experiments with greater confidence that statements of the If p, then q kind *are* what we say they are. It would also seem desirable to test the If p, then q propositions in other settings. One should also look for nonexperimental evidence of the empirical validity of one's hypotheses. So, if it is possible, conditional statements should be studied using both experimental and nonexperimental approaches. The research of Kounin and his colleagues on the influence of teacher variables is impressive and convincing. But how much more impressive and convincing it would be if similar conclusions arise from well-conducted experiments! Conversely, how much more convincing experimental conclusions are if substantiated in well-conducted nonexperimental research.

Replication is always desirable, even necessary. An important point being made is that replication of research does not only mean repetition of the same studies in the same settings. It can and should mean testing empirical implications of theory—interpreting "theory" broadly—in similar and dissimilar situations *and* experimentally and nonexperimentally. It is easier to ask for extensions of research from the laboratory to the field. But researchers should also try to conceive of experimental testing of propositions arrived at nonexperimentally. Of course, this is more difficult and is seldom done. My point is that it *should* be conceived and, when possible, done.

To adopt a firm position that experimental or nonexperimental research is the only road to research heaven is dogmatic guruism. It may be very difficult, perhaps impossible in many cases, to do both experimental and nonexperimental research on the same problem. Can one experimentally manipulate Verba and Nie's participation variable or McClelland's Protestantism, for example? Difficult does not mean impossible, of course. My point is that experimental and nonexperimental possibilities should be explored and exploited if it is possible to do so. Moreover, it should not immediately be assumed that it is *not* possible to do research differently from the way it has been done. There is no one methodological road to scientific validity; there are many roads. And we should choose our roads for their appropriateness to the problems we study. This does not mean, however, that we cannot exploit an approach that is different from what we are used to.

For some stange reason, perhaps the spurious belief in the alleged certitude of science, when people, including scientists, think of science and scientific research, they mistakenly believe there is only one "right" way to approach and do research. Rarely is such a mistake made in music, or art, or building a house. Science, too, has many roads, and experimental and nonexperimental approaches are two such broad roads. Neither is right or wrong. But they *are* different. Our task has been to try to understand the differences and their consequences. We are far from finished with the subject, however. Maybe we will even attain a fair degree of understanding before we are through.

ADDENDUM

Causality and Scientific Research

The study and analysis of ''causal relations'' in research has recently preoccupied social scientists. Economists and econometricians seem to have been the leaders in this work.[22] Simon, a psychologist, has also been a pioneer.[23] Sociologists have written extensively on the subject.[24] The analytic and conceptual movement is productive, as we will see in a later chapter. It is perhaps unfortunate that the word ''cause'' and ''causal relations'' have been used. They imply that science can find the causes of phenomena.

The position taken in this book is that the study of cause and causation is an endless maze. One of the difficulties is that the word ''cause'' has surplus meaning and metaphysical overtones. Perhaps more important, it is not really needed. Scientific research can be done without invoking cause and causal explanations, even though the words and other words that imply cause are almost impossible to avoid and thus will occasionally be used. Blalock points out that causal laws cannot be demonstrated empirically, but that it is helpful to think causally.[25] I agree that causal laws cannot be demonstrated empirically, but am equivocal about thinking causally. There is little doubt that scientists do think causally and that when they talk of a relation between p and q they *hope* or *believe* that p causes q. But no amount of evidence can demonstrate that p *does* cause q.

This position is not so much an objection to causal notions as it is an affirmation that they are not necessary to scientific work. Evidence *can* be brought to bear on the empirical validity of conditional statements of the If p, then q kind, alternative hypotheses can be tested, and probabilistic statements can be made about p and q—and other p's and q's and conditions r, s, and t. Invocation of the word ''cause'' and the expression ''causal relation'' does nothing really constructive. Indeed, it can be misleading.

In expert hands and used with circumspection, path analysis and related methods can help to clarify theoretical and empirical relations.[26] But when their espousal and use imply that causes are sought *and found*, such methods can also be misleading. In sum, the elements of deductive logic in relation to conditional statements, a probabilistic framework and method of work and inference, and the testing of alternative hypotheses are sufficient aids to scientific nonexperimental work without the excess baggage of causal notions and methods presumably geared to strengthening causal inferences. We rest the case with some apt words of Bertrand Russell:

> the word ''cause'' is so inextricably bound up with misleading associations as to make its complete extrusion from the philosophical vocabulary desirable . . . the reason physics has ceased to look for causes is that, in fact, there are no such things. The law of causality . . . is a relic of a bygone age, surviving, like the monarchy, only because it is erroneously supposed to do no harm.[27]

---

[22] See H. Wold and L. Jureen, *Demand Analysis*. New York: Wiley, 1953.

[23] H. Simon, *Models of Men*. New York: Wiley, 1957.

[24] E.g., H. Blalock, *Causal Inferences in Nonexperimental Research*. Chapel Hill, N.C.: University of North Carolina Press, 1961.

[25] *Ibid.*, p. 6.

[26] For an extended discussion of the value and use of path analysis and so-called commonality analysis in studying relations, see F. Kerlinger and E. Pedhazur, *Multiple Regression in Behavioral Research*. New York: Holt, Rinehart and Winston, 1973. The second edition of this book has a more extended discussion of causation and the methods used to study it: E. Pedhazur, *Multiple Regression in Behavioral Research: Explanation and Prediction,* 2d ed. New York: Holt, Rinehart and Winston, 1982, chap. 15.

[27] B. Russell, ''On the Notion of Cause, with Applications to the Free-Will Problem.'' In H. Feigl and M. Brodbeck, eds., *Readings in the Philosophy of Science*. New York: Appleton, 1953, p. 387.

Study Suggestions

1. A social psychologist plans to investigate factors behind anti-Semitism. He believes that people who have had authoritarian parents and authoritarian upbringing tend to be anti-Semitic. Would a research project designed to test this hypothesis be experimental or nonexperimental? Why?

2. An educational psychologist decides to test the hypothesis that intelligence and motivation are the principal determinants of success in school. Would his research most likely be experimental or nonexperimental? Why?

3. An investigator is interested in the relation between role perception and social values.

    (a) Which is the independent variable? The dependent variable?

    (b) Whatever judgment you have made, can you justifiably reverse the variables?

    (c) Do you think a research project designed to investigate this problem would be basically experimental or nonexperimental?

    (d) Can the investigator do two researches, one experimental and one nonexperimental, both designed to test the same hypothesis?

    (e) If your answer to (d) was Yes, will the variables of the two problems be the same? Assuming that the relations in both researches were significant, will the conclusions be substantially the same?

4. Suppose that you want to study the effects of the decisions of boards of education on various aspects of education, such as teacher morale, pupil achievement, relations between teachers and administrators, teacher clique formation. Would your research be experimental or nonexperimental? Why?

5. In the study suggestions of Chapter 2, a number of problems and hypotheses were given. Take each of these problems and hypotheses and decide whether research designed to explore the problems and test the hypotheses would be basically experimental or nonexperimental. Can any of the problems and hypotheses be tackled in both ways?

6. McClelland, in the study described in this chapter, presents data on the electrical production during 1952–1958 of countries high in n Achievement and low in n Achievement.[28] Counting the number of countries in each of the four cells we obtain the results shown in Table 22.1.

Table 22.1   Countries High and Low in n Achievement Whose Electrical Production Was Above or Below Expectation, McClelland Study

	Above Expectation		Below Expectation	
High n Ach	13[a]		7	
		.65		.35
Low n Ach	5		14	
		.26		.70

[a]The cell entries are number of countries that, for example, had high n Achievement and whose electrical output was above expectation (13). The indices in the lower right corners of the cells are percentages (proportions).

Do these results support McClelland's hypothesis? (*Hint:* Calculate χ^2 and C, as in Chapter 10. Use the percentages to help interpret the table.)

    [*Answer:* $\chi^2 = 5.87$, $df = 1$ ($p < .05$); $C = .36$. Yes, the hypothesis is supported.]

7. Sciences differ, among other things, in the degree to which they are experimental or nonexperimental. Psychology is heavily experimental. Sociology is primarily nonexperimental. Research

[28] McClelland, *op. cit.,* p. 100, Table 3.6.

in education is mixed: experimental and nonexperimental. Political science is also mixed. Anthropology is mostly nonexperimental. (Think, too, of economics, astronomy, physics, chemistry, and biology.) Why are some sciences predominantly experimental and others nonexperimental? Explain specifically what you mean.

8. The venturesome student may wish to take a plunge into stimulating, provocative, controversial, and important thinking. The famous Club of Rome report has outraged some observers, startled almost anyone who has read it, and disturbed everyone.[29] Using societally important variables—natural resources, pollution, population, for example—and their complex interactions, ultimate disaster to cities and the world has been predicted. The research on which the conclusions are based is entirely nonexperimental. Try reading the report and perhaps one of the works of the pioneer of the area of study, Professor Forrester of MIT.[30] Do you think that the research's nonexperimental character lowers its credibility?

[29] D. H. Meadows, D. L. Meadows, J. Randers, and W. Behrens, *The Limits to Growth,* 2d ed. New York: Universe Books, 1974.

[30] J. Forrester, *World Dynamics*. Cambridge, Mass.: Wright-Allen Press, 1971.

Chapter 23

Laboratory Experiments, Field Experiments, and Field Studies

SOCIAL SCIENTIFIC research can be divided into four major categories: laboratory experiments, field experiments, field studies, and survey research.[1] This breakdown stems from two sources, the distinction between experimental and nonexperimental research and that between laboratory and field research.

A LABORATORY EXPERIMENT: MILLER STUDIES OF THE LEARNING OF VISCERAL RESPONSES

A brilliant series of experiments by Neal Miller and his colleagues has upset another long-held and well-cherished belief: that learning occurs only with voluntary responses, and that the involuntary autonomic system is subject only to classical conditioning.[2] This means, in effect, that responses like moving the hand and talking can be brought under control and thus taught, but that involuntary responses, like heart rate, intestinal contractions, and blood pressure, cannot be brought under instrumental control and thus not

---

[1] This chapter owes much to L. Festinger and D. Katz, eds., *Research Methods in the Behavioral Sciences*. New York: Holt, Rinehart and Winston, 1953, chaps. 2, 3, 4. Although thirty years old, this book is still a valuable source on many aspects of behavioral research methodology.

[2] N. Miller, "Learning of Visceral and Glandular Responses," *Science,* 168 (1969), 434–445; N. Miller, *Selected Papers*. Chicago: Aldine, 1971, Part XI.

"taught."[3] Miller and his colleagues' work has shown that, through instrumental conditioning, the heart rate can be changed, stomach contractions can be altered, and even urine formation can be increased or decreased! This discovery is of enormous theoretical and practical importance. To show the nature of laboratory experiments, we take one of Miller's interesting and creative experiments.

The idea of the experiment is simple: reward one group of rats when their heart rates go up, and reward another group when their heart rates go down. This is a straightforward example of the two-group design discussed earlier. Miller's big problem was control. There are a number of other causes of changed heart rate—for example, muscular exertion. To control such extraneous variables, Miller and a colleague (Trowill) paralyzed the rats with curare. But if the rats were paralyzed, what could be used as reward? They decided to use direct electrical stimulation of the brain. The dependent variable, heart rate, was continuously recorded with the electrocardiograph. When a small change in heart rate occurred (in the "right" way: up for one group, down for the other), an animal was given an electrical impulse to a reward center of its brain.[4] This was continued until the animals were "trained."

The increases and decreases of heart rate were statistically reliable but small: only five percent in each direction. So Miller and another colleague (DiCara) used the technique known as shaping, which, in this case, means rewarding first small changes and then requiring increasing changes in rate to obtain the rewards. This increased the heart rate changes to an average of 20 percent in either direction. Moreover, further research, using escape from mild shock as reinforcement, showed that the animals remembered what they had learned and "differentiated" the heart responses from other responses.

Miller has been successful in "training" a number of other involuntary responses: intestinal contraction, urine formation, and blood pressure, for example. In short, visceral responses *can* be learned and *can* be shaped. But can the method be used with people? Miller says that he thinks people are as smart as rats, but that it has not yet been completely proved. Although the use of curare might present difficulty, people can be hypnotized, says Miller.

A FIELD EXPERIMENT: WALSTER, CLEARY, AND CLIFFORD'S STUDY OF BIAS IN COLLEGE ADMISSIONS

Do American colleges discriminate against women and black applicants? We used the fine field experiment of Walster, Cleary, and Clifford in Chapter 14 to illustrate factorial

---

[3]To understand Miller's studies, we must define certain psychological terms. In *classical conditioning* a neutral stimulus, inherently unable to produce a certain response, becomes able to by being associated repeatedly with a stimulus inherently capable of doing so. The most famous example is Pavlov's dog salivating at the clicking of a metronome, which had been repeatedly associated with meat powder. In *instrumental conditioning*, a reinforcement given to an organism immediately after it has made a response produces an increment in the response. Pigeons, for example, will peck their beaks bloody after having been subjected to certain forms of instrumental conditioning. In short, reward a response and it will be repeated. Voluntary responses or behavior are thought to be superior, presumably because they are under the control of the individual, whereas involuntary responses are inferior because they are not. It has been believed that involuntary responses can be modified only by classical conditioning and not by instrumental conditioning. In other words, the possibility of "teaching" the heart, the stomach, and the blood is remote, since classical conditioning conditions are difficult to come by. If the organs are subject to instrumental conditioning, however, they can be brought under experimental control, they can be "taught," and they can "learn." For authoritative accounts of both kinds of conditioning and their relation to learning, see E. Hilgard and G. Bower, *Theories of Learning*, 4th ed. Englewood Cliffs, N.J.: Prentice-Hall, 1975, chaps. 3, 7.

[4]Brain research has shown that mild electrical stimulation of a certain part of the brain acts as a reward. See M. Olds and J. Fobes, "The Central Basis of Motivation: Intracranial Self-Stimulation Studies," *Annual Review of Psychology*, 32 (1981), 523–574.

analysis of variance. Hence it is not necessary to labor all the study details here.[5] Recall that the authors randomly selected 240 colleges from a college guide and sent the colleges application letters from fictitious individuals. In the letters, they manipulated applicants' race, sex, and ability levels (three such levels). For example, a candidate might be a *black female* of *high ability,* or a *white male* of *medium ability.* This is, of course, a $2 \times 2 \times 3$ factorial design. The letter to each college was from a "candidate" who represented one cell of the 12 cells of the design. The dependent variable measure was obtained by quantifying the degrees of the colleges' acceptances of candidates. This amounted to a five-point scale: (1) rejection; (2) rejection, but qualified; . . .; (5) acceptance, with encouragement.

Race and sex were found not to be significant. From these results alone one might conclude that there was no bias in admissions. But recall that *the interaction of race and ability was significant.* Although there were no differences in admissions at the high and medium levels of ability, the mean acceptances of men and women at the low ability level were significantly different. The male mean was 3.00, and the female mean was 1.93. (See Table 14.14.) So evidently there *was* discrimination: women were discriminated against at the low ability level!

A FIELD STUDY: NEWCOMB'S BENNINGTON COLLEGE STUDY

In one of the most important studies of the influence on students of a college environment, Newcomb studied the entire student body of Bennington College, about 600 young women, from 1935 to 1939.[6] An unusual facet of the study was Newcomb's attempt to explain both social and personality factors in influencing attitude changes in the students. Although other hypotheses were tested, the principal hypothesis of the Bennington study was that new students would converge on the norms of the college group, and that the more the students assimilated to the college community, the greater would be the change in their social attitudes.

Newcomb used a number of paper-and-pencil attitude scales, written reports on students, and individual interviews. The study was longitudinal and nonexperimental. The independent variable, while not easy to categorize, can be said to be the social norms of Bennington College. The dependent variables were social attitudes and certain behaviors of the students.

Newcomb found significant changes in attitudes between freshmen, on the one hand, and juniors and seniors, on the other. The changes were toward less conservatism on a variety of social issues. For example, the political preferences of juniors and seniors in the 1936 presidential election were much less conservative than those of freshmen and sophomores. Of 52 juniors and seniors, 15 percent preferred Landon (Republican), whereas of 52 freshmen, 62 percent preferred Landon. The percentages of preferences for Roosevelt (Democrat) were 54 percent and 29 percent. The mean scores of all students for four years on a scale designed to measure political and economic conservatism were: freshmen, 74.2; sophomores, 69.4; juniors, 65.9, and seniors, 62.4. Evidently the college had affected the students' attitudes.

[5] E. Walster, T. Cleary, and M. Clifford, "The Effect of Race and Sex on College Admissions," *Journal of Educational Sociology,* 44 (1970), 237–244.

[6] T. Newcomb, *Personality and Social Change.* New York: Holt, Rinehart and Winston, 1943. A number of the Bennington students were later restudied in follow-up research designed to test the permanence of the changes made by Bennington: T. Newcomb, K. Koenig, R. Flacks, and D. Warwick, *Persistence and Change: Bennington College and Its Students After Twenty-Five Years.* New York: Wiley, 1967. In general, it was found that the changes had lasted: evidently Bennington's influence was persistent over the years.

Newcomb asked a ''control'' question: Would these attitudes have changed in other colleges? To answer this question, Newcomb administered his conservatism measures to students of Williams College and Skidmore College. The comparable mean scores of Skidmore students, freshmen through seniors, were: 79.9, 78.1, 77.0, and 74.1. It seems that Skidmore (and Williams) students did not change as much and as consistently over time as did the Bennington students.

CHARACTERISTICS AND CRITERIA OF LABORATORY EXPERIMENTS, FIELD EXPERIMENTS, AND FIELD STUDIES

A *laboratory experiment* is a research study in which the variance of all or nearly all of the possible influential independent variables not pertinent to the immediate problem of the investigation is kept at a minimum. This is done by isolating the research in a physical situation apart from the routine of ordinary living and by manipulating one or more independent variables under rigorously specified, operationalized, and controlled conditions.

Strengths and Weaknesses of Laboratory Experiments

The laboratory experiment has the inherent virtue of the possibility of relatively complete control. The laboratory experimenter can, and often does, isolate the research situation from the life around the laboratory by eliminating the many extraneous influences that may affect the independent and dependent variables.

In addition to situation control, laboratory experimenters can ordinarily use random assignment and can manipulate one or more independent variables. There are other aspects to laboratory control: the experimenter in most cases can achieve a high degree of specificity in the operational definitions of his variables. The relatively crude operational definitions of field situations, such as many of those associated with the measurement of values, attitudes, aptitudes, and personality traits, do not plague the experimentalist, though the definitional problem is never simple. The Miller experiment is a good example. The operational definitions of reinforcement and heart rate change are precise and highly objective.

Closely allied to operational strength is the precision of laboratory experiments. *Precise* means accurate, definite, unambiguous. Precise measurements are made with precision instruments. In variance terms, the more precise an experimental procedure is, the less the error variance. The more accurate or precise a measuring instrument is, the more certain we can be that the measures obtained do not vary much from their ''true'' values. This is the problem of reliability, which will be discussed in a later chapter.

Precise laboratory results are achieved mainly by controlled manipulation and measurement in an environment from which possible ''contaminating'' conditions have been eliminated. Research reports of laboratory experiments usually specify in detail how the manipulations were done and the means taken to control the environmental conditions under which they were done. By specifying exactly the conditions of the experiment, we reduce the risk that subjects may respond equivocally and thus introduce random variance into the experimental situation. Miller's experiment is a model of laboratory experimental precision.

The greatest weakness of the laboratory experiment is probably the lack of strength of independent variables. Since laboratory situations are, after all, situations that are created for special purposes, it can be said that the effects of experimental manipulations are usually weak. Increases and decreases in heart rate by electrical brain reinforcement, while striking, were relatively small. Compare this to the relatively large effects of independent variables in realistic situations. In the Bennington study, for example, the college community apparently had a massive effect. In laboratory research on conformity, only small effects are usually produced by group pressure on individuals. Compare this to the relatively strong effect of a large group majority on an individual group member in a real-life situation. The board of education member, who knows that an action he wants carried goes against the wishes of the majority of his colleagues and perhaps the majority of the community, is under heavy pressure to converge on the norm.

One reason for the preoccupation with laboratory precision and refined statistics is the weakness of laboratory effects. To detect a significant difference in the laboratory requires situations and measures with a minimum of random noise and accurate and sensitive statistical tests that will show relations and significant differences when they exist.

Another weakness is a product of the first: the artificiality of the experimental research situation. Actually, it is difficult to know if artificiality is a weakness or simply a neutral characteristic of laboratory experimental situations. When a research situation is deliberately contrived to exclude the many distractions of the environment, it is perhaps illogical to label the situation with a term that expresses in part the result being sought. The criticism of artificiality does not come from experimenters, who know that experimental situations are artificial; it comes from individuals lacking an understanding of the purposes of laboratory experiments.

The temptation to interpret the results of laboratory experiments incorrectly is great. While Miller's results are believed by social scientists to be highly significant, they can only tentatively be extrapolated beyond the laboratory. Similar results may be obtained in real-life situations, and there is evidence that they do in some cases. But this is not necessarily so. The relations must always be tested anew under nonlaboratory conditions. Miller's research, for instance, will have to be carefully and cautiously done with human beings in hospitals and even in schools.

Although laboratory experiments have relatively high internal validity, then, they lack external validity. Earlier we asked the question: Did X, the experimental manipulation, really make a significant difference? The stronger our confidence in the "truth" of the relations discovered in a research study, the greater the internal validity of the study. When a relation is discovered in a well-executed laboratory experiment, we generally can have considerable confidence in it, since we have exercised the maximum possible control of the independent variable and other possible extraneous independent variables. When Miller "discovered" that visceral responses could be learned and shaped, he could be relatively sure of the "truth" of the relation between reinforcement and visceral response— in the laboratory. He had achieved a high degree of control and of internal validity.

One can say: If I study this problem using field experiments, *maybe* I will find the same relation. This is an empirical, not a speculative, matter; we must put the relation to test in the situation to which we wish to generalize. If a researcher finds that individuals converge on group norms in the laboratory, as Sherif did,[7] does the same or similar phenomenon occur in community groups, faculties, legislative bodies? This lack of external validity is the basis of the objections of many educators to the animal studies of learning theory. Their objections are only valid if an experimenter generalizes from the behavior and learning of laboratory animals to the behavior and learning of children.

---

[7] M. Sherif, "Formation of Social Norms: The Experimental Paradigm." In H. Proshansky and B. Seidenberg, eds., *Basic Studies in Social Psychology*. New York: Holt, Rinehart and Winston, 1965, pp. 461–471. This is a classic laboratory experiment with large implications for both theory and practice.

Capable experimentalists, however, rarely blunder in this fashion—they know that the laboratory is a contrived environment.

Purposes of the Laboratory Experiment

Laboratory experiments have three related purposes. One, they are a means of studying relations under "pure" and uncontaminated conditions. Experimenters ask: Is x related to y? How is it related to y? How strong is the relation? Under what conditions does the relation change? They seek to write equations of the form $y = f(x)$, make predictions on the basis of the function, and see how well and under what conditions the function performs.

A second purpose should be mentioned in conjunction with the first purpose: the testing of predictions derived from theory, primarily, and other research, secondarily. For instance, on the basis of Sherif's norm-convergence finding, one might predict to a number of other laboratory and field experimental situations, as Sherif did in his later studies of boys in camp situations. Asch, though, argued that Sherif's stimulus was ambiguous in the sense that different people would "interpret" it differently.[8] He wondered whether the convergence phenomenon would work with clear stimuli in a more realistic setting. A series of experiments showed that it did.

A third purpose of laboratory experiments is to refine theories and hypotheses, to formulate hypotheses related to other experimentally or nonexperimentally tested hypotheses, and, perhaps most important, to help build theoretical systems. This was one of Miller's and Sherif's major purposes. Although some laboratory experiments are conducted without this purpose, of course, most laboratory experiments are theory-oriented.

The aim of laboratory experiments, then, is to test hypotheses derived from theory, to study the precise interrelations of variables and their operation, and to control variance under research conditions that are uncontaminated by the operation of extraneous variables. As such, the laboratory experiment is one of the great inventions of all time. Although weaknesses exist, they are weaknesses only in a sense that is really irrelevant. Conceding the lack of representativeness (external validity) the well-done laboratory experiment still has the fundamental prerequisite of any research: internal validity.[9]

THE FIELD EXPERIMENT

A field experiment is a research study in a realistic situation in which one or more independent variables are manipulated by the experimenter under as carefully controlled conditions as the situation will permit. The contrast between the laboratory experiment and the field experiment is not sharp: the differences are mostly matters of degree. Sometimes it is hard to label a particular study "laboratory experiment" or "field experiment." Where the laboratory experiment has a maximum of control, most field experiments must operate with less control, a factor that is often a severe handicap.

---

[8] S. Asch, "Studies of Independence and Conformity: I. A. Minority of One against a Unanimous Majority," *Psychological Monographs,* 70 (1956), Whole No. 416; S. Asch, *Social Psychology.* Englewood Cliffs, N.J.: Prentice-Hall, 1952, chap. 16.

[9] In this discussion, guidance on the actual conduct of experiments has been omitted. The reader who wants to go deeper and get practical guidance can profit from a fine and detailed chapter by two social psychologists: E. Aronson and J. Carlsmith, "Experimentation in Social Psychology." In G. Lindzey and E. Aronson, eds., *The Handbook of Social Psychology,* 2d ed. Reading, Mass.: Addison-Wesley, 1968, vol. II, pp. 1–79.

Strengths and Weaknesses of Field Experiments

Field experiments have values that especially recommend them to social psychologists, sociologists, and educators because they are admirably suited to many of the social and educational problems of interest to social psychology, sociology, and education. Because independent variables are manipulated and randomization used, the criterion of control can be satisfied—at least theoretically.

The control of the experimental field situation, however, is rarely as tight as that of the laboratory. We have here both a strength and a weakness. The investigator in a field experiment, though he has the power of manipulation, is always faced with the unpleasant possibility that his independent variables are contaminated by uncontrolled environmental variables. We stress this point because the necessity of controlling extraneous independent variables is particularly urgent in field experiments. The laboratory experiment is conducted in a tightly controlled situation, whereas the field experiment takes place in a natural, often loose, situation. One of the main preoccupations of the field experimenter, then, is to try to make the research situation more closely approximate the conditions of the laboratory experiment. Of course this is often a difficult goal to reach, but if the research situation can be kept tight, the field experiment is powerful because one can in general have greater confidence that relations are indeed what one says they are.

As compensation for dilution of control, the field experiment has two or three unique virtues. The variables in a field experiment usually have a stronger effect than those of laboratory experiments. The effects of field experiments are often strong enough to penetrate the distractions of experimental situations. The principle is: The more realistic the research situation, the stronger the variables. This is one advantage of doing research in educational settings. For the most part, research in school settings is similar to routine educational activities, and thus need not necessarily be viewed as something special and apart from school life. Despite the pleas of many educators for more realistic educational research, there is no special virtue in realism, as realism. Realism simply increases the strength of the variables. It also contributes to external validity, since the more realistic the situation, the more valid are generalizations to other situations likely to be.

Another virtue of field experiments is their appropriateness for studying complex social and psychological influences, processes, and changes in lifelike situations. Lepper, Greene, and Nisbett, for example, studied the effects of extrinsic rewards on children's motivation in a nursery school setting.[10] Deci, who had earlier studied the same problem, used both laboratory experiments and a field experiment.[11] Coch and French, many years ago, manipulated participation of workers in planning, and studied its effect on production, resignations, and aggression.[12]

Field experiments are well-suited both to testing theory and to obtaining answers to practical questions. Whereas laboratory experiments are suited mainly to testing aspects of theories, field experiments are suited both to testing hypotheses derived from theories *and* to finding answers to practical problems. Methods experiments in education, usually practical in purpose, often seek to determine which method among two or more methods is the best for a certain purpose. Industrial research and consumer research depend heavily on field experiments. Much social psychological research, on the other hand, is basically

[10] M. Lepper, D. Greene, and R. Nisbett, "Undermining Children's Intrinsic Interest With Extrinsic Reward: A Test of the 'Overjustification' Hypothesis," *Journal of Personality and Social Psychology,* 23 (1973), 129–137.

[11] E. Deci, "Effects of Externally Mediated Rewards on Intrinsic Motivation," *Journal of Personality and Social Psychology,* 18 (1971), 105–115.

[12] L. Coch and J. French, "Overcoming Resistance to Change," *Human Relations,* 1 (1948), 512–532. (A pioneering and influential study.)

theoretical. Dutton and Lake, in the study of inverse discrimination described in Chapter 14, were heavily influenced by theories of prejudice.[13] The Lepper et al. and the Deci field experiments were also theory-oriented.

Flexibility and applicability to a wide variety of problems are important characteristics of field experiments, the only two limitations being whether one or more independent variables can be manipulated and whether the practical exigencies of the research situation are such that a field experiment can be done on the particular problem under study. Surmounting these two limitations is not easy. When it *can* be done, a wide range of theoretical and practical problems is open to experimentation.

As indicated earlier, the main weaknesses of field experiments are practical. Manipulation of independent variables and randomization are perhaps the two most important problems. They are particularly acute in research in school settings. Manipulation, although quite possible, may often not be practicable because, say, parents object when their children, who happen to have been randomly assigned to a control group, will not get a desirable experimental treatment. Or there may be objection to an experimental treatment because it deprives children of some gratification or puts them into conflict situations.

There is no real reason why randomization cannot be used in field experiments. Nevertheless, difficulties are frequently met. Unwillingness to break up class groups or to allow children to be assigned to experimental groups at random are examples. Even if random assignment is possible and permitted, the independent variable may be seriously blurred, because the effects of the treatments cannot be isolated from other effects. Teachers and children, for example, may discuss what is happening during the course of the experiment. To prevent such muddying of the variables, the experimenter should explain to administrators and teachers the necessity for random assignment and careful control.

An experimental field characteristic of a different nature is to some experimenters a weakness and to others a strength. Field investigators have to be, to some extent at least, socially skilled operators. They should be able to work with people, talk to them, and convince them of the importance and necessity of their research. They should be prepared to spend many hours, even days and weeks, of patient discussion with people responsible for the institutional or community situation in which they are to work. For instance, if they are to work in a rural school system, they should have knowledge of rural as well as general educational problems, and of the particular rural system they wish to study. Some researchers become impatient with these preliminaries, because they are anxious to get the research job done. They find it difficult to spend the time and effort necessary in most practical situations. Others enjoy the inevitable socializing that accompanies field research.[14]

An important obstacle to good design, an obstacle that seems ordinarily to be overlooked, is the attitude of the researcher. For example, the planning of educational research often seems to be characterized by a negative attitude epitomized by such statements as, "That can't be done in schools," "The administrators and teachers won't allow that," and "Experiments can't be done on this problem in that situation." Starting with attitudes like this compromises any good research design before the research even begins. If a research design calls for the random assignment of teachers to classes, and if the lack of such assignment seriously jeopardizes the internal validity of the proposed study, every effort should be made to assign teachers at random. Educators planning research seem to

---

[13] D. Dutton and R. Lake, "Threat of Own Prejudice and Reverse Discrimination," *Journal of Personality and Social Psychology,* 28 (1973), 94–100.

[14] Good advice on handling this aspect of field situations is given by J. French, "Experiments in Field Settings," in Festinger and Katz, *op. cit.,* pp. 118–129, and D. Katz, "Field Studies," *ibid.,* pp. 87–89.

assume that the administrators or the teachers will not permit random assignment. This assumption is not necessarily correct, however.

The consent and cooperation of teachers and administrators can often be obtained if a proper approach, with adequate and accurate orientation, is used, and if explanations of the reasons for the use of specific experimental methods are given. The points being emphasized are these: Design research to obtain valid answers to the research questions. Then, if it is necessary to make the experiment possible, and only then, modify the "ideal" design. With imagination, patience, and courtesy, many of the practical problems of implementation of research design can be satisfactorily solved.

One other weakness inherent in field experimental situations is lack of precision. In the laboratory experiment it is possible to achieve a high degree of precision or accuracy, so that laboratory measurement and control problems are usually simpler than those in field experiments. In realistic situations, there is always a great deal of systematic and random noise. In order to measure the effect of an independent variable on a dependent variable in a field experiment, it is not only necessary to maximize the variance of the manipulated variable and any assigned variables, but also to measure the dependent variable as precisely as possible. But in realistic situations, such as in schools and community groups, extraneous independent variables abound. And measures of dependent variables, unfortunately, are sometimes not sensitive enough to pick up the messages of our independent variables. In other words, the dependent variable measures are often so inadequate they cannot pick up all the variance that has been engendered by the independent variables.

FIELD STUDIES

Field studies are nonexperimental scientific inquiries aimed at discovering the relations and interactions among sociological, psychological, and educational variables in real social structures. In this book, *any* scientific studies, large or small, that systematically pursue relations and test hypotheses, that are nonexperimental, and that are done in life situations like communities, schools, factories, organizations, and institutions will be considered field studies.

The investigator in a field study first looks at a social or institutional situation and then studies the relations among the attitudes, values, perceptions, and behaviors of individuals and groups in the situation. He ordinarily manipulates no independent variables. Before we discuss and appraise the various types of field studies, it will be helpful to consider examples. We have already examined field studies in Chapter 22 and in this chapter: the *Authoritarian Personality* study, the Newcomb Bennington study, and others. We now briefly examine two smaller field studies.

Jones and Cook tested the socially and politically important hypothesis that preferences for social policies to advance racial equality are influenced by racial attitudes. More specifically, individuals with positive attitudes toward blacks will favor *societal change* policies and individuals with negative attitudes toward blacks will favor *self-improvement* policies.[15] They measured attitudes toward blacks with a well-constructed and validated scale (we examine it in a later chapter) and independently by membership in four groups, such membership assumed and shown to be correlated with social attitudes (e.g., the group assumed to have the most favorable attitudes toward blacks had participated in civil

[15] S. Jones and S. Cook, "The Influence of Attitude on Judgments of the Effectiveness of Alternative Social Policy," *Journal of Personality and Social Psychology*, 32 (1975), 767–773. Some of the data of this study was used in Chapter 13.

rights and prointegration activities). The dependent variable, preference for social policy, was measured with a set of 30 policy items, each of which had two alternatives, one favoring social change and the other self-improvement. The hypothesis was supported: attitudes toward blacks evidently influence judgments of effective social policies.

The second smaller field study, part of a larger study by McClelland on the relation between Protestantism and capitalistic growth, was summarized in Chapter 21. Recall that several variables—Protestant-Catholic, need for achievement, and electricity consumption (an index of capitalistic growth or development), among others—were measured in 25 countries in 1925 and 1950. It was found, as predicted, that Protestantism was positively related to capitalistic growth.

Note that the problems of both field studies were attacked nonexperimentally: neither randomization nor experimental manipulation was possible. Note, too, an important difference in the data-gathering methods of the two studies. In the Jones and Cook study, data were collected directly from students at two universities. In the McClelland study, however, data on the variables in the 25 countries were ''indirectly'' collected from published sources, mainly world population statistics. While some might argue that the Jones and Cook study data are stronger than the McClelland data because the former were collected ''directly,'' there is really no difference in principle: both studies are nonexperimental field studies and both are creative and important contributions.

Types of Field Studies

Katz has divided field studies into two broad types: *exploratory* and *hypothesis-testing*.[16] The exploratory type, says Katz, *seeks what is* rather than *predicts relations* to be found. The massive *Equality of Educational Opportunity,* cited in Chapter 22, exemplifies this type of field study. Exploratory studies have three purposes: to discover significant variables in the field situation, to discover relations among variables, and to lay the groundwork for later, more systematic and rigorous testing of hypotheses.

Throughout this book to this point, the use and testing of hypotheses have been emphasized. It is well to recognize, though, that there are activities preliminary to hypothesis-testing in scientific research. In order to achieve the desirable aim of hypothesis-testing, preliminary methodological and measurement investigation must often be done. Some of the finest work of the twentieth century has been in this area. An example is that done by the factor analyst, who is preoccupied with the discovery, isolation, specification, and measurement of underlying dimensions of achievement, intelligence, aptitudes, attitudes, situations, and personality traits.

The second subtype of exploratory field studies, research aimed at discovering or uncovering relations, is indispensable to scientific advance in the social sciences. It is necessary to know, for instance, the correlates of variables. Indeed, the scientific meaning of a construct springs from the relations it has with other constructs. Assume that we have no scientific knowledge of the construct ''intelligence'': we know nothing of its causes or concomitants. For example, suppose that we know nothing whatever about the relation of intelligence to achievement. It is conceivable that we might do a field study in school situations. We might carefully observe a number of boys and girls who are said to be intelligent or nonintelligent by teachers (though here we introduce contamination, because teachers must obviously judge intelligence, in part at least, by achievement). We may notice that a larger number of ''more intelligent'' children come from homes of higher socioeconomic levels; they solve problems in class more quickly than other children; they

[16] Katz, *op. cit,* pp. 75–83.

have a wider vocabulary, and so on. We now have some clues to the nature of intelligence, so that we can attempt to construct a simple measure of intelligence. Note that our "definition" of intelligence springs from what presumably intelligent and nonintelligent children *do*. A similar procedure can be followed with the variable "achievement."

Strengths and Weaknesses of Field Studies

Field studies are strong in realism, significance, strength of variables, theory orientation, and heuristic quality. The variance of many variables in actual field settings is large, especially when compared to the variance of the variables of laboratory experiments. Consider the contrast between the impact of social norms in a laboratory experiment like Sherif's and the impact of these norms in a community where, say, certain actions of teachers are frowned upon and others approved. Consider also the difference between studying cohesiveness in the laboratory where subjects are asked, for example, whether they would like to remain in a group (measure of cohesiveness) and studying the cohesiveness of a school faculty where staying in the group is an essential part of one's professional future. Compare the group atmosphere in the Bennington College Study and that in a field experiment where different atmospheres are engendered by college instructors playing different roles. Variables such as social class, prejudice, conservatism, cohesiveness, and social climate can have strong effects in these studies. The strength of variables is not an unalloyed blessing, however. In a field situation there is usually so much noise in the channel that even though the effects may be strong and the variance great, it is not easy for the experimenter to separate the variables.

The realism of field studies is obvious. Of all types of studies, they are closest to real life. There can be no complaint of artificiality here. (The remarks about realism in field experiments apply, a fortiori, to the realism of field studies.)

Field studies are highly heuristic. One of the research difficulties of a field study is to keep the study contained within the limits of the problem. Hypotheses frequently fling themselves at one. The field is rich in discovery potential. For example, one may wish to test the hypothesis that the social attitudes of board of education members is a determinant of board of education policy decisions. After starting to gather data, however, many interesting notions that can deflect the course of the investigation can arise: the relation between the attitudes of board of education members and their election to the boards, the relation between the scope of men's business and professional interests and their seeking board membership, and the different conceptions of curriculum problems of board members, administrators, teachers, and parents.

Despite these strengths, the field study is a scientific weak cousin of laboratory and field experiments. Its most serious weakness, of course, is its nonexperimental character. Thus statements of relations are weaker than they are in experimental research. To complicate matters, the field situation almost always has a plethora of variables and variance. Think of the many possible independent variables that we can choose as determinants of delinquency or of school achievement. In an experimental study, these variables can be controlled to a large extent, but in a field study they must somehow be controlled by more indirect and less satisfactory means.

Another methodological weakness is the lack of precision in the measurement of field variables. In field studies the problem of precision is more acute, naturally, than in field experiments. The difficulty encountered by Astin (and others) in measuring college environment[17] is one of many similar examples. Administrative environment, for example,

---

[17] A. Astin, *The College Environment*. Washington, D.C.: American Council on Education, 1968.

was measured by students' perceptions of aspects of the environment. Much of the lack of precision is due to the greater complexity of field situations.[18]

Other weaknesses of field studies are practical problems: feasibility, cost, sampling, and time. These difficulties are really *potential* weaknesses—none of them need be a real weakness. The most obvious questions that can be asked are: Can the study be done with the facilities at the investigator's disposal? Can the variables be measured? Will it cost too much? Will it take too much time and effort? Will the subjects be cooperative? Is random sampling possible? Anyone contemplating a field study has to ask and answer such questions. In designing research it is important not to underestimate the large amounts of time, energy, and skill necessary for the successful completion of most field studies. The field researcher needs to be a salesman, administrator, and entrepreneur, as well as investigator.[19]

Study Suggestions

1. Is factorial analysis of variance more likely to be used in laboratory experiments, field experiments, or field studies? Why?

2. In Chapter 15, a study of the comparative effects of marijuana and alcohol was outlined. Suppose such a study is a laboratory experiment. Does that limit its usefulness and generalizability? Would such an experiment differ in generalizability from, say, a laboratory experiment of frustration and aggression?

3. Which kind of study is likely to be more generalizable: laboratory experiment, field experiment, or field study? Why?

4. It has been said that laboratory experiments are artificial, unrealistic, and not too useful to practitioners in the field. Take this position and argue for it. Now, take a stand against this view and argue the new position. In your arguments, bring out the purposes and the strengths and weaknesses of laboratory experiments, especially as compared to field research.

5. Outline plans for the design of a laboratory experiment, a field experiment, and a field study of the same basic problem: the relation between the cohesiveness of a group and its productivity. Keep the designs simple. Do the three designs study the same problem? That is, is the problem altered by the differences in the three kinds of study? How? Which design is "best," do you think?

6. Here are some studies and the chapters they appeared in. Go back to them and refresh your memory. Then identify each as a laboratory experiment, a field experiment, or a field study. Tell why you categorize each study as you do.

Stouffer, 10; Hurlock, 13; Dutton and Lake, 14; Beh and Barratt, 14; Berkowitz, 14; Freedman, 14; Wittrock, 14; Tetlock, 15; Morrow and Smithson, 15; Thorndike, 19; Hoyt, 20; Bandura and Menlove, 21; Suedfeld and Rank, 21; Kounin, 22; Verba and Nie, 22; Bollen, 22.

7. There is considerable controversy over the purpose of research. Two broad views, with variations between, oppose each other. One of these says that the purpose of scientific research is theory or explanation, as pointed out in Chapter 1. The other view, which seems particularly prevalent in education, is that the purpose of research is to help improve human and social conditions, to help find solutions to human and technical problems. In general, the scientist favors the former view, the man-in-the-street the latter view.

Which position do you think you espouse? Why? Is there a rational middle position? If so, why?

8. "The experiment is one of the great inventions of the last century." Do you agree with this statement? If you do, give reasons for your agreement: Why is the statement correct if, indeed, it

---

[18] Studies of organizations, for example, are mostly field studies, and the measurement of organizational variables well illustrates the difficulties. "Organizational Effectiveness" appears to be as complex as "Teacher Effectiveness." For a thorough and enlightening discussion, see: D. Katz and R. Kahn, *The Social Psychology of Organizations,* 2d ed. New York: Wiley, 1978, chap. 8, especially pp. 224–226. This superb book well repays careful reading and study.

[19] For details, see Katz, *op. cit.,* especially pp. 65ff.

is correct? If you do not agree, say why you don't. Before making snap judgments, read and ponder the references given in Study Suggestion 9, below.

9. Unfortunately, there has been much uninformed criticism of experiments. Before pronouncing rational judgments on any complex phenomenon we should first know what we're talking about, and, second, we should know the nature and purpose of the phenomenon we criticize. To help you reach rational conclusions about the experiment and experimentation, the following references are offered as background reading.

BERKOWITZ L., and DONNERSTEIN, E. "External Validity Is More than Skin Deep: Some Answers to Criticisms of Experiments," *American Psychologist,* 3 (1982), 245–257. A penetrating answer to the criticism of experiments as lacking external validity.

KAPLAN, A. *The Conduct of Inquiry*. San Francisco: Chandler, 1964, chap. IV. This chapter called "Experiment" seems to include most controlled observation.

ARONSON, E., and CARLSMITH, J. "Experimentation in Social Psychology." In G. Lindzey and E. Aronson, eds., *The Handbook of Social Psychology,* 2d ed., vol. Two. Reading, Mass.: Addison-Wesley, 1968, chap. 9.

FISHER, R. *The Design of Experiments,* 6th ed. New York: Hafner, 1951. A justly famous book on the statistical basis of inference from experiments. Chapter II is particularly enlightening, including as it does Fisher's classic description of determining whether a lady can, by tasting a cup of tea (with milk), tell whether the milk or the tea was first added to the cup. Pay particular attention to Sections 9 and 10 on randomization.

Chapter 24

Survey Research

SURVEY RESEARCH studies large and small populations (or universes) by selecting and studying samples chosen from the populations to discover the relative incidence, distribution, and interrelations of sociological and psychological variables.[1] Surveys covered by this definition are often called *sample surveys,* probably because survey research developed as a separate research activity, along with the development and improvement of sampling procedures. Surveys, as such, are not new. Social welfare studies were done in England as long ago as the eighteenth century. Survey research in the social scientific sense, however, is quite new—it is a development of the twentieth century.

Survey research is considered to be a branch of social scientific research, which immediately distinguishes it from the status survey. Its procedures and methods have been developed mostly by psychologists, sociologists, economists, political scientists, and statisticians.[2] These individuals have put a rigorous scientific stamp on survey research and, in the process, have profoundly influenced the social sciences.

The definition also links populations and samples. Survey researchers are interested in the accurate assessment of the characteristics of whole populations of people. They want to know, for example, how many persons in the United States vote for a Republican candidate and the relation between such voting and variables like sex, race, religious

[1] This chapter concentrates on the use of survey research in scientific research and neglects so-called status surveys, the aim of which is to learn the status quo rather than to study the relations among variables. There is no intention of derogating status surveys; they are useful, even indispensable. The intention is to emphasize the importance and usefulness of survey research in the scientific study of socially and educationally significant problems. The work of public opinion pollsters, such as Gallup and Roper, is also neglected. For a good account of polls and other surveys, see M. Parten, *Surveys, Polls, and Samples*. New York: Harper & Row, 1950, chap. 1. Though old, this book is still valuable. The current standard text is: D. Warwick and C. Lininger, *The Sample Survey: Theory and Practice*. New York: McGraw-Hill, 1975. This book has the advantage of having been guided by the thinking and practice of the Survey Research Center, University of Michigan. It also has the advantage of having a cross-cultural emphasis.

[2] A. Campbell and G. Katona, "The Sample Survey: A Technique for Social-Science Research." In L. Festinger and D. Katz, *Research Methods in the Behavioral Sciences*. New York: Holt, Rinehart and Winston, 1953, chap. 1.

Table 24.1 Relation Between Race and Trust in People, Campbell et al. Study (in percentages)[a]

	Low Trust	High Trust
Black	72	28
White	38	62

[a]$N = 2070$.

preference, and the like. They want to know the relation between attitudes toward education and public support of school budgets.

Only rarely, however, do survey researchers study whole populations: they study *samples* drawn from populations. From these samples they infer the characteristics of the defined population or universe. The study of samples from which inferences about populations can be drawn is needed because of the difficulties of studying whole populations. Random samples can often furnish the same information as a census (an enumeration and study of an entire population) at much less cost, with greater efficiency, and sometimes greater accuracy!

Sample surveys attempt to determine the incidence, distribution, and interrelations among sociological and psychological variables, and, in so doing, usually focus on people, the vital facts of people, and their beliefs, opinions, attitudes, motivations, and behavior. The social scientific nature of survey research is revealed by the nature of its variables, which can be classified as sociological *facts* and *opinions* and *attitudes*. *Sociological facts* are attributes of individuals that spring from their membership in social groups: sex, income, political and religious affiliation, socioeconomic status, education, age, living expenses, occupation, race, and so on.[3]

The second type of variable is psychological and includes opinions and attitudes, on the one hand, and behavior, on the other. Survey researchers are interested not only in relations among sociological variables; they are more likely to be interested in what people think and do and the relations between sociological and psychological variables. The study of the quality of American life done by the Survey Research Center of the University of Michigan, for instance, reports depressing data on the relation between race and feelings of trust in people, a sociological and a psychological variable.[4] Data are given in Table 24.1. The relation is substantial. Evidently black people feel less trustful of people than whites. As Campbell et al. say (p. 455), "those people who have been least successful in their encounters with society have the least reason to feel trustful of it."

Survey researchers, of course, also study the relations among psychological variables (see, for example, Table 10.3, Chapter 10). But most relations of survey research are those between sociological and psychological variables: between education and tolerance (see Table 10.9), between race and self-esteem (Table 10.11), and between education and sense of political efficacy (Study Suggestion 9, Chapter 10), for example.

TYPES OF SURVEYS

Surveys can be conveniently classified by the following methods of obtaining information: personal interview, mail questionnaire, panel, and telephone. Of these, the personal

---

[3]For a complete description of such personal and social facts, see Parten, *op. cit.*, pp. 169–174.

[4]A. Campbell, P. Converse, and W. Rodgers, *The Quality of American Life*. New York: Russell Sage, Foundation, 1976. I calculated the percentages of Table 24.1 from the reported percentages and frequencies of Campbell et al.'s Table 13–11, p. 455, to show the relation clearly.

interview far overshadows the others as perhaps the most powerful and useful tool of social scientific survey research. These survey types will be briefly described here; in later chapters, when studying methods of data collection, we will study the personal interview in depth.

Interviews and Schedules

The best survey research uses the personal interview as the principal method of gathering information. This is accomplished in part by the careful and laborious construction of a schedule or questionnaire.[5] Schedule information includes factual information, opinions and attitudes, and reasons for behavior, opinions, and attitudes. Interview schedules are difficult to construct; they are time-consuming and relatively costly; but there is no other method that yields the information they do.

The *factual information* gathered in surveys includes the so-called sociological data mentioned previously: sex, marital status, education, income, political preference, religious preference, and the like. Such information is indispensable, since it is used in studying the relations among variables and in checking the adequacy of samples. These data, which are entered on a ''face sheet,'' are called ''face sheet information.'' Face sheet information, at least part of it, is ordinarily obtained at the beginning of the interview. Much of it is neutral in character and helps the interviewer establish rapport with the respondent. Questions of a more personal nature, such as those about income and personal habits, and questions that are more difficult to answer such as the extent of the knowledge or ability of the respondent, can be reserved for later questioning, perhaps at the end of the schedule. The timing must necessarily be a matter of judgment and experience.[6]

Other kinds of factual information include what respondents know about the subject under investigation, what respondents did in the past, what they are doing now, and what they intend to do in the future. After all, unless we observe behavior directly, all data about respondents' behavior must come from them or from other people. In this special sense, past, present, and future behavior can all be classified under the ''fact'' of behavior, even if the behavior is only an intention. A major point of such factual questions is that the respondent presumably knows a good deal about his own actions and behavior. If he says he voted for a school bond issue, we can believe him—unless there is compelling evidence to the contrary. Similarly, we can believe him, perhaps with more reservation (since the event has not happened yet), if he says he is going to vote for a school bond issue.

Just as important, maybe even more important from a social scientific standpoint, are the beliefs, opinions, attitudes, and feelings that respondents have about cognitive objects.[7] Many of the cognitive objects of survey research may not be of interest to the researcher: investments, certain commercial products, political candidates, and the like. Other cognitive objects are more interesting: the United Nations, the Supreme Court, educational practices, integration, Federal aid to education, college students, Jews, and the women's liberation movement.

The personal interview can be helpful in learning respondents' reasons for doing or believing something. When asked reasons for actions, intentions, or beliefs, people may say they have done something, intend to do something, or feel certain ways about some-

---

[5] The term ''schedule'' will be used. It has a clear meaning: the instrument used to gather survey information through personal interview. ''Questionnaire'' has been used to label personal interview instruments and attitudinal or personality instruments. The latter are called ''scales'' in this book.

[6] See Warwick and Lininger, *op. cit.,* pp. 150–151.

[7] *Cognitive object* is an expression used to indicate the object of an attitude. Almost anything can be the object of an attitude, but the term is ordinarily reserved for important social ''objects,'' for example, groups (religious, racial, educational) and institutions (education, marriage, political parties). A more general and probably better term, though one not in general use, is *referent.*

thing. They may say that group affiliations or loyalties or certain events have influenced them. Or they may have heard about issues under investigation via public media of communication. For example, a respondent may say that, while he was formerly opposed to Federal aid to education because he and his political party have always opposed government interference, he now supports Federal aid because he has read a great deal about the problem in newspapers and magazines and has come to the conclusion that Federal aid will benefit American education.

A respondent's desires, values, and needs may influence his attitudes and actions. When saying why he favors Federal aid to education the respondent may indicate that his own educational aspirations were thwarted and that he has always yearned for more education. Or he may indicate that his religious group has, as a part of its value structure, a deep commitment to the education of children. If the individual under study has accurately sounded his own desires, values, and needs—and can express them verbally—the personal interview can be very valuable.

Other Types of Survey Research

The next important type of survey research is the *panel*.[8] A sample of respondents is selected and interviewed, and then reinterviewed and studied at later times. The panel technique enables the researcher to study changes in behaviors and attitudes.

Telephone surveys have little to recommend them beyond speed and low cost. Especially when the interviewer is unknown to the respondent they are limited by possible nonresponse, uncooperativeness, and by reluctance to answer more than simple, superficial questions. Yet telephoning can sometimes be useful in obtaining information essential to a study. Its principal defect, obviously, is the inability to obtain detailed information.

The *mail questionnaire,* another type of survey, has serious drawbacks unless it is used in conjunction with other techniques. Two of these defects are possible lack of response and the inability to check the responses given. These defects, especially the first, are serious enough to make the mail questionnaire worse than useless, except in highly sophisticated hands. Responses to mail questionnaires are generally poor. Returns of less than 40 or 50 percent are common. Higher percentages are rare. At best, the researcher must content himself with returns as low as 50 or 60 percent.

As a result of low returns in mail questionnaires, valid generalizations cannot be made.[9] Although there are means of securing larger returns and reducing deficiencies— follow-up questionnaires, enclosing money, interviewing a random sample of nonrespondents and analyzing nonrespondent data—these methods are costly, time-consuming, and often ineffective. As Parten says, "Most mail questionnaires bring so few returns, and these from such a highly selected population, that the findings of such surveys are almost invariably open to question."[10] The best advice would seem to be not to use mail questionnaires if a better method can possibly be used. If they are used, every effort should be made to obtain returns of at least 80 to 90 percent or more, and lacking such returns, to learn something of the characteristics of the nonrespondents.

THE METHODOLOGY OF SURVEY RESEARCH

Survey research has contributed much to the methodology of the social sciences. Its most important contributions, perhaps, have been to rigorous sampling procedures, the overall

---

[8] See Warwick and Lininger, *op. cit.,* pp. 62ff.

[9] See Parten, *op. cit.,* pp. 391–402, for a discussion of the inadequacies of mail questionnaires and remedies for remediable deficiencies. Also, Warwick and Lininger, *op. cit.,* pp. 131–132.

[10] Parten, *op. cit.,* p. 400.

design and the implementation of the design of studies, the unambiguous definition and specification of the research problem, and the analysis and interpretation of data.

In the limited space of a section of one chapter, it is obviously impossible to discuss adequately the methodology of survey research. Only those parts of the methodology germane to the purposes of this book, therefore, will be outlined: the survey or study design, the so-called flow plan or chart of survey researchers, and the check of the reliability and validity of the sample and the data-gathering methods. (Sampling was discussed in Part Three, analysis in Part Four.)

Survey researchers use a "flow plan" or chart to outline the design and subsequent implementation of a survey.[11] The flow plan starts with the objectives of the survey, lists each step to be taken, and ends with the final report. First, the general and specific problems that are to be solved are as carefully and as completely stated as possible. Since, in principle, there is nothing very different here from the discussion for problems and hypotheses of Chapter 2, we can omit detailed discussion and give one simple hypothetical example. An educational investigator has been commissioned by a board of education to study the attitudes of community members toward the school system. On discussing the general problem with the board of education and the administrators of the school system, the investigator notes a number of more specific problems such as: Is the attitude of the members of the community affected by their having children in school? Are their attitudes affected by their educational level?

One of the investigator's most important jobs is to specify and clarify the problem. To do this well, he should not expect just to ask people what they think of the schools, although this may be a good way to begin if one does not know much about the subject. He should also have specific questions to ask that are aimed at various facets of the problem. Each of these questions should be built into the interview schedule. Some survey researchers even design tables for the analysis of the data at this point in order to clarify the research problem and to guide the construction of interview questions. Since this procedure is recommended, let us design a table to show how it can be used to specify survey objectives and questions.

Take the question: Is attitude related to educational level? The question requires that "attitude" and "educational level" be operationally defined. Positive and negative attitudes will be inferred from responses to schedule questions and items: If, in response to a broad question like, "In general, what do you think of the school system here?" a respondent says, "It is one of the best in this area," it can be inferred that he has a positive attitude toward the schools. Naturally, one question will not be enough. Related questions should be used, too. A definition of "educational level" is quite easy to obtain. It is decided to use three levels: (1) Some College, (2) High School Graduate, and (3) Non-High School Graduate. The analysis paradigm might look like Figure 24.1.

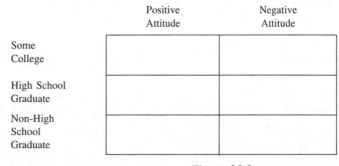

Figure 24.1

[11] Campbell and Katona, *op. cit.*, pp. 39–41.

The virtue of paradigms like this is that the researcher can immediately tell whether he has stated a specific problem clearly and whether the specific problem is related to the general problem. It also gives him some notion as to how many respondents he will need to fill the table cells adequately, as well as provide him guidelines for coding and analysis. In addition, as Katz says, "By actually going through the mechanics of setting out such tables, the investigators are bound to discover complexities of a variable that need more detailed measurement and qualifications of hypotheses in relation to special conditions."[12]

The next step in the flow plan is the sample and the sampling plan. Because sampling is much too complex to be discussed here,[13] we outline only the main ideas. First, the universe to be sampled and studied must be defined. Are all citizens living in the community included: Community leaders? Those citizens paying school taxes? Those with children of school age? Once the universe is defined, a decision is made as to how the sample is to be drawn and how many cases will be drawn. In the best survey research, random samples are used. Because of their high cost and greater difficulty of execution random samples are often bypassed for *quota samples*. In a quota (or quota control) sample, "representativeness" is presumably achieved by assigning quotas to interviewers—so many men and women, so many whites and blacks, and so on. Quota sampling should be avoided: while it *may* achieve representativeness, it lacks the virtues of random sampling.

The next large step in a survey is the construction of the interview schedule and other measuring instruments to be used. This is a laborious and difficult business bearing virtually no resemblance to the questionnaires often hastily put together by neophytes. The main task is to translate the research question into an interview instrument and into any other instruments constructed for the survey. One of the problems of the study, for instance, may be: How are permissive and restrictive attitudes toward the discipline of children related to perceptions of the local school system? Among the questions to be written to assess permissive and restrictive attitudes, one might be: How do you feel children should be disciplined? After drafts of the interview schedule and other instruments are completed, they are pretested on a small representative sample of the universe. They are then revised and put in final form.

The steps outlined above constitute the first large part of any survey. Data collection is the second large part. Interviewers are oriented, trained, and sent out with complete instructions as to whom to interview and how the interview is to be handled. In the best surveys, interviewers are allowed no latitude as to whom to interview. They must interview those individuals and only those individuals designated, generally by random devices. Some latitude may be allowed in the actual interviewing and use of the schedule, but not much. The work of interviewers is also systematically checked in some manner. For example, every tenth interview may be checked by sending another interviewer to the same respondent. Interview schedules are also studied for signs of spurious answering and reporting.

The third large part of the flow plan is analytical. The responses to questions are coded and tabulated. *Coding* is the term used to describe the translation of question responses

---

[12] D. Katz, "Field Studies," in Festinger and Katz, *op. cit.,* pp. 80–81.

[13] See Chapter 8, above. Warwick and Lininger's discussions of sampling are helpful: *op. cit.,* chaps 4, 5. Their Chapter 5, a detailed example of multistage area sampling, is especially helpful. *Area sampling* is the type most used in survey research. First, defined large areas are sampled at random. This amounts to partitioning of the universe and random sampling of the cells of the partition. The partition cells may be areas delineated by grids on maps or aerial photographs of counties, school districts, or city blocks. Then further subarea samples may be drawn at random from the large areas already drawn. Finally, all individuals or families or random samples of individuals and families may be drawn.

and respondent information to specific categories for purposes of analysis.[14] Take the example of Figure 24.1. All respondents must be assigned to one of the three educational-level categories and a number (or other symbol) assigned to each level. Then each person must also be assigned to a "positive attitude" or "negative attitude" category. To aid in the coding, content analysis may be used. Content analysis is an objective and quantitative method for assigning types of verbal and other data to categories (see Chapter 30, below). Coding can mean the analysis of factual response data and then the assignment of individuals to classes or categories, or the assigning of categories to individuals, especially if one is preparing cards for computer analysis. Such cards consist of a large number of columns with a number of cells in each column. The fifth column may be assigned, say, to sex, and the first two cells of the column, or the numbers 0 and 1, used to designate female and male.

Tabulation is the recording of the numbers of types of responses in the appropriate categories, after which statistical analysis follows: percentages, averages, relational indices, and appropriate tests of significance. The analyses of the data are studied, collated, assimilated, and interpreted. Finally, the results of this interpretative process are reported.

Checking Survey Data

Survey research has a unique advantage among social scientific methods: it is often possible to check the validity of survey data. Some of the respondents can be interviewed again, and the results of both interviews checked against each other. It has been found that the reliability of personal factual items, like age and income, is high.[15] The reliability of attitude responses is harder to determine because a changed response can mean a changed attitude. The reliability of average responses is higher than the reliability of individual responses. Fortunately, the researcher is usually more interested in averages, or group measures, than in individual responses.

One way of checking the validity of a measuring instrument is to use an outside criterion. One compares one's results to some outside, presumably valid, criterion. For instance, a respondent tells us he voted in the last election of school board members. We can find out whether he did or not by checking the registration and voting records. Ordinarily, individual behavior is not checked, because information about individuals is hard to obtain, but group information is often available. This information can be used to test to some extent the validity of the survey sample and the responses of the respondents.

A good example of an outside check on survey data is the use of information from the last census. This is particularly useful in large-scale surveys, but it may also help in smaller ones. Proportions of men and women, races, educational levels, age, and so on in the sample and in the U.S. census are compared. In the Verba and Nie study of political participation, for example, the authors report a number of such comparisons.[16] Table 24.2 reports some of them. It is obvious that the sample estimates are accurate: only one of them, Age 20-34, deviates from the Census estimates by more than 2 percent, which is

---

[14] Simple coding is discussed in Warwick and Lininger, *op. cit.*, chap. 9. For detailed discussions of coding and coding problems, instructional materials are available from the Institute for Social Research, University of Michigan, Ann Arbor, Michigan 48104. The Institute also issues bibliographies on survey research and related matters.

[15] Parten, *op. cit.*, pp. 496–498.

[16] S. Verba and N. Nie, *Participation in America: Political Democracy and Social Equality*. New York: Harper & Row, 1972, p. 349.

Table 24.2   Comparison of Sample and Census Data, Verba and Nie Survey[a]

Characteristic	Census	Survey	Deviation[b]
Male	49.2%	48.3%	.9
Black	11.1	13.1	−2.0
Urban	64.0	64.5	− .5
Age 20-34	33.6	29.2	4.4
35-54	36.6	37.3	− .7
Education 0-8	28.7	27.8	.9
> 12	20.5	22.0	−1.5

[a] $N > 2500$. Census estimates for 1967 and 1969 published by the U.S. Bureau of the Census.

[b] Deviation = Census − Survey.

reassuring evidence of the adequacy of the sample. To be sure, the sample was large (>2500), but smaller samples have also been found to be quite accurate.[17]

TWO STUDIES

Many surveys have been done, both good and bad. Most of them would probably not interest the student because they are little more than refined attempts to obtain simple information: studies of presidential voting, of industrial plants, and so on. There are, however, surveys of considerable, even great, interest and significance to behavioral scientists. Two of these are summarized below. They were chosen for their intrinsic interest and because they studied problems that are theoretically and socially important. They also seem to represent a healthy trend toward using survey research to study and understand complex psychological and sociological phenomena. One of them was a large national study (more than 2,500 interviews) and the other a much smaller study done in two suburban districts of Los Angeles (two samples of about 200 each). The latter study also included the "rare luxury of a complete replication."

Verba and Nie: Political Participation in America[18]

Recall that Verba and Nie asked, among other things, how the political participation of citizens of a democracy influences governmental processes. They interviewed more than 2,500 residents of the United States in 200 locales in 1967, selected by an area probability sampling procedure. (Their census-sample comparisons showed generally high agreement.[19]) The main finding was mentioned in Chapter 22: citizen participation does indeed influence political leaders, but it is the more affluent, better-educated, and generally

---

[17] In one study of Detroit done by the University of Michigan, the sample was only 735, but the sample estimates were close to those of the Census of the 1950 census. Detroit Area Study, University of Michigan, *A Social Profile of Detroit*. Ann Arbor: University of Michigan, 1952, p. 36. Campbell and Katona, *op. cit.*, pp. 41–48, discuss methods of checking sample validity and reliability. Warwick and Lininger, *op. cit.*, pp. 311–314, give tables of sampling errors, with an explanation of their statistical meaning and use. We learn, for instance, that reported percentages between 20 and 80 from a sample of 700 have a standard error of 4. To reduce this to 2 requires a sample of 3,000!

[18] Verba and Nie, *op. cit.* The survey was done by the National Opinion Research Center.

[19] *Ibid.*, p. 349, Table A-1.

higher status citizens whose participation is influential. The authors point out that although Americans are not noted for class-based ideology, social status *does* relate to participation.[20] The study was especially characterized by sophisticated measurement and analytic methodology, and by a major disconcerting finding. We will return to it and its methodology in later chapters.

Kinder and Sears: Prejudice and Politics[21]

This study explicitly stated and tested alternative theories of racial prejudice. Indeed, the authors deplored the lack of empirical confrontation between alternative theories in the prejudice literature (p. 414). The study is also unusual because its circumstances "permitted . . . the rare luxury of a complete replication" (albeit with small samples).

The theories of prejudice tested were called symbolic racism and racial threat. *Symbolic racism,* say the authors, is a blend of antiblack sentiment and traditional moral values of the Protestant Ethic. It is resistance to change in the racial status quo based on moral feelings that blacks violate traditional American values of self-reliance, individualism, the work ethic, and discipline. This syndrome of determinants of racial prejudice is the descendant of an older social-cultural learning theory, which emphasized that prejudice was learned by children along with other normative values and attitudes. But, say Kinder and Sears, white America has become, at least in principle, racially egalitarian, and another explanation is therefore necessary.

The alternative explanation, *group conflict theory,* emphasizes the threats that blacks pose to the private lives of whites: moving into white neighborhoods, moving into better jobs displacing whites, insistence on integrated schools and enforced busing and racial mixing of young children, and the threat of rising violence perceived as due to black criminality. The implications of both theories were used to construct measures of personal racial threats and symbolic racism, which were related to the dependent variable, intended votes for two candidates for mayor of Los Angeles in 1969 and 1973, Yorty, a white conservative, and Bradley, a black liberal.

White residents of two suburban communities in Los Angeles were selected in what appears to have been quota sampling. Two samples of adults were interviewed in 1969 and in 1973. The questions asked focused mainly on issues relating to personal threat and symbolic racism. The researchers' analysis indicated that symbolic racism was a more important form of racial prejudice than racial threat. That is, symbolic racism accounted for more of the variance of candidate preference than racial threat. Various control analyses further supported this finding. The authors concluded that "racial attitudes were major determinants of voting in both mayoral elections" (*ibid.,* p. 427), and racial threats to whites' lives were largely irrelevant. These findings and conclusions are highly important both theoretically and practically.

These two studies clearly show a trend toward using survey research as a tool to test theory and hypotheses in contrast to older use in which the emphasis was on finding "what is there." We can expect this trend to continue and to grow, especially in sociology, political science, and education.

---

[20] *Ibid.,* p. 339.
[21] D. Kinder and D. Sears, "Prejudice and Politics: Symbolic Racism versus Racial Threats to the Good Life," *Journal of Personality and Social Psychology,* 40 (1981), 414–431.

APPLICATIONS OF SURVEY RESEARCH TO EDUCATION

The Verba and Nie and the Kinder and Sears studies clearly show the applicability of survey research and its methodology in sociology, social psychology, and political science. Survey research's strong emphases on representative samples, overall design and plan of research, and expert interviewing using carefully and competently constructed interview schedules have had and will continue to have beneficial influence on behavioral research. Despite its evident potential value in all behavioral research fields, survey research has not been used to any great extent where it would seem to have large theoretical and practical value: in education.[22] Its distinctive usefulness in education and educational research seems not to have been realized. This section is therefore devoted to application of survey research to education and educational problems.

Obviously, survey research is a useful tool for educational fact-finding. An administrator, a board of education, or a staff of teachers can learn a great deal about a school system or a community without contacting every child, every teacher, and every citizen. In short, the sampling methods developed in survey research can be very useful. It is unsatisfactory to depend upon relatively hit-or-miss, so-called representative samples based on "expert" judgments. Nor is it necessary to gather data on whole populations; samples are sufficient for many purposes.

Most research in education is done with relatively small nonrandom samples. If hypotheses are supported, they can later be tested with random samples of populations, and if again supported, the results can be generalized to populations of schools, children, and laymen. In other words, survey research can be used to test hypotheses already tested in more limited situations, with the result that external validity is increased.

Survey research seems ideally suited to some of the large controversial issues of education. For example, its ability to handle "difficult" problems like integration and school closings through careful and circumspect interviewing puts it high on the list of research approaches to such problems. Researchers and educators can study the impact of integration and of school closings on communities and their school systems. Interviews of random samples of citizens and teachers of school districts just starting integration or the closing of certain elementary schools because of declining enrollment can provide valuable information on the concerns and fears of citizens so that appropriate measures to inform them and lessen their fears can be taken. The effect of these measures can of course also be studied.

Survey research is probably best adapted to obtaining personal and social facts, beliefs, and attitudes. It is significant that, although hundreds of thousands of words are spoken and written about education and about what people presumably think about education, there is little dependable information on the subject. We simply do not know what people's attitudes toward education are. We have to depend on feature writers and so-called experts for this information. Boards of education frequently depend on administrators and local leaders to tell them what the people think. Will they support an expanded budget next year? What will they think about a merger of adjoining school districts? How will they react to busing white and black children to achieve desegregation?

---

[22] An outstanding example of survey research in education, however, a study that should be read by educational administrators and board of education members, is: N. Gross, W. Mason, and A. McEachern, *Explorations in Role Analysis: Studies of the School Superintendency Role*. New York: Wiley, 1958. A shorter report is: N. Gross, *Who Runs Our Schools?* New York: Wiley, 1958.

ADVANTAGES AND DISADVANTAGES OF SURVEY RESEARCH

Survey research has the advantage of wide scope: a great deal of information can be obtained from a large population. A large population or a large school system can be studied with much less expense than that incurred by a census. While surveys tend to be more expensive than laboratory and field experiments and field studies, for the amount and quality of information they yield they are economical. Furthermore, existing educational facilities and personnel can be used to reduce the costs of the research.

Survey research information is accurate—within sampling error, of course. The accuracy of properly drawn samples is frequently surprising, even to experts in the field. A sample of 600 to 700 individuals or families can give a remarkably accurate portrait of a community—its values, attitudes, and beliefs.

With these advantages go inevitable disadvantages. First, survey information ordinarily does not penetrate very deeply below the surface. The scope of the information sought is usually emphasized at the expense of depth. This seems to be a weakness, however, that is not necessarily inherent in the method. The Verba and Nie and other studies show that it is possible to go considerably below surface opinions. Yet the survey seems best adapted to extensive rather than intensive research. Other types of research are perhaps better adapted to deeper exploration of relations.

A second weakness is a practical one. Survey research is demanding of time and money. In a large survey, it may be months before a single hypothesis can be tested. Sampling and the development of good schedules are major operations. Interviews require skill, time, and money. Surveys on a smaller scale can avoid these problems to some extent, even though it is generally true that survey research demands large investments of time, energy, and money.

Any research that uses sampling is naturally subject to sampling error. While it is true that survey information has been found to be relatively accurate, there is always the one chance in twenty or a hundred that an error more serious than might be caused by minor fluctuations of chance may occur. The probability of such an error can be diminished by building safety checks into a study—by comparing census data or other outside information and by sampling the same population independently.

A potential rather than an actual weakness of this method is that the survey interview can temporarily lift the respondent out of his own social context, which may make the results of the survey invalid. The interview is a special event in the ordinary life of the respondent. This apartness may affect the respondent so that he talks to, and interacts with, the interviewer in an unnatural manner. For example, a mother, when queried about her child-rearing practices, may give answers that reveal methods she would like to use rather than those she *does* use. It is possible for interviewers to limit the effects of lifting respondents out of social context by skilled handling, especially by one's manner and by careful phrasing and asking of questions.[23]

Survey research also requires a good deal of research knowledge and sophistication. The competent survey investigator must know sampling, question and schedule construction, interviewing, the analysis of data, and other technical aspects of the survey. Such knowledge is hard to come by. Few investigators get this kind and amount of experience. As the value of survey research, both large- and small-scale, becomes appreciated, it can be anticipated that such knowledge and experience will be considered, at least in a minimal way, to be necessary for researchers.

[23] C. Cannell and R. Kahn, "Interviewing." In G. Lindzey and E. Aronson, eds., *The Handbook of Social Psychology,* 2d ed. Reading, Mass.: Addison-Wesley, 1968, chap. 15.

Study Suggestions

1. Here are several good examples of survey research. Choose one of them and read the first chapter (or chapters) to learn the problem of the study. Then go to the technical methodological appendix to see how the sampling and interviewing were done. (Most published survey research studies have such appendices.) Try to determine the main variables and their relations.

Studies cited in footnotes 4, 16, 17, 21, 22.

CAMPBELL, A. *White Attitudes toward Black People*. Ann Arbor: Institute for Social Research, University of Michigan, 1971. Changed racial attitudes in America.

FREE, L., and CANTRIL, H. *The Political Beliefs of Americans*. New Brunswick, N. J.: Rutgers University Press, 1967. Ideological and operational views of Americans.

GLOCK, C., and STARK, R. *Christian Beliefs and Anti-Semitism*. New York: Harper & Row, 1966. Religion and prejudice.

LORTIE, D. *Schoolteacher: A Sociological Study*. Chicago: University of Chicago Press, 1975. A valuable and insightful study of teachers.

MILLER, W., and LEVITIN, T. *Leadership and Change: The New Politics and the American Electorate*. Cambridge, Mass.: Winthrop, 1976. The ''New Left'' and the ''Silent Minority.'' Based on Survey Research Center data of 25 years.

QUINN, R., KUHN, R., TABOR, J., and GORDON, L. *The Chosen Few: A Study of Discrimination in Executive Selection*. Ann Arbor, Mich.: Institute for Social Research, University of Michigan, 1968. Anti-Semitism in business.

2. This study suggestion is for students of education. Read as much of the Gross, Mason, and McEachern survey research study (footnote 22) as you can. It is a methodological model for larger-scale educational research. And, of course, it reports a number of interesting findings about superintendents and boards of education and their views. Perhaps most important, it shows that a scientific approach *and* practical concern for educational practice can be combined.

3. Rensis Likert, an outstanding social scientist, a methodological pioneer of survey research, and the founder of the Institute for Social Research of the University of Michigan (of which the Survey Research Center is a part), recently died. Two of his colleagues wrote an obituary in which they described Likert's contributions.[24] It is suggested that students read the obituary, which is virtually an account of the birth and growth of important methodological aspects of survey research, as well as an interesting description of the contributions of this creative and competent individual.

[24] S. Seashore and D. Katz, ''Obituary: Rensis Likert (1903–1981),'' *American Psychologist,* 37 (1982), 851–853.

PART EIGHT

MEASUREMENT

Chapter 25

Foundations of Measurement

"IN ITS broadest sense, measurement is the assignment of numerals to objects or events according to rules."[1] This definition succinctly expresses the basic nature of measurement. To understand it, however, requires the definition and explanation of each important term—a task to which much of this chapter is devoted.

Suppose we ask a judge to stand seven feet away from a group of students. The judge is asked to look at the students and then to estimate the degree to which each of them possesses five attributes: niceness, strength of character, personality, musical ability, and intelligence. The estimates are to be given numerically with a scale of numbers from 1 to 5, 1 indicating a very small amount of the characteristic in question and 5 indicating a great deal of it. In other words, the judge, just by looking at the students, is to assess how "nice" they are, how "strong" their characters are, and so on, using the numbers 1, 2, 3, 4, and 5 to indicate the amounts of each characteristic they possess.

This example may be a little ridiculous. Most of us, however, go through much the same procedure all our lives. We often judge how "nice," how "strong," how "intelligent" people are simply by looking at them and talking to them. It only seems silly when it is given as a serious example of measurement. Silly or serious, it *is* an example of measurement, since it satisfies the definition. The judge assigned numerals to "objects" according to rules. The objects, the numerals, and the rules for the assignment of the numerals to the objects were all specified. The numerals were 1, 2, 3, 4, and 5; the objects were the students; the rules for the assignment of the numerals to the objects were contained in the instructions to the judge. Then the end-product of the work, the numerals, might be used to calculate measures of relation, analyses of variance, and the like.

[1] S. Stevens, "Mathematics, Measurement, and Psychophysics." In S. Stevens, ed., *Handbook of Experimental Psychology*. New York: 1951, p. 1; S. Stevens, "Measurement, Statistics, and the Schemapiric View," *Science*, 161 (1968), 849–856.

The definition of measurement includes no statement about the quality of the measurement procedure. It simply says that, somehow, numerals are assigned to objects or to events. The "somehow," naturally, is important—but not to the definition. Measurement is a game we play with objects and numerals. Games have rules. It is, of course, important for other reasons that the rules be "good" rules, but whether the rules are "good" or "bad," the procedure is still measurement.

Why this emphasis on the definition of measurement and on its "rule" quality? There are three reasons. First, measurement, especially psychological and educational measurement, is misunderstood. It is not hard to understand certain measurements used in the natural sciences—length, weight, and volume, for example. Even measures more removed from common sense can be understood without wrenching elementary intuitive notions too much. But to understand that the measurement of such characteristics of individuals and groups as intelligence, aggressiveness, cohesiveness, and anxiety involves *basically and essentially* the same thinking and general procedure is much harder. Indeed, many say it cannot be done. Knowing and understanding that measurement is the assignment of numerals to objects or events by rule, then, helps to erase erroneous and misleading conceptions of psychological and educational measurement.

Second, the definition tells us that, if rules can be set up on some rational or empirical basis, measurement of anything is *theoretically* possible. This greatly widens the scientist's measurement horizons. He will not reject the possibility of measuring some property because the property is complex and elusive. He understands that measurement is a game that he may or may not be able to play with this or that property at this time. But he never rejects the possibility of playing the game, though he may realistically understand its difficulties.

Third, the definition alerts us to the essential neutral core of measurement and measurement procedures and to the necessity for setting up "good" rules, rules whose virtue can be empirically tested. No measurement procedure is any better than its rules. The rules given in the example above were poor. The procedure was a measurement procedure; the definition was satisfied. But it was a poor procedure for reasons that should become apparent later.

DEFINITION OF MEASUREMENT

To repeat our definition, "measurement is the assignment of numerals to objects or events according to rules." A *numeral* is a symbol of the form: 1, 2, 3, . . . , or I, II, III, ... It has no quantitative meaning unless we give it such a meaning; it is simply a symbol of a special kind. It can be used to label objects, such as baseball players, billiard balls, or individuals drawn in a sample from a universe. We could just as well use the word "symbol" in the definition. It is quite possible, even necessary, to assign symbols to objects or sets of objects according to rules. "Numeral" is used because measurement ordinarily uses numerals which, after being assigned quantitative meaning, become *numbers*. A *number,* then, is a numeral that has been assigned quantitative meaning.

The term "assigned" in the definition means *mapping*. Recall that earlier we talked about mapping the objects of one set onto the objects of another set. A function, *f,* is a rule, a *rule of correspondence*. It is a rule that assigns to each member of one set some one member of another set. The members of the two sets can be any objects at all. In mathematics, the members are generally numbers and algebraic symbols. In research, the members of one set can be individuals, or symbols standing for individuals, and the members

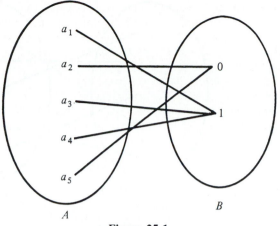

Figure 25.1

of the other set can be numerals or numbers. In most psychological and educational measurement, numerals and numbers are mapped onto, or assigned to, individuals.[2]

The most interesting—and difficult—work of measurement is *the rule*. A *rule* is a guide, a method, a command that tells us what to do. A mathematical rule is f, a function; f is a rule for assigning the objects of one set to the objects of another set. In measurement a rule might say: "Assign the numerals 1 through 5 to individuals according to how nice they are. If an individual is very, very nice, let the number 5 be assigned to him. If an individual is not at all nice, let the number 1 be assigned. Assign to individuals between these limits numbers between the limits." Another rule is one we have already met a number of times: "If an individual is male, assign him a 1. If an individual is female, assign her a 0." Of course, we would have to have a prior rule or set of rules defining male and female.

Assume that we have a set, A, of five persons, three men and two women: a_1, a_3, and a_4 are men; a_2 and a_5 are women. We wish to measure the variable, *sex*. Assuming we have a prior rule that allows us unambiguously to determine sex, we use the rule given in the preceding paragraph: "If a person is male, assign 1; if female, assign 0." Let 0 and 1 be a set. Call it B. Then $B = \{0, 1\}$. The measurement diagram is shown in Figure 25.1.

This procedure is the same as the one we used in Chapter 5 when discussing relations and functions. Evidently measurement is a relation. Since, to each member of A, the domain, one and only one object of B, the range, is assigned, the relation is a function. Are all measurement procedures functions, then? They are, provided the objects being measured are considered the domain and the numerals being assigned to, or mapped onto them, are considered the range.

Here is another way to bring set, relation-function, and measurement ideas together. Recall that a relation is a set of ordered pairs. So is a function. Any measurement procedure, then, sets up a set of ordered pairs, the first member of each pair being the object measured, and the second member the numeral assigned to the object according to the

[2] Usually, in a mapping, the members of the domain are said to be mapped onto members of the range. In order to preserve consistency with the definition of measurement given above and to be able always to conceive of the measurement procedure as a function, the mapping has been turned around. This conception of mapping, furthermore, is consistent with the earlier definition of a function as a rule that assigns to each member of the domain of a set some one member of the range. The rule tells *how* the pairs are to be ordered.

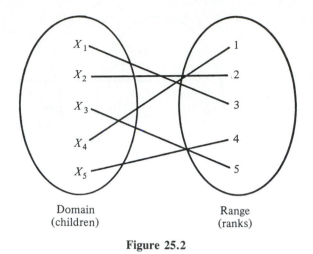

Domain
(children)

Range
(ranks)

Figure 25.2

measurement rule, whatever it is. We can thus write a general equation for any measurement procedure:

$$f = \{(x, y); \; x = \text{any object, and } y = \text{a numeral}\}$$

This is read: "The function, f, or the rule of correspondence, is equal to the set of ordered pairs (x, y) such that x is an object and each corresponding y is a numeral." This is a general rule and will fit any case of measurement.

Let us cite another example to make this discussion more concrete. The events to be measured, the x's, are five children. The numerals, the y's, are the ranks 1, 2, 3, 4, and 5. Assume that f is a rule that instructs a teacher as follows: "Give the rank 1 to the child who has the greatest motivation to do schoolwork. Give the rank 2 to the child who has the next greatest motivation to do schoolwork, and so on to the rank 5 which you should give to the child with the least motivation to do schoolwork." The measurement or the function is shown in Figure 25.2.

Note that f, the rule of correspondence, might have been: "If a child has high motivation for schoolwork, give him a 1, but if a child has low motivation for schoolwork, give him a 0." Then the range becomes $\{0, 1\}$. This simply means that the set of five children has been partitioned into two subsets, to each of which will be assigned, by means of f, the numerals 0 and 1. A diagram of this would look like Figure 25.1 with the set A being the domain and the set B the range.

To return to *rules*. Here is where evaluation comes into the picture. Rules may be "good" or "bad." With "good" rules we have "good," or sound, measurement, other things equal. With "bad" rules we have "bad," or poor, measurement. Many things are easy to measure, because the rules are easy to draw up and follow. To measure sex is easy, for example, since several simple and fairly clear criteria can be used to determine sex and to tell the investigator when to assign 1 and when to assign 0. It is also easy to measure certain other human characteristics: hair color, eye color, height, weight. Unfortunately, most human characteristics are much more difficult to measure, mainly because it is difficult to devise clear rules that are "good." Nonetheless, we must always have rules of some kind in order to measure anything.

MEASUREMENT AND "REALITY" ISOMORPHISM

Measurement can be a meaningless business, as we have seen. How can this be avoided? The definition of sets of objects being measured, the definition of the numerical sets from which we assign numerals to the objects being measured, and the rules of assignment or correspondence have to be tied to "reality." When the hardness of objects is measured, there is little difficulty. If a substance *a* can scratch *b* (and not vice versa), then *a* is harder than *b*. Similarly, if *a* can scratch *b*, and *b* can scratch *c*, then (probably) *a* can scratch *c*. These are empirical matters that are easily tested, so that we can find a rank order of hardness. A set of objects can be measured for its hardness by a few scratch tests, and numerals can be assigned to indicate degrees of hardness. It is said that the measurement procedure and the number system are *isomorphic* to reality.

Isomorphism means identity or similarity of form. The question is asked: Is this set of objects isomorphic to that set of objects? Are the two sets the same or similar in some formal aspect? For example, the two sets of Figure 25.3 are isomorphic as to cardinal number: they both have *three* members. They both have "threeness." In measurement, the question must be asked: Do the measurement procedures being used have some rational and empirical correspondence with "reality"?

To show the nature of this question of isomorphism, we can again use the idea of the correspondence of sets of objects. We may wish to measure the *persistence* of seven individuals. Suppose, also, that I am an omniscient being. I know the exact amount of persistence each individual possesses, that is, I know the "true" persistence values of each individual. (Assume that *persistence* has been adequately defined.) But *you,* the measurer, do not know these "true" values. It is necessary for you to assess the persistence of the individuals in some fallible way and you think you have found such a way. For instance, you might assess persistence by giving the individuals tasks to perform and noting the total time each individual requires to complete a task, or you might note the total number of times he tries to do a task before he turns to some other activity.[3] You use your method and measure the persistence of the individuals. You come out with, say, the seven values 6, 6, 4, 3, 3, 2, 1. Now I know the "true" values. They are: 8, 5, 2, 4, 3, 3, 1. This set of values is "reality." The correspondence of your set to "reality" is shown in Figure 25.4.

In two cases, you have assessed the "true" values exactly. You have "missed" all the others. Only one of these "misses," however, is serious, and there is a fair correspondence between the two rank orders of values. Note, too, that in my omniscience I knew that

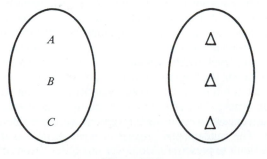

Figure 25.3

[3] N. Feather, "The Study of Persistence," *Psychological Bulletin,* 59 (1962), 94.

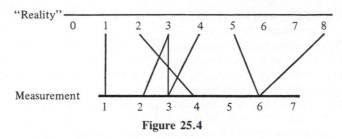

Figure 25.4

the "true" values of persistence run from 0 through 8, whereas your measurement system only encompasses 1 through 7.

While this example is a bit fanciful, it does show in a crude way the nature of the isomorphism problem. The ultimate question to be asked of any measurement procedure is: Is the measurement procedure isomorphic to reality? You were not too far off in measuring persistence. The only trouble is that we rarely discover as simply as this the degree of correspondence to "reality" of our measurements. In fact, we often do not even know whether we are measuring what we are trying to measure! Despite this difficulty, scientists must *test*, in some manner, the isomorphism with "reality" of the measurement numbers games they play.

PROPERTIES, CONSTRUCTS, AND INDICANTS OF OBJECTS

We say we measure objects, but this is not quite true. We measure the properties, or the characteristics, of these objects. Even this qualification is not quite true, however. We actually measure *indicants* of the properties of objects, so that when we say we measure objects we are really saying that we measure indicants of the properties of objects. This is generally true of all science, though the properties of some natural objects are much closer to direct observation than others. For instance, the property of sex associated with animal objects is closely tied to direct observation. As soon as relatively simple physical properties are left behind for more complex and elusive properties—which are of much greater interest to social scientists and educators—direct observation of properties is impossible. Hostility cannot be directly observed, nor can morale, anxiety, intelligence, creativeness, and talent. We must always *infer* these properties or characteristics from observation of presumed indicants of the properties.

Indicant is merely a convenient word used to mean something that points to something else. If a boy continually strikes other boys, we *may* say his behavior is an indicant of his underlying hostility. If someone's hands sweat excessively, we *may* say that he is anxious. A child plays a Schubert impromptu beautifully; we say she has "talent." If a child marks a certain number of objective-type items in an achievement test correctly, we say he has a certain level of achievement. In each of these cases, some identifiable behavior is an indicant of an underlying property. Obviously we are on much shakier ground when making such inferences from observed behavior than when directly observing properties like skin color, size, and sex. To measure a child's cooperativeness, dependency, and imaginativeness is very different from measuring his height, weight, or wrist-bone development. The fundamental process of measurement is the same, but the rules are much more difficult to prescribe. Moreover, the observations of the psychological properties are much further removed from the actual properties than are those of the physical properties. This is perhaps the single greatest difficulty of psychological and educational measurement.

The indicants from which properties are inferred are specified by operational definitions, definitions that specify the activities or "operations" necessary to measure variables or constructs. A *construct* is an invented name for a property. Many constructs have been used in previous chapters: authoritarianism, achievement, social class, intelligence, persistence, and so on.[4] Constructs, commonly and somewhat inaccurately called variables, are defined in two general ways in science: by other constructs and by experimental and measurement procedures. These were earlier called constitutive and operational definitions. An operational definition is necessary in order to measure a property or a construct. This is done by specifying the observations of the behavioral indicants of the properties.

Numerals are assigned to the behavioral indicants of properties. Then, after making observations of the indicants, the numbers (numerals) are substituted for the indicants and analyzed statistically. As an example, consider investigators who are working on the relation between intelligence and honesty. They operationally define *intelligence* as scores on an intelligence test. *Honesty* is operationally defined as observations in a contrived situation permitting pupils to cheat or not to cheat. The intelligence numerals assigned to pupils can be the total number of items correct on the test, or some other form of score. The honesty numerals assigned to pupils are the number of times they did not cheat when they could have cheated. The two sets of numbers may be correlated or otherwise analyzed. The coefficient of correlation, say, is .55, significant at the .01 level. All this is fairly straightforward and quite familiar. What is not so straightforward and familiar is this: if the investigators draw the conclusion that there is a significant positive relation between intelligence and honesty, they are making a large inferential leap from behavior indicants in the form of marks on paper and observations of "cheating" behavior to psychological properties. That they may be mistaken should be quite obvious.

LEVELS OF MEASUREMENT AND SCALING

Levels of measurement, the scales associated with the levels, and the statistics appropriate to the levels are complex, even controversial, problems. The difficulties arise mainly from disagreement over the statistics that can legitimately be used at the different levels of measurement. The Stevens' position and definition of measurement cited earlier is a broad view that, with liberal relaxation, is followed in this text.[5] In the ensuing discussion, we

---

[4] The concepts or constructs under discussion are also called "latent variables." This is an important expression that is being fruitfully used in what has been called analysis of covariance structures, or so-called causal analysis. A *latent variable* is a construct, an unobserved variable, that is presumed to underlie varied behaviors, and that is used to "explain" these behaviors. "Verbal ability," "conservatism," and "anxiety," for example, are latent variables. Their use will be explained later in the book when we study factor analysis and analysis of covariance structures.

[5] A more restrictive—yet defensible—position requires that differences between measures be interpretable as *quantitative differences in the property measured.* "Quantitative," in the view of some experts, means that a difference in magnitude between two attribute values represents a corresponding quantitative difference in the attributes. See L. Jones, "The Nature of Measurement." In R. Thorndike, ed., *Educational Measurement,* 2d ed. Washington, D.C.: American Council on Education, 1971, pp. 335–355. This view, strictly speaking, rules out, *as measurement,* nominal and ordinal scales. I believe that actual measurement experience in the behavioral sciences and education justifies a more relaxed position. Again, it does not matter terribly, provided the student *understands* the general ideas being presented. I recommend that the more advanced student read Torgerson's and Nunnally's fine presentations: W. Torgerson, *Theory and Methods of Scaling.* New York: Wiley, 1958, chaps. 1 and 2; J. Nunnally, *Psychometric Theory,* 2d ed. New York: McGraw-Hill, 1978, chap. 1. An older, outstanding treatise that has strongly influenced this text is: J. Guilford, *Psychometric Methods,* 2d ed. New York: McGraw-Hill, 1954, chap. 1. The curious student will enjoy the collection of articles on the controversy published in R. Kirk, ed., *Statistical Issues: A Reader for the Behavioral Sciences.* Monterey, Calif.: Brooks/Cole, 1972, chap. 2. Readers who intend doing research and who will always be faced with measurement problems should carefully and repeatedly read Nunnally's excellent presentation of the problems and their solution: Nunnally, *op. cit.,* pp. 24–33.

first consider the fundamental scientific and measurement problem of classification and enumeration.

Classification and Enumeration

The first and most elementary step in any measurement procedure is to define the objects of the universe of discourse. Suppose U, the universal set, is defined as all tenth-grade pupils in a certain high school. Next, the properties of the objects of U must be defined. All measurement requires that U be broken down into at least two subsets. The most elementary form of measurement would be to classify or categorize all the objects as possessing or not possessing some characteristic. Say this characteristic is maleness. We break U down into males and nonmales, or males and females. These are of course two *subsets* of U, or a *partitioning* of U. (Recall that partitioning a set consists of breaking it down into subsets that are *mutually exclusive* and *exhaustive*. That is, each set object must be assigned to one subset and one subset only, and all set objects in U must be so assigned.)

What we have done is to classify the objects of interest to us. We have put them into categories: we have partitioned them. The obvious simplicity of this procedure seems to cause difficulty for students. People spend much of their lives categorizing things, events, and people. Life could not go on without such categorizing, yet to associate the process with measurement seems difficult.

After a method of classification has been found, we have in effect a rule for telling which objects of U go into which classes or subsets or partitions. This rule is used and the set objects are put into the subsets. Here are the boys; here are the girls. Easy. Here are the middle-class children; here are the working-class children. Not as easy, but not too hard. Here are the delinquents; here are the nondelinquents. Harder. Here are the bright ones; here are the average ones; here are the dull ones. Much harder. Here are the creative ones; here are the noncreative ones. Very much harder.

After the objects of the universe have been classified into designated subsets, the members of the sets can be counted. In the dichotomous case, the rule for counting was given in Chapter 4: If a member of U has the characteristic in question, say *maleness*, then assign a 1. If the member does not have the characteristic, then assign a 0. (See Figure 25.1.) When set members are counted in this fashion, all objects of a subset are considered to be equal to each other and unequal to the members of other subsets.

Nominal Measurement

There are four general levels of measurement: nominal, ordinal, interval, and ratio. These four levels lead to four kinds of scales. Some writers on the subject admit only ordinal, interval, and ratio measurement, while others say that all four belong to the measurement family. We need not be too fussy about this as long as we understand the characteristics of the different scales and levels.

The rules used to assign numerals to objects define the kind of scale and the level of measurement. The lowest level of measurement is *nominal* measurement (see earlier discussion of categorization). The numbers assigned to objects are numerical without having a number meaning; they cannot be ordered or added. They are *labels* much like the letters used to label sets. If individuals or groups are assigned 1, 2, 3, . . . , these numerals are merely names. For example, baseball and football players are assigned such numbers. Telephones are assigned such numbers. Groups may be given the labels I, II, and III or A_1, A_2, and A_3. We use nominal measurement in our everyday thinking and living. We identify others as "men," "women," "Protestants," "Australians," and so on. At any rate, the symbols assigned to objects, or rather, to the sets of objects, constitute nominal scales. Some experts think this is not measurement, as indicated previously. Such exclusion of nominal measurement would prevent much social scientific research procedure from being called measurement. Since the definition of measurement is satisfied, and since the members of labeled sets can be counted and compared, it would seem that nominal procedures *are* measurement.

The requirements of nominal measurement are simple. All the members of a set are assigned the same numeral and no two sets are assigned the same numeral. Nominal measurement—at least in one simple form—was expressed in Figure 25.1, where the objects of the range, $\{0, 1\}$, were mapped onto the a's, the objects of U, the five people, by the rule: If x is male, assign 1; if x is female, assign 0. This is how nominal measurement is quantified when only a dichotomy is involved. When the partition contains more than two categories, some other method must be used. Basically, nominal measurement quantification amounts to counting the objects in the cells of the subsets or partitions.

Ordinal Measurement

Ordinal measurement requires that the objects of a set can be rank-ordered on an operationally defined characteristic or property. The so-called transitivity postulate must be satisfied: If a is greater than b, and b is greater than c, then a is greater than c. Other symbols or words can be substituted for "greater than," for example, "less than," "precedes," "dominates," and so on. Most measurement in behavioral research depends on this postulate. It must be possible to assert ordinal or rank-order statements like the one just used. That is, suppose we have three objects, a, b, and c, and a is greater than b, and b is greater than c. If we can justifiably say, also, that a is greater than c, then the main condition for ordinal measurement is satisfied. Be wary, however. A relation may *seem* to satisfy the transitivity postulate but may not actually do so. For example, can we always say: a dominates b, and b dominates c; therefore a dominates c? Think of husband, wife, and child. Think, too, of the relations "loves," "likes," "is friendly to," or "accepts." In such cases, transitivity should be demonstrated by the researcher.

The procedure can be generalized in three ways. One, any number of objects of any kind can be measured ordinally simply by extension to a, b, c, . . . , n. (Even though two objects may sometimes be equal, ordinal measurement is still possible.) We simply need to be able to say $a > b > c > \cdots > n$ on some property.

The second extension consists of using combined properties or combined criteria. Instead of using only one property, we can use two or more. For example, instead of ranking a group of college students on academic achievement by grade-point averages, we may wish to rank them on the combined criteria of grade-point average and test scores. (Grade-point averages, too, are composite scores.)

The third extension is accomplished by using criteria other than "greater than." "Less than" occurs to us immediately. "Precedes," "is above," and "is superior to" may be useful criteria. In fact, we might substitute a symbol other than ">" or "<." One such symbol is "○." It can be used to mean any operation, such as those just named, in which the transitivity postulate is satisfied: $a \bigcirc b$ might mean "a precedes b," or "a is subordinate to b," and $a \bigcirc b \bigcirc c$ might mean "a is superior to b, b is superior to c, and a is superior to c."

The numerals assigned to ranked objects are called *rank values*. Let R equal the set of *ranked objects:* $R = \{a > b > \cdots > n\}$. Let R^* equal the set of *rank values:* $R^* = \{1, 2, \ldots, n\}$. We assign the objects of R^* to the objects of R as follows: the largest object is assigned 1, the next in size 2, and so on to the smallest object which is assigned the last numeral in the particular series. If this procedure is used, the rank values assigned are in the reverse order. If, for instance, there are five objects, with a the largest, b the next, through e, the smallest, then:

Objects	R	R*
a	1	5
b	2	4
c	3	3
d	4	2
e	5	1

Of course, one step can be skipped by assigning $R*$ directly: by assigning 5 to a, 4 to b, through 1 to e.

Ordinal numbers indicate rank order and nothing more. The numbers do not indicate absolute quantities, nor do they indicate that the intervals between the numbers are equal. For instance, it cannot be assumed that because the *numerals* are equally spaced the underlying properties they represent are equally spaced. If two subjects have the ranks 8 and 5 and two other subjects the ranks 6 and 3, we cannot say that the differences between the first and second pairs are equal. There is also no way to know that any individual has *none* of the property being measured. Rank-order scales are not equal-interval scales, nor do they have absolute zero points.

Interval Measurement (Scales)

Interval or *equal-interval* scales possess the characteristics of nominal and ordinal scales, especially the rank-order characteristic. In addition, numerically equal distances on interval scales represent equal distances in the property being measured. Thus, suppose that we had measured four objects on an interval scale and gotten the values 8, 6, 5, and 3. Then we can legitimately say that the difference between the first and third objects in the property measured, $8 - 5 = 3$, is equal to the difference between the second and fourth objects, $6 - 3 = 3$. Another way to express the equal-interval idea is to say that the *intervals* can be added and subtracted. An interval scale is assumed as follows:

a	b	c	d	e
1	2	3	4	5

The interval from a to c is $3 - 1 = 2$. The interval from c to d is $4 - 3 = 1$. We can add these two intervals $(3 - 1) + (4 - 3) = 2 + 1 = 3$. Now note that the interval from a to d is $4 - 1 = 3$. Expressed in an equation: $(d - a) = (c - a) + (d - c)$. If these intervals were five pupils measured on an interval scale of achievement, then the differences in achievement between pupils a and c and between b and d would be equal. We could not say, however, that the achievement of d was twice as great as that of pupil b. (Such a statement would require one higher level of measurement.) Note that it is not *quantities* or *amounts* that are added and subtracted. It is *intervals* or *distances*.

Ratio Measurement (Scales)

The highest level of measurement is *ratio measurement,* and the measurement ideal of the scientist is the ratio scale. A ratio scale, in addition to possessing the characteristics of nominal, ordinal, and interval scales, has an absolute or natural zero that has empirical meaning. If a measurement is zero on a ratio scale, then there is a basis for saying that some object has none of the property being measured. Since there is an absolute or natural zero, all arithmetic operations are possible, including multiplication and division. Numbers on the scale indicate the actual amounts of the property being measured. If a ratio scale of achievement existed, then it would be possible to say that a pupil with a scale score of 8 has an achievement twice as great as a pupil with a scale score of 4.

COMPARISONS OF SCALES: PRACTICAL CONSIDERATIONS AND STATISTICS

The basic characteristics of the four types of measurement and their accompanying scales have been discussed. What kinds of scales are used in behavioral and educational research? Mostly nominal and ordinal are used, though the probability is good that many scales and tests used in psychological and educational measurement approximate interval measurement well enough for practical purposes, as we shall see.

First, consider nominal measurement. When objects are partitioned into two, three, or more categories on the basis of group membership—sex, ethnic identification, married-single, Protestant-Catholic-Jew, and so forth—measurement is nominal. When continuous variables are converted to attributes, as when objects are divided into high-low and old-young, we have what can be called quasi-nominal measurement: although capable of at least rank order, the values are in effect collapsed to 1 and 0.

It is instructive to study the numerical operations that are, in a strict sense, legitimate with each type of measurement. With nominal measurement the counting of numbers of cases in each category and subcategory is, of course, permissible. Frequency statistics like χ^2, percentages, and certain coefficients of correlation (contingency coefficients) can be used. This sounds thin. Actually, it is a good deal. A good principle to remember is this: If one cannot use any other method, one can almost always partition or cross-partition subjects. If we are studying the relation between two variables and do not have any way to measure them adequately in an ordinal or interval fashion, some way can probably be found to divide the objects of study into at least two groups. For example, in studying the relation between the motivation of board of education members to become board members and their religion, as Gross and his colleagues did, we may be able to have knowledgeable judges divide the sample of board members into those with "good" motivation and those with "poor" motivation. Then we can cross-partition religion with the motivation dichotomy and thus study the relation.

Intelligence, aptitude, and personality test scores are, *basically and strictly speaking,* ordinal. They indicate with more or less accuracy not the *amounts* of intelligence, aptitude, and personality traits of individuals, but rather the *rank-order positions* of the individuals. To see this, we must realize that ordinal scales do not possess the desirable characteristics of equal intervals or absolute zeroes. Intelligence test scores are examples. It is not possible to say that an individual has zero intelligence. If he is alive, he must have some score above zero. But there is no absolute zero on an intelligence test scale. The zero is arbitrary, and without an absolute zero, addition of *amounts* of intelligence has little meaning, for arbitrary zero points can lead to different sums. On a scale with an arbitrary zero point the following addition is performed: $2 + 3 = 5$. Then the sum is 5 scale units above zero. But if the arbitrary zero point is inaccurate and the "real" zero point is at the scale position 4 scale points lower than the arbitrary zero position, then the former 2 and 3 should really be 6 and 7, and $6 + 7 = 13$!

The lack of a real zero in ordinal scales is not as serious as the lack of equal intervals. Even without a real zero, *distances* within a scale can be added, provided that these

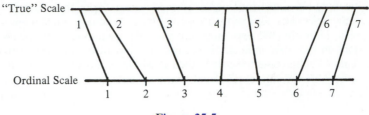

Figure 25.5

distances are equal (empirically). The situation might be somewhat as indicated in Figure 25.5. The scale on the top ("true" scale) indicates the "true" values of a variable. The bottom scale (ordinal scale) indicates the rank-order scale used by an investigator. In other words, an investigator has rank-ordered seven persons quite well, but his ordinal numerals, which *look* equal in interval, are not "true," although they may be fairly accurate representations of the empirical facts.

Strictly speaking, the statistics that can be used with ordinal scales include rank-order measures such as the rank-order coefficient of correlation, ρ, Kendall's W, and rank-order analysis of variance, medians, and percentiles. If only these statistics (and others like them) are legitimate, how can statistics like r, t, and F be used with what are in effect ordinal measures? And they are so used, without a qualm by most researchers.

Although this is a moot point, the situation is not as difficult as it seems. As Torgerson points out, some types of natural origin have been devised for certain types of measurement.[6] In measuring preferences and attitudes, for example, the neutral points (on either side of which are degrees of positive and negative favoring, approving, liking, and preferring) can be considered natural origins. Besides, ratio scales, while desirable, are not absolutely necessary because most of what we need to do in psychological measurement can be done with equal-interval scales.

The lack of equal intervals is more serious since distances *within* a scale theoretically cannot be added without interval equality. Yet, though most psychological scales are basically ordinal, we can with considerable assurance often assume equality of interval. The argument is evidential. If we have, say, two or three measures of the same variable, and these measures are all substantially and linearly related, then equal intervals can be assumed. This assumption is valid because the more nearly a relation approaches linearity, the most nearly equal are the intervals of the scales. This also applies, at least to some extent, to certain psychological measures like intelligence, achievement, and attitude tests and scales.

A related argument is that many of the methods of analysis we use work quite well with most psychological scales. That is, the results we get from using scales and assuming equal intervals are quite satisfactory.

The point of view adopted in this book is, then, a pragmatic one, that the assumption of interval equality works. Still, we are faced with a dilemma: if we use ordinal measures as though they were interval or ratio measures, we *can* err in interpreting data and the relations inferred from data, though the danger is probably not as grave as it has been made out to be. There is no trouble with the numbers, as numbers. *They* do not know the difference between ρ and r or between parametric and nonparametric statistics, nor do they know the assumptions behind their use. But *we* do, or should, know the differences and the consequences of ignoring the differences. On the other hand, if we abide strictly

---

[6]Torgerson, *op. cit.*, p. 30.

by the rules, we cut off powerful modes of measurement and analyses and are left with tools inadequate to cope with the problems we want to solve.[7]

What is the answer, the resolution of the conflict? Part of the answer was given above: it is probable that most psychological and educational scales approximate interval equality fairly well. In those situations in which there is serious doubt as to interval equality, there are technical means for coping with some of the problems. The competent research worker should know something of scaling methods and certain transformations that change ordinal scales into interval scales.[8]

In the state of measurement at present, we cannot be sure that our measurement instruments have equal intervals. It is important to ask the question: How serious are the distortions and errors introduced by treating ordinal measurements as though they were interval measurements? With care in the construction of measuring instruments, and especially with care in the interpretation of the results, the consequences are evidently not serious.

The best procedure would seem to be to treat ordinal measurements as though they were interval measurements, but to be constantly alert to the possibility of *gross* inequality of intervals. As much as possible about the characteristics of the measuring tools should be learned. Much useful information has been obtained by this approach, with resulting scientific advances in psychology, sociology, and education. In short, it is unlikely that researchers will be led seriously astray by heeding this advice, if they are careful in applying it.[9]

(*Note:* Study suggestions for the three chapters of Part 8 appear at the end of Chapter 27.)

---

[7] Again, see Nunnally, *op. cit.,* pp. 24–33, for an enlightened discussion of these and related points.

[8] M. Bartlett, "The Use of Transformations," *Biometrics,* 3 (1947), 39–52 (especially pp. 49–50); Guilford, *op. cit.,* chap. 8. The subject of transformations and their purposes and uses is an important one, but has not been given the attention it deserves. Two authoritative and informative treatments are: G. Snedecor and W. Cochran, *Statistical Methods,* 6th ed. Ames, Iowa: Iowa State University Press, 1967, pp. 325ff.; F. Mosteller and R. Bush, "Selected Quantitative Techniques." In G. Lindzey, ed., *Handbook of Social Psychology,* vol. I. Cambridge, Mass.: Addison-Wesley, 1954, pp. 324–328.

[9] A useful review of the literature on the problem of scales of measurement and statistics is: P. Gardner, "Scales and Statistics," *Review of Educational Research,* 45 (1975), 43–57.

Chapter 26

Reliability

AFTER ASSIGNING numerals to objects or events according to rules, we must face two major problems of measurement: reliability and validity. We have devised a measurement game and have administered the measuring instruments to a group of subjects. We must now ask and answer the questions: What is the reliability of the measuring instrument? What is its validity?

If one does not know the reliability and validity of one's data little faith can be put in the results obtained and the conclusions drawn from the results. The data of the social sciences and education, derived from human behavior and human products, are, as we saw in the last chapter, some steps removed from the properties of scientific interest. Thus their validity can be questioned. Concern for reliability comes from the necessity for dependability in measurement. The data of all psychological and educational measurement instruments contain errors of measurement. To the extent that they do so, to that extent the data they yield will not be dependable.

DEFINITIONS OF RELIABILITY

Synonyms for reliability are: dependability, stability, consistency, predictability, accuracy. Reliable people, for instance, are those whose behavior is consistent, dependable, predictable—what they will do tomorrow and next week will be consistent with what they do today and what they have done last week. They are stable, we say. Unreliable people, on the other hand, are those whose behavior is much more variable. They are unpredictably variable. Sometimes they do this, sometimes that. They lack stability. We say they are inconsistent.

So it is with psychological and educational measurements: they are more or less variable from occasion to occasion. They are stable and relatively predictable or they are unstable and relatively unpredictable; they are consistent or not consistent. If they are reliable, we can depend upon them. If they are unreliable, we cannot depend upon them.

It is possible to approach the definition of reliability in three ways. One approach is epitomized by the question: If we measure the same set of objects again and again with the same or comparable measuring instrument, will we get the same or similar results? This question implies a definition of reliability in *stability, dependability, predictability* terms. It is the definition most often given in elementary discussions of the subject.

A second approach is epitomized by the question: Are the measures obtained from a measuring instrument the ''true'' measures of the property measured? This is an *accuracy* definition. Compared to the first definition, it is further removed from common sense and intuition, but it is also more fundamental. These two approaches or definitions can be summarized in the words *stability* and *accuracy*. As we will see later, however, the accuracy definition implies the stability definition.

There is a third approach to the definition of reliability, an approach that not only helps us better define and solve both theoretical and practical problems but also implies other approaches and definitions. We can inquire how much *error of measurement* there is in a measuring instrument. Recall that here are two general types of variance: systematic and random. *Systematic variance* leans in one direction: scores tend to be all positive or all negative or all high or all low. Error in this case is constant or biased. *Random* or *error variance* is self-compensating: scores tend now to lean this way, now that way. Errors of measurement are random errors. They are the sum of a number of causes: the ordinary random or chance elements present in all measures due to unknown causes, temporary or momentary fatigue, fortuitous conditions at a particular time that temporarily affect the object measured or the measuring instrument, fluctuations of memory or mood, and other factors that are temporary and shifting. To the extent that errors of measurement are present in a measuring instrument, to that extent the instrument is unreliable. In other words, reliability can be defined as the relative absence of errors of measurement in a measuring instrument.

Reliability is the *accuracy* or *precision* of a measuring instrument. A homely example can easily show what is meant. Suppose a sportsman wishes to compare the accuracy of two guns. One is an old piece made a century ago but still in good condition. The other is a modern weapon made by an expert gunsmith. Both pieces are solidly fixed in granite bases and aimed and zeroed in by a sharpshooter. Equal numbers of rounds are fired with each gun. In Figure 26.1, the hypothetical pattern of shots on a target for each gun is shown. The target on the left represents the pattern of shots produced by the older gun. Observe that the shots are considerably scattered. Now observe that the pattern of shots on the target on the right is more closely packed. The shots are closely clustered around the bull's-eye.

Let us assume that numbers have been assigned to the circles of the targets: 3 to the bull's-eye, 2 to the next circle, 1 to the outside circle, and 0 to any shot outside the target. It is obvious that if we calculated measures of variability, say a standard deviation, from the two shot patterns, the old rifle would have a much larger measure of variability than

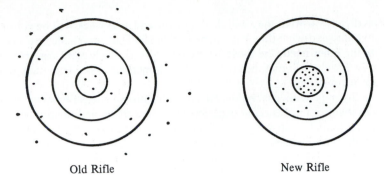

Old Rifle   New Rifle

Figure 26.1

the newer rifle. These measures can be considered reliability indices. The smaller variability measure of the new rifle indicates much less error, and thus much greater accuracy. The new rifle is reliable; the old rifle is less reliable.

Similarly, psychological and educational measurements have greater and lesser reliabilities. A measuring instrument, say an arithmetic achievement test, is given to a group of children—usually only once. Our goal, of course, is a multiple one: we seek to hit the "true" score of each child. To the extent that we miss the "true" scores, to this extent our measuring instrument, our test, is unreliable. The "true," the "real," arithmetic scores of five children, say, are 35, 31, 29, 22, 14. Another researcher does not know these "true" scores. His results are: 37, 30, 26, 24, 15. While he has not in a single case hit the "true" score, he has achieved the same rank order. His reliability and accuracy are surprisingly high.

Suppose that his five scores had been: 24, 37, 26, 15, 30. These are the same five scores, but they have a very different rank order. In this case, the test would be unreliable, because of its inaccuracy. To show all this more compactly, the three sets of scores, with their rank orders, have been set beside each other in Table 26.1. The rank orders of the first and second columns covary exactly. The rank-order coefficient of correlation is 1.00. Even though the test scores of the second column are not the exact scores, they *are* in the same rank order. On this basis, using a rank-order coefficient of correlation, the test is reliable. The rank-order coefficient of correlation between the ranks of the first and third columns, however, is zero, so that the latter test is completely unreliable.

Table 26.1   "True," Reliable, and Unreliable Obtained Test Scores and Rank Orders of Five Children

1 "True" Scores	(Rank)	2 Scores from Reliable Test	(Rank)	3 Scores from Unreliable Test	(Rank)
35	(1)	37	(1)	24	(4)
31	(2)	30	(2)	37	(1)
29	(3)	26	(3)	26	(3)
22	(4)	24	(4)	15	(5)
14	(5)	15	(5)	30	(2)

THEORY OF RELIABILITY

The example given in Table 26.1 epitomizes what we need to know about reliability.[1] It is necessary, now, to formalize the intuitive notions and to outline a theory of reliability. This theory is not only conceptually elegant; it is also practically powerful. It helps to unify measurement ideas and supplies a foundation for understanding various analytic techniques. The theory also ties in nicely with the variance approach emphasized in earlier discussions.

Any set of measures has a total variance, that is, after administering an instrument to a set of objects and obtaining a set of numbers (scores), we can calculate a mean, a standard deviation, and a variance. Let us be concerned here only with the variance. The variance, as seen earlier, is a *total obtained variance*, since it includes variances due to several causes. In general, any total obtained variance (or sum of squares) includes systematic and error variances.

Each person has an obtained score, X_t. (The "t" stands for "total.") This score has two components: a "true" component and an error component. We assume that each person has a "true" score, X_∞. (The "∞" is the infinity sign, and is used to signify "true.") This score would be known only to an omniscient being.[2] In addition to this "true" score, each person has an error score, X_e. The error score is some increment or decrement resulting from several of the factors responsible for errors of measurement.

This reasoning leads to a simple equation basic to the theory:

$$X_t = X_\infty + X_e \tag{26.1}$$

which says, succinctly, that any obtained score is made of two components, a "true" component and an error component. The only part of this definition that gives any real trouble is X_∞, which can be conceived to be the score an individual would obtain if all internal and external conditions were "perfect" and the measuring instrument were "perfect." A bit more realistically, it can be considered to be the mean of a large number of administrations of the test to the same person. Symbolically, $X_\infty = (X_1 + X_2 + \cdots + X_n)/n$.[3]

---

[1] The treatment of reliability in this chapter is based on traditional error theory. See J. Guilford, *Pychometric Methods,* 2d ed. New York: McGraw-Hill, 1954, chaps. 13 and 14. While this theory has been shown to have unnecessary assumptions, it is admirably suited to conveying to the beginning student the basic nature of reliability. For a criticism of the theory, see R. Tryon, "Reliability and Behavior Domain Validity: Reformulation and Historical Critique," *Psychological Bulletin,* 54 (1957), 229–249. In practice, the two approaches arrive at the same formulas. The most recent development of reliability theory and practice, called generalizability theory, emphasizes multivariate (or multifacet) thinking, components of variance analysis, and decision making. An extended discussion of the theory is given in: L. Cronbach, G. Gleser, H. Nanda, and N. Rajaratnam, *The Dependability of Behavioral Measurement: Theory of Generalizability for Scores and Profiles.* New York: Wiley, 1972. (Also see footnote 3, below).

[2] This does not mean that X_∞ may not include properties other than the property being measured. All systematic variance is included in X_∞. The problem of measuring *the* property is a validity problem.

[3] It must be emphasized that the notion of a "true" score is a fiction, albeit a useful fiction. Kaplan calls it "the fiction of the true measure." A. Kaplan, *The Conduct of Inquiry.* San Francisco: Chandler, 1964, p. 202. He points out that the "true measure" is a limit—much as in the calculus—toward which the measures converge (p. 203). Whenever "true score," or X_∞, is used, then, it is understood that the expression is a convenient fiction. Lord and Novick, in their authoritative book on test score theory, define true score as the expected value of an observed score, which can be *interpreted* as the average score an individual "would obtain on infinitely many independent repeated measurements (an unobservable quantity)." F. Lord and M. Novick, *Statistical Theories of Mental Test Scores.* Reading, Mass.: Addison-Wesley, 1968, pp. 30–31. Similar qualifications are to be understood with notions like "true variance" and the correlation between obtained scores and true scores (see below).

With a little simple algebra, Equation 26.1 can be extended to yield a more useful equation in variance terms:

$$V_t = V_\infty + V_e \tag{26.2}$$

Equation 26.2 shows that the total obtained variance of a test is made up of two variance components, a "true" component and an "error" component. If, for example, it were possible to administer the same instrument to the same group 4,367,929 times, and then to calculate the means of each person's 4,367,929 scores, we would have a set of "nearly true" measures of the group. In other words, these means are the X_∞'s of the group. We could then calculate the variance of the X_∞'s yielding V_∞. This value must always be less than V_t, the variance calculated from the obtained set of original scores, the X_t's, because the original scores contain error, whereas the "true," or "nearly true," scores have no error, the error having been washed out by the averaging process. Put differently, if there were no errors of measurement in the X_t's, then $V_t = V_\infty$. But, there are always errors of measurement, and we assume that if we knew the error scores and subtracted them from the obtained scores we would obtain the "true" scores.

We never know the "true" scores nor do we really ever know the error scores. Nevertheless, it is possible to estimate the error variance. By so doing, we can, in effect, substitute in Equation 26.2 and solve the equation. This is the essence of the idea, even though certain assumptions and steps have been omitted from the discussion. A diagram or two may show the ideas more clearly. Let the total variances of two tests be represented by two bars. One test is highly reliable; the other test only moderately so, as shown in Figure 26.2. Tests A and B have the same total variance, but 90 percent of Test A is "true" variance and 10 percent is error variance. Only 60 percent of Test B is "true" variance and 40 percent is error variance. Test A is thus much more reliable than Test B.

Reliability is defined, so to speak, through error: the more error, the greater the unreliability; the less error, the greater the reliability. Practically speaking, this means that if we can estimate the error variance of a measure we can also estimate the measure's reliability. This brings us to two equivalent definitions of reliability:

1. Reliability is the proportion of the "true" variance to the total obtained variance of the data yielded by a measuring instrument.
2. Reliability is the proportion of error variance to the total variance yielded by a measuring instrument subtracted from 1.00, the index 1.00 indicating perfect reliability.

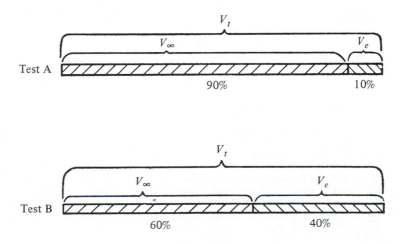

Figure 26.2

It is easier to write these definitions in equation form:

$$r_{tt} = \frac{V_\infty}{V_t} \tag{26.3}$$

$$r_{tt} = 1 - \frac{V_e}{V_t} \tag{26.4}$$

where r_{tt} is the reliability coefficient and the other symbols are as defined before. Equation 26.3 is theoretical and cannot be used for calculation. Equation 26.4 is both theoretical and practical. It can be used both to conceptualize the idea of reliability and to estimate the reliability of an instrument. An alternate equation to (26.4) is:

$$r_{tt} = \frac{V_t - V_e}{V_t} \tag{26.5}$$

This alternate definition of reliability will be useful in helping us to understand what reliability is.

Two Computational Examples

To show the nature of reliability, two examples are given in Table 26.2. One of them, labeled I in the table, is an example of high reliability; the other, labeled II, is an example of low reliability. Note carefully that exactly the same numbers are used in both cases. The only difference is that they are arranged differently. The situation in both cases is this: five individuals have been administered a test of four items. (This is unrealistic, of course, but it will do to illustrate several points.) The data of the five individuals are given in the rows; the sums of the individuals are given to the right of the rows (Σ_t). The sums of the items are given at the bottom of each table (Σ_{it}). In addition, the sums of the individuals on the odd items (Σ_o) and the sums of the individuals on the even items (Σ_e) are given on the extreme right of each subtable. The calculations necessary for two-way analyses of variance are given below the data tables.

To make the examples more realistic, imagine that the data are scores on a six-point scale, say attitudes toward school. A high score means a high favorable attitude, a low score a low favorable (or unfavorable) attitude. (It makes no difference, however, what the scores are. They can even be 1's and 0's resulting from marking items of an achievement test: right = 1, and wrong = 0.) In I, Individual 1 has a high favorable attitude toward school, whereas Individual 5 has a low favorable attitude toward school. These are readily indicated by the sums of the individuals (or the means): 21 and 5. These sums (Σ_t) are the usual scores yielded by tests. For instance, if we wanted to know the mean of the group, we would calculate it as $(21 + 18 + 14 + 10 + 5)/5 = 13.60$.

The variance of these sums provides one of the terms of Equations 26.4 and 26.5, but not the other: V_t, but not V_e. By using the analysis of variance it is possible to calculate both V_t and V_e. The analyses of variance of I and II show how this is done. These calculations need not detain us long, since they are subsidiary to the main issue.

The analysis of variance yields the variances: Between items, Between individuals, and Residual or Error. The F ratios for Items are not significant in I or II. (Note that both mean squares are 2.27. Obviously they must be equal, since they are calculated from the same sums at the bottoms of the two subtables.) Actually, we are not interested in these variances—we only want to remove the variance due to items from the total variance. Our interest lies in the Individual variances and in the Error variances, which are circled in the subtables. The total variance of Equations 26.3, 26.4, and 26.5 is interesting because it

Table 26.2 Demonstration of Reliability and Computation of Reliability Coefficients. Hypothetical Examples

Indi-viduals	Items a	b	c	d	Σ_t	Σ_o	Σ_e	Indi-viduals	Items a	b	c	d	Σ_t	Σ_o	Σ_e
					I: $r_{tt} = .92$								II: $r_{tt} = .45$		
1	6	6	5	4	21	11	10	1	6	4	5	1	16	11	5
2	4	6	5	3	18	9	9	2	4	1	5	4	14	9	5
3	4	4	4	2	14	8	6	3	4	6	4	2	16	8	8
4	3	1	4	2	10	7	3	4	3	6	4	3	16	7	9
5	1	2	1	1	5	2	3	5	1	2	1	2	6	2	4
Σ_{tt}	18	19	19	12	$\Sigma X_t = 68$			Σ_{tt}	18	19	19	12	$\Sigma X_t = 68$		
					$(\Sigma X_t)^2 = 4624$								$(\Sigma X_t)^2 = 4624$		
					$\Sigma X_t^2 = 288$								$\Sigma X_t^2 = 288$		

$$C = \frac{(68)^2}{20} = 231.20 \qquad\qquad C = 231.20$$

$$\text{Total} = 288 - 231.20 = 56.80 \qquad\qquad \text{Total} = 56.80$$

$$\text{Between Items} = \frac{1190}{5} - 231.20 = 6.80 \qquad \text{Between Items} = 6.80$$

$$\text{Between Individuals} = \frac{1086}{4} - 231.20 \qquad \text{Between Individuals} = \frac{1000}{4} - 231.20$$
$$= 40.30 \qquad\qquad = 18.80$$

Source	df	ss	ms	F	Source	df	ss	ms	F
Items	3	6.80	2.27	2.80 (n.s.)	Items	3	6.80	2.27	1 (n.s.)
Individuals	4	40.30	10.08	12.44 (.001)	Individuals	4	18.80	4.70	1.81 (n.s.)
Residual	12	9.70	.81		Residual	12	31.20	2.60	
Total	19	56.80			Total	19	56.80		

By Eq. 26.4:

$$r_{tt} = 1 - \frac{V_e}{V_{\text{ind}}} = 1 - \frac{.81}{10.08} \qquad\qquad r_{tt} = 1 - \frac{2.60}{4.70}$$
$$= .92 \qquad\qquad\qquad = .45$$

By Eq. 26.5:

$$r_u = \frac{V_{\text{ind}} - V_e}{V_{\text{ind}}} = \frac{10.08 - .81}{10.08} \qquad\qquad r_{tt} = \frac{4.70 - 2.60}{4.70}$$
$$= .92 \qquad\qquad\qquad = .45$$

Odd-Even:

$$r_{oe} = .91 \qquad\qquad\qquad r_{oe} = .32$$

is an index of differences between individuals. It is a measure of individual differences. Instead of writing V_t, then, let us write V_{ind}, meaning the variance resulting from individual differences. By using either (26.4) or (26.5), we obtain reliability coefficients of .92

for the data of I and .45 for the data of II. The hypothetical data of I are reliable; those of II are not reliable.

Perhaps the best way to understand this is to go back to Equation 26.3. Now we write $r_{tt} = V_\infty/V_{\text{ind}}$. If we had a direct way to calculate V_∞, we could quickly calculate r_{tt}, but as we saw before, we do not have a direct way. There *is* a way to estimate it, however. If we can find a way to estimate V_e, the error variance, the problem is solved because V_e can be subtracted from V_{ind} to yield an estimate of V_∞. Obviously we can ignore V_∞ and subtract the proportion V_e/V_{ind} from 1 and get r_{tt}. This is perfectly acceptable way to calculate r_{tt} and to conceptualize reliability. Reasoning from $V_{\text{ind}} - V_e$ is perhaps more fruitful and ties in nicely with our earlier discussion of components of variance.

It was said in Chapter 13 that each statistical problem has a total amount of variance and each variance source contributes to this total variance. We translate the reasoning of Chapter 13 to the present problem. In random samples of the same population, V_b and V_w should be statistically equal. But, if V_b, the between-groups variance, is significantly greater than V_w, the within-groups (error) variance, then there is something in V_b over and above chance. That is, V_b includes the variance of V_w and, in addition, some systematic variance.

Similarly, we can say that if V_{ind} is significantly greater than V_e, then there is something in V_{ind} over and above error variance. This excess of variance would seem to be due to individual differences in whatever is being measured. Measurement aims at the "true" scores of individuals. When we say that reliability is the accuracy of a measuring instrument, we mean that a reliable instrument more or less measures the "true" scores of individuals, the "more or less" depending on the reliability of the instrument. That "true" scores are measured can be inferred only from the "true" *differences* between individuals, although neither of these can be directly measured, of course. What we do is to infer the "true" differences from the fallible, empirical, measured differences, which are always to some extent corrupted by errors of measurement.

Now, if there is some way to remove from V_{ind} the effect of errors of measurement, some way to free V_{ind} of error, we can solve the problem easily. We simply subtract V_e from V_{ind} to get an estimate of V_∞. Then the proportion of the "pure" variance to all the variance, "pure" and "impure," is the estimate of the reliability of the measuring instrument. To summarize symbolically:

$$r_{tt} = \frac{V_\infty}{V_{\text{ind}}} = \frac{V_{\text{ind}} - V_e}{V_{\text{ind}}} = 1 - \frac{V_e}{V_{\text{ind}}}$$

The actual calculations are given at the bottom of Table 26.2.

Returning to the data of Table 26.2, let us see if we can "see" the reliability of I and the unreliability of II. Look first at the columns where the totals of the individuals are recorded (Σ_t). Notice that the sums of I have a greater range than those of II: $21 - 5 = 16$ and $16 - 6 = 10$. Given the same individuals, the more reliable a measure the greater the range of the sums of the individuals. Think of the extreme: a completely unreliable instrument would yield sums that are like the sums yielded by random numbers, and, of course, the reliability of random numbers is approximately zero. (The nonsignificant F ratio for Individuals, 1.81, in II indicates that $r_{tt} = .45$ is not statistically significant.)

Now examine the rank orders of the values under the items, *a, b, c,* and *d.* In I, all four rank orders are about the same. Each item of the attitude scale, apparently, is measuring the same thing. To the extent that the individual items yield the same rank orders of individuals, to this extent the test is reliable. The items hang together, so to speak. They are internally consistent. Also, notice that the rank orders of the items of I are about the same as the rank order of the sums.

The rank orders of the item values of II are quite different. The rank orders of a and c agree very well; they are the same as those of I. The rank orders of a and b, a and d, b and d, and c and d, however, do not agree very well. Either the items are measuring different things, or they are not measuring very consistently. This lack of congruence of rank orders is reflected in the totals of the individuals. Although the rank order of these totals is similar to the rank order of the totals of I, the range or variance is considerably less, and there is lack of spread between the sums (for example, the three 16's).

We conclude our consideration of these two examples by considering certain figures in Table 26.2 not considered before. On the right-hand side of both I and II the sums of the odd items (Σ_o) and the sums of the even items (Σ_e) are given. Simply add the values of odd items across the rows: $a + c$: $6 + 5 = 11$, $4 + 5 = 9$, $4 + 4 = 8$, and so forth, in I. Then add the values of the even items: $b + d$: $6 + 4 = 10$, $6 + 3 = 9$, and so forth, in I also. If there were more items, for example, a, b, c, d, e, f, g, then we would add: $a + c + e + g$ for the odd sums, and $b + d + f$ for the even sums. To calculate the reliability coefficient, calculate the product-moment correlation between the odd sums and the even sums, and then correct the resulting coefficient with the Spearman-Brown formula.[4] The odd-even r_{tt}'s for I and II are .91 and .32, respectively, fairly close to the analysis of variance results of .92 and .45. (With more subjects and more items, the estimates will ordinarily be close.)

This simple operation may seem mystifying. To see that this is a variation of the same variance and rank-order theme, let us note, first, the rank order of the sums of the two examples. The rank orders of Σ_o and Σ_e are almost the same in I, but quite different in II. The reasoning is the same as before. Evidently the items are measuring the same thing in I, but in II the two sets of items are not consistent. To reconstruct the variance argument, remember that by adding the sum of the odd items to the sum of the even items for each person the total sum, or $\Sigma_o + \Sigma_e = \Sigma_t$, is obtained.

THE INTERPRETATION OF THE RELIABILITY COEFFICIENT

If r, the coefficient of correlation, is squared, it becomes a coefficient of determination, that is, it gives us the proportion or percentage of the variance shared by two variables. If $r = .90$, then the two variables share $(.90)^2 = 81$ percent of the total variance of the two variables in common. The reliability coefficient is also a coefficient of determination. Theoretically, it tells how much variance of the total variance of a measured variable is "true" variance. If we had the "true" scores and could correlate them with the scores of the measured variable and square the resulting coefficient of correlation, we would obtain the reliability coefficient.

Symbolic representation may make this clear. Let $r_{t\infty}$ be the coefficient of correlation between the obtained scores and the "true" scores, X_∞. The reliability coefficient is defined:

$$r_{tt} = r_{t\infty}^{2} \tag{26.6}$$

Although it is not possible to calculate $r_{t\infty}$ directly, it is helpful to understand the rationale of the reliability coefficient in these theoretical terms.

Another theoretical interpretation is to conceive that each X_∞ can be the mean of a

[4] See any measurement text, for example, A. Anastasi, *Psychological Testing*, 4th ed. New York: Macmillan, 1976, pp. 115–116. The sums of the odd and the sums of the even items are, of course, the sums of only half the items in a test. They are therefore less reliable than the sums of all the items. The Spearman-Brown formula corrects the odd-even coefficient (and other part coefficients) for the lesser number of items used in calculating the coefficient.

large number of X_t's derived from administering the test to an individual a large number of times, other things being equal. The idea behind this notion has been explained before. The first administration of the test yields, say, a certain rank order of individuals. If the second, third, and further measurings all tend to yield approximately the same rank order, then the test is reliable. This is a stability or *test-retest* interpretation of reliability.

Another interpretation is that reliability is the *internal consistency* of a test: the test items are homogeneous. This interpretation in effect boils down to the same idea as other interpretations: accuracy. Take any random sample of items from the test, and any other random and different sample of items for the test. Treat each sample as a separate subtest. Each individual will then have two scores: one X_t for one subsample and another X_t for the other subsample. Correlate the two sets, continuing the process indefinitely. The average intercorrelation of the subsamples (corrected by the Spearman-Brown formula) shows the test's internal consistency.[5] But this means, really, that each subsample, if the test is reliable, succeeds in producing approximately the same rank order of individuals. If it does not, the test is not reliable.

THE STANDARD ERROR OF THE MEAN AND THE STANDARD ERROR OF MEASUREMENT

Two important aspects of reliability are the reliability of means and the reliability of individual measures. These are tied to the standard error of the mean and the standard error of measurement. In research studies, ordinarily, the standard error of the mean—and related statistics like the standard error of the differences between means and the standard error of a correlation coefficient—is the more important of these. Since the standard error of the mean was discussed in considerable detail in an earlier chapter, it is only necessary to say here that the reliability of specific statistics is another aspect of the general problem of reliability. The standard error of measurement, or its square, the standard variance of measurement, needs to be defined and identified, if only briefly. This will be done through use of a simple example.

An investigator measures the attitudes of five individuals and obtains the scores given under the column labeled X_t in Table 26.3. Assume, further, that the "true" attitude scores of the five individuals are those given under the column labeled X_∞. (Remember, however, that we can never know these scores.) It can be seen that the instrument is reliable. While only one of the five obtained scores is exactly the same as its companion "true" score, the differences between those obtained scores that are not the same and the "true" scores are all small. These differences are shown under the column labeled "X_e"; they are "error scores." The instrument is evidently fairly accurate. The calculation of r_{tt} confirms this impression: .71.

A rather direct measure of the reliability of the instrument can be obtained by calculating the variance or the standard deviation of the error scores (X_e). The variance of the error scores and the variances of the X_t and X_∞ scores have been calculated and entered in Table

---

[5] See L. Cronbach, "Coefficient Alpha and the Internal Structure of Tests," *Psychometrika,* 16 (1951), 297–334; Tryon, *op. cit.* The formulas given by Cronbach and Tryon look different from Equations 26.3 and 26.4. They yield the same results, however. The originator of the use of the analysis of variance to estimate reliability seems to have been Hoyt. See C. Hoyt, "Test Reliability Obtained by Analysis of Variance," *Psychometrika,* 6 (1941), 153–160. Ebel extended the use of analysis of variance to ratings and stressed the use of the intraclass coefficient of correlation: R. Ebel, "Estimation of the Reliability of Ratings," *Psychometrika,* 16 (1951), 407–424.

Table 26.3 Hypothetical Reliability and Standard Error of Measurement Example

	X_t	X_∞	X_e
	2	1	1
	1	2	−1
	3	3	0
	3	4	−1
	6	5	1
Σ:	15	15	0
M:	3	3	0
V:	2.80	2.00	.80

$$r_{tt} = 1 - \frac{V_e}{V_t} = 1 - \frac{.80}{2.80} = .71 \qquad r_{t\infty} = .845$$

$$r_{tt} = \frac{V_\infty}{V_t} = \frac{2.00}{2.80} = .71 \qquad\qquad r_{tt} = r^2_{t\infty} = (.845)^2 = .71$$

$$SV_{\mathrm{meas}} = V_t(1 - r_{tt}) = 2.80(1 - .71) = .81$$

$$SE_{\mathrm{meas}} = SD_t\sqrt{1 - r_{tt}} = \sqrt{SV_{\mathrm{meas}}} = \sqrt{.81} = .90$$

26.3. The variance of the error scores we now label, justifiably, *the standard variance of measurement,* which might more accurately be called "the standard variance of errors of measurement." The square root of this statistic is called the *standard error of measurement.* The standard variance of measurement is defined:

$$SV_{\mathrm{meas}} = V_t(1 - r_{tt}) \qquad\qquad (26.7)$$

This statistic can only be calculated, obviously, if we know the reliability coefficient. Note that if there is some way to estimate SV_{meas}, then it is possible to calculate the reliability coefficient. This bears further investigation.

We start with the definition of reliability given earlier: $r_{tt} = V_\infty/V_t = 1 - V_e/V_t$. A little algebraic manipulation yields the standard variance of measurement:

$$r_{tt} = 1 - \frac{V_e}{V_t}$$

$$r_{tt}V_t = V_t - V_e$$

$$V_e = V_t - r_{tt}V_t$$

$$V_e = V_t(1 - r_{tt})$$

The right side of the equation is the same as the right side of Equation 26.7. Therefore $V_e = SV_{\mathrm{meas}}$, or the error variance used earlier in the analysis of variance, *is* the standard variance of measurement. The standard variance of measurement and the standard error of measurement of the example have been calculated in Table 26.3. They are .81 and .90, respectively. As textbooks of measurement show, they can be used to interpret individual test scores. Such interpretation will not be discussed here; these statistics have been included only to show the connection between the original theory and ways of determining reliability.

One more calculation in Table 26.3 needs explanation. If we correlate the X_t, and the

X_∞ scores, we obtain a coefficient of correlation of .845. Now we obtain this coefficient, $r_{t\infty}$, directly, and square it to obtain the reliability coefficient. (See Equation 26.6.) The latter, of course, is the same as before: .71.

THE IMPROVEMENT OF RELIABILITY

The principle behind the improvement of reliability is the one previously called the *maxmincon principle*—in a slightly different form: "Maximize the variance of the individual differences and minimize the error variance." Equation 26.4 clearly indicates the principle. The general procedure follows.

First, write the items of psychological and educational measuring instruments unambiguously. An ambiguous event can be interpreted in more than one way. An ambiguous item permits error variance to creep in because individuals can interpret the item differently. Such interpretations tend to be random, and hence they increase error variance and decrease reliability.

Second, if an instrument is not reliable enough, add more items of equal kind and quality. This will usually, though not necessarily, increase reliability by a predictable amount. Adding more items increases the probability that any individual's X_t is close to his X_∞. This is a matter of the sampling of the property or the item space. With few items, a chance error looms large. With more items, it looms less large. The probability of its being balanced by another random error the other way is greater when there are more items. Summarily, more items increase the probability of accurate measurement. (Remember that each X_t is the sum of the item values for an individual.)

Third, clear and standard instructions tend to reduce errors of measurement. Great care must always be taken, in writing the instructions, to state them clearly. Ambiguous instructions increase error variance. Further, measuring instruments should always be administered under standard, well-controlled, and similar conditions. If the situations of administration differ, error variance can again intrude.

THE VALUE OF RELIABILITY

To be interpretable, a test must be reliable. Unless one can depend upon the results of the measurement of one's variables, one cannot with any confidence determine the relations between the variables. Since unreliable measurement is measurement overloaded with error, the determination of relations becomes a difficult and tenuous business. Is an obtained coefficient of correlation between two variables low because one or both measures are unreliable? Is an analysis of variance F ratio not significant because the hypothesized relation does not exist or because the measure of the dependent variable is unreliable?

Reliability, while not the most important facet of measurement, is still extremely important. In a way, this is like the money problem: the lack of it is the real problem. High reliability is no guarantee of good scientific results, but there can be no good scientific results without reliability. In brief, reliability is a necessary but not sufficient condition of the value of research results and their interpretation.

Chapter 27

Validity

THE SUBJECT of validity is complex, controversial, and peculiarly important in behavioral research. Here perhaps more than anywhere else, the nature of reality is questioned. It is possible to study reliability without inquiring into the meaning of variables. It is not possible to study validity, however, without sooner or later inquiring into the nature and meaning of one's variables.

When measuring certain physical properties and relatively simple attributes of persons, validity is no great problem. There is often rather direct and close congruence between the nature of the object measured and the measuring instrument. The length of an object, for example, can be measured by laying sticks, containing a standard number system in feet or meters, on the object. Weight is more indirect, but nervertheless not difficult: an object placed in a container displaces the container downward. The downward movement of the container is registered on a calibrated index, which reads ''pounds'' or ''ounces.'' With some physical attributes, then, there is little doubt of what is being measured.

On the other hand, suppose an educational scientist wishes to study the relation between intelligence and school achievement or the relation between authoritarianism and teaching style. Now there are no rulers to use, no scales with which to weigh the degree of authoritarianism, no clear-cut physical or behavioral attributes that point unmistakably to teaching style. It is necessary in such cases to invent indirect means to measure psychological and educational properties. These means are often so indirect that the validity of the measurement and its products is doubtful.

TYPES OF VALIDITY

The commonest definition of validity is epitomized by the question: Are we measuring what we think we are measuring? The emphasis in this question is on *what* is being measured. For example, a teacher has constructed a test to measure *understanding* of scientific procedures and has included in the test only *factual* items about scientific proce-dures. The test is not valid, because while it may reliably measure the pupils' *factual knowledge* of scientific procedures, it does not measure their *understanding* of such proce-dures. In other words, it may measure what it measures quite well, but it does not measure what the teacher intended it to measure.

Although the commonest definition of validity was given above, it must immediately be emphasized that there is no one validity. A test or scale is valid for the scientific or practical purpose of its user. Educators may be interested in the *nature* of high school pupils' achievement in mathematics. They would then be interested in *what* a mathematics achievement or aptitude test measures. They might, for instance, want to know the factors that enter into mathematics test performance and their relative contributions to this perfor-mance. On the other hand, they may be primarily interested in knowing the pupils who will probably be successful and those who will probably be unsuccessful in high school mathematics. They may have little interest in *what* a mathematics aptitude test measures. They are interested mainly in successful *prediction*. Implied by these two uses of tests are different kinds of validity. We now examine an extremely important development in test theory: the analysis and study of different kinds of validity.

The most important classification of types of validity is that prepared by a joint committee of the American Psychological Association, the American Educational Re-search Association, and the National Council on Measurements Used in Education.[1] Three types of validity are discussed: *content, criterion-related,* and *construct.* Each of these will be examined briefly, though we put the greatest emphasis on construct validity, since it is probably the most important form of validity from the scientific research point of view.

Content Validity and Content Validation

A university psychology professor has given a course to seniors in which she has empha-sized the understanding of principles of human development. She prepares an objective-type test. Wanting to know something of its validity, she critically examines each of the test's items for its relevance to understanding principles of human development. She also asks two colleagues to evaluate the content of the test. Naturally, she tells the colleagues what it is she is trying to measure. She is investigating the *content validity* of the test.

Content validity is the *representativeness* or *sampling adequacy* of the content—the substance, the matter, the topic—of a measuring instrument. *Content validation* is guided by the question: Is the substance or content of this measure representative of the content or the universe of content of the property being measured? Any psychological or educational property has a theoretical universe of content consisting of all the things that can possibly be said or observed about the property. The members of this universe, U, can be called

---

[1] *Standards for Educational and Psychological Tests.* Washington, D.C.: American Psychological Associa-tion, 1974. An important article that explains in detail the system and thinking of the committee in relation to validity is: L. Cronbach and P. Meehl, "Construct Validity of Psychological Tests," *Psychological Bulletin,* 52 (1955), 281–302. A detailed and definitive more recent statement is: L. Cronbach, "Test Validation." In R. Thorndike, ed., *Educational Measurement,* 2d ed. Washington, D.C.: American Council on Education, 1971, pp. 443–507.

items. The property might be ''arithmetic achievement,'' to take a relatively easy example. U has an infinite number of members: all possible items using numbers, arithmetic operations, and concepts. A test high in content validity would theoretically be a representative sample of U. If it were possible to draw items from U at random in sufficient numbers, then any such sample of items would presumably form a test high in content validity. If U consists of subsets A, B, and C, which are arithmetic operations, arithmetic concepts, and number manipulation, respectively, then any sufficiently large sample of U would represent A, B, and C approximately equally. The test's content validity would be satisfactory.

Ordinarily, and unfortunately, it is not possible to draw random samples of items from a universe of content. Such universes exist only theoretically. True, it is possible and desirable to assemble large collections of items, especially in the achievement area, and to draw random samples from the collections for testing purposes. But the content validity of such collections, no matter how large and how ''good'' the items, is always in question.

If it is not possible to satisfy the definition of content validity, how can a reasonable degree of content validity be achieved? Content validation consists essentially in *judgment*. Alone or with others, one judges the representativeness of the items. One may ask: Does this item measure Property M? To express it more fully one might ask: Is this item representative of the universe of content of M? If U has subsets, such as those indicated above, then one has to ask additional questions; for example: Is this item a member of the subset M_1 or the subset M_2?

Some universes of content are more obvious and much easier to judge than others; the content of many achievement tests, for instance, would seem to be obvious. The content validity of these tests, it is said, can be assumed. While this statement seems reasonable, and while the content of most achievement tests is ''self-validated'' in the sense that the individual writing the test to a degree defines the property being measured (for example, a teacher writing a classroom test of spelling or arithmetic), it is dangerous to assume the adequacy of content validity without systematic efforts to check the assumption. For example, an educational investigator, testing hypotheses about the relations between social studies achievement and other variables, may assume the content validity of a social studies test. The theory from which the hypotheses were derived, however, may require *understanding* and *application* of social studies ideas, whereas the test used may be almost purely factual in content. The test lacks content validity for the purpose. In fact, the investigator is not really testing the stated hypotheses.

Content validation, then, is basically judgmental. The items of a test must be studied, each item being weighed for its presumed representativeness of the universe. This means that each item must be judged for its presumed relevance to the property being measured, which is no easy task. Usually other ''competent'' judges should judge the content of the items. The universe of content must, if possible, be clearly defined; that is, the judges must be furnished with specific directions for making judgments, as well as with specification of what they are judging. Then, some method for pooling independent judgments can be used.[2]

Criterion-Related Validity and Validation

As the unfortunately clumsy name indicates, *criterion-related validity* is studied by comparing test or scale scores with one or more external variables, or criteria, known or

[2] An excellent guide to the content validity of achievement tests is: B. Bloom, ed., *Taxonomy of Educational Objectives, Handbook I: Cognitive Domain*. New York: David McKay, 1956. This is a comprehensive attempt to outline and discuss educational goals in relation to measurement.

believed to measure the attribute under study. When one predicts success or failure of students from academic aptitude measures, one is concerned with criterion-related validity. How well does the test (or tests) predict to graduation or to grade-point average?[3] One does not care so much *what* the test measures as one cares for its predictive ability. In fact, in criterion-related validation, which is often practical and applied research, the basic interest is usually more in the criterion, some practical outcome, than in the predictors. (In basic research this is not so.) The higher the correlation between a measure or measures of academic aptitude and the criterion, say grade-point average, the better the validity. In short and again, the emphasis is on the criterion and its prediction.[4]

The word *prediction* is usually associated with the future. This is unfortunate because, in science, prediction does not necessarily mean *forecast*. One "predicts" from an independent variable to a dependent variable. One "predicts" the existence or nonexistence of a relation; one even "predicts" something that happened in the past! This broad meaning of prediction is the one intended here. In any case, criterion-related validity is characterized by prediction to an *outside* criterion and by checking a measuring instrument, either now or in the future, against some outcome or measure. In a sense, all tests are predictive; they "predict" a certain kind of outcome, some present or future state of affairs. Aptitude tests predict future achievement; achievement tests predict present and future achievement and competence; and intelligence tests predict present and future ability to learn and to solve problems. Even if we measure self-concept, we predict that if the self-concept score is so-and-so, then the individual will be such-and-such now or in the future.

The single greatest difficulty of criterion-related validation is the criterion. Obtaining criteria may even be difficult. What criterion can be used to validate a measure of teacher effectiveness? Who is to judge teacher effectiveness? What criterion can be used to test the predictive validity of a musical aptitude test?

Decision Aspects of Validity

Criterion-related validity, as indicated earlier, is ordinarily associated with practical problems and outcomes. Interest is not so much in what is behind test performance as it is in helping to solve practical problems and to make decisions. Tests are used by the hundreds for the predictive purposes of screening and selecting potentially successful candidates in education, business, and other occupations. Does a test, or a set of tests, materially aid in deciding on the assignment of individuals to jobs, classes, schools, and the like? Any decision is a choice among treatments, assignments, or programs, as Cronbach points out. "To make a decision, one predicts the person's success under each treatment and uses a rule to translate the prediction into an assignment."[5] A test high in criterion-related validity is one that helps investigators make successful decisions in assigning people to treatments, conceiving treatments broadly. An admissions committee or administrator decides to admit or not admit an applicant to college on the basis of a test of academic aptitude. Obviously such use of tests is highly important, and the tests' predictive validity is also highly important. The reader is referred to Cronbach's essay for a good exposition of the decision aspects of tests and validity.

---

[3] Criterion-related validity used to be called *predictive validity*. A related term is *concurrent validity*, which differs from predictive validity in the time dimension: the criterion is measured at about the same time as the predictor. In this sense, the test serves to assess the present status of individuals.

[4] For a discussion of desirable qualities of a criterion, see R. Thorndike and E. Hagen, *Measurement and Evaluation in Psychology and Education*, 4th ed. New York: Wiley, 1977, pp. 61–64.

[5] Cronbach, *op. cit.*, p. 484.

Multiple Predictors and Criteria

Both multiple predictors and multiple criteria can be and are used. Later, when we study multiple regression, we will focus on multiple predictors and how to handle them statistically. Multiple criteria can be handled separately or together, though it is not easy to do the latter. In practical research, a decision must usually be made. If there is more than one criterion, how can we best combine them for decision-making? The relative importance of the criteria, of course, must be considered. Do we want an administrator high in problem-solving ability, high in public relations ability, or both? Which is more important in the particular job? It is highly likely that the use of both multiple predictors and multiple criteria will become common as multivariate methods become better understood and the computer is used routinely in prediction research.

Construct Validity and Construct Validation

Construct validity is one of the most significant scientific advances of modern measurement theory and practice. It is a significant advance because it links psychometric notions and practices to theoretical notions. Measurement experts, when they inquire into the construct validity of tests, usually want to know what psychological or other property or properties can "explain" the variance of tests. They wish to know the "meaning" of tests. If a test is an intelligence test, they want to know what factors lie behind test performance. They ask: What factors or constructs account for variance in test performance? Does this test measure verbal ability and abstract reasoning ability? Does it also "measure" social class membership? They ask, for example, what proportions of the total test variance are accounted for by the constructs verbal ability, abstract reasoning ability, and social class membership. In short, they seek to *explain* individual differences in test scores. Their interest is usually more in the properties being measured than in the tests used to accomplish the measurement.

Researchers generally start with the constructs or variables entering into relations. Suppose that a researcher has discovered a positive correlation between two measures, one a measure of educational traditionalism and the other a measure of the perception of the characteristics associated with the "good" teacher. Individuals high on the traditionalism measure see the "good" teacher as efficient, moral, thorough, industrious, conscientious, and reliable. Individuals low on the traditionalism measure may see the "good" teacher in a different way. The researcher now wants to know *why* this relation exists, what is behind it. To learn why, the meaning of the constructs entering the relation, "perception of the 'good' teacher" and "traditionalism," must be studied. *How* to study these meanings is a construct validity problem.[6]

One can see that construct validation and empirical scientific inquiry are closely allied. It is not simply a question of validating a test. One must try to validate the theory behind the test. Cronbach says that there are three parts to construct validation: suggesting what constructs possibly account for test performance, deriving hypotheses from the theory involving the construct, and testing the hypotheses empirically.[7] This formulation is but a précis of the general scientific approach discussed in Part One.

The significant point about construct validity, that which sets it apart from other types of validity, is its preoccupation with theory, theoretical constructs, and scientific empirical inquiry involving the testing of hypothesized relations. Construct validation in meas-

---

[6] This example was taken from the following research: F. Kerlinger and E. Pedhazur, "Educational Attitudes and Perceptions of Desirable Traits of Teachers," *American Educational Research Journal*, 5 (1968), 543–560.

[7] L. Cronbach, *Essentials of Psychological Testing*, 3d ed. New York: Harper & Row, 1970. p. 143.

urement contrasts sharply with approaches that define the validity of a measure primarily by its success in predicting a criterion. For example, a purely empirical tester might say that a test is valid if it efficiently distinguishes individuals high and low in a trait. *Why* the test succeeds in separating the subsets of a group is of no great concern. It is enough that it does.

Convergence and Discriminability

Note that the testing of alternative hypotheses is particularly important in construct validation because both convergence and discriminability are required. *Convergence* means that evidence from different sources gathered in different ways all indicates the same or similar meaning of the construct. Different methods of measurement should converge on the construct. The evidence yielded by administering the measuring instrument to different groups in different places should yield similar meanings or, if not, should account for differences. A measure of the self-concept of children, for instance, should be capable of similar interpretation in different parts of the country. If it is not capable of such interpretation in some locality, the theory should be able to explain why—indeed, it should predict such a difference.

Discriminability means that one can empirically differentiate the construct from other constructs that may be similar, and that one can point out what is *unrelated* to the construct. We point out, in other words, what other variables are correlated with the construct and how they are so correlated. But we also indicate what variables should be uncorrelated with the construct. We point out, for example, that a scale to measure conservatism should and does correlate substantially with measures of authoritarianism and rigidity—the theory predicts this—but not with measures of social desirability.[8] Let us illustrate these ideas.

A Hypothetical Example of Construct Validation

Let us assume that an investigator is interested in the determinants of creativity and the relation of creativity to school achievement. He notices that the most sociable persons, who exhibit affection for others, also seem to be less creative than those who are less sociable and affectionate. He wants to test the implied relation in a controlled fashion. One of his first tasks is to obtain or construct a measure of the sociable-affectionate characteristic. The investigator, surmising that this combination of traits may be a reflection of a deeper concern of love for others, calls it *amorism*. He assumes that there are individual differences in amorism, that some people have a great deal of it, others a moderate amount, and still others very little.

He must first construct an instrument to measure amorism. The literature gives little help, since scientific psychologists have rarely investigated the fundamental nature of love. Sociability, however, has been measured. The investigator must construct a *new* instrument, basing its content on intuitive and reasoned notions of what amorism is. The reliability of the test, tried out with large groups, runs between .75 and .85.

The question now is whether the test is valid. The investigator correlates the instrument, calling it the *A* scale, with independent measures of sociability. The correlations are moderately substantial, but he needs evidence that the test has construct validity. He deduces certain relations that should and should not exist between amorism and other

---

[8] See F. Kerlinger, "A Social Attitude Scale: Evidence on Reliability and Validity," *Psychological Reports*, 26 (1970), 379–383.

variables. If amorism is a general tendency to love others, then it should correlate with characteristics like cooperativeness and friendliness. Persons high in amorism will approach problems in an ego-oriented manner as contrasted to persons low in amorism, who will approach problems in a task-oriented manner.

Acting on this reasoning, the investigator administers the A scale and a scale to measure subjectivity to a number of tenth-grade students. To measure cooperativeness he observes the classroom behavior of the same group of students. The correlations between the three measures are positive and significant.[9]

Knowing the pitfalls of psychological measurement, the investigator is not satisfied. These positive correlations may be due to a factor common to all three tests, but irrelevant to amorism; for example, the tendency to give "right" answers. (This would probably be ruled out, however, because the observation measure of cooperativeness correlates positively with amorism and subjectivity.) So, taking a new group of subjects, he administers the amorism and subjectivity scales, has the subjects' behavior rated for cooperativeness, and in addition, administers a creativity test that has been found in other research to be reliable.

The investigator states the relation between amorism and creativity in hypothesis form: The relation between the A scale and the creativity measure will be negative and significant. The correlations between amorism and cooperativeness and between amorism and subjectivity will be positive and significant. "Check" hypotheses are also formulated: The correlation between cooperativeness and creativity will not be significant; it will be near zero, but the correlation between subjectivity and creativity will be positive and significant. This last relation is predicted on the basis of previous research findings. The six correlation coefficients are given in the correlation matrix of Table 27.1. The four measures are labeled as follows: A, amorism; B, cooperativeness; C, subjectivity; and D, creativity.

The evidence for the construct validity of the A scale is good. All the r's are as predicted; especially important are the r's between D (creativity) and the other variables. Note that there are three different kinds of prediction: positive, negative, and zero. All three kinds are as predicted. This illustrates what might be called *differential prediction or differential validity*—or discriminability. It is not enough to predict, for instance, that the measure presumably reflecting the target property be positively correlated with one theoretically relevant variable. One should, through deduction from the theory, predict more than one such positive relation. In addition, one should predict zero relations between the principal variable and variables "irrelevant" to the theory. In the example above, al-

Table 27.1 Intercorrelations of Four Hypothetical Measures[a]

	B	C	D
A	.50	.60	$-.30$
B		.40	.05
C			.50

[a] A = amorism; B = cooperativeness; C = subjectivity; D = creativity. Correlation coefficients .25 or greater are significant at the .01 level. $N = 90$.

[9] Note that we would not expect high correlation between the measures. If the correlations were too high, we would then suspect the validity of the A scale. It would be measuring, perhaps, subjectivity or cooperativeness, but not amorism.

though cooperativeness was expected to correlate with amorism, there was no theoretical reason to expect it to correlate at all with creativity.

Another example of a different kind is when an investigator deliberately introduces a measure that would, if it correlates with the variable whose validity is under study, invalidate other positive relations. One bugaboo of personality and attitude scales is the social desirability phenomenon, mentioned earlier. The correlation between the target variable and a theoretically related variable may be because the instruments measuring both variables are tapping social desirability rather than the variables they were designed to tap. One can partly check whether this is so by including a measure of social desirability along with other measures.

Despite all the evidence leading the investigator to believe that the *A* scale has construct validity, he may still be doubtful. So he sets up a study in which he has pupils high and low in amorism solve problems, predicting that pupils low in amorism will solve problems more successfully than those high in amorism. If the data support the prediction, this is further evidence of the construct validity of the amorism measure. It is of course a significant finding in and of itself. Such a procedure, however, is probably more appropriate with achievement and attitude measures. One can manipulate communications, for example, in order to change attitudes. If attitude scores change according to theoretical prediction, this would be evidence of the construct validity of the attitude measure, since the scores would probably not change according to prediction if the measure were not measuring the construct.

The Multitrait-Multimethod Matrix Method

A significant and influential contribution to testing validity is Campbell and Fiske's use of the ideas of convergence and discriminability and correlation matrices to bring evidence to bear on validity.[10] To explain the method, we use some data from a study of social attitudes.[11] It has been found that there are two basic dimensions of social attitudes, which correspond to philosophical, sociological, and political descriptions of liberalism and conservatism. Two different kinds of scales were administered to graduate students of education and groups outside the university in New York, Texas, and North Carolina. One instrument, Social Attitudes Scale, had the usual attitude *statements*, 13 liberal and 13 conservative items. The second instrument, Referents-I, or REF-I, used attitude referents (single words and short phrases: *private property*, *religion*, and *civil rights*, for example) as items, 25 liberal referents and 25 conservative referents.[12]

We have, then, two completely different kinds of attitude instruments, one with referent items and the other with statement items, or Method 1 and Method 2. The two basic dimensions being measured were liberalism (*L*) and conservatism (*C*). Do the *L* and *C* subscales of the two scales measure liberalism and conservatism? Part of the evidence is

[10] D. Campbell and D. Fiske, "Convergent and Discriminant Validation by the Multitrait-Multimethod Matrix," *Psychological Bulletin*, 54 (1959), 81–105.

[11] The data are from one study of a number of studies done to test a structural theory of social attitudes. The theory and supporting evidence are outlined in: F. Kerlinger, "Social Attitudes and Their Criterial Referents: A Structural Theory," *Psychological Review*, 74 (1967), 110–122. The entire series of studies are reported in: F. Kerlinger, *Liberalism and Conservatism: The Nature and Structure of Social Attitudes.* Hillsdale, N.J.: Erlbaum, 1984.

[12] The samples, the scales, and some of the results are described in: F. Kerlinger, "The Structure and Content of Social Attitude Referents: A Preliminary Study," *Educational and Psychological Measurement*, 32 (1972), 613–630. The data reported in Table 27.2 were obtained from a Texas sample, $N = 227$.

Table 27.2 Correlations Between Social Attitude Dimensions Across Two Measurement Methods, Multitrait-Multimethod Approach, Texas Sample, $N = 227$[a]

| | | Method 1 (Referents) | | Method 2 (Statements) | |
		L_1	C_1	L_2	C_2
Method 1 (Referents)	L_1	(.85)			
	C_1	−.07	(.88)		
Method 2 (Statements)	L_2	.53	−.15	(.81)	
	C_2	−.37	.54	−.09	(.82)

[a]Method 1: Referents; Method 2: Statements; L: liberalism; C: conservatism. The diagonal parenthesized entries are internal consistency reliabilities; the italicized entries (*.53* and *.54*) are cross-method *L-L* and *C-C* correlations.

given in Table 27.2, which presents the correlations among the four subscales of the two instruments, as well as the subscale reliability coefficients, calculated from the responses of a Texas sample of 227 graduate students of education to the two scales.

In a multitrait-multimethod analysis, more than one attribute and more than one method are used in the validation process. The results of correlating variables within and between methods can be presented in a so-called multitrait-multimethod matrix. The matrix (matrices) given in Table 27.2 is the simplest possible form of such an analysis : two variables and two methods. Ordinarily one would want more variables. The most important part of the matrix is the diagonal of the cross-method correlations. In Table 27.2, this is the Method 1-Method 2 matrix in the lower left section of the table. The diagonal values should be substantial, since they reflect the magnitudes of the correlations between the same variables measured differently. These values, italicized in the table, are .53 and .54—fairly substantial.

In this example, the theory calls for near-zero or low negative correlations between L and C.[13] The correlation between L_1 and C_1 is −.07 and between L_2 and C_2 is −.09, both in accord with the theory. The cross-correlation between L and C, that is, the correlation between L of Method 1 and C of Method 2, or between L_1 and C_2, is −.37, higher than the theory predicts (an upper limit of −.30 was adopted). With the exception of the cross-correlation of −.37 between L_1 and C_2, then, the construct validity of the social attitudes scale is supported. One will of course want more evidence than the results obtained with one sample. And one will also want an explanation of the substantial cross-method negative correlation between L_1 and C_2. The example, however, illustrates the basic ideas of the multitrait-multimethod approach to validity.

The model of the multitrait-multimethod procedure is an ideal. If possible, it should be followed. Certainly the investigation and measurement of important constructs, like conservatism, aggressiveness, teacher warmth, need for achievement, honesty, and so on, ultimately require it. In many research situations, however, it is difficult or impossible to administer two or more measures of two or more variables to relatively large samples. Though efforts to study validity must always be made, research should not be abandoned just because the full method is not feasible.

[13]Kerlinger, "Social Attitudes and Their Criterial Referents," *op. cit.*

Research Examples of Construct Validation

In a sense, any type of validation is construct validation.[14] Whenever hypotheses are tested, whenever relations are empirically studied, construct validity is involved. Because of its importance, we now examine three research examples of construct validation.

A Measure of Anti-Semitism

In an unusual attempt to validate their measure of anti-Semitism, Glock and Stark used responses to two incomplete sentences about Jews: "It's a shame that Jews . . . ." and "I can't understand why Jews. . . ."[15] Coders considered what each subject had written and characterized the responses as negative, neutral, or positive images of Jews. Each subject, then, was characterized individually as having one of the three different perceptions of Jews. When the responses to the Index of Anti-Semitic Beliefs, the measure being validated, were divided into None, Medium, Medium High, and High Anti-Semitism, the percentages of negative responses to the two open-ended questions were, respectively: 28, 41, 61, 75. This is good evidence of validity, because the individuals categorized None to High Anti-Semitism by the measure to be validated, the Index of Anti-Semitic Beliefs, responded to an entirely different measure of anti-Semitism, the two open-ended questions, in a manner congruent with their categorization by the Index.

Consensual Assessment of Creativity

Expressing dissatisfaction with most attempts to define and measure creativity, Amabile proposed a consensual definition that focused on the judgment of products: "A product or response is creative to the extent that appropriate observers independently agree it is creative. Appropriate observers are those familiar with the domain in which the product was created or the response articulated."[16] The actual measurement method Amabile used was to ask judges to assess the creativity of products produced by individuals using their own criteria of what is creative. The judges should have had experience with the products being judged. For example, to apply the method in the assessment of artistic creativity, Amabile had professional artists and art teachers judge the creativity of collages made by children. (A *collage* is an artistic composition of materials pasted on a surface of some kind.) Let us look at one of her studies, an attempt at construct validation of the method.

Twenty-two young girls, age 7–11 years, were asked to make designs using materials supplied by the researcher: pieces of paper in different sizes and shapes, white cardboard, and glue. Each child received the same materials. The children were told to use the materials in any way they wished to make a design that was "silly." They worked at this for 18 minutes. Then the judges—art teachers, artists, and psychologists (used to provide varying expertise with art)—were told how the designs were produced and asked to judge their creativity using a five-point rating system that produced numerical measures reflecting degrees of creativity. Amabile found substantial to high reliabilities and good agree-

---

[14] J. Loevinger, "Objective Tests as Instruments of Psychological Theory," *Psychological Reports*, 3 (1957), 635–694, Monograph Supplement 9. Loevinger argues that construct validity, from a scientific point of view, is the whole of validity. At the other extreme, Bechtoldt argues that construct validity has no place in psychology. H. Bechtoldt, "Construct Validity: A Critique," *American Psychologist*, 14 (1959), 619–629.

[15] C. Glock and R. Stark, *Christian Beliefs and Anti-Semitism*. New York: Harper & Row, 1966, pp. 125–127.

[16] T. Amabile, "Social Psychology of Creativity: A Consensual Assessment Technique," *Journal of Personality and Social Psychology*, 43 (1982), 997–1013.

ment between the groups of judges. The artist judges were also asked to evaluate the 22 designs on a number of dimensions including creativity, technical goodness, and aesthetic appeal. Certain other measures were also used but they need not concern us.

One of the strong pieces of evidence Amabile offered for the construct validity of the consensual assessment method was the result of a factor analysis of the measures produced by the artist judges.[17] Factor analysis is essentially a method of finding how variables cluster together. Amabile's factor analytic results indicated two independent clusters of variables, which she names "Creativity" and "Technical Goodness." The creativity measures were those that have been associated with artistic creativity—novel idea, novel use, and complexity, for example—and her consensual assessment measure. The Technical Goodness measures were: technical goodness rated globally, organization, neatness, symmetry, and so on. Those variables associated with Creativity clustered together and those variables associated with Technical Goodness clustered together, but the two clusters were separate and different. Had the two kinds of measures appeared together on one cluster, the validity of the consensual method of assessing creativity would have been in doubt because creativity was not supposed to be a function of technical adequacy. The consensual assessment method of measuring creativity evidently passed the construct validity test.

The Measurement of Democracy

What do we mean by "democracy"? The word is used constantly. But what do we mean when we use it? More difficult, how is it measured? Bollen has defined and measured "democracy," used it as a variable, and demonstrated the construct validity of his Index of Political Democracy.[18] He carefully examined previous uses and definitions, explained the theory behind the construct, and extracted from earlier measures important facets of political democracy to construct his measure. It has two large aspects: political liberty and popular sovereignty. These can be called latent variables. Each has three facets: *press freedom*, *freedom of group opposition*, and *government sanctions* (absence of) for political liberties, and *fairness of elections*, *executive selection*, and *legislative selection* for popular sovereignty. It is these six "indicators" that are used to measure the political democracy of countries.[19] Each indicator is operationally defined and a four-point scale used to apply to any country. Popular sovereignty, for instance, is measured by assessing to what extent the elites of a country are accountable to the people: wide franchise, equal weighting of votes, and fair electoral processes. The six indicators are combined into a single index or score.[20]

Through factor analysis (see below) and other procedures, Bollen brought empirical evidence to bear on the reliability and construct validity of the Index. He showed, for

---

[17] The use of factor analysis, a method that usually requires large numbers of subjects (judges, in this case), can be questioned. Since subsequent similar factor analyses produced similar results and since we are here concerned only with the validation method, we omit criticism of the factor analysis.

[18] K. Bollen, "Issues in the Comparative Measurement of Political Democracy," *American Sociological Review*, 45 (1980), 370–390.

[19] "Indicator," or "Social Indicator," is an important term in contemporary social research. Unfortunately, there is little agreement on what indicators are. They have been variously defined as indices of social conditions, statistics, even variables. In Bollen's paper, they are variables. For a discussion of definitions, see R. Jaeger, "About Educational Indicators: Statistics on the Conditions and Trends in Education." In L. Shulman, ed., *Review of Research in Education*, vol. 6. Itasca, Ill.: Peacock, 1978, chap. 7.

[20] See K. Bollen, "Political Democracy and the Timing of Development," *American Sociological Review*, 44 (1979), 572–587, especially Appendix, for a detailed description of the Index and its scoring.

example, that the six indicators are manifestations of an underlying latent variable, which is "political democracy." He also showed that the Index is highly correlated with other measures of democracy. Finally, Index values were calculated for a large number of countries. These values seem to agree with the extent of democracy (on a scale of 0-100) in the countries, for example, U. S., 92.4; Canada, 99.5; Cuba, 5.2; United Arab Republic, 38.7; Sweden, 99.9; Soviet Union, 18.2; Israel, 96.8. Bollen has evidently successfully measured a highly complex and difficult construct.

Other Methods of Construct Validation

In addition to the multitrait-multimethod approach and the methods used in the above studies, there are other methods of construct validation. Any tester is familiar with the technique of correlating items with total scores. In using the technique, the total score is assumed to be valid. To the extent that an item measures the same thing as the total score does, to that extent the item is valid.[21]

In order to study the construct validity of any measure, it is always helpful to correlate the measure with other measures. The amorism example discussed earlier illustrated the method and the ideas behind it. But, would it not be more valuable to correlate a measure with a large number of other measures? How better to learn about a construct than to know its correlates? Factor analysis is a refined method of doing this. It tells us, in effect, what measures measure the same thing and to what extent they measure what they measure.

Factor analysis is a powerful and indispensable method of construct validation. We encountered its use in Amabile's study and pointed out that Bollen used it in his validation of the Index of Political Democracy. Although it has been briefly characterized earlier and will be discussed in detail in a later chapter, its great importance in validating measures warrants characterization here. It is a method for reducing a large number of measures to a smaller number called factors by discovering which ones "go together" (which measures measure the same thing) and the relations between the clusters of measures that go together. For example, we may give a group of individuals twenty tests, each presumed to measure something different. We may find, however, that the twenty tests are really only five measures or factors.

Sorenson, Husek, and Yu, in studying the nature and influence of teacher role expectations, constructed a six-subscale measure of such expectations, the six dimensions having been obtained through interviews with teachers, administrators, and others and from reasoning and role theory.[22] The instrument was made up of 30 teaching problem situations and, in effect, 120 items, 20 for each of the six subscales. The 120 items were intercorrelated and factor-analyzed—a good example of analysis that would not have been possible before the computer—and, in a first study, five of the factors agreed with the designations of five of the six subscales. In a second study and factor analysis, five factors were also found. The five factors seemed to describe the basic dimensions of the teacher's role: disciplinarian, counselor, motivator, referrer, and advice-information giver. In other words, the teacher-role construct and its subordinate constructs were validated by using factor analysis to verify the initial conception of the teacher role.

[21] For a discussion of item analysis, see J. Nunnally, *Psychometric Theory*, 2d ed. New York: McGraw-Hill, 1978, pp. 261ff.

[22] A. Sorenson, T. Husek, and C. Yu, "Divergent Concepts of Teacher Role: An Approach to the Measurement of Teacher Effectiveness," *Journal of Educational Psychology*, 54 (1963), 287–294.

A VARIANCE DEFINITION OF VALIDITY: THE VARIANCE RELATION OF RELIABILITY AND VALIDITY[23]

In the last chapter, reliability was defined as

$$r_{tt} = \frac{V_{\infty}}{V_t} \tag{27.1}$$

the proportion of "true" variance to total variance. It is theoretically and empirically useful to define validity similarly:

$$\text{Val} = \frac{V_{co}}{V_t} \tag{27.2}$$

where Val is the validity; V_{co} the common factor variance; and V_t the total variance of a measure. Validity is thus seen as the proportion of the total variance of a measure that is common factor variance.

Unfortunately, we are not yet in a position to present the full meaning of this definition. An understanding of so-called factor theory is required, but factor theory will not be discussed until later in the book. Despite this difficulty, we must attempt an explanation of validity in variance terms if we are to have a well-rounded view of the subject. Besides, expressing validity and reliability mathematically will unify and clarify both subjects. Indeed, reliability and validity will be seen to be parts of one unified whole.

Common factor variance is the variance of a measure that is shared with other measures. In other words, common factor variance is the variance that two or more tests have in common.

In contrast to the common factor variance of a measure is its *specific variance,* V_{sp}, the systematic variance of a measure that is not shared by any other measure. If a test measures skills that other tests measure, we have common factor variance; if it also measures a skill that no other test does, we have specific variance.

Figure 27.1 expresses these ideas and also adds the notion of error variance. The A and B circles represent the variances of Tests A and B. The intersection of A and B, $A \cap B$, is

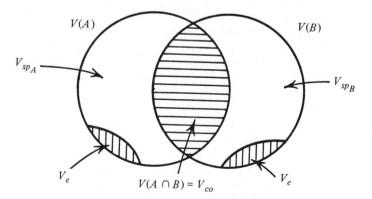

Figure 27.1

[23] The variance treatment of validity presented here is an extension of the treatment of reliability presented in the last chapter. Both treatments follow J. Guilford, *Psychometric Methods*, 2d ed. New York: McGraw-Hill, 1954, pp. 354–357.

the relation of the two sets. Similarly, $V(A \cap B)$ is common factor variance. The specific variances and the error variances of both tests are also indicated.

From this viewpoint, then, and following the variance reasoning outlined in the last chapter, any measure's total variance has several components: *common factor variance, specific variance,* and *error variance.* This is expressed by the equation:

$$V_t = V_{co} + V_{sp} + V_e \qquad (27.3)$$

To be able to talk of proportions of the total variance, we divide the terms of Equation 27.3 by the total variance:

$$\frac{V_t}{V_t} = \frac{V_{co}}{V_t} + \frac{V_{sp}}{V_t} + \frac{V_a}{V_t} \qquad (27.4)$$

How do Equations 27.1 and 27.2 fit into this picture? The first term on the right, V_{co}/V_t, is the right-hand member of (27.2). Therefore validity can be viewed as that part of the total variance of a measure that is not specific variance and not error variance. This is easily seen algebraically:

$$\frac{V_{co}}{V_t} = \frac{V_t}{V_t} - \frac{V_{sp}}{V_t} - \frac{V_e}{V_t} \qquad (27.5)$$

By a definition of the previous chapter, reliability can be defined as

$$r_{tt} = 1 - \frac{V_e}{V_t} \qquad (27.6)$$

This can be written:

$$r_{tt} = \frac{V_t}{V_t} - \frac{V_e}{V_t} \qquad (27.7)$$

The right-hand side of the equations, however, is part of the right-hand side of (27.5). If we rewrite (27.5) slightly, we obtain

$$\frac{V_{co}}{V_t} = \frac{V_t}{V_t} - \frac{V_e}{V_t} - \frac{V_{sp}}{V_t} \qquad (27.8)$$

This must mean, then, that validity and reliability are close variance relations. Reliability is equal to the first two right-hand members of (27.8). So, bringing in (27.1):

$$r_{tt} = \frac{V_t}{V_t} - \frac{V_e}{V_t} = \frac{V_\infty}{V_t} \qquad (27.9)$$

If we substitute in (27.8), we get

$$\frac{V_{co}}{V_t} = \frac{V_\infty}{V_t} - \frac{V_{sp}}{V_t} \qquad (27.10)$$

Thus we see that the proportion of the total variance of a measure is equal to the proportion of the total variance that is "true" variance minus the proportion that is specific variance. Or, the validity of a measure is that portion of the total variance of the measure that shares variance with other measures. Theoretically, valid variance includes no variance due to error, nor does it include variance that is specific to this measure and this measure only.

This can all be summed up in two ways. First, we sum it up in an equation or two. Let us assume that we have a method of determining the common factor variance (or variances) of a test. (Later we shall see that factor analysis is such a method.) For simplicity suppose that there are two sources of common factor variance in a test—and no others. Call these factors A and B. They might be verbal ability and arithmetic ability, or they might be liberal attitudes and conservative attitudes. If we add the variance of A to the variance of B, we obtain the common factor variance of the test, which is expressed by the equations,

$$V_{co} = V_A + V_B \qquad\qquad (27.11)$$

$$\frac{V_{co}}{V_t} = \frac{V_A}{V_t} + \frac{V_B}{V_t} \qquad\qquad (27.12)$$

Then, using (27.2) and substituting in (27.12), we obtain

$$\text{Val} = \frac{V_A}{V_t} + \frac{V_B}{V_t} \qquad\qquad (27.13)$$

The total variance of a test, we said before, includes the common factor variance, the variance specific to the test and to no other test (at least as far as present information goes), and error variance. Equations 27.3 and 27.4 express this. Now, substituting in (27.4) the equality of (27.12), we obtain

$$\frac{V_t}{V_t} = \overbrace{\underbrace{\frac{V_A}{V_t} + \frac{V_B}{V_t} + \frac{V_{sp}}{V_t}}_{r_{tt}}}^{h^2} + \frac{V_e}{V_t} \qquad\qquad (27.14)$$

The first two terms on the right-hand side of (27.14) are associated with the validity of the measure, and the first three terms on the right are associated with the reliability of the measure. These relations have been indicated. Common factor variance, or the validity component of the measure, is labeled h^2 (*communality*), a symbol customarily used to indicate the common factor variance of a test. Reliability, as usual, is labeled r_{tt}.

To discuss all the implications of this formulation of validity and reliability would take us too far astray at this time. All that is needed now is to try to clarify the formulation with a diagram and a brief discussion.

Figure 27.2 is an attempt to express Equation 27.14 diagrammatically. The figure represents the contributions of the different variances to the total variance (taken to be equal to 100 percent). Four variances, three systematic variances and one error variance, comprise the total variance in this theoretical model.[24] The contribution of each of the sources of variance is indicated. Of the total variance, 80 percent is reliable variance. Of the reliable variance, 30 percent is contributed by Factor A and 25 percent by Factor B, and 25 percent is specific to this test. The remaining 20 percent of the total variance is error variance.

The test may be interpreted as quite reliable, since a sizable proportion of the total variance is reliable or "true" variance. The interpretation of validity is more difficult. If there were only one factor, say A, and it contributed 55 percent of the total variance, then we could say that a considerable proportion of the total variance was valid variance. We would know that a good bit of the reliable measurement would be the measurement of the

[24] Naturally, practical outcomes never look this neat. It is remarkable, however, how well the model works. The variance thinking, too, is valuable in conceptualizing and discussing measurement outcomes.

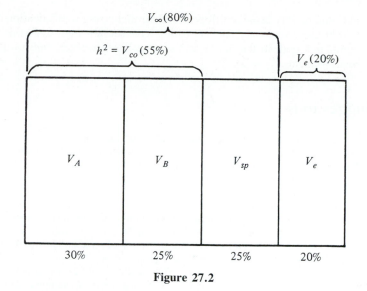

Figure 27.2

property known as *A*. This would be a construct validity statement. Practically speaking, individuals measured with the test would be rank-ordered on *A* with adequate reliability.

With the above hypothetical example, however, the situation is more complex. The test measures two factors, *A* and *B*. There could be three sets of rank orders, one resulting from *A*, one from *B*, and one from *specific*. While repeat reliability might be high, if we thought we were measuring only *A*, to the extent we thought so to this extent the test would not be valid. We might, however, have a score for each individual on *A* and one on *B*. In this case the test would be valid.[25] Indeed, modern developments in measurement indicate that such multiple scores have become more and more a part of accepted procedure.

THE VALIDITY AND RELIABILITY OF PSYCHOLOGICAL AND EDUCATIONAL MEASUREMENT INSTRUMENTS

Poor measurement can invalidate any scientific investigation. Most of the criticisms of psychological and educational measurement, by professionals and laymen alike, center on validity. This is as it should be. Achieving reliability is to a large extent a technical matter. Validity, however, is much more than technique. It bores into the essence of science itself. It also bores into philosophy. Construct validity, particularly, since it is concerned with the nature of ''reality'' and the nature of the properties being measured, is heavily philosophical.

Despite the difficulties of achieving reliable and valid psychological, sociological, and educational measurements, great progress has been made in this century. There is growing understanding that *all* measuring instruments must be critically and empirically examined for their reliability and validity. The day of tolerance of inadequate measurement has ended. The demands imposed by professionals, the theoretical and statistical tools avail-

[25] Note that even if we thought the test was measuring only *A*, predictions to a criterion might well be successful, especially if the criterion had a lot of both *A* and *B* in it. The test could have predictive validity even though its construct validity was questionable.

able and rapidly being developed, and the increasing sophistication of graduate students of psychology, sociology, and education have set new high standards that should be healthy stimulants both to the imaginations of research workers and to developers of scientific measurement.

Study Suggestions

1. The measurement literature is vast. The following references have been chosen for their particular excellence or their relevance to important measurement topics. Some of the discussions, however, are technical and difficult. The student will find elementary discussions of reliability and validity in most measurement texts.

CRONBACH and MEEHL, construct validity article. (See footnote 1 and Mehrens and Ebel, below.) A most important contribution to modern measurement and behavioral research.

CURETON, E. "Measurement Theory." In R. Ebel, V. Noll, and R. Bauer, eds., *Encyclopedia of Educational Research*, 4th ed. New York: Macmillan, 1969, pp. 785–804. A broad and firm overview of measurement, with an emphasis on educational measurement.

GUILFORD and NUNNALLY texts. (Footnotes 21 and 23.) Excellent advanced texts.

Standards for Educational and Psychological Tests. Washington, D.C.: American Psychological Association, 1974. A definitive statement jointly produced by three large associations concerned with measurement.

THORNDIKE, R., ed. *Educational Measurement*, 2d ed. Washington, D.C.: American Council on Education, 1971. An outstanding achievement that follows a distinguished predecessor: E. Lindquist, ed. *Educational Measurement*. Washington, D.C.: American Council on Education, 1951. Both books have excellent chapters on most aspects of educational measurement, including reliability and validity. The reliability chapters in both editions, by Thorndike (1951) and Stanley (1971), have exceptionally good tables (original table by Thorndike) summarizing the possible sources of variance in measures: Table 8, p. 568, 1951 edition; Table 13.1, p. 364, 1971 edition.

TRYON, R. "Reliability and Behavior Domain Validity: A Reformulation and Historical Critique." *Psychological Bulletin*, 54 (1957), 229–249. This is an excellent and important article on reliability. It contains a good worked example.

The following anthologies of measurement articles are valuable sources of the classics in the field. This is especially true of the Mehrens and Ebel and the Jackson and Messick volumes.

ANASTASI, A., ed. *Testing Problems in Perspective*. Washington, D.C.: American Council on Education, 1966.

CHASE, C., and LUDLOW, G., eds. *Readings in Educational and Psychological Measurement*. Boston: Houghton Mifflin, 1966.

JACKSON, D., and MESSICK, S., eds. *Problems in Human Assessment*. New York: McGraw-Hill, 1967.

MEHRENS, W., and EBEL, R., eds. *Principles of Educational and Psychological Measurement*. Skokie, Ill.: Rand McNally, 1967.

2. An important method in validity studies is cross-validation. Advanced students can profit from Mosier's essay in the Chase and Ludlow book mentioned above. A brief summary of Mosier's essay can be found in Guilford, *op. cit.*, p. 406.

3. The more advanced student will also want to know something about response set, a threat to validity, particularly to the validity of personality, attitude, and value items and instruments. *Response sets* are tendencies to respond to items in certain ways—high, low, approve, disapprove, extreme, etc.—regardless of the content of the items. The resulting scores are therefore systematically biased. The literature is extensive and cannot be cited here. An excellent exposition, however, can be found in Nunnally, *op. cit.*, chap. 16, especially pp. 655ff. Advocates of the effects of response sets on measurement instruments are quite strong in their statements. A considerable dash of salt has been thrown on the response-set tail by L. Rorer: "The Great Response-Style Myth," *Psychological Bulletin*, 63 (1965), 129–156.

The position taken in this book is that response sets certainly operate and sometimes have considerable effect but that the strong claims of advocates are exaggerated. Most of the variance in well-constructed measures seems to be due to variables being measured and relatively little to response set. Investigators must be aware of response sets and their possible deleterious effects on measurement instruments, but they should not be afraid to use the instruments. If one were to take too seriously the schools of thought on response set and on what has been called the experimenter effect (in education, the Pygmalion effect), discussed earlier, one would have to abandon behavioral research, except, perhaps, research that can be done with so-called unobtrusive measures.

4. Discuss and criticize the following statements:

(a) "The reliability of my creativity test is .85. I can therefore be reasonably sure that I am measuring creativity."

(b) "My creativity test really measures creativity, because I had an expert on creativity carefully screen all the items of the test."

(c) "Since the reliability of the test of logical thinking is only .40, its validity is negligible.

5. Study the following assertions and decide in each case whether the assertion refers to reliability or validity, or both. Label the type of reliability and validity.

(a) "The test was given twice to the same group. The coefficient of correlation between the scores of the two administrations was .90."

(b) "Four teachers studied the items of a test for their relevance to the objectives of the curriculum."

(c) "The items seem to be a good sample of the item universe."

(d) "Between a test of academic aptitude and grade-point averages, $r = .55$."

(e) "The mean difference between Republicans and Democrats on the conservatism instrument was highly significant."

6. Imagine that you have given a test of six items to six persons. The scores of each person on each item are given below. Say that you have also given another test of six items to six persons. These scores are also given below. The scores of the first test, I, are given on the left; the scores of the second test, II, are given on the right.

I

	Items					
Persons	a	b	c	d	e	f
1	6	6	7	5	6	5
2	6	4	5	5	4	5
3	5	4	7	6	4	3
4	3	2	5	3	4	4
5	2	3	4	4	3	2
6	2	1	3	1	0	2

II

	Items					
Persons	a	b	c	d	e	f
1	6	4	5	6	6	3
2	6	2	7	4	4	4
3	5	6	5	3	4	2
4	3	4	4	5	4	5
5	2	1	7	1	3	5
6	2	3	3	5	0	2

The scores in II are the same as those in I, except that the orders of the scores of Items (b), (c), (d), and (f) have been changed.

(a) Do a two-way analysis of variance of each set of scores. Compare the F ratios and interpret them. Pay special attention to the F ratio for Persons (Individuals).

(b) Compute $r_{tt} = (V_{ind} - V_e)/V_{ind}$ for I and II. Interpret the two r_{tt}'s. Why are they so different?

(c) Add the odd items across the rows; add the even items. Compare the rank orders and the ranges of the odd totals, the even totals, and the totals of all six items. The coefficients of correlation between odd and even items, corrected, are .98 and .30. Explain why they are so different. What do they mean?

(d) Assume that there were 100 persons and 60 items. Would this have changed the procedures and the reasoning behind them? Would the effect of changing the orders of, say, five to ten items have affected the r_{tt}'s as much as in these examples? If not, why not?

[*Answer:* (a) I: $F_{\text{items}} = 3.79$ (.05); $F_{\text{persons}} = 20.44$ (.001); II: $F_{\text{items}} = 1.03$ (*n.s*); $F_{\text{persons}} = 1.91$ (*n.s*). (b) I: $r_{tt} = .95$; II: $r_{tt} = .48$.]

7. An important development of the last decade is criterion-referenced measurement, a large and controversial subject. Since its basic use is in applied educational measurement, and since this book's emphasis is on scientific research in the behavioral sciences generally, it has not been discussed. The following references will be helpful to the student of education:

THORNDIKE and HAGEN text (footnote 4), chap. 6 and pp. 658–661. An elementary discussion.
NITKO, A. "Distinguishing the Many Varieties of Criterion-Referenced Tests," *Review of Educational Research,* 50 (1980), 461–485. Highly useful review.
POPHAM, W. *Criterion-Referenced Measurement.* Englewood Cliffs, N. J.: Prentice-Hall, 1978. A text by a leading exponent.
NUNNALLY text (footnote 21), pp. 265–270. A balanced critical assessment.
HAMBLETON, R., ed. *Contributions to Criterion-Referenced Testing Technology. Applied Psychological Measurement,* 4 (1980), whole issue (No. 4). The whole issue of this journal was devoted to technical problems of criterion-referenced measurement. A valuable source for the deeply interested and committed student.

PART NINE

Methods of Observation and Data Collection

Introduction

To implement general plans of research, methods of data collection must be used. There is always a mutual interplay of problem and method. Problems dictate methods to a considerable extent, but methods—their availability, feasibility, and relevance—also influence problems. Some problems cannot be satisfactorily studied, because methods do not at present exist to collect the data implied by the problems; or existing methods and even those that can be invented may not be capable of yielding the precise data needed. In such cases it may be necessary to alter the problems or perhaps even to abandon them temporarily. At any rate, the problem is the more fundamental consideration.

Methods of observation are systematic and standard procedures for obtaining data. They can be considered extensions of measurement theory and methods. The clue is furnished by the definition of measurement: the assignment of numerals to objects according to rules. In the last analysis, almost all methods have the technical purpose of enabling the researcher to so make observations that symbols or numerals can be assigned to the objects or to the sets of objects under study. Put another way, methods of observation help researchers obtain measures of variables so that they can bring empirical evidence to bear on research questions.

The approach to methods of observation used in this part is dictated by the conviction that such methods can only be learned through experience. It is possible to learn certain principles of schedule construction, but in order to construct an actual schedule, one requires considerable practice in writing and reviewing items and instructions. A book can explain how to interview, but in order to be able to interview, one must interview.

The following chapters, then, have three main purposes. The first is to acquaint the student with the most important observational methods that are available. Graduate students seem to concentrate on two or three methods, perhaps because of lack of familiarity with available methods. This restriction to two or three methods unduly narrows the range of possible problems and inquiry. Thus one of the prime objectives of these chapters is to broaden the student's knowledge of available methods.

The second purpose is to help the student understand the main characteristics and purposes of the methods. Methods differ considerably in what they can and cannot do. Users of methods must know these possibilities if they are to be able to choose methods suited to their problems. Many a good problem has suffered from an inappropriate and inadequate method.

The third purpose is closely related to the second: to indicate, if incompletely, the strengths and weaknesses of the methods. One method may be well suited to a problem, but it may have grave weaknesses that disqualify it. The mail questionnaire is a case in point. A problem may require a wide geographical sampling of schools, which can be easily accomplished by the mail questionnaire. But its well-known weakness would perhaps disqualify it from consideration, unless it were the only possible way to obtain data.

Chapter 28

Interviews and Interview Schedules

THE INTERVIEW is perhaps the most ubiquitous method of obtaining information from people. It has been and is still used in all kinds of practical situations: the lawyer obtains information from a client; the physician learns about a patient; the admissions officer or professor determines the suitability of students for schools, departments, and curricula. Only recently, however, has the interview been used systematically for scientific purposes, both in the laboratory and in the field.

Data-collection methods can be categorized by the degree of their directness. If we wish to know something about people, we can ask them about it directly. They may or may not give us an answer. On the other hand, we may not ask a direct question. We may use an ambiguous stimulus, like a blurred picture, a blot of ink, or a vague question; and then ask for impressions of the stimulus on the assumption that the respondents will give the needed information without knowing they are giving it. This method is highly indirect. Most of the data-collection methods used in psychological and sociological research are relatively direct or moderately indirect. Rarely are highly indirect means used.

Interviews and schedules (questionnaires) are ordinarily quite direct. This is both a strength and a weakness. It is a strength because a great deal of the information needed in social scientific research can be gotten from respondents by direct questions. Though the questions may have to be carefully handled, respondents can, and usually will, give much information directly. There is information, however, of a more difficult nature that respondents may be unwilling, reluctant, or unable to give readily and directly, for example, information on income, sexual relations, and attitudes toward religion and minority groups. In such cases, direct questions may yield data that are invalid. Yet, properly handled, even personal or controversial material can be successfully obtained with interviews and schedules.

The interview is probably man's oldest and most often used device for obtaining information. It has important qualities that objective tests and scales and behavioral observations do not possess. When used with a well-conceived schedule, an interview can obtain a great deal of information, is flexible and adaptable to individual situations, and can often be used when no other method is possible or adequate. These qualities make it especially suitable for research with children.[1] An interviewer can know whether the respondent, especially a child, does not understand a question and can, within limits, repeat or rephrase the question. Questions about hopes, aspirations, and anxieties can be asked in such a way as to elicit accurate information. Most important, perhaps, the interview permits probing into the context and reasons for answers to questions.

The major shortcoming of the interview and its accompanying schedule is practical. Interviews take a lot of time. Getting information from one individual may take as long as an hour or even two hours. This large time investment costs effort and money. So, whenever a more economical method answers the research purposes, interviews should not be used.

INTERVIEWS AND SCHEDULES AS TOOLS OF SCIENCE

For the most part, interviews and schedules have been used simply for gathering so-called facts. The most important use of interviews should be to study relations and to test hypotheses. The interview, in other words, is a psychological and sociological measuring instrument. Perhaps more accurately, the products of interviews, respondents' answers to carefully contrived questions, can be translated into measures of variables. Interviews and interview schedules are therefore subject to the same criteria of reliability, validity, and objectivity as other measuring instruments.

An interview can be used for three main purposes. One, it can be an exploratory device to help identify variables and relations, to suggest hypotheses, and to guide other phases of the research. Two, it can be the main instrument of the research. In this case, questions designed to measure the variables of the research will be included in the interview schedule. These questions are then to be considered as items in a measurement instrument, rather than as mere information-gathering devices. Three, the interview can supplement other methods: follow up unexpected results, validate other methods, and go deeper into the motivations of respondents and their reasons for responding as they do.

In using interviews as tools of scientific research, we must ask the questions: Can data on the research problem be obtained in an easier or better way? To achieve reliability, for example, is not a small problem. Interviewers must be trained; questions must be pretested and revised to eliminate ambiguities and inadequate wording. Is it worth the effort? Validity, too, is no small problem. Special pains must be taken to eliminate interviewer bias; questions must be tested for unknown biases. The particular research problem and the nature of the information sought must, in the last analysis, dictate whether the interview will be used.[2]

---

[1]L. Yarrow, "Interviewing Children." In P. Mussen, ed., *Handbook of Research Methods in Child Development.* New York: Wiley, 1960, chap. 14.

[2]The student will find detailed guidance in: C. Cannell and R. Kahn, "Interviewing." In G. Lindzey and E. Aronson, eds., *The Handbook of Social Psychology,* 2d ed. Reading, Mass.: Addison-Wesley, 1968, vol. II, chap. 15. See, also, D. Warwick and C. Lininger, *The Sample Survey: Theory and Practice.* New York: McGraw-Hill, 1975, chap. 7.

The Interview

The *interview* is a face-to-face interpersonal role situation in which one person, the interviewer, asks a person being interviewed, the respondent, questions designed to obtain answers pertinent to the research problem. There are two broad types of interview: *structured and unstructured* or *standardized and unstandardized*.[3] In the standardized interview, the questions, their sequence, and their wording are fixed. An interviewer may be allowed some liberty in asking questions, but relatively little.[4] This liberty is specified in advance. Standardized interviews use interview schedules that have been carefully prepared to obtain information pertinent to the research problem.

Unstandardized interviews are more flexible and open. Although the research purposes govern the questions asked, their content, their sequence, and their wording are in the hands of the interviewer. Ordinarily no schedule is used. In other words, the unstandardized, nonstructured interview is an open situation in contrast to the standardized, structured interview, which is a closed situation. This does not mean that an unstandardized interview is casual. It should be just as carefully planned as the standardized one. Our concern here is mainly with the standardized interview. It is recognized, however, that many research problems may, and often do, require a compromise type of interview in which the interviewer is permitted to use alternate questions that he judges fit for particular respondents and particular questions.[5]

THE INTERVIEW SCHEDULE

Interviewing itself is an art, but the planning and writing of an interview schedule is even more so. It is unusual for a novice to produce a good schedule, at least without considerable prior study and practice. There are several reasons for this, the main ones probably being the multiple meaning and ambiguity of words, the lack of sharp and constant focus on the problems and hypotheses being studied, a lack of appreciation of the schedule as a measurement instrument, and a lack of necessary background and experience.

Kinds of Schedule Information and Items

Three kinds of information are included in most schedules: face sheet (identification) information, census-type (or sociological) information, and problem information. Except for identification, these types of information were discussed in Chapter 24. The importance of identifying each schedule accurately and completely, however, needs to be mentioned. The careful researcher should learn to identify with letters, numbers, or other symbols, every schedule and every scale. In addition, identifying information for each individual must be systematically recorded.

Two types of schedule items are in common use: *fixed-alternative* (or closed) and

---

[3] Cannell and Kahn, *op. cit.*, pp. 573ff.

[4] *Interviewer's Manual, Survey Research Center,* rev. ed. Ann Arbor: Institute for Social Research, University of Michigan, 1976. Although rather close adherence to the interview schedule has been advocated by experts, a somewhat changed view appears to be relaxing this stricture: the interview is seen as an interaction, an active role relation between interviewer and interviewee, in which the interviewer is even a teacher. See Cannell and Kahn, *op. cit.* See, also, B. Dohrenwend and S. Richardson, "Directiveness and Nondirectiveness in Research Interviewing: A Reformulation of the Problem," *Psychological Bulletin,* 60 (1963), 475–485.

[5] The actual procedure of conducting an interview is not discussed in this book. The reader will find guidance in the study suggestions at the end of the chapter.

open-end (or open). A third type of item, having fixed alternatives, is also used: *scale* items.

Fixed-Alternative Items

Fixed-alternative items, as the name indicates, offer the respondent a choice among two or more alternatives. These items are also called *closed* or *poll* questions. The commonest kind of fixed-alternative item is dichotomous: it asks for Yes-No, Agree-Disagree, and other two-alternative answers. Often a third alternative, Don't Know or Undecided, is added.

Two examples of fixed-alternative items follow:[6]

There are always some people whose ideas are considered bad or dangerous by other people, for instance, somebody who is against all churches and religion. If such a person wanted to make a speech in your city (town, community) against churches and religion, should he be allowed to speak, or not?

Yes. . . . . ☐
No . . . . ☐
Don't know. . . . . ☐

If the school board in your community were to say, some day, that there were no Communists teaching in your schools, would you feel pretty sure it was true, or not?

Would feel it was true. . . . . . . ☐
Would not. . . . . ☐
Don't know . . . . ☐

Although fixed-alternative items have the decided advantages of achieving greater uniformity of measurement and thus greater reliability, of forcing the respondent to answer in a way that fits the response categories previously set up, and of being easily coded, they have certain disadvantages. The major disadvantage is their superficiality: Without probes they do not ordinarily get beneath the response surface. They may also irritate a respondent who finds none of the alternatives suitable. Worse, they can force responses. A respondent may choose an alternative to conceal ignorance. Or he may choose alternatives that do not accurately represent true facts or opinions. These difficulties do not mean that fixed-alternative items are bad and useless. On the contrary, they can be used to good purpose if they are judiciously written, used with probes, and mixed with open items.[7]

Open-End Items

Open or open-end items are an extremely important development in the technique of interviewing. *Open-end questions* are those that supply a frame of reference for respondents' answers, but put a minimum of restraint on the answers and their expression. While their content is dictated by the research problem, they impose no other restrictions on the content and manner of respondent answers. Examples will be given later.

Open-end questions have important advantages, but they have disadvantages, too. If properly written and used, however, these disadvantages can be minimized. Open-end

---

[6]From *Communism, Conformity, and Civil Liberties* by Samuel A. Stouffer. Garden City, N.Y.: Doubleday, 1955, pp. 252 and 256. Copyright © 1955 by Samuel A. Stouffer. Reprinted by permission of Doubleday & Company, Inc.

[7]See Warwick and Lininger, *op. cit.,* pp. 210–215. A *probe* is a device used to find out respondents' information on a subject, their frames of reference, or, more usually, to clarify and ascertain reasons for responses given. Probing increases the "response-getting" power of questions without changing their content. Examples of probes are: "Tell me more about that." "How is that?" "Can you explain that?"

questions are flexible; they have possibilities of depth; they enable the interviewer to clear up misunderstanding (through probing), to ascertain a respondent's lack of knowledge, to detect ambiguity, to encourage cooperation and achieve rapport, and to make better estimates of respondents' true intentions, beliefs, and attitudes. Their use also has another advantage: the responses to open-end questions can suggest possibilities of relations and hypotheses. Respondents will sometimes give unexpected answers that may indicate the existence of relations not originally anticipated.

A special type of open-end question is the *funnel*. Actually, this is a set of questions directed toward getting information on a single important topic or a single set of related topics. The funnel starts with a broad question and narrows down progressively to the important specific point or points.[8] Warwick and Lininger point out that the merits of the funnel is that it allows free response in the earlier questions, narrows down to specific questions and responses, and also facilitates the discovery of respondents' frames of reference.[9] Another form of funnel starts with an open general question and follows this up with specific closed items. The best way to get a feeling for good open-end questions and funnels is to study examples.

To obtain information on child-rearing practices, Sears, Maccoby, and Levin used a number of good open-end and funnel questions. One of them, with the authors' comments in brackets, is:

> All babies cry, of course. [*Note that the interviewer puts the parent at ease about her child's crying.*] Some mothers feel that if you pick up a baby every time it cries, you will spoil it. Others think you should never let a baby cry for very long. [*The frame of reference has been clearly given. The mother is also put at ease no matter how she handles her baby's crying.*] How do you feel about this?
> (a) What did you do about this with *X*?
> (b) How about in the middle of the night?[10]

This funnel question set not only reaches attitudes; it also probes specific practices.

Scale Items

A third type of schedule item is the scale item. A *scale* is a set of verbal items to each of which an individual responds by expressing degrees of agreement or disagreement or some other mode of response. Scale items have fixed alternatives and place the responding individual at some point on the scale. (They will be discussed at greater length in Chapter 29.) The use of scale items in interview schedules is a development of great promise, since the benefits of scales are combined with those of interviews. We can include, for example, a scale to measure attitudes toward education in an interview schedule on the same topic. Scale scores can be obtained in this way for each respondent and can be checked against open-end question data. One can measure the *tolerance of nonconformity,* as Stouffer did, by having a scale to measure this variable embedded in the interview schedule.[11]

In the last decade, survey researchers have increasingly used scale items. They are used heavily, for example, in the large and important survey on the quality of American life done by the Survey Research Center of the University of Michigan.[12] Here is an

[8]*Ibid.,* pp. 137–139.

[9]*Ibid.*

[10]R. Sears, E. Maccoby, and H. Levin, *Patterns of Child Rearing.* New York: Harper & Row, 1957, pp. 491–493.

[11]Stouffer, *op, cit.,* App. C.

[12]A. Campbell, P. Converse, and W. Rodgers, *The Quality of American Life.* New York: Russell Sage Foundation, 1976.

interesting example of an item that combines both open and closed approaches, the latter with a scale item. Note the branching depending on how the respondent answers the "Some people . . . " item. Note, too, the crucial item (C6) on satisfaction with life in the United States.

    C5. Some people say there isn't as much freedom in this country as there ought to be. How about you—how free do you feel to live the kind of life you want—very free, free enough, not very free, or not free at all?

1. VERY FREE	2. FREE ENOUGH	3. NOT VERY FREE	4. NOT FREE AT ALL

    GO TO C6   GO TO C6

C5a. In what way do you feel you aren't very free?_____

    C6. (HAND R CARD 3, WHITE) All things considered, how satisfied are you with life in the United States today? *Which number comes closest to how satisfied or dissatisfied you feel?*[13]

      1   2   3   4   5   6   7

Criteria of Question-Writing

Criteria or precepts of question-writing have been developed through experience and research. Some of the most important of these are given below in the form of questions. Brief comments are appended to the questions. When confronted with the actual necessity of drafting a schedule, the student should consult more extended treatments, since the ensuing discussion, in keeping with the discussion of the rest of the chapter, is intended only as an introduction to the subject.[14]

    1. *Is the question related to the research problem and the research objectives?* Except for factual and sociological information questions, all the items of a schedule should have some research problem function. This means that the purpose of each question is to elicit information that can be used to test the hypotheses of the research.

    2. *Is the type of question appropriate?* Some information can best be obtained with the open-end question—reasons for behavior, intentions, and attitudes. Certain other information, on the other hand, can be more expeditiously obtained with closed questions. If all that is required of a respondent is preferred choice of two or more alternatives, and these alternatives can be clearly specified, it would be wasteful to use an open-end question.[15]

    3. *Is the item clear and unambiguous?* An ambiguous statement or item is one that permits or invites alternative interpretations and differing responses resulting from the alternative interpretations. So-called double-barreled questions are ambiguous, for exam-

---

[13] *Ibid.,* p. 527. In item C6, 1 = highly satisfied, 7 = highly dissatisfied, and 4 = neutral.

[14] For practical guidance, see Warwick and Lininger, *op. cit.,* chap. 6; E. Noelle-Neuman, "Wanted: Rules for Wording Structured Questionnaires," *Public Opinion Quarterly,* 35 (1970), 191–201.

[15] See H. Schuman and S. Presser, "The Open and Closed Question," *American Sociological Review,* 44 (1979), 692–712; Dohrenwend and Richardson, *op. cit.;* Warwick and Lininger, *op, cit.,* pp. 132–140.

ple, because they provide two or more frames of reference rather than only one. Cannell and Kahn give a "good" example of a double-barreled and thus ambiguous question: "How do you feel about the development of a rapid transit system between the central city and the suburbs, and the redevelopment of central city residential areas?"?[16] Respondents, even if not baffled by the complexity and alternatives offered by this question, can hardly respond using a common frame of reference and understanding of what is wanted. But ambiguity can arise from much simpler questions: "How are you and your family getting along this year?" Does the questioner mean finances, marital happiness, health, status, or what?

A great deal of work has been done on item writing. Certain precepts, if followed, help the item writer avoid ambiguity. First, questions that contain more than one idea to which a respondent can react should be avoided. An item like "Do you believe that the educational aims of the modern high school and the teaching methods used to attain these aims are educationally sound?" is an ambiguous question, because the respondent is asked about both educational aims and teaching methods in the same question. Second, avoid ambiguous words and expressions. A respondent might be asked the question, "Do you think the teachers of your school get fair treatment?" This is an ambiguous item because "fair treatment" might refer to several different areas of treatment. The word "fair," too, can mean "just," "equitable," "not too good," "impartial," and "objective." The question needs a clear context, an explicit frame of reference. (Sometimes, however, ambiguous questions are deliberately used to elicit different frames of reference.)

4. *Is the question a leading question?* Leading questions suggest answers. As such, they threaten validity. If you ask a person "Have you read about the local school situation?" you may get a disproportionately large number of "yes" responses, because the question may imply that it is bad not to have read about the local school situation.

5. *Does the question demand knowledge and information that the respondent does not have?* To counter the invalidity of response due to lack of information, it is wise to use information filter questions. Before asking a person what he thinks of UNESCO, first find out whether he knows what UNESCO is and means. Another approach is possible. You can explain UNESCO briefly and then ask the respondent what he thinks of it.

6. *Does the question demand personal or delicate material that the respondent may resist?* Special techniques are needed to obtain information of a personal, delicate, or controversial nature. Ask income and other personal matters late in the interview after rapport has been built up. When asking about something that is socially disapproved, show that some people believe one way and others believe another way. Don't make the respondent in effect disapprove himself.

7. *Is the question loaded with social desirability?* People tend to give responses that are socially desirable, responses that indicate or imply approval of actions or things that are generally considered to be good. We may ask a person about his feelings toward children. Everybody is supposed to love children. Unless we are careful, we will get a stereotyped response about children and love. Also, when we ask if a person votes, we must be careful since everyone is supposed to vote. If we ask respondents their reactions to minority groups, we again run the risk of getting invalid responses. Most educated people, no matter what their "true" attitudes, are aware that prejudice is disapproved. A good question, then, is one in which respondents are not led to express merely socially desirable sentiments. At the same time, one should not question respondents so that they are faced with the necessity of giving socially undesirable responses.

---

[16] Cannell and Kahn, *op. cit.*, p. 559.

THE VALUE OF INTERVIEWS AND INTERVIEW SCHEDULES

The interview, when coupled with an adequate schedule of pretested worth, is a potent and indispensable research tool, yielding data that no other research tool can yield. It is adaptable, capable of being used with all kinds of respondents in many kinds of research, and uniquely suited to exploration in depth. But do its strengths balance its weaknesses? And what is its value in behavioral research when compared to other methods of data collection?

The most natural tool with which to compare the interview is the so-called questionnaire. As noted earlier, "questionnaire" is a term used for almost any kind of instrument that has questions or items to which individuals respond. Although the term is used interchangeably with "schedule," it seems to be associated more with self-administered instruments that have items of the closed- or fixed-alternative type.

The self-administered instrument has certain advantages. With most or all of its items of the closed type, greater uniformity of stimulus and thus greater reliability can be achieved. In this respect, it has the advantages of objective-type, written tests and scales, if they are adequately constructed and pretested. A second advantage is that, if anonymous, honesty and frankness may be encouraged. This kind of instrument can also be administered to large numbers relatively easily. A somewhat dubious advantage is that it can be mailed to respondents. Further, it is economical. Its cost is ordinarily a fraction of that of interviews.

The disadvantages of the self-administered instrument (when mailed) seem to outweigh its advantages. The principal disadvantage is low percentage of returns. A second disadvantage is that it may not be as uniform as its seems. Experience has shown that the same question frequently has different meanings for different people. As we saw, this can be handled in the interview. But we are powerless to do anything about it when the instrument is self-administered. Third, if only closed items are used, the instrument displays the same weaknesses of closed items discussed earlier. On the other hand, if open items are used, the respondent may object to writing the answers, which reduces the sample of adequate responses. Many people cannot express themselves adequately in writing, and many who can express themselves dislike doing so.

Because of these disadvantages, the interview is probably superior to the self-administered questionnaire. (This statement does not include carefully constructed personality and attitude scales.) The best instrument available for sounding people's behavior, future intentions, feelings, attitudes, and reason for behavior would seem to be the structured interview coupled with an interview schedule that includes open-end, closed, and scale items. Of course, the structured interview must be carefully constructed and pretested and be used only by skilled interviewers. The cost in time, energy, and money, and the very high degree of skill necessary for its construction, are its main drawbacks. Once these disadvantages are surmounted, the structured interview is a powerful tool.

ADDENDUM

Examples of the Interview as a Research Tool

This chapter has emphasized the use of the interview in survey research. Its value as a primary or supplementary method in all kinds of studies must be pointed out. When information is difficult to get with other methods and when it is necessary to probe or go deep, the interview can be invaluable. When a new area is being explored, interviewing may be useful to obtain leads on hypotheses, variables, and items. When research is done with small children, interviewing may be the only way to have them communicate. Rather than labor these points, we give examples to supplement those given in the chapter.

In her impressive study of attitudes toward rape mentioned in an earlier chapter, Burt used interviews whose questions were mostly closed and, most important, scales to measure several variables considered to be important in supporting acceptance of rape: sex role stereotypy, adversarial sexual beliefs, and sexual conservatism, for example.[17] The open-ended questions focused on the subjects' experiences with sexual assault, for example: "Have you ever had anyone force sex on you against your will?" Actually, Burt did not use open-ended questions in the usual sense since all her questions required only brief responses with no elaboration. This use of the interview well illustrates what will probably be an increasing trend that we noticed before: generous use of scales in interviews to measure the variables under study. In earlier years the use of scales in interviews was relatively rare. Social scientific researchers today want the advantages of the open-ended question, the closed question, and the scale. Burt's almost exclusive use of closed questions and scales illustrates recent increased preoccupation with the validity and reliability of variable measurement. I think we can also anticipate social scientific researchers' increasing use of scales that are administered to random samples by interviewers working on entirely different research projects. For example, a social attitude scale used in a cross-cultural attitude study was administered to a random sample of The Netherlands by a commercial survey research organization in one of its weekly surveys.[18]

In their study of children's perceptions of social stratification, Simmons and Rosenberg used three-hour interviews as their primary method of determining third- to twelfth-grade children's awareness of stratification and their views of the American opportunity structure.[19] One question aimed at the latter was: "Do all kids in America have the same chance to grow up and get the good things in life, or Do some kids *not* have as good a chance as others, or Don't you know."

Study Suggestions

1. There are valuable references on the interview and the interview schedule. A few are given below. Those marked with an asterisk will probably be of most help to the reader whose knowledge of the field is limited.

> *CANNELL and KAHN; *Warwick and Lininger: see footnote 2, above. *Interviewer's Manual, Survey Research Center, rev. ed. Ann Arbor: Institute for Social Research, University of Michigan, 1976. An excellent guide to the practical aspects of interviewing.
>
> KAHN, R., and CANNELL, C. The Dynamics of Interviewing. New York: Wiley, 1957. An authoritative book based on the University of Michigan Survey Research Center (see above) theory and practice.
>
> RICHARDSON, S., DOHRENWEND, B., and KLEIN, D. Interviewing. New York: Basic Books, 1965.

[17]M. Burt, "Cultural Myths and Support for Rape," *Journal of Personality and Social Psychology,* 38 (1980), 217–230.

[18]F. Kerlinger, C. Middendorp, and J. Amón, "The Structure of Social Attitudes in Three Countries: Tests of a Criterial Referents Theory," *International Journal of Psychology,* 11 (1976), 265–279. My colleagues and I are grateful to Dr. G. C. Schild and the Netherlands Institute of Public Opinion for administering the scale.

[19]R. Simmons and M. Rosenberg, "Functions of Children's Perceptions of the Stratification System," *American Sociological Review,* 36 (1971), 235–249.

2. Good interview schedules are fortunately plentiful. The reader should carefully study two or three of them. Here are six schedules that are both well-constructed and substantively interesting. Note that published schedules usually have extensive methodological discussions accompanying them. The student can learn a good deal about interview scale construction from study of these discussions.

CAMPBELL, A., CONVERSE, P., and RODGERS, W. *The Quality of American Life*. New York: Russell Sage Foundation, 1976, app. B. A long schedule with many scale items and careful interviewer instructions. Also a substantively important study.

FREE, L., and CANTRIL, H. *The Political Beliefs of Americans*. New Brunswick, N. J.: Rutgers University Press, 1967, app. B. Has good questions and probes and fixed-alternative items.

GLOCK, C., and STARK, R. *Christian Beliefs and Anti-Semitism*. New York: Harper & Row, 1966. The complete schedule, mostly with fixed-alternative items, is given at the end of the book.

LORTIE, D. *Schoolteachers: A Sociological Study*. Chicago: University of Chicago Press, 1975, app. B. Particularly valuable to educational researchers. Includes probes and suggestions to interviewers.

STOUFFER, S., *Communism, Conformity, and Civil Liberties*. Garden City, N. Y.: Doubleday, 1955, app. B. This schedule contains many fixed-alternative items and scales especially designed to measure tolerance and perception of Communist threat. See app. C for the scales.

VERBA, S., and NIE, N. *Participation in America: Political Democracy and Social Equality*. New York: Harper & Row, 1972. A valuable and sophisticated study using survey data of 2,549 interviews conducted by the National Opinion Research Center in 1967.

3. The examples given in 2, above, are all survey research, the field of research in which the art and technique of interviewing were developed and used. Interviews, however, can be and have been used in what can be called "normal" studies, studies whose only or main interest is in pursuing relations among variables. The Burt study of attitudes toward rape, discussed earlier, is a good example. Here are four others.

CAMPBELL, A., and SCHUMAN, H. *Racial Attitudes in Fifteen Cities*. Ann Arbor, Michigan: Institute for Social Research, University of Michigan, 1968. A combination of "survey" and attitudinal questions aimed at understanding racial attitudes and their change.

DOOB, A., and MACDONALD, G. "Television Viewing and Fear of Victimization: Is the Relationship Causal?" *Journal of Personality and Social Psychology*, 37 (1979), 170–179.

JACKSON, P., SILBERMAN, M., and WOLFSON, B. "Signs of Personal Involvement in Teachers' Descriptions of Their Students," *Journal of Educational Psychology*, 60 (1969), 22–27. Naturalistic brief interviews whose results were analyzed to obtain evidence of teachers' personal involvement with pupils.

QUINN, R., KAHN, R., TABOR, J., and GORDON, L. *The Chosen Few: A Study of Discrimination in Executive Selection*. Ann Arbor: Institute for Social Research, University of Michigan, 1968. Confidential interviews with executives were used in a study of anti-Semitism.

Chapter 29

Objective Tests and Scales

THE MOST-USED method of observation and data collection in the behavioral sciences is the test or scale. The considerable time researchers spend in constructing or finding measures of variables is well spent because adequate measurement of research variables is at the core of behavioral scientific work. In general, too little attention has been paid to the measurement of the variables of research studies. What good are intriguing and important research problems and sophisticated research design and statistical analysis if the variables of research studies are poorly measured? Fortunately, great progress has been made in understanding psychological and educational measurement theory and in improving measurement practice. In this chapter we examine some of the technology of objective measurement procedures.

OBJECTIVITY AND OBJECTIVE METHODS OF OBSERVATION

Objectivity, a central and essential characteristic of scientific methodology, is easy to define but evidently hard to understand. It is also controversial.[1] *Objectivity* is agreement among expert judges on what is observed. Objective methods of observation are those in which anyone following the prescribed rules will assign the same numerals to objects and

---

[1] For an extended discussion of objectivity, see: F. Kerlinger, *Behavioral Research: A Conceptual Approach*. New York: Holt, Rinehart and Winston, 1979, pp. 9–13 and 262–264. The importance of understanding objectivity in science cannot be overemphasized. It is especially important to understand that scientific objectivity is methodological and has little or nothing to do with objectivity as a presumed characteristic of scientists. Whether a scientist as a person is or is not objective is not the point; the point is that scientific objectivity inheres in methodological procedures characterized by agreement among expert judges—and nothing more.

sets of objects as anyone else. An objective procedure is one in which agreement among observers is at a maximum. In variance terms, observer variance is at a minimum. This means that judgmental variance, the variance due to differences in judges' assignment of numerals to objects, approaches zero.

All methods of observation are inferential: inferences about properties of the members of sets are made on the basis of the numerals assigned to the set members with interviews, tests, scales, and direct observations of behavior. The methods differ in their directness or indirectness, in the degree to which inferences are made from the raw observations. The inferences made by using objective methods of observations are usually lengthy, despite their seeming directness. Most such methods permit a high degree of inter-observer agreement because subjects make marks on paper, the marks being restricted to two or more choices among alternatives supplied by the observer. From these marks on paper the observer infers the characteristics of the individuals and sets of individuals making the marks. In one class of objective methods, the marks on paper are made by the observer (or judge) who looks at the object or objects of measurement and chooses between given alternatives. In this case, too, inferences about the properties of the observed object or objects are made from the marks on paper. The main difference lies in who makes the marks.

It should be recognized that all methods of observation have *some* objectivity. There is not a sharp dichotomy, in other words, between so-called objective methods and other methods of observation. There is, rather, a difference in the degree of objectivity. Again, if we think of degrees of objectivity as degrees of agreement among observers, the ambiguity and confusion often associated with the problem disappear.

We will agree, then, that what are here called objective methods of observation and measurement have no monopoly on objectivity or on inference, but that they are more objective and no less inferential than any other methods of observation and measurement. The methods to be discussed in this chapter will by no means exhaust possible methods, since the subject is large and varied. They are considered only as *measures of variables,* to be viewed and assessed the same as all other measures of variables.

TESTS AND SCALES: DEFINITIONS

A *test* is a systematic procedure in which the individuals tested are presented with a set of constructed stimuli to which they respond, the responses enabling the tester to assign the testees numerals or sets of numerals from which inferences can be made about the testees' possession of whatever the test is supposed to measure. This definition says little more than that a test is a measurement instrument.

A *scale* is a set of symbols or numerals so constructed that the symbols or numerals can be assigned by rule to the individuals (or their behaviors) to whom the scale is applied, the assignment being indicated by the individual's possession of whatever the scale is supposed to measure. Like a test, a scale is a measuring instrument. Indeed, except for the excess meaning associated with *test,* we can see that *test* and *scale* are similarly defined. Strictly speaking, however, *scale* is used in two ways: to indicate a measuring instrument and to indicate the systematized numerals of the measuring instrument. We use it in both senses without worrying too much about fine distinctions. Remember this, however: tests are scales, but scales are not necessarily tests. This can be said because scales do not ordinarily have the meanings of competition and success or failure that tests do. Significantly, we say ''achievement testing,'' not ''achievement scaling''; ''intelligence testing'' and not ''intelligence scaling.''

TYPES OF OBJECTIVE MEASURES

Most of the hundreds, perhaps thousands, of tests and scales can be divided into the following classes: intelligence and aptitude tests, achievement tests, personality measures, attitude and value scales, and miscellaneous objective measures. We discuss each of these types of measure from a research point of view.

Intelligence and Aptitude Tests

In psychological and educational research, a measure of intelligence or aptitude is often needed, either as an independent variable or as a dependent variable. In assessing the effects of educational programs of one kind or another on educational achievement, for instance, it is usually necessary to control intelligence so that the differences found between experimental treatment groups cannot be attributed to differences in intelligence rather than to the treatments. There are a number of good group intelligence tests that researchers can use, perhaps a so-called omnibus test. (An omnibus test is one that has items of different kinds—verbal, numerical, spatial, and others—in one instrument.) These tests are ordinarily highly verbal and correlate substantially with school achievement. Buros' handbooks are useful guides to such tests.[2]

Aptitude is potential ability for achievement. Aptitude tests, although they are used mainly for guidance and counseling, can also be used in research, particularly as control variables. A control variable is one whose effect on a dependent variable may need to be nullified. For example, in studying the effect of a remedial reading program on reading achievement, verbal aptitude may need to be attributed to possible group differences in verbal ability. Similarly, other possible influential variables—numerical and spatial abilities, for instance—may need to be controlled. Aptitude tests can be useful in such cases.

Achievement Tests

Achievement tests measure present proficiency, mastery, and understanding of general and specific areas of knowledge. For the most part, they are measures of the effectiveness of instruction and learning, and, of course, are enormously important in education and educational research. Indeed, in research involving instructional methods, achievement, as we have seen, is often the dependent variable.

Achievement tests can be classified in several ways. For our purposes, we break them down into, first, standardized and specially constructed tests. Standardized tests are published group tests that are based on general educational content common to a large number of educational systems. They are the products of a high degree of professional competence and skill in test-writing and, as such, are usually quite reliable and generally valid. They are also provided with elaborate tables of norms (averages) that can be used for comparative purposes. Specially constructed tests are ordinarily teacher-made tests devised by teachers to measure more limited and specific achievements. They may, of course, also be constructed by educational researchers for measuring limited areas of achievement or proficiency.

---

[2]O. Buros, ed., *The Eighth Mental Measurements Yearbook.* Highland Park, N.J.: Gryphon Press, 1978. See, also, Sax's highly useful presentation on published sources of information about tests: G. Sax, *Principles of Educational and Psychological Measurement and Evaluation,* 2d ed. Belmont, Calif.: Wadsworth, 1980, pp. 339–355.

Standardized achievement tests can also be classified into general and special tests. General tests are typically batteries of tests that measure the most important areas of school achievement: language usage, vocabulary, reading, arithmetic, and social studies. Special achievement tests, as the name indicates, are tests in individual subjects, such as history, science, and English.

Researchers will often have no choice of achievement tests because school systems have already selected them. Given choice, however, they must carefully assess the *kind* of achievement research problems require. Suppose the research variable in a study is achievement in understanding concepts. Many, perhaps most, tests used in schools will not be adequate for measuring this variable. In such cases, researchers can choose a test specifically designed to measure the understanding of concepts, or can devise such tests themselves. The construction of an achievement test is a formidable job, the details of which cannot be discussed here. The student is referred to specialized texts.[3]

Personality Measures

The measurement of personality traits is the most complex problem of psychological measurement. The reason is simple: human personality is extremely complex. For the purposes of measurement, personality can be viewed as the organization of the traits of the individual. A *trait* is a characteristic of an individual revealed through recurring behaviors in different situations. We say an individual is *compulsive,* or has the trait of *compulsivity,* because he is observed to be overly neat in his dress and speech, to be always punctual, to want everything to be very orderly, and to dislike and avoid irregularities.

The major problem in personality measurement is validity. To measure personality traits validly requires knowledge of what these traits are, how they interact and change, and how they relate to each other—a formidable, even forbidding, requirement. The wonder is *not,* as naive critics love to point out, that personality cannot be measured because it is too elusive, too complex, too existential, or that measurement efforts have not been too successful, but rather that some measure of success in so difficult a task *has* been achieved. Nevertheless, the problem of validity is considerable.

There are two general approaches to the construction and validation of personality measures: the *a priori* method and the *construct* or *theoretical* method. In the a priori method, items are constructed to reflect the personality dimension to be measured. Since the introvert is frequently a retiring person, we might write items about his preferring to be alone—shunning parties, for instance—in order to measure introversion. Since the anxious person will probably be nervous and disorganized under stress, we might write items suggesting these conditions in order to measure anxiety. In the a priori method, then, the scale writer collects or writes items that ostensibly measure personality traits.

This approach is essentially that of early personality test writers; it is a content validity method that is still used. While there is nothing inherently wrong with the method— indeed, it will have to be used, especially in the early stages of test and scale construction— the results can be misleading. Items do not always measure what we think they measure. Sometimes we even find that an item we thought would measure, say, social responsibil-

[3]Unfortunately, there are few texts on the construction of tests and scales for research purposes. The many texts and other discussions of measurement focus for the most part on the construction and use of instruments for applied purposes. Researchers who need to construct achievement measures of one kind or another, however, will find excellent guidance in: D. Adkins, *Test Construction: Development and Interpretation of Achievement Tests,* 2d ed. Columbus: Charles E. Merrill, 1974. Researchers who need to construct attitude scales will find Edwards' book invaluable: A. Edwards, *Techniques of Attitude Scale Construction.* New York: Appleton-Century-Crofts, 1957.

ity, actually measures a tendency to agree with socially desirable statements. For this reason, the a priori method, used alone, is insufficient.

The method of validation often used with a priori personality scales is the known-group method. To validate a scale of social responsibility, one might find a group of individuals known to be high in social responsibility, and another known to be low in social responsibility. If the scale differentiates the groups successfully, it is said to have validity.

A priori personality and other measures will continue to be used in behavioral research. Their blind and naive use, however, should be discouraged. Their construct and criterion-related validities must be checked, especially through factor analysis and other empirical means. Measures of personality, as well as other measures, have been used too often merely because users *think* they measure whatever they are said to measure.

The construct or theoretical method of personality measure construction emphasizes the relations of the variable being measured to other variables, the relations prompted by the theory underlying the research. (See Chapter 27.) While scale construction must always to some extent be a priori, the more personality measures are subjected to the tests of construct validity the more faith we can have in them. It is not enough simply to accept the validity of a personality scale, or even to accept its validity because it has successfully differentiated, say, artists from scientists, teachers from non-teachers, normal persons from neurotic persons. Ultimately, its construct validity, its successful use in a wide variety of theoretically predicted relations, must be established.

Attitude Scales

Attitudes, while treated separately here and in most textbook discussions, are really an integral part of personality. (Intelligence and aptitude, too, are considered parts of personality by modern theorists.) Personality measurement, however, is mostly of traits. A *trait* is a relatively enduring characteristic of the individual to respond in a certain manner in all situations. If one is dominant, one exhibits dominant behavior in most situations. If one is anxious, anxious behavior permeates most of one's activities. An *attitude,* on the other hand, is an organized predisposition to think, feel, perceive, and behave toward a referent or cognitive object. It is an enduring structure of beliefs that predisposes the individual to behave selectively toward attitude referents.[4] A *referent* is a category, class, or set of phenomena: physical objects, events, behaviors, even constructs.[5] People have attitudes toward many different things: ethnic groups, institutions, religion, educational issues and practices, the Supreme Court, civil rights, private property, and so on. One has, in other words, an attitude toward something "out there." A trait has subjective reference; an attitude has objective reference. One who has a hostile attitude toward foreigners may be hostile only to foreigners, but one who has the trait *hostility* is hostile toward everyone (at least potentially).

There are three major types of attitude scales: *summated rating scales, equal-appearing interval scales,* and *cumulative (or Guttman) scales.* A summated rating scale (one type of which is called a Likert-type scale) is a set of attitude items, all of which are considered of approximately equal "attitude value," and to each of which subjects re-

---

[4]This definition comes from several sources: D. Krech and R. Crutchfield, *Theory and Problems of Social Psychology.* New York: McGraw-Hill, 1948, p. 152; T. Newcomb, *Social Psychology.* New York: Holt, Rinehart and Winston, 1950, pp. 118–119; F. Kerlinger, "Social Attitudes and Their Criterial Referents: A Structural Theory," *Psychological Review,* 74 (1967), 110–122; M. Rokeach, *Beliefs, Attitudes, and Values.* San Francisco: Jossey-Bass, 1968, p. 112.

[5]R. Brown, *Words and Things.* New York: Free Press, 1958, pp. 7–10.

spond with degrees of agreement or disagreement (intensity). The scores of the items of such a scale are summed, or summed and averaged, to yield an individual's attitude score. As in all attitude scales, the purpose of the summated rating scale is to place an individual somewhere on an agreement continuum of the attitude in question.

It is important to note two or three characteristics of summated rating scales, since many scales share these characteristics. First, *U,* the universe of items, is conceived to be a set of items of equal "attitude value," as indicated in the definition given above. This means that there is no scale of items, as such. One item is the same as any other item in attitude value. The *individuals* responding to items are "scaled"; this "scaling" comes about through the sums (or averages) of the individuals' responses. Any subset of U is theoretically the same as any other subset of U: a set of individuals would be rank-ordered the same using U_2 or U_1.

Second, summated rating scales allow for the *intensity* of attitude expression. Subjects can agree or they can agree strongly. There are advantages to this, as well as disadvantages. The main advantage is that greater variance results. When there are five or seven possible categories of response, it is obvious that the response variance should be greater than with only two or three categories (agree, disagree, no opinion, for example). The variance of summated rating scales, unfortunately, often seems to contain response-set variance. Individuals have differential tendencies to use certain types of responses: extreme responses, neutral responses, agree responses, disagree responses. This response variance confounds the attitude (and personality trait) variance. The individual differences yielded by summated rating attitude scales (and similarly scored trait measures) have been shown to be due in part to response set and other similar extraneous sources of variance.[6]

Here are two summated rating items from a scale constructed by Burt for her study of attitudes toward rape. They were written to measure sex-role stereotyping. A seven-point scale ranging from strongly agree (7) to strongly disagree (1) was used. The values in parentheses (and the values in between) are assigned to the responses indicated.

> There is something wrong with a woman who doesn't want to marry and raise a family. A woman should be a virgin when she marries.[7]

Thurstone *equal-appearing interval scales* are built on different principles. While the ultimate product, a set of attitude items, can be used for the same purpose of assigning individuals attitude scores, equal-appearing interval scales also accomplish the important purpose of scaling the attitude items. *Each item* is assigned a scale value, and the scale value indicates the strength of attitude of an agreement response to the item. The universe of items is considered to be an ordered set; that is, items differ in scale value. The scaling procedure finds these scale values. In addition, the items of the final scale to be used are so selected that the intervals between them are equal, an important and desirable psychometric feature.

The following equal-appearing interval items, with the scale values of the items, are from Thurstone and Chave's scale, Attitude toward the Church:[8]

---

[6]The response-set literature is large and cannot be cited in detail. Nunnally's discussion is well-balanced: J. Nunnally, *Psychometric Theory,* 2d ed. New York: McGraw-Hill, 1978, pp. 655–672. I believe that, while response set is a mild threat to valid measurement, its importance has been overrated and that the available evidence does not justify the strong negative assertions made by response-set enthusiasts. In other words, while one must be conscious of the possibilities and threats, one should certainly not be paralyzed by the somewhat blown-up danger. See *ibid.,* p. 672, and L. Rorer, "The Great Response-Style Myth," *Psychological Bulletin,* 63 (1965), 129–156.

[7]M. Burt, "Cultural Myths and Supports for Rape," *Journal of Personality and Social Psychology,* 38 (1980), 217–230 (p. 222).

[8]L. Thurstone and E. Chave, *The Measurement of Attitude.* Chicago: University of Chicago Press, 1929, pp. 61–63, 78.

I believe the church is the greatest institution in America today. (Scale value: .2)
I believe in religion, but I seldom go to church. (Scale value: 5.4)
I think the church is a hindrance to religion for it still depends upon magic, superstition, and myth. (Scale value: 9.6)

In the Thurstone and Chave scale, the lower the scale value, the more positive the attitude toward the church. The first and third items were the lowest and highest in the scale. The second item, of course, had an intermediate value. The total scale contained 45 items with scale values ranging over the whole continuum. Usually, however, equal-appearing interval scales contain considerably fewer items.

The third type of scale, *the cumulative* or *Guttman scale,* consists of a relatively small set of homogeneous items that are unidimensional (or supposed to be). A *unidimensional* scale measures one variable, and one variable only. The scale gets its name from the cumulative relation between items and the total scores of individuals. For example, we ask four children three arithmetic questions: (a) $28/7 = ?$, (b) $8 \times 4 = ?$, and (c) $12 + 9 = ?$ A child who gets (a) correct is very likely to get the other two correct. The child who misses (a), but gets (b) correct, is likely also to get (c) correct. A child who misses (c), on the other hand, is not likely to get (a) and (b) correct. The situation can be summarized as follows (the table includes the score of the fourth child, who gets none correct):

	(a)	*(b)*	*(c)*	*Total Score*
First Child	1	1	1	3
Second Child	0	1	1	2
Third Child	0	0	1	1
Fourth Child	0	0	0	0

(1 = Correct; 0 = Incorrect)

Note the relation between the *pattern* of item responses and total scores. If we know a child's total score, we can predict his pattern, if the scale is cumulative, just as knowledge of correct responses to the harder items are predictive of the responses to the easier items. Not, too, that both items and persons are scaled.

Similarly, people can be asked various questions about an attitudinal object. If upon analysis the patterns of responses arrange themselves in the manner indicated above (at least fairly closely), then the questions or items are said to be unidimensional. Therefore people can be ranked according to their scale responses.[9]

It is obvious that these three methods of constructing attitude scales are very different. Note that the same or similar methods can be used with other kinds of personality and other scales. The summated rating scale concentrates on the subjects and their places on the scale. The equal-appearing interval scale concentrates on the items and their places on the scale. Interestingly, both types of scales yield about the same results as far as reliability and the placing of individuals in attitudinal rank orders are concerned. Cumulative scales concentrate on the scalability of sets of items and on the scale positions of individuals.

Of the three types of scales, the summated rating scale seems to be the most useful in behavioral research. It is easier to develop, and as indicated above, yields about the same results as the more laboriously constructed equal-appearing interval scale. Used with care and knowledge of its weaknesses, summated rating scales can be adapted to many needs of behavioral researchers. Cumulative scales would seem to be less useful and less generally applicable. If one clear-cut cognitive object is used, a short well-constructed cumulative scale may yield reliable measures of a number of psychological variables: tolerance,

---

[9] For an excellent discussion of cumulative unidimensional scales, see Edwards, *op. cit.,* chap. 7.

conformity, group identification, acceptance of authority, permissiveness, and so on. It should be noted, too, that the method can be improved and altered in various ways.[10]

Value Scales

Values are culturally weighted preferences for things, ideas, people, institutions, and behaviors.[11] Whereas attitudes are organizations of beliefs about things "out there," predispositions to behave toward the objects or referents of attitudes, values express preferences for modes of conduct and end-states of existence.[12] Words like *equality, religion, free enterprise, civil rights,* and *obedience* express values. Simply put, values express the "good," the "bad," the "shoulds," the "oughts" of human behavior. Values put ideas, things, and behaviors on approval–disapproval continua. They imply choices among courses of action and thinking.

To give the reader some flavor of values, here are three items.[13] Individuals can be asked to express their approval or disapproval of the first and second items, perhaps in summated rating form, and to choose from the three alternatives of the third item.

> For his own good and for the good of society, man must be held in restraint by tradition and authority.
> Now more than ever we should strengthen the family, the natural stabilizer of society.
> Which of the following is the most important in living the full life: education, achievement, friendship?

Unfortunately, values have had little scientific study, even though they and attitudes are a large part of our verbal output, and are probably influential determinants of behavior. The measurement of values has thus suffered. Social and educational values will probably become the focus of much more theoretical and empirical work in the next decade, however, since social scientists have become increasingly aware that values are important influences on individual and group behavior.[14]

Miscellaneous Objective Measures

A number of objective measures do not conveniently fall into one of the above categories, although they are closely related to one or more of them. We shall consider several of these measures here to illustrate the variety of work already done and the possible nature of future objective inferential measurement.

Certain scales are important because of their theoretical value and the frequency of their use. The well-known *F* scale is one of these.[15] Designed to measure authoritarianism

---

[10]*Ibid.,* chaps. 7 and 9. Edwards describes how to construct and evaluate cumulative scales, as well as summated rating and equal-appearing interval scales.

[11]C. Kluckhohn et al., "Values and Value-Orientations in the Theory of Action." In T. Parsons and E. Shils, eds., *Toward a General Theory of Action.* Cambridge, Mass.: Harvard University Press, 1952, pp. 388–433.

[12]Rokeach, *op. cit.,* p. 159. The relations between attitudes and values and the definitions of both are still not clear in the literature, perhaps because of neglect of value theory and research.

[13]The first two items were written by the author for a University of Hawaii research project, 1971.

[14]See W. Dukes, "Psychological Studies of Values," *Psychological Bulletin,* 52 (1955), 24–50; R. Hogan, "Moral Conduct and Moral Character," *Psychological Bulletin,* 79 (1973), 217–232; S. Pittel and G. Mendelssohn, "Measurement of Moral Values," *Psychological Bulletin,* 66 (1966), 22–35. A source of values scales is T. Levitin, "Values." In J. Robinson and P. Shaver, eds., *Measures of Psychological Attitudes.* Ann Arbor: Institute for Social Research, University of Michigan, 1969, chap. 7. A highly suggestive and valuable essay appeared thirty years ago; Kluckhohn et al, *op. cit.* Thurstone's essay on values measurement is still important: L. Thurstone, *The Measurement of Values.* Chicago: University of Chicago Press, 1959, chap. 17.

[15]T. Adorno et al., *The Authoritarian Personality.* New York: Harper & Row, 1950.

(*F* originally stood for fascism), it has been called both a personality and an attitude measure. Probably closer to being a personality measure, the *F* scale is a summated rating scale in which subjects are asked to respond to a number of general statements, usually 29 or 30. Here are three such items, agreement with which is supposed to indicate authoritarian trends in the respondent.

> Obedience and respect for authority are the most important virtues children should learn.
> What the youth needs most is strict discipline, rugged determination, and the will to work and fight for family and country.
> Science has its place, but there are many important things that can never possibly be understood by the human mind.[16]

The *F* scale seems to tap broad general attitudes or cores of values, as well as personality traits. Many differences have been found between high- and low-scoring persons and groups.[17] More important, however, are the fruitful theoretical reasoning behind the scale's construction, the empirical approach to an important social and psychological problem, and the stimulus to research in the measurement of complex variables. The *F* scale has fallen into some disrepute under the critical onslaught of psychologists and sociologists because it allegedly does not hold up under the rigorous application of validity criteria. Evidence from a study by Kerlinger and Rokeach, however, seems to indicate that, despite its weaknesses, the *F* scale was well conceived theoretically and well fashioned as a measure of authoritarianism.[18]

The measurement of *interests* is relatively easy. The most important measures are the Strong-Campbell and the Kuder inventories.[19] The reliabilities of both scales are high; the evidence for their validity seems good.

Naturally, there are many other important and useful tests and scales—measures of moral judgment, social responsibility, classroom environment, needs, dominance, and so on. They cannot be discussed here. A few interesting and promising one, however, are mentioned in Study Suggestion 2 at the end of this chapter. Before ending our formal discussion of objective tests and scales, we should examine a new development of considerable potential research importance: social indicators.

SOCIAL AND EDUCATIONAL INDICATORS

Social indicators is the name associated with a relatively new field of considerable interest to behavioral researchers. Definitions are evidently contradictory and unsatisfactory.[20] Indicators seem to have two meanings. One is that they are statistics that reflect social conditions.[21] A second definition is broader: it includes all forms of evidence on techno-

[16] *Ibid.*, pp. 255–257.

[17] J. Kirscht and R. Dillehay, *Dimensions of Authoritarianism: A Review of Research and Theory*. Lexington, Ky.: University of Kentucky Press, 1967.

[18] F. Kerlinger and M. Rokeach, "The Factorial Nature of the F and D Scales," *Journal of Personality and Social Psychology*, 4 (1966), 391–399. The data of this study were reanalyzed and the study replicated by other researchers with essentially the same results: P. Warr, R. Lee, and K. Jöreskog, "A Note on the Factorial Nature of the F and D Scales," *British Journal of Psychology*, 60 (1969), 119–123.

[19] For descriptions of these scales, see Sax, *op. cit.*, pp. 473–490.

[20] R. Jaeger, "About Educational Indicators: Statistics on the Conditions and Trends in Education." In L. Shulman, ed., *Review of Research in Education*, vol. 6. Itasca, Ill.: Peacock, 1978. This chapter is a highly competent exposition on the definition, status, and use of social and educational indicators.

[21] E.g., Bureau of the Census, *Social Indicators III*. Washington, D.C.: Bureau of the Census, 1980; Bureau of the Census, *Social and Economic Characteristics of the Metropolitan and Nonmetropolitan Population; 1977 and 1970*. Washington, D.C.: Bureau of the Census, 1978. The latter publication is a valuable source for sociological and educational researchers, containing as it does comparative statistics on sex, race, education, occupation, and income.

logical and social change, agriculture, mental illness, crime, investments, distribution of wealth, education, and so on.[22] Campbell has emphasized the need for subjective indicators that assess satisfaction with life.[23]

We hazard a definition: *Social indicators* are concepts and associated statistics that reflect social conditions and human status and that under certain conditions can be used as variables in behavioral research. Examples are numerous: occupation, religion, birth rate, divorce, crime, voting, sex, race, unemployment, electricity consumption, alcohol consumption, and so on. Strictly speaking, social indicators are used by action agencies to assess social conditions and social change, to monitor the achievement of governmental social goals, and to study human and social conditions in order to understand and improve them. In this book, however, we stress their potential use as research variables, or as components of latent variables. For example, occupation, education, and income are social indicators that can be combined in some manner to measure the latent variable, "social class." Crime, unemployment, divorce, and other indicators can themselves be used as variables or they can be combined to measure, say, the latent variable "social unrest" or "social malaise." One can say that social indicators "indicate" or point to desirable and undesirable societal conditions that imply desirable and undesirable social trends. And this seems to be their chief meaning and use. They can also be profitably used as observed components of underlying unobserved or latent variables.

Social indicators, as the reader no doubt realizes by now, are usually objective indices calculated from aggregate statistics, statistics obtained from large social, governmental, or organizational units. Literacy, for example, might be reported as 95 percent literacy for such-and-such a population, meaning that 95 percent of that population can read. The use of so-called subjective indicators, however, will probably increase in the next decade. In the Survey Research Center study of the quality of American life mentioned in Chapter 24, for example, respondents were asked rather directly their feelings of well-being (see the questions on freedom and on satisfaction with life in the United States in Chapter 28). In his essay on subjective measures of well-being (see footnote 23), Campbell calls for use of such subjective measures, claiming that they go directly to life experience itself. In any case, both objective and subjective social indicators will probably be used much more in scientific behavioral research in the next decade, especially in multivariate research that explores and tests theories and hypotheses on the complex relations among psychological, sociological, and educational variables.

Educational indicators, similarly, should become increasingly important in scientific multivariate research on educational phenomena. Educational indicators are social indicators or variables that presumably reflect the state of education on national and local levels and, more interesting, the relations among social and educational indicators themselves, their influence on educational achievement, and the assessment of the success of large-scale educational programs. In a sense, large-scale studies like *Equality of Educational Opportunity* depend for their successful prosecution on the intelligent use of both objective and subjective social and educational indicators.

TYPES OF OBJECTIVE SCALES AND ITEMS

Two broad types of items in general use are those in which responses are independent and those in which they are not independent. Independence here means that a person's re-

[22] R. Bauer, ed., *Social Indicators*. Cambridge, Mass.: MIT Press, 1966. This appears to be the pioneer book on indicators.

[23] A. Campbell, "Subjective Measures of Well-Being," *American Psychologist*, 31 (1976), 117–124.

sponse to an item is unrelated to his response to another item. True-false, yes-no, agree-disagree, and Likert items belong to the independent type. The subject responds to each item freely with a range of two or more possible responses from which he can choose one. Nonindependent items, on the other hand, force the respondent to choose one item or alternative that precludes the choice of other items or alternatives. These forms of scales and items are called forced-choice scales and items. The subject is faced with two or more items or subitems and is asked to choose one or more of them according to some criterion, or even criteria.

Two simple examples will show the difference between independent and nonindependent items. First, a set of instructions that allows independence of response might be given to the respondent:

> Indicate beside each of the following statements how much you approve them, using a scale from 1 through 5, 1 meaning "Do not approve at all" and 5 meaning "Approve very much."

A contrasting set of instructions, with more limited choices (nonindependent) might be:

> Forty pairs of statements are given below. From each pair, choose the one you *approve more*. Mark it with a check.

Advantages of independent items are economy and the applicability of most statistical analyses to responses to them. Also, when each item is responded to, a maximum of information is obtained, each item contributing to the variance. Less time is taken to administer independent scales, too, but they may suffer from response-set bias. Individuals can give the same or similar response to each item: they can endorse them all enthusiastically or indifferently depending on their particular response predilections. The substantive variance of a variable, then, can be confounded by response set (but see footnote 6).

The forced-choice type of scale avoids, at least to some extent, response bias. At the same time, though, it suffers from a lack of independence, a lack of economy, and overcomplexity. Forced-choice scales can also strain the subject's endurance and patience, resulting in less cooperation. Still, many experts believe that forced-choice instruments hold great promise for psychological and educational measurement. Other experts are skeptical.

Scales and items, then, can be divided into three types: *agreement-disagreement* (or *approve-disapprove,* or *true-false,* and the like), *rank order,* and *forced choice.* We discuss each of these briefly. Lengthier discussions can be found in the literature.[24]

Agreement-Disagreement Items

There are three general forms of *agreement-disagreement* items:

1. Those permitting one of two possible responses
2. Those permitting one of three or more possible responses.
3. Those permitting more than one choice of three or more possible responses.

The first two of these forms supply alternatives like "agree-disagree"; "yes-no"; "yes-?-no"; "approve-no opinion-disapprove"; "approve strongly-approve-disapprove-disapprove strongly"; "1, 2, 3, 4, 5." Subjects choose one of the supplied responses to report their reactions to the items. In so doing they give reports of themselves or indicate their reactions to items. Most personality and attitude scales use such items.

The third type of scale in this group presents a number of items: subjects are instructed

---

[24] Edwards, *op. cit.,* and J. Guilford, *Psychometric Methods,* 2d ed. New York: McGraw-Hill, 1954.

to indicate those items that describe them, items with which they agree, or simply items that they choose. The adjective check list is a good example. The subject is presented with a list of adjectives, some indicating desirable traits, like *thoughtful, generous,* and *considerate;* and others indicating undesirable traits, like *cruel, selfish,* and *mean.* They are asked to check those adjectives that characterize them. (Of course, this type of instrument can be used to characterize other persons, too.) A better form, perhaps, would be a list with all positive adjectives of known scale values from which subjects are asked to select a specific number of their own personal characteristics. The equal-appearing interval scale and its response system of checking those attitude items with which one agrees is, of course, the same idea. The idea is a useful one, especially with the development of factor scales, scaling methods, and the increasing use of choice methods.

The scoring of agreement-disagreement types of items can be troublesome since not all the items, or the components of the items, receive responses. (With a summated rating scale or an ordinary rating scale subjects usually respond to all items.) In general, however, simple systems of assigning numerals to the various choices can be used. For instance, "agree-disagree" can be 1 and 0; "yes-?-no" can be 1, 0, −1, or, avoiding minus signs: 2, 1, 0. The responses to the summated rating items described earlier are simply assigned 1 through 5 or 1 through 7.

The main thing researchers have to keep in mind is that *the scoring system has to yield interpretable data congruent with the scoring system.* If scores of 1, 0, −1 are used, the data must be capable of a scaled interpretation—that is, 1 is "high" or "most," −1 is "low" or "least," and 0 is in between. A system of 1, 0 can mean high and low or simply presence or absence of an attribute. Such a system can be useful and powerful, as we saw earlier when discussing variables like sex, race, social class, and so on. In sum, the data yielded by scoring systems have to have clearly interpretable meanings in some sort of quantitative sense. The student is referred to Ghiselli's discussion of the meaningfulness of scores.[25]

Various systems for weighting items have been devised, but the evidence indicates that weighted and unweighted scores give much the same results. Students seem to find it hard to believe this. (Note that we are talking about the weighting of *responses* to items.) Although the matter is not completely settled, the evidence is strong that, in tests and measures of sufficient numbers of items—say 20 or more—weighting items differentially does not make much difference in final outcomes. Nor does the different weighting of responses make much difference.[26] It also makes no difference at all, in variance terms, if you transform scoring weights linearly. You may have subjects use a system, +1, 0, −1, and of course, these scores can be used in analysis. But you can add a constant of 1 to each score, yielding 2, 1, 0. The transformed scores are easier to work with, since they have no minus signs.

Rank-Order Items and Scales

The second group of scale and item types is *ordinal* or *rank order,* which is a simple and most useful form of scale or item. A whole scale can be rank-ordered—that is, subjects can be asked to rank all the items according to some specified criterion. We might wish to compare the educational values of administrators, teachers, and parents, for instance. A number of items presumed to measure educational values can be presented to the members of each group with instructions to rank order them according to their preferences.

[25] E. Ghiselli, *Theory of Psychological Measurement.* New York: McGraw-Hill, 1964, pp. 44–49.
[26] See Guilford, *op. cit.,* pp. 447ff.; Nunnally, *op. cit.,* pp. 296–297.

In her study of attitudes toward women's liberation, Taleporos developed a rank-order scale of social problems.[27] Subjects were asked to rank order the following social problems: Drug Addiction, Environmental Pollution, Race Discrimination, Sex Discrimination, Violent Crime, and Welfare. Taleporos expected that the two groups she was studying would rank the social issues similarly except for the issue Sex Discrimination. Her hypothesis was supported. This was a productive use of rank-order scaling.

Rank-order scales have three convenient analytic advantages. One, the scales of individuals can easily be intercorrelated and analyzed. Composite rank orders of groups of individuals can also easily be correlated. Two, scale values of a set of stimuli can be calculated using one of the rank-order methods of scaling.[28] Three, they partially escape response set and the tendency to agree with socially desirable items.

Forced-Choice Items and Scales

The essence of a forced-choice method is that the subject must choose among alternatives that on the surface appear about equally favorable (or unfavorable). Strictly speaking, the method is not new. Pair comparisons and rank-order scales are forced-choice methods. What is different about the forced-choice method, as such, is that the discrimination and preference values of items are determined, and items approximately equal in both are paired. In this way, response set and "item desirability" are to some extent controlled. ("Item desirability" means that one item may be chosen over another simply because it expresses a commonly recognized desirable idea. If a person is asked if he is careless or efficient, he is likely to say he is efficient, even though he *is* careless.)

The method of *paired comparisons* (or *pair comparisons*) has a long and respectable psychometric past. It has, however, been used mostly for purposes of determining scale values.[29] Here we look at paired comparisons as a method of measurement. The essence of the method is that sets of pairs of stimuli, or items of different values on a single continuum or on two different continua or factors, are presented to the subject with instructions to choose one member of each pair on the basis of some stated criterion. The criterion might be: which one better characterizes the subject, or which does the subject prefer. The items of the pairs can be single words, phrases, sentences, or even paragraphs. For example, in his Personal Preference Schedule, Edwards effectively paired statements that expressed different needs.[30] One item measuring the need for autonomy, for instance, is paired with another item measuring the need for change. The subject is asked to choose one of these items. It is assumed that he will choose the item that fits his own needs. A unique feature of the scale is that the social desirability values of the paired members were determined empirically and the pairs matched accordingly. The instrument yields profiles of need scores for each individual.

In some ways, the two types of paired-comparisons technique, (1) the determining of scale values of stimuli, and (2) the direct measurement of variables, are the most satisfying of psychometric methods. They are simple and economical, because there are only two alternatives. Further, a good deal of information can be obtained with a limited amount of material. If, for example, an investigator has only 10 items, say 5 of Variable *A* and 5 of Variable *B*, he can construct a scale of 5 × 5 or 25 items, since each *A* item can

---

[27] E. Taleporos, "Motivational Patterns in Attitudes Towards the Women's Liberation Movement," *Journal of Personality,* 45 (1977), 484–500.

[28] Guilford, *op. cit.,* chap. 8.

[29] *Ibid.,* chap. 7.

[30] A. Edwards, *Personal Preference Schedule, Manual.* New York: Psychological Corp., 1953.

be systematically paired with each *B* item. (The scoring is simple: assign a "1" to *A* or *B* in each item, depending on which alternative the subject chooses.) Most important, paired-comparison items force the subjects to choose. Although this may irk some subjects, especially if they believe that neither item represents what they would choose (that is, choosing between *coward* and *weakling* to categorize oneself), it is really a customary human activity. We must make choices every day of our lives. It can even be argued that agreement-disagreement items are artificial and that choice items are "natural."[31]

Forced-choice items of more than two parts can assume a number of forms with three, four, or five parts, the parts being homogeneous or heterogeneous in favorableness or unfavorableness. We discuss and illustrate only one of these types to demonstrate the principles behind such items. By factor analysis, a procedure known as the critical incidents technique, or some other method, items are gathered and selected. It is usually found that some items discriminate between criterion groups and others do not. Both kinds of items—call them *discriminators* and *irrelevants*—are included in each item set. In addition, *preference values* are determined for each item.

A typical forced-choice item is a tetrad. One useful form of tetrad consists of two pairs of items, one pair high in preference value, the other pair low in preference value, one member of each pair being a discriminator (or valid), and the other member being irrelevant (or not valid). A scheme of such a forced-choice item is

(a) high preference—discriminator
(b) high preference—irrelevant
(c) low preference—discriminator
(d) low preference—irrelevant

A subject is directed to choose the item of the tetrad that he most prefers, or that describes him (or someone else) best, and so on. He is also directed to select the item that is least preferred or least descriptive of himself.

The basic idea behind this rather complex type of item is, as indicated earlier, that response set and social desirability are controlled. The subject cannot tell, theoretically at least, which are the discriminator items and which the irrelevant items; nor can he pick items on the basis of preference values. Thus the tendencies to evaluate oneself (or others) too high or too low is counteracted, and validity is therefore presumably increased.[32]

Here is a forced-choice item of a somewhat different type, constructed by the author for illustrative purposes using items from actual research:

conscientious
agreeable
responsive
sensitive

One of the items (*sensitive*) is an *A* item, and one (*conscientious*) a *B* item. (*A* and *B* refer to adjectival factors.) The other two items are presumably irrelevant. Subjects can be asked to choose the one or two items that are most important for a teacher to have.

Forced-choice methods seem to have great promise. Yet there are technical and psy-

---

[31] In a study of Adler's concept of social interest (valuing things other than self), Crandall used pair comparisons to develop his Social Interest Scale: J. Crandall, "Adler's Concept of Social Interest: Theory, Measurement, and Implications for Adjustment," *Journal of Personality and Social Psychology*, 39 (1980), 481–495. Ninety traits were rated by judges for their relevance to social interest; 48 pairs were then used, one member of each pair having relevance for social interest, the other member not having such relevance. Then, after item analysis to determine the most discriminating items, a 15-item scale was developed. Unfortunately, Crandall does not report the form of the scale. The idea, however, is a good one: he used the strength of paired comparisons to find good items for a final scale.

[32] For further discussion, see Guilford, *op. cit.*, pp. 274ff.

chological difficulties, among which the most important seem to be the lack of independence of items, the perhaps too complex nature of some items, and the resistance of subjects to difficult choices. The reader is referred to Guilford's discussion of the subject: it is authoritative, objective, and brief, and to the reviews by Scott and Zavala.[33]

Ipsative and Normative Measures

A distinction that has become important and that is generally misunderstood in research and measurement is that between normative and ipsative measures. *Normative* measures are the usual kind of measures obtained with tests and scales: they can vary independently—that is, they are relatively unaffected by other measures—and are referred for interpretation to the mean of the measures of a *group,* individuals' sets of measures having different means and standard deviations. *Ipsative* measures, on the other hand, are systematically affected by other measures and are referred for interpretation to the same mean, each *individual's* set of measures having the same mean and standard deviation. To cut through this rather opaque verbiage, just think of a set of ranks, 1 through 5, 1 indicating the "first," "highest," or "most," and 5 indicating "last," "lowest," and "least," with 2, 3, and 4 indicating positions in-between. No matter who uses these ranks, the sum and mean of the ranks is always the same, 15 and 3, and the standard deviation is also always the same, 1.414. Ranks, then, are ipsative measures.

If the values 1, 2, 3, 4, and 5 were available for use to rate, say, five objects, and four people rated the five objects, we might obtain something like the following:

	1	2	2	3
	2	2	1	2
	3	4	5	3
	4	3	5	3
	5	5	4	2
Sum:	15	16	17	13
Mean:	3.00	3.20	3.40	2.60

Note that the sums and means (and standard deviations, too) are different. These are normative measures. Theoretically, with normative measures there are no constraints on the value that individual A can give to object C—except, of course, the numbers 1 through 5.

With ipsative measures, however, the procedure—in this case of ranking—has built-in systematic restraints: each individual must use each of 1, 2, 3, 4, and 5 once and once only, and he must use all of them. This means that when five objects are being ranked and one is given, say, Rank 1, there are only four ranks left to assign. After the next object is assigned 2, there are only three left—and so on until the last object to which 5 *must be* assigned. Similar reasoning applies to other kinds of ipsative procedures and measures: paired comparisons, forced-choice tetrads or pentads, *Q* methodology.

The important limitation on ipsative procedures is that, strictly speaking, the usual statistics are not applicable, since such statistics depend on assumptions that ipsative procedures *systematically* violate. Moreover, the ipsative procedure produces spurious negative correlation between items. In a paired-comparisons instrument, for instance, the selection of one member of a pair automatically excludes the selection of the other mem-

[33] *Ibid.*; W. Scott, "Comparative Validities of Forced-Choice and Single-Stimulus Tests," *Psychological Bulletin,* 70 (1968), 231–244; A. Zavala, "Development of the Forced-Choice Rating Scale Technique," *Psychological Bulletin,* 63 (1965), 117–124.

ber. This means lack of independence and negative correlation among items as a function of the instrumental procedure. Most statistical tests, however, are based on the assumption of independence of the elements entering statistical formulas. And analysis of correlations, as in factor analysis, can be seriously distorted by the negative correlations. Unfortunately, these limitations have not been understood, or they have been overlooked by investigators who, for example, have treated ipsative data normatively.[34]

CHOICE AND CONSTRUCTION OF OBJECTIVE MEASURES

One of the most difficult tasks of the behavioral researcher faced with the necessity of measuring variables is to find his way through a mass of already existing measures. If a good measure of a particular variable exists, there seems to be little point in constructing a new measure. The question is, however: Does a good measure exist? To answer this question may require much search and study. The student should first know what kind of variable he is trying to measure. Some guidance has been attempted with the structure just provided. One must know clearly whether the variable is an aptitude, achievement, personality, attitude, or some other kind of variable. The second step is to consult one or two texts that discuss psychological tests and measures. Next, consult Buros' justly well-known guides. While Buros gives excellent guidance to published tests, many good measures have not been commercially published. Thus the periodical literature may need to be searched. Although many scales are not commercially available, they can be reproduced (with permission) and used for research purposes.

Valuable sources of information on tests and scales are the journals *Psychological Bulletin, Educational and Psychological Measurement, Journal of Educational Measurement,* and *Applied Psychological Measurement.* One can track down measures, too, by checking *Psychological Abstracts,* which includes sections on new tests and measures. Review journals and volumes and handbooks often contain summaries and critiques of new measures: *Annual Review of Psychology, Review of Research in Education, Review of Educational Research, Handbook of Research on Teaching, The Handbook of Social Psychology.*

An investigator may find that no measure exists for measuring what he wants to measure. Or, if a measure exists, he may deem it unsatisfactory for his purpose. Therefore he must construct his own measure—or abandon the variable. The construction of objective tests and scales is a long and arduous task. There are no shortcuts. A poorly constructed instrument may do more harm than good, because it may lead the investigator to erroneous conclusions. The investigator who must construct a new instrument, then, has to follow certain well-recognized procedures and be governed by accepted psychometric criteria.

Tremendous progress has been made in the objective measurement of intelligence, aptitudes, achievement, personality, and attitudes. Opinion is divided, often sharply, on the value of objective measurement, however. The most impressive gain has been made in the objective measurement of intelligence, aptitudes, and achievement. Gains in personality and attitude measurement have not been as impressive. The problem, of course, is validity, especially the validity of personality measures.

Two or three recent developments are most encouraging. One is the increasing realiza-

---

[34] L. Hicks, ''Some Properties of Ipsative, Normative, and Forced-Choice Normative Measures,'' *Psychological Bulletin,* 74 (1970), 167–184. The reader is encouraged to set up a small matrix of ipsative numbers hypothetically generated by responses to a paired-comparisons scale. Use 1's and 0's and calculate the r's between items over individuals.

tion of the complexity of measuring any personality and attitude variables. A second is the technical advances made in doing so. Another closely allied development is the use of factor analysis to help identify variables and to guide the construction of measures. A third development (discussed in Chapter 27) is the increasing knowledge, understanding, and mastery of the validity problem itself, and especially the realization that validity and psychological theory are intertwined.

ADDENDUM

Criterion-Referenced Tests, Latent-Trait Theory, and Controversial Issues in Testing

There are two or three important developments in testing that students of research should know about. We do not elaborate them in this book because they are almost exclusively concerned with the assessment of educational achievement and mental ability. Nevertheless, behavioral researchers have to be aware of them and their importance. We confine this addendum to a few general remarks and recommended references for further study.

The Assessment of Achievement: Criterion-Referenced Tests

The idea of criterion-referenced testing—or content-referenced testing, a preferred designation of some experts—springs from the older notion of mastery learning: the notion of mastery by the individual of defined instructional and learning goals and the assessment of pupil attainment of the goals, or "mastery." In short, the stress is on what the pupil learns, on the criterion of learning set by teacher and pupil, on the goals of instruction. The "usual" criterion in testing is a group norm: the scores of individuals are assessed in relation to group norms—means and percentiles, for instance. Of course, teachers have for hundreds of years tested for mastery. The difference seems to be that pupils were expected to attain the criterion set by the teacher, whereas in the new approach the teacher and the pupil set goals, define task domains, and assess the achievement of the goals. The reader can profit from selective study of one or more of the following references:

> BLOCK, J., and BURNS, R. "Mastery Learning." In L. Shulman, ed., *Review of Research in Education,* vol. 4. Itasca, Ill.: Peacock, 1976, chap. 1. A good review of a controversial subject, with emphasis on research evidence.
>
> BLOOM, B. *Human Characteristics and School Learning.* New York: McGraw-Hill, 1976. Bloom argues eloquently (and controversially) that all children can be taught most things, given enough time and expert teaching.
>
> HAMBLETON, R., ed. *Contributions to Criterion-Referenced Testing Technology.* Whole issue of *Applied Psychological Measurement,* 4 (1980), No. 4.
>
> NITKO, A. "Distinguishing the Many Varieties of Criterion-Referenced Tests." *Review of Educational Research,* 50 (1980), 461–485. Authoritative review by a leading exponent of criterion-referenced testing.
>
> NUNNALLY, J. *Psychometric Theory,* 2d ed. New York: McGraw-Hill, 1978, pp. 265–270, 305–310. A critical and balanced assessment.

Latent Trait Theory and Testing

Latent trait theory is too technical to characterize briefly and adequately. It will probably affect educational and psychological research and thus needs at least to be mentioned. The more advanced student will find the following chapters helpful:

SUBOVIAK, M., and BAKER, F. "Test Theory." In L. Shulman, ed., *Review of Research in Education,* vol. 5. Itasca, Ill.: Peacock, 1977, chap. 7. More technical but clear discussions of criterion-referenced testing (pp. 277–294), test bias (pp. 294–299), and latent trait theory (pp. 299–310).

TRAUB, R., and WOLFE R. "Latent Trait Theories and the Assessment of Educational Achievement." In D. Berliner, ed., *Review of Research in Education,* vol. 9. Washington, D.C.: American Educational Research Association, 1981, chap. 8.

Controversial Issues in Testing

Test theory and practice have become highly controversial, especially the testing of mental ability. The student is directed to the test bias section of the Suboviak and Baker chapter, above, and to the following reference:

BERK, R., ed. *Handbook of Methods for Detecting Test Bias.* Baltimore: Johns Hopkins University Press, 1982.

The most troublesome problem of mental measurement is the heredity-environment issue. What are the relative contributions of heredity and environment to intelligence test scores?[35] Are racial differences innate or acquired? All students of behavioral research should be well-informed on the issues, the arguments, and the evidence. Two good references are:

BLOCK, N., and DWORKIN, G., eds. *The IQ Controversy.* New York: Pantheon, 1976. Valuable readings by leaders in the controversy.

LOEHLIN, J., LINDZEY, G., and SPUHLER, J. *Race Differences in Intelligence.* San Francisco: Freeman, 1975. Balanced, dispassionate treatment of a highly charged and difficult subject.

Professor A. Jensen, a central figure in the controversy, has written an important book on bias in mental testing.[36] Reviews by Bouchard and by Bond of Jensen's book, published in *Applied Psychological Measurement,* 4 (1980), 403–410, are highly recommended because they succinctly and expertly present the basic issues and problems of the controversy.

Study Suggestions

1. Here are a few references that may help students find their way in the large, difficult, but highly important field of objective tests and scales, especially in education.

ADKINS, D. *Test Construction: Development and Interpretation of Achievement Tests,* 2d ed. Columbus: Charles E. Merrill, 1974. An invaluable book for practitioners and researchers.

ANASTASI, A. "Evolving Trait Concepts," *American Psychologist,* 38 (1983), 175–184. Perhaps the best brief presentation available of theories of intelligence.

BLOOM, B., ed. *Taxonomy of Educational Objectives: The Classification of Educational Goals: Handbook I, Cognitive Domain.* New York: David McKay, 1956. This basic and unusual

---

[35] The reader will constantly encounter the expression "IQ," which is used as a virtual equivalent of "intelligence." The IQ, or intelligence quotient, was defined as mental age as determined by an intelligence test divided by the testee's chronological age, multiplied by 100. This quotient has fortunately been abandoned. Forms of standard scores are now used. Although the standard scores are not IQ's nor is "intelligence" equivalent to "IQ," the use of "IQ" by the popular press and even by social scientists seems fixed and ineradicable.

[36] A. Jensen, *Bias in Mental Testing.* New York: Free Press, 1980.

book attempts to lay a foundation for cognitive measurement by classifying educational objectives and by giving numerous precepts and examples. Pages 201–207, which outline the book, are useful to test constructors and educational researchers.

BUROS, O., ed. *The Eighth Mental Measurements Yearbook.* Highland Park, N.J.: Gryphon Press, 1978. Descriptions and reviews of published tests and measures of all kinds. See, also, earlier editions.

HARMAN, H., EKSTROM, R., and FRENCH, J. *Kit of Factor Reference Cognitive Tests.* Princeton, N.J.: Educational Testing Service, 1976. Very useful set of reference tests for researchers in psychology and education. Based on factor analytic studies.

MEHRENS, W., and EBEL, R., eds. *Principles of Educational and Psychological Measurement.* Chicago: Rand McNally, 1967. A valuable collection of many of the classic contributions to measurement and test theory and practice.

2. To gain insight into the rationale and construction of psychological measuring instruments, it is helpful to study relatively complete accounts of their development. The following references describe the development of interesting and important measurement instruments and items.

ALLPORT, G., VERNON, P., and LINDZEY, G. *Study of Values,* rev. ed. *Manual of Directions.* Boston: Houghton Mifflin, 1951.

EDWARDS, A. *Personal Preference Schedule, Manual.* New York: Psychological Corp., 1953. Measures needs in a forced-choice format (pair comparisons).

LIKERT, R. "A Technique for the Measurement of Attitudes." *Archives of Psychology,* no. 140, 1932. Likert's original monograph describing his technique, an important landmark in attitude measurement.

PACE, C. *CUES: College and University Environment Scales. Technical Manual,* 2d ed. Princeton, N.J.: Educational Testing Service, 1969. A well-developed set of five scales to measure aspects of college environment as seen by students. An especially good example of careful and competent scale development.

THURSTONE, L., and CHAVE, E. *The Measurement of Attitude.* Chicago: University of Chicago Press, 1929. This classic describes the construction of the equal-appearing interval scale to measure attitudes toward the church.

VERBA, S. and NIE, N. *Participation in America: Political Democracy and Social Equality.* New York: Harper & Row, 1972. See Appendix C, pp. 365–366, for the measure of socioeconomic status used in the study, and Appendix B, pp. 355–357, for the standard measure of participation used in the study.

WOODMANSEE, J., and COOK, S. "Dimensions of Verbal Racial Attitudes: Their Identification and Measurement." *Journal of Personality and Social Psychology,* 7 (1967), 240–250. Probably the best measure of attitudes toward blacks. The inventory is given in the Robinson, Rusk, and Head volume cited in Study Suggestion 3, below.

3. Here are three useful anthologies of attitude, value, and other scales. Their usefulness inheres not only in the many scales they contain, but also in perspicacious critiques that focus on reliability, validity, and other characteristics of the scales.

ROBINSON, J., RUSK, J., and HEAD, K. *Measures of Political Attitudes.* Ann Arbor: Institute for Social Research, University of Michigan, 1968.

ROBINSON, J., and SHAVER, P. *Measures of Social Psychological Attitudes.* Ann Arbor: Institute for Social Research, University of Michigan, 1969.

SHAW, M., and WRIGHT, J. *Scales for the Measurement of Attitudes.* New York: McGraw–Hill, 1967.

Chapter 30

Available Materials, Projective Methods, and Content Analysis

In this chapter we examine personal and societal products as sources of research data. Personal and societal products are materials, especially verbal materials, produced in the course of living by individuals and groups. The production of materials is also deliberately stimulated by scientists to provide measures of variables. This is the use of available materials, or materials whose creation has been stimulated for scientific purposes, to measure variables of research interest. The method to obtain variable measures from the materials is content analysis. If we study documents already written in order to measure, say, conceptual complexity, we are using available materials. The measures of conceptual complexity (for each document, perhaps) are obtained from the documents by specifying and following operational rules that tell us, in effect, whether a document or a part of it is conceptually complex. Or the rules may even specify the assignment of point-scale numbers to parts of documents. Such rules and procedures are the stuff of content analysis. On the other hand, we may ask children to write stories on given subjects in order to measure a variable or variables of interest. This is material whose production is deliberately stimulated for our purpose, and content analysis is similarly applied to the material. The method can be called projective. We will see what this means shortly. Our purpose, as always, it to understand methods and their use in behavioral research. It is not to master the methods. We do little more, in other words, than open up possibilities for the student of research whose task now is essentially to grasp and comprehend the nature of the complex methods we study rather than to master the methods and their use.[1]

[1] In the first and second editions of this book, the methods of this chapter and the following two chapters were discussed in considerably greater detail than in this edition. Detailed explanations are no longer possible because the methods have developed beyond the point of relatively brief description and explanation. Researchers who want to use content analysis, for instance, will have to give it special study.

AVAILABLE MATERIALS

Uses of Available Materials

A vast store of materials produced by institutions, organizations, and individuals is available for research purposes. Some of the possibilities of these resources are suggested below.

Researchers have to steep themselves in their materials. If they are studying boards of education and their functioning, they must not only know a great deal about education and boards of education generally; they must be quite familiar with the particular boards of education they are going to study. To become familiar with a sample of boards of education they can read the documents produced by the boards and their agents and the official and unofficial documents of the boards' policies, activities, and decisions. Thus the first purpose of the use of available materials is to *explore* the nature of the data and the subjects, to get an insight into the total situation.

A second purpose of available materials is to *suggest hypotheses*. While an investigator may have one or two hypotheses that he has deduced, say, from sociological or psychological theory, the study of available materials, like the minutes of board meetings, may suggest further hypotheses. In reading minutes, for example, an investigator may notice that certain boards seem always to reach unanimous decisions, whereas certain other boards rarely reach unanimous decisions. He may also notice that the boards that reach unanimous decisions also seem to have a higher level of education among their members. This suggests an interesting and perhaps theoretically important hypothesis.

A third use of available materials is to *test hypotheses*. For example, Beale, in his great study of freedom—or rather, lack of freedom—in public schools and teachers' colleges, tested implicit hypotheses on the relation between lack of freedom and other variables.[2] Much of Beale's source data came from available materials: newspapers, periodicals, books, public documents, court decisions, and so on.

Although beset with methodological difficulties, available materials can be deliberately used to test hypotheses. Tetlock, for example, tested Janis' groupthink hypothesis by analyzing the public statements of makers of American foreign policy.[3] He used content analysis, which we examine later, to identify in policy makers' public statements tendencies to treat policy-relevant information in biased ways and tendencies to evaluate one's own group members positively and one's opponents negatively. The statements were obtained from various archives. A more mundane use of available materials is to study trends and changes in social phenomena by examining governmental statistics.[4]

Another use of available materials to check on research findings was mentioned earlier when survey research was discussed: the use of census data to *check sample data*. If one has drawn a random sample of dwellings in a community in order to interview individuals, the accuracy of one's sample should be checked by comparing sociological data of the sample, like income, race, and education, with the same data of the most recent census or with available data in local government offices.

---

[2]H. Beale, *Are American Teachers Free?* New York: Scribner, 1936.

[3]I. Janis, *Victims of Groupthink*. Boston: Houghton Mifflin, 1972. P. Tetlock, "Identifying Victims of Groupthink from Public Statements of Decision Makers," *Journal of Personality and Social Psychology,* 37 (1979), 1314–1324. The essence of the hypothesis is that the intense social pressures toward uniformity in decision-making groups interfere with cognitive efficiency and moral judgment. "Groupthink" occurs when critical analysis takes second place to members' motivations to maintain group solidarity and to avoid disunity.

[4]One of many examples is: Bureau of the Census, *Social and Economic Characteristics of the Metropolitan and Nonmetropolitan Population: 1977 and 1970.* Washington, D.C.: U. S. Dept. of Commerce, Bureau of the Census, 1978. This is a good source of changes in the relations between sex and race and certain population variables like occupation and income.

Census and other official data—voting lists, housing registration, license registration, school censuses, and so on—are also used to help *draw samples*. To draw a random sample of a large geographical area is an expensive and difficult job. But it is not too difficult to draw random samples of single, smaller communities. Some school systems, for example, maintain relatively complete and accurate lists of taxpayers or families with school children. The point is that there are a number of available sources that can be used for drawing samples. Though none of these sources is perfect since records are kept for different purposes, with different degrees of accuracy, by people of different levels of competence, they are better sources of samples than the informed hunches of investigators.

Important Types and Sources of Available Materials

Five or six kinds of available materials seem to be most important for research purposes. Probably the first place to search and make inquiries is the university library. Modern librarians are trained professionals in unearthing materials for study. Use them! *Census and registration data* are often invaluable (see footnote 4), especially for large field studies and survey research. Check with a university library, and write the Superintendent of Documents, U. S. Government Printing Office, Washington, D.C. 20402, and the Bureau of the Census, Washington, D.C. 20233.

Extremely valuable sources of actual data have been stored in data archives for the use of researchers. Again, ask university librarians. There are guides available.[5] Mental achievement test scores of school pupils all over the country have been filed in data bases (see footnote 5). The important Human Relations Area Files contain voluminous data on many contemporary and even ancient societies.[6]

Other important sources of information and data are county clerks' offices (registration data, for example), local school districts, state education departments, and the U. S. Department of Education (Washington, D.C. 20202). Data on foreign countries can ordinarily be obtained from the consulates and embassies of the countries. (Write the appropriate embassy in Washington, D.C., for information.) Useful foreign educational and other information can be obtained from UNESCO, United Nations, New York, N. Y. 10017. Newspaper files and personnel, school records, and personal documents like letters and diaries are also useful sources of information and data.[7] There are, then, many sources of research information. The question is how to find them and use them. The above suggestions may help.[8]

---

[5] See: L. Conger, ''Data Reference Work with Machine Readable Data Files in the Social Sciences,'' *Journal of Academic Librarianship,* 2 (1976), 60–65; *Directory of Online Databases,* Cuadra Associates, 1983; V. Sessions, ed., *Directory of Data Bases in the Social and Behavioral Sciences.* New York: Science Associates/International, 1974; T. Li, *Social Science Reference Sources: A Practical Guide.* Westport, Conn.: Greenwood Press, 1980; E. Sheehy, ed., *Guide to Reference Books,* 9th ed. Chicago: American Library Associates, 1976 (is a guide to guides).

[6] See R. Lagacé, *Nature and Use of HRAF Files: A Research and Teaching Guide.* New Haven: HRAF, Inc., 1974; G. Murdock et al., *Outline of Cultural Materials,* 4th ed. New Haven: HRAF, Inc., 1971. Such files are more and more used in social scientific research, especially in conjunction with computer retrieval and analysis.

[7] G. Allport, *The Use of Personal Documents in Pychological Science.* New York: Social Science Research Council, 1942.

[8] An excellent guide to available materials is: R. Angell and R. Freedman, ''The Use of Documents, Records, Census Materials and Indices.'' In L. Festinger and D. Katz, eds., *Research Methods in the Behavioral Sciences.* New York: Holt, Rinehart and Winston, 1953, chap. 7. Although old, this is one of the only references on the use of available materials in behavioral research. More recent references on data archives are: L. Schoenfeldt, ''Data Archives as Resources for Research, Instruction, and Policy Planning,'' *American Psychologist,* 25 (1970), 609–616; F. Bryant and P. Wortman, ''Secondary Analysis: The Case for Data Archives,'' *American Psychologist,* 33 (1978), 381–387.

PROJECTIVE METHODS

We project some part of ourselves into everything we do. Watch a man walk. Examine an artist's drawings. Study a professor's lecture style. Observe a child play with other children or with toys and dolls. In all these ways human beings express their needs, their drives, their styles of life. If we want to know about people, then we can study *what* they do and the *way* they do it.

People also put part of themselves, their work, their attitudes, and their culture in the materials they create and store. Letters, books, historical records, art objects, artifacts of all kinds express, if indirectly and often remotely, life, society, and culture.

The Idea of Projection

Values, attitudes, needs, and wishes, as well as impulses and motives, are *projected* upon objects and behaviors outside the individual. A hungry individual may invest inedible objects with food properties. An individual with conservative social attitudes may see federal taxes as confiscatory. Each person, then, views the world through his own projective glasses.

It should be possible to study men's motives, emotions, values, attitudes, and needs by somehow getting them to project these internal states onto external objects. This potent idea is behind projective devices of all kinds. A basic principle is that the more unstructured and ambiguous a stimulus, the more a subject can and will project emotions, needs, motives, attitudes, and values. The *structure* of a stimulus, at least from one important point of view, is the degree of choice available to the subject. A highly structured stimulus leaves very little choice: the subject has unambiguous choice among clear alternatives, as in an objective-type achievement test question. A stimulus of low structure has a wide range of alternative choices. It is ambiguous: the subject can "choose" his own interpretation.

Another important characteristic of projective methods is their relative lack of objectivity, in the sense that it is much easier for different observers to come to different conclusions about the responses of the same persons. Recall that one of the powerful advantages of objective methods was that different observers agree on the scoring of responses. Projectives, on the other hand, are used precisely because they lack this desirable characteristic. Although different observers can score the same data quite differently, a serious weakness from the perspective of objectivity, this is a strength from the projection perspective. All tests and measures involve inference, as we have seen. Projective tests and measures require large inferential leaps indeed, larger than those of other methods. Thus their reliability and validity are difficult problems.

A significant virtue of projection and projective methods is that almost anything can be used as a stimulus. In addition to the well-known projective tests, like the Rorschach and the TAT—which will not be stressed in this chapter—the principle of projection can be used in many other ways; drawing pictures, writing essays, using finger paints, playing with dolls and toys, role playing, handwriting, telling stories in response to vague stimuli, associating words to other words, interpreting music.

Projective devices are among the most imaginative and significant creations of psychology. There is little doubt of their power, flexibility, and catholicity. But— and the "but" is a large one—can they be used in scientific research? Are their rather shaky reliability and validity inherent obstacles to their profitable use in research?

CLASSIFICATION OF PROJECTIVE TECHNIQUES

Lindzey's five-way classification of projective methods based on types of responses, first proposed in 1959, is still valid and useful today: association, construction, completion, choice or ordering, and expression.[9]

Association Techniques

These techniques require the subject to respond, at the presentation of a stimulus, with the first thing that comes to mind. The most famous device of this kind is the Rorschach test. The individual is asked by a highly skilled examiner to respond to inkblots of varying shapes and colors. The test is relatively unstructured—inkblots are vague and ambiguous— and allows full play of the subject's reactions and responses. The Rorschach, however, is more useful for clinical work than for research because of the very high skill required of the administrators and scorers of the test and because of its questionable—or at least doubtful—reliability and validity.

Word association methods are more promising. Emotionally tinged words are included with neutral words, and subjects are asked to respond with the first word that comes to mind. Getzels and Jackson, for example, used the technique to measure a presumed aspect of creativity: the ability to shift frames of reference.[10] Among the 25 words used were *arm, bolt, fair, leaf, policy*. Subjects were asked to give as many meanings as possible. The score was the total number of meanings given *and* the number of different categories into which the responses could be put. For instance, a subject might respond to *fair* with beautiful, light, just, equitable, unbiased, legible, average. The score of words produced is 7; the category score might be 4 or 5, depending on the system used.

Construction Techniques

Here the focus is on the *product* of the subject. The subject is required to produce, to construct, something at direction, usually a story or a picture. The stimulus can be simple, like asking children to tell a story about what happened to them yesterday, or complex, like the well-known Thematic Apperception Test (TAT). Generally some sort of standard stimulus is used.

Perhaps the most highly developed use of the construction technique has been the study and measurement of achievement motivation—need achievement, or *n* ach—by McClelland and his colleagues.[11] Subjects were shown four pictures that could be interpreted in a variety of ways. One of these, for example, was a boy sitting before a book, leaning on his left hand, and looking off into space. (Notice the ambiguity and my interpretation: he may be looking at something specific.) They were asked to write, in

---

[9]G. Lindzey, "On the Classification of Projective Techniques," *Psychological Bulletin,* 56 (1959), 158–168. Choice or ordering techniques (see below) are probably not true projective methods. Rather, they seem to be a means of objectifying projective devices. For example, an objective rating scale can be used with the TAT (Thematic Apperception Test), a test in which vague pictures are used as stimuli. The approach taken in this book and in this chapter that the various devices and methods are for the purpose of measuring variables seems not to be stressed in the literature. For an attempt to discuss the use of projectives in research, see J. Zubin, L. Eron, and F. Schumer, *An Experimental Approach to Projective Techniques.* New York: Wiley, 1965. For a thorough review of projective devices, including history, see H. Sargent, "Projective Methods: Their Origins, Theory, and Application in Personality Research," *Psychological Bulletin,* 62 (1945), 257–293.

[10]J. Getzels and P. Jackson, *Creativity and Intelligence.* New York: Wiley, pp. 199–200, 224–225.

[11]D. McClelland et al., *The Achievement Motive.* New York: Appleton, 1953.

about a minute, stories about the pictures. The stories were then scored for achievement imagery and motivation.[12] Other variables were then correlated with n achievement.

In a study of religious beliefs, Cline and Richards used TAT-type pictures with religious overtones and had their subjects tell stories about what was happening, what the people were thinking and feeling, and what would be the outcome.[13] The stories were scored for overall religious commitment, religious conflict, and so on. The average correlation between the projective measures of religious commitment and other measures of such commitment obtained from depth interviews and questionnaire items was .66, quite high for such measures.

Veldman and Menaker invented a remarkably simple yet effective projective device of the construction kind.[14] They simply told their subjects, teacher trainees: "Tell four fictional stories about teachers and their experiences." Judges who read the stories of different samples agreed on six general areas of content: Structural Features, Interest Qualities, Emotional Features, Characters and Activity, Role Identity, and Self-Ability and Competence. Within these areas were subareas, like coherence, realism, and general adjustment. A cluster analysis (a method that determines which variables go together, or are correlated with each other) revealed three basic clusters, which corresponded to professional aspects of teaching, problem-solving, and affective aspects of stories.

Completion Techniques

Schmuck measured the attitudes of school children toward school by having them complete sentences like: "Studying is _____." "This school _____."[15] The completed sentences were rated on a seven-point scale and combined into a single measure (the mean). Schmuck measured attitudes toward self similarly. Completion projective measures supply subjects with a stimulus that is incomplete, the subjects being required to complete it as they wish. It is obvious that responses of completion techniques are simpler than those of association and construction measures, thus simplifying the tasks of scoring and interpretation. The famous sentence-completion method is the best known of such techniques, but other types of completion measures, such as story completion, discussion completion, and others, are possible.

Choice or Ordering Techniques

These methods require simple responses: the subject chooses from among several alternatives, as in a multiple-choice item test, the item or choice that appears most relevant, correct, attractive, and so on. One might wish to measure need for achievement or attitudes toward blacks, for example, and present subjects with sets of pictures or sets of

[12] This research is exceptionally well documented. In *The Achievement Motive,* sample stories and scoring details are given. Moreover, the work has been carried over into other areas. McClelland has even raised the achievement motive of Indian businessmen by teaching them to score stories for n achievement: D. McClelland, "Toward a Theory of Motive Acquisition," *American Psychologist,* 20 (1965), 321–333. In addition, McClelland has used available materials to test his ideas cross-culturally: D. McClelland, *The Achieving Society,* New York: Van Nostrand-Reinhold, 1961.

[13] V. Cline and J. Richards, "A Factor-Analytic Study of Religious Behavior and Belief," *Jornal of Personality and Social Psychology,* 1 (1965), 569–578.

[14] D. Veldman and S. Menaker, "Directed Imagination Method for Projective Assessment of Teacher Candidates," *Journal of Educational Psychology,* 60 (1960), 178–187. There is also a manual with directions for scoring (see *ibid.,* footnote 5, p. 181).

[15] R. Schmuck, "Some Relationships of Peer Liking Patterns in the Classroom to Pupil Attitudes and Achievement," *School Review,* 71 (1963), 337–359.

sentences, each item of which expresses different degrees of achievement motivation or attitude toward blacks. Presumably the subjects, by choosing pictures or sentences they like or approve, will project their own needs for achievement or attitude toward blacks into the pictures or sentences. Of course, such sets of stimuli can also be ranked by subjects and inferences drawn from the rankings.

Expressive Techniques

Expressive projective techniques are similar to construction techniques: subjects are required to form some sort of product out of raw material. But the emphasis is on the *manner* in which they do this—the end product is not important. With construction methods, the content, and perhaps the style, of the story or other product are analyzed. With, say, finger painting or play therapy, it is the process of the activity and not the end product that is important. Subjects *express* their needs, desires, emotions, and motives through working with, manipulating, and interacting with materials, including other people, in a manner or style that uniquely expresses personality.

The principal expressive methods are play, drawing or painting, and role playing. There are, however, other possibilities: working with clay, handwriting, games, and so on. (I suspect that in the near future the expressive possibilities of microcomputers will be used.) The discussion that follows is limited to play techniques and role playing.

In the research use of play techniques, a child is brought into the presence of a variety of toys, often dolls of some kind.[16] He may be told that a set of dolls is a family and that he should play with them and tell a story about them. In their study of the effect of the presence of mothers on the aggressiveness of children, Levin and Turgeon used doll play to measure aggression.[17] Aggression was defined as acts that hurt, irritate, injure, punish, frustrate, or destroy the dolls or equipment. Two scores of aggression were used: total number of aggressive units per session and percent aggression (number of aggressive units divided by total number of units).

Role playing is the acting-out of a personal or social situation for a brief period by two or more individuals who have been assigned specific roles. It holds considerable promise as an experimental method and as an observation tool of behavioral research, though its research use has been limited.[18] The investigator uses an observation system (see Chapter 31) to measure variables. Or experimental variables can be manipulated using the technique. Group processes and interpersonal interaction, especially, can be conveniently studied. Hostility, prejudice, and many other variables can be measured. It has been the experience of role players that they say things they would rarely say under ordinary circumstances. They "come out" with things that surprise even themselves. The method, in other words, tends to bring out motives, needs, and attitudes that are below the social surface. While potent for bringing out emotions and needs, however, it must be recognized that role playing is perhaps an approach more suited to therapeutic and teaching situations than it is to empirical research.[19] The reason is that it is difficult to control role-playing situations so that research variables can be reliably and validly measured. In

[16]H. Levin and E. Wardwell, "The Research Uses of Doll Play," *Psychological Bulletin,* 59 (1962), 27–56.

[17]H. Levin and V. Turgeon, "The Influence of the Mother's Presence on Children's Doll Play Aggression," *Journal of Abnormal and Social Psychology,* 55 (1957), 304–308.

[18]J. Mann, "Experimental Evaluations of Role Playing," *Psychological Bulletin,* 53 (1956), 227–234.

[19]For a skeptical view of role playing as a research method, see C. Spencer, "Two Types of Role Playing: Threats to Internal and External Validity," *American Psychologist,* 33 (1978), 265–268.

this respect, role playing is a poor cousin of the experiment whose main virtue is a high degree of control of extraneous variables (see Chapters 22 and 23).

Yet we must not reject a useful method because it lacks virtues that other methods have. As usual, the nature of research problems and variables should, whenever possible, determine the use of methods of observation. It seems to be too easy to favor methods of observation and analysis because they have characteristics that we find attractive. I repeat: It is the nature of the problems and the variables of the relations studied that, whenever possible, should determine the methods we use. Steiner and Field's study of the effects of role taking on attitudes toward desegregation of schools is a good example of a judicious and fruitful use of role playing.[20] Subjects whose attitudes were for desegregation were put into three-man groups. Two members of each group had similar attitude scores; the third member was an accomplice of the experimenters. The groups were instructed to discuss the desirability of desegregating public schools and to attempt to reach agreement during the 15-minute experimental period. They were urged to take account of the views of a typical Southern segregationist, a typical Northern minister, priest, or rabbi, and a typical member of the National Association for the Advancement of Colored People. Roles were assigned to each group member in half the groups. The experimental subjects in these groups were assigned the Northern clergyman and NAACP roles. The accomplice was always assigned the Southern segregationist role. The treatment for the other 17 groups was the same except that group members were not assigned roles. The results indicated that the role assignment affected group members' perceptions of each other. When specific roles were *not* assigned, for example, subjects yielded more to the segregationist arguments of the accomplice and indicated greater preference for one another (rather than for the accomplice).

VIGNETTES

Various ingenious methods have been invented to measure variables in realistic but unobtrusive ways.[21] One of these methods, called vignettes, has considerable promise in behavioral research. *Vignettes* are brief concrete descriptions of realistic situations so constructed that responses to them—in the form of rating scales, say—will yield measures of variables. As usual, examples will perhaps be more enlightening than formal definition.

Pedhazur, in a study of "pseudoprogressivism" in education, presented his subjects with brief classroom episodes, vignettes that seemed democratic but that actually depicted phony "democratic" behaviors.[22] The instrument elicited the responses he predicted it would.

Alexander and Becker, following factorial design principles, constructed systematically modified descriptions of rape crimes in vignettes.[23] What this means is that the vignettes were so constructed that the sex, age, race, marital status, and so on of the rape victims were systematically varied to assess people's reactions to rape crimes. (The assumption was that respondents' assignment of responsibility to victims and assailants would vary with the descriptions of the victims.)

[20] I. Steiner and W. Field, "Role Assignment and Interpersonal Influence," *Journal of Abnormal and Social Psychology,* 61 (1960), 239–245.

[21] See E. Webb et al., *Unobtrusive Measures: Nonreactive Research in the Social Sciences.* Chicago: Rand McNally, 1966, pp. 75ff.

[22] E. Pedhazur, "Pseudoprogressivism and Assessment of Teacher Behavior," *Educational and Psychological Measurement,* 29 (1969), 377–386.

[23] C. Alexander and H. Becker, "The Use of Vignettes in Survey Research," *Public Opinion Quarterly,* 42 (1978), 93–104.

In her study of students' needs and ratings of teachers, Tetenbaum constructed and used vignette portrayals of twelve teachers.[24] The vignettes contained descriptions of teachers whose orientations were directed toward intellectual challenge and sustained effort in knowledge acquisition, toward support of students and facilitative of interpersonal relationships, and toward the encouragement of competitiveness and assertive leadership of their students. Tetenbaum predicted that student needs for cognitive structure and order, achievement, affiliation, and so on would be related to the different kinds of teachers portrayed in the vignettes, for example, students who had strong needs for affiliation would rate highly those teachers whose orientation was supportive of students.

It should be obvious that vignettes are a combination of expressive and objective ideas and projective methods. As such, they can be expected to be increasingly used in psychological and educational research because, constructed with imagination and ingenuity, they can be interesting to subjects, can measure complex variables, can be good approximations to realistic psychological and social situations. They can also be unobtrusive approaches to sensitive information about the subjects (*e.g.*, prejudiced attitudes, needs, and sexual preferences).

PROJECTIVE TECHNIQUES AND BEHAVIORAL RESEARCH: AN ASSESSMENT

Projective measures are probably the most controversial of psychological measurement instruments. They have been extravagantly praised and extravagantly blamed. In evaluating them, we must not confuse noble sentiments with reliable and valid methods of observation. The position taken in this book is that all methods of observation and measurement must satisfy the same scientific criteria. To argue that a method is valuable because it encompasses the whole personality or plunges into the unconscious mind evades the issue. The fact of the projective matter seems to be that the scientific canons of reliability, validity, and objectivity have not been adequately satisfied. What might a balanced view on projective methods be?

First, projective methods must be considered as methods of observation and measurement, just as any other methods are. As such, their purpose is to assign numerals to objects or events according to rules. The questions to be asked, as always, are: Can the numerals be assigned to the objects reliably? How valid are the procedures?

Second, then, projective methods must be subjected to the same type of reliability testing and empirical validation as any other psychometric procedures. This is not easy to do. Still, it must be done—and done well. Such empirical testing is almost more important with projectives than with other kinds of instruments because of the very long inferential leaps involved.

Third, attempts can and must be made to "objectify the subjective." Projective devices, as we saw earlier, have a large element of subjectivity of interpretation. Objectivity is defined as agreement among observers. This means, to repeat an earlier dictum, that independent and competent judges must agree on the scoring and interpretation of the data yielded by an observation method. How can this be done with projective methods? Suppose an investigator is trying to measure creativity. She shows children a picture and asks them to write a story about it. After the stories are written, she asks judges, whom she has already trained, to read the stories. In addition, she constructs a graphic seven-point rating

---

[24] T. Tetenbaum, "The Role of Student Needs and Teacher Orientations in Student Ratings of Teachers," *American Educational Research Journal*, 12 (1975), 417–433.

scale (or a numerical rating scale) of five items. Each item epitomizes a criterion of creativity as she defines it. Say that two of them are *originality* and *unusual approach*. She now asks her judges to rate the stories of all the children using the rating scale. To the extent that the ratings correlate highly, to this extent she has achieved objectivity. Other objective procedures can similarly be applied to the products of projective tests.[25]

To sum up, projective methods of observation, when considered as psychometric instruments and subjected to the same canons and criteria of scientific measurement as other instruments, and when used with circumspection and care, can be useful tools of behavioral research. A projective instrument should not be used, however, if you have a more objective instrument that adequately measures the same variable. Moreover, it is wise to avoid complex projective techniques, like the Rorschach and the TAT, which require highly specialized training and a good deal of perhaps questionable interpretation. (But note the outstanding use of the TAT by McCelland and his colleagues to measure *n* achievement and other needs.)

CONTENT ANALYSIS[26]

Content analysis is a method of studying and analyzing communications in a systematic, objective, and quantitative manner to measure variables.[27] Much content analysis in the past has not been done to measure variables, as such. Its recent greatly increased use in behavioral research, however, has been to measure variables that could not have been measured without it. This is not to denigrate past use to determine the relative emphasis or frequency of communication phenomena: propaganda, trends, styles, changes in content, readability. In this chapter, however, content analysis is considered as primarily a method of observation and measurement. Instead of observing people's behavior directly, or asking them to respond to scales, or interviewing them, the investigator takes the communications that people have produced and asks questions of the communications. There is a logic and economy about so viewing content analysis. In effect, we take it out of the purely analytic class and put it into the same class as interviews, scales, and other methods of observation. Thus we realize that we are doing nothing essentially different from previous observational activities: we are observing and measuring variables.

[25] In Chapter 27 we cited Amabile's measurement of creativity using what she called a consensual assessment method: T. Amabile, "Social Psychology of Creativity: A Consensual Assessment Technique," *Journal of Personality and Social Psychology,* 43 (1982), 997–1013. Her method is a good example of "objectifying the subjective." It first uses a global subjective approach that instructs judges to assess the creativity of products—collages, for example: a collage, recall, is an artistic composition of materials pasted on a surface of some kind—*using their own criteria of what is creative. The judges must have had experience with the products being judged.* After showing that the procedure was reliable, Amabile analyzed the judgments to determine which objective features of the products predicted the creativity judgments. These features, then, can be useful in future measurement and research. Note that somewhere along the line objective procedures are used; for example, Amabile had the judges rank and rate the collages and analyzed the results quantitatively.

[26] The discussion of this section leans heavily on the older treatments of Berelson and Holsti: B. Berelson, "Content Analysis." In G. Lindzey, ed., *Handbook of Social Psychology.* Reading, Mass.: Addison-Wesley, 1954, vol I, chap. 13; O. Holsti, "Content Analysis." In G. Lindzey and E. Aronson, eds., *The Handbook of Social Psychology,* 2d ed. Reading, Mass.: Addison-Wesley, 1968, vol. II, chap. 16. A more recent treatment of content analysis that emphasizes its use as a method of the measurement of variables is: J. Markoff, G. Shapiro, and S. Weitman, "Toward the Integration of Content Analysis and General Methodology." In D. Heise, ed., *Sociological Methodology 1975.* San Francisco: Jossey-Bass, 1974, chap. 1. Holsti has more recently published a text (see Study Suggestion 1).

[27] A number of definitions of content analysis have been offered by experts. The above definition departs from these by deliberately emphasizing the measurement of variables.

One of the most important characteristics of content analysis is its general applicability, especially now that the use and availability of computers make its application much easier than it used to be. It can be used with the productions of projective methods, with materials deliberately produced for research purposes, and with all kinds of verbal materials. We examine two or three examples from actual research to suggest some of these uses.

Revolutionary Leaders and Conceptual Complexity

Earlier, we cited Suedfeld and Rank's remarkable study of the success of revolutionary leaders.[28] Their hypothesis was that successful revolutionaries were characterized by a conceptually simple level of functioning *before* revolution, but that after takeover of the government, they exhibited greater conceptual complexity. Unsuccessful revolutionary leaders—that is, those leaders who failed in governing *after* the revolution but who had successfully achieved the revolution—were conceptually simple before the revolution and remained conceptually simple after the revolution. Success, the dependent variable, was suitably defined and measured as those individuals who were prominent before the revolution and who held important posts after the revolution until the end of their constitutional terms followed by voluntary retirement, or until natural death. Unsuccessful leaders were those individuals who did not satisfy these requirements. There were nineteen leaders of five countries of whom eleven were successful and eight were unsuccessful. Among the former were Oliver Cromwell, George Washington, Stalin, and Mao Tse-tung. Among the latter were Alexander Hamilton, Trotsky, and Guevara.

Measures of conceptual complexity for each leader were obtained by content analysis of letters, speeches, and documents using the Paragraph Completion Test.[29] The analysis of pre- and postrevolutionary complexity scores supported the hypothesis. The important point in the present context is that the variable conceptual complexity was measured through content analysis of the communications of revolutionary leaders.

Changes in American Motives

In another productive use of both a projective device and content analysis, Veroff and his colleagues measured the achievement, power, and affiliation motives of random samples of American adults in 1957 and again in 1976.[30] They did this by showing the respondents six pictures that had been selected to yield the best distributions of scores on affiliation, power, and achievement imagery. They asked the respondents to tell stories about the pictures—note the projective device—and then content analyzed (coded) the responses,

[28] P. Suedfeld and A. Rank, "Revolutionary Leaders: Long-Term Success as a Function of Changes in Conceptual Complexity," *Journal of Personality and Social Psychology*, 34 (1976), 169–178.

[29] H. Schroder, M. Driver, and S. Streufert, *Human Information Processing*. New York: Holt, Rinehart and Winston, 1967. The system for assessing conceptual complexity is explained in detail in Appendix 2 of this book. An example here, however, may help. Using a seven-point scale, a paragraph is scored 6 (high integration or complexity) if it indicates the simultaneous operation of alternatives and consideration of functional relations between alternatives (p. 189). In contrast, a paragraph (or subunit thereof) is scored 1 (low complexity) if it is generated by a fixed rule and no alternatives are expressed. Here is an example of a 1 response: "Rules are made to be followed. . . . They should not be broken." (p. 190).

[30] J. Veroff, C. Depner, R. Kulka, and E. Douvan, "Comparison of American Motives: 1957 versus 1976," *Journal of Personality and Social Psychology*, 39 (1980), 1249–1262. The authors did not use the expression "content analysis" in their report; they used the term "coding," which is the procedure used by the Survey Research Center, University of Michigan (and elsewhere) to "score" the results of interviews. (See discussion in chap. 24, above.)

which were taken down verbatim by the interviewers. They thus had motive scores for each member of the 1957 sample and for each member of the 1976 sample.

Their analysis of the results suggested that disturbing changes had taken place in American men. There was a decrease in men's affiliation motivation, and no change in their achievement motivation.[31] Women were more achievement-motivated in 1976 than they were in 1957, a finding to be expected in the light of the greatly changed conditions due to the women's liberation movement. Both men's and women's fears of power motivation increased. Veroff et al. say that this reflects increased fear of being controlled by others, a need for autonomy. This study is notable because it successfully used a projective method and content analysis to measure the motives of large random samples of the whole country.

SOME ASPECTS OF METHOD IN CONTENT ANALYSIS

Content analysis, it is clear, can be applied to available materials and to materials especially produced for particular research problems. One can content-analyze letters, diaries, ethnographic materials, newspaper articles and editorials, minutes of meetings, and so on. One can ask children or adults to write autobiographies, stories, essays. As hard as it may be for some people to stomach, essay test questions can be reliably graded using content analysis and the computer. But how is content analysis done? Some ideas were given in the examples above. In addition, a brief introduction to the subject is given below. The student who wants to use content analysis, however, should consult the references given in Study Suggestion 1.

Definition and Categorization of Universe

The first step, as usual, is to define U, the universe of content that is to be analyzed. In Veroff et al.'s study, U was all verbal replies to the questions asked the respondents. Categorization, or the partitioning of U, is perhaps the most important part of the analysis because it is a reflection of the theory or hypotheses being tested. It spells out, in effect, variables of the hypotheses. Veroff et al.'s main categorization seems to have been: achievement, power, affiliation, that is, verbal utterances that could be categorized under one or the other subhead. A great deal of thought, work, and care must go into these first steps.

Units of Analysis

Berelson lists five major units of analysis: words, themes, characters, items, and space-and-time measures.[32] The *word* is the smallest unit. (There can even be smaller units: letters, phonemes, etc.) It is also an easy unit to work with, especially in computer content analysis. An investigator may be studying value words in the writings of high school students. For some reason, he may wish to know the relation between sex or political preference of parents, on the one hand, and the use of value words, on the other hand. The word unit may also be useful in studies of reading. U can ordinarily be clearly defined and

---

[31] The reader who wishes to know more about these motives and their conceptualization and measurement should consult: J. Atkinson, ed., *Motives in Fantasy, Action, and Society*. Princeton, N. J.: Van Nostrand, 1958.

[32] Berelson, *op. cit.*, pp. 508–509.

categorized—for example, value words and nonvalue words; difficult, medium, and easy words. Then the words can simply be counted and assigned to appropriate categories.[33]

The *theme* is a useful though more difficult unit. A *theme* is often a sentence, a proposition about something. Themes are combined into sets of themes. The letters of adolescents or college students may be studied for statements of *self-reference*. This would be the larger theme. The themes making this up might be defined as any sentences that use "I," "me," and other words indicating reference to the writer's self. *Discipline* is an interesting larger theme. *Child training* or *control* is another. Many observers take field notes in a thematic manner. Here is an example from the field notes of an observer in a small village in Japan:

> *Food-Training:* . . . Use cajolery in this family—but it varies. Parents will leave something disliked (if child should be obstreperous about it) out of child's diet.[34]
>
> Informant's first child was fed whenever he cried, and the second child was started out that way; but after one month, informant fed second child on schedule. . . .[35]

It should be emphasized, as Berelson does, that if the themes are complex, content analysis using the theme as the unit of analysis is difficult and perhaps unreliable. Yet it is an important and useful unit because it is ordinarily realistic and close to the original content.

Character and *space-and-time* measures are probably not too useful in behavioral research. The first is simply an individual in a literary production. We might use it in analyzing stories. The second is the actual physical measurement of content: number of inches of space, number of pages, number of paragraphs, number of minutes of discussion, and so on.

Like the theme, the *item* unit is important. It is a whole production: an essay, news story, television program, class recitation or discussion. Getzels and Jackson used short autobiographies to measure creativity.[36] The unit was the item, the whole autobiography. Each autobiography was judged either "creative" or "noncreative." Children can be asked to write projective stories in response to a picture. The whole story of each child can be the unit of analysis. Judges can be trained to use a rating scale to assess the creativity of the stories. Or judges can be trained to assign each story to a creative or noncreative category.

It is likely that the item as a unit of analysis will be particularly useful in behavioral research. As long as pertinent criteria for categorizing a variable can be defined, and as

---

[33] Lest the reader underrate the value of analysis of single words, note that Mosteller and Tukey succeeded in identifying unidentified Federalist papers by Hamilton and Madison (determining whether the author of the unidentified papers was Hamilton or Madison or neither) by using only the words *and, in, of, the,* and *to*—and rather complex statistical analysis: F. Mosteller and J. Tukey, "Data Analysis, Including Statistics." In G. Lindzey and E. Aronson, eds., *The Handbook of Social Psychology,* 2d ed., vol. 2. Reading, Mass.: Addison-Wesley, 1968, pp. 80–203 (147–160). Rokeach and his colleagues also accomplished the same identification goal by analyzing value words and expressions: *freedom, equality, honor, a comfortable life,* for example: M. Rokeach, R. Homant, and L. Penner, "A Value Analysis of the Disputed Federalist Papers," *Journal of Personality and Social Psychology,* 16 (1970), 245–250. The basic method is simple in conception, complex in execution. One instructs the computer to determine the frequencies of the use of certain words in texts of known and disputed authorship. Appropriate statistical comparison of known and disputed texts should then settle the authorship matter. The content analysis is simple; the comparisons and judgments may be complex and difficult, especially if the authors of known and disputed texts espouse similar values, or have similar writing styles, as Hamilton and Madison did.

[34] Center for Japanese Studies, University of Michigan, Okayama Field Station, *863, Niiike,* August 25, 1950 (GB). ("*863*" is the Yale field number; "*Niiike*" is the Japanese village; "GB" is the observer.)

[35] CFJS, UM, OFS, *853,* Takashima, Dec. 18, 1950 (MFN).

[36] Getzels and Jackson, *op. cit.,* pp. 99–103.

long as judges can agree substantially in their ratings, rankings, or assignments, then the item unit is profitable to use. But careful checks on reliability and validity must be made. Judges can wander from the criteria, and they can lose themselves in the masses of reading they must do. Yet it is surprising how much agreement can be reached, even for rather complex material. In judging the creativity of student essays, teacher judges in Hartsdale, New York, achieved agreement coefficients of .70 and .80. Here, again, whole essays were the units.

Quantification

All materials are potentially quantifiable. We can even rank the sonnets of Shakespeare or the last five piano sonatas of Beethoven in the order of our personal preferences, if nothing else. It is true that some materials are not as amenable to quantification as certain other materials. After all, it is much easier to assign numbers to spelling performance than it is to assign numbers to original thinking or creativity. This does not mean, however, that no numbers can be legitimately assigned to children's products on the variables originality and creativity. It is not easy, but it can be done.

There are three or more ways to assign numbers to the objects of the content analysis U. The first and most common of these corresponds to nominal measurement: count the number of objects in each category after assigning each object to its proper category. Suppose we are reading reports of field observers, and we come to a passage, "babies are breast fed until two years of age, then gradually weaned to rice and gruel."[37] This theme might be assigned to the category "Permissive" or the category "Late Weaning." Then, in going through the observer's notes, we assign similar passages to these categories. The quantification would be the counting of the number of themes in each of the categories.

A second form of quantification is *ranking*, or ordinal measurement. If one is working with not too many objects to be ranked—say not more than 30—judges can be asked to rank them according to a specified criterion. Assume that the relations between religiosity and other variables are being studied, and subjects are asked to write on the subject "What I Believe." Judges might be asked to rank the essays on the degree of religious belief. If a large number of essays are involved, they can still be ranked, but a more manageable system than total ranking can be used, for example, 10 or 11 ranks can be made available, and judges can assign the ranks to the essays.

A third form of quantification is *rating*. Children's compositions, for example, can be rated as wholes for degrees of creativity, originality, achievement orientation, interests, values, and other variables.

Certain conditions have to be met before quantification is justified or worthwhile. Berelson has spelled out these conditions.[38] Two of his seven conditions should be noted: (1) to count carefully (or otherwise quantify) when the materials to be analyzed are representative, and (2) to count carefully when the category items appear in the materials in sufficient numbers to justify counting (or otherwise quantifying). The reason for both conditions is obvious: if the materials are not representative or if the category items are relatively infrequent, generalization from statistics calculated from them is unwarranted.

The answer to these two and other conditions, then, is to so select materials or to so have materials produced that quantification is possible. If materials cannot meet the criteria, they can be used only for heuristic and suggestive purposes and not for relating variables to each other.

[37] CFJS, UM, OFS, *853, Niiike,* Aug. 25, 1950.
[38] Berelson, *op. cit.,* pp. 512–514.

THE COMPUTER AND CONTENT ANALYSIS

The computer has profoundly changed content analysis, as it has changed data analysis. Fruitful investigations that could hardly have been conceived a decade ago are now possible. Content analysis is laborious because it involves the scanning of large quantities of materials, not to mention the preliminary work of setting up categories, defining units, and so on. Even with the computer, it can be laborious. Nevertheless, the most onerous aspects of the method are no longer onerous. Potentially at least, then, any problems involving verbal materials can be conceptualized and analyzed for research purposes.

It would take far too much space to describe adequately how the computer can be used in content analysis. Besides, this is one field that is rapidly evolving and changing; it certainly has not yet reached the sort of stability necessary for routine instruction. To give some idea of how the computer is used, and to encourage exploration of possibilities, we briefly describe the computer system known as "The General Inquirer."[39] Then we outline Page's system of grading essays with the computer to illustrate a functioning system.

The General Inquirer is a set of computer programs geared to the content and statistical analysis of verbal materials so generalized that it can be applied to a variety of research problems. Its aim is to free researchers from the details of computer operations and yet to enable them to use the computer flexibly. It locates, counts, tabulates, and analyzes the characteristics of "natural text."

The basis of the system is the "dictionary," which is a large set of words (or short phrases), each word being defined by "tags" or categories. For example, pronouns like *I, me,* and *mine* are tagged "self," and *army, church,* and *administration* are tagged "large-group."[40] These are called first-order tags; they represent the common or manifest meaning of the dictionary words.[41] Second-order tags represent the connotative meanings of words: status connotations and institutional contexts, for example. Holsti gives the example of a dictionary word "teacher," which is tagged with three meanings: job-role, higher-status, academic. The first is a first-order tag, the second and third second-order tags.[42]

Special-purpose dictionaries for a particular research problem are stored in the computer. For example, one such dictionary to analyze verbal materials for need achievement consists of about 800 entries with 14 tags (categories).[43] The rules for scoring materials for achievement imagery developed by McClelland and his colleagues[44] are behind the dictionary and computer program. Say a child has written a story. The whole story is punched on cards and fed into the computer. The computer scans the words in the story, tags those relevant to need achievement, counts them, and does other analyses. In this case the dictionary consists of words like *want, hope, become, gain, compete.* The words *want* and *hope* are tagged "need"; words like *fame* and *honor* are tagged "success."

The computer needs rules that it can use to identify tag sequences that indicate need for achievement. A simple example is when the tags "need" and "compete" appear in

---

[39] P. Stone et al., *The General Inquirer: A Computer Approach to Content Analysis.* Cambridge, Mass.: M.I.T. Press, 1966, especially chap. 3. See, too, Holsti, *op. cit.,* pp. 665ff.

[40] *Ibid.,* p. 666.

[41] Stone et al., *op. cit.,* p. 174.

[42] Holsti, *op. cit.,* p. 666.

[43] Stone et al., *op. cit.,* pp. 191–206.

[44] McClelland et al., *op. cit.*

one sentence.[45] The computer prints out the analysis and, on the basis of rules built into it, arrives at an overall assessment that a passage contains achievement imagery or does not contain it.

An important feature of The General Inquirer is that it has a number of dictionaries that can be used by researchers. The need-for-achievement dictionary just described is one. Another important one is The Harvard Third Psychosociological Dictionary, whose purpose is to provide a computer means of analyzing texts for classifying roles, objects, and dynamic processes. A researcher interested in a particular area can use one or more of these dictionaries to help him build a special dictionary to analyze his own data. For example, if one were interested in values and attitudes, one could provide the first-order words—like *private property, equality,* and *civil rights*—and use parts of The General Inquirer (or other system) to suggest tags or categories.

It is not possible to describe computer content analysis adequately. One has to use a system two or three times with actual problems. But to try to fill in a few of the gaps, let's look at Page's highly effective—and controversial—computer method of grading essays.[46] In one study, Page analyzed 276 essays written by students in grades 8 through 12. Four judges graded the essays for overall quality. These judgments were the criterion in*trins*ic measures, or ''trins,'' as Page calls them. The computer was programmed to measure 30 ap*prox*imation measures, or ''proxes''—again, Page's expression—or various characteristics of the essays: average sentence length, length of essay in words, use of uncommon words, number of commas, and so on. Each of these measures was used in an equation to predict the human ratings of the essays provided by the four judges. What amounts to a coefficient of correlation between a weighted average of the 30 measures and the human judgments was a remarkable .71! Subsequent work confirmed the ability of the computer—rather, the system—to judge and grade essays.

A Cautionary Note

Available materials, projective devices, and content analysis should not be used indiscriminately. It should be obvious that they are not easy to use and that, in most cases, there are better and easier ways to measure variables. If it is possible to use an attitude scale, then trying to measure attitudes with a projective device or the content analysis of available materials seems pointless and wasteful. There are research situations, however, in which certain variables are difficult or impossible to measure. One thinks of trying to measure ethnocentric attitudes in a veterans association. An attitude scale would probably be rejected, but an interview in which opportunities are given respondents to expand on their beliefs about their own groups and other groups might be possible. The results of the interviews can then be content analyzed for expressions of ethnocentricism.

Study Suggestions

1. The following references are useful beginnings in the use of available materials and content analysis.

[45] Stone et al., p. 201.
[46] E. Page, ''Grading Essays by Computer: Progress Report.'' In *Invitational Conference on Testing Problems, 1966.* Princeton, N. J.: Educational Testing Service, 1966, pp. 87–100.

BERELSON and HOLSTI chapters (footnote 26). These chapters are authoritative.

Stone book, chaps. 1 and 2 (footnote 39).

ANGELL, R., and FREEDMAN, R. "The Use of Documents, Records, Census Materials, and Indices." In L. Festinger and D. Katz, eds., *Research Methods in the Behavioral Sciences*. New York: Holt, Rinehart and Winston, 1953, chap. 7. One of the only references on available materials.

HOLSTI, O. *Content Analysis for the Social Sciences and Humanities*. Reading, Mass.: Addison-Wesley, 1969. A competent text.

MARKOFF, J., SHAPIRO, G., and WEITMAN, S. (footnote 26). Very good general chapter that emphasizes the use of content analysis to measure variables. Also has a good discussion of the *The General Inquirer*.

2. Read one or two of the following studies. They show what can be done with knowledge and ingenuity.

ALPER, T., BLANE, H., and ABRAMS, B. "Reactions of Middle and Lower Class Children to Finger Paints as a Function of Class Differences in Child-Training Practices." *Journal of Abnormal and Social Psychology*, 51 (1955), 439–448. A most ingenious and fruitful use of finger paints.

DeCHARMS, R., and MOELLER, G. "Values Expressed in American Children's Readers: 1800–1950." *Journal of Abnormal and Social Psychology*, 64 (1962), 136–142. Study of the values and motives expressed in 150 years of children's readers. The authors tested, among other things, the engaging hypothesis that *achievement motivation* is related to *inventiveness* as expressed by number of patents issued.

HILLER, J., MARCOTTE, D., and MARTIN, T. "Opinionation, Vagueness, and Specificity-Distinction: Essay Traits Measured by Computer." *American Educational Research Journal*, 6 (1969), 271–286. Interesting use of computer analysis of essays; measured three categories of writing style: opinionation-exaggeration, vagueness, specificity-distinctions.

McClelland book (footnote 11). Describes the theoretical and practical development of the famous need-for-achievement measure.

SKINNER, B. "The Alliteration in Shakespeare's Sonnets: A Study in Literary Behavior." *Psychological Record*, 3 (1939), 186–192. Used probability theory and content analysis to study Shakespeare's use of alliteration. Among other things, found that the line contained, on the average, 5.036 syllables, very close to pentameter!

TETLOCK, P. (footnote 3). Interesting but technically difficult.

TETLOCK, P. "Pre- to Postelection Shifts in Presidential Rhetoric: Impression Management or Cognitive Adjustment?" *Journal of Personality and Social Psychology*, 41 (1981), 207–212. Used content analysis of presidential policy statements before and after election to measure conceptual complexity.

WHITING, J., and CHILD, I. *Child Training and Personality*. New Haven: Yale University Press, 1953. Theoretically oriented content analysis study that fruitfully used the Human Relations Area Files (see footnote 6) to test psychoanalytic hypotheses.

WINTER, D., ALPERT, R., and McCLELLAND, D. "The Classic Personal Style." *Journal of Abnormal and Social Psychology*, 67 (1963), 254–265. Content analyzed stories to detect basic "themes" of a private secondary school and imaginative processes of its students. Fascinating.

WINTER, D., and McCLELLAND, D. "Thematic Analysis: An Empirically Derived Measure of the Effects of Liberal Arts Education." *Journal of Educational Psychology*, 70 (1978), 8–16. A modern and imaginative study of an old educational problem.

3. A useful class project would be for a class committee to find sources of available data. One huge source of educational data, for instance, is the data bank of Project Talent with its more than 500 variables and 400,000 secondary school students.[47] The National Center for Educational Statis-

---

[47] See J. Flanagan et al., *Project Talent: Five Years After High School*. Palo Alto: American Institutes for Research and University of Pittsburgh, 1971.

tics (U. S. Dept. of Education) releases data on more than 50,000 upper high-school students. For example, in June 1982, the data tape and codebook for the Twin and Sibling File, which is part of High School and Beyond, a national longitudinal study, was released. Another important source of cultural data is the Human Relations Area Files (footnote 6). (*Note:* A good source for this project is Schoenfeldt's article on data archives, which gives the names, addresses, and brief descriptions of major data archives in the United States and certain other countries—see footnote 8.)

Chapter 31

Observations of Behavior and Sociometry

Everyone observes the actions of others. We look at other persons and listen to them talk. We infer what others mean when they say something, and we infer the characteristics, motivations, feelings, and intentions of others on the basis of these observations. We say, "He is a shrewd judge of people," meaning that his observations of behavior are keen and that we think his inferences of what lies behind the behavior are valid. This day-to-day kind of observation of most people, however, is unsatisfactory for science. Social scientists must also observe human behavior, but they are dissatisfied with uncontrolled observations. They seek reliable and objective observations from which they can draw valid inferences. They treat the observation of behavior as part of a measurement procedure: they assign numerals to objects, in this case human behavioral acts or sequences of acts, according to rules.

This seems simple and straightforward. Yet evidently it is not: there is much controversy and debate about observation and methods of observation. Critics of the point of view that observations of behavior must be rigorously controlled—the point of view espoused in this chapter and elsewhere in this book—claim that it is too narrow and artificial. Instead, say the critics, observations must be naturalistic: observers must be immersed in ongoing realistic and natural situations and must observe behavior as it occurs in the raw, so to speak. As we will see, however, observation of behavior is extremely complex and difficult.

Basically, there are two modes of observation: we can watch people do and say things and we can ask people about their own actions and the behavior of others. The principal ways of getting information are either by experiencing something directly, or by having someone tell us what happened. In this chapter we are concerned mainly with seeing and hearing events and observing behavior, and solving the scientific problems that spring from such observation. We also examine, if briefly, a method for assessing the interactions and interrelations of group members: sociometry. Sociometry is a special and valuable form of observation: group members who of course observe each other record their reactions to each other so that researchers can assess the sociometric status of groups.

PROBLEMS IN OBSERVING BEHAVIOR

The Observer

The major problem of behavioral observation is the observer himself. One of the difficulties with the interview, recall, is the interviewer, because he is part of the measuring instrument. This problem is almost nonexistent in objective tests and scales. In behavioral observation the observer is both a crucial strength and a crucial weakness. Why? The observer must digest the information derived from observations and then make inferences about constructs. He observes a certain behavior, say a child striking another child. Somehow he must process this observation and make an inference that the behavior is a manifestation of the construct "aggression" or "aggressive behavior," or even "hostility." The strength and the weakness of the procedure is the observer's powers of inference. If it were not for inference, a machine observer would be better than a human observer. The strength is that the observer can relate the observed behavior to the constructs or variables of a study: he brings behavior and construct together. One of the recurring difficulties of measurement is to bridge the gap between behavior and construct.[1]

The basic weakness of the observer is that he can make quite incorrect inferences from observations. Take two extreme cases. Suppose, on the one hand, that an observer who is strongly hostile to parochial school education observes parochial school classes. It is clear that his bias may well invalidate the observation. He can easily rate an adaptable teacher as somewhat inflexible because he perceives parochial school teaching as inflexible. Or he may judge the actually stimulating behavior of a parochial school teacher to be dull. On the other hand, assume that an observer can be completely objective and that he knows nothing whatever about public or parochial education. In a sense any observations he makes will not be biased, but they will be inadequate. Observation of human behavior requires competent knowledge of that behavior, and even of the meaning of the behavior.

There is, however, another problem: the observer can affect the objects of observation simply by being part of the observational situation. Actually and fortunately, this is not a severe problem. Indeed, it is more of a problem to the uninitiated, who seem to believe that people will act differently, even artificially, when observed. Observers seem to have little effect on the situations they observe.[2] Individuals and groups seem to adapt rather

---

[1] In their excellent chapter on observation in classrooms, Medley and Mitzel say that the observer should use the least judgment possible: only a judgment "needed to perceive whether the behavior has occurred or not." This means, of course, the least inference possible. While their argument is well taken, it is perhaps too strong. D. Medley and H. Mitzel, "Measuring Classroom Behavior by Systematic Observation." In N. Gage, ed., *Handbook of Research in Teaching*. Skokie, Ill.: Rand McNally, 1963, chap. 6 (see pp. 252–253). K. Weick, "Systematic Observational Methods." In G. Lindzey and E. Aronson, eds., *The Handbook of Social Psychology*, 2d ed. Reading, Mass.: Addison-Wesley, 1968, vol. II, chap. 13, p. 359, supports Medley and Mitzel's view. At the same time, he argues for a more active role of the observer, as Cannell and Kahn argued for a more active role of the interviewer (see Chapter 28).

[2] R. Heyns and R. Lippitt, "Systematic Observational Techniques." In G. Lindzey, ed., *Handbook of Social Psychology*. Cambridge, Mass.: Addison-Wesley, 1954, vol. I, p. 399; Weick, *op. cit.*, pp. 369ff.

quickly to an observer's presence and to act as they would usually act. This does not mean that the observer cannot have an effect. It means that if the observer takes care to be unobtrusive and not to give the people observed the feeling that judgments are being made, then the observer as an influential stimulus is mostly nullified.

Validity and Reliability

On the surface, nothing seems more natural when observing behavior than to believe that we are measuring what we say we are measuring. When an interpretative burden is put on the observer, however, validity may suffer (as well as reliability). The greater the burden of interpretation, the greater the validity problem. (This does not mean, however, that no burden of interpretation should be put on the observer.)

A simple aspect of the validity of observation measures is their predictive power. Do they predict relevant criteria dependably? The trouble, as usual, is in the criteria. Independent measures of the same variables are rare. Can we say that an observational measure of teacher behavior is valid because it correlates positively with superiors' ratings? We might have an independent measure of self-oriented needs, but would this measure be an adequate criterion for observations of such needs?

An important clue to the study of the validity of behavioral observation measures would seem to be construct validity. If the variables being measured by an observational procedure are embedded in a theoretical framework, then certain relations should exist. Do they indeed exist? Suppose our research involves Bandura's self-efficacy theory[3] and that we have constructed an observation system whose purpose is to measure performance competence. The theory says, in effect, that perceived self-efficacy, or the self-perception of competence, affects the competence of a person's actual performance: the higher one's self-efficacy, the higher the performance competence.[4] If we find that self-perception of competence and measures of actual observed competence of doing certain prescribed tasks is positive and substantial, then the hypothesis derived from the theory is supported. But this is also evidence of the construct validity of the observation system.

The reliability of observation systems is a simpler matter, though by no means an easy one. It is often defined as agreement among observers. From this viewpoint, film and tape records can help to achieve very high reliability. Agreement among observers, however, has potential defects. For example, the magnitude of an index of agreement is partly due to chance agreement and thus needs correction. Perhaps the safest course to follow is to use different methods of assessing reliability just as we would with any measures used in behavioral research: agreement of observers, repeat reliability, and the analysis of variance approach.[5]

[3]A. Bandura, "Self-Efficacy Mechanism in Human Agency," *American Psychologist*, 37 (1982), 122–147.
[4]*Ibid.*, p. 122.
[5]Medley and Mitzel, *op. cit.*, pp. 309ff., give a thorough exposition of the reliability of ratings in an analysis of variance framework. But their discussion is difficult, requiring considerable statistical background. (See chap. 26, above.) Hollenbeck discusses reliability of observations when measures are nominal: A. Hollenbeck, "Problems of Reliability in Observational Research." In G. Sackett, ed., *Observing Behavior: Vol. 2. Data Collection and Analysis Methods*. Baltimore: University Park Press, 1978, chap. 5 (pp. 79–98). See, also, Weick, *op. cit.*, pp. 403–406, and G. Rowley, "The Reliability of Observational Measures," *American Educational Research Journal*, 13 (1976), 51–59. Assessing reliability and agreement among observers are especially difficult problems of direct observation because the usual statistics depend on the assumption that measures are independent—and they are often not independent. It is likely that approaches to these problems will change radically in the coming decade with the rapid development of multivariate methods and time-series analysis and the availability of computer programs to expedite both recording and analysis of observational data. Such programs should become available for microcomputers and consequently be convenient and cheap (though perhaps not easy to use).

It is necessary, then, to define fairly precisely and unambiguously what is to be observed. If we are measuring *curiosity*, we must tell the observer what curious behavior is. If *cooperativeness* is being measured, we must somehow tell the observer how cooperative behavior is distinguished from other kinds of behavior. This means that we must provide the observer with some form of operational definition of the variable being measured; we must define the variable behaviorally.

Categories

The fundamental task of the observer is to assign behaviors to categories. From our earlier work on partitioning, recall that categories must be exhaustive and mutually exclusive. To satisfy the exhaustiveness condition, one must first define U, the universe of behaviors to be observed. In some observation systems, this is not hard to do. McGee and Snyder, testing the hypothesis that people who salt their food before they taste it perceive control of behavior as being more from within the individual (dispositional control) than from the environment (situational control), simply observed subjects' salting of food in restaurants.[6] In other observation systems it is more difficult. Many or most of the observation systems cited in the huge anthology of observation instruments, *Mirrors for Behavior*, are complex and hardly easy to use.[7]

In keeping with the emphasis of this book that the purpose of most observation is to measure variables, we cite a classroom observation system from the highly interesting, even creative, work of Kounin and his colleagues.[8] The system reported is more complex than the salt-tasting observation system but much less complex than many classroom observation systems. The variable observed was task-involvement, which was observed by videotaping 596 lessons and then observing playbacks of the tapes to obtain the involvement measures. These measures were categorized as high task-involvement and low task-involvement. The authors also measured continuity in lessons by creating categories that reflected greater or lesser continuity in lessons. When the children's behavior was observed, they used the categories to record the pertinent observed behaviors.

Units of Behavior

What units to use in measuring human behavior is still an unsettled problem. Here one is often faced with a conflict between reliability and validity demands. Theoretically, one can attain a high degree of reliability by using small and easily observed and recorded units. One can attempt to define behavior quite operationally by listing a large number of behavioral acts, and can thus ordinarily attain a high degree of precision and reliability. Yet in so doing one may also have so reduced the behavior that it no longer bears much resemblance to the behavior one intended to observe. Thus validity may be lost.

On the other hand, one can use broad "natural" definitions and perhaps achieve a high degree of validity. One might instruct observers to observe *cooperation* and define

---

[6] M. McGee and M. Snyder, "Attribution and Behavior: Two Field Studies," *Journal of Personality and Social Psychology*, 32 (1975), 185–190. The correlation between food salting and control attribution was .71.

[7] A. Simon and E. Boyer, *Mirrors for Behavior*. Philadelphia: Research for Better Schools, 1970. This work has 14 volumes of behavior observation instruments! Most of these, 67 of 79, are for educational observations. Readers who intend to use behavior observation in their research should consult these volumes, especially vol. 1, which contains a general discussion, pp. 1–24.

[8] J. Kounin and P. Doyle, "Degree of Continuity of a Lesson's Signal System and the Task Involvement of Children," *Journal of Educational Psychology*, 67 (1975), 159–164; J. Kounin and P. Gump, "Signal Systems of Lesson Settings and the Task-Related Behavior of Preschool Children," *Journal of Educational Psychology*, 66 (1974), 554–562. We emphasize the Kounin and Doyle study.

cooperative behavior as "accepting other persons' approaches, suggestions, and ideas; working harmoniously with others toward goals," or some such rather broad definition. If observers have had group experience and understand group processes, then it might be expected that they could validly assess behavior as cooperative and uncooperative by using this definition. Such a broad, even vague, definition enables the observer to capture, if he can, the full flavor of cooperative behavior. But its considerable ambiguity allows differences of interpretation, thus probably lowering reliability.

Some researchers who are strongly operational in their approach insist upon highly specific definitions of the variables observed. They may list a number of specific behaviors for the observer to observe. No others would be observed and recorded. Extreme approaches like this may produce high reliability, but they may also miss part of the essential core of the variables observed. Suppose ten specific types of behavior are listed for *cooperativeness*. Suppose, too, that the universe of possible behaviors consists of 40 or 50 types. Clearly, important aspects of *cooperativeness* will be neglected. While what is measured may be reliably measured, it may be quite trivial or partly irrelevant to the variable *cooperativeness*.

This is the molar-molecular problem of any measurement procedure in the social sciences. The *molar approach* takes larger behavioral wholes as units of observation. Complete interaction units may be specified as observational targets. Verbal behavior may be broken down into complete interchanges between two or more individuals, or into whole paragraphs or sentences. The *molecular approach,* by contrast, takes smaller segments of behavior as units of observation. Each interchange or partial interchange may be recorded. Units of verbal behavior may be words or short phrases. Molar observers start with a general broadly defined variable, as given earlier, and observe and record a variety of behaviors under the one rubric. They depend on experience and knowledge to interpret the meaning of the behavior they observe. Molecular observers, on the other hand, seek to push their own experience, knowledge, and interpretation out of the observational picture. They record what they see—and no more.

Observer Inference

Observation systems differ on another important dimension: the *amount of inference* required of the observer. Molecular systems require relatively little inference. The observer simply notes that an individual does or says something. For example, a system may require the observer to note each interaction unit, which may be defined as any verbal interchange between two individuals. If an interchange occurs, it is noted; if it does not occur, it is not noted. Or a category may be "Strikes another child." Every time one child strikes another it is noted. No inferences are made in such systems—if, of course, it is ever possible to escape inferences (for example, "strikes"). Pure behavior is recorded as nearly as possible.

Observer systems with such low degrees of observer inference are rare. Most systems require some degree of inference. An investigator may be doing research on board of education behavior and may decide that a low inference analysis is suited to the problem and use observation items like "Suggests a course of action," "Interrupts another board member," "Asks a question," "Gives an order to superintendent," and the like. Since such items are comparatively unambiguous, the reliability of the observation system should be substantial.

Systems with higher degrees of inference required of the observer are more common and probably more useful in most research. The high inference observation system gives the observer labeled categories that require greater or lesser interpretation of the observed behavior. For example, suppose that *dominance* is to be measured. It can be defined as attempts by an individual to show intellectual (or other) superiority over other individuals, with little recognition of group goals and the contributions of others. This will of course require a high degree of observer inference, and observers will have to be trained so that there is agreement on what constitutes dominant behavior. Without such training and agreement—and probably observer expertise in group processes—reliability can be endangered.[9] Similar remarks are pertinent when we try to measure many psychological and sociological variables: cooperation, competition, aggressiveness, democracy, verbal aptitude, achievement, and social class, for example.

It is not possible to make flat generalizations on the relative virtues of systems with different degrees of inference. Probably the best advice to the neophyte is to aim at a medium degree of inference. Too vague categories with too little specification of what to observe put an excessive burden on the observer. Different observers can too easily put different interpretations on the same behavior. Too specific categories, while they cut down ambiguity and uncertainty, may tend to be too rigid and inflexible, even trivial. Better than anything else, the student should study various successful systems, paying special attention to the behavior categories and the definitions (instructions) attached to the categories for the guidance of the observer.

Generality or Applicability

Observation systems differ considerably in their *generality*, or degree of *applicability* to research situations other than those for which they were originally designed. Some systems are quite general: they are designed for use with many different research problems. The well-known Bales group interaction analysis is one such general system.[10] This is a low inference system in which all verbal and nonverbal behavior, presumably in any group, can be categorized into one of twelve categories: "shows solidarity," "agrees," "asks for opinion," and so on. The twelve categories are grouped in three larger sets: social-emotional-positive; social-emotional-negative; task-neutral.

Some systems, however, were constructed for particular research situations to measure particular variables. The salting food example, above, is quite specific, hardly applicable in other situations. The Kounin and Doyle system, while specifically constructed for Kounin's research, can be applied in many classroom situations. Indeed, most systems devised for specific research problems can probably be used, often with modification, for other research problems.

I want to emphasize that "small" observation systems can be used to measure specific variables. Suppose, for instance, that the *attentiveness* of elementary school pupils is a key variable in a theory of school achievement. Attentiveness (as a trait or habit) in and of itself has little effect on achievement: let's say the correlation is zero. But, the theory claims, it is a key variable because, with a certain method of teaching, it interacts with the method and has a pronounced indirect effect on achievement. Assuming that this is so, we must measure attentiveness. It seems clear that we will have to observe pupil behavior while the method in question and a "control" method are used. In such a case, we will have to find or devise an observation system that focuses on attentiveness. In assessing the influence of classroom environment, for example, Keeves found it necessary to measure

[9] See Weick, *op. cit.*, pp. 425ff. for a sophisticated discussion of inference in observation. See, too, pp. 428–432 for discussion of biases in observation, and suggested methodological solutions for minimizing the effects of bias. Another valuable source is Heyns and Lippitt, *op. cit.*, pp. 396–403.

[10] R. Bales, *Interaction Process Analysis*. Reading, Mass.: Addison-Wesley, 1951.

attentiveness.[11] He did this by observing students who were required to attend to tasks prescribed by the teacher. Scores that indicated attentiveness or the lack of it were assigned. This "small" observation system was reliable and apparently valid. It is likely that such targeted systems will be increasingly used in behavioral research, especially in education.

Sampling of Behavior

The last characteristic of observations, *sampling*, is, strictly speaking, not a characteristic. It is a way of obtaining observations. Before using an observation system in actual research, when and how the system will be applied must be decided. If classroom behaviors of teachers are to be observed, how will the behaviors be sampled? Will all the specific behaviors in one class period be observed, or will specified samples of specified behaviors be sampled systematically or randomly? In other words, a sampling plan of some kind must be devised and used.

There are two aspects of behavior sampling: *event sampling* and *time sampling.*[12] *Event sampling* is the selection for observation of integral behavioral occurrences or events of a given class.[13] Examples of integral events are temper tantrums, fights and quarrels, games, verbal interchanges on specific topics, classroom interactions between teachers and pupils, and so on. The investigator who is pursuing events must either know when the events are going to occur and be present when they occur, as with classroom events, or wait until they occur, as with quarrels.

Event sampling has three virtues: One, the events are natural lifelike situations and thus possess an inherent validity not ordinarily possessed by time samples. Two, an integral event possesses a continuity of behavior that the more piecemeal behavioral acts of time samples do not possess. If one observes a problem-solving situation from beginning to end, one is witnessing a natural and complete unit of individual and group behavior. By so doing, one achieves a whole and realistic larger unit of individual or social behavior. As we saw in an earlier chapter when field experiments and field studies were discussed, naturalistic situations have an impact and a closeness to psychological and social reality that experiments do not usually have.

A third virtue of event sampling inheres in an important characteristic of many behavioral events: they are sometimes infrequent and rare. For example, one may be interested in decisions made in administrative or legislative meetings. Or one may be interested in the ultimate step in problem solving. Teachers' disciplinary methods may be a variable.

---

[11] J. Keeves, *Educational Environment and Student Achievement*. Melbourne: Australian Council for Educational Research, 1972, pp. 62–65. This study also used a larger carefully conceived and constructed observation system: see pp. 89–100. The focus of the study, however, was on "process" variables: achievement press (*e.g.*, completion of homework), work habits and order, affiliation and warmth in the classroom, and so on. An influential school of thought in educational research emphasizes the importance of climate. Most of the measurement of climate, however, is accomplished with questionnaires that measure climate by asking questions of students and only rarely by direct observation. For a good review see: C. Anderson, "The Search for School Climate: A Review of the Research," *Review of Educational Research*, 52 (1982), 368–420. Another strong influence has been family environment research. Marjoribanks outlines the background and origins of this research: K. Marjoribanks, *Families and Their Learning Environment: An Empirical Analysis*. London: Routledge & Kegan Paul, 1979, chap. 2.

[12] See H. Wright, "Observational Child Study." In P. Mussen, ed., *Handbook of Research Methods in Child Development*. New York: Wiley, 1960, chap. 3. For a review of time sampling, see R. Arrington, "Time Sampling in Studies of Social Behavior: A Critical Review of Techniques and Results with Research Suggestions," *Psychological Bulletin,* 40 (1943), 81–124.

[13] Wright, *op. cit.*, p. 104.

Such events and many others are relatively infrequent. As such, they can easily be missed by time sampling; they therefore require event sampling.[14]

Time sampling is the selection of behavioral units for observation at different points in time. They can be selected in systematic or random ways to obtain samples of behaviors. A good example is teacher behavior. Suppose the relations between certain variables like *teacher alertness, fairness,* and *initiative,* on the one hand, and *pupil initiative* and *cooperativeness,* on the other hand, are studied. We may select random samples of teachers and then take time samples of their behavioral acts. These time samples can be systematic: three five-minute observations at specified times during each of, say, five class hours, the class hours being the first, third, and fifth periods one day and the second and fourth periods the next day. Or they can be random: five five-minute observation periods selected at random from a specified universe of five-minute periods. Obviously, there are many ways that time samples can be set up and selected. As usual, the way such samples are chosen, their length, and their number must be influenced by the research problem.[15]

Time samples have the important advantage of increasing the probability of obtaining representative samples of behavior. This is true, however, only of behaviors that occur fairly frequently. Behaviors that occur infrequently have a high probability of escaping the sampling net, unless huge samples are drawn. Creative behavior, sympathetic behavior, and hostile behavior, for example, may be quite infrequent. Still, time sampling is a positive contribution to the scientific study of human behavior.

Time samples, as implied earlier, suffer from lack of continuity, lack of adequate context, and perhaps naturalness. This is particularly true when small units of time and behavior are used. Still, there is no reason why event sampling and time sampling cannot sometimes be combined. If one is studying classroom recitations, one can draw a random sample of the class periods of one teacher at different times and observe all recitations during the sampled periods, observing each recitation in its entirety.

RATING SCALES[16]

To this point, we have been talking only about the observation of *actual behavior.* Observers look at and listen to the objects of regard directly. They sit in the classroom and observes teacher-pupil and pupil-pupil interactions. Or they may watch and listen to a group of children solving a problem behind a one-way screen. There is another class of behavioral observation, however, that needs to be mentioned. This type of observation

---

[14] If one takes the more active view of observation advocated by Weick (see footnote 1), however, one can arrange situations to ensure more frequent occurrence of rare events.

[15] In a fascinating study of leadership and the power of group influence with small children, Merei points out that time sampling would show only leaders giving orders and the group obeying, whereas prolonged observations would show the inner workings of ordering and obeying. F. Merei, "Group Leadership and Institutionalization," *Human Relations,* 2 (1949), 23–39.

[16] For an excellent discussion of rating scales, see J. Guilford, *Psychometric Methods,* 2d ed. New York: McGraw-Hill, 1954, chap. 11. Nunnally's discussion is also good: J. Nunnally, *Psychometric Theory,* 2d ed. New York: McGraw-Hill, 1978, pp. 594–607.

Although rating scales were mentioned earlier in this book, they were not systematically discussed. In reading what follows, the student should bear in mind that rating scales are really objective scales. As such, they might have been included in Chapter 29. Their discussion was reserved for this chapter because the discussion of Chapter 29 focused mainly on measures responded to by the subject being measured. Rating scales, on the other hand, are measures of individuals and their reactions, characteristics, and behaviors by observers. The contrast, then, is between the subject as he sees himself and the subject as others see him. Rating scales are also used to measure psychological objects, products, and stimuli, such as handwriting, concepts, essays, interview protocols, and projective test materials.

will be called *remembered behavior* or *perceived behavior*. It is conveniently considered under the topic of rating scales.

In measuring remembered or perceived behavior, we ordinarily present observers with an observation system in the form of a scale of some kind and ask them to assess an object on one or more characteristics, the object not being present. In order to do this, they must make assessments on the basis of past observations or on the basis of perceptions of what the observed object is like and how it will behave. A convenient way to measure both actual behavior and perceived or remembered behavior is with rating scales.

A *rating scale* is a measuring instrument that requires the rater or observer to assign the rated object to categories or continua that have numerals assigned to them. Rating scales are perhaps the most ubiquitous of measuring instruments probably because they are seemingly easy to construct and, more important, easy and quick to use. Unfortunately, the apparent ease of construction is deceptive and the ease of use carries a heavy price: lack of validity due to a number of sources of bias that enter into rating measures. Still, with knowledge, skill, and care, ratings can be valuable.

Types of Rating Scales

There are four or five types of rating scales. Two of these types were discussed in Chapter 29: check lists and forced-choice instruments. We consider now only three types and their characteristics. These are the *category rating scale,* the *numerical rating scale,* and the *graphic rating scale.* They are quite similar, differing mainly in details.

The category rating scale presents observers or judges with several categories from which they pick the one that best characterizes the behavior or characteristic of the object being rated. Suppose a teacher's classroom behavior is being rated. One of the characteristics rated, say, is *alertness*. A category item might be:

> How alert is she? (Check one.)
> Very alert
> Alert
> Not alert
> Not at all alert

A different form uses condensed descriptions. Such an item might look like this:

> Is she resourceful? (Check one.)
> Always resourceful; never lacking in ideas
> Resources are good
> Sometimes flounders for ideas
> Unresourceful; rarely has ideas

Numerical rating scales are perhaps the easiest to construct and use. They also yield numbers that can be directly used in statistical analysis. In addition, because the numbers may represent equal intervals in the mind of the observer, they may approach interval measurement.[17] Any of the above category scales can be quickly and easily converted to numerical rating scales simply by affixing numbers before each of the categories. The numbers 3, 2, 1, 0, or 4, 3, 2, 1, can be affixed to the *alertness* item above. A convenient method of numerical rating is to use the same numerical system, say 4, 3, 2, 1, 0, with each item. This is of course the system used in summated-rating attitude scales. In rating scales, it is probably better, however, to give both the verbal description and the numerals.

[17] Guilford, *op. cit.*, p. 264.

In graphic rating scales lines or bars are combined with descriptive phrases. The alertness item, just discussed, could look like this in graphic form:

| Very alert | Alert | Not alert | Not at all alert |

Such scales have many varieties: vertical segmented lines, continuous lines, unmarked lines, lines broken into marked equal intervals (as above), and others. These are probably the best of the usual forms of rating scales. They fix a continuum in the mind of the observer. They suggest equal intervals. They are clear and easy to understand and use. Guilford overpraises them a bit when he says, "The virtues of graphic rating scales are many; their faults are few," but his point is well taken.[18]

Weaknesses of Rating Scales

Ratings have two serious weaknesses, one of them extrinsic, the other intrinsic. The extrinsic defect is that they are seemingly so easy to construct and use that they are used indiscriminately, frequently without knowledge of their intrinsic defects. We will not pause to mention the errors that can creep into the unskillful construction and use of rating scales. Rather, we warn the reader against seizing them for any and all measurement needs. One should first ask the question: Is there a better way to measure my variables? If so, use it. If not, then study the characteristics of good rating scales, work with painstaking care, and subject rating results to empirical test and adequate statistical analysis.[19]

The intrinsic defect of rating scales is their proneness to constant or biased error. This is not new to us, of course. We met this problem when considering response set. With ratings, however, it is particularly threatening to validity. Constant rating error takes several forms, the most pervasive of which is the famous *halo effect*. This is the tendency to rate an object in the constant direction of a general impression of the object. Everyday cases of halo are: believing a man to be virtuous because we like him; giving high praise to Republican presidents and damning Democratic ones.

Halo manifests itself frequently in measurement, especially with ratings. Professors assess the quality of essay test questions higher than they should be because they like the testee. Or they may rate the second, third, and fourth questions higher (or lower) than they should because the first question was well answered (or poorly answered). Teacher evaluation of children's achievement that is influenced by the children's docility or lack of docility is another case of halo. In rating individuals on rating scales, there is a tendency for the rating of one characteristic to influence the ratings of other characteristics. Halo is difficult to avoid. It seems to be particularly strong in traits that are not clearly defined, not easily observable, and that are morally important.[20]

Two important sources of constant error are the error of severity and the error of leniency. The *error of severity* is a general tendency to rate all individuals too low on all characteristics. This is the tough marker: "Nobody gets an *A* in my classes." The *error of leniency* is the opposite general tendency to rate too high. This is the good fellow who loves everybody—and the love is reflected in the ratings.

An exasperating source of invalidity in ratings in the *error of central tendency*, the general tendency to avoid all extreme judgments and rate right down the middle of a rating

---

[18] *Ibid.*, p. 268.
[19] Guilford's advice is invaluable: *ibid.*, pp. 264–268 and 293–296.
[20] *Ibid.*, p. 279.

scale. It manifests itself particularly when raters are unfamiliar with the objects being rated.

There are other less important types of error that will not be considered. More important is how to cope with the types listed above. This is a complex matter that cannot be discussed here. The reader is referred to Guilford's chapter in *Psychometric Methods* where many devices for coping with error are discussed in detail.[21]

Rating scales can and should be used in behavioral research. Their unwarranted, expedient, and unsophisticated use has been rightly condemned. But this should not mean general condemnation. They have virtues that make them valuable tools of scientific research: they require less time than other methods; they are generally interesting and easy for observers to use; they have a very wide range of application; they can be used with a large number of characteristics. It might be added that they can be used as adjuncts to other methods. That is, they can be used as instruments to aid behavioral observations, and they can be used in conjunction with other objective instruments, with interviews, and even with projective measures.

EXAMPLES OF OBSERVATION SYSTEMS

Three or four observation systems were mentioned earlier. Other behavioral observation systems are summarized below to help the student get a feeling for the variety of systems that are possible and the ways in which such systems are constructed and used. In addition, the student may gain further understanding of when behavioral observation is appropriate.

Medley and Mitzel's Classroom Behavior Observation Record

One of the most carefully developed systems of classroom observation is the Observation Schedule and Record (OScAR), which was designed to permit the recording of as many significant aspects as possible of what goes on in classrooms.[22] The individual items were found to group themselves into three relatively independent and reliable dimensions: *Emotional Climate*, *Verbal Emphasis*, and *Social Organization*. That is, the items belonging to each of these dimensions, or factors, were combined and treated as variables. Two items from each of the first two dimensions, respectively, are: "Teacher demonstrates affection for pupil" (positive), "Pupil ignores teacher's question" (negative); "Pupil reads or studies at his seat," "Pupil (or teacher) uses supplementary reading matter." The third dimension reflects social grouping in classes—for example, a class broken up into two or more groups working independently. It can be seen that this is a low inference system.

Medley and Mitzel say that the three dimensions represent what are probably obvious differences between classes, but the OScAR fails to tap aspects of classroom behavior

---

[21] Systematic errors can be dealt with to some extent by statistical means. Guilford has worked out an ingenious method using analysis of variance. The basic idea is that variances due to *subjects, judges,* and *characteristics* are extracted from the total variance of ratings. The ratings are then corrected. An easier method when rating individuals on only one characteristic is two-way (correlated-groups) analysis of variance. Reliability can also be easily calculated. The use of analysis of variance to estimate reliability, as we learned earlier, was Hoyt's contribution. Ebel applied analysis of variance to reliability of ratings. See Guilford, *op. cit.*, pp. 280–288, 383, 395–397; R. Ebel, "Estimation of the Reliability of Ratings," *Psychometrika*, 16 (1951), 407–424.

[22] The system, with research data, is described in Medley and Mitzel, *op. cit.*, pp. 278–286.

related to achievement of cognitive objectives. They are probably too harsh on their own system. The three dimensions of OScAR *are* important.

Time Sampling of Attending and Disruptive Behavior

In their study of the social status of handicapped children, Morrison, Forness, and Mac-Millan used a time-sampling technique to record the behavior of all children in a classroom.[23] This involved observing and recording the behavior of each child in turn during six-second intervals until a minimum of ten intervals of each child's behavior each day had been recorded. As part of this procedure, observations of attending and disruptive behavior were made. Attending behavior was defined as eye contact to teacher, to a reciting peer, or to task materials. Disruptive behavior was defined as activity incompatible with on-task activity: talks to peer when not permitted, hits classmate, and so on. Attending and disruptive behaviors were found to influence teachers' ratings of the students' behavior and academic competence.

Observation and Evaluation of College Teaching

In one of the relatively few—and better—studies of college teachers and teaching, Isaacson and his colleagues, after considerable preliminary work on items and their dimensions or factors, had college students rate and evaluate their teachers based on their remembered observations and impressions.[24] They used a 46-item rating scale and instructed the students to respond according to the frequency of the occurrence of certain behavioral acts and not according to whether the behaviors were desirable or undesirable. Their basic interest was in the dimensions or underlying variables behind the items. They found six such dimensions of which the first they thought to be related to general teaching skill.

Although the six factors are important because they seem to show various aspects of teaching—for example, Structure, which is the instructor's organization of the course and its activities, and Rapport, which is the more interactive aspects of teaching and friendliness—we concentrate on the first. Here are three of the items:

> He put his material across in an interesting way.
> He stimulated the intellectual curiosity of his students.
> He explained clearly and his explanations were to the point.

The most effective item, however, was even more general:

> How would you rate your instructor in general (all-around) teaching ability?
> *a.* An outstanding and stimulating instructor
> *b.* A very good instructor
> *c.* A good instructor
> *d.* An adequate, but not stimulating instructor
> *e.* A poor and inadequate instructor

[23]G. Morrison, S. Forness, and D. MacMillan, "Influences on the Sociometric Ratings of Mildly Handicapped Children: A Path Analysis," *Journal of Educational Psychology*, 75 (1983), 63–74.

[24]R. Isaacson et al., "Dimensions of Student Evaluations of Teaching," *Journal of Educational Psychology*, 55 (1964), 344–351. A number of similar studies have been published since this study appeared, but it is still one of the best, I think. Note that here we have an observation system that was not devised deliberately to measure variables but rather to help evaluate teaching performance. Nevertheless, its two basic dimensions can of course be used as variables in research. A remarkable aspect of studies to evaluate college teachers is that researchers seem not to be aware that the purpose of such observation systems should be the improvement of instruction (or to use their dimensions as research variables) and not for administrative purposes. See F. Kerlinger, "Student Evaluation of University Professors," *School and Society*, 99 (1971), 353–356.

While we may question calling this study and others like it observation studies, there is certainly observation, though it is quite different in being remembered and indirect, global and highly inferential, and, finally, much less systematic in actual observation. We ask students to remember and rate behaviors that they may not have paid particular attention to. Nevertheless, the Isaacson et al. and other studies have shown that this form of observation can be reliably used in instructor and course evaluation.

Behavior Scores (BSs)

There are a number of important observation systems devised to study group interaction. The best-known is the Bales system mentioned earlier. Borgatta, too, devised a system, called Behavior System Scores (BSs), that is virtually an interaction analysis system.[25] It has the virtues of being brief, fairly simple, and based on factor analysis. Its six categories apparently measure two basic dimensions: *Assertiveness* and *Sociability*. Examples of the categories of behavior in each of the factors are: assertions or dominant acts (draws attention, asserts, initiates conversation, etc.) and supportive acts (acknowledges, responds, etc.). Such a system may be useful in behavioral research whose focus is group interaction and behavior—decision-making groups, for example.

ASSESSMENT OF BEHAVIORAL OBSERVATION

There is no doubt whatever that objective observation of human behavior has advanced beyond the rudimentary stage. The advances, like other methodological and measurement advances made in the last ten to twenty years, have been striking. The growth of psychometric and statistical mastery and sophistication has been felt in the observation and assessment of actual and remembered behavior. Social scientific research can and will profit from these advances. Many educational research problems, for example, strongly demand behavior observations: children in classrooms interacting with each other and with teachers, administrators and teachers discussing school problems in staff meetings, boards of education working toward policy decisions. Both basic and applied research, especially research involving group processes and group decisions, can profit from direct observation. And it can be used in field studies, field experiments, and laboratory experiments. Here is a methodological approach that is essentially the same in field and laboratory situations.

The difficulty in using full-scale systems, like Medley and Mitzel's, has undoubtedly discouraged the use of observation in behavioral research. But observations must be used when the variables of research studies are interactive and interpersonal in nature and when we wish to study the relations between actual behavior, like class management techniques or group interaction, and other behaviors or attribute variables. Important as is asking about behavior, there is no substitute for seeing, as directly as possible, what people actually do when confronted with different circumstances and different people. Moreover, in much, perhaps most, behavioral research, it is probably not necessary to use the larger observation systems. As shown earlier, smaller systems can be devised for special research purposes. Keeves' limited system was highly appropriate for his purpose. In any case, scientific behavioral research requires direct and indirect observations of behavior, and the technical means of making such observations are becoming increasingly adequate

[25] E. Borgatta, ''A New Systematic Observation System: Behavior Scores System (BSs System),'' *Journal of Psychological Studies*, 14 (1963), 24–44. Also described briefly by Weick, *op. cit.*, pp. 400–401.

and available. The next decade should see considerable understanding and improvement of methods of observation, as well as their increased meaningful use.

SOCIOMETRY

We constantly assess the people we work with, go to school with, live at home with. We judge them for their suitability to work with us, play with us, live with us. And we base our judgments on our observations of their behavior in different situations. We judge, we say, on the basis of our "experience." The form of measurement we now consider, sociometry, is based on these many informal observations. Again, the method is based on remembered observations and the inevitable judgments we make of people after observing them.

Sociometry and Sociometric Choice

Sociometry is a broad term indicating a number of methods of gathering and analyzing data on the choice, communication, and interaction patterns of individuals in groups. One might say that sociometry is the study and measurement of social choice. It has also been called a means of studying the attractions and repulsions of members of groups.

A person is asked to choose one or more other persons according to one or more criteria supplied by the researcher: With whom would you like to work? With whom would you like to play? He then makes one, two, three, or more choices among the members of his own group (usually) or of other groups. What could be simpler and more natural? The method works well for kindergartners and for atomic scientists.

Sociometric choice should be rather broadly understood: it not only means "choice of people"; it may mean "choice of lines of communication," "choice of lines of influence," or "choice of minority groups." The choices depend upon the instructions and questions given to individuals. Here is a list of sociometric questions and instructions:

With whom would you like to work (play, sit next to, and so on)?
Which two members of this group (age group, class, club, for instance) do you like the most (the least)?
Who are the three best (worst) pupils in your class?
Whom would you choose to represent you on a committee to improve faculty welfare?
What four individuals have the greatest prestige in your organization (class, company, team)?
What two groups of people are the most acceptable (least acceptable) to you as neighbors (friends, business associates, professional associates)?

Obviously, there are many possibilities.[26] In addition, these can be multiplied simply by asking: Who do you think would choose you to . . . ? and Whom do you think the group would choose to . . . ? Subjects can also be asked to rank others using sociometric criteria, providing there are not too many to rank. Or rating scales can be used. Members of a group or organization can be asked to rate each other using one or more criteria. For example, we can phrase the sociometric instructions something like this: "Here is a list of the members of your group. Rate each according to whether you would like to work with him on a committee to draft a set of bylaws. Use the numbers 4, 3, 2, 1, 0—4 meaning you would like to work with him very much, 0 you would not want to work with him at

---

[26] For further discussion, see G. Lindzey and D. Byrne, "Measurement of Social Choice and Interpersonal Attractiveness." In G. Lindzey and E. Aronson, eds., *The Handbook of Social Psychology*, 2d ed. Reading, Mass.: Addison-Wesley, 1968, vol. II, chap. 14.

all, and the other numbers representing intermediate degrees of liking to work with him.'' Clearly, other methods of measurement can be used. The main difference is that sociometry always has such ideas as social choice, interaction, communication, and influence behind it.

METHODS OF SOCIOMETRIC ANALYSIS

There are three basic forms of sociometric analysis: *sociometric matrices*, *sociograms* or *directed graphs*, and *sociometric indices*. Of methods of sociometric analysis, *sociometric matrices*, to be defined presently, perhaps contain the most important possibilities and implications for the behavioral researcher. *Sociograms* are diagrams or charts of the choices made in groups. We shall discuss sociograms or directed graphs very little since they are either used more for practical than for research purposes or their analysis is mathematical and difficult, requiring much more space than we can spare.[27] *Sociometric indices* are single numbers calculated from two or more numbers yielded by sociometric data. They indicate sociometric characteristics of individuals and groups.

Sociometric Matrices[28]

We learned earlier that a *matrix* is a rectangular array of numbers or other symbols. In sociometry we are usually concerned mainly with square, or $n \times n$ matrices, n being equal to the number of persons in a group. Rows of the matrix are labeled i; columns are labeled j; i and j, of course, can stand for any number and any person in the group. If we write a_{ij}, this means the entry in the ith row and jth column of the matrix, or, more simply, any entry in the matrix. It is convenient to write *sociometric matrices*. These are matrices of numbers expressing all the choices of group members in any group.

Suppose a group of five members has responded to the sociometric question, ''With whom would you like to work on such-and-such a project during the next two months? Choose two individuals.'' The responses to the sociometric question are, of course, *choices*. If a group member chooses another group member, the choice is represented by 1. If a group member does not choose another, the lack of choice is represented by 0. (If rejection had been called for, -1 could have been used.) The sociometric matrix of choices, C, of this hypothetical group situation is given in Table 31.1.

It is possible to analyze the matrix in a number of ways. But first let us be sure we know how to read the matrix. It is probably easier to read from left to right, from i to j. Member i chooses (or does not choose) member j. For example, a chooses b and e; c chooses d and e. Sometimes it is convenient to speak passively, ''b was chosen by a, d, and e,'' or ''c was chosen by no one.''

---

[27] See F. Ove, ''A Survey of Statistical Methods for Graph Analysis.'' In S. Leinhardt, ed., *Sociological Methodology 1981*. San Francisco: Jossey-Bass, 1981, chap. 3; S. Fienberg and S. Wasserman, ''Categorical Data Analysis of Single Sociometric Relations.'' In *ibid.*, chap. 4. The latter chapter is important because it shows, among other things, the application of log-linear analysis (see chap. 10, Addendum, above) to sociometric data.

[28] See Lindzey and Byrne, *op. cit.*, pp. 470–473, for a good review of matrix analysis. Explanation of elementary matrix operations and sociometric matrices can be found in: J. Kemeny, J. Snell, and G. Thompson, *Introduction to Finite Mathematics*, 2d ed. Englewood Cliffs, N.J.: Prentice-Hall, 1966, pp. 217–250, 384–406. An old but valuable review of mathematical and statistical methods for analyzing group structure and communication is: M. Glanzer and R. Glaser, ''Techniques for the Study of Group Structure and Behavior: Analysis of Structure,'' *Psychological Bulletin*, 56 (1959), 317–332.

Table 31.1   Sociometric Choice Matrix: Five-member Group, Two-Choice Question[a]

		j				
		a	b	c	d	e
	a	0	1	0	0	1
	b	1	0	0	0	1
i	c	0	0	0	1	1
	d	0	1	0	0	1
	e	1	1	0	0	0
	Σ:	2	3	0	1	4

[a] Individual i *chooses* individual j. That is, the table can be read by rows: b chooses a and e. It can also be read by columns: b *is chosen* by a, d, and e. The sums at the bottom indicate the number of choices each individual receives.

The analysis of a matrix usually begins by studying it to see who chose whom. With a simple matrix this is easy. There are three kinds of choice: *simple* or one-way, *mutual* or two-way, and *no choice*. We look first at simple choices. (This was discussed in the preceding paragraph.) A *simple* one-way choice is where i chooses j, but j does not choose i. In Table 31.1, c chose d, but d did not choose c. We write: $i \rightarrow j$, or $c \rightarrow d$. A *mutual* choice is where i chooses j and j also chooses i. In the table, a chose b and b chose a. We write: $i \leftrightarrow j$, or $a \leftrightarrow b$. We might count mutual choices in Table 31.1: $a \leftrightarrow b$, $a \leftrightarrow e$, $b \leftrightarrow e$.

The extent to which any member is chosen is easily seen by adding the columns of the matrix. Obviously, e is "popular": he was chosen by all the other group members; a and b received 2 and 3 choices, respectively. Evidently c is not at all popular: no one chose him; d is not popular either: he received only 1 choice. If individuals are allowed unlimited choices, that is, if they are instructed to choose any number of other individuals, then the row sums take on meaning.[29] We might call these sums indices of, say, *gregariousness*.

There are other methods of matrix analysis that are potentially useful to researchers. For example, by relatively simple matrix operations one can determine cliques and chains of influence in small and large groups. These matters, however, are beyond the scope of this book.

Sociograms or Directed Graphs

The simplest analyses are like those just discussed. But with a matrix larger than the one in Table 31.1 it is almost impossible to digest the complexities of the choice relations. Here *sociograms* are helpful, provided the group is not too large. We now change the name "sociogram" to "directed graph." This is a more general mathematical term that can be applied to any situation in which i and j are in some relation R. Instead of saying "i chooses j," it is quite possible to say "i influences j," or "i communicates to j," or "i is a friend of j," or "i dominates j." In symbolic shorthand, we can write, generally: iRj. Specifically, we can write for the examples just given: iCj (i chooses j), iIj (i influences j), iCj (i communicates to j), iFj (i is a friend of j), iDj (i dominates j). Any of these

[29] Subjects can be told to choose one, two, three, or more other persons. Three seems to be a common number of choices. The number allowed should be dictated by the research purposes. See Lindzey and Byrne, *op. cit.*, pp. 455–456.

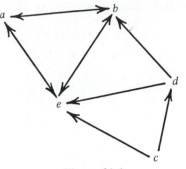

Figure 31.1

interpretations can be depicted by a matrix such as that of Table 31.1 and by a directed graph. A directed graph is given in Figure 31.1.

We see at a glance that e is the center of choice. We might call him a leader. Or we might call him either a likable or competent person. More important, notice that a, b, and e choose each other. This is a clique. We define a *clique* as three or more individuals who mutually choose each other.[30] Looking for more double-headed arrows, we find none. Now we might look for individuals with no arrowheads pointing at them: c is one such individual. We can say that c is not chosen or neglected.

Note that directed graphs and matrices say the same thing. We look at the number of choices a receives by adding the 1's in the a column of the matrix. We get the same information by adding the number of arrowheads pointing at a in the graph. For small and medium-size groups and for descriptive purposes, graphs are excellent means of summarizing group relations. For larger groups (larger than 20 members?) and more analytic purposes, they are not as suitable. They become difficult to construct and to interpret. Moreover, different individuals can draw different graphs with the same data. Matrices are general, and, if handled properly, not too difficult to interpret. Different individuals must, with the same data, write exactly the same matrices.

Sociometric Indices[31]

In sociometry many indices are possible. Three are given below. The student will find others in the literature.

A simple but useful index is:

$$CS_j = \frac{\Sigma c_j}{n - 1} \tag{31.1}$$

where CS_j = the choice status of Person j; Σc_j = the sum of choices in Column j; and n = the number of individuals in the group ($n - 1$ is used because one cannot count the individual himself). For C of Table 31.1, $CS_e = 4/4 = 1.00$ and $CS_a = 2/4 = .50$. How

[30] L. Festinger, S. Schachter, and K. Back, *Social Pressures in Informal Groups*. New York: Harper & Row, 1950, p. 144. This book is not only a report of highly interesting research; it also contains a valuable method for identifying cliques in groups. See, also, Glanzer and Glaser, *op. cit.*, pp. 326–327, which succinctly outlines methods of the multiplication of binary matrices (1,0), whose application yields useful insights into group structure.

[31] The discussion of this section is for the most part based on: C. Proctor and C. Loomis, ''Analysis of Sociometric Data.'' In M. Deutsch, and S. Cook, *Research Methods in Social Relations*. New York: Holt, Rinehart and Winston, 1951, pt. 2, chap. 17.

well or how poorly chosen an individual is is revealed by CS. It is, in short, his *choice status*. It is of course possible to have a choice rejection index. Simply put the number of 0's in any column in the numerator of Equation 31.1.

Group sociometric measures are perhaps more interesting. A measure of the cohesiveness of a group is:

$$Co = \frac{\Sigma(i \leftrightarrow j)}{\dfrac{n(n-1)}{2}} \qquad (31.2)$$

Group cohesiveness is represented by Co and $\Sigma(i \leftrightarrow j) = $ sum of mutual choices (or mutual pairs). This useful index is the proportion of mutual choices to the total number of possible pairs. In a five-member group, the total number of possible pairs is 5 things taken 2 at a time:

$$\binom{5}{2} = \frac{5(5-1)}{2} = 10$$

If, in an unlimited choice situation, there were 2 mutual choices, then $Co = 2/10 = .20$, a rather low degree of cohesiveness. In the case of limited choice, the formula is:

$$Co = \frac{\Sigma(i \leftrightarrow j)}{dn/2} \qquad (31.3)$$

where $d = $ the number of choices each individual is permitted. For C of Table 31.1 $Co = 3/(2 \times 5/2) = 3/5 = .60$, a substantial degree of cohesiveness.

RESEARCH USES OF SOCIOMETRY

Because the data of sociometry seem so different from other kinds of data, students find it difficult to think of sociometric measurement as measurement. There is no doubt that sociometric data are different. But they are the result of observation, *and they are measures*.[32] They are useful, for example, in classifying individuals and groups. In the Bennington College study, Newcomb measured individual prestige by asking students to name five students they would choose as most worthy to represent Bennington College at an important gathering of students from all types of American colleges.[33] He then grouped students by frequency of choice and related this measure of *sociometric prestige* to *political and economic conservatism*. In reading the examples of this section, the student should clearly realize that sociometry is a method of observation and data collection that, like any other method of observation, obtains measures of variables.

Prejudice in Schools

In studying the manifestation of prejudice against blacks and Jews in schools, Smith used the simple procedure of asking all the students of entire grades of high schools to name their five best friends.[34] (Smith calls it "a straightforward approach that has been digni-

[32] For a discussion of the basic measurement aspects of sociometric measures, especially their reliability and validity, see Lindzey and Byrne, *op. cit.*, pp. 475–483.

[33] T. Newcomb, *Personality and Social Change*. New York: Holt, Rinehart and Winston, 1943, pp. 54–55.

[34] M. Smith, "The Schools and Prejudice: Findings." In C. Glock and E. Siegelman, eds., *Prejudice U. S. A.* New York: Praeger, 1969, chap. 5.

fied by the label of 'sociometric method.'") He then collated the responses with the responses of the students named to determine ethnic and religious group membership.[35] The students tended to choose their friends from their own racial and religious groups—hardly surprising. More important, Jews and blacks were not chosen as friends by members of other ethnic and religious groups. White students hardly chose black students at all. While Smith specifically says that he does not want to ascribe his findings to prejudice, it seems clear that "the virtually unpenetrated barrier" between black and white students reflects prejudice. It is evident that a sociometric approach in the study of prejudice can yield important data.

Sociometry and Social Status

In the Morrison et al. study of the determinants of social status among mildly handicapped students cited earlier (footnote 23), social status (the dependent variable) was measured by asking the children in classes to select one of four responses for each of their classmates: a smiling face (acceptance), a straight-mouthed face (no preference), a frowning face (rejection), and a question mark (nonacquaintance). A weighted average score for each child was calculated as follows: 3 = acceptance, 2 = tolerance (no preference), and 1 = rejection. These averages were the social status scores, which were correlated with other variables, *e.g.*, disruptive behavior, teacher rating of behavior, achievement. The two strongest influences on social status were teacher rating of cognition (positive) and student rating of behavior (negative).

Race, Belief, and Sociometric Choice

In a field experiment designed to test Rokeach's controversial hypothesis that differences in beliefs are more influential in determining prejudice than differences in race, Rokeach and Mezei used a realistic employment situation and an ingenious sociometric task.[36] White and black male applicants for various jobs in two mental hospitals were involved individually with four confederates of the experimenters in discussions of rule-oriented and permissive ways of handling patient problems. Two of the confederates were white, two were black; one white and one black confederate espoused the rule-oriented position; the other white and black confederates espoused the permissive position. This arrangement, then, constituted the race and belief conditions. After about 12 minutes of discussion the experimenter came into the room and asked the five individuals—including the experimental subject, of course—to write down the names of two of the four individuals with whom he would most prefer to work. This was, of course, a sociometric task whose purpose was to test the prediction that the subjects would express more preference for those individuals whose opinions they shared than for those of the same race. In general, the prediction was supported.

Sociometry is a simple, economical, and naturalistic method of observation and data collection. Whenever such human actions as choosing, influencing, dominating, and communicating, especially in group situations, are involved, sociometric methods can

[35] Smith says that this procedure—because students had to name names, shed their own anonymity, and respond to personal questions, and because considerable school time was used—stretched the tolerance of administrators and school boards. In fact, one school system ejected the researchers!

[36] M. Rokeach and L. Mezei, "Race and Shared Belief as Factors in Social Choice," *Science*, 151 (1966), 167–172.

usually be used. They have considerable flexibility. If defined broadly, they can be adapted to a wide variety of research in the laboratory and in the field. Their quantification and analysis possibilities, though not generally realized in the literature, are rewarding. The ability to use the simple assignment of 1's and 0's is particularly fortunate, because powerful mathematical methods can be applied to the data with uniquely interpretable and meaningful results. Matrix methods are the outstanding example. With them, one can discover cliques in groups, communication and influence channels, patterns of cohesiveness, connectedness, hierarchization, and so on.

Study Suggestions

1. The student should study one or two behavior observation systems in detail. For students of education, the Medley and Mitzel system will yield high returns. Other students will want to study one or two other systems. The best source for educational systems is Medley and Mitzel's chapter (see footnote 1). It is authoritative and clear with many examples. The two best general references are the Heyns and Lippitt chapter (footnote 2) and the Weick chapter (footnote 1) in the first and second editions of the *Handbook of Social Psychology*. An anthology of 79 observation systems has been published in cooperation with Research for Better Schools, Inc., a regional education laboratory (see footnote 7). The researcher who intends using observations should consult this huge collection of systems. The student of education will find excellent summaries and discussions of educational observation systems in: M. Dunkin and B. Biddle, *The Study of Teaching*. New York: Holt, Rinehart and Winston, 1974. The following articles are valuable: R. Boice, "Observational Skills," *Psychological Bulletin*, 93 (1983), 3–29; J. Herbert and C. Attridge, "A Guide for Developers and Users of Observation Systems and Manuals," *American Educational Research Journal*, 12 (1975), 1–20. Boice points out the lack of training for making observations of behavior and makes suggestions for such training. Herbert and Attridge provide criteria for observation systems. They also point out that knowledge of such systems is limited.

2. Sociometry has been neglected by behavioral researchers and methodologists. As its importance and analytic usefulness become better known and appreciated, and as computer programs are written to handle large amounts of data generated, mathematical and statistical methods of sociometric and related data analysis will probably exert a stronger influence on behavioral research. The student is encouraged to explore mathematical treatments of sociometric data. The Kemeny, Snell, and Thompson reference (footnote 28) is a good introduction, though the student needs knowledge of elementary matrix algebra (which, fortunately, is not difficult). An introduction to the subject is: E. Pedhazur, *Multiple Regression in Behavioral Research: Explanation and Prediction*, 2d ed. New York: Holt, Rinehart and Winston, 1982, Appendix A, pp. 773–783. A highly valuable guide to mathematical and statistical analysis is the following article: M. Glanzer and R. Glaser, "Techniques for the Study of Group Structure and Behavior: I. Analysis of Structure," *Psychological Bulletin*, 56 (1959), 317–332.

3. An investigator, studying the influence patterns of boards of education, obtained the following matrix from one board of education. (Note that this is like an unlimited choice situation because each individual can influence all or none of the members of the group.) Read the matrix: i influences j.

		j				
		a	b	c	d	e
	a	0	0	1	1	0
	b	0	0	0	0	1
i	c	1	0	0	1	0
	d	1	0	1	0	0
	e	0	1	0	0	0

(a) What conclusions can you reach from study of this matrix? Is the board divided? Is there likely to be conflict?

    (b) Draw a graph of the influence situation. Interpret the graph.

    (c) Is there a clique on the board? (Define clique as given in the test.) If so, who are its members?

    (d) What members have the least number of influence channels? Are they, then, much less influential than the other members, other things being equal?

    [*Answers*: (c) Yes: *a, c, d*; (d) *b* and *e*.]

    4. For the situation in Study Suggestion 3, calculate the cohesiveness of the group using Eq. 31.2.

[*Answer*: *Co* = .40.]

Chapter 32

Q Methodology

Q methodology is a general name used by William Stephenson to characterize a set of philosophical, psychological, statistical, and psychometric ideas oriented to research on the individual.[1] *Q technique* is a set of procedures used to implement *Q* methodology. It centers particularly in sorting decks of cards called *Q sorts* and in the correlations among the responses of different individuals to the *Q* sorts.

Persons Correlations and Clusters

Q technique is mainly a sophisticated way of rank-ordering objects (items, stimuli, etc.) and then assigning numerals to subsets of the objects for statistical purposes. Take a set of six items, each item being a characterization of aspects of university or college courses and teaching. Abbreviations of the items are given in Table 32.1. If we ask individual students to rank order the items according to the importance of the aspects of teaching they express, we would expect different rank orders from different individuals. Four students might give the ranks shown in Table 32.1 (1 being the highest rank and 6 the lowest). Suppose, further, that the first two students are person-oriented and the second two task-oriented.

Inspection shows what might have been expected: the two person-oriented students have similar rank orders, as do the two task-oriented students. The rank orders of the person-oriented and task-oriented students, on the other hand, are unlike. To be more

[1]W. Stephenson, *The Study of Behavior*. Chicago: University of Chicago Press, 1953.

Table 32.1 Hypothetical Rank Orders Given to Six Teaching Items by Four Students[a]

	PO-1	PO-2	TO-1	TO-2
Contribution to personal growth	1	1	4	3
Stimulates thinking	2	3	1	2
Value of outside work	3	2	6	6
Instructor's ability to explain	4	6	5	5
Course procedure	6	5	3	4
Course organization	5	4	2	1

[a] PO: Person Orientation; TO: Task Orientation

precise, we calculate rank-order coefficients of correlation between all possible pairs of rankers.[2] This yields a 4 × 4 correlation matrix, as shown in Table 32.2. Note that the clusters (PO-1, PO-2) and (TO-1, TO-2) stand out clearly. The correlations between both pairs are italicized in the table. PO-1 correlates substantially with PO-2 (.77), but virtually zero with TO-1 and TO-2 (−.09 and .03). Similarly, TO-1 and TO-2 correlate highly with each other (.89), but not with PO-1 and PO-2.

This oversimplified example illustrates two of the important basic ideas behind *Q: correlations between persons* and *persons clusters* or *factors*. The usual correlational procedure, loosely called *R* methodology, uses correlations between tests, scales, items, variables. The above example might have been four tests given to six persons, the tests measuring two variables. With *Q*, the four persons break down into two clusters.

Q Sorts and Q Sorting

The example given above used a straightforward rank-order procedure. *Q* technique uses a rank-order procedure of piles or groups of objects. A set of objects—verbal statements, single words, phrases, pictures, musical compositions—is given to an individual to sort into a set of piles according to some criterion. For example, the cards may have typed on them statements about political practices. The subject may be asked to sort the cards according to whether he approves or disapproves the statements on them. With a large number of cards—*Q* sorts usually contain between 60 and 120 cards—it is very difficult

Table 32.2 Correlations Among Person-Oriented and Task-Oriented Students, Table 32.1 Data

	PO-1	PO-2	TO-1	TO-2
PO-1		.77	−.09	.03
PO-2	.77		−.09	.09
TO-1	−.09	−.09		.89
TO-2	.03	.09	.89	

[2] The formula is:

$$rho = \frac{6\Sigma D^2}{n(n^2 - 1)}$$

where *rho* = rank-order coefficient of correlation; *D* = the difference between any pair of ranks; *n* = the number of ranks.

to rank order them. For statistical convenience, the sorter is instructed to put varying numbers of cards in several piles, the whole making up a normal or quasi-normal distribution. Here is a *Q*-sort distribution of 90 items:

Most Approve										Least Approve
3	4	7	10	13	16	13	10	7	4	3
10	9	8	7	6	5	4	3	2	1	0

This is a rank-order continuum from "Most Approve" to "Least Approve" with varying degrees of approval and disapproval between the extremes. The numbers 3, 4, 7, . . . , 7, 4, 3 are the numbers of cards to be placed in each pile. The numbers below the line are the values assigned to the cards in each pile. That is, the 3 cards at the left, "Most Approve," are each assigned 10, the 4 cards in the next pile are assigned 9, and so on through the distribution to the 3 cards at the extreme right, which are assigned 0. The center pile is a neutral pile. The subject is told to put cards that are left over after he has made other choices, cards that seem ambiguous to him or about which he cannot make a decision, into the neutral pile. In brief, this *Q* distribution has 11 piles with varying numbers of cards in each pile, the cards in the piles being assigned values from 0 through 10. Statistical analyses are based on these latter values.

Sorting instructions and the objects sorted vary with the purposes of the research. Subjects can be asked to sort attitudinal statements on an approval-disapproval continuum. They can be asked to sort personality items on a "like me"-"not like me" continuum. Judges can sort behavioral statements to describe an individual or a group. Aesthetic objects, like pictures or abstract drawings, can be sorted according to degree of preference.

The number of cards in a *Q* distribution is determined by convenience and statistical demands. For statistical stability and reliability, the number should probably be not less than 60 (40 or 50 in some rare cases) nor more than 140, in most cases no more than 100. A good range is from 60 to 90 cards.[3]

In part, *Q* distributions are an arbitrary matter. It is possible to use rectangular distributions. That is, we can have the same number of cards in all the piles. Or we can even permit subjects to place the cards in a number of piles where they will. The normal or quasi-normal distribution has advantages, mainly statistical, that make its use desirable. Some *Q*-sort distributions are given in Table 32.3.

Table 32.3 Seven *Q*-Sort Distributions of 80, 70, and 60 Items

n = 80										
2	4	6	9	12	14	12	9	6	4	2
4	6	9		13	16	13		9	6	4
4	6	10		12	16	12		10	6	4
n = 70										
2	3	5	8	11	12	11	8	5	3	2
2	3	4	8	11	14	11	8	4	3	2
n = 60										
2	3	6		11	16	11	6		3	2
2	3	4	7	9	10	9	7	4	3	2

[3] The author has gotten good results with as few as 40 items. These 40 items were culled from a larger pool of items, all of which had been tested. It is rarely necessary or desirable to have more than 90 or 100 items.

A Miniature Q Sort

A semi-realistic example may help to clarify a number of technical points. Suppose we wish to explore educational attitudes. We can assemble a large number of statements from which we select a smaller number to put into a Q sort. We select 10 statements (naturally many more than 10 would actually be required). Subjects are asked to sort the 10 statements into the following distribution:

Most Approve				Least Approve
1	2	4	2	1
4	3	2	1	0

Again, the figures above the line are the numbers of cards in the piles; those below the line are the values assigned to each of the piles.

Suppose four subjects sort the cards as instructed and that the values below the line have been assigned to the cards in the piles. The four sets of values are given in Table 32.4. The numbers in the four columns under a, b, c, and d are the values assigned to the cards in the five piles after the four persons, a, b, c and d, have sorted the cards. By inspection we suspect that the Q sorts of Persons a and b are very similar. The Q sorts of Persons c and d look similar. (With these two pairs of persons, note that the high values and the low values tend to go together.) We can also see that there seems to be little relation between the Q sorts of a and c, b and c, and b and d. To be more precise, we again need to calculate coefficients of correlation.[4]

The r's between the four sets of values of Table 32.4 are given in the correlation matrix of Table 32.5.

The interpretation of these correlations presents no difficulties. Obviously Persons a and b sort the cards very similarly: $r = .92$. Persons c and d, too, are similar: $r = .75$. All the rest of the r's are near zero. Evidently there are two kinds of "types" of persons, insofar as attitudes toward education are concerned: "A-kind" and "B-kind."

Table 32.4 Q-Sort Values of Four Persons: Miniature Q Sort

	Persons			
Items	a	b	c	d
1	2	2	1	1
2	1	1	0	0
3	0	0	3	4
4	2	2	4	2
5	2	1	3	3
6	1	2	2	2
7	3	3	2	2
8	2	2	2	2
9	4	4	2	3
10	3	3	1	1

[4] For a method of calculating r's, see Chapter 6. Note, too, that calculating r's in Q is simpler than usual because all subjects have the same sums of squares, Σx^2, which need to be calculated only once for any Q sort. Only the cross-product term, Σxy, needs to be calculated for each pair of persons. Since microcomputer programs for calculating r's and other common statistics are available—some hand-held calculators even produce r at the touch of a button (after entering the ordered pairs, of course)—we do not here discuss calculations and formulas.

Table 32.5   Correlation Matrix from the Q-Sort Values of Table 32.4

	a	b	c	d
a		.92	−.08	−.08
b	.92		−.17	−.17
c	−.08	−.17		.75
d	−.08	−.17	.75	

To get an idea of what A and B are, we would have to go back to the Q sort and examine the items highly approved by A's and those highly approved by B's. Suppose the three highly approved A items were:

Learning is experimental; the child should be taught to test alternatives before accepting any of them.
No subject is more important than the personalities of the pupils.
Right from the very first grade, teachers must teach the child at his own level and not at the level of the grade he is in.

Suppose the three highly approved B items were:

Learning is essentially a process of increasing one's store of information about the various fields of knowledge.
The curriculum should contain an orderly arrangement of subjects that represent the best of our cultural heritage.
Schools of today are neglecting the three R's.[5]

Obviously, these pairs of people are very different. One, the A pair, seems to favor "progressive" educational notions; the other, the B pair, seems to favor "traditional" educational notions. Perhaps these individuals are "progressives" and "traditionalists."

The miniature example just discussed contains the essential ingredients of much Q analysis. Obviously most Q studies have to have more subjects, even though it is theoretically possible to have a Q study with one individual. Moreover, the impressionistic kind of analysis used would in most cases not be satisfactory. A more objective method of ascertaining clusters of persons, or persons' factors, would have to be used. The highly approved items of clusters of individuals also require a more objective method for their identification. Nevertheless, the example at least outlines the Q correlational method.

THEORY; STRUCTURED AND UNSTRUCTURED Q SORTS; ANALYSIS OF VARIANCE

Unstructured Q Sorts

Most published Q studies have used unstructured Q sorts. An *unstructured* Q sort is a set of items assembled without specific regard to the variables or factors underlying the items. Theoretically, any sample of homogeneous items can be used in an unstructured Q sort. The idea is simple. A large number of statements are taken from various statement sources and put together in a Q sort. The items of an unstructured Q sort are like the items of a

[5]The items are from the author's Q sort on educational attitudes. See F. Kerlinger, "The Attitude Structure of the Individual: A Q-Study of the Educational Attitudes of Professors and Laymen," *Genetic Psychology Monographs,* 53 (1956), 283–329 (see pp. 323–327). The research using the Q sort is described in: F. Kerlinger, *Liberalism and Conservatism: Nature and the Structure of Social Attitudes.* Hillsdale, N. J.: Erlbaum, 1984, chap. 6.

personality or attitude scale: they are selected and used because they presumably measure one broad variable, like neuroticism, attitudes toward blacks, or adjustment.

There is a theoretical infinite population of items, and the hope is that the set of items used by the investigator in his *Q* sort is a representative sample of this item population. One important population of items, used by Rogers and others, is focused on the perception of self and others. A large number of statements about the self is assembled or constructed: "I like people," "I am a failure," "I just can't seem to make up my mind on things," and so on.

Individuals are asked to sort the cards to describe themselves as they think they are, as other people see them, and the like. The cards are sorted into a *Q* distribution, the sorts intercorrelated, and the principal analysis focuses on the correlations among persons and on factor or cluster analysis. Inferences about the efficacy of therapy or training programs are then drawn from the results of the analysis. For example, trainees—in teacher training, the Peace Corps, doctoral programs—sort the cards before, during, and after the training. Assume that there is an "ideal" or criterion *Q* sort available provided by the trainers. One reasons that if the training has been effective—and one of the important results of training is measured by the *Q* sort—then the correlations between the trainees' sorts and the criterion sort are higher after the training than before it.

Correlation approaches have more or less dominated *Q* studies.[6] One of Stephenson's important contributions, the testing of "theory" and the principle of building "theory" into *Q* sorts by means of structured samples of items, has been neglected.[7]

Structured Q Sorts

In a *structured Q sort,* the variables of a "theory," or of a hypothesis or set of hypotheses, are built into a set of items along Fisherian experimental and analysis of variance design principles. What does this mean? An *unstructured Q sort* is a set of items all of which are in one domain—for example, social-values items, self items, teacher-characteristics items—but which are not otherwise differentiated in the *Q* sort or in the analysis. While the items of a structured *Q* sort, on the other hand, are in one domain, they are partitioned in one or more ways. For instance, a child psychologist may be studying moral growth in children. One aspect of his theory implies that as children get older, control of their behavior becomes more internal. A *Q* sort can be structured as *internal-external,* with half the items reflecting internal control and half external control. This is the simplest possible partition of a structured *Q* sort.

To structure a *Q* sort is virtually to build a "theory" into it. Instead of constructing instruments to measure the characteristics of individuals, we construct them to embody or epitomize "theories." In the use of *Q* as Stephenson sees it, individuals as such are not tested; theoretical propositions are tested. Naturally, individuals must do the *Q* sorting. And *Q* sorts can, of course, be used to measure characteristics of individuals. But the basic rationale of *Q*, as Stephenson sees it, is that we have individuals sort the cards not so much to test the individuals as to test "theories" that have been built into the items.

One-Way Structured Q Sorts

Building a theory into a measurement instrument, while not frequent, is not new. A well-known example is the Allport-Vernon-Lindzey *Study of Values,* a values instrument

---

[6]J. Wittenborn, "Contributions and Current Status of *Q* Methodology," *Psychological Bulletin,* 58 (1961), 132–142.

[7]*Ibid.,* pp. 138–139. See Stephenson, *op. cit.,* pp. 66–85.

based on Spranger's theory of six types of men: Theoretical, Economic, Aesthetic, Social, Political, and Religious.[8] The purpose of the instrument is not to test the theory but to measure the values of individuals. If a person is, say, basically a religious "type," he should select items of the Religious category over items of other categories.

The Stephenson approach to the same problem would be to test the Spranger theory. (Note that the *Study of Values* can be used to test the Spranger theory.) A Q sort would be constructed using the Spranger system as a guide. Items would be selected from various sources and specially written to represent the six Spranger values. There would be 10 to 15 Theoretical items, 10 to 15 Aesthetic items, and so forth, making a total of 60 to 90 items in the entire Q sort. Individuals would then be selected to "represent" the six values. For example, the investigator might select ministers and priests (Religious), businessmen (Economic), artists and musicians (Aesthetic), scientists and scholars (Theoretical), and so on.[9]

If the theory is "valid," and if the Q sort adequately expresses the theory, two rather big "ifs," the statistical analyses of the sorts should show the theory's validity. That is, if any individual with "known" values—a minister or priest can be expected to have strong religious values, an artist strong aesthetic values—takes the sort with instructions to place favored or approved statements high and disapproved statements low, we would expect him to place the 10 or 15 statements congruent with his role and its associated values high. Statements associated with other roles and values we would expect him to place lower. If a scientist sorts the cards, we would expect him to place the cards in the Theoretical category high and cards of other categories relatively lower. Naturally, there will be few individuals whose sorts will be so clear-cut. Human beings and their attitudes and values are too complex. But we can expect some such results to occur beyond chance expectation if the theory is valid.

A Q sort suggested by the above considerations can be called a "one-way structured sort," because there is one basis of variable classification.[10] This is directly analogous to simple one-way analysis of variance. To make the matter clear, an example from a research study designed in part to test the Spranger theory in Q fashion can be given. A 90-item Q sort was used. Each item was a single word, each word having been previously categorized by judges in the six Spranger values. There were 15 Theoretical words—*science, knowledge, reason,* and so on; 15 Religious words—*God, church, sermon,* and so on; to a total of six categories and 90 words.

The cards were sorted by a number of persons chosen for their presumed possession of the six values. They were asked to sort the cards according to the degree to which they favored or did not favor the words on the cards. To illustrate the results, here are the mean values in rank order of the sort of one subject, a musician:

a	*s*	*t*	*p*	*e*	*r*
7.13	6.27	6.13	4.73	4.33	1.40

$F = 26.82$, significant at the .001 level. This means that the musician significantly differentiated the six values. What is the pattern of differentiation? The wider spaces indicate

---

[8]G. Allport, P. Vernon, and G. Lindzey, *Study of Values,* rev. ed. Boston: Houghton Mifflin, 1951.

[9]In an interesting Q study of religious attitudes, Broen selected 24 clergymen to represent the full spectrum of religious beliefs and attitudes. There were four representatives of each of five major religious groupings. Broen says that the subjects were selected from churches and institutions known to have religious orientations in the directions of his hypothesized religious categories. W. Broen, "A Factor Analytic Study of Religious Attitudes," *Journal of Abnormal and Social Psychology,* 54 (1957), 176–179.

[10]Stephenson has not stressed the possibility of Q sorts of the one-way type. His Q designs are almost all of the factorial two- and three-way type. There seems to be no reason why one-way designs cannot be used.

significant gaps.[11] Although it is the highest mean, there is no significant gap between Aesthetic and the next highest mean, Social (6.27). In fact, Aesthetic, Social, and Theoretical form a subset which is separated by a significant gap from all the other means. Political and Economic form another subset. Religious, the lowest mean (1.40), is significantly separated from all the other means. Evidently the musician highly favors Aesthetic, Social, and Theoretical words, and strongly disfavors Religious words. From this analysis we may perhaps draw inferences as to her value system, at least insofar as the measurement system allows. Independent knowledge of the subject confirmed this analysis.

If a set of stimuli can be categorized in this fashion, a one-way structured Q sort may be possible to construct and desirable to use. Small theories and hypotheses can be tested in this manner by having subjects of known values, attitudes, personality, roles, and so forth sort the cards. The student should realize that in addition to the analysis of variance structured sort approach, correlation analysis is always applicable. Simply correlate the Q sorts of different persons, and disregard the structure built into the sort.

Two-Way (Factorial) Structured Q Sorts

Many theories and hypotheses that can be structured along the lines of analysis of variance paradigms have the potentiality of being tested with Q methods. The Spranger example just discussed is a case in point. Other one-way examples might be: introversion-extroversion; oral eroticism-anal eroticism; progressivism-traditionalism; liberalism-conservatism; open mindedness-closed mindedness; and so on. But how about more complex theories and hypotheses? Taking the next logical step, we add another dimension or variable to the Q paradigm. This makes a two-variable Q sort and a two-variable or factorial analysis of variance design. The Q sort is structured in two ways rather than one. This means that every item in the Q sort reflects facets of the two variables. A little reflection will show that this can often be quite difficult.

To illustrate two-way structured sorts, the paradigm of an 80-item sort to explore social attitudes and to test a structural "theory" of attitudes is given in Table 32.6.[12] The means of a known conservative individual are also given in the table.

First note the Q-sort structure. The two main variables are *Attitudes* and *Abstractness*. *Attitudes* is partitioned into Liberal (L) and Conservative (C), *Abstractness* into Abstract (A) and Specific (S). Any item of the Q sort must fit into one of the four cells of the cross partition. Any attitude item must be either Conservative or Liberal and at the same time either Abstract of Specific. The more important variable is *Attitudes*. The second variable, *Abstractness,* was incorporated into the structure because it was conjectured that both liberals and conservatives would react differently to the abstractness-specificity of items.

---

[11] A simple way to do this test is to calculate the standard error of the difference between means. The formula is

$$SE_{M_i - M_j} = \sqrt{V_w \left(\frac{1}{n_i} + \frac{1}{n_j} \right)}$$

where V_w = within-groups variance (from the analysis of variance). Multiply this value by 2:

$$2\sqrt{2.34 \left(\frac{1}{15} + \frac{1}{15} \right)} = 2\sqrt{2.34 \times 1.33} = 2 \times .558 = 1.12$$

Any difference equal to or greater than 1.12 is significant. Perhaps a more legitimate but more conservative test is Scheffé's. See Chapter 13, Study Suggestion 6. Also see A. Edwards, *Statistical Methods,* 2d ed. New York: Holt, Rinehart and Winston, 1967, pp. 265–269.

[12] F. Kerlinger, "A Q Validation of the Structure of Social Attitudes," *Educational and Psychological Measurement,* 32 (1972), 987–995. The theory tested is discussed in: F. Kerlinger, "Social Attitudes and Their Criterial Referents: A Structural Theory," *Psychological Review,* 74 (1967), 110–122.

Table 32.6 A Two-way Structured Q Sort with the Means of a Known
Conservative

		Attitudes		
		Liberal (*L*)	Conservative (*C*)	Means
Abstractness	Abstract (*A*)	3.15	4.70	3.93
	Specific (*S*)	2.45	5.70	4.07
	Means	2.80	5.20	$M_t = 4.00$

For example, a conservative might strongly endorse *specific* conservative items, while
another conservative might endorse *abstract* conservative items—and similarly for liberals. Whether the structure is valid is, of course, an empirical matter. At any rate, here are
four items, one for each of the cells of Table 32.6. The labels correspond to those given in
the table and on page 514.

social equality (LA)
Supreme Court (LS)
competition (CA)
private property (CS)

The data of this individual's sort can be analyzed with analysis of variance, provided
we use care and circumspection in the interpretation of the data. (The questionable nature
of using analysis of variance with Q-sort data will be discussed later.) The analysis of
variance to use, of course, is the factorial type. The individual whose data (means) are in
the table is a "known" conservative who evidently favors conservative referents of the
specific kind. The *L* and *C* means are 2.80 and 5.20, a difference of 2.40, which is
significant at the .01 level. The difference between the *A* and *S* means (3.93 and 4.07) is
not significant.

Much more interesting, note the Specific row means: 2.45 and 5.70. Contrast this with
the Abstract row means: 3.15 and 4.70. The two differences lead to an interaction *F* ratio
of 5.23, significant at the .05 level. Although we should treat .05-level differences with
caution, these results indicate the subject's preference for conservative and specific referents. Of the four referents given above, he would probably rank *private property* above
the others. Since we knew that this individual was conservative before we started, this is
some small confirmation of the validity of the reasoning that went into the *Q* sort.

The use of the *abstractness* dimension in this sort was not dictated by theory; it was
purely exploratory. A number of individuals (14 out of 33), however, had significant
interaction *F* ratios, which indicates that it makes a difference to many individuals
whether referents are abstract or specific. This may even mean that we would have to talk
about abstract and specific liberalism and conservatism. It may also mean that conservatives tend to favor specific referents, while liberals favor abstract referents. Despite these
findings, significant interactions are ordinarily not expected; the principal interest in *Q* is
ordinarily in the main effects.[13] Nevertheless, there is no compelling reason why interactions cannot be predicted on the basis of theory or hunch and deliberately studied just as
in experimental work in learning and teaching.

Before leaving structured sorts, it should be mentioned that *Q* designs are not limited
to the simple 2 × 2 case shown above. Other combinations—3 × 2, 4 × 3, 2 × 4—are
possible. Three- and four-variable designs are also possible, if not too practicable. Another possibility, mentioned in an earlier chapter, is the application of the structure idea to

---

[13] See Stephenson, *op. cit.,* pp. 103 and 163–164. There are a number of interesting structured *Q* sorts in this
volume and in Stephenson's later book: W. Stephenson, *The Play Theory of Mass Communication.* Chicago:
University of Chicago Press, 1967.

objective tests and scales. The items of the referents Q sort can be put into summated-rating scale form, for instance, and scored and analyzed accordingly.[14]

FACTOR ANALYSIS AND FACTOR ARRAYS IN Q METHODOLOGY

The impossibility of doing justice to Q methodology without discussing factor analysis is nowhere more evident than in describing factor arrays, the final technical step of a Q study. One of the strong points of Q methodology is its analytic possibilities. Of these possibilities, factor arrays are very important. A *factor array* is a Q sort constructed from factor analytic results. Conceive factors as similar clusters of objects—in this case persons, or rather, the responses of persons. Those individuals who respond to a Q sort similarly will form clusters of persons. Oversimplified, conceive of summing the responses of the individuals of a cluster to any Q-sort item. If we do this for every item in a Q sort, we will have sums for all items. These sums will, of course, vary a great deal. They can be rank-ordered and then fitted into the original Q distribution.[15] This "new" synthetic Q sort is literally a description of the factor, which can be directly interpreted. Usually, only the top and bottom two or three piles of the Q distribution are used for interpretative purposes. Factor arrays are calculated similarly for each factor.

A Q Study of Perceptions of Teacher Behaviors

In a Q study of the relation between attitudes toward education and teachers' perceptions of desirable teaching behaviors, Sontag used an 80-item Q sort whose items were brief descriptions of a large variety of teaching behaviors.[16] Half of 80 elementary and secondary school teachers were instructed to sort the behaviors according to their desirability for elementary teachers and the other half according to their desirability for secondary teachers. The Q-sort results for each group were factor analyzed separately and factor arrays calculated. Four factors were obtained in each analysis. These factor arrays are complete 80-item Q sorts that describe a weighted average of the relative values the teachers put on the behaviors. Four of the highest values for two of the elementary-teacher behavior factors, with the names of the factors, are:

Concern for Students
Provides individualized material for pupils as required.
Shows sincere concern when confronted with personal problems of pupils.
Teaches students to be sensitive to the needs of others.
Takes advantage of student interest in planning lessons.

Structure and Subject Matter
Presents well-planned lessons.
Is consistent in administering discipline.
In his presentations, shows competent knowledge of subject matter.
Adheres to rules he sets up.

One can readily get a feeling for the underlying themes behind the items, even with these few items. Ordinarily, more positive items are needed to identify and interpret the

---

[14] Some of the possibilities have been described in: F. Kerlinger, "*Q* Methodology in Behavioral Research." In S. Brown and D. Brenner, eds., *Science, Psychology, and Communication: Essays Honoring William Stephenson*. New York: Teachers College Press, 1972, chap. 1.

[15] For details of calculating factor arrays, see Stephenson, *The Study of Behavior*, pp. 176–179.

[16] M. Sontag, "Attitudes Toward Education and Perception of Teacher Behaviors," *American Educational Research Journal*, 5 (1968), 385–402.

arrays. In addition, the negative ends of the arrays can and often should be used, since they may be helpful in interpretation. Note, too, that the Q sorts of new subjects can be correlated with the arrays, a valuable procedure that has rarely been used. The correlations can be used to identify the factor predispositions of students, teachers in training and in service, administrators, and so on. This kind of use can be particularly valuable in studies of attitude, value, belief, and perception (or judgment) change. The perceptions or judgments of desirable teacher characteristics and behaviors before and after, say, special training can be correlated with "ideal" perceptions of the trainers, as indicated earlier, or with the factor arrays.

STRENGTHS AND WEAKNESSES OF Q METHODOLOGY

Like factor analysis, which it uses liberally, Q methodology is controversial. It has been highly praised and harshly criticized. The truth of the critical matter is probably that the method is not as powerful and all-embracing as Stephenson has claimed it to be, nor is it as poor and defective as some critics have said it is. It is probably safe to say that Q is a flexible and useful tool in the armamentarium of the psychological and educational investigator. It also has defects, however, as we shall see.

The main strength of Q is its affinity to theory. This simple-sounding statement conceals complex ideas. It means that if a theory, or aspects of a theory, can be expressed in categories and if items that express the categories can be produced, then Q can be a powerful approach to testing theory. Its principal analytic procedure to accomplish this is factor analysis of the Q profiles of individuals and thus the "discovery" of persons' factors. If the theory is empirically valid, then the persons' factors should correspond to the major variables of the theory. For example, look again at the paradigm of Table 32.6 in which liberalism-conservatism was one of the categories of a Q sort and abstract-specific was the other. Suppose we believe that many people are favorable to liberal ideas when they are abstract and that many other people are favorable to conservative ideas when they are specific. A Q sort with a structure like that of Table 32.6 and, of course, items that fit the four cells can be constructed and administered to known conservatives and known liberals. If the theoretical idea just expressed is correct for substantial numbers of liberals and conservatives, then analysis of variance and factor analysis of the Q-sort data should show this. A substantial number of the sample should have significant F ratios, and at least two of the factors of the persons' factor analysis should have these "abstract liberals" and "specific conservatives" on them.[17]

Another strength of Q is its suitability for intensive study of the individual. One person can sort a Q sort many times to study, say, attitude change or changes in perception of self under the impact of educational or other programs. The data of the sortings can be analyzed objectively without sacrificing the richness of the usual clinical and case study methods.

Q can also be used to test the effects of independent variables on complex dependent variables. One difficulty in studying attitude change under the impact of communication, interaction, and other change agents is that the effects are not simple. Ordinarily the

---

[17] This is a dicey prediction, indeed, because one expects the factor analysis and the analysis of variance results to agree in all particulars. While the results should agree in general if the theory holds, it is unrealistic to expect them to agree in all particulars. The example, however, illustrates what is meant by the affinity of Q and theory. Theories that can be tested with Q are *structural* theories, that is, they are explanation of the relations among the elements or variables of a phenomenon under study. For a discussion of different kinds of theories in behavioral science and research, see Kerlinger, *Liberalism and Conservatism: The Nature and Structure of Social Attitudes, op. cit.,* chap. 2.

attitude mean of an experimental group is expected to increase or decrease under the impact of the independent variable or variables. With Q, we can rather sensitively assess such changes of individuals by using analysis of variance and factor analysis of the data of structured Q sorts. Although they have hardly been used, such methods hold promise for experimental studies.

Two related strengths of Q are its heuristic quality and its usefulness in exploratory research. Q seems to be helpful in turning up new ideas, new hypotheses. Stephenson's work perhaps best illustrates this quality. One gets the feeling of a curious mind turning up interesting ideas while working with Q. Q's exploratory power is shown to some extent by the attitude referents Q study outlined above. One can start to get an empirical purchase on slippery problems like the abstractness of attitudes and values.

An important potential of Q mentioned above is the construction and use of factor arrays. Properly constructed factor arrays are "new" Q sorts that reflect the factors from which they are calculated. Although their value and usefulness in behavioral research will be discussed later, we mention here their two principal uses. One, they greatly aid in the interpretation of persons' factors. One sees, so to speak, the verbal or other expression of whatever it is that is common to the group of individuals of the factor. A byproduct of this advantage is that the arrays can be a strong aid in scale construction. The high items of factor arrays should make good scale items. Indeed they have been used to advantage in constructing educational and social attitude scales.[18] The second use of factor arrays is as "prototypes" of factors that can be administered to individuals to assess their attitudinal and other agreement with the factors. This second use will also be discussed later.

As usual, disadvantages accompany advantages. First, take the sampling of persons. One can rarely work with sufficiently large samples in Q. It is not a method well-suited to cross-sectional or large sample purposes. One does not draw a random sample of persons for study with Q. While Stephenson argues the point vigorously, there is no escaping the inability of the investigator using Q to generalize to populations of individuals. Q therefore requires cross-sectional supplementation. No matter how promising Q results may be, one cannot escape the necessity of testing theory on larger numbers of individuals.[19]

Q has been adversely criticized, mostly on statistical grounds.[20] Remember that most statistical tests assume independence. This means that the response to one item should not be affected by the responses to other items. In Q the placement of one card somewhere on the continuum should not affect the placement of other cards. If Q placements affect each other, then the independence assumption is violated. Q is an ipsative, forced-choice procedure, and it will be recalled that such procedures violate the independence assumption: the placement of one Q card affects the placement of other cards. It is, after all, a rank-order method.

The real question is: How serious is the violation of the assumption? Is it serious enough to invalidate the use of correlation and analysis of variance procedures? There is no doubt that in an 80-item sort, there are not really 79 degrees of freedom. Thus, to some extent at least, the analysis of variance procedure is vitiated. It is doubtful, however, that too much is risked in Q statistical situations, if there is a fairly large number of items. One can perhaps fall back on Fisher's advice given long ago: raise the requirements for statisti-

---

[18] See *ibid.*, chaps. 6 and 7.

[19] Stephenson has argued vigorously against this point of view: *The Study of Behavior*, pp. 193–194, 218.

[20] D. Sundland, "The Construction of Q Sorts: A Criticism," *Psychological Review*, 69 (1962), 62–64; L. Cronbach and G. Gleser, "William Stephenson. *The Study of Behavior: Q-Technique and Its Methodology.* Chicago: University of Chicago Press, 1953," *Psychometrika*, 19 (1954), 327–330 (book review).

cal significance. Instead of accepting the .05 level in Q sorts, require the .01 level of significance. In most cases of Q statistical significance encountered by the author, F ratios are so high they leave little doubt as to statistical significance.[21]

Another criticism of Q has focused on the forced-choice feature of Q sorting. It has been said that the forced procedure is unnatural, that it requires the subject to conform to an unreasonable requirement. Furthermore, important information on elevation and scatter is said to be lost. This means, for example, that two individuals can correlate highly because their profiles are alike. Yet these two individuals might be quite unlike: one might be high on a scale and the other low on the scale. (The computation of r takes no account of mean differences, or differences in level or elevation.) The Q procedure throws away levels differences between individuals.

On the constraint argument, all psychometric procedures are constraints on the individual. Because an individual feels constrained in sorting Q sorts, however, is no really good reason for declaring the procedure invalid. Most such inferences are probably made by critics who *think* forced procedures constrain the individual. In the experience of the author and his students, very few individuals complain about the procedure. Most of them, indeed, seem to enjoy it. Livson and Nichols say that the Q sorter is his own worst critic and that researchers should not be unduly alarmed by adverse sorter criticisms of the method.[22] They recommend use of the forced procedure after careful study of alternatives.

The evidence on the relative merits of forced and unforced Q sorts is mixed. Many years ago Block found forced sorting equal or superior to unforced procedures.[23] Jones, on the other hand, found the forced procedure wanting.[24] Brown much more recently concluded from his studies and experience that results are little affected by different distributions and forced and unforced procedures.[25] I believe that *for its purpose* the forced sorting procedure is useful. Whether the distribution of items is normal, rectangular, or otherwise is not so important, though quasi-normal distributions seem to work well. The important thing is to force individuals to make discriminations that they often will not make unless required to do so.

The criticism on the loss of information in Q sorting through lack of elevation and scatter is more serious.[26] The argument is too complex to discuss here. The reader should realize, however, that every time a coefficient of correlation is computed, the elevation

---

[21] It is well, however, to bear the independence stricture in mind. Instructions to subjects should not encourage lack of independence. That is, tell subjects that they can always move any card or cards from one pile to another right to the end of the sorting procedure. Moreover, one should not use Q-sort ''scores'' normatively. That is, one should not use the values assigned to the Q piles (see the Q-sort distributions of 90 items given earlier and the numbers assigned to the piles) as though they were scores of individuals on a variable, add them across persons, and use them in statistical tests of significance.

[22] N. Livson and T. Nichols, ''Discrimination and Reliability in Q-Sort Personality Descriptions,'' *Journal of Abnormal and Social Psychology,* 52 (1956), 159–165. The author recalls an amusing and instructive incident. Colleagues had been asked to sort a 90-item unstructured Q sort the items of which were single words. One colleague, a philosopher, complained about the procedure. When he had finished, he said the procedure was highly questionable, and that if he had to do it over again the results would certainly be quite different. He did the sort again *eleven months later*. The coefficient of correlation between the first and second sorts was .81!

[23] J. Block, ''A Comparison of Forced and Unforced Q-Sorting Procedures,'' *Educational and Psychological Measurement,* 16 (1956), 481–493.

[24] A. Jones, ''Distribution of Traits in Current Q-Sort Methodology,'' *Journal of Abnormal and Social Psychology,* 53 (1956), 90–95.

[25] S. Brown, *Political Subjectivity: Applications of Q Methodology in Political Science.* New Haven: Yale University Press, 1980, pp. 201–203, 288–289.

[26] See L. Cronbach and G. Gleser, ''Assessing Similarity Between Profiles,'' *Psychological Bulletin,* 50 (1953), 456–473.

(mean) and scatter (standard deviation) of the sets of scores are lost. *Q* is not unique here. *Q* is unique, however, in systematically using a procedure that sacrifices level and scatter. All individuals have the same *general* mean and the same *general* standard deviation.

The practical answer is simple to state but not simple to implement: when elevation and scatter are important, do not use ipsative measures. If you are comparing the mean performances of two groups, for example, ipsative scores are of course inappropriate.[27] If, on the other hand, mean differences are not important but the relations among variables *within* individuals or groups are important, then ipsative scores may well be appropriate. In the last analysis, the experience and judgment of the researcher are the final arbiters of whether *Q* sorting should be used.

Q METHODOLOGY IN SOCIAL SCIENTIFIC AND EDUCATIONAL RESEARCH

Although it is possible, and sometimes desirable, to use *Q* to assess the effects of experimental manipulations, simpler procedures are usually more appropriate. This stricture applies whenever a hypothesis is tested by comparing the central tendencies, variabilities, or relative frequencies of characteristics of groups of individuals. *Q* can profitably be used for comparing the characteristics of groups of individuals only when comparing the relations *within* the groups. For example, we might test a hypothesis that two specified groups of individuals, categorized on the basis of holding different values or attitudes, will also cluster together similarly on some other measure presumably related to the values or attitudes.

Some research problems lend themselves nicely to *Q*. Complex aesthetic judgments and preferences are examples. Stephenson, in a brilliant *tour de force,* applied the structured *Q*-sort idea to artistic judgments.[28] He used actual squares and rectangles juxtaposed in various ways as items in a *Q* sort. Three variables were built into the sort: *shape dominance* (regular-irregular), *shape concentration* (overlapping-not overlapping), and *color*. He used an artist, himself, and graduate students as subjects, and made statistical predictions based on an aesthetic theory.

Getzels and Csikszentmihalyi followed a related and equally interesting procedure.[29] They had art students, all of whom were highly competent but of differing degrees of artistic talent, produce 31 drawings under controlled conditions. Then they had experts (artists) and nonexperts (graduate students) judge the drawings on *craftmanship, originality,* and *overall aesthetic value* by *Q* sorting the drawings. That is, each judge (total of 20 judges) sorted or rated the drawings three times. Correlations between *Q* sorts enabled the authors to conclude, among other things, that artists differed as much among themselves in judgments as laymen, but that they evidently related originality more to overall value than did the laymen. Both studies are themselves creative and original uses of *Q* to study the complex and highly elusive problem of aesthetic judgment. It is difficult to conceive a better empirical approach to the problem.

As indicated earlier, *Q* can be used to open up new areas, to test preliminary theories, to explore heuristic hunches. The problem of creativity has been tackled up to now almost entirely with large *N* cross-sectional methods. Following the lead of the two aesthetic

---

[27] This stricture has often been disregarded with unknown consequences. See footnote 21, above.

[28] Stephenson, *The Study of Behavior*, pp. 128ff.

[29] J. Getzels and M. Czikszentmihalyi, ''Aesthetic Opinion: An Empirical Study,'' *Pubic Opinion Quarterly,* 30 (1969), 34–45.

judgment studies just described, study of the stubborn but fascinating problem of creativity can be tackled. One might take a Guilford theory of convergent-divergent thinking or a Barron originality theory and explore them with Q.[30] Complex areas, especially psychological areas where intensive study of the individual is required, do not always yield too readily to large N approaches. Q methods, adequately used, should be useful in laying some of the research foundations in these areas.

One of the most valuable outcomes of a successful Q study is the factor array idea discussed earlier. A factor array, recall, is a "new" Q sort constructed from factor analytic results. The items of an array have Q values calculated from the Q sorts of the persons loaded on a factor. These items and their array values express the essence or content of a persons' factor. They epitomize the variable that the persons on the persons' factor share to a substantial degree. They form, in other words, a prototype. They can be used in a number of ways, even experimental. One of the most important is to assess the "agreement" with the prototype of untested individuals. For example, arrays can be calculated for the two factors, Concern for Students and Structure and Subject Matter, that Sontag found in his perceptions of teacher behaviors study outlined earlier (see the examples of items of the arrays given earlier). If we were studying, say, success in teaching and had found that those teachers high on Structure and Subject Matter tended to be successful, then we might use the prototype Q sort with teacher trainees. Perhaps further study of those individuals whose sorts correlate substantially with the prototype may help us learn more of the psychological and other characteristics that seem to be characteristic of "good" teachers. Or we can assess the influence of a teacher-training program by having trainees sort prototype Q sorts before, during, and after the training. Toward which prototype does the program lead students? The research potential of factor arrays seems to be great. Maybe researchers in education and psychology should pay more attention to their possibilities.

Although it cannot replace the methods discussed earlier in this book, Q methodology has a valuable contribution to make to behavioral research. In competent and imaginative hands it has an important place, perhaps mainly in opening up new areas of research. It is not well-suited to testing hypotheses over large numbers of individuals, nor can it be used too well with large samples.[31] One can rarely generalize to populations from Q persons samples. Indeed, one usually does not wish to do so. Rather, one tests theories on small sets of individuals carefully chosen for their "known" or presumed possession of some significant characteristic or characteristics. One explores unknown and unfamiliar areas and variables for their identity, their interrelations, and their functioning. Used thus, Q is an important and unique approach to the study of psychological, sociological, and educational phenomena.[32]

---

[30] J. Guilford, "Three Faces of Intellect," *American Psychologist,* 14 (1959), 469–479; F. Barron, "Complexity-Simplicity as a Personality Dimension," *Journal of Abnormal and Social Psychology,* 48 (1953), 163–172; "The Disposition toward Originality," *Journal of Abnormal and Social Psychology,* 51 (1955), 478–485.

[31] At least one adaptation of the Q idea, more or less minus its ipsative feature, has been worked out so that some of the advantages of Q can be obtained in large-sample surveys. See, for example, E., Cataldo et al., "Card Sorting as a Technique for Survey Interviewing," *Public Opinion Quarterly,* 34 (1970), 202–215. In addition, it is possible to construct pencil-and-paper measures that incorporate Q ideas. See D. Jackson and C. Bidwell, "A Modification of Q-Technique," *Educational and Psychological Measurement,* 29 (1959), 221–232; H. Webster, "A Forced-Choice Figure Preference Test Based on Factorial Design," *Educational and Psychological Measurement,* 29 (1959), 45–54. Both methods are ingenious and potentially effective.

[32] For a supplementary discussion in considerable depth of the place of Q in behavioral research, see Kerlinger, "Q Methodology in Behavioral Research," *op. cit.*

Study Suggestions

1. There are unfortunately very few widely available references on Q methodology. Brown's book cited in footnote 25 has valuable technical discussions with examples from Q research. To learn the mechanics of Q, students are advised to work with the examples and Q sorts that Stephenson included in *Study of Behavior*. The Jung Q sort he gives on pp. 83–85 is useful. Type the items on 3×5 cards. Use the distribution on p. 72, and record on the backs of the cards the categories I and E. (Stephenson uses a for Introversion and b for Extroversion for the items given on pp. 83–85.) Sort the cards to describe yourself. Have friends and fellow students do the same. Try to include both introverted and extroverted friends (according to your best judgment). Intercorrelate the sorts.[33] Try a simple cluster analysis by grouping persons with high r's together. After some practice you will acquire a knack for doing this. Next, try calculating one-way analysis of variance for each person using the categorization Introversion-Extroversion. Do the differences between the I and E means agree with your original judgments?

2. To learn something about the building of structured sorts, study Stephenson's Q testing of aesthetic preference in *The Study of Behavior*, pp. 128–141. Then try structuring some problem of interest to yourself. Write or select the items and try out the sort with friends or with other members of your class.

3. Pick 12 prominent political names, six Republicans and six Democrats. Type the names on sheets in random order. Ask some individuals whom you know to be Republicans and Democrats to rank order the names according to their preference for the individuals. Intercorrelate the ranks using the rank-order coefficient of correlation. Enter the *rho*'s in a correlation matrix. Can you identify the individuals who have rank ordered the names by the intercorrelations? Do the political party preferences show in the correlations? Is this like Q methodology? (See Table 32.1 and accompanying discussion.)

4. Intercorrelate the data of Table 32.4. Do you get the correlation matrix of Table 32.5? Substitute other persons (and, of course, other variables) and interpret the matrix.

5. Here is an easy and perhaps interesting class exercise. Have the following 12 attitude referents typed and reproduced: *civil rights, children's interests, Supreme Court, poverty program, Jews, socialized medicine; private property, education as intellectual training, subject matter, free enterprise, school discipline, religion.* The first six referents have been found to be liberal referents and the last six to be conservative referents (see text). Select ten members of the class at random to rank order the referents according to positive and negative feelings about them. (Rank 1, for instance, can be "strongly positive" and Rank 12 "strongly negative.") Then intercorrelate the rank orders using the rank-order coefficient of correlation (see footnote 2) to produce a 10×10 correlation matrix. See if any of the class members cluster together judged by substantial correlations ($\geq$ .40). Are there two clusters? If so, go back to the original rank orders of the members of the cluster to identify what is common to the cluster members. (A simple way to do this is to add the values given each item by the members of a cluster. Then rank order these sums. The nature of the cluster may be deduced from its rank order on this sums set of ranks.)

(*Note:* If the attitudes of the ten individuals are homogeneous, you may obtain only one cluster. It may be necessary to go outside the class for greater heterogeneity of attitudes.)

---

[33] It is useful, in recording an individual's Q-sort data, to write the values of the pile placements on the backs of the cards with the individual's initials, being careful to record the initials and numbers of an individual in the same relative position on each card. With structured sorts, record the structure category symbols on the back of each card. Number the faces of the cards with random numbers 1 through n, n being the number of cards in the deck. There are more elaborate systems for sorting and recording data—for example, racks for sorting and scoring sheets for entering pile placement values—but these are not recommended.

PART TEN

MULTIVARIATE APPROACHES AND ANALYSIS

Introduction

M ultivariate thinking has profoundly changed behavioral research, and in the coming decade will be even more influential than it has been in the last decade. To understand why, we must examine in some depth multivariate methods of conceiving research and of analyzing research data. The subject is not easy. But it is by no means unapproachable. Our purpose, as usual, is to try to understand the underlying nature and meaning of multivariate analysis methods in relation to research problems of psychology, sociology, education, and related behavioral disciplines. In order to understand, of course, we must also learn, to some extent at least, how to do multivariate analysis. As we will see later when we study the computer, it is not enough to have a smattering of the methods and to let the computer do the rest. We must penetrate the surface and know, both intuitively and analytically, the rationale and working of multivariate research problems and their analysis.

Multivariate analysis is a general term used to describe a group of mathematical and statistical methods whose purpose is to analyze multiple measures of N individuals: multiple regression, multivariate analysis of variance, canonical correlation, discriminant analysis, factor analysis, and analysis of covariance structures. Much behavioral research is multivariate in nature. The phenomena we wish to study and explain are complex: memory, achievement, learning, intelligence, creativity, organizational productivity, cognitive complexity, attitude structure, and many others. Many variables influence such phenomena, and multivariate methods are ways of studying multiple influences of several independent variables on one or more dependent variables. Multivariate methods, then, mirror the actual complexity of behavioral "reality." They make it possible for the behavioral scientist to probe more deeply and realistically into phenomena. The influence is profound: the very nature of the problems that behavioral scientists study changes radically.

Because they are the basic ingredients, so to speak, of most multivariate methods, we examine multiple regression and factor analysis in more depth and detail than we do other multivariate methods. Chapter 33 examines the foundations of multiple regression and the interpretation of its results, and Chapter 34 explores its application to analysis of variance and covariance and its use in path analysis. In Chapter 34 we also briefly examine discriminant analysis, canonical correlation, and multivariate analysis of variance. Unfortunately, we have the space to do little more than characterize these analytic methods. Chapter 35 on factor analysis is one of the most important in the book. It attempts to present some idea of the sweep and even grandeur of the queen of methodologies, factor analysis. Finally, in Chapter 36 we face our greatest challenge: analysis of covariance structures. In this most ambitious approach, virtually all other multivariate methods, but especially factor analysis and multiple regression, are combined and generalized and the powerful idea of latent variables used as a functional part of the system. We end the substantive and methodological discussion of the book fittingly, in other words, with consideration of an analytic system that makes possible the conceptualization and empirical testing of complex behavioral theories and alternative hypotheses.

Chapter 33

Multiple Regression Analysis: Foundations

Multiple regression analysis is a method for studying the effects and the magnitudes of the effects of more than one independent variable on one dependent variable using principles of correlation and regression. We turn immediately to research and defer explanation until later.

TWO RESEARCH EXAMPLES

How are air pollution and socioeconomic status related to mortality from respiratory ailments? Lave and Seskin, in their study of English and American data, used multiple regression analysis to answer the question.[1] In their studies in English boroughs, they assessed the presumed effects of air pollution and socioeconomic status, as independent variables, on mortality rates of lung cancer, bronchitis, and pneumonia, as dependent variables.

The overall effect of the two independent variables on the dependent variable is expressed by the square of a correlation coefficient called the coefficient of multiple correlation, or R^2. This coefficient's interpretation is similar to that of r^2, which we discussed much earlier.[2] It is the proportion of the variance of the dependent variable, in this case

---

[1] L. Lave and E. Seskin, "Air Pollution and Human Health," *Science*, 169 (1970), 723–733.

[2] Recall that squaring a correlation coefficient yields an estimate of the amount of variance shared by two variables. This notion is used a great deal in regression analysis.

mortality, accounted for by the two independent variables. The R^2's between mortality due to bronchitis, on the one hand, and air pollution and socioeconomic status, on the other hand, ranged from .30 to .78 in different samples in England and Wales, indicating substantial relations. The R^2's for the dependent variables, lung cancer and pneumonia mortalities, were similar. Multiple regression also enables the researcher to learn something of the relative influences of independent variables. In most of the samples, air pollution was more important than socioeconomic status. As a "control" analysis, Lave and Seskin studied other cancers that would presumably not be affected by air pollution. The R^2's were consistently lower, as expected. Extension of the research to metropolitan areas in the United States yielded similar results.[3]

In a study of the prediction of high school GPA (grade-point average), Holtzman and Brown used two independent variable measures: study habits and attitudes (SHA) and scholastic aptitude (SA).[4] The correlations between high school GPA (the dependent variable) and SHA and SA in grade 7 ($N = 1684$) were .55 and .61. The correlation between SHA and SA was .32. How much more variance was accounted for by adding the scholastic-aptitude measure to the study-habits measure? If we combine SHA and SA optimally to predict GPA, we obtain a correlation of .72. The answer to the question, then, is $.72^2 - .55^2 = .52 - .30 = .22$, or 22 percent more of the variance of GPA is accounted for by adding SA to SHA.

These are examples of multiple regression analysis. The basic idea is the same as simple correlation except that k, where k is greater than 1, independent variables are used to predict the dependent variable. In simple regression analysis, a variable, X, is used to predict another variable, Y. In multiple regression analysis, variables $X_1, X_2, \ldots, X_k$ are used to predict Y. The method and the calculations are done in a manner to give the "best" prediction possible, given the correlations among all the variables. In other words, instead of saying: If X, then Y, we say: If $X_1, X_2, \ldots, X_k$, then Y, and the results of the calculations tell us how "good" the prediction is and approximately how much of the variance of Y is accounted for by the "best" linear combination of the independent variables.

SIMPLE REGRESSION ANALYSIS

We say that we study the regression of Y scores on X scores. We wish to study how the Y scores "go back to," how they "depend upon," the X scores. Galton, who first worked out the notion of correlation, got the idea from the notion of "regression toward mediocrity," a phenomenon observed in studies of inheritance. (The symbol r used for the coefficient of correlation originally meant "regression.") Tall men will tend to have shorter sons, and short men taller sons. The sons' heights, then, tend to "regress to," or "go back to," the mean of the population. Statistically, if we want to predict Y from X and the correlation between X and Y is zero, then our best prediction is to the mean. That is, for any given X, say X_7, we can only predict the mean of Y. The higher the correlation, however, the better the prediction. If $r = 1.00$, then prediction is perfect. To the extent

---

[3] Students should bear in mind our earlier discussions of the difficulty in interpreting nonexperimental results (Chapter 22). Lave and Seskin, however, have built a strong case, even though some of their interpretation was questionable. At this point, it would be wise for readers to turn back to the discussion, "Multivariate Relations and Regression," in Chapter 5.

[4] W. Holtzman and W. Brown, "Evaluating the Study Habits and Attitudes of High School Students," *Journal of Educational Psychology*, 59 (1968), 404–409.

that the correlation departs from 1.00, to that extent predictions from X to Y are less than perfect. If we plot the X and Y values when $r = 1.00$, they will all lie on a straight line. The higher the correlation, the closer the plotted values will be to the regression line (see Chapter 5).

To illustrate and explain the notion of statistical regression, we use two fictitious examples with simple numbers. The numbers used in the two examples are the same except that they are arranged differently.[5] The examples are given in Table 33.1. In the example on the left, labeled A, the correlation between the X and Y values is .90, while in the example on the right, labeled B, the correlation is 0. Certain calculations necessary for regression analysis are also given in the table: the sums and means, the deviation sums of squares of X and Y ($\Sigma x^2 = \Sigma X^2 - (\Sigma X)^2/n$), the deviation cross products ($\Sigma xy = \Sigma XY - (\Sigma X)(\Sigma Y)/n$), and certain regression values to be explained shortly.

First, note the difference between the A and B sets of scores. They differ only in the order of the scores of the second or X columns. The two different orders produce very different correlations between the X and Y scores. In the A set, $r = .90$, and in the B set, $r = .00$. Second, note the statistics at the bottom of the table. Σx^2 and Σy^2 are the same in both A and B, but Σxy is 9 in A and 0 in B. Let us concentrate on the A set of scores.

The basic equation of simple linear regression is:

$$Y' = a + bX \tag{33.1}$$

Table 33.1 Regression Analysis of Two Sets of Scores

A.		$r = .90$				B.		$r = .00$		
Y	X	XY	Y'	d		Y	X	XY	Y'	d
1	2	2	1.2	$-.2$		1	5	5	3	-2
2	4	8	3.0	-1.0		2	2	4	3	-1
3	3	9	2.1	$.9$		3	4	12	3	0
4	5	20	3.9	$.1$		4	6	24	3	1
5	6	30	4.8	$.2$		5	3	15	3	2
Σ: 15	20	69		0		15	20	60		0
M: 3	4		$\Sigma d^2 = 1.90$			3	4		$\Sigma d^2 = 10.00$	
Σ^2:55	90					55	90			

$\Sigma y^2 = 55 - \dfrac{(15)^2}{5} = 10$ $\qquad\qquad$ $\Sigma y^2 = 55 - \dfrac{(15)^2}{5} = 10$

$\Sigma x^2 = 90 - \dfrac{(20)^2}{5} = 10$ $\qquad\qquad$ $\Sigma x^2 = 90 - \dfrac{(20)^2}{5} = 10$

$\Sigma xy = 69 - \dfrac{(15)(20)}{5} = 9$ $\qquad\qquad$ $\Sigma xy = 60 - \dfrac{(15)(20)}{5} = 0$

$b = \dfrac{\Sigma xy}{\Sigma x^2} = \dfrac{9}{10} = .90$ $\qquad\qquad$ $b = \dfrac{0}{10} = 0$

$a = \bar{Y} - b\bar{X} = 3 - (.90)(4) = -.60$ $\qquad\qquad$ $a = 3 - (0)(4) = 3$

$Y' = a + bx = -.60 + .90X$ $\qquad\qquad$ $Y' = 3 + (0)X$

---

[5] These examples are taken from Chapter 15, where, in considering the analysis of variance, we studied the effect on the F test of the correlation between experimental groups.

where X = the scores of the independent variable, a = intercept constant, b = regression coefficient, and Y' = predicted scores of the dependent variable. A regression equation is a prediction formula: Y values are predicted from X values. The correlation between the observed X and Y values in effect determines how the prediction equation "works." The intercept constant, a, and the regression coefficient, b, will be explained shortly.

The two sets of X and Y values of Table 33.1 are plotted in Figure 33.1. Lines have been drawn in each plot to "run through" the plotted points. If we had a way of placing these lines so that they would simultaneously be as close to all the points as possible, then the lines should express the regression of Y on X. The line in the left plot, where r = .90, runs close to the plotted XY points. In the right plot, however, where r = .00, it is not possible to run the line close to all the points. The points, after all, are in effect placed randomly, since r = .00.

The correlations between X and Y, r = .90 and r = .00, determine the slopes of the regression lines (when the standard deviations are equal, as they are in this case). The *slope* indicates the change in Y with a change of one unit of X. In the r = .90 example, with a change of 1 in X, we predict a change of .90 in Y. (This is expressed trigonometrically as the length of the line opposite the angle made by the regression line divided by the length of the line adjacent to the angle. In Figure 33.1, if we drop a perpendicular from the regression line—the point where the X and Y means intersect, for example—to a line drawn horizontally from the point where the regression line intersects the Y axis, or at Y = −.60, then 3.6/4.0 = .90. A change of 1 in X means a change of .90 in Y.[6])

The plot of the X and Y values of Example B, right part of Figure 33.1, is quite different. In Example A, one can rather easily and visually draw a line through the points and achieve a fairly accurate approximation to the regression line. But in Example B this is hardly possible. We can draw the line only by using other guidelines, which we get to shortly. Another important thing to note is the scatter or dispersion of the plotted points around the two regression lines. In Example A, they cling rather closely to the line. If r = 1.00, they would all be on the line. When r = .00, on the other hand, they scatter widely about the line. The lower the correlation, the greater the scatter.

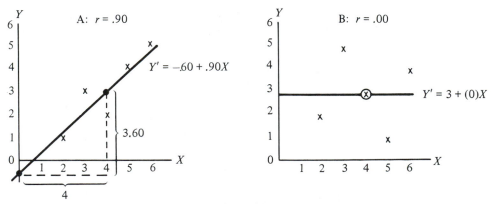

Figure 33.1

[6] Raw scores have been used for most of the examples in this chapter because they fit our purposes better. A thorough treatment of regression, however, requires discussions using deviation scores and standard scores. The emphasis here, as elsewhere in the book, is on research uses of the methods and techniques and not on statistics as such. The student should supplement his study, therefore, with good basic discussions of simple and multiple regression. See the references in the study suggestions at the end of the next chapter.

In order to calculate the regression statistics of the two examples, we must calculate the deviation sums of squares and cross products. This has been done at the bottom of Table 33.1. The formula for the *slope*, or *regression coefficient*, *b*, is:

$$b = \frac{\Sigma xy}{\Sigma x^2} \tag{33.2}$$

The two *b*'s are .90 and .00. The *intercept constant, a,* is calculated with the formula:

$$a = \bar{Y} - b\bar{X} \tag{33.3}$$

The *a*'s for the two examples are $-.60$ and 3; e.g., for Example A, $a = 3 - (.90)(4) = -.60$. The intercept constant is the point where the regression line intercepts the Y axis. To draw the regression line, lay a ruler between the intercept constant on the Y axis and the point where the mean of Y and the mean of X meet. (In Figure 33.1, these points are indicated with small circles.)

The final steps in the process, at least as far as it will be taken here, are to write regression equations and then, using the equations, calculate the predicted values of Y, or Y', given the X values. The two equations are given in the last line of Table 33.1. First look at the regression equation for $r = .00$: $Y' = 3 + (0)X$. This means, of course, that all the predicted Y's are 3, the mean of Y. When $r = 0$, the best prediction is the mean, as indicated earlier. When $r = 1.00$, at the other extreme, the reader can see that one can predict exactly: one simply adds a, the constant, to the X scores. When $r = .90$, prediction is less than perfect and one predicts Y' values calculated with the regression equation. For example, to predict the first Y' score, we calculate:

$$Y'_1 = -.60 + (.90)(2) = 1.20$$

The predicted scores of the A and B sets have been given in Table 33.1. (See columns labeled Y'.) Note an important point: If, for Example A, we plot the X and the predicted Y, or Y', values, the plotted points all lie on the regression line. That is, the regression line of the figure represents the set of predicted Y values, given the X values and the correlation between the X and the observed Y values.

We can now calculate the predicted values of Y. The higher the correlation, the more accurate the prediction. The accuracy of the predictions of the two sets of scores can be clearly shown by calculating the differences between the original Y values and the predicted Y values, or $Y - Y' = d$, and then calculating the sums of squares of these differences. Such differences are called *residuals*. In Table 33.1, the two sets of residuals and their sums of squares have been calculated (see columns labeled d). The two values of Σd^2, 1.90 for A and 10.00 for B, are quite different, just as the plots in Figure 33.1 are quite different: that of the B, or $r = .00$, set is much greater than that of the A, or $r = .90$, set. That is, the higher the correlation, the smaller the deviations from prediction and thus the more accurate the prediction.

MULTIPLE LINEAR REGRESSION

The method of multiple linear regression extends the ideas presented in the preceding section to more than one independent variable. From knowledge of the values of two or more independent variables, $X_1, X_2, \ldots, X_k$, we want to predict to a dependent variable, Y. Earlier in the book we talked about the great need to assess the influence of several variables on a dependent variable. We can, of course, predict from verbal aptitude, say, to reading achievement, or from conservatism to ethnic attitudes. But how much more powerful it would be if we could predict from verbal aptitude together with other variables known or thought to influence reading—for example, achievement motivation and attitude toward school work. Theoretically, there is no limit to the number of variables we can use, but there are practical limits. Although only two independent variables are used in the example that follows, the principles apply to any number of independent variables.

An Example

Take one of the problems just mentioned. Suppose we had reading achievement (RA), verbal aptitude (VA), and achievement motivation (AM) scores on 20 eighth-grade pupils. We want to predict to reading achievement, Y, from verbal aptitude, X_1, and achievement motivation, X_2. Or, we want to calculate the regression of reading achievement on *both* verbal aptitude and achievement motivation. If the scores on verbal aptitude and achievement motivation were standard scores, we might average them, treat the averages as one composite independent variable, and calculate the regression statistics as we did earlier. We might not do too badly either. But there is a better way.

Suppose the X_1, verbal aptitude, X_2, achievement motivation, and Y, reading achievement, scores of the 20 subjects and the sums, means, and raw score sums of squares are those of Table 33.2 (Disregard the Y' and d columns for the moment.) We need to calculate the deviation sums of squares, the deviation cross products, the standard deviations $[\sqrt{\Sigma x^2/(N-1)}]$, and the correlations among the three variables. These are the basic

Table 33.2   Fictitious Example: Reading Achievement (Y), Verbal Aptitude (X_1), and Achievement Motivation (X_2) Scores

Y	X_1	X_2	Y'	$Y - Y' = d$
2	2	4	3.0305	−1.0305
1	2	4	3.0305	−2.0305
1	1	4	2.3534	−1.3534
1	1	3	1.9600	−.9600
5	3	6	4.4944	.5056
4	4	6	5.1715	−1.1715
7	5	3	4.6684	2.3316
6	5	4	5.0618	.9382
7	7	3	6.0226	.9774
8	6	3	5.3455	2.6545
3	4	5	4.7781	−1.7781
3	3	5	4.1010	−1.1010
6	6	9	7.7059	−1.7059
6	6	8	7.3125	−1.3125
10	8	6	7.8799	2.1201
9	9	7	8.9504	.0496
6	10	5	8.8407	−2.8407
6	9	5	8.1636	−2.1636
9	4	7	5.5649	3.4351
10	4	7	5.5649	4.4351
Σ: 110	99	104		0
M: 5.50	4.95	5.20		
Σ²: 770.0	625.0	600.0		81.6091

Table 33.3 Deviation Sums of Squares and Cross Products, Correlation
Coefficients, and Standard Deviations of Data of Table 33.2[a]

	y	x_1	x_2
y	165.00	100.50	39.00
x_1	.6735	134.95	23.20
x_2	.3946	.2596	59.20
s	2.9469	2.6651	1.7652

[a]The tabled entries are as follows. The first line gives, successively, Σy^2, the
deviation sum of squares of Y, the cross product of the deviations of X_1 and Y, or $\Sigma x_1 y$,
and finally $\Sigma x_2 y$. The entries in the second and third lines, on the diagonal or above,
are $\Sigma x_1{}^2$, $\Sigma x_1 x_2$, and (in the lower right corner) $\Sigma x_2{}^2$. The italicized entries *below* the
diagonal are the correlation coefficients. The standard deviations are given in the last
line.

statistics that are calculated for almost any set of data. They are given in Table 33.3.[7] The
sums of squares and cross products are given in the diagonal (from upper left to lower
right) and above it, and the correlations are given below the diagonal. The r's of prime
interest are those of the two independent variables with the dependent variable, r_{y1} and
r_{y2}, .6735 and .3946. With these routine calculations out of the way, we can concentrate
on the basic notions of multiple regression.

The fundamental regression equation is:

$$Y' = a + b_1 X_1 + \cdots + b_k X_k \qquad (33.4)$$

The symbols have the same meaning as those of the simple regression equation, except
that there are k independent variables and k regression coefficients. Somehow, a and the
b's must be calculated from knowledge of the X's and Y. These calculations are the most
complex of multiple regression analysis. For only two independent variables, algebraic
formulas given in statistics books can be used.[8] The calculation of a, once the b's are
found, is straightforward. The problem is the calculation of the b's when there are more
than two independent variables. Only the general ideas behind the calculations will be
explained, since the details would take us too far from our central concern.[9]

What we have, in effect, is a set of linear equations, one equation for each independent variable. The objective of the determination of the b's of Equation 33.4 is to find
those b values that will minimize the sums of squares of the residuals. This is the so-called
principle of least squares. The calculus provides the method of differentiation for doing
this. If used, it yields a set of simultaneous linear equations called *normal* equations (no
relation to the normal distribution). A convenient form of these equations contains the
coefficients of correlation among all the independent variables and between the indepen-

[7]The calculations are not done here because their mechanics were covered in earlier chapters. The student
should do them and note that he will probably obtain results slightly different from those reported above. Such
differences are due to rounding errors—an ever-present problem in multivariate analysis. In fact, the results of
this problem, obtained on a desk calculator, are slightly different from those obtained by computer.

[8]See E. Pedhazur, *Multiple Regression in Behavioral Research: Explanation and Prediction*, 2d ed. New
York: Holt, Rinehart and Winston, 1982, p. 51.

[9]See *ibid.*, chap. 3, for complete discussions of both the ideas and the calculations. The "data" used in
Tables 33.2 and 33.3 are identical to those in Pedhazur, *ibid.*, Tables 3.1 and 3.2, pp. 49–50. They are also the
same as in the first edition: F. Kerlinger and E. Pedhazur, *Multiple Regression in Behavioral Research*. New
York: Holt, Rinehart and Winston, 1973, pp. 49–50.

dent variables and the dependent variable and a set of weights called beta weights, β_j, which will be explained later (they are like the b weights). The normal equations for the above problem are:

$$r_{11}\beta_1 + r_{12}\beta_2 = r_{y1}$$
$$r_{21}\beta_1 + r_{22}\beta_2 = r_{y2}$$

(33.5)

where β_j = beta weights; r_{ij} = the correlations among the independent variables; and r_{yj} = the correlations between the independent variables and the dependent variable, Y. (Note that $r_{12} = r_{21}$, and that $r_{11} = r_{22} = 1.00$. Note, too, that Equation 33.5 can be extended to any number of independent variables.)

Probably the best way—certainly the most elegant way—to solve the equations for the β_j is to use matrix algebra. Unfortunately, knowledge of matrix algebra cannot be assumed. So the actual solution of the equations must be omitted. The solution yields the following beta weights: $\beta_1 = .6123$ and $\beta_2 = .2357$. The b weights are then obtained from the following formula:

$$b_j = \beta_j \frac{s_y}{s_j}$$

(33.6)

where s_j = standard deviations of variables 1 and 2 (see Table 33.3) and s_y = standard deviation of Y. Substituting in Equation 33.6 we obtain:

$$b_1 = (.6123)\left(\frac{2.9469}{2.6651}\right) = .6771$$

$$b_2 = (.2357)\left(\frac{2.9469}{1.7652}\right) = .3934$$

To obtain the intercept constant, extend Equation 33.3 to two independent variables:

$$a = \bar{Y} - b_1\bar{X}_1 - b_2\bar{X}_2$$
$$a = 5.50 - (.6771)(4.95) - (.3934)(5.20) = .1027$$

Finally, we write the complete regression equation:

$$Y' = a + b_1X_1 + b_2X_2$$
$$Y' = .1027 + .6771X_1 + .3934X_2$$

Substituting the observed values of X_1 and X_2 of Table 33.2, the predicted values of Y, or Y', are obtained. For example, calculate the predicted Y's for the fifth and twentieth subjects:

$$Y'_5 = .1027 + (.6771)(3) + (.3934)(6) = 4.4944$$
$$Y'_{20} = .1027 + (.6771)(4) + (.3934)(7) = 5.5649$$

These values and the other eighteen values are given in the fourth column of Table 33.2. The fifth column of the table gives the deviations from regression, or the residuals, $Y_i - Y'_i = d_i$. For example, the residuals for Y_5 and Y_{20} are:

$$d_5 = Y_5 - Y'_5 = 5 - 4.4944 = .5056$$
$$d_{20} = Y_{20} - Y'_{20} = 10 - 5.5649 = 4.4351$$

Note that one deviation is small and the other large. The residuals are given in the last column of Table 33.2. Most of them are relatively small, and about half are positive and half negative.

The sum of squares due to regression can now be calculated, but the regression of Y

on X_1 *and* X_2 must be considered. Square each of the Y' values of the fourth column of Table 33.2 and sum:

$$(3.0305)^2 + \cdots + (5.5649)^2 = 688.3969$$

Now use the usual formula for the deviation sum of squares (see chap. 13):

$$\Sigma y'^2 = 688.3969 - \frac{(110)^2}{20} = 83.3969$$

Similarly, calculate the sum of squares of the residuals:

$$\Sigma d^2 = (-1.0305)^2 + \cdots + (4.4351)^2 = 81.6091^{10}$$

As a check, calculate:

$$ss_{reg} + ss_{res} = ss_t$$
$$83.3969 + 81.6091 = 165.0060$$

The regression and residual sums of squares are not usually calculated in this way. They were so calculated here to show just what these quantities are. Had the formulas that are ordinarily used been used, we might not have clearly seen that the regression sum of squares is the sum of squares of the Y' values calculated by using the regression equation. We also might not have seen clearly that the residual sum of squares is the sum of squares calculated with the d's of the fifth column of Table 33.2. Recall, too, that the a and the b's (or β's) of the regression equation were calculated to satisfy the least-squares principle, that is, to minimize the d's, or errors of prediction—or, rather, to minimize the sum of the squares of the errors of prediction. To summarize: The regression sum of squares expresses that portion of the total sum of squares of Y that is due to the regression of Y, the dependent variable, on X_1 and X_2, the independent variables, and the residual sum of squares expresses that portion of the total sum of squares of Y that is *not* due to the regression.

The reader may wonder: Why bother with this complicated procedure of determining the regression weights? Is it necessary to invoke a least-squares procedure? Why not just average the X_1 and X_2 values and call the means of the individual X_1 and X_2 values the predicted Y's? The answer is that it might work quite well. Indeed, in this case it would work very well, almost as well, in fact, as the full regression procedure. But it might *not* work too well. The trouble is that you do not really know when it will work well and when it will not. The regression procedure always "works," other things equal. It always minimizes the squared errors of prediction. Notice that in both cases linear equations are used and that only the coefficients differ:

Regression equation: $Y' = a + b_1X_1 + b_2X_2$
Mean equation: $Y' = \frac{1}{2}X_1 + \frac{1}{2}X_2$

Of the innumerable possible ways of weighting X_1 and X_2, which should be chosen if the least-squares principle is not used? It is conceivable, of course, that one has prior knowledge or some reason for weighting X_1 and X_2. X_1 may be the scores on some test that has been found to be highly successful in prediction. X_2 may be a successful predictor, too, but not as successful as X_1. Therefore one may decide to weight X_1 very heavily, say four times as much as X_2. The equation would be: $Y' = 4X_1 + X_2$. And this might

---

[10] This is a "good" example of the errors that cumulate through rounding. The actual regression sum of squares, calculated by computer, is 83.3909, an error of .006. Note, however, that even though the residuals were calculated from the hand-calculated predicted Y's, the sum of squares of the residuals is exactly that produced by the computer, 81.6091.

work well. The trouble is that seldom do we have prior knowledge, and even when we do, it is rather imprecise. How can the decision to weight X_1 four times as much as X_2 be reached? An educated guess can be made. The regression method is not a guess, however. It is a precise method based on the data and on a powerful mathematical principle. It is in this sense that the calculated regression weights are "best."

The regression and residual sums of squares can be calculated more readily than indicated above. The formulas are:

$$ss_{reg} = b_1 \Sigma x_1 y + \cdots + b_k \Sigma x_k y \qquad (33.7)$$
$$ss_{res} = ss_t - ss_{reg} \qquad (33.8)$$

In the present case, (33.7) becomes:

$$ss_{reg} = b_1 \Sigma x_1 y + b_2 \Sigma x_2 y$$

This is easily calculated by substituting the two b values calculated above and the cross products given in Table 33.3.

$$ss_{reg} = (.6771)(100.50) + (.3934)(39.00) = 83.3912$$
$$ss_{res} = 165.0 - 83.3912 = 81.6088$$

Within errors of rounding, these are the values calculated directly from the fourth and fifth columns of Table 33.2. (Note the "most accurate" values given by a computer: $ss_{reg} = 83.3909$ and $ss_{res} = 81.6091$, which of course total to $ss_t = \Sigma y^2 = 165.0$.)

THE MULTIPLE CORRELATION COEFFICIENT

If the ordinary product-moment coefficient of correlation between the predicted values, Y', and the observed values of Y are calculated, we obtain an index of the magnitude of the relation between, on the one hand, a least-squares composite of X_1 and X_2, and, on the other hand, Y. This index is called the *multiple correlation coefficient, R*. Although in this chapter it is usually written as R for the sake of brevity, a more satisfactory way to write it is with subscripts: $R_{y.12\ldots k}$, or, in this case, $R_{y.12}$. The theory of multiple regression seems to be especially elegant when we consider the multiple correlation coefficient. It is one of the links that bind together the various aspects of multiple regression and analysis of variance. The formula for R that expresses the first sentence of this paragraph is:

$$R = \frac{\Sigma yy'}{\sqrt{\Sigma y^2 \Sigma y'^2}} \qquad (33.9)$$

Its square is calculated:

$$R^2 = \frac{(\Sigma yy')^2}{\Sigma y^2 \Sigma y'^2} \qquad (33.10)$$

Using the Y and Y' values of Table 33.2, we obtain: $R^2 = .5054$ and $R = \sqrt{.5054} = .7109$.[11]

[11] Calculating these values is a good exercise. We already have $\Sigma y^2 = 165$. Then calculate:

$$\Sigma y'^2 = \Sigma Y'^2 - \frac{(\Sigma Y')^2}{N} = 688.3969 - \frac{(110)^2}{20} = 83.3969$$

and

$$\Sigma yy' = \Sigma YY' - \frac{(\Sigma Y)(\Sigma Y')}{N} = 688.3939 - \frac{(110)(110)}{20} = 83.3939$$

It can be shown algebraically that $\Sigma y'^2$ equals $\Sigma yy'$. The difference of .003 is due to rounding errors.

R, then, is the highest possible correlation between a least-squares linear composite of the independent variables and the observed dependent variable. R^2, analogous to r^2, indicates that portion of the variance of the dependent variable, Y, due to the independent variables in concert. R, unlike r, varies only from 0 to 1.00; it does not have negative values.

Two other important conclusions can be reached by calculating the correlations of the residuals, d_i, of Table 33.2, with X_1 and X_2, on the one hand, and with Y, on the other hand. The correlations of the residuals with X_1 and X_2 are both zero. This is not surprising when it is realized that, by definition, the residuals are that part of Y not accounted for by X_1 and X_2. That is, when the Y' values are subtracted from the Y values, that portion due to the regression of Y on X_1 and X_2 is taken from them. Whatever is left over, then, is unrelated to either X_1 or X_2. (If the student will take the trouble to calculate the correlation between the d vector—a vector is a single set of measures, either in a column or a row—and either the X_1 or the X_2 vector, he will convince himself of this fact.[12]) An important research implication of this generalization will be discussed later when actual research examples are summarized and discussed.

The correlation of the residuals, d_i, of Table 33.2 with the original Y values also helps to clarify matters. This correlation is: $r_{dy} = .7033$, and its square is: $r_{dy}^2 = (.7033)^2 = .4946$. If this latter value is added to the R^2 calculated earlier, the result is interesting: $R^2 + r_{dy}^2 = .5054 + .4946 = 1.0000$. And this will always be true. The total variance of Y is represented by 1.0000. The variance of Y due to Y's regression on X_1 and X_2 is .5054. The variance of Y not due to the regression of Y on X_1 and X_2 can be calculated: $1.0000 - .5054 = .4946$, which is, of course, the value of r_{dy}^2 just calculated directly. The meaning of r_{dy}^2 can be seen in two ways. The direct calculation of the correlation shows that the residuals constitute that part of the variance of Y not due to the regression of Y on X_1 and X_2. In the present case, 51 percent ($R^2 = .51$) of the variance of the reading achievement (Y) of the 20 pupils is accounted for by a least-squares linear combination of verbal aptitude (X_1) and achievement motivation (X_2). But 49 percent of the variance is due to other variables and to error. After discussing more usual ways to calculate R and R^2, we will again consider the proportion or percentage interpretation of R^2.

In sum, R^2 is an estimate of the proportion of the variance of the dependent variable, Y, accounted for by the independent variables, X_j. R, the multiple correlation coefficient, is the product-moment correlation between the dependent variable and another variable produced by a least-squares combination of the independent variables. Its square is interpreted analogously to the square of an ordinary correlation coefficient. It differs from the ordinary coefficient, however, in taking values only from 0 to 1. R is not as useful and interpretable as R^2, and henceforth R^2 will be used almost exclusively in subsequent discussion.

The proportion or percentage interpretation of R^2 becomes clearer if a sum of squares formula is used:

$$R^2 = \frac{ss_{\text{reg}}}{ss_t} \tag{33.11}$$

where ss_t is, as usual, the total sum of squares of Y, or Σy_t^2. Substituting the regression

[12] Don't underestimate the importance of doing such calculations and pondering their meaning. This is especially important in helping to understand multiple regression and other multivariate techniques. It can be a serious mistake to let the computer do everything for us, especially with package programs. Use a programmable calculator-computer or a microcomputer. For the simpler statistics, like r and the various sums of squares, write relatively simple programs, store them on floppy disks of microcomputers or on the plastic slides of programmable calculators, and use them when needed. The nature and use of the computer, especially the microcomputer or the so-called personal computer, will be discussed in more detail in Appendix B.

sum of squares calculated earlier by Formula 33.7, and the total sum of squares from Table 33.3, we obtain:

$$R^2 = \frac{83.3912}{165.0000} = .5054$$

And R^2 is seen to be that part of the Y sum of squares associated with the regression of Y on the independent variables. As with all proportions, multiplying it by 100 converts it to a percentage.

Formula 33.11 provides another link to the analysis of variance. In Chapter 13 on the foundations of analysis of variance, a formula for calculating E, the so-called correlation ratio, was given (Formula 13.4). Square that formula:

$$E^2 = \frac{ss_b}{ss_t}$$

where ss_b = the between-groups sum of squares, and ss_t = total sum of squares. ss_b is the sum of squares due to the independent variable. ss_{reg} is the sum of squares due to regression. Both terms refer to the sum of squares of a dependent variable due to an independent variable or to independent variables.[13]

TESTS OF STATISTICAL SIGNIFICANCE

Earlier we studied the simple regression of Y on X. To test the statistical significance of simple regression, we can assess the significance of the correlation coefficient between X and Y, r_{xy}, by referring to an appropriate table.[14] Tests of statistical significance in multiple regression, though more complex, are based on the relatively simple idea of comparing variances (or mean squares) as in analysis of variance. The same questions asked many times before must be asked again: Can this R^2 have arisen by chance? Or does it depart sufficiently from chance expectation that it can be said to be "significant"? Similar questions can be asked about individual regression coefficients. In this chapter and the next, F tests will be used almost exclusively. They fit in nicely with both regression analysis and analysis of variance, and they are both conceptually and computationally simple.[15]

---

[13] It should be noted that R and R^2 can be and are often inflated. Therefore, R^2 should be interpreted conservatively. If the sample is large, say over 200, there is little cause for concern. If the sample is small, however, it is wise to reduce the calculated R^2 by a few points. A so-called shrinkage formula can be used:

$$R_c^2 = 1 - (1 - R^2)\left(\frac{N-1}{N-n}\right)$$

where R_c^2 = shrunken or corrected R^2; N = size of sample; n = total number of variables in the analysis. Using this formula, the R^2 in the example reduces to .45.

[14] E.g., G. Snedecor and W. Cochran, *Statistical Methods*, 6th ed. Ames, Iowa: Iowa State University Press, 1967, Table A 11, p. 557. A readily available and useful book of statistical tables is: R. Burington and D. May, *Handbook of Probability and Statistics with Tables*, 2d ed. New York: McGraw-Hill, 1970. It should be pointed out, however, that statistical tables are probably obsolescent because routines for calculating the p's (probabilities) of r's, F, and t ratios, and other statistics can be and are written for computer programs, *e.g.*, N. Jaspen, "The Calculation of Probabilities Corresponding to Values of z, t, F and Chi Square," *Educational and Psychological Measurement*, 25 (1965), 877–880.

[15] Consideration of t tests of regression coefficients must be omitted because they require matrix algebra calculations beyond our reach. A t test of a regression coefficient, if significant, indicates that the regression weight differs significantly from zero, which means that the variable with which it is associated contributes significantly to the regression, the other independent variables being taken into account.

One is expressed by Equations 33.12a and 33.12b:

$$F = \frac{ss_{reg}/df_1}{ss_{res}/df_2} \tag{33.12a}$$

$$F = \frac{ss_{reg}/k}{ss_{res}/(N-k-1)} \tag{33.12b}$$

where ss_{reg} = sum of squares due to regression; ss_{res} = residual or error sum of squares; k = number of independent variables; N = sample size. If df_1 and df_2, the degrees of freedom for the numerator and denominator of the F ratio in Equation 33.12a, are defined, Equation 33.12b results. It is important because it is a formula to test the significance of any multiple regression problem. Using the values calculated earlier for the example of Table 33.2, now calculate:

$$F = \frac{83.3912/2}{81.6091/(20 - 2 - 1)} = \frac{41.6956}{4.8005} = 8.686$$

Note that the idea expressed by this formula is in the same family of ideas as analysis of variance. The numerator is the mean square due to the regression, analogous to the between-groups mean square, and the denominator is the mean square *not* due to regression, which is used as an error term, analogous to the within-groups mean square, or error variance. The basic principle, again, is always the same: variance due to the regression of Y on $X_1, X_2, \ldots X_k$, or, in analysis of variance, due to the experimental effects, is evaluated against variance presumably due to error or chance. This basic notion, elaborated at length in earlier chapters, can be expressed:

$$\frac{\text{regression variance}}{\text{error variance}} : \frac{\text{experimental variance}}{\text{error variance}}$$

Another formula for F is:

$$F = \frac{R^2/k}{(1 - R^2)/(N - k - 1)} \tag{33.13}$$

where k and N are the same as above. For the same example:

$$F = \frac{.5054/2}{(1 - .5054)/(20 - 2 - 1)} = \frac{.2527}{.0291} = 8.684$$

which is the same as the F value obtained with Equation 33.12, within errors of rounding. At 2 and 17 degrees of freedom, it is significant at the .01 level. This formula is particularly useful when our research data are only in the form of correlation coefficients. In such a case, the sums of squares required by Equation 33.12 may not be known. Much regression analysis can be done using only the matrix of correlations among all the variables, independent and dependent. Such analysis is beyond the scope of this book. Nevertheless, the student of research should be aware of the possibility.[16]

INTERPRETATION OF MULTIPLE REGRESSION STATISTCS

The interpretation of multiple regression statistics can be complex and difficult. Indeed, the interpretation of multivariate analysis statistics is in general considerably more diffi-

[16] See Pedhazur, *op. cit.*, pp. 57–58.

cult than the interpretation of the univariate statistics studied earlier. We therefore go into the interpretation of the statistics of our example in some depth.

Statistical Significance of the Regression and R^2

The F ratio of 8.684 calculated above tells us that the regression of Y on X_1 and X_2, expressed by $R^2_{y.12}$, is statistically significant. The probability that an F ratio this large will occur by chance is less than .01 (it is actually about .003), which means that the relation between Y and a least-squares combination of X_1 and X_2 could probably not have occurred by chance.

$R = .71$ can be interpreted much like an ordinary coefficient of correlation, except that the values of R range from 0 to 1.00, unlike r, which ranges from -1.00 through 0 to 1.00. $R^2 = .71^2 = .51$ is more meaningful and useful, however. It means that 51 percent of the variance of Y is accounted for, or "determined," by X_1 and X_2 in combination. It is accordingly called a *coefficient of determination*.

Relative Contributions to Y of the X's

Let us ask, somewhat diffidently, a more difficult question: What are the relative contributions of X_1 and X_2, of verbal aptitude and achievement motivation, to Y, reading achievement? The restricted scope of this book does not permit an examination of the answers to this question in the detail it deserves.[17]

One would think that the regression weights, b or β, would provide us with a ready means of identifying the relative contributions of independent variables to a dependent variable. And they do, but only roughly and sometimes misleadingly. Earlier it was said that the regression coefficient b is called the *slope*. The slope of the regression line is at the rate of b units of Y for one unit of X. In the little problem A of Table 33.1, for instance, $b = .90$. Thus, as said earlier, with a change of 1 unit in X we predict a change of .90 in Y. In multiple regression, however, straightforward interpretation like this is not so easy because there is more than one b. Nevertheless, we can say, *for present pedagogical purposes,* that if X_1 and X_2 have about the same scale of values—in the example of Table 33.2, the values of X_1 and X_2 are in the approximate range of 1 to 10—the b's are weights that show roughly the relative importance of X_1 and X_2. In the present case, the regression formula is:

$$Y' = .1027 + .6771X_1 + .3934X_2$$

We can say that X_1, verbal aptitude, is weighted more heavily than X_2, achievement motivation. This happens to be true in this case, but it may not always be true, especially with more independent variables.

Regression coefficients, unfortunately for interpretative purposes, are not stable. They change with different samples and with addition or subtraction of independent variables to the analysis.[18] There is no absolute way to interpret them. If the correlations among the

[17] The problem of the relative contribution of independent variables to a dependent variable or variables is one of the most complex and difficult of regression analysis. It seems that no really satisfactory solution exists, at least when the independent variables are correlated. Nevertheless, the problem cannot be neglected. The reader should bear in mind, however, that considerable reservation must be attached to the above and later discussions. The technical and substantive problems of interpretation of multiple regression analysis are discussed in two or three of the references given in Study Suggestion 1 at the end of the next chapter.

[18] See R. Darlington, "Multiple Regression in Psychological Research and Practice," *Psychological Bulletin*, 69 (1968), 161–182; R. Gordon, "Issues in Multiple Regression," *American Journal of Sociology*, 73 (1968), 592–612; Pedhazur, *op. cit.*, pp. 63–64, chap. 8.

independent variables are all zero or near-zero, interpretation is greatly simplified. But many or most variables that are correlated with a dependent variable are also correlated among themselves. The example of Table 33.3 shows this: the correlation between X_1 and X_2 is .26, a modest correlation, to be sure. Such intercorrelations are often higher, however. And the higher they are, the more unstable the interpretation situation.

The ideal predictive situation is when the correlations between the independent variables and the dependent variable are high, and the correlations among the independent variables are low. This principle is important. The more the independent variables are intercorrelated, the more difficult the interpretation. Among other things, one has greater difficulty telling the relative influence on the dependent variable of the independent variables. Examine the two fictitious correlation matrices of Table 33.4 and the accompanying R^2's. In the two matrices, the independent variables, X_1 and X_2, are correlated .87 and .43, respectively, with the dependent variable, Y. But the correlations between the independent variables are different in the two cases. In matrix A, $r_{12} = .50$, a substantial correlation. In matrix B, however, $r_{12} = 0$.

The contrast between the R^2's is dramatic: .76 for A and .94 for B. Since, in B, X_1 and X_2 are not correlated, any correlations they have with Y contribute to the prediction and the R^2.[19] When the independent variables are correlated, as in matrix A ($r_{12} = .50$), some of the common variance of Y and X_1 is also shared with X_2. In short, X_1 and X_2 are to some extent redundant in predicting Y. In matrix B there is no such redundancy.

The situation is clarified, perhaps, by Figure 33.2. Let the circles stand for the total variance of Y, and let this total variance be 1.00. Then the portions of the variance of Y accounted for by X_1 and X_2 can be depicted. In both circles, the horizontal hatching indicates the variance accounted for by X_1, or V_{X_1}, and the vertical hatching X_2, or V_{X_2}. (The variances remaining after V_{X_1} and V_{X_2} are the residual variances, labeled V_{res} in the figure.) In B, V_{X_1} and V_{X_2} do not overlap. In A, however, V_{X_1} and V_{X_2} overlap. Simply because $r_{12} = 0$ in B and $r_{12} = .50$ in A, the predictive power of the independent variables is much greater in B than in A. This is, of course, reflected by the R^2's: .76 in A and .94 in B.

While this is a contrived and artificial example, it has the virtue of showing the effect of correlation between the independent variables, and thus it illustrates the principle enunciated above. It also reflects the difficulty of interpreting the results of most regression analysis, since in much research the independent variables are correlated. And when more independent variables are added, interpretation becomes still more complex and difficult. A central problem is: How does one sort out the relative effects of the different

Table 33.4 Multiple Regression Examples With and Without Correlations Between Independent Variables

A				B		
1	2	Y		1	2	Y
1.00	.50	.87		1.00	0	.87
.50	1.00	.43		0	1.00	.43
.87	.43	1.00		.87	.43	1.00

$R^2_{y.12} = .76$ $\qquad\qquad\qquad\qquad$ $R^2_{y.12} = .94$

[19] When the correlations between the independent variables are exactly zero, as in matrix B, then R^2 is easy to calculate. It is simply the sum of the squares of the r's between each independent variable and the dependent variable: $(.87)^2 + (.43)^2 = .94$.

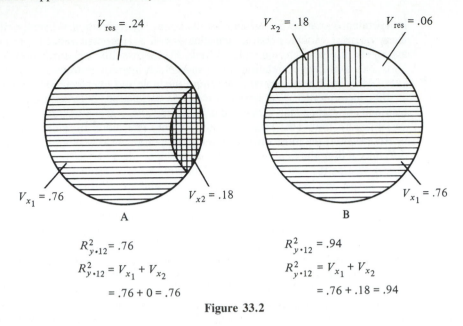

$V_{res} = .24$ $V_{x_2} = .18$ $V_{res} = .06$

$V_{x_1} = .76$ $V_{x2} = .18$ $V_{x_1} = .76$

A   B

$R^2_{y \cdot 12} = .76$ $R^2_{y \cdot 12} = .94$

$R^2_{y \cdot 12} = V_{x_1} + V_{x_2}$ $R^2_{y \cdot 12} = V_{x_1} + V_{x_2}$

$= .76 + 0 = .76$ $= .76 + .18 = .94$

Figure 33.2

X's on Y? The answer is also complex. There are ways of doing so, some more satisfying than others, but none completely satisfactory.[20]

OTHER ANALYTIC AND INTERPRETATIVE PROBLEMS

A number of problems in multiple regression analysis cannot in this book be discussed in the detail they deserve. Two or three, however, must be mentioned because of the increasing importance of multiple regression in behavioral research. One, mentioned earlier, is the problem of regression weights. In this chapter and the next, the discussion has been confined to b weights, because in most research uses of regression we predict with raw or deviation scores, and b's are used with such scores. So-called beta, or β, weights, on the other hand, are used with standard scores. They are called *standard partial regression coefficients*. "Standard" means that they would be used if all variables were in standard-score form. "Partial" means that the effects of variables other than the one to which the

[20] Perhaps the most satisfactory way, at least in the author's opinion and experience, is to calculate so-called squared semipartial correlations (also called part correlations). These are calculated with the formula:

$$SP^2 = R^2_{y.12...k} - R^2_{y.12...(k-1)}$$

or in the present case, for B:

$$SP^2 = R^2_{y.12} - R^2_{y.1} = .94 - .76 = .18$$

which indicates the contribution to the variance of Y of X_2 *after X_1 has been taken into account*. The same calculation for A yields: $.76 - .76 = 0$, which indicates that X_2 contributes nothing to the variance of Y, after X_1 has been taken into account. (Actually, there is a slight increase that emerges only with a large number of decimal places.)

The student is referred to the articles by Darlington and Gordon cited earlier for discussions of the problems involved. Kerlinger and Pedhazur also discuss the problem in considerable detail and relate it to research examples: Kerlinger and Pedhazur, *op. cit.*, pp. 70–72, *et passim*.

weight applies are held constant. For example, $\beta_{y1.23}$, or β_1 in a three-variable (independent variable) problem, is the standard partial regression weight, which expresses the change in Y due to change in X_1, with variables 2 and 3 held constant.[21] The b weights, too, are partial regression coefficients, but they are not in standard form.

Another problem is that in any given regression, R, R^2, and the regression weights will be the same no matter what the order of the variables. If one or more variables are added or subtracted from the regression, however, these values will change. And regression weights can change from sample to sample. In other words, there is no absolute quality about them. One cannot say, for instance, that because verbal and numerical aptitudes have, say, regression weights of .60 and .50 in one set of data, they will have the same values in another set.

Another important point is that there usually is limited usefulness to adding new variables to a regression equation. Because many variables of behavioral research are correlated, the principle illustrated by the data of Table 33.4 and discussed earlier operates so as to decrease the usefulness of additional variables. If one finds three or four independent variables that are substantially correlated with a dependent variable and not highly correlated with each other, one is lucky. But it becomes more and more difficult to find other independent variables that are not in effect redundant with the first three or four. If $R^2_{y.123} = .50$, then it is unlikely that $R^2_{y.1234}$ will be much more than .55, and $R^2_{y.12345}$ will probably not be more than .56 or .57. We have a regression law of diminishing returns, which will be illustrated in the next section when actual research results are discussed.[22]

It was said above that R, R^2, and the regression coefficients remain the same, if the same variables are entered in different orders. This should not be taken to mean, however, that the order in which variables enter the regression equation does not matter. On the contrary, order of entry can be very important. When the independent variables are correlated, the relative amount of variance of the dependent variable that each independent variable accounts for or contributes can change drastically with different orders of entry of the variables. With the A data of Table 33.4, for example, if we reverse the order of X_1 and X_2, their relative contributions change rather markedly. With the original order, X_2 contributed nothing to R^2, whereas with the order reversed X_2 becomes X_1 and contributes 19 percent $[r^2 = (.43)^2 = .19]$ to the total R^2, and the original X_1, which becomes X_2, contributes 57 percent $(.19 + .57 = .76)$. The order of variables, while making no difference in the final R^2 and thus in overall prediction, is a major research problem.

---

[21] A second meaning, used in theoretical work, is that β is the population regression weight which b estimates. We omit this meaning. β's can be translated into b's with the formula:

$$b_j = \beta_j \frac{s_y}{s_j}$$

where s_y = standard deviation of Y and s_j = standard deviation of variable j.

[22] When independent variables are added, one notes how much they add to R^2 and tests their statistical significance. The formula for doing so, much like formula 33.13, is:

$$F = \frac{(R^2_{y.12\ldots k_1} - R^2_{y.12\ldots k_2})/(k_1 - k_2)}{(1 - R^2_{y.12\ldots k_1})/(N - k_1 - 1)}$$

where k_1 = number of independent variables of the larger R^2, k_2 = number of independent variables of the smaller R^2, and N = number of cases. This formula will be used later. Although an F calculated like this may be statistically significant, especially with a large sample, the actual increase in R^2 may be quite small. In an example presented later in the chapter (Layton and Swanson's study), the addition of a sixth independent variable yielded a statistically significant F ratio, but the actual increase in R^2 was .0147! The difference between the R^2's in the numerator is the squared semipartial correlation coefficient mentioned in footnote 20.

RESEARCH EXAMPLES

DDT and Bald Eagles

One of the several controversies over despoliation of the environment by commercial interests and the opposition and protests of environmentalist groups has focused on the use of DDT. One effect of DDT spraying has been the decimation of bird species. For example, reproduction of the bald eagle population was seriously affected. In December 1972, DDT spraying was banned by the Environmental Protection Agency. Grier, in a study of the effect of the ban on bald eagle reproduction, reported the average number of young eagles per geographical area for the years 1966 through 1981.[23] His regression (and other) analyses of the reproduction averages (means) before and after the ban showed that the two slopes, or b coefficients, differed significantly. From 1966 to 1974, $b = -.07$, indicating a decrease in reproduction over the years, but from 1973 to 1981 $b = .07$, indicating an increase. (Both b's were statistically significant.)[24] The two regressions have been plotted in Figure 33.3. The plot portrays the regression of mean eagle young per geographical area on the years 1966 through 1974 (before the DDT ban)[25] and the years 1975–1981 (after the ban). The sharp difference between the two relations or slopes is dramatic.

Aptitudes and High School Rank

We take the data of a relatively simple study to show in some detail the importance of the order of entry of independent variables. Layton and Swanson used the subtests of the

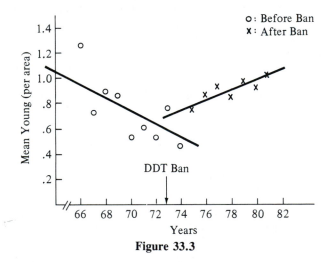

Figure 33.3

---

[23] J. Grier, "Ban of DDT and Subsequent Recovery of Reproduction in Bald Eagles," *Science*, 218 (1982), 1232–1234.

[24] The method of comparing slopes statistically is given in Pedhazur, *op. cit.*, pp. 438ff. The simple regressions are calculated using years as the independent variable and reproduction rates as the dependent variable. The correlation before the DDT ban was -.74, but after the ban it was .80 (my calculations).

[25] The regression before the ban was calculated through 1974 because the effect of the ban could not have been expected to manifest itself for about a year. Grier did his calculation through 1973 (Grier, *op. cit.*, footnote 11).

Differential Aptitude Test to predict rank in high school.[26] Using the correlation matrix that Layton and Swanson calculated among the six DAT subtests and high school rank (628 boys in 27 schools), three different orders of entry were used in multiple regression analyses.

To simplify matters, we report only the results with the first four of the six DAT subtests: Verbal Reasoning (VR), Numerical Aptitude (NA), Abstract Reasoning (AR), and Space Relations (SR). And we report only the R^2's of the first variable entered and the differences between the successive $\bar{R}^2$'s—that is $R^2_{y.1}$, $R^2_{y.12} - R^2_{y.1}$, $R^2_{y.123} - R^2_{y.12}$, and $R^2_{y.1234} - R^2_{y.123}$. These differences show the contributions, respectively, of X_1 alone, of X_2 after subtracting the effect of X_1, of X_3 after subtracting the effect of X_1 and X_2, and, finally, of X_4 after subtracting the effect of X_1, X_2, and X_3. These indices are squared semipartial (part) correlations (see footnotes 20 and 22). They can be interpreted, with circumspection, as indices of the variance contributions of each of the variables—in that particular order.

The squared semipartial correlations, which are percentages of the total variance (with the particular order of entry of the variables), are given in Table 33.5. The differences are pronounced. VR, for instance, which accounts for 31 percent of the total variance (with all six independent variables) in the first order of entry, accounts for only 5 percent in the third order. AR, which accounts for almost none of the variance in the first order when it is the third independent variable, jumps to 20 percent in the second order when it is the first independent variable. Obviously, the order of entry of variables in the regression equation is highly important. The reader should note other similar differences—for example, VR.

If readers feel a bit baffled by the problem of the order of entry of variables, they can hardly be blamed. Indeed, they have company among experts in the field. Actually, there is no "correct" method for determining the order of variables. A researcher may decide that he will let the computer choose the variables in order of the size of their contributions to the variance of Y. For some problems this may be satisfactory; for others, it may not. As always, there is no substitute for depth of knowledge of the research problem and concomitant knowledge and use of the theory behind the problem. *In other words, the research problem and the theory behind the problem should determine the order of entry of variables in multiple regression analysis.*

In one problem, for instance, intelligence may be a variable that is conceived as acting in concert with other variables, compensatory methods and social class, say, to produce changes in verbal achievement. Intelligence would then probably enter the equation after compensatory methods and before (or after) social class. A researcher doing this would be

Table 33.5 Squared Semipartial Correlations with Different Orders of Entry of Variables, Differential Aptitude Tests and High School Ranks, Layton and Swanson Study[a]

Order 1:	VR .31	NA .07	AR .00	SR .00
Order 2:	AR .20	VR .13	NA .05	SR .00
Order 3:	SR .13	AR .09	NA .12	VR .05

[a] VR: Verbal Reasoning; NA: Numerical Ability; AR: Abstract Reasoning; SR: Space Relations. $R^2 = .41$ (for six variables).

[26] W. Layton and E. Swanson, "Relationship of Ninth Grade Differential Aptitude Test Scores to Eleventh Grade Test Scores and High School Rank," *Journal of Educational Psychology,* 49 (1958), 153–155. Layton and Swanson also used two other measures which are ignored here. The multiple regression analysis reported above was done by the author.

influenced by the notion of interaction: the compensatory methods differ in their effects at different levels of intelligence. Suppose, however, that the researcher wants only to control intelligence, to eliminate its influence on verbal achievement. The theory underlying his reasoning may say nothing about an interaction between intelligence and other variables. But the researcher *knows* that it will certainly influence verbal achievement and he wants its influence eliminated *before* the effects of compensatory education and social class are assessed. In this case he would treat intelligence as a covariate and enter it into the regression equation first.

Earlier in this book it was said: "Design is data discipline." The design of research and the analysis of data spring from the demands of research problems. Again, the order of entry of independent variables into the regression equation is determined by the research problem and the design of the research, which is itself determined by the research problem.

Although the order of entry of variables and the changes in regression weights that can occur with different samples are difficult problems, one must remember that regression weights do not change with different orders of entry. This is a real compensation, especially useful in prediction. In many research problems, for example, the relative contribution of variables is not a major consideration. In such cases, one wants the total regression equation and its regression weights mainly for prediction and for assessing the general nature of the regression situation.

Determinants of Political Development and Multicollinearity

As an illustration of an entirely different kind of research and data and of the effect of high correlations among independent variables—and thus high redundancy of predictors—consider a study of regression of political development (of 77 nations), Y, on communication, X_1, urbanization, X_2, education, X_3, and agriculture, X_4.[27] The lowest r between independent variables was .69 and the highest .88. There is obviously considerable redundancy. This is clearly shown by calculating $R^2_{y.1}$, $R^2_{y.12}$, $R^2_{y.123}$, and $R^2_{y.1234}$. They are: .66, .67, .67, .67! Efficiency of prediction is as good with one independent variable, X_1, as it is with all four independent variables! This state of high correlations among independent variables is called *multicollinearity*, a dread word because it means instability of regression coefficients and other statistical difficulties.

Equality of Educational Opportunity in American and in Poland

We now examine two highly important studies of equality of educational opportunity, one in the United States and the other in Poland.[28] We study the first of these, the justly famous Coleman Report, in some depth because it is interesting, instructive, and highly controversial, and because it is perhaps the most important single and massive educational study of three decades.

One of the basic purposes of the study was to explain school achievement, or rather, inequality in school achievement. Multiple regression analysis was used in a complex manner to help do this. The researchers chose as one of their most important dependent

[27] P. Cutright, "National Political Development: Measurement and Analysis," *American Sociological Review*, 27 (1963), 229–245. Although Cutright supplied regression statistics, I calculated the R^2's reported above. The student can profit from studying Cutright's solutions to interesting measurement problems.

[28] J. Coleman et al., *Equality of Educational Opportunity*. Washington, D.C.: Dept. of Health, Education, and Welfare, Office of Education (U.S. Govt. Printing Office), 1966; A. Firkowska et al., "Cognitive Development and Social Policy," *Science*, 200 (1978), 1357–1362.

variable measures verbal ability or skill (VA). Some 60 independent variable measures were correlated with VA. From the many correlations reported by the authors, several were selected from those for the total Northern white and black samples (in Appendix 9.10), and multiple regression analyses were done.

Five independent variables were chosen to predict to VA because of their presumed importance. They are listed in the footnote of Table 33.6. The R^2's, beta weights, β, and the squared semipartial correlations (SP^2) of the regression analysis of two samples of more than 100,000 each of Northern white and Northern black twelfth-grade pupils are given in Table 33.6. In addition to the comparisons between the white and black sample results, the variables have been entered into the regression equation in three different orders of entry. The R^2's and the β's for the three orders, of course, are the same, since changing the order does not change R^2 and the β's, as we learned earlier.

Most of the variance of verbal ability appears to be due to Self-Concept, a measure constructed from three questions, the answers to which reveal how the pupil perceives himself (*e.g.,* "I sometimes feel that I just can't learn"). Study the SP^2's and see that this is true in all orders of entry for whites (.214, .139, .218). It is less true for blacks (.111, .063, .120). The only other variable that accounts for a substantial amount of variance ($\geq$ .10) is Control of Environment, CE, which is another variable involving the concept of self and adding the notion of control over one's fate. Here whites and blacks are similar, except that CE appears to be somewhat weightier for blacks.

One of the most interesting comparisons is that between kinds of variables. SC and CE are both "subjective" variables: the pupil projects his own image. The other variables are

Table 33.6 Multiple Regression Analysis: R^2's, Beta Weights, and Squared Semipartial Correlations, Selected Variables from *Equality of Educational Opportunity*

	VAT[a]	PPE	SC	PW	CE	R^2
White:						
β	.033	.074	.396	.069	.198	
SP^2	.001	.007	.214	.006	.034	.262
Black:						
β	.079	−.019	.265	.161	.277	
SP^2	.016	.000	.111	.020	.070	.217

	CE	PW	SC	PPE	VAT	
White:						
β	.198	.069	.396	.074	.033	
SP^2	.114	.003	.139	.005	.001	.262
Black:						
β	.277	.161	.265	−.019	.079	
SP^2	.120	.028	.063	.000	.005	.217

	PW	SC	CE	PPE	VAT	
White:						
β	.069	.396	.198	.074	.033	
SP^2	.004	.218	.035	.005	.001	.262
Black:						
β	.161	.265	.277	−.019	.079	
SP^2	.021	.120	.070	.000	.005	.217

[a] VAT: Verbal Ability, Teacher; PPE: Per Pupil Expenditure; SC: Self-Concept; PW: Proportion White; CE: Control of Environment.

"objective": they are external to the pupil; they are part of the objective environment, so to speak. This was an important finding of the study. Where things like tracking (homogeneous grouping) and school facilities accounted for little of the variance in achievement, the so-called attitude variables, two of which were SC and CE, accounted for more variance for both white and black pupils than any other variables in the study.[29]

The Warsaw Study is highly important not only because it is a good example of multiple regression analysis but also because it was an attempt to assess the effects of a massive effort by a government to achieve educational equality, among other things. After the World War II destruction of Warsaw, the government attempted to equalize social conditions and educational opportunity by spreading people over different parts of the city. One of the objectives of the policy was to reduce differences in ability and achievement due to social class. In other words, if equalization of extrinsic factors of the environment was accomplished, this should help to wipe out differences in mental performance: the correlation between social class and intelligence should be zero. The researchers used two kinds of variables: intrinsic and extrinsic. The latter were presumably equalized by the policy. Intrinsic variables were parental occupation, parental education, and others. All children born in 1963 and then (1974) living in Warsaw (about 13,000) were tested using a well-known nonverbal intelligence test.

Among the many analyses done, we are here concerned only with two of them. In the multiple regression analysis, the researchers created and analyzed composite district, school, and family variables. The first two were those presumably affected by the equalization policy. It was believed that the effects of the variables the children bring with them to school, the family set, would also be equalized. The researchers entered the sets of variables in three different orders into multiple regression analyses. Summary R^2 results are given in Table 33.7. The data in the table are essentially squared semipartial correlations (see footnotes 20 and 22), which are of course affected by the order of entry of the variables in the regression equation. The total R^2, $R_{y.123}^2$, was .106. The important coefficients in testing the equalization effects are those of the second data column, the SP^2's.

Table 33.7 Results of Multiple Regression Analyses of Environmental and Family Variables, Warsaw Study

Order of Entry	Variable Set Entered	Squared Semipartial Coefficients, SP^2	Total R^2
1	District	.016	
2	School	.006	.106
3	Family	*.084*[a]	
1	School	.013	
2	Family	*.092*	.106
3	District	.001	
1	Family	*.103*	
2	District	.002	.106
3	School	.001	

[a]The family variable set coefficients are italicized. They indicate the percentages of the total variance of the dependent variable that the family variable set accounts for, in that order of variable entry. These data were adapted from Firkowska et al., *op. cit.*, Table 5.

[29]Coleman et al., *op. cit.*, pp. 319–325. The beta weights in Table 33.6 bear careful study. Since they were calculated from very large samples, they are less likely to be unstable. And they accurately reflect the relative importance of the five variables. The contrast between whites and blacks on self-concept is particularly interesting. See *ibid.*, Table 3.26.1.

The district and school variable sets, no matter the order of entry, amounted to only .02 (.016 + .006 = .022). As the authors say (p. 1361), the contribution of extrinsic variables was minor. The program was apparently successful in equalizing the *extrinsic* school and district variables. But the *intrinsic* family variables, again no matter the order of entry, accounted for most of the total R^2: between .08 and .10. Alas, the heroic attempt to annihilate the influence of what the child brings with him failed. As the authors say a bit wistfully,

> Despite this social policy of equalization, the association persists in a form characteristic of more traditional societies. Indeed, contrary to expectation, those associations are as strong as many reported in large-scale studies from Western societies . . . societal changes over a generation have failed to override forces that determine the social class distribution of mental performance.[30]

MULTIPLE REGRESSION ANALYSIS AND SCIENTIFIC RESEARCH[31]

Multiple regression is close to the heart of scientific investigation. It is also fundamental in statistics and inference, and is tightly tied to basic and powerful mathematical methods. From the researcher's point of view, moreover, it is useful and practical: it does its analytic job successfully and efficiently. In explaining these strong and sweeping statements, it may be possible to clarify what we have already learned.

The scientist is concerned, basically, with propositions of the If *p*, then *q* kind. Such propositions "explain" phenomena. When we say, "If positive incentive, then higher achievement," we are to some extent "explaining" achievement. But this is hardly enough. Even if supported by a good deal of empirical evidence, it does not go very far in explaining achievement. In addition to other if-then statements of a similar kind, the scientist must ask more complex questions. He may ask, for example, under what conditions the statement, "If positive incentive, then higher achievement," is valid. Is it true of black children as well as white children? Is it true of children of both lower and higher intelligence? To test such statements and to advance knowledge, scientists in effect write statements of the kind, If *p*, then *q*, under conditions *r, s,* and *t*, where *p* is an independent variable, *q* a dependent variable, and *r, s,* and *t* other independent variables. Other kinds of statements can, of course, be written—*e.g.*, If *p* and *r*, then *q*. In such a case *p* and *r* are two independent variables, both of which are required for *q*.

The point of all this is that multiple regression can successfully handle such cases. In most behavioral research there is usually one dependent variable, though we are theoretically not restricted to only one. Consequently, multiple regression is a general method of analyzing much behavioral research data. Certain other methods of analysis can be considered special cases of multiple regression. The most prominent is analysis of variance, all types of which can be conceptualized and accomplished with multiple regression analysis.

It was said earlier that all control is control of variance. Multiple regression analysis can be conceived as a refined and powerful method of "controlling" variance. It accom-

---

[30]*Ibid.*, p. 1362. Note that the multiple regression analysis was supported by another analysis. The authors worked out a global index of parental education occupation, which ran from 0 through 12 (see their Table 3 and accompanying discussion). They calculated the mean scores of about 13,000 children on the intelligence test used for each level of this "home background" index (see their Table 6). The correlation between the index values and mean intelligence test scores was .98 (my calculation)!

[31]Some of the material in this section was published in my essay, "Research in Education." In R. Ebel, V. Noll, and R. Bauer, eds., *Encyclopedia of Educational Research,* 4th ed. New York: Macmillan, 1969, pp. 1127–1144. Note that whenever the expression "If *p*, then *q*" appears, it should be taken to mean "If *p*, then *probably q*.

plishes this the same way analysis of variance does: by estimating the magnitudes of different sources of influence on Y, different sources of variance of Y, through analysis of the interrelations of all the variables. It tells how much of Y is presumably due to X_1, X_2 . . . , X_k. It gives some idea of the relative amounts of influence of the X's. And it furnishes tests of the statistical significance of combined influences of X's on Y and of the separate influence of each X. In short, multiple regression analysis is an efficient and powerful hypothesis-testing and inference-making technique, since it helps scientists study, with relative precision, complex interrelations between independent variables and a dependent variable, and thus helps them "explain" the presumed phenomenon represented by the dependent variable.[32]

[32] Study suggestions for this chapter are given at the end of the next chapter.

Chapter 34

Multiple Regression, Analysis of Variance, and Other Multivariate Methods

Close examination shows the conceptual bases underlying different approaches to data analysis to be the same or similar. The symmetry of the fundamental ideas has great aesthetic appeal, and is nowhere more interesting and appealing than in multiple regression and analysis of variance. Earlier, in discussing the foundations of analysis of variance, the similarity of the principles and structures of analysis of variance and so-called correlational methods was brought out. We now link the two approaches and, in the process, show that analysis of variance can be done using multiple regression. In addition, the linking of the two approaches will happily yield unexpected bonuses. We will see, for example, that certain analytic problems that are intractable with analysis of variance—or at least difficult and certainly inappropriate—are quite easily conceptualized and accomplished by the judicious and flexible use of multiple regression. Because of space limitation and because the book's purpose is not to teach the mechanics of statistical methods and approaches, the discussion will be quite limited: some of what is said must be taken on faith. Nevertheless, even at a somewhat limited level of discourse we will find that certain difficult problems associated with analysis of variance—analysis of covariance, pretest and posttest data, unequal numbers of cases in cells (of factorial designs), and the handling of both experimental and nonexperimental data—are naturally and easily handled with multiple regression analysis.

ONE-WAY ANALYSIS OF VARIANCE AND MULTIPLE REGRESSION ANALYSIS

Suppose an experiment has been done with three methods of presenting verbal materials to ninth-grade children. The dependent variable is comprehension measured by an objective test of the materials. Suppose the results were those given in Table 34.1. Obviously an analysis of variance can be and should be done. The analysis of variance results are given at the bottom of the table.[1] The F ratio is 18, which, at 2 and 12 degrees of freedom, is significant at the .01 level. The effect of the experimental treatment is clearly significant. $\eta^2 = ss_b/ss_t = 90/120 = .75$. The relation between the experimental treatment and comprehension is strong.

Now, transfer our thinking from an analysis of variance framework to a multiple regression framwork. Can we obtain $\eta^2 = .75$ "directly"? The independent variable, methods, can be conceived as membership in the three experimental groups, A_1, A_2, and A_3. This membership can be expressed by 1's and 0's: if a subject is a member of A_1,

Table 34.1 Fictitious Data and One-way Analysis of Variance Results, Three Experimental Groups

	A_1	A_2	A_3	
	4	7	1	
	5	8	2	
	6	9	3	
	7	10	4	
	8	11	5	
Y:	30	45	15	$\Sigma Y_t = 90$
M:	6	9	3	$(\Sigma Y_t)^2 = 8100$
				$M_t = 6$
				$\Sigma Y_t^2 = 660$

$$C = \frac{8100}{15} = 540$$

$$ss_t = 660 - 540 = 120$$

$$ss_b = \frac{30^2}{5} + \frac{45^2}{5} + \frac{15^2}{5} - 540 = 630 - 540 = 90$$

Source	df	ss	ms	F
Between Groups	2	90.0	45.0	18.0(.01)
Within Groups	12	30.0	2.5	
Total	14	120.0		

[1] Students are urged to do the calculations of the examples of this chapter. This is urgently necessary for full understanding of important points to be made in the chapter. For example, do the analysis of variance calculations of Table 34.1 and the multiple regression calculations of the problem in Table 34.2. Study and ponder the results of both analyses. Do *not* leave it to a computer program, which you may not understand. Work through the examples of Part 10 whenever possible. If you *do* succumb to the temptation to use one of the large computer or microcomputer packages, be wary. The quality of statistical software for microcomputers (and large computers) is sometimes questionable.

Table 34.2 Regression Layout and Calculations, Table 34.1 Data

	Y	X_1	X_2
A_1	4	1	0
	5	1	0
	6	1	0
	7	1	0
	8	1	0
A_2	7	0	1
	8	0	1
	9	0	1
	10	0	1
	11	0	1
A_3	1	0	0
	2	0	0
	3	0	0
	4	0	0
	5	0	0
Σ:	90	5	5
M:	6	.3333	.3333
Σ^2:	660	5	5

assign a 1; if a member of A_2 or of A_3, assign a 0. Or we can assign 1's to A_2 membership and 0's to the members of the other two groups. The basic results will be the same.[2]

The regression analysis layout of the data of Table 34.1 is given in Table 34.2. Treat the 15 dependent variable measures in the column labeled Y as a single set of scores. Treat the "scores" of X_1 and X_2 similarly, except that the 1's and 0's indicate group membership. The members of A_1 have been assigned 1's in the column X_1, while the members of A_2 and A_3 have been assigned 0 (second column). The members of A_2 have been assigned 1's in the third column, X_2, while the members of A_1 and A_3 have been assigned 0's. One may ask: Where is A_3 in the table? When coding experimental groups, there are only $k - 1$ coded vectors, where $k =$ the number of experimental treatments (in this case $k = 3$). Expressed differently, there is one coded vector for each degree of freedom. Recall from our earlier discussion of analysis of variance that the between-groups degrees of freedom was $k - 1$. In this case there are three treatments, A_1, A_2, and A_3 and $k = 3$. Therefore there are $k - 1 = 2$ coded vectors. These vectors of 1's and 0's are called *dummy variables*.[3] They fully express the three experimental treatments.

Now, do a multiple regression analysis of the data in Table 34.2 just as in the last chapter. The sums of squares and cross products necessary for the analysis are given in

---

[2] Indeed, use any two different numbers, for instance—1 and 10 or 31 and 5, or any two random numbers, and the basic results will be the same. The assignment of 1's and 0's however, has interpretative advantages that will be mentioned later. See J. Cohen, "Multiple Regression as a General Data-Analytic System," *Psychological Bulletin*, 70 (1968), 426–443.

[3] D. Suits, "Use of Dummy Variables in Regression Equations," *Journal of the American Statistical Association*, 52 (1967), 548–551. For full discussions of coding variables for multiple regression analysis, see F. Kerlinger and E. Pedhazur, *Multiple Regression in Behavioral Research*. New York: Holt, Rinehart and Winston, 1973, chaps. 6–7, or E. Pedhazur, *Multiple Regression in Behavioral Research: Explanation and Prediction*, 2d ed. New York: Holt, Rinehart and Winston, 1982, chaps. 9–10. The latter reference is more thorough than the former.

Table 34.3 Sums of Squares and Cross Products of Data of Table 34.2[a]

	x_1	x_2	y
x_1	3.3333	−1.6667	0
x_2		3.3333	15.0000
y			120.0000

[a]The values on the diagonal are the deviation sums of squares: $\Sigma x_1{}^2$, $\Sigma x_2{}^2$, $\Sigma y_t{}^2$. The remaining three values above the diagonal are the deviation cross products: $\Sigma x_1 x_2$, $\Sigma x_1 y$, and $\Sigma x_2 y$.

Table 34.3.[4] To calculate the regression and residual sums of squares, use Formulas 33.10 and 33.11 of the last chapter (given here with the numbering of this chapter):

$$ss_{reg} = b_1 x_1 y + b_2 x_2 y \tag{34.1}$$
$$ss_{res} = ss_y - ss_{reg} \tag{34.2}$$

We have in Table 34.3 all the above values except b_1 and b_2, the regression coefficients and a, the intercept. There are two or three ways to calculate the b's, but they are beyond the scope of our treatment.[5] So, we accept them on faith: $b_1 = 3$ and $b_2 = 6$. The intercept, a, is calculated

$$a = \bar{Y} - b_1 \bar{X}_1 - b_2 \bar{X}_2 \tag{34.3}$$
$$= 6 - (3)(.3333) - (6)(.3333) = 3.$$

The sums of cross products are given in Table 34.3: $\Sigma x_1 y = 0$ and $\Sigma x_2 y = 15$. Substituting in 34.1 and 34.2, we obtain:

$$ss_{reg} = (3)(0) + (6)(15) = 90.$$
$$ss_{res} = 120 - 90 = 30.$$

To calculate R^2, use Formula 33.14 of Chapter 33 (with a new number):

$$R^2 = \frac{ss_{reg}}{ss_t} \tag{34.4}$$

$$= \frac{90.}{120.} = .75$$

and

$$R = \sqrt{.75} = .8660$$

Finally, calculate the F ratio using Formula 33.16, again with a new number:

$$F = \frac{R^2/k}{(1 - R^2)/(N - k - 1)} \tag{34.5}$$

[4]For example,

$$\Sigma x_1{}^2 = (1^2 + 1^2 + \cdots + 0^2) - \frac{5^2}{15} = 5 - 1.6667 = 3.3333$$

$$\Sigma x_2 y = (0)(4) + (0)(5) + \cdots + (0)(5) - \frac{(5)(90)}{15} = 45 - 30 = 15$$

$$\Sigma x_1 x_2 = (1)(0) + (1)(0) + \cdots + (0)(0) - \frac{(5)(5)}{15} = 0 - 1.6667 = -1.6667$$

[5]See Kerlinger and Pedhazur, op. cit., p. 34 and chap. 4.

where k = number of independent variables and N = number of cases. Substituting:

$$F = \frac{.75/2}{(1 - .75)/(15 - 2 - 1)} = \frac{.375000}{.020833} = 18.$$

Another formula for F can be borrowed from the previous chapter:

$$F = \frac{ss_{\text{reg}}/df_1}{ss_{\text{res}}/df_2} = \frac{ss_{\text{reg}}/k}{ss_{\text{res}}/(N - k - 1)}$$

$$= \frac{90/2}{30/(15 - 2 - 1)} = \frac{45.00}{2.50} = 18.$$

This F ratio is then checked in an F table (see Kerlinger and Pedhazur, App. D), at $df = 2$, 12. The entry at $p = .05$ is 3.88 and at $p = .01$ it is 6.93. Since F of 18 calculated above is greater than 6.93, the regression is statistically significant, and R^2 is statistically significant.

Check the multiple regression values calculated with those obtained earlier from the analysis of variance. The values of the sums of squares, the mean squares, and F are the same. R^2 also equals η^2. In addition, the values of a and the b's tell us something about the data. $a = 3$ is the mean of the group-assigned zeroes in both coded vectors. $b_1 = 3$ is the difference between the means of A_1 and A_3, the group-assigned zeroes in both vectors: $6 - 3 = 3$. b_2 is the difference between the means of A_2 and A_3: $9 - 3 = 6$. The means of the three groups are easily found by using the regression equation:

$$Y' = a + b_1 X_1 + b_2 X_2$$
$$\overline{Y}_{A_1} = 3 + (3)(1) + (6)(0) = 6$$
$$\overline{Y}_{A_2} = 3 + (3)(0) + (6)(1) = 9$$
$$\overline{Y}_{A_3} = 3 + (3)(0) + (6)(0) = 3$$

Note that even though A_3 was not coded—it had no coded vector of its own—its mean is easily recovered by substituting 0's for X_1 and X_2.

The argument on the relation between multiple regression analysis and analysis of variance can be summarized by listing parallel formulas. This has been done in Table 34.4. The only unfamiliar formula is the first one in the analysis of variance column. It is an adaptation of similar formulas used in theoretical discussions of analysis of variance. It is merely the same kind of formula as the multiple regression prediction formula and has a similar interpretation based on the different contributions of treatments (A, B, etc.) to the scores of individuals. Note the e (for error) in the first equations of each column of the table. Its presence is always recognized. The rest of the table is obvious and needs no explanation.

Table 34.4 Parallel Formulations of Multiple Regression Analysis and Analysis of Variance[a]

Multiple Regression Analysis	Analysis of Variance
$Y' = a + b_1 X_1 + \cdots + b_k X_k + e$	$Y = M_{\text{pop}} + A + B + e$
$ss_t = ss_{\text{reg}} + ss_{\text{res}}$	$ss_t = ss_b + ss_w$
$R^2 = ss_{\text{reg}}/ss_t$	$\eta^2 = ss_b/ss_t$
$F = \dfrac{ss_{\text{reg}}/df_1}{ss_{\text{res}}/df_2}$	$F = \dfrac{ss_b/df_1}{ss_w/df_2}$

[a] M_{pop} = mean of population; A and B = treatment conditions in analysis of variance; e = error. The remaining symbols are defined in the text. (See discussion of the general linear model in Chapter 13.)

While it has been shown that multiple regression analysis accomplishes what one-way analysis of variance does, can it be said that there is any real advantage to using the regression method? Actually the calculations are more involved. Why do it, then? The answer is that with the kinds of data of the example above there is no practical advantage beyond aesthetic nicety and conceptual clarification. But when research problems are more complex—when, for example, interactions, covariates (*e.g.*, intelligence test scores), nominal variables (sex, social class), and nonlinear components (X^2, X^3) are involved—the regression procedure has decided advantages. Indeed, many research analytic problems that analysis of variance cannot handle readily or at all can be fairly readily accomplished with multiple regression analysis. Factorial analysis of variance, analysis of covariance, and, indeed, all forms of analysis of variance can also be done with regression analysis. Since it is not our purpose to teach statistics and the mechanics of analysis, we refer the reader to appropriate discussions like those cited in footnote 3. We will explain in the next section, however, the nature of highly important methods of coding variables and their use in analysis.

CODING AND DATA ANALYSIS

Before enlarging the discussion of multiple regression and analysis of variance, we need to know something about different ways of coding experimental treatments for multiple regression analysis. A *code* is a set of symbols that is assigned to a set of objects for various reasons. In multiple regression analysis, *coding* is the assignment of numbers to the members of a population or sample to indicate group or subset membership according to a rule determined by an independent means. When some characteristic or aspect of the members of a population or sample is objectively defined, it is then possible to create a set of ordered pairs, the first members of which constitute the dependent variable, Y, and the second members numerical indicators of subset or group membership.

In the preceding discussion of the coding of experimental treatments in the multiple regression analogue of one-way analysis of variance, 1's and 0's were used. Vectors of 1's and 0's are correlated. In Table 34.3, for instance, the sum of the cross products, $\Sigma x_1 x_2$, is -1.6667, and $r_{12} = -.50$. Such 1 and 0, or *dummy*, coding works quite well. It is possible to use other forms of coding, however. One of these, *effects* coding, consists of assigning $\{1, 0, -1\}$ or $\{1, -1\}$ to experimental treatments. Although a useful method, it will be discussed only briefly.

To clarify matters, the coding of the data of Table 34.2, a multiple regression analogue of the one-way analysis of variance of the data of Table 34.1, with three experimental groups or treatments, is laid out in Table 34.5. Under the heading "Dummy" is given the

Table 34.5 Examples of Dummy, Effect, and Orthogonal Coding of Experimental Treatments[a]

Groups	Dummy		Effects		Orthogonal	
	X_1	X_2	X_1	X_2	X_1	X_2
A_1	1	0	1	0	0	2
	1	0	1	0	0	2
A_2	0	1	0	1	-1	-1
	0	1	0	1	-1	-1
A_3	0	0	-1	-1	1	-1
	0	0	-1	-1	1	-1
	$r_{12} = -.50$		$r_{12} = .50$		$r_{12} = .00$	

[a] In the dummy coding, A_3 is a control group. In the orthogonal coding, A_2 is compared to A_3, and A_1 is compared to A_2 *and* A_3, or $(A_2 + A_3)/2$.

dummy coding of Table 34.5, using only two subjects per experimental group. Since there are two degrees of freedom, or $k - 1 = 3 - 1 = 2$, there are two column vectors labeled X_1 and X_2. The dummy coding assignment has already been explained: a 1 indicates that a subject is a member of the experimental group against which the 1 is placed, and a 0 that the subject is not a member of the experimental group.

Under the "Effects" column, the coding is seen to be $\{1, 0, -1\}$. Effects coding is virtually the same as dummy coding—indeed, it has been called dummy coding—except that one experimental group, usually the last, is always assigned -1's. If the n's of the experimental groups are equal, the sums of the columns of the codes equal zero. The vectors, however, are not systematically uncorrelated. The correlation between the two columns under "Effects" in Table 34.5, for example, is .50. (Contrast this with the correlation between the dummy code columns: $r = -.50$.)

Each of these two systems of coding has its own characteristics. Two of the characteristics of dummy coding were discussed in the previous section. One of the characteristics of effects coding, on the other hand, is that the intercept constant, a, yielded by the multiple regression analysis will equal the grand mean, or M_t, of Y. For the data of Table 34.2, the intercept constant is 6.00, which is the mean of all the Y scores.

The third form of coding is *orthogonal* coding. (It is also called "contrasts" coding, but some contrasts coding can be nonorthogonal.) As its name indicates, the coded vectors are orthogonal or uncorrelated. If an investigator's main interest is in specific contrasts between means rather than the overall F test, orthogonal coding can provide the needed contrasts. In any set of data, a number of contrasts can be made. This is, of course, particularly useful in analysis of variance. The rule is that only contrasts that are orthogonal to each other, or independent, are made. For example, in Table 34.5, the coding of the last set of vectors is orthogonal: each of the vectors totals to zero and the sum of their products is zero, or

$$(0 \times 2) + (0 \times 2) + (-1)(-1) + \cdots + (1)(-1) = 0$$

r_{12} is also equal to zero.

Instead of the dummy coding of Table 34.2, suppose we now use orthogonal coding. Suppose we decide to test A_2 against A_3, or $M_{A_2} - M_{A_3}$, and also test A_1 against A_2 and A_3, or $M_{A_1} - (M_{A_2} + M_{A_3})/2$. X_1 is then coded $(0, -1, 1)$ and X_2 is coded $(2, -1, -1)$, as shown by the orthogonal coding of Table 34.5. The interested reader grounded in analysis of variance can follow up such possibilities.[6]

No matter what kind of coding is used, R^2, F, the sums of squares, the standard errors of estimate, and the predicted Y's will be the same (the means of the experimental groups). The intercept constant, the regression weights, and the t tests of b weights will be different. Strictly speaking, it is not possible to recommend one method over another; each has its purposes. At first, it is probably wise for the student to use the simplest method, dummy coding, or 1's and 0's. He should fairly soon use effects coding, however. Finally, orthogonal coding can be tried and mastered.[7]

The simplest use of coding is to indicate nominal variables, particularly dichotomies. Some variables are "natural" dichotomies: sex, public school-parochial school, conviction-no conviction, vote for-vote against. All these can be scored $(1, 0)$ and the resulting vectors analyzed as though they were continuous score vectors. Most variables are continuous, or potentially so, however, even though they can always be treated as dichotomous. In any case, the use of $(1, 0)$ vectors for dichotomous variables in multiple regression is highly useful.

[6]Cohen, *op. cit.*, pp. 428–434, especially pp. 432–434. For a detailed discussion, see Kerlinger and Pedhazur, *op. cit.*, chap. 7.

[7]Before using orthogonal coding to any extent, the student should study the topic of comparisons of means. See W. Hays, *Statistics*, 3d ed. New York: Holt, Rinehart and Winston, 1981, chap. 12.

With nominal variables that are not dichotomies one can still use (1, 0) vectors. One simply creates a (1, 0) vector for each subset but one of a category or partition. Suppose the category A is partitioned into A_1, A_2, A_3, say Protestant, Catholic, Jew. Then a vector is created for Protestants, each of which is assigned a 1; the Catholics and Jews are assigned 0. Another vector is created for Catholics: each Catholic is assigned 1; Protestants and Jews are assigned 0. It would, of course, be redundant to create a third vector for Jews. The number of vectors is $k - 1$, where $k =$ the number of subsets of the partition or category.

While sometimes convenient or necessary, partitioning a continuous variable into a dichotomy or trichotomy throws information away. If, for example, an investigator dichotomizes intelligence, ethnocentrism, cohesiveness of groups, or any other variable that can be measured with a scale that even approximates equality of interval, he is discarding information. To reduce a set of values with a relatively wide range to a dichotomy is to reduce its variance and thus its possible correlation with other variables. A good rule of research data analysis, therefore, is: *Do not reduce continuous variables to partitioned variables* (dichotomies, trichotomies, etc.) unless compelled to do so by circumstances or the nature of the data (seriously skewed, bimodal, etc.).

FACTORIAL ANALYSIS OF VARIANCE, ANALYSIS OF COVARIANCE, AND RELATED ANALYSES

Factorial Analysis of Variance and Correlation Among Independent Variables

It is with factorial analysis of variance, analysis of covariance, and nominal variables that we begin to appreciate the advantages of multiple regression analysis. We do little more here than comment on the use of coded vectors in factorial analysis of variance. Exceptionally full discussions can found in Pedhazur's exhaustive work.[8] We will, however, explain the basic reason why multiple regression analysis is often better than factorial analysis of variance.

The underlying difficulty in research and analysis is that the independent variables in which we are interested are correlated. Analysis of variance, however, assumes that they are uncorrelated. If we have, say, two experimental independent variables and subjects are assigned at random to the cells of a factorial design, we can assume that the two independent variables are not correlated—by definition. And factorial analysis of variance is appropriate. But if we have two nonexperimental variables and the two experimental variables, we cannot assume that all four independent variables are uncorrelated. Although there are ways to analyze such data with analysis of variance, they are cumbersome and "unnatural." Moreover, if there are unequal n's in the groups, analysis of variance becomes still more inappropriate because unequal n's also introduce correlations between independent variables. The analytic procedure of multiple regression, on the other hand, takes cognizance, so to speak, of the correlations among the independent variables as well as between the independent variables and the dependent variable. This means that multiple regression can effectively analyze both experimental and nonexperimental data, separately or together. Moreover, continuous and categorical variables can be used together.

When subjects have been assigned at random to the cells of a factorial design and other things are equal, there isn't much benefit from using multiple regression. But when the n's

[8] Pedhazur, *op. cit.*, chap. 9.

of the cells are unequal, and one wants to include one, two, or more control variables—like intelligence, sex, and social class—then multiple regression should be used. This point is most important. In analysis of variance, the addition of control variables is difficult and clumsy. With multiple regression, however, the inclusion of such variables is easy and natural: each of them is merely another vector of scores, another X_j!

Analysis of Covariance

Analysis of covariance (*not* analysis of covariance structures, which we study later) is a particularly good example of the value of a multiple regression approach because it is hard and cumbersome in the analysis of variance framework and easily and readily grasped and done in a regression framework. What analysis of covariance does in its traditional application[9] is to test the significance of the differences among means after taking into account or controlling initial mean differences between the experimental groups on a so-called *covariate*, a variable that is correlated with the dependent variable. (This correlation is taken into account.) In the multiple regression approach, however, the covariate's influence is controlled just as though it were any independent variable whose influence on the dependent variable has to be controlled. The covariate can be a pretest or a variable whose influence must be "removed" statistically.

It has been found in large-scale studies by Prothro and Grigg and by McClosky that people's agreement with social issues is greater the more abstract the issue.[10] Suppose a political scientist believes that authoritarianism has a good deal to do with this relation, that the more authoritarian the person, the more he agrees with abstract social assertions. In order to study the relation between abstractness and agreement, he will have to control authoritarianism. In other words, the political scientist is interested in studying the relation between abstractness of issues and statements, on the one hand, and agreement with such issues and statements, on the other hand. He is not at this point interested in authoritarianism and agreement; he needs, rather, to control the influence of authoritarianism on agreement. Authoritarianism is the covariate.

The political scientist devises three experimental treatments, A_1, A_2, and A_3, different levels of abstractness of materials. He obtains responses from 15 subjects who have been assigned randomly to the three experimental groups, five in each group. Before the experiment begins the investigator administers the F (authoritarianism) scale to the 15 subjects and uses these measures as a covariate. He wishes to control the possible influence of authoritarianism on agreement. This is a fairly straightforward analysis of covariance problem in which we test the significance of the differences among the three agreement means after correcting the means for the influence of authoritarianism and taking into account the correlation between authoritarianism and agreement. We now do the analysis of covariance using multiple regression analysis.

First, the data are presented in the usual analysis of covariance way in Table 34.6. In analysis of covariance one does separate analyses of variance on the X scores, the Y scores, and the cross products of the X and Y scores, XY. Then, using regression analysis, one calculates sums of squares and mean squares of the errors of estimate of the total and the within groups and, finally, the adjusted between groups. Since the concern here is not with the usual analysis of covariance procedure, we do not do these calculations. Instead, we proceed immediately to a multiple regression approach to the analysis.

---

[9] See Hays, *op. cit.*, pp. 524–530.

[10] H. McClosky, "Consensus and Ideology in American Politics," *American Political Science Review*, 58 (1964), 361–382; J. Prothro and C. Grigg, "Fundamental Principles of Democracy: Bases of Agreement and Disagreement," *Journal of Politics*, 22 (1960), 276–294.

Table 34.6 Fictitious Analysis of Covariance Problem, Three Experimental Groups and One Covariate

			Treatments			
A_1			A_2		A_3	
X	Y		X	Y	X	Y
12	12		6	9	12	15
11	12		9	9	10	12
10	11		11	13	4	9
12	10		14	14	4	8
10	12		2	5	8	11

The data of Table 34.6, arranged for multiple regression analysis, are given in Table 34.7. As usual, there is one vector for the dependent variable, Y. A second vector, X_1, is the covariate. The remaining two vectors, X_2 and X_3, represent the experimental treatments A_1 and A_2. (It is not necessary to have a vector for A_3, since there is only one vector for each degree of freedom, and there are only two degrees of freedom.)

A regression analysis yields: $R^2_{y.123} = .8612$ and $R^2_{y.1} = .7502$. To test the significance of the differences among the means of A_1, A_2, and A_3, after adjusting for the effect of X_1, the variance in Y due to the covariate is subtracted from the total variance accounted for by the regression of Y on variables X_1, X_2, and X_3: $R^2_{y.123} - R^2_{y.1}$. This reminder is then tested:

$$F = \frac{(R^2_{y.123} - R^2_{y.1})/(k_1 - k_2)}{(1 - R^2_{y.123})/(N - k_1 - 1)} \tag{34.6}$$

where k_1 = the number of independent variables associated with $R^2_{y.123}$, the larger R^2, and k_2 = the number of independent variables associated with $R^2_{y.1}$, the smaller R^2. Thus:

Table 34.7 Fictitious Analysis of Covariance Data of Table 34.6 Arranged for Multiple Regression Analysis[a]

	Y	X_1	X_2	X_3
	12	12	1	0
	12	11	1	0
A_1	11	10	1	0
	10	12	1	0
	12	10	1	0
	9	6	0	1
	9	9	0	1
A_2	13	11	0	1
	14	14	0	1
	5	2	0	1
	15	12	0	0
	12	10	0	0
A_3	9	4	0	0
	8	4	0	0
	11	8	0	0

[a]Y = dependent variable; X_1 = covariate; X_2 = treatment A_1; X_3 = treatment A_2.

$$F = \frac{(.8612 - .7502)/(3 - 1)}{(1 - .8612)/(15 - 3 - 1)} = \frac{.0555}{.0126} = 4.405$$

which, at 2 and 11 degrees of freedom, is significant at the .05 level. (Note that an ordinary one-way analysis of variance of the three groups, without taking the covariate into account, yields a nonsignificant F ratio.) $R^2_{y.23}$, or the variance of Y accounted for by the regression on variables 2 and 3 (the experimental treatments), after allowing for the correlation of variable 1 and Y, is .1110. While this is not a strong relation, especially compared with the massive correlation between the covariate, authoritarianism, and Y ($r^2_{1y} = .75$), it is not inconsequential. Evidently abstractness of issues influences agreement responses: the more abstract the issues, the greater the agreement.[11]

The analysis of covariance, then, is seen to be simply a variation on the theme of multiple regression analysis. And in this case it happens to be easier to conceptualize than the rather elaborate analysis of covariance procedure—especially if there is more than one covariate. The covariate is nothing but an independent variable. Moreover, a variable considered as a covariate in one study can easily be considered as an independent variable in another study. Cohen neatly says, "one man's main effect is another man's covariate."[12]

The beauty, power, and general applicability of multiple regression emerge rather clearly in this example. And it should be borne in mind that two, even three, covariates can be easily handled with multiple regression. With two covariates and two other independent variables, for instance, we simply write the F ratio:

$$F = \frac{(R^2_{y.1234} - R^2_{y.12})/(k_1 - k_2)}{(1 - R^2_{y.1234})/(N - k_1 - 1)}$$

Carry the reasoning a step further. The use of analysis of covariance with factorial designs is complex. It is simpler with multiple regression analysis. Take a 2×2 factorial design and one covariate. We have, then, the following "variables":

Y	X_1	X_2	X_3	$X_4 = X_2 X_3$
Dependent variable	Covariate	Treatment A	Treatment B	Interaction: $A \times B$

Each of the X's has one degree of freedom, and the analysis proceeds like any multiple regression analysis except at the end when the effect of X_1, the covariate, is subtracted. The remaining "variables," X_2, X_3, and X_4, are then analyzed and the results interpreted.

DISCRIMINANT ANALYSIS, CANONICAL CORRELATION, MULTIVARIATE ANALYSIS OF VARIANCE, AND PATH ANALYSIS

Canonical correlation and discriminant analysis address themselves to two important research questions. One, what is the relation between two *sets* of data with several independent variables and several dependent variables? Two, how can individuals best be assigned to groups on the basis of several variables? Canonical correlation analysis

---

[11] Authoritarianism is unlikely to have a correlation with Y of .87. The example was deliberately contrived to show how a strong influence like X_1 can be controlled and the influence of the remaining variables (in this case experimental treatments) evaluated. Note that Formula 34.6 can be used in any multiple regression analysis; it is not limited to analysis of covariance or other experimental methods.

[12] Cohen, *op. cit.*, p. 439.

addresses itself to the first question, and discriminant analysis to the second. As one would expect from the name, multivariate analysis of variance is the multivariate counterpart of analysis of variance: the influence of k independent experimental variables on m dependent variables is assessed. Path analysis is more a graphic and heuristic aid than a multivariate method. As such, it has great usefulness, especially for helping to clarify and conceptualize multivariate problems.

Discriminant Analysis

A discriminant function is a regression equation with a dependent variable that represents group membership. The function maximally discriminates the members of the group; it tells us to which group each member probably belongs. In short, if we have two or more independent variables and the members of, say, two groups, the discriminant function gives the ''best'' prediction, in the least-squares sense, of the ''correct'' group membership of each member of the sample. The discriminant function, then, can be used to assign individuals to groups on the basis of their scores on two or more measures. From the scores on the two or more measures, the least-squares ''best'' composite score is calculated. If this is so, then, the higher the R^2 the better the prediction of group membership. In other words, *when dealing with two groups*, the discriminant function is nothing more than a multiple regression equation with the dependent variable a nominal variable (coded 0, 1) representing group membership. (With three or more groups, however, discriminant analysis goes beyond multiple regression methods.[13])

Discriminant analysis can be used to study the relations among variables in different populations or samples. Suppose we have ratings of administrators on administrative performance and we also have found, through the In-Basket Test, that three kinds of performance are important.[14] We wish to know how successful and unsuccessful administrators, as judged by an independent criterion, perform on the three tests, which are Ability to Work With Others (X_1), Motivation for Administrative Work (X_2), and General Professional Skill (X_3). Suppose the discriminant regression equation were: $Y' = .06X_1 + .45X_2 + .30X_3$. From this equation, we can form the tentative conclusion that Ability to Work With Others seems unimportant compared to Motivation for Administrative Work and General Professional Skill. In other words, the discriminant equation gives us a profile picture of the difference between successful and unsuccessful administrators as measured by the In-Basket Test.

Canonical Correlation[15]

It is not too large a conceptual step from multiple regression analysis with one dependent variable to multiple regression analysis with more than one dependent variable. Computationally, however, it is a considerable step. We will not, therefore, supply the actual calculations. The regression analysis of data with k independent variables and m dependent variables is called *canonical correlation* analysis. The basic idea is that, through

[13] The reader will find excellent guidance in: M. Tatsuoka, *Discriminant Analysis: The Study of Group Differences*. Champaign, Ill.: Institute for Personality and Ability Testing, 1970.

[14] J. Hemphill, D. Griffiths, and N. Frederiksen, *Administrative Performance and Personality*. New York: Teachers College Press, 1962.

[15] For reasons that we will not now discuss, canonical correlation analysis can be considered obsolescent. We will, however, examine it briefly because one or two of its aspects need to be understood, the most important of which is that a traditional multivariate view terms it a generalization of multiple regression: the relations among k x variables, on the one hand, and m y variables, on the other hand.

least-squares analysis, two linear composites are formed, one for the independent variables, X_j, and one for the dependent variables, Y_j. The correlation between these two composites is the canonical correlation. And, like R, it will be the maximum correlation possible given the particular sets of data. It should be clear that what has been called until now multiple regression analysis is a special case of canonical analysis. In view of practical limitations on canonical analysis, it might be better to say that canonical analysis is a generalization of multiple regression analysis.

Tetenbaum studied the relations between, on the one hand, personality measures of the needs for order, achievement, and affiliation and, on the other hand, control, intellectuality, dependency, and ascendancy as shown in ratings of teachers by graduate students.[16] The general hypothesis tested was that the personality needs would be related to the teacher ratings. They were. The three needs were related to three sources of covariation in the teacher ratings. As predicted, students' rating of teachers were influenced by their needs. (See below for comments on multiple sources of covariation.)

The second use of canonical analysis comes from a study by Walberg of the relations between five sets of independent variables consisting of measures of the social environment of learning, student biographical items, and miscellaneous variables (dogmatism, authoritarianism, intelligence, and so on), on the one hand, and a set of dependent variables consisting of cognitive and noncognitive measures of learning.[17] Separate analyses were run between each set of independent variables and the set of dependent variables. Of the five sets of independent variables, three predicted significantly to the learning criteria.

One interesting result was the canonical correlation between the learning environment variables—Intimacy, Friction, Formality, and so on—and the dependent learning variables—Science Understanding, Science Interest, and so on. The canonical R was .61, indicating a fairly substantial relation between the linear composites of the two sets of variables.

In order to understand the significance of what is theoretically perhaps Walberg's most important finding, the reader should know that, as we found out in earlier discussions, there can be more than one source of variation in a set of data. Similarly, there can be more than one source of covariation in the two sets of variables being analyzed by canonical correlation. If there is more than one source, then more than one canonical correlation can be found.

Walberg found that 15 of the independent variables each correlated significantly with the set of dependent variables collectively. In a separate canonical analysis of these two sets of variables, two statistically significant canonical correlations were found: .64 and .60.[18] The first canonical variate or component was produced by the independent variables positively correlated with the cognitive learning gains of Physics Achievement, Science Understanding, and Science Processes. The second variate was produced by the gains on noncognitive dependent variables: Science Interest, Physics Interest, and Physics Activities. In short, Walberg was able, through canonical analysis, to present a highly condensed generalization, as he calls it, about the relations between cognitive learning, noncognitive learning, and a variety of environmental and other variables related to learning.

[16] T. Tetenbaum, ''The Role of Student Needs and Teacher Orientations in Student Ratings of Teachers,'' *American Educational Research Journal*, 12 (1975), 417–433.

[17] H. Walberg, ''Predicting Class Learning: An Approach to the Class as a Social System,'' *American Educational Research Journal*, 6 (1969), 529–542.

[18] The nature of canonical analysis is such that when the second linear component is calculated, it is orthogonal to the first component. Thus the above canonical correlations reflect two independent sources of variance in the data.

Multivariate Analysis of Variance

As one might suspect, analysis of variance has its multivariate counterpart, multivariate analysis of variance, which enables researchers to assess the effects of k independent variables on m dependent variables. Like its univariate companion, which we examined in some detail earlier, it is or should be used for experimental data. We forego further discussion here except to say that, as in all or most multivariate analysis, the results of multivariate analysis of variance are sometimes difficult to interpret because the difficulties mentioned earlier of assessing the relative importance of variables in this influence on one dependent variable, as in multiple regressive analysis, are often compounded in multivariate analysis of variance, canonical correlation, and discriminant analysis.[19]

Path Analysis

Path analysis is a form of applied multiple regression analysis that uses path diagrams to guide problem conceptualization or to test complex hypotheses. Through its use one can calculate the direct and indirect influences of independent variables on a dependent variable. These influences are reflected in so-called path coefficients, which are actually standardized regression coefficients (beta, B). Moreover, one can test different path models for their congruence with observed data.[20] While path analysis has been and is an important analytic and heuristic method, it is doubtful that it will continue to be used to help test models for their congruence with obtained data. Rather, its value will be as a heuristic method to aid conceptualization and the formation of complex hypotheses. The testing of such hypotheses, however, will probably be done with analytic tools more powerful and more appropriate for such testing. Let us look at an example to give a general idea of the approach.

Consider the two models, a and b, of Figure 34.1[21] Suppose we are trying to "explain" achievement, x_4, in the figure, or GPA, grade-point average. I believe that model a is "correct"; you believe, however, that model b is "correct." Model a says, in effect, that SES and intelligence both influence x_3, n achievement, or need for achievement, and that x_3 influences x_4, GPA or achievement. Well and good! I believe, in other words, that model a best expresses the relations among the four variables. On the other hand, you believe that model b is a better representation. It adds a direct influence of x_2, intelligence, on x_4, achievement (note the paths from x_2 to x_4 and from x_2 to x_3 to x_4). Which model is "correct"? It is possible in path analysis to test the two models. From the calculated path coefficients one produces two correlation matrices, R_a and R_b. Each of these is compared to the original four-by-four matrix, R, and the one whose correlations are closer to those of R is a "better" model. (It is possible, of course, that both models produce much the same results or that neither does.)

The calculations of the path coefficients are easy. Take model a. We calculate, first, the regression of x_3 on x_1 and x_2. This will yield the two path coefficients p_{31} and p_{32}, which are the same as the beta weights, β_1 and β_2. Second, calculate the regression of x_4 on x_3, which yields p_{43}, or β_{43}. (In addition, error terms are also calculated. We ignore them here.) From these path coefficients one calculates the R matrix they imply and

---

[19] See Pedhazur, *op. cit.* chaps. 17–18. For another very good discussion of multivariate analysis of variance, see J. Bray and S. Maxwell, "Analyzing and Interpreting Significant MANOVAs," *Review of Educational Research*, 52 (1982), 340–367.

[20] A complete and detailed exposition of path analysis can be found in Pedhazur, *op. cit.*, chap. 15.

[21] The example is *ibid.*, p. 601.

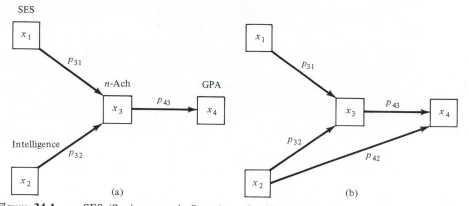

Figure 34.1 x_1: SES (Socioeconomic Status); x_2: Intelligence; x_3: n-Ach, or Need for Achievement; x_4: GPA, or Grade-Point Average (Achievement)

related statistics.[22] These are the ideas behind path analysis. We will return to such ideas when we study analysis of covariance structures in Chapter 36, a much more satisfying and scientifically rigorous approach to testing alternative models.

MULTIVARIATE ANALYSIS AND BEHAVIORAL RESEARCH

Although our study of multivariate methods has been rather superficial, we must still stop to place them into the research scheme of things and to evaluate them. Should we abandon analysis of variance, for example, simply because multiple regression can accomplish all that analysis of variance can—and more? Some such implication has perhaps been picked up by the reader. Isn't multiple regression analysis *really* unsuited to experimental data because it is a so-called correlational method (which it is only in part)? Other important questions can and should be asked and answered, especially at this time in the development of behavioral science research. We are at the point, perhaps, of an important transition. Since Sir Ronald Fisher invented and expounded the analysis of variance in the 1920s and 1930s, the method, or rather, approach, has had great influence on behavioral research, particularly in psychology. Are we now about to leave this stage? Have we entered a "multivariate stage"? If so, it can have an enormously important influence on the kind and quality of research done by psychologists, sociologists, and educators during the next decade. Obviously we can't handle all such questions in a textbook. But we should at least try to open the door to the student.

Should the analysis of variance approach be supplanted by multiple regression analysis? I don't think it should. But is this merely a sentimental clinging to something I have found interesting and satisfying? Perhaps. But there is more to it than that. There is little point to using multiple regression in the ordinary analysis of variance problem situation: random assignment of subjects to experimental treatments; equal or proportional n's in the cells; one, two, or three independent variables. Another argument for analysis of variance is its usefulness in teaching. Multiple regression analysis, while elegant and powerful, lacks the structural heuristic quality of analysis of variance. There is nothing quite so

[22]Pedhazur gives all details of the calculations. Students are urged to study his discussion and examples.

effective in teaching and learning research as drawing paradigms of the designs using analysis of variance analytic partitioning.

The answer is that both methods should be taught and learned. The additional demands on both teacher and student are inevitable, just as the development, growth, and use of inferential statistics earlier in the century made their teaching and learning inevitable. Multiple regression and other multivariate methods, however, will no doubt suffer some of the lack of understanding, even opposition, that inferential statistics has suffered. Even today there are psychologists, sociologists, and educators who know little about inferential statistics or modern analysis, and who even oppose their learning and use. This is part of the social psychology and pathology of the subject, however. While there will no doubt be cultural lag, the ultimate acceptance of these powerful tools of analysis is probably assured.

Multivariate methods, as we have seen, are not easy to use and to interpret. This is due not only to their complexity; it is due even more to the complexity of the phenomena that behavioral scientists work with. One of the drawbacks of educational research, for instance, has been that the enormous complexity of a school or a classroom could not adequately be handled by the too-simple methods used. Scientists, naturally, can never mirror the ''real'' world with their methods of observation and analysis. They are forever bound to simplifications of the situations and problems they study. They can never ''see things whole,'' just as no human being can see and understand the whole of anything. But multivariate methods mirror psychological, sociological, and educational reality better than simpler methods, and they enable researchers to handle larger portions of their research problems. In educational research, the days of the simple methods experiment with an experimental group and a control group are almost over. In sociological research, the reduction of much valuable data to frequency and percentage crossbreaks will decrease relative to the whole body of sociological research.

Most important of all, the healthy future of behavioral research depends on the healthy development of psychological, sociological, and other theories to help explain the relations among behavioral phenomena. By definition, theories are interrelated sets of constructs or variables. Obviously, multivariate methods are well adapted to testing fairly complex theoretical formulations, since their very nature is the analysis of several variables at once. Indeed, the development of behavioral theory must go hand-in-hand, even depend upon, the assimilation, mastery, and intelligent use of multivariate methods.

Study Suggestions

1. Unfortunately, completely satisfactory elementary treatments of multiple regression are scarce, especially if one expects concomitant regression treatment of analysis of variance. Perhaps satisfactory elementary treatment of such a complex subject is not possible. The following references on multiple regression and other multivariate methods may be helpful.

KERLINGER, F., and PEDHAZUR, E. *Multiple Regression in Behavioral Research*. New York: Holt, Rinehart and Winston, 1973. A text that attempts to enhance understanding of multiple regression and its research uses by providing as simple an exposition as possible and many examples with simple numbers. Also has a complete multiple regression computer program (Appendix D).

COOLEY, W., and LOHNES, P. *Multivariate Data Analysis*. New York: Wiley, 1971. Although more difficult than its predecessor, its computer routines (in Fortran) can be adapted to different installations. It is also an important textbook.

LEWIS-BECK, M. *Applied Regression: An Introduction*. Beverly Hills: Sage Publications, 1980. One of the Sage manuals of quantitative applications. A good workable treatment that covers most essential points.

PEDHAZUR, E. *Multiple Regression in Behavioral Research: Explanation and Prediction*, 2d ed. New York: Holt, Rinehart and Winston, 1982. The revision of the Kerlinger and Pedhazur text. It is, however, much more detailed and thorough. *Highly recommended.*

SNEDECOR, G., and COCHRAN, G. *Statistical Methods*, 6th ed. Ames, Iowa: Iowa State University Press, 1967. Chaps. 6 and 13 are pertinent—and very good, indeed.

TATSUOKA, M. *Multivariate Analysis: Techniques for Educational and Psychological Research*. New York: Wiley, 1971. This clearly written middle-level book has little discussion of multiple regression, but competently attacks many important multivariate problems.

TATSUOKA, M. *Discriminant Analysis: The Study of Group Differences*. Champaign, Ill.: Institute for Personality and Ability Testing, 1970. An excellent manual. *Highly recommended.*

After the student and researcher have mastered the elements of multiple regression analysis and have had some experience with actual problems, the following references provide sophisticated guidance in the use of multiple regression analysis and, more important, the interpretation of data.

COHEN, J. "Multiple Regression as a General Data-Analytic System." *Psychological Bulletin*, 70 (1968), 426–433. Successfully shows the relation between multiple regression and analysis of variance and also suggests general research uses of multiple regression.

DARLINGTON, R. "Multiple Regression in Psychological Research and Practice." *Psychological Bulletin*, 69 (1968), 161–182. Excellent, highly sophisticated, and sobering discussion of multiple regression.

RULON, P., and BROOKS, W. "On Statistical Tests of Group Differences." In D. Whitla, ed., *Handbook of Measurement and Assessment in Behavioral Sciences*. Reading, Mass.: Addison-Wesley, 1968, chap. 2. Lean exposition of the relations among a wide range of tests of statistical significance. *Highly recommended* (for the advanced student).

The following books are fundamental: they emphasize the theoretical and mathematical bases of multivariate methods.

GREEN, P. *Mathematical Tools for Applied Multivariate Analysis*. New York: Academic Press, 1976. An outstanding book on the mathematical basis of multivariate analysis. *Highly recommended.*

KENNY, D. *Correlation and Causality*. New York: Wiley, 1979. Worth many hours of study.

2. Suppose that a social psychologist has two correlation matrices:

$$
\begin{array}{ccc}
 & X_1 & X_2 & Y \\
X_1 & 1.00 & 0 & .70 \\
X_2 & 0 & 1.00 & .60 \\
Y & .70 & .60 & 1.00 \\
 & & A &
\end{array}
\qquad
\begin{array}{ccc}
 & X_1 & X_2 & Y \\
X_1 & 1.00 & .40 & .70 \\
X_2 & .40 & 1.00 & .60 \\
Y & .70 & .60 & 1.00 \\
 & & B &
\end{array}
$$

(a) Which matrix, A or B, will yield the higher R^2? Why?
(b) Calculate the R^2 of matrix A.
[*Answers:* (a) Matrix A; (b) $R^2 = .85$]

3. Cutright, in a study of the effect of communication, urbanization, education, and agriculture on the political development of 77 nations, found a multiple correlation of .82.[23] The correlations between each of the independent variables and the dependent variable were high: .81, .69, .74, and −.72. But the intercorrelations among the independent variables were also high—mostly in the .70's and .80's. What conclusions can you reach about the relations between the independent and dependent variables? The beta weights were (for the four independent variables): .65, .19, .02, and

---

[23] P. Cutright, "National Political Development: Measurement and Analysis," *American Sociological Review*, 27 (1963), 229–245.

.00. How much dependence can be put on these weights? What would happen if we reversed the order of entry of the independent variables?

4. Here are three sets of simple fictitious data, laid out for an analysis of variance. Lay out the data for multiple regression analysis, and calculate as much of the regression analysis as possible. Use dummy coding (1, 0), as in Table 34.2. The b coefficients are: $b_1 = 3$; $b_2 = 6$.

A_1	A_2	A_3
7	12	5
6	9	2
5	10	6
9	8	3
8	11	4

Imagine that A_1, A_2, and A_3 are three methods of changing racial attitudes and that the dependent variable is a measure of change with higher scores indicating more change. Interpret the results. [*Answers: a* = 4; R^2 = .75; F = 18, with df = 2, 12; ss_{reg} = 90; ss_t = 120. Note that these fictitious data are really the scores of Table 34.2 with 1 added to each score. Compare the various regression and analysis of variance statistics, above, with those calculated with the data of Table 34.2]

5. Using the data of Table 33.2 in Chapter 33, calculate the sums of each X_1 and X_2 pair. Correlate these sums with the Y scores. Compare the square of this correlation with $R^2_{y.12}$ = .51 (r^2 = .70^2 = .49). Since the two values are quite close, why shouldn't we simply use the averages of the independent variables and not bother with the complexity of multiple regression analysis?

6. Here are several interesting studies that have effectively used multiple regression, path analysis, and discriminant analysis. Read one or two of them carefully. Those marked with an asterisk are perhaps easier than the others.

BACHMAN, J., and O'MALLEY, P. "Self-Esteem in Young Men: A Longitudinal Analysis of the Impact of Educational and Occupational Attainment." *Journal of Personality and Social Psychology*, 35 (1977), 365–380. An outstanding educational study that used path analysis. Results contrary to expectation.

CLEARY, T. "Test Bias: Prediction of Grades of Negro and White Students in Integrated Colleges." *Journal of Educational Measurement*, 5 (1968), 115–124. An ingenious use of multiple regression to detect test bias.

*FIRKOWSKA, A., et al. "Cognitive Development and Social Policy." *Science*, 200 (1978), 1357–1362. The Warsaw study summarized earlier in the book.

*FISCHER, C. "The City and Political Psychology." *American Political Science Review*, 69 (1975), 559–571. Used path analysis to study sense of political efficacy.

*HILLER, J., FISHER, G., and KAESS, W. "A Computer Investigation of Verbal Characteristics of Effective Classroom Lecturing." *American Educational Research Journal*, 6 (1969), 661–675. Although marred methodologically, has highly interesting multiple regression results on college lecturing. Unusual and potentially effective use of residual scores to control unwanted variables. (*Special Question*: Why would a researcher want to analyze residual scores?)

KEEVES, J. *Educational Environment and Student Achievement*. Melbourne: Australian Council for Educational Research, 1972. Impressive Australian study that used multiple regression, canonical correlation, and path analysis.

*MARJORIBANKS, K. "Ethnic and Environmental Influences on Mental Abilities." *American Journal of Sociology*, 78 (1972), 323–337. An interesting use of the addition and subtraction of R^2's to assess the relative influence of variables, especially of the environment and ethnicity. (But see Pedhazur, *op. cit.*, chap. 7.)

*PAGE, R., and KEITH, T. "Effects of U. S. Private Schools: A Technical Analysis of Two Recent Claims." *Educational Researcher*, 10 (1981), 7–17. Questioned Coleman's private school findings. Used path analysis.

RIGHTMIRE, G. "Multivariate Analysis of an Early Hominid Metacarpal from Swartkrans." *Science*, 176 (1972), 159–161. Used discriminant analysis to distinguish human and chimpanzee fossil bones.

Chapter 35

Factor Analysis

BECAUSE of its power, elegance, and closeness to the core of scientific purpose, factor analysis can be called the queen of analytic methods. In this chapter we explore what factor analysis is and why and how it is done. In the exploration we will also examine old and new researches in which factor analysis has been a central methodology.

Factor analysis serves the cause of scientific parsimony. It reduces the multiplicity of tests and measures to greater simplicity. It tells us, in effect, what tests or measures belong together—which ones virtually measure the same thing, in other words, and how much they do so. It thus reduces the number of variables with which the scientist must cope. It also helps the scientist locate and identify unities or fundamental properties underlying tests and measures.

A *factor* is a construct, a hypothetical entity, a latent variable that is assumed to underlie tests, scales, items, and, indeed, measures of almost any kind. A number of factors have been found to underlie intelligence, for example: verbal ability, numerical ability, abstract reasoning, spatial reasoning, memory, and others. Similarly, aptitude, attitude, and personality factors have been isolated and identified. Even nations and people have been factored!

FOUNDATIONS

A Hypothetical Example

Suppose we administer six tests to a large number of seventh-grade pupils. We suspect that the six tests are measuring not six but some smaller number of variables. The tests are: *vocabulary, reading, synonyms, numbers, arithmetic* (standardized test), *arithmetic*

Table 35.1 *R* Matrix: Coefficients of Correlation Among Six Tests

		V	R	S	N	AS	AT
Cluster I	V		.72	.63	.09	.09	.00
	R	.72		.57	.15	.16	.09
	S	.63	.57		.14	.15	.09
	N	.09	.15	.14		.57	.63
	AS	.09	.16	.15	.57		.72
	AT	.00	.09	.09	.63	.72	

Cluster II

(teacher-made test). The names of these tests indicate their nature. We label them, respectively, *V, R, S, N, AS, AT.* (The last two tests, though both arithmetic, have different content. We assume a good reason for including both of them in our little test battery.) After the tests are administered and scored, coefficients of correlation are calculated between each test and every other test. We lay out the *r*'s in a correlation matrix (usually called *R* matrix). The matrix is given in Table 35.1.

Recall that a matrix is any rectangular array of numbers (or symbols). Correlation matrices are always square and symmetric. This is because the lower half of the matrix below the diagonal (from upper left to lower right) is the same as the upper half of the matrix. That is, the coefficients in the lower half are identical to those in the upper half, except for their arrangement. (Note that the top row is the same as the first column, the second row the same as the second column, and so on.)

The problem before us is expressed in two questions: How many underlying variables, or factors, are there? What are the factors? They are presumed to be underlying unities behind the test performances reflected in the correlation coefficients. If two or more tests are substantially correlated, then the tests share variance. They have common factor variance. They are measuring something in common.

The first question in this case is easy to answer. There are two factors. This is indicated by the two clusters of *r*'s, circled and labeled I and II in Table 35.1. Note that *V* correlates with *R*, .72; *V* with *S*, .63; and *R* with *S*, .57. *V, R*, and *S* appear to be measuring something in common. Similarly, *N* correlates with *AS*, .57, and with *AT*, .63; and *AS* correlates with *AT*, .72. *N, AS*, and *AT* are measuring something in common. It is important to note, however, that the tests in Cluster I, though themselves intercorrelated, are not to any great extent correlated with the tests in Cluster II. Likewise, *N, AS*, and *AT*, though themselves intercorrelated, are not substantially correlated with the tests *V, R*, and *S*. What is measured in common by the tests in Cluster I is evidently not the same as what is measured in common by the tests of Cluster II. There appear to be two clusters or factors in the matrix.[1]

By inspecting the *R* matrix, we have determined that there are two factors underlying these tests. The second question (What are the factors?) is almost always more difficult. When we ask what the factors are, we seek to name them. We want *constructs* that explain the underlying unities or common factor variances of the factors. We ask what is common to the tests *V, R*, and *S*, on the one hand, and to the tests *N, AS*, and *AT*, on the other hand. *V, R*, and *S* are vocabulary, reading, and synonym tests. All three involve words, to a large extent. Perhaps the underlying factor is *verbal ability*. We name the factor *Verbal*, or

---

[1] In this presentation, occasional oversimplifications and somewhat unrealistic examples are used. For example, the *R* matrix of Table 35.1 is unrealistic. All the tests would be positively correlated, and the two factors would probably emerge. In addition, clusters, while similar to factors, are not factors. For simplicity and pedagogy, however, we risk these oversimplifications.

V. N, AS, and *AT* all involve numerical or arithmetic operations. Suppose we named this factor *Arithmetic*. A friend points out to us that test *N* does not really involve arithmetic operations, since it consists mostly of manipulating numbers nonarithmetically. We overlooked this in our eagerness to name the underlying unity. Anyway, we now name the factor *Numerical*, or *Number*, or *N*. There is no inconsistency: all three tests involve numbers and numerical manipulation and operation.

   Both questions have been answered: there are two factors, and they are named *Verbal*, *V*, and *Numerical*, *N*. It must be hastily and urgently pointed out, however, that neither question is ever finally answered in actual factor analytic research. This is especially true in early investigations of a field. The number of factors can change in subsequent investigations using the same tests. One of the *V* tests may also have some variance in common with another factor, say *K*. If a test measuring *K* is added to the matrix, a third factor may emerge. Perhaps more important, the name of a factor may be incorrect. Subsequent investigation using these *V* tests and other tests may show that *V* is not now common to all the tests. The investigator must then find another construct, another source of common factor variance. In short, factor names are tentative; they are hypotheses to be tested in further factor analytic and other kinds of research.[2]

Factor Matrices and Factor Loadings

If a test measures one factor only, it is said to be *factorially "pure."* To the extent that a test measures a factor, it is said to be *loaded* on the factor, or saturated with the factor. Factor analysis is not really complete unless we know whether a test is factorially "pure" and how saturated it is with a factor. If a measure is not factorially pure, we usually want to know what other factors pervade it. Some measures are so complex that it is difficult to tell just what they measure. A good example is teacher grades, or grade-point averages. If a test contains more than one factor, it is said to be *factorially complex.*

   Some tests and measures are factorially quite complex. The Stanford-Binet Intelligence Test, the Otis intelligence tests, and the *F* (authoritarianism) scale are examples. A desideratum of scientific investigation is to have pure measures of variables. If a measure of numerical ability is not factorially pure, how can we have confidence that a relation between numerical ability and school achievement, say, is really the relation we think it is? If the test measures both numerical ability and verbal reasoning, doubt is thrown upon relations studied with its help.

   To solve these and other problems, we need an objective method to determine the number of factors, the tests loaded on the various factors, and the magnitude of the loadings. There are several factor analytic methods to accomplish these purposes. We discuss one of these later.

   One of the final outcomes of a factor analysis is called a *factor matrix,* a table of coefficients that expresses the relations between the tests and the underlying factors. The factor matrix yielded by factor analyzing the data of Table 35.1 with the principal factors method, one of the several methods available, is given in Table 35.2.[3] The entries in the table are called *factor loadings.* They can be written a_{ij}, meaning the loading *a* of test *i* on factor *j*. In the second line, .79 is the factor loading of test *R* on factor *A*.[4] In the fourth

[2]Nunnally's excellent chapter on factor analysis is well worth study: J. Nunnally, *Psychometric Theory*, 2d ed. New York: McGraw-Hill, 1978, chap. 10.

   [3]Actually, factor analytic methods do not yield final solutions like that in Table 35.2. They yield solutions that require what is called "rotation of axes." Rotation will be discussed later.

   [4]Some factor analysts label final solution factors I, II, . . . , or I', II', ... In this chapter we label unrotated factors I, II, . . . and rotated (final solution) factors *A, B,* . . . .

line, .70 is the factor loading of test *N* on factor *B*. Test *AS* has the following loadings: .10 on factor *A* and .79 on factor *B*.

Factor loadings are not hard to interpret. They range from -1.00 through 0 to $+1.00$, like correlation coefficients. They are interpreted similarly. In short, they express the correlations *between the tests and the factors*. For example, test *V* has the following correlations with factors *A* and *B*, respectively: .83 and .01. Evidently test *V* is highly loaded on *A*, but not at all on *B*.[5] Tests *V*, *R*, and *S* are loaded on *A* but not on *B*. Tests *N*, *AS*, and *AT* are loaded on *B* but not on *A*. All the tests are "pure."

The entries in the last column are called *communalities*, or h^2's. They are the sums of squares of the factor loadings of a test or variable. For example, the communality of test *R* is $(.79)^2 + (.10)^2 = .63$. The communality of a test or variable is its common factor variance. This will be explained later when we discuss factor theory.

Before going further, we should again note that this example is unrealistic. Factor matrices rarely present such a clear-cut picture. Indeed, the factor matrix of Table 35.2 was "known." The author first wrote the matrix given in Table 35.3. If this matrix is multiplied by itself, the *R* matrix of Table 35.1 (with diagonal values) will be obtained. In this case, all that is necessary to obtain *R* is to multiply each row by every other row. For example, multiply row *V* by row *R*: $(.90)(.80) + (.00)(.10) = .72$; row *V* by row *S*: $(.90)(.70) + (.00)(.10) = .63$; row *S* by row *AS*: $(.70)(.10) + (.10)(.80) = .15$; and so on. The resulting *R* matrix was then factor-analyzed.[6]

It is instructive to compare Tables 35.2 and 35.3. Note the discrepancies. They are small. That is, the fallible factor analytic method cannot perfectly reproduce the "true" factor matrix. It estimates it. In this case the fit is close because of the deliberate simplicity of the problem. Real data are not so obliging. Moreover, we never know the "true" factor matrix. If we did, there would be no need for factor analysis. We always estimate

Table 35.2 Factor Matrix of Data of Table 35.1, Rotated Solution[a]

Tests	A	B	h^2
V	.83	.01	.70
R	.79	.10	.63
S	.70	.10	.50
N	.10	.70	.50
AS	.10	.79	.63
AT	.01	.83	.70

[a]See text for identification of the tests. "Significant" loadings are italicized. See footnotes to Table 35.5.

[5]Unfortunately, there is no generally accepted standard error of factor loadings. A crude rule is to use the standard error of *r*—or, easier, to find the *r* that is significant for the *N* of the study. For example, with $N = 200$, an *r* of about .18 is significant at the .01 level. Some factor analysts in some studies do not bother with loadings less than .30, or even .40. Others do. The loadings considered "significant" in Table 35.2 are italicized. The use of $1/\sqrt{N}$ as the standard error of factor loadings is recommended in: N. Cliff and C. Hamburger, "The Study of Sampling Errors in Factor Analysis by Means of Artificial Experiments," *Psychological Bulletin*, 68 (1967), 430–445. A more conservative formula—that is, it yields larger standard errors—is given in: H. Harman, *Modern Factor Analysis*, 3d ed. Chicago: University of Chicago Press, 1976, p. 443. Both formulas must be used with circumspection. With large *N* (>400), the two estimates are close.

[6]This matrix multiplication operation springs from what is called the basic equation of factor analysis: $R = FF'$, which says succinctly in matrix symbols what was said more laboriously above. A thorough understanding of factor analysis requires a good understanding of matrix algebra. Thurstone has written an excellent exposition: L. Thurstone, *Multiple Factor Analysis*. Chicago: University of Chicago Press, 1947, chap. II. See, too, the Kerlinger and Pedhazur, Pedhazur, and Tatsuoka, references, Study Suggestion 1, Chapter 34.

Table 35.3 Original Factor Matrix from Which the R Matrix of Table 35.1 Was Derived

Tests	A	B	h^2
V	.90	.00	.81
R	.80	.10	.65
S	.70	.10	.50
N	.10	.70	.50
AS	.10	.80	.65
AT	.00	.90	.81

the factor matrix from the correlation matrix. The complexity and fallibility of research data frequently make this estimation a difficult business.

Some Factor Theory

In Chapter 27 we wrote an equation that expresses sources of variance in a measure (or test):

$$V_t = V_{co} + V_{sp} + V_e \qquad (35.1)$$

where V_t = total variance of a measure; V_{co} = common factor variance, or the variance that two or more measures share in common; V_{sp} = specific variance, or the variance of the measure that is not shared with any other measure, that is, variance of that measure and no other; V_e = error variance.

The common factor variance V_{co} was broken down into two sources of variance, A and B, two factors (see Equation 27.11):

$$V_{co} = V_A + V_B \qquad (35.2)$$

V_A might be verbal ability variance, and V_B might be numerical ability variance.

This is reasonable if we think of the sums of squares of factor loadings of any test:

$$h_i^2 = a_i^2 + b_i^2 + \cdots + k_i^2 \qquad (35.3)$$

where a_i^2, b_i^2, . . . are the squares of the factor loadings of test i, and h_i^2 is the communality of test i. But $h_i^2 = V_{co}$. Therefore $V(A) = a^2$ and $V(B) = b^2$, and Equation 35.2 is tied to real factor analytic operations.

But there may, of course, be more than two factors. The generalized equation is

$$V_{co} = V_A + V_B + \cdots + V_k \qquad (35.4)$$

Substituting in Equation 35.1, we obtain

$$V_t = V_A + V_B + \cdots + V_K + V_{sp} + V_e \qquad (35.5)$$

Dividing through by V_t we find a proportional representation:

$$\frac{V_t}{V_t} = 1.00 = \overbrace{\frac{V_A}{V_t} + \frac{V_B}{V_t} + \cdots + \frac{V_K}{V_t}}^{h^2} + \underbrace{\frac{V_{sp}}{V_t} + \frac{V_e}{V_t}}_{r_{tt}} \qquad (35.6)$$

The h^2 and r_{tt} parts of the equation have been labeled as they were in Chapter 27. This equation has beauty. It ties tightly together measurement theory and factor

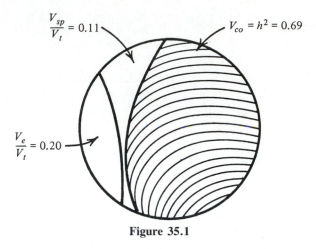

Figure 35.1

theory.[7] h^2 is the proportion of the total variance that is common factor variance. r_{tt} is the proportion of the total variance that is reliable variance. V_e/V_t is the proportion of the total variance that is error variance. In Chapter 27 an equation like this enabled us to tie reliability and validity together. Now, it shows us the relation between factor theory and measurement theory. We see, in brief, that *the main problem of factor analysis is to determine the variance components of the total common factor variance*.

Take test V in Table 35.2. A glance at Equation 35.6 shows us, among other things, that the reliability of a measure is always greater than, or equal to, its communality. Test V's reliability, then, is at least .70. Suppose $r_{tt} = .80$. Since $V_t/V_t = 1.00$, we can fill in all the terms:

$$\frac{V_t}{V_t} = 1.00 = \overbrace{(.83)^2 + (.01)^2}^{h^2 = .69} + \overbrace{.11}^{V_{sp}} + \overbrace{.20}^{V_e}$$
$$\underbrace{\hspace{5cm}}_{r_{tt} = .80}$$

Test V, then, has a high proportion of common factor variance and a low proportion of specific variance.

The proportions can be seen clearly in a circle diagram. Let the area of the circle equal the total variance, or 1.00 (100 percent of the area), in Figure 35.1. The three variances have been indicated by blocking out areas of the circle. V_{co}, or h^2, for example, is 69 percent, V_{sp} is 11 percent, and V_e is 20 percent of the total variance.

A factor analytic investigation including test V would tell us mainly about V_{co}, the common factor variance. It would tell us the proportion of the test's total variance that is common factor variance and would give us clues to its nature by telling us which other tests share the same common factor variance and which do not.[8]

Graphical Representation of Factors and Factor Loadings

The student of factor analysis must learn to think spatially and geometrically if he is to grasp the essential nature of the factor approach. There are two or three good ways to do

[7] See J. Guilford, *Psychometric Methods*, 2d ed. New York: McGraw-Hill, 1954. pp. 354–357, and Thurstone, *op. cit.*, chap. II.

[8] See Figure 27.1 in Chapter 27 for a diagrammatic two-test illustration of these notions.

this. A table of correlations can be represented by the use of vectors and the angles between them. We here use a more common method. We treat the row entries of a factor matrix as coordinates and plot them in geometric space. In Figure 35.2 the factor matrix entries of Table 35.2 have been plotted.

The two factors, A and B, are laid out at right angles to each other. These are called *reference axes*. Appropriate factor loading values are indicated on each of the axes. Then each test's loadings are treated as coordinates and plotted. For example, test R's loadings are (.79, .10). Go out .79 on A and up .10 on B. This point has been indicated in Figure 35.2 by a circled letter indicating the test. Plot the coordinates of the other five tests similarly.

The factor structure can now be clearly seen. Each test is highly loaded on one factor but not on the other. They are all relatively "pure" measures of their respective factors. A seventh point has been indicated in Figure 35.2 by a circled cross in order to illustrate a presumed test that measures both factors. Its coordinates are (.60, .50). This means that the test is loaded on both factors, .60 on A and .50 on B. It is not "pure." Factor structures of this simplicity and clarity, where the factors are orthogonal (the axes at right angles to each other), the test loadings substantial and "pure," almost no tests loaded on two or more factors, and only two factors, are not common.

Most published factor analytic studies report more than two factors. Four, five, even nine, ten, and more factors have been reported. Graphical representation of such factor structures in one graph is, of course, not possible. Factor analysts customarily plot factors two at a time, though it is possible to plot three at a time. It must be admitted, however, that it is difficult to visualize or keep in mind complex n-dimensional structures. One therefore visualizes two-dimensional structures and generalizes to n dimensions algebraically.[9]

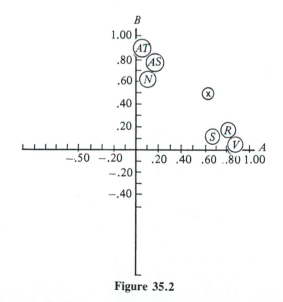

Figure 35.2

[9]One of the fortunate aspects of computer factor analysis programs is that such factor plotting is easily possible. In the widely available BMDP and SAS factor analysis programs, for example, one can instruct the computer to print the plots one wishes to see. W. Dixon, ed., *BMDP Statistical Software 1981*. Berkeley: University of California Press, 1981, Program P4M, Factor Analysis, p. 497; *SAS User's Guide 1979 Edition*. Cary, N.C.: SAS Institute, 1979, Program Factor, p. 204. It is highly likely, too, that the expanded memories of microcomputers will make factor plotting possible in the near future.

EXTRACTION AND ROTATION OF FACTORS, FACTOR SCORES, AND SECOND-ORDER FACTOR ANALYSIS

There are a number of methods of factor analyzing a correlation matrix: principal factors, centroid, diagonal, maximum likelihood, multiple group, minres, image, alpha, and so on.[10] We cannot discuss all these methods. Our purpose is elementary basic understanding. Therefore, we describe the method that is used the most at present and that is widely available at computer installations: the principal factors method.

The reader may ask: Why not use a comparatively simple cluster method like the inspection approach used earlier instead of a complex method like the principal factors method? Cluster methods can be used and have been recommended. They depend upon our identifying clusters and presumed factors by finding interrelated groups of correlation coefficients or other measures of relation. In Table 35.1, the clusters are easy to find. In most *R* matrices, however, the clusters cannot be so easily identified. More objective and precise methods are needed.

The Principal Factors Method[11]

The principal factors method is mathematically satisfying because it yields a mathematically unique solution of a factor problem. Perhaps its major solution feature is that it extracts a maximum amount of variance as each factor is calculated. In other words, the first factor extracts the most variance, the second the next most variance, and so on.

To show the logic of the principal factors method without considerable mathematics is difficult. One can achieve a certain intuitive understanding of the method, however, by approaching it geometrically. Conceive tests or variables as points in *m*-dimensional space. Variables that are highly and positively correlated should be near each other and away from variables with which they do not correlate. If this reasoning is correct, there should be swarms of points in space. Each of these points can be located in the space if suitable axes are inserted into the space, one axis for each dimension of the *m* dimensions. Then any point's location is its multiple identification obtained by reading its coordinates on the *m* axes. The factor problem is to project axes through neighboring swarms of points and to so locate these axes that they "account for" as much of the variances of the variables as possible.

Imagine the room you are sitting in to have swarms of points in various parts of its three-dimensional space. Imagine that some of the points cluster together in the upper right center of the room (from your vantage point). Now imagine another cluster of points at another point in the room, say in the lower right center. Part of the problem is to locate axes—three axes in this case, since the room is three-dimensional—so as to identify and appropriately label the swarms and the points in the swarms.

We can demonstrate these ideas with a simple two-dimensional example. Suppose we have five tests. These tests, let us say, are situated in two-dimensional space as indicated in Figure 35.3. The closer two points are, the more they are related. The problem is to determine: (1) how many factors there are; (2) what tests are loaded on what factors; and (3) the magnitudes of the test loadings.

The problem will now be solved in two different ways, each interesting as well as instructive. First, we solve directly from the points themselves. Follow these directions. Draw a vertical line three units to the left of point 3. Draw a horizontal line one unit below

---

[10] Harman, *op. cit.*, Part II.

[11] See *ibid.*, chap. 8. This is a thorough exposition, with computational and analytic details.

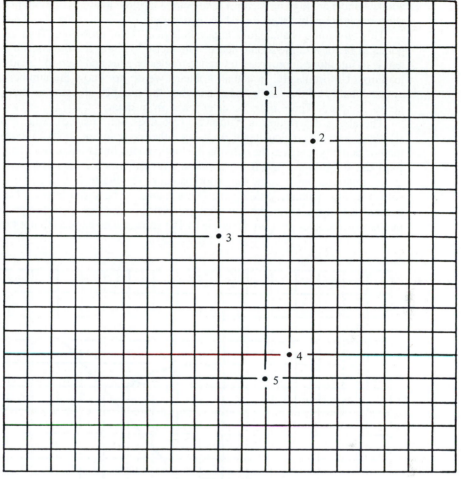

Figure 35.3

point 3. Label these reference axes I and II. Now read off the coordinates of each point, for instance, point 2 is (.70, .50), point 4 is (.60, −.40). Write a "factor matrix" with these five pairs of values.

Rotate the axes orthogonally and clockwise so that axis I goes between points 4 and 5. Axis II, of course, will go between Points 1 and 2. (The use of a protractor is recommended: the rotation should be approximately 40 degrees.) Label these "new" rotated axes *A* and *B*. Cut a strip of four-to-the-inch graph paper. (The points are plotted on this size graph paper.) Count the base of each square as .10 (.10 = 1/4 inch; ten units, of course, equal 1.00). Using the strip as a measure, measure the distances of the points on the new axes. For example, point 2 should be close to (.22, .83), and point 5 should be close to (.71, −.06). (It does not make too much difference if there are small discrepancies.) The original (I and II) and rotated (*A* and *B*) axes and the five points are shown in Figure 35.4.

Now write both factor matrices, unrotated and rotated. They are given in Table 35.4. The problem is solved: There are two factors. Points (tests) 1 and 2 are high on factor *B*, points 4 and 5 are high on factor A, and point 3 has low loadings on both factors. The three questions originally asked have been answered.

This procedure is analogous to psychological factor problems. Tests are conceived as points in factor m-dimensional space. The factor loadings are the coordinates. The problem is to introduce appropriate reference frames or axes and then to "read off" the factor loadings. Unfortunately, in actual problems we do not know the number of factors (the dimensionality of the factor space and thus the number of axes) or the location of the points in space. These must be determined from data.

The above description is figurative. One does not "read off" factor loadings from reference axes; one calculates them using rather complex methods. The principal factors method actually involves the solution of simultaneous linear equations. The roots obtained from the solution are called *eigenvalues*. *Eigenvectors* are also obtained; after suitable transformation, they become the factor loadings. The fictitious R matrix of Table 35.1 was solved in this manner, yielding the factor matrix to be given later in Table 35.5. Most computer analysis programs use principal factors solutions. And the programs given in published computer program texts use it. The student who expects to use factor analysis to

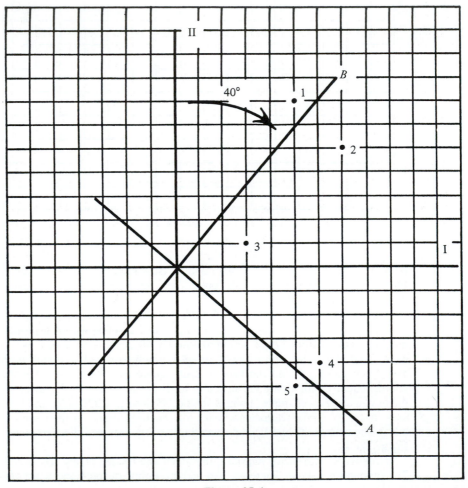

Figure 35.4

Table 35.4 Unrotated and Rotated Factor Matrices, Point-Distance Problem

	Unrotated			Rotated	
Points	I	II	Points	A	B
1	.50	.70	1	−.07	.86
2	.70	.50	2	.22	.83
3	.30	.10	3	.17	.27
4	.60	−.40	4	.72	.08
5	.50	−.50	5	.71	−.06

any extent should study the method carefully and at least understand what it does. There is nothing quite so dangerous and self-defeating as using computer programs blindly. This is especially true in factor analysis.[12]

Rotation and Simple Structure

Most factor analytic methods produce results in a form that is difficult or impossible to interpret. Thurstone argued that it was necessary to rotate factor matrices if one wanted to interpret them adequately.[13] He pointed out that original factor matrices are arbitrary in the sense that an infinite number of reference frames (axes) can be found to reproduce any given R matrix.[14] A principal factors matrix and its loadings account for the common factor variance of the test scores, but they do not in general provide scientifically meaningful structures. It is the configurations of tests or variables in factor space that are of fundamental concern. In order to discover these configurations adequately, the arbitrary reference axes must be rotated. In other words, we assume that there are unique and "best" positions for the axes, "best" ways to view the variables in n-dimensional space.

There is no intention here of reifying constructs, variables, or factors. Factors are simply structures or patterns produced by covariances of measures. What is meant by "best way to view the variables" is the most parsimonious, the simplest way. A "best" way can be predicted from theory and hypotheses, as Guilford did in his structure of intellect theory and research,[15] or as Cattell did in his theory of crystallized and fluid intelligence,[16] or as Thurstone and Thurstone did in their extensive studies of primary mental abilities (see *Research Examples,* below).[17] Or a "best" way may be discovered from a structure so clear and strong as almost to compel belief in its validity and "reality."

[12] It is possible, perhaps probable, that the principal factors solution will be replaced in the next decade by other methods. Harman (*op. cit.,* pp. 174ff.) thinks that his minres (minimum residual) method, an approach quite different from the principal factors method—and equally if not more complex—will perhaps replace it. The most likely outcome will be that several excellent methods will be readily available, so that researchers can select methods to suit problems.

[13] Thurstone, *op. cit.,* pp. 508–509.

[14] *Ibid.,* p. 93.

[15] J. Guilford, *The Nature of Human Intelligence.* New York: McGraw-Hill, 1967. For a distinguished evaluation of this important book, see J. Carroll's review: *American Educational Research Journal,* 5 (1968), 249–256.

[16] R. Cattell, "Theory of Fluid and Crystallized Intelligence: A Critical Experiment, *Journal of Educational Psychology,* 54 (1963), 1–22.

[17] L. Thurstone and T. Thurstone, *Factorial Studies of Intelligence.* Chicago: University of Chicago Press, 1941 (reprinted 1968, Psychometric Society). For a clear, concise, and informative review of the different factor theories of intelligence, see P. Vernon, *Intelligence: Heredity and Environment.* San Francisco: Freeman, 1979, chap. 4.

Among Thurstone's important contributions, his invention of the ideas of simple structure and factor axes rotation are perhaps the most important. With them he laid down relatively clear guidelines for achieving psychologically meaningful and interpretable factor analytic solutions. In Table 35.2 we reported a factor matrix obtained from the R matrix of Table 35.1. This was the final *rotated* matrix and not the matrix originally produced by the factor analysis. The *unrotated* matrix originally produced by the principal factors method is given on the left side of Table 35.5. The rotated factors are reproduced on the right side of the table. The communalities (h^2) are also given. They are the same for both matrices.

If we try to interpret the unrotated matrix on the left of the table, we run into trouble. It can be said that all the tests are loaded on a general factor, I, and that the second factor, II, is bipolar. (A *bipolar factor* is one that has substantial positive and negative loadings.) This would amount to saying that all the tests measure the same thing (factor I), but that the first three measure the negative aspect of whatever the second three measure (factor II). But aside from the ambiguous nature of such an interpretation, we know that the reference axes, I and II, and consequently the factor loadings, are arbitrary. Look at the factor plot of Figure 35.2. There are two clearly defined clusters of tests clinging closely to the axes A and B. There is no general factor here, nor is there a bipolar factor. The second major problem of factor analysis, therefore, is to discover a unique and compelling solution or position of the reference axes.

Plot the loadings of I and II, and we "see" the original unrotated structure. This has been done in Figure 35.5. Now swing the axes so that I goes as near as possible to the *V, R,* and *S* points and, at the same time, II goes as near as possible to the *N, AS,* and *AT* points. A rotation of 45 degrees will do nicely. We then obtain essentially the structure of Figure 35.2. That is, the new rotated positions of the axes and the positions of the six tests are the same as the positions of the axes and tests of Figure 35.2. The structure simply leans to the right. Turn the figure so that the B of the B axis points directly up and this becomes clear. It is now possible to read off the new rotated factor loadings on the rotated axes. (The reader can confirm this by reading off and writing down the loadings of the tests on the rotated axes of Figure 35.5.) Since the axes are kept at a 90-degree angle, this is called an *orthogonal* rotation.

This example, though unrealistic, may help the reader understand that factor analysts search for the unities that presumably underlie test performances. Spatially conceived, they search out the relations among variables "out there" in multidimensional factor

Table 35.5 Unrotated and Rotated Factor Matrices, R Matrix of Table 35.1[a]

Tests	Unrotated		Rotated		h^2
	I	II	A	B	
V	.60	−.58	.83	.01	.70
R	.63	−.49	.79	.10	.63
S	.56	−.43	.70	.10	.50
N	.56	.43	.10	.70	.50
AS	.63	.49	.10	.79	.63
AT	.60	.58	.01	.83	.70

[a] Significant loadings (≥ .30) are italicized. Note that the A and B vectors are reversed in this table. The h^2's calculated from the unrotated and rotated values are slightly different, owing to errors of rounding, *e.g.*, $.60^2 + .58^2 = .70$ and $.83^2 + .01^2 = .69$. The correct computer values have been used in the table (and in Table 35.2).

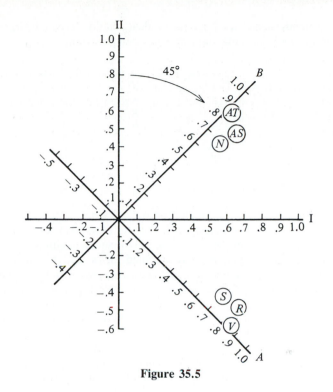

Figure 35.5

space. Through knowledge of the empirical relations among tests or other measures, they probe in factor space with reference axes until they find the unities or relations among relations—if they exist.

To guide rotations, Thurstone laid down five principles or rules of simple structure.[18] The rules are applicable to both orthogonal and oblique rotations, though Thurstone emphasized the oblique case. (Oblique rotations are those in which the angles between axes are acute or obtuse.) The simple structure principles are as follows:

1. Each row of the factor matrix should have at least one loading close to zero.
2. For each column of the factor matrix there should be at least as many variables with zero or near-zero loadings as there are factors.
3. For every pair of factors (columns) there should be several variables with loadings in one factor (column) but not in the other.
4. When there are four or more factors, a large proportion of the variables should have negligible (close to zero) loadings on any pair of factors.
5. For every pair of factors (columns) of the factor matrix there should be only a small number of variables with appreciable (nonzero) loadings in both columns.

In effect, these criteria call for as "pure" variables as possible, that is, each variable loaded on as few factors as possible, and *as many zeros as possible in the rotated factor matrix*. In this way the simplest possible interpretation of the factors can be achieved. In other words, rotation to achieve simple structure is a fairly objective way to achieve variable simplicity or to reduce variable complexity.

---

[18] Thurstone, *op. cit.*, p. 335; Harman, *op. cit.*, pp. 97–99.

To understand this, imagine an ideal solution in which simple structure is "perfect." It might look like this, say, in a three-factor solution:

Tests	A	B	C
1	X	0	0
2	X	0	0
3	X	0	0
4	0	X	0
5	0	X	0
6	0	X	0
7	0	0	X
8	0	0	X
9	0	0	X

X's indicate substantial factor loadings, O's near-zero loadings. Of course, such "perfect" factor structures are rare. It is more likely that some of the tests have loadings on more than one factor. Still, good approximations to simple structure have been achieved, especially in well-planned and executed factor analytic studies.

Before leaving the subject of factor rotations it must be pointed out that there are a number of rotational methods. The two main types of rotation are called "orthogonal" and "oblique." *Orthogonal* rotations maintain the independence of factors, that is, the angles between the axes are kept at 90 degrees. If we rotate factors I and II orthogonally, for instance, we swing both axes together, maintaining the right angle between them. This means that the correlation between the factors is zero. The rotation just performed in Figure 35.5 was orthogonal. If we had four factors, we would rotate I and II, I and III, I and IV, II and III, and so on, maintaining right angles between each pair of axes. Some researchers prefer to rotate orthogonally. Others insist that orthogonal rotation is unrealistic, that actual factors are not usually uncorrelated, and that rotations should conform to psychological "reality."[19]

Rotations in which the factor axes are allowed to form acute or obtuse angles are called *oblique*. Obliqueness, of course, means that factors are correlated. There is no doubt that factor structures can be better fitted with oblique axes and the simple structure criteria better satisfied. Some researchers might object to oblique factors because of the possible difficulty of comparing factor structures from one study to another. We leave this controversial subject with two remarks. One, the type of rotation seems to be a matter of taste. Two, the reader should understand both types of rotation to the extent that he can interpret both kinds of factors. He should be particularly careful when confronted with the results of oblique solutions. They contain peculiarities and subtleties not present in orthogonal solutions.

Second-Order Factor Analysis

Second-order factor analysis is a highly important but neglected approach to complex data analysis and hypothesis-testing. When factors are rotated obliquely, there are correlations between factors. In a provocative factor analytic and canonical correlation study of the redundancy present in student test scores, Lohnes and Marshall extracted two factors from 21 ability and achievement tests.[20] The unrotated factor loadings of eight of their measures, four ability tests and four grades (English, arithmetic, social studies, science), have

---

[19] See Thurstone, *op. cit.,* pp. 139–140.

[20] P. Lohnes and T. Marshall, "Redundancy in Student Records," *American Educational Research Journal,* 2 (1965), 19–23.

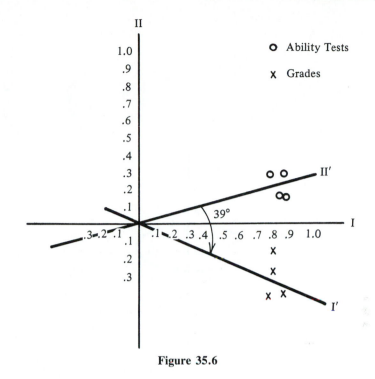

Figure 35.6

been plotted in Figure 35.6. The axes have been rotated obliquely so that they will go through the two clusters of loadings. There is an acute angle of about 39 degrees between the rotated axes, now labeled I' and II'. Any angle other than 90 degrees between axes means correlation between factors. In this case, the correlation is approximately .78, quite high.

Imagine this situation multiplied over six, eight, or ten factors: there would be a set of correlations among the factors. Factor analyze these correlations and we have second-order factor analysis, which is a method of finding the factors behind the factors. The famous "g" of intelligence testing is evidently a second-order factor. Whenever large numbers of ability tests are factor analyzed, the correlations among the tests are usually positive. Factor analyze them and some such pattern, as in Figure 35.6, though more complex, emerges. Calculate the correlations between the factors and again factor analyze and a single factor, perhaps "g," may emerge.

Are there second-order attitude factors? In a large study of social attitudes, which was the R-methodological counterpart of a Q study outlined in Chapter 32, Kerlinger administered a 50-item summated-rating scale, each item of which was a single word or short phrase (attitude referents or objects)—*private property, religion, civil rights, Social Security,* for example—to several large samples in different parts of the country.[21] The item responses of a combined sample of Texas and North Carolina teachers, $N = 530$, were intercorrelated and factor analyzed with the principal factors method. Six factors were obtained and rotated obliquely to simple structure. Three of these factors consisted of presumably conservative referents (*e.g., moral standards in education, religion, subject*

[21] F. Kerlinger, "The Structure and Content of Social Attitude Referents: A Preliminary Study," *Educational and Psychological Measurement,* 32 (1972), 613–630.

	A	*B*	Type
I	.71	.09	C
II	−.22	.64	L
III	.19	.61	L
IV	−.13	.65	L
V	.78	.04	C
VI	.68	−.12	C

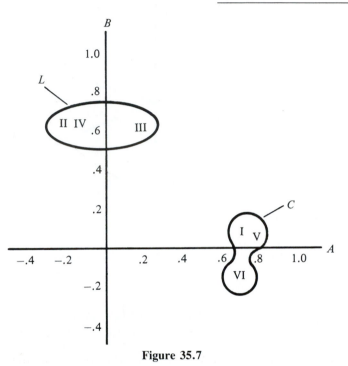

Figure 35.7

matter), and the other three factors liberal referents (*e.g., civil rights, children's interests, Supreme Court*).

The correlations among the factors were themselves factor analyzed with the principal factors method. Two factors were obtained and rotated orthogonally to simple structure. The rotated factor matrix is given in Figure 35.7, together with the identifications of the types of factors, *C* (Conservatism) and *L* (Liberalism). The factor loadings are also plotted. The evidence is so clear that it needs little elaboration. There are two clear, relatively orthogonal (uncorrelated) second-order factors, one of which has conservative referent factors, while the other has liberal referent factors.[22]

---

[22] There are no elementary guides to second-order factor analysis. The best available discussion is the oldest: Thurstone, *Multiple Factor Analysis,* pp. 215, 432–434. A second-order factor analysis computer program can be put together as follows. Use a standard program to factor analyze the *R* matrix. Use an oblique rotation program to rotate the factors. Have the computer create a file of the correlations among the factors (see Thurstone formula, *ibid.,* p. 433). Then use the factor analysis program to factor this matrix. You will need a program that accepts *R* matrices as input, of course. In my book on social attitudes, factors and second-order factor analysis are explained in two places: F. Kerlinger, *Liberalism and Conservatism: The Nature and Structure of Social Attitudes.* Hillsdale, N.J.: Erlbaum, 1984, chap. 4 and Appendix A. The example given above (footnote 21) and a number of other examples like it are discussed at length in this book.

Factor Scores

While second-order factor analysis is more oriented toward basic and theoretical research, another technique of factor analysis, so-called factor scores or measures, is eminently practical, though not without theoretical significance. *Factor scores* are measures of individuals on factors. Suppose, like Lohnes and Marshall, we found two factors underlying 21 ability and grade measures. Instead of using all 21 scores of groups of children in research, why not use just two scores calculated from the factors? Lohnes and Marshall recommend just this, pointing out the redundancy in the usual scores of pupils. These factor scores are, in effect, weighted averages, weighted according to the factor loadings.

Here is an oversimplified example. Suppose the factor matrix of Table 35.2 were actual data and that we want to calculate the A and B factor scores of an individual. The raw scores of one individual on the six tests, say, are: 7, 5, 5, 3, 4, 2. We multiply these scores by the related factor loadings, first for factor A and then for factor B, as follows:

$$A: F_A = (.83)(7) + (.79)(5) + (.70)(5) + (.10)(3) + (.10)(4) + (.01)(2)$$
$$= 13.98$$
$$B: F_B = (.01)(7) + (.10)(5) + (.10)(5) + (.70)(3) + (.79)(4) + (.83)(2)$$
$$= 7.99$$

The individual's "factor scores" are $F_A = 13.98$ and $F_B = 7.99$. We can, of course, calculate other individuals' "factor scores" similarly.

This is not the best way to calculate factor scores.[23] The example was made up to convey the idea of such scores as weighted sums or averages, the weights being the factor loadings. In any case, the method, though not extensively used in the past, has great potential for complex behavioral research. Instead of using many separate test scores, fewer factor scores can be used. An excellent real example is described by Mayeske, who participated in the reanalysis of the data of the Coleman report, *Equality of Educational Opportunity*.[24]

First, the scores of fifth-grade students on five achievement tests were weighted with principal component weights (loadings) and added to obtain an overall achievement composite scores (as in the above example). This was the dependent variable in many subsequent analyses. Second, the intercorrelations of sets of student variables and school variables were factor analyzed. Then "factor scores" were calculated to form indices—for example, socioeconomic status, attitude toward life, training of teacher, experience of teacher. These scores were used in multiple regression and other analyses. In short, more than 400 variables were reduced to 31 "factor variables" calculated from the data of over 130,000 students in 923 schools, thus achieving considerable parsimony and increasing the reliability and validity of the measures.

RESEARCH EXAMPLES

Most factor analytic studies have factored intelligence, aptitude, and personality tests and scales, the tests or scales themselves being intercorrelated and factor analyzed. The Thurstone example, below, is an excellent example; indeed, it is a classic. Persons, or the responses of persons, as we saw in Chapter 32, can also be factored. The variables entered into the correlation and factor matrices, in fact, can be tests, scales, persons, items,

---

[23] For better methods, see Harman, *op. cit.,* chap. 16.

[24] G. Mayeske, "Teacher Attributes and School Achievement." In *Do Teachers Make a Difference?* Washington, D.C.: U.S. Government Printing Office, 1970, pp. 100–119.

concepts, or whatever can be intercorrelated. The studies given below have been selected not to represent factor analytic investigations in general, but rather to familiarize the student with different uses of factor analysis.

Thurstone Factorial Study of Intelligence

Thurstone and Thurstone, in their monumental work on intelligence factors and their measurement, factor analyzed 60 tests plus the three variables chronological age, mental age, and sex.[25] The analysis was based on the test responses of 710 eighth-grade pupils to the 60 tests. It revealed essentially the same set of so-called primary factors that had been found in previous studies.

The Thurstones chose the three best tests for each of seven of the ten primary factors. Six of these tests seemed to have stability at different age levels sufficient for practical school use. They then revised and administered these tests to 437 eighth-grade school children. The main purpose of the study was to check the factor structure of the tests. In other words, they predicted that the same primary factors of intelligence put into the 21 tests would emerge from a new factor analysis on a new sample of children.

The rotated factor matrix (oblique rotation) is given in Table 35.6. This is a remarkable validation of the primary factors. The seven factors and their loadings are almost exactly as predicted. (See, especially, the italicized loadings.)

Table 35.6 Oblique Rotated Factor Matrix, Thurstone and Thurstone Study[a]

Tests	P	N	W	V	S	M	R
Identification Numbers	*42*	*40*	05	−02	−07	−06	−06
Faces	*45*	17	−06	04	20	05	02
Mirror Reading	*36*	09	19	−02	05	−01	09
First Names	−02	09	02	00	−05	*53*	10
Figure Recognition	*20*	−10	02	−02	10	*31*	07
Word-Number	02	13	−03	00	01	*58*	−04
Sentences	00	01	−03	*66*	−08	−05	13
Vocabulary	−01	02	05	*66*	−04	02	02
Completion	−01	00	−01	*67*	15	00	−01
First Letters	12	−03	*63*	03	−02	00	−00
4-Letter Words	−02	−05	*61*	−01	08	−01	04
Suffixes	04	03	*45*	18	−03	03	−08
Flags	−04	05	03	−01	*68*	00	01
Figures	02	−06	01	−02	*76*	−02	−02
Cards	07	−03	−03	03	*72*	02	−03
Addition	01	*64*	−02	01	05	01	−02
Multiplication	01	*67*	01	−03	−05	02	02
3-Higher	−05	*38*	−01	06	20	−05	16
Letter Series	−03	03	03	02	00	02	*53*
Pedigrees	02	−05	−03	22	−03	05	*44*
Letter Group	06	06	13	−04	01	−06	*42*

[a]Decimal points are omitted. *P* = Perception; *N* = Number; *W* = Word Fluency; *V* = Verbal; *S* = Space; *M* = Memory; *R* = Reasoning.

[25] Thurstone and Thurstone, *op. cit.* The student interested in factor analysis and the testing of intelligence can profit greatly from study of this fine monograph.

Fluid and Crystallized Intelligence

One of the most active, important, and controversial problems of behavioral scientific and practical interest is the nature of mental abilities. Different theories with different amounts and kinds of evidence to support them have been propounded by some of the ablest psychologists of the century: Spearman, Thurstone, Burt, Thorndike, Guilford, Cattell, and others. There can be no doubt whatever of the high scientific and practical importance of the problem. We have alluded, if only briefly, to the work and thinking of Thurstone and Guilford. We now describe, also briefly, one among the many factor analytic studies of Raymond Cattell.[26]

The famous general factor of intelligence, g, can be shown to be a second-order factor that runs through most tests of mental ability. Cattell believes, in effect, that there are two g's, or two aspects of g: crystallized and fluid. *Crystallized intelligence* is exhibited by cognitive performances in which "skilled judgment habits" have become fixed or crystallized owing to the earlier application of general learning ability to such performances. The well-known verbal and number factors are examples. *Fluid intelligence,* on the other hand, is exhibited by performances characterized more by adaptation to new situations, the "fluid" application of general ability, so to speak. Such ability is more characteristic of creative behavior than is crystallized intelligence. If tests are factor analyzed and the correlations among the factors found are themselves factored (second-order factor analysis), then both crystallized and fluid intelligence should emerge as second-order factors.

Cattell administered Thurstone's primary abilities tests and a number of his own mental ability and personality tests to 277 eighth-grade children, factor analyzed the 44 variables, and rotated the obtained 22 factors (probably too many) to simple structure. The correlations among these factors were themselves factored, yielding eight second-order factors. (Recall that oblique rotations yield factors that are correlated.) Although Cattell

Table 35.7 Part of Second-order Factor Matrix, Cattell Fluid and Crystallized Intelligence Study[a]

	F_1 (g_f)	F_2 (g_c)
Thurstone Tests		
Verbal	.15	*.46*
Spatial	*.32*	.14
Reasoning	.08	*.50*
Number	.05	*.59*
Fluency	.07	.09
Cattell Tests		
Series	*.35*	*.43*
Classification	*.63*	− .02
Matrices	*.50*	.10
Topology	*.51*	.09

[a] g_f: general factor, fluid; g_c: general factor, crystallized. Italics supplied by the author (FNK). These are only two of Cattell's eight factors.

[26] Cattell, *op. cit.* For a penetrating critique of this study, see L. Humphreys, "Critique of Cattell's 'Theory of Fluid and Crystallized Intelligence: A Critical Experiment,'" *Journal of Educational Psychology,* 58 (1967), 129–136.

included a number of personality variables, we concentrate only on the first two factors, fluid intelligence and crystallized intelligence. He reasoned that Thurstone's tests, since they measure crystallized cognitive abilities, should load on one general factor, and that his own culture-fair tests, since they measure fluid ability, should load on another factor. They did. The two sets of factor loadings are given in Table 35.7, together with the names of the tests. The two factors also were correlated positively ($r = .47$), as predicted.

This study demonstrates the power of an astute combination of theory, test construction, and factor analysis. Similar to Guildford's equally astute conceptualization and analysis of convergent, divergent, and other factors mentioned earlier, it is a significant contribution to psychological knowledge of an extremely complex and important subject.

Factors of Political Participation

It is not often that factor analysis of the responses of random samples of subjects has been done. Indeed, Thurstone even said that representative samples should *not* be used in factor analytic studies.[27] Verba and Nie, in a large sophisticated study of political participation in the United States, report factors obtained from a random sample of over 3,000 citizens.[28] A distinction between exploratory factor analysis and confirmatory factor analysis is increasingly made in the literature. *Exploratory factor analysis* is usually the use of factor analysis to learn the factors underlying a set of variables or measures. *Confirmatory factor analysis* is the use of factor analysis to test hypotheses about the factor structures of sets of data. In confirmatory factor analysis, in other words, one sets up a model that reflects aspects of a theory, and then somehow sees whether the model fits the observed data. The Thurstone and Thurstone model examined earlier is a good example. The factors were predicted before the data were gathered and the factor analysis done.[29] The point of this disquisition is that Verba and Nie's study of political participation is clearly and consciously confirmatory factor analysis. They say, for instance,

> it is important to be clear on what we are *not* doing. We are not looking to see what clusterings among political acts we find. Rather, we are looking to see whether the clustering we expect to find, given our analysis of the alternative characteristics of the modes of activity, is indeed found.[30]

Verba and Nie's analysis of political activity led them to believe that four modes of such activity lie behind political participation: citizen-initiated contacts, voting, campaign activity, and cooperative activity.[31] These are conceived to be different if related ways that citizens can influence their government. The authors designed a questionnaire by constructing several measures for each of the four modes of political activity: persuade others how to vote, contribute money to party or candidate, contact local officials, for example. There were thirteen of these measures that formed the questionnaire adminis-

---

[27] Thurstone, *Multiple Factor Analysis,* p. xii. The wisdom of Thurstone's words was shown in a cross-cultural study in which a referent attitude scale was administered to a random sample of the Netherlands and also to a separate sample of University of Amsterdam students. The student factors were clear and readily interpretable, but those of the random sample were much less clear and difficult to interpret. See F. Kerlinger, C. Middendorp, and J. Amón, ''The Structure of Social Attitudes in Three Countries: Tests of a Criterial Referent Theory,'' *International Journal of Psychology,* 11 (1976), 265–279. (Also reported in Kerlinger, *Liberalism and Conservatism: The Nature and Structure of Social Attitudes,* chap. 7.)

[28] S. Verba and N. Nie, *Participation in America: Political Democracy and Social Equality.* Copyright © 1972 by Sidney Verba and Norman H. Nie. Reprinted by permission of Harper & Row, Publishers, Inc. The obliquely rotated factor matrix of Table 35.8 is their Table 4–3, p. 65.

[29] For an excellent discussion of the two approaches, see S. Mulaik, *The Foundations of Factor Analysis.* New York: McGraw-Hill, 1972, pp. 361–366.

[30] Verba and Nie, *op. cit.,* p. 57.

[31] *Ibid.,* pp. 51–54.

Table 35.8 Rotated Oblique Factor Matrix, Thirteen Political Activities, Verba and Nie Study

Participation Variable	Campaign Activity I	Voting II	Cooperative Activity III	Contacting IV
1. Persuade others how to vote	.53	.15	.14	.27
2. Actively work for party or candidate	.75	.11	.20	.11
3. Attend political meeting or rally	.74	.12	.17	.08
4. Contribute money to party or candidate	.64	.10	−.07	.23
5. Membership in political clubs	.74	.04	.18	−.03
6. Voted in 1964 Presidential election	.11	.89	.06	.06
7. Voted in 1960 Presidential election	.10	.88	.05	.04
8. Frequency of voting in local elections	.18	.81	.12	.11
9. Work with others on local problems	.15	.13	.71	.23
10. Form group to work on local problem	.14	.02	.82	.01
11. Active membership in community organizations	.25	.14	.47	.34
12. Contact local officials	.15	.06	.28	.60
13. Contact state and national officials	.15	.07	.04	.82

tered to the national sample (see Table 35.8). Verba and Nie calculated the 13-by-13 correlation matrix (given in their Table 4-1, p. 58), factor analyzed the R matrix, and obliquely rotated the four factors obtained. Their rotated factor matrix is given in Table 35.8, which is their Table 4-3 (*ibid.*, p. 65).

The research question is clearly answered. There are four factors, each of which has substantial loadings precisely where predicted. For example, the researchers predicted that Items 9, 10, and 11 would appear together on the same factor with substantial loadings, and that (in effect) no other items would appear on that factor. In the column or factor, "Cooperative Activity," Items 9, 10, and 11 have substantial loadings of .71, .82, and .47, and none of the other items has similar loadings. The predictions for the other factors were also supported. Indeed, this is a remarkable example of happy and intelligent use of theory—the political participation variables and their predicted factor structure—and factor analysis to test the theory.

In and of itself, this is a major contribution. But Verba and Nie were also using factor analysis to help construct measures of political participation to use as both dependent and independent variables in further analyses. For example, they wished to study the effects of social status on political participation. To obtain a measure of participation or political activity, they used the four factors (of Table 35.8) and a composite variable. Our purpose is not served by going into further detail. We simply wished to show the power and effectiveness of factor analysis and of bringing theoretical and measurement thinking and factor analysis together.

FACTOR ANALYSIS AND SCIENTIFIC RESEARCH

Factor analysis has two basic purposes: to explore variable areas in order to identify the factors presumably underlying the variables; and, as in all scientific work, to test hypotheses about the relations among variables. The first purpose is well known and fairly well accepted. The second purpose is not so well known nor so well accepted.

In conceptualizing the first purpose, the exploratory or reductive purpose, one should keep construct validity and constitutive definitions in mind. Factor analysis can be conceived as a construct validity tool. Recall that validity was defined in Chapter 27 as common-factor variance. Since the main preoccupation of factor analysis is common-factor variance, by definition it is firmly tied to measurement theory. Indeed, this tie was expressed earlier in the section headed "Some Factor Theory," where equations were written to clarify factor analytic theory. (See, especially, Equation 35.6.)

Recall, too, that construct validity seeks the "meaning" of a construct through the relations between the construct and other constructs. In Part One, when types of definitions were discussed, we learned that constructs could be defined in two ways: by operational definitions and by constitutive definitions. Constitutive definitions are definitions that define constructs with other constructs. Essentially this is what factor analysis does. It may be called a constitutive meaning method, since it enables the researcher to study the constitutive meanings of constructs—and thus their construct validity.

The measures of three variables, say, may share something in common. This something itself is a variable, presumably a more basic entity than the variables used to isolate and identify it. We give this new variable a name; in other words, we construct a hypothetical entity. Then, to inquire into the "reality" of the variable we may systematically devise a measure of it and test its "reality" by correlating data obtained with the measure with data from other measures theoretically related to it. Factor analysis helps us check our theoretical expectations.

Part of the basic life-stuff of any science is its constructs. Old constructs continue to be used; new ones are constantly being invented. Note some of the general constructs directly pertinent to behavioral and educational research: achievement, intelligence, learning, aptitude, attitude, problem-solving ability, needs, interests, creativity, conformity. Note some of the more specific variables important in behavioral research: test anxiety, verbal ability, traditionalism, convergent thinking, arithmetic reasoning, political participation, and social class. Clearly, a large portion of scientific behavioral research effort has to be devoted to what might be called construct investigation or construct validation. This requires factor analysis.

When we talk about relations we talk about the relations between constructs: intelligence and achievement, authoritarianism and ethnocentricism, reinforcement and learning, organizational climate and administrative performance—all these are relations between highly abstract constructs or latent variables. Such constructs usually have to be operationally defined to be studied. Factors are latent variables, of course, and the major scientific factor analytic effort in the past has been to identify the factors and occasionally use the factors in measuring variables in research. Rarely have deliberate attempts been made to assess the effects of latent variables on other variables. With recent advances and developments in multivariate thinking and methodology, however, it is clear that it is now possible to assess the influence of latent variables on each other. This important development will be discussed and illustrated in the next chapter on analysis of covariance structures. We will find there that the scientist can obtain indices of the magnitudes and statistical significance of the effects of latent variables on other latent variables. If this is so, then factor analysis becomes even more important in identifying the latent variables or factors, and the scientist has to exercise great care in the interpretation of data in which the influences of latent variables are assessed.

Many research areas, then, can well be preceded by factor analytic explorations of the variables of the area. This does not mean that a number of tests are thrown together and given to any samples that happen to be available. Factor analytic investigations, both exploratory and hypothesis-testing, have to be painstakingly planned. Variables that may be influential have to be controlled—sex, education, social class, intelligence, and so on.[32] Variables are not put into a factor analysis just to put them in. They must have legitimate purpose. If, for instance, one cannot control intelligence by sample selection, one can include a measure of intelligence (verbal, perhaps) in the battery of measures. By identifying intelligence variance, one has in a sense controlled intelligence. One can learn whether one's measures are contaminated by response biases by including response-bias measures in factor analyses.

The second major purpose of factor analysis is to test hypotheses. One aspect of hypothesis-testing has already been hinted: one can put tests or measures into factor analytic batteries deliberately to test the identification and nature of factors. The design of such studies has been well outlined by Thurstone, Cattell, Guilford, and others. First, factors are "discovered." Their nature is inferred from the tests that are loaded on them. This "nature" is set up as a hypothesis. New tests are constructed and given to new samples of subjects. The data are factor analyzed. If the factors emerge *as predicted,* the hypothesis is to this extent confirmed, the factors would seem to have "reality." This will certainly not end the matter. One will have to test, among other things, the factors' relations to other factors. One will have to place the factors, as constructs, in a nomological network of constructs.

A less well-known use of factor analysis as a hypothesis-testing method is in testing experimental hypotheses.[33] One may hypothesize that a certain method of teaching reading changes the ability patterns of pupils, so that verbal intelligence is not as potent an influence as it is with other teaching methods. An experimental study can be planned to test this hypothesis. The effects of the teaching methods can be assessed by factor analyses of a set of tests given before and after the different methods were used. Woodrow tested a similar hypothesis when he gave a set of tests before and after practice in seven tests: adding, subtracting, anagrams, and so on.[34] He found that factor loading patterns *did* change after practice.

In considering the scientific value of factor analysis, the reader must be cautioned against attributing "reality" and uniqueness to factors. The danger of reification is great. It is easy to name a factor and then to believe there is a reality behind the name. But giving a factor a name does not give it reality. Factor names are simply attempts to epitomize the essence of factors. They are always tentative, subject to later confirmation or disconfirmation. Then, too, factors can be produced by many things. Anything that introduces correlation between variables "creates" a factor. Differences in sex, education, social and cultural background, and intelligence can cause factors to appear. Factors also differ—at least to some extent—with different samples. Response sets or test forms may cause factors to appear. Despite these cautions, it must be said that factors do repeatedly emerge with different tests, different samples, and different conditions. When this happens, we have fair assurance that there is an underlying variable that we are successfully measuring.

There are serious criticisms of factor analysis. The major valid ones center around the indeterminacy of how many factors to extract from a correlation matrix and the problem of how to rotate factors. Another difficulty that bothers critics and devotees alike is what can

---

[32] J. Guilford, "Factorial Angles to Psychology," *Psychological Review,* 68 (1961), 1–20. This is an important article that any investigator who uses factor analysis should study.

[33] B. Fruchter, "Manipulative and Hypothesis-Testing Factor-Analytic Experimental Designs." In R. Cattell, ed., *Handbook of Multivariate Experimental Psychology.* Skokie, Ill.: Rand McNally, 1966, chap. 10.

[34] H. Woodrow, "The Relation between Abilities and Improvement with Practice," *Journal of Educational Psychology,* 29 (1938), 215–230.

be called the communality problem, or what quantities to put into the diagonal of the *R* matrix before factoring. In an introductory chapter, these problems cannot be discussed. The reader is referred to the discussions of Cattell, Guilford, Harman, and Thurstone. A criticism of a different order seems to bother educators and sociologists and some psychologists. This takes two or three forms that seem to boil down to distrust, sometimes profound, combined with antipathy toward the method due to its complexity and, strangely enough, its objectivity.

The argument runs something like this. Factor analysts throw a lot of tests together into a statistical machine and get out factors that have little psychological or sociological meaning. The factors are simply artifacts of the method. They are averages that correspond to no psychological reality, especially the psychological reality of the individual, other than that in the mind of the factor analyst.[35] Besides, you can't get any more out of a factor analysis than you put into it.

The argument is basically irrelevant. To say that factors have no psychological meaning and that they are averages is both true and untrue. If the argument were valid, no scientific constructs would have any meaning. They are all, in a sense, averages. They are all inventions of the scientist. This is simply the lot of science. The basic criterion of the "reality" of any construct, any factor, is its empirical, scientific "reality." If, after uncovering a factor, we can successfully predict relations from theoretical presuppositions and hypotheses, then the factor has "reality." There is no more reality to a factor than this, just as there is no more reality to an atom than its empirical manifestations.

The argument about only getting out what is put into a factor analysis is meaningless as well as irrelevant. No competent factor analytic investigator would ever claim more than this. But this does not mean that nothing is discovered in factor analysis. Quite the contrary. The answer is, of course, that we get nothing more out of a factor analysis than we put into it, but that we do not know *all* we put into it. Nor do we know what tests or measures share common factor variance. Nor do we know the relations between factors. Only study and analysis can tell us these things. We may write an attitude scale that we believe measures a single attitude. A factor analysis of the attitude items, naturally, cannot produce factors that are not in the items. But it can show us, for example, that there are two or three sources of common variance in a scale that we thought to be unidimensional. Similarly, a scale that we believe measures authoritarianism may be shown by factor analysis to measure intelligence, dogmatism, and other variables.

If we examine empirical evidence rather than opinion, we must conclude that factor analysis is one of the most powerful tools yet devised for the study of complex areas of behavioral scientific concern. Indeed, factor analysis is one of the creative inventions of the century, just as intelligence testing, conditioning, reinforcement theory, the operational definition, the notion of randomness, measurement theory, research design, multivariate analysis, the computer, and theories of learning, personality, development, organizations, and society are.[36]

It is fitting that this chapter conclude with some words of a great psychological scientist, teacher, and factor analyst, Louis Leon Thurstone:

> As scientists, we have the faith that the abilities and personalities of people are not so complex as the total enumeration of attributes that can be listed. We believe that these traits are made up of a smaller number of primary factors or elements that combine in various ways to make a long list of traits. It is our ambition to find some of these elementary abilities and traits. . . .

[35] See G. Allport, *Pattern and Growth in Personality*. New York: Holt, Rinehart and Winston, 1961, pp. 329–330; G. Allport, *Personality*. New York: Holt, Rinehart and Winston, 1937, pp. 242–248.
[36] K. Deutsch, J. Platt, and D. Senghaas, "Conditions Favoring Major Advances in Social Science," *Science*, 171 (1971), 450–459.

All scientific work has this in common, that we try to comprehend nature in the most parsimonious manner. An explanation of a set of phenomena or of a set of experimental observations gains acceptance only in so far as it gives us intellectual control or comprehension of a relatively wide variety of phenomena in terms of a limited number of concepts. The principle of parsimony is intuitive for anyone who has even slight aptitude for science. The fundamental motivation of science is the craving for the simplest possible comprehension of nature, and it finds satisfaction in the discovery of the simplifying uniformities that we call scientific laws.[37]

ADDENDUM

Sample Size and Replication

Two desiderata, even necessities, of factor analysis are large samples and replication. A general rule is: Use as large samples as possible. Like any statistical procedure, factor analysis is subject to measurement and sampling error, and the reliable identification of factors and factor loadings requires large N's to wash out error variance. This is especially true for item factor analysis, because item intercorrelations are usually lower and less reliable than test intercorrelations. A loose but not bad rule-of-thumb might be: ten subjects for each variable (item, measure, etc.).

Replication is too seldom practiced in any research. And it is particularly needed in factor analytic studies. The "reality" of factors is much more compelling if found in two or three different and large samples. Factor loadings and patterns of loadings, like regression coefficients—which, by the way, they *are*—are often unstable, especially in smaller samples. A good rule is: Replicate all studies. This does not mean literal duplication of studies. Indeed, the word "replication" means doing additional studies based on the same problems and variables but with minor, sometimes major, variations. For example, the measurement instrument of an original study may have been found wanting. A replication of the study done with another sample and an improved instrument and similar results would be compelling evidence of the empirical validity of the original results.

Study Suggestions

1. Fortunately, there are good, even excellent, books and articles on factor analysis. Unfortunately, there is as yet no satisfactory and up-to-date book written at an elementary level. So, to learn factor analysis, one has to work hard at it, using more advanced texts. It is suggested that the student who will not take a course in factor analysis use either the Harman (footnote 5) or the Thurstone (footnote 6) text or both. Both are definitive but rather difficult.

2. The more advanced student will find the following selected articles valuable:

ANASTASI, A. "On the Formation of Psychological Traits." *American Psychologist,* 10 (1970), 899–910. Very good review of (mostly) factor analytic studies of traits and their development.

CARROLL, J. "Ability and Task Difficulty in Cognitive Psychology." *Educational Researcher,* 10 (1981), 11–21. In criticizing Jensen's use and interpretation of the first unrotated factor as a general factor—a common practice, by the way—Carroll settles the issue of what a general factor is.

COAN, R. "Facts, Factors, and Artifacts: The Quest for Psychological Meaning." *Psychological Review,* 71 (1964), 123–140. A good general theoretical article on factor analysis, with discussion of the interpretation of factors.

[37]L. Thurstone, *The Measurement of Values*. Chicago: University of Chicago Press, 1959, p. 8.

GORSUCH, R. "A Comparison of Biquartimin, Maxplane, Promax, and Varimax." *Educational and Psychological Measurement,* 30 (1970), 861–872. Compared four methods of rotation (three oblique and one orthogonal) and found the results to be much the same. The oblique procedures were better than the orthogonal (varimax), and Promax was the best.[38]

GUERTIN, W. "Do the Different Methods of Factor Analysis Still Give Almost Identical Results?" *Perceptual and Motor Skills,* 33 (1971), 600–602. Another study of different factor analysis methods; again, they yield similar results.

LINN, R. "A Monte Carlo Approach to the Number of Factors Problem." *Psychometrika,* 33 (1968), 37–71. Detailed and competent treatment of the number-of-factors problem.

MONTANELLI, R., and HUMPHREYS, L. "Latent Roots of Random Data Correlation Matrices with Squared Multiple Correlations on the Diagonal: A Monte Carlo Study." *Psychometrika,* 41 (1976), 341–348. Excellent random correlation and regression method on the number-of-factors problem.

OVERALL, J. "Note on the Scientific Status of Factors." *Psychological Bulletin,* 61 (1964), 270–276. Excellent, even brilliant, analysis of basic factor analytic notions.

PETERSON, D. "Scope and Generality of Verbally Defined Personality Factors." *Psychological Review,* 72 (1965), 48–59. Very convincing on the number-of-factors problem.

THOMPSON, J. "Meaningful and Unmeaningful Rotation of Factors." *Psychological Bulletin,* 59 (1962), 211–223. Good article on one of the difficult problems of factor analysis; calls for both objective machine rotation and judgmental rotation.

3. The individual who wishes a broad overview—with considerable specificity, however—has a few excellent sources available. Among the following general references, the French monograph and the French et al. reference test kit are valuable. Rather well-established cognitive factors are named, described, and illustrated. The kit is very valuable.

FRENCH, J. "The Description of Aptitude and Achievement Tests in Terms of Rotated Factors." *Psychometric Monographs,* no. 5. Chicago: University of Chicago Press, 1951. An exhaustive review, with data, of many factor analytic studies of aptitude and achievement.

FRENCH, J., EKSTROM, R., and PRICE, L. *Manual for Kit of Reference Tests for Cognitive Factors.* Princeton, N. J.: Educational Testing Service, 1963.

NUNNALLY, J. *Psychometric Theory,* 2d ed. New York: McGraw-Hill, 1978, chap. 10. The late Professor Nunnally's synthesis and critique of factor analysis: excellent.

4. As usual, there is no substitute for the study of actual research uses of methods. The student should, therefore, read two or three good factor analytic studies. Select from those cited in the chapter or from the following:

ISAACSON, R., et al. "Dimensions of Student Evaluation of Teaching." *Journal of Educational Psychology,* 55 (1964), 344–351. A competent study of the factors behind student evaluations of instructors. The first factor is important.

KERLINGER, F., and ROKEACH, M. "The Factorial Nature of the F and D Scales." *Journal of Personality and Social Psychology,* 4 (1966), 391–399. An attempt to clarify a difficult area of measurement: authoritarianism and dogmatism. This study has had the benefit of a thorough replication, which included reanalysis of the original data and a new study on 421 graduate and undergraduate students: P. Warr, R. Lee, and K. Jöreskog, "A Note on the Factorial Nature of the *F* and *D* Scales." *British Journal of Psychology,* 60 (1969), 119–123.

LONGABAUGH, R. "The Structure of Interpersonal Behavior." *Sociometry,* 29 (1966), 441–460. Use of factor analysis in cross-cultural observations of interpersonal behavior.

REILLY, R. "Factors in Graduate Student Performance." *American Educational Research Journal,* 13 (1976), 125–138. Found factors underlying graduate student performance.

[38] A. Hendrickson and P. White, "PROMAX: A Quick Method for Rotation to Oblique Simple Structure," *British Journal of Statistical Psychology,* 17 (1964), 65–70.

THURSTONE, L. "A Factorial Study of Perception." *Psychometric Monographs,* no. 4. Chicago: University of Chicago Press, 1944. Another Thurstone pioneering and classic study.

5. Here is a small fictitious correlation matrix, with the tests labeled.

	1	2	3	4	5	6
1. Vocabulary		.70	.22	.20	.15	.25
2. Analogies	.70		.15	.26	.12	.30
3. Addition	.22	.15		.81	.21	.10
4. Multiplication	.20	.26	.81		.31	.29
5. Recall First Names	.15	.12	.21	.31		.72
6. Recognize Figures	.25	.30	.10	.29	.72	

(a) Do an "armchair" factor analysis. That is, by inspection of the matrix determine how many factors there probably are and which tests are on what factors.

(b) Name the factors. How sure are you of your names? What would you do to be more sure of your conclusions?

6. Since this chapter was completed, an excellent book on factor analysis has been published: R. Gorsuch, *Factor Analysis.* Hillsdale, N.J.: Erlbaum, 1983. The book is scholarly, authoritative, up-to-date. One of its great virtues is that it thoroughly explores the most difficult and troublesome problems of factor analysis. Gorsuch not only explains the technical ideas but also cites theoretical contributions and empirical investigations of the problems. *Highly recommended* as a reference work for behavioral researchers.

Chapter 36

Analysis of Covariance Structures

IN THIS long and involved dissertation on the foundations of behavioral research, we have often talked of the importance of theory and the testing of theory. We have from time to time stressed the purpose of scientific research as formulating explanations of natural phenomena and submitting implications of the explanations to empirical test. In this chapter, we study and try to understand a highly developed and sophisticated conceptual and analytic system to model and test scientific behavioral theories: analysis of covariance structures. To do this, we focus largely on the powerful mathematical-statistical system and computer program LISREL (*Li*near *S*tructural *Rel*ations), conceived and developed by Jöreskog and his colleagues to set up and analyze covariance structures.[1]

Unfortunately, analysis of covariance structures and LISREL are hard to learn and to use. The difficulty, it must be confessed, is to explain the system in language comprehensible to nonmathematical readers and, at the same time, to stay within the purposes and confines of this book. So the discussion is limited to presenting and explaining the bare mathematical skeleton of the system and how and why it is used. Fortunately, our subject is closely related to the discussions of multiple regression analysis and factor analysis of Chapters 33, 34, and 35.

---

[1] K. Jöreskog and D. Sörbom, *LISREL-V: Analysis of Linear Structural Relationships by Maximum Likelihood and Least Squares Methods*. Uppsala, Sweden: University of Uppsala, 1981 (henceforth we refer to this book as the *Manual*); K. Jöreskog and D. Sörbom, *Advances in Factor Analysis and Structural Equation Models* (edited by J. Magidson). Cambridge, Mass.: Abt Books, 1979. The latter reference is a collection of papers by Jöreskog and Sörbom. The former reference is the manual that accompanies the fifth version of the computer program LISREL.

COVARIANCE STRUCTURES, LATENT VARIABLES, AND TESTING THEORY

Analysis of covariance structures can be viewed as a combination of factor analysis and multiple regression analysis. Its most important strength is that the effects of latent variables on each other and on observed variables can be assessed. A *latent variable*, recall, is a construct or hypothetical "entity": intelligence, verbal ability, spatial ability, prejudice, anxiety, achievement. Latent variables, of course, are unobserved variables whose "reality" we assume or infer from observed variables or indicators. Factors are latent variables, constructs we invent to help explain observed behavior. This is perhaps too abstract. Let's examine an example from actual research.[2] It has the virtues of familiarity and relative simplicity.

TESTING ALTERNATIVE FACTOR HYPOTHESES: DUALITY VERSUS BIPOLARITY OF SOCIAL ATTITUDES

Recall that there are two general views of the social attitudes we generally associate with liberalism and conservatism. One view, the much more commonly held one among both scientists and laymen, is that liberal and conservative issues and people are opposed to each other: what the liberal is for the conservative is against, and vice versa. This was earlier expressed as a bipolar theory. It implies one dimension of attitudes, with liberal issues and people at one end and conservative issues and people at the other end:

Liberalism   Conservatism

|————————————————————————————————|

The contrasting theory, hypothesis, or conception of social attitudes says, in effect, that liberal issues and ideas are in general different and virtually independent of conservative issues and ideas. Liberalism and conservatism, to use the abstract names of the latent variables, are not necessarily opposed to each other: they are two separate and independent ideologies or sets of related beliefs that can be expressed as orthogonal dimensions:

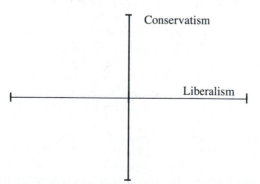

This conception of the structure of social attitudes is a dualistic one.

The two contrasting "theories" of the structure of social attitudes can be expressed by the two factor matrices, A and B, given in Table 36.1. These can be called "target"

[2]F. Kerlinger, "The Structure and Content of Social Attitude Referents: A Preliminary Study," *Educational and Psychological Measurement*, 32 (1972), 613–630.

Table 36.1 Factor Analytic Structures Implied by the Dualistic Hypothesis *(A)* and the Bipolar Hypothesis *(B)*[a]

Scales	(A) Dualistic I	II	Type	Scales	(B) Bipolar I	Type
1	+	0	C	1	+	C
2	+	0	C	2	+	C
3	+	0	C	3	+	C
4	0	+	L	4	−	L
5	0	+	L	5	−	L
6	0	+	L	6	−	L

[a] +: indicates positive factor loadings; −: indicates negative factor loadings; 0: zero loadings. *L*: liberal scales; *C*: conservative scales. I and II are the ξ_1 and ξ_2 of Figure 36.1.

matrices because they are set up to express contrasting analyses. Suppose we have administered six social attitude scales to a large heterogeneous sample of individuals. Scales 1, 2, and 3 are conservative scales, and scales 4, 5, and 6 are liberal scales. The responses of the sample to the six scales were correlated and factor analyzed, say. The results of the factor analysis that the duality and bipolarity theories imply are given in the table. The +'s indicate substantial and positive loadings, the −'s indicate substantial and negative loadings, and the 0's indicate near-zero loadings. The dualistic theory *(A)*, of course, implies two orthogonal factors, and the bipolarity theory *(B)* implies one factor with substantial positive and negative loadings. *A* and *B* of the table succinctly express the two models implied by the two theories. If we plotted the "loadings" of the duality theory, they would look like those of Figure 35.7 in Chapter 35, whereas the plot of the bipolarity theory loadings can be plotted on a single axis, with the positive loadings at one end of the axis and the negative loadings at the other end.

Researchers who use analysis of covariance structures like to picture models in path diagrams. The path diagrams for the two factor models are given in Figure 36.1. (See Chapter 34 for a discussion of path diagrams.) $x_1, x_2, \ldots, x_6$ are the observed variables, x_1, x_2, and x_3 measures of conservatism, and x_4, x_5, and x_6 measures of liberalism. Observed variables are indicated by boxes, unobserved, latent variables, or factors by circles. In *A*, ξ_1 (Xsi) and ξ_2 stand for conservatism and liberalism. They are assumed to influence the *x*'s: thus the arrows. λ_{11} (lambda), λ_{21}, λ_{31} are the factor loadings of factor I, which, since x_1, x_2, and x_3 are conservative measures, we call "conservatism," and λ_{42}, λ_{52}, and λ_{62} and factor II, which we call "liberalism." δ_1 (delta), $\ldots$, δ_6 are the error terms; $\phi_{21} = r_{12}$ is the correlation between ξ_1 and ξ_2, or factors I and II. Since the theory says that conservatism and liberalism are separate and distinct factors, we predict $\phi_{21} = 0$.

The bipolarity theory diagram, *B*, is easier to explain. We have, of course, the same six *x*'s, or observed variables and the same six δ's or error terms. We also have six λ's or factor loadings. There is only one factor, or ξ. In *A*, the duality model, there are twelve λ's or factor loadings, but six of them are predicted to be positive and substantial and the rest are constrained to be zero. "Constrained," or "fixed" values are maintained during the computations. In *B*, the bipolarity model, there are six factor loadings, three of them positive (the path arrows are marked +) and the three negative (marked −). In other words, we predict the two factor matrices of Table 36.1, except that in the table we only use +'s and −'s rather than λ's.

To determine which of the two models is closer to empirical "reality," we must test

(A) Duality Theory

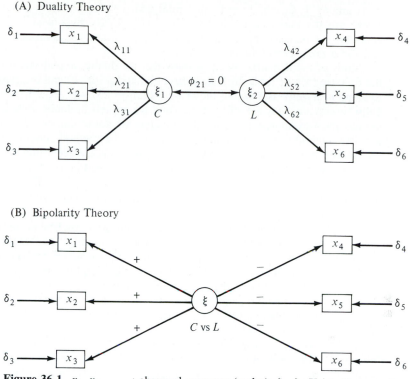

(B) Bipolarity Theory

Figure 36.1 $x_1, x_2, \ldots$: observed measures (scales); ξ_1, ξ_2: Xsi 1: Conservatism *(C)*; Xsi 2: Liberalism *(L)*; $\lambda_{11}, \lambda_{21}, \ldots$: lambda's, factor loadings; $\delta_1, \delta_2, \ldots$: delta 1, delta 2, . . . : error terms

each of them separately and then test one against the other. This is done using the information or the data we have: the correlations among the observed variables, $x_1, \ldots, x_6$. This matrix of correlations, **R**, is a covariance matrix. It is given in Table 36.2. Variables (or attitude scales) 1, 2, and 3 are measures of conservatism, and variables 4, 5, and 6 are measures of liberalism. The duality hypothesis predicts substantial and positive correla-

Table 36.2 Observed Correlations Among Six Attitude Scales[a]

	Scales						Attitude Designation
	1	2	3	4	5	6	
1	1.000						*C*
2	.569	1.000					*C*
3	.388	.548	1.000				*C*
4	−.237	−.157	−.199	1.000			*L*
5	.107	.151	.087	.385	1.000		*L*
6	−.148	−.026	−.225	.433	.370	1.000	*L*

[a] Variables 1, 2, and 3 are measures of conservatism *(C)*; variables 4, 5, and 6 are measures of liberalism *(L)*. The predicted positive and substantial correlations under the duality hypothesis are italicized. All other correlations are predicted to be zero (except, of course, the diagonal entries). $N = 530$.

tions among 1, 2, and 3, and substantial and positive correlations among 4, 5, and 6. These are the italicized *r*'s in the table. The duality hypothesis also predicts zero or near-zero *r*'s between the *C* variables (1, 2, and 3) and the *L* variables (4, 5, and 6). We call these *cross-correlations*.

Study of the **R** matrix seems to show that the duality hypothesis is supported because the italicized *r*'s in Table 36.2 are substantial and positive, and the cross-correlations are low and near-zero. But two of the cross *r*'s are $-.237$ and $-.225$. Although not statistically significant, they are still not zero and we are left in doubt. Besides, this example is simple; most examples encountered in practice are not so simple. In other words, we need a better method to test the duality hypothesis. The method actually used in analysis of covariance structures is as follows. The data are analyzed according to the model setup, in this case the duality model: two orthogonal factors (see Figure 36.1). From the parameters estimated by the data analysis, factor analysis in this case, an **R** matrix is calculated by using the estimated parameters of the theoretical model. This is done by writing equations for each of the *x*'s.

To help us clearly understand what is done and why, we first set up the two theories in path diagrams. Behavioral researches who use "modeling" or "causal modeling," as it is called, use path diagrams to help conceptualize the research problems they are studying and, almost more important, to learn the empirical implications of theories under test. I strongly recommend that students try to set up any research problem under study in a path diagram. It forces one to conceptualize and bring out the basic structures of problems. In any case, the duality and bipolarity "theories" of social attitudes have been set up in the two path diagrams, *A* and *B*, of Figure 36.1. It is customary in such path diagrams to use squares for observed variables and circles for unobserved or latent variables. Single-headed arrows are used to indicate influences, double-headed arrows to indicate correlations. In other words, the path diagrams used in analysis of covariance structures follow much the same principles and practices of path analysis discussed earlier.

To set up the equation of a model, we "define" each variable that is at the end of an arrow. For example, from Figure 36.1, *A*, we write for x_{11} and for x_{52}:[3]

$$x_{11} = \lambda_{11} \, \xi_1 + \delta_1 \tag{36.1}$$

$$x_{52} = \lambda_{52} \, \xi_2 + \delta_5 \tag{36.2}$$

The values or parameters to be estimated are: λ_{11} and δ_1 and λ_{52} and δ_5. ξ_1 and ξ_2, of course, are latent variables or factors I and II, and thus are not estimated. Their "effects," or λ_{11} and λ_{52}, *are* estimated. Naturally, we must have six equations since there are six *x*'s. These are written as matrices:[4]

$$\begin{pmatrix} x_1 \\ x_2 \\ x_3 \\ x_4 \\ x_5 \\ x_6 \end{pmatrix} = \begin{pmatrix} \lambda_{11} & 0 \\ \lambda_{21} & 0 \\ \lambda_{31} & 0 \\ 0 & \lambda_{42} \\ 0 & \lambda_{52} \\ 0 & \lambda_{62} \end{pmatrix} \begin{pmatrix} \xi_1 \\ \xi_2 \end{pmatrix} + \begin{pmatrix} \delta_1 \\ \delta_2 \\ \delta_3 \\ \delta_4 \\ \delta_5 \\ \delta_6 \end{pmatrix} \tag{36.3}$$

or, in matrix notation:

$$\mathbf{x} = \mathbf{\Lambda}_x \, \boldsymbol{\xi} + \boldsymbol{\delta} \tag{36.4}$$

[3] Double subscripts of variables are necessary to identify them unambiguously. In the duality model, the factor loadings need two subscripts *i* and *j*, where *i* is the row (variables) designation and *j* is the column (factor) designation. Look at the factor matrix a; Table 36.3. The λ's (lambda) have two subscripts, *e.g.*, λ_{32} means lambda, the factor loading of the third row ($i = 3$) and the second column ($j = 2$).

[4] The necessity of knowing matrix algebra should be apparent. The reader who does not know matrix algebra can take the development on faith.

Table 36.3 Factor Matrices of (a) Ordinary Factor Analysis and (b) LISREL Constrained Factor Analysis

	a. Ordinary Factor Analysis			b. LISREL Constrained Factor Analysis		
Variables	I	II	Variables	I	II	Type[a]
1	λ_{11}	λ_{12}	1	λ_{11}	0	C
2	λ_{21}	λ_{22}	2	λ_{21}	0	C
3	λ_{31}	λ_{32}	3	λ_{31}	0	C
4	λ_{41}	λ_{42}	4	0	λ_{42}	L
5	λ_{51}	λ_{52}	5	0	λ_{52}	L
6	λ_{61}	λ_{62}	6	0	λ_{62}	L

[a]C: Conservative; L: Liberal.

where **x** is the vector of x variables, Λ_x is the lambda-x matrix, ξ is the unobserved variables matrix and δ is the vector of error terms. This is called the *measurement equation*. (Λ_x, lambda x, is the factor matrix. The λ's [lambda's] are the factor loadings. In Chapter 35, we used a's, but in this chapter we use the symbols of LISREL.)

The computational task of LISREL is to solve this set of simultaneous equations for the λ's and the δ's. The x's are observed. In Chapter 35 on factor analysis, the main computational task was to calculate *all* the factor loadings of the factor loading matrix. If we do a principal factors factor analysis of the present problem, for instance, twelve factor loadings would be estimated: λ_{11}, λ_{12}, λ_{21}, λ_{22}, . . . , λ_{61}, λ_{62}. The problem in the LISREL framework, however, is different because we have specified that six factor loadings, or λ's, are to be estimated; the remaining loadings are constrained to be 0's under the duality hypothesis. To be sure we see and understand the difference, we set out the two factor matrices in Table 36.3. Note that there are twelve factor loadings to be calculated in a, ordinary factor analysis, and only six loadings to be calculated in b, the LISREL solution constrained by the 0's because of the duality hypothesis.

The difference between the two approaches is striking—and very important. In ordinary factor analysis all the factor loadings are estimated, but in analysis of covariance structures only those factor loadings germane to the hypothesis are estimated. All the rest are constrained to be zero—a perfect simple structure, by the way. To emphasize the points being made, the actual estimated parameters are given in Table 36.4. The final

Table 36.4 Obtained Factor Matrices (a) Conventional (Rotated) and (b) LISREL Constrained Factors[a]

	a. Conventional Factors			b. LISREL Constrained Factors		
Variables	I	II	Variables	I	II	Type
1	.69	.19	1	.65	0	C
2	.70	.33	2	.87	0	C
3	.68	.14	3	.63	0	C
4	−.44	.51	4	0	.71	L
5	−.05	.64	5	0	.54	L
6	−.36	.55	6	0	.63	L

[a]The conventional factor analysis was the principal factors method with varimax rotation; the LISREL method was maximum likelihood. All loadings of b are statistically significant. The correlation between the two factors was −.15, statistically not significant.

rotated factors of an ordinary factor analysis are given in a, and the LISREL constrained solution is given in b. You may well ask: What happens to the factor loadings where the 0's are in b? The point is that b expresses the "pure" form of the duality hypothesis. As said earlier, the computer is instructed to do the calculations keeping the 0's of Tables 36.3 and 36.4 intact. But how about the fairly large negative loadings, $-.44$ and $-.36$ in a, the conventional factor analysis? Both are substantial, negative, and statistically significant, contrary to the duality hypothesis. They are deviations from the duality model. The key question, then, is: Are the deviations large enough to invalidate the hypothesis, which specifies 0's? We will return to this point shortly.

The model of Figure 36.1, A, and Equation 36.3 requires calculation of the error terms, δ_i (delta). The six error terms were calculated, but we are not interested in the method of calculation. Much more interesting and relevant to the duality hypothesis is the estimation of variances and covariances of the Φ (phi) matrix because it expresses the relations between ξ_1 and ξ_2, the factors. Remember that the duality hypothesis included the correlation between the two factors: it will be zero or close to zero. Look back at Figure 36.1, A, and note that, in accordance with the duality hypothesis $\phi_{21} = r_{12} = 0$. While r_{12} can be constrained to be zero, we chose, instead, to let LISREL estimate ϕ_{21} for reasons to be given later. The variances of ξ_1 and ξ_2 were set equal to 1.00, $\phi_{11} = \phi_{22} = 1.00$, and r_{12} or ϕ_{21} was "free." (When a parameter is "free" in LISREL, the program estimates its value.)

$r_{12} = -.15$, not statistically significant. So, in effect, the two factors are orthogonal, which is consistent with the duality hypothesis. Recall that the theory says that conservatism and liberalism are separate and independent dimensions of social attitudes. This means, of course, that the correlation between them is zero (or close to zero).

The crucial question, however, is: Is the whole model congruent with the data? The whole model of the duality hypothesis is expressed by Figure 36.1, A, and by equations 36.3. Following the rules of LISREL, we instruct the computer to estimate the six factor loadings, $\lambda_{11}, \lambda_{21}, \lambda_{31}, \lambda_{42}, \lambda_{52}, \lambda_{62}$ of the factor matrix Λ_x, while maintaining the zero constraints in the matrix. We also specify that the error terms of the six equations of 36.3 be calculated. We must also specify what the relations between the two factors will be; therefore we must instruct the computer what to do with the phi (Φ) matrix. We set $\phi_{11} = \phi_{22} = 1.00$. These are the diagonal entries of Φ, which are the variances of ξ_1 and ξ_2. We also instruct the computer to estimate ϕ_{21} (which is r_{12}). Following an iterative procedure the computer estimates the 13 values we have specified to be estimated: $\lambda_{11}, \lambda_{21}, \lambda_{31}, \lambda_{42}, \lambda_{52}, \lambda_{62}; \delta_1, \delta_2, \delta_3, \delta_4, \delta_5, \delta_6; \phi_{21}$, using the correlations among the six variables (Table 36.2) as input data.[5] It also constrains the zeroes of Table 36.3 and sets the phi's: $\phi_{11} = \phi_{22} = 1.00$. The factor loadings, or λ_{ij}, are given in Table 36.4, b, and $\phi_{21} = r_{12} = -.15$. The six error terms are: .58, .25, .61, .50, .71, and .60. Are these values congruent with the data, or alternatively, does the duality model "fit" the data?

The core idea behind the assessment of the "goodness of fit" of a theoretical model is simple and powerful. Use the estimated parameter values and the constrained values to calculate a predicted correlation matrix, $\mathbf{R}^*$, and then compare this predicted matrix to the obtained or observed correlation matrix, $\mathbf{R}$. This can be done by subtracting $\mathbf{R}^*$ from $\mathbf{R}$, or $\mathbf{R} - \mathbf{R}^*$. This matrix of differences is called a *residual matrix*.[6] The residual matrix under the duality hypothesis is given above the diagonal of Table 36.5. Study of these

---

[5]There are a number of other important methodological points we do not discuss. One of these is the assumptions behind the analysis. To do maximum likelihood analysis, for example, it must be assumed that the distribution of the x variables is multivariate normal. Another assumption or requirement is identification: the LISREL problem must be set up so that all estimated parameters can be identified.

[6]The matrix R^* can in this case be generated by multiplying the rows of Table 36.4: $r_{12} = (.65)(.87) + (0)(0) = .57; r_{13} = (.65)(.63) + (0)(0) = .41; r_{23} = (.57)(.41) + (0)(0) = .55;$ and so on.

Table 36.5 Residuals Calculated from the Duality Hypothesis Model (Above Diagonal) and from the Bipolarity Hypothesis Model (Below Diagonal)[a]

	1	2	3	4	5	6	Type
1		.003	−.021	−.167	.161	−.085	C
2	.009		.003	−.063	.223	.058	C
3	−.047	.010		−.131	.139	−.164	C
4	−.070	.050	−.038		.002	−.016	L
5	.024	.048	.007	.416		.028	L
6	−.049	.096	−.130	.396	.388		L

[a]The diagonal values are all zero. χ^2 (duality) = 10.15 (p = .26), df = 8; χ^2 (bipolarity) = 28.00 (p = .001), df = 9. *rms* (duality) = .093, *rms* (bipolarity) = .158; χ^2 (bipolarity) − χ^2 (duality) = 28.00 − 10.15 = 17.85, df = 1, p < .001.

residuals shows that they are, with one exception, small. An average of the squared residuals is used to assess goodness of fit: *rms* = .093, which is a good fit (.10 or .11 or less).[7] χ^2 can also be calculated. In general, if χ^2 is significant, the fit is not good; if χ^2 is not significant, the fit is "good." χ^2 for the duality model is 10.15, which, at 8 degrees of freedom, is not significant.[8] The duality model is therefore congruent with the data.

We are after the ideas behind the method. The principle is: *The smaller the residuals, the better the fit; the larger the residuals, the poorer the fit.* If the hypothesis or model is empirically valid, the less the model-generated covariance (correlation) matrix, **R***, will differ from the observed correlation matrix, **R**. Both situations are reflected in the matrix of residuals, **R** − **R***, and in measures, like *rms*, that reflect the magnitudes of the residuals. Again, the larger the residuals, the poorer the fit. (The LISREL program obligingly prints the residual matrix.)

The empirical implications of the bipolarity hypothesis are depicted in Figure 36.1, *B*. There is of course only one factor, ξ, the conservatism measures, x_1, x_2, and x_3 are marked "+", and those for x_4, x_5, and x_6 are marked "−," consistent with the bipolarity hypothesis. That is, we expect one bipolar factor with the conservative measures having positive signs and the liberal measures negative signs (or vice versa). The six LISREL-estimated factor loadings (on one factor) were: .67, .83, .65, −.25, .12, −.15. χ^2 = 28.00, df = 9, p < .01. The residuals are reported in Table 36.5, below the diagonal. The substantial values of .416, .396, and .388 stand out. And they are supported by *rms* = .16, which of course means the residuals are large, considerably larger than the duality test residuals. It is obvious on all counts that the fit is poor.

[7]Jöreskog and Sörbom, LISREL Manual, p. I.41; H. Harman, *Modern Factor Analysis*, 3d ed. Chicago: University of Chicago Press, 1976, p. 343. The formulas of the two sources appear to differ. Jöreskog and Sörbom include the diagonal zero values; Harman does not. This makes the former *rms* smaller than the latter *rms*. Since the diagonal values are always zero when reproducing an R matrix, Harman's formula is more conservative.

[8]The trouble with χ^2 is that its magnitude is a function of the sample size N. With large N, χ^2 will almost certainly be significant, even though the fit is quite good. See P. Bentler, "Causal Modeling," *Annual Review of Psychology*, 31 (1980), 419–456 (especially p. 428). Bentler discusses this problem and suggests the use of coefficients that do not depend on sample size and, perhaps more important, suggests the use of the difference in χ^2 values in testing alternative models. We so contrast the duality and bipolarity models below. Bentler's review is excellent. Another problem in this example is that the x's were not really tests; they were six obliquely rotated factors. And the correlation matrix analyzed by LISREL contained the correlations among these factors. Since the correlations among the factors were in effect obtained by correlating each pair of factors over the 50 items, N = 50 was used. Had the original N of 530 been used—N = 530 *was* used to calculate the correlations among all 59 items—certain results would have been quite different. For our purpose of illustrating LISREL, the difference doesn't matter.

The factor loadings are interesting and informative. Those of the three conservative measures, x_1, x_2, and x_3, are positive and substantial, but those of the liberal measures are all low. Evidently the one-factor model is inadequate: the three liberal measures are "lost." The χ^2 is also significant, indicating a lack of fit. Now look at the residuals in the lower half of Table 36.5. Note carefully that the residuals for r_{45}, r_{46}, and r_{56} are substantial: .416, .396, and .388. The correlations among the liberal measures, x_4, x_5, and x_6, were "missed" by the one-factor solution, the model for the bipolarity hypothesis. It seems that the bipolarity model has not succeeded too well. The duality model, on the other hand, made out well on all counts.

We now make a final test: we directly compare the two models. This is done through the χ^2's. The χ^2 for the bipolarity model was 28.00, at 9 degrees of freedom, while the χ^2 for the duality model was 10.15, at 8 degrees of freedom. Recall that earlier we had the computer estimate r_{12}, or ϕ_{21}, even though, strictly speaking, we should have "fixed" it at zero, or $\phi_{21} = 0$, since the pure duality model predicts orthogonal factors. One of the main reasons for doing this was to "use up" one degree of freedom so that the χ^2's of the two models could be compared. The direct test is $\chi^2_{\text{bip}} - \chi^2_{\text{du}}$, or $28.00 - 10.15 = 17.85$. The degrees of freedom are also subtracted: $9 - 8 = 1$. Had we not estimated ϕ_{21}, the degrees of freedom for both models would have been the same, making a χ^2 comparison impossible. $\chi^2 = 17.85$, at $df = 1$, is evaluated. It is highly significant, which indicates the superiority of the duality hypothesis (since the bipolarity model χ^2 is significantly larger than the duality model χ^2). If there is no significant difference between the χ^2's of the two models, then the bipolarity hypothesis is as "good" (or as "poor") as the duality hypothesis. One cannot then infer that one hypothesis is more satisfactory than the other. Remember that a model that is congruent with the data will have a χ^2 that is not significant. If the difference between the χ^2's is significant, on the other hand, one can then infer that the model with the larger χ^2 is less satisfactory than the model with the smaller χ^2. Another way of putting it is that the difference χ^2, if significant, tests the importance of the parameters that differentiate the models.[9]

LATENT VARIABLE INFLUENCES: THE FULL LISREL SYSTEM

In the above attitude example only one part of the LISREL system was used. If ordinary first-order factor analysis is done this is all that is necessary. The most interesting problems, however, study the relations between independent variables and dependent variables. Only the x part of the system was used above. There is much more to the system, however. LISREL has an x part, a y part, and a highly important part that relates the x and y parts. Before discussing the formal properties of the system, let's examine a simple fictitious example. We lay out the path diagram of the example to have something con-

---

[9]This is difficult to show and explain the way the problem has been done. A more elegant approach is as follows. Set up the duality model as it has been done above. Then set up the bipolarity model exactly the same except for the Φ matrix. For the duality model estimate Φ_{21}, as above. This will yield a χ^2 with $df = 8$. Now set up the bipolarity model fixing $\Phi_{21} = 1.00$, with $df = 9$. This will yield exactly the same parameter estimates as if the program had been told that there was only one factor, except that the one-factor loadings will appear on two factors. Since the correlation between the two factors is 1.00, the net effect is the same as with one factor. The test of the alternative hypotheses, $\chi^2_{\text{bip}} - \chi^2_{\text{du}}$, will be the same as that given above, but it is now clear that the two models differ only in the one parameter, ϕ_{21}. This is one of the reasons for estimating ϕ_{21}, or r_{12}, in the duality model: for a test of alternative hypotheses, there must be a difference in degrees of freedom. Moreover, one model must be a subset of the other model. This means that both models estimate the same parameters except (in this case) for one parameter.

crete to refer to. The example is a small model of ability and achievement. We say, in effect: Verbal Ability and Numerical Ability influence Achievement positively. Although perhaps not terribly interesting, the example has the virtue of being obvious and easily understood. No attempt is made to test alternative hypotheses here even though there are a number of possibilities. We seek only to convey the essence of the system.

The three parts of the system mentioned above are expressed in the following equations:[10]

Measurement Equations:

$$x: \quad \mathbf{x} = \mathbf{\Lambda}_x \boldsymbol{\xi} + \boldsymbol{\delta} \tag{36.4}$$

$$y: \quad \mathbf{y} = \mathbf{\Lambda}_y \boldsymbol{\eta} + \boldsymbol{\epsilon} \tag{36.5}$$

Structural Equation:

$$\boldsymbol{\eta} \text{ and } \boldsymbol{\xi}: \mathbf{B}\boldsymbol{\eta} = \mathbf{\Gamma}\boldsymbol{\xi} + \boldsymbol{\zeta} \tag{36.6}$$

We are familiar with 36.4, the x measurement equation. It succinctly expresses factor analysis, as we have seen. The y measurement equation, 36.5, is identical in form to the x measurement equation. It therefore also expresses factor analysis. Indeed the factor analysis of the attitude example could have been done with the y measurement equation. Both equations express the relations between measured or observed variables x and y and latent or unobserved variables: x and $\boldsymbol{\xi}$ and $\mathbf{\Lambda}_x$ go together, and y, $\boldsymbol{\eta}$, and $\mathbf{\Lambda}_y$ go together. That is, the latent variables ξ and η underlie the observed variables x and y, and the entries of $\mathbf{\Lambda}_x$ and $\mathbf{\Lambda}_y$, the factor loadings, λ, say "how much" ξ and η underlie the x and y measures.

The so-called structural equation, 36.6, is the most interesting and perhaps most important part of the system.[11] It relates the latent variables, ξ of the x system and η of the y-system, to each other. Look at this system and its function from a regression point of view. First, regard the x-side of Figure 36.2. We have four tests: Verbal Test 1, Verbal Test 2, Numerical Test 1, and Numerical Test 2, x_1, x_2, x_3, and x_4. We calculate the four-by-four correlation matrix and factor analyze it, and obtain the two factors ξ_1 and ξ_2, as in Figure 36.2. The lambda-x, $\mathbf{\Lambda}_x$, matrix ordinarily contains the factor loadings: λ_{11}, λ_{12}, λ_{21}, λ_{22}, λ_{31}, λ_{32}, λ_{41}, λ_{42}. In our case it will contain only four of these, the four in Figure 36.2: λ_{11}, λ_{21}, λ_{32}, and λ_{42}. The other lambdas will be set at zero as we did earlier with the attitude duality hypothesis:

Tests	I	II
1	λ_{11}	0
2	λ_{21}	0
3	0	λ_{32}
4	0	λ_{42}

[10] The Greek symbols used in LISREL are: $\mathbf{\Lambda}_x$, lambda x, $\mathbf{\Lambda}_y$: lambda y; ξ: xi, η: eta, δ: delta, ϵ: epsilon, $\mathbf{B}$: beta, β: beta, lower case; $\mathbf{\Gamma}$: gamma, γ: gamma, lower case, ζ: zeta. Each of these symbols stands for a matrix, or, in two cases, for latent variables. We use the Greek symbols because students who undertake to learn LISREL will have to learn the Greek symbols anyway. Note that $\mathbf{\Gamma}$ is capital gamma and γ lower-case gamma. In addition, the matrix $\mathbf{\Phi}$ (phi) is used but not in the above equations.

[11] In the LISREL-V version of the system, Equation 36.6 is written a little differently: $\boldsymbol{\eta} = \mathbf{B}\,\boldsymbol{\eta} + \mathbf{\Gamma}\,x + \boldsymbol{\zeta}$. This was done for a minor technical reason and is not as conceptually clear as Equation 36.6, which we use because it clearly shows the relation between the latent variables, η and ϵ, to each other.

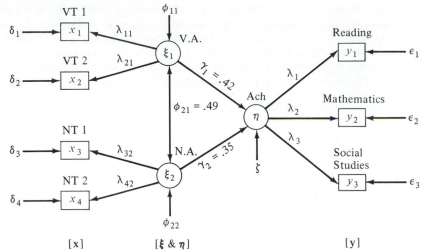

Figure 36.2 Influence of Ability on Achievement: Fictitious Example. VT 1: Verbal Test 1; VT 2: Verbal Test 2; NT 1: Numerical Test 1; NT 2: Numerical Test 2; V.A.: Verbal Ability; N.A.: Numerical Ability

The λ's are regression coefficients. The regression equation for x_1 is:

$$x_1 = \lambda_{11}\xi_1 + \delta_1$$

We seek the regression of x_1 on ξ_1, just as in Chapter 33 we sought the regression of y on x, or y on $x_1, x_2, \ldots$. The factor loadings λ serve the same function as the regression coefficients, b or β, of Chapter 33. The same reasoning applies to the y side of Figure 36.2: we write the regression of y_1 on η:

$$y_1 = \lambda_1\eta + \epsilon_1$$

There are in LISREL two separate factor analysis or regression systems: one on the x side and one on the y side. Either side can be used for confirmatory or hypothesis-testing factor analysis as when we tested the duality and bipolarity hypotheses using the x side of the LISREL system. The same hypothesis-testing could have been done with the y side of the system. What is more interesting and innovative, however, is to ask and answer research questions about the regression of the latent variable (or variables) η on the latent variable (or variables) ξ. We ask, in effect, about the relations between ξ and η, or the regression of η on ξ, considering the ξ's as independent variables and the η's as dependent variables. This is what the structural equation 36.6 does.

The research problem of Figure 36.2 can be expressed as the multivariate relation between the independent variables and the dependent variables. It might be approached, for instance, using canonical correlation, which would express the overall relation between the x's and the y's. But canonical correlation is not capable of refining the relations: it pursues the $x - y$ relation using *all* the y's. It is ordinarily not concerned, moreover, with the latent variables. The model and hypotheses implied by Figure 36.2 say, in effect, that the x variables reflect two factors, Verbal Ability (ξ_1: x_1 and x_2) and Numerical Ability (ξ_2: x_3 and x_4). The latent variables are Verbal Ability, ξ_1, and Numerical Ability, ξ_2. The three achievement variables are Reading, y_1, Mathematics, y_2, and Social Studies, y_3. They are presumed to measure one factor, Achievement—in other words, a one-factor hypothesis. Note carefully that hypotheses that are not satisfactory in the sense that they are not congruent with the data can easily be stated, invalidating the whole model. For example, the y variables, which we said measured reflections of *one* factor or latent variables, might be incorrect. Perhaps two factors are necessary. That is, Figure 36.2 has one factor, η, for Achievement. But there may really be two factors, η_1, and η_2. After all, y_1 is a reading test and y_2 is a mathematics tests, and we know that these are usually two different factors. If so, then the model of Figure 36.2 is deficient.

Setting Up the LISREL Matrices

We finally arrive at the crucial relation: that between ξ_1 and ξ_2, the latent independent variables, and η, the latent dependent variable. Our substantive hypothesis may state that Verbal Ability, ξ_1, and Numerical Ability, ξ_2, both influence Achievement, η.

This is not too fascinating a hypothesis but one amenable to example and explanation. In order to test it, we must set up the problem and model of Figure 36.2 in matrices. This is a crucial and difficult step in LISREL. At the risk of provoking boredom, let us pursue the ideas and set them up in equations and matrix equations, after spelling out the individual variable equations. First, the x equations. The equation for x_1 is repeated here: $x_1 = \lambda_{11}\xi_1 + \delta_1$. Similarly, x_2, x_3, and x_4 are set up:

$$
\begin{aligned}
x_1 &= \lambda_{11}\,\xi_1 + \delta_1 \\
x_2 &= \lambda_{21}\,\xi_1 + \delta_2 \\
x_3 &= \lambda_{32}\,\xi_2 + \delta_3 \\
x_4 &= \lambda_{42}\,\xi_2 + \delta_4
\end{aligned}
\tag{36.7}
$$

For LISREL specification we write the same equations in matrix form:

$$
\begin{pmatrix} x_1 \\ x_2 \\ x_3 \\ x_4 \end{pmatrix} = \begin{pmatrix} \lambda_{11} & 0 \\ \lambda_{21} & 0 \\ 0 & \lambda_{32} \\ 0 & \lambda_{42} \end{pmatrix} \begin{pmatrix} \xi_1 \\ \xi_2 \end{pmatrix} + \begin{pmatrix} \delta_1 \\ \delta_2 \\ \delta_3 \\ \delta_4 \end{pmatrix}
\tag{36.7a}
$$

(Students should pause here, study Figure 36.2 and Equations 36.7 and 36.7a, and try to understand their meaning.)

The y-side is a bit easier:

$$
\begin{aligned}
y_1 &= \lambda_1\,\eta + \epsilon_1 \\
y_2 &= \lambda_2\,\eta + \epsilon_2 \\
y_3 &= \lambda_3\,\eta + \epsilon_3
\end{aligned}
\tag{36.8}
$$

In matrix form:

$$
\begin{pmatrix} y_1 \\ y_2 \\ y_3 \end{pmatrix} = \begin{pmatrix} \lambda_1 \\ \lambda_2 \\ \lambda_3 \end{pmatrix}\eta + \begin{pmatrix} \epsilon_1 \\ \epsilon_2 \\ \epsilon_3 \end{pmatrix}
\tag{36.8a}
$$

The structural equation matrices must also be set up. The structural equation was given in 36.6; it is repeated here for convenience:

$$
\mathbf{B}\,\boldsymbol{\eta} = \boldsymbol{\Gamma}\,\boldsymbol{\xi} + \boldsymbol{\zeta}
\tag{36.9}
$$

η is the latent variable of the y-side of the problem, and ξ is the latent variable (or variables) of the x-side. $\mathbf{B}$ (beta) and $\boldsymbol{\Gamma}$ (gamma) are coefficient or weight matrices. ζ (zeta) is a matrix of so-called disturbance terms, or errors in the structural equation. Let's write out the individual equation:

$$
\boldsymbol{\eta} = \gamma_1\,\xi_1 + \gamma_2\,\xi_2 + \zeta_1
\tag{36.10}
$$

Notice that $\mathbf{B}$, the beta matrix, has dropped out since there is only one η. $\mathbf{B}$ spells out the relations among the η or latent y variables if there is more than one η. For example, if we had two η's, or η_1 and η_2, it may well be that η_1 influences η_2, and we would want to assess this influence.

As usual, we must write Equation 36.10 in matrix form so that it can be prepared for LISREL analysis:

$$\boldsymbol{\eta} = (\gamma_1 \quad \gamma_2)\begin{pmatrix} \xi_1 \\ \xi_2 \end{pmatrix} + \boldsymbol{\zeta} \tag{36.10a}$$

The parameters γ_1 and γ_2 (gamma 1 and gamma 2) are the most important part of the problem because they estimate the effects of the latent variables, Verbal Ability (ξ_1) and Numerical Ability (ξ_2), on Achievement (η). The three sets of equations, 36.7a, 36.8a, and 36.10a, then, spell out the LISREL problem.[12]

A fictitious correlation matrix was synthesized so that the LISREL solution would support the model of the path diagram of Figure 36.2 and the equations written on the basis of the diagram.[13] The results were very nice, indeed. $\chi^2 = 7.85$, which, at 11 degrees of freedom, is not significant ($p = .73$). The model fits: it is congruent with the data. $rms = .03$, a low value indicating that the residuals were small. Other indices calculated by LISREL all supported the conclusion that the model was satisfactory. (This is no great achievement, of course: I set up the example so that the solution would be satisfactory!)

Although the parameters of the x and y factor analyses (or regression analyses) are also satisfactory, they are not reported because our interest is in testing the model for congruence with the data, in this case a correlation matrix, and in assessing the relations between the latent variables ξ_1 and ξ_2, or Verbal Ability and Numerical Ability, on the one hand, and η, Achievement, on the other hand. The Γ coefficients, γ_1 and γ_2, express these influences. The values were $\gamma_1 = .42$ and $\gamma_2 = .35$, both statistically significant ($p < .01$), Verbal Ability and Numerical Ability have moderate positive and statistically significant "influences" on Achievement. In the language of Chapter 33, the regression of η, Achievement, on ξ_1, Verbal Ability, and ξ_2, Numerical Ability, is moderate and statistically significant. LISREL also calculates what is in effect R^2 for the structural equation: $R^2_{\eta.\xi_1\xi_2} = .437$.[14] This is a moderate to substantial relation. It can be interpreted as the proportion of variance of the y variables, as expressed by the dependent latent variable, η, accounted for by the latent independent variables, ξ_1 and ξ_2. This index, then, is a multivariate expression of the multiple regression of η on ξ_1 and ξ_2.

It was said earlier that analysis of covariance structures and LISREL, the computer program to do the necessary complex computations, are difficult, hard to learn, and hard to use. Why bother with it, then? Can't the factor analyses and the regression analyses be

---

[12] We do not try to explain how this is done since it is almost purely technical and would probably require another chapter.

[13] This is by no means easy to do because one can easily write correlations some of which are inconsistent with each other. In such cases LISREL will either stop or yield nonsense. In this case I was lucky: the solution was just what I wanted.

[14] The calculation is accomplished by using the idea developed in Chapter 26 of calculating reliability using the error term: $r_{tt} = 1 - V_e/V_t$ (see Equation 26.4, Chapter 26). It is also based on the theory of matrices and determinants. In LISREL, note that error in the structural equation is provided by the matrix Ψ (psi), whose individual terms are ζ's, zetas. In the present example there is only one ζ. Thus the calculation of $R^2_{\eta.\xi_1\xi_2} = 1 - |\Psi|/\text{cov}(\eta) = 1 - (.382/.679) = .437$ is easy. $|\Psi|$ means "the determinant of the matrix psi." The values .382 and .679 are recovered from the computer output. See Jöreskog and Sörbom, LISREL Manual, p. I.38, for definition of the formula and P. Green, *Methodological Tools for Applied Multivariate Analysis.* New York: Academic Press, 1976, pp. 122–124, for a discussion of a generalized variance measure, which is the basis of the above equation.

done separately with far less wear and tear on the behavioral scientist? Yes and no. The separate factor analyses of the y and x variables can certainly be done separately: indeed, psychometric and factor analytic study should be done before LISREL is used. But the general regression analysis just described obviously cannot be done separately because it depends on the x and y analyses. One may of course try various approaches to the analysis of the data. But there appears to be no simple way to study sets of complex relations and to test the congruence of theoretical models with observed data. The ideas of analysis of covariance structures are mathematically and statistically powerful, conceptually penetrating, and aesthetically satisfying. The conception of LISREL and other computer programs[15] are highly ingenious, productive, and creative achievements. They are, at the present writing, the highest development of behavioral scientific and analytic thinking, a development that brings psychological and sociological theory and multivariate mathematical and statistical analysis together into a unique and powerful synthesis that will probably revolutionize behavioral research. It is in this sense that analysis of covariance structures is said to be the culmination of contemporary methodology.

RESEARCH STUDIES

In the relatively short time that analysis of covariance structures and LISREL have been functional and available—since the early and middle 1970s—the approach has been fruitfully used in a number of fields. Some of these studies are LISREL reanalyses of existing data; others are studies that were conceived with analysis of covariance structures in mind. (See Study Suggestion 2 at the end of the chapter.) The first study of attitude structure discussed in this chapter was only one of twelve sets of attitude data that were reanalyzed using LISREL. Most of the evidence supported the duality hypothesis.[16] Jöreskog and his colleagues have reanalyzed the data of a number of psychological and sociological studies.[17] The first study described in detail below is a LISREL reanalysis of the data of a large study of political participation in America, a study discussed in considerable detail in Chapter 35.

Bentler and Woodward used LISREL to reanalyze Head Start data—with depressing results.[18] They found that the Head Start program had no significant effects on the Head Start children's cognitive abilities. Judd and Millburn studied the attitude structure of the general public of the United States.[19] Using panel data from surveys done in 1972, 1974, and 1976, they investigated Converse's contention that the general public does not have meaningful and stable social attitudes. They found that the noneducated public *does* have consistent ideological predispositions.

[15] The present discussion of LISREL seems to imply that the work of Jöreskog and his colleagues is a unique contribution. Not so. Many others have contributed to the field, and Jöreskog has explicitly and repeatedly cited the sources of his work and acknowledges his indebtedness. And there will certainly be further developments and other computer programs. Jöreskog appears to be the first analyst, however, to bring psychometric theory and practice, factor analysis, regression theory, and computer analysis into a productive and functional synthesis.

[16] F. Kerlinger, "Analysis of Covariance Structure Tests of a Criterial Referents Theory of Attitudes," *Multivariate Behavioral Research*, 15 (1980), 403–422.

[17] One of the best articles is also one of the earliest. The computer program was called ACOVS: K. Jöreskog, "Analyzing Psychological Data by Structural Analysis of Covariance Matrices." In K. Jöreskog and D. Sörbom, *Advances, op. cit.*, chap. 3. Later examples of Jöreskog reanalyses have appeared in the five or six LISREL manuals.

[18] P. Bentler and J. Woodward, "A Head Start Reevaluation: Positive Effects Are Not Yet Demonstrable," *Evaluation Quarterly*, 2 (1978), 493–510.

[19] C. Judd and M. Milburn, "The Structure of Attitude Systems in the General Public: Comparisons of a Structural Equation Model," *American Sociological Review*, 45 (1980), 627–643.

Verba and Nie: Political Participation in America

In Chapter 35 we reported the factor analysis of the correlations among 13 variables of political participation. These variables are shown in Table 36.6. Recall that Verba and Nie reasoned from political theory that there should be four factors behind the 13 variables.[20] These factors are also given in Table 36.6. Recall that we said that this study was confirmatory factor analysis and cited the authors' emphasis of this point (see their p. 57). It seemed that they were correct in their structural hypothesis, and we applauded their careful and competent work. But factor analysis has been criticized for its lack of rigor, among other things. Can we put Verba and Nie's structural hypothesis to a more rigorous test? Let's use LISREL on the problem.[21]

The correlations among the 13 political variables are given above the diagonal of Table 36.6.[22] The LISREL model that follows from the theoretical discussion of Verba and Nie is given in Figure 36.3. $x_1, x_2, \ldots, x_{13}$ are the observed variables, with their error terms. $\delta_1, \delta_2, \ldots, \delta_{13}$. $\xi_1, \xi_2, \xi_3,$ and ξ_4 are the four hypothesized factors. $\phi_{21}, \ldots, \phi_{43}$ are the correlations among the factors. Remember that when the factors are correlated, the solution is oblique. The program instructed the computer to calculate the correlations among the parameters of Figure 36.3 and then to use the parameters to calculate a predicted correlation matrix $\mathbf{R}^*$. Finally, to assess the adequacy of the fit of the model of the four oblique factors of Figure 36.3, $\mathbf{R} - \mathbf{R}^*$, the differences or residuals, and various "fit" statistics were calculated.

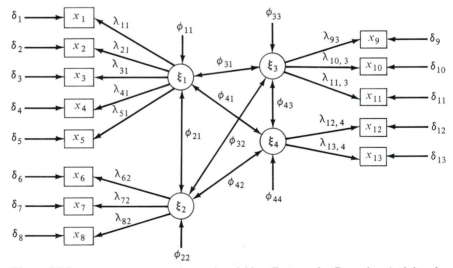

Figure 36.3 $x_1, x_2, \ldots, x_{13}$: observed variables; Factors: ξ_1: Campaign Activity; ξ_2: Voting; ξ_3: Cooperative Activity; ξ_4: Contacting ϕ_{ij}: correlations among factors

---

[20]S. Verba and N. Nie, *Participation in America: Political Democracy and Social Equality*. New York: Harper & Row, 1972, chap. 3 and pp. 57ff.

[21]It is emphasized that Verba and Nie did not use LISREL and are in no way responsible for this analysis or its conceptualization and interpretation.

[22]These correlations were reported by Verba and Nie, *op. cit.*, p. 58, Table 4-1. The residuals obtained in the LISREL analysis are given below below the diagonal. They will be discussed shortly.

Table 36.6 Correlations Among Thirteen Political Variables, Verba and Nie Study, Above Diagonal; Residuals, Below Diagonal

	Variables[a,b]												
	1	2	3	4	5	6	7	8	9	10	11	12	13
1	1.00	.47	.35	.27	.27	.21	.19	.24	.24	.23	.22	.24	.23
2	.05	1.00	.50	.36	.46	.19	.19	.27	.31	.24	.27	.26	.22
3	−.03	−.01	1.00	.37	.45	.20	.18	.25	.23	.24	.30	.25	.21
4	−.03	−.03	.01	1.00	.36	.17	.17	.20	.21	.12	.24	.20	.20
5	−.07	.01	.03	.04	1.00	.14	.13	.18	.22	.22	.29	.17	.19
6	.04	−.04	−.01	.01	−.05	1.00	.71	.64	.18	.10	.19	.13	.14
7	.03	−.03	−.02	.02	−.05	.01	1.00	.60	.17	.09	.18	.11	.12
8	.09	.07	.07	.06	.02	−.01	−.01	1.00	.22	.14	.23	.17	.18
9	.01	.01	−.05	−.01	−.03	−.01	−.01	.06	1.00	.38	.34	.29	.23
10	.04	−.02	.01	−.06	.01	−.06	−.06	.00	.05	1.00	.28	.22	.19
11	.01	−.02	.04	.04	.06	.01	.01	.08	−.03	−.03	1.00	.26	.27
12	.04	−.01	.01	.01	−.05	−.02	−.03	.04	.01	−.01	.00	1.00	.23
13	.05	−.02	−.01	.03	−.01	.00	−.01	.06	−.02	−.02	.04	.00	1.00

[a] 1. Persuade others how to vote; 2. Actively work for party or candidate; 3. Attend political meeting or rally; 4. Contribute money to party or candidate; 5. Membership in political clubs; 6. Voted in 1964 Presidential election; 7. Voted in 1960 Presidential election; 8. Frequency of voting in local elections; 9. Work with others on local problems; 10. Form a group to work on local problems; 11. Active membership in community problem-solving organizations; 12. Contact local officials; 13. Contact state and national officials.

[b] Factors: 1-5: Campaign Activity; 6-8: Voting; 9-11: Cooperative Activity; 12-13: Contacting. The correlations among the variables of the predicted factors are outlined in the triangles.

The overall results support Verba and Nie's model of four oblique factors, even though the χ^2 of 406.64, at $df = 59$, is highly significant. The large χ^2 is clearly due to the very large N of 3,000, and is thus not a good measure of fit. (An identical solution with a reduced N of 300 produced a $\chi^2 = 40.54$, which is not significant.) The root mean square residual was: $rms = .03$. This small index merely reflected the generally small residuals, which are shown below the diagonal of Table 36.6. A goodness-of-fit index, also calculated by LISREL, was .97, very high. In short, the fit of the model of Figure 36.3 is good.[23] Verba and Nie's theoretical reasoning and measurement procedure seemed to have been sound. They have significantly contributed to understanding of the political process and to the nature and meaning of participation in the political process.

Maruyama and Miller: Effects of Desegregated Classrooms

In the face of contradictory findings on the presumed effects of desegregated classrooms on the achievement of minority group children, Maruyama and Miller used analysis of covariance structures and LISREL to reanalyze data of Lewis and St. John.[24] Lewis and St. John thought that their path analytic results supported the transmission of values hypothesis, which asserts, in effect, that the norms and values of middle-class, achievement-oriented white students will be accepted and internalized by black children if the middle-class children befriend them. But other contrary evidence that seemed to support

[23] The correlation between the third and fourth factors, as estimated by ϕ_{43}, is very high: .88. It is possible, therefore, that a three-factor model might have provided as good a fit.

[24] G. Maruyama and N. Miller, "Reexamination of Normative Influence Processes in Desegregated Classrooms," *American Educational Research Journal*, 16 (1979), 273–283; R. Lewis and N. St. John, "Contribution of Cross-Racial Friendship to Minority Group Achievement in Desegregated Classrooms," *Sociometry*, 37 (1974), 79–91.

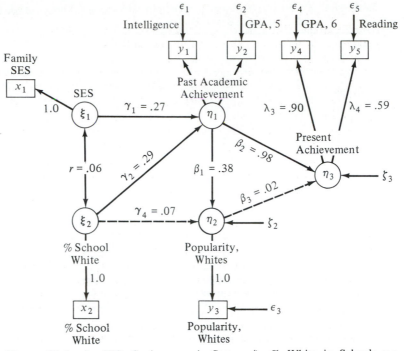

Figure 36.4 ξ_1: SES: Socioeconomic Status; ξ_2: % White in School; η_1: Achievement Past; η_2: Popularity with Whites; η_3: Achievement, present

the notion that achievement influences peer acceptance prompted Maruyama and Miller to reanalyze Lewis and St. John's data. In other words, is the influence from peer acceptance to achievement, or is it from achievement to peer acceptance? The relation and the theory behind it are theoretically and practically important. One of the major justifications for desegregation is that white peer acceptance of black children will affect the achievement of the black children.

The LISREL model used is given in Figure 36.4. Careful attention is necessary: this is the most complex model we have yet encountered. It is also interesting and instructive, and we will use it here to reinforce earlier discussion and to make two or three new methodological points. What is important are the relations and implied influences among the latent variables, but especially among the y latent variables, η_1: Past Achievement, η_2: Popularity with whites, and η_3: Present Achievement. The solid arrows in Figure 36.4 indicate significant influences, which are epitomized by γ (gamma) or β (beta) coefficients. Broken arrows indicate statistically not-significant coefficients. I have kept Maruyama and Miller's diagram and have only changed it slightly in conformity with earlier usage in this chapter. I have also inserted the coefficients' values to facilitate discussion and interpretation.

$\chi^2 = 4.88$, which, at 5 degrees of freedom, is not significant. The model fits. (The authors do not report *rms* or other indices of fit. Had the size of the sample been larger—it was $N = 154$—the χ^2 would probably have been significant.) The γ coefficients are not important for our purpose; so we concentrate on the relations among the latent η (eta) variables: η_1: Past Academic Achievement expresses the observed variables y_1: Intelligence, and y_2: GPA, 5, or Grade-Point Average, Grade 5; η_2: Popularity with Whites; and

η_3: Present Achievement, which expresses the observed variables y_4: GPA, or Grade-Point Average, Grade 6, and y_5: Reading. We must now discuss an aspect of LISREL that we skimped earlier: the nature and use of the B (beta) matrix and the directional (regression) coefficients β.

Earlier it was said that our main interest is usually focused on the influences of the ξ (Xsi) latent variables on the η (eta) latent variables, as expressed by the Γ (gamma) coefficient matrix: γ_{11}, γ_{21}, etc. That is, the γ's express the influences of the ξ's, or independent latent variables, on the η's, or dependent latent variables. Some problems, however, do not quite fit into this usual mold, and the present problem is a case in point. When a latent variable is an "intermediary" variable, a variable that is influenced by another independent latent variable and that, in turn, influences a dependent variable, then it must be treated as a dependent latent variable, η. Look at the middle horizontal layer of Figure 36.4 and note the influence sequence: $\xi_1 \xrightarrow{\gamma} \eta_1 \xrightarrow{\beta} \eta_3$. ξ_1 influences η_1, and η_1 influences η_3. The magnitudes of the influences are expressed by the γ and the β. η_1 influences η_3, which is expressed by a β coefficient. The B, or beta, matrix contains the β (beta) coefficients, which express the influence of one η on one or more other η's. Earlier in this chapter we mentioned the difference between the x and y parts of the LISREL system. The Φ (phi) matrix contains ϕ coefficients that do *not* express the influence of one ξ on one or more other ξ's. They are only covariances or, in our case, correlations. In short, the β's are regression coefficients and the Φ's are correlations. Therefore, if a latent variable is an "intermediary" variable, it has to be designated as an η latent variable.

If the cultural transmission hypothesis is correct, then black children's acceptance by white children should influence the black children's achievement positively and substantially. But β_3 in Figure 36.4 is only .02. To make these crucial relations quite clear, we reproduce the η latent variables in Figure 36.5. Notice that the influence of Past Achievement, η_1, on Present Achievement, η_3, is strong, $\beta_2 = .98$, as we would expect. But the influence of Popularity, η_2, on Present Achievement, η_3, is virtually zero, $\beta_3 = .02$. And the influence of Past Achievement, η_1, on Popularity, η_2, is moderate and statistically significant, $\beta_1 = .38$. Maruyama and Miller conclude, then, that the cultural transmission hypothesis is not correct, *and that achievement influences popularity or acceptance by whites*.

Readers should study Figures 36.4 and 36.5 carefully and understand clearly what was done. As said earlier, the example is important theoretically and practically. It casts doubt on the influential cultural transmission hypothesis as an explanation of minority children's achievement in desegregated classrooms. It suggests that white pupils' acceptance of black children springs from black pupils' achievement. One cannot of course accept these findings as conclusive. We have used the study analysis to help explain analysis of covari-

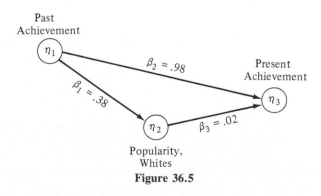

Figure 36.5

ance structures and LISREL analysis. We are *not* saying that the results are definitive or conclusive. The sample was only 154 black pupils in desegregated classrooms. The results *are* suggestive, however, and the research should be replicated with larger samples, in different parts of the country, and with other variables.

CONCLUSIONS—AND RESERVATIONS

It would be wrong to create the impression in the reader's mind that all problems attacked with analysis of covariance structures and LISREL work out as well as those described in this chapter, or that LISREL should be used with all multivariate research problems. Quite the contrary. The purpose of this final section of the chapter is to try to put the subject into reasonable perspective.

Let's ask the most difficult question first: When should the procedure be used? As usual with such questions, it is hard to say clearly and unambiguously when it should be used. One precept that is fairly safe is that it should *not* be used routinely or for ordinary statistical analysis and calculations. For instance, it should not be used to factor analyze a set of data to "discover" the factors behind the variables of the set. It is simply not suited to exploratory factor analysis or to testing mean differences between groups or subgroups of data. If it is possible to use a simpler procedure and obtain answers to research questions, like multiple regression, discriminant analysis, or analysis of variance, then using LISREL is pointless. That inappropriate use will be attempted is obvious. LISREL has recently been added to the SPSS package, which means, among other things, that it will be used often. Unlike many other procedures, LISREL is hard to use because its appropriate use requires rather difficult conceptualization, technical understanding of measurement theory, multiple regression, and factor analysis. The same was true, if to a lesser extent, of the use of factor analysis. Yet factor analysis has been "successfully" integrated into the body of behavioral research methodology, but too often poorly used. The nature of computer packages almost makes this inevitable. One of their purposes is to make easy what is essentially not easy. So I suspect that we will be seeing the publication of many studies that have used LISREL—inadequately. In short, LISREL should only be used at a relatively late stage of a research program when "crucial" tests of complex hypotheses are needed.

Analysis of covariance structures and LISREL[25] are most suited to the study and analysis of complex structural theoretical models in which complex chains of reasoning are used to tie theory to empirical research. Under certain conditions and limitations, the system is a powerful means of testing alternative explanations of behavioral phenomena. It is *not* well-suited to testing the statistical significance of ordinary statistics. And it is not well-suited to computer hacking. (See Appendix B on the computer.) To solve a covariance structures problem adequately usually requires a good deal of preliminary thought and analysis—away from the computer.

Another use to which LISREL can well be put is checking on complex results from other analyses. In the past decade, for example, path analysis has been used to analyze the data of many research problems. While path analysis is a useful approach to research problems—it is particularly helpful in conceptualizing the problems—it cannot accom-

---

[25] I am uncomfortable referring to LISREL so often because it *is* a computer program and as such cannot bear the full weight of scientific discussion. At present, however, it is the only widely available and functional computer program of its kind, but this does not mean that there will not be other structural analysis programs, one or two of which may well displace LISREL.

plish what LISREL can. Maruyama and Miller made this point when they discussed why they used LISREL to reanalyze the desegregation data of Lewis and St. John. LISREL often has the capability of neatly settling research hypotheses issues when other methods cannot do so. Yet it is not a generally applicable methodology.

There are often technical difficulties in using LISREL. We have already discussed large and significant χ^2's with large numbers of subjects, and have suggested remedies, especially study of residuals and the use of R^2's and coefficients of determination which the latest versions of LISREL (LISREL-V and VI) calculate and report, and the use of coefficients that do not depend on sample size.[26] Another remedy is the testing of alternative hypotheses when the problem permits such testing.

One of the most difficult problems is identification. A model being tested must be overidentified. This means that there must be more data points, usually variances and covariances, than parameters estimated.[27] If there are p x variables and q y variables— let's say $p = 3$ and $q = 2$—then there can be no more than t parameters estimated from the data, where $t = \frac{1}{2}(p + q)(p + q + 1)$. If $p = 3$ and $q = 2$, then $t = \frac{1}{2}(3 + 2)(3 + 2 + 1) = 15$, and no more than 15 parameters can be estimated in a model. There are other conditions that can make a model not identifiable, but it is extremely difficult to specify them in advance.[28]

The commonest technical difficulty is closely related to identification. For any one or combination of reasons a problem may not run and may announce that ''something'' is wrong. But what? On the other hand, the computer run may be completed, but some of the parameters may not make sense. For example, negative variances may be reported. Why? Anyone who has used LISREL to any extent is familiar with the lugubrious messages the computer announces. When an expert is consulted, the answer is invariably: ''There is something wrong with the model.'' Yes, of course! But what? And, naturally, theoretical models often do not fit: ''There is something wrong with the model!'' And, too, there is the frequent occurrence of the computer analysis that works beautifully, but the statistics indicate that the researcher's model doesn't fit. Is the theory wrong? If one is strongly committed to a theoretical position, it may be hard to admit this. In any case, one has to check several possibilities. One, the model doesn't fit because it was poorly or incorrectly conceptualized. Two, it doesn't fit because the LISREL user made a mistake (or two, or three) in using the system. Three, the computer analysis won't work because there are flaws in the data (strong multicollinearity in a correlation matrix, for example). And four, the model doesn't fit because the theory from which it was derived is wrong or is inapplicable.

Inadequate measurement is a limitation of much behavioral research. The technical difficulty of measuring psychological and sociological variables is still not appreciated by researchers in psychology, sociology, and education. It is not easy to devise tests and scales to measure psychological and sociological constructs; it is also not easy to do the psychometric research necessary to establish the reliability and validity of the measures used. It is even more difficult, evidently, to admit that one's measures are deficient. Too often in behavioral research measures in common use are accepted and used without question. And rarely are assumptions about study variables questioned. If we are measuring, say, authoritarianism we assume that part of the latent variable authoritarianism is anti-authoritarianism (whatever that is). Early in this chapter and in Chapter 35 we studied

---

[26] Bentler's discussion of these problems and their remedies is helpful: Bentler, *op. cit.*, pp. 427–429.
[27] *Ibid.*, p. 426; Jöreskog and Sörbom, LISREL Manual, pp. I.20–I.24.
[28] Fortunately, the program announces when a model being run cannot be identified. Yet to know why is often a mystery.

research that sprang from questioning the commonly held assumption that conservatism and liberalism are logical and empirical opposites. Unfortunately, a number of studies have been done—and marred—by measurement of social attitudes based on this assumption.[29] Similarly, other studies have been marred, perhaps ruined, both by incorrect assumptions and inadequate measurement.

An analytic methodology, no matter how well-conceived and powerful, cannot make up for measures whose reliability and validity are unsatisfactory. Validity by assumption is a particularly severe threat to scientific conclusions because measurement procedures are not questioned or tested: their reliability and validity are assumed. It is a poor factor analysis that emerges from factoring what is in effect sloppy choice or construction of tests and scales. Similarly, it is poor use of analysis of covariance structures when some or all of the measures used have little sound technical basis in psychometric theory and empirical research. The point being made should be strongly emphasized: Elegant procedures applied to poor data gathered without regard to theory and logical analysis cannot produce anything of scientific value.

Another difficulty for users of LISREL is that modern multivariate structural analysis is quite different from most earlier statistical analysis. The preoccupation of classical statistics was assessing whether observed mean differences in an analysis of variance or the joint and separate contributions of independent variables in a multiple regression analysis were statistically significant. With structural modeling, however, implications of a theory are built into a model that reflects the theory and its implications: latent variables are included, their relations and effects assessed, and the whole structure of relations subjected to simultaneous test. The test or tests are based on the congruence of the hypothesized model with the obtained data. It is not surprising that researchers experience logical, technical, and theoretical failures. Indeed, it is surprising that models can be and are successfully tested given the complexity and even delicacy of the undertaking.

There seems to be no reasonable alternative, however. Science requires the formulation of theories *and* their empirical testing. Behavioral science and research deal with psychological and sociological explanations of complex human and social phenomena. They therefore require both complex theories in which sets of observed and latent variables are related to each other *and* complex methods of conceptualizing and analyzing the data that are produced by controlled observation and measurement of the sets of variables. To date, multivariate analysis and analysis of covariance structures seem to be the most promising ways to accomplish the goals of behavioral science. That they will pose many difficult, even intractable, methodological problems is obvious. That they will yield both theoretical and practical advances and benefits has already been demonstrated in this chapter.

Despite the difficulties and reservations mentioned above, there can be little doubt that analysis of covariance structures and the LISREL system that implements it are outstanding and highly valuable and useful contributions to scientific behavioral research. We conclude this chapter—and the book—by saying that their use and influence will be strong and salutary influences on the development of psychological and sociological theory and its testing and on the material advance of scientific behavioral research in general.[30]

---

[29] See F. Kerlinger, *Liberalism and Conservatism: The Nature and Structure of Social Attitudes*. Hillsdale, N.J.: Erlbaum, 1984, chap. 5.

[30] I wish to thank Prof. A. Mittman, University of Oregon, and Prof. G. Mellenbergh, University of Amsterdam, for their critical reading of this chapter.

Study Suggestions

1. There are as yet no readily accessible discussions of analysis of covariance structures in the literature. Perhaps there never will be. The subject presupposes knowledge of matrix algebra, factor analysis, and multiple regression analysis. For some of Jöreskog's papers—almost all of which are difficult—see the book *Advances* cited in footnote 1. To use the LISREL program, the most recent Jöreskog and Sörbom manual, also cited in footnote 1, is recommended. It is much easier to understand and use than earlier manuals. Perhaps the best and clearest exposition of the system is Bentler's *Annual Review* article (see footnote 8). Another helpful exposition is: W. Saris, "Linear Structural Relationships," *Quality and Quantity,* 14 (1980), 205–224. Saris and Stronkhorst have written a useful introductory text: W. Saris & L. Stronkhorst, *Causal Modelling in Nonexperimental Research*. Amsterdam: Sociometric Research Foundation, 1984. Jöreskog's presidential address to the Psychometric Society is also excellent—but not easy: K. Jöreskog, "Structural Analysis of Covariance and Correlation Matrices," *Psychometrika,* 43 (1978), 443–447. Researchers who have used analysis of covariance structures and LISREL will profit from Cliff's skeptical and cautionary article: N. Cliff, "Some Cautions Concerning the Application of Causal Modeling Methods," *Multivariate Behavioral Research,* 18 (1983), 115–126. After saying that analysis of covariance structures is perhaps the most important and influential statistical revolution of the social sciences, Cliff also says,

> Initially, these methods seemed to be a great boon to social science research, but there is some danger that they may instead become a disaster, a disaster because they seem to encourage one to suspend his normal critical faculties. Somehow the use of one of these computer procedures lends an air of unchallengeable sanctity to conclusions that would otherwise be subjected to the most intense scrutiny.

I agree with Cliff and will return to the danger he mentions in Appendix B on the computer and its use by behavioral researchers.

2. Here are five research studies that have profitably used analysis of covariance structures.

GEISELMAN, R., WOODWARD, J., and BEATTY, J. "Individual Differences in Verbal Memory Performance: A Test of Alternative Information Processing Models." *Journal of Experimental Psychology: General*, 111 (1982), 109–134. A sophisticated cognitive psychological study of short-term and long-term memory. Found that memory recall was a dualistic process.

JUDD, C., and MILBURN, M. "The Structure of Attitude Systems in the General Public: Comparisons of a Structural Equation Model." *American Sociological Review,* 45 (1980), 627–643. Complex study that showed that Converse's statements about the general public not having attitude structure is incorrect. Based on national survey data collected in 1972, 1974, and 1976 by the Survey Research Center of the University of Michigan.

HILL, P., and McGAW, B. "Testing the Simplex Assumption Underlying Bloom's Taxonomy." *American Educational Research Journal,* 18 (1981), 93–101. The authors competently tested a hierarchical model of Bloom's well-known classification of cognitive behaviors.

KERLINGER, F. "Analysis of Covariance Structures Tests of a Criterial Referents Theory of Attitudes." *Multivariate Behavioral Research,* 15 (1980), 403–422. The larger report of which the chapter example was one part.

WOLFLE, L., and ROBERTSHAW, D. "Effects of College Attendance on Locus of Control." *Journal of Personality and Social Psychology,* 43 (1982), 802–810. Interesting and well-done study of data from a national longitudinal study of the high school class of 1972.

APPENDICES

Appendix A

Historical and Methodological Research

THE LIMITS of this book forbid adequate discussion of two important and very different kinds of research: *historical research* and what will be called *methodological research*. This appendix will acquaint the reader with the nature of historical and methodological research and point out the part they play in social scientific and educational research.

HISTORICAL RESEARCH[1]

Historical research is the critical investigation of events, developments, and experiences of the past, the careful weighing of evidence of the validity of sources of information on the past, and the interpretation of the weighed evidence. The historical investigator, like other investigators, then, collects data, evaluates the data for validity, and interprets the data. Actually, the historical method, or *historiography,* differs from other scholarly activity only in its subject matter, the past, and the peculiarly difficult interpretive task imposed by the elusive nature of the subject matter.

Historical research is important in behavioral research. The roots of behavioral disciplines have to be understood if behavioral scientists are to be able to put their theories and research in appropriate contexts. This is perhaps more so in disciplines like sociology, economics, and political science than it is in psychology. Nevertheless, even the psychologist must know psychology's origins, since theories develop almost always in a context of earlier theories and research. Reinforcement theory, for example, developed from earlier work by Pavlov, Thorndike, and others, and psychologists of today must use this earlier work as a cognitive stratum, so to speak, from which they do their work.

[1] I wish to thank Professor David Madsen for expert help and guidance with the historiographical literature and in pointing out trends in historiography.

Education is a particularly good example of the virtue of historical research. The virtue of historical research in the behavioral sciences probably springs mainly from the need to do present work with earlier work as a cognitive context. In education, however, historical research per se has great value, because it is necessary to know and understand educational accomplishments and trends of the past in order to gain perspective on present and future directions. To understand contemporary movements like the ungraded classroom, the so-called British system, and community control, for example, one should understand progressivism and its roots in Froebel, Rousseau, Dewey, and even Freud. That one has to search for historical roots is nicely shown by the current emphasis on "hard-core" learning, which is understood to be a very old point of view. Psychology and education nicely come together here: hard-core learning is in part the old razor-strop theory of the mind revivified and dressed up in modern clothes. The "British system" is seen to be a version of what Dewey and Parker preached and practiced early in the century.

If we look at one or two canons of historiography, we may be able to understand why historiographical discipline is valuable in and of itself and also valuable for the social scientist. One of the basic rules of research in history is: Always use primary sources. A *primary source* is the original repository of an historical datum, like an original record kept of an important occasion, an eyewitness description of an event, a photograph, minutes of organization meetings, and so on. A *secondary source* is an account or record of an historical event or circumstance one or more steps removed from an original repository. Instead of the minutes of an organization meeting, for example, one uses a newspaper account of the meeting. Instead of studying and citing the original report of a research, one studies and cites someone else's account and digest of it.

To use secondary sources when primary sources are available is a major historiographical error. And with good reason. Materials and data, especially those about human beings and their activities, are changed and often distorted in transmission. Reputable historians never completely trust secondary sources, though they of course study them and weigh them for their validity. (Often they are forced to use them for lack of primary sources.) The dangers of distortion and consequent erroneous interpretation are too great.

The precept of the primary source is a good one for behavioral investigators. While the sheer mass of published studies is so great that one has to depend upon secondary sources, such as competent digests and abstracts, one should always attempt to study primary sources, especially of important studies in one's own field. This suggestion applies to both the scientist and the practitioner. If the precept of the primary source were taken more seriously, fewer erroneous generalizations would gain currency.

Two other canons of historiography are expressed by the terms *external criticism* and *internal criticism*. The historian critically examines the sources of data for their genuineness, or more accurately, for their validity. Is the document or source genuine? Did X really write this paper? If X wrote the paper, was he a competent and truthful witness? This is *external criticism*. *Internal criticism* is preoccupied with the *content* of the source or document and its meaning. Are the statements made accurate representations of the historical facts? A document may survive external criticism and still be suspect as evidence. There may be no doubt of the "true" author or recorder of events—and he may be competent. Wittingly or unwittingly, however, he may have distorted the truth. Internal criticism, in brief, seeks the "true" meaning and value of the content of sources of data.

Social scientific and educational investigators obviously use both external and internal criticism, but particularly internal criticism. If an author of a research report comes to an erroneous conclusion because of inadequate statistical analysis or interpretation, for example, it is clearly the task of other scientists to correct the error. There is a well-known study on transfer of training whose authors seemed to have erred in the interpretation of their data. The study was well done. Its conception and execution were imaginative and competent. But the conclusions and the interpretation of the data are questionable, because of inadequate statistical analysis and inadequate interpretation of the statistical analysis that was done. Any investigator can make, and does make, such errors. This is not the point. The point is that the study has been reproduced in anthologies and cited in texts as evidence of the effect of knowledge of principles on the transfer of learning. Perhaps the conclusion *is* correct. But this study did not yield adequate evidence of its correctness. Careful internal criticism of research studies is clearly needed.

The contributions to knowledge of the educational historian have been many and important. The history of education and historical research in education have declined, in part because of the impact of scientific research.[2] Early in the century, historical and related inquiry occupied a large part of educational attention. After the investigations of men like Thorndike, Terman, and others, however, historical inquiry was subordinated to scientific research. Despite a contemporary recrudescence of historical inquiry among historians in schools of education, the history of education never recovered. This is most unfortunate. Without good history and good historians, a discipline can lose perspective, not to mention the serious consequences on the intellectual development of students of education of this neglect, even derogation, in education of the philosophy and history of education. Rigorous historiography is needed, just as good scientific research is needed.

The following excerpt from a report of a committee of historians on historiography summarizes the importance of historiography to the social sciences:

> Historiography has a necessary relevance to all the social sciences, to the humanities, and to the formulation of public and private policies, because (1) all the data used in the social sciences, in the humanities, and in the formulation of public and private policies are drawn from records of, experience in, or writing about the past; because (2) all policies respecting human affairs, public or private, and all generalizations of a nonstatistical character in the social sciences and in the humanities involve interpretations of or assumptions about the past; and because (3) all workers in the social sciences and in the humanities are personalities of given times, places, and experience whose thinking is consequently in some measure conditioned and determined by the historical circumstances of their lives and experiences.[3]

METHODOLOGICAL RESEARCH

Methodological research is controlled investigation of the theoretical and applied aspects of measurement, mathematics and statistics, and ways of obtaining and analyzing data. Without methodological research, modern behavioral research would still be in the research dark ages. Like historical research, it is an extremely important part of the body scientific. This strong statement is made to counteract the somewhat negative sentiments that many professionals in psychology, sociology, and education seem to hold about methodological research.

Methodology is called "mere" methodology. The methodologist is called a "mere" methodologist. This is a curious state of affairs. Some of the most competent, imaginative, and creative men in modern psychology, sociology, and education have been and are methodologists. Indeed, it is almost impossible to do outstanding research, though one can do acceptable research, without being something of a methodologist. It is needless to pursue the prejudice further. My point is that methodological research is a vital and absolutely indispensable part of behavioral research. Let us look at what the methodological researcher does and see why these statements have been made.

Perhaps the largest and most rigorous areas of psychological and educational methodological research are measurement and statistical analysis. The methodologist—and it should be emphasized that good behavioral researchers have to be, to some extent, measurement methodologists—is preoccupied with theoretical and practical problems of identifying and measuring psychological variables. These problems have a number of aspects. Reliability and validity, in and of themselves, are large areas of preoccupation and inves-

---

[2]M. Borrowman, "History of Education." In C. Harris, ed., *Encyclopedia of Educational Research,* 3d ed. New York: Macmillan, 1960, pp. 661–668. (See especially pp. 663–664.)

[3]Social Science Research Council, *Theory and Practice in Historical Study: A Report of the Committee on Historiography.* New York: Social Science Research Council, 1946, pp. 134–135.

tigation. Then there are the theoretical and practical problems of the construction of measuring instruments: scaling, item writing, item analysis, and so on. A methodologist can easily spend a lifetime on any one of these aspects of measurement.

Statisticians long ago turned their talents to solving the problem of the objective evaluation of research data. Their contributions were considered at length earlier and need not be repeated here. It is significant to add, however, that some of the most outstanding methodological contributions of statistics have come from applied researchers—Fisher and Thurstone, to name only two.

The application of mathematics to social scientific research is well developed. Applications of set theory and probability theory were discussed early in this book. Later in the book we saw how important matrix theory and algebra are, especially in multivariate analysis.[4] Analysis of covariance structures and log-linear models and analysis are two highly important examples of the application of advanced mathematical and statistical ideas to the solution of complex multivariate problems. The prospects of further applications of modern mathematics and logic are most promising—and exciting.

The third large area of methodological research, investigations of methods of data collection and analysis, has thrived for many years. This area includes interviews and the construction of interview schedules, content analysis, methods of sampling, systematic observational techniques, and other methods. An example or two may help the student appreciate the significance of such work.

Interviews can yield biased data. The study of the causes and prevention of biases in the schedule and in the interview situation, if successful, can help investigators increase the validity of their data. Which is the more reliable of two methods of direct observation of behavior: the observation and recording of small clearly defined acts of individuals or of larger molar units of behavior? What method of analysis of the content of written documents or of interview material yields the most reliable and valid results? Such questions and many others are being successfully answered by methodologists.

REFERENCES

Some readers may wish to pursue historical and methodological inquiry further. Readers should also know that the point of view of this appendix is more or less a traditional one. Some critics would therefore take issue with it. One of the best single sources on historiography is the Social Science Research Council monograph cited in footnote 3. Here are four books, three of which express a wide variety of views on history and historiography.

Except for textbooks (like this one), which usually lack critical focus and depth, books on the general topic of methodology—that is, books that examine methodology itself—seem not to have been published.[5] The best single source for original contributions to the methodology of behavioral research is probably the *Psychological Bulletin*. There has hardly been a recent development in statistics, methods of observation, and general analytic approaches that has not appeared in the *Bulletin*.

BEST, J., ed. *Historical Inquiry in Education: A Research Agenda.* Washington, D.C.: American Educational Research Association, 1983. Varied views on the history of education in a book published by the American Educational Research Association.

DOLLAR, C., and JENSEN, R. *Historian's Guide to Statistics.* New York: Holt, Rinehart and Winston, 1971. Statistics text written specifically for historians. In addition to statistics

---

[4] For an excellent book on the mathematical bases of multivariate analysis, see: P. Green, *Mathematical Tools for Applied Multivariate Analysis.* New York: Academic Press, 1976.

[5] This statement is true only when methodology is conceived technically, that is, methods of observation, data collection, sampling, statistical analysis, and so on. Broader aspects of methodology, such as objectivity, operationism, inference, the nature of "reality," and so on, have of course been considered by philosophers of science. American behavioral researchers tend to be preoccupied with the technical aspects of methodology. European behavioral researchers, however, tend to be more concerned about philosophical issues.

itself, has valuable discussions of information retrieval, content analysis, computer use, and available archives of data in the United States.

HIGHAM, J., and CONKIN, P., eds. *New Directions in American Intellectual History*. Baltimore: Johns Hopkins University Press, 1979. Particularly good on modern developments in history.

KAMMEN, M., ed. *The Past Before Us: Contemporary Historical Writing in the United States*. Ithaca: Cornell University Press, 1980. Another reference on newer trends in historical writing.

Appendix B

The Computer and Behavioral Research[1]

THE COMPUTER has become an integral and highly important part of both the conception and the methodology of research in the behavioral disciplines. Its central role makes it imperative that we examine, if too briefly and superficially, the major characteristics of the modern high-speed computer. We will also explore the influence of computers, computer programs, and computer uses on behavioral research and research findings and on the work of behavioral researchers.

Another purpose of this appendix is practical: to guide the reader in computer analysis of research data. In doing so, we will consider the use of the large university computer and computer installation and the use of the microcomputer. Computer analysis has been done mostly on the large computer using so-called package programs like BMDP, SAS, SPSS, and the like. The remarkable technical development of microcomputers—often called personal computers—and their increased power and decreasing cost, however, are radically changing analysis and analytic practices. Within five years or so, students of behavioral research will either own microcomputers or have them readily available on university campuses. The future of much, perhaps most, behavioral data analysis lies with the microcomputer. Part of the discussion of this appendix, therefore, will be on microcomputers and their uses.

[1] I am deeply indebted to the following individuals of the computing centers of New York University, the University of Amsterdam, and the University of Oregon for their help with computer programs and problems: M. Goldstein, H. Walowitz, E. Kolchin, E. Friedman, R. Malchie, N. Smith, B. Holland, C. van de Wijgaart, L. Störm, and R. Haller. I am in large debt to my former colleague, Prof. N. Jaspen, who long ago needled my professional conscience until I overcame a curious resistance to learning programming. I want also to express my thanks to Prof. R. Rankin and to G. Rankin and S. Goff for expert and generous help and guidance in the complex and mysterious world of the microcomputer, and for critical reading of this appendix. If the appendix is deficient, of course, it is their fault and not mine.

THE NATURE OF THE COMPUTER

The high-speed electronic digital computer has profoundly influenced behavioral research. Research projects that would not have been attempted years ago because of the sheer bulk of necessary calculations to manipulate and analyze the data of the projects are now readily approached because the computer does the tedious work of complex analyses accurately, efficiently, and rapidly. The intent of this appendix is to indicate the importance, even indispensability, of computers in behavioral research, and to stimulate students to learn enough of the computer and computer techniques to understand both the large computer and the microcomputer.

Important Computer Characteristics

The computer is an elaborate complex of word- and number-processing electronic hardware whose chief characteristics are tremendous speed, large memory, generality or universality, easy ability to do thousands of repetitive operations of all kinds with a high degree of accuracy, reliability, flexibility, and what will be called "ductility."

High Speed

Everyone has heard that computers are fast. Few people can really grasp how fast they are. They are faster than almost anything we work with. In 1972 Kemeny said that a computer is a million times faster than a human being.[2] Here is an example. Appendix C of this book reports one sample of 4,000 random numbers between 1 and 100. I had the computer generate four such samples of 4,000 numbers each, calculate the means, standard deviations, and correlations of the 40 "variables" in each of the samples of random numbers like those of Appendix C. That is, Appendix C reports only the first of four samples for each of which the random numbers were generated, and 40 means, 40 standard deviations, and 780 correlation coefficients calculated. This is 16,000 random numbers, 160 means, 160 standard deviations, and 3,120 correlation coefficients. In addition, the means of the four sets of means were rank ordered from high to low. The recorded time for all the computations was 11.1 seconds![3]

Curious and skeptical readers may wonder why such high speeds are desirable. After all, what practical difference does it make if a computer takes seconds, minutes, or even hours to do a given problem? The answer is complex and we here give only two reasons, the two that are probably the most important for behavioral researchers. Psychologists, sociologists, and other behavioral researchers are more and more using multivariate procedures to analyze their data and even to help conceptualize the research problems they study. Factor analysis and multiple regression analysis have become common, and other multivariate methods like discriminant analysis, multivariate analysis of variance, analysis of covariance structures, and log-linear models are used increasingly. Such methods are virtually impossible to use without the high-speed computer because they require complex analysis requiring thousands of computations. Without very high computer speeds the computations become awkward and cumbersome, if not impossible.

A second reason for high speed is that many computer users now work in time-sharing systems. *Time-sharing* is just what the expression says: many users work at terminals and

---

[2] J. Kemeny, *Man and the Computer*. New York: Scribner's, 1972, p. 14.

[3] Such remarkably fast computing times are obtained with larger computers. The typical microcomputer, if its memory is sufficient to accommodate large problems, takes much longer. For example, I had a well-known microcomputer generate 15 sets of 100 random digits 1 through 9, "bias" some of the digits, and then calculate means, standard deviations, sums of squares, and correlations among the 15 "variables." The calculations took well over an hour. Don't misjudge microcomputer speed, however. The microcomputer I used was not very fast. Yet even the one-hour time is fast compared to the computing time of earlier computers. For discussions of computer speed and its desirability, see Kemeny, *op. cit.*, pp. 14ff.; C. Evans, *The Micro Millenium*. New York: Washington Square Press, 1979, pp. 54–57.

share the available time. (A terminal is a special keyboard with a screen, like a TV screen, both connected to a large computer either directly or indirectly by means of what is called a modem, which makes it possible to communicate with the computer over the telephone.) To make it possible for as many as a hundred users to use the same computer more or less at the same time, the computer must be very fast.

Let's compare time-sharing with what is called a batch system, which used to be the major way researchers used the computer. This comparison may clarify the power of time-sharing, a "direct" interactive relationship with the computer, and the need for high speed. In the batch system, computer users type (punch) their programs and data on cards and submit decks of such cards to a clerk who puts the cards into a card reader. After the cards are read, the program and data are stored on tape or disk, and the job is put on a waiting list to be processed by the central processor. One job after another is processed by the central computer in a serial fashion: it is, therefore, a serial system. No matter how fast or how slow the computer is, the system works the same way: one job after another.

A time-sharing system, on the other hand, handles many jobs "simultaneously" and rapidly. Generally speaking, each job is allocated a certain number of computer instructions for a given time unit. When a job's turn comes up, the computer performs the number of operations that the job is allocated, stores the results, and goes on to the next job. A job may not use its allocated time; in this case the time can be given to the next job. For example, suppose I type in at my terminal the commands and data for my job, and the computer accepts the job (after checking the legitimacy of my identification and time allocation) and processes, say, n operations of my job. Now suppose you type in another job at your terminal. The system starts processing your job after it has done the n operations of my job. It then processes, say, m operations of your job. It may then go on to another job or return to my job. Suppose it returns to my job, finishes it, and stores it in a "waiting" memory (waiting to be printed). Then it goes on to another job similarly.

Let us say that your job and my job are finished and in the "waiting" memory waiting their turns to be printed—or maybe aborted (if something was wrong with them). The computer of course goes on to other jobs and similarly stores the results in memory. And so it goes for as many as 100 jobs! For such a system to be successful, the computer must be very, very fast and must be programmed efficiently. It is possible in a well-designed time-sharing system for the computer to process 100 jobs in ten seconds! This description is of course oversimplified; it serves, however, to show how it works.[4] It should also be obvious that the computer has to be fast, efficient, and tireless.

Large Memory

A second basic characteristic of the modern computer is large memory. The processing of verbal or numerical data requires large amounts of storage. A computer can work without large memory, but it would be slow, inefficient, and perhaps inaccurate. When computers were first made, computing was done piecemeal, so to speak. One phase of a job was completed, and the results of this phase were fed into the computer (with cards or tape) for further computing. These results might then be fed in for further computing. And so on.

It is extremely difficult to know clearly who is responsible for the basic conception of the modern computer as a self-contained, self-regulating, and general purpose machine. Two mathematical geniuses of the century, Alan Turing and John von Neumann, how-

---

[4]Most large computer systems use another computer to "administer" and monitor the job process. For a lively description and the rationale of the development of an actual time-sharing system at Dartmouth College by one of its pioneers, see Kemeny, *op. cit.,* chap. 3. Note that you can enter an analytic job in, say, half an hour and, if you have made no errors, have the results printed on your own printer—assuming you have a printer and it has been suitably set up with your terminal—in a few minutes! So can I. If either of us has made one or more errors, the system will abort the work and tell us what and where the errors are! Anyone who has spent years using the batch system and first successfully uses the terminal learns the difference—dramatically. An authoritative account of the original development of time-sharing at MIT is given by M. Denicoff, "Sophisticated Software: The Road to Science and Utopia," in M. Dertouzos and J. Moses, eds., *The Computer Age: A Twenty-Year View*. Cambridge, Mass. MIT Press, 1979, pp. 370ff.

ever, saw that the piecemeal system described above was inadequate and formulated and helped implement the principle of the computer being able to do within itself all the procedures and processes necessary for computing.[5] This means that when the computer has finished, say, one phase of a job, it stores the results and goes on to the next computing phase. When it needs the stored results for further computations, it retrieves them from memory. Thus was the modern idea of computer programs born! Turing and von Neumann proposed that a set of instructions to the computer be stored in its memory so that it can always "know" what to do. The program stored in the internal memory of the computer, in other words, should be the computer director. Then the machine need not pause for further instructions. The end result is a faster, more efficient, and virtually error-free device. The idea, of course, is that computers have to be completely self-regulating: give the complete instructions for any procedure to the computer so that they are stored internally, and so write them that the computer can continue to compute to the end without interruption. If these instructions require "data" to operate on, store these data, too, in the internal memory, or at least make the data easily available to the computer. Obviously, computers need capacious memories.

Universality

A third basic characteristic of modern computers is *universality*. This means that computers are general purpose machines: they can be programmed to solve any problem that is solvable. The first computers were built for specific purposes, for example, to calculate the trajectories of artillery shells or to solve sets of equation. Such computers are limited. When the early computers were being developed, it was realized (by von Neumann primarily) that computers should be universal Turing machines. Turing had shown that a machine that could do a few basic operations could, in principle, do any calculations.[6] What this boils down to is this: modern computers can in principle be instructed ("programmed") to do all kinds of operations and calculations. They are, in short, "general" or "universal" machines.

Flexibility

Flexibility is really a characteristic of the use of the computer. What is meant is that there are several ways to write a program to accomplish a given end. Virtually identical results can be achieved with different instructions. That is, the way computers work permits flexibility of programming. This means that you and I can write different programs to calculate analysis of variance, say, and both our programs will yield the same results (assuming, of course, that both programs are "correct," a very large assumption indeed).

Ductility

The last important characteristic of the computer to be discussed here is what I will call *ductility*, which, loosely defined, means tractability or obedience. A computer will do

---

[5] For von Neumann's thinking and work, see the fine book of Goldstine: H. Goldstine, *The Computer: From Pascal to von Neumann*. Princeton: Princeton University Press, 1972. Hodges has written an exhaustive biography of Turing with detailed accounts of his thinking on the computer and his influence on von Neumann (see footnote 6, below). Weizenbaum's explanation of Turing's ideas is detailed and clear (again, see footnote 6).

[6] This is difficult to explain. Weizenbaum explains it in detail with examples: J. Weizenbaum, *Computer Power and Human Reason: From Judgment to Calculation*. San Francisco: Freeman, 1976, pp. 51ff. Turing was a member of a small group of mathematicians who during World War II succeeded in breaking the secret code the German high command used to transmit orders to field commanders, thus materially helping the British war effort. For a fascinating but sad account of Turing's brilliant thinking, work, and life, see A. Hodges, *Alan Turing: The Enigma*. New York: Simon and Schuster, 1983. von Neumann seems to have gotten his ideas for a modern computer from Turing.

precisely what it is told to do. If a programmer solves a difficult problem brilliantly, the computer will perform "brilliantly." If the programmer programs incorrectly, the machine will faithfully and obediently make the errors the programmer has told it to make—unless the errors are such that programming rules are broken, in which case the job will be stopped and the programmer given an appropriate message. (With trivial kinds of errors, modern computers will continue to compute. Such errors are "venial" sins. The machine only aborts the computations when errors are "mortal" sins.) This is a great strength because it means that computers are highly reliable. The researcher can therefore depend on the machine's "logic" and accuracy—within the finite limitations of the machine.[7]

COMPUTER PROGRAMS AND LANGUAGES

A *computer program* is a set of instructions, in some sort of machine or intermediary language, that tells the machine how to read in and print out data, what operations to perform, and how to perform them to analyze the data.[8] Programs are usually written in one or another program language that uses condensed forms of English commands. Such intermediary languages are needed since machine language, essentially binary, is difficult and error-prone. Researchers and programmers need to be able to write instructions in a language that is readily comprehended by themselves and by others. There are a number of such languages: FORTRAN, BASIC, PASCAL, ALGOL, COBOL, and so on.[9] FORTRAN (*For*mula *Tran*slation) is one of the most used. Some version or other of FORTRAN can be found in most computer installations of the world. Let us look at FORTRAN briefly; later we will discuss BASIC because it is the program language most used by microcomputers.

An important need of researchers is to communicate with computers. It is possible to program a machine "directly" in machine language. This is very difficult, tedious, error-prone, as already indicated. It is much easier to use a verbal computer language like FORTRAN and have the computer "translate" the English program language into machine language. The computer does this at the behest of a program called a *compiler*. In any case, the invention of computer languages like FORTRAN, PASCAL, and BASIC was a major breakthrough. It made the computer available to all researchers provided they knew the "language." FORTRAN, for instance, is an intermediary language that researchers and programmers use to communicate their wishes to computers. The researcher writes his program in FORTRAN (or other language) and communicates the program to the computer by typing it on cards and submitting the cards to be fed to the computer as computer input (a batch job), or by typing it into computer memory at a terminal.

---

[7] Despite this rather strong statement, it must be remembered that computers often produce wrong results for one or more of several reasons. If, for example, the input data are large numbers and sums of squares and cross products are computed, the accuracy limitations of the machine can be exceeded. Most computers have a double-precision feature that doubles accuracy (and is slower). A frequent source of errors is incorrectly typed (punched) input. Just think: one incorrect decimal can throw off the accuracy of a whole set of data. The moral is that all input and output should be checked for accuracy. Programs should have the options for users to print all input data, intermediate results, and output data. Then users should check, say, a random sample of five or ten percent of the input cases and calculate some of the intermediate and final results using another means of computation. *Researchers must constantly guard against machine and human error*.

[8] This definition emphasizes quantitative data and numerical analysis because such data and analysis are most often encountered in behavioral research. Computer programs, however, are by no means limited to numerical analysis. Indeed, we have seen that the modern computer is a universal machine: it can in principle solve any problem that is solvable, numerical and nonnumerical. In earlier chapters we learned that content analysis focuses on the analysis of verbal materials. Modern word processors are computer programs that make it possible to type verbal materials into computer memories, recall and edit the materials, and print them on an external printer.

[9] See the following book for authoritative discussions of the characteristics and the invention and development of computer languages from the beginning of such languages in the early 1950s: R. Wexelblatt, ed., *History of Programming Languages*. New York: Academic Press, 1981.

FORTRAN and BASIC

FORTRAN, among other things, uses several English commands like DO, GO TO, READ, WRITE, CALL, CONTINUE, and IF. These commands mean what they say: they tell the machine to do this, do that, go to this instruction, read that instruction, and write (print) the outcome. The power and flexibility of this seemingly simple language cannot be exaggerated. There is almost no numerical or logical operation that cannot be accomplished with it.[10]

Some computer experts say that the programming languages of the future are "structured" languages. PASCAL is a prominent and much-used structured language. Yet one cannot be sure. Perlis, in his view of the future of computer languages, says, "FORTRAN, glorious and persistent weed that it is, not only survives, but its users become increasingly committed to it, even though theirs is a love-hate relationship."[11] Because of its worldwide use and availability, FORTRAN has become dominant, even though PASCAL is thought to be a more satisfactory language. Perlis points out that even in China, where one might expect independence of Western views and usage, FORTRAN is becoming dominant! PASCAL is perhaps more difficult to learn and to use than FORTRAN and much more difficult than BASIC. One of its great strengths is that it can handle both quantitative and verbal materials. FORTRAN is strong in quantitative analysis but weak in verbal analysis. We now turn to an easy computer language, BASIC, mainly because it is the common language of the microcomputer.[12] It is an effective language, even though not admired by computer specialists.

BASIC was invented by Kemeny and his colleagues at Dartmouth College so that typical college students could learn it easily.[13] Kemeny says that he and his colleagues envisaged millions of people writing their own programs. So they deliberately kept BASIC simple, "easy for the layman to learn and that facilitated communication between man and machine."

The reader who intends to do research is strongly urged to explore the possibility of learning FORTRAN, BASIC, or other widely used computer languages. To use the computer intelligently demands knowledge of programming. Many researchers and most students believe that they can depend entirely on professional programmers, "expert" student assistants, and so-called package programs. Such dependence has pitfalls; indeed, it can be disastrous! Many professional programmers are not familiar enough with the purposes and analytic tools of behavioral research to be able to help solve many analytic problems adequately. And package programs frequently lack desirable and necessary analyses, or they do so much that their output can be confusing, even irrelevant, to the

---

[10] This description omits consideration of the creation and manipulation of "files" and having FORTRAN or other programs already in the computer memory so that the files can be readily used with a few commands. Another omission is the necessity of learning and using a special installation language for editing files. Suppose, for instance, that you have a program you have written in BASIC to do analysis of variance and you want to add, say, one or two formulas to calculate indices of the magnitude of relations. An editing procedure is necessary to do this. This procedure, also a program, is called into action, and you edit your program with its help. A *file* is any program or set of data, each with a name, that is in the computer memory and that you can invoke and use. For information on the creation and editing of files at your installation, consult the appropriate people at the installation.

[11] A. Perlis, "Current Research Frontiers in Computer Science," in Dertouzos and Moses, *op cit.* pp. 422–436 (p. 427).

[12] That BASIC will remain the language of the microcomputer is of course problematical. It is now, but this may change. I doubt it because BASIC is not only easy to learn and use; it is also powerful enough for most computing purposes in the behavioral sciences. And, as Kemeny points out, it is nicely suited to man-machine interaction. Some computer experts deplore its use, but this may be due to specialist admiration for more structured languages. See S. Papert, "Computers and Learning," in Dertouzos and Moses, *op. cit.,* pp. 73–86, for a rather violent attack on BASIC. Papert attributes the use of BASIC to the QWERTY phenomenon, the persistence of the present typewriter keyboard not because it has an adequate rationale but because it is widely used and many people have learned it.

[13] Kemeny, *op. cit.,* chap. 3.

demands of research problems. For example, an analysis of variance program may not include relational indices such as omega-squared or the coefficient of intraclass correlation. And most package programs do not include intermediary statistics in their outputs so that one can calculate such indices. Moreover, it is easy for novices—even initiates—to use an analysis of variance program that has error terms (residual mean squares) that are inappropriate for their problems. While professional programmers are usually highly competent people, many of them do not know the reasons for many statistical procedures, nor would it be economical for them to adapt package programs or to write new programs for such special needs.

One of the most difficult problems associated with computer work, then, is communication between researcher and programmer. It is perhaps unrealistic to expect researchers to be highly expert in programming. But it is even more unrealistic to expect professional programmers to understand the substance and methodology of behavioral science analysis. The best solution of the problem of communication between scientist and programmer is clear: the scientist must learn at least enough about programming to enable him to talk knowledgeably and intelligently to the programmer. The researcher can learn to do this in a matter of months, whereas it would take the programmer years to learn enough about behavioral science and behavior science analysis to communicate at the researcher's level.

THE COMPUTER AND BEHAVIORAL RESEARCH

The computer has revolutionized behavioral research and will continue to have a strong influence in the next decade. This has been made clear, I hope, in earlier chapters. Research problems that could not have been tackled two decades ago are now easily possible. This is especially so of problems that require the complex analysis of many variables and very large amounts of repetitive calculations. The use of factor analysis used to be infrequent, for example. Today, reports of research in which factor analysis has been used either as the principal analysis or as a subsidiary analysis are common. Similarly, multiple regression analysis has become almost as common as analysis of variance. Log-linear analysis, which we examined briefly in Chapter 10 (Addendum), is unthinkable without the computer. It is even highly unlikely that Goodman and others would have developed the theory and the extensive methodology without knowing that its tedious calculations could be done by a computer.

The computer has increased the demands on researchers and on the faculties of institutions who educate and train researchers. Mathematical and statistical ignorance, too much a part of the past, is no longer possible. Faculty and administration of universities will have to recognize the necessity—not the desirability, the necessity—of providing adequate education and training in mathematics, statistics, and computer usage.

Content Analysis, Word Processing, Computer Searches

One or two aspects of the computer's impact other than numerical analysis need to be mentioned if the reader is to comprehend how far-reaching and deep the impact of the computer has been and will continue to be. Perhaps the most important development is the computer's versatility and applicability to research problems that require the analysis of verbal materials.[14] In Chapter 30, for instance, we found that content analysis can be a highly useful approach to the measurement of complex and elusive variables. Conceptual complexity itself is one such variable. With content analysis programs, such as those discussed in Chapter 30 and no doubt increasingly available in the next decade as the rich research possibilities are realized, all kinds of verbal materials can be effectively analyzed: children's stories and textbooks, editorials, projective materials, interview proto-

---

[14]Examples of the increasing use in psychology of content analysis have been mentioned in earlier chapters.

cols, essays, speeches, and so forth. Attitudes, motives, creativity, and historical and philosophical trends are present possibilities, though still not well-developed research preoccupations.[15]

The historian, the language specialist, the psychologist, the sociologist, and the political scientist can now analyze historical materials, literary productions, and political records in a number of ways. Research like McClelland's pursuit of achievement and its determinants in the present and the past can be extended and enhanced by using computer methods of document search and analysis.[16]

The tedious and time-consuming business of literature searches to find references pertinent to a subject has been a scholarly imperative for centuries. It is now possible— indeed, necessary in view of the vast amounts of books and articles published in all fields—to have a computer search the literature and note references that are presumably pertinent to a subject. The service is available in many university libraries for modest fees. One can go the university (or other) library and request that a search be made for references on such-and-such a subject. The librarian will ask for several key words or expressions so that the search can be made practicable. One cannot, for instance, just request searches for studies of intelligence or achievement. One has to narrow requests to pertinent aspects of such broad subjects. Here is an example.

About five years ago, I needed a computer search for reference works on attitudes so that I could update my knowledge of theory and research in the field. To ask for a search of "attitude," however, would be disastrous: the computer would undoubtedly find thousands of references, most of them irrelevant. I was given a form that asked for key words. I supplied such terms as "structure," "attitude structure," "bipolarity," and "attitude bipolarity." The computer searched the literature that had been "banked" in computer memory—not all journals, of course, are banked—and printed out a list of books and articles that had the key words in the titles. Even with the keyword limitation, the list was large. I was asked whether I wanted summaries of any of the articles. I studied the list, eliminated most of the references, and requested summaries of a few articles. Later I requested full copies of five or six articles. The computer saved me weeks of library work, most of it unfruitful. And note: the requests were made in Amsterdam, but the computer search itself was done in California![17]

The Computer Imperative

The possibilities of computer use and application are fascinating—and seemingly endless. Scholars and researchers in all fields can be enormously helped by this general purpose information-transforming machine with its incredible speed, large memory, generality, great flexibility, and obliging ductility. It is obvious that the many uses and applications of the computer will be the source of endless argument about the computer's great benefits *and* its deleterious effects. For scholars and researchers, however, it goes much further than this: Scholars in almost all disciplines have no choice: they *must* master, use, and *understand* the computer. Indeed, it can be said that scholars and researchers will be obsolescent, even obsolete, if they do not understand and use the computer in their work.

Some will say that this is an extreme view. I don't think it is. Much of the avoidance by scholars of the computer is due to lack of understanding and a curious fear that the

[15] I think that within four or five years some word-processor programs for microcomputers may include sophisticated content analysis possibilities. The best microcomputers will have sufficient memories and speed to handle content analysis. The real challenge will be researcher imagination and ingenuity.

[16] D. McClelland, *The Achieving Society*. Princeton, N. J.: Van Nostrand, 1961, especially chap. 4. In a study of drinking, McClelland used the General Inquirer computer-based system mentioned in Chapter 30 to study folk-tale themes associated with drinking: D. McClelland et al., "A Cross-Cultural Study of Folk Content and Drinking," *Sociometry,* 29 (1966), 308–333.

[17] I am grateful to my former colleague, Dr. Harrie Vorst, for his expert help with the computer search, and to the Faculty of the Social Sciences of the University of Amsterdam for making the search possible.

computer will "take over" and somehow hurt scholars and scholarly work. It is no doubt true that misuse of computers can hurt scholars and their work. But most of the beliefs about computers and computer destruction of human values is nonsense. The computer can only get out of hand through ignorance, avoidance, and misuse. *We* are the masters. *We* use the computer. And we must master and use it not because it is fashionable to do so but because modern communication and research demand that we do so. If scholars refuse to work with computers for whatever reason, then they abandon the important policy determinations that shape the future and the future use of the powerful technology that is transforming scholarly work and research. To leave such determinations in the hands of computer specialists and technicians and academic administrators is to abandon a large part of the scholarly and research enterprise.

PACKAGE PROGRAMS: FAITH AND SKEPTICISM

Package programs are integrated and coordinated sets of statistical (and other) programs that have been prepared so that researchers who have minimal computer and programming knowledge can organize and analyze research data with comparative ease. A large proportion of the computer jobs of university computing centers are done with such packages. And their authority seems to be generally accepted and unquestioned. (I have seen research reports that have even cited a computer package program as an authority, presumably, on multiple regression.) They are therefore important. Unfortunately, there seem to have been few intensive and critical reviews and systematic tests of the programs of these packages. Most users seem to accept their worth on faith. The main criteria for use seem to be ready availability and ease of use. I emphasize that package programs must be used with great care and that any particular program be checked for accuracy and adequate documentation. An important and seemingly obvious question to ask is: Does this program do what I want and need it to do?[18] Yet it is highly likely that this question is rarely asked and virtually never answered!

If one is skeptical of the virtues of large and unmonitored sets of programs, what can one offer instead? The answer is not simple, and it is probably unpalatable to many or most computer users. Let us first be clear on the sources of unease with package programs. The principal and underlying danger is that we slide too easily into letting the programs do our real work for us, and more important for the future of scientific behavioral research, we reinforce the tendency of ourselves and our students to escape the necessity of knowing as clearly as possible what we are doing. This means, as I tried to point out earlier, that we have to learn the rationale and the methods of calculating the statistical procedures and tests we use. We have to know how to interpret the results of statistical manipulations and tests. And we have to be constantly aware that a complex computer package can in no way make up for inadequate data due to faulty methods of observation, poor measurement, inadequate research design, and lack of independence of observations and measures. Worse, it may conceal these fundamental weaknesses.

When we have run a factor analysis program, we have to know enough factor analytic theory so that we can intelligently instruct the program what kind of factor analysis to do, how many factors to rotate, what the method of factor rotation should be. We should also know what factor loadings and factor scores are, and we should be able to judge the "success" of factor solutions, as well as how to interpret the results. To use a factor

---

[18] In the only published account I have seen of a comparative assessment of the factor analysis programs of the three leading packages, SPSS, BMDP, and SAS, MacCallum found SAS the most satisfactory, BMDP the next most satisfactory, and SPSS the least satisfactory. Very significantly, MacCallum found that the programs were so constructed that the user can leave many decisions to the computer, a situation he rightly deplored. R. MacCallum, "A Comparison of Factor Analysis Programs in SPSS, BMDP, and SAS," *Psychometrika*, 48 (1983), 223–231. The journal editor added a note that this review was the first of a new type of paper to be published by the journal: evaluative descriptions of widely distributed computer programs. This is a commendable policy.

analysis program and to let the program assume control of what happens and then to try to extract meaning from the results is hardly appealing. This does not necessarily mean that we are technical masters of the many ramifications of factor analysis, but it does mean that we have a fair grasp of the technical principles behind the various forms of statistical analysis, the mathematics of the general linear model, and, most important, that we are committed to the principle that we ourselves analyze research data and draw conclusions from the results. We do not put our whole dependence on computer experts, on graduate student assistants, and on computer package programs. This is based on the principle that analysis is part of the research problem and the research design and plan to obtain answers to the problem. It is not something farmed out to technicians and assistants and the computer itself.

This position is evidently at considerable variance with much actual practice. It is thus controversial. MacCallum, in the review of package programs cited above, was forced to conclude that the factor analysis program of one of the packages he studied could not be recommended to users. He emphasized that the programs of the computer packages he reviewed were so constructed that the user can leave many important choices of methods to the program.[19] His point is well-taken.

Etzioni has pointed out the possible deleterious effects of microcomputers on scientific practice.[20] He deplored the increasing trend to do scientific work "by what is in effect, a trial-and-error search, rather than a focused effort. Such a development would be a latter-day repeat performance of the impact of the introduction of prepackaged computer programs on some branches of the social sciences." He points out that finding new variables to study group differences requires considerable intellectual, not mechanical, effort—less use of prepackaged programs and more of scientific creativity. What he means, I think, is that the ready availability and ease of use of microcomputers makes it very easy for the researcher to plunge into analysis without having thoroughly studied problems and their implications and ramifications. Finally, Etzioni stresses the need for training graduate students to recognize the danger of letting the computer set the direction of their work and the need for reflection and thought. To this excellent advice I would add the need for behavioral science and education faculties to recognize the danger and, even more important, the need for adequate study and learning of both faculty and graduate students of the research methodology necessary to do adequate scientific behavioral research.

A HORTATORY CONCLUSION

Sermons are bores. More important, they probably have little effect except to produce yawns and exasperation. In providing students of research with recommendations on how best to use the computer, one is certainly inclined to deliver a sermon because the fascination and power of these remarkable machines have a seductive influence that is extremely hard to resist and that can lead to marked lowering of scientific criteria and standards. This is part of the power that Weizenbaum talked about, especially when he described hackers and hacking. It is what Etzioni talked about when he deplored the danger of mindless use of computers.

Suppose one agrees that there is a danger to science, scientists, and research; what do students do both to use the computer and to avoid the dangers inherent in its use? How can we avoid the danger Etzioni stressed of losing the essential core of science and research through trial-and-error use of the computer rather than the use of focused intellectual effort on research problems? I risk the boredom of sermonizing by suggesting two or three things one can do.

---

[19] MacCallum (*ibid.*, p. 230) is referring to the defaults built into large computer programs. So when users do not really know much about, say, factor analysis or multiple regression, they can let the program "decide" how to analyze the data—by default.

[20] A. Etzioni, "Effects of Small Computers on Scientists," *Science,* 189 (1975), editorial.

One and most important, remember that the basic purpose of behavioral science and research is psychological and sociological theory, explanation of human behavior. Anything that interferes with the pursuit of theory is a threat to science. I won't belabor how the computer can be such a threat since I've already done so earlier.

Two, behavioral researchers should learn at least one computer language, perhaps FORTRAN because it is used everywhere and is always available (maybe not a good argument!), or BASIC because it is easily learned (again, maybe not a good argument!), it is quite adequate for statistical analysis, and it is, at least at present and in the immediate future, the language of the microcomputer. Psychologically, the successful writing of programs is an enormous boost to one's scientific morale, so often beaten down in our highly technical, budget- and market-oriented surroundings. Yet it is not only writing programs; computer language is one of the most important keys to mastering the computer and to solving analytic problems. For example, if one knows FORTRAN or BASIC, one can build quite powerful programs by using the subroutines provided by various sources.[21] One writes input and output statements and calls the subroutines as needed.

Three, total dependence on statisticians and computer specialists is unwise. Behavioral researchers have to have sufficient methodological competence to do most things themselves. Technical people are indispensable, but they usually know little about science and research. The behavioral scientist, in other words, has to know enough of statistical analysis and computer technology to be able to use technicians as resources rather than as preceptors. The microcomputer can help greatly in developing self-sufficiency and competence in analysis—if we are constantly alert to the seductiveness of any powerful mechanical tool. It's so easy to lose oneself in hacking! And so hard to hew to research problems, to understand the difficult demands of measurement, and to master the intricacies of statistical analysis!

Computers, then, are extremely useful, obedient, and reliable servants, but one must always remember that their facile output can never substitute for competent and imaginative theoretical, research design, and analytic thinking. Despite the dangers, however, the reader is urged to explore and learn to use this enormously fascinating and powerful analytic tool. One thing is certain: researchers who learn a little FORTRAN or BASIC and who put two or three programs through a machine complex successfully will never again be the same. They have participated in one of the most interesting and exciting adventures they will ever experience. The main problem will then be to maintain the balance and discretion to keep the machine where it belongs: in the background and not the foreground of research activity.

ADDENDUM

Users of computers, large and small, should know something of their absorbing history and evolution. The following references are suggested for their interest and their quality.

BRADSHAW, G., LANGLEY, P., and SIMON, H. "Studying Scientific Discovery by Computer Simulation," *Science*, 222 (1983), 971–975. An account of a remarkable achievement: the successful simulation of scientific discovery itself.

BRANSCOMB, L. "Information: The Ultimate Frontier," *Science*, 203 (1979), 143–147. Interesting and disturbing futuristic essay on the influence of the computer: no more letter post, printing with jet inks (already with us), and so on.

DAVIS, R. "Evolution of Computers and Computing," *Science*, 195 (1977), 1096–1102. Very good essay on the history of computers and computing.

[21] For example, D. McCracken, *A Guide to Fortran IV Programming*, 2d ed. New York: Wiley, 1972. In this excellent guide, McCracken provides several valuable FORTRAN routines. Ruckdeschel has published BASIC subroutines that can be useful in building analysis programs: F. Ruckdeschel, *BASIC Scientific Subroutines*. Peterborough, N.H.: Byte/McGraw-Hill, 1981. See, also, J. Kemeny and T. Kurtz, *BASIC Programming*, 3d ed. New York: Wiley, 1980.

DERTOUZOS, M., and MOSES, J., eds. *The Computer Age: A Twenty-Year View.* Cambridge, Mass.: MIT Press, 1979. An important book. Its authors are contemporary leaders of computer science, mostly from the Massachusetts Institute of Technology (MIT). Is especially valuable because of its extended discussions of artificial intelligence (AI), perhaps the most controversial computer development.

EVANS, C. *The Micro Millenium.* New York: Washington Square Press, 1979. Interesting and potentially controversial. An optimistic view, more or less, of the computer future. (Cf. Weizenbaum's book, below, for a more critical view.)

GOLDSTINE, H. *The Computer from Pascal to von Neumann.* Princeton: Princeton University Press, 1972. Very good to excellent book by one of the leading figures in the development and manufacture of the computer. Is especially interesting on von Neumann's thinking and work by a man who worked with von Neumann.

GREEN, B. *Digital Computers in Research.* New York: McGraw-Hill, 1963. Though old, this is a very good book on computers, computer usage, and behavioral science applications.

KEMENY, J. *Man and the Computer.* New York: Scribner's, 1972. Excellent book by a distinguished mathematician and college president. Gives the history of the Dartmouth College computer project, time-sharing, and the language BASIC.

KIDDER, T. *The Soul of a New Machine.* New York: Little, Brown, 1981 (Avon, 1982, pb). Interesting, informative, and well-written account of the building of a new computer.

TURING, A. "Can a Machine Think?" In J. Newman, ed., *The World of Mathematics,* vol. 4. New York: Simon and Schuster, 1956, pp. 2099–2123. Justly famous essay by a mathematical genius.

WEIZENBAUM, J. *Computer Power and Human Reason.* San Francisco: Freeman, 1976. Brilliant critical book by a leading computer scientist.

WEXELBLATT, R., ed. *History of Programming Languages.* New York: Wiley, 1981. Remarkable book: history of the evolution and development of computer languages told, in large part, by the individuals who took part in the thinking and events.

The student who wants to learn a computer language will of course need help. Here are good guides to BASIC and FORTRAN.

KEMENY, J., and KURTZ, T. *BASIC Programming,* 3d ed. New York: Wiley, 1980. An excellent manual by the two main inventors of BASIC. Has examples of useful programs.

McCRACKEN, D. *A Guide to FORTRAN-IV Programming,* 2d ed. New York: Wiley, 1972. Standard and excellent guide to FORTRAN. Has useful examples.

A highly useful tool for behavioral researchers is the programmable hand-held calculator-computer. Advanced models make the calculation of many statistical procedures easily possible. Programs can be written and recorded on small plastic slides, which can be used again and again.

It is well to bear in mind always that many analyses do not require a large computer; they can easily be done with a desk calculator. Indeed, a useful precept might be: Don't use the large computer unless you have to. Most analyses of variance and multiple regression analyses can be done with a programmable calculator or a microcomputer. In less than half a decade, many or most behavioral researchers will have their own microcomputers, and good statistical and mathematical programs will be readily available. Readers are cautioned, however, not to accept and buy too easily sets of statistical programs for microcomputers. They may be untested—and expensive. During the next half decade, too, reviews of package programs for both large and small computers will appear in the better journals. Until you are fairly sure of the adequacy of a program, use it with circumspection and care—or not at all.

Appendix C

Random Numbers and Statistics[1]

THIS APPENDIX contains 4000 random numbers organized in 40 sets of 100 each. The numbers are whole numbers evenly distributed in the range 0 through 100. The appendix has three purposes: to supply random numbers and statistics for the text and for the study suggestions of earlier chapters; to give readers at least some more-or-less direct experience with random numbers; and to demonstrate randomness with simple statistics. To achieve the third purpose, basic statistics calculated from the 40 sets of numbers, treating the sets as variables, are also given below: means, variances, standard deviations, and the intercorrelations of the 40 ''variables.''

Random numbers, or rather pseudorandom numbers,[2] can be generated in a number of ways. One can take the square roots of numbers to several decimal places and extract the middle numbers from each number. Or one can copy the numbers produced by the spins of a roulette wheel. Probably the best way is to use the computer and an addition or multiplication process to produce large numbers and then take parts of these numbers as random numbers. The 4000 numbers given below were produced by such a method.

---

[1] I am grateful to Mr. Edward Friedman, Associate Research Scientist, Computing Center, Courant Institute of Mathematical Sciences, New York University, for his help with the program that generated the random numbers given in this appendix. The actual random number computer program used as a subroutine was RANFNYU, a CIMS Computing Center routine.

[2] Oddly enough, numbers generated by a computer are generated with a completely determined calculation. They are thus called *pseudorandom numbers*.

Green and Lohnes and Cooley discuss the method, which is called the *power residue method*.[3]

RANCAL, the random number computer program used, generates k sets of N random numbers each. k and N are read into the computer. In this case $k = 40$ and $N = 100$. The program also calculates the means and standard deviations of each of the 40 sets as well as the mean and standard deviation of all 4000 numbers. The statistics are given below. Since the random properties of the numbers were discussed in Chapter 12, they need not be discussed here. It is, of course, possible to test the randomness of the numbers in a number of ways.[4] One can count the frequencies of odd and even numbers, or the frequencies of any arbitrarily defined groups of numbers, such as 0-9, 10-19, etc., and then do chi-square analysis to test the significance of departures from chance expectations. We now describe a more interesting test.

RANCAL calculates the intercorrelations of the k (=40) sets of random numbers. Since the numbers are presumably random, the correlations among the 40 sets should hover around zero with occasional r's in the .10's and .20's, but rarely in the .30's (plus and minus). With $N = 100$, an r of .197 is significant at the .05 level and an r of .256 at the .01 level. The number of r's equal to or greater than .197 and the number of r's equal to or greater than .256 were counted. Since 5 percent of the total number of r's $[k(k - 1)/2 = (40)(39)/2 = 780]$ is 39 (780 × .05), we can expect to find about 39 r's equal to or greater than .197. Similarly, 1 percent of the 780 r's, or about 8, can be expected to be equal to or greater than .256.

To provide a better test, three different additional samples of 4000 numbers each were generated with RANCAL, and the r's counted as above. The results of counting the r's in the four samples are given in Table C.1. The departures from chance expectations are not significant (by chi-square test). Most of the r's hover around zero. The highest r of the $4 \times 780 = 3120$ r's is $-.35$. The numbers appear to be random by this test. It would be profitable for the student to make up other tests and use them on the data given below. The importance of understanding and gaining experience with random processes, random numbers, and Monte Carlo methods cannot be overemphasized.[5]

Table C.1 Frequencies of Correlation Coefficients Calculated Between 40 Sets of Pseudorandom Numbers in Four Samples of 4000 Numbers Each

	Samples				
	1	2	3	4	Expected
.05 level (≥ .197)	46	45	29	48	39
.01 level (≥ .256)	12	8	11	13	8
Highest r's	−.33	.31	−.35	−.31	

[3] B. Green, *Digital Computers in Research*. New York: McGraw-Hill, 1963, chap. 9; P. Lohnes and W. Cooley, *Introduction to Statistical Procedures: With Computer Exercises*. New York: Wiley, 1968, chap. 5. Green's discussion is clear and informative—and surprising (about how hard it is to generate random numbers that are really random); Lohnes and Cooley display all the arithmetic to take the mystery out of the procedure.

[4] See Rand Corporation, *A Million Random Digits with 100,000 Normal Deviates*. New York: Free Press, 1955, pp. xiff., for a good discussion of a number of actual tests. This is an excellent set of random numbers. In addition, behavioral scientists should read this perhaps classic account of the pains taken to produce random numbers and the difficulties encountered in doing so.

[5] Readers who wish to generate their own pseudorandom numbers should consult the computer specialists at their computer installations. Random number routines are widely available. The reader will have to write the basic program in which to insert the random number program. This is not hard to do, nor is the writing of the program to calculate the usual statistics. Readers who have not learned to program can have a computer specialist do the job, though this sacrifices a good bit of fun. Readers who either own a microcomputer or have access to one can generate random numbers easily since the major machines have random number functions that users can activate with a few simple BASIC commands. It will then be necessary to calculate statistics with the numbers and, of course, to print the results.

RANDOM NUMBERS

1	53	95	67	80	79	93	28	69	25	78	13	24	100	62	62	21	11	4	54
2	62	12	27	41	5	4	19	34	84	78	71	45	73	79	33	57	29	58	75
3	90	16	47	72	20	60	70	71	2	67	21	65	7	39	58	81	64	11	70
4	10	59	4	76	80	6	82	20	60	92	33	61	76	83	73	12	84	43	90
5	32	17	36	64	8	30	80	95	61	33	65	5	39	88	36	44	42	43	5
6	54	71	27	89	41	53	60	10	2	91	76	95	98	91	64	65	23	57	16
7	10	60	18	77	34	59	28	99	15	11	70	34	27	78	67	19	97	30	23
8	42	20	24	36	78	58	82	81	49	91	35	53	30	92	57	19	97	40	58
9	73	55	87	48	49	97	60	92	27	78	2	55	29	76	99	21	45	72	56
10	21	56	41	23	58	57	49	49	70	33	6	79	95	3	70	38	26	26	5
11	9	60	37	99	6	41	69	97	18	44	100	18	46	3	90	57	22	82	15
12	63	26	41	8	21	38	15	63	38	100	68	89	24	39	19	29	93	97	40
13	98	72	9	45	69	50	7	86	5	80	0	8	28	96	45	0	0	13	95
14	87	89	65	22	98	55	86	9	66	43	64	55	80	30	15	99	26	25	71
15	5	91	68	44	67	2	71	96	15	73	78	3	12	87	53	9	11	12	21
16	75	93	62	49	95	82	30	81	24	4	11	36	71	96	49	47	65	48	28
17	76	15	55	38	29	0	8	20	71	42	81	51	44	76	93	42	87	89	38
18	26	76	93	84	8	40	96	69	84	82	89	5	16	43	34	37	64	39	14
19	8	35	6	83	76	8	87	81	13	33	14	86	38	23	33	22	58	47	60
20	59	73	37	6	26	44	0	24	89	24	78	80	20	8	19	31	32	53	40
21	87	94	75	45	72	15	39	100	46	99	59	12	22	95	76	18	27	73	88
22	5	74	8	91	37	5	13	55	13	7	19	24	76	4	25	93	78	9	50
23	49	82	39	40	51	15	71	53	68	86	50	93	31	22	64	77	46	17	28
24	2	25	92	97	41	39	98	100	99	67	44	0	99	93	31	69	26	72	56
25	59	41	49	100	13	0	15	33	82	61	28	59	83	8	17	76	24	58	91
26	40	13	20	51	81	15	12	45	16	57	47	54	92	60	70	55	98	12	90
27	80	25	91	36	83	59	19	9	47	61	84	89	98	18	11	56	99	3	26
28	48	33	7	70	61	95	51	32	89	87	72	6	40	88	52	44	19	96	95
29	89	5	7	93	48	60	69	97	61	21	87	68	20	4	61	63	75	8	76
30	97	64	36	36	99	98	23	18	66	28	58	48	34	18	64	71	48	90	63
31	59	73	71	62	66	34	17	41	32	65	50	73	82	7	20	85	1	65	74
32	88	75	43	66	66	38	56	31	25	36	26	91	36	100	88	42	74	27	36
33	34	16	43	38	50	28	34	14	41	2	6	97	56	73	75	17	56	31	100
34	14	61	81	2	69	73	3	89	79	64	67	80	75	5	66	77	97	30	88
35	15	39	5	99	29	36	25	40	46	28	34	63	75	18	21	23	13	85	15
36	68	49	1	55	11	6	63	23	50	33	80	34	82	20	66	48	27	16	86
37	1	72	18	84	84	86	61	41	22	61	45	36	37	16	20	28	98	36	72
38	58	73	55	11	9	96	81	84	21	34	50	92	65	91	69	33	23	4	77
39	91	63	65	63	70	90	57	20	9	13	28	77	72	0	12	30	48	6	28
40	39	45	31	74	91	85	29	45	98	15	11	50	26	16	36	76	1	40	76
41	94	12	62	59	14	42	32	75	41	41	0	58	5	78	89	48	35	1	78
42	3	33	41	22	45	37	65	3	96	27	62	77	16	97	81	78	26	48	94
43	58	2	83	10	100	50	98	57	32	65	31	87	84	45	0	90	42	78	9
44	29	73	79	48	66	72	32	1	100	3	2	61	35	0	88	100	45	42	16
45	55	9	63	66	31	5	8	72	4	85	5	44	4	98	2	79	40	44	96
46	52	13	44	91	39	85	22	33	4	29	52	6	82	77	25	0	46	100	41
47	31	52	65	63	88	78	21	35	28	22	91	84	4	30	14	0	97	92	63
48	44	38	76	99	38	67	60	95	67	68	17	18	46	76	83	5	8	20	87
49	84	47	44	4	67	22	89	78	44	84	66	15	56	0	90	21	25	88	99
50	71	50	78	48	65	74	21	24	2	23	65	94	51	82	67	16	35	91	100
51	42	47	97	81	10	99	40	15	63	77	89	10	32	92	86	32	9	33	79
52	3	70	75	49	90	92	62	0	47	90	78	63	44	60	13	55	38	64	60
53	31	6	46	39	27	93	81	79	100	94	43	39	79	2	18	82	40	30	56

RANDOM NUMBERS (*continued*)

44	59	90	78	83	4	97	61	52	75	91	76	98	40	41	2	56	78	62	79	16
20	79	78	68	31	25	30	97	31	82	51	72	23	58	27	17	69	94	75	68	79
4	79	44	47	7	74	34	55	28	90	19	35	15	27	66	20	26	81	37	61	63
71	82	28	21	61	31	92	100	75	22	31	11	5	74	38	84	78	69	70	24	77
88	81	13	63	15	47	92	20	62	5	60	44	83	22	50	59	80	29	12	71	11
0	90	52	26	90	49	31	68	29	58	10	13	8	54	63	58	7	29	25	38	80
60	0	22	11	12	54	50	93	25	69	54	2	60	4	53	16	80	45	30	72	51
13	39	42	25	3	97	64	100	55	24	7	30	58	96	5	30	55	23	39	53	27
24	16	33	50	84	12	65	4	30	48	56	97	74	33	90	0	5	99	3	60	53
89	49	0	68	57	53	91	66	81	53	83	15	81	17	65	0	47	8	65	77	61
38	73	97	74	9	35	82	66	34	84	14	28	36	24	87	76	96	89	34	9	29
91	70	41	95	83	33	25	33	94	44	39	43	23	53	15	54	81	74	31	17	94
24	92	51	11	11	37	91	21	87	89	89	9	68	26	79	43	16	19	89	66	82
87	22	39	97	26	50	12	86	22	65	70	94	86	38	11	60	57	16	41	46	20
32	57	72	16	35	27	51	91	43	58	61	6	62	50	24	11	19	73	14	42	48
8	91	58	40	55	32	7	86	84	95	59	53	70	54	25	96	38	43	5	2	4
51	88	65	83	80	66	91	9	68	30	63	28	75	64	90	11	80	94	99	35	54
77	95	100	52	99	86	81	65	85	21	9	68	57	34	30	29	61	33	49	0	11
36	97	89	20	59	52	9	76	75	52	82	45	65	89	88	39	93	71	55	29	67
32	32	23	57	74	49	17	97	49	71	0	73	11	78	58	58	34	20	30	43	40
41	31	99	37	31	24	89	35	14	14	73	26	59	10	35	75	4	34	38	0	63
85	98	71	37	53	67	75	9	56	95	71	58	15	70	36	19	49	45	18	36	2
25	2	17	69	68	56	44	100	55	80	26	87	85	52	76	40	61	50	68	72	7
25	71	42	28	22	96	76	19	63	97	5	98	44	82	35	0	33	26	68	75	7
25	3	2	76	87	10	18	23	69	93	27	35	39	8	70	79	48	30	65	65	63
27	95	66	23	91	78	86	27	98	16	30	79	82	7	23	41	81	8	32	8	8
67	21	24	80	60	44	42	48	77	84	63	0	30	98	86	100	14	55	86	71	13
62	12	100	82	5	17	62	65	100	63	9	88	88	48	70	64	81	29	71	62	67
92	37	35	40	70	25	86	34	54	53	95	45	62	32	83	60	48	0	44	94	22
57	15	14	24	26	65	29	38	85	99	17	63	8	87	100	28	82	67	65	10	81
85	23	19	45	61	48	98	84	51	63	70	33	6	49	38	55	78	94	26	4	29
40	33	92	18	9	54	51	40	24	82	6	79	51	52	9	38	18	13	16	86	42
84	32	25	33	52	26	78	83	44	0	81	63	29	23	97	64	6	63	74	29	77
82	52	87	25	63	11	67	93	99	61	39	94	16	38	87	3	25	25	49	22	68
43	88	70	92	44	23	73	62	47	60	45	32	6	90	100	29	26	31	39	32	93
78	74	89	9	23	66	62	83	28	34	87	92	99	60	23	79	82	6	62	2	75
39	67	100	71	8	19	29	0	24	95	26	46	1	2	68	40	8	3	99	19	6
93	3	37	95	14	84	27	67	46	61	88	65	55	20	58	89	100	74	77	28	30
89	94	6	58	72	73	16	86	19	95	49	37	58	49	5	51	55	90	22	3	37
1	88	15	60	27	55	0	83	96	36	53	80	47	63	53	58	95	55	25	67	58
70	20	98	38	93	67	35	35	40	38	44	2	48	66	86	47	74	48	87	71	21
59	77	82	54	1	63	24	64	31	31	14	49	71	92	36	55	72	74	13	99	31
17	21	92	92	47	5	29	6	27	62	72	35	48	56	92	76	75	45	23	91	15
18	48	67	36	37	57	12	97	12	95	8	77	61	32	6	66	47	66	0	24	26
75	91	59	66	15	41	19	100	33	23	64	50	83	57	78	38	55	48	97	5	62
35	46	93	11	9	56	82	97	53	18	86	83	94	8	40	14	39	93	51	42	80
87	46	73	55	82	18	76	67	43	76	22	82	1	78	19	94	56	38	8	37	28
87	2	42	65	27	16	22	60	18	78	33	73	74	13	2	42	64	89	86	72	9
100	32	86	30	50	92	48	55	70	35	20	54	43	20	13	39	76	59	7	51	19
35	61	31	75	8	81	58	67	50	28	17	77	32	56	82	56	60	98	80	21	49
69	50	7	61	78	15	60	79	47	73	51	99	27	39	7	32	7	85	14	22	76
63	92	17	100	2	40	93	83	89	88	20	1	14	43	75	65	65	63	53	81	57
31	81	84	62	41	59	4	46	56	100	58	26	51	32	8	24	99	30	36	32	59

RANDOM NUMBERS *(continued)*

54	69	27	97	71	52	38	45	35	14	74	40	96	40	88	38	67	44	81	5
55	2	76	36	72	7	28	55	13	31	78	67	98	50	25	94	39	71	28	0
56	3	4	20	8	63	33	69	31	69	32	35	18	23	84	69	64	13	43	86
57	79	55	89	1	25	68	100	58	44	92	73	29	70	47	3	51	37	24	24
58	99	6	65	35	66	98	66	47	47	22	1	54	94	13	0	31	40	55	69
59	46	98	1	46	43	86	42	91	63	1	93	84	51	8	79	47	54	85	90
60	6	14	71	51	7	10	79	41	58	3	27	33	74	67	18	94	4	57	99
61	92	31	31	40	12	19	74	73	20	94	33	41	40	74	79	42	23	41	29
62	87	8	68	74	61	66	94	27	71	81	37	82	83	7	8	46	65	63	37
63	50	48	52	100	68	75	38	65	59	57	78	24	29	52	24	98	78	48	77
64	67	96	52	88	76	79	16	12	42	33	35	50	54	69	21	57	62	21	84
65	54	42	22	99	28	90	74	46	26	13	48	45	99	3	38	94	86	53	41
66	99	51	72	2	75	81	92	71	85	26	77	73	23	14	2	46	7	13	2
67	35	63	58	46	91	44	56	26	59	56	21	91	19	83	6	61	47	53	10
68	81	98	63	17	77	45	47	96	25	38	23	26	80	20	47	40	39	14	71
69	90	47	44	40	40	9	60	62	13	79	39	0	99	57	37	39	2	8	42
70	29	30	16	54	83	76	50	0	61	100	51	74	78	15	9	16	17	22	44
71	47	94	70	80	51	26	11	78	34	29	10	55	90	42	4	6	83	72	95
72	69	14	17	73	79	25	71	14	52	98	77	82	15	25	8	34	38	80	82
73	54	58	47	9	0	6	36	94	27	3	18	5	36	98	74	36	30	8	87
74	24	63	57	91	8	58	38	29	72	5	56	71	81	50	67	59	41	9	17
75	14	24	69	85	97	51	68	80	16	92	59	72	97	23	89	44	16	71	19
76	86	21	31	59	72	17	77	45	43	29	34	97	67	45	23	88	91	68	12
77	5	28	80	31	99	77	39	23	69	0	15	49	100	2	22	64	73	92	53
78	29	71	48	4	87	32	17	90	89	9	99	34	58	8	61	73	98	48	89
79	90	94	19	80	70	36	2	17	48	63	82	39	85	26	65	27	81	69	83
80	62	66	48	74	86	6	66	41	15	65	6	41	85	57	84	64	70	39	64
81	67	54	3	54	23	40	25	95	93	55	59	46	77	55	49	82	26	8	87
82	75	27	62	15	81	36	22	26	69	42	44	91	55	0	84	48	68	65	5
83	70	19	7	100	94	53	81	76	73	40	22	58	49	42	96	18	66	89	8
84	75	7	9	20	58	92	41	42	79	26	91	44	63	87	45	21	23	15	6
85	55	70	10	23	25	73	91	72	29	47	93	58	21	75	80	52	9	12	36
86	83	42	62	53	55	12	11	54	19	2	45	43	67	13	5	74	30	93	11
87	94	20	76	23	65	72	55	27	44	19	10	72	50	67	83	18	67	22	49
88	51	10	72	9	59	47	66	32	17	6	75	8	54	22	37	3	46	83	95
89	99	50	22	2	92	9	98	9	40	23	34	8	63	58	49	31	70	39	83
90	9	12	3	23	2	0	82	75	36	63	71	19	78	26	66	63	16	75	7
91	20	40	50	29	51	82	81	47	73	69	74	100	80	37	14	67	1	90	92
92	90	92	54	52	74	0	88	71	45	49	38	54	80	2	85	42	75	47	20
93	25	6	92	30	19	31	22	41	0	22	79	87	84	61	6	19	67	97	60
94	13	12	94	76	29	61	50	67	29	76	27	70	97	16	83	88	100	22	48
95	91	77	51	3	92	85	46	22	0	58	84	64	87	93	94	94	13	98	41
96	29	12	39	35	32	47	30	81	40	32	37	8	48	81	50	77	18	39	7
97	43	96	86	14	91	24	22	85	16	51	42	37	41	100	94	76	45	50	67
98	57	44	72	45	87	21	7	29	26	82	69	99	10	39	76	29	11	17	85
99	63	10	10	76	7	75	19	91	2	31	45	94	54	72	10	48	52	7	12
100	34	28	11	95	4	82	51	7	69	53	93	36	81	66	93	88	15	73	54
12	13	98	21	39	36	74	39	83	77	79	37	89	4	20	21	91	98	90	37	49
39	31	69	14	22	50	40	54	12	71	98	25	26	20	61	52	93	90	76	46	19
53	10	28	46	41	29	74	46	64	39	4	47	55	98	22	69	9	15	34	94	16
29	95	79	80	35	0	9	65	42	99	69	90	22	16	34	81	44	3	24	96	70
20	59	12	35	63	52	35	2	56	40	85	2	85	2	58	26	94	48	0	85	70
2	19	26	78	95	1	4	72	81	80	60	49	67	32	10	28	90	72	25	28	53
37	40	96	68	6	95	55	82	16	36	58	68	68	69	7	11	31	17	39	82	85

RANDOM NUMBERS (continued)

1	0	13	31	19	63	90	75	17	33	49	13	54	32	26	66	38	1	7	35	16
63	88	20	20	75	16	70	26	75	22	48	6	1	89	99	21	48	6	9	67	85
64	93	100	50	95	76	94	84	25	67	98	94	23	75	40	33	86	87	76	24	98
95	13	66	49	11	48	20	54	51	65	63	33	98	80	13	84	70	85	93	74	22
18	35	10	64	79	70	5	55	92	41	92	14	63	52	94	56	5	40	55	50	17
40	62	28	72	82	81	51	7	45	9	26	47	34	47	47	95	45	38	82	85	20
33	7	97	68	76	44	73	73	0	80	55	84	77	74	27	5	17	57	75	63	2
15	60	83	28	56	78	9	27	52	79	68	90	48	12	51	55	77	48	10	55	21
58	1	28	1	64	50	28	8	69	70	96	26	100	6	31	89	0	31	91	5	23
71	94	59	17	43	50	34	12	14	45	30	79	63	76	72	18	67	87	47	90	93
73	24	19	13	98	0	64	44	90	20	13	66	81	97	81	11	38	7	37	93	64
97	82	87	98	29	97	69	24	62	100	12	28	84	86	10	69	25	66	93	21	57
2	23	76	42	76	87	64	99	5	7	13	33	19	18	37	96	73	95	91	24	24
17	85	42	29	80	53	92	6	44	100	18	24	31	5	6	37	63	93	42	5	97
83	42	53	54	93	63	19	59	30	80	75	8	91	48	79	2	40	6	56	57	60
30	3	41	73	63	76	18	82	8	13	30	78	45	43	77	77	99	98	40	14	82
64	7	19	80	64	4	34	30	65	63	11	72	20	15	22	30	82	77	51	87	61
90	24	25	98	38	79	45	84	30	49	64	98	48	25	14	0	12	63	67	12	77
20	40	25	87	45	88	52	19	33	17	63	60	62	46	12	59	99	5	88	74	89
87	62	78	25	71	57	6	98	59	79	34	20	77	87	83	12	74	29	12	16	99
54	10	53	29	37	82	5	77	54	4	69	7	40	18	32	85	37	73	42	49	49
45	35	11	73	30	16	3	75	56	58	98	46	93	58	96	29	73	6	71	8	46
69	17	54	7	86	29	18	86	98	5	56	78	0	78	24	34	73	95	11	44	36
72	60	78	88	27	45	80	66	25	37	73	7	67	29	27	12	90	60	97	15	94
93	9	58	84	88	90	73	47	49	53	95	62	28	11	61	0	91	49	32	82	28
74	75	27	81	28	48	4	65	87	69	32	14	46	52	52	36	21	13	70	24	76
36	42	53	92	96	19	52	38	2	22	47	26	94	34	57	81	28	49	74	68	50
93	76	77	19	31	74	40	5	0	23	61	15	11	82	35	77	9	28	11	32	30
54	75	23	75	34	69	93	93	20	29	78	24	71	92	75	70	60	80	88	21	11
72	99	15	97	27	48	50	88	2	89	57	18	25	7	100	80	84	97	84	18	53
99	6	34	98	33	77	44	86	95	0	30	34	91	25	98	77	14	95	100	84	19
94	13	95	44	22	63	18	88	37	89	95	98	80	72	72	71	66	13	33	24	12
48	56	64	63	75	27	69	63	29	51	59	22	83	2	33	32	91	78	53	45	63
7	66	52	91	70	34	54	25	71	91	12	41	39	35	37	66	52	80	1	33	94
77	83	71	83	68	55	85	11	69	32	10	30	54	73	21	43	68	65	83	26	90
95	28	92	53	63	46	36	45	62	24	39	65	100	85	12	69	3	72	55	43	5
54	59	91	34	52	75	87	95	30	97	33	57	69	37	7	62	65	36	9	57	73
76	13	93	41	42	27	80	85	61	11	42	44	51	38	59	85	91	51	79	14	26
59	84	46	41	29	7	44	63	27	29	41	39	76	88	46	46	65	72	62	92	67
15	91	53	78	85	78	77	80	36	89	88	84	60	42	55	48	99	44	66	77	27

	MEAN	VARIANCE	ST. DEV.
1	51.8400	895.8144	29.9302
2	46.2000	809.3200	28.4486
3	47.6900	740.6539	27.2150
4	51.8300	872.7611	29.5425
5	53.2100	877.5659	29.6237
6	48.8700	903.9131	30.0651
7	49.6400	778.8704	27.9082
8	51.3700	889.7331	29.8284
9	45.0700	771.7251	27.7799

	MEAN	VARIANCE	ST. DEV.
10	49.2800	872.3016	29.5348
11	48.8700	777.5731	27.8850
12	53.0800	860.2136	29.3294
13	56.5100	773.0099	27.8031
14	47.9900	1110.2299	33.3201
15	49.3700	913.6531	30.2267
16	49.0200	714.0396	26.7215
17	45.6800	842.0776	29.0186
18	47.0400	853.3384	29.2120
19	53.5100	977.2499	31.2610
20	52.7400	853.4924	29.2146
21	50.0600	1001.1564	31.6411
22	53.9500	907.7475	30.1288
23	53.6100	737.3779	27.1547
24	49.3100	807.4139	28.4150
25	49.1600	673.9544	25.9606
26	50.2200	855.3316	29.2461
27	58.3600	877.1904	29.6174
28	49.5700	709.7051	26.6403
29	55.4400	868.3664	29.4681
30	49.4300	791.3851	28.1316
31	48.5200	847.9296	29.1192
32	52.9400	802.3564	28.3259
33	46.7900	784.6259	28.0112
34	48.3300	881.4611	29.6894
35	47.2900	759.3059	27.5555
36	55.5100	854.5499	29.2327
37	52.3900	907.8379	30.1303
38	49.9500	851.3275	29.1775
39	46.0000	817.7800	28.5969
40	47.6500	815.1475	28.5508

Appendix D

The Research Report

THIS APPENDIX has two purposes: to outline some of the main points of report writing and to cite appropriate references to guide the reader.

THE PURPOSE

The purpose of the research report is to tell readers the problem investigated, the methods used to solve the problem, the results of the investigation, and the conclusions inferred from the results. It is not the function of the investigator to *convince* the reader of the virtue of the research. Rather, it is to *report,* as expeditiously and clearly as possible, what was done, why it was done, the outcome of the doing, and the investigator's conclusions. The report should be so written that readers can reach their own conclusions as to the adequacy of the research and the validity of the reported results and conclusions.

To achieve this purpose is not easy. The writer must strive for the right blend of detail and brevity, for objectivity, and for clarity in presentation. Perhaps the best criterion question is: Can another investigator replicate the research by following the research report? If not, due to incomplete or inadequate reporting of methodology or to lack of clarity in presentation, then the report is inadequate.[1]

---

[1] The realities of publishing and its costs limit the above statement. Book publishers and journal editors do not have the space available to make it possible to publish enough details of research studies so that they can be replicated. Indeed, the constraints on editors are such that they can hardly publish sufficient details of research for readers to make informed judgments of the methodological adequacy of the studies. Nevertheless, the criterion question should always be kept in mind.

THE STRUCTURE

The structure of the research report is simple. It is almost the same as the structure of the research itself: the problem, the methodology, the results. Here is a general outline:

I. Problem
   1. Theory, hypotheses, definitions
   2. Previous research; the literature
II. Methodology-Data Collection
   1. Sample and sampling method
   2. How hypotheses were tested (methodology), experimental procedures, instrumentation
   3. Measurement of variables
   4. Methods of analysis, statistics
   5. Pretesting and pilot studies
III. Results, Interpretation, and Conclusions

THE PROBLEM

The problem section differs greatly in different reports. In theses and books, it is usually long and detailed. In published research reports, it is kept to a minimum (see footnote 1). The basic precept, though seemingly obvious, is not easy to follow: Tell readers what the research problem is. Tell it to them in question form. For example, What effect does equalized extrinsic environment have on the mental status of school children?[2] Does past experience with materials have a negative effect on problem-solving involving the materials?[3] How do social attitudes influence judgments of the effectiveness of social policies?[4]

The statement of the general problem is usually not precise and operational. Rather, it sets the general stage for the reader. The subproblems, however, should be more precise. They should have implications for testing. For example: Can a person conversing with others manipulate conversation by agreeing or disagreeing with the others, or by paraphrasing what they have said?[5] The Jones and Cook statement given in the preceding paragraph is made more operational by specifying the social attitudes and the judgments of social policies affecting blacks: Do attitudes toward blacks affect recommendations of social policies for improving black welfare? Do individuals with positive attitudes toward blacks recommend societal change, and do individuals with negative attitudes recommend that blacks improve themselves?

Some report writers, rather than state the problems, state the general and specific hypotheses. A good practice would seem to be to state the broader general problem and then to state the hypotheses, both general and specific. The reader is referred to Chapter 2 for examples. Whatever way is used, bear in mind the main purpose of informing the reader of the main area of investigation and the specific propositions that were tested.

At some point in the problem discussion the variables should be defined, or at least mentioned or generally characterized, with more specific definitions given later. Variable definition was discussed at length in Chapter 3 and need not be repeated here, except for the admonition: Inform the reader not only of the variables but also what you mean by them. Define in general and operational terms, giving justification for your definitions.

[2] A. Firkowska, A. Ostrowska, M. Sokolowska, Z. Stein, M. Susser, and I. Wald, "Cognitive Development and Social Policy," *Science,* 200 (1978), 1357–1362. (Note again that my problem statements are often, perhaps usually, different from the authors'.)

[3] H. Birch and H. Rabinowitz, "The Negative Effect of Previous Experience on Productive Thinking," *Journal of Experimental Psyxchology,* 41 (1951), 121–125.

[4] S. Jones and S. Cook, "The Influence of Attitude on Judgments of the Effectiveness of Social Policy," *Journal of Personality and Social Psychology,* 32 (1975), 767–773.

[5] W. Verplanck, "The Control of the Content of Conversation: Reinforcement of Statements of Opinion," *Journal of Abnormal and Social Psychology,* 51 (1955), 668–676. The statement is an operational expression of reinforcement theory.

There are two main reasons for discussing the general and research literature related to the research problem. The first of these is the more important: to explain and clarify the theoretical rationale of the problem. Suppose, like Haslerud and Meyers, one were interested in investigating the relative effectiveness for transfer of self-discovery of principles by learners and systematic enunciation of the principles to learners.[6] Since the problem is in part a transfer of training problem, one would have to discuss transfer and some of the literature on transfer, but especially that part of the literature pertinent to this problem. One may well want to discuss to some extent philosophical and pedagogical writings on the theory of formal discipline, for instance. In this manner the investigator provides a general picture of the research topic and fits his problem into the general picture.

A second reason for discussing the literature is to tell the reader what research has and has not been done on the problem. Obviously, the investigator must show that his particular investigation has not been done before. The underlying purpose, of course, is to locate the present research in the existing body of research on the subject and to point out what it contributes to the subject.

Methodology-Data Collection

The function of the methodology-data collection section of the research report, of course, is to tell the reader what was done to solve the problem. Meticulous care must be exercised to so report that the criterion of replicability is satisfied. That is, it should be possible for another investigator to reproduce the research, to reanalyze the data, or to arrive at unambiguous conclusions as to the adequacy of the methods and data collection. In books and theses there can be little question of the applicability of the criterion. In research journal reports, unfortunately, the criterion is difficult, sometimes even impossible, to satisfy. Owing to lack of journal space, investigators are forced to condense reports in such a way that it is sometimes difficult to reconstruct and evaluate what a researcher has done. (See footnote 1.) Yet the criterion remains a good one and should be kept in mind when tackling the methodology section.

The first part of the methodology-data collection section should tell what sample or samples were used, how they were selected, and why they were so selected. If eighth-grade pupils were used, the reason for using them should be stated. If the samples were randomly selected, this should be said. The method of random sampling should also be specified. If pupils were assigned at random to experimental groups, this should be reported. If they were not, this, too, should be reported with reasons for the lack of such assignment.

The method of testing the hypotheses should be reported in detail. If the study has been experimental, the manner in which the independent variable(s) has been manipulated is described. This description includes instruments used, instructions to the subjects, control precautions, and the like. If the study has been nonexperimental, the procedures used to gather data are outlined.

The report of any empirical study must include an account of the measurement of the variables of the study. This may be accomplished in few sentences in some studies. For example, in an experiment with one independent variable and a dependent variable whose measurement is simple, all that may be necessary is a brief description of the measurement of the dependent variable. Such measurement may entail only the counting of responses. In other studies, the description of the measurement of the variables may take up most of the methodology section. A factor analytic study, for instance, may require lengthy descriptions of measurement instruments and how they were used. Such descriptions will, of course, include justification of the instruments used, as well as evidence of their reliability and validity.

An account of the data analysis methods used is sometimes put into the methodology

---

[6]G. Haslerud and S. Meyers, "The Transfer Value of Given and Individually Derived Principles," *Journal of Educational Psychology*, 49 (1958), 293–298.

section, sometimes in the analysis-interpretation section. It is probably better to include these methods in the methodology section, though space can sometimes be saved the other way. Whichever practice is followed, the analysis methods must be outlined and justified. Since most of the common methods of analysis are well known, it is ordinarily sufficient to say, for example, that a $2 \times 3 \times 3$ factorial analysis of variance was done, or that χ^2 was used, or that principal-factors factor analysis with orthogonal rotations was used. If an unusual method of analysis is used, or if a common method is used in an unusual way, the investigator should describe what was done in sufficient detail to enable a competent reader to understand it. If space is at a premium, as it usually is, sometimes a reference to a technical source of the analytic method is sufficient. Lately, there has been a tendency to cite computer program packages (BMDP, SPSS, and others) as reference sources. This practice cannot be recommended because it assumes that the programs and their manuals are legitimate and accurate sources of methodology. It is better practice to state the method and the original source, or a well-recognized source (e.g., Harman's *Modern Factor Analysis* for, say, rotation of factors) that explains the method and its rationale.

In many investigations, pilot studies and pretesting are used. (Indeed, they should be used in most studies.) If so, what was done and the outcome of what was done are reported. If the pilot study was solely for trying out the instruments or the variable manipulation method on a small scale, little need be said. If, however, the pilot study or the pretesting supplied actual research data, the reader is entitled to know methodological details.

Results, Interpretation, Conclusions

This part of the report, though logically a unit, is often broken down into two or three sections. We treat it here as one section, since the interpretation of results and the conclusions drawn from the results are so often reported together in journal research reports. In a thesis or book, however, it may be desirable to separate the data from their interpretation and from the conclusions.

The results or data of a research study are the raw materials for the solution of the research problem. The data and their analysis are the hypothesis-testing stuff of research. Methodology and data collection are tools used to obtain the raw material of hypothesis-testing, the data. The main question in this: Do the data support or not support the hypotheses? It cannot be emphasized enough that methodology, data collection, and analysis are selected and used for the purpose of testing the operational hypotheses deduced from the general research questions. Therefore the report writer must be exceptionally careful to report his results as accurately and completely as possible, informing the reader how the results bear on the hypotheses.

Before writing this part of the report, it is helpful to reduce the data and the results of the data analysis to condensed form, particularly tables. The data should be thoroughly digested and understood before writing. The answer to the question, Do the data support the hypotheses? must be clearly answered before writing the results section. While writing, one must be constantly on guard against wandering from the task at hand, the solution of the research problem. Everything written must be geared to letting the data bear on the problem and the hypotheses.[7]

Somewhere in the final section of the research report the limitations and weaknesses of the study should be discussed. This can be overdone, of course. All scientific work has weaknesses, and many pages can be written belaboring a study's weaknesses. Still, the major limitations, which, of course, may have been mentioned earlier when discussing the

---

[7] In the report of an experimental phase of a larger complex study, the writer and a colleague evidently lost sight of this precept. A severe but perspicacious critic who read the final report noted that the basic hypothesis of the experiments *had not really been tested*. Unfortunately, the critic was right. The experimental project had to be scrapped! For an account of the research and the project's demise, see F. Kerlinger, *Liberalism and Conservatism: The Nature and Structure of Social Attitudes*. Hillsdale, N. J.: Lawrence Erlbaum Associates, 1984, chap. 12.

problem or the methodology, should be pointed out. This is done, not to show humility or one's technical competence, but rather to enable the reader to judge the validity of the conclusions drawn from the data and the general worth of the study.

Limitations of social scientific and educational research generally come from sampling and subject assignment inadequacies, methodological weaknesses, and statistical deficiencies. Lack of random sampling, as we have seen, limits the conclusions to the particular sample used. Lack of random assignment casts doubt on the adequacy of the control of independent variables and thus on the conclusions. Statistical deficiencies, similarly, can lead to incorrect conclusions. Deficiencies in measurement always affect conclusions, too. If a measurement instrument, perhaps through no fault of the writer, is only moderately reliable, a finding may be ambiguous and inconclusive. More important, the questionable validity of an instrument may seriously affect conclusions.

These matters have been discussed in the text and need no further elaboration here. It may be added, however, that the writing of the conclusions is naturally affected by the recognized and acknowledged limitations and weaknesses. Moreover, readers can hardly be expected to judge the validity of research conclusions without knowing both the positive and the negative aspects of whatever was done. It is the professional responsibility of the researcher, then, to inform readers of both the strengths and the weaknesses of the research.

THE WRITING

It is not easy to write simply and clearly. One has to work at it. One should realize that almost no writer can escape the necessity of constant revision by reorganizing and paring—deleting circumlocutions, redundancies, and other verbal fat. Suggestions for better research report writing follow.

Although research reports should be fairly detailed, there is no need to waste words. State the problem, the methodology, and the results as clearly, simply, and briefly as possible. Avoid hackneyed expressions like "in terms of," "with respect to," "with reference to," "give consideration to," and the like. Delete unnecessary words and expressions when revising. For example, sentences with expressions like "the fact of the matter is," "owing to the fact that," and "as to whether" can always be revised to remove such clumsy inelegancies. For good advice on simplicity and clarity, study Strunk and White's little classic, *The Elements of Style*. Nicholson's book is most helpful.[8]

Writing scholarly papers and research reports requires a certain amount of routine drudgery that few of us like. Bibliographies, footnotes, tables, figures, and other mechanical details, however, cannot be escaped. Yet a little systematic study can help solve most problems. That is, do not wait until you sit down to write and then find out how to handle footnotes and other mechanical details. Get a good reference book or two and study and lay out footnote and bibliographical forms, tables, figures, and headings. Put three or four types of footnote entries on 3-by-5 cards. Similarly, learn two or three methods of laying out tables. Lay out skeleton tables. Then use these samples when writing. In short, put much of the drudgery and doubt behind you by mastering the elements of the methods, instead of impeding your writing by constant interruptions to check on how to do things.

Presentation of statistical results and analyses gives students considerable trouble. Hit the problem head-on. Perhaps the best way to do this is to study statistical presentation in two or three good journals, like the *Journal of Personality and Social Psychology,* the *Journal of Educational Psychology,* the *American Educational Research Journal,* and the *American Sociological Review*. The style manual of the American Psychological Association (see References) has been adopted by all psychology journals and a number of education journals. Although a bit fussy, it is an excellent guide, especially to statistical and tabular presentation. Turabian's manual is another good guide.

The purpose of statistical, tabular, and other condensed presentation should be kept in

[8] See the references at the end of this appendix.

mind. A statistical table, for instance, should clearly tell the reader what the data essentially say. This does not mean, of course, that a statistical table can stand by itself. Its purpose is to illuminate and clarify the textual discussion. The text carries the story; the table helps make the text clear and gives the statistical evidence for assertions made in the text. The text may say, for example, "The three experimental groups differed significantly in achievement," and the tables will report the statistical data—means, standard deviations, F ratios, levels of significance—to support the assertion. There is often no need for a table. If a hypothesis has been tested by calculating one, two, or three coefficients of correlation, these can simply be reported in the text without tabular presentation.

A fairly safe generalization to guide one in writing research reports is: first drafts are not adequate. In other words, almost any writing, as said earlier, improves upon revision. It is almost always possible to simplify first-draft language and to delete unnecessary words, phrases, and even sentences and paragraphs. A first rule, then, is to go over any report with a ruthless pencil toward the end of greater simplicity, clarity, and brevity. With experience this not only becomes possible; it becomes easier.

If an adequate outline has been used, there should be little problem with the organization of a research paper. Yet sometimes it is necessary to reorganize a report. One may find, for example, that one has discussed something at the end of the report that was not anticipated in the beginning. Reorganization is required. In any case, the possibility of improvement in communication through reorganization should always be kept in mind.

Anyone's research writing can be improved in two ways: by letting something one has written sit for a few weeks, and by having someone else read and criticize one's work. It is remarkable what a little time will do for one's objectivity and critical capacity. One sees obvious blemishes that somehow one could not see before. Time helps salve the ego, too. Our precious inventions do not seem so precious after a few weeks or months. We can be much more objective about them.

The second problem is harder. It is hard to take criticism, but the researcher must learn to take it. Scientific research is one of the most complex of human activities. Writing research reports is not easy, and no one can be expected to be perfect. It should be accepted and routine procedure, therefore, to have colleagues read our reports. It should be accepted routine, too, to accept our readers' criticisms in the spirit in which we should have asked for them. There is of course no obligation to change a manuscript in line with criticism. But there is an obligation to give each criticism the serious, careful, and objective attention it deserves. Doctoral students have to consider seriously the criticisms of their sponsors—whether or not they like them or agree with them. All scholarly and scientific writers, however, should voluntarily learn the discipline of subjecting their work to their peers. They should learn that the complex business of communicating scholarly and scientific work is difficult and demanding, and that in the long run they can only profit from competent criticism and careful revision.

SOME USEFUL REFERENCES

A Manual of Style, 13th ed. Chicago: University of Chicago Press, 1982. A basic reference that should be consulted for moot points—hyphenation, capitalization, tables, types, and so forth.

American Psychological Association. *Publication Manual of the American Psychological Asociation,* 3rd ed. Washington, D.C.: American Psychological Association, 1983. The basic manual for writers of reports in psychological journals. Particularly good for mechanical details such as tables, typing, and the like.

CAMPBELL, W. *Form and Style: Theses, Reports, Term Papers,* 5th ed. Boston: Houghton Mifflin, 1978. A useful reference for thesis writers.

NICHOLSON, M. *A Dictionary of American-English Usage.* New York: Oxford University Press, 1957. A valuable American revision of Fowler's classic, *A Dictionary of English Usage.* Anyone who plans to write much should get this book.

SCHMID, C. *Statistical Graphics: Design Principles and Practices*. New York: Wiley, 1983. In writing reports, we have paid too little attention to the graphic presentation of statistical data. This book discusses and illustrates the principles of good graphic procedures.

STRUNK, W., and WHITE, E. *The Elements of Style*, 3rd ed. New York: Macmillan, 1979. This little gem, which every writer should own, is dedicated to clarity, brevity, and simplicity.

TURABIAN, K. *A Manual for Writers of Term Papers, Theses, and Dissertations*, 4th ed. Chicago: University of Chicago Press, 1973. An excellent, invaluable reference. Can well be called the handbook of the doctoral student. It is based on the *Manual of Style*.

Name Index

Subject Index